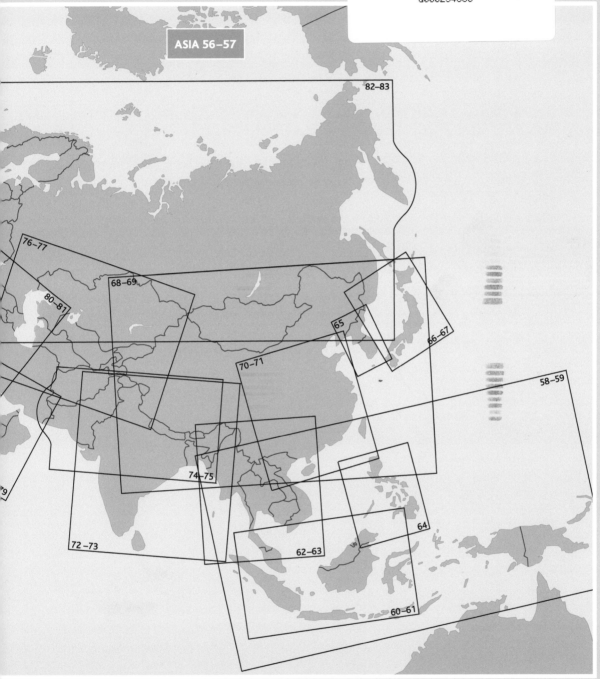

ASIA 56–57

82–83

76–77

68–69

80–81

65

66–67

70–71

58–59

74–75

79

72–73

64

62–63

60–61

# THE TIMES

# WORLD ATLAS

Times Books, 77-85 Fulham Palace Road, London W6 8JB

*The Times* is a registered trademark of Times Newspapers Ltd

First published 2005
Reprinted with changes 2006

Copyright © HarperCollins*Publishers* 2006
Maps © CollinsBartholomew Ltd 2006

Globes pp30-32
Copyright © 1993 Digital Wisdom Inc.

Printed in Hong Kong

British Library Cataloguing in Publication Data.
A catalogue record for this book is available from the British Library.

ISBN-13 978-0-00-721354-2
ISBN-10 0-00-721354-9

All mapping in this atlas is generated from Collins Bartholomew digital databases.
Collins Bartholomew, the UK's leading independent geographical information supplier,
can provide a digital, custom, and premium mapping service to a variety of markets.
For further information:
Tel: +44 (0) 141 306 3752
e-mail: collinsbartholomew@harpercollins.co.uk

or visit our website at: www.collinsbartholomew.com

www.harpercollins.co.uk
*visit the book lover's website*

# THE TIMES

# WORLD ATLAS

TIMES BOOKS
London

# CONTENTS

## THE WORLD TODAY

6–29    STATES AND TERRITORIES OF THE WORLD

30–33   CONTINENTS AND OCEANS

34–35   CLIMATE

36–37   ENVIRONMENT

38–39   POPULATION AND CITIES

40–41   TELECOMMUNICATIONS

## ATLAS OF THE WORLD

42–43   INTRODUCTION TO ATLAS OF THE WORLD

44–45   **WORLD** PHYSICAL FEATURES

46–47   **WORLD** COUNTRIES

**48–49    OCEANIA    1:40 000 000**

50–51   AUSTRALIA    1:16 000 000

52–53   AUSTRALIA Southeast    1:6 000 000

54    NEW ZEALAND    1:6 000 000

55    ANTARCTICA    1:36 000 000

**56–57    ASIA    1:44 000 000**

58–59   SOUTHEAST ASIA    1:20 000 000

60–61   MALAYSIA AND INDONESIA West    1:9 600 000

62–63   CONTINENTAL SOUTHEAST ASIA    1:9 600 00

64    PHILIPPINES    1:9 600 00

65    NORTH KOREA AND SOUTH KOREA    1:5 200 00

66–67   JAPAN    1:6 000 00

68–69   CHINA AND MONGOLIA    1:20 000 00

70–71   CHINA Central    1:9 600 00

72–73   SOUTH ASIA    1:12 000 00

74–75   PAKISTAN, INDIA North AND BANGLADESH    1:9 600 00

76–77   CENTRAL ASIA    1:12 000 00

78–79   ARABIAN PENINSULA    1:9 600 00

80–81   EAST MEDITERRANEAN    1:9 600 00

82–83   RUSSIAN FEDERATION    1:24 000 00

**84–85    EUROPE    1:20 000 00**

86–87   EUROPEAN RUSSIAN FEDERATION    1:12 000 00

88–89   NORTHEAST EUROPE    1:4 800 00

90–91   UKRAINE AND MOLDOVA    1:4 800 00

92–93   SCANDINAVIA AND ICELAND    1:6 000 00

94–95   BRITISH ISLES    1:4 800 00

| Pages | Title | Scale |
|---|---|---|
| 6 | SCOTLAND | 1:2 400 000 |
| 7 | IRELAND | 1:2 400 000 |
| 8–99 | ENGLAND AND WALES | 1:2 400 000 |
| 00–101 | NORTHWEST EUROPE | 1:2 400 000 |
| 02–103 | CENTRAL EUROPE | 1:4 800 000 |
| 04–105 | FRANCE AND SWITZERLAND | 1:4 800 000 |
| 06–107 | SPAIN AND PORTUGAL | 1:4 800 000 |
| 08–109 | ITALY AND THE BALKANS | 1:4 800 000 |
| 10–111 | SOUTHEAST EUROPE | 1:4 800 000 |
| **12–113** | **AFRICA** | **1:36 000 000** |
| 14–115 | NORTHWEST AFRICA | 1:16 000 000 |
| 16–117 | NORTHEAST AFRICA | 1:16 000 000 |
| 18–119 | CENTRAL AFRICA | 1:12 000 000 |
| 20–121 | SOUTHERN AFRICA | 1:12 000 000 |
| 22–123 | REPUBLIC OF SOUTH AFRICA | 1:6 000 000 |
| **24–125** | **NORTH AMERICA** | **1:32 000 000** |
| 26–127 | CANADA | 1:20 000 000 |
| 28–129 | CANADA West | 1:9 600 000 |
| 30–131 | CANADA East | 1:9 600 000 |
| 132–133 | UNITED STATES OF AMERICA | 1:16 000 000 |
| 134–135 | USA West | 1:6 400 000 |
| 136–137 | USA North Central | 1:6 400 000 |
| 138–139 | USA Northeast | 1:6 400 000 |
| 140–141 | USA Southeast | 1:6 400 000 |
| 142–143 | USA South Central | 1:6 400 000 |
| 144–145 | MEXICO | 1:9 600 000 |
| 146–147 | CENTRAL AMERICA AND THE CARIBBEAN | 1:12 000 000 |
| **148–149** | **SOUTH AMERICA** | **1:28 000 000** |
| 150–151 | SOUTH AMERICA North | 1:16 000 000 |
| 152–153 | SOUTH AMERICA South | 1:16 000 000 |
| 154–155 | BRAZIL Southeast | 1:6 000 000 |

**OCEANS**

| Pages | Title | Scale |
|---|---|---|
| 156–157 | PACIFIC OCEAN | 1:72 000 000 |
| 158 | ATLANTIC OCEAN | 1:72 000 000 |
| 159 | INDIAN OCEAN | 1:72 000 000 |
| 160 | ARCTIC OCEAN | 1:36 000 000 |

**161–224 INDEX**

**6** All independent countries and populated dependent and disputed territories are included in this list of the states and territories of the world; the list is arranged in alphabetical order by the conventional name form. For independent states, the full name is given below the conventional name, if this is different; for territories, the status is given. The capital city name is the same form as shown on the reference maps.

The statistics used for the area and population are the latest available and include estimates. The information on languages and religions is based on the latest information on 'de facto' speakers of the language or 'de facto' adherents to the religion. The information available on languages and religions varies greatly from country to country. Some countries include questions in censuses, others do not, in which case best estimates are used. The order of the languages and religions reflect their relative importance within the country; generally, languages or religions are included when more than one per cent of the population are estimated to be speakers or adherents.

Membership of selected international organizations is shown for each independent country. Territories are not shown as having separate memberships of these organizations.

## ABBREVIATIONS

### Currencies

| | |
|---|---|
| CFA | Communauté Financière Africaine |
| CFP | Comptoirs Français du Pacifique |

### Organizations

| | |
|---|---|
| APEC | Asia-Pacific Economic Cooperation |
| ASEAN | Association of Southeast Asian Nations |
| CARICOM | Caribbean Community |
| CIS | Commonwealth of Independent States |
| Comm. | The Commonwealth |
| EU | European Union |
| OECD | Organization of Economic Cooperation and Development |
| OPEC | Organization of Petroleum Exporting Countries |
| SADC | Southern African Development Community |
| UN | United Nations |

## AFGHANISTAN
### Islamic State of Afghanistan

| | | | |
|---|---|---|---|
| Area Sq Km | 652 225 | Religions | Sunni Muslim, Shi'a Muslim |
| Area Sq Miles | 251 825 | | |
| Population | 23 897 000 | Currency | Afghani |
| Capital | Kābul | Organizations | UN |
| Languages | Dari, Pushtu, Uzbek, Turkmen | Map page | 76–77 |

## ALBANIA
### Republic of Albania

| | | | |
|---|---|---|---|
| Area Sq Km | 28 748 | Religions | Sunni Muslim, Albanian Orthodox, Roman Catholic |
| Area Sq Miles | 11 100 | | |
| Population | 3 166 000 | | |
| Capital | Tirana (Tiranë) | Currency | Lek |
| Languages | Albanian, Greek | Organizations | UN |
| | | Map page | 109 |

## ALGERIA
### People's Democratic Republic of Algeria

| | | | |
|---|---|---|---|
| Area Sq Km | 2 381 741 | Religions | Sunni Muslim |
| Area Sq Miles | 919 595 | Currency | Algerian dinar |
| Population | 31 800 000 | Organizations | OPEC, UN |
| Capital | Algiers (Alger) | Map page | 114–115 |
| Languages | Arabic, French, Berber | | |

## American Samoa
### United States Unincorporated Territory

| | | | |
|---|---|---|---|
| Area Sq Km | 197 | Religions | Protestant, Roman Catholic |
| Area Sq Miles | 76 | | |
| Population | 67 000 | Currency | United States dollar |
| Capital | Fagatogo | Map page | 49 |
| Languages | Samoan, English | | |

## ANDORRA
### Principality of Andorra

| | | | |
|---|---|---|---|
| Area Sq Km | 465 | Religions | Roman Catholic |
| Area Sq Miles | 180 | Currency | Euro |
| Population | 71 000 | Organizations | UN |
| Capital | Andorra la Vella | Map page | 104 |
| Languages | Spanish, Catalan, French | | |

## ANGOLA
### Republic of Angola

| | | | |
|---|---|---|---|
| Area Sq Km | 1 246 700 | Religions | Roman Catholic, Protestant, traditional beliefs |
| Area Sq Miles | 481 354 | | |
| Population | 13 625 000 | | |
| Capital | Luanda | Currency | Kwanza |
| Languages | Portuguese, Bantu, local languages | Organizations | SADC, UN |
| | | Map page | 120 |

# Anguilla
United Kingdom Overseas Territory

| | | | |
|---|---|---|---|
| Area Sq Km | 155 | Religions | Protestant, Roman Catholic |
| Area Sq Miles | 60 | | |
| Population | 12 000 | Currency | East Caribbean dollar |
| Capital | The Valley | Map page | 147 |
| Languages | English | | |

# ANTIGUA AND BARBUDA

| | | | |
|---|---|---|---|
| Area Sq Km | 442 | Religions | Protestant, Roman Catholic |
| Area Sq Miles | 171 | | |
| Population | 73 000 | Currency | East Caribbean dollar |
| Capital | St John's | Organizations | CARICOM, Comm., UN |
| Languages | English, creole | Map page | 147 |

# ARGENTINA
Argentine Republic

| | | | |
|---|---|---|---|
| Area Sq Km | 2 766 889 | Religions | Roman Catholic, Protestant |
| Area Sq Miles | 1 068 302 | | |
| Population | 38 428 000 | Currency | Argentinian peso |
| Capital | Buenos Aires | Organizations | UN |
| Languages | Spanish, Italian, Amerindian languages | Map page | 152–153 |

# ARMENIA
Republic of Armenia

| | | | |
|---|---|---|---|
| Area Sq Km | 29 800 | Religions | Armenian Orthodox |
| Area Sq Miles | 11 506 | Currency | Dram |
| Population | 3 061 000 | Organizations | CIS, UN |
| Capital | Yerevan (Erevan) | Map page | 81 |
| Languages | Armenian, Azeri | | |

# Aruba
Self-governing Netherlands Territory

| | | | |
|---|---|---|---|
| Area Sq Km | 193 | Religions | Roman Catholic, Protestant |
| Area Sq Miles | 75 | | |
| Population | 100 000 | Currency | Aruban florin |
| Capital | Oranjestad | Map page | 147 |
| Languages | Papiamento, Dutch, English | | |

# Ascension
Dependency of St Helena

| | | | |
|---|---|---|---|
| Area Sq Km | 88 | Religions | Protestant, Roman Catholic |
| Area Sq Miles | 34 | | |
| Population | 1 122 | Currency | Pound sterling |
| Capital | Georgetown | Map page | 113 |
| Languages | English | | |

# AUSTRALIA
Commonwealth of Australia

| | | | |
|---|---|---|---|
| Area Sq Km | 7 692 024 | Religions | Protestant, Roman Catholic, Orthodox |
| Area Sq Miles | 2 969 907 | | |
| Population | 19 731 000 | Currency | Australian dollar |
| Capital | Canberra | Organizations | APEC, Comm., OECD, UN |
| Languages | English, Italian, Greek | Map page | 50–51 |

## Australian Capital Territory (Federal Territory)

| | | | |
|---|---|---|---|
| Area Sq Km | 2 358 | Population | 321 680 |
| Area Sq Miles | 910 | Capital | Canberra |

## Jervis Bay Territory (Territory)

| | | | |
|---|---|---|---|
| Area Sq Km | 73 | Population | 611 |
| Area Sq Miles | 28 | | |

## New South Wales (State)

| | | | |
|---|---|---|---|
| Area Sq Km | 800 642 | Population | 6 609 304 |
| Area Sq Miles | 309 130 | Capital | Sydney |

## Northern Territory (Territory)

| | | | |
|---|---|---|---|
| Area Sq Km | 1 349 129 | Population | 200 019 |
| Area Sq Miles | 520 902 | Capital | Darwin |

## Queensland (State)

| | | | |
|---|---|---|---|
| Area Sq Km | 1 730 648 | Population | 3 635 121 |
| Area Sq Miles | 668 207 | Capital | Brisbane |

## South Australia (State)

| | | | |
|---|---|---|---|
| Area Sq Km | 983 482 | Population | 1 514 854 |
| Area Sq Miles | 379 725 | Capital | Adelaide |

## Tasmania (State)

| | | | |
|---|---|---|---|
| Area Sq Km | 68 401 | Population | 472 931 |
| Area Sq Miles | 26 410 | Capital | Hobart |

## Victoria (State)

| | | | |
|---|---|---|---|
| Area Sq Km | 227 416 | Population | 4 822 663 |
| Area Sq Miles | 87 806 | Capital | Melbourne |

## Western Australia (State)

| | | | |
|---|---|---|---|
| Area Sq Km | 2 529 875 | Population | 1 906 114 |
| Area Sq Miles | 976 790 | Capital | Perth |

# AUSTRIA
Republic of Austria

| | | | |
|---|---|---|---|
| Area Sq Km | 83 855 | Religions | Roman Catholic, Protestant |
| Area Sq Miles | 32 377 | | |
| Population | 8 116 000 | Currency | Euro |
| Capital | Vienna (Wien) | Organizations | EU, OECD, UN |
| Languages | German, Croatian, Turkish | Map page | 102–103 |

# AZERBAIJAN
Azerbaijani Republic

| | | | |
|---|---|---|---|
| Area Sq Km | 86 600 | Religions | Shi'a Muslim, Sunni Muslim, Russian and Armenian Orthodox |
| Area Sq Miles | 33 436 | | |
| Population | 8 370 000 | | |
| Capital | Baku (Bakı) | Currency | Azerbaijani manat |
| Languages | Azeri, Armenian, Russian, Lezgian | Organizations | CIS, UN |
| | | Map page | 81 |

**Azores** (Arquipélago dos Açores)
Autonomous Region of Portugal

| | | | |
|---|---|---|---|
| Area Sq Km | 2 300 | Religions | Roman Catholic, Protestant |
| Area Sq Miles | 888 | | |
| Population | 242 073 | Currency | Euro |
| Capital | Ponta Delgada | Map page | 112 |
| Languages | Portuguese | | |

 **THE BAHAMAS**
Commonwealth of The Bahamas

| | | | |
|---|---|---|---|
| Area Sq Km | 13 939 | Religions | Protestant, Roman Catholic |
| Area Sq Miles | 5 382 | | |
| Population | 314 000 | Currency | Bahamian dollar |
| Capital | Nassau | Organizations | CARICOM, Comm., UN |
| Languages | English, creole | | |
| | | Map page | 146–147 |

 **BAHRAIN**
Kingdom of Bahrain

| | | | |
|---|---|---|---|
| Area Sq Km | 691 | Religions | Shi'a Muslim, Sunni Muslim, Christian |
| Area Sq Miles | 267 | | |
| Population | 724 000 | Currency | Bahraini dinar |
| Capital | Manama (Al Manāmah) | Organizations | UN |
| | | Map page | 79 |
| Languages | Arabic, English | | |

 **BANGLADESH**
People's Republic of Bangladesh

| | | | |
|---|---|---|---|
| Area Sq Km | 143 998 | Religions | Sunni Muslim, Hindu |
| Area Sq Miles | 55 598 | Currency | Taka |
| Population | 146 736 000 | Organizations | Comm., UN |
| Capital | Dhaka (Dacca) | Map page | 75 |
| Languages | Bengali, English | | |

 **BARBADOS**

| | | | |
|---|---|---|---|
| Area Sq Km | 430 | Religions | Protestant, Roman Catholic |
| Area Sq Miles | 166 | | |
| Population | 270 000 | Currency | Barbados dollar |
| Capital | Bridgetown | Organizations | CARICOM, Comm., UN |
| Languages | English, creole | | |
| | | Map page | 147 |

 **BELARUS**
Republic of Belarus

| | | | |
|---|---|---|---|
| Area Sq Km | 207 600 | Religions | Belorussian Orthodox, Roman Catholic |
| Area Sq Miles | 80 155 | | |
| Population | 9 895 000 | Currency | Belarus rouble |
| Capital | Minsk | Organizations | CIS, UN |
| Languages | Belorussian, Russian | Map page | 88–89 |

 **BELGIUM**
Kingdom of Belgium

| | | | |
|---|---|---|---|
| Area Sq Km | 30 520 | Religions | Roman Catholic, Protestant |
| Area Sq Miles | 11 784 | | |
| Population | 10 318 000 | Currency | Euro |
| Capital | Brussels (Bruxelles) | Organizations | EU, OECD, UN |
| Languages | Dutch (Flemish), French (Walloon), German | Map page | 100 |

 **BELIZE**

| | | | |
|---|---|---|---|
| Area Sq Km | 22 965 | Religions | Roman Catholic, Protestant |
| Area Sq Miles | 8 867 | | |
| Population | 256 000 | Currency | Belize dollar |
| Capital | Belmopan | Organizations | CARICOM, Comm., UN |
| Languages | English, Spanish, Mayan, creole | | |
| | | Map page | 147 |

 **BENIN**
Republic of Benin

| | | | |
|---|---|---|---|
| Area Sq Km | 112 620 | Religions | Traditional beliefs, Roman Catholic, Sunni Muslim |
| Area Sq Miles | 43 483 | | |
| Population | 6 736 000 | | |
| Capital | Porto-Novo | Currency | CFA franc |
| Languages | French, Fon, Yoruba, Adja, local languages | Organization | UN |
| | | Map page | 114 |

 **Bermuda**
United Kingdom Overseas Territory

| | | | |
|---|---|---|---|
| Area Sq Km | 54 | Religions | Protestant, Roman Catholic |
| Area Sq Miles | 21 | | |
| Population | 82 000 | Currency | Bermuda dollar |
| Capital | Hamilton | Map page | 125 |
| Languages | English | | |

 **BHUTAN**
Kingdom of Bhutan

| | | | |
|---|---|---|---|
| Area Sq Km | 46 620 | Religions | Buddhist, Hindu |
| Area Sq Miles | 18 000 | Currency | Ngultrum, Indian rupee |
| Population | 2 257 000 | | |
| Capital | Thimphu | Organizations | UN |
| Languages | Dzongkha, Nepali, Assamese | Map page | 75 |

 **BOLIVIA**
Republic of Bolivia

| | | | |
|---|---|---|---|
| Area Sq Km | 1 098 581 | Religions | Roman Catholic, Protestant, Baha'i |
| Area Sq Miles | 424 164 | | |
| Population | 8 808 000 | Currency | Boliviano |
| Capital | La Paz/Sucre | Organizations | UN |
| Languages | Spanish, Quechua, Aymara | Map page | 152 |

 **Bonaire**
part of Netherlands Antilles

| | | | |
|---|---|---|---|
| Area Sq Km | 288 | Religions | Roman Catholic, Protestant |
| Area Sq Miles | 111 | | |
| Population | 10 114 | Currency | Netherlands Antilles guilder |
| Capital | Kralendijk | | |
| Languages | Dutch, Papiamento | Map page | 147 |

**Bonin Islands** (Ogasawara-shotō)
part of Japan

| | | | |
|---|---|---|---|
| Area Sq Km | 104 | Religions | Shintoist, Buddhist, Christian |
| Area Sq Miles | 40 | | |
| Population | 2 300 | Currency | Yen |
| Capital | Omura | Map page | 69 |
| Languages | Japanese | | |

## BOSNIA-HERZEGOVINA
Republic of Bosnia and Herzegovina

| | | | |
|---|---|---|---|
| Area Sq Km | 51 130 | Religions | Sunni Muslim, Serbian |
| Area Sq Miles | 19 741 | | Orthodox, Roman |
| Population | 4 161 000 | | Catholic, Protestant |
| Capital | Sarajevo | Currency | Marka |
| Languages | Bosnian, Serbian, | Organizations | UN |
| | Croatian | Map page | 109 |

## BOTSWANA
Republic of Botswana

| | | | |
|---|---|---|---|
| Area Sq Km | 581 370 | Religions | Traditional beliefs, |
| Area Sq Miles | 224 468 | | Protestant, Roman |
| Population | 1 785 000 | | Catholic |
| Capital | Gaborone | Currency | Pula |
| Languages | English, Setswana, | Organizations | Comm., SADC, UN |
| | Shona, local | Map page | 120 |
| | languages | | |

## BRAZIL
Federative Republic of Brazil

| | | | |
|---|---|---|---|
| Area Sq Km | 8 514 879 | Religions | Roman Catholic, |
| Area Sq Miles | 3 287 613 | | Protestant |
| Population | 178 470 000 | Currency | Real |
| Capital | Brasília | Organizations | UN |
| Languages | Portuguese | Map page | 150–151 |

## BRUNEI
State of Brunei Darussalam

| | | | |
|---|---|---|---|
| Area Sq Km | 5 765 | Religions | Sunni Muslim, Buddhist, |
| Area Sq Miles | 2 226 | | Christian |
| Population | 358 000 | Currency | Brunei dollar |
| Capital | Bandar Seri Begawan | Organizations | APEC, ASEAN, |
| Languages | Malay, English, | | Comm., UN |
| | Chinese | Map page | 61 |

## BULGARIA
Republic of Bulgaria

| | | | |
|---|---|---|---|
| Area Sq Km | 110 994 | Religions | Bulgarian Orthodox, |
| Area Sq Miles | 42 855 | | Sunni Muslim |
| Population | 7 897 000 | Currency | Lev |
| Capital | Sofia (Sofiya) | Organizations | UN |
| Languages | Bulgarian, Turkish, | Map page | 110 |
| | Romany, | | |
| | Macedonian | | |

## BURKINA
Democratic Republic of Burkina Faso

| | | | |
|---|---|---|---|
| Area Sq Km | 274 200 | Religions | Sunni Muslim, |
| Area Sq Miles | 105 869 | | traditional beliefs, |
| Population | 13 002 000 | | Roman Catholic |
| Capital | Ouagadougou | Currency | CFA franc |
| Languages | French, Moore | Organizations | UN |
| | (Mossi), Fulani, local | Map page | 114 |
| | languages | | |

## BURUNDI
Republic of Burundi

| | | | |
|---|---|---|---|
| Area Sq Km | 27 835 | Religions | Roman Catholic, |
| Area Sq Miles | 10 747 | | traditional beliefs, |
| Population | 6 825 000 | | Protestant |
| Capital | Bujumbura | Currency | Burundian franc |
| Languages | Kirundi (Hutu, | Organizations | UN |
| | Tutsi), French | Map page | 119 |

## CAMBODIA
Kingdom of Cambodia

| | | | |
|---|---|---|---|
| Area Sq Km | 181 000 | Religions | Buddhist, Roman |
| Area Sq Miles | 69 884 | | Catholic, Sunni |
| Population | 14 144 000 | | Muslim |
| Capital | Phnum Pénh | Currency | Riel |
| | (Phnom Penh) | Organizations | ASEAN, UN |
| Languages | Khmer, Vietnamese | Map page | 63 |

## CAMEROON
Republic of Cameroon

| | | | |
|---|---|---|---|
| Area Sq Km | 475 442 | Religions | Roman Catholic, |
| Area Sq Miles | 183 569 | | traditional beliefs, |
| Population | 16 018 000 | | Sunni Muslim, |
| Capital | Yaoundé | | Protestant |
| Languages | French, English, | Currency | CFA franc |
| | Fang, Bamileke, | Organizations | Comm., UN |
| | local languages | Map page | 118 |

## CANADA

| | | | |
|---|---|---|---|
| Area Sq Km | 9 984 670 | Religions | Roman Catholic, |
| Area Sq Miles | 3 855 103 | | Protestant, Eastern |
| Population | 31 510 000 | | Orthodox, Jewish |
| Capital | Ottawa | Currency | Canadian dollar |
| Languages | English, French, | Organizations | APEC, Comm., |
| | local languages | | OECD, UN |
| | | Map page | 126–127 |

Alberta (Province)

| | | | |
|---|---|---|---|
| Area Sq Km | 661 848 | Population | 3 113 600 |
| Area Sq Miles | 255 541 | Capital | Edmonton |

British Columbia (Province)

| | | | |
|---|---|---|---|
| Area Sq Km | 944 735 | Population | 4 141 300 |
| Area Sq Miles | 364 764 | Capital | Victoria |

Manitoba (Province)

| | | | |
|---|---|---|---|
| Area Sq Km | 647 797 | Population | 1 150 800 |
| Area Sq Miles | 250 116 | Capital | Winnipeg |

New Brunswick (Province)

| | | | |
|---|---|---|---|
| Area Sq Km | 72 908 | Population | 756 700 |
| Area Sq Miles | 28 150 | Capital | Fredericton |

Newfoundland and Labrador (Province)

| | | | |
|---|---|---|---|
| Area Sq Km | 405 212 | Population | 531 600 |
| Area Sq Miles | 156 453 | Capital | St John's |

Northwest Territories (Territory)

| | | | |
|---|---|---|---|
| Area Sq Km | 1 346 106 | Population | 41 400 |
| Area Sq Miles | 519 734 | Capital | Yellowknife |

##  CANADA

**Nova Scotia (Province)**

| | | | |
|---|---|---|---|
| Area Sq Km | 55 284 | Population | 944 800 |
| Area Sq Miles | 21 345 | Capital | Halifax |

**Nunavut (Territory)**

| | | | |
|---|---|---|---|
| Area Sq Km | 2 093 190 | Population | 28 700 |
| Area Sq Miles | 808 185 | Capital | Iqaluit (Frobisher Bay) |

**Ontario (Province)**

| | | | |
|---|---|---|---|
| Area Sq Km | 1 076 395 | Population | 12 068 300 |
| Area Sq Miles | 415 598 | Capital | Toronto |

**Prince Edward Island (Province)**

| | | | |
|---|---|---|---|
| Area Sq Km | 5 660 | Population | 139 900 |
| Area Sq Miles | 2 185 | Capital | Charlottetown |

**Québec (Province)**

| | | | |
|---|---|---|---|
| Area Sq Km | 1 542 056 | Population | 7 455 200 |
| Area Sq Miles | 595 391 | Capital | Québec |

**Saskatchewan (Province)**

| | | | |
|---|---|---|---|
| Area Sq Km | 651 036 | Population | 1 011 800 |
| Area Sq Miles | 251 366 | Capital | Regina |

**Yukon Territory (Territory)**

| | | | |
|---|---|---|---|
| Area Sq Km | 482 443 | Population | 29 900 |
| Area Sq Miles | 186 272 | Capital | Whitehorse |

##  Canary Islands (Islas Canarias)
Autonomous Community of Spain

| | | | |
|---|---|---|---|
| Area Sq Km | 7 447 | Languages | Spanish |
| Area Sq Miles | 2 875 | Religions | Roman Catholic |
| Population | 1 694 477 | Currency | Euro |
| Capital | Santa Cruz de Tenerife/Las Palmas | Map page | 114 |

##  CAPE VERDE
Republic of Cape Verde

| | | | |
|---|---|---|---|
| Area Sq Km | 4 033 | Religions | Roman Catholic, Protestant |
| Area Sq Miles | 1 557 | | |
| Population | 463 000 | Currency | Cape Verde escudo |
| Capital | Praia | Organizations | UN |
| Languages | Portuguese, creole | Map page | 46 |

##  Cayman Islands
United Kingdom Overseas Territory

| | | | |
|---|---|---|---|
| Area Sq Km | 259 | Religions | Protestant, Roman Catholic |
| Area Sq Miles | 100 | | |
| Population | 40 000 | Currency | Cayman Islands dollar |
| Capital | George Town | Map page | 146 |
| Languages | English | | |

##  CENTRAL AFRICAN REPUBLIC

| | | | |
|---|---|---|---|
| Area Sq Km | 622 436 | Religions | Protestant, Roman Catholic, traditional beliefs, Sunni Muslim |
| Area Sq Miles | 240 324 | | |
| Population | 3 865 000 | | |
| Capital | Bangui | Currency | CFA franc |
| Languages | French, Sango, Banda, Baya, local languages | Organizations | UN |
| | | Map page | 118 |

## Ceuta
Autonomous Community of Spain

| | | | |
|---|---|---|---|
| Area Sq Km | 19 | Religions | Roman Catholic, Muslim |
| Area Sq Miles | 7 | | |
| Population | 71 505 | Currency | Euro |
| Capital | Ceuta | Map page | 106 |
| Languages | Spanish, Arabic | | |

## CHAD
Republic of Chad

| | | | |
|---|---|---|---|
| Area Sq Km | 1 284 000 | Religions | Sunni Muslim, Roman Catholic, Protestant, traditional beliefs |
| Area Sq Miles | 495 755 | | |
| Population | 8 598 000 | | |
| Capital | Ndjamena | Currency | CFA franc |
| Languages | Arabic, French, Sara, local languages | Organizations | UN |
| | | Map page | 115 |

##  Chatham Islands
part of New Zealand

| | | | |
|---|---|---|---|
| Area Sq Km | 963 | Religions | Protestant |
| Area Sq Miles | 372 | Currency | New Zealand dollar |
| Population | 717 | Map page | 49 |
| Capital | Waitangi | | |
| Languages | English | | |

## CHILE
Republic of Chile

| | | | |
|---|---|---|---|
| Area Sq Km | 756 945 | Religions | Roman Catholic, Protestant |
| Area Sq Miles | 292 258 | | |
| Population | 15 805 000 | Currency | Chilean peso |
| Capital | Santiago | Organizations | APEC, UN |
| Languages | Spanish, Amerindian languages | Map page | 152–153 |

## CHINA
People's Republic of China

| | | | |
|---|---|---|---|
| Area Sq Km | 9 584 492 | Religions | Confucian, Taoist, Buddhist, Christian, Sunni Muslim |
| Area Sq Miles | 3 700 593 | | |
| Population | 1 289 161 000 | | |
| Capital | Beijing (Peking) | Currency | Yuan, Hong Kong dollar, Macao pataca |
| Languages | Mandarin, Wu, Cantonese, Hsiang, regional languages | Organizations | APEC, UN |
| | | Map page | 68–69 |

**Anhui (Province)**

| | | | |
|---|---|---|---|
| Area Sq Km | 139 000 | Population | 59 860 000 |
| Area Sq Miles | 53 668 | Capital | Hefei |

**Bejing (Municipality)**

| | | | |
|---|---|---|---|
| Area Sq Km | 16 800 | Population | 13 820 000 |
| Area Sq Miles | 6 487 | Capital | Beijing (Peking) |

**Chongqing (Municipality)**

| | | | |
|---|---|---|---|
| Area Sq Km | 23 000 | Population | 30 900 000 |
| Area Sq Miles | 8 880 | Capital | Chongqing |

**Fujian (Province)**

| | | | |
|---|---|---|---|
| Area Sq Km | 121 400 | Population | 34 710 000 |
| Area Sq Miles | 46 873 | Capital | Fuzhou |

**ansu (Province)**

| | | | |
|---|---|---|---|
| Area Sq Km | 453 700 | Population | 25 620 000 |
| rea Sq Miles | 175 175 | Capital | Lanzhou |

**uangdong (Province)**

| | | | |
|---|---|---|---|
| Area Sq Km | 178 000 | Population | 86 420 000 |
| rea Sq Miles | 68 726 | Capital | Guangzhou (Canton) |

**uangxi Zhuangzu Zizhiqu (Autonomous Region)**

| | | | |
|---|---|---|---|
| Area Sq Km | 236 000 | Population | 44 890 000 |
| rea Sq Miles | 91 120 | Capital | Nanning |

**uizhou (Province)**

| | | | |
|---|---|---|---|
| Area Sq Km | 176 000 | Population | 35 250 000 |
| rea Sq Miles | 67 954 | Capital | Guiyang |

**ainan (Province)**

| | | | |
|---|---|---|---|
| Area Sq Km | 34 000 | Population | 7 870 000 |
| rea Sq Miles | 13 127 | Capital | Haikou |

**ebei (Province)**

| | | | |
|---|---|---|---|
| Area Sq Km | 187 700 | Population | 67 440 000 |
| rea Sq Miles | 72 471 | Capital | Shijiazhuang |

**eilongjiang (Province)**

| | | | |
|---|---|---|---|
| Area Sq Km | 454 600 | Population | 36 890 000 |
| rea Sq Miles | 175 522 | Capital | Harbin |

**enan (Province)**

| | | | |
|---|---|---|---|
| Area Sq Km | 167 000 | Population | 92 560 000 |
| rea Sq Miles | 64 479 | Capital | Zhengzhou |

**ong Kong (Special Administrative Region)**

| | | | |
|---|---|---|---|
| Area Sq Km | 1 075 | Population | 6 780 000 |
| rea Sq Miles | 415 | Capital | Hong Kong |

**ubei (Province)**

| | | | |
|---|---|---|---|
| Area Sq Km | 185 900 | Population | 60 280 000 |
| rea Sq Miles | 71 776 | Capital | Wuhan |

**unan (Province)**

| | | | |
|---|---|---|---|
| Area Sq Km | 210 000 | Population | 64 400 000 |
| rea Sq Miles | 81 081 | Capital | Changsha |

**angsu (Province)**

| | | | |
|---|---|---|---|
| Area Sq Km | 102 600 | Population | 74 380 000 |
| rea Sq Miles | 39 614 | Capital | Nanjing |

**angxi (Province)**

| | | | |
|---|---|---|---|
| Area Sq Km | 166 900 | Population | 41 400 000 |
| rea Sq Miles | 64 440 | Capital | Nanchang |

**in (Province)**

| | | | |
|---|---|---|---|
| Area Sq Km | 187 000 | Population | 27 280 000 |
| rea Sq Miles | 72 201 | Capital | Changchun |

**aoning (Province)**

| | | | |
|---|---|---|---|
| Area Sq Km | 147 400 | Population | 42 380 000 |
| rea Sq Miles | 56 911 | Capital | Shenyang |

**Macao (Special Administrative Region)**

| | | | |
|---|---|---|---|
| Area Sq Km | 17 | Population | 440 000 |
| Area Sq Mile | 7 | | |

**Nei Mongol Zizhiqu (Inner Mongolia) (Autonomous Region)**

| | | | |
|---|---|---|---|
| Area Sq Km | 1 183 000 | Population | 23 760 000 |
| Area Sq Miles | 456 759 | Capital | Hohhot |

**Ningxia Huizu Zizhiqu (Autonomous Region)**

| | | | |
|---|---|---|---|
| Area Sq Km | 66 400 | Population | 5 620 000 |
| Area Sq Miles | 25 637 | Capital | Yinchuan |

**Qinghai (Province)**

| | | | |
|---|---|---|---|
| Area Sq Km | 721 000 | Population | 5 180 000 |
| Area Sq Miles | 278 380 | Capital | Xining |

**Shaanxi (Province)**

| | | | |
|---|---|---|---|
| Area Sq Km | 205 600 | Population | 36 050 000 |
| Area Sq Miles | 79 383 | Capital | Xi'an |

**Shandong (Province)**

| | | | |
|---|---|---|---|
| Area Sq Km | 153 300 | Population | 90 790 000 |
| Area Sq Miles | 59 189 | Capital | Jinan |

**Shanghai (Municipality)**

| | | | |
|---|---|---|---|
| Area Sq Km | 6 300 | Population | 16 740 000 |
| Area Sq Miles | 2 432 | Capital | Shanghai |

**Shanxi (Province)**

| | | | |
|---|---|---|---|
| Area Sq Km | 156 300 | Population | 32 970 000 |
| Area Sq Miles | 60 348 | Capital | Taiyuan |

**Sichuan (Province)**

| | | | |
|---|---|---|---|
| Area Sq Km | 569 000 | Population | 83 290 000 |
| Area Sq Miles | 219 692 | Capital | Chengdu |

**Tianjin (Municipality)**

| | | | |
|---|---|---|---|
| Area Sq Km | 11 300 | Population | 10 010 000 |
| Area Sq Miles | 4 363 | Capital | Tianjin |

**Xinjiang Uygur Zizhiqu (Sinkiang) (Autonomous Region)**

| | | | |
|---|---|---|---|
| Area Sq Km | 1 600 000 | Population | 19 250 000 |
| Area Sq Miles | 617 763 | Capital | Ürümqi |

**Xizang Zizhiqu (Tibet) (Autonomous Region)**

| | | | |
|---|---|---|---|
| Area Sq Km | 1 228 400 | Population | 2 620 000 |
| Area Sq Miles | 474 288 | Capital | Lhasa |

**Yunnan (Province)**

| | | | |
|---|---|---|---|
| Area Sq Km | 394 000 | Population | 42 880 000 |
| Area Sq Miles | 152 124 | Capital | Kunming |

**Zhejiang (Province)**

| | | | |
|---|---|---|---|
| Area Sq Km | 101 800 | Population | 46 770 000 |
| Area Sq Miles | 39 305 | Capital | Hangzhou |

STATES AND TERRITORIES

 ## Christmas Island
Australian External Territory

| | | | |
|---|---|---|---|
| Area Sq Km | 135 | Religions | Buddhist, Sunni |
| Area Sq Miles | 52 | | Muslim, Protestant, |
| Population | 1 560 | | Roman Catholic |
| Capital | The Settlement | Currency | Australian dollar |
| Languages | English | Map page | 58 |

 ## Cocos Islands (Keeling Islands)
Australian External Territory

| | | | |
|---|---|---|---|
| Area Sq Km | 14 | Religions | Sunni Muslim, |
| Area Sq Miles | 5 | | Christian |
| Population | 632 | Currency | Australian dollar |
| Capital | West Island | Map page | 58 |
| Languages | English | | |

## COLOMBIA
Republic of Colombia

| | | | |
|---|---|---|---|
| Area Sq Km | 1 141 748 | Religions | Roman Catholic, |
| Area Sq Miles | 440 831 | | Protestant |
| Population | 44 222 000 | Currency | Colombian peso |
| Capital | Bogotá | Organizations | APEC, UN |
| Languages | Spanish, Amerindian | Map page | 150 |
| | languages | | |

 ## COMOROS
Union of the Comoros

| | | | |
|---|---|---|---|
| Area Sq Km | 1 862 | Religions | Sunni Muslim, Roman |
| Area Sq Miles | 719 | | Catholic |
| Population | 768 000 | Currency | Comoros franc |
| Capital | Moroni | Organizations | UN |
| Languages | Comorian, French, | Map page | 121 |
| | Arabic | | |

## CONGO
Republic of the Congo

| | | | |
|---|---|---|---|
| Area Sq Km | 342 000 | Religions | Roman Catholic, |
| Area Sq Miles | 132 047 | | Protestant, traditional |
| Population | 3 724 000 | | beliefs, Sunni Muslim |
| Capital | Brazzaville | Currency | CFA franc |
| Languages | French, Kongo, | Organizations | UN |
| | Monokutuba, local | Map page | 118 |
| | languages | | |

 ## CONGO, DEMOCRATIC REPUBLIC OF THE

| | | | |
|---|---|---|---|
| Area Sq Km | 2 345 410 | Religions | Christian, Sunni |
| Area Sq Miles | 905 568 | | Muslim |
| Population | 52 771 000 | Currency | Congolese franc |
| Capital | Kinshasa | Organizations | SADC, UN |
| Languages | French, Lingala, | Map page | 118–119 |
| | Swahili, Kongo, | | |
| | local languages | | |

 ## Cook Islands
Self-governing New Zealand Territory

| | | | |
|---|---|---|---|
| Area Sq Km | 293 | Religions | Protestant, Roman |
| Area Sq Miles | 113 | | Catholic |
| Population | 18 000 | Currency | New Zealand dollar |
| Capital | Avarua | Map page | 49 |
| Languages | English, Maori | | |

## COSTA RICA
Republic of Costa Rica

| | | | |
|---|---|---|---|
| Area Sq Km | 51 100 | Religions | Roman Catholic, |
| Area Sq Miles | 19 730 | | Protestant |
| Population | 4 173 000 | Currency | Costa Rican colón |
| Capital | San José | Organizations | UN |
| Languages | Spanish | Map page | 146 |

## CÔTE D'IVOIRE
Republic of Côte d'Ivoire

| | | | |
|---|---|---|---|
| Area Sq Km | 322 463 | Religions | Sunni Muslim, Roma |
| Area Sq Miles | 124 504 | | Catholic, traditonal |
| Population | 16 631 000 | | beliefs, Protestant |
| Capital | Yamoussoukro | Currency | CFA franc |
| Languages | French, creole, Akan, | Organizations | UN |
| | local languages | Map page | 114 |

 ## CROATIA
Republic of Croatia

| | | | |
|---|---|---|---|
| Area Sq Km | 56 538 | Religions | Roman Catholic, |
| Area Sq Miles | 21 829 | | Serbian Orthodox, |
| Population | 4 428 000 | | Sunni Muslim |
| Capital | Zagreb | Currency | Kuna |
| Languages | Croatian, Serbian | Organizations | UN |
| | | Map page | 109 |

## CUBA
Republic of Cuba

| | | | |
|---|---|---|---|
| Area Sq Km | 110 860 | Religions | Roman Catholic, |
| Area Sq Miles | 42 803 | | Protestant |
| Population | 11 300 000 | Currency | Cuban peso |
| Capital | Havana (La Habana) | Organizations | UN |
| Languages | Spanish | Map page | 146 |

 ## Curaçao
part of Netherlands Antilles

| | | | |
|---|---|---|---|
| Area Sq Km | 444 | Religions | Roman Catholic, |
| Area Sq Miles | 171 | | Protestant |
| Population | 126 816 | Currency | Netherlands Antilles |
| Capital | Willemstad | | guilder |
| Languages | Dutch, Papiamento | Map page | 147 |

 ## CYPRUS
Republic of Cyprus

| | | | |
|---|---|---|---|
| Area Sq Km | 9 251 | Religions | Greek Orthodox, |
| Area Sq Miles | 3 572 | | Sunni Muslim |
| Population | 802 000 | Currency | Cyprus pound |
| Capital | Nicosia (Lefkosia) | Organizations | Comm., UN |
| Languages | Greek, Turkish, | Map page | 80 |
| | English | | |

## CZECH REPUBLIC

| | | | |
|---|---|---|---|
| Area Sq Km | 78 864 | Religions | Roman Catholic, Protestant |
| Area Sq Miles | 30 450 | | |
| Population | 10 236 000 | Currency | Czech koruna |
| Capital | Prague (Praha) | Organizations | UN |
| Languages | Czech, Moravian, Slovakian | Map page | 102–103 |

## DENMARK
Kingdom of Denmark

| | | | |
|---|---|---|---|
| Area Sq Km | 43 075 | Religions | Protestant |
| Area Sq Miles | 16 631 | Currency | Danish krone |
| Population | 5 364 000 | Organizations | EU, OECD, UN |
| Capital | Copenhagen (København) | Map page | 93 |
| Languages | Danish | | |

## DJIBOUTI
Republic of Djibouti

| | | | |
|---|---|---|---|
| Area Sq Km | 23 200 | Religions | Sunni Muslim, Christian |
| Area Sq Miles | 8 958 | | |
| Population | 703 000 | Currency | Djibouti franc |
| Capital | Djibouti | Organizations | UN |
| Languages | Somali, Afar, French, Arabic | Map page | 117 |

## DOMINICA
Commonwealth of Dominica

| | | | |
|---|---|---|---|
| Area Sq Km | 750 | Religions | Roman Catholic, Protestant |
| Area Sq Miles | 290 | | |
| Population | 79 000 | Currency | East Caribbean dollar |
| Capital | Roseau | Organizations | CARICOM, Comm., UN |
| Languages | English, creole | | |
| | | Map page | 147 |

## DOMINICAN REPUBLIC

| | | | |
|---|---|---|---|
| Area Sq Km | 48 442 | Religions | Roman Catholic, Protestant |
| Area Sq Miles | 18 704 | | |
| Population | 8 745 000 | Currency | Dominican peso |
| Capital | Santo Domingo | Organizations | UN |
| Languages | Spanish, creole | Map page | 147 |

## Easter Island (Isla de Pascua)
part of Chile

| | | | |
|---|---|---|---|
| Area Sq Km | 171 | Religions | Roman Catholic |
| Area Sq Miles | 66 | Currency | Chilean peso |
| Population | 3 791 | Map page | 157 |
| Capital | Hanga Roa | | |
| Languages | Spanish | | |

## EAST TIMOR
Democratic Republic of East Timor

| | | | |
|---|---|---|---|
| Area Sq Km | 14 874 | Religions | Roman Catholic |
| Area Sq Miles | 5 743 | Currency | United States dollar |
| Population | 778 000 | Organisations | UN |
| Capital | Dili | Map page | 59 |
| Languages | Portuguese, Tetun, English | | |

## ECUADOR
Republic of Ecuador

| | | | |
|---|---|---|---|
| Area Sq Km | 272 045 | Religions | Roman Catholic |
| Area Sq Miles | 105 037 | Currency | United States dollar |
| Population | 13 003 000 | Organizations | APEC, UN |
| Capital | Quito | Map page | 150 |
| Languages | Spanish, Quechua, Amerindian languages | | |

## EGYPT
Arab Republic of Egypt

| | | | |
|---|---|---|---|
| Area Sq Km | 1 000 250 | Religions | Sunni Muslim, Coptic Christian |
| Area Sq Miles | 386 199 | | |
| Population | 71 931 000 | Currency | Egyptian pound |
| Capital | Cairo (Al Qāhira) | Organizations | UN |
| Languages | Arabic | Map page | 116 |

## EL SALVADOR
Republic of El Salvador

| | | | |
|---|---|---|---|
| Area Sq Km | 21 041 | Religions | Roman Catholic, Protestant |
| Area Sq Miles | 8 124 | | |
| Population | 6 515 000 | Currency | El Salvador colón, United States dollar |
| Capital | San Salvador | | |
| Languages | Spanish | Organizations | UN |
| | | Map page | 146 |

## EQUATORIAL GUINEA
Republic of Equatorial Guinea

| | | | |
|---|---|---|---|
| Area Sq Km | 28 051 | Religions | Roman Catholic, traditional beliefs |
| Area Sq Miles | 10 831 | | |
| Population | 494 000 | Currency | CFA franc |
| Capital | Malabo | Organizations | UN |
| Languages | Spanish, French, Fang | Map page | 118 |

## ERITREA
State of Eritrea

| | | | |
|---|---|---|---|
| Area Sq Km | 117 400 | Religions | Sunni Muslim, Coptic Christian |
| Area Sq Miles | 45 328 | | |
| Population | 4 141 000 | Currency | Nakfa |
| Capital | Asmara | Organizations | UN |
| Languages | Tigrinya, Tigre | Map page | 116 |

## ESTONIA
Republic of Estonia

| | | | |
|---|---|---|---|
| Area Sq Km | 45 200 | Religions | Protestant, Estonian and Russian Orthodox |
| Area Sq Miles | 17 452 | | |
| Population | 1 323 000 | Currency | Kroon |
| Capital | Tallinn | Organizations | UN |
| Languages | Estonian, Russian | Map page | 88 |

## ETHIOPIA
Federal Democratic Republic of Ethiopia

| | | | |
|---|---|---|---|
| Area Sq Km | 1 133 880 | Religions | Ethiopian Orthodox, Sunni Muslim, traditional beliefs |
| Area Sq Miles | 437 794 | | |
| Population | 70 678 000 | | |
| Capital | Addis Ababa (Ādīs Ābeba) | Currency | Birr |
| | | Organizations | UN |
| Languages | Oromo, Amharic, Tigrinya, local languages | Map page | 117 |

STATES AND TERRITORIES

 **Falkland Islands**
United Kingdom Overseas Territory

| | | | |
|---|---|---|---|
| Area Sq Km | 12 170 | Religions | Protestant, Roman Catholic |
| Area Sq Miles | 4 699 | | |
| Population | 3 000 | Currency | Falkland Islands pound |
| Capital | Stanley | | |
| Languages | English | Map page | 153 |

 **Faroe Islands**
Self-governing Danish Territory

| | | | |
|---|---|---|---|
| Area Sq Km | 1 399 | Religions | Protestant |
| Area Sq Miles | 540 | Currency | Danish krone |
| Population | 47 000 | Map page | 94 |
| Capital | Tórshavn (Thorshavn) | | |
| Languages | Faroese, Danish | | |

 **FIJI**
Sovereign Democratic Republic of Fiji

| | | | |
|---|---|---|---|
| Area Sq Km | 18 330 | Religions | Christian, Hindu, Sunni Muslim |
| Area Sq Miles | 7 077 | | |
| Population | 839 000 | Currency | Fiji dollar |
| Capital | Suva | Organizations | UN, Comm. |
| Languages | English, Fijian, Hindi | Map page | 49 |

 **FINLAND**
Republic of Finland

| | | | |
|---|---|---|---|
| Area Sq Km | 338 145 | Religions | Protestant, Greek Orthodox |
| Area Sq Miles | 130 559 | | |
| Population | 5 207 000 | Currency | Euro |
| Capital | Helsinki (Helsingfors) | Organizations | EU, OECD, UN |
| Languages | Finnish, Swedish | Map page | 92–93 |

 **FRANCE**
French Republic

| | | | |
|---|---|---|---|
| Area Sq Km | 543 965 | Religions | Roman Catholic, Protestant, Sunni Muslim |
| Area Sq Miles | 210 026 | | |
| Population | 60 144 000 | | |
| Capital | Paris | Currency | Euro |
| Languages | French, Arabic | Organizations | EU, OECD, UN |
| | | Map page | 104–105 |

 **French Guiana**
French Overseas Department

| | | | |
|---|---|---|---|
| Area Sq Km | 90 000 | Religions | Roman Catholic |
| Area Sq Miles | 34 749 | Currency | Euro |
| Population | 178 000 | Map page | 151 |
| Capital | Cayenne | | |
| Languages | French, creole | | |

**French Polynesia**
French Overseas Territory

| | | | |
|---|---|---|---|
| Area Sq Km | 3 265 | Religions | Protestant, Roman Catholic |
| Area Sq Miles | 1 261 | | |
| Population | 244 000 | Currency | CFP franc |
| Capital | Papeete | Map page | 49 |
| Languages | French, Tahitian, Polynesian languages | | |

 **GABON**
Gabonese Republic

| | | | |
|---|---|---|---|
| Area Sq Km | 267 667 | Religions | Roman Catholic, Protestant, traditona beliefs |
| Area Sq Miles | 103 347 | | |
| Population | 1 329 000 | | |
| Capital | Libreville | Currency | CFA franc |
| Languages | French, Fang, local languages | Organizations | UN |
| | | Map page | 118 |

 **Galapagos Islands** (Islas Galápagos)
part of Ecuador

| | | | |
|---|---|---|---|
| Area Sq Km | 8 010 | Religions | Roman Catholic |
| Area Sq Miles | 3 093 | Currency | United States dollar |
| Population | 18 640 | Map page | 125 |
| Capital | Puerto Baquerizo Moreno | | |
| Languages | Spanish | | |

 **THE GAMBIA**
Republic of The Gambia

| | | | |
|---|---|---|---|
| Area Sq Km | 11 295 | Religions | Sunni Muslim, Protestant |
| Area Sq Miles | 4 361 | | |
| Population | 1 426 000 | Currency | Dalasi |
| Capital | Banjul | Organizations | Comm., UN |
| Languages | English, Malinke, Fulani, Wolof | Map page | 114 |

**Gaza**
semi-autonomous region

| | | | |
|---|---|---|---|
| Area Sq Km | 363 | Religions | Sunni Muslim, Shi'a Muslim |
| Area Sq Miles | 140 | | |
| Population | 1 203 591 | Currency | Israeli shekel |
| Capital | Gaza | Map page | 80 |
| Languages | Arabic | | |

 **GEORGIA**
Republic of Georgia

| | | | |
|---|---|---|---|
| Area Sq Km | 69 700 | Religions | Georgian Orthodox, Russian Orthodox, Sunni Muslim |
| Area Sq Miles | 26 911 | | |
| Population | 5 126 000 | | |
| Capital | T'bilisi | Currency | Lari |
| Languages | Georgian, Russian, Armenian, Azeri, Ossetian, Abkhaz | Organizations | CIS, UN |
| | | Map page | 81 |

 **GERMANY**
Federal Republic of Germany

| | | | |
|---|---|---|---|
| Area Sq Km | 357 022 | Religions | Protestant, Roman Catholic |
| Area Sq Miles | 137 847 | | |
| Population | 82 476 000 | Currency | Euro |
| Capital | Berlin | Organizations | EU, OECD, UN |
| Languages | German, Turkish | Map page | 102 |

**GHANA**
Republic of Ghana

| | | | |
|---|---|---|---|
| Area Sq Km | 238 537 | Religions | Christian, Sunni Muslim, traditional beliefs |
| Area Sq Miles | 92 100 | | |
| Population | 20 922 000 | | |
| Capital | Accra | Currency | Cedi |
| Languages | English, Hausa, Akan, local languages | Organizations | Comm., UN |
| | | Map page | 114 |

## Gibraltar
United Kingdom Overseas Territory

| | | | |
|---|---|---|---|
| Area Sq Km | 7 | Religions | Roman Catholic, Protestant, Sunni Muslim |
| Area Sq Miles | 3 | | |
| Population | 27 000 | | |
| Capital | Gibraltar | Currency | Gibraltar pound |
| Languages | English, Spanish | Map page | 106 |

## GREECE
Hellenic Republic

| | | | |
|---|---|---|---|
| Area Sq Km | 131 957 | Religions | Greek Orthodox, Sunni Muslim |
| Area Sq Miles | 50 949 | | |
| Population | 10 976 000 | Currency | Euro |
| Capital | Athens (Athina) | Organizations | EU, OECD, UN |
| Languages | Greek | Map page | 111 |

## Greenland
Self-governing Danish Territory

| | | | |
|---|---|---|---|
| Area Sq Km | 2 175 600 | Religions | Protestant |
| Area Sq Miles | 840 004 | Currency | Danish krone |
| Population | 57 000 | Map page | 127 |
| Capital | Nuuk (Godthåb) | | |
| Languages | Greenlandic, Danish | | |

## GRENADA

| | | | |
|---|---|---|---|
| Area Sq Km | 378 | Religions | Roman Catholic, Protestant |
| Area Sq Miles | 146 | | |
| Population | 80 000 | Currency | East Caribbean dollar |
| Capital | St George's | Organizations | CARICOM, Comm., UN |
| Languages | English, creole | | |
| | | Map page | 147 |

## Guadeloupe
French Overseas Department

| | | | |
|---|---|---|---|
| Area Sq Km | 1 780 | Religions | Roman Catholic |
| Area Sq Miles | 687 | Currency | Euro |
| Population | 440 000 | Map page | 147 |
| Capital | Basse-Terre | | |
| Languages | French, creole | | |

## Guam
United States Unincorporated Territory

| | | | |
|---|---|---|---|
| Area Sq Km | 541 | Religions | Roman Catholic |
| Area Sq Miles | 209 | Currency | United States dollar |
| Population | 163 000 | Map page | 59 |
| Capital | Hagåtña | | |
| Languages | Chamorro, English, Tagalog | | |

## GUATEMALA
Republic of Guatemala

| | | | |
|---|---|---|---|
| Area Sq Km | 108 890 | Religion | Roman Catholic, Protestant |
| Area Sq Miles | 42 043 | | |
| Population | 12 347 000 | Currency | Quetzal, United States dollar |
| Capital | Guatemala City | | |
| Languages | Spanish, Mayan languages | Organizations | UN |
| | | Map page | 146 |

## Guernsey
United Kingdom Crown Dependency

| | | | |
|---|---|---|---|
| Area Sq Km | 78 | Religions | Protestant, Roman Catholic |
| Area Sq Miles | 30 | | |
| Population | 62 701 | Currency | Pound sterling |
| Capital | St Peter Port | Map page | 95 |
| Languages | English, French | | |

## GUINEA
Republic of Guinea

| | | | |
|---|---|---|---|
| Area Sq Km | 245 857 | Religions | Sunni Muslim, traditional beliefs, Christian |
| Area Sq Miles | 94 926 | | |
| Population | 8 480 000 | | |
| Capital | Conakry | Currency | Guinea franc |
| Languages | French, Fulani, Malinke, local languages | Organizations | UN |
| | | Map page | 114 |

## GUINEA-BISSAU
Republic of Guinea-Bissau

| | | | |
|---|---|---|---|
| Area Sq Km | 36 125 | Religions | Traditional beliefs, Sunni Muslim, Christian |
| Area Sq Miles | 13 948 | | |
| Population | 1 493 000 | | |
| Capital | Bissau | Currency | CFA franc |
| Languages | Portuguese, crioulo, local languages | Organizations | UN |
| | | Map page | 114 |

## GUYANA
Co-operative Republic of Guyana

| | | | |
|---|---|---|---|
| Area Sq Km | 214 969 | Religions | Protestant, Hindu, Roman Catholic, Sunni Muslim |
| Area Sq Miles | 83 000 | | |
| Population | 765 000 | | |
| Capital | Georgetown | Currency | Guyana dollar |
| Languages | English, creole, Amerindian languages | Organizations | CARICOM, Comm., UN |
| | | Map page | 150 |

## HAITI
Republic of Haiti

| | | | |
|---|---|---|---|
| Area Sq Km | 27 750 | Religions | Roman Catholic, Protestant, Voodoo |
| Area Sq Miles | 10 714 | | |
| Population | 8 326 000 | | |
| Capital | Port-au-Prince | Currency | Gourde |
| Languages | French, creole | Organizations | CARICOM, UN |
| | | Map page | 147 |

## HONDURAS
Republic of Honduras

| | | | |
|---|---|---|---|
| Area Sq Km | 112 088 | Religions | Roman Catholic, Protestant |
| Area Sq Miles | 43 277 | | |
| Population | 6 941 000 | Currency | Lempira |
| Capital | Tegucigalpa | Organizations | UN |
| Languages | Spanish, Amerindian languages | Map page | 147 |

## HUNGARY
Republic of Hungary

| | | | |
|---|---|---|---|
| Area Sq Km | 93 030 | Religions | Roman Catholic, Protestant |
| Area Sq Miles | 35 919 | | |
| Population | 9 877 000 | Currency | Forint |
| Capital | Budapest | Organizations | OECD, UN |
| Languages | Hungarian | Map page | 103 |

 ## ICELAND
Republic of Iceland

| | | | |
|---|---|---|---|
| Area Sq Km | 102 820 | Religions | Protestant |
| Area Sq Miles | 39 699 | Currency | Icelandic króna |
| Population | 290 000 | Organizations | OECD, UN |
| Capital | Reykjavík | Map page | 92 |
| Languages | Icelandic | | |

 ## INDIA
Republic of India

| | | | |
|---|---|---|---|
| Area Sq Km | 3 064 898 | Religions | Hindu, Sunni Muslim, |
| Area Sq Miles | 1 183 364 | | Shi'a Muslim, Sikh, |
| Population | 1 065 462 000 | | Christian |
| Capital | New Delhi | Currency | Indian rupee |
| Languages | Hindi, English, many | Organizations | Comm., UN |
| | regional languages | Map page | 72–73 |

 ## INDONESIA
Republic of Indonesia

| | | | |
|---|---|---|---|
| Area Sq Km | 1 919 445 | Religions | Sunni Muslim, |
| Area Sq Miles | 741 102 | | Protestant, Roman |
| Population | 219 883 000 | | Catholic, Hindu, |
| Capital | Jakarta | | Buddhist |
| Languages | Indonesian, local | Currency | Rupiah |
| | languages | Organizations | APEC, ASEAN, |
| | | | OPEC, UN |
| | | Map page | 58–59 |

 ## IRAN
Islamic Republic of Iran

| | | | |
|---|---|---|---|
| Area Sq Km | 1 648 000 | Religions | Shi'a Muslim, Sunni |
| Area Sq Miles | 636 296 | | Muslim |
| Population | 68 920 000 | Currency | Iranian rial |
| Capital | Tehrān | Organizations | OPEC, UN |
| Languages | Farsi, Azeri, Kurdish, | Map page | 81 |
| | regional languages | | |

## IRAQ
Republic of Iraq

| | | | |
|---|---|---|---|
| Area Sq Km | 438 317 | Religions | Shi'a Muslim, Sunni |
| Area Sq Miles | 169 235 | | Muslim, Christian |
| Population | 25 175 000 | Currency | Iraqi dinar |
| Capital | Baghdād | Organizations | OPEC, UN |
| Languages | Arabic, Kurdish, | Map page | 81 |
| | Turkmen | | |

## IRELAND

| | | | |
|---|---|---|---|
| Area Sq Km | 70 282 | Religions | Roman Catholic, |
| Area Sq Miles | 27 136 | | Protestant, |
| Population | 3 956 000 | Currency | Euro |
| Capital | Dublin | Organizations | EU, OECD, UN |
| | (Baile Átha Cliath) | Map page | 97 |
| Languages | English, Irish | | |

## Isle of Man
United Kingdom Crown Dependency

| | | | |
|---|---|---|---|
| Area Sq Km | 572 | Religions | Protestant, Roman |
| Area Sq Miles | 221 | | Catholic |
| Population | 75 000 | Currency | Pound sterling |
| Capital | Douglas | Map page | 98 |
| Languages | English | | |

## ISRAEL
State of Israel

| | | | |
|---|---|---|---|
| Area Sq Km | 20 770 | Religions | Jewish, Sunni Muslim, |
| Area Sq Miles | 8 019 | | Christian, Druze |
| Population | 6 433 000 | Currency | Shekel |
| Capital | Jerusalem* | Organizations | UN |
| | (Yerushalayim) | Map page | 80 |
| | (El Quds) | | |
| Languages | Hebrew, Arabic | | |

*De facto capital. Disputed.

 ## ITALY
Italian Republic

| | | | |
|---|---|---|---|
| Area Sq Km | 301 245 | Religions | Roman Catholic |
| Area Sq Miles | 116 311 | Currency | Euro |
| Population | 57 423 000 | Organizations | EU, OECD, UN |
| Capital | Rome (Roma) | Map page | 108–109 |
| Languages | Italian | | |

 ## JAMAICA

| | | | |
|---|---|---|---|
| Area Sq Km | 10 991 | Religions | Protestant, Roman |
| Area Sq Miles | 4 244 | | Catholic |
| Population | 2 651 000 | Currency | Jamaican dollar |
| Capital | Kingston | Organizations | CARICOM, Comm. |
| Languages | English, creole | | UN |
| | | Map page | 146 |

## Jammu and Kashmir
Disputed territory (India/Pakistan)

| | | | |
|---|---|---|---|
| Area Sq Km | 222 236 | Map page | 74–75 |
| Area Sq Miles | 85 806 | | |
| Population | 13 000 000 | | |
| Capital | Srinagar | | |

 ## JAPAN

| | | | |
|---|---|---|---|
| Area Sq Km | 377 727 | Religions | Shintoist, Buddhist, |
| Area Sq Miles | 145 841 | | Christian |
| Population | 127 654 000 | Currency | Yen |
| Capital | Tōkyō | Organizations | APEC, OECD, UN |
| Languages | Japanese | Map page | 66–67 |

 ## Jersey
United Kingdom Crown Dependency

| | | | |
|---|---|---|---|
| Area Sq Km | 116 | Religions | Protestant, Roman |
| Area Sq Miles | 45 | | Catholic |
| Population | 87 186 | Currency | Pound sterling |
| Capital | St Helier | Map page | 95 |
| Languages | English, French | | |

 ## JORDAN
Hashemite Kingdom of Jordan

| | | | |
|---|---|---|---|
| Area Sq Km | 89 206 | Religions | Sunni Muslim, |
| Area Sq Miles | 34 443 | | Christian |
| Population | 5 473 000 | Currency | Jordanian dinar |
| Capital | 'Ammān | Organizations | UN |
| Languages | Arabic | Map page | 80 |

## Juan Fernández Islands
part of Chile

| | | | |
|---|---|---|---|
| Area Sq Km | 179 | Religions | Roman Catholic, Protestant |
| Area Sq Miles | 69 | | |
| Population | 633 | Currency | Chilean peso |
| Capital | San Juan Bautista | Map page | 157 |
| Languages | Spanish, Amerindian languages | | |

## KAZAKHSTAN
Republic of Kazakhstan

| | | | |
|---|---|---|---|
| Area Sq Km | 2 717 300 | Religions | Sunni Muslim, Russian Orthodox, Protestant |
| Area Sq Miles | 1 049 155 | | |
| Population | 15 433 000 | Currency | Tenge |
| Capital | Astana (Akmola) | Organizations | CIS, UN |
| Languages | Kazakh, Russian, Ukrainian, German, Uzbek, Tatar | Map page | 76–77 |

## KENYA
Republic of Kenya

| | | | |
|---|---|---|---|
| Area Sq Km | 582 646 | Religions | Christian, traditional beliefs |
| Area Sq Miles | 224 961 | | |
| Population | 31 987 000 | Currency | Kenyan shilling |
| Capital | Nairobi | Organizations | Comm., UN |
| Languages | Swahili, English, local languages | Map page | 119 |

## KIRIBATI
Republic of Kiribati

| | | | |
|---|---|---|---|
| Area Sq Km | 717 | Religions | Roman Catholic, Protestant |
| Area Sq Miles | 277 | | |
| Population | 88 000 | Currency | Australian dollar |
| Capital | Bairiki | Organizations | Comm., UN |
| Languages | Gilbertese, English | Map page | 49 |

## KUWAIT
State of Kuwait

| | | | |
|---|---|---|---|
| Area Sq Km | 17 818 | Religions | Sunni Muslim, Shi'a Muslim, Christian, Hindu |
| Area Sq Miles | 6 880 | | |
| Population | 2 521 000 | | |
| Capital | Kuwait (Al Kuwayt) | Currency | Kuwaiti dinar |
| Languages | Arabic | Organizations | OPEC, UN |
| | | Map page | 78 |

## KYRGYZSTAN
Kyrgyz Republic

| | | | |
|---|---|---|---|
| Area Sq Km | 198 500 | Religions | Sunni Muslim, Russian Orthodox |
| Area Sq Miles | 76 641 | | |
| Population | 5 138 000 | Currency | Kyrgyz som |
| Capital | Bishkek (Frunze) | Organizations | CIS, UN |
| Languages | Kyrgyz, Russian, Uzbek | Map page | 77 |

## LAOS
Lao People's Democratic Republic

| | | | |
|---|---|---|---|
| Area Sq Km | 236 800 | Religions | Buddhist, traditional beliefs |
| Area Sq Miles | 91 429 | | |
| Population | 5 657 000 | Currency | Kip |
| Capital | Vientiane (Viangchan) | Organizations | ASEAN, UN |
| | | Map page | 62–63 |
| Languages | Lao, local languages | | |

## LATVIA
Republic of Latvia

| | | | |
|---|---|---|---|
| Area Sq Km | 63 700 | Religions | Protestant, Roman Catholic, Russian Orthodox |
| Area Sq Miles | 24 595 | | |
| Population | 2 307 000 | | |
| Capital | Rīga | Currency | Lats |
| Languages | Latvian, Russian | Organizations | UN |
| | | Map page | 88 |

## LEBANON
Republic of Lebanon

| | | | |
|---|---|---|---|
| Area Sq Km | 10 452 | Religions | Shi'a Muslim, Sunni Muslim, Christian |
| Area Sq Miles | 4 036 | | |
| Population | 3 653 000 | Currency | Lebanese pound |
| Capital | Beirut (Beyrouth) | Organizations | UN |
| Languages | Arabic, Armenian, French | Map page | 80 |

## LESOTHO
Kingdom of Lesotho

| | | | |
|---|---|---|---|
| Area Sq Km | 30 355 | Religions | Christian, traditional beliefs |
| Area Sq Miles | 11 720 | | |
| Population | 1 802 000 | Currency | Loti, South African rand |
| Capital | Maseru | | |
| Languages | Sesotho, English, Zulu | Organizations | Comm., SADC, UN |
| | | Map page | 123 |

## LIBERIA
Republic of Liberia

| | | | |
|---|---|---|---|
| Area Sq Km | 111 369 | Religions | Traditional beliefs, Christian, Sunni Muslim |
| Area Sq Miles | 43 000 | | |
| Population | 3 367 000 | | |
| Capital | Monrovia | Currency | Liberian dollar |
| Languages | English, creole, local languages | Organizations | UN |
| | | Map page | 114 |

## LIBYA
Socialist People's Libyan Arab Jamahiriya

| | | | |
|---|---|---|---|
| Area Sq Km | 1 759 540 | Religions | Sunni Muslim |
| Area Sq Miles | 679 362 | Currency | Libyan dinar |
| Population | 5 551 000 | Organizations | OPEC, UN |
| Capital | Tripoli (Ṭarābulus) | Map page | 115 |
| Languages | Arabic, Berber | | |

## LIECHTENSTEIN
Principality of Liechtenstein

| | | | |
|---|---|---|---|
| Area Sq Km | 160 | Religions | Roman Catholic, Protestant |
| Area Sq Miles | 62 | | |
| Population | 34 000 | Currency | Swiss franc |
| Capital | Vaduz | Organizations | UN |
| Languages | German | Map page | 105 |

## LITHUANIA
Republic of Lithuania

| | | | |
|---|---|---|---|
| Area Sq Km | 65 200 | Religions | Roman Catholic, Protestant, Russian Orthodox |
| Area Sq Miles | 25 174 | | |
| Population | 3 444 000 | | |
| Capital | Vilnius | Currency | Litas |
| Languages | Lithuanian, Russian, Polish | Organizations | UN |
| | | Map page | 88 |

### Lord Howe Island
part of Australia

| | | | |
|---|---|---|---|
| Area Sq Km | 17 | Religions | Protestant, |
| Area Sq Miles | 6 | | Roman Catholic |
| Population | 397 | Currency | Australian dollar |
| Languages | English | Map page | 51 |

### LUXEMBOURG
Grand Duchy of Luxembourg

| | | | |
|---|---|---|---|
| Area Sq Km | 2 586 | Religions | Roman Catholic |
| Area Sq Miles | 998 | Currency | Euro |
| Population | 453 000 | Organizations | EU, OECD, UN |
| Capital | Luxembourg | Map page | 100 |
| Languages | Letzeburgish, German, French | | |

### MACEDONIA (F.Y.R.O.M.)
Republic of Macedonia

| | | | |
|---|---|---|---|
| Area Sq Km | 25 713 | Religions | Macedonian Orthodox, |
| Area Sq Miles | 9 928 | | Sunni Muslim |
| Population | 2 056 000 | Currency | Macedonian denar |
| Capital | Skopje | Organizations | UN |
| Languages | Macedonian, Albanian, Turkish | Map page | 111 |

### MADAGASCAR
Republic of Madagascar

| | | | |
|---|---|---|---|
| Area Sq Km | 587 041 | Religions | Traditional beliefs, |
| Area Sq Miles | 226 658 | | Christian, Sunni |
| Population | 17 404 000 | | Muslim |
| Capital | Antananarivo | Currency | Malagasy ariary, |
| Languages | Malagasy, French | | Malagasy franc |
| | | Organizations | UN |
| | | Map page | 121 |

### Madeira
Autonomous Region of Portugal

| | | | |
|---|---|---|---|
| Area Sq Km | 779 | Religions | Roman Catholic, |
| Area Sq Miles | 301 | | Protestant |
| Population | 242 603 | Currency | Euro |
| Capital | Funchal | Map page | 114 |
| Languages | Portuguese | | |

### MALAWI
Republic of Malawi

| | | | |
|---|---|---|---|
| Area Sq Km | 118 484 | Religions | Christian, traditional |
| Area Sq Miles | 45 747 | | beliefs, Sunni Muslim |
| Population | 12 105 000 | Currency | Malawian kwacha |
| Capital | Lilongwe | Organizations | Comm.,SADC, UN |
| Languages | Chichewa, English, local languages | Map page | 121 |

### MALAYSIA
Federation of Malaysia

| | | | |
|---|---|---|---|
| Area Sq Km | 332 965 | Religions | Sunni Muslim, |
| Area Sq Miles | 128 559 | | Buddhist, |
| Population | 24 425 000 | | Hindu, Christian, |
| Capital | Kuala Lumpur/ | | traditional beliefs |
| | Putrajaya | Currency | Ringgit |
| Languages | Malay, English, Chinese, Tamil, local languages | Organizations | APEC, ASEAN, Comm., UN |
| | | Map page | 60–61 |

### MALDIVES
Republic of the Maldives

| | | | |
|---|---|---|---|
| Area Sq Km | 298 | Religions | Sunni Muslim |
| Area Sq Miles | 115 | Currency | Rufiyaa |
| Population | 318 000 | Organizations | Comm., UN |
| Capital | Male | Map page | 56 |
| Languages | Divehi (Maldivian) | | |

### MALI
Republic of Mali

| | | | |
|---|---|---|---|
| Area Sq Km | 1 240 140 | Religions | Sunni Muslim, |
| Area Sq Miles | 478 821 | | traditional beliefs, |
| Population | 13 007 000 | | Christian |
| Capital | Bamako | Currency | CFA franc |
| Languages | French, Bambara, local languages | Organizations | UN |
| | | Map page | 114 |

### MALTA
Republic of Malta

| | | | |
|---|---|---|---|
| Area Sq Km | 316 | Religions | Roman Catholic |
| Area Sq Miles | 122 | Currency | Maltese lira |
| Population | 394 000 | Organizations | Comm., UN |
| Capital | Valletta | Map page | 84 |
| Languages | Maltese, English | | |

### MARSHALL ISLANDS
Republic of the Marshall Islands

| | | | |
|---|---|---|---|
| Area Sq Km | 181 | Religions | Protestant, Roman |
| Area Sq Miles | 70 | | Catholic |
| Population | 53 000 | Currency | United States dollar |
| Capital | Delap-Uliga-Djarrit | Organizations | UN |
| Languages | English, Marshallese | Map page | 48 |

### Martinique
French Overseas Department

| | | | |
|---|---|---|---|
| Area Sq Km | 1 079 | Religions | Roman Catholic, |
| Area Sq Miles | 417 | | traditional beliefs |
| Population | 393 000 | Currency | Euro |
| Capital | Fort-de-France | Map page | 147 |
| Languages | French, creole | | |

### MAURITANIA
Islamic Arab and African Republic of Mauritania

| | | | |
|---|---|---|---|
| Area Sq Km | 1 030 700 | Religions | Sunni Muslim |
| Area Sq Miles | 397 955 | Currency | Ouguiya |
| Population | 2 893 000 | Organizations | UN |
| Capital | Nouakchott | Map page | 114 |
| Languages | Arabic, French, local languages | | |

### MAURITIUS
Republic of Mauritius

| | | | |
|---|---|---|---|
| Area Sq Km | 2 040 | Religions | Hindu, Roman |
| Area Sq Miles | 788 | | Catholic, Sunni |
| Population | 1 221 000 | | Muslim |
| Capital | Port Louis | Currency | Mauritius rupee |
| Languages | English, creole, Hindi, Bhojpuri, French | Organizations | Comm., SADC, UN |
| | | Map page | 113 |

## Mayotte
French Territorial Collectivity

| | | | |
|---|---|---|---|
| Area Sq Km | 373 | Religions | Sunni Muslim, Christian |
| Area Sq Miles | 144 | | |
| Population | 170 879 | Currency | Euro |
| Capital | Dzaoudzi | Map page | 121 |
| Languages | French, Mahorian | | |

## Melilla
Autonomous Community of Spain

| | | | |
|---|---|---|---|
| Area Sq Km | 13 | Languages | Spanish, Arabic |
| Area Sq Miles | 5 | Religions | Roman Catholic, Muslim |
| Population | 66 411 | | |
| Capital | Melilla | Currency | Euro |
| | | Map page | 114 |

## MEXICO
United Mexican States

| | | | |
|---|---|---|---|
| Area Sq Km | 1 972 545 | Religions | Roman Catholic, Protestant |
| Area Sq Miles | 761 604 | | |
| Population | 103 457 000 | Currency | Mexican peso |
| Capital | Mexico City | Organizations | APEC, OECD, UN |
| Languages | Spanish, Amerindian languages | Map page | 144–145 |

## MICRONESIA, FEDERATED STATES OF

| | | | |
|---|---|---|---|
| Area Sq Km | 701 | Religions | Roman Catholic, Protestant |
| Area Sq Miles | 271 | | |
| Population | 109 000 | Currency | United States dollar |
| Capital | Palikir | Organizations | UN |
| Languages | English, Chuukese, Pohnpeian, local languages | Map page | 48 |

## MOLDOVA
Republic of Moldova

| | | | |
|---|---|---|---|
| Area Sq Km | 33 700 | Religions | Romanian Orthodox, Russian Orthodox |
| Area Sq Miles | 13 012 | | |
| Population | 4 267 000 | Currency | Moldovan leu |
| Capital | Chişinău (Kishinev) | Organizations | CIS, UN |
| Languages | Romanian, Ukrainian, Gagauz, Russian | Map page | 90 |

## MONACO
Principality of Monaco

| | | | |
|---|---|---|---|
| Area Sq Km | 2 | Religions | Roman Catholic |
| Area Sq Miles | 1 | Currency | Euro |
| Population | 34 000 | Organizations | UN |
| Capital | Monaco-Ville | Map page | 105 |
| Languages | French, Monégasque, Italian | | |

## MONGOLIA

| | | | |
|---|---|---|---|
| Area Sq Km | 1 565 000 | Religions | Buddhist, Sunni Muslim |
| Area Sq Miles | 604 250 | | |
| Population | 2 594 000 | Currency | Tugrik (tögrög) |
| Capital | Ulan Bator (Ulaanbaatar) | Organizations | UN |
| Languages | Khalka (Mongolian), Kazakh, local languages | Map page | 68–69 |

## Montserrat
United Kingdom Overseas Territory

| | | | |
|---|---|---|---|
| Area Sq Km | 100 | Religions | Protestant, Roman Catholic |
| Area Sq Miles | 39 | | |
| Population | 4 000 | Currency | East Caribbean dollar |
| Capital | Plymouth | Organizations | CARICOM |
| Languages | English | Map page | 147 |

## MOROCCO
Kingdom of Morocco

| | | | |
|---|---|---|---|
| Area Sq Km | 446 550 | Religions | Sunni Muslim |
| Area Sq Miles | 172 414 | Currency | Moroccan dirham |
| Population | 30 566 000 | Organizations | UN |
| Capital | Rabat | Map page | 114 |
| Languages | Arabic, Berber, French | | |

## MOZAMBIQUE
Republic of Mozambique

| | | | |
|---|---|---|---|
| Area Sq Km | 799 380 | Religions | Traditional beliefs, Roman Catholic, Sunni Muslim |
| Area Sq Miles | 308 642 | | |
| Population | 18 863 000 | | |
| Capital | Maputo | Currency | Metical |
| Languages | Portuguese, Makua, Tsonga, local languages | Organizations | Comm., SADC, UN |
| | | Map page | 121 |

## MYANMAR
Union of Myanmar

| | | | |
|---|---|---|---|
| Area Sq Km | 676 577 | Religions | Buddhist, Christian, Sunni Muslim |
| Area Sq Miles | 261 228 | | |
| Population | 49 485 000 | Currency | Kyat |
| Capital | Rangoon (Yangôn) | Organizations | ASEAN, UN |
| Languages | Burmese, Shan, Karen, local languages | Map page | 62–63 |

## NAMIBIA
Republic of Namibia

| | | | |
|---|---|---|---|
| Area Sq Km | 824 292 | Religions | Protestant, Roman Catholic |
| Area Sq Miles | 318 261 | | |
| Population | 1 987 000 | Currency | Namibian dollar |
| Capital | Windhoek | Organizations | Comm., SADC, UN |
| Languages | English, Afrikaans, German, Ovambo, local languages | Map page | 121 |

## NAURU
Republic of Nauru

| Area Sq Km | 21 | Religions | Protestant, Roman |
|---|---|---|---|
| Area Sq Miles | 8 | | Catholic |
| Population | 13 000 | Currency | Australian dollar |
| Capital | Yaren | Organizations | Comm., UN |
| Languages | Nauruan, English | Map page | 48 |

## NEPAL
Kingdom of Nepal

| Area Sq Km | 147 181 | Religions | Hindu, Buddhist, |
|---|---|---|---|
| Area Sq Miles | 56 827 | | Sunni Muslim |
| Population | 25 164 000 | Currency | Nepalese rupee |
| Capital | Kathmandu | Organizations | UN |
| Languages | Nepali, Maithili, | Map page | 75 |
| | Bhojpuri, English, | | |
| | local languages | | |

## NETHERLANDS
Kingdom of the Netherlands

| Area Sq Km | 41 526 | Religions | Roman Catholic, |
|---|---|---|---|
| Area Sq Miles | 16 033 | | Protestant, Sunni |
| Population | 16 149 000 | | Muslim |
| Capital | Amsterdam/ | Currency | Euro |
| | The Hague | Organizations | EU, OECD, UN |
| | ('s-Gravenhage) | Map page | 100 |
| Languages | Dutch, Frisian | | |

## Netherlands Antilles
Self-governing Netherlands Territory

| Area Sq Km | 800 | Religions | Roman Catholic, |
|---|---|---|---|
| Area Sq Miles | 309 | | Protestant |
| Population | 221 000 | Currency | Netherlands Antilles |
| Capital | Willemstad | | guilder |
| Languages | Dutch, Papiamento, | Map page | 147 |
| | English | | |

## New Caledonia
French Overseas Territory

| Area Sq Km | 19 058 | Religions | Roman Catholic, |
|---|---|---|---|
| Area Sq Miles | 7 358 | | Protestant, Sunni |
| Population | 228 000 | | Muslim |
| Capital | Nouméa | Currency | CFP franc |
| Languages | French, local | Map page | 48 |
| | languages | | |

## NEW ZEALAND

| Area Sq Km | 270 534 | Religions | Protestant, Roman |
|---|---|---|---|
| Area Sq Miles | 104 454 | | Catholic |
| Population | 3 875 000 | Currency | New Zealand dollar |
| Capital | Wellington | Organizations | APEC, Comm., |
| Languages | English, Maori | | OECD, UN |
| | | Map page | 54 |

## NICARAGUA
Republic of Nicaragua

| Area Sq Km | 130 000 | Religions | Roman Catholic, |
|---|---|---|---|
| Area Sq Miles | 50 193 | | Protestant |
| Population | 5 466 000 | Currency | Córdoba |
| Capital | Managua | Organizations | UN |
| Languages | Spanish, Amerindian | Map page | 146 |
| | languages | | |

## NIGER
Republic of Niger

| Area Sq Km | 1 267 000 | Religions | Sunni Muslim, |
|---|---|---|---|
| Area Sq Miles | 489 191 | | traditional beliefs |
| Population | 11 972 000 | Currency | CFA franc |
| Capital | Niamey | Organizations | UN |
| Languages | French, Hausa, | Map page | 115 |
| | Fulani, local | | |
| | languages | | |

## NIGERIA
Federal Republic of Nigeria

| Area Sq Km | 923 768 | Religions | Sunni Muslim, |
|---|---|---|---|
| Area Sq Miles | 356 669 | | Christian, traditional |
| Population | 124 009 000 | | beliefs |
| Capital | Abuja | Currency | Naira |
| Languages | English, Hausa, | Organizations | Comm., OPEC, UN |
| | Yoruba, Ibo, Fulani, | Map page | 115 |
| | local languages | | |

## Niue
Self-governing New Zealand Overseas Territory

| Area Sq Km | 258 | Religions | Christian |
|---|---|---|---|
| Area Sq Miles | 100 | Currency | New Zealand dollar |
| Population | 2 000 | Map page | 48 |
| Capital | Alofi | | |
| Languages | English, Polynesian | | |

## Norfolk Island
Australian External Territory

| Area Sq Km | 35 | Religions | Protestant, Roman |
|---|---|---|---|
| Area Sq Miles | 14 | | Catholic |
| Population | 2 037 | Currency | Australian dollar |
| Capital | Kingston | Map page | 48 |
| Languages | English | | |

## Northern Mariana Islands
United States Commonwealth

| Area Sq Km | 477 | Religions | Roman Catholic |
|---|---|---|---|
| Area Sq Miles | 184 | Currency | United States dollar |
| Population | 79 000 | Map page | 59 |
| Capital | Capitol Hill | | |
| Languages | English, Chamorro, | | |
| | local languages | | |

## NORTH KOREA
People's Democratic Republic of North Korea

| Area Sq Km | 120 538 | Religions | Traditional beliefs, |
|---|---|---|---|
| Area Sq Miles | 46 540 | | Chondoist, Buddhist |
| Population | 22 664 000 | Currency | North Korean won |
| Capital | P'yŏngyang | Organizations | UN |
| Languages | Korean | Map page | 65 |

## NORWAY
Kingdom of Norway

| | | | |
|---|---|---|---|
| Area Sq Km | 323 878 | Religions | Protestant, Roman |
| Area Sq Miles | 125 050 | | Catholic |
| Population | 4 533 000 | Currency | Norwegian krone |
| Capital | Oslo | Organizations | OECD, UN |
| Languages | Norwegian | Map page | 92–93 |

## OMAN
Sultanate of Oman

| | | | |
|---|---|---|---|
| Area Sq Km | 309 500 | Religions | Ibadhi Muslim, Sunni |
| Area Sq Miles | 119 499 | | Muslim |
| Population | 2 851 000 | Currency | Omani riyal |
| Capital | Muscat (Masqat) | Organizations | UN |
| Languages | Arabic, Baluchi, | Map page | 79 |
| | Indian languages | | |

## PAKISTAN
Islamic Republic of Pakistan

| | | | |
|---|---|---|---|
| Area Sq Km | 803 940 | Religions | Sunni Muslim, Shi'a |
| Area Sq Miles | 310 403 | | Muslim, Christian, |
| Population | 153 578 000 | | Hindu |
| Capital | Islamabad | Currency | Pakistani rupee |
| Languages | Urdu, Punjabi, | Organizations | Comm., UN |
| | Sindhi, Pushtu, | Map page | 74 |
| | English | | |

## PALAU
Republic of Palau

| | | | |
|---|---|---|---|
| Area Sq Km | 497 | Religions | Roman Catholic, |
| Area Sq Miles | 192 | | Protestant, traditional |
| Population | 20 000 | | beliefs |
| Capital | Koror | Currency | United States dollar |
| Languages | Palauan, English | Organizations | UN |
| | | Map page | 59 |

## PANAMA
Republic of Panama

| | | | |
|---|---|---|---|
| Area Sq Km | 77 082 | Religions | Roman Catholic, |
| Area Sq Miles | 29 762 | | Protestant, Sunni |
| Population | 3 120 000 | | Muslim |
| Capital | Panama City | Currency | Balboa |
| Languages | Spanish, English, | Organizations | UN |
| | Amerindian | Map page | 146 |
| | languages | | |

## PAPUA NEW GUINEA
Independent State of Papua New Guinea

| | | | |
|---|---|---|---|
| Area Sq Km | 462 840 | Religions | Protestant, Roman |
| Area Sq Miles | 178 704 | | Catholic, traditional |
| Population | 5 711 000 | | beliefs |
| Capital | Port Moresby | Currency | Kina |
| Languages | English, Tok Pisin | Organizations | Comm., UN |
| | (creole), local | Map page | 59 |
| | languages | | |

## PARAGUAY
Republic of Paraguay

| | | | |
|---|---|---|---|
| Area Sq Km | 406 752 | Religions | Roman Catholic, |
| Area Sq Miles | 157 048 | | Protestant |
| Population | 5 878 000 | Currency | Guaraní |
| Capital | Asunción | Organizations | UN |
| Languages | Spanish, Guaraní | Map page | 152 |

## PERU
Republic of Peru

| | | | |
|---|---|---|---|
| Area Sq Km | 1 285 216 | Religions | Roman Catholic, |
| Area Sq Miles | 496 225 | | Protestant |
| Population | 27 167 000 | Currency | Sol |
| Capital | Lima | Organizations | APEC, UN |
| Languages | Spanish, Quechua, | Map page | 150 |
| | Aymara | | |

## PHILIPPINES
Republic of the Philippines

| | | | |
|---|---|---|---|
| Area Sq Km | 300 000 | Religions | Roman Catholic, |
| Area Sq Miles | 115 831 | | Protestant, Sunni |
| Population | 79 999 000 | | Muslim, Aglipayan |
| Capital | Manila | Currency | Philippine peso |
| Languages | English, Filipino, | Organizations | APEC, ASEAN, UN |
| | Tagalog, Cebuano, | Map page | 64 |
| | local languages | | |

## Pitcairn Islands
United Kingdom Overseas Territory

| | | | |
|---|---|---|---|
| Area Sq Km | 45 | Religions | Protestant |
| Area Sq Miles | 17 | Currency | New Zealand dollar |
| Population | 51 | Map page | 49 |
| Capital | Adamstown | | |
| Languages | English | | |

## POLAND
Polish Republic

| | | | |
|---|---|---|---|
| Area Sq Km | 312 683 | Religions | Roman Catholic, |
| Area Sq Miles | 120 728 | | Polish Orthodox |
| Population | 38 587 000 | Currency | Złoty |
| Capital | Warsaw (Warszawa) | Organizations | OECD, UN |
| Languages | Polish, German | Map page | 103 |

## PORTUGAL
Portuguese Republic

| | | | |
|---|---|---|---|
| Area Sq Km | 88 940 | Religions | Roman Catholic, |
| Area Sq Miles | 34 340 | | Protestant |
| Population | 10 062 000 | Currency | Euro |
| Capital | Lisbon (Lisboa) | Organizations | EU, OECD, UN |
| Languages | Portuguese | Map page | 106 |

## Puerto Rico
United States Commonwealth

| | | | |
|---|---|---|---|
| Area Sq Km | 9 104 | Religions | Roman Catholic, |
| Area Sq Miles | 3 515 | | Protestant |
| Population | 3 879 000 | Currency | United States dollar |
| Capital | San Juan | Map page | 147 |
| Languages | Spanish, English | | |

## QATAR
State of Qatar

| | | | |
|---|---|---|---|
| Area Sq Km | 11 437 | Religions | Sunni Muslim |
| Area Sq Miles | 4 416 | Currency | Qatari riyal |
| Population | 610 000 | Organizations | OPEC, UN |
| Capital | Doha (Ad Dawḩah) | Map page | 79 |
| Languages | Arabic | | |

### Réunion
French Overseas Department

| | | | |
|---|---|---|---|
| Area Sq Km | 2 551 | Religions | Roman Catholic |
| Area Sq Miles | 985 | Currency | Euro |
| Population | 756 000 | Map page | 113 |
| Capital | St-Denis | | |
| Languages | French, creole | | |

### Rodrigues Island
part of Mauritius

| | | | |
|---|---|---|---|
| Area Sq Km | 104 | Religions | Christian |
| Area Sq Miles | 40 | Currency | Rupee |
| Population | 36 306 | Map page | 159 |
| Capital | Port Mathurin | | |
| Languages | English, creole | | |

### ROMANIA

| | | | |
|---|---|---|---|
| Area Sq Km | 237 500 | Religions | Romanian Orthodox, |
| Area Sq Miles | 91 699 | | Protestant, Roman |
| Population | 22 334 000 | | Catholic |
| Capital | Bucharest (Bucureşti) | Currency | Romanian leu |
| Languages | Romanian, | Organizations | UN |
| | Hungarian | Map page | 110 |

### RUSSIAN FEDERATION

| | | | |
|---|---|---|---|
| Area Sq Km | 17 075 400 | Religions | Russian Orthodox, |
| Area Sq Miles | 6 592 849 | | Sunni Muslim, |
| Population | 143 246 000 | | Protestant |
| Capital | Moscow (Moskva) | Currency | Russian rouble |
| Languages | Russian, Tatar, | Organizations | APEC, CIS, UN |
| | Ukrainian, local | Map page | 82–83 |
| | languages | | |

### RWANDA
Republic of Rwanda

| | | | |
|---|---|---|---|
| Area Sq Km | 26 338 | Religions | Roman Catholic, |
| Area Sq Miles | 10 169 | | traditional beliefs, |
| Population | 8 387 000 | | Protestant |
| Capital | Kigali | Currency | Rwandan franc |
| Languages | Kinyarwanda, | Organizations | UN |
| | French, English | Map page | 119 |

### Saba
part of Netherlands Antilles

| | | | |
|---|---|---|---|
| Area Sq Km | 13 | Religions | Roman Catholic, |
| Area Sq Miles | 5 | | Protestant |
| Population | 1 387 | Currency | Netherlands Antilles |
| Capital | Bottom | | guilder |
| Languages | Dutch, English | Map page | 147 |

### St Barthélémy
Dependency of Guadeloupe

| | | | |
|---|---|---|---|
| Area Sq Km | 21 | Religions | Roman Catholic |
| Area Sq Miles | 8 | Currency | Euro |
| Population | 6 852 | Map page | 147 |
| Capital | Gustavia | | |
| Languages | French, creole | | |

### St Helena
United Kingdom Overseas Territory

| | | | |
|---|---|---|---|
| Area Sq Km | 121 | Religions | Protestant, Roman |
| Area Sq Miles | 47 | | Catholic, |
| Population | 5 644 | Currency | St Helena pound |
| Capital | Jamestown | Map page | 113 |
| Languages | English | | |

### ST KITTS AND NEVIS
Federation of St Kitts and Nevis

| | | | |
|---|---|---|---|
| Area Sq Km | 261 | Religions | Protestant, Roman |
| Area Sq Miles | 101 | | Catholic |
| Population | 42 000 | Currency | East Caribbean doll |
| Capital | Basseterre | Organizations | CARICOM, Comm., |
| Languages | English, creole | | UN |
| | | Map page | 147 |

### ST LUCIA

| | | | |
|---|---|---|---|
| Area Sq Km | 616 | Religions | Roman Catholic, |
| Area Sq Miles | 238 | | Protestant |
| Population | 149 000 | Currency | East Caribbean doll |
| Capital | Castries | Organizations | CARICOM, Comm., |
| Languages | English, creole | | UN |
| | | Map page | 147 |

### St Martin
Dependency of Guadeloupe

| | | | |
|---|---|---|---|
| Area Sq Km | 54 | Religions | Roman Catholic |
| Area Sq Miles | 21 | Currency | Euro |
| Population | 29 078 | Map page | 147 |
| Capital | Marigot | | |
| Languages | French, creole | | |

### St Pierre and Miquelon
French Territorial Collectivity

| | | | |
|---|---|---|---|
| Area Sq Km | 242 | Religions | Roman Catholic |
| Area Sq Miles | 93 | Currency | Euro |
| Population | 6 000 | Map page | 131 |
| Capital | St-Pierre | | |
| Languages | French | | |

### ST VINCENT AND THE GRENADINES

| | | | |
|---|---|---|---|
| Area Sq Km | 389 | Religions | Protestant, Roman |
| Area Sq Miles | 150 | | Catholic |
| Population | 120 000 | Currency | East Caribbean doll |
| Capital | Kingstown | Organizations | CARICOM, Comm., |
| Languages | English, creole | | UN |
| | | Map page | 147 |

### SAMOA
Independent State of Samoa

| | | | |
|---|---|---|---|
| Area Sq Km | 2 831 | Religions | Protestant, Roman |
| Area Sq Miles | 1 093 | | Catholic |
| Population | 178 000 | Currency | Tala |
| Capital | Apia | Organizations | Comm., UN |
| Languages | Samoan, English | Map page | 49 |

## SAN MARINO
Republic of San Marino

| | | | |
|---|---|---|---|
| Area Sq Km | 61 | Religions | Roman Catholic |
| Area Sq Miles | 24 | Currency | Euro |
| Population | 28 000 | Organizations | UN |
| Capital | San Marino | Map page | 108 |
| Languages | Italian | | |

## SÃO TOMÉ AND PRÍNCIPE
Democratic Republic of São Tomé and Príncipe

| | | | |
|---|---|---|---|
| Area Sq Km | 964 | Religions | Roman Catholic, Protestant |
| Area Sq Miles | 372 | | |
| Population | 161 000 | Currency | Dobra |
| Capital | São Tomé | Organizations | UN |
| Languages | Portuguese, creole | Map page | 113 |

## SAUDI ARABIA
Kingdom of Saudi Arabia

| | | | |
|---|---|---|---|
| Area Sq Km | 2 200 000 | Religions | Sunni Muslim, Shi'a Muslim |
| Area Sq Miles | 849 425 | | |
| Population | 24 217 000 | Currency | Saudi Arabian riyal |
| Capital | Riyadh (Ar Riyāḍ) | Organizations | OPEC, UN |
| Languages | Arabic | Map page | 78–79 |

## SENEGAL
Republic of Senegal

| | | | |
|---|---|---|---|
| Area Sq Km | 196 720 | Religions | Sunni Muslim, Roman Catholic, traditional beliefs |
| Area Sq Miles | 75 954 | | |
| Population | 10 095 000 | | |
| Capital | Dakar | Currency | CFA franc |
| Languages | French, Wolof, Fulani, local languages | Organizations | UN |
| | | Map page | 114 |

## SERBIA AND MONTENEGRO

| | | | |
|---|---|---|---|
| Area Sq Km | 102 173 | Religions | Serbian Orthodox, Montenegrin Orthodox, Sunni Muslim |
| Area Sq Miles | 39 449 | | |
| Population | 10 527 000 | | |
| Capital | Belgrade (Beograd) | Currency | Serbian dinar, Euro |
| Languages | Serbian, Albanian, Hungarian | Organizations | UN |
| | | Map page | 109 |

## SEYCHELLES
Republic of the Seychelles

| | | | |
|---|---|---|---|
| Area Sq Km | 455 | Religions | Roman Catholic, Protestant |
| Area Sq Miles | 176 | | |
| Population | 81 000 | Currency | Seychelles rupee |
| Capital | Victoria | Organizations | Comm., SADC, UN |
| Languages | English, French, creole | Map page | 113 |

## SIERRA LEONE
Republic of Sierra Leone

| | | | |
|---|---|---|---|
| Area Sq Km | 71 740 | Religions | Sunni Muslim, traditional beliefs |
| Area Sq Miles | 27 699 | | |
| Population | 4 971 000 | Currency | Leone |
| Capital | Freetown | Organizations | Comm., UN |
| Languages | English, creole, Mende, Temne, local languages | Map page | 114 |

## SINGAPORE
Republic of Singapore

| | | | |
|---|---|---|---|
| Area Sq Km | 639 | Religions | Buddhist, Taoist, Sunni Muslim, Christian, Hindu |
| Area Sq Miles | 247 | | |
| Population | 4 253 000 | | |
| Capital | Singapore | Currency | Singapore dollar |
| Languages | Chinese, English, Malay, Tamil | Organizations | APEC, ASEAN, Comm., UN |
| | | Map page | 60 |

## Sint Eustatius
part of Netherlands Antilles

| | | | |
|---|---|---|---|
| Area Sq Km | 21 | Religions | Protestant, Roman Catholic |
| Area Sq Miles | 8 | | |
| Population | 2 829 | Currency | Netherlands Antilles guilder |
| Capital | Oranjestad | | |
| Languages | Dutch, English | Map page | 147 |

## Sint Maarten
part of Netherlands Antilles

| | | | |
|---|---|---|---|
| Area Sq Km | 34 | Religions | Protestant, Roman Catholic |
| Area Sq Miles | 13 | | |
| Population | 31 882 | Currency | Netherlands Antilles guilder |
| Capital | Philipsburg | | |
| Languages | Dutch, English | Map page | 147 |

## SLOVAKIA
Slovak Republic

| | | | |
|---|---|---|---|
| Area Sq Km | 49 035 | Religions | Roman Catholic, Protestant, Orthodox |
| Area Sq Miles | 18 933 | | |
| Population | 5 402 000 | Currency | Slovakian koruna |
| Capital | Bratislava | Organizations | UN |
| Languages | Slovakian, Hungarian, Czech | Map page | 103 |

## SLOVENIA
Republic of Slovenia

| | | | |
|---|---|---|---|
| Area Sq Km | 20 251 | Religions | Roman Catholic, Protestant |
| Area Sq Miles | 7 819 | | |
| Population | 1 984 000 | Currency | Tólar |
| Capital | Ljubljana | Organizations | UN |
| Languages | Slovene, Croatian, Serbian | Map page | 108–109 |

## SOLOMON ISLANDS

| | | | |
|---|---|---|---|
| Area Sq Km | 28 370 | Religions | Protestant, Roman Catholic |
| Area Sq Miles | 10 954 | | |
| Population | 477 000 | Currency | Solomon Islands dollar |
| Capital | Honiara | Organizations | Comm., UN |
| Languages | English, creole, local languages | Map page | 48 |

## SOMALIA
Somali Democratic Republic

| | | | |
|---|---|---|---|
| Area Sq Km | 637 657 | Religions | Sunni Muslim |
| Area Sq Miles | 246 201 | Currency | Somali shilling |
| Population | 9 890 000 | Organizations | UN |
| Capital | Mogadishu (Muqdisho) | Map page | 117 |
| Languages | Somali, Arabic | | |

## SOUTH AFRICA, REPUBLIC OF

| | | | |
|---|---|---|---|
| Area Sq Km | 1 219 080 | Religions | Protestant, Roman Catholic, Sunni Muslim, Hindu |
| Area Sq Miles | 470 689 | | |
| Population | 45 026 000 | | |
| Capital | Pretoria (Tshwane) /Cape Town | Currency | Rand |
| | | Organizations | Comm., SADC, UN |
| Languages | Afrikaans, English, nine official local languages | Map page | 122–123 |

## SOUTH KOREA
Republic of Korea

| | | | |
|---|---|---|---|
| Area Sq Km | 99 274 | Religions | Buddhist, Protestant, Roman Catholic |
| Area Sq Miles | 38 330 | | |
| Population | 47 700 000 | Currency | South Korean won |
| Capital | Seoul (Sŏul) | Organizations | APEC, UN |
| Languages | Korean | Map page | 65 |

## SPAIN
Kingdom of Spain

| | | | |
|---|---|---|---|
| Area Sq Km | 504 782 | Religions | Roman Catholic |
| Area Sq Miles | 194 897 | Currency | Euro |
| Population | 41 060 000 | Organizations | EU, OECD, UN |
| Capital | Madrid | Map page | 106–107 |
| Languages | Castilian, Catalan, Galician, Basque | | |

## SRI LANKA
Democratic Socialist Republic of Sri Lanka

| | | | |
|---|---|---|---|
| Area Sq Km | 65 610 | Religions | Buddhist, Hindu, Sunni Muslim, Roman Catholic |
| Area Sq Miles | 25 332 | | |
| Population | 19 065 000 | | |
| Capital | Sri Jayewardenepura Kotte | Currency | Sri Lankan rupee |
| | | Organizations | Comm., UN |
| Languages | Sinhalese, Tamil, English | Map page | 73 |

## SUDAN
Republic of the Sudan

| | | | |
|---|---|---|---|
| Area Sq Km | 2 505 813 | Religions | Sunni Muslim, traditional beliefs, Christian |
| Area Sq Miles | 967 500 | | |
| Population | 33 610 000 | | |
| Capital | Khartoum | Currency | Sudanese dinar |
| Languages | Arabic, Dinka, Nubian, Beja, Nuer, local languages | Organizations | UN |
| | | Map page | 116–117 |

## SURINAME
Republic of Suriname

| | | | |
|---|---|---|---|
| Area Sq Km | 163 820 | Religions | Hindu, Roman Catholic, Protestant, Sunni Muslim |
| Area Sq Miles | 63 251 | | |
| Population | 436 000 | | |
| Capital | Paramaribo | Currency | Suriname guilder |
| Languages | Dutch, Surinamese, English, Hindi | Organizations | CARICOM, UN |
| | | Map page | 151 |

## Svalbard
part of Norway

| | | | |
|---|---|---|---|
| Area Sq Km | 61 229 | Religions | Protestant |
| Area Sq Miles | 23 641 | Currency | Norwegian krone |
| Population | 2 515 | Map page | 82 |
| Capital | Longyearbyen | | |
| Languages | Norwegian | | |

## SWAZILAND
Kingdom of Swaziland

| | | | |
|---|---|---|---|
| Area Sq Km | 17 364 | Currency | Emalangeni, South African rand |
| Area Sq Miles | 6 704 | | |
| Population | 1 077 000 | Organizations | Comm., SADC, UN |
| Capital | Mbabane | Map page | 123 |
| Languages | Swazi, English | | |
| Religions | Christian, traditional beliefs | | |

## SWEDEN
Kingdom of Sweden

| | | | |
|---|---|---|---|
| Area Sq Km | 449 964 | Religions | Protestant, Roman Catholic |
| Area Sq Miles | 173 732 | | |
| Population | 8 876 000 | Currency | Swedish krona |
| Capital | Stockholm | Organizations | EU, OECD, UN |
| Languages | Swedish | Map page | 92–93 |

## SWITZERLAND
Swiss Confederation

| | | | |
|---|---|---|---|
| Area Sq Km | 41 293 | Religions | Roman Catholic, Protestant, |
| Area Sq Miles | 15 943 | | |
| Population | 7 169 000 | Currency | Swiss franc |
| Capital | Bern (Berne) | Organizations | OECD, UN |
| Languages | German, French, Italian, Romansch | Map page | 105 |

## SYRIA
Syrian Arab Republic

| | | | |
|---|---|---|---|
| Area Sq Km | 185 180 | Religions | Sunni Muslim, Shi'a Muslim, Christian |
| Area Sq Miles | 71 498 | | |
| Population | 17 800 000 | Currency | Syrian pound |
| Capital | Damascus (Dimashq) | Organizations | UN |
| Languages | Arabic, Kurdish, Armenian | Map page | 80 |

## TAIWAN
Republic of China

| | | | |
|---|---|---|---|
| Area Sq Km | 36 179 | Religions | Buddhist, Taoist, Confucian, Christian |
| Area Sq Miles | 13 969 | | |
| Population | 22 548 009 | Currency | Taiwan dollar |
| Capital | T'aipei | Organizations | APEC |
| Languages | Mandarin, Min, Hakka, local languages | Map page | 71 |

## TAJIKISTAN
Republic of Tajikistan

| | | | |
|---|---|---|---|
| Area Sq Km | 143 100 | Religions | Sunni Muslim |
| Area Sq Miles | 55 251 | Currency | Somoni |
| Population | 6 245 000 | Organizations | CIS, UN |
| Capital | Dushanbe | Map page | 77 |
| Languages | Tajik, Uzbek, Russian | | |

## TANZANIA
United Republic of Tanzania

| | | | |
|---|---|---|---|
| Area Sq Km | 945 087 | Religions | Shi'a Muslim, Sunni Muslim, traditional beliefs, Christian |
| Area Sq Miles | 364 900 | | |
| Population | 36 977 000 | | |
| Capital | Dodoma | Currency | Tanzanian shilling |
| Languages | Swahili, English, Nyamwezi, local languages | Organizations | Comm., SADC, UN |
| | | Map page | 119 |

## THAILAND
Kingdom of Thailand

| | | | |
|---|---|---|---|
| Area Sq Km | 513 115 | Religions | Buddhist, Sunni Muslim |
| Area Sq Miles | 198 115 | | |
| Population | 62 833 000 | Currency | Baht |
| Capital | Bangkok (Krung Thep) | Organizations | APEC, ASEAN, UN |
| | | Map page | 62–63 |
| Languages | Thai, Lao, Chinese, Malay, Mon-Khmer languages | | |

## TOGO
Republic of Togo

| | | | |
|---|---|---|---|
| Area Sq Km | 56 785 | Religions | Traditional beliefs, Christian, Sunni Muslim |
| Area Sq Miles | 21 925 | | |
| Population | 4 909 000 | | |
| Capital | Lomé | Currency | CFA franc |
| Languages | French, Ewe, Kabre, local languages | Organizations | UN |
| | | Map page | 114 |

## Tokelau
New Zealand Overseas Territory

| | | | |
|---|---|---|---|
| Area Sq Km | 10 | Religions | Christian |
| Area Sq Miles | 4 | Currency | New Zealand dollar |
| Population | 2 000 | Map page | 49 |
| Capital | none | | |
| Languages | English, Tokelauan | | |

## TONGA
Kingdom of Tonga

| | | | |
|---|---|---|---|
| Area Sq Km | 748 | Religions | Protestant, Roman Catholic |
| Area Sq Miles | 289 | | |
| Population | 104 000 | Currency | Pa'anga |
| Capital | Nuku'alofa | Organizations | Comm., UN |
| Languages | Tongan, English | Map page | 49 |

## TRINIDAD AND TOBAGO
Republic of Trinidad and Tobago

| | | | |
|---|---|---|---|
| Area Sq Km | 5 130 | Religions | Roman Catholic, Hindu, Protestant, Sunni Muslim |
| Area Sq Miles | 1 981 | | |
| Population | 1 303 000 | | |
| Capital | Port of Spain | Currency | Trinidad and Tobago dollar |
| Languages | English, creole, Hindi | | |
| | | Organizations | CARICOM, Comm., UN |
| | | Map page | 147 |

## Tristan da Cunha
Dependency of St Helena

| | | | |
|---|---|---|---|
| Area Sq Km | 98 | Religions | Protestant, Roman Catholic |
| Area Sq Miles | 38 | | |
| Population | 284 | Currency | Pound sterling |
| Capital | Settlement of Edinburgh | Map page | 113 |
| Languages | English | | |

## TUNISIA
Republic of Tunisia

| | | | |
|---|---|---|---|
| Area Sq Km | 164 150 | Religions | Sunni Muslim |
| Area Sq Miles | 63 379 | Currency | Tunisian dinar |
| Population | 9 832 000 | Organizations | UN |
| Capital | Tunis | Map page | 115 |
| Languages | Arabic, French | | |

## TURKEY
Republic of Turkey

| | | | |
|---|---|---|---|
| Area Sq Km | 779 452 | Religions | Sunni Muslim, Shi'a Muslim |
| Area Sq Miles | 300 948 | | |
| Population | 71 325 000 | Currency | Turkish lira |
| Capital | Ankara | Organizations | OECD, UN |
| Languages | Turkish, Kurdish | Map page | 80 |

## TURKMENISTAN
Republic of Turkmenistan

| | | | |
|---|---|---|---|
| Area Sq Km | 488 100 | Religions | Sunni Muslim, Russian Orthodox |
| Area Sq Miles | 188 456 | | |
| Population | 4 867 000 | Currency | Turkmen manat |
| Capital | Ashgabat (Ashkhabad) | Organizations | CIS, UN |
| Languages | Turkmen, Uzbek, Russian | Map page | 76 |

## Turks and Caicos Islands
United Kingdom Overseas Territory

| | | | |
|---|---|---|---|
| Area Sq Km | 430 | Religions | Protestant |
| Area Sq Miles | 166 | Currency | United States dollar |
| Population | 21 000 | Map page | 147 |
| Capital | Grand Turk | | |
| Languages | English | | |

## TUVALU

| | | | |
|---|---|---|---|
| Area Sq Km | 25 | Religions | Protestant |
| Area Sq Miles | 10 | Currency | Australian dollar |
| Population | 11 000 | Organizations | Comm. |
| Capital | Vaiaku | Map page | 49 |
| Languages | Tuvaluan, English | | |

## UGANDA
### Republic of Uganda

| | | | |
|---|---|---|---|
| Area Sq Km | 241 038 | Religions | Roman Catholic, Protestant, Sunni Muslim, traditional beliefs |
| Area Sq Miles | 93 065 | | |
| Population | 25 827 000 | | |
| Capital | Kampala | | |
| Languages | English, Swahili, Luganda, local languages | Currency | Ugandan shilling |
| | | Organizations | Comm., UN |
| | | Map page | 119 |

## UKRAINE
### Republic of Ukraine

| | | | |
|---|---|---|---|
| Area Sq Km | 603 700 | Religions | Ukrainian Orthodox, Ukrainian Catholic, Roman Catholic |
| Area Sq Miles | 233 090 | | |
| Population | 48 523 000 | | |
| Capital | Kiev (Kyiv) | Currency | Hryvnia |
| Languages | Ukrainian, Russian | Organizations | CIS, UN |
| | | Map page | 90–91 |

## UNITED ARAB EMIRATES
### Federation of Emirates

| | | | |
|---|---|---|---|
| Area Sq Km | 77 700 | Religions | Sunni Muslim, Shi'a Muslim |
| Area Sq Miles | 30 000 | | |
| Population | 2 995 000 | Currency | United Arab Emirates dirham |
| Capital | Abu Dhabi (Abū Ẓabī) | | |
| | | Organizations | OPEC, UN |
| Languages | Arabic, English | Map page | 79 |

### Abu Dhabi (Abū Ẓabī) (Emirate)

| | | | |
|---|---|---|---|
| Area Sq Km | 67 340 | Population | 1 248 000 |
| Area Sq Miles | 26 000 | Capital | Abu Dhabi (Abū Ẓabī) |

### Ajman (Emirate)

| | | | |
|---|---|---|---|
| Area Sq Km | 259 | Population | 189 000 |
| Area Sq Miles | 100 | Capital | Ajman |

### Dubai (Emirate)

| | | | |
|---|---|---|---|
| Area Sq Km | 3 885 | Population | 971 000 |
| Area Sq Miles | 1 500 | Capital | Dubai |

### Fujairah (Emirate)

| | | | |
|---|---|---|---|
| Area Sq Km | 1 165 | Population | 103 000 |
| Area Sq Miles | 450 | Capital | Fujairah |

### Ras al Khaimah (Emirate)

| | | | |
|---|---|---|---|
| Area Sq Km | 1 684 | Population | 179 000 |
| Area Sq Miles | 650 | Capital | Ras al Khaimah |

### Sharjah (Emirate)

| | | | |
|---|---|---|---|
| Area Sq Km | 2 590 | Population | 551 000 |
| Area Sq Miles | 1 000 | Capital | Sharjah |

### Umm al Qaiwain (Emirate)

| | | | |
|---|---|---|---|
| Area Sq Km | 777 | Population | 49 000 |
| Area Sq Miles | 300 | Capital | Umm al Qaiwain |

## UNITED KINGDOM
### of Great Britain and Northern Ireland

| | | | |
|---|---|---|---|
| Area Sq Km | 243 609 | Religions | Protestant, Roman Catholic, Muslim |
| Area Sq Miles | 94 058 | | |
| Population | 58 789 194 | Currency | Pound sterling |
| Capital | London | Organizations | Comm., EU, OECD, UN |
| Languages | English, Welsh, Gaelic | | |
| | | Map page | 94–95 |

### England (Constituent country)

| | | | |
|---|---|---|---|
| Area Sq Km | 130 433 | Population | 49 138 831 |
| Area Sq Miles | 50 360 | Capital | London |

### Northern Ireland (Province)

| | | | |
|---|---|---|---|
| Area Sq Km | 13 576 | Population | 1 685 267 |
| Area Sq Miles | 5 242 | Capital | Belfast |

### Scotland (Constituent country)

| | | | |
|---|---|---|---|
| Area Sq Km | 78 822 | Population | 5 062 011 |
| Area Sq Miles | 30 433 | Capital | Edinburgh |

### Wales (Principality)

| | | | |
|---|---|---|---|
| Area Sq Km | 20 778 | Population | 2 903 085 |
| Area Sq Miles | 8 022 | Capital | Cardiff |

## UNITED STATES OF AMERICA
### Federal Republic

| | | | |
|---|---|---|---|
| Area Sq Km | 9 826 635 | Religions | Protestant, Roman Catholic, Sunni Muslim, Jewish |
| Area Sq Miles | 3 794 085 | | |
| Population | 294 043 000 | | |
| Capital | Washington D.C. | Currency | United States dollar |
| Languages | English, Spanish | Organizations | APEC, OECD, UN |
| | | Map page | 132–133 |

### Alabama (State)

| | | | |
|---|---|---|---|
| Area Sq Km | 135 765 | Population | 4 486 508 |
| Area Sq Miles | 52 419 | Capital | Montgomery |

### Alaska (State)

| | | | |
|---|---|---|---|
| Area Sq Km | 1 717 854 | Population | 643 786 |
| Area Sq Miles | 663 267 | Capital | Juneau |

### Arizona (State)

| | | | |
|---|---|---|---|
| Area Sq Km | 295 253 | Population | 5 456 453 |
| Area Sq Miles | 113 998 | Capital | Phoenix |

### Arkansas (State)

| | | | |
|---|---|---|---|
| Area Sq Km | 137 733 | Population | 2 710 079 |
| Area Sq Miles | 53 179 | Capital | Little Rock |

### California (State)

| | | | |
|---|---|---|---|
| Area Sq Km | 423 971 | Population | 35 116 033 |
| Area Sq Miles | 163 696 | Capital | Sacramento |

## Colorado (State)

| | | | |
|---|---|---|---|
| Area Sq Km | 269 602 | Population | 4 506 542 |
| Area Sq Miles | 104 094 | Capital | Denver |

## Connecticut (State)

| | | | |
|---|---|---|---|
| Area Sq Km | 14 356 | Population | 3 460 503 |
| Area Sq Miles | 5 543 | Capital | Hartford |

## Delaware (State)

| | | | |
|---|---|---|---|
| Area Sq Km | 6 446 | Population | 807 385 |
| Area Sq Miles | 2 489 | Capital | Dover |

## District of Columbia (District)

| | | | |
|---|---|---|---|
| Area Sq Km | 176 | Population | 570 898 |
| Area Sq Miles | 68 | Capital | Washington |

## Florida (State)

| | | | |
|---|---|---|---|
| Area Sq Km | 170 305 | Population | 16 713 149 |
| Area Sq Miles | 65 755 | Capital | Tallahassee |

## Georgia (State)

| | | | |
|---|---|---|---|
| Area Sq Km | 69 700 | Population | 5 126 000 |
| Area Sq Miles | 26 911 | Capital | Atlanta |

## Hawaii (State)

| | | | |
|---|---|---|---|
| Area Sq Km | 28 311 | Population | 1 244 898 |
| Area Sq Miles | 10 931 | Capital | Honolulu |

## Idaho (State)

| | | | |
|---|---|---|---|
| Area Sq Km | 216 445 | Population | 1 341 131 |
| Area Sq Miles | 83 570 | Capital | Boise |

## Illinois (State)

| | | | |
|---|---|---|---|
| Area Sq Km | 149 997 | Population | 12 600 620 |
| Area Sq Miles | 57 914 | Capital | Springfield |

## Indiana (State)

| | | | |
|---|---|---|---|
| Area Sq Km | 94 322 | Population | 6 159 068 |
| Area Sq Miles | 36 418 | Capital | Indianapolis |

## Iowa (State)

| | | | |
|---|---|---|---|
| Area Sq Km | 145 744 | Population | 2 936 760 |
| Area Sq Miles | 56 272 | Capital | Des Moines |

## Kansas (State)

| | | | |
|---|---|---|---|
| Area Sq Km | 213 096 | Population | 2 715 884 |
| Area Sq Miles | 82 277 | Capital | Topeka |

## Kentucky (State)

| | | | |
|---|---|---|---|
| Area Sq Km | 104 659 | Population | 4 092 891 |
| Area Sq Miles | 40 409 | Capital | Frankfort |

## Louisiana (State)

| | | | |
|---|---|---|---|
| Area Sq Km | 134 265 | Population | 4 482 646 |
| Area Sq Miles | 51 840 | Capital | Baton Rouge |

## Maine (State)

| | | | |
|---|---|---|---|
| Area Sq Km | 91 647 | Population | 1 294 464 |
| Area Sq Miles | 35 385 | Capital | Augusta |

## Maryland (State)

| | | | |
|---|---|---|---|
| Area Sq Km | 32 134 | Population | 5 458 137 |
| Area Sq Miles | 12 407 | Capital | Annapolis |

## Massachusetts (State)

| | | | |
|---|---|---|---|
| Area Sq Km | 27 337 | Population | 6 427 801 |
| Area Sq Miles | 10 555 | Capital | Boston |

## Michigan (State)

| | | | |
|---|---|---|---|
| Area Sq Km | 250 493 | Population | 10 050 446 |
| Area Sq Miles | 96 716 | Capital | Lansing |

## Minnesota (State)

| | | | |
|---|---|---|---|
| Area Sq Km | 225 171 | Population | 5 019 720 |
| Area Sq Miles | 86 939 | Capital | St Paul |

## Mississippi (State)

| | | | |
|---|---|---|---|
| Area Sq Km | 125 433 | Population | 2 871 782 |
| Area Sq Miles | 48 430 | Capital | Jackson |

## Missouri (State)

| | | | |
|---|---|---|---|
| Area Sq Km | 180 533 | Population | 5 672 579 |
| Area Sq Miles | 69 704 | Capital | Jefferson City |

## Montana (State)

| | | | |
|---|---|---|---|
| Area Sq Km | 380 837 | Population | 909 453 |
| Area Sq Miles | 147 042 | Capital | Helena |

## Nebraska (State)

| | | | |
|---|---|---|---|
| Area Sq Km | 200 346 | Population | 1 729 180 |
| Area Sq Miles | 77 354 | Capital | Lincoln |

## Nevada (State)

| | | | |
|---|---|---|---|
| Area Sq Km | 286 352 | Population | 2 173 491 |
| Area Sq Miles | 110 561 | Capital | Carson City |

## New Hampshire (State)

| | | | |
|---|---|---|---|
| Area Sq Km | 24 216 | Population | 1 275 056 |
| Area Sq Miles | 9 350 | Capital | Concord |

## New Jersey (State)

| | | | |
|---|---|---|---|
| Area Sq Km | 22 587 | Population | 8 590 300 |
| Area Sq Miles | 8 721 | Capital | Trenton |

**STATES AND TERRITORIES**

## UNITED STATES OF AMERICA
Federal Republic

**New Mexico (State)**

| | | | |
|---|---|---|---|
| Area Sq Km | 314 914 | Population | 1 855 059 |
| Area Sq Miles | 121 589 | Capital | Santa Fe |

**New York (State)**

| | | | |
|---|---|---|---|
| Area Sq Km | 141 299 | Population | 19 157 532 |
| Area Sq Miles | 54 556 | Capital | Albany |

**North Carolina (State)**

| | | | |
|---|---|---|---|
| Area Sq Km | 139 391 | Population | 8 320 146 |
| Area Sq Miles | 53 819 | Capital | Raleigh |

**North Dakota (State)**

| | | | |
|---|---|---|---|
| Area Sq Km | 183 112 | Population | 634 110 |
| Area Sq Miles | 70 700 | Capital | Bismarck |

**Ohio (State)**

| | | | |
|---|---|---|---|
| Area Sq Km | 116 096 | Population | 11 421 267 |
| Area Sq Miles | 44 825 | Capital | Columbus |

**Oklahoma (State)**

| | | | |
|---|---|---|---|
| Area Sq Km | 181 035 | Population | 3 493 714 |
| Area Sq Miles | 69 898 | Capital | Oklahoma City |

**Oregon (State)**

| | | | |
|---|---|---|---|
| Area Sq Km | 254 806 | Population | 3 521 515 |
| Area Sq Miles | 98 381 | Capital | Salem |

**Pennsylvania (State)**

| | | | |
|---|---|---|---|
| Area Sq Km | 119 282 | Population | 12 335 091 |
| Area Sq Miles | 46 055 | Capital | Harrisburg |

**Rhode Island (State)**

| | | | |
|---|---|---|---|
| Area Sq Km | 4 002 | Population | 1 069 725 |
| Area Sq Miles | 1 545 | Capital | Providence |

**South Carolina (State)**

| | | | |
|---|---|---|---|
| Area Sq Km | 82 931 | Population | 4 107 183 |
| Area Sq Miles | 32 020 | Capital | Columbia |

**South Dakota (State)**

| | | | |
|---|---|---|---|
| Area Sq Km | 199 730 | Population | 761 063 |
| Area Sq Miles | 77 116 | Capital | Pierre |

**Tennessee (State)**

| | | | |
|---|---|---|---|
| Area Sq Km | 109 150 | Population | 5 797 289 |
| Area Sq Miles | 42 143 | Capital | Nashville |

**Texas (State)**

| | | | |
|---|---|---|---|
| Area Sq Km | 695 622 | Population | 21 779 893 |
| Area Sq Miles | 268 581 | Capital | Austin |

**Utah (State)**

| | | | |
|---|---|---|---|
| Area Sq Km | 219 887 | Population | 2 316 256 |
| Area Sq Miles | 84 899 | Capital | Salt Lake City |

**Vermont (State)**

| | | | |
|---|---|---|---|
| Area Sq Km | 24 900 | Population | 616 592 |
| Area Sq Miles | 9 614 | Capital | Montpelier |

**Virginia (State)**

| | | | |
|---|---|---|---|
| Area Sq Km | 110 784 | Population | 7 293 542 |
| Area Sq Miles | 42 774 | Capital | Richmond |

**Washington (State)**

| | | | |
|---|---|---|---|
| Area Sq Km | 184 666 | Population | 6 068 996 |
| Area Sq Miles | 71 300 | Capital | Olympia |

**West Virginia (State)**

| | | | |
|---|---|---|---|
| Area Sq Km | 62 755 | Population | 1 801 873 |
| Area Sq Miles | 24 230 | Capital | Charleston |

**Wisconsin (State)**

| | | | |
|---|---|---|---|
| Area Sq Km | 169 639 | Population | 5 441 196 |
| Area Sq Miles | 65 498 | Capital | Madison |

**Wyoming (State)**

| | | | |
|---|---|---|---|
| Area Sq Km | 253 337 | Population | 498 703 |
| Area Sq Miles | 97 814 | Capital | Cheyenne |

## URUGUAY
Oriental Republic of Uruguay

| | | | |
|---|---|---|---|
| Area Sq Km | 176 215 | Religions | Roman Catholic, Protestant, Jewish |
| Area Sq Miles | 68 037 | | |
| Population | 3 415 000 | Currency | Uruguayan peso |
| Capital | Montevideo | Organizations | UN |
| Languages | Spanish | Map page | 153 |

## UZBEKISTAN
Republic of Uzbekistan

| | | | |
|---|---|---|---|
| Area Sq Km | 447 400 | Religions | Sunni Muslim, Russian Orthodox |
| Area Sq Miles | 172 742 | | |
| Population | 26 093 000 | Currency | Uzbek som |
| Capital | Tashkent | Organizations | CIS, UN |
| Languages | Uzbek, Russian, Tajik, Kazakh | Map page | 76–77 |

## Wallis and Futuna Islands
French Overseas Territory

| | | | |
|---|---|---|---|
| Area Sq Km | 274 | Religions | Roman Catholic |
| Area Sq Miles | 106 | Currency | CFP franc |
| Population | 15 000 | Map page | 49 |
| Capital | Matā'utu | | |
| Languages | French, Wallisian, Futunian | | |

## VANUATU
Republic of Vanuatu

| | | | |
|---|---|---|---|
| Area Sq Km | 12 190 | Religions | Protestant, Roman Catholic, traditional beliefs |
| Area Sq Miles | 4 707 | | |
| Population | 212 000 | | |
| Capital | Port Vila | Currency | Vatu |
| Languages | English, Bislama (creole), French | Organizations | Comm., UN |
| | | Map page | 48 |

## West Bank
Disputed Territory

| | | | |
|---|---|---|---|
| Area Sq Km | 5 860 | Religions | Sunni Muslim, Jewish, Shi'a Muslim, Christian |
| Area Sq Miles | 2 263 | | |
| Population | 2 303 660 | Currency | Jordanian dinar, Isreali shekel |
| Capital | none | | |
| Languages | Arabic, Hebrew | Map page | 80 |

## VATICAN CITY
Vatican City State

| | | | |
|---|---|---|---|
| Area Sq Km | 0.5 | Religions | Roman Catholic |
| Area Sq Miles | 0.2 | Currency | Euro |
| Population | 472 | Map page | 108 |
| Capital | Vatican City | | |
| Languages | Italian | | |

## Western Sahara
Disputed territory (Morocco)

| | | | |
|---|---|---|---|
| Area Sq Km | 266 000 | Religions | Sunni Muslim |
| Area Sq Miles | 102 703 | Currency | Moroccan dirham |
| Population | 308 000 | Map page | 114 |
| Capital | Laâyoune | | |
| Languages | Arabic | | |

## VENEZUELA
Republic of Venezuela

| | | | |
|---|---|---|---|
| Area Sq Km | 912 050 | Religions | Roman Catholic, Protestant |
| Area Sq Miles | 352 144 | | |
| Population | 25 699 000 | Currency | Bolívar |
| Capital | Caracas | Organizations | OPEC, UN |
| Languages | Spanish, Amerindian languages | Map page | 150 |

## YEMEN
Republic of Yemen

| | | | |
|---|---|---|---|
| Area Sq Km | 527 968 | Religions | Sunni Muslim, Shi'a Muslim |
| Area Sq Miles | 203 850 | | |
| Population | 20 010 000 | Currency | Yemeni riyal |
| Capital | Şan'a' | Organizations | UN |
| Languages | Arabic | Map page | 78–79 |

## VIETNAM
Socialist Republic of Vietnam

| | | | |
|---|---|---|---|
| Area Sq Km | 329 565 | Religions | Buddhist, Taoist, Roman Catholic, Cao Dai, Hoa Hoa |
| Area Sq Miles | 127 246 | | |
| Population | 81 377 000 | | |
| Capital | Ha Nôi (Hanoi) | Currency | Dong |
| Languages | Vietnamese, Thai, Khmer, Chinese, local languages | Organizations | APEC, ASEAN, UN |
| | | Map page | 62–63 |

## ZAMBIA
Republic of Zambia

| | | | |
|---|---|---|---|
| Area Sq Km | 752 614 | Religions | Christian, traditional beliefs |
| Area Sq Miles | 290 586 | | |
| Population | 10 812 000 | Currency | Zambian kwacha |
| Capital | Lusaka | Organizations | Comm., SADC, UN |
| Languages | English, Bemba, Nyanja, Tonga, local languages | Map page | 120–121 |

## Virgin Islands (U.K.)
United Kingdom Overseas Territory

| | | | |
|---|---|---|---|
| Area Sq Km | 153 | Religions | Protestant, Roman Catholic |
| Area Sq Miles | 59 | | |
| Population | 21 000 | Currency | United States dollar |
| Capital | Road Town | Map page | 147 |
| Languages | English | | |

## ZIMBABWE
Republic of Zimbabwe

| | | | |
|---|---|---|---|
| Area Sq Km | 390 759 | Religions | Christian, traditional beliefs |
| Area Sq Miles | 150 873 | | |
| Population | 12 891 000 | Currency | Zimbabwean dollar |
| Capital | Harare | Organizations | SADC, UN |
| Languages | English, Shona, Ndebele | Map page | 121 |

## Virgin Islands (U.S.)
United States Unincorporated Territory

| | | | |
|---|---|---|---|
| Area Sq Km | 352 | Religions | Protestant, Roman Catholic |
| Area Sq Miles | 136 | | |
| Population | 111 000 | Currency | United States dollar |
| Capital | Charlotte Amalie | Map page | 147 |
| Languages | English, Spanish | | |

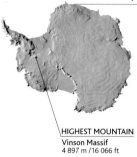

## ANTARCTICA
Total Land Area
12 093 000 sq km
4 669 292 sq miles
(excluding ice shelves)

HIGHEST MOUNTAIN
Vinson Massif
4 897 m / 16 066 ft

## OCEANIA
Total land area
8 844 516 sq km
3 414 887 sq miles
(includes New Guinea and
Pacific Island nations)

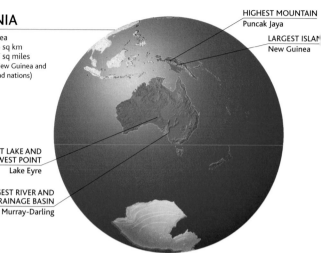

HIGHEST MOUNTAIN
Puncak Jaya

LARGEST ISLAND
New Guinea

LARGEST LAKE AND
LOWEST POINT
Lake Eyre

LONGEST RIVER AND
LARGEST DRAINAGE BASIN
Murray-Darling

| HIGHEST MOUNTAINS | HEIGHT metres | feet | LARGEST ISLANDS | AREA sq km | sq miles | LARGEST LAKES | AREA sq km | sq miles | LONGEST RIVERS | LENGTH km | miles |
|---|---|---|---|---|---|---|---|---|---|---|---|
| Puncak Jaya | 5 030 | 16 502 | New Guinea | 808 510 | 312 167 | Lake Eyre | 0–8 900 | 0–3 436 | Murray-Darling | 3 750 | 2 330 |
| Puncak Trikora | 4 730 | 15 518 | South Island | 151 215 | 58 384 | Lake Torrens | 0–5 780 | 0–2 232 | Darling | 2 739 | 1 702 |
| Puncak Mandala | 4 700 | 15 420 | North Island | 115 777 | 44 702 | | | | Murray | 2 589 | 1 608 |
| Puncak Yamin | 4 595 | 15 075 | Tasmania | 67 800 | 26 178 | | | | Murrumbidgee | 1 690 | 1 050 |
| Mt Wilheim | 4 509 | 14 793 | | | | | | | Lachlan | 1 480 | 919 |

## ASIA
Total Land Area
45 036 492 sq km
17 388 686 sq miles

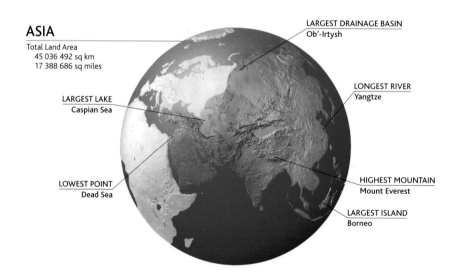

LARGEST DRAINAGE BASIN
Ob'-Irtysh

LONGEST RIVER
Yangtze

LARGEST LAKE
Caspian Sea

LOWEST POINT
Dead Sea

HIGHEST MOUNTAIN
Mount Everest

LARGEST ISLAND
Borneo

| HIGHEST MOUNTAINS | HEIGHT metres | feet | LARGEST ISLANDS | AREA sq km | sq miles | LARGEST LAKES | AREA sq km | sq miles | LONGEST RIVERS | LENGTH km | miles |
|---|---|---|---|---|---|---|---|---|---|---|---|
| Mt Everest | 8 848 | 29 028 | Borneo | 745 561 | 287 863 | Caspian Sea | 371 000 | 143 244 | Yangtze | 6 380 | 3 964 |
| K2 | 8 611 | 28 251 | Sumatra | 473 606 | 182 860 | Lake Baikal | 30 500 | 11 776 | Ob'-Irtysh | 5 568 | 3 460 |
| Kangchenjunga | 8 586 | 28 169 | Honshū | 227 414 | 87 805 | Lake Balkhash | 17 400 | 6 718 | Yenisey-Angara-Selenga | 5 550 | 3 448 |
| Lhotse | 8 516 | 27 939 | Celebes | 189 216 | 73 057 | Aral Sea | 17 158 | 6 625 | Yellow | 5 464 | 3 395 |
| Makalu | 8 463 | 27 765 | Java | 132 188 | 51 038 | Ysyk-Köl | 6 200 | 2 393 | Irtysh | 4 440 | 2 759 |

# EUROPE

Total Land Area
9 908 599 sq km
3 825 731 sq miles

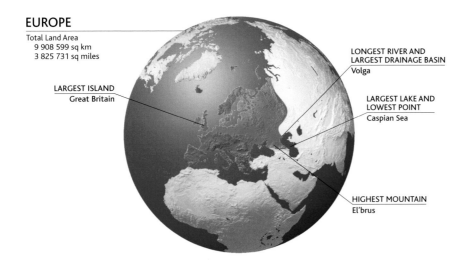

LARGEST ISLAND
Great Britain

LONGEST RIVER AND
LARGEST DRAINAGE BASIN
Volga

LARGEST LAKE AND
LOWEST POINT
Caspian Sea

HIGHEST MOUNTAIN
El'brus

| HIGHEST MOUNTAINS | HEIGHT | | LARGEST ISLANDS | AREA | | LARGEST LAKES | AREA | | LONGEST RIVERS | LENGTH | |
|---|---|---|---|---|---|---|---|---|---|---|---|
| | metres | feet | | sq km | sq miles | | sq km | sq miles | | km | miles |
| El'brus | 5 642 | 5 642 | Great Britain | 218 476 | 84 354 | Caspian Sea | 371 000 | 143 244 | Volga | 3 688 | 2 291 |
| Gora Dykh-Tau | 5 204 | 17 073 | Iceland | 102 820 | 39 699 | Lake Ladoga | 18 390 | 7 100 | Danube | 2 850 | 1 770 |
| Shkhara | 5 201 | 17 063 | Novaya Zemlya | 90 650 | 35 000 | Lake Onega | 9 600 | 3 706 | Dnieper | 2 285 | 1 419 |
| Kazbek | 5 047 | 16 558 | Ireland | 83 045 | 32 064 | Vänern | 5 585 | 2 156 | Kama | 2 028 | 1 260 |
| Mont Blanc | 4 808 | 15 774 | Spitsbergen | 37 814 | 14 600 | Rybinskoye Vdkhr. | 5 180 | 2 000 | Don | 1 931 | 1 199 |

# AFRICA

Total Land Area
30 343 578 sq km
11 715 721 sq miles

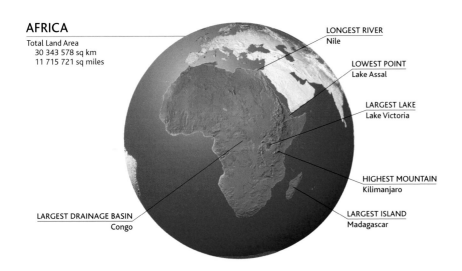

LONGEST RIVER
Nile

LOWEST POINT
Lake Assal

LARGEST LAKE
Lake Victoria

HIGHEST MOUNTAIN
Kilimanjaro

LARGEST DRAINAGE BASIN
Congo

LARGEST ISLAND
Madagascar

| HIGHEST MOUNTAINS | HEIGHT | | LARGEST ISLANDS | AREA | | LARGEST LAKES | AREA | | LONGEST RIVERS | LENGTH | |
|---|---|---|---|---|---|---|---|---|---|---|---|
| | metres | feet | | sq km | sq miles | | sq km | sq miles | | km | miles |
| Kilimanjaro | 5 892 | 19 331 | Madagascar | 587 040 | 226 657 | Lake Victoria | 68 800 | 26 564 | Nile | 6 695 | 4 160 |
| Mt Kenya | 5 199 | 17 057 | | | | Lake Tanganyika | 32 900 | 12 702 | Congo | 4 667 | 2 900 |
| Margherita Peak | 5 110 | 16 765 | | | | Lake Nyasa | 30 044 | 11 600 | Niger | 4 184 | 2 599 |
| Meru | 4 565 | 14 977 | | | | Lake Volta | 8 485 | 3 276 | Zambezi | 2 736 | 1 700 |
| Ras Dejen | 4 533 | 14 872 | | | | Lake Turkana | 6 475 | 2 500 | Webi Shabeelle | 2 490 | 1 547 |

# CONTINENTS AND OCEANS

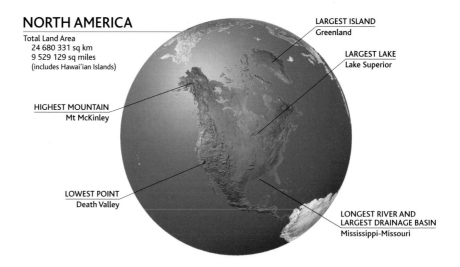

## NORTH AMERICA

Total Land Area
24 680 331 sq km
9 529 129 sq miles
(includes Hawai'ian Islands)

LARGEST ISLAND
Greenland

LARGEST LAKE
Lake Superior

HIGHEST MOUNTAIN
Mt McKinley

LOWEST POINT
Death Valley

LONGEST RIVER AND
LARGEST DRAINAGE BASIN
Mississippi-Missouri

| HIGHEST MOUNTAINS | HEIGHT metres | feet | LARGEST ISLANDS | AREA sq km | sq miles | LARGEST LAKES | AREA sq km | sq miles | LONGEST RIVERS | LENGTH km | miles |
|---|---|---|---|---|---|---|---|---|---|---|---|
| Mt McKinley | 6 194 | 20 321 | Greenland | 2 175 600 | 840 004 | Lake Superior | 82 100 | 31 699 | Mississippi-Missouri | 5 969 | 3 709 |
| Mt Logan | 5 959 | 19 550 | Baffin Island | 507 451 | 195 928 | Lake Huron | 59 600 | 23 012 | Mackenzie-Peace-Finlay | 4 241 | 2 635 |
| Pico de Orizaba | 5 747 | 18 855 | Victoria Island | 217 291 | 83 897 | Lake Michigan | 57 800 | 22 317 | Missouri | 4 086 | 2 539 |
| Mt St Elias | 5 489 | 18 008 | Ellesmere Island | 196 236 | 75 767 | Great Bear Lake | 31 328 | 12 095 | Mississippi | 3 765 | 2 339 |
| Volcán Popocatépetl | 5 452 | 17 887 | Cuba | 110 860 | 42 803 | Great Slave Lake | 28 568 | 11 030 | Yukon | 3 185 | 1 979 |

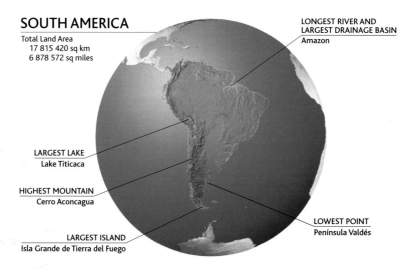

## SOUTH AMERICA

Total Land Area
17 815 420 sq km
6 878 572 sq miles

LONGEST RIVER AND
LARGEST DRAINAGE BASIN
Amazon

LARGEST LAKE
Lake Titicaca

HIGHEST MOUNTAIN
Cerro Aconcagua

LOWEST POINT
Península Valdés

LARGEST ISLAND
Isla Grande de Tierra del Fuego

| HIGHEST MOUNTAINS | HEIGHT metres | feet | LARGEST ISLANDS | AREA sq km | sq miles | LARGEST LAKES | AREA sq km | sq miles | LONGEST RIVERS | LENGTH km | miles |
|---|---|---|---|---|---|---|---|---|---|---|---|
| Cerro Aconcagua | 6 959 | 22 831 | Isla Grande de Tierra del Fuego | 47 000 | 18 147 | Lake Titicaca | 8 340 | 3 220 | Amazon | 6 516 | 4 049 |
| Nevado Ojos del Salado | 6 908 | 22 664 | Isla de Chiloé | 8 394 | 3 240 | | | | Río de la Plata-Paraná | 4 500 | 2 796 |
| Cerro Bonete | 6 872 | 22 546 | East Falkland | 6 760 | 2 610 | | | | Purus | 3 218 | 1 999 |
| Cerro Pissis | 6 858 | 22 500 | West Falkland | 5 413 | 2 090 | | | | Madeira | 3 200 | 1 988 |
| Cerro Tupungato | 6 800 | 22 211 | | | | | | | Sao Francisco | 2 900 | 1 802 |

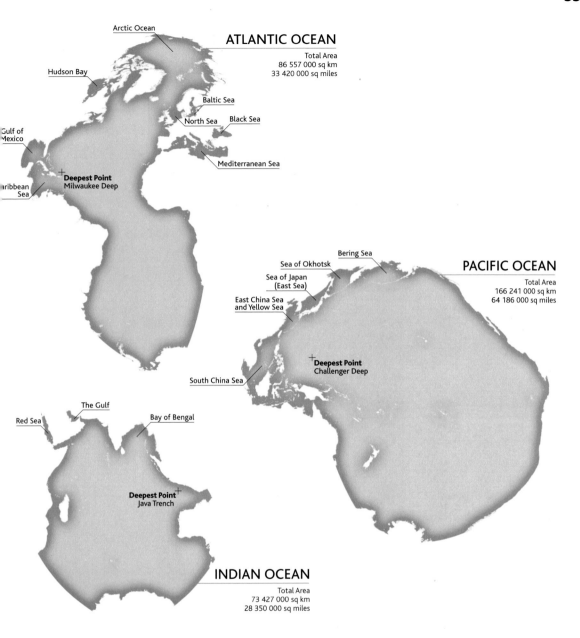

## ATLANTIC OCEAN

Total Area
86 557 000 sq km
33 420 000 sq miles

Arctic Ocean

Hudson Bay

Baltic Sea

North Sea    Black Sea

Gulf of
Mexico

Mediterranean Sea

Caribbean
Sea

**Deepest Point**
Milwaukee Deep

## PACIFIC OCEAN

Total Area
166 241 000 sq km
64 186 000 sq miles

Bering Sea

Sea of Okhotsk

Sea of Japan
(East Sea)

East China Sea
and Yellow Sea

**Deepest Point**
Challenger Deep

South China Sea

The Gulf

Bay of Bengal

Red Sea

**Deepest Point**
Java Trench

## INDIAN OCEAN

Total Area
73 427 000 sq km
28 350 000 sq miles

| ATLANTIC OCEAN | AREA | | DEEPEST POINT | |
|---|---|---|---|---|
| | sq km | sq miles | metres | feet |
| Extent | 86 557 000 | 33 420 000 | 8 605 | 28 231 |
| Arctic Ocean | 9 485 000 | 3 662 000 | 5 450 | 17 880 |
| Caribbean Sea | 2 512 000 | 970 000 | 7 680 | 25 196 |
| Mediterranean Sea | 2 510 000 | 969 000 | 5 121 | 16 800 |
| Gulf of Mexico | 1 544 000 | 596 000 | 3 504 | 11 495 |
| Hudson Bay | 1 233 000 | 476 000 | 259 | 849 |
| North Sea | 575 000 | 222 000 | 661 | 2 168 |
| Black Sea | 508 000 | 196 000 | 2 245 | 7 365 |
| Baltic Sea | 382 000 | 147 000 | 460 | 1 509 |

| INDIAN OCEAN | AREA | | DEEPEST POINT | |
|---|---|---|---|---|
| | sq km | sq miles | metres | feet |
| Extent | 73 427 000 | 28 350 000 | 7 125 | 23 376 |
| Bay of Bengal | 2 172 000 | 839 000 | 4 500 | 14 763 |
| Red Sea | 453 000 | 175 000 | 3 040 | 9 973 |
| The Gulf | 238 000 | 92 000 | 73 | 239 |

| PACIFIC OCEAN | AREA | | DEEPEST POINT | |
|---|---|---|---|---|
| | sq km | sq miles | metres | feet |
| Extent | 166 241 000 | 64 186 000 | 10 920 | 35 826 |
| South China Sea | 2 590 000 | 1 000 000 | 5 514 | 18 090 |
| Bering Sea | 2 261 000 | 873 000 | 4 150 | 13 615 |
| Sea of Okhotsk | 1 392 000 | 537 000 | 3 363 | 11 033 |
| Sea of Japan (East Sea) | 1 013 000 | 391 000 | 3 743 | 12 280 |
| East China Sea and Yellow Sea | 1 202 000 | 464 000 | 2 717 | 8 913 |

## MAJOR CLIMATIC REGIONS AND SUB-TYPES

Winkel Tripel Projection

1:120 000 000

Köppen classification system

**A** Rainy climate with no winter: coolest month above 18°C (64.4°F).

**B** Dry climates; limits are defined by formulae based on rainfall effectiveness:
- **BS** Steppe or semi-arid climate.
- **BW** Desert or arid climate.

***C** Rainy climates with mild winters: coolest month above 0°C (32°F), but below 18°C (64.4°F); warmest month above 10°C (50°F).

***D** Rainy climates with severe winters: coldest month below 0°C (32°F); warmest month above 10°C (50°F).

**E** Polar climates with no warm season: warmest month below 10°C (50°F).
- **ET** Tundra climate: warmest month below 10°C (50°F) but above 0°C (32°F).
- **EF** Perpetual frost: all months below 0°C (32°F).

**a** Warmest month above 22°C (71.6°F).

**b** Warmest month below 22°C (71.6°F).

**c** Less than four months over 10°C (50°F).

**d** As 'c', but with severe cold: coldest month below -38°C (-36.4°F).

**f** Constantly moist rainfall throughout the year.

***h** Warmer dry: all months above 0°C (32°F).

***k** Cooler dry: at least one month below 0°C (32°F).

**m** Monsoon rain: short dry season, but is compensated by heavy rains during rest of the year.

**n** Frequent fog.

**s** Dry season in summer.

*** Modification of Köppen definition**

| | |
|---|---|
| ● | World weather extremes- see table |

**Polar**

| | |
|---|---|
| EF | Ice cap |
| ET | Tundra |

**Cooler humid**

| | |
|---|---|
| Dc Dd | Subarctic |
| Db | Continental cool summer |
| Da | Continental warm summer |

**Warmer humid**

| | |
|---|---|
| Cb Cc | Temperate |
| Ca | Humid subtropical |
| Cs | Mediterranean |

**Dry**

| | |
|---|---|
| BS | Steppe |
| BW | Desert |

**Tropical humid**

| | |
|---|---|
| Aw As | Savanna |
| Af Am | Rain forest |

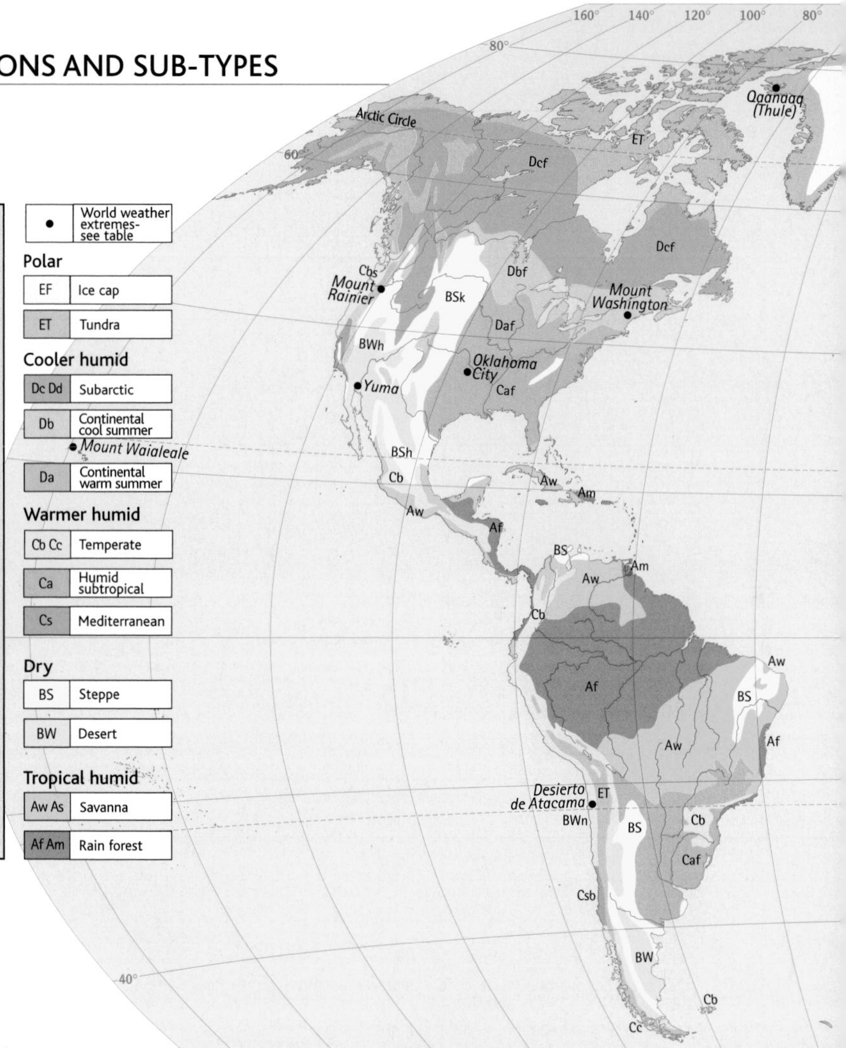


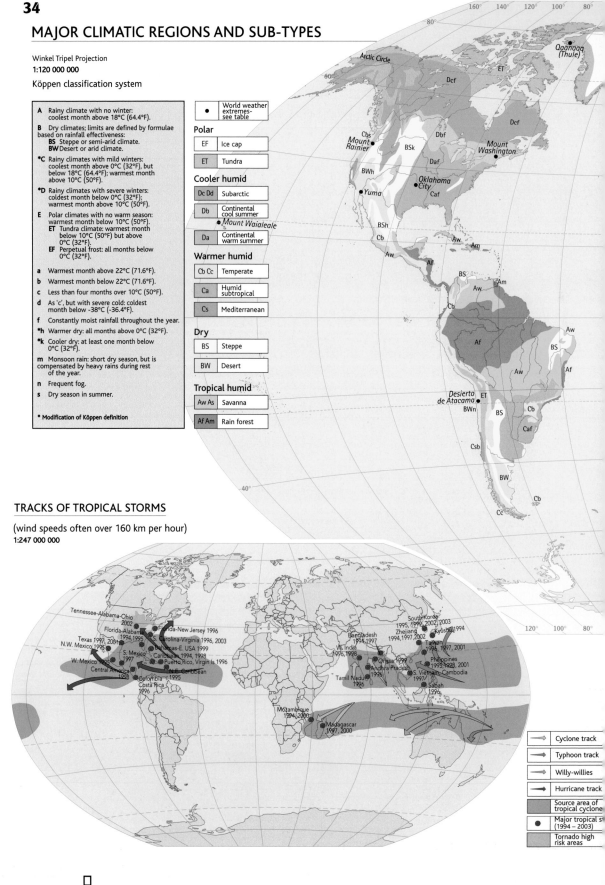

## TRACKS OF TROPICAL STORMS

(wind speeds often over 160 km per hour)

1:247 000 000

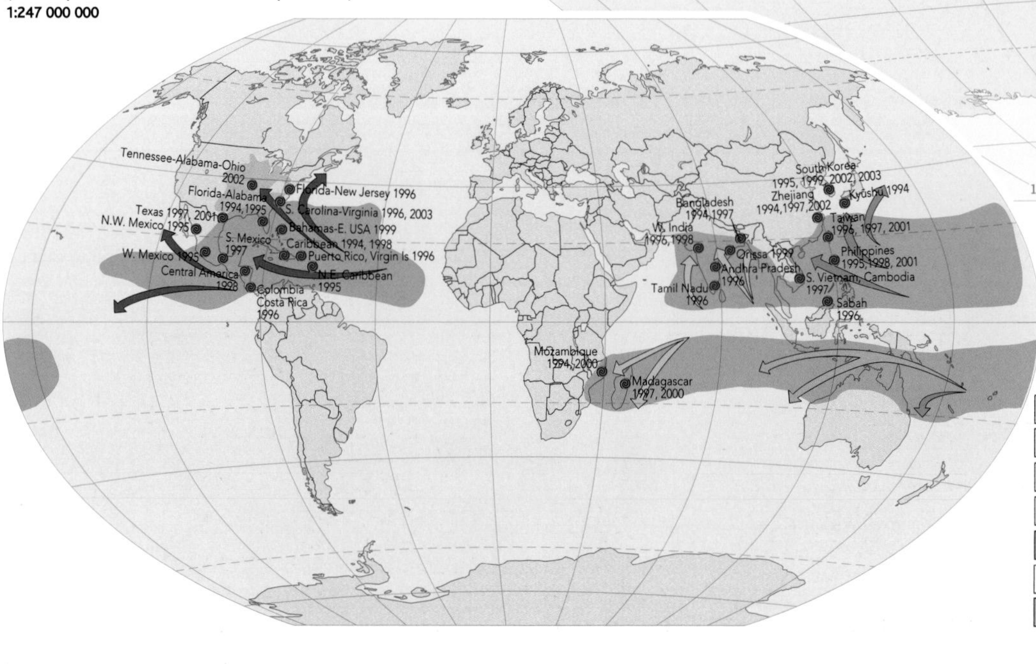


| | |
|---|---|
| → | Cyclone track |
| → | Typhoon track |
| → | Willy-willies |
| → | Hurricane track |
| | Source area of tropical cyclone |
| ● | Major tropical s (1994 – 2003) |
| | Tornado high risk areas |

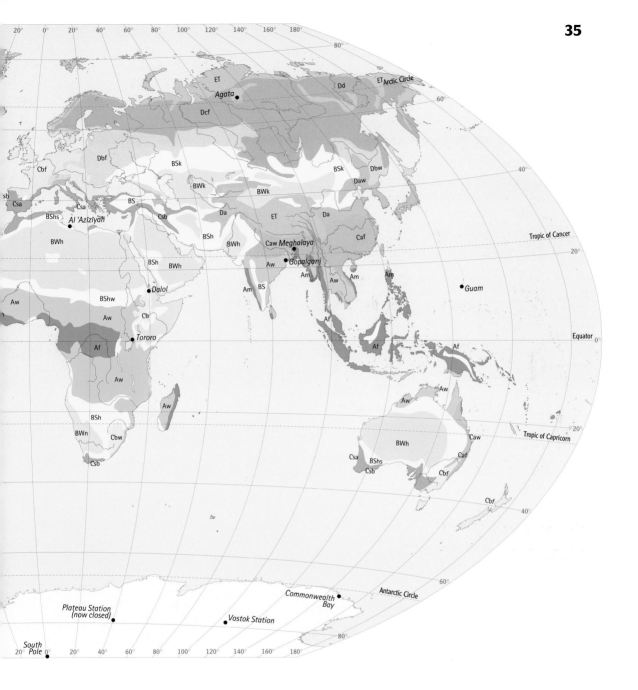

# WORLD WEATHER EXTREMES

| | | | | |
|---|---|---|---|---|
| Highest shade temperature | 57.8°C/136°F **Al 'Azīzīyah**, Libya (13th September 1922) | Highest surface wind speed | | |
| Hottest place – Annual mean | 34.4°C/93.9°F **Dalol**, Ethiopia | High altitude | 372 km per hour/231 miles per hour **Mount Washington**, New Hampshire, USA (12th April 1934) | |
| Driest place – Annual mean | 0.1 mm/0.004 inches **Atacama Desert**, Chile | Low altitude | 333 km per hour/207 miles per hour **Qaanaaq (Thule)**, Greenland (8th March 1972) | |
| Most sunshine – Annual mean | 90% **Yuma**, Arizona, USA (over 4 000 hours) | Tornado | 512 km per hour/318 miles per hour **Oklahoma City**, Oklahoma, USA (3rd May 1999) | |
| Least sunshine | Nil for 182 days each year, **South Pole** | Greatest snowfall | 31 102 mm/1 224.5 inches **Mount Rainier**, Washington, USA (19th February 1971–18th February 1972) | |
| Lowest screen temperature | -89.2°C/-128.6°F **Vostok Station**, Antarctica (21st July 1983) | Heaviest hailstones | 1 kg/2.21 lb **Gopalganj**, Bangladesh (14th April 1986) | |
| Coldest place – Annual mean | -56.6°C/-69.9°F **Plateau Station**, Antarctica | Thunder-days Average | 251 days per year **Tororo**, Uganda | |
| Wettest place – Annual mean | 11 873 mm/467.4 inches **Meghalaya**, India | Highest barometric pressure | 1 083.8 mb **Agata**, Siberia, Rus. Fed. (31st December 1968) | |
| Most rainy days | Up to 350 per year **Mount Waialeale**, Hawaii, USA | Lowest barometric pressure | 870 mb 483 km/300 miles west of **Guam**, Pacific Ocean (12th October 1979) | |
| Windiest place | 322 km per hour/200 miles per hour in gales, **Commonwealth Bay**, Antarctica | | | |

© Collins Bartholomew Ltd

**ENVIRONMENT**

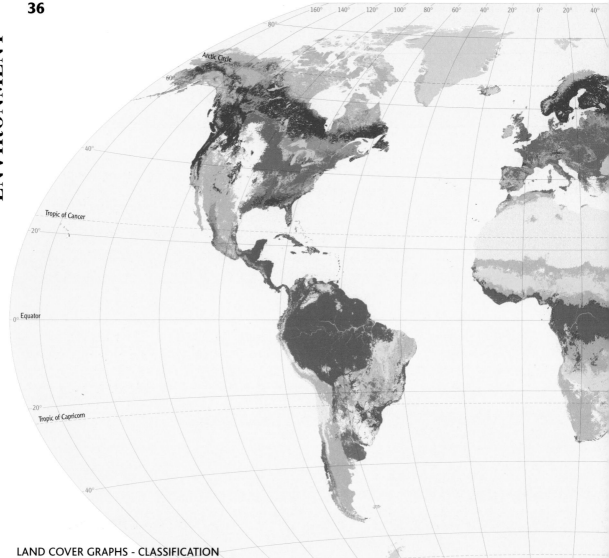

## LAND COVER GRAPHS - CLASSIFICATION

| CLASS DESCRIPTION | IGBP CLASSES |
|---|---|
| Forest/Woodland | Evergreen needleleaf forest |
| | Evergreen broadleaf forest |
| | Deciduous needleleaf forest |
| | Deciduous broadleaf forest |
| | Mixed forest |
| Shrubland | Closed shrublands |
| | Open shrublands |
| Grass/Savanna | Woody savannas |
| | Savannas |
| | Grasslands |
| Wetland | Permanent wetlands |
| Crops/Mosaic | Croplands |
| | Cropland/Natural vegetation mosaic |
| Urban | Urban and built-up |
| Snow/Ice | Snow and Ice |
| Barren | Barren or sparsely vegetated |

## GLOBAL LAND COVER COMPOSITION

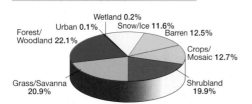

Wetland 0.2%
Urban 0.1%
Snow/Ice 11.6%
Barren 12.5%
Forest/Woodland 22.1%
Crops/Mosaic 12.7%
Grass/Savanna 20.9%
Shrubland 19.9%

## CONTINENTAL LAND COVER COMPOSITION

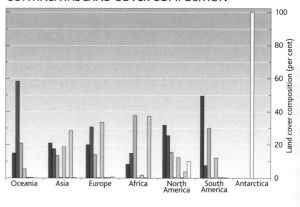

Land cover composition (per cent)

Oceania   Asia   Europe   Africa   North America   South America   Antarctica

# WORLD LAND COVER

Winkel Tripel Projection
**1:120 000 000**

| | |
|---|---|
| | Water bodies |
| | Evergreen needleleaf forest |
| | Evergreen broadleaf forest |
| | Deciduous needleleaf forest |
| | Deciduous broadleaf forest |
| | Mixed forest |
| | Closed shrublands |
| | Open shrublands |
| | Woody savannas |
| | Savannas |
| | Grasslands |
| | Permanent wetlands |
| | Croplands |
| | Urban and build-up |
| | Cropland/Natural vegetation mosaic |
| | Snow and Ice |
| | Barren or sparsely vegetated |

# ENVIRONMENTAL IMPACTS

Winkel Tripel Projection
**1:247 000 000**

Percentage change
in forest area, 1990–2000

| | |
|---|---|
| | -2.0 – -9.0 |
| | -0.4 – -1.9 |
| | no significant change |

Threat of desertification

| | |
|---|---|
| | very high risk |

Coral reefs at risk

| | |
|---|---|
| • | high risk |

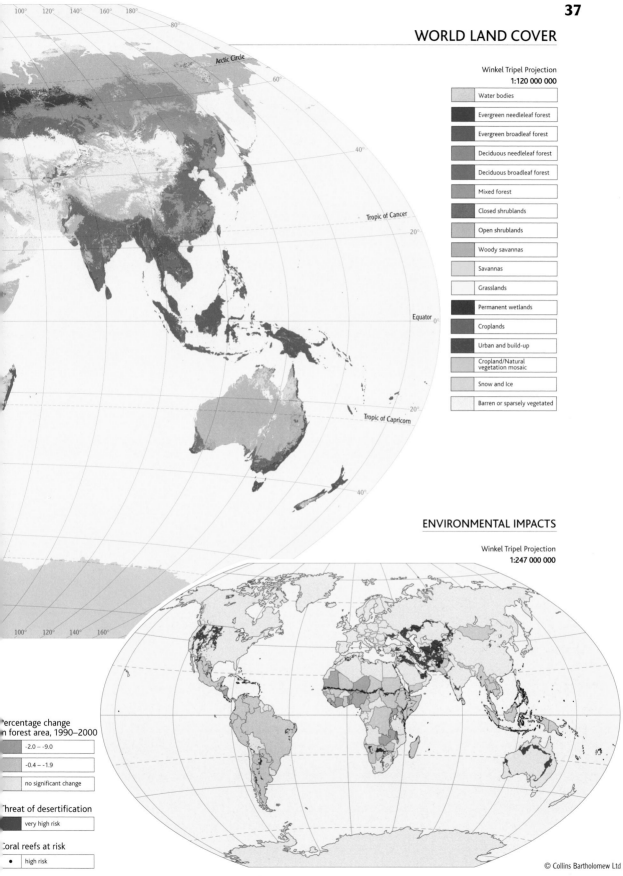

# WORLD POPULATION DISTRIBUTION AND THE WORLD'S MAJOR CITIES

Winkel Tripel Projection

**1:120 000 000**

## Population Density

per sq mile

| 1 250 | 250 | 62.5 | 2.5 | 0 |
|---|---|---|---|---|

Inhabitants — Uninhabited

| 500 | 100 | 25 | 1 | 0 |
|---|---|---|---|---|

per sq km

## Major Urban Agglomerations

| ● | 5 million–10 million |
|---|---|
| ● | 10 million–20 million |
| ○ | over 20 million |

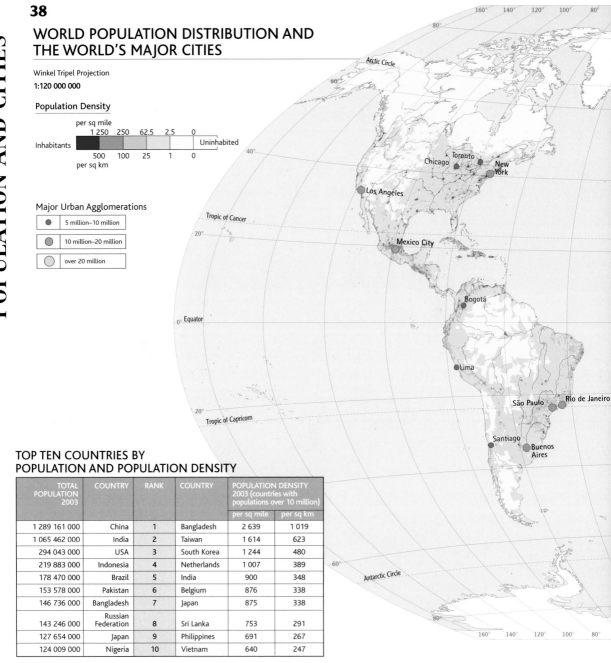

## TOP TEN COUNTRIES BY POPULATION AND POPULATION DENSITY

| TOTAL POPULATION 2003 | COUNTRY | RANK | COUNTRY | POPULATION DENSITY 2003 (countries with populations over 10 million) | |
|---|---|---|---|---|---|
| | | | | per sq mile | per sq km |
| 1 289 161 000 | China | 1 | Bangladesh | 2 639 | 1 019 |
| 1 065 462 000 | India | 2 | Taiwan | 1 614 | 623 |
| 294 043 000 | USA | 3 | South Korea | 1 244 | 480 |
| 219 883 000 | Indonesia | 4 | Netherlands | 1 007 | 389 |
| 178 470 000 | Brazil | 5 | India | 900 | 348 |
| 153 578 000 | Pakistan | 6 | Belgium | 876 | 338 |
| 146 736 000 | Bangladesh | 7 | Japan | 875 | 338 |
| 143 246 000 | Russian Federation | 8 | Sri Lanka | 753 | 291 |
| 127 654 000 | Japan | 9 | Philippines | 691 | 267 |
| 124 009 000 | Nigeria | 10 | Vietnam | 640 | 247 |

## KEY POPULATION STATISTICS FOR MAJOR REGIONS

| | POPULATION 2003 (millions) | GROWTH (per cent) | INFANT MORTALITY RATE | TOTAL FERTILITY RATE | LIFE EXPECTANCY (years) | % AGED 60 OR OVER | |
|---|---|---|---|---|---|---|---|
| | | | | | | 2000 | 2050 |
| World | 6 301 | 1.2 | 56 | 2.7 | 65 | 10 | 21 |
| More developed regions | 1 203 | 0.3 | 8 | 1.6 | 76 | 19 | 32 |
| Less developed regions | 5 098 | 1.5 | 61 | 2.9 | 63 | 8 | 20 |
| Africa | 851 | 2.2 | 89 | 4.9 | 49 | 5 | 10 |
| Asia | 3 823 | 1.3 | 53 | 2.6 | 67 | 9 | 23 |
| Europe | 726 | -0.1 | 9 | 1.4 | 74 | 20 | 35 |
| Latin America and the Caribbean | 543 | 1.4 | 32 | 2.5 | 70 | 8 | 24 |
| North America | 326 | 1.0 | 7 | 2.1 | 77 | 16 | 26 |
| Oceania | 32 | 1.2 | 26 | 2.3 | 74 | 13 | 25 |

Except for population (2003) and % aged 60 and over figures, the data are annual averages projected for the period 2000–2005.

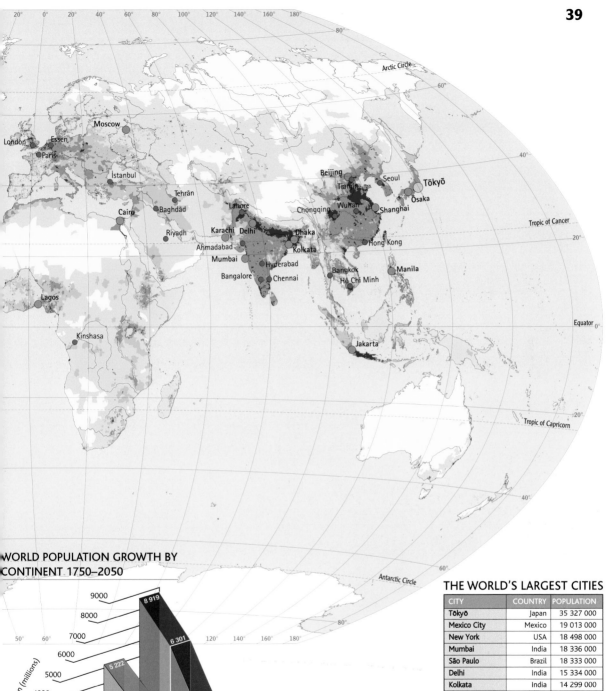

20° 0° 20° 40° 60° 80° 100° 120° 140° 160° 180°

Arctic Circle

London
Essen
Paris
Moscow
İstanbul
Tehrān
Baghdād
Cairo
Riyadh
Lahore
Karachi  Delhi
Ahmadabad
Mumbai
Bangalore
Hyderabad
Chennai
Kolkata
Dhaka
Beijing
Tianjin
Wuhan
Chongqing
Shanghai
Seoul
Tōkyō
Ōsaka
Hong Kong
Bangkok
Hồ Chí Minh
Manila
Jakarta
Lagos
Kinshasa

Tropic of Cancer
Equator 0°
Tropic of Capricorn

Antarctic Circle

## WORLD POPULATION GROWTH BY CONTINENT 1750–2050

Population (millions)

9000 — 8 919
8000
7000 — 6 301
6000
5000 — 5 222
4000 — 3 823
3000
2000 — 2 519 1 803
1 650

Year: 2003, 1950, 1900, 1850, 1800, 1750

Continents: Oceania, North America, Europe, Latin America and the Caribbean, Africa, Asia, World

## THE WORLD'S LARGEST CITIES

| CITY | COUNTRY | POPULATION |
|---|---|---|
| Tōkyō | Japan | 35 327 000 |
| Mexico City | Mexico | 19 013 000 |
| New York | USA | 18 498 000 |
| Mumbai | India | 18 336 000 |
| São Paulo | Brazil | 18 333 000 |
| Delhi | India | 15 334 000 |
| Kolkata | India | 14 299 000 |
| Buenos Aires | Argentina | 13 349 000 |
| Jakarta | Indonesia | 13 194 000 |
| Shanghai | China | 12 665 000 |
| Dhaka | Bangladesh | 12 560 000 |
| Los Angeles | USA | 12 146 000 |
| Karachi | Pakistan | 11 819 000 |
| Rio de Janeiro | Brazil | 11 469 000 |
| Ōsaka | Japan | 11 286 000 |
| Cairo | Egypt | 11 146 000 |
| Lagos | Nigeria | 11 135 000 |
| Beijing | China | 10 849 000 |
| Manila | Philippines | 10 677 000 |
| Moscow | Russian Fed. | 10 672 000 |

© Collins Bartholomew Ltd

**TELECOMMUNICATIONS**

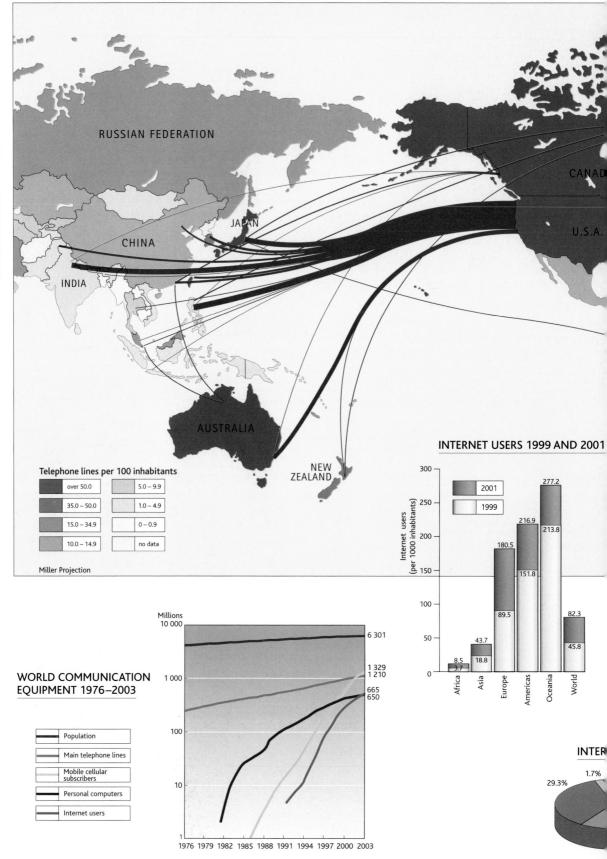

RUSSIAN FEDERATION

CANAD

JAPAN

U.S.A.

CHINA

INDIA

AUSTRALIA

NEW
ZEALAND

**Telephone lines per 100 inhabitants**

| | |
|---|---|
| over 50.0 | 5.0 – 9.9 |
| 35.0 – 50.0 | 1.0 – 4.9 |
| 15.0 – 34.9 | 0 – 0.9 |
| 10.0 – 14.9 | no data |

Miller Projection

**INTERNET USERS 1999 AND 2001**

Internet users (per 1000 inhabitants)

2001
1999

| | 2001 | 1999 |
|---|---|---|
| Africa | 8.5 | 3.7 |
| Asia | 43.7 | 18.8 |
| Europe | 180.5 | 89.5 |
| Americas | 216.9 | 151.8 |
| Oceania | 277.2 | 213.8 |
| World | 82.3 | 45.8 |

**WORLD COMMUNICATION
EQUIPMENT 1976–2003**

Millions
10 000

6 301

1 329
1 210

665
650

| | |
|---|---|
| ▬ | Population |
| ▬ | Main telephone lines |
| ▬ | Mobile cellular subscribers |
| ▬ | Personal computers |
| ▬ | Internet users |

1976 1979 1982 1985 1988 1991 1994 1997 2000 2003

**INTER**

1.7%

29.3%

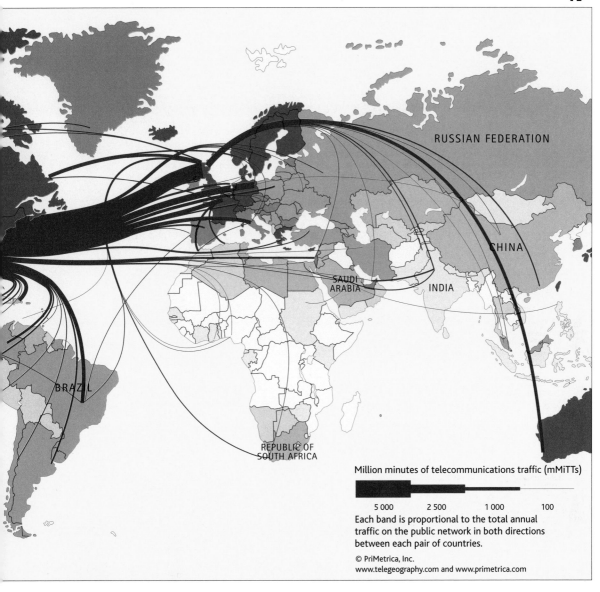

RUSSIAN FEDERATION

CHINA

SAUDI
ARABIA

INDIA

BRAZIL

REPUBLIC OF
SOUTH AFRICA

Million minutes of telecommunications traffic (mMiTTs)

| 5 000 | 2 500 | 1 000 | 100 |

Each band is proportional to the total annual
traffic on the public network in both directions
between each pair of countries.

© PriMetrica, Inc.
www.telegeography.com and www.primetrica.com

## TELEPHONE MAIN LINES

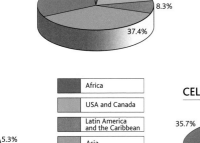

1.2%  2.0%  20.1%
31.0%
8.3%
37.4%

## TOP 10 INTERNET SERVICE PROVIDERS (ISPs)

| INTERNET SERVICE PROVIDER | WEB ADDRESS | SUBSCRIBERS |
|---|---|---|
| AOL (USA) | www.aol.com | 20 500 000 |
| T-Online (Germany) | www.t-online.de | 4 151 000 |
| Nifty-Serve (Japan) | www.nifty.com | 3 500 000 |
| EarthLink (USA) | www.earthlink.com | 3 122 000 |
| Biglobe (Japan) | www.biglobe.ne.jp | 2 720 000 |
| MSN (USA) | www.msn.com | 2 700 000 |
| Chollian (South Korea) | www.chollian.net | 2 000 000 |
| Tin.it (Italy) | www.tin.it | 1 990 000 |
| Freeserve (UK) | www.freeserve.com | 1 575 000 |
| AT&T WorldNet (USA) | www.att.net | 1 500 000 |

RS

1.1%
5.3%
.2%

| | Africa |
| | USA and Canada |
| | Latin America and the Caribbean |
| | Asia |
| | Europe |
| | Oceania |

## CELLULAR SUBSCRIBERS

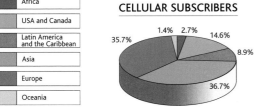

1.4%  2.7%  14.6%
35.7%
8.9%
36.7%

# MAP POLICIES AND ABBREVIATIONS

## Place Names

The spelling of place names on maps has always been a matter of great complexity, because of the variety of the world's languages and the systems used to write them down. There is no standard way of spelling names or of converting them from one alphabet, or symbol set, to another. Instead, conventional ways of spelling have evolved in each of the world's major languages, and the results often differ significantly from the name as it is spelled in the original language. Familiar examples of English conventional names include Munich (München), Florence (Firenze) and Moscow (from the transliterated form, Moskva).

In this atlas, local name forms are used where these are in the Roman alphabet, though for major cities, and main physical features, conventional English names are given first. The local forms are those which are officially recognized by the government of the country concerned, usually as represented by its official mapping agency. This is a basic principle laid down by the United Kingdom government's Permanent Committee on Geographical Names (PCGN) and the equivalent United States Board on Geographic Names, (BGN). Prominent English-language and historic names are not neglected, however. These, and significant superseded names and alternate spellings, are included in brackets on the maps where space permits, and are cross-referenced in the index.

Country names are shown in conventional English form and include any recent changes promulgated by national governments and adopted by the United Nations. The names of continents, oceans, seas and under-water features in international waters also appear in English throughout the atlas, as do those of

other international features where such an English form exists and is in common use. International features are defined as features crossing one or more international boundary.

## Boundaries

The status of nations, their names and their boundaries, are shown in this atlas as they are at the time of going to press, as far as can be ascertained. Where an international boundary symbol appears in the sea or ocean it does not necessarily infer a legal maritime boundary, but shows which offshore islands belong to which country. The extent of island nations is shown by a short boundary symbol at the extreme limits of the area of sea or ocean within which all land is part of that nation.

Where international boundaries are the subject of dispute it may be that no portrayal of them will meet with the approval of any of the countries involved, but it is not seen as the function of this atlas to try to adjudicate between the rights and wrongs of political issues. Although reference mapping at atlas scales is not the ideal medium for indicating the claims of many separatist and irredentist movements, every reasonable attempt is made to show where an active territorial dispute exists, and where there is an important difference between 'de facto' (existing in fact, on the ground) and 'de jure' (according to law) boundaries. This is done by the use of a different symbol where international boundaries are disputed, or where the alignment is unconfirmed, to that used for settled international boundaries. Ceasefire lines are also shown by a separate symbol. For clarity, disputed boundaries and areas are annotated where this is considered necessary. The atlas aims to take a strictly neutral viewpoint of all such cases, based on advice from expert consultants.

## Map Projections

Map projections have been selected specifically for the area and scale of each map, or suite of maps. As the only way to show the Earth with absolute accuracy is on a globe, all map projections are compromise. Some projections seek to maintain correct area relationships (equal area projections), true distances and bearings from a point (equidistant projections) or correct angles and shapes (conformal projections); others attempt to achieve a balance between these properties. The choice of projections used in this atlas has been made on an individual continental and regional basis. Projections used, and their individual parameters, have been defined to minimize distortion and to reduce scale errors as much as possible. The projection used is indicated at the bottom left of each map page.

## Scale

In order to directly compare like with like throughout the world it would be necessary to maintain a single scale throughout the atlas. However, the desirability of mapping the more densely populated areas of the world at larger scales, and other geographical considerations, such as the need to fit a homogeneous physical region within a uniform rectangular page format, mean that a range of scales have been used. Scales for continental maps range between 1:25 000 000 and 1:55 000 000, depending on the size of the continental land mass being covered. Scales for regional maps are typically in the range 1:15 000 000 to 1:25 000 000. Mapping for most countries is at scales between 1:6 000 000 and 1:12 000 000, although for the more densely populated areas of Europe the scale increases to 1:3 000 000.

## ABBREVIATIONS

| Arch. | Archipelago | | | L. | Lake | | | Ra. | Range | | mountain range |
|---|---|---|---|---|---|---|---|---|---|---|---|
| B. | Bay | | | | Loch | (Scotland) | lake | S. | South, Southern | | |
| | Bahia, Baía | Portuguese | bay | | Lough | (Ireland) | lake | | Salar, Salina, | | |
| | Bahía | Spanish | bay | | Lac | French | lake | | Salinas | Spanish | salt pan, salt pans |
| | Baie | French | bay | | Lago | Portuguese, Spanish | lake | Sa | Serra | Portuguese | mountain range |
| C. | Cape | | | M. | Mys | Russian | cape, point | | Sierra | Spanish | mountain range |
| | Cabo | Portuguese, | | Mt. | Mount | | | Sd | Sound | | |
| | | Spanish | cape, headland | | Mont | French | hill, mountain | S.E. | Southeast, | | |
| | Cap | French | cape, headland | Mt. | Mountain | | | | Southeastern | | |
| Co | Cerro | Spanish | hill, peak, summit | Mte | Monte | Portuguese, Spanish | hill, mountain | St | Saint | | |
| E. | East, Eastern | | | Mts | Mountains | | | | Sankt | German | |
| Est. | Estrecho | Spanish | strait | | Monts | French | hills, mountains | | Sint | Dutch | saint |
| G. | Gebel | Arabic | hill, mountain | N. | North, Northern | | | Sta | Santa | Italian, Portuguese, | |
| Gt | Great | | | O. | Ostrov | Russian | island | | | Spanish | saint |
| I. | Island, Isle | | | Pk | Puncak | Indonesian, Malay | hill, mountain | Ste | Sainte | French | saint |
| | Ilha | Portuguese | island | Pt | Point | | | Str. | Strait | | |
| | Islas | Spanish | island | Pta | Punta | Italian, Spanish | cape, point | Tk | Teluk | Indonesian, Malay | bay, gulf |
| Is | Islands, Isles | | | R. | River | | | Tg | Tanjong, Tanjung | Indonesian, Malay | cape, point |
| | Islas | Spanish | islands | | Rio | Portuguese | river | Vdkhr. | Vodokhranilishche | Russian | reservoir |
| Kep. | Kepulauan | Indonesian | islands | | Río | Spanish | river | W. | West, Western | | |
| Khr. | Khrebet | Russian | mountain range | | Rivière | French | river | | Wadi, Wâdi, Wādī | Arabic | watercourse |

# MAP SYMBOLS

## Land and Water Features

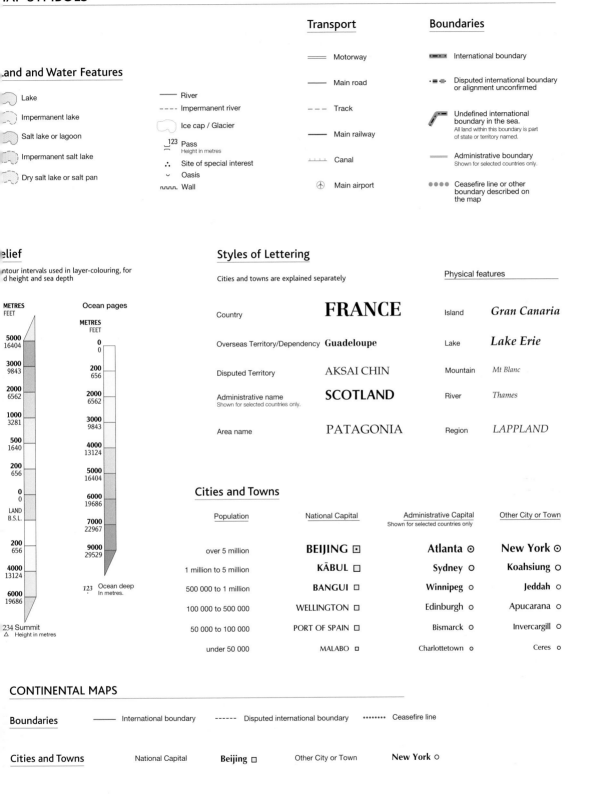

- Lake
- Impermanent lake
- Salt lake or lagoon
- Impermanent salt lake
- Dry salt lake or salt pan

— River
---- Impermanent river
Ice cap / Glacier
123 Pass
    Height in metres
∴ Site of special interest
⌄ Oasis
Wall

## Transport

═══ Motorway
─── Main road
– – – Track
─── Main railway
┼┼┼ Canal
✈ Main airport

## Boundaries

International boundary
Disputed international boundary or alignment unconfirmed
Undefined international boundary in the sea. All land within this boundary is part of state or territory named.
Administrative boundary Shown for selected countries only.
Ceasefire line or other boundary described on the map

## Relief

Contour intervals used in layer-colouring, for land height and sea depth

| METRES FEET | Ocean pages METRES FEET |
|---|---|
| 5000 16404 | 0 0 |
| 3000 9843 | 200 656 |
| 2000 6562 | 2000 6562 |
| 1000 3281 | 3000 9843 |
| 500 1640 | 4000 13124 |
| 200 656 | 5000 16404 |
| 0 0 | 6000 19686 |
| LAND B.S.L. | 7000 22967 |
| 200 656 | 9000 29529 |
| 4000 13124 | |
| 6000 19686 | 123 Ocean deep In metres. |

234 Summit △ Height in metres

## Styles of Lettering

Cities and towns are explained separately

| | | Physical features | |
|---|---|---|---|
| Country | **FRANCE** | Island | *Gran Canaria* |
| Overseas Territory/Dependency | **Guadeloupe** | Lake | *Lake Erie* |
| Disputed Territory | AKSAI CHIN | Mountain | *Mt Blanc* |
| Administrative name Shown for selected countries only. | **SCOTLAND** | River | *Thames* |
| Area name | PATAGONIA | Region | *LAPPLAND* |

## Cities and Towns

| Population | National Capital | Administrative Capital Shown for selected countries only | Other City or Town |
|---|---|---|---|
| over 5 million | **BEIJING** ⊡ | **Atlanta** ⊙ | **New York** ⊙ |
| 1 million to 5 million | **KĀBUL** ☐ | **Sydney** ○ | **Koahsiung** ⊙ |
| 500 000 to 1 million | **BANGUI** ☐ | **Winnipeg** ○ | **Jeddah** ⊙ |
| 100 000 to 500 000 | WELLINGTON ☐ | Edinburgh ○ | Apucarana ○ |
| 50 000 to 100 000 | PORT OF SPAIN ☐ | Bismarck ○ | Invercargill ○ |
| under 50 000 | MALABO ☐ | Charlottetown ○ | Ceres ○ |

# CONTINENTAL MAPS

## Boundaries

─── International boundary    ----- Disputed international boundary    ········ Ceasefire line

## Cities and Towns

National Capital  **Beijing** ☐   Other City or Town  **New York** ○

# WORLD PHYSICAL FEATURES

Winkel Tripel Projection

## EARTH'S DIMENSIONS

| | |
|---|---|
| Mass | $5.974 \times 10^{21}$ tonnes |
| Total area | 509 450 000 sq km / 196 699 746 sq miles |
| Land area | 148 721 936 sq km / 57 421 861 sq miles |
| Water area | 360 728 064 sq km / 139 277 885 sq miles |
| Volume | $1\ 083\ 207 \times 10^6$ cu km / $259\ 911 \times 10^6$ cu miles |

## HIGHEST MOUNTAINS

| | LOCATION | HEIGHT | |
|---|---|---|---|
| | | metres | feet |
| Mt Everest | China/Nepal | 8 848 | 29 028 |
| K2 | China/Jammu and Kashmir | 8 611 | 28 251 |
| Kangchenjunga | India/Nepal | 8 586 | 28 169 |
| Lhotse | China/Nepal | 8 516 | 27 939 |
| Makalu | China/Nepal | 8 463 | 27 765 |

## LARGEST ISLANDS

| | LOCATION | AREA | |
|---|---|---|---|
| | | sq km | sq miles |
| Greenland | North America | 2 175 600 | 840 004 |
| New Guinea | Oceania | 808 510 | 312 167 |
| Borneo | Asia | 745 561 | 287 863 |
| Madagascar | Africa | 587 040 | 266 657 |
| Baffin Island | North America | 507 451 | 195 928 |

Equatorial diameter 12 756 km / 7 927 miles
Polar diameter 12 714 km / 7 901 miles
Equatorial circumference 40 075 km / 24 903 miles
Meridional circumference 40 008 km / 24 861 miles

1: 100 800 000

## LARGEST LAKES

| | LOCATION | AREA | |
|---|---|---|---|
| | | sq km | sq miles |
| Caspian Sea | Asia/Europe | 371 000 | 143 244 |
| Lake Superior | North America | 82 100 | 31 699 |
| Lake Victoria | Africa | 68 800 | 26 564 |
| Lake Huron | North America | 59 600 | 23 012 |
| Lake Michigan | North America | 57 800 | 22 317 |

## LONGEST RIVERS

| | LOCATION | LENGTH | |
|---|---|---|---|
| | | km | miles |
| Nile | Africa | 6 695 | 4 160 |
| Amazon | South America | 6 516 | 4 049 |
| Yangtze | Asia | 6 380 | 3 965 |
| Mississippi-Missouri | North America | 5 969 | 3 709 |
| Ob'-Irtysh | Asia | 5 568 | 3 460 |

© Collins Bartholomew Ltd

# WORLD COUNTRIES

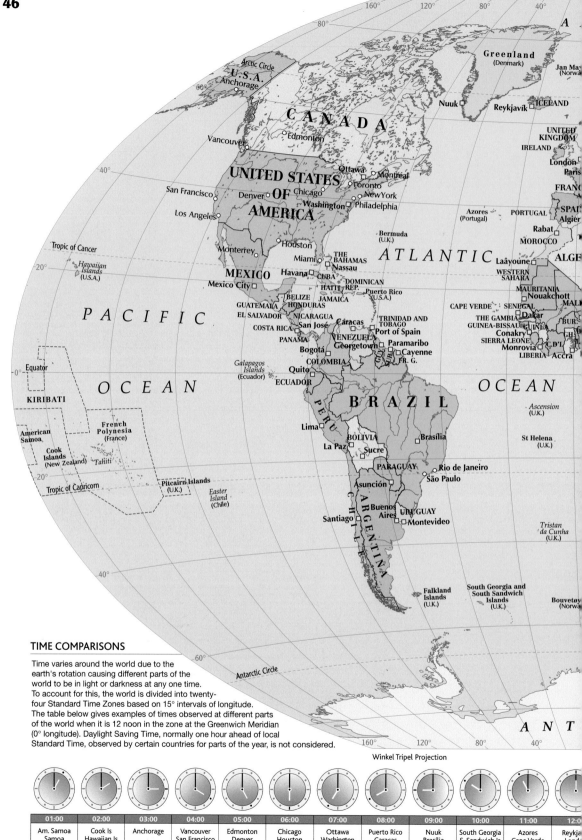

Greenland (Denmark)

Jan May (Norwa

ICELAND
Reykjavík

Arctic Circle

U.S.A.
Anchorage

Nuuk

UNITED
KINGDOM
IRELAND

London
Paris

CANADA

Edmonton

Vancouver

FRANC

Ottawa  Montreal

Azores
(Portugal)

PORTUGAL  SPAI
Algier
Rabat
MOROCCO

ALGE

UNITED STATES
OF
AMERICA

Toronto
Chicago  NewYork
Washington  Philadelphia

Denver

San Francisco

Los Angeles

Bermuda
(U.K.)

Tropic of Cancer

Hawaiian
Islands
(U.S.A.)

Monterrey

Houston

Miami
THE
BAHAMAS
Nassau

Laâyoune
WESTERN
SAHARA

ATLANTIC

MEXICO
Mexico City

Havana  CUBA
HAITI  DOMINICAN
REP.
JAMAICA  Puerto Rico
(U.S.A.)

MAURITANIA
Nouakchott
MAL

PACIFIC

GUATEMALA  BELIZE
HONDURAS
EL SALVADOR  NICARAGUA
COSTA RICA  San José

CAPE VERDE  SENEGAL
THE GAMBIA  Dakar
GUINEA-BISSAU GUINEA
Conakry
SIERRA LEONE
Monrovia  C. D'I
LIBERIA  Accra

TRINIDAD AND
TOBAGO
Caracas  Port of Spain
PANAMA  VENEZUELA
Bogotá  Georgetown  Paramaribo
Cayenne
COLOMBIA  FR. G.

BUR

OCEAN

Galapagos
Islands
(Ecuador)

Quito
ECUADOR

KIRIBATI

OCEAN

BRAZIL

Ascension
(U.K.)

Equator

PERU

Lima

American
Samoa

French
Polynesia
(France)

St Helena
(U.K.)

BOLIVIA
La Paz  Sucre

Brasília

Cook
Islands
(New Zealand)  Tahiti

PARAGUAY

Rio de Janeiro
São Paulo

Tropic of Capricorn

Pitcairn Islands
(U.K.)

Easter
Island
(Chile)

Asunción

ARGENTINA

Santiago

Buenos
Aires  URUGUAY
Montevideo

Tristan
da Cunha
(U.K.)

Falkland
Islands
(U.K.)

South Georgia and
South Sandwich
Islands
(U.K.)

Bouvetøy
(Norwa

Antarctic Circle

ANT

## TIME COMPARISONS

Time varies around the world due to the
earth's rotation causing different parts of the
world to be in light or darkness at any one time.
To account for this, the world is divided into twenty-
four Standard Time Zones based on 15° intervals of longitude.
The table below gives examples of times observed at different parts
of the world when it is 12 noon in the zone at the Greenwich Meridian
(0° longitude). Daylight Saving Time, normally one hour ahead of local
Standard Time, observed by certain countries for parts of the year, is not considered.

Winkel Tripel Projection

| 01:00 | 02:00 | 03:00 | 04:00 | 05:00 | 06:00 | 07:00 | 08:00 | 09:00 | 10:00 | 11:00 | 12:0 |
|---|---|---|---|---|---|---|---|---|---|---|---|
| Am. Samoa
Samoa | Cook Is
Hawaiian Is
Tahiti | Anchorage | Vancouver
San Francisco
Los Angeles
Pitcairn Is | Edmonton
Denver | Chicago
Houston
Monterrey
Mexico City
Easter Island | Ottawa
Washington
Havana
Bogotá
Lima | Puerto Rico
Caracas
La Paz
Asunción | Nuuk
Brasília
Rio de Janeiro
Buenos Aires | South Georgia
S. Sandwich Is | Azores
Cape Verde | Reykja
Lond
Raba
Nouakc
Accr |

ARCTIC OCEAN

Svalbard (Norway)

RUSSIAN FEDERATION

Magadan

Arctic Circle

FINLAND
ESTONIA
LATVIA
LITH.
BELARUS
Moscow
Yekaterinburg
Omsk
Novosibirsk
UKRAINE
MO.
ROMANIA
BULGARIA
GEOR.
T'bilisi
Astana
KAZAKHSTAN
Ulan Bator
MONGOLIA
Harbin
N. KOREA
P'yŏngyang
Seoul
JAPAN
Istanbul
TURKEY
ANKARA
ARM.
AZ.
UZBEK.
Dushanbe
KYR.
TURKM.
TAJIK.
CHINA
Beijing
Tianjin
S. KOREA
Tōkyō
Osaka
CYP.
SYRIA
LEB.
ISR.
Baghdad
IRAQ
JOR.
Tehrān
IRAN
Kabul
AFGHAN-
ISTAN
Islamabad
New
Delhi
Lanzhou
Xi'an
Wuhan
Shanghai
Chengdu
Chongqing
PACIFIC

Cairo
EGYPT
Amman
Riyadh
SAUDI
ARABIA
U.A.E.
Muscat
PAKISTAN
Karachi
NEPAL
Kathmandu
BHUTAN
BANGLA-
DESH
Dhaka
MYANMAR
(BURMA)
Ha Nôi
Hong Kong
T'aipei
TAIWAN
Tropic of Cancer
OCEAN

Khartoum
SUDAN
ERITREA
Asmara
YEMEN
San'ā'
DJIBOUTI
OMAN
INDIA
Mumbai
Vientiane
Rangoon
THAILAND
Bangkok
CAM-
BODIA
Manila
PHILIPPINES
Northern
Mariana
Islands
(U.S.A.)
MARSHALL
ISLANDS

N'djamena
Addis
Ababa
ETHIOPIA
SOMALIA
Chennai
SRI
LANKA
BRUNEI
FEDERATED STATES
OF MICRONESIA

C.A.R.
Bangui
UGANDA
DEM.
REP.
CONGO
KENYA
Nairobi
Dodoma
TANZANIA
SEYCHELLES
MALDIVES
British Indian
Ocean Territory
(U.K.)
Kuala Lumpur
Putrajaya
MALAYSIA
SINGAPORE
PALAU
NAURU
KIRIBATI

Lilongwe
ZAMBIA
MOZAMBIQUE
COMOROS
INDIAN
Christmas
Island
(Australia)
Cocos
Islands
(Australia)
INDONESIA
Jakarta
EAST
TIMOR
PAPUA
NEW
GUINEA
Port
Moresby
SOLOMON
ISLANDS
TUVALU
SAMOA

Harare
ZIMBABWE
MADAGASCAR
MAURITIUS
Antananarivo
Réunion
(France)
Coral Sea
Islands
Territory
(Aust.)
VANUATU
FIJI

BOTS-
WANA
Maputo
SWAZILAND
LESOTHO
Pretoria
Maseru
REP. OF
SOUTH AFRICA
OCEAN
AUSTRALIA
Brisbane
New
Caledonia
(France)
Tropic of Capricorn
Norfolk
Island
(Australia)

French Southern
and Antarctic Lands
Îles Kerguélen
(France)
Perth
Sydney
Canberra

Wellington
NEW
ZEALAND

ANTARCTICA

## Abbreviations

| | | | | | | |
|---|---|---|---|---|---|---|
| A. | ANDORRA | CZ.R. | CZECH REPUBLIC | M. | MACEDONIA |
| AL. | ALBANIA | DEN. | DENMARK | MO. | MOLDOVA |
| ARM. | ARMENIA | EQ.G. | EQUATORIAL GUINEA | NETH. | NETHERLANDS |
| AUS. | AUSTRIA | FR.G. | FRENCH GUIANA | NI. | NIGERIA |
| AZ. | AZERBAIJAN | GEOR. | GEORGIA | Q. | QATAR |
| B. | BURUNDI | GER. | GERMANY | R. | RWANDA |
| BE. | BENIN | GH. | GHANA | S. | SERBIA AND MONTENEGRO |
| BEL. | BELGIUM | GUY. | GUYANA | SLA. | SLOVAKIA |
| B.H. | BOSNIA-HERZEGOVINA | HUN. | HUNGARY | SL. | SLOVENIA |
| BN. | BAHRAIN | ISR. | ISRAEL | SUR. | SURINAME |
| BUR. | BURKINA | JOR. | JORDAN | SW. | SWITZERLAND |
| CAM. | CAMEROON | K. | KUWAIT | T. | TOGO |
| C.A.R. | CENTRAL AFRICAN REPUBLIC | KYR. | KYRGYZSTAN | TAJIK. | TAJIKISTAN |
| C.D'I. | CÔTE D'IVOIRE | LEB. | LEBANON | TURKM. | TURKMENISTAN |
| CR. | CROATIA | LITH. | LITHUANIA | U.A.E. | UNITED ARAB EMIRATES |
| CYP. | CYPRUS | LUX. | LUXEMBOURG | UZBEK. | UZBEKISTAN |

1: 100 800 000

| 13:00 | 14:00 | 15:00 | 16:00 | 17:00 | 18:00 | 19:00 | 20:00 | 21:00 | 22:00 | 23:00 | 24:00 |
|---|---|---|---|---|---|---|---|---|---|---|---|
| Oslo Paris Algiers Abuja Kinshasa | Kiev Ankara Cairo Harare Cape Town | Moscow Baghdād Riyadh Addis Ababa Dodoma | T'bilisi Muscat Seychelles Mauritius | Yekaterinburg Islamabad Karachi | Omsk Dhaka | Ha Nôi Bangkok Jakarta | Ulaanbaatar Beijing Manila Singapore Perth | P'yŏngyang Tōkyō Palau | Port Moresby Brisbane Canberra | Magadan Solomon Is New Caledonia | Marshall Is Tuvalu Fiji Wellington |

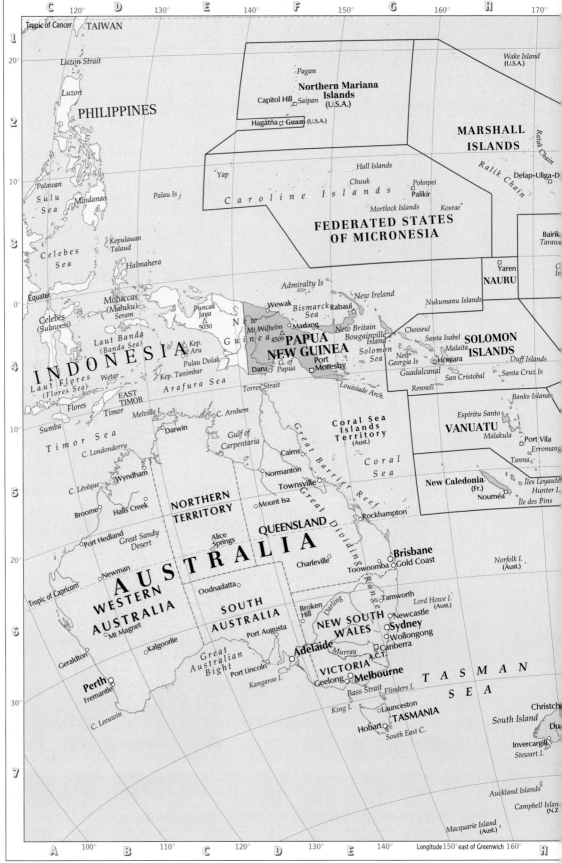

Lambert Azimuthal Equal Area Projection

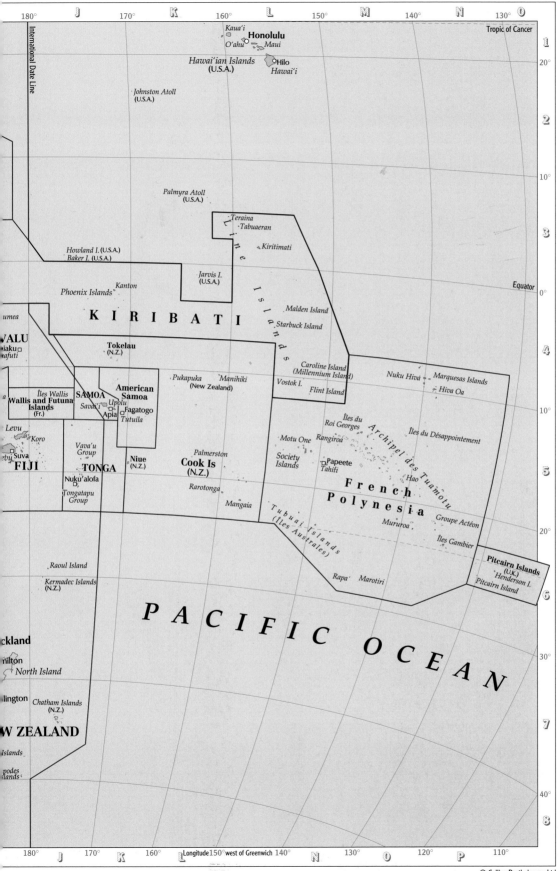

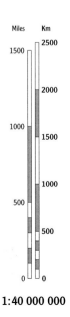

J · K · L · M · N · O

Tropic of Cancer

International Date Line

*Kaua'i*
**Honolulu**
*O'ahu* · *Maui*
**Hawai'ian Islands**
**(U.S.A.)** · *Hilo*
*Hawai'i*

20°

*Johnston Atoll*
*(U.S.A.)*

2

10°

*Palmyra Atoll*
*(U.S.A.)*

3

*Teraina*
*Tabuaeran*

*Kiritimati*

*Howland I.* (U.S.A.)
*Baker I.* (U.S.A.)

*Jarvis I.*
*(U.S.A.)*

Equator

0°

*Phoenix Islands* · *Kanton*

**K I R I B A T I**

*Line Islands*

*Malden Island*

*Starbuck Island*

**VALU**
*iaku*
*afuti*

*Tokelau*
*(N.Z.)*

4

*Caroline Island*
*(Millennium Island)*

*Nuku Hiva* · *Marquesas Islands*

*Pukapuka* · *Manihiki*
**(New Zealand)**

*Vostok I.*

*Flint Island*

*Hiva Oa*

*Îles Wallis*
**Wallis and Futuna**
**Islands**
**(Fr.)**

**SAMOA**
*Savai'i* · *Upolu*
*Apia*

**American**
**Samoa**
*Fagatogo*
*Tutuila*

*Îles du*
*Roi Georges*

*Archipel des Tuamotu*

*Îles du Désappointement*

*Levu*
*Koro*

*Motu One* · *Rangiroa*

*vu* *Suva*

**FIJI**

*Vava'u*
*Group*

**Niue**
**(N.Z.)**

*Palmerston*

**Cook Is**
**(N.Z.)**

*Society*
*Islands*

*Papeete*
*Tahiti*

5

*Hao*

**F r e n c h**

**TONGA**

*Nuku'alofa*

*Rarotonga*

**P o l y n e s i a**

*Groupe Actéon*

*Tongatapu*
*Group*

*Mangaia*

*Mururoa*

10°

*Tubuai Islands*
*(Îles Australes)*

*Îles Gambier*

20°

**Pitcairn Islands**
**(U.K.)**
*Henderson I.*

*Raoul Island*

*Rapa* · *Marotiri*

*Pitcairn Island*

6

*Kermadec Islands*
*(N.Z.)*

**P A C I F I C**

**O C E A N**

*ckland*

*ilton*
*North Island*

30°

*lington* · *Chatham Islands*
*(N.Z.)*

**W ZEALAND**

7

*Islands*

*podes*
*lands*

40°

8

Miles · Km

2500

1500

2000

2000

1000

1500

1000

500

500

500

0 · 0

**1:40 000 000**

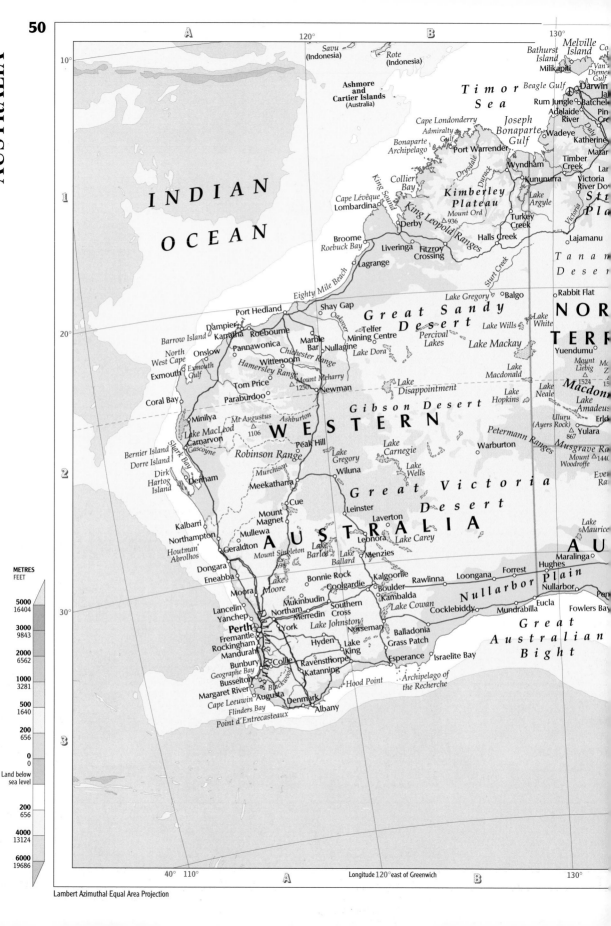

AUSTRALIA

**INDIAN**

**OCEAN**

Savu (Indonesia)
Rote (Indonesia)

*Timor Sea*

Ashmore and Cartier Islands (Australia)

Bathurst Island
Melville Island
Milikapiti
Van Diemen Gulf
Beagle Gulf
Darwin
Rum Jungle
Adelaide River
Wadeye
Katherine
Matar

Cape Londonderry
Admiralty Gulf
Bonaparte Archipelago
Port Warrender
Joseph Bonaparte Gulf
Wyndham
Kununurra
Timber Creek
Victoria River Do

Collier Bay
Cape Lévêque
Lombardina
King Sound
*Kimberley Plateau*
Mount Ord △ 936
Derby
Turkey Creek
Lake Argyle
Halls Creek
Lajamanu

Broome
Roebuck Bay
Liveringa
Fitzroy Crossing
*King Leopold Ranges*
*Drysdale*
*Durack*

Eighty Mile Beach
Lagrange
Sturt Creek
*Tanan Deser*

Port Hedland
Shay Gap
*Great Sandy Desert*
Lake Gregory
Balgo
Rabbit Flat

Dampier
Karratha
Roebourne
Pannawonica
Marble Bar
Nullagine
Mining Centre
Telfer
Percival Lakes
Lake Wills
Lake White
Lake Mackay

**NOR TERR**

North West Cape
Onslow
Barrow Island
Chichester Range
Lake Dora
Yuendumu

Exmouth
Exmouth Gulf
*Hamersley Range*
Wittenoom
Mount Meharry △ 1250
Lake Disappointment
Lake Hopkins
Mount Liebig △ 1524
*Macdon*

Coral Bay
Tom Price
Paraburdoo
Newman
*Gibson Desert*
Lake Macdonald
Lake Neale
Lake Amadeus

Mt Augustus △ 1106
Ashburton
Uluru (Ayers Rock) △ 867
Yulara
Erld

Minilya
Lake MacLeod
Carnarvon
Gascoyne
*Robinson Range*
Peak Hill
*WESTERN*
Lake Carnegie
Warburton
*Petermann Ranges*
*Musgrave Ra*
Mount Woodroffe △ 1440

Bernier Island
Dorre Island
Shark Bay
Murchison
Lake Gregory
Wiluna
Lake Wells

Dirk Hartog Island
Denham
Meekatharra
*Great Victoria*
Eve Ra

Cue
Leinster
*Desert*
Lake Maurice

Kalbarri
Mount Magnet
Laverton
*AUSTRALIA*
Lake Carey
Leonora
Maralinga

Northampton
Mullewa
Mount Singleton △ 698
Leonora
Menzies
Hughes
Maralinga

Houtman Abrolhos
Geraldton
Lake Barlee
Lake Ballard
*AU*
Nullarbor

Dongara
Eneabba
Bonnie Rock
Coolgardie
Kalgoorlie
Boulder
Rawlinna
Loongana
Forrest
Hughes
Nullarbor

Moora
Mukinbudin
Kambalda
*Nullarbor Plain*
Eucla
Cocklebiddy
Mundrabilla
Fowlers Bay

Lancelin
Yanchep
Northam
Southern Cross
Lake Cowan
Cocklebiddy
*Great*

**Perth**
Fremantle
Rockingham
Mandurah
York
Merredin
Lake Johnston
Norseman
Balladonia
Grass Patch
*Australian Bight*

Bunbury
Collie
Hyden
Lake King
Esperance
Israelite Bay

Busselton
Geographe Bay
Ravensthorpe
Katanning
Hood Point
Archipelago of the Recherche

Margaret River
Cape Leeuwin
Augusta
*Blackwood*
Denmark
Albany
Flinders Bay
Point d'Entrecasteaux

120°
130°
10°
20°
30°

40° 110°
Longitude 120° east of Greenwich
130°

Lambert Azimuthal Equal Area Projection

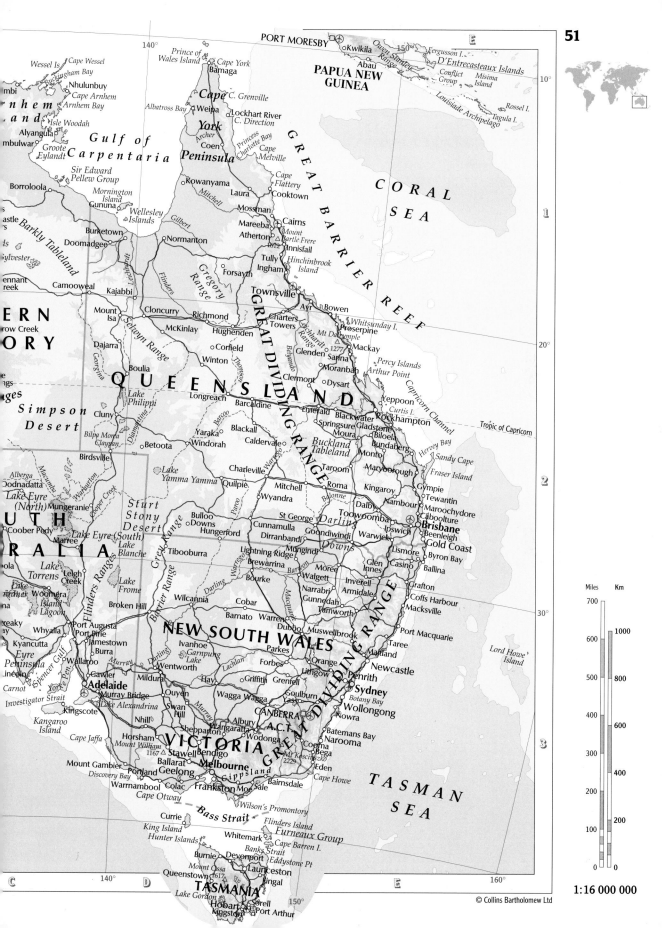

PORT MORESBY
Kwikila    Owen Stanley Range    Fergusson I.
Abau    D'Entrecasteaux Islands
**PAPUA NEW GUINEA**    Conflict Group    Misima Island
   10°
   Louisiade Archipelago    Rossel I.
   Tagula I.

Wessel Is    Cape Wessel
Prince of Wales Island    Cape York
Bamaga
mbi    Buckingham Bay
Nhulunbuy
**rnhem**    Cape Arnhem    Arnhem Bay
**l and**    Isle Woodah
**Cape**    C. Grenville
Albatross Bay    Weipa    Lockhart River
Alyangula    **York**    C. Direction
mbulwar    Archer    Princess Bay
Groote    Coen    Charlotte Bay    Cape Melville
Eylandt    **Peninsula**
Sir Edward Pellew Group
Borroloola
Mornington Island
Gununa    Cape Flattery
**Castle**    Wellesley Islands    Cooktown
**ds**    Burketown    Mossman
**ylvester**    Doomadgee    Mareeba    Cairns
**C O R A L**
Rowanyama    Laura    Atherton    Mount Bartle Frere 1612
**S E A**

*Gulf of*
*Carpentaria*

**G R E A T   B A R R I E R   R E E F**

**rn**    Normanton    Innisfail
**row Creek**    Tully
**ory**    Forsayth    Ingham    Hinchinbrook Island
**ennant**    Camooweal
**reek**    Kajabbi    **Townsville**
Mount Isa    Cloncurry    Richmond    Ayr    Bowen
Charters Towers    Proserpine    Whitsunday I.
McKinlay    Hughenden    Mt Dalrymple
Dajarra    Mackay
Corfield    Glenden    Sarina
**ges**    Boulia    Winton    Clermont    Moranbah
20°
Percy Islands
*Simpson*    **Q U E E N S L A N D**    Dysart    Arthur Point
*Desert*    Lake Philippi    Longreach    Barcaldine    Capricorn Channel
Cluny    Emerald    Blackwater    Rockhampton    Curtis I.
Yaraka    Blackall    Springsure    Gladstone
Bilpa Morea    Windorah    Caldervale    Moura    Biloela
Claypan    Betoota    **Buckland Tableland**    Bundaberg
Birdsville    Charleville    Taroom    Monto    Hervey Bay    Sandy Cape
Lake Yamma Yamma    Maryborough    Fraser Island
**Odnadatta**    Quilpie    Mitchell    Roma    Kingaroy    Gympie
*Lake Eyre*    Wyandra    Dalby    Nambour    Tewantin
*(North)*    Mungeranie    Toowoomba    Maroochydore
**Coober Pedy**    Bulloo Downs    St George    Caboolture
Marree    Hungerford    Cunnamulla    Goondiwindi    Ipswich    **Brisbane**
Lake Eyre (South)    Dirranbandi    Warwick    Beenleigh
**SOUTH**    Leigh Creek    Lightning Ridge    Mungindi    **Gold Coast**
**RALIA**    Lake Blanche    Tibooburra    Moree    Glen Innes    Lismore
*Lake Torrens*    Brewarrina    Narrabri    Casino    Byron Bay
**ola**    Bourke    Walgett    Inverell    Ballina
Lake Frome    Gunnedah    Armidale    Grafton
**reaky**    Woomera    Wilcannia    Cobar    Tamworth    Coffs Harbour
Whyalla    Broken Hill    Barnato    Warren    Macksville
30°
**Eyre**    Port Augusta    **NEW SOUTH WALES**    Port Macquarie
**Peninsula**    Port Pirie    Ivanhoe    Dubbo    Muswellbrook    Taree
Kyancutta    Jamestown    Garnpung Lake    Parkes    Lord Howe Island
**Lincoln**    Burra    Orange    Maitland
**s**    Wallaroo    Forbes    Newcastle
Carnot    Wentworth    Lithgow    Penrith
Gawler    Hay    Grenfell    **Sydney**
**Adelaide**    Mildura    Griffith    Botany Bay
Kingscote    Murray Bridge    Ouyen    Wagga Wagga    Yass    Wollongong
*Kangaroo Island*    Lake Alexandrina    Swan Hill    Goulburn    Nowra
Cape Jaffa    Nhill    **CANBERRA**    Batemans Bay
Horsham    Shepparton    **A.C.T.**    Narooma
Mount William    Wangaratta    Albury    Cooma    Bega
Mount Gambier    Stawell    Bendigo    Wodonga    Mt Kosciuszko 2229
Discovery Bay    Ballarat    **VICTORIA**    Eden
Warrnambool    Portland    Geelong    **Melbourne**    Cape Howe
Colac    Frankston    Gippsland    Sale
Cape Otway    Moe    Bairnsdale    **T A S M A N**
Wilson's Promontory    **S E A**
*Bass Strait*
Currie    Flinders Island    Furneaux Group
King Island    Whitemark    Cape Barren I.
Hunter Islands    Banks Strait    Eddystone Pt
Burnie    Devonport    Ringal
Mount Ossa 1617    Launceston
Queenstown    **TASMANIA**
Lake Gordon    Sorell    Port Arthur
150°    **Hobart**    Kingston

140°    150°    160°

Miles    Km
700 — 1000
600 — 800
500 — 600
400 — 400
300
200 — 200
100
0 — 0

**1:16 000 000**

**AUSTRALIA Southeast**

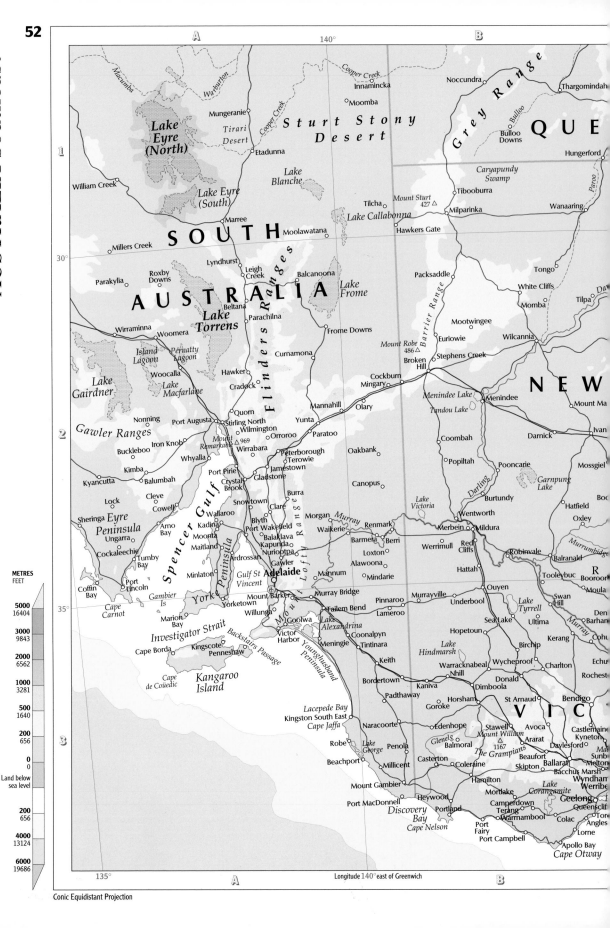

A  140°  B

**QUE**

Grey Range

Noccundra · Thargomindah

Innamincka

Cooper Creek

Moomba

Sturt Stony
Desert

Bulloo
Downs

Mungeranie

Tirari
Desert

Lake
Eyre
(North)

Etadunna

Lake
Blanche

Hungerford

Caryapundy
Swamp

Tiboooburra

William Creek

Lake Eyre
(South)

Tilcha

Mount Sturt
427 △

Milparinka

Wanaaring

Marree

Moolawatana

Hawkers Gate

**SOUTH**

Millers Creek

Lyndhurst

Leigh
Creek

Balcanoona

Lake
Frome

Packsaddle

White Cliffs

Tongo

Momba

Tilpa

Parakylia

Roxby
Downs

Beltana

Parachilna

Barrier Range

Mootwingee

**AUSTRALIA**

Lake
Torrens

Wirraminna

Woomera

Hawker

Cradock

Curnamona

Frome Downs

Mount Robe
486 △

Euriowie

Wilcannia

Island
Lagoon

Pernatty
Lagoon

Woocalla

Lake
Macfarlane

Quorn

Mannahill

Broken
Hill

Stephens Creek

**NEW**

Lake
Gairdner

Flinders Ranges

Port Augusta

Stirling North

Wilmington

Yunta

Olary

Cockburn
Mingary

Menindee Lake

Menindee

Mount Ma

**Gawler Ranges**

Nonning

Mount
Remarkable △ 969

Wirrabara

Orroroo

Paratoo

Oakbank

Tandou Lake

Darnick

Ivan

Buckleboo

Iron Knob

Whyalla

Peterborough
Terowie

Coombah

Popiltah

Pooncarie

Mossgiel

Kimba

Jamestown
Gladstone

Canopus

Darling

Burtundy

Garnpung
Lake

Hatfield

Oxley

Kyancutta

Balumbah

Port Pirie
Crystal
Brook

Burra

Clare

Morgan

Murray

Lake
Victoria

Wentworth

Boo

Lock

Cleve
Cowell

Snowtown

Blyth

Waikerie

Renmark

Merbein

Mildura

Red
Cliffs

Hatfield

Sheringa

**Eyre
Peninsula**

Wallaroo

Kadina

Port Wakefield

Balaklava

Barmera

Berri

Werrimull

Robinvale

Balranald

**Murrumbidge**

Ungarra

Arno
Bay

Moonta

Maitland

Kapunda
Nuriootpa

Loxton

Hattah

Tooleybuc

**R**

Cockaleechie

Tumby
Bay

Ardrossan

Gawler

Mannum

Alawoona

Mindarie

Boorooro

Moula

**Spencer Gulf**

Minlaton

**Adelaide**

Murray Bridge

Ouyen

Swan
Hill

Den

Coffin
Bay

Port
Lincoln

Gulf St
Vincent

Mount Barker

Murrayville

Underbool

Lake
Tyrrell

Ultima

Barhan

Cape
Carnot

Gambier
Is

**York Peninsula**

Yorketown

Willunga

Tailem Bend

Pinnaroo

Lameroo

Sea Lake

Hopetoun

Kerang

Echu

Marion
Bay

Investigator Strait

Goolwa

Victor
Harbor

Lake
Alexandrina

Meningie

Coonalpyn

Tintinara

Keith

Lake
Hindmarsh

Birchip

Wycheproof

Charlton

Rochest

Cape Borda

Kingscote

Penneshaw

Backstairs Passage

Younghusband Peninsula

Warracknabeal

Nhill

Donald

Dimboola

St Arnaud

Bendigo

**Kangaroo
Island**

Cape
de Coüedic

Bordertown

Kaniva

Padthaway

Horsham

Goroke

**VIC**

Lacepede Bay

Kingston South East

Cape Jaffa

Naracoorte

Edenhope

Stawell

Mount William
△ 1167

Avoca

Castlemaine

Kyneton

Daylesford

Robe

Lake
George

Penola

Glenelg

Balmoral

**The Grampians**

Ararat

Beaufort

Skipton

Ballarat

Sunb

Melton

Beachport

Millicent

Casterton

Coleraine

Bacchus Marsh

Wyndham

Werribe

Mount Gambier

Hamilton

Mortlake

Lake
Corangamite

Terang

Geelong

Queensclif

Discovery
Bay

Heywood

Portland

Camperdown

Warrnambool

Colac

Tor

Angles

Port MacDonnell

Cape Nelson

Port
Fairy

Port Campbell

Lorne

Apollo Bay

**Cape Otway**

135°  A  Longitude 140° east of Greenwich  B

Conic Equidistant Projection

**METRES**
FEET

5000
16404

3000
9843

2000
6562

1000
3281

500
1640

200
656

0
0

Land below
sea level

200
656

4000
13124

6000
19686

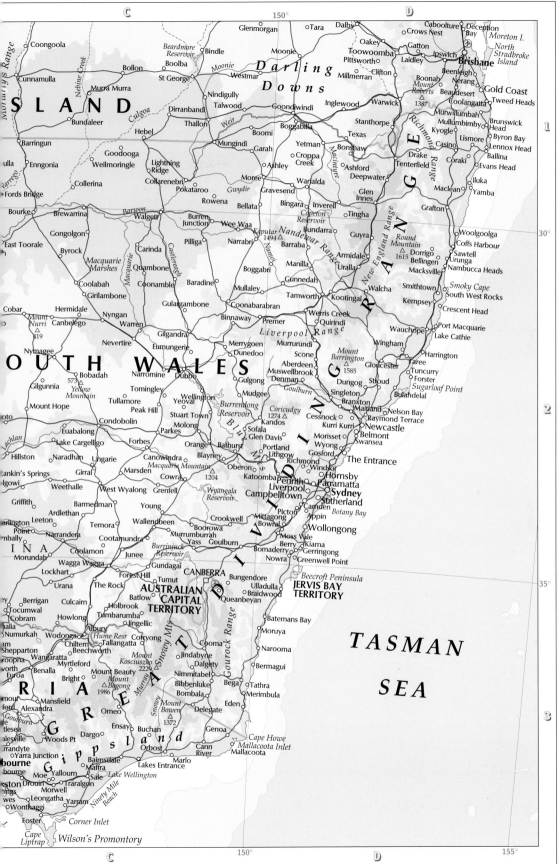

MORANS I. *North Stradbroke Island*
Moreton I.

Glenmorgan  Tara  Dalby  Crows Nest  Caboolture  Deception Bay
Moonie  Oakey  Gatton  Ipswich  **Brisbane**
Bollon  Westmar  Toowoomba  Laidley  Beenleigh  Nerang
Boolba  Pittsworth  Clifton  Boonah  Beaudesert  Gold Coast
St George  Millmerran  Mount Roberts 1387  Coolangatta  Tweed Heads
Bindle  Goondiwindi  Inglewood  Warwick  Stanthorpe  Murwillumbah  Brunswick Head
Dirranbandi  Talwood  Texas  Bonshaw  Tenterfield  Kyogle  Byron Bay
Thallon  Boomi  Yetman  Croppa Creek  Ashford  Drake  Casino  Lennox Head
Mungindi  Garah  Ashley  Deepwater  Glen Innes  Coraki  Ballina

**SLAND**
Cunnamulla  Murra Murra
Barringun  Goodooga  Weilmoringle
Ennngonia  Collerina  Lightning Ridge  Collarenebri  Pokataroo  Rowena  Bellata
Fords Bridge  Moree  Gravesend  Bingara  Inverell  Tingha  Grafton
Bourke  Brewarrina  Walgett  Burren Junction  Wee Waa  Bundarra  Guyra  Woolgoolga
Gongolgon  Pilliga  Narrabri  Barraba  Armidale  Dorrigo  Coffs Harbour
East Toorale  Byrock  Carinda  Quambone  Boggabri  Manilla  Uralla  Bellingen  Sawtell
Coolabah  Coonamble  Baradine  Mullaley  Gunnedah  Walcha  Smithtown  Macksville
Girilambone  Hermidale  Nyngan  Warren  Gulargambone  Coonabarabran  Tamworth  Kootingal  Kempsey  South West Rocks
Cobar  Mount Nurri 419  Canbelego  Gilgandra  Binnaway  Premier  Werris Creek  Quirindi  Wauchope  Crescent Head
Nymagee  Nevertire  Eumungerie  Merrygoen  Dunedoo  Murrurundi  Wingham  Port Macquarie
Bobadah  Narromine  Dubbo  Gulgong  Scone  Mount Barrington 1585  Gloucester  Taree  Lake Cathie
Gilgunnia 573  Yellow Mountain  Tomingley  Wellington  Mudgee  Aberdeen  Dungog  Stroud  Tuncurry  Harrington
Mount Hope  Tullamore  Yeoval  Muswellbrook  Denman  Singleton  Bulahdelah  Forster
Condobolin  Peak Hill  Stuart Town  Molong  Burrendong Reservoir  Goulburn  Branxton  Sugarloaf Point
Euabalong  Parkes  Coricudgy 1274  Kandos  Cessnock  Maitland  Nelson Bay
Lake Cargelligo  Forbes  Glen Davis  Sofala  Kurri Kurri  Raymond Terrace
Naradhan  Ungarie  Orange  Portland  Lithgow  Morisset  Newcastle
Hillston  Marsden  Canowindra  Blayney  Richmond  Windsor  Wyong  Belmont
Rankin's Springs  Girral  Cowra  Oberon  Katoomba  Penrith  Gosford  Swansea
Weethalle  West Wyalong  Grenfell  Macquarie Mountain 1204  Liverpool  Hornsby  The Entrance
Griffith  Barmedman  Young  Wyangala Reservoir  Campbelltown  Parramatta  **Sydney**  Sutherland
Ardlethan  Temora  Crookwell  Picton  Camden  Botany Bay
Leeton  Wallendbeen  Boorowa  Mittagong  Appin  Wollongong
Narrandera  Cootamundra  Yass  Goulburn  Bowral  Kiama
Coolamon  Junee  Gundagai  Moss Vale  Berry  Gerringong
Morundah  Wagga Wagga  Burrinjuck Reservoir  Bomaderry  Greenwell Point
Lockhart  Forest Hill  **CANBERRA**  Bungendore  Nowra
Urana  The Rock  Tumut  Batlow  Ulladulla  Beecroft Peninsula
Berrigan  Culcairn  **AUSTRALIAN CAPITAL TERRITORY**  Braidwood  **JERVIS BAY TERRITORY**
Tocumwal  Holbrook  Queanbeyan
Cobram  Howlong  Tumbarumba  Batemans Bay
Numurkah  Wodonga  Corryong  Jingellic  Moruya
Shepparton  Chiltern  Tallangatta  Cooma  Narooma
Wangaratta  Beechworth  Jindabyne  Bermagui
Euroa  Benalla  Myrtleford  Mount Kosciuszko 2229  Dalgety  Bega
Bright  Mount Beauty  Nimmitabel  Bibbenluke  Tathra
**RIA**  Mansfield  Mount Bogong 1986  Bombala  Merimbula
Alexandra  Omeo  Mount Bowen 1372  Delegate  Eden
Woods Pt  Dargo  Ensay  Buchan  Genoa
Yarra Junction  Omeo  Orbost  Cann River  Cape Howe
**bourne**  Bairnsdale  Lakes Entrance  Marlo  Mallacoota Inlet
Moe  Yallourn  Maffra  Sale  Mallacoota
Drouin  Traralgon  Morwell  Lake Wellington
Leongatha  Yarram  *Ninety Mile Beach*
Wonthaggi
Foster  *Corner Inlet*
Cape Liptrap  *Wilson's Promontory*

*Darling Downs*
*Richmond Range*
*New England Range*
*Nandewar Range*
*Liverpool Range*
*GREAT DIVIDING RANGE*
*Macquarie Marshes*
*Gippsland*
*Snowy Mts*

**TASMAN SEA**

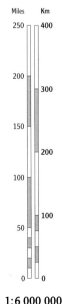

Miles  Km
250  400
200  300
150  200
100  100
50
0  0

**1:6 000 000**

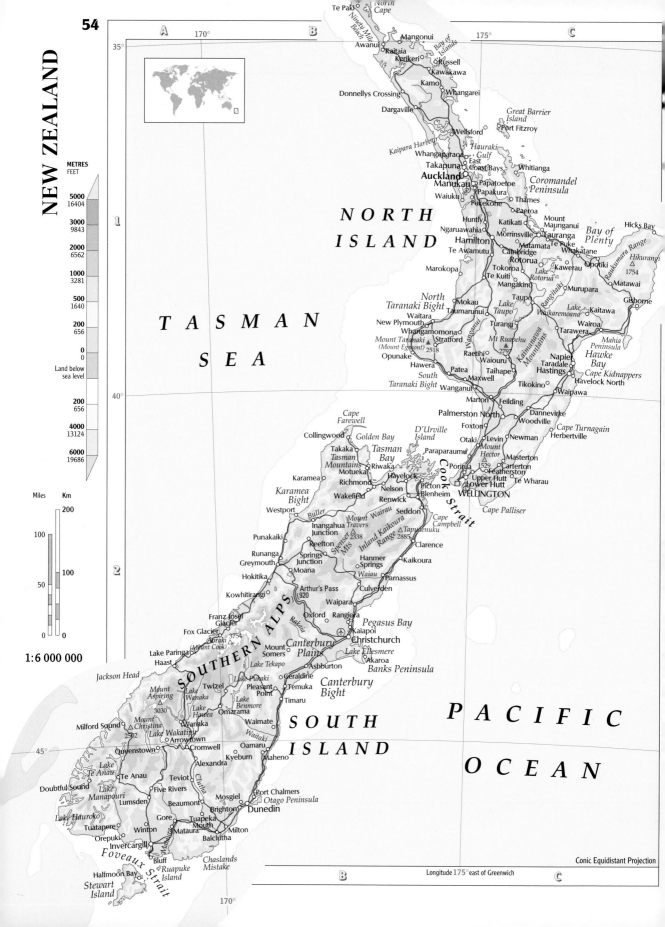

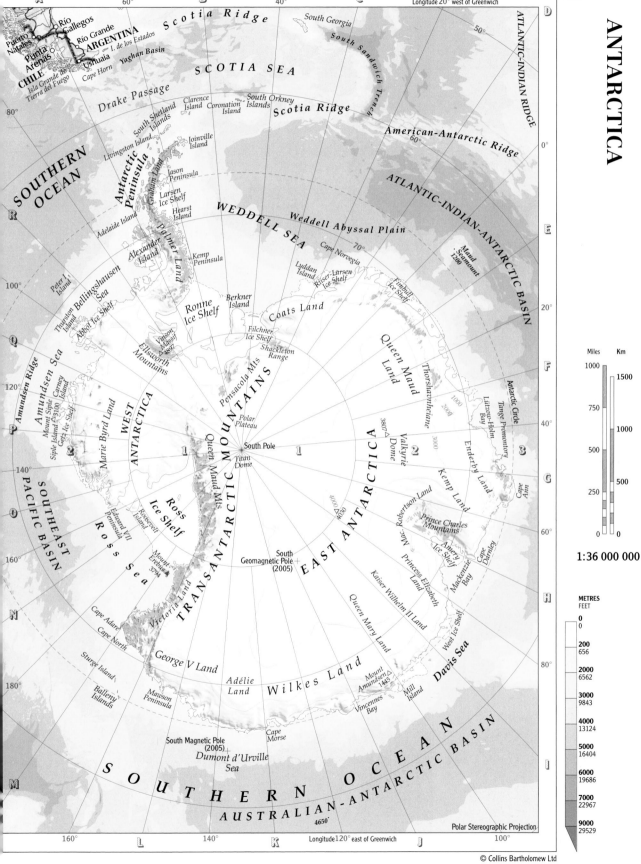

A  B  C  Longitude 20° west of Greenwich  D

Río Gallegos
Puerto Natales
Río Grande
ARGENTINA
I. de los Estados
Punta Arenas
Ushuaia
Yaghan Basin
CHILE
Isla Grande de Tierra del Fuego
Cape Horn

Scotia Ridge
South Georgia
South Sandwich Trench

SCOTIA SEA

Drake Passage
Clarence Island
Coronation Island
South Orkney Islands
Scotia Ridge

80°
SOUTHERN OCEAN

South Shetland Islands
Joinville Island
Livingston Island
Antarctic Peninsula
Graham Land
Jason Peninsula
Larsen Ice Shelf
Hearst Island

American-Antarctic Ridge
60°
0°

R
ATLANTIC-INDIAN-ANTARCTIC BASIN

WEDDELL SEA
Weddell Abyssal Plain
70°
Maud Seamount 1200

Adelaide Island
Palmer Land
Alexander Island
Kemp Peninsula
Lyddan Island
Riiser-Larsen Ice Shelf
Fimbull Ice Shelf
Cape Norvegia

Peter I Island
Thurston Island
Bellingshausen Sea
Abbot Ice Shelf

Ronne Ice Shelf
Berkner Island
Coats Land

Queen Maud Land

20°
F

Vinson Massif 4897
Ellsworth Mountains
Filchner Ice Shelf
Shackleton Range
Thorshavnheiane

Antarctic Circle
Tange Promontory
Lützow-Holm Bay

Amundsen Sea
Mount Siple
Carney Island
Siple Island 3110
Getz Ice Shelf

WEST ANTARCTICA
Marie Byrd Land

Pensacola Mts
TRANSANTARCTIC MOUNTAINS
Queen Maud Mts

Polar Plateau
South Pole
Titan Dome

Valkyrie Dome 3807
2000
1000
3000

Enderby Land
Cape Ann

G

Ross Ice Shelf
Edward VII Peninsula
Roosevelt Island

EAST ANTARCTICA

Kemp Land
Mac. Robertson Land
Prince Charles Mountains
Amery Ice Shelf
Cape Darnley

Mount Erebus 3794

South Geomagnetic Pole (2005)

4000
Princess Elizabeth Land
Mackenzie Bay

Ross Sea
Victoria Land
Cape Adare
Cape North

Kaiser Wilhelm II Land
Queen Mary Land
West Ice Shelf
Davis Sea

George V Land
Adélie Land
Wilkes Land
Mount Amundsen 1445
Mill Island
Vincennes Bay

SOUTHEAST PACIFIC BASIN

Sturge Island
Balleny Islands
Mawson Peninsula
Cape Morse

South Magnetic Pole (2005)
Dumont d'Urville Sea

SOUTHERN OCEAN

AUSTRALIAN-ANTARCTIC BASIN
4650

160°  140°  120° east of Greenwich  100°

Polar Stereographic Projection

© Collins Bartholomew Ltd

Miles / Km
1000
750
500
250
0
1500
1000
500
0

1:36 000 000

METRES FEET
| 0 | 0 |
| 200 | 656 |
| 2000 | 6562 |
| 3000 | 9843 |
| 4000 | 13124 |
| 5000 | 16404 |
| 6000 | 19686 |
| 7000 | 22967 |
| 9000 | 29529 |

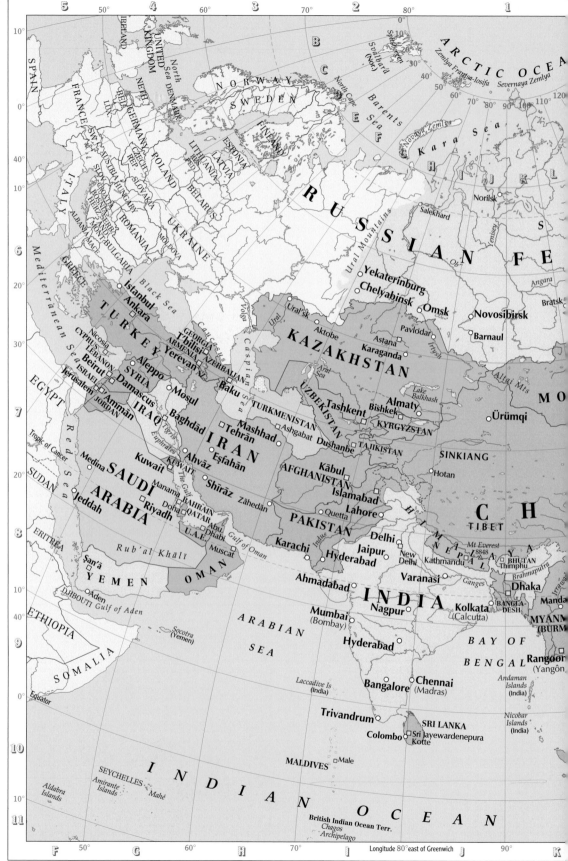

Two Point Equidistant Projection

1:44 000 000

© Collins Bartholomew Ltd

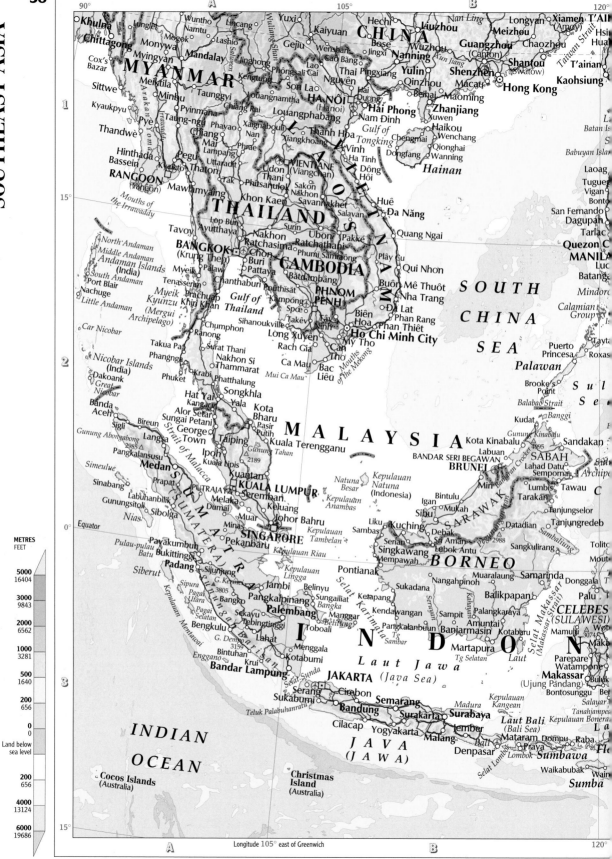

Albers Equal Area Conic Projection

A    100°    B

Phangnga
Ban Khok Kloi
Thalang
Phuket
Krabi
Thung Song
Nakhon Si Thammarat
Khao Chum Thong
**THAILAND**
Trang
Phatthalung
*Thale Luang*
Hat Yai
Songkhla
Satun
Sadao
Pattani
*Langkawi*
Kangar
Yala
Narathiwat
Alor Setar
Rangae
Kota Bharu
Sungai Petani
*Pinang*
Butterworth
Pasir Putih
George Town
Kuala Kerai
**MALAYSIA**
Taiping
Kuala Kangsar
Kuala Terengganu
Ipoh
*Gunung Tahan* △2189
*Tasik Kenyir*
Dungun
**PENINSULAR**
Kampar
Kuala Lipis
Cukai
**MALAYSIA**
Teluk Intan
Bagan Datuk
Kuantan
**KUALA LUMPUR**
Klang
Temerluh
Pekan
PUTRAJAYA
Bahau
Padang Endau
Tanjungbalai
Labuhanbilik
Seremban
Mersing
Melaka
Segamat
Keluang
Bagansiapiapi
Muar
Dumai
Batu Pahat
Duri
Bengkalis
**SINGAPORE**
Johor Bahru

*Mui Ca Mau*  Năm Căn  *Côn Son*
**VIETNAM**

**SOUTH CHI**

Phangnga

*Andaman Sea*

*Pulau We*  Sabang
Banda Aceh
Sigli
Bireun
Lhokseumawe
Calang
Takengon
Peureula
Langsa
*Gunung Abongabong* △2985
Pangkalansusu
Blangkejeren
Belawan
*Gunung Leuser* △3145
Binjai
**Medan**
Tapaktuan
Tebingtinggi
**Pematangsiantar**
Kisaran
Sidikalang
Prapat
*Danau Toba*
Labuhanbilik
Singkil
Balige
Sibolga
Rantauprapat
Gunungsitoli
Gunungtua
*Simeulue*
Sinabang
*Pulau-pulau Banyak*
**Nias**
Sirombu
Padangsidimpuan

*Strait of Malacca*

*Laut*
*Natuna Besar*
*Kepulauan Anambas*
Panarik
*Jemaja*
*Kepulauan Natuna (Indonesia)*
*Selat Serasan*
Liku
Sem
Kuch
Sambas
Pemangkat
Siluas
Singkawang
Bengkaya
Mempawah
Ngabang
*Kepulauan Tambelan (Indonesia)*
Pontianak
Balaibe
Kubu

Telukdalam
Hutanapan
Natal
Minas
Daludalu
Airbangis
Talu
Pekanbaru
Bangkinang

**SUMATRA**
*Rokan*
*(SUMATERA)*

*Bintan*
Tanjungpinang
*Kepulauan Riau*

0°   Equator   Telo
*Tanahmasa*
*Tanahbala*
*Pulau-pulau Batu*
Payakumbuh
*Kampar*
Tembilahan
*Lingga*
Daik
*Kepulauan Lingga*
Telukbatang

Kagologolo
Padangpanjang
Bukittinggi
**Padang**
Solok
Sijunjung
Rengat
*Singkep*
Kualatungal
*Pulau-pulau Karimata*
Sukadan
Ketapan

*Siberut*
Painan
Muarabungo
*Batanghari*
Simpang
Jambi
Belinyu
Sungailiat
Suk

Muarasiberut
△3805
*Gunung Kerinci*
Muaratembesi
Mentok
Pangkalpinang
*Bangka*
Kendaw

*Sipura*
Kaliet
Sungaipenuh
Bangko
Sarolangun
*Selat Bangka*
Rajik
Koba
Tanjungpandan
Manggar
Tanj
Sa

*Pagai Utara*
Mukomuko
Surulangun
Plaju
Toboali
*Dendang*

*Pagai Selatan*
Buriat
Sekayu
*Musi*
**Palembang**
*Belitung*

*Kepulauan Mentawai*
Lubuklinggau
Tebingtinggi
Kayuagung
Prabumulih

Curup
Lahat

*Mega*
Bengkulu
*Gunung Dempo* ▲ 3159
Martapura
Menggala

Bintuhan
*Gunung Resag* △2232
Kotabumi
**IND**
**LAUT**
**(JAV**

*Enggano*
Krui
Kotaagung
Metro

Tanjung Cina
Bandar Lampung
*Tanjung Indramayu*
Krakatau
Serang
**JAKARTA**

*Teluk Semangka*
*Sebesi*
Rangkasbitung
Karawang
Cirebon
Pekalor

*Selat Sunda*
*Panaitan*
*Deli*
Bogor △3019
**Bandung**
Garut
Tegal
*Gunung Slamet* △3428
Temanggu

*Teluk Palabuhanratu*
Sindangbarang
Ciamis
Cilacap
Kebum

**INDIAN OCEAN**

**JAVA**
**(JAWA**

METRES / FEET

5000 / 16404
3000 / 9843
2000 / 6562
1000 / 3281
500 / 1640
200 / 656
0 / 0
Land below sea level
200 / 656
4000 / 13124
6000 / 19686

**MALAYSIA AND INDONESIA West**

**C** 120° **D**

Palawan · Rio Tuba
Balabac
*Bugsuk*
*Balabac*
*Balabac Strait*
*Banggi*
**S U L U**
**S E A**

Roxas Oroquieta
Liloy Ozamiz Iligan
Siocon
*Zamboanga* Pagadian
*Peninsula*
Zamboanga Cotabato
Isabela *Moro* Datu Piang
*Sulu* Basilan *Gulf*
*Archipelago* Lebak

**S E A**
Kudat
Kanibongan
*Mapin*

Kota Belud
Kota *Turtle Islands*
Kinabalu *(Philippines)*
*Gunung*
*Kinabalu* Ranau Sandakan
△4095 Tambisan
Beaufort *Gunung Trus Madi* Lamag
Labuan △2649 Lahad
Tenom Kuamut Datu Balimbing
**BANDAR SERI** *Tawitawi*
**BEGAWAN** Tomani **SABAH** Semporna *Sibutu*
**BRUNEI** Lawas Pensiangan
Kuala Belait Lumbis Tawau
Lutong Seria *Bukit Harden* Mensalong
Miri 2136

Jolo *Jolo* Siasi
**PHILIPPINES**

**C E L E B E S**

**S E A**

Bintulu Labang Long Kubuang Tarakan
Akah
Igan Mukah Tanjungselor
Sibu Belaga Kapit
Saratok
Debak Datadian Tanjungredeb
Sri Aman △2988

**M SARAWAK**

**B O R N E O**

Putusibau
Semitau
Sintang

Longiram
Muaralaung
Tewah Muarateweh Samboja
Rantaupanjang Samarinda
Palangkaraya Balikpapan
Sampit Tanahgrogot
Kualapembuang Kandangan Tanjung
Amuntai
Banjarmasin Martapura Kotabaru
Pagatan *Sebuku*
*Tanjung* *Laut*
*Puting* *Tanjung*
*Selatan*

**I  N**  **O**  **N E S I A**

*Kepulauan*
*Laut Kecil*

*Tolitoli* Kwandang

**Semenanjung Minahasa**
Moutong Gorontalo
Sidoan *Kepulauan*
*Togian*
*Tanjung*
*Teluk* *Pangkalsiang*
Tomali *Tomini* *Togian*
Donggala *Batudaka*
Luwuk
Palu Tataba *Peleng*
Mapane Poso
Uekuli *Kepulauan*
Tenteno Kolonedale *Banggi*
*Teluk Towori* *Banggai*
Babana
Mamuju Masamba *Manui*
*Gandadiwata* *Bukit* △3074 Wotu
Sambo Rantepao
Majene Makale Palopo
Polewali Malamala
Anabanua
Parepare Kolaka Kendari
Singkang *Wowoni*
Watampone Raha
Maros Sinjai *Muna* *Buton*
*G. Lompobattang*
**Makassar** △2871
Ujung Pandang Bulukumba Baubau
Bontosunggu *Salayar*
Benteng *Batuata*

**C E L E B E S**
**(SULAWESI)**

*A   W   A*

*(E A)*
*pulau*
*unjawa* *Bawean*
*Tanjung*
*Bugel*

S Pati Tuban **Madura**
Purwodadi Bangkalan Sumenep Arjasa
arang **Surabaya** *Genteng Raas*
arta Jombang *Selat Madura* Situbondo
Pasuruan
Madiun **Malang** Banyuwangi
akarta *G. Semeru G. Raung*
Ngunut *3676* Singaraja
Lumajang Jember *332* Mataram
Denpasar Gianyar Praya
**Bali** *Selat Lombok* **Lombok** Taliwang

*Masalembu*
*Besar*

*Kepulauan*
*Kangean*

*Laut Bali*
*(Bali Sea)* **Sumbawa**
*Gunung*
*Tambora* △2821
Alas Dompu
Sumbawabesar Raba
Plampang
**Sumba** Waikabubak

*Sabalana*
*Tanahjampea* *Kalao*
*Kalaotoa*
*Kepulauan Bonerate*
*Kepulauan*
*Tengah*

**Laut Flores**
*(Flores Sea)* *Kepulauan*
*Solor*
Reo **Flores** Larantuka
Labuhanbajo Maumere Labala
Ruteng Bajawa
Ende
*Selat Sumba* **Laut Sawu**
Memboro *(Savu Sea)*
Waingapu

0°

1

2

10°

**C** 120° **D**

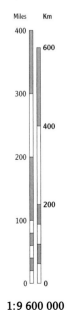

Miles Km
400
600
300
400
200
200
100
0 0

**1:9 600 000**

# CONTINENTAL SOUTHEAST ASIA

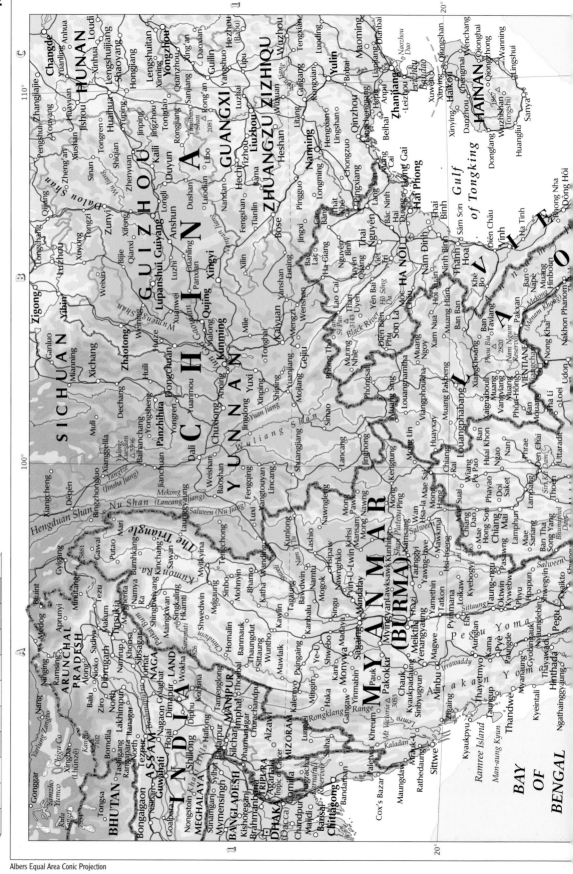

Albers Equal Area Conic Projection

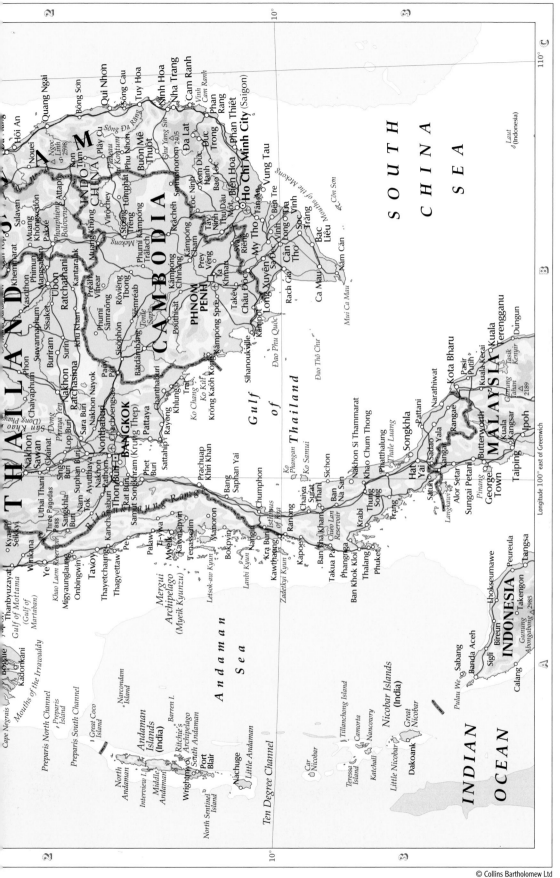

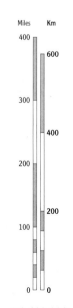

1:9 600 000

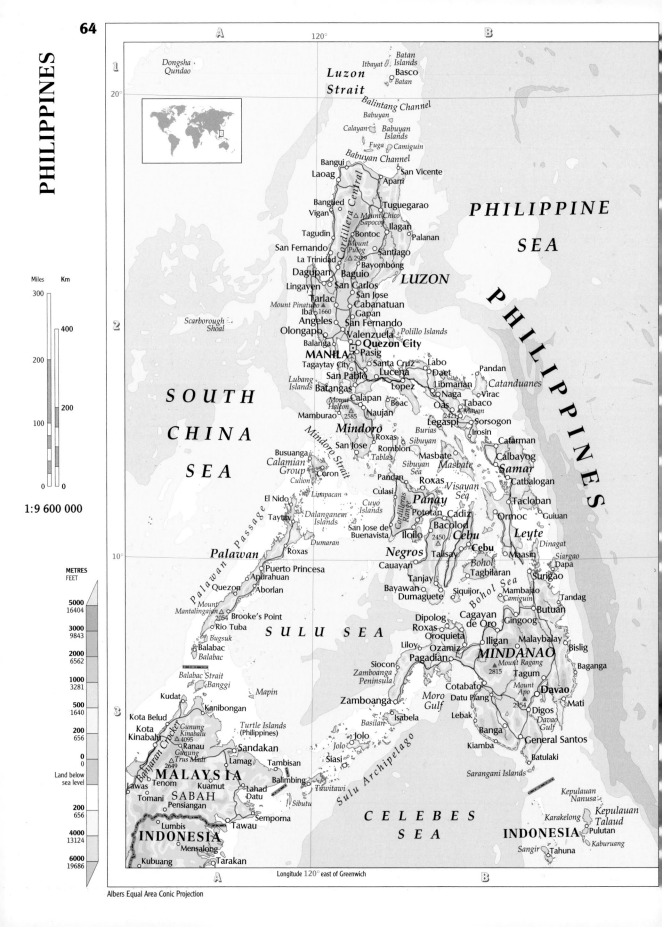

**PHILIPPINES**

Miles   Km

300

200          400

100          200

0            0

**1:9 600 000**

METRES
FEET

5000
16404

3000
9843

2000
6562

1000
3281

500
1640

200
656

0
0

Land below
sea level

200
656

4000
13124

6000
19686

Albers Equal Area Conic Projection

Longitude 120° east of Greenwich

Dongsha
Qundao

*Luzon
Strait*

Batan
Islands
Itbayat    Basco
Batan

*Balintang Channel*
Babuyan
Calayan    Babuyan
Islands
Fuga  Camiguin

*Babuyan Channel*
Bangui    San Vicente
Laoag    Aparri

Bangued    Tuguegarao
Vigan    Mount Chico
Sapocoy    Ilagan    Palanan
Tagudin    Bontoc
San Fernando    Santiago
La Trinidad    Mount
Pulog    Bayombong
Dagupan    △2929
Lingayen    Baguio    **LUZON**
Tarlac    San Carlos
San Jose
Mount Pinatubo    Cabanatuan
Iba    1660    Gapan
Angeles    San Fernando
Olongapo    Valenzuela    Polillo Islands
Balanga    Quezon City
**MANILA**    Pasig
Tagaytay City    Santa Cruz    Labo
San Pablo    Lucena    Daet    Pandan
Batangas    Lopez    Libmanan    *Catanduanes*
Lubang    Calapan    Naga    Virac
Islands    Boac    Oas    Tabaco
Mount    Naujan    Mayon    Sorsogon
Halton    Legaspi    △2421
Mamburao    2585    Irosin
*Mindoro*    Burias
Roxas    Sibuyan
San Jose    Romblon    Masbate
*Tablas*    Catarman
Busuanga    Pandan    *Masbate*    Calbayog
*Calamian
Group*    Coron    Culasi    Roxas    **Samar**
Culion    *Sibuyan
Sea*    Catbalogan
Limnacan    *Cuyo
Islands*    *Visayan
Sea*    Tacloban
El Nido    *Dalanganem
Islands*    Pototan    Cadiz    Ormoc    Guiuan
Taytay    San Jose de    Bacolod    Cebu    **Leyte**
Buenavista    Iloilo    △2450    **Cebu**    Dinagat
Dumaran    **Negros**    Talisay    Maasin    *Siargao*
Roxas    Cauayan    *Bohol*    Dapa
**Palawan**    Tanjay    Tagbilaran    Surigao
Puerto Princesa    Bayawan    Siquijor    *Bohol
Sea*    Mambajao    Tandag
Apurahuan    Dumaguete    Camiguin
Aborlan    Butuan

**SOUTH
CHINA
SEA**

Scarborough
Shoal

*Mindoro Strait*

*Palawan Passage*

Mount
Mantalingajan
2054    Brooke's Point
Rio Tuba
Bugsuk
Balabac
Balabac    *Banggi*    *Mapin*

*Balabac Strait*

Kudat
Kanibongan
Kota Belud
Kota
Kinabalu    Gunung
Kinabalu
Ranau    △4095
Gunung
Trus Madi    Sandakan
Lamag    △2649
Tambisan
Tenom    Balimbing
Kuamut
Lawas    Kuamut
**MALAYSIA**
**SABAH**    Lahad
Pensiangan    Datu    *Sibutu*    *Tawitawi*
Lumbis    Tawau    Semporna
**INDONESIA**    Mensalong
Kubuang    Tarakan

Dipolog
Roxas    Iligan    Malaybalay
Liloy    Oroquieta    Cagayan    Gingoog
Siocon    Ozamiz    de Oro    **MINDANAO**
Zamboanga    Pagadian    Mount Ragang
Peninsula    △2815    Bislig
Zamboanga    Cotabato    Mount
Datu Piang    Apo    Baganga
Isabela    Lebak    △2954    **Davao**
*Basilan*    Banga    Digos    Mati
Jolo    Kiamba    Davao
Siasi    General Santos    Gulf
Jolo    *Sulu Archipelago*    Batulaki
Sarangani Islands

*Siocon*
*Moro
Gulf*

**SULU SEA**

Turtle Islands
(Philippines)

**CELEBES
SEA**    **INDONESIA**

Sangir    Tahuna

*Kepulauan
Nanusa*
Karakelong    *Kepulauan
Talaud*
Pulutan
Kaburuang

*PHILIPPINE

SEA*

*PHILIPPINES*

*Panay*

*Cardillera
Range*

*Cardillera Central*

*Banjaran Crocker*

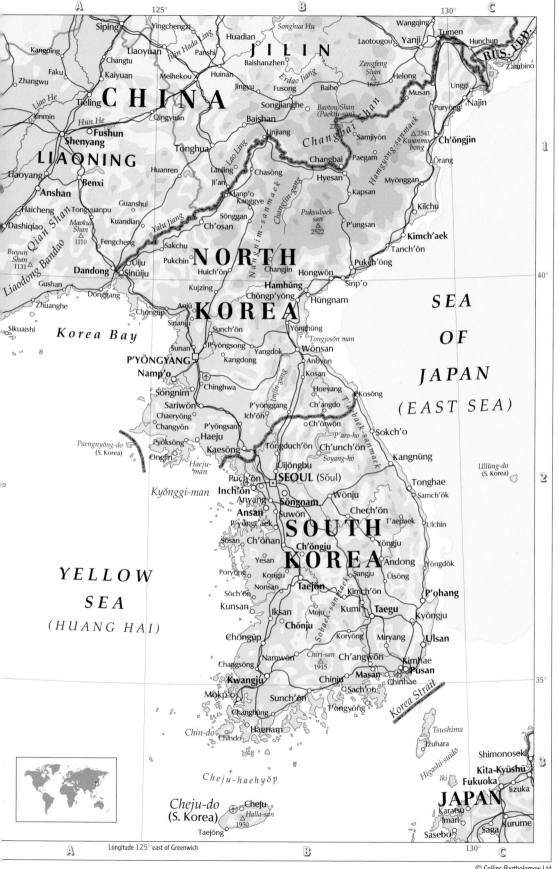
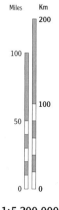

# JAPAN

Sakhalin

Korsakov
Novikovo
Zaliv
Aniva
Mys Aniva
Gornozavodsk
Ostrov
Moneron

Mys Kril'on
La Pérouse Strait
Soya-misaki
Rebun-tō
Rishiri-tō

Shiretoko-misaki
Abashiri-wan
Rausu
Shibetsu
Nemuro
Bekkai

Monbetsu
Kitami
Kussharo-ko
Meaken-dake
1503
Kushiro
Abashiri
Asahi-dake
2290
Obihiro
Ashoro
Hiroo
Erimo-misaki
Samani

Nayoro
Hidaka-sanmyaku

HOKKAIDŌ

Teshio
Wakkanai
Teshio-gawa
Rumoi
Asahikawa
Takikawa
Ebetsu
Otaru
Ishikari-wan
Iwanai
Shakotan-misaki
Shakotan-hantō
Suttsu
Okushiri-tō

Ashibetsu
Bibai
Iwamizawa
Yūbari
Chitose
Sapporo
Shikotsu-ko
Toya-ko
Date
Mori
Yakumo
Esashi
O-shima

Tomakomai
Muroran
Uchiura-wan
(Volcano Bay)
Hakodate
Oma
Shimokita-hantō
Matsumae

Svetlaya

Amgu

Terney

Kamenka
Rudnaya Pristan'

Dal'negorsk

RUSSIAN
FEDERATION
Sikhote-Alin'

Bikin
Iman
Bikin
Luchegorsk
Dal'nerechensk
Vostok
Lesozavodsk
Kirovskiy

Spassk-Dal'niy
Ussuri
Khorol
Yaroslavskiy
Mikhaylovka
Ussuriysk
Artem
Ugolovye
Slavyanka
Vladivostok
Zaliv
Petra Velikogo
Zarubino

Arsen'yev
Chuguyevka
Kavalerovo
Lazo
Smolyoninovo
Kamen-Rybolov
Bol'shoy Kamen
Partizansk
Vrangel'
Nakhodka
Preobrazheniye

SEA

OF

JAPAN

(EAST SEA)

CHINA

Shuangyashan
Baoqing
Qitaihe
Boli
Linkou
Wanda Shan

Jixi
Mishan
Lake
Khanka
Mudan Jiang
Muling
Mudanjiang
Suifenhe
Poganichnyy

Yilan
Fangzheng
Changting
Helong
Yanji
Zhangguangcai Ling
Laoye Ling
Wangqing
Tumen
Hunchun
Najin
Unggi
Kaimma-bong
251

Dongfanghong
Hulin

Pinan Ling

NORTH
KOREA

Ch'ŏngjin
Myŏnggan
Kilchu
Kimch'aek

Aomori
Hachinohe
Kuji
Miyako
Kamaishi
Kesennuma
Hirosaki
Towada
Ninohe
Morioka
Kitakami-gawa
Kitakami
Hanamaki
Ichinoseki
Noshiro
Odate
Kazuno
Iwate-san
2041
Oga
Oga-hantō
Akita
Honjō
Yokote
Honjō
Sakata

Tsugaru-kaikyō
Mutsu-wan
Shiriya-zaki
Mutsu

METRES
FEET

5000
16404

3000
9843

2000
6562

1000
3281

500
1640

200
656

0
0

Land below
sea level

200
656

4000
13124

6000
19686

Albers Equal Area Conic Projection

© Collins Bartholomew Ltd

1:6 000 000

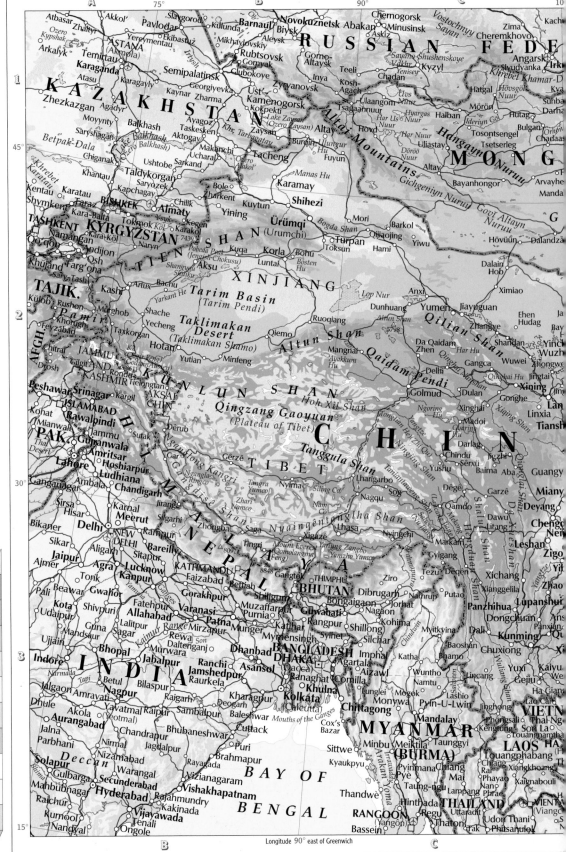

METRES
FEET

| 5000 | 16404 |
| 3000 | 9843 |
| 2000 | 6562 |
| 1000 | 3281 |
| 500 | 1640 |
| 200 | 656 |
| 0 | 0 |

Land below
sea level

| 200 | 656 |
| 4000 | 13124 |
| 6000 | 19686 |

RUSSIAN FEDE

Atbasar  Akkol'  Slavgorod  Barnaul  Novokuznetsk  Abakan  Chernogorsk  Vostochnyy  Zima  Cheremkhovo  Kach
Ozero  Zhaltyr  Pavlodar  Biysk  Minusinsk  Askiz  Sayan  Angarsk  Irk
Kypshak  (Akmola)  Ekibastuz  Mikhaylovskiy  Gorno-  Teeli  Sayano-Shushenskoye  Khrebet Khamar-D  Kya
Arkalyk  ASTANA  Yereymentau  Rubtsovsk  Altaysk  Kyzyl  Chadan  Hatgal  Hövsgöl  Subha
Karaganda  Temirtau  Gornyak  Inya  Kosh-  Nuur  Mörön  Darha
Zhezkazgan  Karagayly  Georgiyevka  Ust'-  Zyryanovsk  Agach  Ulaangom  Uvs Nuur  Hutag
Agadyr'  Kaynar  Zharma  Kamenogorsk  Tsagaannuur  Hyargas  Tosontsengel  Bulgan  Orhon
Moyynty  Balkhash  Ayagoz  Lake Zaysan  Altay  Nuur  Uliastay  Darha
Betpak-Dala  Saryshagan  Taskesken  (Ozero Zaysan)  Burqin  Ulungur  Har Us  Nuur  Tsetserleg  MONG
Chiganak  Ushtobe  Sarkand  Aktogay  Tacheng  Hu  Fuyun  Döröö  Bayanhongor  Arvayhe
Khantau  Taldykorgan  Ozero  Manas Hu  Altay  Nuur  Govĭ-Altayn  Manda
Kentau  Saryözek  Alakol'  Karamay  Gichgeniyn Nuruu  Nuruu  G
Karatau  Kapchagay  Bole  Shihezi  Bayanhongor
Shymkent  Faraz  Chilik  Zharkent  Mori  Hövüün  Dalandz
TASHKENT  BISHKEK  Almaty  Kuytun  Barkol  Yiwu  Yinch
Kara-Balta  Yining  Ürümqi  Bogda Shan  Hami  Wuzh
Namangan  Tokmok  Kegen  (Urumchi)  Turpan  Qijiaojing  Zhongwe
O'qon  Naryn  Karakol  Korla  Toksun  Dalain  Xining

KAZAKHSTAN

MONG

TIEN SHAN

XINJIANG

Tarim Basin
(Tarim Pendi)

Taklimakan
Desert
(Taklimakan Shamo)

Altun Shan

Qilian Shan

Qaidam Pendi

KUNLUN SHAN

Qingzang Gaoyuan
(Plateau of Tibet)

CHIN

TIBET

Tanggula Shan

Nyainqentanglha Shan

HIMALAYA

MYANMAR
(BURMA)

INDIA

Deccan

BAY OF
BENGAL

THAILAND

LAOS

VIETN

Albers Equal Area Conic Projection

# CHINA Central

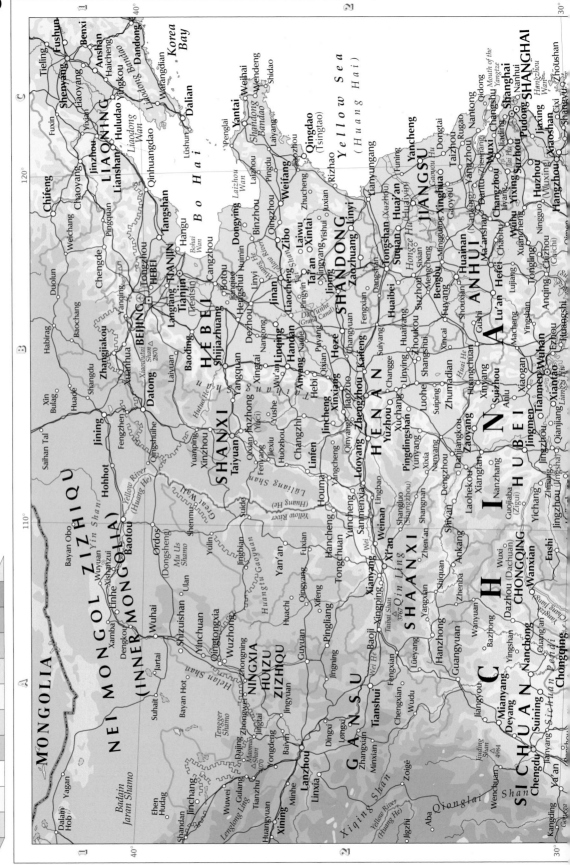

METRES
FEET

| | |
|---|---|
| 5000 | 16404 |
| 3000 | 9843 |
| 2000 | 6562 |
| 1000 | 3281 |
| 500 | 1640 |
| 200 | 656 |
| 0 | 0 |

Land below
sea level

| | |
|---|---|
| 200 | 656 |
| 4000 | 13124 |
| 6000 | 19686 |

Albers Equal Area Conic Projection

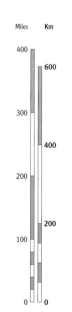

1:9 600 000

© Collins Bartholomew Ltd

# SOUTH ASIA

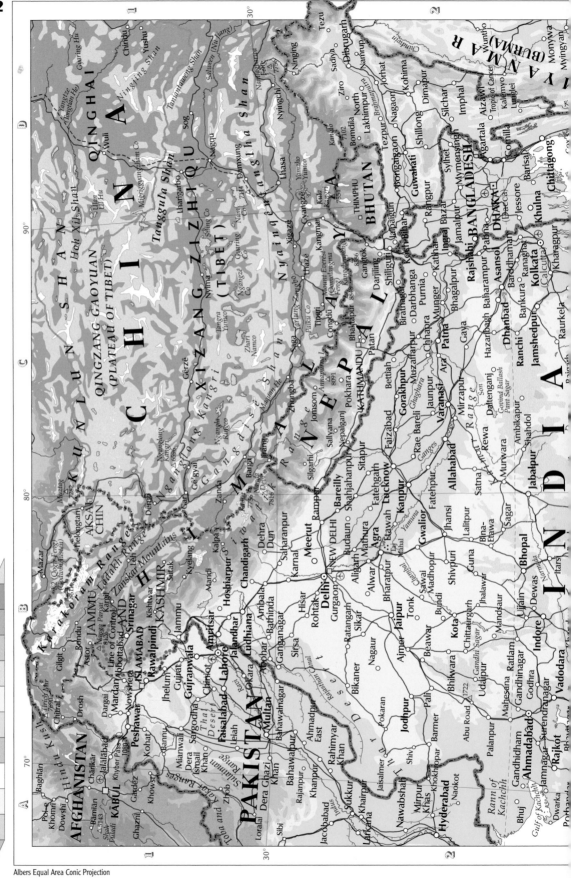

METRES
FEET

| 5000 | 16404 |
| 3000 | 9843 |
| 2000 | 6562 |
| 1000 | 3281 |
| 500 | 1640 |
| 200 | 656 |
| 0 | 0 |

Land below
sea level

| 200 | 656 |
| 4000 | 13124 |
| 6000 | 19686 |

Albers Equal Area Conic Projection

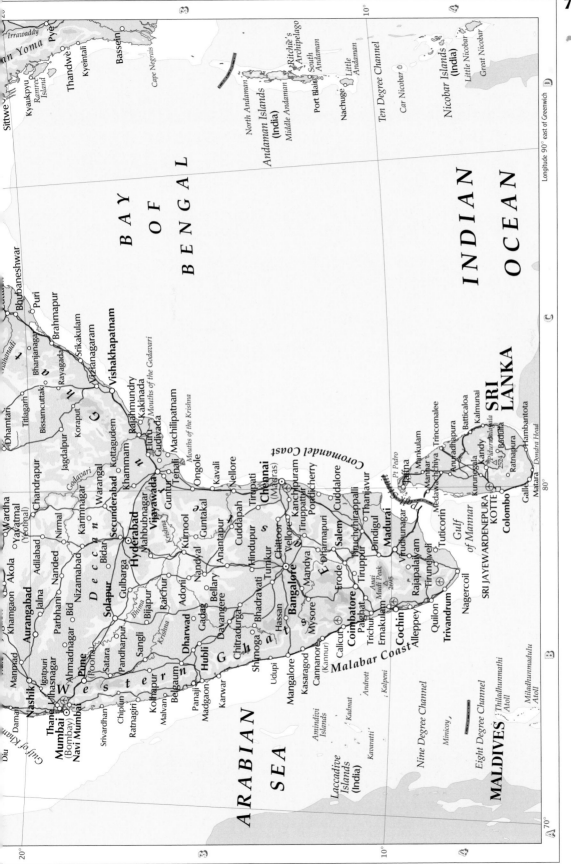

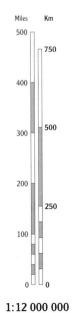

Irrawaddy
Pye
an Yoma
Kyaukpyu
Ramree
Island
Thandwe
Kyeintali
Bassein
Cape Negrais
Sittwe
North Andaman
Andaman Islands
(India)
Ritchie's
Archipelago
Middle Andaman
South
Andaman
Port Blair
Nachugê
Little
Andaman
Ten Degree Channel
Car Nicobar
Nicobar Islands
(India)
Little Nicobar
Great Nicobar

**B A Y**

**O F**

**B E N G A L**

**I N D I A N**

**O C E A N**

Longitude 90° east of Greenwich

Bhubaneshwar
Puri
Brahmapur
Bhanjanagar
Rayagada
Srikakulam
Titlagarh
Vizianagaram
**Vishakhapatnam**
Bissamcuttack
Koraput
Jagdalpur
Kottagudem
Mouths of the Godavari
Chandrapur
Godavari
Warangal
Rajahmundry
Kakinada
Eluru
Machilipatnam
Khammam
Gudivada
Nirmal
Vijayawada
Tenali
Mouths of the Krishna
**Secunderabad**
Guntur
Ongole
Karimnagar
**Hyderabad**
Krishna
Nellore
Kavali
Nizamabad
Bidar
Mahbubnagar
Kurnool
Kavali
Coromandel Coast
Gulbarga
Nandyal
Anantapur
Cuddapah
Tirupati
**Chennai**
(Madras)
Raichur
Adoni
Bellary
Hindupur
Chittoor
Kanchipuram
Ratchur
Gadag
Davangere
Tumkur
Vellore
Pondicherry
Cuddalore
Hubli
Chitradurga
**Bangalore**
Dharmapuri
**Salem**
Tiruchchirappalli
Thanjavur
Shimoga
Hassan
Mandya
Erode
Tiruppur
Dindigul
**Madurai**
**Coimbatore**
Mysore
Palghat
Trichur
Virudhunagar
Rajapalayam
Tirunelveli
**Cochin**
Alleppey
Tuticorin
Quilon
**Trivandrum**
Nagercoil
Mangalore
Kasaragod
(Kannur)
Calicut

Malabar Coast

**SRI**
**LANKA**
Jaffna
Pt Pedro
Mankulam
Trincomalee
Mannar
Anuradhapura
Batticaloa
Kalmunai
Kurunegala
Kandy
Ratnapura
**SRI JAYEWARDENEPURA**
**KOTTE**
**Colombo**
Galle
Matara
Dondra Head

Gulf
of Mannar

**A R A B I A N**

**S E A**

Laccadive
Islands
(India)

Amindivi
Islands

Nine Degree Channel

Minicoy

Eight Degree Channel

**MALDIVES**

Thiladhunmathi
Atoll
Miladhunmadulu
Atoll

| Miles | Km |
|---|---|
| 500 | 750 |
| 400 | 500 |
| 300 | |
| 200 | 250 |
| 100 | |
| 0 | 0 |

1:12 000 000

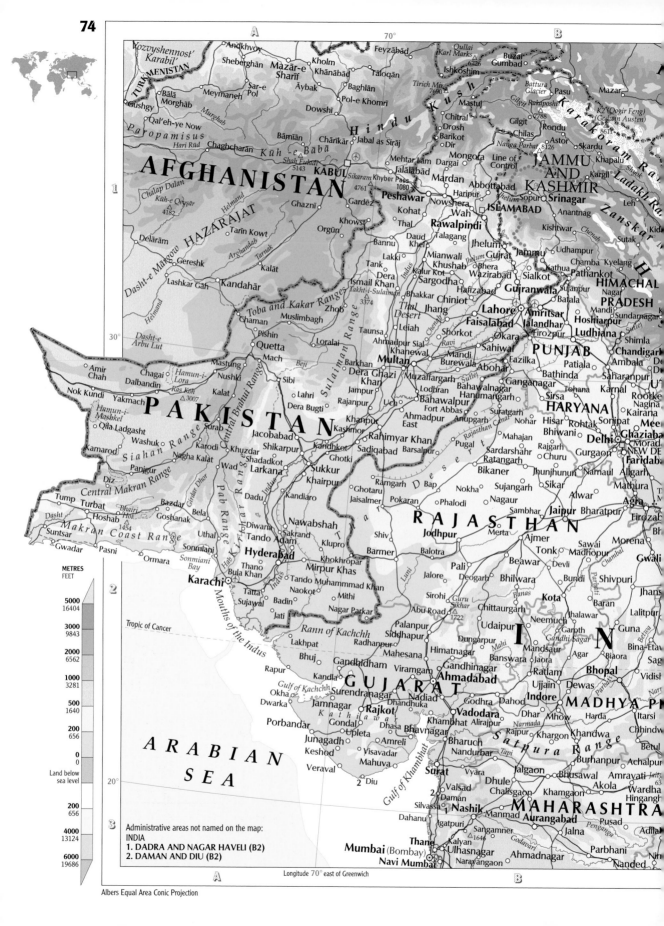

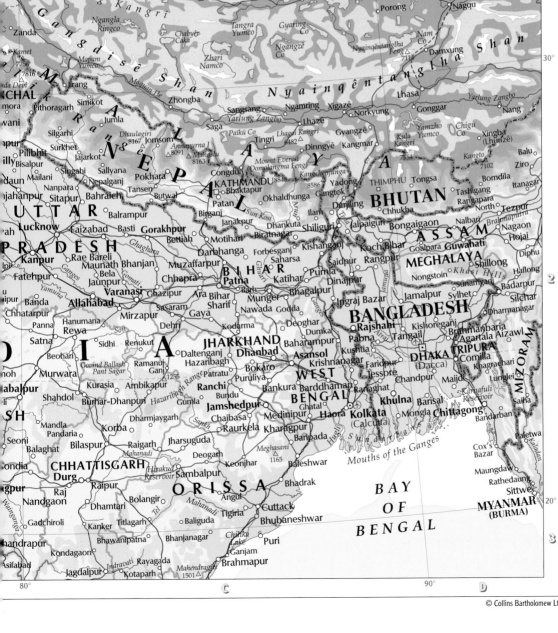

PAKISTAN, INDIA North AND BANGLADESH

1:9 600 000

© Collins Bartholomew Ltd

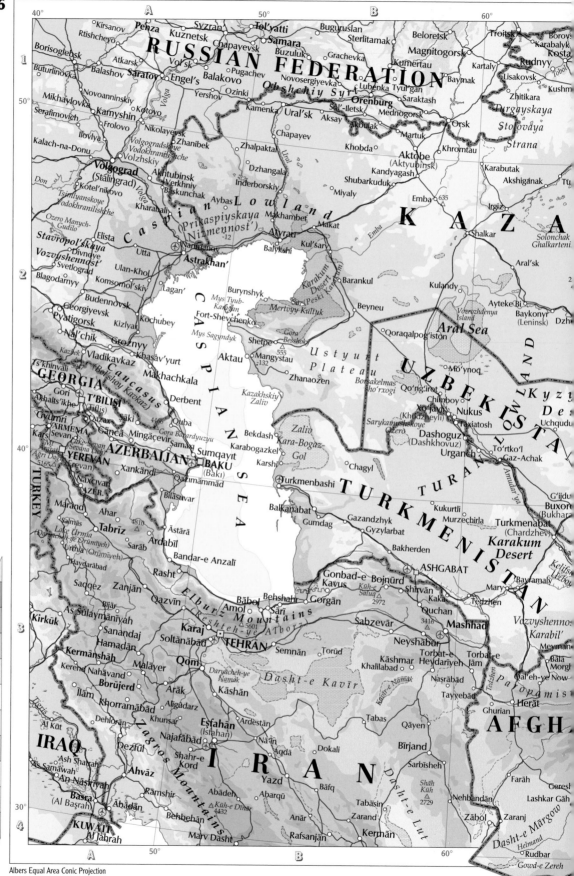

**METRES**
FEET

| | |
|---|---|
| **5000** | 16404 |
| **3000** | 9843 |
| **2000** | 6562 |
| **1000** | 3281 |
| **500** | 1640 |
| **200** | 656 |
| **0** | 0 |
| | Land below sea level |
| **200** | 656 |
| **4000** | 13124 |
| **6000** | 19686 |

Albers Equal Area Conic Projection

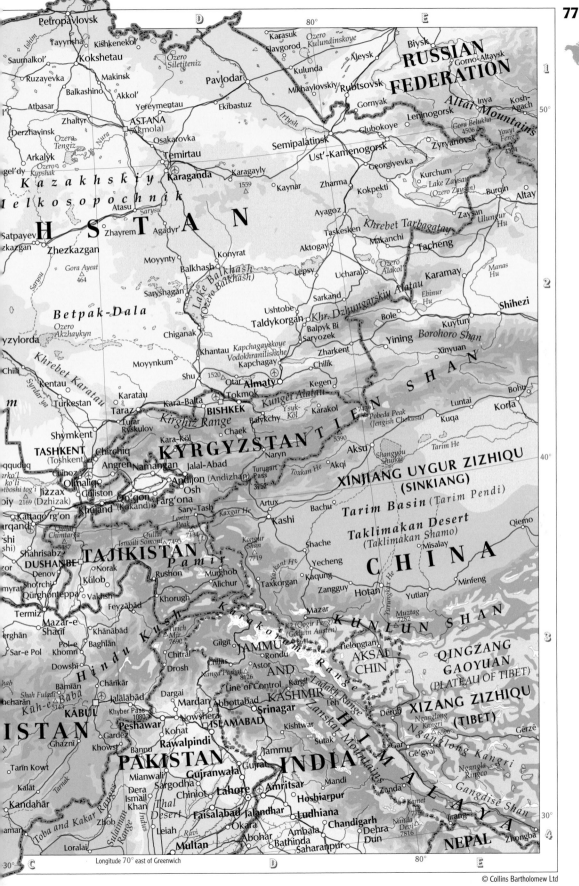

RUSSIAN
FEDERATION

*Altai Mountains*

Petropavlovsk
Tayynsha
Kishkenekol'
Karasuk
Slavgorod
*Ozero Kulundinskoye*
Aleysk
Biysk
Gorno-Altaysk
Inya
Kosh-Agach

Saumalkol'
Kokshetau
Kulunda
Mikhaylovskiy
Rubtsovsk
Gornyak
Leninogorsk
*Gora Belukha 4506*
50°

Ruzayevka
Makinsk
Akkol'
Yereymentau
Pavlodar
*Irtysh*
Georgiyevka
Zyryanovsk
Youyi Feng
4374

Atbasar
Zhaltyr
ASTANA
(Akmola)
Osakarovka
Ekibastuz
Ust'-Kamenogorsk
Kurchum
Lake Zaysan
(Ozero Zaysan)
Burqin
Altay

Derzhavinsk
*Ozero Tengiz*
Temirtau
Karaganda
*1559*
Kaynar
Semipalatinsk
Kokpekti
Zaysan
Ulungur
Hu

Arkalyk
*Kazakhskiy*
Atasu
Zhayrem
Agadyr'
Kaynar
Zharma
Ayagoz
*Khrebet Tarbagatay*
Taskesken
Makanchi
Tacheng
Manas
Hu

*Melkosopochnik*
ngel'dy
H S T A N
Konyrat
Balkhash
Lepsy
Ucharal
*Ozero Alakol'*
Karamay
Shihezi
2

Satpayev
zkazgan
Zhezkazgan
*Gora Ayeat 464*
Moyynty
Balkhash
*Lake Balkhash (Ozero Balkhash)*
Saryshagan
Sarkand
Bole
Ebinur Hu
Kuytun
*Borohoro Shan*

yzylorda
*Betpak-Dala*
*Ozero Akzhaykyn*
Chiganak
Ushtobe
Taldykorgan
*Khr. Dzhungarskiy Alatau*
Balpyk Bi
Saryozek
Yining
Xinyuan
Bohu

Chiili
*Khrebet Karatau*
Moyynkum
Khantau
*Kapchagayskoye Vodokhranilishche*
Kapchagay
Zharkent
Chilik
Kuqa
Korla

Kentau
Karatau
Shu
*1520*
Otar
Almaty
Kegen
*T I E N   S H A N*
Luntai

Turkestan
Taraz
Kara-Balta
Tokmok
*Kungei Alatau*
Karakol
*Pobeda Peak (Jengish Chokusu)*
*7439*
Kuqa

TASHKENT
(Toshkent)
Chirchiq
Ryskulov
*Kirghiz Range*
BISHKEK
Balykchy
*Ysyk-Köl*
*5390*
Aksu
*Tarim He*
Korla

Angren
Namangan
Jalal-Abad
Chaek
Naryn
Akqi
*XINJIANG UYGUR ZIZHIQU*
*(SINKIANG)*

Olmaliq
Andijon (Andizhan)
Osh
*Turugart Pass 3752*
Artux
Bachu
*Tarim Basin (Tarim Pendi)*

Chinoz
*2169 (Dzhizak)*
Qo'qon (Kokand)
Farg'ona
Sary-Tash
*Kaxgar He*
Kashi
Shache
*Taklimakan Desert (Taklimakan Shamo)*
Qiemo

Jizzax
Khujand
*Lenin Peak 7134*
Misalay

Kattaqo'rg'on
*Qullai Chimtarga 5487*
*Qullai Ismoili Somoni 7495*
*Konsur Shan 7719*
Yecheng
Shache
C H I N A

Shahrisabz
DUSHANBE
Denov
Norak
*Pamir*
Murghob
Taxkorgan
Zangguy
Hotan
Yutian
Minfeng

Qürghonteppa
Kúlob
Khorugh
Alichur
Mazar
*K U N L U N   S H A N*

Termiz
Vakhsh
Feyzābād
*Karakoram Range*
Muztag
7282
*QINGZANG GAOYUAN (PLATEAU OF TIBET)*

Mazar-e Sharif
Khānābād
*Hindu Kush*
Gilgit
*K2 (Qogir Feng/Godwin Austen) 8611*
Tielongtan
*AKSAI CHIN*

Pol-e Khomri
Baghlān
*Tirich Mir 7690*
Chitral
JAMMU
Rondu
Derub
*XIZANG ZIZHIQU*
Gérzê

Dowshi
Bāmiān
Chārikār
Drosh
Astor
AND
*Nganglong Kangri 6596*
(TIBET)

*Kūh-e Bābā*
*Shah Fuladi 5143*
Jalālābād
Dargai
*Nanga Parbat 8126*
*Line of Control*
Kargil
KASHMIR
Leh
*Ngangzê*
Ge'gyai

KĀBUL
*Khyber Pass 1080*
Peshawar
Mardan
Abbottabad
Srinagar
*Zanskar Mountains*
*Ladakh Range*
Gar
*Ngangla Ringco*

I S T A N
Ghaznī
Gardez
Khowst
Kohat
Nowshera
ISLAMABAD
Kishtwar
Sutak
*H I M A L A Y A*

Rawalpindi
Banpu
Jammu
*Ngangla Ringco*

Tarīn Kowt
PAKISTAN
Gujranwala
Gujrat
I N D I A
*Gangdisê Shan*

Kalāt
Mianwali
Sargodha
Chiniot
Lahore
Amritsar
Hoshiarpur
Mandi
*Kamet 7816*
Jirang
NEPAL
Zhongba

Kandahār
Dera Ismail Khan
Faisalabad
Jalandhar
Ludhiana
Chandigarh
Dehra Dun
*Nanda Devi 7816*

Loralai
*Sulaiman Range*
Leiah
Okara
Abohar
Ambala
Saharanpur
30°

aman
*Toba and Kakar Ranges*
Multan
Bathinda

30°

Miles
Km
500
750
400
300
500
200
250
100
0
0

© Collins Bartholomew Ltd

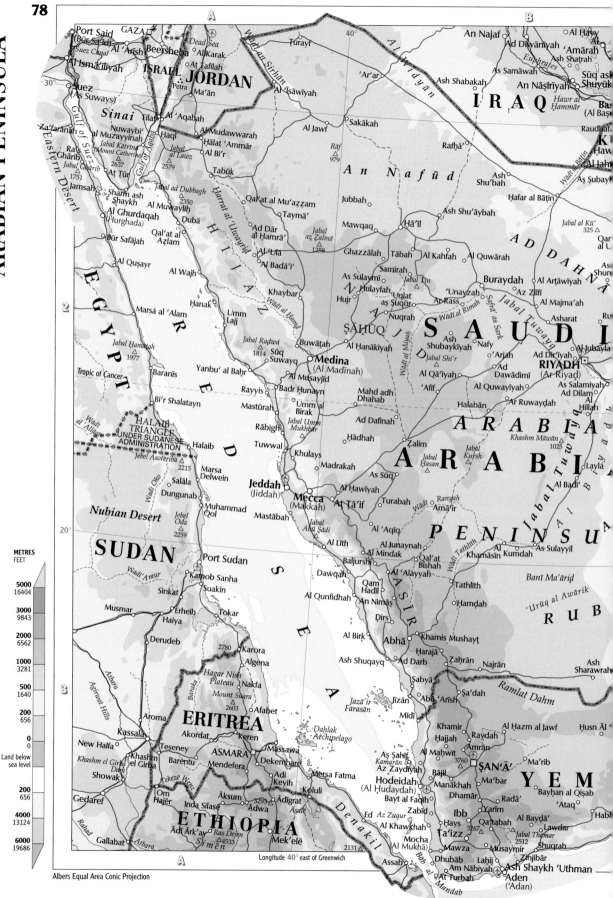

ARABIAN PENINSULA

Port Said
(Būr Saʿīd)
GAZA
Suez Canal
Al ʿArīsh
Beersheba
Dead Sea
Al Karak
At Tafīlah
ISRAEL
JORDAN
Petra
Maʿān
Suez
(As Suways)
Sinai
Eilat
Al ʿAqabah
Al Mudawwarah
Ḥālat ʿAmmār
Turayf
Wādī as Sirḥān
40°
Al Wīdyān
An Najaf
Ad Dīwānīyah
Ash Shatrah
AMĀRAH
ʿArʿar
Ash Shabakah
As Samāwah
An Nāṣirīyah
Hawr al
Ḥammār
(Al Baṣ
IRAQ
Baṣ
Al Ḥayy

Nuwaybiʿ
Al Muzayyinah
Jabal Katrīnā
(Mount Catherine)
2637
Raʾs
Ghārib
Jabal Gharib
1751
Jamsah
Haql
Jabal
al Lawz
2579
Al Biʿr
Tabūk
Zaʿfaranah
Eastern Desert
Gulf of Suez
Gulf of Aqaba
Al Jawf
Sakākah
Rāf
979
Rafḥāʾ
An Nafūd
Ash
Shuʿbah
Ḥafar al Bāṭin
Wādī al Bāṭin
Raudhat
Hawr
Aṣ Ṣubayḥ
Al Jah

Sharm ash
Shaykh
Al Muwayliḥ
Dubā
Jabal ad Dubbagh
2350
Qalʿat al Muʿaẓẓam
Taymāʾ
Mawqaq
Ḥāʾil
Ash Shuʿaybah
Jabal al Kūʾ
325
Qar
al U

At Ṭūr
Al Ghurdaqah
(Hurghada)
Qalʿat al
Azlam
Ad Dār
al Ḥamrāʾ
Jabal
az Zalmā
1258
Al ʿUlā
Al Badāʾiʿ
Ghazzālah
Tābah
Samīrah
Al Kahfah
Al Quwārah
Buraydah
Az Zilfī
Al Majmaʿah
Asharat
Jabal al Kū
AD DAHNĀ
Al Shun

Būr Safājah
Al Quṣayr
HIJAZ
Al Wajh
Khaybar
As Sulaymī
Ḥulayfah
Jabal Tin
Hujr
ʿUqlat
aṣ Ṣuqūr
Nuqrah
Ar Rass
ʿUnayzah
Nafy
Shubaykīyah
Jabal Shiʿr
Safrā as Sark
Jabal Tuwayq

Harrat al ʿUwayriḍ
Hanak
Umm
Lajj
Marsā al ʿAlam
Wādī al Ḥamḍ
Jabal Ḥamāṭah
1977
Jabal Raḍwā
1814
Sūq
Suwayq
Buwāṭah
Medina
(Al Madīnah)
Al Ḥanākīyah
NAJD
SAUDI
Al Qāʿīyah
ʿAriah
Ad
Dawādimī
Ad Dirʿīyah
RIYADH
(Ar Riyāḍ)
As Salamiyah
Ad Dilam
Al
Hillan

Tropic of Cancer
Baranīs
Bi'r Shalatayn
Yanbuʿ al Bahr
Al Musayjīd
Badr Ḥunayn
Rayyis
Mastūrah
Mahd adh
Dhahab
ʿAfīf
Al Quwayyīyah
Halabān
Ḥādhah
ARABIA
Ar Ruwaydah
Al Badī
Layla

HALAIB
TRIANGLE
UNDER SUDANESE
ADMINISTRATION
Jebel Asoteriba
2215
Halaib
Marsa
Delwein
Rābigh
Tuwwal
Khulays
Madrakah
Umm
Mukhbar
Umm
Birak
Ad Dafīnah
Ẓalim
Jabal
Ḥasan
Jabal
Kursh
Khashm Māwān
1025
ARABI
Jabal Tuwayq

Wadi al Allaqi
Salâla
Dungunab
Muhammad
Qol
Jeddah
(Jiddah)
Mecca
(Makkah)
At Ṭāʾif
As Sūq
Al Ḥawīyah
Turabah
Wādī
Amʿir
Ranyah
Al Badī
PENINSUL

Nubian Desert
Jebel
Oda
2259
Mastābah
Jabal
Abū Sadi
Al Lith
Al ʿAqīq
At Tathlīth
As Sulayyil
Banī Maʿāriḍ

20°
SUDAN
Port Sudan
Al Junaynah
Al Mindak
Qalʿat al
Bīshah
Al ʿAlāyyah
Khamāsīn
Al Kumdah
Tathlīth
ʿUrūq al Awārik
RUB

Kamob Sanha
Suakin
Wadi Amur
Baljurshi
Dawqah
Qam
Hadīl
An Nimāṣ
Hamdāh
Ash
Sharawrah

Sinkat
Erheib
Musmar
Haiya
2780
Karora
Al Birk
Abhā
Khamis Mushayṭ
Najrān

Tokar
Algena
Ash Shuqayq
Ad Darb
Ḥarajā
Zahrān
Ramlat Dahm

Derudeb
Hagar Nish
Plateau
Nakfa
Mount Suara
2603
Afabet
Jazāʾir
Farasān
Jizan
Midī
Sabyā
Abū ʿArīsh
Saʿdah
Husn Āl
Al Ḥazm al Jawf

Aroma
ERITREA
Akordat
Keren
Massawa
Dahlak
Archipelago
Khamir
Ḥajjah
Raydah
ʿAmrān
Maʾrib

Kassala
Teseney
ASMARA
Mendefera
Dekemhare
Mersa Fatma
Aṣ Ṣahīr
Kamarān
Az Zaydīyah
Al Maḥwīt
ʿAmrān
3760
ṢANʿĀʾ
Maʾbar
YEM

New Halfa
Khashm el Girba
Dam
Khashm
el Girba
Barentu
Adi
Keyih
Koluli
Hodeidah
(Al Ḥudaydah)
Manākhah
Dhamār
Radāʾ
Bayḥan al Qiṣāb
ʿAtaq
Habl

Showak
Gedaref
Om
Hajēr
Āksum
Ādigrat
Bayt al Faqīh
Zabīd
Az Zuqur
Ibb
Yarīm
Jabal Thamar
2512
Lawdar
Shuqrah

Inda Silase
3293
Aṣale
Ed
Al Khawkhah
Ḥays
Qaʿṭabah
Al Bayḍāʾ

Rahad
Gallabat
Atbara
Ādī Ārkʾay
Simen
4533
Ras Dejen
Mekʼelē
Adwa
2131
Denakil
Mocha
Al Mukhāʾ
Mawza
Taʿizz
3267
Jabal Thamar
2512
Musaymir
Zinjibar

ETHIOPIA
Assab
Bāb al
Mandab
Dhubāb
Aḥ Ṭurbah
Laḥij
Am Nābiyah
Ash Shaykh ʿUthman
Aden
(ʿAdan)

Longitude 40° east of Greenwich
Albers Equal Area Conic Projection

METRES
FEET
5000
16404
3000
9843
2000
6562
1000
3281
500
1640
200
656
0
0
Land below
sea level
200
656
4000
13124
6000
19686

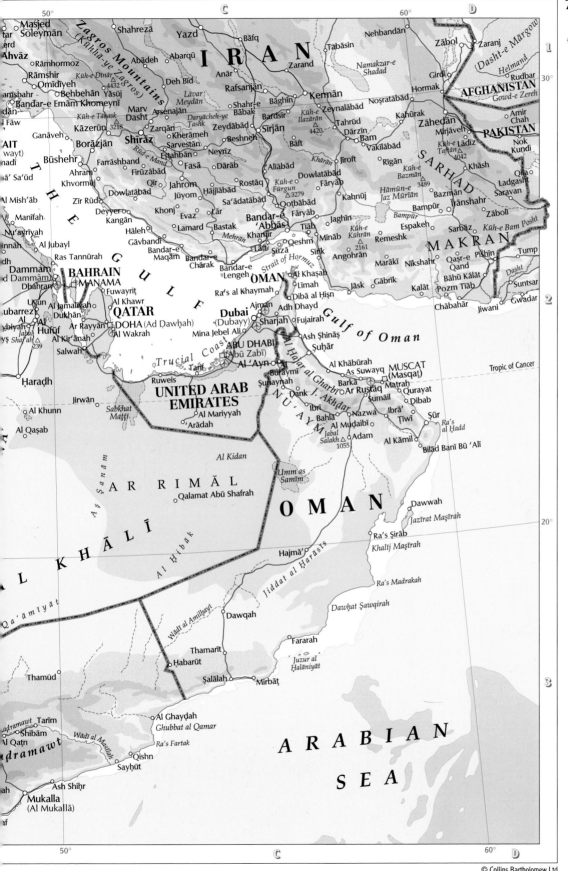

Maşjed Soleymān
Ahvāz
Rāmhormoz
Rāmshir
Omīdīyeh
Bandar-e Emām Khomeynī
Fāw
Ganāveh
Būshehr
Sa'ūd
Al Mish'āb
Manīfah
Nu'ayrīyah
Al Jubayl
Ras Tannūrah
Dammām
Dhahran
BAHRAIN
MANAMA
Fuwayriţ
Al Khawr
QATAR
DOHA (Ad Dawḩah)
Ar Rayyān
Al Wakrah
Al Kir'ānah
Salwah
Haradh
Jirwān
Al Khunn
Al Qaşab

**Zagros Mountains (Kūhhā-ye Zagros)**
Shahreza
Abādeh
Rāmhormoz
Behbehān
Deh Bīd
Rafsanjān
Anār
Shahr-e Bābak
Kahūrak
Kermān
Zeynalābād
Noşratābād
Zāhedān
Mīrjāveh
Kāzerūn
Marv Dasht
Arsenajān
Zeydābād
Bardsīr
Tahrūd
Dārzīn
Borāzjān
Shīrāz
Zarqān
Sīrjān
Bāft
Bam
Vakīlābād
Rīgān
Khāsh
Ladgasht
Ahram
Khvormūj
Firūzābād
Fasā
Dārāb
Aliābād
Dowlatābād
Fāryāb
Kahnūj
Bāzmān
Īrānshahr
Zāboli
Deyyer
Kangān
Hāleh
Gāvbandi
Bandar-e Maqām
Bandar-e Chārak
Bandar-e Lengeh
Lāft
Qeshm
Sūzā
Sīrīk
Angohrān
Marākī
Nīkshahr
Qaşr-e Qand
Bāhū Kalāt
Pishīn
Tump
Jāsk
Gābrīk
Kalāt
Pozm Tīāb
Suntsar
Chābahār
Jiwani
Gwadar

IRAN
AFGHANISTAN
PAKISTAN
SARHAD
MAKRAN
OMAN
Ra's al Khaymah
Dibā al Ḩişn
Dubai (Dubayy)
Sharjah
Ajman
Fujairah
ABU DHABI (Abū Zabī)
Al 'Ayn
UNITED ARAB EMIRATES
Trucial Coast
Tarīf
Ruweis
Al Mariyyah
Arādah
Al Kidan
Sabkhat Maţţī
Umm as Samīm
ŞAR RIMĀL
Qalamat Abū Shafrah
OMAN
Dawwah
Jazīrat Maşīrah
Ra's Şīrāb
Khalīj Maşīrah
Hajma'
Jiddat al Ḩarāsīs
Ra's Madrakah
Dawḩat Şawqirah
Dawqah
Fararah
Thamarīt
Ḩabarūt
Şalālah
Mīrbāţ
Juzur al Ḩalāniyāt
Al Ghaydah
Ghubbat al Qamar
Ra's Fartak
Qishn
Sayḩūt
Ash Shiḩr
Mukalla (Al Mukallā)

AL KHĀLĪ
Al Hibak
Qa'āmīyāt

ARABIAN SEA

Tropic of Cancer

MUSCAT (Masqaţ)

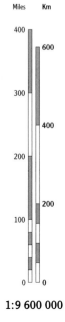

Miles    Km
400
                600
300
                400
200
                200
100
0       0

1:9 600 000

# EAST MEDITERRANEAN

**METRES** **FEET**

| 5000 | 16404 |
|------|-------|
| 3000 | 9843 |
| 2000 | 6562 |
| 1000 | 3281 |
| 500 | 1640 |
| 200 | 656 |
| 0 | 0 |

Land below sea level

| 200 | 656 |
| 4000 | 13124 |
| 6000 | 19686 |

Longitude 30° east of Greenwich

Albers Equal Area Conic Projection

cherkassk
v-na-Donu
vograd

l'sk

RUSSIAN
FEDERATION

oretsk
opotkin    Ipatovo    Divnoye
         Stavropol'skaya
'urban   Stavropol'
vir      Vozvyshennost'    Budennovsk
Labinsk  Nevinnomyssk
op       Cherkessk    Georgiyevsk
Karachayevsk  Pyatigorsk   Prokhladnyy
         Kislovodsk    Mozdok
A(      Nal'chik   Groznyy   Khasav'yurt
El'brus        Alagir  Vladikavkaz
5642     U
Sokhumi  (BOL'SHOY KAVKAZ)   Buynaksk
Tqvarch'eli                   Izberbash
Zugdidi                       Derbent
K'ut'aisi   GEORGIA    T'elavi
P'ot'i   Samtredia  Gori
'umi    Akhalts'ikhe   T'BILISI
        Akhalk'alak'        Zaqatala
Artvin  Ardahan   Rust'avi   Säki
Kackar                       Quba
Dagi   Yusufeli  Gyumri  Qazax  Mingäçevir
3932                 Gäncä
Oltu                         Göyçay  Şamaxı
        Kars   Sevan         ARMENIA  AZERBAIJAN
Horasan  Sarıkamış  YEREVAN  Ağdam
rzurum          (Erevan)  Ararat
Ağrı   Iğdır  Mt.Ararat  Xankändi  Äli Bäyrämlı
Hınıs  Tutak  Doğubeyazıt  AZER.  Salyan
       Patnos   Erciş   Mäkü   Sisian  Biläsuvar
Malazgirt            Naxçıvan   Cälilabad
Muş   Ahlat  4058  Khvoy   Länkäran
Tatvan          Marand  Ahar   Ästärä
Bitlis  Lake Van  Salmas  4810  Ardabıl
arbakır (Van Gölü)  Van  Sarab
       Siirt  Başkale   Tabriz
Şırnak  Hakkari  Urmia  Maragheh
Mardin  Şemdinli  Haydarabad  Mıäneh
Qämishli  Al 'Amadiyah  Miandowab
akho  Dahük   Oshnoviyeh  Mahabad  Zanjan  Qazvın
       Tall  As Sulaymaniyah  Saqqez
Asakah  'Afar   Arbil   Bıjar   Abhar
Mosul                           Karaj
az                    Sanandaj
Mayadın  Ash  Kirkük   Halabja  Qorveh
        Sharqat         Hamadan
Al Hadithah  Bayji  Tuz Khurmatü  Kangavar  Soltanabad
Hit   Tikrit  Qasr-e  Ravansar
bah   Samarra'  Shırın  Kerend  Malayer   Arak
Al Muqdadiyah  Eslamabad-e  Nahavand
Ar Ramadı  Ba'qübah  Gharb  İlam  Borujerd  Dow
Hawr al Habbaniyah  Al Kazimiyah  Khorramabad  Rud
bah   BAGHDAD   Dehloran   Aligudarz
Buhayrat ar  Al Küt  Dezful  Daran
Razazah  Karbala  Shushtar  Shahr-e
IRAQ  Hillah  Al Hayy  Masjed  Kord
      An Najaf  Al 'Amarah  Soleyman
Widyan  Ad Diwaniyah  Susangerd  Ahvaz
      As Samawah  Ramshir  Ramhormoz
ar    An Nasiriyah  Khorramshahr  Omıdiyeh  Yasuj
      Süq ash  Shuyükh  Bandar-e  Behbehan
RABIA  Rafha'  Basra  Emam Khomeyni  Kazerun
n Nafud  (Al Basrah)  Abadan  KUWAIT  Borazjan
      Raudhatain  Al Faw  Ganaveh  Shiraz
Ash   Hawalli  KUWAIT  Büshehr  Farrashband
Shu'bah  Al Jahrah  (Al Kuwayt)  Ahram
      Al Ahmadı  Mına' Sa'ud
Aş Şubayhiyah  Dowlatabad

KAZAKHSTAN

Karakum
Desert
(Peski Karakum)

UZBEKISTAN

TURKMENISTAN

IRAN

Balykshi
Sor
Donyztau
Barankul

Burynshyk
Beyneu

Mys Tyub-
Karagan   Fort-Shevchenko
         Shetpe   Gora
         Besshoky  555
Mangystau
Aktau    132
Kuryk    Zhanaozen

Kazakhskiy
Zaliv
Sarykamyshskoye
Ozero

Bekdash  Zaliv
Kara-Bogaz-  Chagyl
Gol
Karabogazkel'  Karshi

Turkmenbashi  Dzhanga
Cheleken  Dzhebel  Balkanabat
Gumdag        Gazandzhyk
Ostrov        Gyzylarbat
Ogurchinskiy  Garrygala

Gomishan  Gonbad-e
Behshahr  Gorgan  Kavus
Babol  Sarı  Mayamey
Amol        Emamrud
         Damghan

Elburz Mountains
(Reshteh-ye Alborz)

TEHRAN   Semnan   Torüd

Soltanabad   Dasht-e Kavir

Qom   Daryacheh-ye
      Namak       Jandaq

Kashan

Ardestan
Golpayegan  Na'ın   Dokali
Khunsar
Najafabad  Esfahan  Aqda  Meybod
Küh-e  (Isfahan)
Garbosh
4294   Shahreza  Yazd
              Abarqü  Bafq
Abadeh  Anar
Küh-e  Deh Bid
Dınar
4432   Lavar  Shahr-e
       Meydan  Babak
Marv  Arsenajan  Abadeh Tashk
Dasht       Daryacheh-ye Tashk
Küh-e Täbask  Kherämeh  Beshneh
Zarqan  Sarvestan  Neyrız
Shiraz  Estahban
Qır    Jahrom  Darab
       Hajjiabad  Rostaq

Volga

CASPIAN    SEA

© Collins Bartholomew Ltd

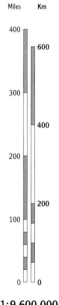

Miles   Km

400
        600

300
        400

200
        200

100

0       0

1:9 600 000

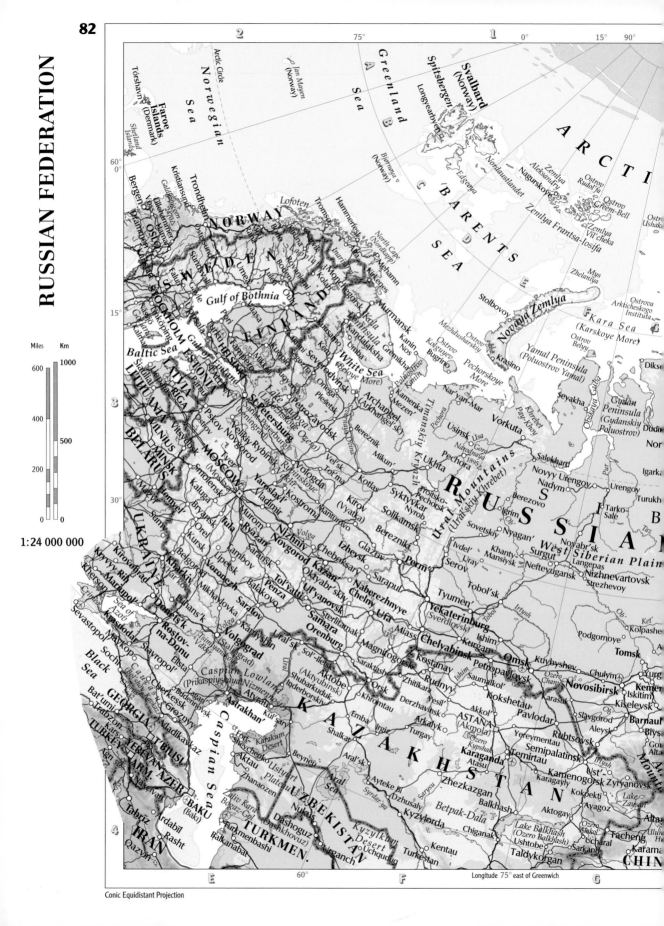

OCEAN

Chukchi Sea

Bering Strait

U.S.A.

Arctic Circle

St Laurence Island

Wrangel Island (Ostrov Vrangelya)

New Siberia Islands (Novosibirskiye Ostrova)

East Siberian Sea (Vostochno-Sibirskoye More)

Laptev Sea (More Laptevykh)

Shmidta

Ostrov Komsomolets

Ostrov Oktyabr'skoy Revolyutsii

Ostrov Bol'shevik

Proliv Vil'kitskogo

Chelyuskin

Taymyr Peninsula (Poluostrov Taymyr)

Ozero Taymyr

Khatanga

Kheta

Mayskoye

Kotuy

Saskylakh

Popigay

Kotuy

Yessey

SIBERIA

FEDERATION

Central Siberian Plateau

Tura

Taymura

Podkamennaya Tunguska

Severo-Yeniseyskiy

Chunya

Vanavara

Tembenchi

Boguchany

ibirsk

Angara

Uyar

Nizhneudinsk

Tulun

Zima

Kansk

Zaozernyy

Vostochnyy Sayan

Kyzyl

Uvs Nuur

Hövsgöl Nuur

MONGOLIA

Gichgeniyn Nuruu

Altay

Uliastay

Hyargas Nuur

Tsetserleg

Bayanhongor

Arvayheer

Möron

Tosontsengel

Dzuunmod

ULAN BATOR (Ulaanbaatar)

Darhan

Bulgan

Sühbaatar

Erdenet

Mandalgovi

GOBI

Saynshand

Choybalsan

Baruun-Urt

Uliastai

Erenhot

Chengde

Chifeng

Xilinhot

Tongliao

Chengde

Jinzhou

Shenyang

Benxi

Anshan

Dandong

CHINA

Chongjin

N. KOREA

PYONGYANG

Kimch'aek

Hamhung

Wonsan

SEOUL

S. KOREA

© Collins Bartholomew Ltd

METRES / FEET

| 5000 | 16404 |
| 3000 | 9843 |
| 2000 | 6562 |
| 1000 | 3281 |
| 500 | 1640 |
| 200 | 656 |
| 0 | 0 |
| Land below sea level | |
| 200 | 656 |
| 4000 | 13124 |
| 6000 | 19686 |

# EUROPE

A    40°    B    30°    20°    C    10°    D    0°    E    10°    F    20°

Bear I.
(Nor.)

**Greenland**
(Denmark)

Arctic Circle

2

60°

Denmark Strait

Jan Mayen
(Nor.)

**ICELAND**
Reykjavik

NORWEGIAN
SEA

Tron

3

Faroe
Islands
(Den.)
Tórshavn

Trondheim

Gulf of Bo

Shetland
Islands

Bergen

Oslo

Stockh

Orkney
Islands

Vänern

Gotland

50°

SCOTLAND

NORTH
SEA

Gothenburg

Baltic Sea

Glasgow
Edinburgh

DENMARK
Copenhagen
Malmö

RUS.

N. Belfast
IRELAND

UNITED
KINGDOM

POLAN

IRELAND
Dublin
Manchester

NETHERLANDS
Amsterdam
Hannover

Hamburg

Berlin

Poznań
Warsaw

Łódź

WALES
ENGLAND
Birmingham

The Hague

Essen

GERMANY

Prague

Kato

Cardiff
London

Brussels

CZECH
REPUBLIC

English Channel
Channel Is
(U.K.)

BELGIUM

Frankfurt

Vienna

SLOVAK
Bratislava

Buda

**LIE.**    LIECHTENSTEIN
**MACE.**    MACEDONIA

4

Seine

Luxembourg
LUXEMBOURG

Rhine

Munich

Danube

AUSTRIA
S

HUNGARY

Paris

Loire

SLOVENIA
Ljubljana

Zagreb

Bay
of Biscay

FRANCE

Bern LIE.
SWITZERLAND

Lyon
Mont Blanc
4808

A
L
P

CROATIA
Belgra

Cape Finisterre

Bordeaux

Rhône

Milan

SAN
MARINO

BOSNIA-
HERZ.
Sarajevo

SERB
AND
MONTEN

40°

Bilbao

Pyrenees

Turin

Adriatic Sea

Oporto

Andorra
la Vella
ANDORRA

Marseille
MONACO

ITALY

PORTUGAL
SPAIN

Madrid

Barcelona

Corsica

VATICAN
CITY
Rome

Skop

Tirana
ALBANIA

Lisbon

Valencia

Balearic Islands

Sardinia

Naples

Cabo de
São Vicente

5

Seville

Gibraltar
(U.K.)

MEDITERR

Palermo

Sicily

Ionian
Sea

MOROCCO

ALGERIA

TUNISIA

MALTA
Valletta

MEDITERRANEAN SEA

A

10°    D    Greenwich 0° meridian    E    10°    F    20°

Chamberlin Trimetric Projection

ATLANTIC
OCEAN

# H 40° I 50° J 60° K 70° L 80° M

BARENTS
SEA

*Novaya
Zemlya*

*Ostrov
Kolguyev*

Vorkuta

*Ob'*

2

3

n d Murmansk

*White Sea*

Archangel

Syktyvkar

RUSSIAN FEDERATION

*Ural Mountains*

*Lake
Onega*

Perm

*Lake
Ladoga*

elsinki

St Petersburg

50°

NIA

Yaroslavl'

*Volga*

Nizhniy
Novgorod

Kazan'

nn

Moscow

Orenburg

A

Ryazan'

Samara

A

KAZAKHSTAN

Minsk

4

BELARUS

Voronezh

Saratov

Homyel'

*Aral Sea*

Kiev

Kharkiv

*Don*

Volgograd

UZBEKISTAN

U K R A I N E

Donets'k

*Volga*

Dnipropetrovs'k

Rostov
na-Donu

Astrakhan

*C a s p i a n   S e a*

40°

MOLDOVA

Chișinău

*Dnieper*

*Sea
of Azov*

Krasnodar

TURKMENISTAN

Odesa

MANIA

*C a u c a s u s*

Bucharest

*Black Sea*

GEORGIA

Groznyy

ofia

AZERBAIJAN

5

LGARIA

ARMENIA

AZER.

İstanbul

essaloniki

T U R K E Y

I R A N

*egean
Sea*

CE

Athens

*Euphrates*

30°

*Crete*

CYPRUS

SYRIA

IRAQ

*Tigris*

LEBANON

G 30° H 40° I 50° J

© Collins Bartholomew Ltd

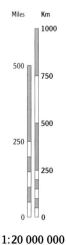

Miles    Km

1000

500      750

500

250      250

0        0

1:20 000 000

# EUROPEAN RUSSIAN FEDERATION

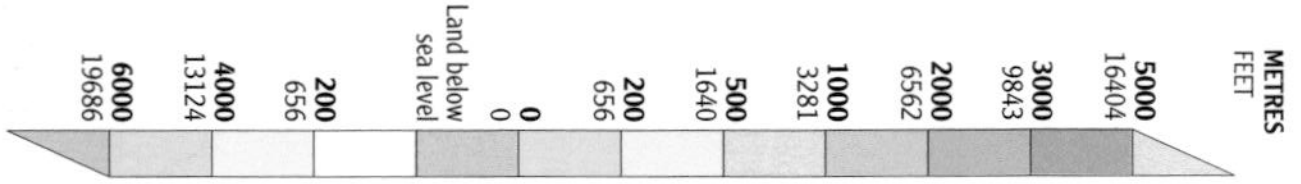

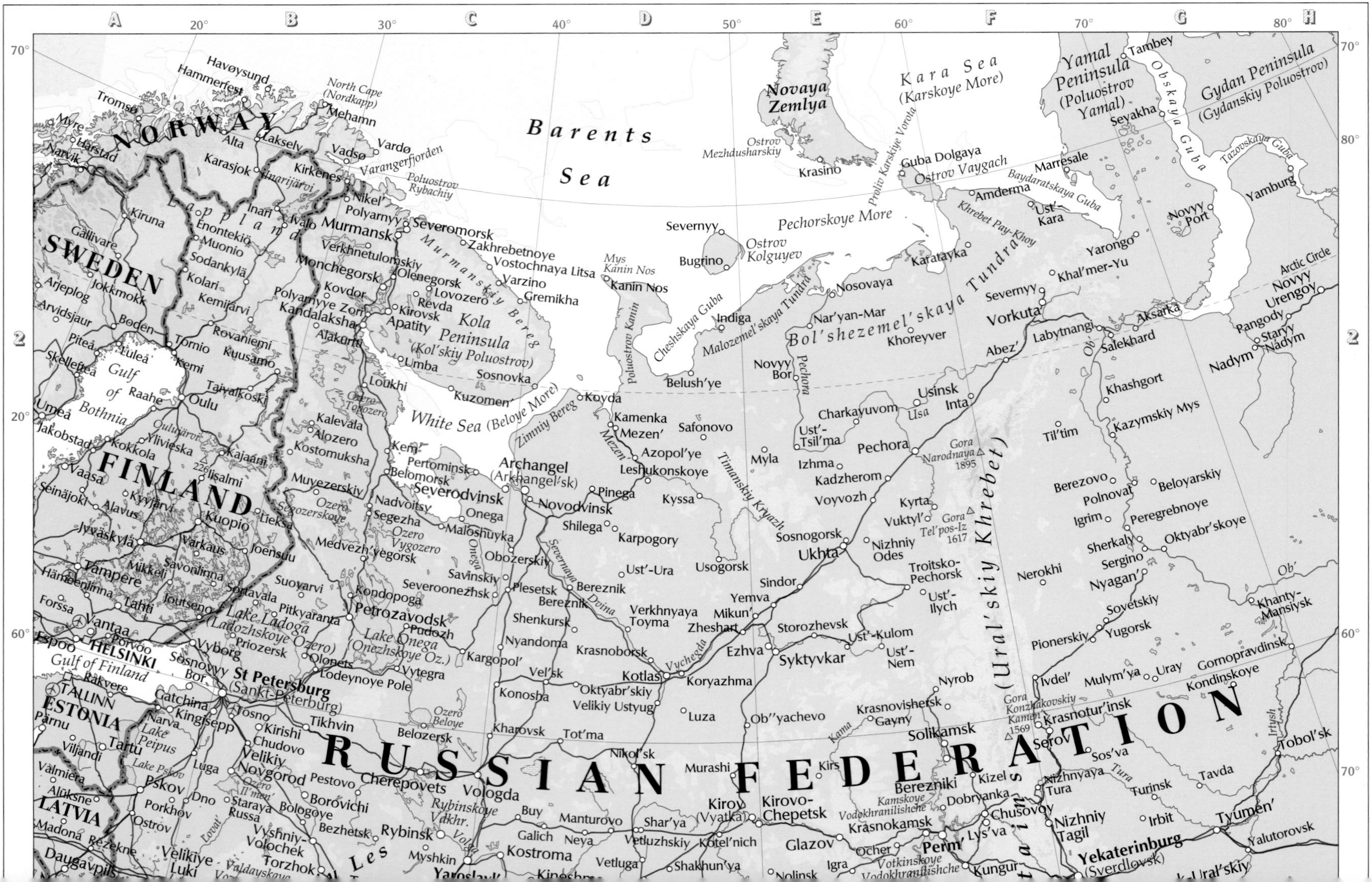

**RUSSIAN FEDERATION**

**NORWAY**

**SWEDEN**

**FINLAND**

**ESTONIA**

**LATVIA**

Barents Sea

Kara Sea (Karskoye More)

Novaya Zemlya

White Sea (Beloye More)

Pechorskoye More

Obskaya Guba

Gulf of Bothnia

Gulf of Finland

Lake Ladoga

Lake Onega

Yamal Peninsula (Poluostrov Yamal)

Gydan Peninsula (Gydanskiy Poluostrov)

Kola Peninsula (Kol'skiy Poluostrov)

Kanin Peninsula (Poluostrov Kanin)

Bol'shezemel'skaya Tundra

Malozemel'skaya Tundra

Ural Mountains (Ural'skiy Khrebet)

Timanskiy Kryazh

Murmanskiy Bereg

Zimniy Bereg (Beloye More)

Arctic Circle

Conic Equidistant Projection

**METRES / FEET**

| METRES | FEET |
|---|---|
| 5000 | 16404 |
| 3000 | 9843 |
| 2000 | 6562 |
| 1000 | 3281 |
| 500 | 1640 |
| 200 | 656 |
| 0 | 0 |

Land below sea level

| 200 | 656 |
| 4000 | 13124 |
| 6000 | 19686 |

St Petersburg (Sankt-Peterburg)

Murmansk, Arkhangel'sk (Archangel), Severodvinsk, Pechora, Ukhta, Vorkuta, Salekhard, Naryan-Mar, Syktyvkar, Kirov, Vologda, Cherepovets, Novgorod, Velikiy, Yekaterinburg (Sverdlovsk), Perm', Nizhniy Tagil, Khanty-Mansiysk, Tyumen', Tobol'sk, Petrozavodsk, HELSINKI, TALLINN, Oulu

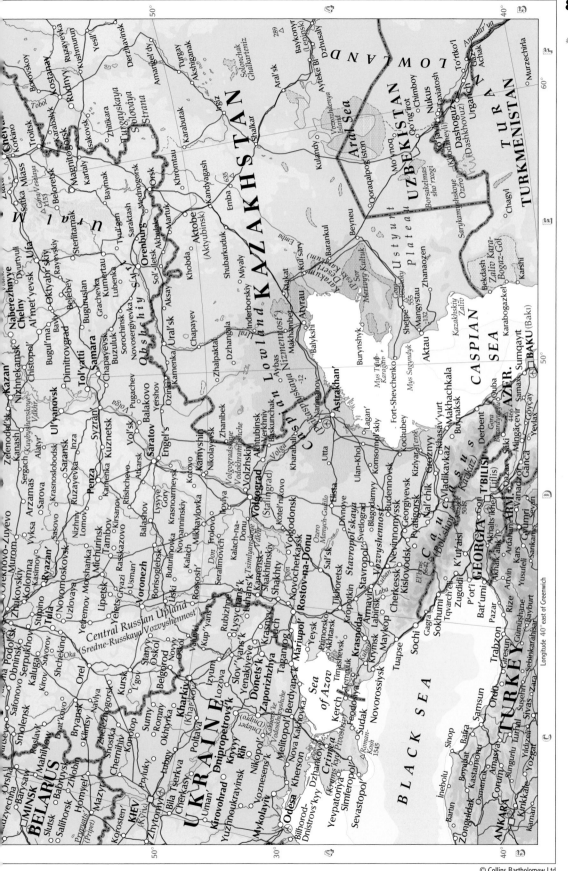

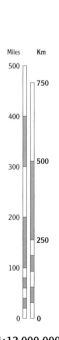

Miles / Km

1:12 000 000

**NORTHEAST EUROPE**

FINLAND

Kouvola
Anjalankoski
Mäntsälä
Järvenpää
Tuusula
Vantaa
Hamina
Espoo
Porvob
Lovisa
Kotka
Vyborgskiy Zal.
Vyborg
Zelenogorsk
Kirkkonummi
HELSINKI
(Helsingfors)
Ostrov
Gogland
Ostrov
Moshchnyy
Lomonos
Petrodvor

Uppsala
Norrtälje
Mariehamn
Korpo
Ekenäs
Hanko
Åland
Islands
Kökar
**SWEDEN**
Sollentuna
Märsta
Åkersberga
Täby
**STOCKHOLM**
Tumba
Västerhaninge
Nynäshamn

Gulf of Finland

TALLINN
Paldiski
Keila
Kehra
Rakvere
Kohtla-
Järve
Sillamäe
Narva
Maardu
Loksa
Vaida
Tapa
Kiviõli
Jõhvi
Narvskoye
Vdkhr.
Kingisepp
Volos
Slantsy
Os'mino
Sive
Mshins

Kalana
Kärdla
Vormsi
Turba
Rapla
Rakke
Emumägi
166
Raja
Vasknarva
Hiiumaa
Emmaste
Kalna
Muhu
Virtsu
Haapsalu
Paide
Põltsamaa
**ESTONIA**
Jõgeva
Gdov
Lake
Peipus
Plyussa

Mustjala
Orissaare
Pärnu
Viljandi
Tartu
Ülenurme
Elva
Yamm
Strugi-
Krasny
Kuressaare
Vändra
Võrtsjärv
Mõisaküla
200

**Saaremaa**
Sääre
Kihnu
Valga
Põlva
Pechory
Pskov
Porkhov
Slavkov'

BALTIC SEA

Visby
Slite
Gotland
(Sweden)
Klintehamn
Gotska
Sandön
Fårö

Irbe Strait
Ruhnu
Salacgrīva
Valka
Võru
Palkino
Dedov'

Ovišrags
Mazirbe
Kolkasrags
Limbaži
Valmiera
Smiltene
Alūksne
Ostrov
Chikhache

Ventspils
Dundaga
Roja
Gulf of
Riga
Saulkrasti
Cēsis
Rauna
Gulbene
Balvi
Pytalovo
Novorzl

Pāvilosta
Akmeņrags
Kuldīga
Tukums
Garkalne
Sigulda
Elkas kalns
265
Madona
Kārsava
Pushkinskiye
Gory
Krasnogorodskoye
Opochka

Liepāja
Aizpute
Skrunda
Saldus
Dobele
Jūrmala
**RIGA**
Olaine
Ogre
Iecava
Aizkraukle
Koknese
Barkava
Viļāni
Mežvidi
Ludza
Pustoshka

Nīca
Mažeikiai
Naujoji
Akmenė
Bauska
Jelgava
Birži
Jēkabpils
Līvāni
Preiļi
Rēzekne
Sebezh

Skuodas
Venta
Kuršėnai
Pasvalys
Viski
Dagda
Kraslava
Rasony
Yezyarysh'

Kretinga
Plungė
Telšiai
**Šiauliai**
Pakruojis
Rokiškis
Daugavpils
Zarasai
Druya
Vyerkhnyadzvinsk

Klaipėda
Gargždai
Medvėgalio
kalnis
235
Kelmė
Radviliškis
Kupiškis
Dūkštas
Braslaw
Myory
Navapolatsk
Hara

**LITHUANIA**
Šilalė
Raseiniai
Panevėžys
Visaginas
Nevaišiu
kalnis
289
Sharkawshchyna
Polatsk
Obal'

Courland
Lagoon
Kintai
Silutė
Pagėgiai
Kelmė
Kėdainiai
Ukmergė
Utena
Ignalina
Molėtai
Varapayeva
Ushachy
Shumilina

Nida
Mys Taran
Svetlogorsk
Zelenogradsk
Sovetsk
Neman
Jurbarkas
Šakiai
Jonava
Širvintos
Švenčionys
Pastavy
Narach
Hlybokaye
Byeshankov'

Gulf of
Gdańsk
Svetlyy
Baltiysk
Kaliningrad
Chernyakhovsk
Vilkaviškis
Grigiškės
**VILNIUS**
Astravyets
Myadzyel
Lyepyel'
Sya
Chashniki

Frombork
Mamonovo
Gvardeysk
Gusev
Kybartai
Prienai
Trakai
Ashmyany
Smarhon'
Dokshytsy
Byahoml'
Kokha
Talachyn

Braniewo
Bagrationovsk
Ozersk
Marijampolė
Alytus
Salčininkai
Varėna
Vilyeyka
Plyeshchanitsy

**RUS. FED.**
Elbląg
Bartoszyce
Korsze
Gołdap
Lazdijai
Sejny
Merkinė
Voranava
Maladzyechna
Barysaw
Zhodzina
Bartoszyce

Malbork
Pasłęk
Dobre
Miasto
Węgorzewo
Giżycko
Olecko
Suwałki
Druskininkai
Lida
Valozhyn
Zaslawye
Smalyavichy
Byalynichy
Byerazino

Kwidzyn
Ostróda
Olsztyn
Ełk
Augustów
Shchuchyn
Navahrudak
Iwye
Dzyarzhynsk
Uskhodni
**MINSK**
345
Smilavichy
Chervyen'
Mar''ina Horka
Klicha

Iława
Nidzica
Szczytno
Jezioro
Śniardwy
Grajewo
Mońki
Masty
Byarozawka
Karelichy
Stowbtsy
Asipovichy
Babrujsk

Brodnica
Działdowo
Mława
Łomża
Vawkavysk
Zel'va
Baranavichy
Nyasvizh
Kapyl'
Staryya
Darohi
Klichaw

Dylewska
Góra
312
Pojezierze
Mazurskie
Ostrów
Mazowiecka
Białystok
Slonim
Lyakhavichy
Klyetsk
Slutsk
Hlusk
Byaryezina
Zhl

Ciechanów
Zambrów
Svislach
Ivatsevichy
Nyasvizh
Saliharsk
Lyuban'
Svyetlah
Rahac

Wyszków
Hajnówka
Pruzhany
Hantsavichy
Mal'kavichy
Aktsyabrski
Kapatkyevichy
Kalinkavichy

**POLAND**
Nizina
Mazowiecka
Płock
Legionowo
**WARSAW**
(Warszawa)
Węgrów
Bug
Siedlce
Byaroza
Tsyelyakhany
Dzyatlavichy
Zhytkavichy
Pyetrykaw
Kuznetsov's'k
Mazyr
Khoy

Kutno
Pruszków
Łowicz
Minsk
Mazowiecki
Biała
Podlaska
Łuków
Zhabinka
Drahichyn
Ivanava
Luninyets
Dayyd-Haradok
Vasilyevich'

Zgierz
Skierniewice
Mazowiecka
Vistula
(Wisła)
Radzyń
Brest
Kobryn
Pina
Pinsk
Zarichne
Stolin
Lyel'chytsy
Yel'sk
Narow

Łódź
Tomaszów
Mazowiecki
Mazowiecka
Dęblin
Parczew
Lubartów
Malaryta
Lyubeshiv
Prypyats' (Pripet)
Dubrovytsya
Klesiv

Piotrków
Trybunalski
Pionki
Radom
Puławy
Chełm
Ratne
Zarichne
Manevychi
220
Samy
Rokytne
Ovruch
Polis'

Końskie
Skarżysko-
Kamienna
Starachowice
Ostrowiec
Świętokrzyski
Krasnystaw
Liuboml'
Kovel'
Turiys'k
Styr
Luhyny
Narodychi

Kielce
Łysica
611
**UKRA**

METRES
FEET

5000 / 16404
3000 / 9843
2000 / 6562
1000 / 3281
500 / 1640
200 / 656
0 / 0
Land below
sea level
200 / 656
4000 / 13124
6000 / 19686

Longitude 25° east of Greenwich

Conic Equidistant Projection

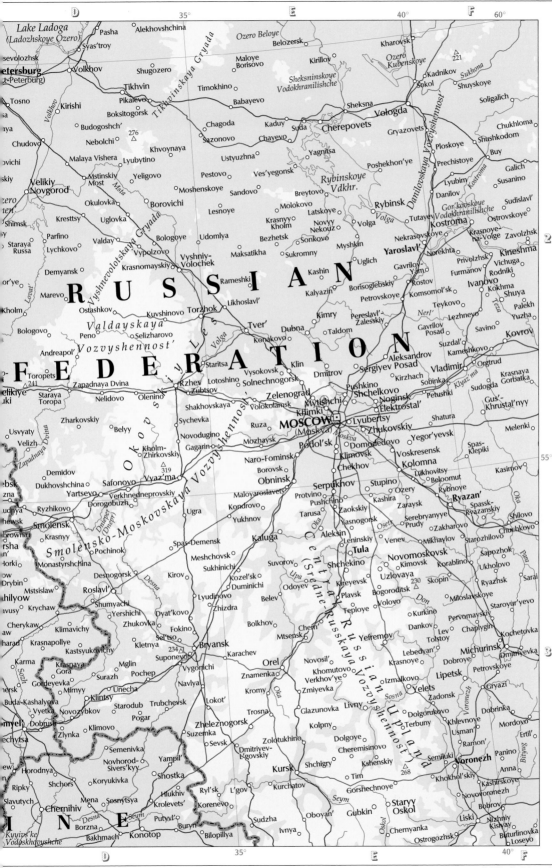

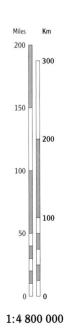

**1:4 800 000**

UKRAINE AND MOLDOVA

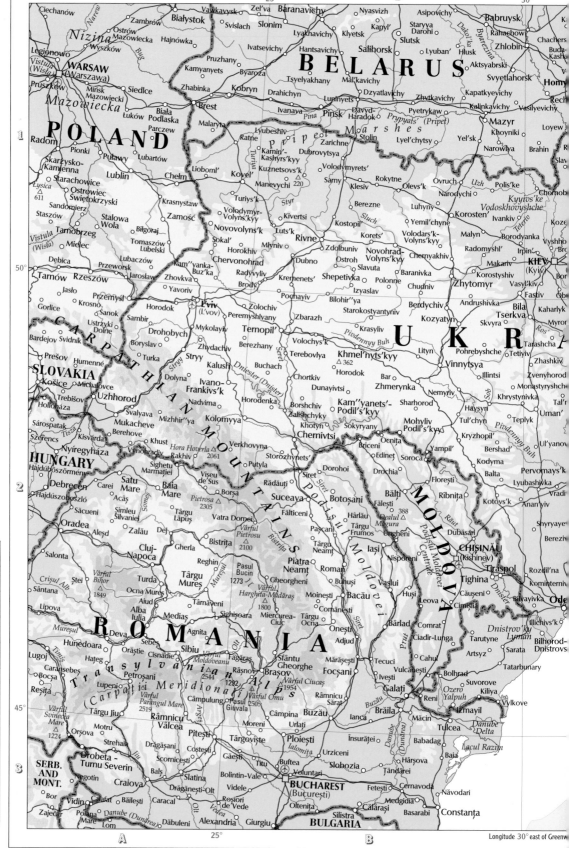

Conic Equidistant Projection

Longitude 30° east of Greenw

**METRES**
FEET

5000 16404
3000 9843
2000 6562
1000 3281
500 1640
200 656
0
Land below sea level
200 656
4000 13124
6000 19686

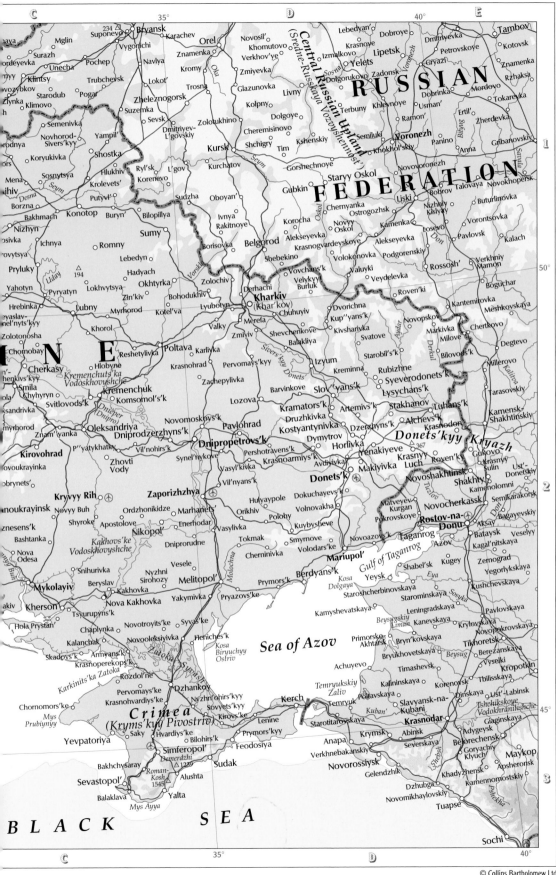

1:4 800 000

© Collins Bartholomew Ltd

# SCANDINAVIA AND ICELAND

Branner

**RUS. FED.**

FINLAND

NORWAY

SWEDEN

**BOTHNIA**

NORWEGIAN SEA

## ICELAND
### AT THE SAME SCALE

Vatnajökull

Bakkaflói

Hofsjökull

Langjökull

Mýrdalsjökull

Húnaflói

Faxaflói

REYKJAVÍK

Arctic Circle

| METRES | FEET |
| --- | --- |
| 5000 | 16404 |
| 3000 | 9843 |
| 2000 | 6562 |
| 1000 | 3281 |
| 500 | 1640 |
| 200 | 656 |
| 0 | 0 |
| Land below sea level | |
| 200 | 656 |
| 4000 | 13124 |
| 6000 | 19686 |

Conic Equidistant Projection

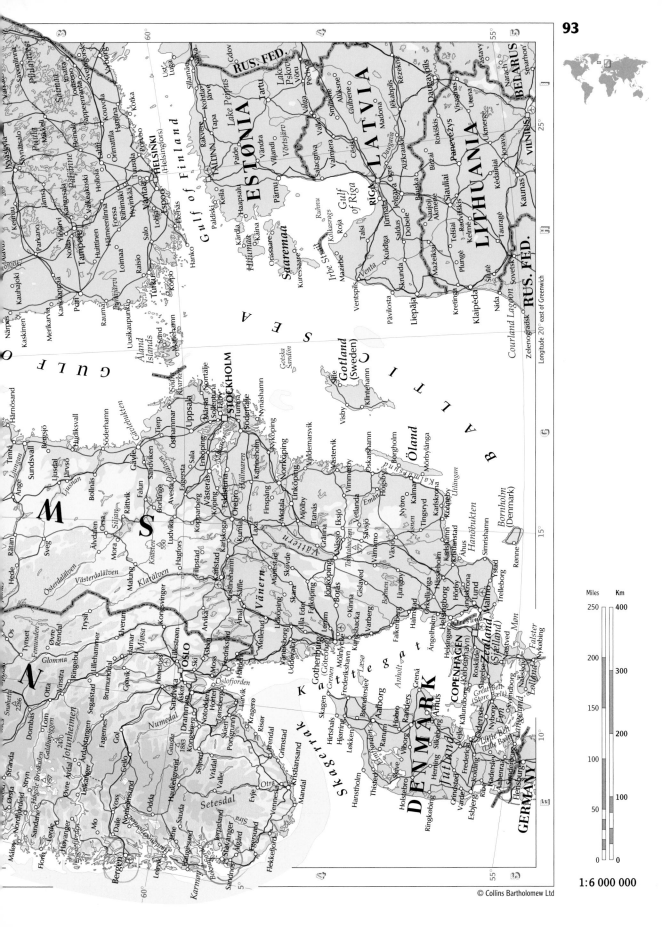

RUS. FED.

ESTONIA

LATVIA

LITHUANIA

BELARUS

VILNIUS

Gulf of Finland

HELSINKI
(Helsingfors)

Gulf of Riga

RĪGA

Saaremaa

Hiiumaa

Irbe Strait

Courland Lagoon

Zelenogradsk

RUS. FED.

Longitude 20° east of Greenwich

BALTIC

SEA

Gotland
(Sweden)

Bornholm
(Denmark)

Öland

Kalmarsund

Hanöbukten

GULF OF

Åland
Islands

STOCKHOLM

Uppsala

Gävle

S

M

N

OSLO

Oslofjorden

Vänern

Vättern

Kattegat

Skagerrak

Gothenburg
(Göteborg)

COPENHAGEN
København

Zealand
(Sjælland)

DENMARK

Jutland

GERMANY

Bergen

Stavanger

Kristiansand

Little Belt
(Lille Bælt)

Great Belt
(Store Bælt)

© Collins Bartholomew Ltd

| Miles | Km |
|---|---|
| 250 | 400 |
| 200 | 300 |
| 150 | 200 |
| 100 | 100 |
| 50 | |
| 0 | 0 |

1:6 000 000

N O R T H

S E A

Shetland
Islands

Herna Ness
Unst
Yell
Fetlar
Isbister
Lerwick
Mainland
Foula ◦
Sumburgh Head
◦ Fair Isle

Orkney Islands
Westray
Sanday
Rousay
Kirkwall
Mainland
Stromness
Hoy
John o'Groats
Pentland Firth
Wick
Thurso
Helmsdale

Peterhead
Fraserburgh
Banff
Huntly
Elgin
Grantown-
on-Spey
Inverurie
Aberdeen
Dee
Montrose
Arbroath
Dundee
St Andrews
Forfar
Brechin
Ballater
Crieff
Perth
Pitlochry
1124 △

SCOTLAND
Grampian Mountains
Kingussie
Aviemore
Nairn
Inverness
Dingwall
Moray Firth

Tongue
Durness
Cape
Wrath
Hope △ 927
Loch
Shin
Ullapool
An Teallach △ 1062
Scourie
Ben Eighe △ 1183 Loch
Ness
Fort Augustus
Spean Bridge
Fort William
Ben Nevis △ 1344

Butt of
Lewis
Stornoway
799 △
Isle of
Lewis
Harris
Kyle of
Lochalsh
Portree
Skye
Gairloch
The Minch
Little Minch
Rum
Coll
Tiree

North Uist
Benbecula
South Uist
Barra
Outer Hebrides

St Kilda

A T L A N T I C

O C E A N

Faroe Islands
(Denmark)
Norðoyar
Klaksvik
Borðoy
Eysturoy
882
Streymoy
Vestmanna
Miðvágur
Vágar
TÓRSHAVN
Sandur
Sandoy
Suðuroy
Vágur

Rockall

Conic Equidistant Projection

METRES
FEET

5000
16404
3000
9843
2000
6562
1000
3281
500
1640
200
656
0
0
Land below
sea level
200
656
4000
13124
6000
19686

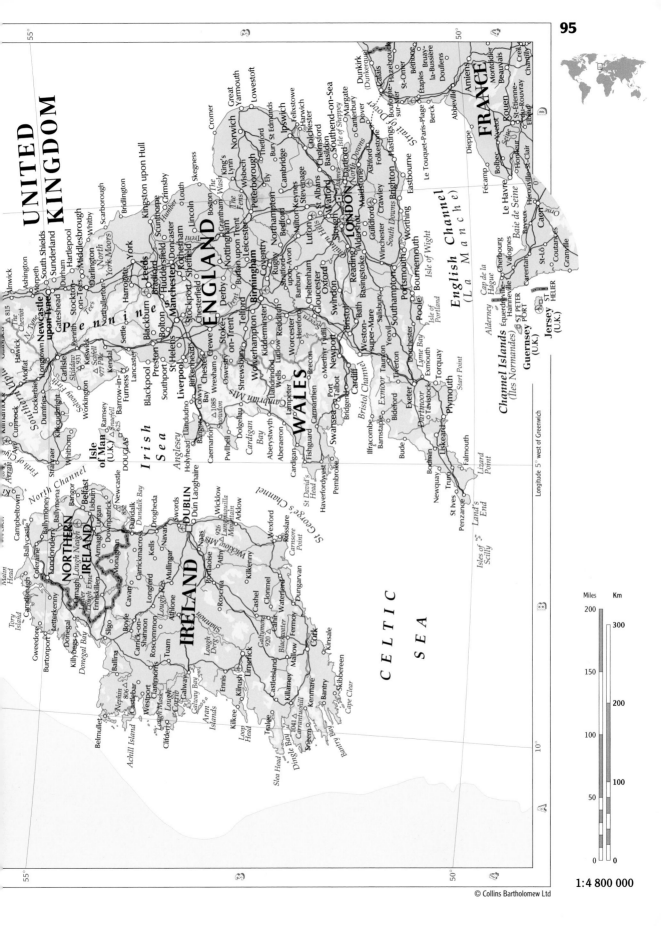

UNITED KINGDOM

FRANCE

ENGLAND

WALES

IRELAND

NORTHERN IRELAND

CELTIC SEA

English Channel (La Manche)

Irish Sea

North Channel

St George's Channel

Bristol Channel

Channel Islands (Îles Normandes)

Guernsey (U.K.)

Jersey (U.K.)

Isle of Man (U.K.)

Longitude 5° west of Greenwich

Miles
200

150

100

50

Km
300

200

100

0   0

1:4 800 000

© Collins Bartholomew Ltd

ATLANTIC OCEAN

North Ronaldsay
Westray
Rousay Eday Sanday
Birsay Loth
Stronsay
**Orkney Islands** Mainland Shapinsay
Stromness Kirkwall
Ward Hill △ Gritley
479
Hoy Scapa Flow
Longhope South Ronaldsay Burwick
Pentland Firth
Dunnet Head John o' Groats
Duncansby Head

Herma Ness
Unst
Haroldswick
Yell
Isbister Ronas Hill △ Ulsta Fetlar
450
Hillswick Toft
St Magnus Bay Papa Stour Mainland Walls Whalsay
Foula Lerwick
Scalloway Bressay
**Shetland Islands**
Sumburgh 60°
Sumburgh Head
2° Fair Isle

Cape Wrath
Durness
Butt of Lewis
Port Ness (Port Nis)
Ben Hope △ 927 Tongue Thurso
Scourie Naver Thurso Wick
Carloway West Loch Roag Stornoway Altnaharra Kinbrace Dunbeath
**Isle of Lewis** Loch a' Tuath Ben More Assynt △ 998 Loch Shin Helmsdale
Clisham △ 799 Lochinver Lairg Golspie
Tarbert Point of Stoer Cassley Dornoch
**Harris** Loch Broom Ullapool Dornoch Firth
Leverburgh An Teallach △ 1062 Tarbat Ness

**North Uist** Gairloch Invergordon Cromarty Lossiemouth Rosehearty Fraserburgh
Lochmaddy Loch Maree Ben Wyvis △ 1046 Alness Cromarty Firth Banff Macduff Rattray Head
Sound of Harris Achnasheen Dingwall Black Isle Nairn Elgin Buckie Aberchirder Peterhead
**Benbecula** Torridon Fortrose Forres Rothes Keith Turriff Mintlaw Boddam
Uig Loch Torridon Beauly Inverness Findhorn Huntly Dufftown Ellon Oldmeldrum
**South Uist** Stromeferry Carn Eighe △ 1183 Beauly Spey Inverurie Dyce
Beinn Mhòr △ 620 **Skye** Kyle of Lochalsh Drumnadrochit Strathspey Alford Kintore Westhill Aberdeen
Lochboisdale Dunvegan Portree Glen More Loch Ness Aviemore Grantown-on-Spey Don
**Barra** Sligachan Broadford Fort Augustus Monadhliath Mountains Kingussie Cairngorm Mountains Ben Macdui △ 1309 Dee Banchory Stonehaven
Castlebay Sgurr Alasdair △ 993 Ardvasar Garry Newtonmore Lochnagar △ 1155 Ballater Inverbervie
Mingulay Mallaig Dalwhinnie Braemar North Esk Edzell Laurencekirk
Point of Ardnamurchan Arisaig Fort William Ben Nevis △ 1344 Spean Bridge Glen Shee Brechin Montrose
**Rum** Salen Glenfinnan Kinlochleven **S C O T L A N D** Blair Atholl Pitlochry Kirriemuir Forfar Arbroath
**Eigg** Loch Shiel Glencoe △ 1150 Rannoch Moor Aberfeldy Blairgowrie Sidlaw Hills Carnoustie
**Coll** Arinagour Tobermory Bidean nam Bian Ben Lawers △ 1214 Dunkeld Dundee Bell Rock
Tiree Lochaline Morvern Loch Linnhe Tay Loch Tay Killin Tayport St Andrews
Scarinish **Mull** Ben More △ 966 Connel Tyndrum Ben More △ 1174 Earn Crieff Perth Fife Ness
Iona Oban Dalmally Crianlarich Callander Cupar Anstruther
Fionnphort Loch Awe Inveraray Ben Lomond △ 974 Aberfoyle Stirling Glenrothes Buckhaven
Scarba Loch Lomond Forth Alloa Kirkcaldy North Berwick
Colonsay **Jura** Crinan Lochgilphead Helensburgh Dumbarton Dunfermline Cowdenbeath East Linton Dunbar
Beinn an Oir △ 785 Greenock Alexandria Cumbernauld Falkirk Edinburgh Haddington
Port Askaig Tarbert Rothesay **Glasgow** Airdrie Bathgate Livingston Musselburgh Eyemouth Berwick-upon-Tweed
**Islay** Bute Clydebank Coatbridge Dalkeith Holy Island (Lindisfarne)
Portnahaven Gigha Johnstone Paisley Motherwell Penicuik Duns
Port Ellen Lochranza Newton Mearns Hamilton Peebles Galashiels Coldstream
Mull of Oa Ardrossan Saltcoats East Kilbride Lanark Biggar Melrose Kelso Wooler Bamburgh
Goat Fell △ 874 Irvine Kilmarnock Newtown St Boswells Jedburgh The Cheviot △ 815 Alnwick
**Kintyre** Brodick **Arran** Troon Prestwick Muirkirk Selkirk Hawick Teviot Rothbury Amble
Campbeltown Ayr Cumnock Broad Law △ 840 **Southern Uplands** Langholm Cheviot Hills Otterburn Ashington
Rathlin Island Maybole Sanquhar Moffat Teviothead Kielder Water Morpeth
Giant's Causeway Mull of Kintyre Dalmellington Thornhill Nith Liddel Bedlington
Portrush Ballycastle Cushendun Girvan Merrick △ 843 New Galloway Dumfries Lockerbie Longtown Haltwhistle Hexham **Newcastle upon Tyne**
Portstewart Coleraine Ballantrae Newton Stewart Castle Douglas Annan Carlisle Brampton Gateshead Consett
Limavady Ballymoney Trostan △ 554 Cairnryan Wigtown Dalbeattie Silloth Alston △ 893 Cross Fell Durham
Dungiven Ballymena Antrim Hills Stranraer Portpatrick Kirkcudbright Maryport Cockermouth Penrith Skiddaw △ 931 Bishop Auckland
Cullybackey Larne Luce Bay Whithorn Workington △ Newton Aycliffe
**NORTHERN IRELAND** Magherafelt Whitehead Carrickfergus Drummore Solway Firth **ENGLAND**
Lough Neagh Newtownabbey Bangor Donaghadee Mull of Galloway Spennymoor

Milleur Point North Channel

**NORTH SEA**

**Firth of Forth**
**Firth of Tay**
**Firth of Clyde**
Sound of Jura
Firth of Lorn
Moray Firth
The Minch
Little Minch
Inner Sound
Cuillin Sound
Sound of Arisaig
Luce Bay

**Outer Hebrides**

1
2
3
A 6° B 4° C D
58°
56°
Longitude 4° west of Greenwich
2°
Conic Equidistant Projection

METRES FEET
5000 16404
3000 9843
2000 6562
1000 3281
500 1640
200 656
0 0
Land below sea level
200 656
4000 13124
6000 19686

**IRELAND**

ATLANTIC OCEAN

SCOTLAND

*Jura*
*Islay*
Port Askaig
Portnahaven
*Gigha*
Port Ellen
*Mull of Oa*
*Kintyre*
Campbeltown
*Mull of Kintyre*
Ballycastle

North Channel

*Malin Head*
Malin
Carndonagh
*Giant's Causeway*
*Rathlin Island*
*Inishowen*
Portstewart
Portrush
Coleraine
Cushendun
*Antrim Hills*
*Trostan 554*
West Town *Tory Island*
*Tory Sound*
Falcarragh
*Lough Foyle*
Limavady
Ballycastle
*Bloody Foreland*
Brinlack
Gweedore
Buncrana
Dungiven
Ballymoney
Larne
Bunbeg
*Errigal 752*
Ramelton
Londonderry
Cullybackey
Ballymena
Whitehead
*Aran Island*
Burtonport
Letterkenny
Ballyclare
Carrickfergus
Lifford
Newtownabbey
Antrim
Bangor
*Gweebarra Bay*
Glenties
Strabane
Newtownstewart
Cookstown
Magherafelt
Newtownabbey
Donaghadee
Newtownards
Malin More
*Blue Stack Mts 676*
Castlederg
*Lough Neagh*
Belfast
*Strangford Lough*
*Rossan Point*
Donegal
Omagh
Dungannon
Lisburn
Dunmurry
Saintfield
Killybegs
Fintona
Dromore
Ballyshannon
Portaferry
Ardglass
*Donegal Bay*
Bundoran
*Lower Lough Erne*
Portadown
Armagh
Ballynahinch
Downpatrick
Enniskillen
*Upper Lough Erne*
Rathfriland
Newcastle
*Dundrum Bay*
*Slieve Donard 85*
*Benwee Head*
*Erris Head*
Sligo
Dromahair
Lisnaskea
Monaghan
Keady
*Mourne Mts*
Belmullet
Ballycastle
*Killala Bay*
*Sligo Bay*
Swanlinbar
Newtownbutler
Clones
Newry
Kilkeel
*The Mullet*
Killala
Colooney
Castleblayney
Warrenpoint
*Carlingford Lough*
*Lough Conn*
Ballina
*Lough Allen*
Belturbet
Cootehill
Dundalk
Greenore
*Blacksod Bay*
*Nephin 806*
*Slieve Gamph*
*Moy*
Carrick-on-Shannon
Shercock
Carrickmacross
*Dundalk Bay*
Dunany Point
*Achill Island*
*Nephin Beg Range*
*Lough Gara*
Boyle
Cavan
Kingscourt
Ardee
*Clare Island*
*Clew Bay*
Westport
Castlebar
Ballaghaderreen
Granard
*Lough Sheelin*
Kells
Navan
Drogheda
Louisburgh
*Croagh Patrick 765*
Ballyhaunis
Castlerea
Longford
Castlepollard
Athboy
Duleek
Balbriggan
*Inishbofin*
Leenane
Ballinrobe
Roscommon
Mullingar
Trim
Skerries
CONNAUGHT
*Partry Mts*
Tuam
*Mount Bellew*
*Lough Ree*
*Inny*
*Boyne*
Swords
Clifden
*Lough Mask*
Athlone
Moate
Clara
Kilcock
*Slyne Head*
Oughterard
*Suck*
Enfield
Leixlip
*Connemara*
*Lough Corrib*
Athenry
Ballinasloe
Edenderry
Naas
DUBLIN
(Baile Átha Cliath)
*Gorumna Island*
Galway
Loughrea
Tullamore
*Bog of Allen*
Lucan
Dún Laoghaire
*Galway Bay*
Portumna
Birr
LEINSTER
Newbridge
Bray
*Inishmore*
*Aran Islands*
*Burren*
Lisdoonvarna
*Lough Derg*
Roscrea
Portarlington
Kildare
Enniskerry
Greystones
Ennistymon
Mountmellick
Portlaoise
*Wicklow Mts*
*Hag's Head*
*Liscannor Bay*
Ennis
Nenagh
Templemore
Athy
*Lungnaquilla Mountain 926*
Ashford
Wicklow
Spanish Point
Killaloe
Carlow
Tullow
*Wicklow Head*
Kilkee
Newmarket-on-Fergus
Thurles
Baltinglass
Shillelagh
Arklow
Kilrush
Limerick
Kilkenny
Leighlinbridge
*Loop Head*
Tarbert
Adare
*Golden Vale*
Cashel
Muine Bheag
*Mount Leinster 795*
Bunclody
Gorey
*Mouth of the Shannon*
Foynes
Tipperary
Callan
*Blackstairs Mts*
Ferns
*Cahore Point*
*Kerry Head*
Listowel
Newcastle West
Thomastown
Graiguenamanagh
Enniscorthy
*Brandon Mountain*
Tralee
Abbeyfeale
Rathlurc
*Galtymore 920*
Fethard
Clonmel
New Ross
Wexford
*Wexford Harbour*
*Slea Head*
*Dingle*
Castleisland
Newtown
Mitchelstown
Carrick-on-Suir
Rosslare
*Dingle Bay*
Killorglin
Newmarket
Fermoy
*Blackwater*
Lismore
Waterford
Rosslare Harbour
*Carnsore Point*
*Valencia Island*
*Carrantuohill 1041*
Killarney
*Boggeragh Mts*
Mallow
Dungarvan
Tramore
*Waterford Harbour*
*Helvick Head*
Cahersiveen
*Macgillycuddy's Reeks*
*Lough Leane*
Blarney
Cork
Youghal
Waterville
Kenmare
Macroom
*Comeragh Mountains*
Midleton
Sheem
*Knockaboy 707*
*Lee*
Passage West
Cobh
*Kenmare River*
*Caha Mts*
Ballineen
Bandon
Kinsale
Cahermore
Dunmanway
*Bandon*
*Dursey Island*
Bantry
Clonakilty
*Old Head of Kinsale*
*Bantry Bay*
Skibbereen
Schull
Baltimore
*Mizen Head*
*Cape Clear*

*St George's Channel*

CELTIC SEA

MUNSTER
ULSTER
NORTHERN IRELAND
IRELAND

Miles   Km
60   100
40   50
20
0   0

1 : 2 400 000

METRES   FEET
5000   16404
3000   9843
2000   6562
1000   3281
500   1640
200   656
0   0
Land below sea level
200   656
4000   13124
6000   19686

Longitude 8° west of Greenwich

© Collins Bartholomew Ltd

# ENGLAND AND WALES

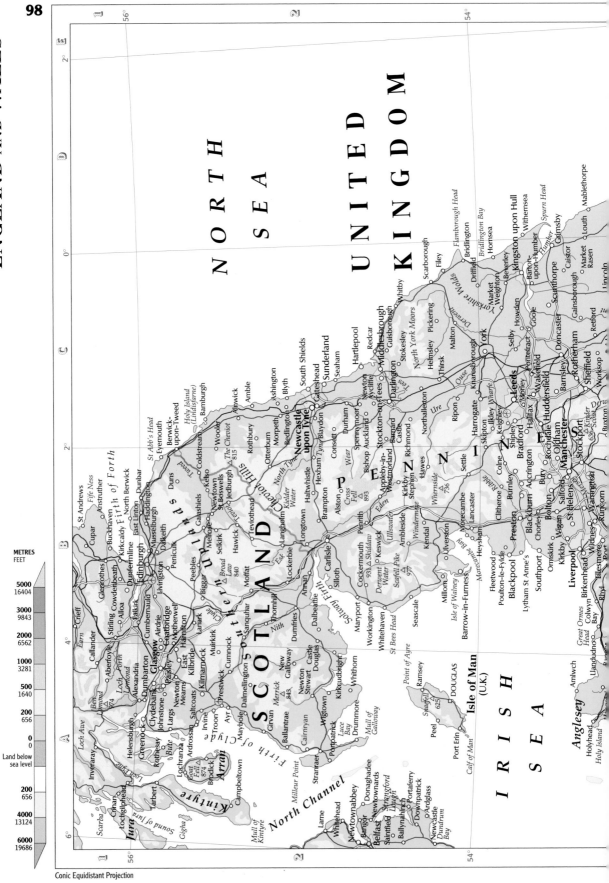

**METRES**
FEET

5000
16404

3000
9843

2000
6562

1000
3281

500
1640

200
656

0
0

Land below
sea level

200
656

4000
13124

6000
19686

Conic Equidistant Projection

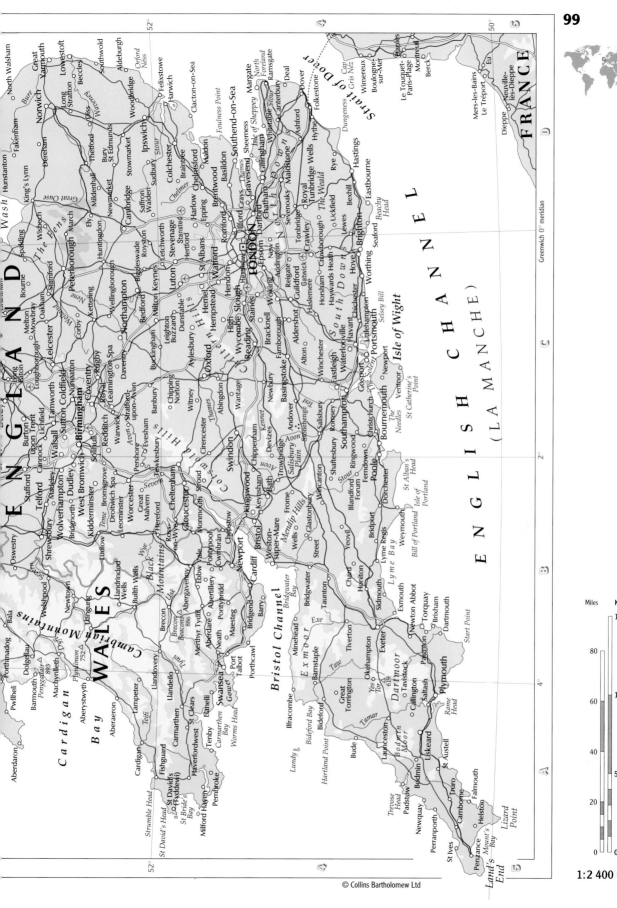

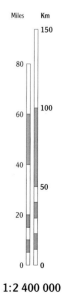

© Collins Bartholomew Ltd

1:2 400 000

**NORTHWEST EUROPE**

*N O R T H*

*S E A*

West Frisian Islands

Schiermonnikoog
Ameland
Terschelling
West-Terschelling
Hollum
Oost-Vlieland
Vlieland
Texel
Den Burg
Marsdiep

East Frisian Islands
Spiekeroog
Langeoog
Norderney
Juist
Borkum
Norden
Norderney
Westerholt
Wittr
OSTFRIESLA

Den Helder
Wieringerwerf
Schagen
Nieuwe-Niedorp
Heerhugowaard
Bergen
Alkmaar
Castricum
Beverwijk
IJmuiden
Zaandam
Zandvoort
Haarlem
Hillegom
Noordwijk-Binnen
Katwijk aan Zee
Alphen aan den Rijn
Leiden
THE HAGUE
('s-Gravenhage)
Hook of Holland
(Hoek van Holland)
Delft
Rotterdam
Vlaardingen
Hellevoetsluis
Scharendijke
Burgh-
Haamstede
Westkapelle
Koudekerke
Knokke-Heist
Zeebrugge
Blankenberge
Ostend
(Oostende)
Nieuwpoort
Zedelgem
Veurne
Diksmuide
Roeselare
Ieper
Kortrijk
Menen
Roubaix
Lille
Villeneuve-
d'Ascq

Harlingen
Witmarsum
Bolsward
Sneek
Sloten
IJsselmeer
Enkhuizen
Hoorn
Berkhout
Purmerend
AMSTERDAM
Amstelveen
Hilversum
Waddinxveen
Gouda
Schoonhoven
Capelle aan
de IJssel
Spijkenisse
Middelharnis
Zierikzee
Oosterschelde
Middelburg
Goes
Vlissingen
Hoogerheide
Breskens
Terneuzen
Philippine
Kapellen
Maldegem
St-Laureins
Eeklo
Brugge
(Bruges)
Torhout
Tielt
Wingene
Deinze
Zulte
Oudenaarde
Ronse
Ath

Den Helder
Wieringerwerf
Wolvega
Steenwijk
Meppel
Kraggenburg
Emmeloord
Urk
Creil
Kampen
Lelystad
Dronten
Zwolle
Ommen
Kloosterhaar
Hardenberg
Coevorden
Groß-Hesepe
Lingen
(Ems)
Fürste
Nordhorn
Rheine
Ibb
Gronau
(Westfalen)
Steinfurt
Greven

Wadenzee
Eemskanaal
Groningen
Winschoten
(Ostfriesland)
Appingedam
Delfzijl
Emden
Leer
Weste
Aurich
Wies
Hinte
Bedum
Hoogezand-
Sappemeer
Veendam
Stadskanaal
Assen
Beilen
Hoogeveen
Emmen
Haren (Ems)
Meppen
Sustrum
Löningen
Papenbo
Frieso
Walchum
Strücklingen
(Saterland)

Leeuwarden
Franeker
Reduzum
Drachten
Heerenveen
Dokkum
Kollum
Oenkerk
Burdaard
Ferwert
Eenrum
Uithuizen

Edam
Heerde
Raalte
Apeldoorn
Deventer
Zutphen
Doesburg
Hoog-
Keppel
Winterswijk
Doetinchem
Borken
Dülmen
Coesfeld
Havixbeck
Velen
Bocholt
MÜNSTERLAND
Haltern
Recklinghausen
Gelsenkirchen
Bottrop
Essen
Bochum
Dort
Wesel
Dinslaken
Duisburg
Moers
Mülheim an der Ruhr
Krefeld
Ratingen
Düsseldorf
Neuss
Mönchengladbach
Viersen

NETHERLANDS

Deventer
Harderwijk
Nijverdal
Almelo
Oldenzaal
Borne
Hengelo
Enschede
Eibergen
Ahaus

Driemond
Naarden
Nijkerk
Amersfoort
Barneveld
Ede
Veenendaal
Wageningen
Nieuwegein
Utrecht
Torenberg
107 △
Torenberg
Apeldoorn
Doetinchem
Zevenaar
Andelst
Arnhem
Nijmegen
Kleve
Goch
Kevelaer
Wachtendonk
Venlo
Tegelen
Geldern
Kempen

Culemborg
Tiel
Waal
Neder Rijn
Gorinchem
Dordrecht
Oss
Wijchen
's-Hertogenbosch
Wanroij
St Anthonis
Uden
Erp
Boxmeer
Deurne
Venray
Horst
Roermond
Herkenbosch
Sittard
Stein
Heerlen

Oosterhout
Waalwijk
Tilburg
Eindhoven
Helmond
Asten
Weert
Maaseik
Maastricht
Aachen

Zevenbergen
Roosendaal
Breda
Etten-Leur
Best
Boxtel
Valkenswaard
Luyksgestel
Hechtel
Hamont
Bree
Beringen
Genk
Maaseik

BELGIUM

Antwerp
(Anvers)
St-Niklaas
Lille
Turnhout
Geel
Bocholt
Lommel
Hasselt
Maastricht
Tongeren
Borgloon
Sittard

Meetkerke
Zandvliet
Brecht
Westmalle
Schilde
Schoten
Kapellen
Willebroek
Lier
Mechelen
Aarschot
Diest
Hasselt
Tienen
Leuven

Dendermonde
Wichelen
Aalst
Vilvoorde
Schaerbeek
Anderlecht
BRUSSELS
(Bruxelles)
Uccle
Halle
Waterloo
Nivelles
Genappe
Tongeren
Michelen
Eschweiler
Kerkrade
Herzogenrath
Heerlen
Bergheim (Erft)
Grevenbroich
Bergisch Gladbach
Leverkusen
Dormagen
Cologne (Köln)
Hürth
Düren
Kerpen
Wergberg
Hückelhoven
Erkelenz
Wuppertal
Hilden
Solingen
Remscheid
Lüdenscheid
Gummersbach
Attendo
Iser
Froden
Hagen
Wesel
Siegen

Ghent
(Gent)
Evergem
Lokeren
Zele

Lille
Mouscron
Tournai
Péruwelz
Ath
Soignies
Lens
Nivelles
Fleurus
Namur
Andenne
Huy
Liège
Seraing
Verviers
Spa
Malmédy
St-Vith
Raeren
Stolberg
(Rheinland)
Bonn
Königswinter
Altenki
Weste
Hennef (Sieg)
St Augustin
Troisdorf
Meckenheim
Bad Neuenahr-
Ahrweiler
Blankenheim
Adenau
Mayen
Koblenz
Neuwied
Andernach
Mülheim-
Kärlich
Mont
Lahnstein

Lens
Douai
Valenciennes
Maubeuge
Aulnoye-
Aymeries
Cambrai
Caudry
Avesnes-
sur-Helpe
La Capelle

Boussu
Mons
Frameries
Thuin
Charleroi
Châtelet
Montignies-
le-Tilleul
Beaumont
Philippeville
Hastière-
Lavaux
Dinant
Ciney
Assesse
Durbuy
Marche-
en-Famenne
Rochefort
La Roche-
en-Ardenne
Vielsalm
St-Hubert
Houffalize
Thommen
Clervaux
Neuerburg
Bitburg
Clervaux
Bastogne
Arzfeld
Prüm
Gerolstein
Hillesheim
Dahlem
Daun
Mayen
Cochem
Manderscheid
Blankenrath
Wittlich
Bernkastel-Kues
Mosel
Simme
(Huns
Emmels
Bo
am Ha

Hohe
Venn
Eifel
Rhine (Rhein)
Kyll
Salm
Erbeskopf
818 △
Idar-Oberstein
Donner

BELGIUM

Cambrai
Caudry
Bohain-en-
Vermandois
La Capelle
Avesnes-
sur-Helpe
Couvin
Beauraing
Fumay
Rocroi
Montherme
Bièvre
Vresse
Bouillon
Paliseul
Neufchâteau
Libramont
Wiltz
Ettelbruck
Redange
Mersch
Echternach
Trier
Konz
Reinsfeld
Saarburg
Kell
Morbach
Idar-Oberstein
Wolfstei
Nohfelden
Bad Kreuzna

LUXEMBOURG

St-Quentin
Péronne
Guise
Vervins
Marle
Montcornet
Chauny
Tergnier
Serre
Signy-
l'Abbaye
316 △
Rozoy-
sur-Serre
Charleville-
Mézières
Sedan
Carignan
Omont
Mouzon
Stenay
Virton
Arlon
Esch-
sur-Alzette
Pétange
Esch-
sur-Alzette
LUXEMBOURG
Redange
Differdange
Dudelange
Thionville
Hayange
Florange
Rombas
Mettlach
Merzig
Saarlouis
Homburg
Neunkirchen
Kaisersl
St Wendel

FRANCE

Noyon
Laon
Rethel
Attichy
Soissons
Courmelles
Fismes
Villers-
Cotterêts
Tinqueux
Reims
Bétheny
Guignicourt
Vouziers
Dun-sur-
Meuse
Longuyon
Spincourt
Consenvoye

Aisne
Oise
Chauny
Marle
Montcornet

Longitude 6° east of Greenwich

Conic Equidistant Projection

METRES
FEET

5000
16404

3000
9843

2000
6562

1000
3281

500
1640

200
656

0
0

Land below
sea level

200
656

4000
13124

6000
19686

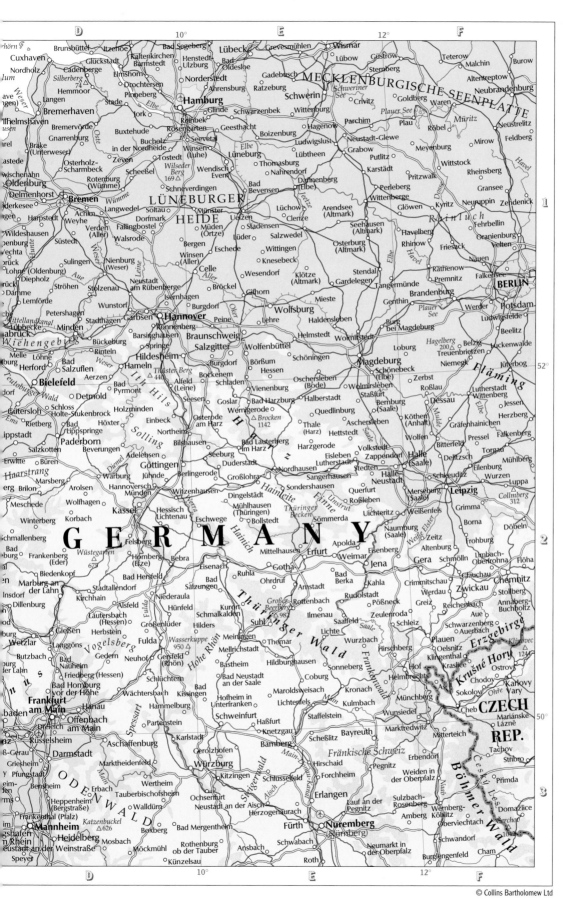

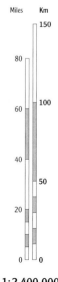

**Miles** **Km**

150

80 100

60

40 50

20

0 0

1:2 400 000

CENTRAL EUROPE

NORTH SEA

DENMARK

NETHERLANDS

GERMANY

BELGIUM

LUXEMBOURG

FRANCE

LORRAINE

SWITZERLAND

BAVARIA

CZECH

AUSTRIA

ITALY

AMSTERDAM
THE HAGUE ('s-Gravenhage)
BRUSSELS (Bruxelles)
BERLIN
Hamburg
Bremen
Hannover
Potsdam
BERN
Stuttgart
Munich (München)
Nuremberg (Nürnberg)
Mannheim
Frankfurt am Main
Cologne (Köln)
Düsseldorf
Dortmund
Essen
Duisburg
Leipzig

Longitude 10° east of Greenwich

METRES
FEET

5000
16404

3000
9843

2000
6562

1000
3281

500
1640

200
656

0
0

Land below
sea level

200
656

4000
13124

6000
19686

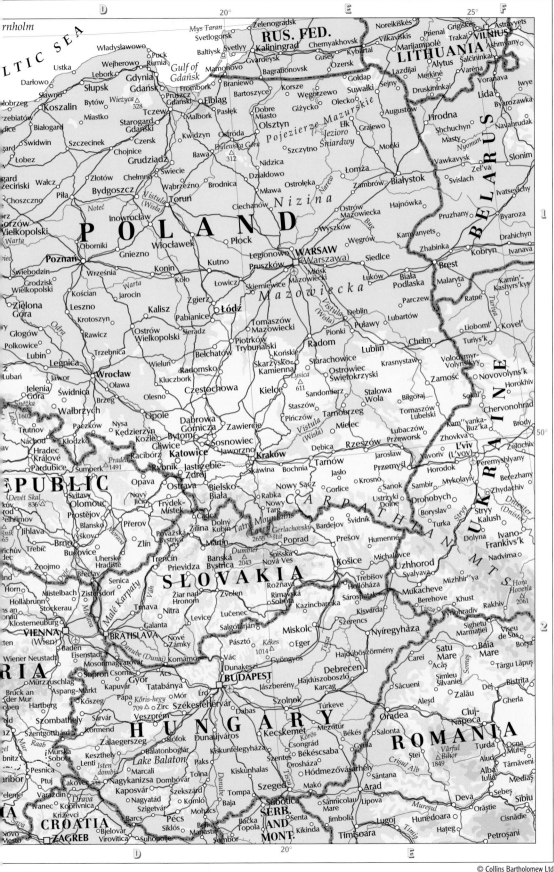

1:4 800 000

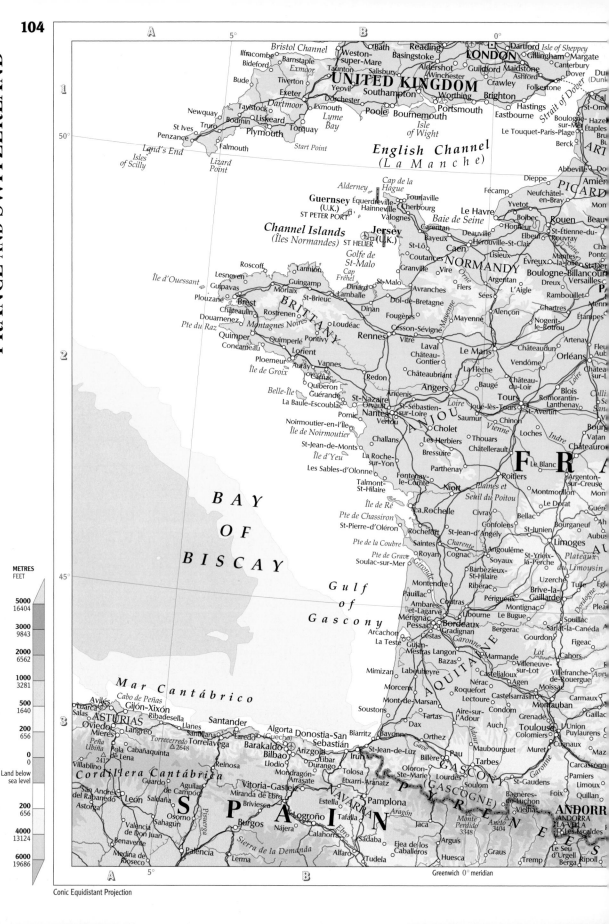

FRANCE AND SWITZERLAND

**A** 5° **B** 0°

UNITED KINGDOM

Bristol Channel
Ilfracombe
Barnstaple
Bideford
*Exmoor*
Weston-super-Mare
Bath
Reading
Basingstoke
Dartford *Isle of Sheppey*
LONDON
Gillingham Margate
Canterbury
Du
(Dunk

Bude
Tiverton
Yeovil
Salisbury
Aldershot
Guildford Maidstone
Crawley
Ashford
Dover
Folkestone

Newquay
Tavistock
Exeter
*Dartmoor*
Winchester
Southampton
Worthing
Brighton
Hastings
Eastbourne
*Strait of Dover*
Cal
St-Om

Truro
Bodmin
Liskeard
Plymouth
Torquay
*Lyme Bay*
Poole
Bournemouth
Portsmouth
*Isle of Wight*
Boulogne-sur-Mer
Étaples
Berck
ART

Penzance
Falmouth
*Land's End*
*Lizard Point*
*Start Point*
*English Channel*
*(La Manche)*
Dieppe
Abbeville
Amie
PICARD

*Isles of Scilly*

*Alderney*
*Cap de la Hague*
Tourlaville
Cherbourg
Le Havre
Fécamp
Neufchâtel-en-Bray
Mon

Guernsey (U.K.)
ST PETER PORT
Equerdreville
Hainneville
Valognes
*Baie de Seine*
Bolbec
Honfleur
Elbeuf
Rouen
Beau

Channel Islands
*(Îles Normandes)*
Jersey (U.K.)
ST HELIER
Carentan
Bayeux
Deauville
St-Lô
Coutances
Caen
Hérouville-St-Clair
St-Étienne-du-Rouvray
Cha

*Golfe de St-Malo*
*Cap Fréhel*
Granville
Vire
*Orne*
NORMANDY
Lisieux
Évreux
Mantes-la-Jolie
Versailles
St-De

Roscoff
Lannion
Guingamp
St-Malo
Dinard
Avranches
Flers
Argentan
Sées
L'Aigle
Dreux
Rambouillet
P

Lesneven
St-Brieuc
Lamballe
Dinan
Dol-de-Bretagne
Fougères
Mayenne
Alençon
Chartres
Nogent-le-Rotrou
Menn
Étampes

*Île d'Ouessant*
Guipavas
Morlaix
BRITTANY
Loudéac
*Mayenne*
Laval
Le Mans
Châteaudun
Artenay
Orléans
Fleu

Plouzané
Brest
Châteaulin
Rostrenen
Pontivy
Cesson-Sévigné
Vitré
Château-Gontier
La Flèche
Vendôme
Château-sur-l

Douarnenez
*Montagnes Noires*
Quimperlé
Rennes
Châteaubriant
Baugé
Château-du-Loir
Tours
Blois
Château

*Pte du Raz*
Quimper
Lorient
Vannes
Redon
Angers
Saumur
Joué-lès-Tours
St-Avertin
Romorantin-Lanthenay
Colli
San

Concarneau
Ploemeur
Auray
*Île de Groix*
Carnac
Quiberon
*Belle-Île*
Guérande
La Baule-Escoublac
St-Nazaire
Pornic
ANJOU
Vertou
Cholet
Les Herbiers
Thouars
Châtellerault
Chinon
Loches
*Vienne*
*Indre*
Châteaurou
Bourg
Vatan

Noirmoutier-en-l'Île
*Île de Noirmoutier*
St-Jean-de-Monts
*Île d'Yeu*
Challans
La Roche-sur-Yon
Bressuire
Parthenay
Fontenay-le-Comte
F R A
Le Blanc
Argenton-sur-Creuse
Mon

Les Sables-d'Olonne
Talmont-St-Hilaire
Niort
Poitiers
Montmorillon
Le Dorat
Guére

*Île de Ré*
*Plaines et Seuil du Poitou*
Civray
Bellac
Bourganeuf
Ah
Aubus

**BAY**
*Pte de Chassiron*
La Rochelle
Rochefort
St-Jean-d'Angély
Confolens
St-Junien
Limoges
AU

**OF**
St-Pierre-d'Oléron
*Charente*
Angoulême
St-Yrieix-la-Perche
*Plateaux du Limousin*

**BISCAY**
*Pte de la Coubre*
Saintes
Royan
Cognac
Soyaux
Barbezieux-St-Hilaire
Uzerche
Tulle
Égl

*Pte de Grave*
Soulac-sur-Mer
Montendre
Riberac
Périgueux
Brive-la-Gaillarde
Montignac
Plea

50°

45°

*Gulf of Gascony*
Pauillac
Blaye
Coutras
Libourne
Le Bugue
Sarlat-la-Canéda
Figeac
*Dordogne*
Souillac
Gourdon

Ambarès-et-Lagrave
Mérignac
Bordeaux
Bergerac
Marmande
*Lot*
Cahors

Arcachon
La Teste
Pessac
Gradignan
Cestas
Gujan-Mestras Langon
Bazas
Villeneuve-sur-Lot
Agen
Villefranche-de-Rouergue
Moissac
Carmaux

Mimizan
Labouheyre
Morcenx
Nérac
Roquefort
Castelsarrasin
Condom
Lectoure
Montauban
Gaillac

Soustons
Mont-de-Marsan
Aire-sur-l'Adour
Auch
Grenade
Toulouse
Colomiers
Union
Puylaurens

Avilés
*Cabo de Peñas*
Gijón-Xixón
*Mar Cantábrico*
Santander
Algorta Donostia-San Sebastián
Biarritz
Dax
Tartas
Bayonne
Orthez
Pau
Maubourguet
Muret
Cugnaux
Maz

Luarca
Salas
Oviedo
Ribadesella
Llanes
Santillana
Torrelavega
Laredo
(Guecho)
Barakaldo
Arizgoiti
Bilbao
St-Jean-de-Luz
Billère
Tarbes
Carcassonn

Mieres
ASTURIAS
Langreo
*Torrecerredo 2648*
Eibar
Durango
Irun
Oloron-Ste-Marie
Lourdes
Bagnères-de-Luchon
Foix
Pamiers
Limou

Peña Ubiña
Pola de Lena
Cabañaquinta
*2417*
Reinosa
Llodio
Mondragón
Arrasate
Etxarri-Aranatz
Soulom
St-Gaudens
Vielha
*Aneto 3404*
ANDORR

Villablino
*Cordillera Cantábrica*
Vitoria-Gasteiz
NAVARA
Pamplona
*Monte Perdido 3348*
ANDORRA LA VELLA

San Andrés del Rabanedo
Guardo
Aguilar de Campóo
Miranda de Ebro
Estella
*Aragón*
Jaca
*PYRENEES*
Les Escaldes

León
Saldaña
Briviesca
*Ebro*
Tafalla
Logroño
Calahorra
Sadaba
Arguis
Graus
La Seu d'Urgell
Berga
Ripoll

Astorga
Sahagún
Osorno
*Pisuerga*
Burgos
Nájera
Ejea de los Caballeros
Huesca
Tremp

Valencia de Don Juan
SPAIN
*Sierra de la Demanda*
Alfaro
Tudela

Benavente
Medina de Ríoseco
Palencia
Lerma

1

2

3

*Greenwich 0° meridian*

Conic Equidistant Projection

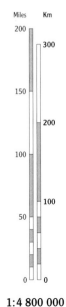

1:4 800 000

© Collins Bartholomew Ltd

# SPAIN AND PORTUGAL

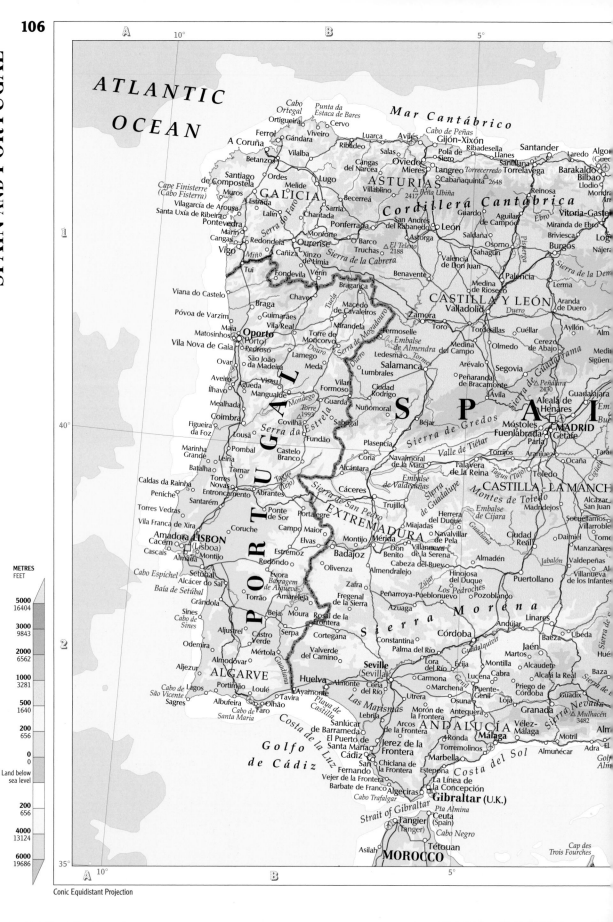

**ATLANTIC OCEAN**

*Mar Cantábrico*

Cabo Ortegal
Punta da Estaca de Bares
Ortigueira
Cervo
Ferrol
Gándara
Viveiro
Ribadeo
Luarca
Avilés
Gijón-Xixón
Santander
A Coruña
Vilalba
Salas
Ribadesella
Llanes
Laredo
Algo
(Guec
Betanzos
Cangas del Narcea
Oviedo
Mieres
Pola de Siero
Torrecerredo 2648
Torrelavega
Santillana
Barakaldo
Bilbao
Santiago de Compostela
Ordes
Melide
Lugo
**ASTURIAS**
Villablino
Cabañaquinta △2648
Llodio
Mondra
Vitoria-Gaste
Cape Finisterre
(Cabo Fisterra)
Muros
Estrada
Becerreá
Peña Ubiña 2417
Peña Ubiña
Reinosa
Aguilar de Campóo
Briviesca
Log
Vilagarcía de Arousa
Lalín
Chantada
San Andrés del Rabanedo
Guardo
Vitoria-Gaste
Miranda de Ebro
Santa Uxía de Ribeira
Pontevedra
Sarria
Ponferrada
León
Saldaña
Osorno
Burgos
Nájera
Marín
Redondela
Monforte
Barco
Truchas
El Teleno 2188
Astorga
Sahagún
Palencia
Lerma
Cangas
Cañiza
Ourense
Valencia de Don Juan
**Cordillera Cantábrica**
Vigo
Tui
Xinzo de Limia
Sierra de la Cabrera
Benavente
Medina de Rioseco
Aranda de Duero
Fondevila
Verín
Bragança
Zamora
**CASTILLA Y LEÓN**
Valladolid
*Duero*
Viana do Castelo
Braga
Chaves
Macedo de Cavaleiros
Toro
Tordesillas
Cuéllar
Ayllón
Póvoa de Varzim
Guimarães
Vila Real
Mirandela
Hermisende
Medina del Campo
Olmedo
Cerezo de Abajo
Maia
Torre de Moncorvo
*Embalse de Almendra*
Ledesma
Arévalo
Segovia
Sierra de Guadarrama
Matosinhos
**Oporto (Porto)**
Lamego
*Douro*
Salamanca
Peñaranda de Bracamonte
Peñalara 2430
Guadalajara
Vila Nova de Gaia
Pedroso
Meda
Lumbrales
Ávila
Alcalá de Henares
São João da Madeira
Vilar Formoso
Ciudad Rodrigo
Nuñomoral
Sierra de Gredos
Madrid
Ovar
Aveiro
Viseu
Guarda
Béjar
Plasencia
Móstoles
Getafe
Ílhavo
Águeda
Mangualde
Sabugal
**MADRID**
Mealhada
Covilhã
Fundão
Coria
Valle de Tiétar
Torrijos
Aranjuez
Ocaña
Coimbra
Figueira da Foz
Lousã
**Serra da Estrela**
Torre 1993
Castelo Branco
Alcántara
Navalmoral de la Mata
Talavera de la Reina
Toledo
Tara
Marinha Grande
Pombal
Leiria
*Tagus (Tejo)*
Cáceres
**CASTILLA - LA MANCH**
Batalha
Tomar
Abrantes
Trujillo
Sierra de Guadalupe
Montes de Toledo
Madridejos
Alcázar San Juan
Caldas da Rainha
Torres Novas
Entroncamento
Sierra de San Pedro
Herrera del Duque
Embalse de Cijara
Villarroble
Peniche
Santarém
Ponte de Sor
Portalegre
**EXTREMADURA**
Miajadas
Navalvillar de Pela
Ciudad Real
Daimiel
Tome
Torres Vedras
Coruche
Campo Maior
Mérida
Manzanares
Vila Franca de Xira
Amadora
Cacém
**LISBON (Lisboa)**
Montijo
Elvas
Estremoz
Montijo
Don Benito
Villanueva de la Serena
Almadén
Jabalón
Valdepeñas
Cascais
Almada
Redondo
Badajoz
Olivenza
Almendralejo
Cabeza del Buey
Hinojosa del Duque
Puertollano
Villanueva de los Infantes
Cabo Espichel
Setúbal
Alcácer do Sal
Barragem de Alqueva
Évora
Zafra
Peñarroya-Pueblonuevo
Los Pedroches
Pozoblanco
Baía de Setúbal
Grândola
Torrão
Amareleja
Fregenal de la Sierra
Azuaga
**Sierra Morena**
Linares
Sines
Cabo de Sines
Beja
Moura
Rosal de la Frontera
Constantina
Córdoba
Andújar
Baeza
Úbeda
Aljustrel
Castro Verde
Serpa
Cortegana
**Sierra**
Palma del Río
Jaén
Martos
Sierra de
Hué
Odemira
Mértola
Valverde del Camino
*Guadalquivir*
Écija
Montilla
Cabra
Alcaudete
Almodóvar
**ALGARVE**
Huelva
Almonte
**Seville (Sevilla)**
Lora del Río
Carmona
Lucena
Puente-Genil
Priego de Córdoba
Baza
Aljezur
Portimão
Loulé
Ayamonte
Coria del Río
Utrera
Marchena
Osuna
Loja
Guadix
Cabo de São Vicente
Lagos
Tavira
Olhão
*Guadiana*
Playa de Castilla
Las Marismas
Morón de la Frontera
Antequera
Granada
**Sierra Nevada**
Sagres
Albufeira
Cabo de Santa Maria
Sanlúcar de Barrameda
Lebrija
Arcos de la Frontera
**ANDALUCÍA**
Vélez-Málaga
Mulhacén 3482
Alm
El Puerto de Santa María
Jerez de la Frontera
Ronda
Málaga
Motril
Almuñécar
Adra
El
*Golfo de Cádiz*
*Costa de la Luz*
Cádiz
Chiclana de la Frontera
Torremolinos
Marbella
Estepona
**Costa del Sol**
Golf
Alm
San Fernando
Vejer de la Frontera
La Línea de la Concepción
Barbate de Franco
Algeciras
**Gibraltar (U.K.)**
Cabo Trafalgar
Strait of Gibraltar
Pta Almina
Ceuta (Spain)
Cabo Negro
Cap des Trois Fourches
Asilah
Tangier (Tanger)
Tétouan
**MOROCCO**

*PORTUGAL*
*SPAIN*

Conic Equidistant Projection

**FRANCE**

Arcachon
La Teste
Gujan-Mestras
Gradignan
Garonne
Marmande
Figeac
Villefranche-de-Rouergue
Espalion
Marvejols
Mende
Les-Vans
Pierrelatte
Valréas
Nyons
Sisteron
Digne-les-Bains

Mimizan
Labouheyre
Bazas
Cahors
Villeneuve-sur-Lot
Lot
Rodez
Sévérac-le-Château
Florac
Bagnols-sur-Cèze
Bollène
Orange
Carpentras

Morcenx
Nérac
Castellalou
Agen
Moissac
Montauban
Gaillac
Millau
Aveyron
Carmaux
Albi
Alès
Ganges
Uzès
Avignon
Cavaillon
Salon-de-Provence
Manosque
Draguignan

Mont-de-Marsan
Roquefort
Castelsarrasin
Condom
Lectoure
Colomiers
Castres
Lodève
Cévennes
Nîmes
Arles
Aix-en-Provence
Marignane
Aubagne
Fréjus

Soustons
Aire-sur-l'Adour
Dax
Auch
Toulouse
Puylaurens
Mazamet
Vauvert
Montpellier
Sète
Châteauneuf-les-Martigues
Marseille
Toulon
St-Tropez

Biarritz
Bayonne
Orthez
Pau
Tarbes
Cugnaux
Muret
Béziers
Agde
Golfe du Lion
La Ciotat
Six-Fours-les-Plages
Cap Sicié
Hyères

St-Jean-de-Luz
Irún
Billère
St-Gaudens
Pamiers
Carcassonne
Narbonne
Durban-Corbières
Étang de Leucate

Oloron-Ste-Marie
Lourdes
Soulom
Bagnères-de-Luchon
Foix
Limoux
Quillan
Rivesaltes
Perpignan
Port-Vendres

**PYRENEES**

Pamplona
Jaca
Monte Perdido 3348
Aneto 3404
Vielha
**ANDORRA**
**ANDORRA LA VELLA**
Les Escaldes
Prades
Céret
Cap de Creus

**NAVARRA**
Sádaba
Ejea de los Caballeros
Huesca
Arguís
Le Seu d'Urgell
Figueres
Banyoles
Cap de Begur

Tudela
Tarazona
Graus
Berga
Ripoll
Olot
Torroella de Montgrí

Alagón
**Zaragoza**
Barbastro
Monzón
Tremp
Torelló
Vic
Salt
Girona
Costa Brava

**ARAGÓN**
Quinto
Binéfar
Tárrega
Manresa
Igualada
**CATALUÑA**
Sabadell
Mataró
Palamós

Cariñena
Escatrón
Lleida
Valls
Martorell
Santa Coloma de Gramanet
Blanes

Daroca
Calamocha
Fraga
Caspe
Reus
**Barcelona**
El Prat de Llobregat

Molina de Aragón
Monreal del Campo
Alcañiz
Gandesa
Tortosa
Tarragona
Costa Dorada
Vilanova i la Geltrú

Perales del Alfambra
Morella
Amposta
Golf de Sant Jordi

Teruel
Peñarroya 2019
Sant Carles de la Ràpita
Vinaròs

Sarrión
Torreblanca

Sierra de Javalambre
Alcora
Castelló de la Plana
Costa del Azahar

**Minorca (Menorca)**
Punta Nati
Ciutadella de Menorca
Mercadal
Mahón

**Majorca (Mallorca)**
Cap de Formentor
Pollença
Alcúdia
Sa Pobla

Santa Cruz de Moya
Vall de Uxó
Burriana
Sóller
Sa Cabaneta
Cap des Freu

Utiel
Lliria
Sagunto
Sa Dragonera
Calvià
Palma de Mallorca
Manacor
Félanitx

Manises
Burjassot
**Valencia**
Torrent
Catarroja
Cabrera
Cap de ses Salines

Requena
Sueca
Golfo de Valencia

Algemesí
Cullera

Carcaixent
Gandía
**Ibiza (Eivissa)**

Albacete
Xàtiva
Oliva
San Juan Bautista
Santa Eulalia del Río

Almansa
Ontinyent
Denia
San Antonio Abad
Ibiza (Eivissa)

Yecla
Villena
Ibi
Alcoy-Alcoi
Cabo de la Nao
San Francisco Javier

Hellín
Elda
Benidorm
Altea
Formentera

Jumilla
Novelda
La Vila Joiosa
Villajoyosa

Cieza
Crevillente
**Alicante**

Molina de Segura
Orihuela
Elche
Elx

Alcantarilla
Torrevieja
Costa Blanca

**Murcia**
Cartagena
Cabo de Palos

Alhama de Murcia
Mazarrón
Golfo de Mazarrón

Lorca
Águilas

**BALEARIC ISLANDS**
**(ISLAS BALEARES)**
**(Spain)**

**MEDITERRANEAN SEA**

Cabo de Gata

Ténès
Djebel Bissa
Gouraya
Tipasa
Koléa
Aïn Taya
Dellys
Boumerdes
Bejaïa
Jijel

**ALGIERS (Alger)**
Larba
Blida
Médéa
Bouira
Tizi Ouzou
Bougaa
Sétif

Sidi Ali
Ouled Farès
Aïn Defla
1157
Miliana
Berrouaghia
Sour el Ghozlane
Bordj Bou Arréridj
Aïn Azel

Mostaganem
Aïn Tédélés
Ech Chélif
Khemis Miliana
Ksar el Boukhari
Sidi Aïssa
M'Sila

Gap Carbon
Arzew
Relizane
Bordj Bounaama
Barika

**Oran**
Oued Tlélat
Zemmora
Tissemsilt
Mahdia
Zenzach
Bou Saâda
M'Oukal

Beni-Saf
Aïn Temouchent
Sig
Mohammadia
Mascara
Tiaret

**ALGERIA**

Miles | Km

200
150
100
50
0

300
200
100
0

Greenwich 0° meridian

1:4 800 000

ITALY AND THE BALKANS

Conic Equidistant Projection

METRES
FEET

5000
16404

3000
9843

2000
6562

1000
3281

500
1640

200
656

0
0

Land below
sea level

200
656

4000
13124

6000
19686

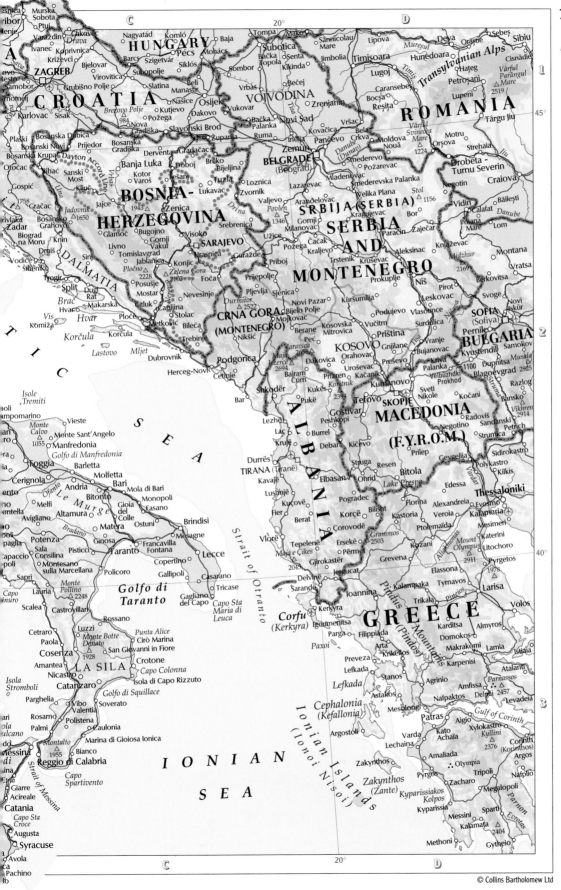

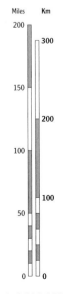

**Miles** **Km**

1:4 800 000

© Collins Bartholomew Ltd

# SOUTHEAST EUROPE

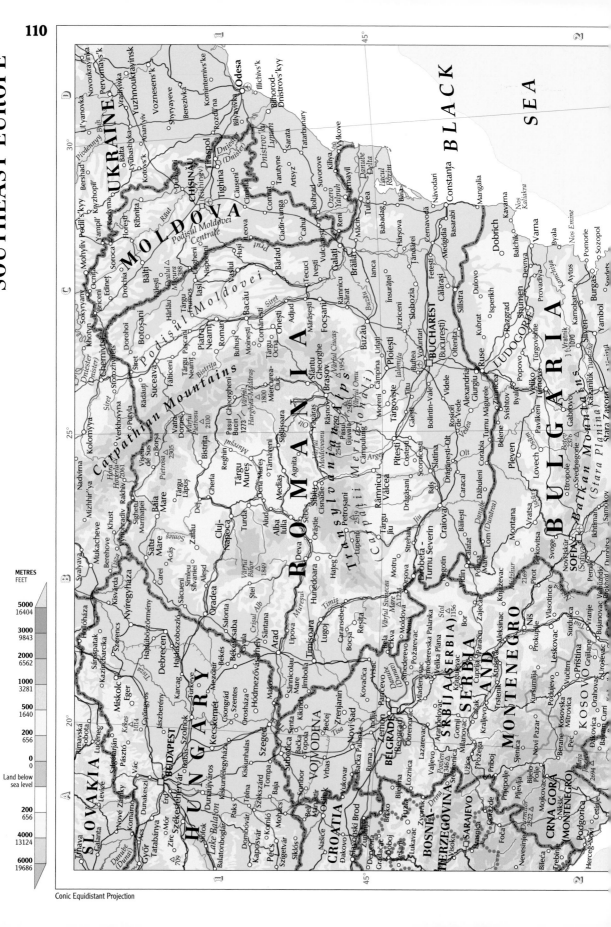

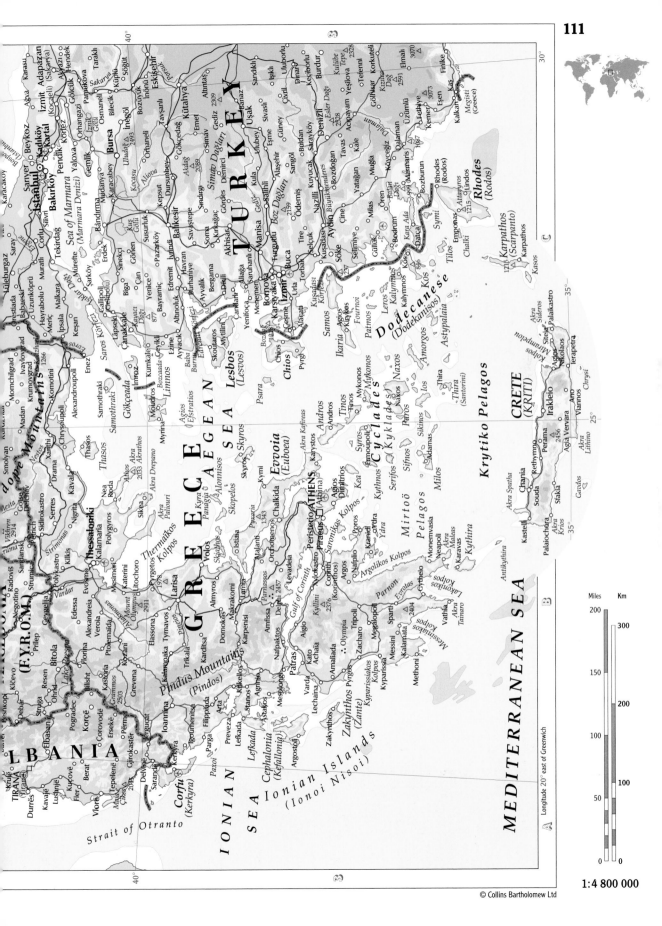

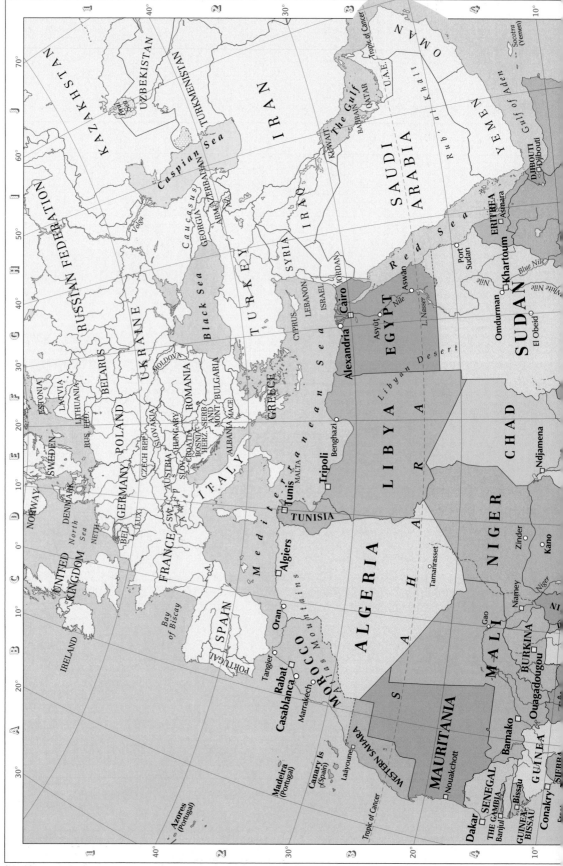

Oblated Stereographic Projection

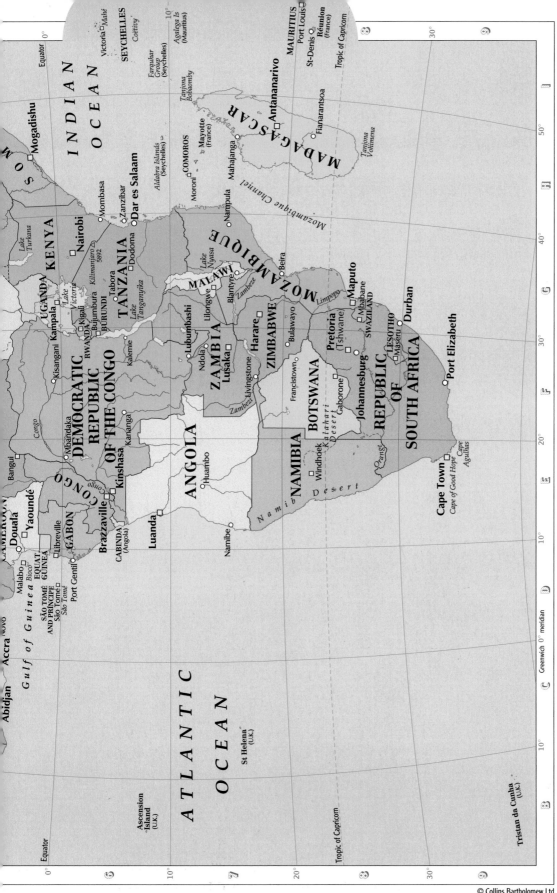

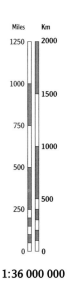

1:36 000 000

© Collins Bartholomew Ltd

**NORTHWEST AFRICA**

20° A 10°

SPAIN
Gibraltar · Almería · Carta
Gibraltar (U.K.) · Málaga
Strait of Gibraltar · Mostaganem
Tangier (Tanger) · Ceuta (Spain) · Oran · Sidi Bel Abbès
Larache · Tétouan · Melilla (Spain)
Ksar el Kebir · Sidi Kacem · Oujda · Tlemcen · Saïc
Ben Slimane · Taourirt · Bay
RABAT · Meknès · Fès (Fez) · Taza · Taourirt
Casablanca · El Jadida · Oued Zem · MOROCCO
Safi · Khouribga · Beni Mellal · Hauts Plateaux
El Kelaâ des Srarhna · Bouârfa · Aïn Sefra
Essaouira · Marrakech · Haut Atlas (High Atlas)
Jbel Toubkal 4167 · Er Rachidia · Figuig (Saha
Taroudannt · ATLAS MOUNTAINS · Grand Erg
Agadir · Ouarzazate · Béchar · Occident
Tiznit · Anti Atlas · Zagora · Abadla · Beni-Abbès · El Hom
Sidi Ifni · Hammada du Drâa · Tabelbala · Timimo
Guelmine · Ksabi · Platea
Tan-Tan · Erg Iabès · Adrar · Sbaa
LAÂYOUNE · Al Mahbas · Tindouf · Bordj Flye Ste-Marie · ALGI
Es Semara · El Eglab · Reggane · Aoulef · In
Boujdour · Chegga · Chenachane · Sebkha Azzel Matti · Sebk
WESTERN SAHARA · Post Weygand
Galtat Zemmour · Aïn Ben Tili
Skaymat · Bir Mogreïn · Erg Iguidi
Ad Dakhla · Tropic of Cancer · Tiguesmat · El Ha · Taoudenni · Oued Ilaferh
Awserd · Zouérat · El Hammâmi · Erg Chech · Bordj Mokhtar
Tichla · Fdérik · Maqteïr · Taudenni · Adrar d
Choûm · Guelb er Richât 485 · Tanezrouft · Aguelhok
Nouâdhibou · Atâr · OURÂNE · Aoukâr · Ifoghas
Akchâr · Akjoujt · Araouane · Kidal
Nouâmghâr · MAURITANIA · Anéfis
NOUAKCHOTT · Tidjikja · Dhar Tichît · Mazouâd
Boutilimit · Moudjéria · Tichît · MALI
Tiguent · Magta Lahjar · HÔD · Oualâta · Timbuktu (Tombouctou)
Aleg · Dhar Oualâta · Lac Faguibine · Gao
Rosso · Bogué · Ayoûn el Atroûs · IRÎGUI · Gourma-Rharous · Ménaka
St-Louis · Dagana · Kaédi · Kiffa · Néma · Ansongo
Louga · Linguère · Mbout · Sélibabi · Bassikounou · Goundam · Lac Niangay · Hombori
Dara · Matam · Nioro · Ballé · Nara · Youvarou · Nampala · Mopti · Douentza
DAKAR · Thiès · SENEGAL · Yélimané · Diéma · Kogoni · Bandiagara · Gorom
Mbour · Fatick · Bakel · Sandaré · Boron · Niono · Djenné · BURKINA
Kaolack · Kaffrine · Goudiri · Kidira · Bafoulabé · Kolokani · Ségou · Ouahigouya · Dori
BANJUL · Tambacounda · Kayes · Kita · Koulikoro · San · Tougan · Filin
Brikama · THE GAMBIA · Georgetown · Satadougou · BAMAKO · Dioïla · Koutiala · OUAGADOUGOU · NIAM
Ziguinchor · Kolda · Kédougou · Kangaba · Sikasso · Bobo-Dioulasso · Fada-N'Gourma · Tenkodogo
GUINEA-BISSAU · Gabú · Koundara · Siguiri · Kouroussa · Orodara · Léo · Pô · Bawku · Forga
BISSAU · Buba · Koubia · Dinguiraye · Dabola · Kolondiéba · Banfora · Koudougou · Gayéri · Diapa
Bolama · Cacine · Labé · Pita · Kankan · Kadiolo · Minnian · Manga · Zorgo · Kantcha
Fria · Boké · Fouta Djallon · Mamou · Faranah · Kérouané · Fékéssédougou · Gaoua · Wa · Bolgatanga · Dapaong · BEN
Dubréka · Kindia · Kissidougou · Dienné · Korhogo · Bouna · Tamale · Yendi · Kara · Natitingou
CONAKRY · GUINEA · Macenta · Odienné · Touba · Séguéla · Bondoukou · GHANA · Bimbila · Bassila · Sokodé
FREETOWN · Makeni · Kailahun · Beyla · Nzérékoré · Man · Katiola · CÔTE D'IVOIRE · Salaga · Savalou · Abeo
SIERRA LEONE · Magburaka · Lola · Bouaké · Sunyani · Kintampo · Kete Krachi · PORTO-N
Bonthe · Zimmi · Gbarnga · Daloa · YAMOUSSOUKRO · Mampong · Atakpamé · Aného
MONROVIA · LIBERIA · Tapeta · Gagnoa · Divo · Bongouanou · Abengourou · Kumasi · Kofondua · LOMÉ · Slave Co
Harbel · Buchanan · Zwedru · Lakota · Tiassalé · Aboisso · Obuasi · Adzopé · ACCRA · Tema
River Cess · Greenville · Sassandra · Abidjan · Tarkwa · Winneba
Barclayville · Harper · San-Pédro · Tabou · Grand-Lahou · Sekondi · Cape Coast · Bigh
Cape Palmas · Three Points · Axim · Gold Coast · of Ben

ATLANTIC OCEAN
Madeira (Portugal) · FUNCHAL
Canary Islands (Islas Canarias) (Spain)
La Palma · SANTA CRUZ DE TENERIFE · Lanzarote
Pico del Teide 3718 · Tenerife · Fuerteventura · Jandía
La Gomera · El Hierro 807 · Gran Canaria
LAS PALMAS DE GRAN CANARIA

GULF OF GUINEA

**METRES / FEET**
5000 / 16404
3000 / 9843
2000 / 6562
1000 / 3281
500 / 1640
200 / 656
0 / 0
Land below sea level
200 / 656
4000 / 13124
6000 / 19686

Lambert Azimuthal Equal Area Projection

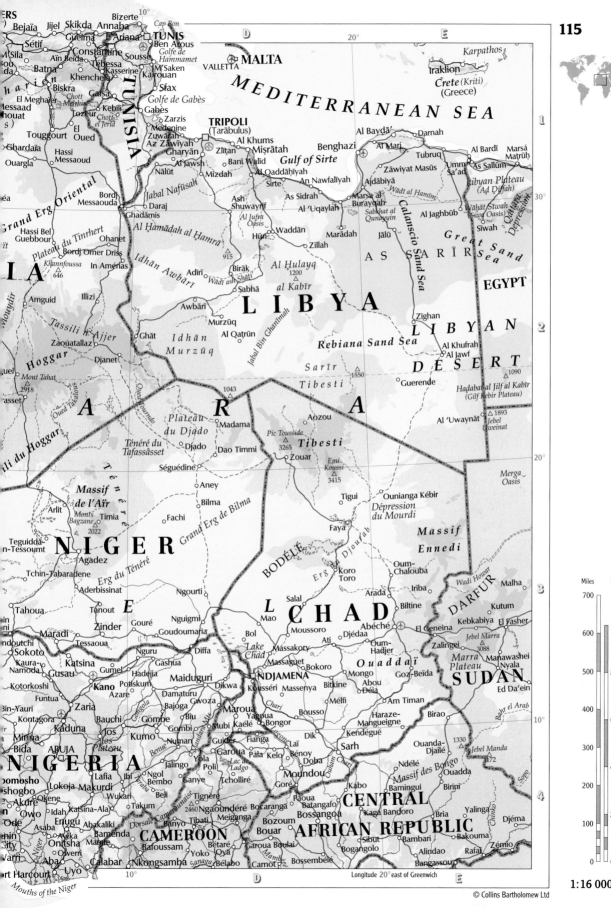

**115**

ERS
Bejaïa  Jijel  Skikda  Annaba  Bizerte
Sétif  Guelma  L'Ariana  TUNIS  Cap Bon
Sila  Aïn Beïda  Constantine  Ben Arous
ou  Batna  Sousse  VALLETTA  **MALTA**
harian  El Meghaïer  Khenchela  M'Saken  *Karpathos*
Messaad  Biskra  Gafsa  Kairouan  *Iraklion*
houat  El Meghaïer  Tozeur  Sfax  *Crete (Kriti)*
Ouargla  Kebili  Golfe de Gabès  *(Greece)*

## MEDITERRANEAN SEA

Touggourt  El Oued  Medenine  Zarzis  Al Baydā'  Darnah
Ghardaïa  Hassi  Zuwārah  Al Khums  Benghazi  Marsā
  Messaoud  Az Zāwiyah  Zlītan  Misrātah  Al Marj  Tubruq  Al Bardī  Matrūḥ
Gharyān  Banī Walīd  **Gulf of Sirte**  Zāwiyat Masūs  Umm  As Sallūm
Bordj  Al Jawsh  Mizdah  Sirte  An Nawfalīyah  Ajdābiyā  Sa'ad  *Libyan Plateau*
  Messaouda  Daraj  Ghadāmis  As Sidrah  Marsā al  Wādī al Hamīm  (Ad Diffah)
  *Jabal Nafūsah*  Ash  Al 'Uqaylah  Burayqah  Wāḥāt Sīwah
Hassi Bel  Bordj Omer Driss  Shuwayrif  Sabkhat al  Al Jaghbūb  (Siwa Oasis)
  Guebbour  *Al Ḥamādah al Ḥamrā'*  Waddān  Qunayyin  Sīwah  Qattara
  Khannfoussa  *Al Jufra*  Marādah  Jālū  As  *Great Sand*  Depression
  646  *Oasis*  Zillah  *Sand Sea*  **EGYPT**
Amguid  In Aménas  Adiri  Birāk  *al Kabir*  Zighan  *Sea*
Tassili n'Ajjer  Sabhā  **LIBYA**  **L I B Y A N**
Zaouatallaz  Awbārī  Murzūq  Al Khufrah
Hoggar  Ghāt  Al Qatrūn  Rebiana Sand Sea  Al Jawf  **D E S E R T**
Mont Tahat  *Idhān*  *Sarīr*  Guerende  Hadabah al Jilf al Kabīr  1090
2918  Djanet  *Murzūq*  1550  (Gilf Kebir Plateau)
  A  *Tibesti*  R  Al 'Uwaynāt  1893
1043  Madama  Aozou  A  *Jebel Uweinat*
  *Plateau*  *Pic Toussíde*  *Tibesti*
  *du Djado*  3265  Zouar
Djado  Dao Timmi  *Emi*  *Merga*
Ténéré du  *Koussi*  *Oasis*
  Tafassâsset  Séguédine  Aney  3415
Massif  Bilma  Tigui  Ounianga Kébir
de l'Aïr  Fachi  *Dépression*
Arlit  Monts  *Grand Erg de Bilma*  Faya  *du Mourdi*  *Massif*
  Bagzane  Timia  *Ennedi*
  2022  **N I G E R**  *BODÉLÉ*  Oum-
Teguidda-  Agadez  *Erg*  Chalouba  *Wadi Howar*  Malha
n-Tessoumt  *Erg du Ténéré*  *Koro*  Iriba
Tchin-Tabaradene  Aderbissinat  Ngourti  *Toro*  Arada  Biltine  **DARFUR**  Kutum
Tahoua  Salal  **CHAD**  El Geneina  Kebkabiya  El Fasher
Tanout  Mao  Moussoro  Abéché  Zalingei  *Jebel Marra*
Zinder  Gouré  Nguigmi  Bol  Ati  Djédaa  Oum-  3088  Manawashei
Maradi  Tessaoua  *Lake*  Massakory  Hadjer  *Marra*  Nyala
Sokoto  Nguru  Diffa  *Chad*  Bokoro  Mongo  Abou  Goz-Beïda  *Plateau*
Katsina  Gumel  Gashua  Massaguet  *Ouaddaï*  Déia  **S U D A N**
Kano  Potiskum  Maiduguri  **NDJAMENA**  Bitkine  Am Timan  Ed Da'ein
Azare  Hadejia  Dikwa  Kousséri  Massenya  Mélfi
Funtua  Damaturu  Gwoza  Maroua  Bousso  Haraze-  Birao
Kotorkoshi  Bauchi  Gombe  Bajoga  Yagoua  Bongor  Dik  Mangueigne
Zaria  Biu  Mubi  Kaélé  Laï  Kendégué  Ouanda-  1330  *Jebel Manda*
Kaduna  Jos  Kumo  Numan  Guider  Fianga  Sarh  Djalé  1172
Minna  *Jos*  Gombi  Garoua  Pala  Kelo  Ndélé  *Massif des Bongo*
Bida  **ABUJA**  *Plateau*  Jalingo  Yola  Poli  Bénoy  Doba  Goré  Bamingui  Ouadda
**NIGERIA**  Lafia  Ibi  Ngol  Bembo  Ganye  Tcholliré  Moundou  Kabo  Birini
omosho  Lokoja  Makurdi  Wukari  Beli  Tignère  Paoua  Bozoum  Kaga Bandoro  Yalinga
shogbo  Okene  Idah  Katsina-Ala  Takum  2460  Ngaoundéré  Bocaranga  Batangafo  Bria  Djéma
Akure  Owo  Enugu  Abakaliki  Bamenda  Tibati  Meiganga  Bossangoa  Bambari  Bakouma
Ode  Asaba  Awka  *Dorsale Camerounaise*  Banyo  Yoko  Qya  Bélabo  **CENTRAL**  Bozoum  Sibut  Alindao
nin  Onitsha  **CAMEROON**  Bafoussam  Bétaré  Garoua Boulaï  **AFRICAN REPUBLIC**  Bogangolo  Bangassou
rri  Aba  Calabar  Nkongsamba  Yoko  Bélabo  Carnot  Bossembélé  Rafaï  Zémio
t Harcourt  Uyo  *Canaga*  Bambari  Bambari
*Mouths of the Niger*

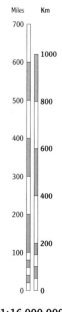

Miles  Km
700  1000
600
500  800
400  600
300
200  400
100  200
0  0

**1:16 000 000**

© Collins Bartholomew Ltd

# NORTHEAST AFRICA

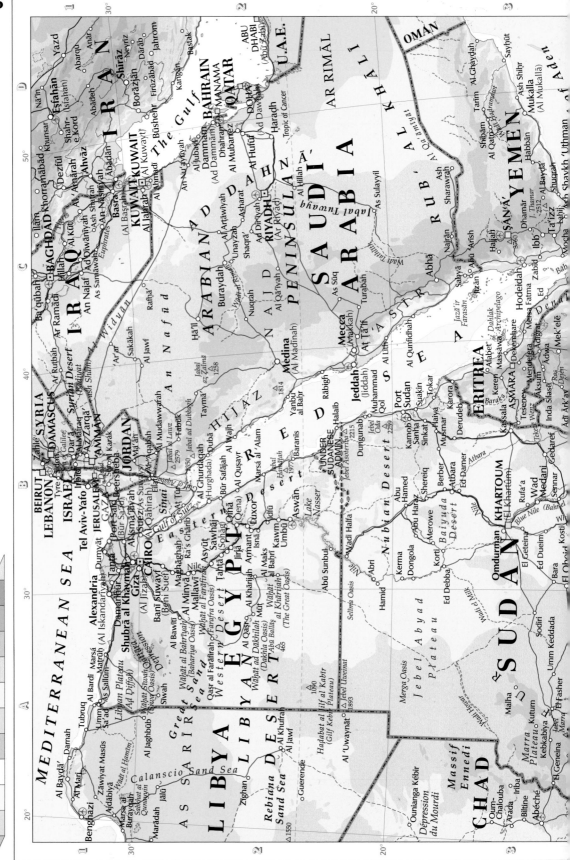

METRES / FEET

| | |
|---|---|
| 5000 | 16404 |
| 3000 | 9843 |
| 2000 | 6562 |
| 1000 | 3281 |
| 500 | 1640 |
| 200 | 656 |
| 0 | 0 |
| Land below sea level | |
| 200 | 656 |
| 4000 | 13124 |
| 6000 | 19686 |

Lambert Azimuthal Equal Area Projection

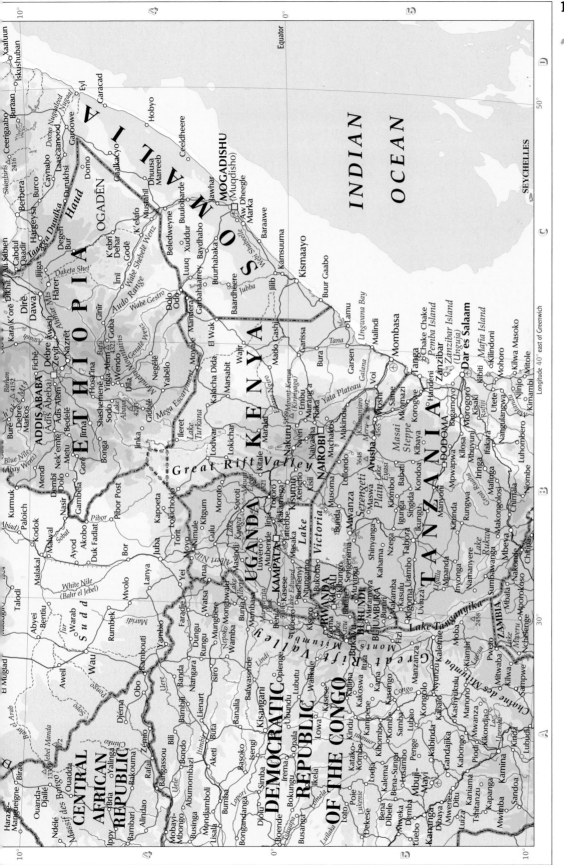

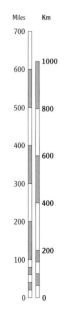

1:16 000 000

© Collins Bartholomew Ltd

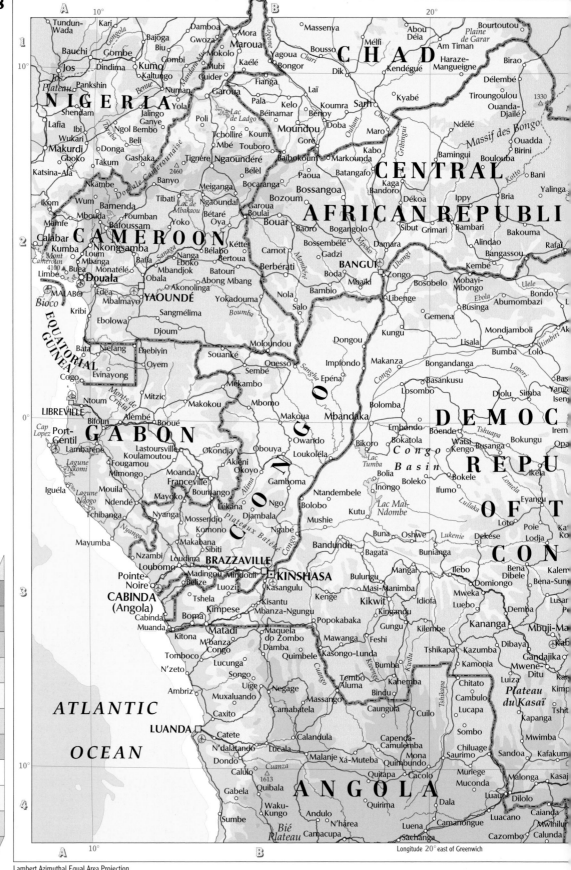

## Map labels

**CHAD**

**CENTRAL AFRICAN REPUBLI**

**NIGERIA**

**CAMEROON**

**EQUATORIAL GUINEA**

**GABON**

**CONGO**

**DEMOC REPU OF T CON**

**ATLANTIC OCEAN**

**ANGOLA**

Tundun-Wada, Kari, Bauchi, Gombe, Biu, Gombi, Jos, Dindima, Kumo, Kaltungo, Pankshin, Jos Plateau, Shendam, Lafia, Ibi, Wukari, Makurdi, Gboko, Katsina-Ala, Donga, Takum, Ikom, Wum, Nkambe, Mbouda, Bamenda, Mamfe, Calabar, Kumba, Loum, Mbanga, Nkongsamba, Mont Cameroun 4100, Buea, Limbe, MALABO, Bioco, Douala, Edéa, Kribi, Ebolowa, Bata, Niefang, Ebebiyin, Cogo, Evinayong, Oyem, Mitzic, Ntoum, LIBREVILLE, Bifoun, Alembé, Booué, Cap Lopez, Port-Gentil, Lambaréné, Lastoursville, Koulamoutou, Fougamou, Mimongo, Iguéla, Lagune Nkomi, Mouila, Ndendé, Tchibanga, Mayumba, Nzambi, Loubomo, Pointe-Noire, CABINDA (Angola), Cabinda, Muanda, Kitona, Matadi, Tomboco, N'zeto, Ambriz, LUANDA, Catete, N'dalatando, Dondo, Caxito, Calulo, Gabela, Waku-Kungo, Sumbe, Quibala, Andulo, N'harea, Camacupa, Bié Plateau, Camanongue, Sachanga

## Scale

| METRES | FEET |
|---|---|
| 5000 | 16404 |
| 3000 | 9843 |
| 2000 | 6562 |
| 1000 | 3281 |
| 500 | 1640 |
| 200 | 656 |
| 0 | 0 |

Land below sea level

| 200 | 656 |
|---|---|
| 4000 | 13124 |
| 6000 | 19686 |

Longitude 20° east of Greenwich

Lambert Azimuthal Equal Area Projection

# SOUTHERN AFRICA

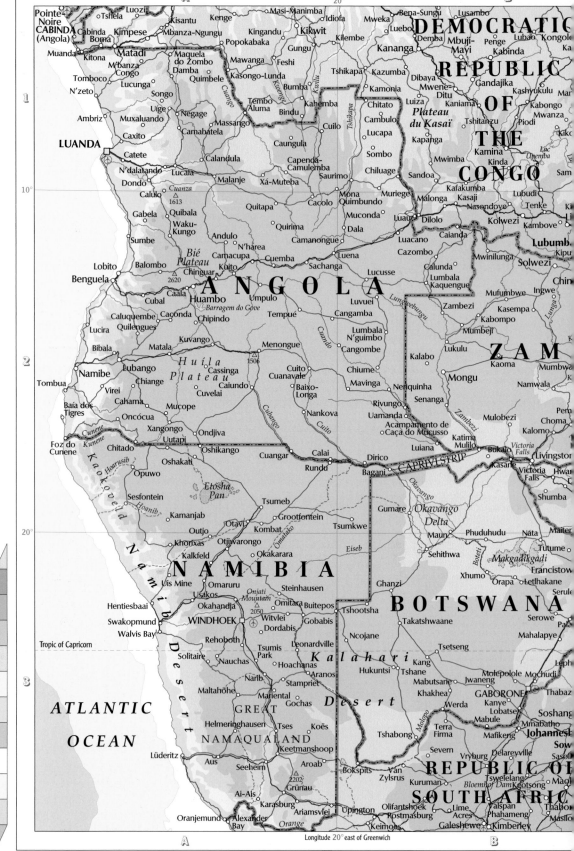

Lambert Azimuthal Equal Area Projection

INDIAN OCEAN

TANZANIA

MALAWI

MOZAMBIQUE

MBABWE

COMOROS

MORONI □  Njazidja (Grande Comore)

DZAOUDZI

Mayotte (France)

MADAGASCAR

ANTANANARIVO

INDIAN OCEAN

INDIAN OCEAN

Tropic of Capricorn

SWAZILAND

MBABANE

MAPUTO

HARARE

LILONGWE

DODOMA

LUSAKA

Miles  Km

500    750

400    500

300    250

200

100

0      0

1:12 000 000

© Collins Bartholomew Ltd

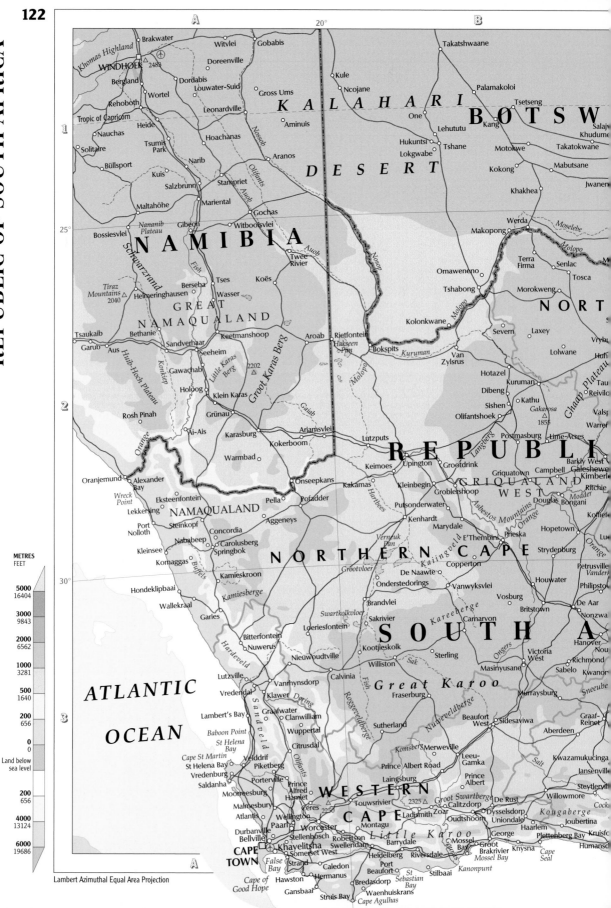

# REPUBLIC OF SOUTH AFRICA

**METRES** | **FEET**

5000 | 16404
3000 | 9843
2000 | 6562
1000 | 3281
500 | 1640
200 | 656
0 | 0
Land below
sea level
200 | 656
4000 | 13124
6000 | 19686

Lambert Azimuthal Equal Area Projection

A                    20°                    B

Brakwater
Khomas Highland
Witvlei
Gobabis
Takatshwaane

WINDHOEK
2483
Doreenville
Kule
Palamakoloi
Tsetseng

Bergland
Dordabis
Louwater-Suid
Ncojane
Kang
Salaj
Khudume

Wortel
Gross Ums
One
Lehututu
Takatokwane

Rehoboth
Leonardville
Hukuntsi
Tshane
Motokwe
Mabutsane

Tropic of Capricorn
Heide
Hoachanas
Aminuis
Lokgwabe
Kokong
Jwane

Nauchas
Tsumis Park
Narib
Aranos
Khakhea

Solitaire
Bullsport

Kuis
Salzbrunn
Stampriet
Gochas
Werda
Makopong

Maltahöhe
Mariental
Witbooisvlei

**N A M I B I A**

Nananib Plateau
Gibeon
Terra Firma
Senlac

Bossiesvlei
Twee Rivier
Omaweneno
Tosca

Schwarzrand
Fish
Tses
Koës
Tshabong
Morokweng

Tiraz Mountains
2040
Berseba
Wasser
Kolonkwane

Helmeringhausen
**N O R T**

**G R E A T**
Severn
Laxey
Vryb

**N A M A Q U A L A N D**
Keetmanshoop
Aroab
Rietfontein
Bokspits
Van Zylsrus
Hotazel
Lolwane
Hu

Tsaukaib
Bethanie
Sandverhaar
Kuruman

Garub
Aus
Seeheim
Gawachab
2202
Dibeng
Kuruman
Tau
Reivilo

Holoog
Klein Karas
Gaiab
Sishen
Kathu
1855
Valsp
Warrel

Rosh Pinah
Grünau
Ariamsvlei
Lutzputs
Olifantshoek
Postmasburg
Lime-Acres
Barkly West
Kimber

Ai-Ais
Karasburg
Kokerboom
**R E P U B L I**
Campbell
Galeshewe
Ritchie

Warmbad
Keimoes
Upington
Grootdrink
Griquatown
Douglas
Bongani
Koffief

Oranjemund
Alexander Bay
Onseepkans
Kakamas
Kleinbegin
Groblershoop
**G R I Q U A L A N D**
Hopetown

Wreck Point
Eksteenfontein
Pella
Pofadder
Putsonderwater
**W E S T**
Lu

Lekkersing
Aggeneys
Kenhardt
Prieska
Strydenburg

Port Nolloth
Steinkopf
Concordia
Marydale
E'Thembini

Kleinsee
Nababeep
Carolusberg
Springbok
Copperton
Petrusville
Vanderl

Komaggas
Kamieskroon
**N O R T H E R N   C A P E**
Houwater
Philipsto

Hondeklipbaai
De Naawte
Vanwyksvlei
Vosburg
De Aar
Nonzwa

Wallekraal
Garies
Onderstedorings
Britstown
Hanover
Nou

Bitterfontein
Brandvlei
Carnarvon
Victoria West
Richmond
Kwanor

Nuwerus
Sakrivier
Sterling
Masinyusane
Sabelo

Nieuwoudtville
Williston
**S O U T H   A**
Kootjieskolk
Calvinia
**G r e a t   K a r o o**
Fraserburg
Murraysburg
Graaf-Reinet

Lutzville
Vanrhynsdorp
Klawer
Sutherland
Beaufort West
Sidesaviwa
Aberdeen

Vredendal
Graafwater
Clanwilliam
Merweville
Leeu-Gamka

Lambert's Bay
Wuppertal
Komsberg
Prince Albert Road
Kwazamukucinga

Citrusdal
Jansenville

St Helena Bay
Velddrif
Piketberg
Prince Albert
Steytlerv

Vredenburg
Porterville
Laingsburg
Willowmore

Saldanha
Moorreesburg
Prince Alfred Hamlet
2325
De Rust
Joubertina

Malmesbury
Atlantis
Ceres
2250
Ladismith
Zoar
Calitzdorp
Dysselsdorp
Uniondale

Wellington
Montagu
Oudtshoorn

**A T L A N T I C**
**O C E A N**

Paarl
Worcester
**W E S T E R N**
Groot Swartberge
George
Plettenberg Bay

Stellenbosch
Robertson
**C A P E**
Montagu
**L i t t l e   K a r o o**
Mossel Bay
Knysna

Bellville
Khayelitsha
Somerset West
Swellendam
Heidelberg
Barrydale
Riversdale
Brakrivier

**CAPE TOWN**
Strand
Caledon
Port Beaufort
Stilbaai

False Bay
Hawston
Hermanus
Bredasdorp
Waenhuiskrans

Cape of Good Hope
Gansbaai
Struis Bay
Cape Agulhas

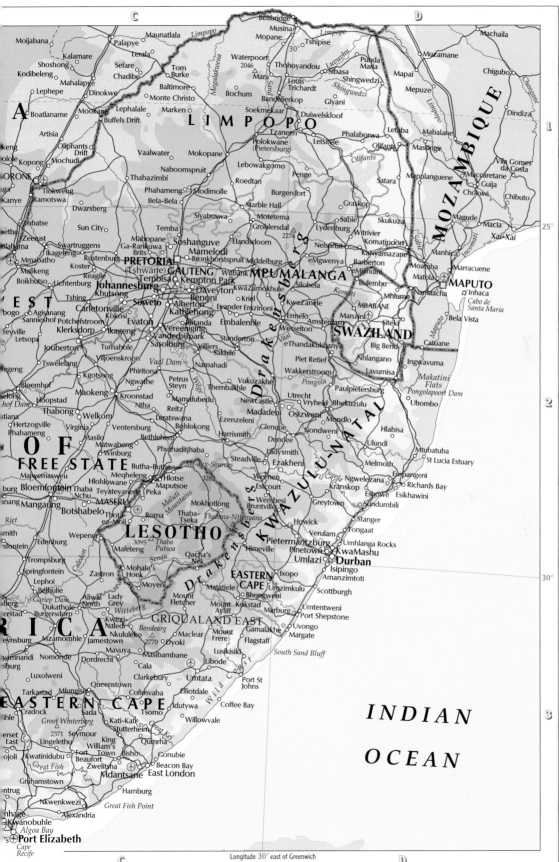

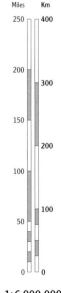

1:6 000 000

© Collins Bartholomew Ltd

ICELAND

Arctic Circle

Denmark Strait

Ammassalik

Jan Mayen (Nor.)

Kong Christian IX Land

Kong Frederik VI Kyst

NEWFOUNDLAND AND LABRADOR

St John's
C. Race
Cabot Strait
St Pierre and Miquelon (Fr.)
Newfoundland
Labrador
Sea

Greenland
(Denmark)

Kong Christian X Land

Kong Frederik VIII Land

Kong Knud Land

Baffin
Bay

Davis Strait

Nuuk

Sisimiut

Gulf of St Lawrence
Île d'Anticosti
PRINCE EDWARD ISLAND
Charlottetown
NEW SCOTIA
BRUNSWICK
Fredericton

QUÉBEC

Québec

Montréal

Baffin Island

Hudson Strait

Iqaluit

Kuujjuaq

Inukjuak

Chisasibi

ONTARIO

Ellesmere Island

Foxe
Basin

NUNAVUT

Repulse Bay

Southampton I.

Coats I.

Mansel I.

Belcher Is.

Hudson
Bay

Churchill

Thunder Bay
Lake Superior
MICHIG

Queen Elizabeth
Islands

Parry Islands

Melville Island

Devon Island

Somerset Island

Prince of Wales Island

Boothia
Pen.

Bathurst Inlet

MANITOBA

Winnipeg

Lake Winnipeg

MINNESOTA
St Paul
Minneapolis

Banks Island

Victoria Island

Amundsen Gulf

Coronation Gulf

Great Bear Lake

Great Slave Lake

Yellowknife

SASKATCHEWAN

Lake Athabasca

Regina

Saskatoon

NORTH DAKOTA
Bismarck

SOUTH DAKOTA
Pierre

ARCTIC OCEAN

Beaufort
Sea

Sachs Harbour

NORTHWEST
TERRITORIES

Peace

ALBERTA

Edmonton

Calgary

C A N A D A

Mackenzie

Inuvik

Rapid City

WYOMING

Barrow

YUKON
TERRITORY

Whitehorse

BRITISH COLUMBIA

Prince George

Kamloops

MONTANA
Helena
Billings

R O C K Y   M O U N T A I N

Fairbanks

Mt McKinley
6194

U.S.A.
ALASKA

Yukon

Vancouver

Seattle
WASHINGTON
Olympia

IDAHO
Boise

Salt Lake City

Arctic Circle

RUS.
FED.

Nome

Anchorage

Juneau

Vancouver Island
Victoria

Portland
Salem
OREGON

Columbia

Reno
Carson City

Bering Str.

St Lawrence I.

Gulf of
Alaska

Alexander
Archipelago

Queen Charlotte
Islands

CALI

Sacramento

San Francisco

St Matthew I.

Nunivak I.

Kodiak I.

Pribilof Is

Alaska Pen.

Bering
Sea

Aleutian Islands

90°
80°
70°
60°
50°

Arctic Circle

70°

80°

70°

60°

50°

40°

10°
20°
30°
40°
50°
60°
70°
80°
90°
100°
110°
120°
130°
140°
150°
160°
170°

A
B
C
D

1
2
3
4

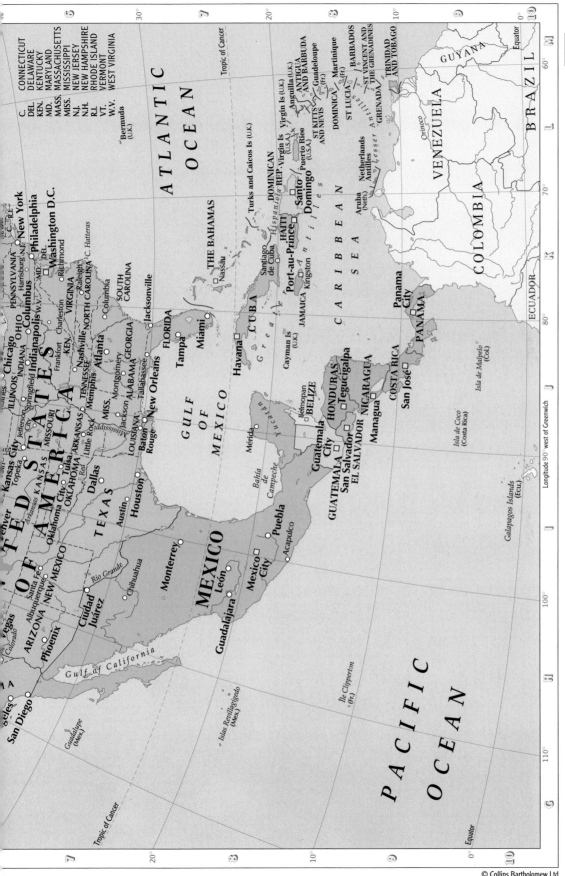

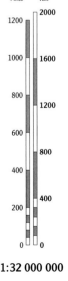

1:32 000 000

© Collins Bartholomew Ltd

Lambert Azimuthal Equal Area Projection

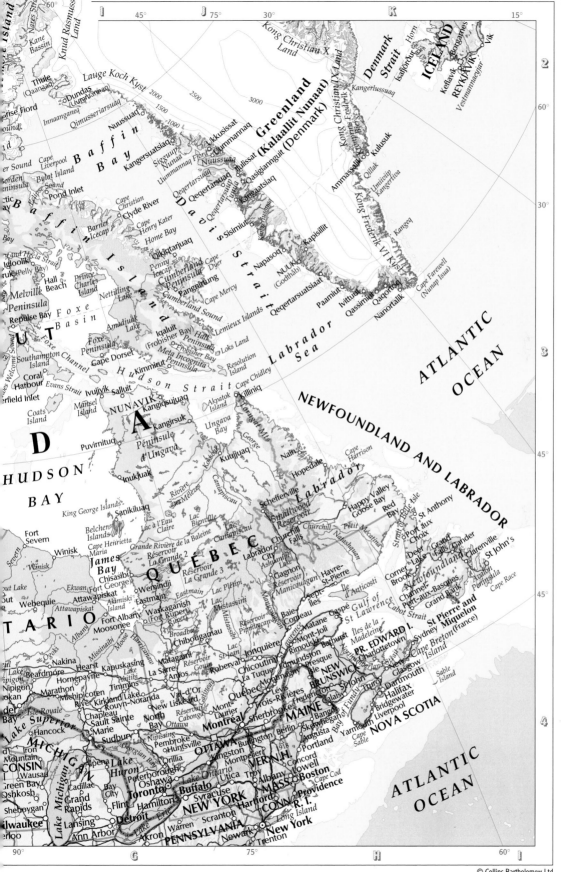

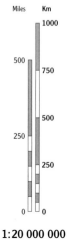

1:20 000 000

© Collins Bartholomew Ltd

PACIFIC

OCEAN

METRES
FEET

5000
16404

3000
9843

2000
6562

1000
3281

500
1640

200
656

0
0

Land below
sea level

200
656

4000
13124

6000
19686

Lambert Azimuthal Equal Area Projection

Longitude 120° west of Greenwich

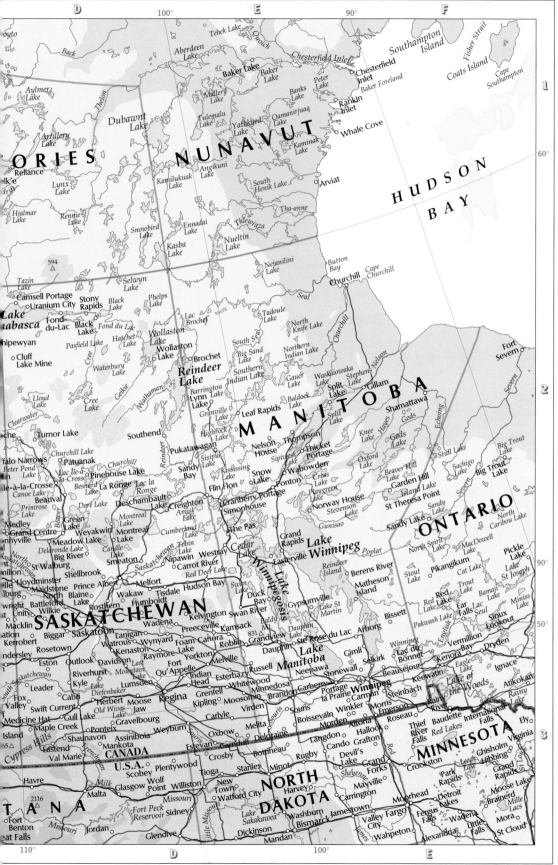

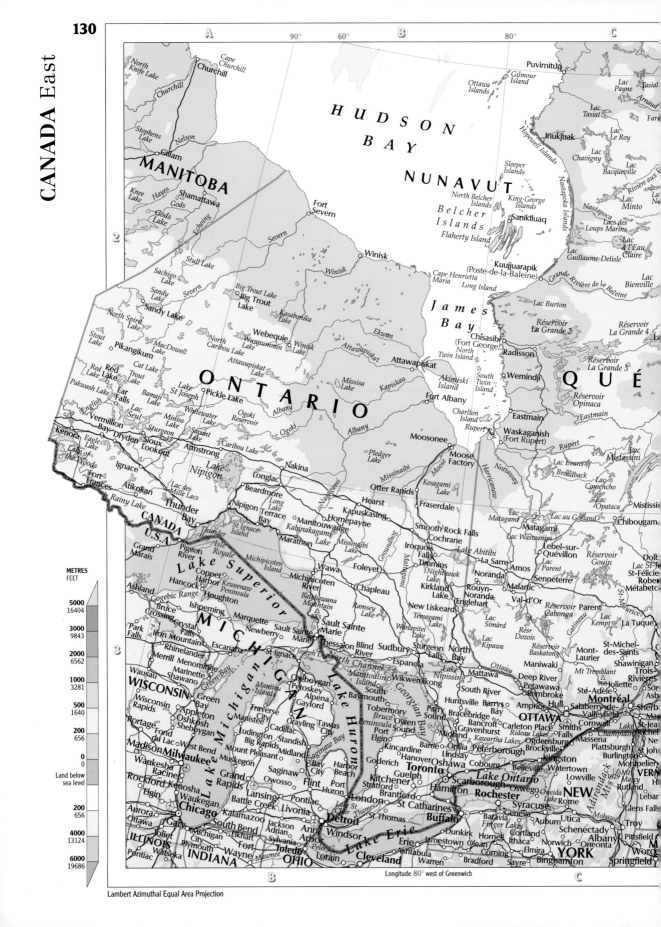

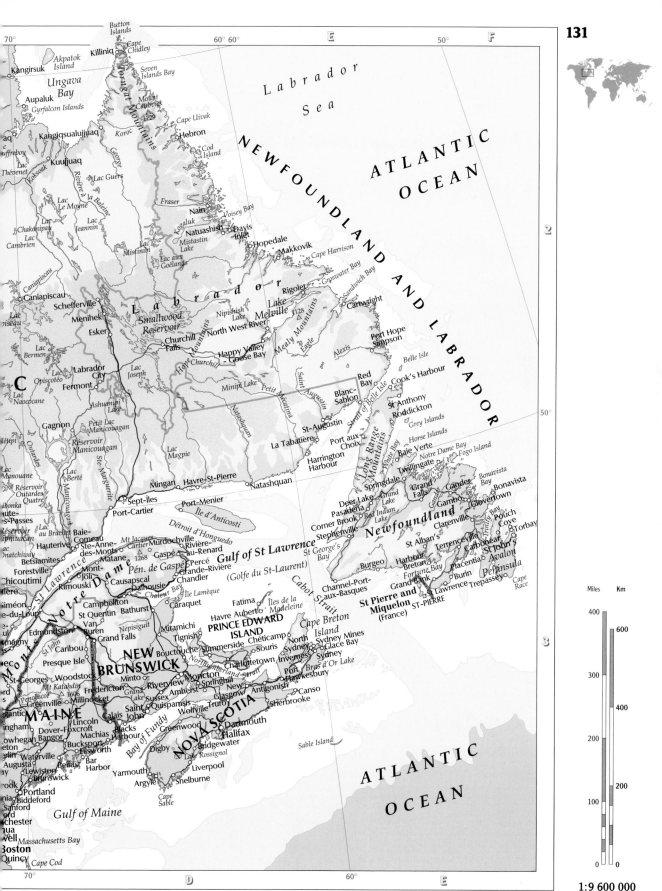

Button Islands

70°  60°  60°  E  50°  F

Akpatok Island
Kangirsuk
Killiniq
Cape Chidley

*Ungava Bay*

Aupaluk
Gyrfalcon Islands

aq
uffreboy
Lac
Thévenet
Kangiqsualujjuaq
Kuujjuaq
Koroc
George
Rivière à la Baleine
Cape Uivak
Hebron
Cod Island

*Labrador Sea*

Koksoak
Lac Guers
Fraser
Nain
Voisey Bay
Natuashish
Mistastin Lake
Davis Inlet
Hopedale
Makkovik

Lac
Le Moyne
Lac Jeannin
Lac aux Goélands

Lac
Chakonipau
Lac
Cambrien
Lac Mistinibi

Cape Harrison

*NEWFOUNDLAND AND LABRADOR*

*ATLANTIC OCEAN*

Caniapiscau
Scefferville
Menihek
Esker
Lac
iseau

Lac
Bermen

Nipishish Lake
Lake Melville
1128
North West River
Mealy Mountains

*L a b r a d o r*

Smallwood Reservoir
Churchill Falls
Happy Valley - Goose Bay

Hope Mountains
Churchill
Eagle

Rigolet
Grosswater Bay
Sandwich Bay
Cartwright

Port Hope Simpson

Belle Isle

Alexis

Lac
Opiscotéo
Labrador City
Fermont

Lac Joseph
Minipi Lake
Petit Mécatina
Saint Augustin

Red Bay
Blanc-Sablon
Cook's Harbour
St Anthony
Roddickton

Strait of Belle Isle

50°

Lac
Naococane
Gagnon
Ashuanipi Lake
Petit Lac Manicouagan

Réservoir Manicouagan

St-Augustin
La Tabatière
Port aux Choix
Grey Islands

Lac Magpie

Harrington Harbour

Baie Verte
Horse Islands
Fogo Island
Notre Dame Bay
Bonavista Bay

Lac
Manouane
Réservoir Outardes Quatre
Lac Berté
Lac au Brochet

Mingan
Havre-St-Pierre
Natashquan

Springdale
Grand Falls
White Bay
Twillingate
Gander
Bonavista

onka
aute-
s-Passes
Baie-Comeau
Hauterive
Betsiamites
Forestville

Sept-Îles
Port-Cartier
Port-Menier
Île d'Anticosti
Détroit d'Honguedo

Deer Lake
Pasadena
Corner Brook
Grand Lake
Red Indian Lake

*Newfoundland*

St Alban's
Clarenville
Gloverton

Trinity Bay
Pouch Cove
Torbay

natchiway
Chicoutimi

Mt Jacques Cartier
Murdochville
Rivière-au-Renard
Gaspé
Grande-Rivière
Chandler

Stephenville

St George's Bay

Terrenceville
Carbonear
St John's

Avalon Peninsula

iéon
-du-Loup
ière

Hauterive
Mont-joli
Rimouski
Matane
1268
Pén. de Gaspé
Percé

*Gulf of St Lawrence*

(Golfe du St-Laurent)

Burgeo
Harbour Breton
Placentia

St Lawrence
Trepassey
Cape Race

St-Quentin
Bathurst
Campbellton
Causapscal
Dalhousie
Chaleur Bay
Île Lamèque
Caraquet

Fatima
Îles de la Madeleine
Havre Aubert

Channel-Port-aux-Basques
Grand Bank
Fortune Bay
Burin

Cabot Strait

St Pierre and Miquelon
(France)
ST-PIERRE

Edmundston
St John
Van Buren
Nepisiguit
Grand Falls
Mitamichi
Tignish

PRINCE EDWARD ISLAND

Cape Breton Island

Magny
St-Georges
St John
Caribou
Presque Isle
Woodstock

Minto
Grand Lake
Fredericton
Riverview
Springhill

Bouctouche
Summerside
Charlottetown
Chéticamp
North Sydney
Inverness
Sydney Mines
Sydney
Glace Bay

NEW BRUNSWICK

Northumberland Strait

Souris

Port Hawkesbury
Bras d'Or Lake

rd
St-Georges
Mt Katahdin
1606
Greenville
Millinocket
Penobscot

Moncton
Sussex
Amherst
New Glasgow
Antigonish
Canso

MAINE

Quispamsis
Saint John
Truro

NOVA SCOTIA

Sherbrooke

ngham
Dover-Foxcroft
Bangor
Lincoln
Machias
Calais
Blacks Harbour
Wolfville
Greenwood
Bridgewater
Halifax
Dartmouth

eton
rlin
Waterville
Ellsworth
Bay of Fundy
Digby
Lake Rossignol
Liverpool

Sable Island

Augusta
ook
Belfast
Bar Harbor
Yarmouth
Argyle
Shelburne

*ATLANTIC OCEAN*

ia
Portland
Biddeford
Sanford
ord
chester
qua
well
**Boston**
Quincy

Cape Sable

*Gulf of Maine*

Massachusetts Bay
Cape Cod

70°  D  60°  E

© Collins Bartholomew Ltd

Miles  Km

400  600
300  400
200  200
100
0  0

1:9 600 000

# UNITED STATES OF AMERICA

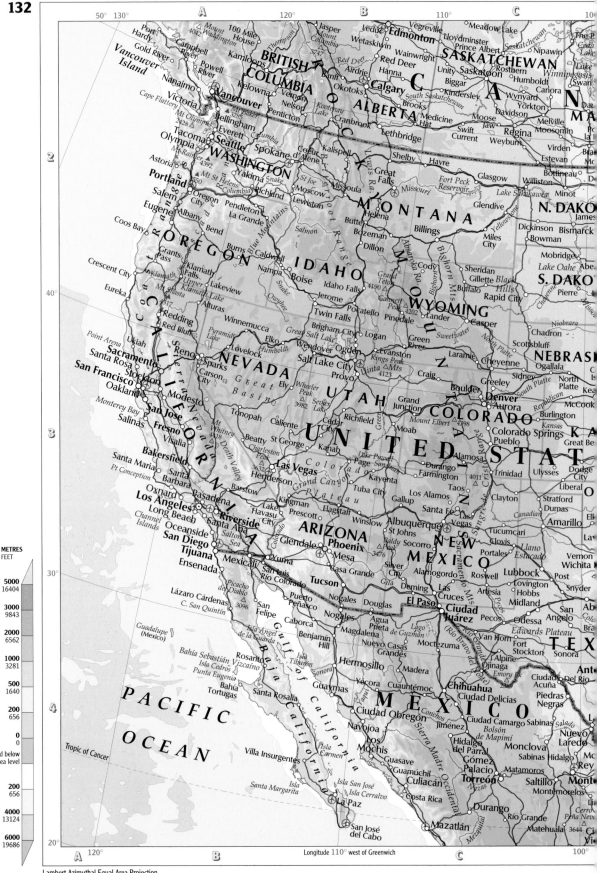

**METRES**
FEET

| 5000 | 16404 |
| 3000 | 9843 |
| 2000 | 6562 |
| 1000 | 3281 |
| 500 | 1640 |
| 200 | 656 |
| 0 | 0 |

Land below
sea level

| 200 | 656 |
| 4000 | 13124 |
| 6000 | 19686 |

**PACIFIC**

**OCEAN**

Tropic of Cancer

Lambert Azimuthal Equal Area Projection

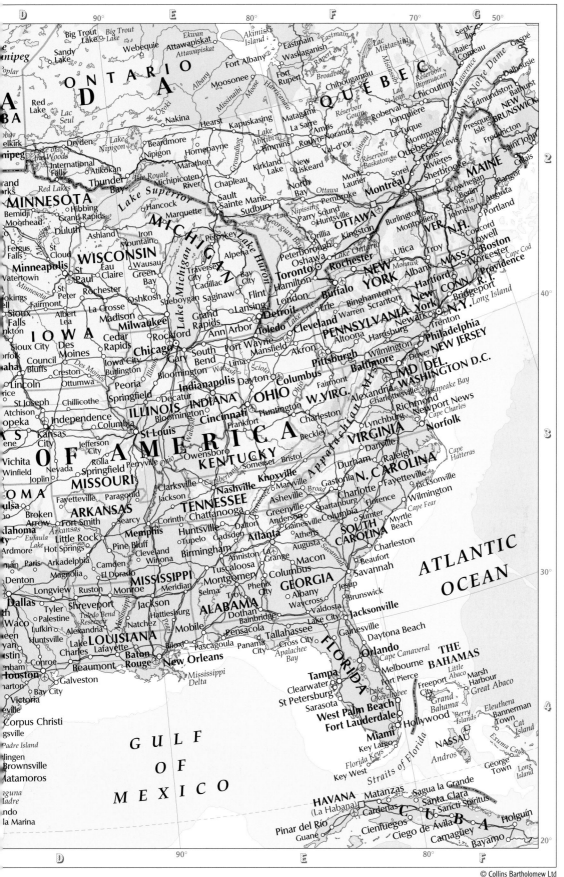

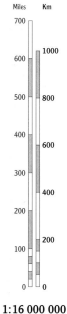

1:16 000 000

© Collins Bartholomew Ltd

# USA West

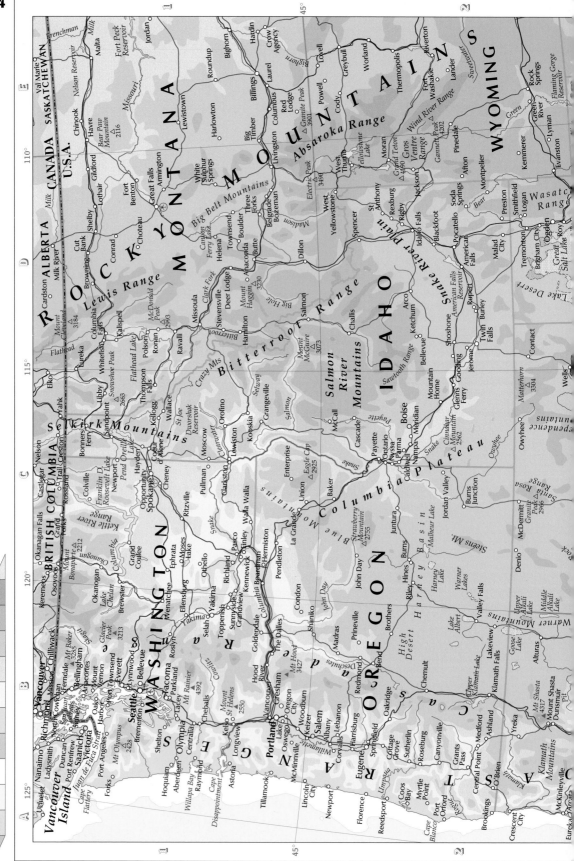

**CANADA**
**U.S.A.**

**SASKATCHEWAN**

Val Marie
Frenchman
Milk
Milk River
Nelson Reservoir
Fort Peck Reservoir
Malta
Jordan
Missouri

**ALBERTA**
Cardston
Milk River
Cut Bank
Browning
Conrad
Chinook
Havre
Lothair
Gildford
Shelby
Choteau
Fort Benton
Great Falls

**R O C K Y**

Mount Cleveland 3184
**Lewis Range**

**BRITISH COLUMBIA**
Castlegar
Nelson
Trail
Creston
Rossland
Grand Forks
Yahk
Bonners Ferry
Sandpoint

**Selkirk Mountains**

Libby
Whitefish
Kalispell
Snowshoe Peak 2663
Columbia Falls
Eureka

**Flathead Lake**
Polson
Ronan
Thompson Falls
Ravalli

**M O N T A N A**

White Sulphur Springs
Lewistown
Harlowton
Roundup
Big Timber
Livingston

**Big Belt Mountains**
Boulder
Townsend
Canyon Ferry Lake
Helena
Three Forks
Belgrade
Bozeman

**Absaroka Range**

**M O U N T A I N S**

Billings
Laurel
Columbus
Red Lodge
Granite Peak 3901
Cody

Bighorn
Hardin
Crow Agency
Lowell
Greybull
Worland
Thermopolis
Fort Washakie
Lander

**WYOMING**

Rock Springs
Green River
Flaming Gorge Reservoir
Lyman
Evanston
Kemmerer
Afton
Montpelier

**Wind River Range**
Grand Teton 4190
Pinedale
Jackson
Moran

**Gros Ventre Range**

Gannett Peak 4202

Bear
Soda Springs
Preston
Logan
Smithfield
Ogden

**Wasatch Range**

**Great Salt Lake**
**Lake Desert**

Tremonton
Brigham City
Malad City

Pocatello
Blackfoot
American Falls
American Falls Reservoir
Rupert

**Snake River Plain**

**I D A H O**

Idaho Falls
Rigby
Rexburg
St Anthony
Spencer

Salmon
Challis
McCall
Cascade

**Salmon River Mountains**

**Sawtooth Range**
Stanley
Ketchum
Bellevue
Shoshone
Gooding
Jerome
Twin Falls
Burley

Matterhorn 3304
Wells
Contact
Owyhee

**Independence Mountains**

**Santa Rosa Range**
Granite Peak 2946
McDermitt
Denio

**Bitterroot Range**

Deer Lodge
Anaconda
Butte
Dillon

Mount Haggin 3230

**Big Hole**

Stevensville
Hamilton
Darby

Merritt McGuire 3073

**WASHINGTON**

Vancouver
Nanaimo
Ladysmith
Chemainus
Duncan
Sidney
Saanich
Victoria

**Vancouver Island**

Ucluelet
Port Renfrew
Port Angeles
Forks
Cape Flattery

**Juan de Fuca Strait**

Blaine
Bellingham
Anacortes
Oak Harbor
Mount Vernon
Port Townsend
Everett
Edmonds
Seattle
Bremerton
Tacoma
Parkland

Mt Baker 3285
Glacier Peak 3213

**C a s c a d e**

Mount Olympus 2428
Shelton
Olympia
Centralia
Chehalis
Hoquiam
Aberdeen
Raymond

**Willapa Bay**
Cape Disappointment

Skagit

**Ross L.**

Wenatchee
Chelan
Brewster
Okanogan

Mount Baker 3285

Mt Rainier 4392
Mt St Helens 2550
Mt Adams 3742

Roslyn
Ellensburg
Cle Elum
Yakima
Selah
Toppenish

**R a n g e**

Mt Hood 3427
Hood River
The Dalles

Longview
Kelso
Castle Rock
Woodland

Portland
Gresham
Oregon City
Lake Oswego
Newberg
McMinnville
Salem
Keizer
Woodburn

**O R E G O N**

Albany
Corvallis
Lebanon
Sweet Home
Eugene
Springfield
Cottage Grove
Oakridge

Roseburg
Sutherlin
Myrtle Creek
Canyonville
Grants Pass
Medford
Ashland

Mount Shasta 4317
Mount Shasta
Dunsmuir
Yreka
Klamath Falls

**Klamath Mountains**

McKinleyville
Eureka

**C A**

**Columbia Plateau**

Spokane
Opportunity
Hayden
Coeur d'Alene
Kellogg
Wallace
Cheney

**St Joe**
St Maries
Clarkia

Moscow
Pullman
Colfax
Lewiston
Clarkston

**Clearwater**
Orofino
Kooskia
Grangeville
Kamiah

**Selway**

Enterprise
Union
La Grande
Baker

**Blue Mountains**

Eagle Cap 2925

**Snake**

Richland
Pasco
Kennewick
Finley
Hermiston
Boardman
Pendleton

**Columbia**

Condon
Shaniko
Madras
Prineville
Redmond
Bend

**Deschutes**

**High Desert**

John Day
Dayville

Burns
Hines
Riley

**Harney Basin**
Malheur Lake
Harney Lake

Steens Mt.

Jordan Valley
Juntura
Burns Junction

Nyssa
Ontario
Parma
Caldwell
Nampa
Meridian
Boise
Payette
Emmett

Cinnabar Mountain 2562
Mountain Home
Glenns Ferry
Mountain Home

Owyhee

**Warner Mountains**

Valley Falls
Lakeview
Alturas

**Warner Lakes**
Lake Abert
Summer Lake

**Goose Lake**

Upper Klamath Lake
Chiloquin
Chemult
Crescent

**C A S**

Brothers
Brookings

Reedsport
Coos Bay
Myrtle Point
Port Orford
Cape Blanco
Crescent City

Coquille
North Bend
Bandon

Florence
Newport
Lincoln City
Tillamook
Astoria

Umpqua

**Willamette**

**West Yellowstone**
West Thumb
Yellowstone
Electric Peak 3490

Greybull

**Yellowstone Range**
2116
Bear Paw Mountain

**Crazy Mts**
Bighorn

Crow Agency
Armington
Armington

Lowell
Powell
Roundup

**Flathead**

**Clark Fork**
Missoula
McDonald Peak 2993

**Bitterroot**

**Cont. Divide**

**Pend Oreille**
Newport
Franklin D Roosevelt Lake
Colville

**Kettle River Range**

Mount Bonaparte 2212
Okanagan Falls
Keremeos
Osoyoos
Oliver

Okanogan
Lake Chelan

Grand Coulee
Moses Lake
Othello
Ephrata

Ritzville
Walla Walla

**SELKIRK MOUNTAINS**

Dworshak Reservoir

Cascade

Payette

**Snake River Plain**

Ontario

Vale

**METRES / FEET scale bar:**

| METRES | FEET |
|--------|------|
| 5000 | 16404 |
| 3000 | 9843 |
| 2000 | 6562 |
| 1000 | 3281 |
| 500 | 1640 |
| 200 | 656 |
| 0 | 0 |
| Land below sea level | |
| 200 | 656 |
| 4000 | 13124 |
| 6000 | 19686 |

1:6 400 000

USA North Central

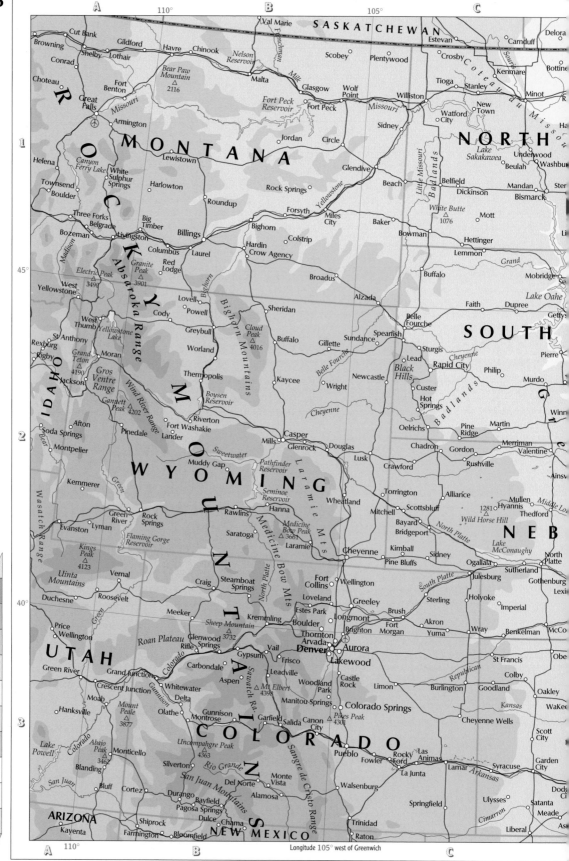

**METRES**
FEET

5000 / 16404
3000 / 9843
2000 / 6562
1000 / 3281
500 / 1640
200 / 656
0 / 0
Land below
sea level
200 / 656
4000 / 13124
6000 / 19686

Lambert Azimuthal Equal Area Projection

Longitude 105° west of Greenwich

**SASKATCHEWAN**

**MONTANA**

**NORTH**

**SOUTH**

**WYOMING**

**NEB**

**UTAH**

**COLORADO**

**ROCKY MOUNTAINS**

**IDAHO**

**ARIZONA**

**NEW MEXICO**

Val Marie, Estevan, Carnduff, Delora, Crosby, Kenmare, Bottine, Minot, Tioga, Stanley, New Town, Watford City, Williston, Scobey, Plentywood, Wolf Point, Fort Peck, Glasgow, Malta, Chinook, Havre, Gildford, Cut Bank, Browning, Shelby, Lothair, Conrad, Choteau, Fort Benton, Great Falls, Armington, Helena, Townsend, Boulder, Three Forks, Belgrade, Bozeman, Livingston, Columbus, Laurel, Billings, Big Timber, Harlowton, Lewistown, Roundup, Jordan, Circle, Glendive, Beach, Baker, Bowman, Hettinger, Lemmon, Buffalo, Faith, Dupree, Belle Fourche, Sundance, Spearfish, Sturgis, Lead, Rapid City, Newcastle, Custer, Hot Springs, Oelrichs, Chadron, Crawford, Alliance, Torrington, Scottsbluff, Mitchell, Bayard, Bridgeport, Cheyenne, Pine Bluffs, Sidney, Kimball, Ogallala, Sutherland, Julesburg, Sterling, Holyoke, Imperial, Wray, Yuma, Akron, Brush, Fort Morgan, Greeley, Longmont, Boulder, Brighton, Thornton, Arvada, Denver, Aurora, Lakewood, Castle Rock, Limon, Burlington, Goodland, Oakley, Colby, Woodland Park, Colorado Springs, Manitou Springs, Pikes Peak 4301, Cheyenne Wells, Pueblo, Rocky Ford, Las Animas, Lamar, Syracuse, Garden City, Fowler, La Junta, Walsenburg, Trinidad, Raton, Springfield, Ulysses, Satanta, Meade, Liberal, Cimarron

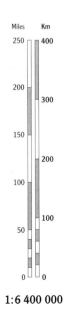

1:6 400 000

Lambert Azimuthal Equal Area Projection

METRES
FEET

5000
16404

3000
9843

2000
6562

1000
3281

500
1640

200
656

0
0

Land below
sea level

200
656

4000
13124

6000
19686

Longitude 85° west of Greenwich

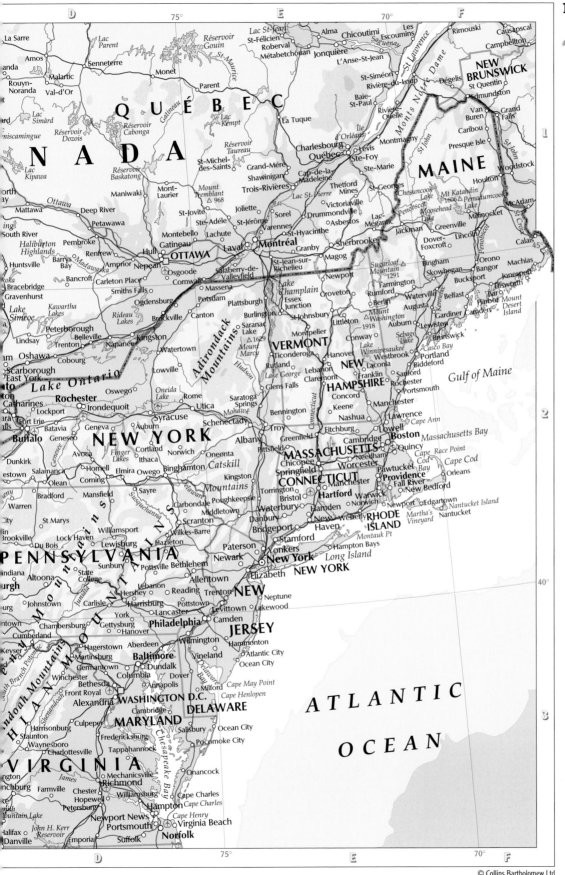

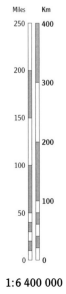

QUÉBEC

NADA

NEW BRUNSWICK

MAINE

La Sarre
Amos
Rouyn-Noranda
Malartic
Val-d'Or
Lac Simard
Réservoir Dozois
miscamingue
Lac Kipawa
orth ay
Ottawa
Mattawa
South River
Haliburton Highlands
Huntsville
Bracebridge
Gravenhurst
Lindsay
Oshawa
Scarborough
East York
o
Catharines
Buffalo
Dunkirk
estown
Olean
Warren
City
Brookville
urgh
town
urg

Senneterre
Monet
Parent
Réservoir Gouin
St-Félicien
St-Maurice
Réservoir Cabonga
Maniwaki
Deep River
Petawawa
Renfrew
Pembroke
Barrys Bay
Madawaska
Bancroft
Carleton Place
Smiths Falls
Peterborough
Kawartha Lakes
Lake Simcoe
Cobourg
Belleville
Napanee
Trenton
Kingston
Watertown
Lake Ontario
Rochester
Irondequoit
Lockport
Batavia
Geneva
Geneseo
Avoca
Hornell
Corning
Elmira
Bradford
Mansfield
St Marys
Williamsport
Lock Haven
Lewisburg
Altoona
State College
Sunbury
Lebanon
Carlisle
Harrisburg
York
Lancaster
Gettysburg
Hanover
Chambersburg

Réservoir Baskatong
Mont-Laurier
Ste-Adèle
St-Jovite
Mount Tremblant △968
Montebello
Lachute
Hull
OTTAWA
Gatineau
Nepean
Osgoode
Salaberry-de-Valleyfield
Cornwall
Massena
Potsdam
Ogdensburg
Brockville
Canton
Rideau Lakes
Adirondack Mountains
Saranac Lake
Plattsburgh
Burlington
Montpelier
△1629
Mount Marcy
Hudson
Syracuse
Oneida Lake
Rome
Mohawk
Utica
Schenectady
Saratoga Springs
Troy
Albany
NEW YORK
Cortland
Ithaca
Owego
Binghamton
Catskill
Kingston
Poughkeepsie
Middletown
Scranton
Wilkes-Barre
Hazleton
PENNSYLVANIA
Pottsville
Bethlehem
Allentown
Reading
Pottstown
Trenton
Philadelphia
Camden

Lac St-Jean
Alma
Chicoutimi
Les Escoumins
Roberval
Jonquière
Métabetchouan
L'Anse-St-Jean
La Tuque
St-Siméon
Rivière-du-Loup
Baie-St-Paul
Rivière-Ouelle
Île d'Orléans
Charlesbourg
Québec
Lévis
Ste-Foy
Montmagny
Cap-de-la-Madeleine
St-Pierre
Trois-Rivières
Lac St-Pierre
Victoriaville
Thetford Mines
St-Georges
Drummondville
Asbestos
Lac-Mégantic
Jackman
Granby
Sherbrooke
Magog
Newport
Sugarloaf Mountain 1291
Lake Champlain
Essex Junction
St-Johnsbury
Mount Washington 1918
Littleton
Berlin
Conway
VERMONT
Ticonderoga
Hanover
Lebanon
Claremont
NEW HAMPSHIRE
Rutland
Lake George
Glens Falls
Bennington
Concord
Keene
Nashua
Greenfield
Fitchburg
Pittsfield
Chicopee
Springfield
Worcester
CONNECTICUT
Torrington
Bristol
Hartford
Waterbury
Danbury
Bridgeport
Stamford
Yonkers
Newark
Elizabeth
NEW
Levittown
Lakewood
Neptune
JERSEY
Hammonton
Vineland
Atlantic City
Ocean City

Rimouski
Causapscal
Campbellton
St Quentin
Edmundston
Van Buren
Caribou
Grand Falls
Presque Isle
Woodstock
Mt Katahdin 1606
Pemadumcook Lake
Millinocket
McAdam
St Croix
Chesuncook Lake
Moosehead Lake
Greenville
Dover-Foxcroft
Lincoln
Bingham
Skowhegan
Bangor
Orono
Farmington
Rumford
Waterville
Augusta
Auburn
Lewiston
Gardiner
Belfast
Camden
Bar Harbor
Mount Desert Island
Brunswick
Casco Bay
Portland
Westbrook
Biddeford
Sebago Lake
Lake Winnipesaukee
Laconia
Rochester
Sanford
Portsmouth
Gulf of Maine
Lawrence
Lowell
Cape Ann
Manchester
Cambridge
Boston
Massachusetts Bay
MASSACHUSETTS
Needham
Quincy
Cape Cod Bay
Cape Race Point
Cape Cod
Providence
Pawtucket
Orleans
Manchester
Fall River
New Bedford
Newport
RHODE ISLAND
Warwick
Norwich
New West
Haven erly
Martha's Vineyard
Edgartown
Nantucket Island
Nantucket
Montauk Pt
Hampton Bays
NEW YORK
Long Island
New York

Troy
Cohoes
Oneonta
Norwich

Gardiner
Penobscot

ATLANTIC

OCEAN

Baltimore
Dundalk
Columbia
Aberdeen
Hagerstown
Martinsburg
Germantown
Winchester
Bethesda
Front Royal
WASHINGTON D.C.
Alexandria
Cambridge
MARYLAND
Culpeper
DELAWARE
Dover
Milford
Cape May Point
Cape Henlopen
Annapolis
Delaware Bay
Hammonton
Vineland
Atlantic City
Ocean City
Keyser
Cumberland
South Branch Potomac
Harrisonburg
Staunton
Waynesboro
Charlottesville
VIRGINIA
James
Mechanicsville
Richmond
Williamsburg
Chester
Hopewell
Petersburg
Hampton
Cape Charles
Cape Charles
Cape Henry
Newport News
Portsmouth
Virginia Beach
Norfolk
Suffolk
Emporia
Danville
Halifax
John H. Kerr Reservoir
Farmville
ington
nchburg
Salisbury
Pocomoke City
Ocean City
Onancock
Chesapeake Bay
Tappahannock
Fredericksburg
Wilmington
Vineland
NEW JERSEY
Princeton

Miles | Km
250 | 400
200 | 300
150 | 200
100 | 100
50
0 | 0

1:6 400 000

© Collins Bartholomew Ltd

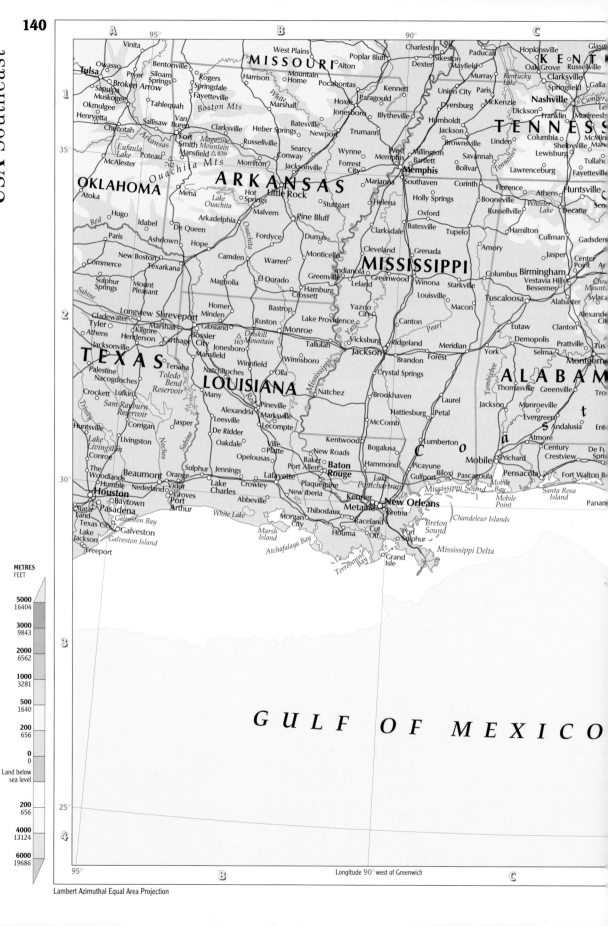

Lambert Azimuthal Equal Area Projection

METRES
FEET

5000 16404
3000 9843
2000 6562
1000 3281
500 1640
200 656
0 0
Land below sea level
200 656
4000 13124
6000 19686

GULF OF MEXICO

Longitude 90° west of Greenwich

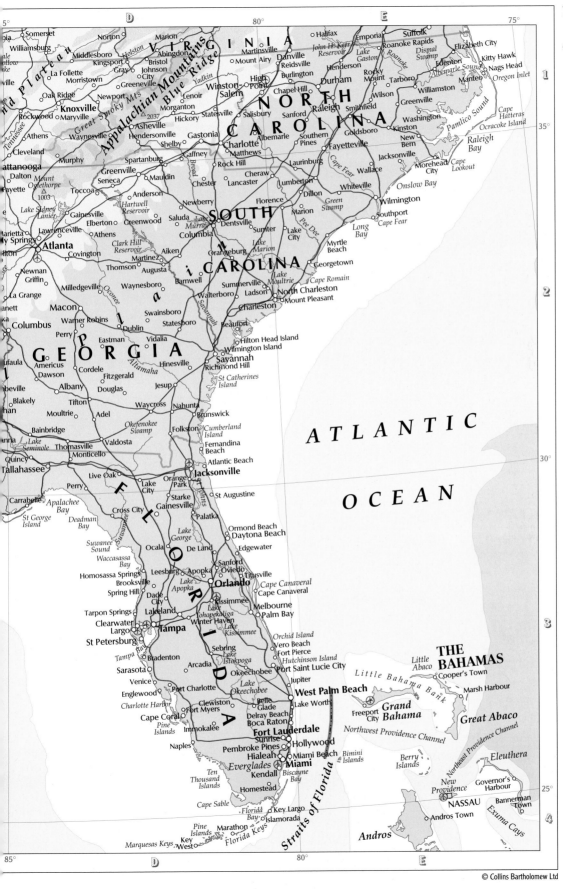

**141**

## North Carolina / South Carolina / Georgia / Florida

5°  D  80°  E  75°

**VIRGINIA**

Somerset
Williamsburg
Middlesboro  Kingsport  Johnson City
La Follette  Morristown
Oak Ridge  **Knoxville**  Maryville
Rockwood  Newport
Athens  Waynesville
Cleveland
attanooga  Dalton
Fayette  Murphy
**Mount Oglethorpe**  1003

Norton  Marion  Halifax  Emporia  Suffolk
Abingdon  Martinsville  Danville  Roanoke Rapids
Holston  Mount Airy  Reidsville  Roanoke  Elizabeth City
Gray  Burlington  Henderson  Edenton  Kitty Hawk  Nags Head
Greeneville  Durham  Rocky Mount  Manteo
Morganton  Salisbury  Raleigh  Smithfield  Wilson  Greenville  Williamston  Washington  Cape Hatteras
Hickory  Statesville  Sanford  Kinston  New Bern  Ocracoke Island

**NORTH CAROLINA**

**SOUTH CAROLINA**

**GEORGIA**

**FLORIDA**

**ATLANTIC OCEAN**

**THE BAHAMAS**

**NASSAU**

Andros

Miles  Km

1:6 400 000

© Collins Bartholomew Ltd

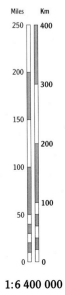

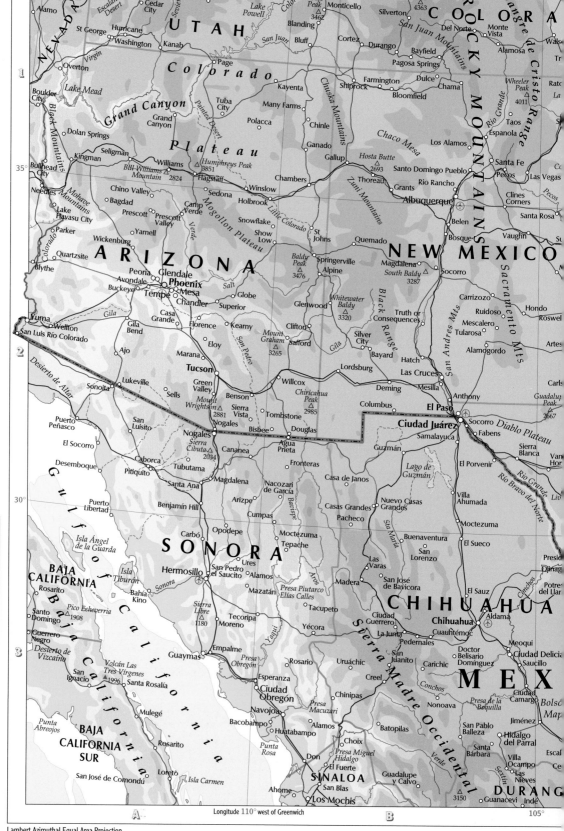

USA South Central

NEVADA

UTAH

COLORADO

ROCKY MOUNTAINS

Sangre de Cristo Range

Caliente
Alamo
St George
Washington
Overton
Boulder City
Kingman
Bullhead City
Needles
Lake Havasu City
Parker
Quartzsite
Blythe

Parowan
Cedar City
Hurricane
Kanab
Page

Escalante
Escalante Desert

Lake Powell

Colorado

Abajo Peak
3462
Monticello
Blanding
Bluff
Cortez

Uncompahgre Peak
4363
Silverton
Del Norte
Durango
Bayfield
Pagosa Springs

Pueblo
Monte Vista
Alamosa
Wals
Tr

Grand Canyon

San Juan

Tuba City

Kayenta

Many Farms

San Juan Mountains

Wheeler Peak
4011
Taos
Espanola

Rato
La

Dolan Springs

Plateau

Grand Canyon

Painted Desert

Polacca

Chinle

Chuska Mountains

Shiprock
Farmington
Bloomfield
Dulce
Chama

Chaco Mesa

Los Alamos

Santa Fe
Pecos
Las Vegas
Clines Corners
Pecos

Colorado

Seligman
Kingman
Bill Williams Mountain 2824

Williams
Flagstaff
Humphreys Peak 3851

Sedona

Winslow
Holbrook

Little Colorado

Ganado
Gallup

Hosta Butte
2693
Thoreau
Grants
Rio Rancho

Santo Domingo Pueblo
Albuquerque
Belen
Bosque

Santa Rosa
Vaughn
Su

Chino Valley
Bagdad
Prescott
Prescott Valley
Yarnell
Wickenburg

Camp Verde

Snowflake
Show Low

St Johns

Chambers

Zuni Mountains

Mogollon Plateau

Verde

ARIZONA

Peoria
Glendale
Avondale
Phoenix
Buckeye
Tempe
Mesa
Chandler

Globe
Salt
Superior

Baldy Peak 3476
Springerville
Alpine

South Baldy 3287
Magdalena
Socorro

NEW MEXICO

Quemado

Carrizozo

Sacramento Mts

Yuma
Wellton
San Luis Río Colorado

Gila

Casa Grande
Florence
Eloy

Gila Bend

Marana

Ajo

Kearny

Clifton
Safford
Mount Graham 3265

San Pedro

Glenwood

Whitewater Baldy 3320

Silver City
Bayard
Hatch

Truth or Consequences

Black Range

Gila

San Andres Mts

Ruidoso
Mescalero
Tularosa
Alamogordo

Hondo
Roswell

Artes

Tucson

Lordsburg
Las Cruces
Deming
Mesilla
Anthony

El Paso

Guadalup Peak 2667

Carls

Desierto de Altar

Sonoita
Lukeville
Sells

Green Valley
Mount Wrightson 2881
Sierra Vista

Benson
Tombstone

Willcox

Chiricahua Peak 2985

Columbus

Ciudad Juárez

Socorro
Fabens

Diablo Plateau

Sierra Blanca
Van Hor

San Luisito
Nogales
Sierra Cibuta 2034
Nogales
Bisbee
Douglas
Agua Prieta
Cananea

Samalayuca
Guzmán

El Porvenir

Rio Grande

Puerto Peñasco
El Socorro

Caborca
Tubutama
Santa Ana
Magdalena

Fronteras

Casa de Janos

Villa Ahumada

Rio Bravo del Norte

Liv

Desemboque
Pitiquito

Nacozari de García
Arizpe

Casas Grandes
Nuevo Casas Grandes
Pacheco

Moctezuma

Presi
Ojina

Puerto Libertad

Benjamín Hill

Cumpas

Bavispe

El Sueco

SONORA

Carbó
Opodepe
Tepache

Moctezuma

Las Varas
San Lorenzo

Buenaventura

Sta Maria

Potre
del Llar

Gulf of California

Isla Ángel de la Guarda

Ures
Tepache

Hermosillo

San Pedro el Saucito

Alamos
Mazatán

Aros

Madera

San José de Bavicora

El Sauz

CHIHUAHUA

BAJA CALIFORNIA

Rosarito

Isla Tiburón

Bahía Kino

Sonora

Presa Piutarco Elías Calles
Tacupeto

Ciudad Guerrero

La Junta

Chihuahua

Aldama

Pico Echeverria 1908
Santo Domingo

Sierra Libre 1180

Tecoripa Moreno

Yécora

Sierra Madre Occidental

Pedernales

Cuauhtémoc

Doctor Belisario Domínguez

Meoqui
Ciudad Delicia
Saucillo

MEX

Guerrero Negro

Desierto de Vizcaíno

Guaymas
Empalme

Presa Obregón

Rosario

Uruáchic

Creel

Conchos

Carichic

Ciudad Camargo
Bols
Map

Volcán Las Tres Vírgenes 1996
Santa Rosalía

Esperanza
Ciudad Obregón

Chinipas

Nonoava

Presa de la Boquilla
San Pablo Balleza

Ciudad Jiménez

Escal

San Ignacio

Baja California

Navojoa

Bacobampo

Presa Macuzari

Batopilas

San Juanito

Doctor

San Bárbara
Villa Ocampo
Las Nieves

Hidalgo del Parral

Punta Abreojos

BAJA CALIFORNIA SUR

Mulegé

Rosarito

Alamos
Choix
El Fuerte

Presa Miguel Hidalgo

Guadalupe y Calvo

Verde

Setin

DURANG

San José de Comondú

Loreto

Isla Carmen

Punta Rosa

Don
San Blas
Ahome
Los Mochis

SINALOA

3150
Guanacevi
Inde

Lambert Azimuthal Equal Area Projection

METRES
FEET

5000 / 16404
3000 / 9843
2000 / 6562
1000 / 3281
500 / 1640
200 / 656
0 / 0
Land below sea level
200 / 656
4000 / 13124
6000 / 19686

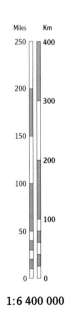

1:6 400 000

MEXICO

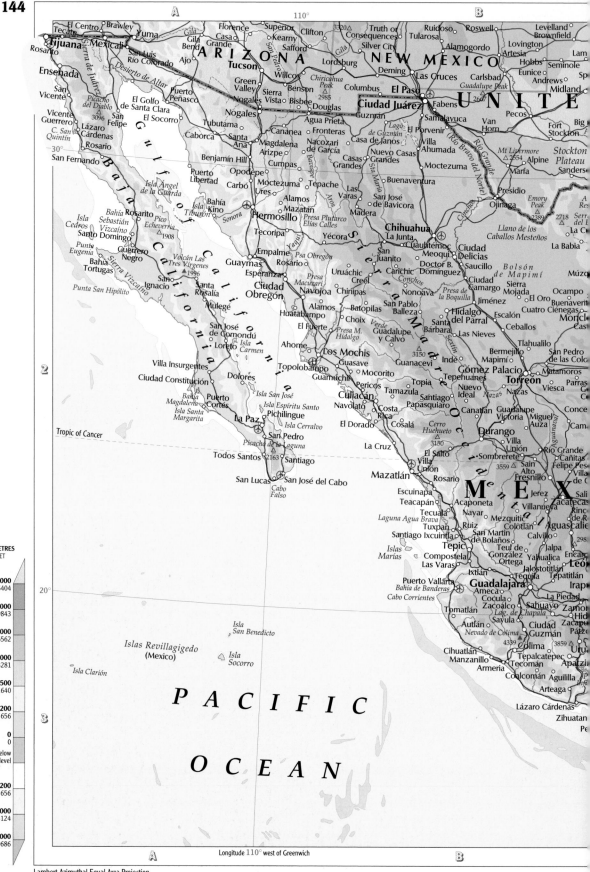

Lambert Azimuthal Equal Area Projection

**CENTRAL AMERICA AND THE CARIBBEAN**

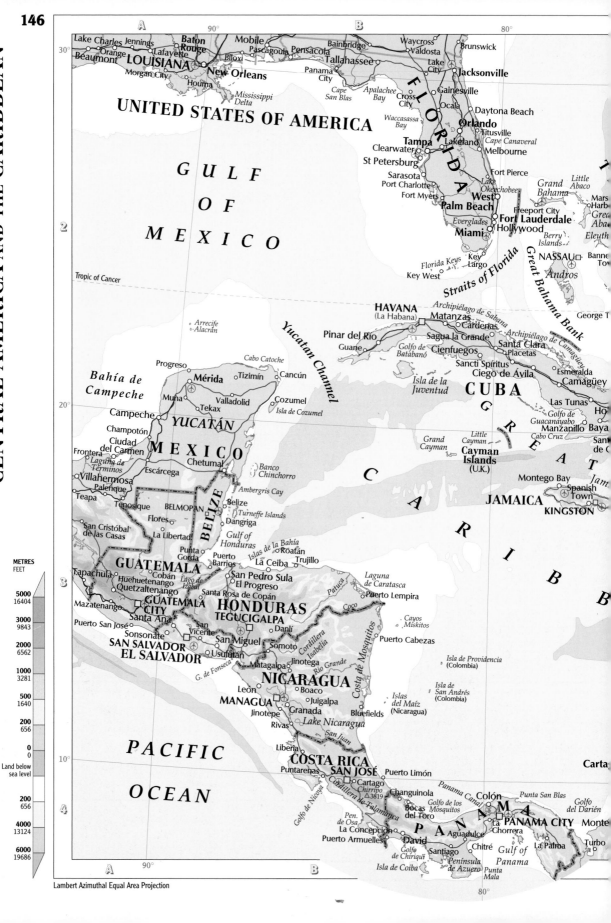

Lambert Azimuthal Equal Area Projection

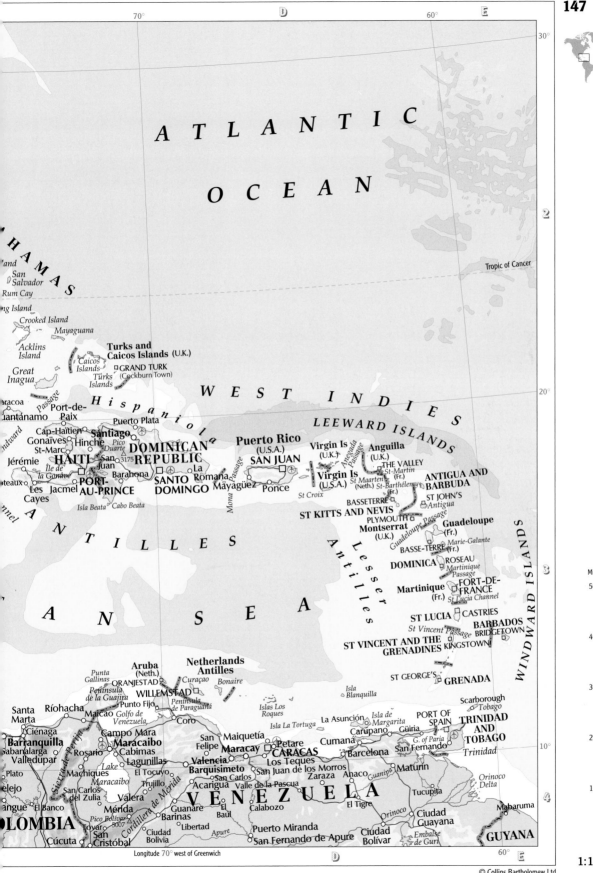

A T L A N T I C

O C E A N

Tropic of Cancer

30°

20°

*BAHAMAS*

*land*
*San*
*Salvador*
*Rum Cay*

*ng Island*

*Crooked Island*
*Mayaguana*

*Acklins*
*Island*

*Great*
*Inagua*

**Turks and**
**Caicos Islands** (U.K.)

*Caicos*
*Islands*
□GRAND TURK
*Türks* (Cockburn Town)
*Islands*

W E S T   I N D I E S

*racoa*
*antanamo*

*Passage*

Port-de-
Paix

*Windward*

*Hispaniola*

Puerto Plata

Cap-Haïtien
Gonaïves Hinche Santiago *Pico*
St-Marc *Duarte*
Jérémie *Île de* San 3175
*la Gonâve* Juan
**HAITI**
PORT-
AU-PRINCE

Les Jacmel
Cayes

*Isla Beata* *Cabo Beata*

**DOMINICAN**
**REPUBLIC**

Barahona

**SANTO**
**DOMINGO**

La
Romana

*Mona Passage*

L E E W A R D   I S L A N D S

**Puerto Rico**
(U.S.A.)
**SAN JUAN**

Mayagüez
Ponce

*St Croix*

Virgin Is
(U.K.)

**Virgin Is**
(U.S.A.)

*Anegada Passage*

Anguilla
(U.K.)
□THE VALLEY
*St-Martin*
*(Fr.)*
St Maarten *St-Barthélemy*
(Neth.) *(Fr.)*

BASSETERRE
**ST KITTS AND NEVIS**
PLYMOUTH
**Montserrat**
(U.K.)

*Guadeloupe Passage*

BASSE-TERRE

**ANTIGUA AND**
**BARBUDA**
ST JOHN'S
*Antigua*

**Guadeloupe**
(Fr.)
*Marie-Galante*
(Fr.)

**DOMINICA** ROSEAU
*Martinique*
*Passage*

*L e s s e r*

**Martinique**
(Fr.)

**FORT-DE-**
**FRANCE**
*St Lucia Channel*

**ST LUCIA** ○CASTRIES

*St Vincent Passage*

**ST VINCENT AND THE**
**GRENADINES**

*A n t i l l e s*

**BARBADOS**
BRIDGETOWN

KINGSTOWN

*W I N D W A R D   I S L A N D S*

ST GEORGE'S ○ **GRENADA**

A   N   T   I   L   L   E   S

*channel*

*teaux*

*nel*

A N

S E A

**Netherlands**
**Antilles**
*Curaçao*
*Bonaire*

**Aruba**
(Neth.)
ORANJESTAD
WILLEMSTAD

*Isla*
*Blanquilla*

*Punta*
*Gallinas*
*Peninsula*
*de la Guajira*
Punto Fijo

Santa
Marta
Ríohacha
Maicao

*Golfo de*
*Venezuela*
Coro

*Peninsula*
*de Paraguaná*

*Islas Los*
*Roques*

*Isla La Tortuga*

*Isla de*
La Asunción *Margarita*

Scarborough
○ *Tobago*

PORT OF
SPAIN

**TRINIDAD**
**AND**
**TOBAGO**

Ciénaga
**Barranquilla**
abanalarga
Valledupar
*Plato*
elejo
ángue ○El Banco
 OLOMBIA

Campo Mara
**Maracaibo**
Cabimas
*Lake*
Lagunillas *Maracaibo*
Machiques El Tocuyo
San Carlos
del Zulia Trujillo
Valera
*Pico Bolivar*
**Mérida** 5007

*Cordillera de Mérida*

San
Cristóbal

*Sierra de Perijá*

San
Felipe **Maracay**
**Valencia** □**CARACAS**
**Barquisimeto** Los Teques
San Carlos San Juan de los Morros
Acarigua Valle de la Pascua
Zaraza Anaco
**VENEZUELA**
Barinas
Guanare El Tigre
Libertad *Apure* Calabozo
San
Tovar *Baúl* Puerto Miranda
Ciudad
Bolivia San Fernando de Apure

Maiquetía
**Petare**

Cumaná
Barcelona

Carúpano Güiria

*G. of Paria*
San Fernando
*Trinidad*

Maturín

*Orinoco*
*Delta*

Tucupita

*Guanipa*

*Orinoco*

Ciudad
Guayana
Ciudad
Bolívar *Embalse*
*de Guri*

Mabaruma

**GUYANA**

*Caribbean Sea*

10°

Longitude 70° west of Greenwich

60°

1:12 000 000

© Collins Bartholomew Ltd

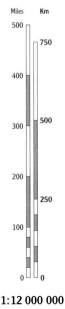

Miles   Km

500   750

400   500

300   250

200   100

0   0

# SOUTH AMERICA

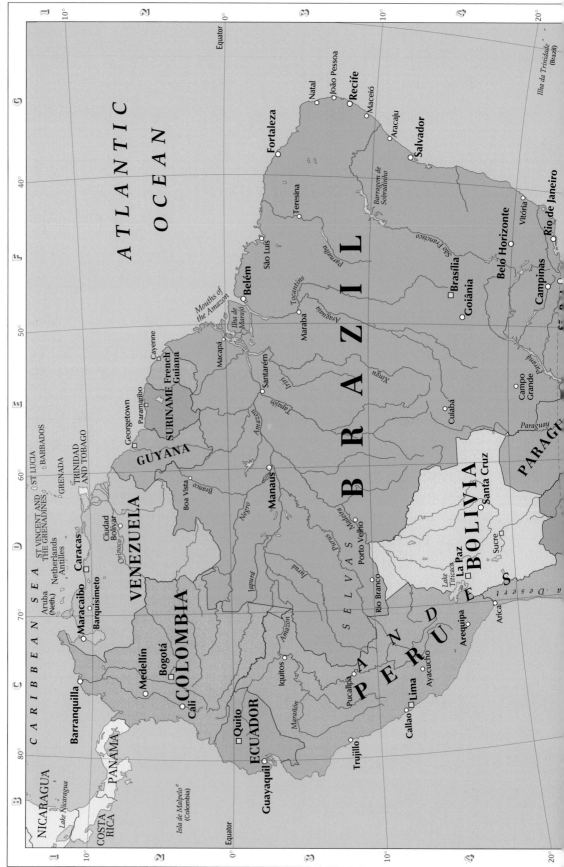

Bi-Polar Oblique Projection

**ATLANTIC**

**OCEAN**

**CARIBBEAN SEA**

NICARAGUA

Lake Nicaragua

COSTA RICA

PANAMA

Isla de Malpelo
(Colombia)

Equator

Barranquilla

Maracaibo

Barquisimeto

ST LUCIA

BARBADOS

ST VINCENT AND
THE GRENADINES

GRENADA

Netherlands
Antilles

Aruba
(Neth.)

Caracas

TRINIDAD
AND TOBAGO

Ciudad
Bolívar

Orinoco

VENEZUELA

Georgetown

Paramaribo

Cayenne

French
Guiana

SURINAME

GUYANA

Boa Vista

Branco

Negro

Medellín

Bogotá

Cali

COLOMBIA

Quito

ECUADOR

Guayaquil

Iquitos

Marañón

Amazon

Japurá

Juruá

Pucallpa

Trujillo

Callao

Lima

Ayacucho

Arequipa

Arica

PERU

ANDES

SELVAS

Rio Branco

Porto Velho

Madeira

Purus

Manaus

Madeira

Tapajós

Teodoro

Santarém

Macapá

Ilha de
Marajó

Mouths of
the Amazon

Belém

Marabá

São Luís

Teresina

Tocantins

Araguaia

Xingu

Parnaíba

Fortaleza

Natal

João Pessoa

Recife

Maceió

Aracaju

Salvador

BRAZIL

Barragem de
Sobradinho

São Francisco

Brasília

Goiânia

Belo Horizonte

Vitória

Campinas

Rio de Janeiro

Campo
Grande

Cuiabá

Paraná

Paraguay

Paraguay

PARAGUAY

BOLIVIA

Santa Cruz

Sucre

La Paz

Lake
Titicaca

Desert

Atacama

Ilha da Trindade
(Brazil)

Equator

10°

0°

10°

20°

80°

70°

60°

50°

40°

10°

0°

10°

20°

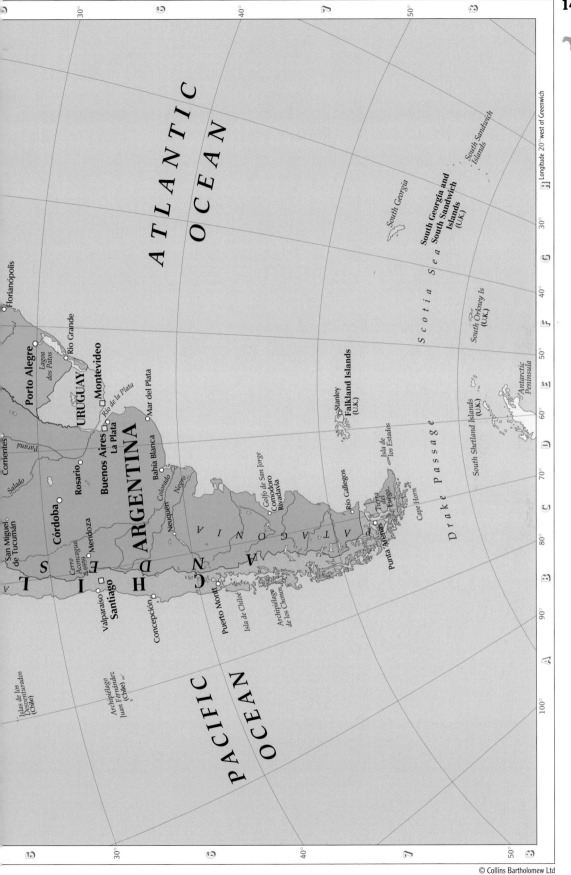

ATLANTIC
OCEAN

South Sandwich
Islands

South Georgia

South Georgia and
South Sandwich
Islands
(U.K.)

S c o t i a   S e a

South Orkney Is
(U.K.)

Florianópolis

Porto Alegre

Lagoa
dos Patos

Rio Grande

URUGUAY

Montevideo

Río de la Plata

Mar del Plata

La Plata

Buenos Aires

Rosario

Corrientes

Paraná

Salado

Córdoba

San Miguel
de Tucumán

Mendoza

ARGENTINA

Bahía Blanca

Colorado

Negro

Neuquén

P A T A G O N I A

Golfo de San Jorge

Comodoro
Rivadavia

Río Gallegos

Isla de
los Estados

Tierra del
Fuego

Cape Horn

D r a k e   P a s s a g e

Stanley
Falkland Islands
(U.K.)

South Shetland Islands
(U.K.)

Antarctic
Peninsula

Cerro
Aconcagua
6959

CHILE

ANDES

Valparaíso

Santiago

Concepción

Puerto Montt

Isla de Chiloé

Archipiélago
de los Chonos

Punta Arenas

PACIFIC
OCEAN

Islas de los
Desventurados
(Chile)

Archipiélago
Juan Fernández
(Chile)

© Collins Bartholomew Ltd

Miles

Km

2000

1200

1000

1500

800

1000

600

400

500

200

0

0

1:28 000 000

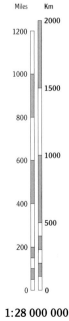

**SOUTH AMERICA** North

Lambert Azimuthal Equal Area Projection

Longitude 70° west of Greenwich

PACIFIC OCEAN

**VENEZUELA**

**COLOMBIA**

**ECUADOR**

**PERU**

**BOLIVIA**

**PANAMA**

GRENADA  
ST GEORGE'S  
TRINIDAD AND TOB  
PORT OF SP

Netherlands Antilles  
Aruba (Neth.)  
Curaçao  
WILLEMSTAD

Punta Gallinas  
Punto Fijo  
Golfo de Venezuela  
Coro  
Isla de Margarita  
La Asunción  
Tobago  
Scarbo  
San Fernand

Santa Marta  
Ríohacha  
Maracaibo  
San Felipe  
CARACAS  
Maiquetía  
Los Teques  
Cumana  
Carúpano  
Güiria

Barranquilla  
Sabanalarga  
Campo Mara  
Cabimas  
Barquisimeto  
Valencia  
Maracay  
Barcelona  
Anaco  
Maturín  
Tucupita  
Orinoco Delta

Cartagena  
Valledupar  
Sincelejo  
Magangue  
El Banco  
Lake Maracaibo  
Machiques  
Valera  
Acarigua  
Guanare  
Zaraza  
El Tigre

Colón  
PANAMA CITY  
Golfo del Darién  
Montería  
Mérida  
5007  
Pico Bolívar  
Barinas  
El Baúl  
Calabozo  
Valle de la Pascua  
Ciudad Bolívar  
Ciudad Guayana  
Maba  
Baramann

Panama Canal  
Aguadulce  
La Palma  
Turbo  
Tovar  
San Cristóbal  
San Fernando de Apure  
El Callao  
Tumereng

Chitré  
Gulf of Panama  
Bucaramanga  
Cúcuta  
Pamplona  
Arauca  
Puerto Páez  
La Paragua  
Angel Falls  
Mt Roraima  
2810

Punta Mala  
Medellín  
Socorro  
5493  
Sierra Nevada del Cocuy  
Tunja  
Meta  
Puerto Nuevo  
Puerto Ayacucho  
El Gran Sabana  
Pakaraima Mountains  
Normandia

Quibdó  
Manizales  
Pereira  
Armenia  
Zipaquirá  
BOGOTÁ  
Villavicencio  
Bisinaca  
Puerto Inírida  
Cerro Marahuaca 2579  
Serra Parima  
Boa Vista

Buenaventura  
Ibagué  4560  
Cerro El Nevado  
Arrecifal  
Orinoco  
Serra Grande  1150  
Caracarai

Cali  6750  
Palmira  
Neiva  
San José del Guaviare  
Guaviare  
Mesa de Yambi  
Pico da Neblina  3014  
Nova Paraíso

Popayán  
Tumaco  
Pasto  
Mocoa  
Florencia  
Caquetá  
Mitú  
Apaporis  
Uaupés  
Tapurucuara  
Repres. de Ball

Esmeraldas  
Ibarra  
Ipiales  
Puerto Leguizamo  
Lérida  
Negro  
Barcelos

QUITO  
Equator  0°  
Nueva Loja  
Volcán Cotopaxi 5896  
Napo  
La Pedrera  
Fonte Boa  
Maraã  
Unini  
Manacapuru  
Itacoa

Chone  
Ambato  
Cabo Pantoja  
El Encanto  
Pamar  
Japurá  
Maraã  
Amazon Amazonas  
Codajás  
Beruri  
Auta

Manta  
Portoviejo  
Chimborazo 6310  
Riobamba  
Río Tigre  
Curaray  
Putumayo  
Santa Clara  
Tonantins  
Santo Antônio do Içá  
Coari  
Bor

Pajón  
Alausí  
Azogues  
Tigre  
Leticia  
Tabatinga  
Carauari  
Purus  
Novo Aripuanã

Guayaquil  
Cuenca  
Gualaceo  
Amazon Amazonas  
Benjamim Constant  
Tapauá  
Manicoré

Isla Puná  
Machala  
Tumbes  
Pastaza  
Nauta  
Iquitos  
Yavari  
Itui  
Jutaí  
Juruá  
Madeira

Golfo de Guayaquil  
Macará  
Loja  
Marañón  
Barranca  
Requena  
Irunepé  
Lábrea  
Barr  
São Ma

Talara  
Sullana  
Piura  
Catacaos  
Jaén  
Chachapoyas  
Lagunas  
Yurimaguas  
Pauini  
Humaitá  
Aripuanã

Sechura  
Olmos  
Rioja  
Tarapoto  
Contamana  
Ipixuna  
Boca do Acre  
Porto Velho  
Theodore Roosevelt

Pta Negra  
Chiclayo  
Cajamarca  
Cordillera Oriental  
Ucayali  
Cruzeiro do Sul  
Tarauacá  
Feijó  
Sena Madureira  
Porto Acre  
Ariquemes  
Jarú  
Aripuanã  
Juír

Pacasmayo  
Otuzco  
Huallaga  
Pucallpa  
Puerto Portillo  
Iaco  
Xapuri  
Rio Branco  
Abunã  
Guayaramerín  
Pimenta Bueno  
Vilhena

Trujillo  
Huaráz  
Huánuco  
Atalaya  
Alerta  
Cobija  
Riberalta  
Mamoré  
Costa Marques

Chimbote  
Huarmey  
Yerupajá 6634  
Cerro de Pasco  
Madeira  
Guaporé  
Serra dos Pare

Barranca  
Huacho  
La Merced  
Huancayo  
Madre de Dios  
Machupicchu  
Puerto Maldonado  
Exaltación  
Mategua  
Branco

Huaral  
Callao  
LIMA  
Huancavelica  
Cordillera Vilcabamba  
Cusco (Cuzco)  
Inambari  
Sandia  
Santa Ana de Yacuma  
Puerto Alegre  
Mato Grosso

San Vicente de Cañete  
Ayacucho  
Abancay  
Antabamba  
Yanaoca  
Sicuani  
Ayaviri  
San Borja  
Ascensión  
Pontes-e-Lacerda  
Po Esperidi

Chincha Alta  
Pisco  
Ica  
Coracora  
Nudo Coropuna 6425  
Juliaca  
Lake Titicaca  
Santa Ana  
Trinidad  
Loreto  
Puerto Frey

Nazca  
Marcona  
Chuquibamba  
Arequipa  
BOLIVIA  
San Ignacio  
San Pedro  
El Cerro

PACIFIC OCEAN  
Chala  
Camana  
Moquegua  
Colquiri  
Cordillera Oriental  
Montero  
Warnes  
Santa Cruz  
Bañados del Izozog

Mollendo  
Ilo  
Tacna  
Arica  
Nevado Sajama 6542  
Oruro  
Huanui  
Corque  
Pampa Grande  
Cochabamba  
Cabezas  
Tuca

LA PAZ

**METRES / FEET**

| METRES | FEET |
|---|---|
| 5000 | 16404 |
| 3000 | 9843 |
| 2000 | 6562 |
| 1000 | 3281 |
| 500 | 1640 |
| 200 | 656 |
| 0 | 0 |

Land below sea level

| | |
|---|---|
| 200 | 656 |
| 4000 | 13124 |
| 6000 | 19686 |

Cordillera Occidental  
Cordillera Central  
Cordillera Oriental  
Cordillera de Perijá  
Serranía de Perijá  
Llanos  
Guiana Highlands  
SELVAS

## ATLANTIC OCEAN

GETOWN
dise
New Amsterdam
Totness
PARAMARIBO
Albina   St-Laurent-du-Maroni
Brokopondo   Sinnamary
Professor van   Kourou
Blommestein Mee   CAYENNE
SURINAME   Guisanbourg
French   Oiapoque
Guiana
△ Juliana Top   Inini
1230
Pontoetoe

Serra Tumucumaque

Lourenço
Calçoene   Ilha de
Amapá   Maracá

Mouths of the
Amazon

Macapá
Porto Santana   Ilha
Mazagão   Caviana
Chaves   Cabo
Arere   Paru   Maguarinho   Salinópolis
Serra   Almeirim   Ilha de   Bragança
ximina   Parauaquara 359△   Breves   Marajó   Viseu
Óbidos   Portel   Belém   Cururupu
Juruti   Monte   Breves   Muaná   Castanhal
a   Alegre   Cametá   Acará   Pinheiro   São Luís
tituba   Santarém   Viana   Parnaíba   Camocim
Altamira   Tucuruí   Santa   Bacabal   Itapicuru   Luzilândia
Itaituba   Represa   Luzia   Codó   Mirim   Tianguá   Caucaia   Fortaleza
Tucuruí   Pedreiras   Piripiri   Sobral   Cascavel
Jacundá   Pres. Dutra   Caxias   Campo Maior   Canindé   Aracati
Maraba   Grajaú   Timon   Teresina   Crateús   Quixadá   Macau   Touros
Araras   Imperatriz   Barra do   Buriti Bravo   Boa   Ponta
Serra   Tocantinópolis   Corda   Palmeiras   Taua   Viagem   Mossoró   do Calcanhar
Xinguara   Porto Franco   Açude Boa   Floriano   Iguatu   Icó   Natal
Manuelzinho   Araguaína   Esperança   Jerumenha   Picos   Juazeiro   Campina
Balsas   Uruçuí   Oeiras   Crato   do Norte   Grande   João
BRAZIL   Conceição   Carolina   Canto do Buriti   Paulistana   Salgueiro   Jaboatão   Pessoa
do Araguaia   São Raimundo   Floresta   Caruaru   Recife
Santa Maria   Pedro   Nova   Nonato   Cabo
Serra   das Barreiras   Afonso   Caracol   Remanso   Petrolina   Paulo   Garanhuns
do Cachimbo   Gilbués   Juazeiro   Afonso   Rio Largo
Peixoto de   Palmas   Corrente   Senhor do Bonfim   Maceió
Azevedo   Porto Nacional   Barragem de   Monte Santo   Arapiraca
Ilha do   Dianópolis   Sobradinho   Xique   Lagarto
Bananal   Xique   Irecê   Jacobina   Aracaju
dos   São   Gurupi   Natividade   Ibotirama   Feira   Serrinha
Félix   Barreiras   de Santana   Estância
Porto Artur   Cavalcante   Santana   Bom Jesus   Itaberaba   Alagoinhas
Diamantino   Porangatu   Correntina   da Lapa   Camaçari
Rosário Oeste   Uruaçu   Posse   Jequié   Santo Antônio de Jesus
rra do Bugres   Represa   Brumado   Salvador
Cuiabá   Barra do   Serra da Mesa   Guanambi   Ipiaú
Garças   Niquelândia   Itabuna   Ubaitaba
Rondonópolis   Iporá   Formosa   Januária   Vitória da   Ilhéus
Goiás   Anápolis   Arinos   Espinosa   Conquista   Itapetinga
res   Alto   Trindade   Luziânia   Janaúba   Salinas   Una
Garças   Vianópolis   Unaí   Montes   Porto Seguro
Itiquira   Paraúna   Goiânia   Claros   Almenara
to   Jatai   Araguari   Paracatu   Teófilo   Alcobaça
umbá   Coxim   Itumbiara   Jequitaí   Otôni
Rio Verde de Mato Grosso   Uberlândia   Patos
de Minas

Equator 0°

Miles   Km
500   800
400   600
300   400
200
100   200
0   0

1:16 000 000

© Collins Bartholomew Ltd

SOUTH AMERICA South

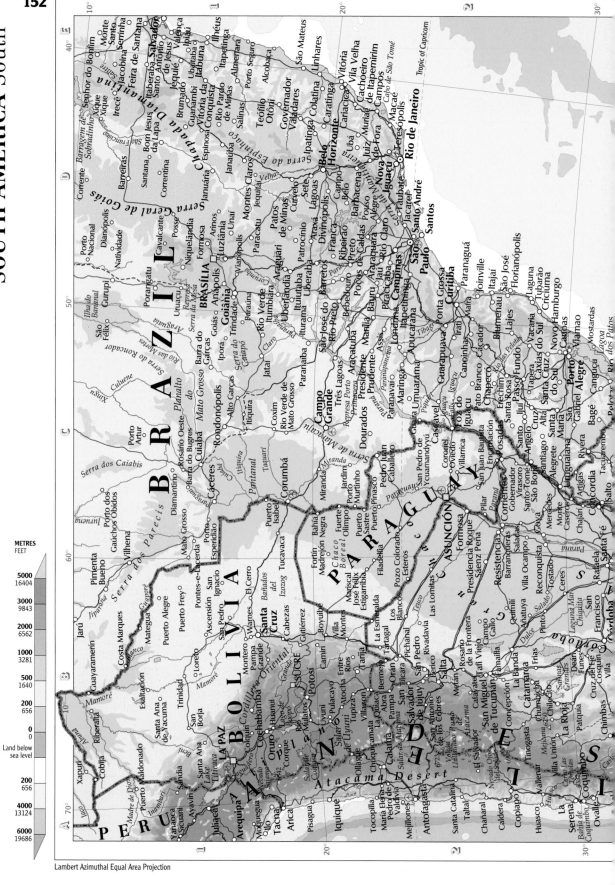

METRES
FEET

5000 16404
3000 9843
2000 6562
1000 3281
500 1640
200 656
0 0
Land below
sea level
200 656
4000 13124
6000 19686

Lambert Azimuthal Equal Area Projection

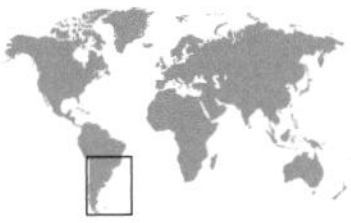

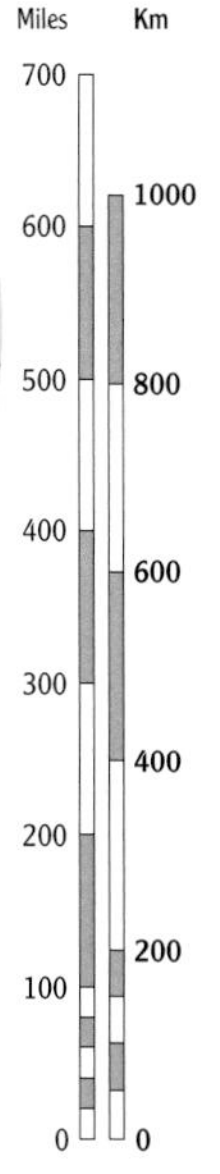

ATLANTIC

OCEAN

**South Georgia**
(U.K.)
Grytviken
Cape
Alexandra
Mount Paget
2934
Cape
Disappointment

Longitude 50° west of Greenwich

**Falkland Islands**
(U.K.)
STANLEY
Darwin
West
Falkland
East
Falkland
Port
Stephens
Isla de
los Estados

Estrecho de Le Maire
Cape
Horn

URUGUAY
MONTEVIDEO
La Plata de la Plata
Las Minas
Rocha
Punta del Este
Florida
Pando
Quilmes
Bahía
Samborombón
Pinamar
Villa Gesell
**Mar del Plata**
Cabo Corrientes
Necochea

BUENOS AIRES
Lomas de Zamora
Pilar
Quino
Junín
Arroyos
Las Flores
Azul
Tandil
Benito Juárez
Tres
Arroyos
Punta
Alta
*Bahía Blanca*
Coronel
Suárez
Coronel
Pringles
Olavarría
Pigüé

ARGENTINA

Villa
Mercedes
General
Alvear
Laboulaye
San
Rafael
Santa
Rosa
General
Acha
Pico
Salado
Chadileo
Puelén
Neuquén
Cipolletti
General Roca
Choele
Choel
Río
Colorado
Viedma
*Negro*
Río
San Antonio
Oeste
Stroeder
Punta
Rasa
*Península
Valdés*
*Golfo San Matías*
Maquinchao
Sierra Grande
Puerto
Madryn
Trelew
Rawson
Gangán
Las
Plumas
*Chubut*
*Chico*
*Cabo Dos Bahías*
Comodoro Rivadavia
*Golfo
de
San Jorge*
Sarmiento
Caleta
Olivia
Pico
Truncado
*Cabo Tres Puntas*
Deseado
*Desado*
Punta Medanosa
San
Julián
Puerto Santa Cruz
*Bahía
Grande*
Río
Gallegos
Gobernador
Gregores
*Santa Cruz*
Río Grande
Porvenir
Ushuaia

CHILE
SANTIAGO
Valparaíso
Rancagua
Puente Alto
Curicó
Talca
Linares
Parral
Chillán
Talcahuano
Concepción
Coronel
Lebu
Los Ángeles
Carahue
Temuco
Victoria
Valdivia
La Unión
Osorno
Puerto
Montt
Ancud
Castro
*Isla
de Chiloé*
Quellón
*Golfo de
Penas*
Puerto Aisén
Puerto
Cisnes
Coihaique
Cochrane
*Península
de Taitao*
*Archipiélago
de los
Chonos*
*Isla
Wellington*
*Isla
Campana*
*Archipiélago de
la Reina Adelaida*
San Carlos
de Bariloche
El Bolsón
Esquel
Nueva
Lubecka
Paso
Río Mayo
*Lago Buenos
Aires*
*Lago
San Martín*
*Lago
Viedma*
El Calafate
*Lago
Argentino*
Tres
Lagos
PATAGONIA
Punta
Arenas
Puerto
Natales

Miles    Km
700  1000
600
500   800
400   600
300
200   400
100   200
0    0

**1:16 000 000**

© Collins Bartholomew Ltd

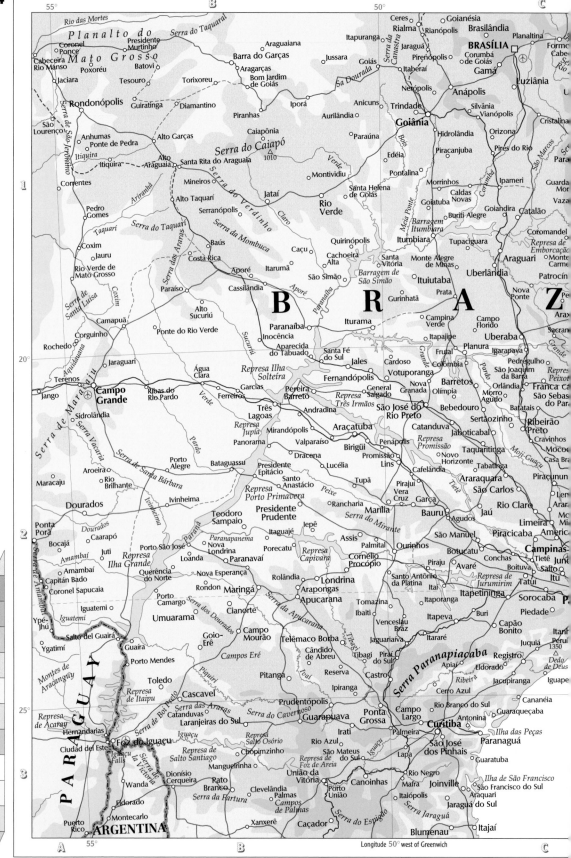

METRES
FEET

5000
16404

3000
9843

2000
6562

1000
3281

500
1640

200
656

0
0

Land below
sea level

200
656

4000
13124

6000
19686

Lambert Azimuthal Equal Area Projection

Longitude 50° west of Greenwich

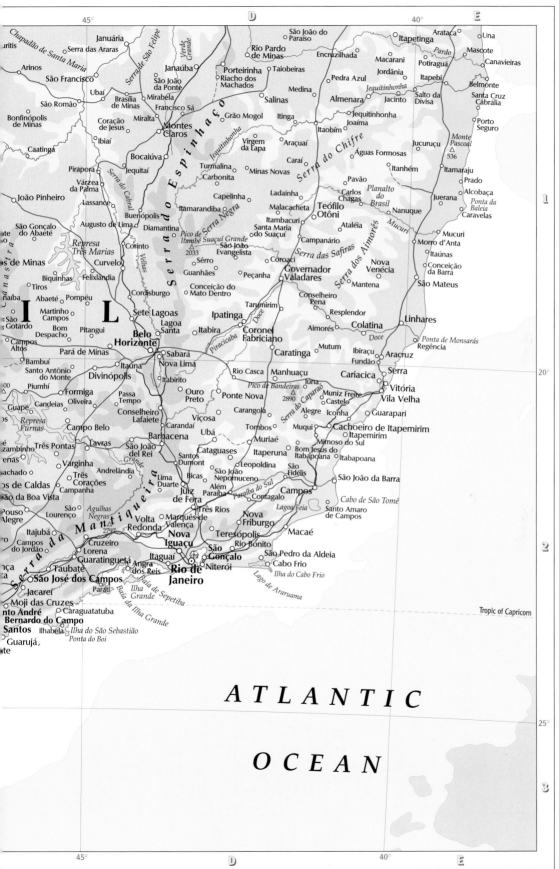

Chapadão de Santa Maria
uritis
Januária
Serra das Araras
Arinos
São Francisco
Ubaí
São Romão
Bonfinópolis de Minas
Caatinga
João Pinheiro
de Minas
Piracicaba
Várzea da Palma
Lassance
São Gonçalo do Abaeté
Augusto de Lima
de Minas
Represa Três Marias
Corinto
Biquinhas
Tiros
Felixlândia
Abaeté
Pompéu
Martinho Campos
São Gotardo
Bom Despacho
Pitangui
Campos Altos
Pará de Minas
Bambuí
Santo Antônio do Monte
Piumhí
Formiga
Guapé
Candeias
Oliveira
Represa Furnas
Campo Belo
Três Pontas
Lavras
zambinho
enas
Varginha
Andrelândia
Machado
Três Corações
Campanha
os de Caldas
ão da Boa Vista
São Lourenço
Pouso Alegre
Itajubá
Campos do Jordão
ça
São José dos Campos
Taubaté
Jacareí
Moji das Cruzes
nto André
Bernardo do Campo
Santos
Guarujá
te

Januába
São João da Ponte
Mirabéla
Brasília de Minas
Francisco Sá
Coração de Jesus
Miralta
Montes Claros
Ibiaí
Bocaiúva
Pirapora
Jequitaí
Buenópolis
Diamantina
Cordisburgo
Guanhães
Sete Lagoas
Lagoa Santa
Sabará
Nova Lima
Itabira
Belo Horizonte
Itaúna
Itabirito
Divinópolis
Passa Tempo
Ouro Preto
Conselheiro Lafaiete
Carandaí
Barbacena
São João del Rei
Santos Dumont
Lima Duarte
Bicas
Juiz de Fora
Além Paraíba
Tres Rios
Marqués de Valença
Volta Redonda
Nova Iguaçu
Teresópolis
Cruzeiro
Lorena
Guaratinguetá
Itaguaí
São Gonçalo
Niterói
Angra dos Reis
Rio de Janeiro
Parati
Baía da Ilha Grande
Ilhabela
Ilha do São Sebastião
Ponta do Boi

Serra de São Felipe
Verde Grande
Porteirinha
Riacho dos Machados
Grão Mogol
Capelinha
Itamarandiba
Diamantina
Pico de Serra Grande
Itambé Suaçuí Grande
2033
Sêrro
Conceição do Mato Dentro
Ipatinga
Coronel Fabriciano
Caratinga
Rio Casca
Ponte Nova
Viçosa
Carangola
Tombos
Muriaé
Cataguases
Itaperuna
Leopoldina
São João Nepomuceno
Paraíba
Contagalo
Três Rios
Nova Friburgo
Rio Bônito
São Pedro da Aldeia
Cabo Frio
Ilha do Cabo Frio
Lago de Araruama

São João do Paraíso
Rio Pardo de Minas
Taiobeiras
Salinas
Medina
Grão Mogol
Itinga
Virgem da Lapa
Araçuaí
Caraí
Minas Novas
Turmalina
Carbonita
Ladainha
Malacacheta
Itambacuri
Santa Maria do Suaçuí
São João Evangelista
Coroaci
Peçanha
Tarumirim
Doce
Governador Valadares
Itabira
Aimorés
Mutum
Ibiraçu
Fundão
Manhuaçu
Tuna
Pico de Bandeiras
2890
Serra do Caparaó
Alegre
Muqui
Mimoso do Sul
Bom Jesus do Itabápoana
São Fidélis
Campos
Lagoa Feia
Santo Amaro de Campos
Macaé

Itapetinga
Macarani
Jordânia
Pedra Azul
Almenara
Jequitinhonha
Joaíma
Itaobím
Águas Formosas
Pavão
Carlos Chagas
Teófilo Otôni
Ataléia
Campanário
Nanuque
Conselheiro Pena
Resplendor
Colatina
Doce
Serra
Cariacica
Vitória
Vila Velha
Muniz Freire
Castelo
Iconha
Guarapari
Cachoeiro de Itapemirim
Itapemirim
São João da Barra

Serra do Chifre
Serra das Safiras
Nova Venécia
Mantena
Serra dos Aimorés
São Mateus
Aracruz
Ponta de Monsarás
Regência

Arataca
Una
Mascote
Canavieiras
Potiraguá
Itapebi
Belmonte
Santa Cruz Cabrália
Salto da Divisa
Jacinto
Porto Seguro
Jucuruçu
Monte Pascoal
536
Itanhém
Itamaraju
Prado
Alcobaça
Caravelas
Ponta da Baleia
Mucuri
Morro d'Anta
Itaúnas
Conceição da Barra
Juerana

Pardo
Jequitinhonha
Planalto do Brasil
Mucuri

1

20°

2

Tropic of Capricorn

*A T L A N T I C*

*O C E A N*

3

25°

© Collins Bartholomew Ltd

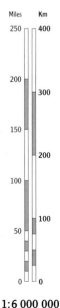

Miles   Km
250  —  400
200  —  300
150  —  200
100  —  100
50  —
0  —  0

1:6 000 000

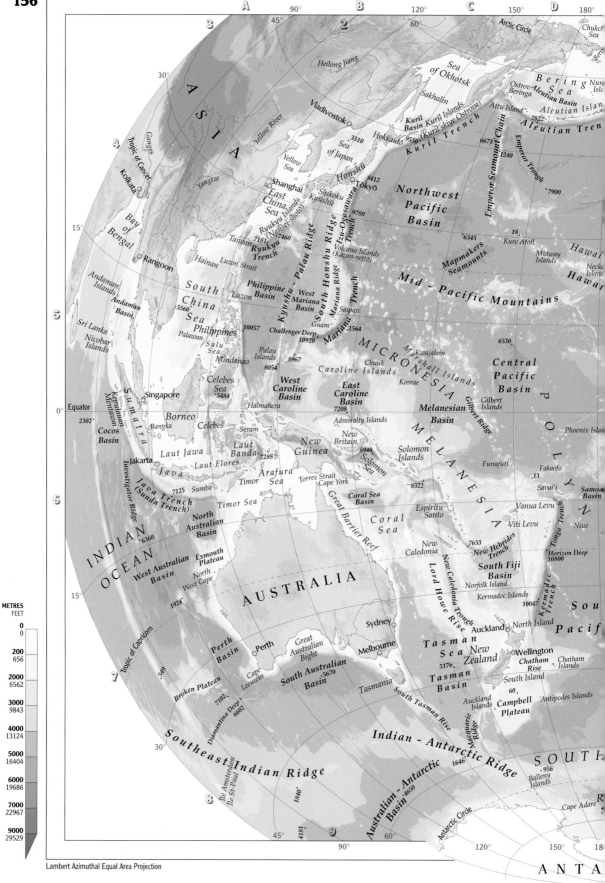

Lambert Azimuthal Equal Area Projection

**METRES / FEET**

| METRES | FEET |
|---|---|
| 0 | 0 |
| 200 | 656 |
| 2000 | 6562 |
| 3000 | 9843 |
| 4000 | 13124 |
| 5000 | 16404 |
| 6000 | 19686 |
| 7000 | 22967 |
| 9000 | 29529 |

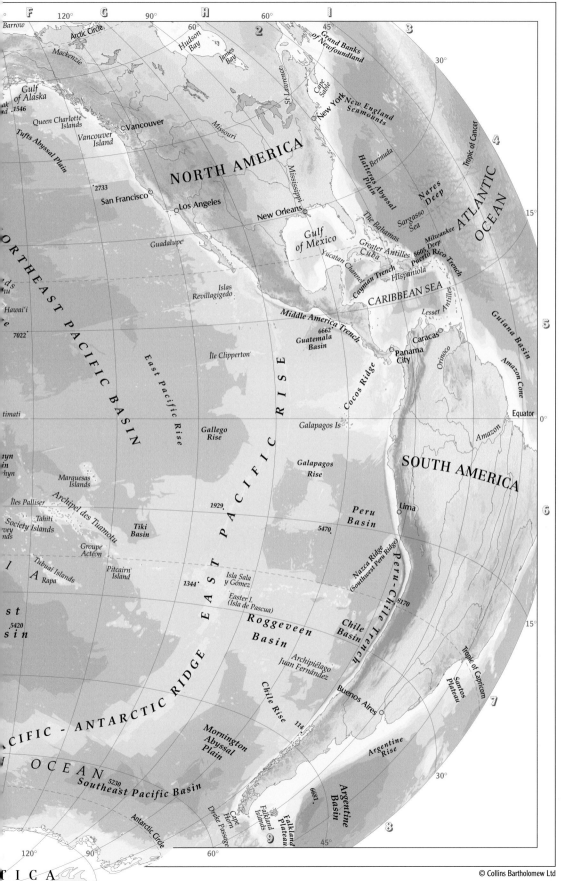

Barrow
120° F
90° G
60° H
60°
45° I
30°

Arctic Circle
Mackenzie
Hudson Bay
James Bay
St Lawrence
Grand Banks of Newfoundland

Gulf of Alaska
.1546
Cape Sable
New York
New England Seamounts
Tropic of Cancer
4

Queen Charlotte Islands
Vancouver
Vancouver Island
Missouri
Bermuda
Hatteras Abyssal Plain
Nares Deep

Tufts Abyssal Plain
NORTH AMERICA
ATLANTIC OCEAN
15°

.2733
San Francisco
Los Angeles
Mississippi
The Bahamas
Sargasso Sea
Milwaukee 8605 Deep
Puerto Rico Trench

New Orleans
Gulf of Mexico
Greater Antilles
Cuba
Yucatan Channel
Cayman Trench
Hispaniola
Lesser Antilles

Guadalupe
Islas Revillagigedo
CARIBBEAN SEA
Guiana Basin
5

Hawai'i
7022
NORTHEAST PACIFIC BASIN
Middle America Trench
Guatemala Basin
6662
Caracas
Panama City
Orinoco
Amazon Cone
Equator
0°

timati
East Pacific Rise
Île Clipperton
Cocos Ridge
Galapagos Is
Amazon

Gallego Rise
SOUTH AMERICA

Marquesas Islands
EAST
Galapagos Rise

Îles Palliser
Archipel des Tuamotu
1929
Peru Basin
Lima
6

Society Islands
Tahiti
Tiki Basin
5470
Nazca Ridge (Southwest Peru Ridge)

Groupe Actéon
PACIFIC
1344
Isla Sala y Gómez
Peru-Chile Trench
8170

Tubuai Islands
Rapa
Pitcairn Island
Easter I. (Isla de Pascua)
Chile Basin
15°

5420
RISE
Roggeveen Basin
Archipiélago Juan Fernández
Tropic of Capricorn
Santos Plateau
7

PACIFIC - ANTARCTIC RIDGE
Chile Rise
114
Buenos Aires

Mornington Abyssal Plain
Argentine Rise
30°

OCEAN
5230
Southeast Pacific Basin
6687
Argentine Basin
Falkland Plateau

Antarctic Circle
Cape Horn
Drake Passage
Falkland Islands
8

120°
90°
60°
45° 9

TICA

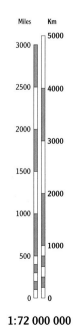

Miles    Km

3000     5000

2500     4000

2000     3000

1500     2000

1000     1000

500

0        0

**1:72 000 000**

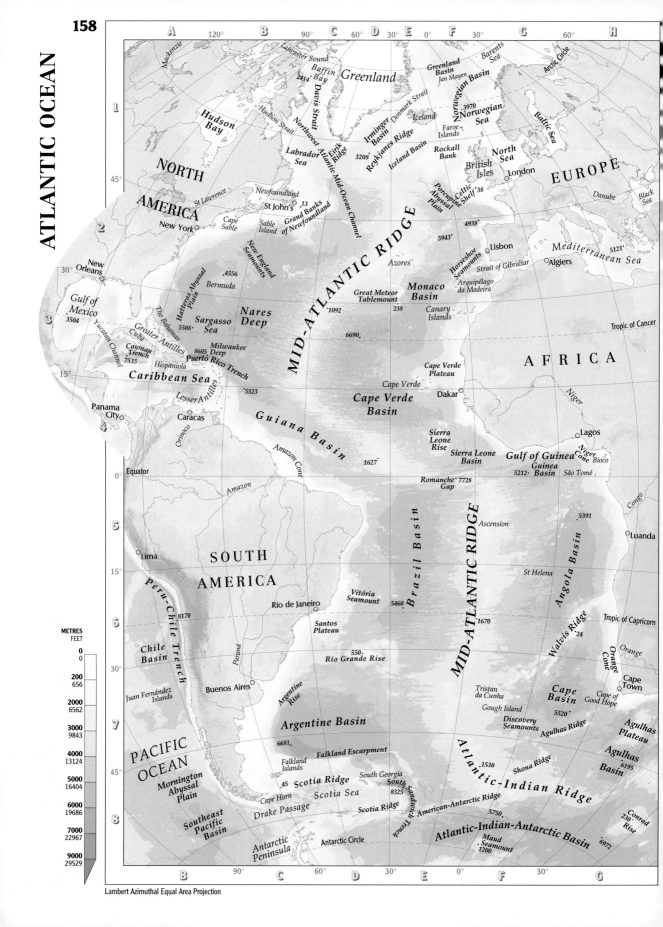

**ATLANTIC OCEAN**

Mackenzie

**A** 120° **B** 90° **C** 60° **D** 30° **E** 0° **F** 30° **G** 60° **H**

Lancaster Sound

Baffin Bay
2414

Davis Strait

Greenland Basin
Jan Mayen

Greenland

Barents Sea

Arctic Circle

Hudson Bay

Hudson Strait

Northwest Atlantic Mid-Ocean Channel

Eirik Ridge

Irminger Basin

Denmark Strait

Iceland

Norwegian Basin
3970

Baltic Sea

**1**

45°

Labrador Sea

3208

Reykjanes Ridge

Iceland Basin

Faroe Islands

Norwegian Sea

**NORTH**

**AMERICA**

St Lawrence

Newfoundland

St John's

.13

Grand Banks of Newfoundland

Rockall Bank

Porcupine Abyssal Plain

Celtic Shelf .38

British Isles

London

North Sea

**EUROPE**

Danube

Black Sea

**2**

30°

New York

Cape Sable

Sable Island

4938

Lisbon

Mediterranean Sea

5121

New Orleans

.4556

Bermuda

New England Seamounts

Azores

5943

Horseshoe Seamounts

Strait of Gibraltar

Algiers

**MID-ATLANTIC RIDGE**

Great Meteor Tablemount

Monaco Basin

238

Arquipélago da Madeira

Gulf of Mexico
3504

The Bahamas

Hatteras Abyssal Plain

Nares Deep

.1092

Canary Islands

**AFRICA**

Yucatan Channel

Greater Antilles

Cuba

5508

Sargasso Sea

6690.

Tropic of Cancer

**3**

Cayman Trench
7535

Milwaukee Deep
8605

Puerto Rico Trench

Cape Verde Plateau

Hispaniola

Cape Verde

Dakar

**Caribbean Sea**

Lesser Antilles

.5523

Cape Verde Basin

Panama City

Caracas

Orinoco

**G u i a n a   B a s i n**

Sierra Leone Rise

Sierra Leone Basin

Lagos

Niger

Niger Cone
Bioco

**4**

15°

Amazon Cone

1627.

Guinea Basin
5212.

Gulf of Guinea

São Tomé

Equator

Amazon

Romanche Gap 7728

Congo

**SOUTH**

**AMERICA**

Amazon

Lima

**B r a z i l   B a s i n**

Ascension

5391

Luanda

**5**

15°

Peru-Chile Trench

Vitória Seamount

5460.

St Helena

**Angola Basin**

**MID-ATLANTIC RIDGE**

Rio de Janeiro

Santos Plateau

1670.

Tropic of Capricorn

Walvis Ridge

.24

**6**

8170

Chile Basin

Paraná

550.

Rio Grande Rise

Orange Cone

Orange

Cape Town

**7**

30°

Juan Fernández Islands

Buenos Aires

Argentine Rise

Tristan da Cunha

**Cape Basin**

Cape of Good Hope

5520.

Agulhas Plateau

Gough Island

Discovery Seamounts

Agulhas Ridge

**Argentine Basin**

6681.

.1530

Shona Ridge

**Agulhas Basin**
.6195

**PACIFIC**

**OCEAN**

Falkland Islands

Falkland Escarpment

South Georgia

South Sandwich Trench

**Atlantic-Indian Ridge**

**8**

Mornington Abyssal Plain

45

Scotia Ridge

South Sandwich Islands

8325

American-Antarctic Ridge

5750.

Conrad Rise
230

Southeast Pacific Basin

Cape Horn

Drake Passage

Scotia Sea

Scotia Ridge

**Atlantic-Indian-Antarctic Basin**

.6972

Antarctic Peninsula

Antarctic Circle

Maud Seamount
1200

**B** 90° **C** 60° **D** 30° **E** 0° **F** 30° **G**

METRES / FEET

| METRES | FEET |
|---|---|
| 0 | 0 |
| 200 | 656 |
| 2000 | 6562 |
| 3000 | 9843 |
| 4000 | 13124 |
| 5000 | 16404 |
| 6000 | 19686 |
| 7000 | 22967 |
| 9000 | 29529 |

Lambert Azimuthal Equal Area Projection

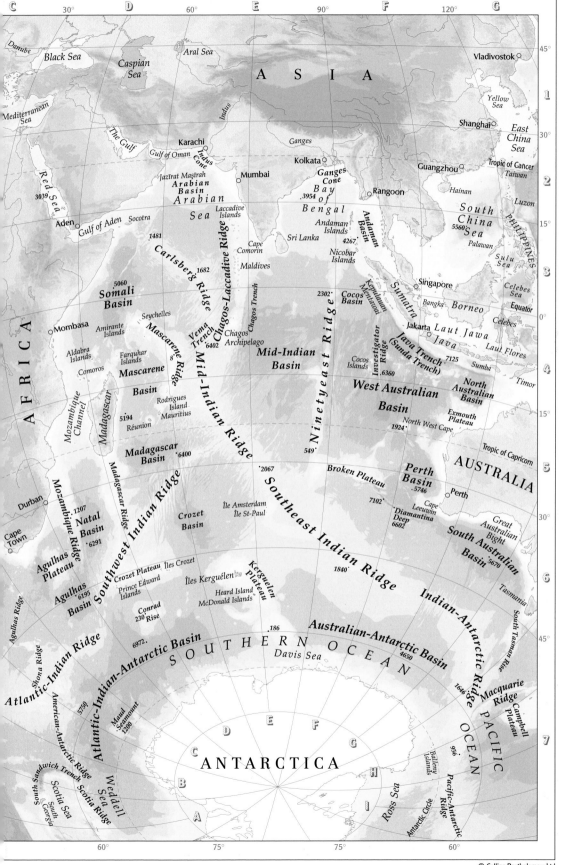

**INDIAN OCEAN**

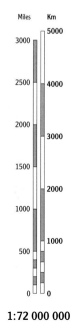

1:72 000 000

© Collins Bartholomew Ltd

# ARCTIC OCEAN

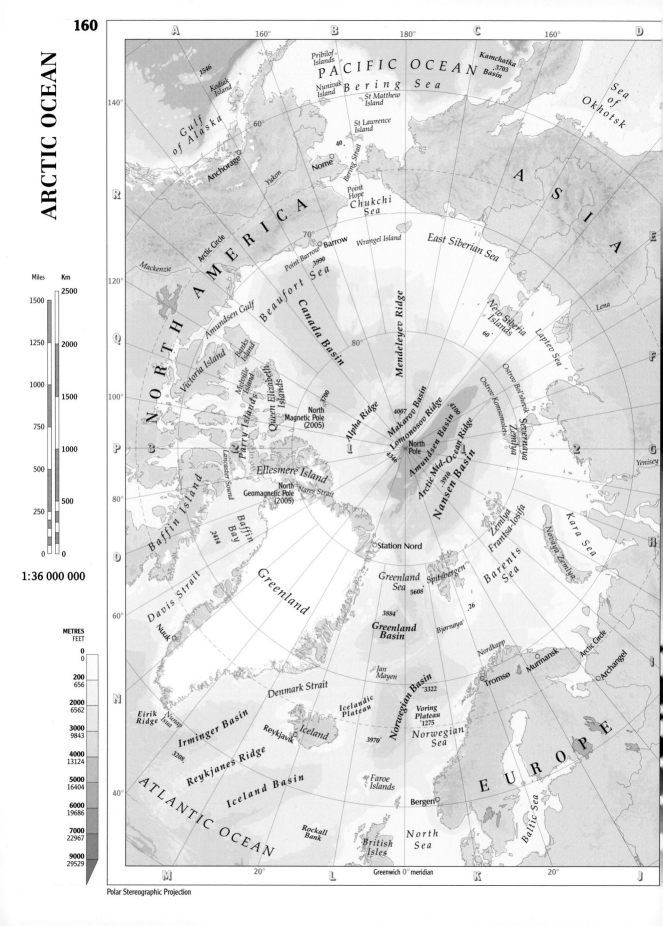

Miles    Km

1500 — 2500

1250 — 2000

1000 — 1500

750 —

500 — 1000

250 — 500

0 — 0

**1:36 000 000**

METRES
FEET

0 / 0

200 / 656

2000 / 6562

3000 / 9843

4000 / 13124

5000 / 16404

6000 / 19686

7000 / 22967

9000 / 29529

Polar Stereographic Projection

PACIFIC OCEAN

Pribilof Islands

Nunivak Island   *Bering Sea*

Kamchatka Basin .3703

St Matthew Island

St Lawrence Island

*Sea of Okhotsk*

.1546

Kodiak Island

*Gulf of Alaska*

60°

140°

Anchorage

40.

Nome

Bering Strait

Point Hope

*Chukchi Sea*

A S I A

160°   B   180°   C   160°   D

Yukon

Arctic Circle

*Mackenzie*

70°

Point Barrow   Barrow

Wrangel Island

East Siberian Sea

New Siberia Islands

Lena

120°

3990

*Beaufort Sea*

Amundsen Gulf

*Canada Basin*

Mendeleyev Ridge

60

Laptev Sea

Ostrov Bol'shevik

N O R T H   A M E R I C A

80°

Victoria Island

Banks Island

Melville Island

Parry Islands

Queen Elizabeth Islands

3700

North Magnetic Pole (2005)

Alpha Ridge

4007

Makarov Basin

Lomonosov Ridge

4100

Ostrov Komsomolets

Severnaya Zemlya

Kara Sea

100°

Lancaster Sound

North Pole

4346

Amundsen Basin

Arctic Mid-Ocean Ridge

3910

Nansen Basin

Zemlya Frantsa-Iosifa

Novaya Zemlya

Ellesmere Island

North Geomagnetic Pole (2005)

Nares Strait

80°

*Baffin Island*

*Baffin Bay*

2414

Station Nord

Davis Strait

*Greenland*

Greenland Sea

5608

Spitsbergen

*Barents Sea*

60°

3884.

**Greenland Basin**

Bjørnøya

.26

Nuuk

Nordkapp

Tromsø   Murmansk

Arctic Circle

Archangel

E U R O P E

*Jan Mayen*

Denmark Strait

Icelandic Plateau

*Norwegian Basin* .3322

Voring Plateau .1275

Eirik Ridge

Nunap Isua

*Irminger Basin*

Reykjavik   Iceland

3970.

*Norwegian Sea*

Bergen

Reykjanes Ridge

Iceland Basin

3208.

40°

*North Sea*

Baltic Sea

A T L A N T I C   O C E A N

Rockall Bank

*British Isles*

*Faroe Islands*

Greenwich 0° meridian

20°   L   K   20°   J

# INTRODUCTION TO THE INDEX

The index includes all names shown on the maps in the Atlas of the World. Names are referenced by page number and by a grid reference. The grid reference correlates to the alphanumeric values which appear within each map frame. Each entry also includes the country or geographical area in which the feature is located. Entries relating to names appearing on insets are indicated by a small box symbol: ▫, followed by a grid reference if the inset has its own alphanumeric values.

Name forms are as they appear on the maps, with additional alternative names or name forms included as cross-references which refer the user to the entry for the map form of the name. Names beginning with Mc or Mac are alphabetized exactly as they appear. The terms Saint, Sainte, Sankt, etc, are abbreviated to St, Ste, St, etc, but alphabetized as if in the full form.

Names of physical features beginning with generic geographical terms are permuted – the descriptive term is placed after the main part of the name. For example, Lake Superior is indexed as Superior, Lake; Mount Everest as Everest, Mount. This policy is applied to all languages.

Entries, other than those for towns and cities, include a descriptor indicating the type of geographical feature. Descriptors are not included where the type of feature is implicit in the name itself.

Administrative divisions are included to differentiate entries of the same name and feature type within the one country. In such cases, duplicate names are alphabetized in order of administrative division. Additional qualifiers are also included for names within selected geographical areas.

## INDEX ABBREVIATIONS

| | | | | | | |
|---|---|---|---|---|---|---|
| admin. div. | administrative division | g. | gulf | Port. | Portugal |
| Afgh. | Afghanistan | Ger. | Germany | prov. | province |
| Alg. | Algeria | Guat. | Guatemala | pt | point |
| Arg. | Argentina | hd | headland | r. | river |
| Austr. | Australia | Hond. | Honduras | r. mouth | river mouth |
| aut. comm. | autonomous community | i. | island | reg. | region |
| aut. reg. | autonomous region | imp. l. | impermanent lake | resr | reservoir |
| aut. rep. | autonomous republic | Indon. | Indonesia | rf | reef |
| Azer. | Azerbaijan | is. | islands | Rus. Fed. | Russian Federation |
| b. | bay | isth. | isthmus | S. | South |
| B.I.O.T. | British Indian Ocean Territory | Kazakh. | Kazakhstan | salt l. | salt lake |
| | | Kyrg. | Kyrgyzstan | sea chan. | sea channel |
| Bangl. | Bangladesh | l. | lake | Serb. and Mont. | Serbia and Montenegro |
| Bol. | Bolivia | lag. | lagoon | special admin. reg. | special administrative region |
| Bos.-Herz. | Bosnia Herzegovina | Lith. | Lithuania | | |
| Bulg. | Bulgaria | Lux. | Luxembourg | str. | strait |
| c. | cape | Madag. | Madagascar | Switz. | Switzerland |
| Can. | Canada | Maur. | Mauritania | Tajik. | Tajikistan |
| C.A.R. | Central African Republic | Mex. | Mexico | Tanz. | Tanzania |
| Col. | Colombia | Moz. | Mozambique | terr. | territory |
| Czech Rep. | Czech Republic | mt. | mountain | Thai. | Thailand |
| Dem. Rep. Congo | Democratic Republic of Congo | mts | mountains | Trin. and Tob. | Trinidad and Tobago |
| | | mun. | municipality | Turkm. | Turkmenistan |
| depr. | depression | N. | North | U.A.E. | United Arab Emirates |
| des. | desert | Neth. | Netherlands | U.K. | United Kingdom |
| Dom. Rep. | Dominican Republic | Neth. Antilles | Netherland Antilles | Ukr. | Ukraine |
| Equat. Guinea | Equatorial Guinea | Nic. | Nicaragua | union terr. | union territory |
| | | N.Z. | New Zealand | Uru. | Uruguay |
| esc. | escarpment | Pak. | Pakistan | U.S.A. | United States of America |
| est. | estuary | Para. | Paraguay | Uzbek. | Uzbekistan |
| Eth. | Ethiopia | pen. | peninsula | val. | valley |
| Fin. | Finland | Phil. | Philippines | Venez. | Venezuela |
| for. | forest | plat. | plateau | vol. | volcano |
| Fr. Guiana | French Guiana | P.N.G. | Papua New Guinea | vol. crater | volcanic crater |
| Fr. Polynesia | French Polynesia | Pol. | Poland | | |

### A

93 E4 Aabenraa Denmark
100 C2 Aachen Ger.
93 E4 Aalborg Denmark
102 C2 Aalen Ger.
100 B2 Aalst Belgium
93 I3 Äänekoski Fin.
105 C2 Aarau Switz.
100 B2 Aarschot Belgium
70 A2 Aba China
119 D2 Aba Dem. Rep. Congo
115 C4 Aba Nigeria
81 C2 Ābādān Iran
81 D2 Abādeh Iran
81 D3 Ābādeh Ţashk Iran
114 B1 Abadla Alg.
155 C1 Abaeté Brazil
Abagnar Qi China see Xilinhot
135 E3 Abajo Peak U.S.A.
115 C4 Abakaliki Nigeria
83 H3 Abakan Rus. Fed.
150 B4 Abancay Peru
81 D2 Abarqū Iran
66 D2 Abashiri Japan
66 D2 Abashiri-wan b. Japan
59 D3 Abau P.N.G.
Abaya, Lake Eth. see
Lake Abaya
Àbay Wenz r. Eth. see
Blue Nile
83 H3 Abaza Rus. Fed.
108 A2 Abbasanta Sardinia Italy
104 C1 Abbeville France
141 C2 Abbeville AL U.S.A.
140 B3 Abbeville LA U.S.A.
97 B2 Abbeyfeale Ireland
55 K2 Abbot Ice Shelf Antarctica
74 B1 Abbottabad Pak.
115 E3 Abéché Chad
114 B4 Abengourou Côte d'Ivoire
114 C4 Abeokuta Nigeria
99 A3 Aberaeron U.K.
96 C2 Aberchirder U.K.
Abercorn Zambia see Mbala
99 B4 Aberdare U.K.
99 A3 Aberdaron U.K.
53 D2 Aberdeen Austr.
122 B3 Aberdeen S. Africa
96 C2 Aberdeen U.K.
139 D3 Aberdeen MD U.S.A.
137 D1 Aberdeen SD U.S.A.
134 B1 Aberdeen WA U.S.A.
129 E1 Aberdeen Lake Can.
96 C2 Aberfeldy U.K.
96 B2 Aberfoyle U.K.
99 B4 Abergavenny U.K.
Abergwaun U.K. see Fishguard
Aberhonddu U.K. see Brecon
143 C2 Abernathy U.S.A.
134 B2 Abert, Lake U.S.A.
Abertawe U.K. see Swansea
Aberteifi U.K. see Cardigan
99 B4 Abertillery U.K.
99 A3 Aberystwyth U.K.
86 F2 Abez' Rus. Fed.
78 B3 Abhā Saudi Arabia
81 C2 Abhar Iran
Abiad, Bahr r. Sudan/Uganda see
White Nile
114 B4 Abidjan Côte d'Ivoire
137 D3 Abilene KS U.S.A.
143 D2 Abilene TX U.S.A.
99 C4 Abingdon U.K.
138 C3 Abingdon U.S.A.
91 D3 Abinsk Rus. Fed.
130 B3 Abitibi, Lake Can.
Åbo Fin. see Turku
74 B1 Abohar India
114 B4 Aboisso Côte d'Ivoire
114 C4 Abomey Benin
60 A1 Abongabong, Gunung mt. Indon.
118 B2 Abong Mbang Cameroon
64 A3 Aborlan Phil.
115 D3 Abou Déia Chad
106 B2 Abrantes Port.
152 B2 Abra Pampa Arg.
142 A3 Abreojos, Punta pt Mex.
116 B2 'Abri Sudan
136 A2 Absaroka Range mts U.S.A.
81 C1 Abşeron Yarımadası pen. Azer.
78 B3 Abū 'Arīsh Saudi Arabia
116 A2 Abū Ballāş hill Egypt
79 C2 Abu Dhabi U.A.E.
116 B3 Abu Hamed Sudan
116 B3 Abu Haraz Sudan
115 C4 Abuja Nigeria
81 C2 Abū Kamāl Syria
118 C2 Abumombazi Dem. Rep. Congo
152 B1 Abunã r. Bol.
150 C2 Abunã Brazil
74 B2 Abu Road India
78 B2 Abū Şādi, Jabal hill Saudi Arabia
116 B2 Abū Sunbul Egypt
116 A3 Abu Zabad Sudan
Abū Zabī U.A.E. see Abu Dhabi
117 A4 Abyei Sudan
145 B2 Acambaro Mex.
120 B2 Acampamento de Caça do
Mucusso Angola
106 B1 A Cañiza Spain
144 B2 Acaponeta Mex.
145 C3 Acapulco Mex.
151 E3 Acará Brazil

154 A3 Acaray, Represa de resr Para.
150 C2 Acarigua Venez.
110 B1 Acâş Romania
145 C3 Acatlan Mex.
145 C3 Acayucán Mex.
114 B4 Accra Ghana
98 B3 Accrington U.K.
74 B2 Achalpur India
97 A2 Achill Island Ireland
101 D1 Achim Ger.
96 B2 Achnasheen U.K.
91 D2 Achuyevo Rus. Fed.
111 C3 Acıpayam Turkey
109 C3 Acireale Sicily Italy
147 C2 Acklins Island Bahamas
153 A3 Aconcagua, Cerro mt. Arg.
106 B1 A Coruña Spain
108 A2 Acqui Terme Italy
103 D2 Ács Hungary
49 N6 Actéon, Groupe is Fr. Polynesia
145 C2 Actopán Mex.
143 D2 Ada U.S.A.
Adabazar Turkey see Adapazarı
79 C2 Adam Oman
111 B3 Adamas Greece
135 B3 Adams Peak U.S.A.
'Adan Yemen see Aden
80 B2 Adana Turkey
111 D2 Adapazarı Turkey
97 B2 Adare Ireland
55 M2 Adare, Cape Antarctica
108 A1 Adda r. Italy
78 B2 Ad Dafinah Saudi Arabia
78 B2 Ad Dahnā' des. Saudi Arabia
79 B2 Ad Dahnā' des. Saudi Arabia
114 A2 Ad Dakhla Western Sahara
Ad Dammām Saudi Arabia see
Dammam
78 A2 Ad Dār al Ḥamrā' Saudi Arabia
78 B3 Ad Darb Saudi Arabia
78 B2 Ad Dawādimī Saudi Arabia
Ad Dawḥah Qatar see Doha
Aḍ Ḍiffah Egypt/Libya see Libyan Plateau
78 B2 Ad Dilam Saudi Arabia
78 B2 Ad Dir'īyah Saudi Arabia
117 B4 Addis Ababa Eth.
81 C2 Ad Dīwānīyah Iraq
141 D2 Adel U.S.A.
52 A2 Adelaide Austr.
55 A3 Adelaide Island Antarctica
50 C1 Adelaide River Austr.
101 D2 Adelebsen Ger.
55 K2 Adélie Land Antarctica
78 B3 Aden Yemen
116 C3 Aden, Gulf of Somalia/Yemen
100 C2 Adenau Ger.
115 C3 Aderbissinat Niger
79 C2 Adh Dhayd U.A.E.
59 C3 Adi i. Indon.
116 B3 Ādī Ārk'ay Eth.
108 B1 Adige r. Italy
116 B3 Ādīgrat Eth.
78 A3 Adi Keyih Eritrea
74 B3 Adilabad India
115 D2 Adirī Libya
139 E2 Adirondack Mountains U.S.A.
Ādīs Ābeba Eth. see Addis Ababa
117 B4 Ādīs Alem Eth.
80 B2 Adıyaman Turkey
110 C1 Adjud Romania
50 B1 Admiralty Gulf Austr.
128 A2 Admiralty Island U.S.A.
59 D3 Admiralty Islands P.N.G.
73 B3 Adoni India
104 B3 Adour r. France
106 C2 Adra Spain
114 B2 Adrar Alg.
138 C2 Adrian MI U.S.A.
143 C1 Adrian TX U.S.A.
108 B2 Adriatic Sea Europe
116 B3 Ādwa Eth.
83 K2 Adycha r. Rus. Fed.
91 D3 Adygeysk Rus. Fed.
114 B4 Adzopé Côte d'Ivoire
111 B3 Aegean Sea Greece/Turkey
101 D1 Aerzen Ger.
106 B1 A Estrada Spain
116 B3 Afabet Eritrea
Affreville Alg. see Khemis Miliana
76 C3 Afghanistan country Asia
78 B2 'Afīf Saudi Arabia
136 A2 Afton U.S.A.
80 B2 Afyon Turkey
115 C3 Agadez Niger
114 B1 Agadir Morocco
77 D2 Agadyr' Kazakh.
113 I7 Agalega Islands Mauritius
Agana Guam see Hagåtña
74 B2 Agar India
119 D2 Agaro Eth.
75 D2 Agartala India
81 C2 Ağdam Azer.
105 C3 Agde France
104 C3 Agen France
122 A2 Aggeneys S. Africa
111 C3 Agia Vervara Greece
111 B3 Agios Dimitrios Greece
111 C3 Agios Efstratios i. Greece
111 C3 Agios Kirykos Greece
111 C3 Agios Nikolaos Greece
78 A3 Agirwat Hills Sudan
123 C2 Agisanang S. Africa
110 B1 Agnita Romania

74 B2 Agra India
81 C2 Ağrı Turkey
Ağrı Dağı mt. Turkey see
Ararat, Mount
108 B3 Agrigento Sicily Italy
111 B3 Agrinio Greece
109 C2 Agropoli Italy
87 E3 Agryz Rus. Fed.
144 B2 Agua Brava, Laguna lag. Mex.
154 B2 Água Clara Brazil
145 C3 Aguada Mex.
146 B4 Aguadulce Panama
144 B2 Aguanaval r. Mex.
144 B1 Agua Prieta Mex.
144 B2 Aguascalientes Mex.
155 D1 Águas Formosas Brazil
154 C2 Águeda Brazil
106 B1 Águeda Port.
114 C3 Aguelhok Mali
106 C1 Aguilar de Campóo Spain
107 C2 Águilas Spain
144 B3 Aguililla Mex.
122 B3 Agulhas, Cape S. Africa
158 F7 Agulhas Basin sea feature
Southern Ocean
155 D2 Agulhas Negras mt. Brazil
158 F7 Agulhas Plateau sea feature
Southern Ocean
158 F7 Agulhas Ridge sea feature
S. Atlantic Ocean
111 C2 Ağva Turkey
81 C2 Ahar Iran
100 C1 Ahaus Ger.
81 C2 Ahlat Turkey
100 C2 Ahlen Ger.
74 B2 Ahmadabad India
74 B3 Ahmadnagar India
74 B2 Ahmadpur East Pak.
74 B1 Ahmadpur Sial Pak.
117 C4 Ahmar Mountains Eth.
Ahmedabad India see
Ahmadabad
Ahmednagar India see
Ahmadnagar
144 B2 Ahome Mex.
81 D3 Ahram Iran
101 E1 Ahrensburg Ger.
104 C2 Ahun France
93 F4 Åhus Sweden
81 C2 Ahvāz Iran
Ahvenanmaa is Fin. see
Åland Islands
122 A2 Ai-Ais Namibia
80 B2 Aigialousa Cyprus
111 B3 Aigio Greece
Aihui China see Heihe
Aijal India see Aizawl
141 D2 Aiken U.S.A.
155 D1 Aimorés Brazil
155 D1 Aimorés, Serra dos hills Brazil
105 D2 Ain r. France
107 C2 Aïn Azel Alg.
115 C1 Aïn Beïda Alg.
114 B2 'Aïn Ben Tili Maur.
107 D2 Aïn Defla Alg.
114 B1 Aïn Sefra Alg.
136 D2 Ainsworth U.S.A.
Aintab Turkey see Gaziantep
107 D2 Aïn Taya Alg.
107 D2 Aïn Tédélès Alg.
107 C2 Aïn Temouchent Alg.
115 C3 Aïr, Massif de l' mts Niger
60 A1 Airbangis Indon.
128 C2 Airdrie Can.
96 C3 Airdrie U.K.
104 B3 Aire-sur-l'Adour France
101 E3 Aisch r. Ger.
128 A1 Aishihik Lake Can.
100 A3 Aisne r. France
59 D3 Aitape P.N.G.
137 E1 Aitkin U.S.A.
110 B1 Aiud Romania
105 D3 Aix-en-Provence France
Aix-la-Chapelle Ger. see Aachen
105 D2 Aix-les-Bains France
75 D2 Aizawl India
88 C2 Aizkraukle Latvia
88 B2 Aizpute Latvia
67 C3 Aizu-wakamatsu Japan
105 D3 Ajaccio Corsica France
Ajayameru India see Ajmer
115 E1 Ajdābiyā Libya
79 C2 'Ajman U.A.E.
74 B2 Ajmer India
Ajmer-Merwara India see Ajmer
142 A2 Ajo U.S.A.
119 D2 Āk'ak'ī Beseka Eth.
Akamagaseki Japan see
Shimonoseki
54 B2 Akaroa N.Z.
87 E3 Akbulak Rus. Fed.
80 B2 Akçakale Turkey
114 A3 Akchâr reg. Maur.
111 C3 Akdağ mt. Turkey
80 B2 Akdağmadeni Turkey
88 A2 Åkersberga Sweden
118 C2 Aketi Dem. Rep. Congo
81 C1 Akhalk'alak'i Georgia
81 C1 Akhalts'ikhe Georgia
79 C2 Akhdar, Jabal mts Oman
111 C3 Akhisar Turkey
87 D4 Akhtubinsk Rus. Fed.
118 B3 Akiéni Gabon
130 B2 Akimiski Island Can.
66 D3 Akita Japan

114 A3 Akjoujt Maur.
Akkerman Ukr. see
Bilhorod-Dnistrovs'kyy
77 D1 Akkol' Kazakh.
Ak-Mechet Kazakh. see Kyzylorda
88 B2 Akmeņrags pt Latvia
Akmola Kazakh. see Astana
Akmolinsk Kazakh. see Astana
67 B4 Akō Japan
117 B4 Akobo Sudan
74 B2 Akola India
118 B2 Akonolinga Cameroon
78 A3 Akordat Eritrea
131 D1 Akpatok Island Can.
77 D2 Akqi China
92 □A3 Akranes Iceland
111 B2 Akrathos, Akra pt Greece
136 C2 Akron CO U.S.A.
138 C2 Akron OH U.S.A.
75 B1 Aksai Chin terr. Asia
80 B2 Aksaray Turkey
86 F2 Aksarka Rus. Fed.
76 B1 Aksay Kazakh.
91 D2 Aksay Rus. Fed.
80 B2 Akşehir Turkey
76 C2 Akshiganak Kazakh.
77 E2 Aksu China
116 B3 Āksum Eth.
76 B2 Aktau Kazakh.
76 B1 Aktobe Kazakh.
77 D2 Aktogay Kazakh.
88 C3 Aktsyabrski Belarus
Aktyubinsk Kazakh. see Aktobe
67 B4 Akune Japan
115 C4 Akure Nigeria
92 □B2 Akureyri Iceland
Akyab Myanmar see Sittwe
111 D2 Akyazı Turkey
77 C2 Akzhaykyn, Ozero salt l. Kazakh.
140 C2 Alabama r. U.S.A.
140 C2 Alabama state U.S.A.
140 C2 Alabaster U.S.A.
111 C3 Alaçatı Turkey
145 D2 Alacrán, Arrecife rf Mex.
81 C1 Alagir Rus. Fed.
151 F4 Alagoinhas Brazil
107 C1 Alagón Spain
78 B2 Al Aḥmadī Kuwait
77 E2 Alakol', Ozero salt l. Kazakh.
92 J2 Alakurtti Rus. Fed.
78 B3 Al 'Alayyah Saudi Arabia
81 C2 Al 'Amādīyah Iraq
81 C2 Al 'Amārah Iraq
80 A2 Al 'Āmirīyah Egypt
143 C3 Alamitos, Sierra de los mt. Mex.
135 C3 Alamo U.S.A.
142 B2 Alamogordo U.S.A.
144 A2 Alamos Mex.
144 B2 Alamos Mex.
144 B2 Alamos r. Mex.
136 B3 Alamosa U.S.A.
Åland Fin. see Åland Islands
93 G3 Åland Islands is Fin.
80 B2 Alanya Turkey
Alappuzha India see Alleppey
80 B2 Al 'Aqabah Jordan
78 B2 Al 'Aqiq Saudi Arabia
107 C2 Alarcón, Embalse de resr Spain
80 B2 Al 'Arish Egypt
78 B2 Al Arţāwīyah Saudi Arabia
61 C2 Alas Indon.
111 C3 Alaşehir Turkey
128 A2 Alaska state U.S.A.
124 D4 Alaska, Gulf of U.S.A.
126 B3 Alaska Peninsula U.S.A.
126 C3 Alaska Range mts U.S.A.
81 C2 Ālāt Azer.
87 D3 Alatyr' Rus. Fed.
150 B3 Alausí Ecuador
93 H3 Alavus Fin.
52 B2 Alawoona Austr.
79 C2 Al 'Ayn U.A.E.
108 A2 Alba Italy
107 C2 Albacete Spain
78 A2 Al Badā'i' Saudi Arabia
78 B2 Al Badī' Saudi Arabia
110 B1 Alba Iulia Romania
109 C2 Albania country Europe
50 A3 Albany Austr.
130 B2 Albany r. Can.
141 D2 Albany GA U.S.A.
139 E2 Albany NY U.S.A.
134 B2 Albany OR U.S.A.
115 E1 Al Bardī Libya
Al Başrah Iraq see Basra
51 D1 Albatross Bay Austr.
116 A2 Al Bawīţī Egypt
115 E1 Al Baydā' Libya
78 B3 Al Baydā' Yemen
141 D1 Albemarle U.S.A.
141 E1 Albemarle Sound sea chan. U.S.A.
108 A2 Albenga Italy
51 C2 Alberga watercourse Austr.
119 D2 Albert, Lake
Dem. Rep. Congo/Uganda
128 C2 Alberta prov. Can.
100 B2 Albert Kanaal canal Belgium
137 E2 Albert Lea U.S.A.
117 B4 Albert Nile r. Sudan/Uganda
123 C3 Alberton S. Africa
Albertville Dem. Rep. Congo see
Kalemie
105 D2 Albertville France
104 C3 Albi France
151 D2 Albina Suriname

| | | |
|---|---|---|
| 78 A2 | Al Bi'r Saudi Arabia | |
| 78 B3 | Al Birk Saudi Arabia | |
| 78 B2 | Al Biyāḍḥ *reg.* Saudi Arabia | |
| | Alborz, Reshteh-ye Iran *see* | |
| | Elburz Mountains | |
| 107 C2 | Albox Spain | |
| 106 B2 | Albufeira Port. | |
| 142 B1 | Albuquerque U.S.A. | |
| 79 C2 | Al Buraymī Oman | |
| 53 C3 | Albury Austr. | |
| 106 B2 | Alcácer do Sal Port. | |
| 106 C1 | Alcalá de Henares Spain | |
| 106 C2 | Alcalá la Real Spain | |
| 108 B3 | Alcamo *Sicily* Italy | |
| 107 C1 | Alcañiz Spain | |
| 106 B2 | Alcántara Spain | |
| 107 C2 | Alcantarilla Spain | |
| 106 C2 | Alcaraz Spain | |
| 106 C2 | Alcaraz, Sierra de *mts* Spain | |
| 106 C2 | Alcaudete Spain | |
| 106 C2 | Alcázar de San Juan Spain | |
| | Alcazarquivir Morocco *see* | |
| | Ksar el Kebir | |
| 91 D2 | Alchevs'k Ukr. | |
| 155 E1 | Alcobaça Brazil | |
| 107 C1 | Alcora Spain | |
| 107 C2 | Alcoy-Alcoi Spain | |
| 107 D2 | Alcúdia Spain | |
| 113 H6 | Aldabra Islands Seychelles | |
| 142 B3 | Aldama Mex. | |
| 145 C2 | Aldama Mex. | |
| 83 J3 | Aldan Rus. Fed. | |
| 83 J2 | Aldan *r.* Rus. Fed. | |
| 99 D3 | Aldeburgh U.K. | |
| 95 C4 | Alderney *i.* Channel Is | |
| 99 C4 | Aldershot U.K. | |
| 114 A3 | Aleg Maur. | |
| 155 D2 | Alegre Brazil | |
| 152 C2 | Alegrete Brazil | |
| 89 D1 | Alekhovshchina Rus. Fed. | |
| 89 E2 | Aleksandrov Rus. Fed. | |
| | Aleksandrovsk Ukr. *see* | |
| | Zaporizhzhya | |
| 83 K3 | Aleksandrovsk-Sakhalinskiy | |
| | Rus. Fed. | |
| 82 E1 | Aleksandry, Zemlya *i.* Rus. Fed. | |
| | Alekseyevka Kazakh. *see* Akkol' | |
| 91 D1 | Alekseyevka Rus. Fed. | |
| 91 D1 | Alekseyevka Rus. Fed. | |
| 89 E3 | Aleksin Rus. Fed. | |
| 109 D2 | Aleksinac Serb. and Mont. | |
| 118 B3 | Alèmbé Gabon | |
| 155 D2 | Além Paraíba Brazil | |
| 93 F3 | Ålen Norway | |
| 104 C2 | Alençon France | |
| 80 B2 | Aleppo Syria | |
| 150 B4 | Alerta Peru | |
| 128 B2 | Alert Bay Can. | |
| 105 C3 | Alès France | |
| 110 B1 | Aleşd Romania | |
| 108 A2 | Alessandria Italy | |
| | Alessio Albania *see* Lezhë | |
| 93 E3 | Ålesund Norway | |
| 156 D2 | Aleutian Basin *sea feature* | |
| | Bering Sea | |
| 124 A4 | Aleutian Islands U.S.A. | |
| 83 L3 | Alevina, Mys *c.* Rus. Fed. | |
| 128 A2 | Alexander Archipelago *is* U.S.A. | |
| 122 A2 | Alexander Bay S. Africa | |
| 140 C2 | Alexander City U.S.A. | |
| 55 A2 | Alexander Island Antarctica | |
| 53 C3 | Alexandra Austr. | |
| 54 A3 | Alexandra N.Z. | |
| 153 E5 | Alexandra, Cape S. Georgia | |
| | Alexander Land *r.* Rus. Fed. *see* | |
| | Aleksandry, Zemlya | |
| 111 B2 | Alexandreia Greece | |
| 116 A1 | Alexandria Egypt | |
| 110 C2 | Alexandria Romania | |
| 123 C3 | Alexandria S. Africa | |
| 96 B3 | Alexandria U.K. | |
| 140 B2 | Alexandria *LA* U.S.A. | |
| 137 D1 | Alexandria *MN* U.S.A. | |
| 139 D3 | Alexandria *VA* U.S.A. | |
| 52 A3 | Alexandrina, Lake Austr. | |
| 111 C2 | Alexandroupoli Greece | |
| 131 E2 | Alexis *r.* Can. | |
| 128 B2 | Alexis Creek Can. | |
| 77 E1 | Aleysk Rus. Fed. | |
| 107 C1 | Alfaro Spain | |
| 81 C2 | Al Fāw Iraq | |
| 80 B3 | Al Fayyūm Egypt | |
| 101 D2 | Alfeld (Leine) Ger. | |
| 155 C2 | Alfenas Brazil | |
| 96 C2 | Alford U.K. | |
| | Al Fujayrah U.A.E. *see* Fujairah | |
| | Al Furāt *r.* Iraq/Syria *see* Euphrates | |
| 93 E4 | Ålgård Norway | |
| 106 B2 | Algarve *reg.* Port. | |
| 106 B2 | Algeciras Spain | |
| 107 C2 | Algemesí Spain | |
| 78 A3 | Algena Eritrea | |
| | Alger Alg. *see* Algiers | |
| 114 C2 | Algeria *country* Africa | |
| 79 C3 | Al Ghaydah Yemen | |
| 108 A2 | Alghero *Sardinia* Italy | |
| 116 B2 | Al Ghurdaqah Egypt | |
| 79 B2 | Al Ghwaybiyah Saudi Arabia | |
| 115 C1 | Algiers Alg. | |
| 123 C3 | Algoa Bay S. Africa | |
| 137 E2 | Algona U.S.A. | |
| 106 C1 | Algorta Spain | |
| | Algueirao Moz. *see* Hacufera | |
| 81 C2 | Al Ḩadīthah Iraq | |
| 79 C2 | Al Ḩajar al Gharbī *mts* Oman | |
| 115 E2 | Al Ḩamādah al Ḩamrā' *plat.* Libya | |
| 107 C2 | Alhama de Murcia Spain | |
| 80 A2 | Al Ḩammām Egypt | |
| 78 B2 | Al Ḩanākīyah Saudi Arabia | |
| 81 C2 | Al Ḩasakah Syria | |
| 78 B2 | Al Ḩawiyah Saudi Arabia | |
| 81 C2 | Al Ḩayy Iraq | |
| 78 B3 | Al Ḩazm al Jawf Yemen | |
| 79 C3 | Al Ḩibāk *des.* Saudi Arabia | |
| | Al Ḩillah Iraq *see* Hillah | |
| 78 B2 | Al Ḩillah Saudi Arabia | |
| 79 B2 | Al Ḩinnāh Saudi Arabia | |
| | Al Ḩudaydah Yemen *see* Hodeidah | |
| 79 B2 | Al Ḩufūf Saudi Arabia | |
| 115 D2 | Al Ḩulayq al Kabir *hills* Libya | |
| 79 C2 | 'Alīābād Iran | |
| 111 C3 | Aliağa Turkey | |
| 111 B3 | Aliakmonas *r.* Greece | |
| 81 C2 | Äli Bayramlı Azer. | |
| 107 C2 | Alicante Spain | |
| 143 D3 | Alice U.S.A. | |
| 109 C3 | Alice, Punta *pt* Italy | |
| 51 C2 | Alice Springs Austr. | |
| 77 D3 | Alichur Tajik. | |
| 74 B2 | Aligarh India | |
| 81 C2 | Alīgūdarz Iran | |
| 69 E1 | Alihe China | |
| 118 B3 | Alima *r.* Congo | |
| 118 C2 | Alindao C.A.R. | |
| 111 C3 | Aliova *r.* Turkey | |
| 74 B2 | Alirajpur India | |
| 117 C3 | Ali Sabieh Djibouti | |
| 78 A1 | Al 'Īsāwīyah Saudi Arabia | |
| | Al Iskandarīyah Egypt *see* | |
| | Alexandria | |
| 116 B1 | Al Ismā'īlīyah Egypt | |
| 123 C3 | Aliwal North S. Africa | |
| 115 E2 | Al Jaghbūb Libya | |
| 78 B2 | Al Jahrah Kuwait | |
| 79 C2 | Al Jamalīyah Qatar | |
| 115 E2 | Al Jawf Libya | |
| 78 A2 | Al Jawf Saudi Arabia | |
| 115 D1 | Al Jawsh Libya | |
| 106 B2 | Aljezur Port. | |
| | Al Jīzah Egypt *see* Giza | |
| 79 B2 | Al Jubayl Saudi Arabia | |
| 78 B2 | Al Jubaylah Saudi Arabia | |
| 115 D2 | Al Jufra Oasis Libya | |
| 78 B2 | Al Junaynah Saudi Arabia | |
| 106 B2 | Aljustrel Port. | |
| 78 B2 | Al Kahfah Saudi Arabia | |
| 79 C2 | Al Kāmil Oman | |
| 80 B2 | Al Karak Jordan | |
| 81 C2 | Al Kāẓimīyah Iraq | |
| 78 B2 | Al Khābūrah Oman | |
| 78 B2 | Al Khamāsīn Saudi Arabia | |
| 116 B2 | Al Khārijah Egypt | |
| 79 C2 | Al Khaşab Oman | |
| 78 B3 | Al Khawkhah Yemen | |
| 79 C2 | Al Khawr Qatar | |
| 115 E2 | Al Khufrah Libya | |
| 115 D1 | Al Khums Libya | |
| 79 B2 | Al Khunn Saudi Arabia | |
| 79 C2 | Al Kidan *well* Saudi Arabia | |
| 79 C2 | Al Kir'ānah Qatar | |
| 100 B1 | Alkmaar Neth. | |
| 81 C2 | Al Kūt Iraq | |
| | Al Kuwayt Kuwait *see* Kuwait | |
| | Al Lādhiqīyah Syria *see* Latakia | |
| 75 C2 | Allahabad India | |
| 83 K2 | Allakh-Yun' Rus. Fed. | |
| 78 A2 | 'Allāqī, Wādī al *watercourse* Egypt | |
| 139 D2 | Allegheny *r.* U.S.A. | |
| 139 C3 | Allegheny Mountains U.S.A. | |
| 97 B1 | Allen, Lough *l.* Ireland | |
| 145 B2 | Allende Mex. | |
| 145 B2 | Allende Mex. | |
| 139 D2 | Allentown U.S.A. | |
| 73 B4 | Alleppey India | |
| 101 D1 | Aller *r.* Ger. | |
| 136 C2 | Alliance *NE* U.S.A. | |
| 138 C2 | Alliance *OH* U.S.A. | |
| 78 B2 | Al Līth Saudi Arabia | |
| 96 C2 | Alloa U.K. | |
| 131 C3 | Alma Can. | |
| | Alma-Ata Kazakh. *see* Almaty | |
| 106 B2 | Almada Port. | |
| 106 C2 | Almadén Spain | |
| | Al Madīnah Saudi Arabia *see* | |
| | Medina | |
| 80 B2 | Al Mafraq Jordan | |
| 114 B2 | Al Mahbas Western Sahara | |
| 78 B3 | Al Maḩwīt Yemen | |
| 78 B2 | Al Majma'ah Saudi Arabia | |
| 116 B2 | Al Maks al Baḩri Egypt | |
| | Al Manāmah Bahrain *see* Manama | |
| 135 B2 | Almanor, Lake U.S.A. | |
| 107 C2 | Almansa Spain | |
| 80 B2 | Al Manşūrah Egypt | |
| 79 C2 | Al Mariyyah U.A.E. | |
| 115 E1 | Al Marj Libya | |
| 77 D2 | Almaty Kazakh. | |
| | Al Mawşil Iraq *see* Mosul | |
| 81 C2 | Al Mayādīn Syria | |
| 106 C1 | Almazán Spain | |
| 151 D3 | Almeirim Brazil | |
| 100 C1 | Almelo Neth. | |
| 155 D1 | Almenara Brazil | |
| 106 B1 | Almendra, Embalse de *resr* Spain | |
| 106 B2 | Almendralejo Spain | |
| 106 C2 | Almería Spain | |
| 106 C2 | Almería, Golfo de *b.* Spain | |
| 87 E3 | Al'met'yevsk Rus. Fed. | |
| 78 B2 | Al Mindak Saudi Arabia | |
| 116 B2 | Al Minyā Egypt | |
| 79 B2 | Al Mish'āb Saudi Arabia | |
| 106 B2 | Almodôvar Port. | |
| 106 B2 | Almonte Spain | |
| 75 B2 | Almora India | |
| 79 B2 | Al Mubarrez Saudi Arabia | |
| 79 C2 | Al Muḍaibī Oman | |
| 80 B3 | Al Mudawwarah Jordan | |
| | Al Mukallā Yemen *see* Mukalla | |
| | Al Mukhā Yemen *see* Mocha | |
| 106 C2 | Almuñécar Spain | |
| 81 C2 | Al Muqdādīyah Iraq | |
| 78 A2 | Al Musayjid Saudi Arabia | |
| 78 A2 | Al Muwayliḩ Saudi Arabia | |
| 111 B3 | Almyros Greece | |
| 96 B2 | Alness U.K. | |
| 98 C2 | Alnwick U.K. | |
| 62 A1 | Along India | |
| 111 B3 | Alonnisos *i.* Greece | |
| 59 C3 | Alor *i.* Indon. | |
| 59 C3 | Alor, Kepulauan *is* Indon. | |
| 60 B1 | Alor Setar Malaysia | |
| | Alor Star Malaysia *see* Alor Setar | |
| | Alost Belgium *see* Aalst | |
| 59 E3 | Alotau P.N.G. | |
| 86 C2 | Alozero Rus. Fed. | |
| 138 C1 | Alpena U.S.A. | |
| 160 Q1 | Alpha Ridge *sea feature* | |
| | Arctic Ocean | |
| 100 B1 | Alphen aan den Rijn Neth. | |
| 142 B2 | Alpine *AZ* U.S.A. | |
| 143 C2 | Alpine *TX* U.S.A. | |
| 84 E4 | Alps *mts* Europe | |
| 79 B3 | Al Qa'āmīyat *reg.* Saudi Arabia | |
| 115 D1 | Al Qaddāḩīyah Libya | |
| | Al Qāhirah Egypt *see* Cairo | |
| 78 B2 | Al Qā'iyah Saudi Arabia | |
| 81 C2 | Al Qāmishlī Syria | |
| 80 B2 | Al Qaryatayn Syria | |
| 79 B2 | Al Qaşab Saudi Arabia | |
| 116 A2 | Al Qaşr Egypt | |
| 79 B3 | Al Qaṭn Yemen | |
| 115 D2 | Al Qaṭrūn Libya | |
| 106 B2 | Alqueva, Barragem de Portugal | |
| 80 B2 | Al Qunayṭirah Syria | |
| 78 B3 | Al Qunfidhah Saudi Arabia | |
| 116 B2 | Al Quşayr Egypt | |
| 78 B2 | Al Quwārah Saudi Arabia | |
| 78 B2 | Al Quwayīyah Saudi Arabia | |
| 101 D2 | Alsfeld Ger. | |
| 98 B2 | Alston U.K. | |
| 92 H2 | Alta Norway | |
| 92 H2 | Altaelva *r.* Norway | |
| 68 B1 | Altai Mountains Asia | |
| 141 D2 | Altamaha *r.* U.S.A. | |
| 151 D3 | Altamira Brazil | |
| 109 C2 | Altamura Italy | |
| 144 A1 | Altar, Desierto de *des.* Mex. | |
| 77 E2 | Altay China | |
| 68 C1 | Altay Mongolia | |
| 105 D2 | Altdorf Switz. | |
| 107 C2 | Altea Spain | |
| 92 H1 | Alteidet Norway | |
| 101 F2 | Altenburg Ger. | |
| 100 C2 | Altenkirchen (Westerwald) Ger. | |
| 101 F1 | Altentreptow Ger. | |
| 111 C3 | Altınoluk Turkey | |
| 111 D3 | Altıntaş Turkey | |
| 152 B1 | Altiplano *plain* Bol. | |
| 96 B1 | Altnaharra U.K. | |
| 154 B3 | Alto Araguaia Brazil | |
| 106 B1 | Alto del Moncayo *mt.* Spain | |
| 154 B1 | Alto Garças Brazil | |
| 121 C2 | Alto Ligonha Moz. | |
| 121 C2 | Alto Molócuè Moz. | |
| 99 C4 | Alton U.K. | |
| 137 E3 | Alton U.S.A. | |
| 129 E3 | Altona Can. | |
| 139 D2 | Altoona U.S.A. | |
| 154 B1 | Alto Sucuriú Brazil | |
| 154 B1 | Alto Taquarí Brazil | |
| 102 C2 | Altötting Ger. | |
| 68 C2 | Altun Shan *mt.* China | |
| 68 B2 | Altun Shan *mts* China | |
| 134 B2 | Alturas U.S.A. | |
| 143 D2 | Altus U.S.A. | |
| 88 C2 | Alūksne Latvia | |
| 78 A2 | Al 'Ulá Saudi Arabia | |
| 115 D1 | Al 'Uqaylah Libya | |
| | Al Uqşur Egypt *see* Luxor | |
| 91 C2 | Alushta Ukr. | |
| 115 E2 | Al 'Uwaynāt Libya | |
| 143 D1 | Alva U.S.A. | |
| 145 C3 | Alvarado Mex. | |
| 93 F3 | Älvdalen Sweden | |
| 93 F3 | Alvdalen *vil.* Sweden | |
| 92 H2 | Älvsbyn Sweden | |
| 78 A2 | Al Wajh Saudi Arabia | |
| 79 C2 | Al Wakrah Qatar | |
| 74 B2 | Alwar India | |
| 81 C2 | Al Widyān *plat.* Iraq/Saudi Arabia | |
| | Alxa Youqi China *see* Ehen Hudag | |
| | Alxa Zuoqi China *see* Bayan Hot | |
| 51 C2 | Alyangula Austr. | |
| 88 B3 | Alytus Lith. | |
| 136 C1 | Alzada U.S.A. | |
| 101 D3 | Alzey Ger. | |
| 50 C2 | Amadeus, Lake *salt flat* Austr. | |
| 127 H2 | Amadjuak Lake Can. | |
| 106 B2 | Amadora Port. | |
| 78 B2 | Amā'ir Saudi Arabia | |
| 67 A4 | Amakusa-Shimo-shima *i.* Japan | |
| 93 F4 | Åmål Sweden | |
| 111 B3 | Amaliada Greece | |
| 59 D3 | Amamapare Indon. | |
| 154 A1 | Amambaí Brazil | |
| 154 B2 | Amambaí *r.* Brazil | |
| 154 A2 | Amambaí, Serra de *hills* | |
| | Brazil/Para. | |
| 69 E3 | Amami-Ō-shima *i.* Japan | |
| 69 E3 | Amami-shotō *is* Japan | |
| 77 C1 | Amangel'dy Kazakh. | |
| 109 C3 | Amantea Italy | |
| 123 D3 | Amanzimtoti S. Africa | |
| 151 D2 | Amapá Brazil | |
| 106 B2 | Amareleja Port. | |
| 88 B2 | Āmari Estonia | |
| 143 C1 | Amarillo U.S.A. | |
| 108 B2 | Amaro, Monte *mt.* Italy | |
| 80 B1 | Amasya Turkey | |
| 150 D2 | Amazon *r.* S. America | |
| 151 E2 | Amazon, Mouths of the Brazil | |
| | Amazonas *r.* S. America *see* | |
| | Amazon | |
| 157 I5 | Amazon Cone *sea feature* | |
| | S. Atlantic Ocean | |
| 74 B1 | Ambala India | |
| 121 □D3 | Ambalavao Madag. | |
| 121 □D2 | Ambanja Madag. | |
| 104 B3 | Ambarès-et-Lagrave France | |
| 150 B3 | Ambato Ecuador | |
| 121 □D2 | Ambato Boeny Madag. | |
| 121 □D3 | Ambato Finandrahana Madag. | |
| 121 □D2 | Ambatolampy Madag. | |
| 121 □D2 | Ambatondrazaka Madag. | |
| 101 E3 | Amberg Ger. | |
| 146 B3 | Ambergris Cay *i.* Belize | |
| 75 C2 | Ambikapur India | |
| 121 □D2 | Ambilobe Madag. | |
| 98 C2 | Amble U.K. | |
| 98 B2 | Ambleside U.K. | |
| 121 □D3 | Amboasary Madag. | |
| 121 □D2 | Ambodifotatra Madag. | |
| 121 □D3 | Ambohidratrimo Madag. | |
| 121 □D2 | Ambohimahasoa Madag. | |
| | Amboina Indon. *see* Ambon | |
| 59 C3 | Ambon Indon. | |
| 59 C3 | Ambon *i.* Indon. | |
| 121 □D3 | Ambositra Madag. | |
| 121 □D3 | Ambovombe Madag. | |
| 135 C4 | Amboy U.S.A. | |
| | Ambre, Cap d' *c.* Madag. *see* | |
| | Bobaomby, Tanjona | |
| 120 A1 | Ambriz Angola | |
| | Ambrizete Angola *see* N'zeto | |
| 86 F2 | Amderma Rus. Fed. | |
| | Amdo China *see* Lharigarbo | |
| 145 B2 | Amealco Mex. | |
| 144 B2 | Ameca Mex. | |
| 100 B1 | Ameland *i.* Neth. | |
| 154 C2 | Americana Brazil | |
| 55 D4 | American-Antarctic Ridge | |
| | *sea feature* S. Atlantic Ocean | |
| 134 D2 | American Falls U.S.A. | |
| 134 D2 | American Falls Reservoir U.S.A. | |
| 135 D2 | American Fork U.S.A. | |
| 49 J5 | American Samoa *terr.* | |
| | S. Pacific Ocean | |
| 141 D2 | Americus U.S.A. | |
| 100 B1 | Amersfoort Neth. | |
| 55 H2 | Amery Ice Shelf Antarctica | |
| 137 E2 | Ames U.S.A. | |
| 111 B3 | Amfissa Greece | |
| 83 J2 | Amga Rus. Fed. | |
| 66 C1 | Amgu Rus. Fed. | |
| 115 C2 | Amguid Alg. | |
| 83 K3 | Amgun' *r.* Rus. Fed. | |
| 131 D2 | Amherst Can. | |
| 104 C2 | Amiens France | |
| 79 C3 | Amilḩayt, Wādī al *r.* Oman | |
| 73 B3 | Amindivi Islands India | |
| 122 A1 | Aminuis Namibia | |
| 74 A2 | Amir Chah Pak. | |
| 129 D2 | Amisk Lake Can. | |
| 143 C3 | Amistad Reservoir Mex./U.S.A. | |
| 98 A3 | Amlwch U.K. | |
| 80 B2 | 'Ammān Jordan | |
| 127 J2 | Ammassalik Greenland | |
| 78 B3 | Am Nābiyah Yemen | |
| 81 D2 | Amol Iran | |
| 111 C3 | Amorgos *i.* Greece | |
| 140 C2 | Amory U.S.A. | |
| 130 C2 | Amos Can. | |
| | Amoy China *see* Xiamen | |
| 121 □D3 | Ampanihy Madag. | |
| 155 C2 | Amparo Brazil | |
| 121 □D2 | Ampasimanolotra Madag. | |
| 107 D1 | Amposta Spain | |
| 78 B3 | Amrān Yemen | |
| | Amraoti India *see* Amravati | |
| 74 B2 | Amravati India | |
| 74 B2 | Amreli India | |
| 74 B1 | Amritsar India | |
| 100 B1 | Amstelveen Neth. | |
| 100 B1 | Amsterdam Neth. | |
| 123 D2 | Amsterdam S. Africa | |
| 156 A8 | Amsterdam, Île *i.* Indian Ocean | |
| 103 C2 | Amstetten Austria | |
| 115 E3 | Am Timan Chad | |
| 76 B2 | Amudar'ya *r.* Asia | |
| 126 F1 | Amund Ringnes Island Can. | |
| 55 J3 | Amundsen, Mount Antarctica | |
| 160 H1 | Amundsen Basin *sea feature* | |
| | Arctic Ocean | |
| 126 F2 | Amundsen Gulf Can. | |
| 55 P2 | Amundsen Ridge *sea feature* | |
| | Southern Ocean | |
| 55 P2 | Amundsen Sea Antarctica | |
| 61 C2 | Amuntai Indon. | |

Amur r. China/Rus. Fed. see Heilong Jiang
78 A3 'Amur, Wadi watercourse Sudan
61 D2 Anabanua Indon.
83 I2 Anabar r. Rus. Fed.
83 I2 Anabarskiy Zaliv b. Rus. Fed.
150 C2 Anaco Venez.
134 D1 Anaconda U.S.A.
134 B1 Anacortes U.S.A.
143 D1 Anadarko U.S.A.
80 B1 Anadolu Dağları mts Turkey
83 M2 Anadyr' Rus. Fed.
83 M2 Anadyr' r. Rus. Fed.
81 C2 'Ānah Iraq
145 B2 Anáhuac Mex.
73 B3 Anai Mudi Peak India
121 □D2 Analalava Madag.
121 □D3 Analavelona mts Madag.
60 B1 Anambas, Kepulauan is Indon.
137 E2 Anamosa U.S.A.
80 B2 Anamur Turkey
67 B4 Anan Japan
73 B3 Anantapur India
74 B1 Anantnag Jammu and Kashmir
90 B2 Anan'yiv Ukr.
91 D3 Anapa Rus. Fed.
154 C1 Anápolis Brazil
81 D2 Anār Iran
152 B2 Añatuya Arg.
65 B2 Anbyon N. Korea
104 B2 Ancenis France
126 C2 Anchorage U.S.A.
108 B2 Ancona Italy
153 A4 Ancud Chile
Anda China see Daqing
93 E3 Åndalsnes Norway
106 C2 Andalucía reg. Spain
Andalusia reg. Spain see Andalucía
140 C2 Andalusia U.S.A.
159 F3 Andaman Basin sea feature Indian Ocean
73 D3 Andaman Islands India
63 A2 Andaman Sea Indian Ocean
121 □D2 Andapa Madag.
100 B2 Andelst Neth.
92 G2 Andenes Norway
100 B2 Andenne Belgium
100 B2 Anderlecht Belgium
105 D2 Andermatt Switz.
126 D2 Anderson r. Can.
126 C2 Anderson AK U.S.A.
138 B2 Anderson IN U.S.A.
141 D2 Anderson SC U.S.A.
148 C3 Andes mts S. America
77 D2 Andijon Uzbek.
121 □D2 Andilamena Madag.
121 □D2 Andilanatoby Madag.
Andizhan Uzbek. see Andijon
74 A1 Andkhvoy Afgh.
121 □D2 Andoany Madag.
Andong China see Dandong
65 B2 Andong S. Korea
104 C3 Andorra country Europe
104 C3 Andorra la Vella Andorra
99 C4 Andover U.K.
154 B2 Andradina Brazil
89 D2 Andreapol' Rus. Fed.
155 D2 Andrelândia Brazil
143 C2 Andrews U.S.A.
109 C2 Andria Italy
121 □D3 Androka Madag.
Andropov Rus. Fed. see Rybinsk
146 C2 Andros i. Bahamas
111 B3 Andros Greece
111 B3 Andros i. Greece
141 E4 Andros Town Bahamas
73 B3 Andrott i. India
90 B1 Andrushivka Ukr.
92 G2 Andselv Norway
106 C2 Andújar Spain
120 A2 Andulo Angola
114 C3 Anéfis Mali
147 D3 Anegada Passage Virgin Is (U.K.)
114 C4 Aného Togo
107 D1 Aneto mt. Spain
115 D3 Aney Niger
83 H3 Angara r. Rus. Fed.
68 C1 Angarsk Rus. Fed.
93 G3 Ånge Sweden
Angel, Salto del waterfall Venez. see Angel Falls
144 A2 Ángel de la Guarda, Isla i. Mex.
64 B2 Angeles Phil.
150 C2 Angel Falls Venez.
93 F4 Ängelholm Sweden
92 G3 Ångermanälven r. Sweden
104 B2 Angers France
129 E1 Angikuni Lake Can.
52 B3 Anglesea Austr.
98 A3 Anglesey i. U.K.
121 C2 Angoche Moz.
79 C2 Angohrän Iran
120 A2 Angola country Africa
138 B2 Angola U.S.A.
158 F6 Angola Basin sea feature S. Atlantic Ocean
128 A2 Angoon U.S.A.
104 C2 Angoulême France
155 D2 Angra dos Reis Brazil
77 D2 Angren Uzbek.
147 D3 Anguilla terr. West Indies
75 C2 Angul India
93 F4 Anholt i. Denmark
71 B3 Anhua China

70 B2 Anhui prov. China
154 B1 Anhumas Brazil
Anhwei prov. China see Anhui
154 C1 Anicuns Brazil
66 A1 Aniva, Mys c. Rus. Fed.
66 D1 Aniva, Zaliv b. Rus. Fed.
88 C1 Anjalankoski Fin.
104 B2 Anjou reg. France
65 B2 Anjü N. Korea
70 A2 Ankang China
80 B2 Ankara Turkey
121 □D3 Ankazoabo Madag.
121 □D2 Ankazobe Madag.
137 E2 Ankeny U.S.A.
102 C1 Anklam Ger.
121 □D2 Ankofa mt. Madag.
70 B2 Anlu China
55 G3 Ann, Cape Antarctica
139 E2 Ann, Cape U.S.A.
89 F3 Anna Rus. Fed.
115 C1 Annaba Alg.
101 F2 Annaberg-Buchholtz Ger.
80 B2 An Nabk Syria
78 B2 An Nafūd des. Saudi Arabia
150 D2 Annai Guyana
81 C2 An Najaf Iraq
63 B2 Annam Highlands mts Laos/Vietnam
96 C3 Annan U.K.
139 D3 Annapolis U.S.A.
75 C2 Annapurna I mt. Jammu and Kashmir/Nepal
138 C2 Ann Arbor U.S.A.
150 D2 Anna Regina Guyana
An Nás Ireland see Naas
81 C2 An Nāşiriyah Iraq
115 D1 An Nawfaliyah Libya
105 C2 Annecy France
78 B3 An Nimāş Saudi Arabia
71 A3 Anning China
140 C2 Anniston U.S.A.
105 C2 Annonay France
79 B2 An Nu'ayriyah Saudi Arabia
121 □D2 Anorontany, Tanjona hd Madag.
111 C3 Ano Viannos Greece
71 B3 Anpu China
70 B2 Anqing China
65 B2 Ansan S. Korea
101 E3 Ansbach Ger.
70 C1 Anshan China
71 A3 Anshun China
78 A1 An Sirhān, Wādī watercourse Saudi Arabia
143 D2 Anson U.S.A.
114 C3 Ansongo Mali
96 C2 Anstruther U.K.
150 B4 Antabamba Peru
80 B2 Antakya Turkey
121 □E2 Antalaha Madag.
80 B2 Antalya Turkey
80 B2 Antalya Körfezi g. Turkey
121 □D2 Antananarivo Madag.
55 A2 Antarctic Peninsula Antarctica
96 B2 An Teallach mt. U.K.
106 C2 Antequera Spain
142 B2 Anthony U.S.A.
114 B2 Anti Atlas mts Morocco
105 D3 Antibes France
131 D3 Anticosti, Île d' i. Can.
131 D3 Antigonish Can.
147 D3 Antigua i. Can.
147 D3 Antigua and Barbuda country West Indies
145 C2 Antiguo-Morelos Mex.
111 B3 Antikythira i. Greece
Antioch Turkey see Antakya
49 I8 Antipodes Islands N.Z.
An t-Ob U.K. see Leverburgh
152 A2 Antofagasta Chile
154 C3 Antonina Brazil
António Enes Moz. see Angoche
97 C1 Antrim U.K.
97 C1 Antrim Hills U.K.
121 □D2 Antsalova Madag.
Antseranana Madag. see Antsirañana
121 □D2 Antsirabe Madag.
121 □D2 Antsirañana Madag.
121 □D2 Antsohihy Madag.
100 B2 Antwerp Belgium
Antwerpen Belgium see Antwerp
An Uaimh Ireland see Navan
74 B2 Anupgarh India
73 C4 Anuradhapura Sri Lanka
Anvers Belgium see Antwerp
68 C2 Anxi China
51 C3 Anxious Bay Austr.
70 B2 Anyang China
65 B2 Anyang S. Korea
108 B2 Anzio Italy
67 C4 Aoga-shima i. Japan
66 D2 Aomori Japan
54 B2 Aoraki N.Z.
108 A1 Aosta Italy
114 B2 Aoukâr reg. Mali/Maur.
115 D2 Aozou Chad
141 D3 Apalachee Bay U.S.A.
150 B2 Apaporis r. Col.
154 B2 Aparecida do Tabuado Brazil
64 B2 Aparri Phil.
86 C2 Apatity Rus. Fed.
144 B3 Apatzingán Mex.
100 B1 Apeldoorn Neth.
100 C1 Apen Ger.

108 A2 Apennines mts Italy
49 J5 Apia Samoa
154 C2 Apiaí Brazil
64 B3 Apo, Mount vol. Phil.
101 E2 Apolda Ger.
52 B3 Apollo Bay Austr.
141 D3 Apopka U.S.A.
141 D3 Apopka, Lake U.S.A.
154 B1 Aporé Brazil
154 B1 Aporé r. Brazil
138 A1 Apostle Islands U.S.A.
80 B2 Apostolos Andreas, Cape Cyprus
91 C2 Apostolove Ukr.
133 F3 Appalachian Mountains U.S.A.
Appennino mts Italy see Apennines
53 D2 Appin Austr.
100 C1 Appingedam Neth.
98 B2 Appleby-in-Westmorland U.K.
138 B2 Appleton U.S.A.
108 B2 Aprilia Italy
62 A1 Aprunyi India
91 D3 Apsheronsk Rus. Fed.
Apsheronskaya Rus. Fed. see Apsheronsk
154 B2 Apucarana Brazil
154 B2 Apucarana, Serra da hills Brazil
64 A3 Apurahuan Phil.
147 D4 Apure r. Venez.
53 C2 Aqaba, Gulf of Asia
100 C1 Aqqikkol Hu salt l. China
154 A1 Aquidauana r. Brazil
104 B3 Aquitaine reg. France
75 C2 Ara India
117 A4 Arab, Bahr el watercourse Sudan
Arabian Gulf Asia see The Gulf
78 B2 Arabian Peninsula Saudi Arabia
56 B4 Arabian Sea Indian Ocean
151 F4 Aracaju Brazil
154 A2 Aracanguy, Montes de hills Para.
151 F3 Aracati Brazil
154 B2 Araçatuba Brazil
155 D1 Aracruz Brazil
155 D1 Araçuaí Brazil
110 B1 Arad Romania
115 E3 Arada Chad
79 C2 'Arādah U.A.E.
59 C3 Arafura Sea Austr./Indon.
154 B1 Aragarças Brazil
107 C1 Aragón r. Spain
107 C1 Aragón reg. Spain
151 E3 Araguaia r. Brazil
154 B1 Araguaína Brazil
151 E3 Araguaína Brazil
154 C1 Araguari Brazil
67 C3 Arai Japan
115 C2 Arak Alg.
81 C2 Arāk Iran
62 A1 Arakan Yoma mts Myanmar
81 C1 Arak's r. Armenia/Turkey
76 C2 Aral Sea salt l. Kazakh./Uzbek.
76 C2 Aral'sk Kazakh.
Aral'skoye More salt l. Kazakh./Uzbek. see Aral Sea
106 C1 Aranda de Duero Spain
109 D2 Arandelovac Serb. and Mont.
97 B1 Aran Island Ireland
97 B2 Aran Islands Ireland
106 C1 Aranjuez Spain
122 A1 Aranos Namibia
143 D3 Aransas Pass U.S.A.
67 B4 Arao Japan
114 B3 Araouane Mali
151 F3 Arapiraca Brazil
154 B2 Arapongas Brazil
154 C3 Araquari Brazil
78 B1 'Ar'ar Saudi Arabia
154 B2 Araraquara Brazil
151 D3 Araras Brazil
154 C2 Araras Brazil
154 B1 Araras, Serra das hills Brazil
154 B3 Araras, Serra das mts Brazil
81 C2 Ararat Armenia
52 B3 Ararat Austr.
81 C2 Ararat, Mount Turkey
155 D2 Araruama, Lago de lag. Brazil
155 E1 Arataca Brazil
Aratürük China see Yiwu
150 B2 Arauca Col.
154 C1 Araxá Brazil
81 C2 Arbil Iraq
129 E2 Arborg Can.
96 C2 Arbroath U.K.
74 A2 Arbu Lut, Dasht-e des. Afgh.
104 B3 Arcachon France
141 D3 Arcadia U.S.A.
134 B2 Arcata U.S.A.
145 B3 Arcelia Mex.
86 D2 Archangel Rus. Fed.
51 D1 Archer r. Austr.
49 M5 Archipel des Tuamotu is Fr. Polynesia
149 B6 Archipiélago Juan Fernández S. Pacific Ocean
134 D2 Arco U.S.A.
106 C2 Arcos de la Frontera Spain
127 G2 Arctic Bay Can.
Arctic Institute Islands Rus. Fed. see Arkticheskogo Instituta, Ostrova
160 J1 Arctic Mid-Ocean Ridge sea feature Arctic Ocean
160 Arctic Ocean
126 D2 Arctic Red r. Can.

81 C2 Ardabīl Iran
81 C1 Ardahan Turkey
93 E3 Årdalstangen Norway
97 C2 Ardee Ireland
100 B3 Ardennes plat. Belgium
135 B3 Arden Town U.S.A.
81 D2 Ardestān Iran
97 D1 Ardglass U.K.
53 C2 Ardlethan Austr.
143 D2 Ardmore U.S.A.
96 A2 Ardnamurchan, Point of U.K.
52 A2 Ardrossan Austr.
96 B3 Ardrossan U.K.
96 B2 Ardvasar U.K.
135 B3 Arena, Point U.S.A.
93 E4 Arendal Norway
100 B2 Arendonk Belgium
101 E1 Arendsee (Altmark) Ger.
150 B4 Arequipa Peru
151 D3 Arere Brazil
106 C1 Arévalo Spain
108 B2 Arezzo Italy
108 B2 Argenta Italy
104 B2 Argentan France
153 B4 Argentina country S. America
158 D7 Argentina Basin sea feature S. Atlantic Ocean
157 I8 Argentine Rise sea feature S. Atlantic Ocean
153 A5 Argentino, Lago l. Arg.
104 C2 Argenton-sur-Creuse France
110 C2 Argeş r. Romania
74 A1 Arghandab r. Afgh.
111 B3 Argolikos Kolpos b. Greece
111 B3 Argos Greece
111 B3 Argostoli Greece
107 C1 Arguís Spain
69 E1 Argun' r. China/Rus. Fed.
131 D3 Argyle Can.
50 B1 Argyle, Lake Austr.
Argyrokastron Albania see Gjirokastër
Ar Horqin Qi China see Tianshan
93 F4 Århus Denmark
122 A2 Ariamsvlei Namibia
152 A1 Arica Chile
96 A2 Arinagour U.K.
155 C1 Arinos Brazil
150 D4 Aripuanã Brazil
150 C3 Aripuanã r. Brazil
150 C3 Ariquemes Brazil
154 B1 Ariranhá r. Brazil
96 B2 Arisaig U.K.
96 B2 Arisaig, Sound of sea chan. U.K.
104 B3 Arizgoiti Spain
142 A2 Arizona state U.S.A.
144 A1 Arizpe Mex.
78 B2 'Arjah Saudi Arabia
61 C1 Arjasa Indon.
92 G2 Arjeplog Sweden
140 B2 Arkadelphia U.S.A.
77 C1 Arkalyk Kazakh.
140 B2 Arkansas r. U.S.A.
140 B1 Arkansas state U.S.A.
137 D3 Arkansas City U.S.A.
Arkhangel'sk Rus. Fed. see Archangel
97 C2 Arklow Ireland
102 C1 Arkona, Kap c. Ger.
82 G1 Arkticheskogo Instituta, Ostrova is Rus. Fed.
105 C3 Arles France
143 D2 Arlington U.S.A.
138 B2 Arlington Heights U.S.A.
115 C3 Arlit Niger
100 B3 Arlon Belgium
97 C1 Armagh U.K.
116 B2 Armant Egypt
87 D4 Armavir Rus. Fed.
81 C1 Armenia country Asia
150 B2 Armenia Col.
Armenopolis Romania see Gherla
144 B3 Armeria Mex.
53 D2 Armidale Austr.
134 D1 Armington U.S.A.
130 B2 Armstrong Can.
91 C2 Armyans'k Ukr.
Armyanskaya S.S.R. admin. reg. Asia see Armenia
Arnaoutis, Cape Cyprus see Arnauti, Cape
130 D2 Arnaud r. Can.
80 D2 Arnauti, Cape Cyprus
100 B2 Arnhem Neth.
51 C1 Arnhem, Cape Austr.
51 C1 Arnhem Bay Austr.
51 C1 Arnhem Land reg. Austr.
108 B2 Arno r. Italy
52 A2 Arno Bay Austr.
130 C2 Arnprior Can.
101 D2 Arnsberg Ger.
101 E2 Arnstadt Ger.
122 A2 Aroab Namibia
154 B2 Aroeira Brazil
101 D2 Arolsen Ger.
78 A3 Aroma Sudan
108 A1 Arona Italy
144 B2 Aros r. Mex.
Arquipélago dos Açores aut. reg. N. Atlantic Ocean see Azores
Arrah India see Ara
81 C2 Ar Ramādī Iraq
96 B3 Arran i. U.K.
80 B2 Ar Raqqah Syria

105 C1 Arras France
78 B2 Ar Rass Saudi Arabia
79 C2 Ar Rayyān Qatar
150 C2 Arrecifal Col.
145 C3 Arriagá Mex.
79 C2 Ar Rimāl *reg.* Saudi Arabia
Ar Riyāḍ Saudi Arabia *see* Riyadh
54 A2 Arrowtown N.Z.
135 B3 Arroyo Grande U.S.A.
145 C3 Arroyo Seco Mex.
79 C2 Ar Rustāq Oman
81 C2 Ar Ruṭbah Iraq
78 B2 Ar Ruwaydah Saudi Arabia
81 D3 Arsenaján Iran
66 B2 Arsen'yev Rus. Fed.
111 B3 Arta Greece
144 B3 Arteaga Mex.
66 B2 Artem Rus. Fed.
91 D2 Artemivs'k Ukr.
104 C2 Artenay France
142 C2 Artesia U.S.A.
51 E2 Arthur Point Austr.
54 B2 Arthur's Pass N.Z.
152 C3 Artigas Uru.
129 D1 Artillery Lake Can.
123 C1 Artisia Botswana
104 C1 Artois *reg.* France
90 B2 Artsyz Ukr.
Artur de Paiva Angola *see* Kuvango
77 D3 Artux China
81 C1 Artvin Turkey
59 C3 Aru, Kepulauan *is* Indon.
119 D2 Arua Uganda
147 D3 Aruba *terr.* West Indies
75 C2 Arun *r.* Nepal
119 D3 Arusha Tanz.
136 B3 Arvada U.S.A.
68 C1 Arvayheer Mongolia
129 E1 Arviat Can.
92 G2 Arvidsjaur Sweden
93 F4 Arvika Sweden
108 A2 Arzachena *Sardinia* Italy
87 D3 Arzamas Rus. Fed.
107 C2 Arzew Alg.
100 C2 Arzfeld Ger.
Arzila Morocco *see* Asilah
101 F2 Aš Czech Rep.
115 C4 Asaba Nigeria
66 D2 Asahi-dake *vol.* Japan
66 D2 Asahikawa Japan
78 B3 Āsalē *l.* Eth.
75 C2 Asansol India
117 C3 Āsayita Eth.
130 C3 Asbestos Can.
152 B1 Ascensión Bol.
113 B6 Ascension *i.* S. Atlantic Ocean
145 D3 Ascensión, Bahía de la *b.* Mex.
101 D3 Aschaffenburg Ger.
100 C2 Ascheberg Ger.
101 E2 Aschersleben Ger.
108 B2 Ascoli Piceno Italy
119 D2 Āsela Eth.
92 G3 Åsele Sweden
111 B2 Asenovgrad Bulg.
78 B2 Asharat Saudi Arabia
50 A2 Ashburton *watercourse* Austr.
54 B2 Ashburton N.Z.
140 B2 Ashdown U.S.A.
141 D1 Asheville U.S.A.
53 D1 Ashford Austr.
97 C2 Ashford Ireland
99 D4 Ashford U.K.
76 B3 Ashgabat Turkm.
66 D2 Ashibetsu Japan
98 C2 Ashington U.K.
67 B4 Ashizuri-misaki *pt* Japan
Ashkhabad Turkm. *see* Ashgabat
136 D3 Ashland *KS* U.S.A.
138 C3 Ashland *KY* U.S.A.
138 C2 Ashland *OH* U.S.A.
134 B2 Ashland *OR* U.S.A.
138 A1 Ashland *WI* U.S.A.
53 C1 Ashley Austr.
88 C3 Ashmyany Belarus
66 D2 Ashoro Japan
81 C2 Ash Shabakah Iraq
78 B3 Ash Sharawrah Saudi Arabia
Ash Shāriqah U.A.E. *see* Sharjah
81 C2 Ash Sharqāṭ Iraq
81 C2 Ash Shaṭrah Iraq
78 B3 Ash Shaykh 'Uthman Yemen
79 B3 Ash Shiḥr Yemen
79 C2 Ash Shināṣ Oman
78 B2 Ash Shu'aybah Saudi Arabia
78 B2 Ash Shubaykīyah Saudi Arabia
78 B2 Ash Shu'bah Saudi Arabia
78 B3 Ash Shumlūl Saudi Arabia
78 B3 Ash Shuqayq Saudi Arabia
115 D2 Ash Shuwayrif Libya
138 C2 Ashtabula U.S.A.
131 D2 Ashuanipi Lake Can.
75 B3 Asifabad India
106 B2 Asilah Morocco
108 A2 Asinara, Golfo dell' *b. Sardinia* Italy
108 A2 Asinara, Isola *i. Sardinia* Italy
82 G3 Asino Rus. Fed.
88 C3 Asipovichy Belarus
78 B2 'Asir *reg.* Saudi Arabia

93 F4 Asker Norway
93 F4 Askim Norway
68 C1 Askiz Rus. Fed.
116 B3 Asmara Eritrea
93 F4 Åsnen *l.* Sweden
116 B3 Asoteriba, Jebel *mt.* Sudan
103 D2 Aspang-Markt Austria
136 B3 Aspen U.S.A.
143 C2 Aspermont U.S.A.
54 A2 Aspiring, Mount N.Z.
116 C3 Assab Eritrea
78 B3 Aṣ Ṣaḥif Yemen
Aṣ Ṣaḥrā' al Gharbīyah *des.* Egypt *see* Western Desert
Aṣ Ṣaḥrā' ash Sharqīyah *des.* Egypt *see* Eastern Desert
78 B2 As Salamiyah Saudi Arabia
116 A1 As Sallūm Egypt
75 D2 Assam *state* India
81 C2 As Samāwah Iraq
79 C2 Aş Şanām *reg.* Saudi Arabia
115 E2 As Sarir *reg.* Libya
108 A3 Assemini *Sardinia* Italy
100 C1 Assen Neth.
100 B2 Assesse Belgium
115 D1 As Sidrah Libya
129 D2 Assiniboia Can.
128 C2 Assiniboine, Mount Can.
154 B2 Assis Brazil
78 B2 Aṣ Ṣubayhī Kuwait
81 C2 As Sulaymānīyah Iraq
78 B2 As Sulaymī Saudi Arabia
78 B2 As Sulayyil Saudi Arabia
78 B2 As Sūq Saudi Arabia
80 B2 As Suwaydā' Syria
79 C2 As Suwayq Oman
As Suways Egypt *see* Suez
111 B3 Astakos Greece
77 D1 Astana Kazakh.
81 C2 Āstārā Iran
100 B2 Asten Neth.
108 A2 Asti Italy
74 B1 Astor Jammu and Kashmir
72 B1 Astor Jammu and Kashmir
106 B1 Astorga Spain
134 B1 Astoria U.S.A.
Astrabad Iran *see* Gorgān
87 D4 Astrakhan' Rus. Fed.
Astrakhan' Bazar Azer. *see* Cälilabad
88 C3 Astravyets Belarus
Astrida Rwanda *see* Butare
106 B1 Asturias *reg.* Spain
111 C3 Astypalaia *i.* Greece
152 C2 Asunción Para.
116 B2 Aswān Egypt
116 B2 Asyūṭ Egypt
Atacama, Desierto de *des.* Chile *see* Atacama Desert
152 B2 Atacama, Puna de *plat.* Arg.
152 B2 Atacama, Salar de *salt flat* Chile
152 B2 Atacama Desert *des.* Chile
114 C4 Atakpamé Togo
111 B3 Atalanti Greece
150 B4 Atalaya Peru
155 D1 Ataléia Brazil
77 D2 Atamyrat Turkm.
78 B3 'Ataq Yemen
114 A2 Atâr Maur.
135 B3 Atascadero U.S.A.
77 D2 Atasu Kazakh.
116 B3 Atbara Sudan
116 B3 Atbara *r.* Sudan
77 C1 Atbasar Kazakh.
140 B3 Atchafalaya Bay U.S.A.
137 D3 Atchison U.S.A.
Ateransk Kazakh. *see* Atyrau
108 B2 Aterno *r.* Italy
108 B2 Atessa Italy
100 A2 Ath Belgium
128 C2 Athabasca Can.
129 C2 Athabasca *r.* Can.
129 D2 Athabasca, Lake Can.
97 B2 Athboy Ireland
97 B2 Athenry Ireland
111 B3 Athens Greece
140 C2 Athens *AL* U.S.A.
141 D2 Athens *GA* U.S.A.
138 C3 Athens *OH* U.S.A.
141 D1 Athens *TN* U.S.A.
143 D2 Athens *TX* U.S.A.
51 D1 Atherton Austr.
Athina Greece *see* Athens
97 C2 Athlone Ireland
111 B3 Athos *mt.* Greece
97 C2 Athy Ireland
115 D3 Ati Chad
130 B3 Atikokan Can.
87 D3 Atkarsk Rus. Fed.
137 D3 Atlanta U.S.A.
141 D2 Atlantic U.S.A.
141 D3 Atlantic Beach U.S.A.
139 E3 Atlantic City U.S.A.
55 Atlantic-Indian-Antarctic Basin *sea feature* S. Atlantic Ocean
158 E8 Atlantic-Indian Ridge *sea feature* Southern Ocean
158 Atlantic Ocean
122 A3 Atlantis S. Africa
114 B1 Atlas Mountains Africa
114 C1 Atlas Saharien *mts* Alg.
128 A2 Atlin Can.
128 A2 Atlin Lake Can.
140 C2 Atmore U.S.A.

152 B2 Atocha Bol.
143 D2 Atoka U.S.A.
75 C2 Atrai *r.* India
80 B2 Aṭ Ṭafīlah Jordan
78 B2 Aṭ Ṭā'if Saudi Arabia
63 B2 Attapu Laos
111 C3 Attavyros *mt.* Greece
130 B2 Attawapiskat Can.
130 B2 Attawapiskat *r.* Can.
130 B2 Attawapiskat Lake Can.
100 C2 Attendorn Ger.
100 A3 Attichy France
116 B2 Aṭ Ṭūr Egypt
78 B3 At Turbah Yemen
135 B3 Atwater U.S.A.
76 B2 Atyrau Kazakh.
105 D3 Aubagne France
105 C3 Aubenas France
126 D2 Aubry Lake Can.
140 C2 Auburn *AL* U.S.A.
135 B3 Auburn *CA* U.S.A.
138 B2 Auburn *IN* U.S.A.
139 E2 Auburn *ME* U.S.A.
137 D2 Auburn *NE* U.S.A.
139 D2 Auburn *NY* U.S.A.
104 C2 Auch France
54 B1 Auckland N.Z.
48 H9 Auckland Islands N.Z.
117 C4 Aude Range *mts* Eth.
101 F2 Aue Ger.
101 F2 Auerbach Ger.
102 C2 Augsburg Ger.
50 A3 Augusta Austr.
109 C3 Augusta *Sicily* Italy
141 D2 Augusta *GA* U.S.A.
137 D3 Augusta *KS* U.S.A.
139 F2 Augusta *ME* U.S.A.
155 D1 Augusto de Lima Brazil
103 E1 Augustów Pol.
50 A2 Augustus, Mount Austr.
100 A2 Aulnoye-Aymeries France
Aumale Alg. *see* Sour el Ghozlane
62 A2 Aunglan Myanmar
122 B2 Auob *watercourse* Namibia/S. Africa
131 D2 Aupaluk Can.
74 B3 Aurangabad India
104 B2 Auray France
100 C1 Aurich Ger.
154 B1 Aurilândia Brazil
104 C3 Aurillac France
136 C3 Aurora *CO* U.S.A.
138 B2 Aurora *IL* U.S.A.
137 E3 Aurora *MO* U.S.A.
137 D2 Aurora *NE* U.S.A.
122 A2 Aus Namibia
138 C2 Au Sable *r.* U.S.A.
137 E2 Austin *MN* U.S.A.
135 C3 Austin *NV* U.S.A.
143 D2 Austin *TX* U.S.A.
Australes, Îles *is* Fr. Polynesia *see* Tubuai Islands
50 B2 Australia *country* Oceania
55 K4 Australian-Antarctic Basin *sea feature* Southern Ocean
53 C3 Australian Capital Territory *admin. div.* Austr.
102 C2 Austria *country* Europe
150 D3 Autazes Brazil
144 B3 Autlán Mex.
105 C2 Autun France
104 C3 Auvergne *reg.* France
105 C2 Auvergne, Monts d' *mts* France
105 C2 Auxerre France
105 D2 Auxonne France
105 C2 Avallon France
131 E3 Avalon Peninsula Can.
154 C2 Avaré Brazil
91 D2 Avdiyivka Ukr.
106 B1 Aveiro Port.
109 B2 Avellino Italy
108 B2 Aversa Italy
100 A2 Avesnes-sur-Helpe France
93 G3 Avesta Sweden
104 C3 Aveyron *r.* France
108 B2 Avezzano Italy
96 C2 Aviemore U.K.
109 C2 Avigliano Italy
105 C3 Avignon France
106 C1 Ávila Spain
106 B1 Avilés Spain
52 B3 Avoca Austr.
139 D2 Avoca U.S.A.
109 C3 Avola *Sicily* Italy
99 C4 Avon *r. England* U.K.
99 B4 Avon *r. England* U.K.
99 B3 Avon *r. England* U.K.
142 A2 Avondale U.S.A.
104 B2 Avranches France
54 B1 Awanui N.Z.
119 D2 Awasa Eth.
117 C4 Āwash Eth.
117 C4 Āwash *r.* Eth.
115 D2 Awbārī Libya
117 C4 Aw Dheege Somalia
96 B2 Awe, Loch *l.* U.K.
117 A4 Aweil Sudan
115 C4 Awka Nigeria
114 A2 Awserd Western Sahara
126 F1 Axel Heiberg Island Can.
114 B4 Axim Ghana
150 B4 Ayacucho Peru
77 E2 Ayagoz Kazakh.
Ayaguz Kazakh. *see* Ayagoz

68 B2 Ayakkum Hu *salt l.* China
106 B2 Ayamonte Spain
83 K3 Ayan Rus. Fed.
150 B4 Ayaviri Peru
74 A1 Āybak Afgh.
76 A2 Aybas Kazakh.
91 D2 Aydar *r.* Turkey
77 C2 Aydarko'l ko'li *l.* Uzbek.
111 C3 Aydın Turkey
77 C2 Ayeat, Gora *hill* Kazakh.
Ayers Rock *hill* Austr. *see* Uluṟu
83 I2 Aykhal Rus. Fed.
99 C4 Aylesbury U.K.
106 C1 Ayllón Spain
129 C1 Aylmer Lake Can.
117 B4 Ayod Sudan
83 M2 Ayon, Ostrov *i.* Rus. Fed.
114 B3 'Ayoûn el 'Atroûs Maur.
51 D1 Ayr Austr.
96 B3 Ayr U.K.
98 A2 Ayre, Point of Isle of Man
76 C2 Ayteke Bi Kazakh.
110 C2 Aytos Bulg.
145 C3 Ayutla Mex.
63 B2 Ayutthaya Thai.
111 C3 Ayvacık Turkey
111 C3 Ayvalık Turkey
91 C3 Ayya, Mys *pt* Ukr.
114 B3 Azaouâd *reg.* Mali
114 B3 Azaouagh, Vallée de *watercourse* Mali/Niger
115 D3 Azare Nigeria
Azbine *mts* Niger *see* Aïr, Massif de l'
81 C1 Azerbaijan *country* Asia
Azerbaydzhanskaya S.S.R. *admin. reg.* Asia *see* Azerbaijan
150 B3 Azogues Ecuador
86 D2 Azopol'ye Rus. Fed.
112 A2 Azores *aut. reg.* N. Atlantic Ocean
91 D2 Azov Rus. Fed.
91 D2 Azov, Sea of Rus. Fed./Ukr.
Azraq, Bahr el *r.* Sudan *see* Blue Nile
106 B2 Azuaga Spain
146 B4 Azuero, Península de *pen.* Panama
153 C3 Azul Arg.
108 A3 Azzaba Alg.
Az Zahrān Saudi Arabia *see* Dhahran
80 B2 Az Zaqāzīq Egypt
80 B2 Az Zarqā' Jordan
115 D1 Az Zāwiyah Libya
78 B3 Az Zaydīyah Yemen
114 C2 Azzel Matti, Sebkha *salt pan* Alg.
78 B2 Az Zilfi Saudi Arabia
78 B3 Az Zuqur *i.* Yemen

**B**

117 C4 Baardheere Somalia
77 C3 Bābā, Kūh-e *mts* Afgh.
111 C3 Baba Burnu *pt* Turkey
110 C2 Babadag Romania
111 C2 Babaeski Turkey
116 C3 Bāb al Mandab *str.* Africa/Asia
61 C2 Babana Indon.
119 C1 Babanusa Sudan
59 C3 Babar *i.* Indon.
119 D3 Babati Tanz.
89 E2 Babayevo Rus. Fed.
59 C2 Babeldaob *i.* Palau
128 B2 Babine *r.* Can.
128 B2 Babine Lake Can.
59 C3 Babo Indon.
81 D2 Bābol Iran
122 A3 Baboon Point S. Africa
88 C3 Babruysk Belarus
Babu China *see* Hezhou
64 B2 Babuyan *i.* Phil.
64 B2 Babuyan Channel Phil.
64 B2 Babuyan Islands Phil.
151 E3 Bacabal Brazil
145 D3 Bacalar Mex.
59 C3 Bacan *i.* Indon.
110 C1 Bacău Romania
52 B3 Bacchus Marsh Austr.
77 D3 Bachu China
129 E1 Back *r.* Can.
109 C1 Bačka Palanka Serb. and Mont.
109 C1 Bačka Topola Serb. and Mont.
52 A3 Backstairs Passage Austr.
62 B1 Bac Lac Vietnam
63 B3 Bac Liêu Vietnam
62 B1 Băc Ninh Vietnam
142 B3 Bacobampo Mex.
64 B2 Bacolod Phil.
130 C2 Bacqueville, Lac *l.* Can.
Bada China *see* Xilin
70 A1 Badain Jaran Shamo *des.* China
106 B2 Badajoz Spain
75 D2 Badarpur India
101 D2 Bad Berka Ger.
101 D2 Bad Berleburg Ger.
101 E1 Bad Bevensen Ger.
101 D3 Bad Dürkheim Ger.
100 C2 Bad Ems Ger.
103 D2 Baden Austria
102 B2 Baden-Baden Ger.
101 E2 Bad Harzburg Ger.
101 D2 Bad Hersfeld Ger.

102 C2 **Bad Hofgastein** Austria
101 D2 **Bad Homburg vor der Höhe** Ger.
101 D1 **Bad Iburg** Ger.
74 A2 **Badin** Pak.
**Bādiyat ash Shām** des. Asia see Syrian Desert
101 E2 **Bad Kissingen** Ger.
100 C3 **Bad Kreuznach** Ger.
136 C1 **Badlands** reg. ND U.S.A.
136 C2 **Badlands** reg. SD U.S.A.
101 E2 **Bad Lauterberg im Harz** Ger.
101 D2 **Bad Lippspringe** Ger.
101 D3 **Bad Mergentheim** Ger.
101 D2 **Bad Nauheim** Ger.
100 C2 **Bad Neuenahr-Ahrweiler** Ger.
101 E2 **Bad Neustadt an der Saale** Ger.
101 E1 **Bad Oldesloe** Ger.
101 D2 **Bad Pyrmont** Ger.
78 A2 **Badr Ḥunayn** Saudi Arabia
101 D1 **Bad Salzuflen** Ger.
101 E2 **Bad Salzungen** Ger.
102 C2 **Bad Schwartau** Ger.
101 E1 **Bad Segeberg** Ger.
73 C4 **Badulla** Sri Lanka
101 D1 **Bad Zwischenahn** Ger.
106 C2 **Baeza** Spain
114 A3 **Bafatá** Guinea-Bissau
127 H2 **Baffin Bay** sea Can./Greenland
127 H2 **Baffin Island** Can.
118 B2 **Bafia** Cameroon
114 A3 **Bafing** r. Guinea/Mali
114 A3 **Bafoulabé** Mali
118 B2 **Bafoussam** Cameroon
81 D2 **Bāfq** Iran
80 B1 **Bafra** Turkey
79 C2 **Bāft** Iran
119 C2 **Bafwasende** Dem. Rep. Congo
119 D3 **Bagamoyo** Tanz.
**Bagan Datoh** Malaysia see Bagan Datuk
60 B1 **Bagan Datuk** Malaysia
64 B3 **Baganga** Phil.
120 B2 **Bagani** Namibia
60 B1 **Bagansiapiapi** Indon.
118 B3 **Bagata** Dem. Rep. Congo
91 E2 **Bagayevskiy** Rus. Fed.
142 A2 **Bagdad** U.S.A.
152 A3 **Bagé** Brazil
81 C2 **Baghdād** Iraq
79 C1 **Bāghīn** Iran
77 C3 **Baghlān** Afgh.
104 C3 **Bagnères-de-Luchon** France
105 C3 **Bagnols-sur-Cèze** France
**Bago** Myanmar see Pegu
88 B3 **Bagrationovsk** Rus. Fed.
**Bagrax** China see Bohu
64 B2 **Baguio** Phil.
115 C3 **Bagzane, Monts** mts Niger
146 C2 **Bahamas, The** country West Indies
75 C2 **Baharampur** India
**Bahariya Oasis** Egypt see Bahrīyah, Wāḥāt al
60 B1 **Bahau** Malaysia
74 B2 **Bahawalnagar** Pak.
74 B2 **Bahawalpur** Pak.
**Bahia** Brazil see Salvador
146 B3 **Bahía, Islas de la** is Hond.
153 B3 **Bahía Blanca** Arg.
144 A2 **Bahía Kino** Mex.
152 C2 **Bahía Negra** Para.
144 A2 **Bahía Tortugas** Mex.
117 B3 **Bahir Dar** Eth.
79 C2 **Bahlā** Oman
75 C2 **Bahraich** India
79 C2 **Bahrain** country Asia
116 A2 **Bahrīyah, Wāḥāt al** Egypt
79 D2 **Bāhū Kālāt** Iran
89 D3 **Bahushewsk** Belarus
110 C2 **Baia** Romania
120 A2 **Baía dos Tigres** Angola
110 B1 **Baia Mare** Romania
118 B2 **Baïbokoum** Chad
69 E1 **Baicheng** China
**Baidoa** Somalia see Baydhabo
**Baie-aux-Feuilles** Can. see Tasiujaq
131 D3 **Baie-Comeau** Can.
**Baie-du-Poste** Can. see Mistissini
131 C3 **Baie-St-Paul** Can.
131 E3 **Baie Verte** Can.
62 A1 **Baihanchang** China
65 B1 **Baihe** China
69 D2 **Baikal, Lake** Rus. Fed.
**Baile Átha Cliath** Ireland see Dublin
110 B2 **Băileşti** Romania
68 C2 **Baima** China
141 D2 **Bainbridge** U.S.A.
**Baingoin** China see Porong
48 I3 **Bairiki** Kiribati
**Bairin Youqi** China see Daban
53 C3 **Bairnsdale** Austr.
65 B1 **Baishan** Jilin China
65 B1 **Baishanzhen** Jilin China
120 A2 **Baixo-Longa** Angola
70 A2 **Baiyin** China
116 B3 **Baiyuda Desert** Sudan
103 D2 **Baja** Hungary
144 A1 **Baja California** pen. Mex.
61 C2 **Bajawa** Indon.
78 B3 **Bājil** Yemen
115 C3 **Bajoga** Nigeria
109 D2 **Bajram Curri** Albania
114 A3 **Bakel** Senegal

135 C3 **Baker** CA U.S.A.
140 B2 **Baker** LA U.S.A.
136 C1 **Baker** MT U.S.A.
134 C2 **Baker** OR U.S.A.
134 B1 **Baker, Mount** vol. U.S.A.
129 E1 **Baker Foreland** hd Can.
49 J3 **Baker Island** terr. N. Pacific Ocean
129 E1 **Baker Lake** Can.
129 E1 **Baker Lake** l. Can.
135 C3 **Bakersfield** U.S.A.
**Bakharden** Turkm. see Bakherden
91 C3 **Bakhchysaray** Ukr.
76 B3 **Bakherden** Turkm.
91 C1 **Bakhmach** Ukr.
**Bakhmut** Ukr. see Artemivs'k
**Bākhtarān** Iran see Kermānshāh
**Bakı** Azer. see Baku
111 C2 **Bakırköy** Turkey
92 □C2 **Bakkaflói** b. Iceland
118 C2 **Bakouma** C.A.R.
81 C1 **Baku** Azer.
99 B3 **Bala** U.K.
64 A3 **Balabac** Phil.
64 A3 **Balabac** i. Phil.
61 C1 **Balabac Strait** Malaysia/Phil.
75 C2 **Balaghat** India
60 C2 **Balaiberkuak** Indon.
52 A2 **Balaklava** Austr.
91 C3 **Balaklava** Ukr.
91 D2 **Balakliya** Ukr.
87 D3 **Balakovo** Rus. Fed.
76 C3 **Bālā Morghāb** Afgh.
145 C3 **Balancán** Mex.
111 C3 **Balan Dağı** hill Turkey
64 B2 **Balanga** Phil.
87 D3 **Balashov** Rus. Fed.
**Balaton, Lake** Hungary see Lake Balaton
103 D2 **Balatonboglár** Hungary
150 D3 **Balbina, Represa de** resr Brazil
97 C2 **Balbriggan** Ireland
52 A2 **Balcanoona** Austr.
110 C2 **Balchik** Bulg.
54 A3 **Balclutha** N.Z.
143 D2 **Balcones Escarpment** U.S.A.
129 E1 **Baldock Lake** Can.
138 D2 **Baldwin** U.S.A.
129 D2 **Baldy Mountain** hill Can.
142 B2 **Baldy Peak** U.S.A.
**Baleares, Islas** is Spain see Balearic Islands
107 D2 **Balearic Islands** is Spain
155 E1 **Baleia, Ponta da** pt Brazil
130 C2 **Baleine, Grande Rivière de la** r. Can.
131 D2 **Baleine, Rivière à la** r. Can.
75 C2 **Baleshwar** India
50 B2 **Balgo** Austr.
79 B3 **Bālḥaf** Yemen
61 C2 **Bali** i. Indon.
60 A1 **Balige** Indon.
75 C2 **Baliguda** India
111 C3 **Balıkesir** Turkey
61 C2 **Balikpapan** Indon.
64 A3 **Balimbing** Phil.
59 D3 **Balimo** P.N.G.
102 B2 **Balingen** Ger.
64 B2 **Balintang Channel** Phil.
**Bali Sea** Indon. see Laut Bali
78 B3 **Baljurshi** Saudi Arabia
76 B3 **Balkanabat** Turkm.
110 B2 **Balkan Mountains** Bulg./Serb. and Mont.
77 C1 **Balkashino** Kazakh.
77 D2 **Balkhash** Kazakh.
77 D2 **Balkhash, Lake** Kazakh.
**Balkhash, Ozero** l. Kazakh. see Balkhash, Lake
**Balla Balla** Zimbabwe see Mbalabala
96 B2 **Ballachulish** U.K.
50 B3 **Balladonia** Austr.
97 B2 **Ballaghaderreen** Ireland
92 G2 **Ballangen** Norway
96 B3 **Ballantrae** U.K.
52 B3 **Ballarat** Austr.
50 B2 **Ballard, Lake** salt flat Austr.
96 C2 **Ballater** U.K.
114 B3 **Ballé** Mali
55 M3 **Balleny Islands** Antarctica
53 D1 **Ballina** Austr.
97 B1 **Ballina** Ireland
97 B2 **Ballinasloe** Ireland
97 B2 **Ballineen** Ireland
143 D2 **Ballinger** U.S.A.
97 B2 **Ballinrobe** Ireland
97 C1 **Ballycastle** Ireland
97 C1 **Ballycastle** U.K.
97 D1 **Ballyclare** U.K.
97 B2 **Ballyhaunis** Ireland
97 C1 **Ballymena** U.K.
97 C1 **Ballymoney** U.K.
97 D1 **Ballynahinch** U.K.
97 B1 **Ballyshannon** Ireland
95 B2 **Ballyvoy** U.K.
52 B3 **Balmoral** Austr.
143 C2 **Balmorhea** U.S.A.
120 A2 **Balombo** Angola
52 D2 **Balonne** r. Austr.
74 B2 **Balotra** India
77 D2 **Balpyk Bi** Kazakh.
75 C2 **Balrampur** India
52 B2 **Balranald** Austr.
110 B2 **Balş** Romania

151 E3 **Balsas** Brazil
145 C3 **Balsas** Mex.
145 B3 **Balsas** r. Mex.
90 B2 **Balta** Ukr.
90 B2 **Bălţi** Moldova
93 G4 **Baltic Sea** g. Europe
80 B2 **Balţīm** Egypt
97 B3 **Baltimore** Ireland
123 C1 **Baltimore** S. Africa
139 D3 **Baltimore** U.S.A.
97 C2 **Baltinglass** Ireland
88 A3 **Baltiysk** Rus. Fed.
75 D2 **Balu** India
52 A2 **Balumbah** Austr.
88 C2 **Balvi** Latvia
77 D2 **Balykchy** Kyrg.
87 E4 **Balykshi** Kazakh.
79 C2 **Bam** Iran
71 A3 **Bama** China
51 D1 **Bamaga** Austr.
130 A2 **Bamaji Lake** Can.
114 B3 **Bamako** Mali
118 C2 **Bambari** C.A.R.
101 E3 **Bamberg** Ger.
119 C2 **Bambili** Dem. Rep. Congo
118 B2 **Bambio** C.A.R.
119 C2 **Bambouti** C.A.R.
155 C2 **Bambuí** Brazil
98 C2 **Bamburgh** U.K.
118 B2 **Bamenda** Cameroon
77 C3 **Bāmiān** Afgh.
118 C2 **Bamingui** C.A.R.
79 D2 **Bampūr** Iran
79 C2 **Bampūr** watercourse Iran
152 B1 **Bañados del Izozog** swamp Bol.
119 C2 **Banalia** Dem. Rep. Congo
71 A3 **Banan** China
151 D4 **Bananal, Ilha do** i. Brazil
74 B2 **Banas** r. India
111 C3 **Banaz** Turkey
62 B2 **Ban Ban** Laos
97 C1 **Banbridge** U.K.
99 C3 **Banbury** U.K.
96 C2 **Banchory** U.K.
130 C3 **Bancroft** Can.
**Bancroft** Zambia see Chililabombwe
119 C2 **Banda** Dem. Rep. Congo
75 C2 **Banda** India
59 C3 **Banda, Kepulauan** is Indon.
59 C3 **Banda, Laut** Indon.
60 A1 **Banda Aceh** Indon.
**Bandar** India see Machilipatnam
**Bandar Abbas** Iran see Bandar-e 'Abbās
75 D2 **Bandarban** Bangl.
79 C2 **Bandar-e 'Abbās** Iran
81 C2 **Bandar-e Anzalī** Iran
79 C2 **Bandar-e Chārak** Iran
81 C2 **Bandar-e Emām Khomeynī** Iran
79 C2 **Bandar-e Lengeh** Iran
79 C2 **Bandar-e Maqām** Iran
**Bandar-e Pahlavī** Iran see Bandar-e Anzalī
**Bandar-e Shāhpūr** Iran see Bandar-e Emām Khomeynī
60 B2 **Bandar Lampung** Indon.
61 C1 **Bandar Seri Begawan** Brunei
**Banda Sea** Indon. see Banda, Laut
155 D2 **Bandeiras, Pico de** mt. Brazil
123 C1 **Bandelierkop** S. Africa
144 B2 **Banderas, Bahía de** b. Mex.
114 B3 **Bandiagara** Mali
111 C2 **Bandırma** Turkey
**Bandjarmasin** Indon. see Banjarmasin
97 B3 **Bandon** Ireland
97 B3 **Bandon** r. Ireland
118 B3 **Bandundu** Dem. Rep. Congo
60 B2 **Bandung** Indon.
128 C2 **Banff** Can.
96 C2 **Banff** U.K.
114 B3 **Banfora** Burkina
64 B3 **Banga** Phil.
73 B3 **Bangalore** India
118 C2 **Bangassou** C.A.R.
61 C2 **Banggai** Indon.
59 C3 **Banggai, Kepulauan** is Indon.
61 C2 **Banggai, Kepulauan** is Indon.
61 C1 **Banggi** i. Sabah Malaysia
**Banghāzī** Libya see Benghazi
60 B2 **Bangka** i. Indon.
60 B2 **Bangka, Selat** sea chan. Indon.
61 C2 **Bangkalan** Indon.
60 B1 **Bangkinang** Indon.
60 B2 **Bangko** Indon.
63 B2 **Bangkok** Thai.
75 C2 **Bangladesh** country Asia
97 D1 **Bangor** Northern Ireland U.K.
98 A3 **Bangor** Wales U.K.
139 F2 **Bangor** U.S.A.
63 A2 **Bang Saphan Yai** Thai.
64 B2 **Bangued** Phil.
118 B2 **Bangui** C.A.R.
64 B2 **Bangui** Phil.
121 B2 **Bangweulu, Lake** Zambia
80 B2 **Banhā** Egypt
62 B2 **Ban Huai Khon** Thai.
118 C2 **Bani** C.A.R.
80 B3 **Banī Mazār** Egypt
116 B2 **Banī Suwayf** Egypt
115 D1 **Banī Walīd** Libya
80 B2 **Bāniyās** Syria
109 C2 **Banja Luka** Bos.-Herz.
61 C2 **Banjarmasin** Indon.

114 A3 **Banjul** Gambia
63 A3 **Ban Khok Kloi** Thai.
128 A2 **Banks Island** B.C. Can.
126 D2 **Banks Island** N.W.T. Can.
48 H5 **Banks Islands** Vanuatu
129 E1 **Banks Lake** Can.
54 B2 **Banks Peninsula** N.Z.
51 D4 **Banks Strait** Austr.
75 C2 **Bankura** India
62 A1 **Banmauk** Myanmar
62 B2 **Ban Mouang** Laos
97 C1 **Bann** r. U.K.
62 B2 **Ban Napè** Laos
63 A3 **Ban Na San** Thai.
146 C2 **Bannerman Town** Bahamas
**Banningville** Dem. Rep. Congo see Bandundu
71 A4 **Ban Nong Kung** Thai.
74 B1 **Bannu** Pak.
103 D2 **Banská Bystrica** Slovakia
111 B2 **Bansko** Bulg.
74 B2 **Banswara** India
62 B2 **Ban Taviang** Laos
63 A3 **Ban Tha Kham** Thai.
62 A2 **Ban Tha Song Yang** Thai.
63 B2 **Ban Tôp** Laos
97 B3 **Bantry** Ireland
97 B3 **Bantry Bay** Ireland
60 A1 **Banyak, Pulau-pulau** is Indon.
118 B2 **Banyo** Cameroon
107 D1 **Banyoles** Spain
61 C2 **Banyuwangi** Indon.
**Banzyville** Dem. Rep. Congo see Mobayi-Mbongo
**Bao'an** China see Shenzhen
70 B1 **Baochang** China
70 B2 **Baoding** China
70 A2 **Baoji** China
63 B2 **Bao Lôc** Vietnam
66 B1 **Baoqing** China
118 B2 **Baoro** C.A.R.
62 A1 **Baoshan** China
70 B1 **Baotou** China
65 B1 **Baotou Shan** mt. China/N. Korea
74 B2 **Bap** India
81 C2 **Ba'qūbah** Iraq
109 C2 **Bar** Serb. and Mont.
90 B2 **Bar** Ukr.
116 B3 **Bara** Sudan
117 C4 **Baraawe** Somalia
147 C2 **Baracoa** Cuba
53 C2 **Baradine** Austr.
147 C3 **Barahona** Dom. Rep.
116 B3 **Baraka** watercourse Eritrea/Sudan
106 C1 **Barakaldo** Spain
61 C1 **Baram** r. Sarawak Malaysia
150 D2 **Baramanni** Guyana
89 D3 **Baran'** Belarus
74 B2 **Baran** India
88 C3 **Baranavichy** Belarus
116 B2 **Baranis** Egypt
90 B1 **Baranivka** Ukr.
76 B2 **Barankul** Kazakh.
128 A2 **Baranof Island** U.S.A.
**Baranowicze** Belarus see Baranavichy
59 C3 **Barat Daya, Kepulauan** is Indon.
155 D2 **Barbacena** Brazil
147 E3 **Barbados** country West Indies
107 D1 **Barbastro** Spain
106 B2 **Barbate de Franco** Spain
123 D2 **Barberton** S. Africa
104 B2 **Barbezieux-St-Hilaire** France
51 D2 **Barcaldine** Austr.
107 D1 **Barcelona** Spain
150 C1 **Barcelona** Venez.
105 D3 **Barcelonnette** France
150 C3 **Barcelos** Brazil
114 B4 **Barclayville** Liberia
51 C2 **Barcoo** watercourse Austr.
**Barcoo Creek** watercourse Austr. see Cooper Creek
103 D2 **Barcs** Hungary
92 □B3 **Bárðarbunga** mt. Iceland
75 C2 **Barddhaman** India
103 E2 **Bardejov** Slovakia
**Bardera** Somalia see Baardheere
79 C2 **Bardsīr** Iran
75 B2 **Bareilly** India
82 D1 **Barents Sea** Arctic Ocean
78 A3 **Barentu** Eritrea
72 C1 **Barga** China
108 B2 **Barga** Italy
75 C2 **Barh** India
52 B3 **Barham** Austr.
139 F2 **Bar Harbor** U.S.A.
109 C2 **Bari** Italy
107 C2 **Barika** Alg.
74 B1 **Barikot** Afgh.
150 B2 **Barinas** Venez.
75 C2 **Baripada** India
75 D2 **Barisal** Bangl.
60 B2 **Barisan, Pegunungan** mts Indon.
61 C2 **Barito** r. Indon.
79 C2 **Barkā** Oman
88 C2 **Barkava** Latvia
74 A2 **Barkhan** Pak.
51 C1 **Barkly Tableland** reg. Austr.
122 B2 **Barkly West** S. Africa
68 C2 **Barkol** China
110 C1 **Bârlad** Romania
105 D2 **Bar-le-Duc** France
50 A2 **Barlee, Lake** salt flat Austr.
109 C2 **Barletta** Italy

Bennett Island
167

53 C2 Barmedman Austr.
Barmen-Elberfeld Ger. see Wuppertal
74 B2 Barmer India
52 B2 Barmera Austr.
99 A3 Barmouth U.K.
101 D1 Barmstedt Ger.
98 C2 Barnard Castle U.K.
53 B2 Barnato Austr.
82 G3 Barnaul Rus. Fed.
127 H2 Barnes Icecap Can.
100 B1 Barneveld Neth.
98 C3 Barnsley U.K.
99 A4 Barnstaple U.K.
Barnstaple Bay U.K. see Bideford Bay
141 D2 Barnwell U.S.A.
Baroda India see Vadodara
150 C1 Barquisimeto Venez.
96 A2 Barra i. U.K.
53 D2 Barraba Austr.
151 D4 Barra do Bugres Brazil
151 E3 Barra do Corda Brazil
154 B1 Barra do Garças Brazil
150 D3 Barra do São Manuel Brazil
Barraigh i. U.K. see Barra
150 B4 Barranca Peru
150 B3 Barranca Peru
152 C2 Barranqueras Arg.
150 B1 Barranquilla Col.
105 D3 Barre des Ecrins mt. France
151 E4 Barreiras Brazil
63 A2 Barren Island India
154 C2 Barretos Brazil
128 C2 Barrhead Can.
130 C3 Barrie Can.
128 B2 Barrière Can.
52 B2 Barrier Range hills Austr.
53 D2 Barrington, Mount Austr.
129 D2 Barrington Lake Can.
53 C1 Barringun Austr.
97 C2 Barrow r. Ireland
126 B2 Barrow U.S.A.
126 B2 Barrow, Point U.S.A.
51 C2 Barrow Creek Austr.
98 B2 Barrow-in-Furness U.K.
50 A2 Barrow Island Austr.
126 F2 Barrow Strait Can.
99 B4 Barry U.K.
122 B3 Barrydale S. Africa
130 C3 Barrys Bay Can.
74 B2 Barsalpur India
101 D1 Barsinghausen Ger.
135 C4 Barstow U.S.A.
105 C2 Bar-sur-Aube France
102 C1 Barth Ger.
80 B1 Bartın Turkey
51 D1 Bartle Frere, Mount Austr.
143 D1 Bartlesville U.S.A.
137 D2 Bartlett NE U.S.A.
140 C1 Bartlett TN U.S.A.
98 C3 Barton-upon-Humber U.K.
103 E1 Bartoszyce Pol.
61 C2 Barung i. Indon.
69 D1 Baruun-Urt Mongolia
91 D2 Barvinkove Ukr.
53 C2 Barwon r. Austr.
88 C3 Barysaw Belarus
118 B2 Basankusu Dem. Rep. Congo
110 C2 Basarabi Romania
64 B1 Basco Phil.
105 D2 Basel Switz.
71 C3 Bashi Channel Taiwan
91 C2 Bashtanka Ukr.
64 B3 Basilan i. Phil.
99 D4 Basildon U.K.
99 C4 Basingstoke U.K.
81 C2 Başkale Turkey
130 C3 Baskatong, Réservoir resr Can.
Basle Switz. see Basel
118 C2 Basoko Dem. Rep. Congo
81 C2 Basra Iraq
128 C2 Bassano Can.
114 C4 Bassar Togo
63 A2 Bassein Myanmar
147 D3 Basse-Terre Guadeloupe
147 D3 Basseterre St Kitts and Nevis
114 B3 Bassikounou Maur.
114 C4 Bassila Benin
51 D3 Bass Strait Austr.
79 C2 Bastak Iran
101 E2 Bastheim Ger.
75 C2 Basti India
105 D3 Bastia Corsica France
100 B2 Bastogne Belgium
140 B2 Bastrop U.S.A.
Basuo China see Dongfang
Basutoland country Africa see Lesotho
118 A2 Bata Equat. Guinea
146 B2 Batabanó, Golfo de b. Cuba
83 J2 Batagay Rus. Fed.
154 B2 Bataguassu Brazil
74 B1 Batala India
106 B2 Batalha Port.
64 B1 Batan i. Phil.
118 B2 Batangafo C.A.R.
64 B2 Batangas Phil.
60 B2 Batanghari r. Indon.
64 B1 Batan Islands Phil.
154 C2 Batatais Brazil
139 D2 Batavia U.S.A.
91 D2 Bataysk Rus. Fed.
130 B3 Batchawana Mountain hill Can.
50 C1 Batchelor Austr.
63 B2 Bătdâmbâng Cambodia
118 B3 Batéké, Plateaux Congo
53 D3 Batemans Bay Austr.
140 B1 Batesville AR U.S.A.
140 C2 Batesville MS U.S.A.
89 D2 Batetskiy Rus. Fed.
99 B4 Bath U.K.
96 C3 Bathgate U.K.
74 B1 Bathinda India
53 C2 Bathurst Austr.
131 D3 Bathurst Can.
Bathurst Gambia see Banjul
126 E2 Bathurst Inlet Can.
126 E2 Bathurst Inlet inlet Can.
50 C1 Bathurst Island Austr.
126 F1 Bathurst Island Can.
78 B1 Bāṭin, Wādī al watercourse Asia
53 C3 Batlow Austr.
81 C2 Batman Turkey
115 C1 Batna Alg.
140 B2 Baton Rouge U.S.A.
144 B2 Batopilas Mex.
118 B2 Batouri Cameroon
154 B1 Batovi Brazil
Batrā' tourist site Jordan see Petra
92 I1 Båtsfjord Norway
73 C4 Batticaloa Sri Lanka
109 B2 Battipaglia Italy
128 D2 Battle r. Can.
138 B2 Battle Creek U.S.A.
135 C2 Battle Mountain U.S.A.
74 B1 Battura Glacier Jammu and Kashmir
117 B4 Batu mt. Eth.
60 A2 Batu, Pulau-pulau is Indon.
61 D2 Batuata i. Indon.
61 D2 Batudaka i. Indon.
64 B3 Batulaki Phil.
Batum Georgia see Bat'umi
81 C1 Bat'umi Georgia
60 B1 Batu Pahat Malaysia
61 D2 Baubau Indon.
115 C3 Bauchi Nigeria
137 E1 Baudette U.S.A.
Baudouinville Dem. Rep. Congo see Moba
104 B2 Baugé France
105 D2 Baume-les-Dames France
154 C2 Bauru Brazil
154 B1 Baús Brazil
88 B2 Bauska Latvia
102 C1 Bautzen Ger.
102 C2 Bavaria reg. Ger.
144 B2 Bavispe r. Mex.
87 E3 Bavly Rus. Fed.
62 A1 Bawdwin Myanmar
61 C2 Bawean i. Indon.
114 B3 Bawku Ghana
Baxian China see Banan
146 C2 Bayamo Cuba
Bayan Gol China see Dengkou
68 C1 Bayanhongor Mongolia
70 A2 Bayan Hot China
70 A1 Bayan Obo China
136 C2 Bayard NE U.S.A.
142 B2 Bayard NM U.S.A.
64 B3 Bayawan Phil.
81 C1 Bayburt Turkey
138 C2 Bay City MI U.S.A.
143 D3 Bay City TX U.S.A.
86 F2 Baydaratskaya Guba Rus. Fed.
117 C4 Baydhabo Somalia
104 B2 Bayeux France
136 B3 Bayfield U.S.A.
78 B3 Bayḥan al Qiṣab Yemen
Bay Islands is Hond. see Bahía, Islas de la
81 C2 Bayjī Iraq
Baykal, Ozero l. Rus. Fed. see Baikal, Lake
Baykal Range mts Rus. Fed. see Baykal'skiy Khrebet
83 I3 Baykal'skiy Khrebet mts Rus. Fed.
76 C2 Baykonyr Kazakh.
87 E3 Baymak Rus. Fed.
64 B2 Bayombong Phil.
104 B3 Bayonne France
76 C3 Bayramaly Turkm.
111 C3 Bayramiç Turkey
101 E3 Bayreuth Ger.
78 B3 Bayt al Faqīh Yemen
143 D3 Baytown U.S.A.
106 C2 Baza Spain
106 C2 Baza, Sierra de mts Spain
76 A2 Bazardyuzyu, Gora mt. Azer./Rus. Fed.
104 B3 Bazas France
74 A2 Bazdar Pak.
70 A2 Bazhong China
79 D2 Bazmān Iran
79 D2 Bazmān, Kūh-e mt. Iran
Bé, Nossi i. Madag. see Nosy Bé
136 C1 Beach U.S.A.
52 B3 Beachport Austr.
99 D4 Beachy Head hd U.K.
123 C3 Beacon Bay S. Africa
50 B1 Beagle Gulf Austr.
121 □D2 Bealanana Madag.
121 □D3 Beampingaratra mts Madag.
134 D2 Bear r. U.S.A.
130 B3 Beardmore Can.
53 C1 Beardmore Reservoir Austr.
Bear Island i. Arctic Ocean see Bjørnøya
134 E1 Bear Paw Mountain U.S.A.
147 C3 Beata, Cabo c. Dom. Rep.
147 C3 Beata, Isla i. Dom. Rep.
137 D2 Beatrice U.S.A.
135 C3 Beatty U.S.A.
53 D1 Beaudesert Austr.
52 B3 Beaufort Austr.
61 C1 Beaufort Sabah Malaysia
141 D2 Beaufort U.S.A.
126 D2 Beaufort Sea Can./U.S.A.
122 B3 Beaufort West S. Africa
96 B2 Beauly U.K.
96 B2 Beauly r. U.K.
100 B2 Beaumont Belgium
54 A3 Beaumont N.Z.
143 E2 Beaumont U.S.A.
105 C2 Beaune France
100 B2 Beauraing Belgium
129 E2 Beauséjour Can.
104 C2 Beauvais France
129 D2 Beauval Can.
129 D2 Beaver r. Can.
135 D3 Beaver U.S.A.
128 A1 Beaver Creek Can.
138 B2 Beaver Dam U.S.A.
129 E2 Beaver Hill Lake Can.
138 B1 Beaver Island U.S.A.
128 C2 Beaverlodge Can.
74 B2 Beawar India
154 C2 Bebedouro Brazil
101 D2 Bebra Ger.
99 D3 Beccles U.K.
109 D1 Bečej Serb. and Mont.
106 B1 Becerreá Spain
114 B1 Béchar Alg.
Bechuanaland country Africa see Botswana
138 C3 Beckley U.S.A.
117 B4 Bedelē Eth.
99 C3 Bedford U.K.
138 B3 Bedford U.S.A.
98 C2 Bedlington U.K.
100 C1 Bedum Neth.
53 C3 Beechworth Austr.
53 D2 Beecroft Peninsula Austr.
101 F1 Beelitz Ger.
53 D1 Beenleigh Austr.
80 B2 Beersheba Israel
Be'ér Sheva' Israel see Beersheba
143 D3 Beeville U.S.A.
121 □D2 Befandriana Avaratra Madag.
53 C3 Bega Austr.
107 D1 Begur, Cap de c. Spain
81 D2 Behbehān Iran
81 D2 Behshahr Iran
69 E1 Bei'an China
71 A3 Beihai China
70 B2 Beijing China
100 C1 Beilen Neth.
118 B2 Béinamar Chad
96 B3 Beinn an Oir hill U.K.
96 A2 Beinn Mhòr hill U.K.
Beinn na Faoghlia i. U.K. see Benbecula
121 C2 Beira Moz.
80 B2 Beirut Lebanon
123 C1 Beitbridge Zimbabwe
106 B2 Beja Port.
115 C1 Bejaïa Alg.
106 B1 Béjar Spain
74 A2 Beji r. Pak.
76 B2 Bekdash Turkm.
103 E2 Békés Hungary
103 E2 Békéscsaba Hungary
121 □D3 Bekily Madag.
66 D2 Bekkai Japan
114 B4 Bekwai Ghana
75 C2 Bela India
74 A2 Bela Pak.
123 C1 Bela-Bela S. Africa
118 B2 Bélabo Cameroon
109 D2 Bela Crkva Serb. and Mont.
61 C1 Belaga Sarawak Malaysia
88 C3 Belarus country Europe
121 C3 Bela Vista Moz.
60 A1 Belawan Indon.
83 M2 Belaya r. Rus. Fed.
103 D1 Bełchatów Pol.
Belchatow Pol. see Bełchatów
130 C2 Belcher Islands Can.
87 E3 Belebey Rus. Fed.
117 C4 Beledweyne Somalia
118 B2 Bélèl Cameroon
151 E3 Belém Brazil
142 B2 Belen U.S.A.
110 C2 Belene Bulg.
89 E3 Belev Rus. Fed.
97 D1 Belfast U.K.
139 F2 Belfast U.S.A.
136 C1 Belfield U.S.A.
105 D2 Belfort France
73 B3 Belgaum India
Belgian Congo country Africa see Congo, Democratic Republic of the
100 B2 Belgium country Europe
91 D1 Belgorod Rus. Fed.
109 D2 Belgrade Serb. and Mont.
134 D1 Belgrade U.S.A.
115 D4 Beli Nigeria
109 C1 Beli Manastir Croatia
60 B2 Belinyu Indon.
60 B2 Belitung i. Indon.
118 B3 Belize Angola
146 B3 Belize Belize
146 B3 Belize country Central America
83 K1 Bel'kovskiy, Ostrov i. Rus. Fed.
128 B2 Bella Bella Can.
104 C2 Bellac France
128 B2 Bella Coola Can.
73 B3 Bellary India
53 C1 Bellata Austr.
138 C2 Bellefontaine U.S.A.
136 C2 Belle Fourche U.S.A.
136 C2 Belle Fourche r. U.S.A.
141 D3 Belle Glade U.S.A.
104 B2 Belle-Île i. France
131 E2 Belle Isle i. Can.
131 E2 Belle Isle, Strait of Can.
130 C3 Belleville Can.
138 B3 Belleville IL U.S.A.
137 D3 Belleville KS U.S.A.
134 D2 Bellevue ID U.S.A.
134 B1 Bellevue WA U.S.A.
Bellin Can. see Kangirsuk
53 D2 Bellingen Austr.
134 B1 Bellingham U.S.A.
55 R2 Bellingshausen Sea Antarctica
105 D2 Bellinzona Switz.
96 C2 Bell Rock i. U.K.
108 B1 Belluno Italy
122 A3 Bellville S. Africa
53 D2 Belmont Austr.
155 E1 Belmonte Brazil
146 B3 Belmopan Belize
97 B1 Belmullet Ireland
69 E1 Belogorsk Rus. Fed.
121 □D3 Beloha Madag.
155 D1 Belo Horizonte Brazil
138 B2 Beloit U.S.A.
86 C2 Belomorsk Rus. Fed.
89 E3 Beloomut Rus. Fed.
91 D3 Belorechensk Rus. Fed.
Belorechenskaya Rus. Fed. see Belorechensk
87 E3 Beloretsk Rus. Fed.
Belorussia country Europe see Belarus
Belorusskaya S.S.R. admin. reg. Europe see Belarus
Belostok Pol. see Białystok
121 □D2 Belo Tsiribihina Madag.
86 F2 Beloyarskiy Rus. Fed.
89 E1 Beloye, Ozero l. Rus. Fed.
Beloye More sea Rus. Fed. see White Sea
89 E1 Belozersk Rus. Fed.
52 A2 Beltana Austr.
143 D2 Belton U.S.A.
Bel'ts' Moldova see Bălţi
Bel'tsy Moldova see Bălţi
97 C1 Belturbet Ireland
77 E2 Belukha, Gora mt. Kazakh./Rus. Fed.
86 D2 Belush'ye Rus. Fed.
138 B2 Belvidere U.S.A.
51 D2 Belyando r. Austr.
89 D2 Belyy Rus. Fed.
82 F2 Belyy, Ostrov i. Rus. Fed.
101 F1 Belzig Ger.
137 E1 Bemidji U.S.A.
118 C3 Bena Dibele Dem. Rep. Congo
53 C3 Benalla Austr.
Benares India see Varanasi
115 D1 Ben Arous Tunisia
118 C3 Bena-Sungu Dem. Rep. Congo
106 B1 Benavente Spain
96 A2 Benbecula i. U.K.
134 B2 Bend U.S.A.
123 C3 Bendearg mt. S. Africa
Bender Moldova see Tighina
Bendery Moldova see Tighina
52 B3 Bendigo Austr.
121 C2 Bene Moz.
102 C2 Benešov Czech Rep.
109 B2 Benevento Italy
73 C3 Bengal, Bay of sea Indian Ocean
70 B2 Bengbu China
115 E1 Benghazi Libya
60 B1 Bengkalis Indon.
60 B1 Bengkayang Indon.
60 B2 Bengkulu Indon.
120 A2 Benguela Angola
Benha Egypt see Banhā
96 B1 Ben Hope hill U.K.
152 B1 Beni r. Bol.
119 C2 Beni Dem. Rep. Congo
114 B1 Beni-Abbès Alg.
107 C2 Benidorm Spain
114 B1 Beni Mellal Morocco
114 C3 Benin country Africa
114 C4 Benin, Bight of g. Africa
115 C4 Benin City Nigeria
107 C2 Beni-Saf Alg.
Beni Suef Egypt see Banī Suwayf
153 C3 Benito Juárez Arg.
150 C3 Benjamim Constant Brazil
144 A1 Benjamín Hill Mex.
59 C3 Benjina Indon.
136 C2 Benkelman U.S.A.
96 B2 Ben Lawers mt. U.K.
96 B2 Ben Lomond hill U.K.
96 C2 Ben Macdui mt. U.K.
96 A2 Ben More hill U.K.
96 B2 Ben More mt. U.K.
54 B2 Benmore, Lake N.Z.
96 B1 Ben More Assynt hill U.K.
128 A2 Bennett Can.
83 K1 Bennetta, Ostrov i. Rus. Fed.
Bennett Island Rus. Fed. see Bennetta, Ostrov

96 B2 Ben Nevis mt. U.K.
139 E2 Bennington U.S.A.
123 C2 Benoni S. Africa
115 D4 Bénoy Chad
101 B3 Bensheim Ger.
114 B1 Ben Slimane Morocco
142 A2 Benson U.S.A.
61 D2 Benteng Indon.
117 A4 Bentiu Sudan
138 B2 Benton Harbor U.S.A.
140 B1 Bentonville U.S.A.
63 B2 Bên Tre Vietnam
115 C4 Benue r. Nigeria
97 B1 Benwee Head hd Ireland
96 B2 Ben Wyvis mt. U.K.
70 C1 Benxi China
Beograd Serb. and Mont. see Belgrade
75 C2 Beohari India
114 B4 Béoumi Côte d'Ivoire
67 B4 Beppu Japan
109 C2 Berane Serb. and Mont.
109 C2 Berat Albania
59 D3 Berau, Teluk b. Indon.
116 B3 Berber Sudan
117 C3 Berbera Somalia
118 B2 Berbérati C.A.R.
104 C1 Berck France
91 D2 Berdyans'k Ukr.
90 B2 Berdychiv Ukr.
90 A2 Berehove Ukr.
59 D3 Bereina P.N.G.
129 E2 Berens River Can.
137 D2 Beresford U.S.A.
91 D2 Berezanskaya Rus. Fed.
90 A2 Berezhany Ukr.
90 C2 Berezivka Ukr.
90 B1 Berezne Ukr.
86 D2 Bereznik Rus. Fed.
86 E3 Berezniki Rus. Fed.
Berezov Rus. Fed. see Berezovo
86 F2 Berezovo Rus. Fed.
107 D1 Berga Spain
111 C3 Bergama Turkey
108 A1 Bergamo Italy
102 C1 Bergen Ger.
101 D1 Bergen Ger.
100 B1 Bergen Neth.
93 E3 Bergen Norway
100 B2 Bergen op Zoom Neth.
104 C3 Bergerac France
100 C2 Bergheim (Erft) Ger.
100 C2 Bergisch Gladbach Ger.
122 A1 Bergland Namibia
93 G3 Bergsjö Sweden
92 H2 Bergsviken Sweden
Berhampur India see Baharampur
83 M3 Beringa, Ostrov i. Rus. Fed.
100 B2 Beringen Belgium
124 A4 Bering Sea N. Pacific Ocean
124 B3 Bering Strait Rus. Fed./U.S.A.
100 C1 Berkel r. Neth.
135 B3 Berkeley U.S.A.
100 B1 Berkhout Neth.
55 T2 Berkner Island Antarctica
110 B2 Berkovitsa Bulg.
92 I1 Berlevåg Norway
101 F1 Berlin Ger.
139 E2 Berlin U.S.A.
101 E2 Berlingerode Ger.
53 D3 Bermagui Austr.
144 B2 Bermejillo Mex.
152 B2 Bermejo Bol.
131 D2 Bermen, Lac l. Can.
125 L6 Bermuda terr. N. Atlantic Ocean
105 D2 Bern Switz.
101 E2 Bernburg (Saale) Ger.
127 G2 Bernier Bay Can.
50 A2 Bernier Island Austr.
100 C3 Bernkastel-Kues Ger.
121 □D3 Beroroha Madag.
52 B2 Berri Austr.
115 C1 Berriane Alg.
53 C3 Berrigan Austr.
107 D2 Berrouaghia Alg.
53 D2 Berry Austr.
146 C2 Berry Islands Bahamas
122 A2 Berseba Namibia
101 C1 Bersenbrück Ger.
90 B2 Bershad' Ukr.
131 D2 Berté, Lac l. Can.
118 B2 Bertoua Cameroon
150 C3 Beruri Brazil
98 B2 Berwick-upon-Tweed U.K.
91 C2 Beryslav Ukr.
121 □D2 Besalampy Madag.
105 D2 Besançon France
81 D3 Beshneh Iran
129 E2 Besnard Lake Can.
140 C2 Bessemer U.S.A.
76 B2 Besshoky, Gora hill Kazakh.
100 B2 Best Neth.
121 □D2 Betafo Madag.
106 B1 Betanzos Spain
118 B2 Bétaré Oya Cameroon
122 A2 Bethanie Namibia
100 B3 Bétheny France
139 D3 Bethesda U.S.A.
123 C2 Bethlehem S. Africa
139 D2 Bethlehem U.S.A.
123 C3 Bethulie S. Africa
105 C1 Béthune France
121 □D3 Betioky Madag.
51 D2 Betoota Austr.

77 D2 Betpak-Dala plain Kazakh.
121 □D3 Betroka Madag.
131 D3 Betsiamites Can.
121 □D2 Betsiboka r. Madag.
137 E2 Bettendorf U.S.A.
75 C2 Bettiah India
74 B2 Betul India
74 B2 Betwa r. India
99 B3 Betws-y-coed U.K.
100 C2 Betzdorf Ger.
136 C1 Beulah U.S.A.
98 C3 Beverley U.K.
101 D2 Beverungen Ger.
100 B1 Beverwijk Neth.
99 D4 Bexhill U.K.
111 C2 Beykoz Turkey
114 B4 Beyla Guinea
76 B2 Beyneu Kazakh.
80 B1 Beypazarı Turkey
Beyrouth Lebanon see Beirut
80 B2 Beyşehir Turkey
80 B2 Beyşehir Gölü l. Turkey
91 D2 Beysug r. Rus. Fed.
91 D2 Beysugskiy Liman lag. Rus. Fed.
88 C2 Bezhanitsy Rus. Fed.
89 E2 Bezhetsk Rus. Fed.
105 C3 Béziers France
Bhadgaon Nepal see Bhaktapur
75 C2 Bhadrak India
73 B3 Bhadravati India
75 C2 Bhagalpur India
74 A2 Bhairi Hol mt. Pak.
74 B1 Bhakkar Pak.
75 C2 Bhaktapur Nepal
62 A1 Bhamo Myanmar
75 C3 Bhanjanagar India
74 B2 Bharatpur India
74 B2 Bharuch India
75 C3 Bhavnagar India
75 C3 Bhawanipatna India
123 D2 Bhekuzulu S. Africa
74 B1 Bhera Pak.
74 B2 Bhilwara India
73 B3 Bhima r. India
74 B2 Bhind India
74 B2 Bhiwani India
123 C3 Bhongweni S. Africa
74 B2 Bhopal India
75 C2 Bhubaneshwar India
Bhubaneswar India see Bhubaneshwar
74 A2 Bhuj India
62 A2 Bhumiphol Dam Thai.
74 B2 Bhusawal India
75 D2 Bhutan country Asia
62 B2 Bia, Phou mt. Laos
Biafra, Bight of g. Africa see Benin, Bight of
59 C3 Biak Indon.
59 C3 Biak i. Indon.
103 E1 Biała Podlaska Pol.
103 D1 Białogard Pol.
103 E1 Białystok Pol.
109 C3 Bianco Italy
74 B2 Biaora India
104 B3 Biarritz France
105 D2 Biasca Switz.
66 D2 Bibai Japan
120 A2 Bibala Angola
53 C3 Bibbenluke Austr.
102 B2 Biberach an der Riß Ger.
155 C2 Bicas Brazil
73 B3 Bid India
115 C4 Bida Nigeria
73 B3 Bidar India
139 E2 Biddeford U.S.A.
96 B2 Bidean nam Bian mt. U.K.
99 A4 Bideford U.K.
99 A4 Bideford Bay U.K.
101 D2 Biedenkopf Ger.
105 D2 Biel Switz.
101 D1 Bielefeld Ger.
108 A1 Biella Italy
103 D1 Bielsko-Biała Pol.
63 B2 Biên Hoa Vietnam
130 C2 Bienville, Lac l. Can.
120 A2 Bié Plateau Angola
100 B3 Bièvre Belgium
118 B3 Bifoun Gabon
111 C2 Biga Turkey
134 C1 Big Belt Mountains U.S.A.
123 D2 Big Bend Swaziland
129 D2 Biggar Can.
96 C3 Biggar U.K.
99 C3 Biggleswade U.K.
134 D1 Big Hole r. U.S.A.
134 E1 Bighorn r. U.S.A.
136 B1 Bighorn U.S.A.
136 B2 Bighorn Mountains U.S.A.
143 C2 Big Lake U.S.A.
138 B2 Big Rapids U.S.A.
129 D2 Big River Can.
129 E2 Big Sand Lake Can.
137 D2 Big Sioux r. U.S.A.
143 C2 Big Spring U.S.A.
134 E1 Big Timber U.S.A.
130 B2 Big Trout Lake Can.
130 A2 Big Trout Lake l. Can.
109 C2 Bihać Bos.-Herz.
75 C2 Bihar state India
75 C2 Bihar Sharif India
110 B1 Bihor, Vârful mt. Romania
114 A3 Bijagós, Arquipélago dos is Guinea-Bissau

73 B3 Bijapur India
81 C2 Bijār Iran
109 C2 Bijeljina Bos.-Herz.
109 C2 Bijelo Polje Serb. and Mont.
71 A3 Bijie China
74 B2 Bikaner India
66 B1 Bikin Rus. Fed.
66 B1 Bikin r. Rus. Fed.
118 B3 Bikoro Dem. Rep. Congo
79 C2 Bilād Banī Bū 'Alī Oman
75 C2 Bilaspur India
81 C2 Biläsuvar Azer.
90 C2 Bila Tserkva Ukr.
63 A2 Bilauktaung Range mts Myanmar/Thai.
106 C1 Bilbao Spain
109 C2 Bileća Bos.-Herz.
111 C2 Bilecik Turkey
103 E1 Biłgoraj Pol.
119 D3 Bilharamulo Tanz.
90 C2 Bilhorod-Dnistrovs'kyy Ukr.
119 C2 Bili Dem. Rep. Congo
83 M2 Bilibino Rus. Fed.
109 D2 Bilisht Albania
104 B3 Billère France
134 E1 Billings U.S.A.
99 B4 Bill of Portland hd U.K.
142 A1 Bill Williams Mountain U.S.A.
115 D3 Bilma Niger
51 E2 Biloela Austr.
91 C2 Bilohirs'k Ukr.
90 B1 Bilohir"ya Ukr.
91 C1 Bilopillya Ukr.
91 D2 Bilovods'k Ukr.
140 C2 Biloxi U.S.A.
51 C2 Bilpa Morea Claypan salt flat Austr.
101 E2 Bilshausen Ger.
115 E3 Biltine Chad
90 C2 Bilyayivka Ukr.
114 C4 Bimbila Ghana
141 E3 Bimini Islands Bahamas
74 B2 Bina-Etawa India
59 C3 Binaija, Gunung mt. Indon.
53 C1 Bindle Austr.
118 B3 Bindu Dem. Rep. Congo
121 C2 Bindura Zimbabwe
107 D1 Binefar Spain
120 B2 Binga Zimbabwe
53 D1 Bingara Austr.
100 C3 Bingen am Rhein Ger.
114 B4 Bingerville Côte d'Ivoire
139 F1 Bingham U.S.A.
139 D2 Binghamton U.S.A.
115 D2 Bin Ghanimah, Jabal hills Libya
81 C2 Bingöl Turkey
62 A1 Bingzhongluo China
60 A1 Binjai Indon.
53 C2 Binnaway Austr.
60 B1 Bintan i. Indon.
60 B2 Bintuhan Indon.
61 C1 Bintulu Sarawak Malaysia
115 C3 Bin-Yauri Nigeria
70 B2 Binzhou China
118 A2 Bioco i. Equat. Guinea
109 C2 Biograd na Moru Croatia
155 C1 Biquinhas Brazil
115 D2 Birāk Libya
118 C1 Birao C.A.R.
75 C2 Biratnagar Nepal
52 B3 Birchip Austr.
128 C2 Birch Mountains Can.
51 C2 Birdsville Austr.
80 B2 Birecik Turkey
Birendranagar Nepal see Surkhet
60 A1 Bireun Indon.
75 C2 Birganj Nepal
117 B3 Birhan mt. Eth.
154 B2 Birigüi Brazil
118 C2 Birini C.A.R.
76 B3 Birjand Iran
98 B3 Birkenhead U.K.
99 C3 Birmingham U.K.
140 C2 Birmingham U.S.A.
114 A2 Bîr Mogreïn Maur.
115 C3 Birnin-Kebbi Nigeria
115 C3 Birnin Konni Niger
69 E1 Birobidzhan Rus. Fed.
97 C2 Birr Ireland
96 C1 Birsay U.K.
78 A2 Bi'r Shalatayn Egypt
88 B2 Biržai Lith.
75 B2 Bisalpur India
142 B2 Bisbee U.S.A.
104 A2 Biscay, Bay of sea France/Spain
141 D3 Biscayne Bay U.S.A.
102 C2 Bischofshofen Austria
77 D2 Bishkek Kyrg.
123 C3 Bisho S. Africa
135 C3 Bishop U.S.A.
98 C2 Bishop Auckland U.K.
69 E1 Bishui China
150 C2 Bisinaca Col.
115 C1 Biskra Alg.
64 B3 Bislig Phil.
136 C1 Bismarck U.S.A.
59 D3 Bismarck Archipelago is P.N.G.
59 D3 Bismarck Sea P.N.G.
107 D2 Bissa, Djebel mt. Alg.
114 A3 Bissau Guinea-Bissau
129 E2 Bissett Can.
128 C2 Bistcho Lake Can.
110 B1 Bistrița Romania
110 C1 Bistrița r. Romania
100 C2 Bitburg Ger.

105 D2 Bitche France
115 D3 Bitkine Chad
81 C2 Bitlis Turkey
111 B2 Bitola Macedonia
Bitolj Macedonia see Bitola
109 C2 Bitonto Italy
101 F2 Bitterfeld Ger.
122 A3 Bitterfontein S. Africa
134 D1 Bitterroot r. U.S.A.
134 C1 Bitterroot Range mts U.S.A.
89 E3 Bityug r. Rus. Fed.
115 D3 Biu Nigeria
67 C3 Biwa-ko l. Japan
77 E1 Biysk Rus. Fed.
Bizerta Tunisia see Bizerte
115 C1 Bizerte Tunisia
92 □A2 Bjargtangar hd Iceland
92 G3 Bjästa Sweden
109 C1 Bjelovar Croatia
92 G2 Bjerkvik Norway
Björneborg Fin. see Pori
82 C1 Bjørnøya Arctic Ocean
114 B3 Bla Mali
137 E3 Black r. U.S.A.
51 D2 Blackall Austr.
98 B3 Blackburn U.K.
134 D2 Blackfoot U.S.A.
102 B2 Black Forest mts Ger.
136 C2 Black Hills U.S.A.
96 B2 Black Isle pen. U.K.
129 D2 Black Lake Can.
129 D2 Black Lake l. Can.
99 B4 Black Mountains hills U.K.
142 A1 Black Mountains U.S.A.
98 B3 Blackpool U.K.
142 B2 Black Range mts U.S.A.
62 B1 Black River r. Vietnam
138 A2 Black River Falls U.S.A.
134 C2 Black Rock Desert U.S.A.
138 C3 Blacksburg U.S.A.
80 B1 Black Sea Asia/Europe
131 D3 Blacks Harbour Can.
97 A1 Blacksod Bay Ireland
97 C2 Blackstairs Mountains hills Ireland
114 B4 Black Volta r. Africa
51 D2 Blackwater Austr.
97 C2 Blackwater r. Ireland
128 B1 Blackwater Lake Can.
50 A3 Blackwood r. Austr.
87 D4 Blagodarnyy Rus. Fed.
111 B2 Blagoevgrad Bulg.
69 E1 Blagoveshchensk Rus. Fed.
129 D2 Blaine Lake Can.
137 D2 Blair U.S.A.
96 C2 Blair Atholl U.K.
96 C2 Blairgowrie U.K.
141 D2 Blakely U.S.A.
105 D2 Blanc, Mont mt. France/Italy
153 B3 Blanca, Bahía b. Arg.
52 A1 Blanche, Lake salt flat Austr.
152 B1 Blanco r. Bol.
134 B2 Blanco, Cape U.S.A.
131 E2 Blanc-Sablon Can.
92 □A2 Blanda r. Iceland
99 B4 Blandford Forum U.K.
135 E3 Blanding U.S.A.
107 D1 Blanes Spain
60 A1 Blangkejeren Indon.
100 A2 Blankenberge Belgium
100 C2 Blankenheim Ger.
100 C2 Blankenrath Ger.
147 D3 Blanquilla, Isla i. Venez.
103 D2 Blansko Czech Rep.
121 C2 Blantyre Malawi
97 B3 Blarney Ireland
98 C2 Blaydon U.K.
53 C2 Blayney Austr.
54 B2 Blenheim N.Z.
115 C1 Blida Alg.
130 B3 Blind River Can.
123 C2 Bloemfontein S. Africa
123 C2 Bloemhof S. Africa
123 C2 Bloemhof Dam S. Africa
104 C2 Blois France
92 □A2 Blönduós Iceland
97 B1 Bloody Foreland pt Ireland
142 B1 Bloomfield U.S.A.
138 B3 Bloomington IL U.S.A.
138 B3 Bloomington IN U.S.A.
102 B2 Bludenz Austria
137 E2 Blue Earth U.S.A.
138 C3 Bluefield U.S.A.
146 B3 Bluefields Nic.
53 C2 Blue Mountains Austr.
134 C1 Blue Mountains U.S.A.
116 B3 Blue Nile r. Eth./Sudan
126 E2 Bluenose Lake Can.
138 C3 Blue Ridge mts U.S.A.
128 C2 Blue River Can.
97 B1 Blue Stack Mountains hills Ireland
54 A3 Bluff N.Z.
135 E3 Bluff U.S.A.
154 C3 Blumenau Brazil
52 A2 Blyth Austr.
98 C2 Blyth U.K.
135 D4 Blythe U.S.A.
140 C1 Blytheville U.S.A.
114 A4 Bo Sierra Leone
64 B2 Boac Phil.
146 B3 Boaco Nic.
151 E3 Boa Esperança, Açude resr Brazil
134 C1 Boardman U.S.A.

Brezhnev 169

123 C1 Boatlaname Botswana
151 F3 Boa Viagem Brazil
150 C2 Boa Vista Brazil
53 C2 Bobadah Austr.
71 B3 Bobai China
121 □D2 Bobaomby, Tanjona c. Madag.
114 B3 Bobo-Dioulasso Burkina
121 B3 Bobonong Botswana
Bobriki Rus. Fed. see Novomoskovsk
89 F3 Bobrov Rus. Fed.
91 C1 Bobrovytsya Ukr.
91 C2 Bobrynets' Ukr.
121 □D3 Boby mt. Madag.
150 C3 Boca do Acre Brazil
155 D1 Bocaiúva Brazil
154 A2 Bocajá Brazil
118 B2 Bocaranga C.A.R.
141 D3 Boca Raton U.S.A.
146 B4 Bocas del Toro Panama
103 E2 Bochnia Pol.
100 B2 Bocholt Belgium
100 C2 Bocholt Ger.
100 C2 Bochum Ger.
123 C1 Bochum S. Africa
101 E1 Bockenem Ger.
110 B1 Bocşa Romania
118 B2 Boda C.A.R.
83 I3 Bodaybo Rus. Fed.
96 D2 Boddam U.K.
115 D3 Bodélé reg. Chad
92 H2 Boden Sweden
Bodensee l. Ger./Switz. see Constance, Lake
99 A4 Bodmin U.K.
99 A4 Bodmin Moor moorland U.K.
92 F2 Bodø Norway
111 C3 Bodrum Turkey
118 C3 Boende Dem. Rep. Congo
63 A2 Bogale Myanmar
140 C2 Bogalusa U.S.A.
114 B3 Bogandé Burkina
118 B2 Bogangolo C.A.R.
80 B2 Boğazlıyan Turkey
68 B2 Bogda Shan mts China
53 D1 Boggabilla Austr.
53 D2 Boggabri Austr.
97 B2 Boggeragh Mountains hills Ireland
Boghari Alg. see Ksar el Boukhari
59 D3 Bogia P.N.G.
100 B3 Bogny-sur-Meuse France
97 C2 Bog of Allen reg. Ireland
53 C3 Bogong, Mount Austr.
60 B2 Bogor Indon.
89 E3 Bogoroditsk Rus. Fed.
150 B2 Bogotá Col.
83 G3 Bogotol Rus. Fed.
Bogoyavlenskoye Rus. Fed. see Pervomayskiy
83 H3 Boguchany Rus. Fed.
91 E2 Boguchar Rus. Fed.
114 A3 Bogué Maur.
70 B2 Bo Hai g. China
100 A3 Bohain-en-Vermandois France
70 B2 Bohai Wan b. China
Bohemian Forest mts Ger. see Böhmer Wald
123 C2 Bohlokong S. Africa
101 F3 Böhmer Wald mts Ger.
91 D1 Bohodukhiv Ukr.
64 B3 Bohol i. Phil.
64 B3 Bohol Sea Phil.
77 E2 Bohu China
155 C2 Boi, Ponta do pt Brazil
123 C2 Boikhutso S. Africa
154 B3 Boi Preto, Serra de hills Brazil
154 B1 Bois r. Brazil
126 D2 Bois, Lac des l. Can.
134 C2 Boise U.S.A.
143 C1 Boise City U.S.A.
129 D3 Boissevain Can.
123 C2 Boitumelong S. Africa
154 C2 Boituva Brazil
101 E1 Boizenburg Ger.
76 B3 Bojnūrd Iran
75 C2 Bokaro India
118 B3 Bokatola Dem. Rep. Congo
114 A3 Boké Guinea
118 C3 Bokele Dem. Rep. Congo
93 E4 Boknafjorden sea chan. Norway
115 D3 Bokoro Chad
63 A2 Bokpyin Myanmar
89 D2 Boksitogorsk Rus. Fed.
122 B2 Bokspits S. Africa
118 C3 Bokungu Dem. Rep. Congo
115 D3 Bol Chad
114 A3 Bolama Guinea-Bissau
75 C2 Bolangir India
104 C2 Bolbec France
77 E2 Bole China
118 B3 Boleko Dem. Rep. Congo
114 B3 Bolgatanga Ghana
90 B2 Bolhrad Ukr.
66 B1 Boli China
118 B3 Bolia Dem. Rep. Congo
92 H3 Boliden Sweden
110 C2 Bolintin-Vale Romania
137 E3 Bolivar MO U.S.A.
140 C1 Bolivar TN U.S.A.
150 B2 Bolívar, Pico mt. Venez.
152 B1 Bolivia country S. America
89 E3 Bolkhov Rus. Fed.
105 C3 Bollène France
93 G3 Bollnäs Sweden
53 C1 Bollon Austr.
101 E2 Bollstedt Ger.
93 F4 Bolmen l. Sweden
118 B3 Bolobo Dem. Rep. Congo
108 B2 Bologna Italy
89 D2 Bologovo Rus. Fed.
89 D2 Bologoye Rus. Fed.
123 C2 Bolokanang S. Africa
118 B2 Bolomba Dem. Rep. Congo
63 B2 Bolovens, Phouphieng plat. Laos
108 B2 Bolsena, Lago di l. Italy
83 H1 Bol'shevik, Ostrov i. Rus. Fed.
86 E2 Bol'shezemel'skaya Tundra lowland Rus. Fed.
83 L2 Bol'shoy Aluy r. Rus. Fed.
66 B2 Bol'shoy Kamen' Rus. Fed.
Bol'shoy Kavkaz mts Asia/Europe see Caucasus
83 K2 Bol'shoy Lyakhovskiy, Ostrov i. Rus. Fed.
Bol'shoy Tokmak Kyrg. see Tokmok
Bol'shoy Tokmak Ukr. see Tokmak
100 B1 Bolsward Neth.
98 B3 Bolton U.K.
80 B1 Bolu Turkey
59 E3 Bolubolu P.N.G.
92 □A2 Bolungarvík Iceland
108 B1 Bolzano Italy
118 B3 Boma Dem. Rep. Congo
53 D2 Bomaderry Austr.
53 C3 Bombala Austr.
Bombay India see Mumbai
155 C1 Bom Despacho Brazil
75 D2 Bomdila India
154 B1 Bom Jardim de Goiás Brazil
151 E4 Bom Jesus da Lapa Brazil
155 D2 Bom Jesus do Itabapoana Brazil
115 D1 Bon, Cap c. Tunisia
147 D3 Bonaire i. Neth. Antilles
134 C1 Bonaparte, Mount U.S.A.
50 B1 Bonaparte Archipelago is Austr.
131 E3 Bonavista Can.
131 E3 Bonavista Bay Can.
118 C2 Bondo Dem. Rep. Congo
114 B4 Bondoukou Côte d'Ivoire
Bône Alg. see Annaba
61 D2 Bonerate, Kepulauan is Indon.
155 C1 Bonfinópolis de Minas Brazil
117 B4 Bonga Eth.
75 D2 Bongaigaon India
118 C2 Bongandanga Dem. Rep. Congo
122 B2 Bongani S. Africa
118 C2 Bongo, Massif des mts C.A.R.
121 □D2 Bongolava mts Madag.
115 D3 Bongor Chad
114 B4 Bongouanou Côte d'Ivoire
63 B2 Bông Sơn Vietnam
143 D2 Bonham U.S.A.
105 D3 Bonifacio Corsica France
108 A2 Bonifacio, Strait of France/Italy
69 F3 Bonin Islands is Japan
100 C2 Bonn Ger.
134 C1 Bonners Ferry U.S.A.
105 D2 Bonneville France
50 A3 Bonnie Rock Austr.
129 C2 Bonnyville Can.
108 A2 Bonorva Sardinia Italy
53 D1 Bonshaw Austr.
61 C1 Bontang Indon.
114 A4 Bonthe Sierra Leone
64 B2 Bontoc Phil.
61 C2 Bontosunggu Indon.
123 C3 Bontrug S. Africa
53 C1 Boolba Austr.
52 B2 Booligal Austr.
53 C1 Boomi Austr.
53 D1 Boonah Austr.
137 E2 Boone U.S.A.
140 C2 Booneville U.S.A.
137 E3 Boonville U.S.A.
52 B2 Booroorban Austr.
53 C2 Boorowa Austr.
117 C3 Boosaaso Somalia
126 G2 Boothia, Gulf of Can.
126 F2 Boothia Peninsula Can.
118 B3 Booué Gabon
100 C2 Boppard Ger.
144 B2 Boquilla, Presa de la resr Mex.
109 D2 Bor Serb. and Mont.
117 B4 Bor Sudan
80 B2 Bor Turkey
93 F4 Borås Sweden
81 D3 Borāzjān Iran
150 D3 Borba Brazil
104 B3 Bordeaux France
126 E1 Borden Island Can.
127 G2 Borden Peninsula Can.
52 B3 Bordertown Austr.
107 D2 Bordj Bou Arréridj Alg.
107 D2 Bordj Bounaama Alg.
114 B2 Bordj Flye Ste-Marie Alg.
115 C1 Bordj Messaouda Alg.
114 C2 Bordj Mokhtar Alg.
Bordj Omar Driss Alg. see Bordj Omer Driss
115 C2 Bordj Omer Driss Alg.
94 B1 Borðoy i. Faroe Is
Borgå Fin. see Porvoo
92 □A3 Borgarnes Iceland
143 C1 Borger U.S.A.
93 G4 Borgholm Sweden
100 B2 Borgloon Belgium
108 A1 Borgosesia Italy
87 D3 Borisoglebsk Rus. Fed.
89 E2 Borisoglebskiy Rus. Fed.
91 D1 Borisovka Rus. Fed.
119 C2 Bo River Post Sudan
100 C2 Borken Ger.
92 G2 Borkenes Norway
100 C1 Borkum Ger.
100 C1 Borkum i. Ger.
93 G3 Borlänge Sweden
101 F2 Borna Ger.
100 C1 Borne Neth.
61 C1 Borneo i. Asia
93 F4 Bornholm i. Denmark
111 C3 Bornova Turkey
90 B1 Borodyanka Ukr.
77 E2 Borohoro Shan mts China
114 B3 Boron Mali
89 D2 Borovichi Rus. Fed.
89 E2 Borovsk Rus. Fed.
76 C1 Borovskoy Kazakh.
51 C1 Borroloola Austr.
110 B1 Borşa Romania
76 B2 Borsakelmas sho'rxogi salt marsh Uzbek.
90 B2 Borshchiv Ukr.
69 D1 Borshchovochnyy Khrebet mts Rus. Fed.
101 E1 Börßum Ger.
Bortala China see Bole
81 C2 Borūjerd Iran
90 A2 Boryslav Ukr.
90 C1 Boryspil' Ukr.
91 C1 Borzna Ukr.
69 D1 Borzya Rus. Fed.
109 C1 Bosanska Dubica Bos.-Herz.
109 C1 Bosanska Gradiška Bos.-Herz.
109 C2 Bosanska Krupa Bos.-Herz.
109 C1 Bosanski Novi Bos.-Herz.
109 C2 Bosansko Grahovo Bos.-Herz.
71 A3 Bose China
123 C2 Boshof S. Africa
109 C2 Bosnia-Herzegovina country Europe
118 B2 Bosobolo Dem. Rep. Congo
111 C2 Bosporus str. Turkey
142 B2 Bosque U.S.A.
118 B2 Bossangoa C.A.R.
118 B2 Bossembélé C.A.R.
140 B2 Bossier City U.S.A.
122 A2 Bossiesvlei Namibia
68 B2 Bosten Hu l. China
99 C3 Boston U.K.
139 E2 Boston U.S.A.
140 B1 Boston Mountains U.S.A.
53 D2 Botany Bay Austr.
120 B3 Boteti r. Botswana
110 B2 Botev mt. Bulg.
80 A1 Botevgrad Bulg.
92 G3 Bothnia, Gulf of Fin./Sweden
110 C1 Botoşani Romania
70 B2 Botou China
123 C2 Botshabelo S. Africa
120 B3 Botswana country Africa
109 C3 Botte Donato, Monte mt. Italy
136 C1 Bottineau U.S.A.
100 C2 Bottrop Ger.
154 C2 Botucatu Brazil
114 B4 Bouaké Côte d'Ivoire
118 B2 Bouar C.A.R.
114 B1 Bouârfa Morocco
131 D3 Bouctouche Can.
107 E2 Bougaa Alg.
48 G4 Bougainville Island P.N.G.
Bougie Alg. see Bejaïa
114 B3 Bougouni Mali
100 B3 Bouillon Belgium
107 D2 Bouira Alg.
114 A2 Boujdour Western Sahara
50 B3 Boulder Austr.
136 B2 Boulder CO U.S.A.
134 D1 Boulder MT U.S.A.
135 D3 Boulder City U.S.A.
Boulhaut Morocco see Ben Slimane
51 C2 Boulia Austr.
104 C2 Boulogne-Billancourt France
104 C1 Boulogne-sur-Mer France
118 C2 Boulouba C.A.R.
118 B3 Boumango Gabon
118 B2 Boumba r. Cameroon
107 D2 Boumerdes Alg.
114 B4 Bouna Côte d'Ivoire
114 B4 Boundiali Côte d'Ivoire
134 D2 Bountiful U.S.A.
49 I8 Bounty Islands N.Z.
114 B3 Bourem Mali
104 C2 Bourganeuf France
105 D2 Bourg-en-Bresse France
104 C2 Bourges France
Bourgogne reg. France see Burgundy
105 D2 Bourgoin-Jallieu France
53 C2 Bourke Austr.
99 C3 Bourne U.K.
99 C4 Bournemouth U.K.
118 C1 Bourtoutou Chad
115 C1 Bou Saâda Alg.
115 D3 Bousso Chad
100 A2 Boussu Belgium
114 A3 Boutilimit Maur.
128 C3 Bow r. Can.
Bowa China see Muli
51 D2 Bowen Austr.
53 C3 Bowen, Mount Austr.
129 C3 Bow Island Can.
138 B3 Bowling Green KY U.S.A.
137 E3 Bowling Green MO U.S.A.
138 C2 Bowling Green OH U.S.A.
136 C1 Bowman U.S.A.
53 D2 Bowral Austr.
101 D3 Boxberg Ger.
100 B2 Boxtel Neth.
80 B1 Boyabat Turkey
71 B3 Boyang China
97 B2 Boyle Ireland
97 C2 Boyne r. Ireland
136 B2 Boysen Reservoir U.S.A.
152 B2 Boyuibe Bol.
111 C3 Bozburun Turkey
111 C3 Bozcaada i. Turkey
111 C3 Bozdağ mt. Turkey
111 C3 Boz Dağları mts Turkey
111 C3 Bozdoğan Turkey
134 D1 Bozeman U.S.A.
118 B2 Bozoum C.A.R.
111 D3 Bozüyük Turkey
109 C2 Brač i. Croatia
130 C3 Bracebridge Can.
131 D3 Brachet, Lac au l. Can.
93 G3 Bräcke Sweden
99 C4 Bracknell U.K.
109 C2 Bradano r. Italy
141 D3 Bradenton U.S.A.
98 C3 Bradford U.K.
139 D2 Bradford U.S.A.
143 D2 Brady U.S.A.
96 C2 Braemar U.K.
106 B1 Braga Port.
151 E3 Bragança Brazil
106 B1 Bragança Port.
155 C2 Bragança Paulista Brazil
89 D3 Brahin Belarus
75 D2 Brahmanbaria Bangl.
75 C3 Brahmapur India
62 A1 Brahmaputra r. China/India
53 C3 Braidwood Austr.
110 C1 Brăila Romania
137 E1 Brainerd U.S.A.
99 D4 Braintree U.K.
100 B2 Braives Belgium
101 D1 Brake (Unterweser) Ger.
122 A1 Brakwater Namibia
98 B2 Brampton U.K.
101 D1 Bramsche Ger.
150 C3 Branco r. Brazil
101 F1 Brandenburg Ger.
129 E3 Brandon Can.
140 C2 Brandon U.S.A.
97 A2 Brandon Mountain hill Ireland
122 B3 Brandvlei S. Africa
103 D1 Braniewo Pol.
130 B3 Brantford Can.
53 D2 Branxton Austr.
131 D3 Bras d'Or Lake Can.
155 D1 Brasil, Planalto do plat. Brazil
154 C1 Brasilândia Brazil
154 C1 Brasília Brazil
155 D1 Brasília de Minas Brazil
88 C2 Braslaw Belarus
110 C1 Braşov Romania
103 D2 Bratislava Slovakia
83 H3 Bratsk Rus. Fed.
102 C2 Braunau am Inn Austria
101 E1 Braunschweig Ger.
92 □A2 Brautarholt Iceland
Bravo del Norte, Río r. Mex./U.S.A. see Rio Grande
135 C4 Brawley U.S.A.
97 C2 Bray Ireland
150 D2 Brazil country S. America
158 E6 Brazil Basin sea feature S. Atlantic Ocean
143 D3 Brazos r. U.S.A.
118 B3 Brazzaville Congo
109 C2 Brčko Bos.-Herz.
96 C2 Brechin U.K.
100 B2 Brecht Belgium
143 D2 Breckenridge U.S.A.
103 D2 Břeclav Czech Rep.
99 B4 Brecon U.K.
99 B4 Brecon Beacons reg. U.K.
100 B2 Breda Neth.
122 B3 Bredasdorp S. Africa
102 B2 Bregenz Austria
92 H1 Breivikbotn Norway
92 E3 Brekstad Norway
101 D1 Bremen Ger.
101 D1 Bremerhaven Ger.
Bremersdorp Swaziland see Manzini
134 B1 Bremerton U.S.A.
101 D1 Bremervörde Ger.
143 D2 Brenham U.S.A.
108 B1 Brennero Italy
102 C2 Brenner Pass Austria/Italy
99 D4 Brentwood U.K.
108 B1 Brescia Italy
100 A2 Breskens Neth.
108 B1 Bressanone Italy
96 □ Bressay i. U.K.
104 B2 Bressuire France
88 B3 Brest Belarus
104 B2 Brest France
Brest-Litovsk Belarus see Brest
Bretagne reg. France see Brittany
140 C3 Breton Sound b. U.S.A.
151 D3 Breves Brazil
53 C1 Brewarrina Austr.
134 C1 Brewster U.S.A.
89 E2 Breytovo Rus. Fed.
Brezhnev Rus. Fed. see Naberezhnyye Chelny

**109** C1 **Brezovo Polje** hill Croatia
**118** C2 **Bria** C.A.R.
**105** D3 **Briançon** France
**90** B2 **Briceni** Moldova
**Brichany** Moldova see Briceni
**99** B4 **Bridgend** U.K.
**139** E2 **Bridgeport** CT U.S.A.
**136** C2 **Bridgeport** NE U.S.A.
**147** E3 **Bridgetown** Barbados
**131** D3 **Bridgewater** Can.
**99** B3 **Bridgnorth** U.K.
**99** B4 **Bridgwater** U.K.
**99** B4 **Bridgwater Bay** U.K.
**98** C2 **Bridlington** U.K.
**98** C2 **Bridlington Bay** U.K.
**99** B4 **Bridport** U.K.
**105** D2 **Brig** Switz.
**134** D2 **Brigham City** U.S.A.
**53** C3 **Bright** Austr.
**54** B3 **Brighton** N.Z.
**99** C4 **Brighton** U.K.
**136** C3 **Brighton** CO U.S.A.
**138** C2 **Brighton** MI U.S.A.
**105** D3 **Brignoles** France
**114** A3 **Brikama** Gambia
**101** D2 **Brilon** Ger.
**109** C2 **Brindisi** Italy
**97** B1 **Brinlack** Ireland
**53** D1 **Brisbane** Austr.
**99** B4 **Bristol** U.K.
**139** E2 **Bristol** CT U.S.A.
**141** D1 **Bristol** TN U.S.A.
**99** A4 **Bristol Channel** est. U.K.
**128** B2 **British Columbia** prov. Can.
**British Guiana** country S. America
see Guyana
**British Honduras** country
Central America see Belize
**56** C6 **British Indian Ocean Territory**
terr. Indian Ocean
**British Solomon Islands** country
S. Pacific Ocean see
Solomon Islands
**123** C2 **Brits** S. Africa
**122** B3 **Britstown** S. Africa
**104** B2 **Brittany** reg. France
**104** C2 **Brive-la-Gaillarde** France
**106** C1 **Briviesca** Spain
**99** B4 **Brixham** U.K.
**103** D2 **Brno** Czech Rep.
**Broach** India see Bharuch
**141** D1 **Broad** r. U.S.A.
**130** C2 **Broadback** r. Can.
**53** C3 **Broadford** Austr.
**96** B2 **Broadford** U.K.
**96** C3 **Broad Law** hill U.K.
**136** B1 **Broadus** U.S.A.
**129** D2 **Brochet** Can.
**129** D2 **Brochet, Lac** l. Can.
**101** E1 **Bröckel** Ger.
**101** E2 **Brocken** mt. Ger.
**126** E1 **Brock Island** Can.
**130** C3 **Brockville** Can.
**127** G2 **Brodeur Peninsula** Can.
**96** B3 **Brodick** U.K.
**103** D1 **Brodnica** Pol.
**90** B1 **Brody** Ukr.
**143** D1 **Broken Arrow** U.S.A.
**137** D2 **Broken Bow** U.S.A.
**52** B2 **Broken Hill** Austr.
**Broken Hill** Zambia see Kabwe
**159** F6 **Broken Plateau** sea feature
Indian Ocean
**151** D2 **Brokopondo** Suriname
**99** B3 **Bromsgrove** U.K.
**93** E4 **Brønderslev** Denmark
**123** C2 **Bronkhorstspruit** S. Africa
**92** F2 **Brønnøysund** Norway
**64** A3 **Brooke's Point** Phil.
**140** B2 **Brookhaven** U.S.A.
**134** B2 **Brookings** OR U.S.A.
**137** D2 **Brookings** SD U.S.A.
**128** C2 **Brooks** Can.
**126** C2 **Brooks Range** mts U.S.A.
**141** D3 **Brooksville** U.S.A.
**139** D2 **Brookville** U.S.A.
**96** B2 **Broom, Loch** inlet U.K.
**50** B1 **Broome** Austr.
**134** B2 **Brothers** U.S.A.
**Broughton Island** Can. see
Qikiqtarjuaq
**90** C1 **Brovary** Ukr.
**143** D2 **Brownfield** U.S.A.
**128** C3 **Browning** U.S.A.
**140** C1 **Brownsville** TN U.S.A.
**143** D3 **Brownsville** TX U.S.A.
**143** D2 **Brownwood** U.S.A.
**92** □A2 **Brú** Iceland
**104** C1 **Bruay-la-Bussière** France
**138** B1 **Bruce Crossing** U.S.A.
**130** B3 **Bruce Peninsula** Can.
**103** D2 **Bruck an der Mur** Austria
**Bruges** Belgium see Brugge
**100** A2 **Bruint** India
**62** A1 **Brûlé** Can.
**128** C2 **Brûlé** Can.
**151** E4 **Brumado** Brazil
**93** F3 **Brumunddal** Norway
**61** C1 **Brunei** country Asia
**Brunei** Brunei see
**Bandar Seri Begawan**
**102** C2 **Brunico** Italy
**Brünn** Czech Rep. see Brno
**101** D1 **Brunsbüttel** Ger.
**141** D2 **Brunswick** GA U.S.A.

**139** F2 **Brunswick** ME U.S.A.
**53** D1 **Brunswick Head** Austr.
**123** D2 **Bruntville** S. Africa
**136** C2 **Brush** U.S.A.
**100** B2 **Brussels** Belgium
**Bruxelles** Belgium see Brussels
**143** D3 **Bryan** U.S.A.
**89** D3 **Bryansk** Rus. Fed.
**91** D2 **Bryn'kovskaya** Rus. Fed.
**91** D2 **Bryukhovetskaya** Rus. Fed.
**103** D1 **Brzeg** Pol.
**Brześć nad Bugiem** Belarus see
Brest
**114** A3 **Buba** Guinea-Bissau
**111** C3 **Buca** Turkey
**80** B2 **Bucak** Turkey
**150** B2 **Bucaramanga** Col.
**90** B2 **Buchach** Ukr.
**53** C3 **Buchan** Austr.
**114** A4 **Buchanan** Liberia
**110** C2 **Bucharest** Romania
**101** D1 **Bucholz in der Nordheide** Ger.
**110** C1 **Bucin, Pasul** pass Romania
**101** D1 **Bückeburg** Ger.
**142** A2 **Buckeye** U.S.A.
**96** C2 **Buckhaven** U.K.
**96** C2 **Buckie** U.K.
**99** C3 **Buckingham** U.K.
**51** C1 **Buckingham Bay** Austr.
**51** D2 **Buckland Tableland** reg. Austr.
**52** A2 **Buckleboo** Austr.
**139** F2 **Bucksport** U.S.A.
**103** D2 **Bučovice** Czech Rep.
**Bucureşti** Romania see
Bucharest
**89** D3 **Buda-Kashalyova** Belarus
**103** D2 **Budapest** Hungary
**75** B2 **Budaun** India
**108** A2 **Buddusò** Sardinia Italy
**99** A4 **Bude** U.K.
**87** D4 **Budennovsk** Rus. Fed.
**Budennoye** Rus. Fed. see
Krasnogvardeyskoye
**89** D3 **Budogoshch'** Rus. Fed.
**108** A2 **Budoni** Sardinia Italy
**Budweis** Czech Rep. see
České Budějovice
**118** A2 **Buea** Cameroon
**135** B4 **Buellton** U.S.A.
**150** B2 **Buenaventura** Col.
**144** B2 **Buenaventura** Mex.
**Buena Vista** i. N. Mariana Is see
Tinian
**106** C1 **Buendia, Embalse de** resr Spain
**155** D1 **Buenópolis** Brazil
**153** C3 **Buenos Aires** Arg.
**153** A4 **Buenos Aires, Lago** l. Arg./Chile
**139** D2 **Buffalo** NY U.S.A.
**136** C1 **Buffalo** SD U.S.A.
**143** D2 **Buffalo** TX U.S.A.
**136** B2 **Buffalo** WY U.S.A.
**129** D2 **Buffalo Narrows** Can.
**121** C3 **Buffalo Range** Zimbabwe
**122** A2 **Buffels** watercourse S. Africa
**123** C1 **Buffels Drift** S. Africa
**110** C2 **Buftea** Romania
**103** E1 **Bug** r. Pol.
**61** C2 **Bugel, Tanjung** pt Indon.
**109** C2 **Bugojno** Bos.-Herz.
**86** D2 **Bugrino** Rus. Fed.
**64** A3 **Bugsuk** i. Phil.
**87** E3 **Bugul'ma** Rus. Fed.
**87** E3 **Buguruslan** Rus. Fed.
**121** C2 **Buhera** Zimbabwe
**110** C1 **Buhuşi** Romania
**99** B3 **Builth Wells** U.K.
**69** D1 **Buir Nur** l. Mongolia
**120** A3 **Buitepos** Namibia
**109** D2 **Bujanovac** Serb. and Mont.
**119** C3 **Bujumbura** Burundi
**69** D1 **Bukachacha** Rus. Fed.
**120** B2 **Bukalo** Namibia
**119** C3 **Bukavu** Dem. Rep. Congo
**Bukhara** Uzbek. see Buxoro
**60** B2 **Bukittinggi** Indon.
**119** D3 **Bukoba** Tanz.
**103** D1 **Bukowiec** hill Pol.
**59** C3 **Bula** Indon.
**59** C3 **Buryn'** Ukr.
**53** C1 **Bulahdelal** Austr.
**121** B3 **Bulawayo** Zimbabwe
**111** C3 **Buldan** Turkey
**123** D2 **Bulembu** Swaziland
**68** C1 **Bulgan** Mongolia
**110** C2 **Bulgaria** country Europe
**54** B2 **Buller** r. N.Z.
**142** A1 **Bullhead City** U.S.A.
**52** B1 **Bulloo** watercourse Austr.
**52** B1 **Bulloo Downs** Austr.
**122** A1 **Bullsport** Namibia
**61** D2 **Bulukumba** Indon.
**118** B3 **Bulungu** Dem. Rep. Congo
**118** B3 **Bumba** Dem. Rep. Congo
**118** C2 **Bumba** Dem. Rep. Congo
**62** A1 **Bumhkang** Myanmar
**118** B3 **Buna** Dem. Rep. Congo
**97** B1 **Bunbeg** Ireland
**50** A3 **Bunbury** Austr.
**97** C2 **Bunclody** Ireland
**97** C1 **Buncrana** Ireland
**119** D3 **Bunda** Tanz.
**51** E2 **Bundaberg** Austr.
**53** C1 **Bundaleer** Austr.
**53** C2 **Bundarra** Austr.
**74** B2 **Bundi** India
**97** B1 **Bundoran** Ireland

**75** C2 **Bundu** India
**53** C3 **Bungendore** Austr.
**119** D2 **Bungoma** Kenya
**67** B4 **Bungo-suidō** sea chan. Japan
**119** D2 **Bunia** Dem. Rep. Congo
**118** C3 **Buninga** Dem. Rep. Congo
**63** B2 **Buôn Mê Thuôt** Vietnam
**119** D3 **Bura** Kenya
**117** C3 **Buraan** Somalia
**Burang** China see Jirang
**78** B2 **Buraydah** Saudi Arabia
**101** D2 **Burbach** Ger.
**117** C4 **Burco** Somalia
**100** B1 **Burdaard** Neth.
**111** D3 **Burdwan** India see Barddhaman
**117** B3 **Burē** Eth.
**99** D3 **Bure** r. U.K.
**69** E1 **Bureinskiy Khrebet** mts Rus. Fed.
**101** D2 **Büren** Ger.
**Bureya Range** mts Rus. Fed. see
Bureinskiy Khrebet
**110** C2 **Burgas** Bulg.
**101** E1 **Burg bei Magdeburg** Ger.
**101** E1 **Burgdorf** Ger.
**101** E1 **Burgdorf** Ger.
**131** E3 **Burgeo** Can.
**123** C3 **Burgersdorp** S. Africa
**123** D1 **Burgersfort** S. Africa
**100** A2 **Burgh-Haamstede** Neth.
**101** F3 **Burglengenfeld** Ger.
**145** C2 **Burgos** Mex.
**106** C1 **Burgos** Spain
**105** C2 **Burgundy** reg. France
**111** C3 **Burhaniye** Turkey
**74** B2 **Burhanpur** India
**75** C2 **Burhar-Dhanpuri** India
**101** D1 **Burhave (Butjadingen)** Ger.
**154** C2 **Buri** Brazil
**60** B2 **Buriai** Indon.
**64** B2 **Burias** i. Phil.
**131** E3 **Burin** Can.
**63** B2 **Buriram** Thai.
**154** C1 **Buriti Alegre** Brazil
**151** E3 **Buriti Bravo** Brazil
**155** C1 **Buritis** Brazil
**107** C2 **Burjassot** Spain
**143** D2 **Burkburnett** U.S.A.
**51** C1 **Burketown** Austr.
**114** B3 **Burkina** country Africa
**134** D2 **Burley** U.S.A.
**136** C3 **Burlington** CO U.S.A.
**137** E2 **Burlington** IA U.S.A.
**141** E1 **Burlington** NC U.S.A.
**139** E2 **Burlington** VT U.S.A.
**Burma** country see Myanmar
**134** B2 **Burney** U.S.A.
**51** D4 **Burnie** Austr.
**98** B3 **Burnley** U.K.
**134** C2 **Burns** U.S.A.
**134** C2 **Burns Junction** U.S.A.
**128** B2 **Burns Lake** Can.
**137** E2 **Burnsville** U.S.A.
**101** F1 **Burow** Ger.
**77** E2 **Burqin** China
**52** A2 **Burra** Austr.
**109** D2 **Burrel** Albania
**97** B2 **Burren** reg. Ireland
**53** C2 **Burrendong Reservoir** Austr.
**53** C2 **Burren Junction** Austr.
**107** C2 **Burriana** Spain
**53** C2 **Burrinjuck Reservoir** Austr.
**144** B2 **Burro, Serranías del** mts Mex.
**111** C2 **Bursa** Turkey
**116** B2 **Bûr Safâjah** Egypt
**Bûr Sa'îd** Egypt see Port Said
**Bûr Sa'îd** Egypt see Port Said
**Bûr Sudan** Sudan see Port Sudan
**130** C2 **Burton, Lac** l. Can.
**97** B1 **Burtonport** Ireland
**99** C3 **Burton upon Trent** U.K.
**52** B2 **Burtundy** Austr.
**59** C3 **Buru** i. Indon.
**119** C3 **Burundi** country Africa
**119** C3 **Bururi** Burundi
**96** C1 **Burwick** U.K.
**98** B3 **Bury** U.K.
**91** C1 **Bury St Edmunds** U.K.
**99** D3 **Bury St Edmunds** U.K.
**118** C3 **Busanga** Dem. Rep. Congo
**81** D3 **Büshehr** Iran
**119** D3 **Bushenyi** Uganda
**Bushire** Iran see Büshehr
**118** C2 **Businga** Dem. Rep. Congo
**50** A3 **Busselton** Austr.
**143** C3 **Bustamante** Mex.
**108** A1 **Busto Arsizio** Italy
**64** A2 **Busuanga** Phil.
**118** C2 **Buta** Dem. Rep. Congo
**119** C3 **Butare** Rwanda
**96** B3 **Bute** i. U.K.
**119** C2 **Butembo** Dem. Rep. Congo
**123** C2 **Butha-Buthe** Lesotho
**139** D2 **Butler** U.S.A.
**59** C3 **Buton** i. Indon.
**134** D1 **Butte** U.S.A.
**60** B1 **Butterworth** Malaysia
**96** A1 **Butt of Lewis** hd U.K.
**129** E2 **Button Bay** Can.
**131** D1 **Button Islands** Can.
**64** B3 **Butuan** Phil.
**89** F3 **Buturlinovka** Rus. Fed.
**75** C2 **Butwal** Nepal
**101** D2 **Butzbach** Ger.

**117** C4 **Buulobarde** Somalia
**117** C5 **Buur Gaabo** Somalia
**117** C4 **Buurhabaka** Somalia
**78** A2 **Buwâṭah** Saudi Arabia
**76** C3 **Buxoro** Uzbek.
**101** D1 **Buxtehude** Ger.
**98** C3 **Buxton** U.K.
**89** F2 **Buy** Rus. Fed.
**87** D4 **Buynaksk** Rus. Fed.
**111** C3 **Büyükmenderes** r. Turkey
**65** A1 **Buyun Shan** mt. China
**74** B2 **Buzai Gumbad** Afgh.
**110** C1 **Buzău** Romania
**110** C1 **Buzău** r. Romania
**121** C2 **Búzi** Moz.
**87** E3 **Buzuluk** Rus. Fed.
**88** C3 **Byahoml'** Belarus
**110** C2 **Byala** Bulg.
**110** C2 **Byala** Bulg.
**88** C3 **Byalynichy** Belarus
**88** B3 **Byarezina** r. Belarus
**88** B3 **Byaroza** Belarus
**88** C3 **Byarozawka** Belarus
**103** D1 **Bydgoszcz** Pol.
**Byelorussia** country Europe see
Belarus
**88** C3 **Byerazino** Belarus
**88** C3 **Byeshankovichy** Belarus
**89** D3 **Bykhaw** Belarus
**127** G2 **Bylot Island** Can.
**53** C2 **Byrock** Austr.
**53** D1 **Byron Bay** Austr.
**83** J2 **Bytantay** r. Rus. Fed.
**103** D1 **Bytom** Pol.
**103** D1 **Bytów** Pol.

**C**

**120** A2 **Caála** Angola
**154** B2 **Caarapó** Brazil
**155** C1 **Caatinga** Brazil
**144** B2 **Caballos Mesteños, Llano de los**
plain Mex.
**106** B1 **Cabañaquinta** Spain
**64** B2 **Cabanatuan** Phil.
**117** C3 **Cabdul Qaadir** Somalia
**154** A1 **Cabeceira Rio Manso** Brazil
**154** C1 **Cabeceiras** Brazil
**106** B2 **Cabeza del Buey** Spain
**152** B1 **Cabezas** Bol.
**150** B1 **Cabimas** Venez.
**120** A1 **Cabinda** Angola
**118** B3 **Cabinda** prov. Angola
**151** F3 **Cabo** Brazil
**155** D2 **Cabo Frio** Brazil
**155** D2 **Cabo Frio, Ilha do** i. Brazil
**130** C3 **Cabonga, Réservoir** resr Can.
**53** D1 **Caboolture** Austr.
**150** B3 **Cabo Pantoja** Peru
**121** C2 **Cabora Bassa, Lake** resr Moz.
**144** A1 **Caborca** Mex.
**131** D3 **Cabot Strait** Can.
**106** C2 **Cabra** Spain
**155** D1 **Cabral, Serra do** mts Brazil
**107** D2 **Cabrera** i. Spain
**106** B1 **Cabrera, Sierra de la** mts Spain
**129** D2 **Cabri** Can.
**107** C2 **Cabriel** r. Spain
**154** B2 **Caçador** Brazil
**109** D2 **Čačak** Serb. and Mont.
**108** A2 **Caccia, Capo** c. Sardinia Italy
**106** B2 **Cacém** Port.
**151** D4 **Cáceres** Brazil
**106** B2 **Cáceres** Spain
**128** B2 **Cache Creek** Can.
**114** A3 **Cacheu** Guinea-Bissau
**151** D3 **Cachimbo, Serra do** hills Brazil
**154** B1 **Cachoeira Alta** Brazil
**155** D2 **Cachoeiro de Itapemirim** Brazil
**114** A3 **Cacine** Guinea-Bissau
**120** A2 **Cacolo** Angola
**120** A2 **Caconda** Angola
**154** B1 **Caçu** Brazil
**103** D2 **Čadca** Slovakia
**101** D1 **Cadenberge** Ger.
**145** B2 **Cadereyta** Mex.
**138** B2 **Cadillac** U.S.A.
**64** B2 **Cadiz** Phil.
**106** B2 **Cádiz** Spain
**106** B2 **Cádiz, Golfo de** g. Spain
**128** C2 **Cadotte Lake** Can.
**104** B2 **Caen** France
**Caerdydd** U.K. see Cardiff
**Caerfyrddin** U.K. see Carmarthen
**Caergybi** U.K. see Holyhead
**98** A3 **Caernarfon** U.K.
**99** A3 **Caernarfon Bay** U.K.
**Caernarvon** U.K. see Caernarfon
**152** B2 **Cafayate** Arg.
**154** C1 **Cafelândia** Brazil
**64** B2 **Cagayan de Oro** Phil.
**108** B2 **Cagli** Italy
**108** A3 **Cagliari** Sardinia Italy
**108** A3 **Cagliari, Golfo di** b. Sardinia Italy
**120** A2 **Cahama** Angola
**97** B3 **Caha Mountains** hills Ireland
**97** A3 **Cahermore** Ireland
**97** B3 **Cahersiveen** Ireland
**97** C2 **Cahir** Ireland
**Cahora Bassa, Lago de** resr Moz.
see Cabora Bassa, Lake
**97** C2 **Cahore Point** Ireland
**104** C3 **Cahors** France

90 B2 **Cahul** Moldova
121 C2 **Caia** Moz.
151 D4 **Caiabis, Serra dos** *hills* Brazil
120 B2 **Caianda** Angola
154 B1 **Caiapó, Serra de** *mts* Brazil
154 B1 **Caiapônia** Brazil
147 C2 **Caicos Islands** Turks and Caicos Is
96 C2 **Cairngorm Mountains** U.K.
96 B3 **Cairnryan** U.K.
51 D1 **Cairns** Austr.
116 B1 **Cairo** Egypt
**Caisleán an Bharraigh** Ireland *see* Castlebar
98 C3 **Caistor** U.K.
120 A2 **Caiundo** Angola
150 B3 **Cajamarca** Peru
109 C1 **Čakovec** Croatia
123 C3 **Cala** S. Africa
115 C4 **Calabar** Nigeria
110 B2 **Calabozo** Venez.
110 B2 **Calafat** Romania
153 A5 **Calafate** Arg.
107 C1 **Calahorra** Spain
120 A1 **Calai** Angola
104 C1 **Calais** France
139 F1 **Calais** U.S.A.
152 B2 **Calama** Chile
64 A2 **Calamian Group** *is* Phil.
107 C1 **Calamocha** Spain
120 A2 **Calandula** Angola
60 A1 **Calang** Indon.
115 E1 **Calanscio Sand Sea** *des.* Libya
64 B2 **Calapan** Phil.
110 C2 **Călăraşi** Romania
107 C1 **Calatayud** Spain
64 B2 **Calayan** *i.* Phil.
64 B2 **Calbayog** Phil.
151 F3 **Calcanhar, Ponta do** *pt* Brazil
151 D2 **Calçoene** Brazil
**Calcutta** India *see* Kolkata
106 B2 **Caldas da Rainha** Port.
154 B1 **Caldas Novas** Brazil
152 A2 **Caldera** Chile
51 D2 **Caldervale** Austr.
134 C2 **Caldwell** U.S.A.
123 C3 **Caledon** *r.* Lesotho/S. Africa
122 A3 **Caledon** S. Africa
153 B4 **Caleta Olivia** Arg.
98 A1 **Calf of Man** *i.* Isle of Man
128 C2 **Calgary** Can.
150 B2 **Cali** Col.
73 B3 **Calicut** India
135 D3 **Caliente** U.S.A.
135 B2 **California** *state* U.S.A.
144 A1 **California, Gulf of** *g.* Mex.
135 B3 **California Aqueduct** *canal* U.S.A.
81 C2 **Cälilabad** Azer.
122 B3 **Calitzdorp** S. Africa
145 C2 **Calkiní** Mex.
52 B1 **Callabonna, Lake** *salt flat* Austr.
135 C3 **Callaghan, Mount** U.S.A.
97 C2 **Callan** Ireland
96 B2 **Callander** U.K.
150 B4 **Callao** Peru
99 A4 **Callington** U.K.
108 B3 **Caltagirone** *Sicily* Italy
108 B3 **Caltanissetta** *Sicily* Italy
120 A1 **Calulo** Angola
120 B2 **Calunda** Angola
120 A2 **Caluquembe** Angola
117 D3 **Caluula** Somalia
105 D3 **Calvi** *Corsica* France
107 D2 **Calvià** Spain
144 B2 **Calvillo** Mex.
122 A3 **Calvinia** S. Africa
109 C2 **Calvo, Monte** *mt.* Italy
120 A1 **Camabatela** Angola
151 F4 **Camaçari** Brazil
144 B2 **Camacho** Mex.
120 A2 **Camacupa** Angola
146 C2 **Camagüey** Cuba
146 C2 **Camagüey, Archipiélago de** *is* Cuba
150 B4 **Camana** Peru
120 B2 **Camanongue** Angola
154 B1 **Camapuã** Brazil
145 C2 **Camargo** Mex.
63 B3 **Ca Mau** Vietnam
**Cambay** India *see* Khambhat
63 B2 **Cambodia** *country* Asia
99 A4 **Camborne** U.K.
105 C1 **Cambrai** France
99 B3 **Cambrian Mountains** *hills* U.K.
138 C2 **Cambridge** Can.
54 C1 **Cambridge** N.Z.
99 D3 **Cambridge** U.K.
139 E2 **Cambridge** *MA* U.S.A.
139 D3 **Cambridge** *MD* U.S.A.
137 E1 **Cambridge** *MN* U.S.A.
138 C2 **Cambridge** *OH* U.S.A.
126 E2 **Cambridge Bay** Can.
131 D2 **Cambrien, Lac** *l.* Can.
120 B1 **Cambulo** Angola
53 D2 **Camden** Austr.
140 B2 **Camden** *AR* U.S.A.
139 F2 **Camden** *ME* U.S.A.
139 D3 **Camden** *NJ* U.S.A.
137 E3 **Camdenton** U.S.A.
137 E3 **Cameron** U.S.A.
118 B2 **Cameroon** *country* Africa
118 A2 **Cameroun, Mont** *vol.* Cameroon
151 E3 **Cametá** Brazil
64 B2 **Camiguin** *i.* Phil.
64 B3 **Camiguin** *i.* Phil.
152 B2 **Camiri** Bol.

151 E3 **Camocim** Brazil
51 C1 **Camooweal** Austr.
63 A3 **Camorta** *i.* India
153 A4 **Campana, Isla** *i.* Chile
155 D1 **Campanário** Brazil
122 B2 **Campanha** Brazil
122 B2 **Campbell** S. Africa
54 B2 **Campbell, Cape** N.Z.
48 H9 **Campbell Island** N.Z.
156 D9 **Campbell Plateau** *sea feature*
  S. Pacific Ocean
128 B2 **Campbell River** Can.
138 B3 **Campbellsville** U.S.A.
131 D3 **Campbellton** Can.
53 D2 **Campbelltown** Austr.
96 B3 **Campbeltown** U.K.
145 C3 **Campeche** Mex.
145 C3 **Campeche, Bahía de** *g.* Mex.
52 B3 **Camperdown** Austr.
110 C1 **Câmpina** Romania
151 F3 **Campina Grande** Brazil
154 C2 **Campinas** Brazil
154 C1 **Campina Verde** Brazil
108 B2 **Campobasso** Italy
155 C2 **Campo Belo** Brazil
154 C1 **Campo Florido** Brazil
152 B2 **Campo Gallo** Arg.
154 B2 **Campo Grande** Brazil
154 C3 **Campo Largo** Brazil
151 E3 **Campo Maior** Brazil
106 B2 **Campo Maior** Port.
150 B1 **Campo Mara** Venez.
109 C2 **Campomarino** Italy
151 C2 **Campo Mourão** Brazil
155 D2 **Campos** Brazil
155 C1 **Campos Altos** Brazil
155 C2 **Campos do Jordão** Brazil
110 C1 **Câmpulung** Romania
142 A2 **Camp Verde** U.S.A.
63 B2 **Cam Ranh** Vietnam
63 B2 **Cam Ranh, Vinh** *b.* Vietnam
**Cam Ranh Bay** Vietnam *see*
  Cam Ranh, Vinh
128 C2 **Camrose** Can.
129 D2 **Camsell Portage** Can.
111 C3 **Çan** Turkey
126 F2 **Canada** *country* N. America
160 A2 **Canada Basin** *sea feature*
  Arctic Ocean
143 C1 **Canadian** U.S.A.
143 D1 **Canadian** *r.* U.S.A.
111 C2 **Çanakkale** Turkey
144 A1 **Cananea** Mex.
154 C2 **Cananéia** Brazil
114 A2 **Canary Islands** *terr.*
  N. Atlantic Ocean
154 C1 **Canastra, Serra da** *mts* Goiás
  Brazil
155 C1 **Canastra, Serra da** *mts*
  Minas Gerais Brazil
144 B2 **Canatlán** Mex.
141 D3 **Canaveral, Cape** U.S.A.
155 E1 **Canavieiras** Brazil
53 C2 **Canbelego** Austr.
53 C3 **Canberra** Austr.
145 D2 **Cancún** Mex.
111 C3 **Çandarlı** Turkey
155 C2 **Candeias** Brazil
145 C3 **Candelaria** Mex.
154 B2 **Cândido de Abreu** Brazil
129 D2 **Candle Lake** Can.
137 D1 **Cando** U.S.A.
120 A2 **Cangamba** Angola
106 B1 **Cangas** Spain
106 B1 **Cangas del Narcea** Spain
120 B2 **Cangombe** Angola
152 C3 **Canguçu** Brazil
70 B2 **Cangzhou** China
131 D2 **Caniapiscau** Can.
131 D2 **Caniapiscau** *r.* Can.
131 C2 **Caniapiscau, Lac** *l.* Can.
**Caniçado** Moz. *see* Guija
108 B3 **Canicattì** *Sicily* Italy
151 F3 **Canindé** Brazil
144 B2 **Cañitas de Felipe Pescador** Mex.
80 B1 **Çankırı** Turkey
128 C2 **Canmore** Can.
96 A2 **Canna** *i.* U.K.
73 B3 **Cannanore** India
105 D3 **Cannes** France
99 B3 **Cannock** U.K.
53 C3 **Cann River** Austr.
152 C2 **Canoas** Brazil
129 D2 **Canoe Lake** Can.
154 B3 **Canoinhas** Brazil
136 B3 **Canon City** U.S.A.
52 B2 **Canopus** Austr.
129 D2 **Canora** Can.
53 C2 **Canowindra** Austr.
131 D3 **Canso** Can.
**Cantabrian Mountains** Spain *see*
  Cantábrica, Cordillera
**Cantabrian Sea** Spain *see*
  Cantábrico, Mar
106 C1 **Cantábrica, Cordillera** *mts* Spain
106 B1 **Cantábrico, Mar** *sea feature* Spain
99 D4 **Canterbury** U.K.
54 B2 **Canterbury Bight** *b.* N.Z.
54 B2 **Canterbury Plains** N.Z.
63 B2 **Cân Thơ** Vietnam
151 E3 **Canto do Buriti** Brazil
**Canton** China *see* Guangzhou
137 E2 **Canton** *MO* U.S.A.
140 C2 **Canton** *MS* U.S.A.
139 D2 **Canton** *NY* U.S.A.

138 C2 **Canton** *OH* U.S.A.
143 C1 **Canyon** U.S.A.
134 D1 **Canyon Ferry Lake** U.S.A.
134 B2 **Canyonville** U.S.A.
62 B1 **Cao Bằng** Vietnam
109 C2 **Capaccio** Italy
154 C2 **Capão Bonito** Brazil
155 D2 **Caparaó, Serra do** *mts* Brazil
139 E1 **Cap-de-la-Madeleine** Can.
51 D1 **Cape Barren Island** Austr.
158 F7 **Cape Basin** *sea feature*
  S. Atlantic Ocean
52 A3 **Cape Borda** Austr.
131 D3 **Cape Breton Island** Can.
141 D3 **Cape Canaveral** U.S.A.
139 D3 **Cape Charles** U.S.A.
114 B4 **Cape Coast** Ghana
139 E2 **Cape Cod Bay** U.S.A.
141 D3 **Cape Coral** U.S.A.
127 G2 **Cape Dorset** Can.
141 E2 **Cape Fear** *r.* U.S.A.
137 F3 **Cape Girardeau** U.S.A.
155 D1 **Capelinha** Brazil
100 B2 **Capelle aan de IJssel** Neth.
**Capelongo** Angola *see* Kuvango
139 E3 **Cape May Point** U.S.A.
120 A1 **Capenda-Camulemba** Angola
122 A3 **Cape Town** S. Africa
158 E3 **Cape Verde** *country*
  N. Atlantic Ocean
158 D4 **Cape Verde Basin** *sea feature*
  N. Atlantic Ocean
51 D1 **Cape York Peninsula** Austr.
147 C3 **Cap-Haïtien** Haiti
151 E3 **Capim** *r.* Brazil
154 A2 **Capitán Bado** Para.
58 D1 **Capitol Hill** N. Mariana Is
154 B2 **Capivara, Represa** *resr* Brazil
109 C2 **Čapljina** Bos.-Herz.
109 B3 **Capo d'Orlando** *Sicily* Italy
108 A2 **Capraia, Isola di** *i.* Italy
108 A2 **Caprara, Punta** *pt* Sardinia Italy
108 B2 **Capri, Isola di** *i.* Italy
51 E2 **Capricorn Channel** Austr.
120 B2 **Caprivi Strip** *reg.* Namibia
143 C2 **Cap Rock Escarpment** U.S.A.
143 C1 **Capulin** U.S.A.
150 B2 **Caquetá** *r.* Col.
110 B2 **Caracal** Romania
150 C2 **Caracarai** Brazil
150 C1 **Caracas** Venez.
151 E3 **Caracol** Brazil
155 C2 **Caraguatatuba** Brazil
153 A3 **Carahue** Chile
155 D1 **Caraí** Brazil
151 D3 **Carajás, Serra dos** *hills* Brazil
155 D2 **Carandaí** Brazil
155 D2 **Carangola** Brazil
110 B1 **Caransebeş** Romania
131 D3 **Caraquet** Can.
146 B3 **Caratasca, Laguna de** *lag.* Hond.
155 D1 **Caratinga** Brazil
150 B2 **Carauari** Brazil
107 C2 **Caravaca de la Cruz** Spain
155 E1 **Caravelas** Brazil
129 E3 **Carberry** Can.
144 A2 **Carbó** Mex.
108 A3 **Carbonara, Capo** *c.* Sardinia Italy
136 B3 **Carbondale** *CO* U.S.A.
138 B3 **Carbondale** *IL* U.S.A.
139 D2 **Carbondale** *PA* U.S.A.
131 E2 **Carbonear** Can.
155 D1 **Carbonita** Brazil
107 C2 **Carcaixent** Spain
104 C3 **Carcassonne** France
128 A1 **Carcross** Can.
146 B2 **Cárdenas** Cuba
145 C3 **Cárdenas** Mex.
99 B4 **Cardiff** U.K.
99 A3 **Cardigan** U.K.
99 A3 **Cardigan Bay** U.K.
154 C2 **Cardoso** Brazil
128 C3 **Cardston** Can.
110 B1 **Carei** Romania
104 B2 **Carentan** France
50 B2 **Carey, Lake** *salt flat* Austr.
155 D2 **Cariacica** Brazil
146 B3 **Caribbean Sea** N. Atlantic Ocean
128 B2 **Cariboo Mountains** Can.
139 F1 **Caribou** U.S.A.
130 B2 **Caribou Lake** Can.
128 C2 **Caribou Mountains** Can.
144 B2 **Carichic** Mex.
100 B3 **Carignan** France
53 C2 **Carinda** Austr.
107 C1 **Cariñena** Spain
130 C3 **Carleton Place** Can.
123 C2 **Carletonville** S. Africa
135 C2 **Carlin** U.S.A.
97 C1 **Carlingford Lough** *inlet*
  Ireland/U.K.
138 B3 **Carlinville** U.S.A.
98 B2 **Carlisle** U.K.
139 D2 **Carlisle** U.S.A.
155 D1 **Carlos Chagas** Brazil
97 C2 **Carlow** Ireland
96 A1 **Carloway** U.K.
135 C4 **Carlsbad** *CA* U.S.A.
142 C2 **Carlsbad** *NM* U.S.A.
129 D3 **Carlyle** Can.
128 A1 **Carmacks** Can.
129 E3 **Carman** Can.
99 A4 **Carmarthen** U.K.
99 A4 **Carmarthen Bay** U.K.
104 C3 **Carmaux** France

145 C3 **Carmelita** Guat.
144 A2 **Carmen, Isla** *i.* Mex.
155 C1 **Carmo do Paranaíba** Brazil
**Carmona** Angola *see* Uíge
106 B2 **Carmona** Spain
104 B2 **Carnac** France
50 A2 **Carnarvon** Austr.
122 B3 **Carnarvon** S. Africa
97 C1 **Carndonagh** Ireland
129 D3 **Carnduff** Can.
50 B2 **Carnegie, Lake** *salt flat* Austr.
96 B2 **Carn Eighe** *mt.* U.K.
55 S2 **Carney Island** Antarctica
73 D4 **Car Nicobar** *i.* India
118 B2 **Carnot** C.A.R.
52 A2 **Carnot, Cape** Austr.
96 C2 **Carnoustie** U.K.
97 C2 **Carnsore Point** Ireland
151 E3 **Carolina** Brazil
49 L4 **Caroline Island** Kiribati
59 D2 **Caroline Islands** N. Pacific Ocean
122 A3 **Carolusberg** S. Africa
103 D2 **Carpathian Mountains** Europe
**Carpaţii Meridionali** *mts* Romania
  *see* Transylvanian Alps
51 C1 **Carpentaria, Gulf of** Austr.
105 D3 **Carpentras** France
108 B2 **Carpi** Italy
141 D3 **Carrabelle** U.S.A.
97 B3 **Carrantuohill** *mt.* Ireland
108 B2 **Carrara** Italy
97 C1 **Carrickfergus** U.K.
97 C1 **Carrickmacross** Ireland
97 B2 **Carrick-on-Shannon** Ireland
97 C2 **Carrick-on-Suir** Ireland
137 D1 **Carrington** U.S.A.
143 D3 **Carrizo Springs** U.S.A.
142 B2 **Carrizozo** U.S.A.
137 E2 **Carroll** U.S.A.
141 C2 **Carrollton** U.S.A.
129 D2 **Carrot River** Can.
135 C3 **Carson City** U.S.A.
135 C3 **Carson Sink** *l.* U.S.A.
**Carstensz-top** *mt.* Indon. *see*
  Jaya, Puncak
150 B1 **Cartagena** Col.
107 C2 **Cartagena** Spain
146 B4 **Cartago** Costa Rica
54 C2 **Carterton** N.Z.
137 E3 **Carthage** *MO* U.S.A.
143 E2 **Carthage** *TX* U.S.A.
131 E2 **Cartwright** Can.
151 F3 **Caruarú** Brazil
150 C1 **Carúpano** Venez.
52 B1 **Caryapundy Swamp** Austr.
114 B1 **Casablanca** Morocco
154 C2 **Casa Branca** Brazil
144 B1 **Casa de Janos** Mex.
142 A2 **Casa Grande** U.S.A.
108 A1 **Casale Monferrato** Italy
109 C2 **Casarano** Italy
144 B1 **Casas Grandes** Mex.
134 C2 **Cascade** U.S.A.
134 B2 **Cascade Range** *mts* Can./U.S.A.
106 B2 **Cascais** Port.
151 F3 **Cascavel** Brazil
154 B2 **Cascavel** Brazil
139 F2 **Casco Bay** U.S.A.
108 B2 **Caserta** Italy
97 C2 **Cashel** Ireland
153 B3 **Casilda** Arg.
53 D1 **Casino** Austr.
**Casnewydd** U.K. *see* Newport
107 C1 **Caspe** Spain
136 B2 **Casper** U.S.A.
76 A2 **Caspian Lowland**
  Kazakh./Rus. Fed.
81 C2 **Caspian Sea** Asia/Europe
**Cassaigne** Alg. *see* Sidi Ali
154 C2 **Cássia** Brazil
128 B2 **Cassiar** Can.
128 A2 **Cassiar Mountains** Can.
154 B1 **Cassilândia** Brazil
120 A2 **Cassinga** Angola
108 B2 **Cassino** Italy
96 B2 **Cassley** *r.* U.K.
151 E3 **Castanhal** Brazil
152 B3 **Castaño** *r.* Arg.
144 B2 **Castaños** Mex.
104 C3 **Casteljaloux** France
105 D3 **Castellane** France
107 C2 **Castelló de la Plana** Spain
155 D2 **Castelo** Brazil
106 B2 **Castelo Branco** Port.
104 C3 **Castelsarrasin** France
108 B3 **Castelvetrano** *Sicily* Italy
52 B3 **Casterton** Austr.
108 B2 **Castiglione della Pescaia** Italy
106 C2 **Castilla - La Mancha** *reg.* Spain
106 C1 **Castilla y León** *reg.* Spain
97 B2 **Castlebar** Ireland
96 A2 **Castlebay** U.K.
97 C1 **Castleblayney** Ireland
97 C1 **Castlederg** U.K.
96 C3 **Castle Douglas** U.K.
128 C3 **Castlegar** Can.
97 B2 **Castleisland** Ireland
52 B3 **Castlemaine** Austr.
97 C2 **Castlepollard** Ireland
97 B2 **Castlerea** Ireland
53 C2 **Castlereagh** *r.* Austr.
136 B3 **Castle Rock** U.S.A.
128 C2 **Castor** Can.
104 C3 **Castres** France
100 B1 **Castricum** Neth.

**147** D3 **Castries** St Lucia
**154** C2 **Castro** Brazil
**153** A4 **Castro** Chile
**106** B2 **Castro Verde** Port.
**109** C3 **Castrovillari** Italy
**150** A3 **Catacaos** Peru
**155** D2 **Cataguases** Brazil
**154** C1 **Catalão** Brazil
**Catalonia** reg. Spain see **Cataluña**
**107** D1 **Cataluña** reg. Spain
**152** B2 **Catamarca** Arg.
**64** B2 **Catanduanes** i. Phil.
**154** C2 **Catanduva** Brazil
**154** B3 **Catanduvas** Brazil
**109** C3 **Catania** Sicily Italy
**109** C3 **Catanzaro** Italy
**64** B2 **Catarman** Phil.
**107** C2 **Catarroja** Spain
**64** B2 **Catbalogan** Phil.
**145** C3 **Catemaco** Mex.
**120** A1 **Catete** Angola
**Catherine, Mount** mt. Egypt see **Kātrīna, Jabal**
**147** C2 **Cat Island** Bahamas
**130** A2 **Cat Lake** Can.
**145** D2 **Catoche, Cabo** c. Mex.
**139** E2 **Catskill Mountains** U.S.A.
**123** D2 **Catuane** Moz.
**64** B3 **Cauayan** Phil.
**131** D2 **Caubvick, Mount** Can.
**150** B2 **Cauca** r. Col.
**151** F3 **Caucaia** Brazil
**81** C1 **Caucasus** mts Asia/Europe
**100** A2 **Caudry** France
**109** C3 **Caulonia** Italy
**120** A1 **Caungula** Angola
**150** C2 **Caura** r. Venez.
**131** D3 **Causapscal** Can.
**90** B2 **Căuşeni** Moldova
**105** D3 **Cavaillon** France
**151** A1 **Cavalcante** Brazil
**114** B4 **Cavally** r. Côte d'Ivoire
**97** C2 **Cavan** Ireland
**154** B3 **Cavernoso, Serra do** mts Brazil
**151** D2 **Caviana, Ilha** i. Brazil
**Cawnpore** India see **Kanpur**
**151** E3 **Caxias** Brazil
**152** C2 **Caxias do Sul** Brazil
**120** A1 **Caxito** Angola
**151** D2 **Cayenne** Fr. Guiana
**146** B3 **Cayman Islands** terr. West Indies
**158** C3 **Cayman Trench** sea feature
Caribbean Sea
**117** C4 **Caynabo** Somalia
**120** B2 **Cazombo** Angola
**Ceará** Brazil see **Fortaleza**
**Ceatharlach** Ireland see **Carlow**
**144** B2 **Ceballos** Mex.
**64** B2 **Cebu** Phil.
**64** B2 **Cebu** i. Phil.
**108** B2 **Cecina** Italy
**137** F2 **Cedar** r. U.S.A.
**135** D3 **Cedar City** U.S.A.
**137** E2 **Cedar Falls** U.S.A.
**129** D2 **Cedar Lake** Can.
**137** E2 **Cedar Rapids** U.S.A.
**144** A2 **Cedros, Isla** i. Mex.
**51** C3 **Ceduna** Austr.
**117** C4 **Ceeldheere** Somalia
**117** C3 **Ceerigaabo** Somalia
**108** B3 **Cefalù** Sicily Italy
**145** B2 **Celaya** Mex.
**61** D2 **Celebes** i. Indon.
**156** C5 **Celebes Sea** Indon./Phil.
**145** C2 **Celestún** Mex.
**101** E1 **Celle** Ger.
**95** B3 **Celtic Sea** Ireland/U.K.
**59** D3 **Cenderawasih, Teluk** b. Indon.
**140** C2 **Center Point** U.S.A.
**150** B2 **Central, Cordillera** mts Col.
**150** B4 **Central, Cordillera** mts Peru
**64** B2 **Central, Cordillera** mts Phil.
**Central African Empire** country
Africa see **Central African Republic**
**118** C2 **Central African Republic** country
Africa
**74** A2 **Central Brahui Range** mts Pak.
**137** D2 **Central City** U.S.A.
**138** B3 **Centralia** IL U.S.A.
**134** B1 **Centralia** WA U.S.A.
**74** A2 **Central Makran Range** mts Pak.
**156** D5 **Central Pacific Basin** sea feature
Pacific Ocean
**134** B2 **Central Point** U.S.A.
**Central Provinces** state India see
**Madhya Pradesh**
**59** D3 **Central Range** mts P.N.G.
**89** E3 **Central Russian Upland** hills
Rus. Fed.
**83** I2 **Central Siberian Plateau** plat.
Rus. Fed.
**140** C2 **Century** U.S.A.
**Ceos** i. Greece see **Kea**
**111** B3 **Cephalonia** i. Greece
**Ceram** i. Indon. see **Seram**
**Ceram Sea** Indon. see **Laut Seram**
**101** F3 **Čerchov** mt. Czech Rep.
**152** B2 **Ceres** Arg.
**154** C1 **Ceres** Brazil
**122** A3 **Ceres** S. Africa
**105** C3 **Céret** France
**106** C1 **Cerezo de Abajo** Spain
**109** C2 **Cerignola** Italy
**Cerigo** i. Greece see **Kythira**
**110** C2 **Cernavodă** Romania

**145** C2 **Cerralvo** Mex.
**144** B2 **Cerralvo, Isla** i. Mex.
**145** B2 **Cerritos** Mex.
**154** C2 **Cerro Azul** Brazil
**145** C2 **Cerro Azul** Mex.
**150** B4 **Cerro de Pasco** Peru
**105** D3 **Cervione** Corsica France
**106** B1 **Cervo** Spain
**108** B2 **Cesena** Italy
**108** B2 **Cesenatico** Italy
**88** C2 **Cēsis** Latvia
**102** C2 **České Budějovice** Czech Rep.
**101** F3 **Český Les** mts Czech Rep./Ger.
**111** C3 **Çeşme** Turkey
**53** D2 **Cessnock** Austr.
**104** B2 **Cesson-Sévigné** France
**104** B3 **Cestas** France
**109** C2 **Cetinje** Serb. and Mont.
**109** C3 **Cetraro** Italy
**106** B2 **Ceuta** N. Africa
**105** C3 **Cévennes** mts France
**Ceylon** country Asia see **Sri Lanka**
**79** D2 **Chābahār** Iran
**75** C1 **Chabyêr Caka** salt l. China
**150** B3 **Chachapoyas** Peru
**89** D3 **Chachersk** Belarus
**63** B2 **Chachoengsao** Thai.
**152** C2 **Chaco Boreal** reg. Para.
**142** B1 **Chaco Mesa** plat. U.S.A.
**115** D3 **Chad** country Africa
**115** D3 **Chad, Lake** Africa
**68** C1 **Chadaasan** Mongolia
**68** C1 **Chadan** Rus. Fed.
**123** C1 **Chadibe** Botswana
**136** C2 **Chadron** U.S.A.
**Chadyr-Lunga** Moldova see
**Ciadîr-Lunga**
**77** D2 **Chaek** Kyrg.
**65** B2 **Chaeryŏng** N. Korea
**74** A2 **Chagai** Pak.
**77** C3 **Chaghcharān** Afgh.
**89** E2 **Chagoda** Rus. Fed.
**56** I10 **Chagos Archipelago** is B.I.O.T.
**159** E4 **Chagos-Laccadive Ridge**
sea feature Indian Ocean
**159** E4 **Chagos Trench** sea feature
Indian Ocean
**76** B2 **Chagyl** Turkm.
**75** C2 **Chaibasa** India
**63** B2 **Chainat** Thai.
**63** A3 **Chaiya** Thai.
**63** B2 **Chaiyaphum** Thai.
**152** C3 **Chajarí** Arg.
**119** D3 **Chake Chake** Tanz.
**131** D3 **Chakonipau, Lake** Can.
**150** B4 **Chala** Peru
**74** A1 **Chalap Dalan** mts Afgh.
**121** C2 **Chaláua** Moz.
**131** D3 **Chaleur Bay** inlet Can.
**74** B2 **Chalisgaon** India
**111** C3 **Chalki** i. Greece
**111** B3 **Chalkida** Greece
**143** C3 **Chalk Mountains** U.S.A.
**104** B2 **Challans** France
**134** D2 **Challis** U.S.A.
**105** C2 **Châlons-en-Champagne** France
**Châlons-sur-Marne** see
**Châlons-en-Champagne**
**105** C2 **Chalon-sur-Saône** France
**101** F3 **Cham** Ger.
**142** B1 **Chama** U.S.A.
**121** C2 **Chama** Zambia
**74** A1 **Chaman** Pak.
**74** B1 **Chamba** India
**74** B2 **Chambal** r. India
**137** D2 **Chamberlain** U.S.A.
**142** B1 **Chambers** U.S.A.
**139** D3 **Chambersburg** U.S.A.
**105** D2 **Chambéry** France
**121** C2 **Chambeshi** Zambia
**121** B2 **Chambeshi** r. Zambia
**Chamdo** China see **Qamdo**
**105** D2 **Chamonix-Mont-Blanc** France
**105** C2 **Champagne** reg. France
**138** B2 **Champaign** U.S.A.
**139** E2 **Champlain, Lake** Can./U.S.A.
**145** C3 **Champotón** Mex.
**Chanak** Turkey see **Çanakkale**
**152** A2 **Chañaral** Chile
**Chanda** India see **Chandrapur**
**126** C2 **Chandalar** r. U.S.A.
**140** C3 **Chandeleur Islands** U.S.A.
**74** B1 **Chandigarh** India
**131** D3 **Chandler** Can.
**142** A2 **Chandler** U.S.A.
**75** D2 **Chandpur** Bangl.
**75** B3 **Chandrapur** India
**63** B2 **Chang, Ko** i. Thai.
**Chang** China see **Rong'an**
**121** C3 **Changane** r. Moz.
**121** C2 **Changara** Moz.
**65** B1 **Changbai** China
**65** B1 **Changbai Shan** mts
China/N. Korea
**Changchow** China see **Zhangzhou**
**Changchow** China see **Changzhou**
**69** E2 **Changchun** China
**71** B3 **Changde** China
**65** B2 **Ch'angdo** N. Korea
**70** B2 **Changge** China
**71** C3 **Changhua** Taiwan
**65** B3 **Changhŭng** S. Korea
**Chang Jiang** r. China see **Yangtze**
**Changjiang Kou** r. mouth China
see **Yangtze, Mouth of the**

**65** B1 **Changjin** N. Korea
**65** B1 **Changjin-gang** r. N. Korea
**Changkiang** China see **Zhanjiang**
**Changning** China see **Xunwu**
**Ch'ang-pai Shan** mts
China/N. Korea see **Changbai Shan**
**71** B3 **Changsha** China
**70** C2 **Changshu** China
**65** B2 **Changsŏng** S. Korea
**Changteh** China see **Changde**
**71** B3 **Changting** Fujian China
**66** A2 **Changting** Heilong. China
**65** B1 **Changtu** China
**146** B4 **Changuinola** Panama
**65** B2 **Ch'angwŏn** S. Korea
**65** B2 **Changyŏn** N. Korea
**70** B2 **Changyuan** China
**70** B2 **Changzhi** China
**70** B2 **Changzhou** China
**111** B3 **Chania** Greece
**95** C4 **Channel Islands** English Chan.
**135** C4 **Channel Islands** U.S.A.
**131** E3 **Channel-Port-aux-Basques** Can.
**106** B1 **Chantada** Spain
**63** B2 **Chanthaburi** Thai.
**104** C2 **Chantilly** France
**137** D3 **Chanute** U.S.A.
**82** G3 **Chany, Ozero** salt l. Rus. Fed.
**70** B2 **Chaohu** China
**71** B3 **Chaoyang** Guangdong China
**Chaoyang** China see **Huinan**
**70** C1 **Chaoyang** Liaoning China
**71** B3 **Chaozhou** China
**144** B2 **Chapala, Laguna de** l. Mex.
**76** B1 **Chapayev** Kazakh.
**87** D3 **Chapayevsk** Rus. Fed.
**152** C2 **Chapecó** Brazil
**141** E1 **Chapel Hill** U.S.A.
**130** B3 **Chapleau** Can.
**89** E3 **Chaplygin** Rus. Fed.
**91** C2 **Chaplynka** Ukr.
**Chapra** India see **Chhapra**
**145** B2 **Charcas** Mex.
**99** B4 **Chard** U.K.
**Chardzhev** Turkm. see
**Turkmenabat**
**Chardzhou** Turkm. see
**Turkmenabat**
**104** B2 **Charente** r. France
**118** B1 **Chari** r. Cameroon/Chad
**77** C3 **Chārīkār** Afgh.
**86** E2 **Charkhlik** China see **Ruoqiang**
**100** B2 **Charleroi** Belgium
**139** D3 **Charles, Cape** U.S.A.
**139** E1 **Charlesbourg** Can.
**137** E2 **Charles City** U.S.A.
**138** B3 **Charleston** IL U.S.A.
**137** F3 **Charleston** MO U.S.A.
**141** E2 **Charleston** SC U.S.A.
**138** C3 **Charleston** WV U.S.A.
**135** C3 **Charleston Peak** U.S.A.
**51** D2 **Charleville** Austr.
**105** C2 **Charleville-Mézières** France
**138** B1 **Charlevoix** U.S.A.
**141** D1 **Charlotte** U.S.A.
**141** D3 **Charlotte Harbor** b. U.S.A.
**139** D3 **Charlottesville** U.S.A.
**131** D3 **Charlottetown** Can.
**52** B3 **Charlton** Austr.
**130** C2 **Charlton Island** Can.
**51** D2 **Charters Towers** Austr.
**104** C2 **Chartres** France
**128** C2 **Chase** Can.
**88** C3 **Chashniki** Belarus
**54** A3 **Chaslands Mistake** c. N.Z.
**65** B1 **Chasŏng** N. Korea
**104** B2 **Chassiron, Pointe de** pt France
**104** B2 **Chateaubriant** France
**104** C2 **Château-du-Loir** France
**104** C2 **Châteaudun** France
**104** B2 **Château-Gontier** France
**104** C2 **Châteaulin** France
**105** D3 **Châteauneuf-les-Martigues**
France
**104** C2 **Châteauneuf-sur-Loire** France
**104** C2 **Châteauroux** France
**105** D2 **Château-Thierry** France
**100** B2 **Châtelet** Belgium
**104** C2 **Châtellerault** France
**138** C2 **Chatham** Can.
**99** D4 **Chatham** U.K.
**49** J8 **Chatham Islands** N.Z.
**105** C2 **Châtillon-sur-Seine** France
**141** D2 **Chattahoochee** r. U.S.A.
**141** C1 **Chattanooga** U.S.A.
**63** B2 **Châu Đôc** Vietnam
**62** A1 **Chauk** Myanmar
**105** C2 **Chaumont** France
**105** C2 **Chauny** France
**Chau Phu** Vietnam see **Châu Đôc**
**151** E3 **Chaves** Brazil
**106** B1 **Chaves** Port.
**130** C2 **Chavigny, Lac** l. Can.
**89** D3 **Chavusy** Belarus
**89** E2 **Chayevo** Rus. Fed.
**86** E3 **Chaykovskiy** Rus. Fed.
**140** C2 **Cheaha Mountain** hill U.S.A.
**102** C1 **Cheb** Czech Rep.
**87** D3 **Cheboksary** Rus. Fed.
**138** C1 **Cheboygan** U.S.A.
**65** B2 **Chech'ŏn** S. Korea
**140** A1 **Checotah** U.S.A.
**Chefoo** China see **Yantai**

**126** B2 **Chefornak** U.S.A.
**114** B2 **Chegga** Maur.
**121** C2 **Chegutu** Zimbabwe
**134** B1 **Chehalis** U.S.A.
**65** B3 **Cheju** S. Korea
**65** B3 **Cheju-do** i. S. Korea
**65** B3 **Cheju-haehyŏp** sea chan. S. Korea
**89** E2 **Chekhov** Rus. Fed.
**Chekiang** prov. China see **Zhejiang**
**134** B1 **Chelan, Lake** U.S.A.
**81** D2 **Cheleken** Turkm.
**107** D2 **Chélif, Oued** r. Alg.
**103** E1 **Chełm** Pol.
**99** D3 **Chelmer** r. U.K.
**103** D1 **Chełmno** Pol.
**99** D3 **Chelmsford** U.K.
**99** B4 **Cheltenham** U.K.
**87** F3 **Chelyabinsk** Rus. Fed.
**83** H1 **Chelyuskin** Rus. Fed.
**101** F2 **Chemnitz** Ger.
**Chemulpo** S. Korea see **Inch'ŏn**
**134** B2 **Chemult** U.S.A.
**74** B2 **Chenab** r. India/Pak.
**114** B2 **Chenachane** Alg.
**134** C1 **Cheney** U.S.A.
**Chengchow** China see **Zhengzhou**
**70** B1 **Chengde** China
**70** A2 **Chengdu** China
**Chengjiang** China see **Taihe**
**71** B4 **Chengmai** China
**Chengshou** China see **Yingshan**
**Chengtu** China see **Chengdu**
**70** A2 **Chengxian** China
**Chengxiang** China see **Wuxi**
**Chengxiang** China see **Mianning**
**Chengyang** China see **Juxian**
**73** C3 **Chennai** India
**Chenstokhov** Pol. see
**Częstochowa**
**71** B3 **Chenzhou** China
**99** B4 **Chepstow** U.K.
**141** E2 **Cheraw** U.S.A.
**104** B2 **Cherbourg** France
**Cherchen** China see **Qiemo**
**89** E3 **Cheremisinovo** Rus. Fed.
**68** C1 **Cheremkhovo** Rus. Fed.
**89** E2 **Cherepovets** Rus. Fed.
**91** C2 **Cherkasy** Ukr.
**87** D4 **Cherkessk** Rus. Fed.
**89** E3 **Chern'** Rus. Fed.
**91** C1 **Chernihiv** Ukr.
**90** B2 **Cherninivka** Ukr.
**90** B2 **Chernivtsi** Ukr.
**68** C1 **Chernogorsk** Rus. Fed.
**90** B1 **Chernyakhiv** Ukr.
**88** B3 **Chernyakhovsk** Rus. Fed.
**89** E3 **Chernyanka** Rus. Fed.
**69** D1 **Chernyshevsk** Rus. Fed.
**83** I2 **Chernyshevskiy** Rus. Fed.
**Chernyy Rynok** Rus. Fed. see
**Kochubey**
**137** D2 **Cherokee** U.S.A.
**83** L2 **Cherskiy** Rus. Fed.
**83** K2 **Cherskogo, Khrebet** mts
Rus. Fed.
**91** E2 **Chertkovo** Rus. Fed.
**Chervonoarmeyskoye** Ukr. see
**Vil'nyans'k**
**Chervonoarmiys'k** Ukr. see
**Krasnoarmiys'k**
**Chervonoarmiys'k** Ukr. see
**Radyvyliv**
**90** A1 **Chervonohrad** Ukr.
**88** C3 **Chervyen'** Belarus
**89** D3 **Cherykaw** Belarus
**139** D3 **Chesapeake Bay** U.S.A.
**86** D2 **Cheshskaya Guba** b. Rus. Fed.
**98** B3 **Chester** U.K.
**138** B3 **Chester** IL U.S.A.
**141** D2 **Chester** SC U.S.A.
**139** D3 **Chester** VA U.S.A.
**98** C3 **Chesterfield** U.K.
**137** E3 **Chesterfield** U.S.A.
**129** E1 **Chesterfield Inlet** Can.
**129** E1 **Chesterfield Inlet** inlet Can.
**139** E1 **Chesuncook Lake** U.S.A.
**108** A3 **Chetaïbi** Alg.
**131** D3 **Chéticamp** Can.
**145** D3 **Chetumal** Mex.
**128** B2 **Chetwynd** Can.
**98** B2 **Cheviot Hills** U.K.
**119** D2 **Che'w Bahir** salt l. Eth.
**136** C2 **Cheyenne** U.S.A.
**136** C2 **Cheyenne** r. U.S.A.
**136** C3 **Cheyenne Wells** U.S.A.
**75** C2 **Chhapra** India
**75** C2 **Chhatarpur** India
**75** C2 **Chhattisgarh** state India
**74** B2 **Chhindwara** India
**75** C2 **Chhukha** Bhutan
**71** C3 **Chiai** Taiwan
**62** A2 **Chiang Dao** Thai.
**120** A2 **Chiange** Angola
**62** A2 **Chiang Mai** Thai.
**62** A2 **Chiang Rai** Thai.
**145** C3 **Chiapa** Mex.
**108** A1 **Chiavenno** Italy
**69** F2 **Chiba** Japan
**70** B3 **Chibi** China
**Chibizovka** Rus. Fed. see
**Zherdevka**
**121** C3 **Chiboma** Moz.
**130** C2 **Chibougamau** Can.
**123** D1 **Chibuto** Moz.
**138** B2 **Chicago** U.S.A.

128 A2 **Chichagof Island** U.S.A.
99 C4 **Chichester** U.K.
50 A2 **Chichester Range** *mts* Austr.
143 D1 **Chickasha** U.S.A.
106 B2 **Chiclana de la Frontera** Spain
150 B3 **Chiclayo** Peru
153 B4 **Chico** *r.* Arg.
153 B4 **Chico** *r.* Arg.
135 B3 **Chico** U.S.A.
139 E2 **Chicopee** U.S.A.
64 B2 **Chico Sapocoy, Mount** Phil.
131 C3 **Chicoutimi** Can.
131 D1 **Chidley, Cape** Can.
63 A3 **Chieo Lan Reservoir** Thai.
108 B2 **Chieti** Italy
145 C3 **Chietla** Mex.
70 B1 **Chifeng** China
155 D1 **Chifre, Serra do** *mts* Brazil
121 C2 **Chifunde** Moz.
77 D2 **Chiganak** Kazakh.
145 C3 **Chignahuapán** Mex.
121 C3 **Chigubo** Moz.
62 A1 **Chigu Co** *l.* China
144 B2 **Chihuahua** Mex.
77 C2 **Chiili** Kazakh.
88 C3 **Chikhachevo** Rus. Fed.
67 C3 **Chikuma-gawa** *r.* Japan
128 B2 **Chilanko** *r.* Can.
74 B1 **Chilas** Jammu and Kashmir
143 C2 **Childress** U.S.A.
153 A3 **Chile** *country* S. America
158 C6 **Chile Basin** *sea feature* S. Pacific Ocean
153 A3 **Chilecito** Arg.
157 G8 **Chile Rise** *sea feature* S. Pacific Ocean
77 D2 **Chilik** Kazakh.
75 C3 **Chilika Lake** India
121 B2 **Chililabombwe** Zambia
128 B2 **Chilko** *r.* Can.
128 B2 **Chilko Lake** Can.
153 A3 **Chillán** Chile
138 B2 **Chillicothe** *IL* U.S.A.
137 E3 **Chillicothe** *MO* U.S.A.
138 C3 **Chillicothe** *OH* U.S.A.
128 B3 **Chilliwack** Can.
153 A4 **Chiloé, Isla de** *i.* Chile
145 C3 **Chilpancingo** Mex.
53 C3 **Chiltern** Austr.
99 C4 **Chiltern Hills** U.K.
120 B1 **Chiluage** Angola
71 C3 **Chilung** Taiwan
119 D3 **Chimala** Tanz.
121 C2 **Chimanimani** Zimbabwe
152 B3 **Chimbas** Arg.
150 B3 **Chimborazo** *mt.* Ecuador
150 B3 **Chimbote** Peru
76 B2 **Chimboy** Uzbek.
 **Chimishliya** Moldova *see* **Cimişlia**
 **Chimkent** Kazakh. *see* **Shymkent**
121 C2 **Chimoio** Moz.
77 C3 **Chimtargha, Qullai** *mt.* Tajik.
68 C2 **China** *country* Asia
145 C2 **China** Mex.
150 B4 **Chincha Alta** Peru
128 C2 **Chinchaga** *r.* Can.
145 D3 **Chinchorro, Banco** *sea feature* Mex.
121 C2 **Chinde** Moz.
65 B3 **Chindo** S. Korea
65 B3 **Chin-do** *i.* S. Korea
68 C2 **Chindu** China
62 A1 **Chindwin** *r.* Myanmar
65 B2 **Chinghwa** N. Korea
121 B2 **Chingola** Zambia
120 A2 **Chinguar** Angola
65 B2 **Chinhae** S. Korea
121 C2 **Chinhoyi** Zimbabwe
 **Chini** India *see* **Kalpa**
 **Chining** China *see* **Jining**
74 B1 **Chiniot** Pak.
144 B2 **Chinipas** Mex.
65 B2 **Chinju** S. Korea
118 C2 **Chinko** *r.* C.A.R.
142 B1 **Chinle** U.S.A.
71 B3 **Chinmen** Taiwan
 **Chinnamp'o** N. Korea *see* **Namp'o**
67 C3 **Chino** Japan
135 C4 **Chino** U.S.A.
104 C2 **Chinon** France
134 E1 **Chinook** U.S.A.
142 A2 **Chino Valley** U.S.A.
77 C2 **Chinoz** Uzbek.
121 C2 **Chinsali** Zambia
108 B1 **Chioggia** Italy
111 C3 **Chios** Greece
111 C3 **Chios** *i.* Greece
121 C2 **Chipata** Zambia
120 A2 **Chipindo** Angola
 **Chipinga** Zimbabwe *see* **Chipinge**
121 C3 **Chipinge** Zimbabwe
73 B3 **Chiplun** India
99 B4 **Chippenham** U.K.
138 A2 **Chippewa Falls** U.S.A.
99 C4 **Chipping Norton** U.K.
 **Chipuriro** Zimbabwe *see* **Guruve**
145 D3 **Chiquimula** Guat.
77 C2 **Chirchiq** Uzbek.
121 C3 **Chiredzi** Zimbabwe
142 B2 **Chiricahua Peak** U.S.A.
146 B4 **Chiriquí, Golfo de** *b.* Panama
65 B2 **Chiri-san** *mt.* S. Korea
146 B4 **Chirripo** *mt.* Costa Rica
121 B2 **Chirundu** Zimbabwe
130 C2 **Chisasibi** Can.
137 E1 **Chisholm** U.S.A.

90 B2 **Chisimaio** Somalia *see* **Kismaayo**
87 E3 **Chişinau** Moldova
69 D1 **Chistopol'** Rus. Fed.
120 A2 **Chita** Rus. Fed.
 **Chitado** Angola
121 C2 **Chitaldrug** India *see* **Chitradurga**
120 B1 **Chitambo** Zambia
121 C1 **Chitato** Angola
121 C3 **Chitipa** Malawi
 **Chitobe** Moz.
 **Chitor** India *see* **Chittaurgarh**
66 D2 **Chitose** Japan
73 B3 **Chitradurga** India
74 B1 **Chitral** Pak.
146 B4 **Chitré** Panama
75 C2 **Chittagong** Bangl.
74 B2 **Chittaurgarh** India
73 B3 **Chittoor** India
 **Chittorgarh** India *see* **Chittaurgarh**
121 C2 **Chitungwiza** Zimbabwe
120 B2 **Chiume** Angola
121 C2 **Chivhu** Zimbabwe
70 B2 **Chizhou** China
 **Chkalov** Rus. Fed. *see* **Orenburg**
101 F2 **Chodov** Czech Rep.
153 B3 **Choele Choel** Arg.
 **Chogori Feng** *mt.* China/Jammu and Kashmir *see* **K2**
48 G4 **Choiseul** *i.* Solomon Is
144 B2 **Choix** Mex.
102 C1 **Chojna** Pol.
103 D1 **Chojnice** Pol.
117 B3 **Ch'ok'ē Mountains** Eth.
 **Chokue** Moz. *see* **Chókwé**
83 K2 **Chokurdakh** Rus. Fed.
121 C3 **Chókwé** Moz.
104 B2 **Cholet** France
145 C3 **Cholula** Mex.
120 B2 **Choma** Zambia
 **Chomo** China *see* **Yadong**
102 C1 **Chomutov** Czech Rep.
83 I2 **Chona** *r.* Rus. Fed.
65 B2 **Ch'ōnan** S. Korea
58 A2 **Chon Buri** Thai.
150 A3 **Chone** Ecuador
65 B1 **Chong'an** China *see* **Wuyishan**
65 B1 **Ch'ŏngjin** N. Korea
65 B2 **Chŏngju** N. Korea
65 B2 **Ch'ŏngju** S. Korea *see* **Chŏngup**
70 A3 **Chŏngp'yŏng** N. Korea
70 A2 **Chongqing** China
65 B2 **Chongqing** *mun.* China
121 B2 **Chŏngup** S. Korea
71 A3 **Chongwe** Zambia
65 B2 **Chongzuo** China
153 A4 **Chŏnju** S. Korea
 **Chonos, Archipiélago de los** *is* Chile
154 B3 **Chopimzinho** Brazil
98 B3 **Chorley** U.K.
91 C1 **Chornobay** Ukr.
90 C1 **Chornobyl'** Ukr.
91 C2 **Chornomors'ke** Ukr.
90 B2 **Chortkiv** Ukr.
65 B2 **Ch'ŏrwŏn** S. Korea
65 B1 **Ch'osan** N. Korea
67 C3 **Chōshi** Japan
153 A3 **Chos Malal** Arg.
103 D1 **Choszczno** Pol.
134 C1 **Choteau** U.S.A.
114 A2 **Choûm** Maur.
69 D1 **Choybalsan** Mongolia
69 D1 **Choyr** Mongolia
54 B2 **Christchurch** N.Z.
99 C4 **Christchurch** U.K.
127 H2 **Christian, Cape** Can.
123 C2 **Christiana** S. Africa
 **Christianshåb** Greenland *see* **Qasigiannguit**
54 A2 **Christina, Mount** N.Z.
58 B3 **Christmas Island** *terr.* Indian Ocean
111 C3 **Chrysi** *i.* Greece
111 B2 **Chrysoupoli** Greece
 **Chu** Kazakh. *see* **Shu**
 **Chubarovka** Ukr. *see* **Polohy**
153 B4 **Chubut** *r.* Arg.
89 F3 **Chuchkovo** Rus. Fed.
90 B1 **Chudniv** Ukr.
89 D2 **Chudovo** Rus. Fed.
126 C2 **Chugach Mountains** U.S.A.
67 B4 **Chūgoku-sanchi** *mts* Japan
 **Chuguchak** China *see* **Tacheng**
66 B2 **Chuguyevka** Rus. Fed.
91 D2 **Chuhuyiv** Ukr.
 **Chukchi Peninsula** Rus. Fed. *see* **Chukotskiy Poluostrov**
160 J3 **Chukchi Sea** *sea* Rus. Fed./U.S.A.
89 F2 **Chukhloma** Rus. Fed.
83 N2 **Chukotskiy Poluostrov** *pen.* Rus. Fed.
 **Chulaktau** Kazakh. *see* **Karatau**
135 C4 **Chula Vista** U.S.A.
82 G3 **Chulym** Rus. Fed.
152 B2 **Chumbicha** Arg.
83 K3 **Chumikan** Rus. Fed.
63 A2 **Chumphon** Thai.
65 B2 **Ch'unch'ŏn** S. Korea
 **Chungking** China *see* **Chongqing**
 **Ch'ungmu** S. Korea *see* **T'ongyŏng**
71 C3 **Chungyang Shanmo** *mts* Taiwan
83 H2 **Chunya** *r.* Rus. Fed.
119 D3 **Chunya** Tanz.
150 B4 **Chuquibamba** Peru
152 B2 **Chuquicamata** Chile

105 D2 **Chur** Switz.
62 A1 **Churachandpur** India
83 J2 **Churapcha** Rus. Fed.
129 E2 **Churchill** Can.
129 E2 **Churchill** *r. Man.* Can.
131 D2 **Churchill** *r. Nfld and Lab.* Can.
129 E2 **Churchill, Cape** Can.
131 D2 **Churchill Falls** Can.
129 E2 **Churchill Lake** Can.
74 B2 **Churu** India
142 B1 **Chuska Mountains** U.S.A.
86 E3 **Chusovoy** Rus. Fed.
131 C3 **Chute-des-Passes** Can.
48 G3 **Chuuk** *is* Micronesia
62 B1 **Chuxiong** China
63 B2 **Chu Yang Sin** *mt.* Vietnam
91 C2 **Chymyshliya** Moldova *see* **Cimişlia**
 **Ciadar-Lunga** Moldova *see* **Ciadîr-Lunga**
90 B2 **Ciadîr-Lunga** Moldova
60 B2 **Ciamis** Indon.
60 B2 **Cianjur** Indon.
154 B3 **Cianorte** Brazil
142 A2 **Cibuta, Sierra** *mt.* Mex.
103 E1 **Cide** Turkey
103 E1 **Ciechanów** Pol.
147 C3 **Ciego de Ávila** Cuba
147 C3 **Ciénaga** Col.
146 B2 **Cienfuegos** Cuba
107 C2 **Cieza** Spain
106 C2 **Cigüela** *r.* Spain
80 B2 **Cihanbeyli** Turkey
144 B3 **Cihuatlán** Mex.
106 C2 **Cijara, Embalse de** *resr* Spain
109 C2 **Çikes, Maja e** *mt.* Albania
60 B2 **Cilacap** Indon.
143 C1 **Cimarron** *r.* U.S.A.
90 B2 **Cimişlia** Moldova
108 B2 **Cimone, Monte** *mt.* Italy
 **Câmpina** Romania *see* **Câmpina**
 **Câmpulung** Romania *see* **Câmpulung**
60 B2 **Cina, Tanjung** *c.* Indon.
138 C3 **Cincinnati** U.S.A.
 **Cinco de Outubro** Angola *see* **Xá-Muteba**
111 C3 **Çine** Turkey
100 B2 **Ciney** Belgium
134 C2 **Cinnabar Mountain** U.S.A.
145 C3 **Cintalapa** Mex.
 **Ciping** China *see* **Jinggangshan**
153 B3 **Cipolletti** Arg.
126 C2 **Circle** *AK* U.S.A.
136 B1 **Circle** *MT* U.S.A.
60 B2 **Cirebon** Indon.
99 C4 **Cirencester** U.K.
108 A1 **Ciriè** Italy
109 C3 **Cirò Marina** Italy
110 B1 **Cisnădie** Romania
109 C2 **Čitluk** Bos.-Herz.
122 A3 **Citrusdal** S. Africa
135 B3 **Citrus Heights** U.S.A.
110 C1 **Ciucaş, Vârful** *mt.* Romania
145 B2 **Ciudad Acuña** Mex.
145 B3 **Ciudad Altamirano** Mex.
150 C2 **Ciudad Bolívar** Venez.
147 C4 **Ciudad Bolivia** Venez.
144 B2 **Ciudad Camargo** Mex.
144 A2 **Ciudad Constitución** Mex.
145 C3 **Ciudad Cuauhtémoc** Mex.
145 C3 **Ciudad del Carmen** Mex.
154 B3 **Ciudad del Este** Para.
144 B2 **Ciudad Delicias** Mex.
145 C2 **Ciudad de Valles** Mex.
150 C2 **Ciudad Guayana** Venez.
142 B3 **Ciudad Guerrero** Mex.
144 B3 **Ciudad Guzmán** Mex.
145 C3 **Ciudad Hidalgo** Mex.
145 C3 **Ciudad Ixtepec** Mex.
144 B1 **Ciudad Juárez** Mex.
145 C2 **Ciudad Madero** Mex.
145 C2 **Ciudad Mante** Mex.
145 C2 **Ciudad Mier** Mex.
144 B2 **Ciudad Obregón** Mex.
106 C2 **Ciudad Real** Spain
145 C2 **Ciudad Río Bravo** Mex.
106 B1 **Ciudad Rodrigo** Spain
 **Ciudad Trujillo** Dom. Rep. *see* **Santo Domingo**
145 C2 **Ciudad Victoria** Mex.
107 D1 **Ciutadella de Menorca** Spain
108 B1 **Cividale del Friuli** Italy
108 B2 **Civitanova Marche** Italy
108 B2 **Civitavecchia** Italy
104 C2 **Civray** France
111 C3 **Çivril** Turkey
70 C2 **Cixi** China
99 D4 **Clacton-on-Sea** U.K.
128 C2 **Claire, Lake** Can.
105 C2 **Clamecy** France
140 C2 **Clanton** U.S.A.
122 A3 **Clanwilliam** S. Africa
97 A2 **Clara** Ireland
52 A2 **Clare** Austr.
138 C2 **Clare** U.S.A.
97 A2 **Clare Island** Ireland
139 E2 **Claremont** U.S.A.
97 B2 **Claremorris** Ireland
54 B2 **Clarence** N.Z.
55 B3 **Clarence Island** Antarctica
131 E3 **Clarenville** Can.
128 C2 **Claresholm** Can.

137 D2 **Clarinda** U.S.A.
144 A3 **Clarión, Isla** *i.* Mex.
123 C3 **Clarkebury** S. Africa
134 C1 **Clark Fork** *r.* U.S.A.
141 D2 **Clark Hill Reservoir** U.S.A.
138 C3 **Clarksburg** U.S.A.
140 B2 **Clarksdale** U.S.A.
134 C1 **Clarkston** U.S.A.
140 B1 **Clarksville** *AR* U.S.A.
140 C1 **Clarksville** *TN* U.S.A.
154 B1 **Claro** *r.* Brazil
143 C1 **Claude** U.S.A.
143 C1 **Clayton** U.S.A.
97 B3 **Clear, Cape** Ireland
126 C3 **Cleare, Cape** U.S.A.
137 E2 **Clear Lake** U.S.A.
135 B3 **Clear Lake** *l.* U.S.A.
128 C2 **Clearwater** Can.
129 C2 **Clearwater** *r.* Can.
141 D3 **Clearwater** U.S.A.
134 C1 **Clearwater** *r.* U.S.A.
143 D2 **Cleburne** U.S.A.
101 E1 **Clenze** Ger.
51 D2 **Clermont** Austr.
105 C2 **Clermont-Ferrand** France
100 C3 **Clervaux** Lux.
52 A2 **Cleve** Austr.
140 B2 **Cleveland** *MS* U.S.A.
138 C2 **Cleveland** *OH* U.S.A.
141 D1 **Cleveland** *TN* U.S.A.
134 D1 **Cleveland, Mount** U.S.A.
154 B3 **Clevelândia** Brazil
97 B2 **Clew Bay** Ireland
141 D3 **Clewiston** U.S.A.
97 A2 **Clifden** Ireland
53 D1 **Clifton** Austr.
142 B2 **Clifton** U.S.A.
142 B1 **Clines Corners** U.S.A.
128 B2 **Clinton** Can.
137 E2 **Clinton** *IA* U.S.A.
137 E3 **Clinton** *MO* U.S.A.
143 D1 **Clinton** *OK* U.S.A.
125 H8 **Clipperton, Île** *terr.* N. Pacific Ocean
96 A2 **Clisham** *hill* U.K.
98 B3 **Clitheroe** U.K.
97 B3 **Clonakilty** Ireland
51 D2 **Cloncurry** Austr.
97 C1 **Clones** Ireland
97 C2 **Clonmel** Ireland
101 D1 **Cloppenburg** Ger.
137 E1 **Cloquet** U.S.A.
136 B2 **Cloud Peak** U.S.A.
135 C3 **Clovis** *CA* U.S.A.
143 C2 **Clovis** *NM* U.S.A.
 **Cluain Meala** Ireland *see* **Clonmel**
129 D2 **Cluff Lake Mine** Can.
110 B1 **Cluj-Napoca** Romania
51 C2 **Cluny** Austr.
105 D2 **Cluses** France
54 A3 **Clutha** *r.* N.Z.
96 B3 **Clyde** *r.* U.K.
96 B3 **Clyde, Firth of** *est.* U.K.
96 B3 **Clydebank** U.K.
127 H2 **Clyde River** Can.
144 B3 **Coalcomán** Mex.
128 C3 **Coaldale** U.S.A.
135 C3 **Coalinga** U.S.A.
128 B2 **Coal River** Can.
150 B2 **Coari** Brazil
150 B2 **Coari** *r.* Brazil
141 D2 **Coastal Plain** U.S.A.
128 B2 **Coast Mountains** Can.
134 B2 **Coast Ranges** *mts* U.S.A.
96 B3 **Coatbridge** U.K.
129 F1 **Coats Island** Can.
55 C2 **Coats Land** *reg.* Antarctica
145 C3 **Coatzacoalcos** Mex.
146 A3 **Cobán** Guat.
53 C2 **Cobar** Austr.
97 B3 **Cóbh** Ireland
152 B1 **Cobija** Bol.
 **Coblenz** Ger. *see* **Koblenz**
130 C3 **Cobourg** Can.
50 C1 **Cobourg Peninsula** Austr.
53 C3 **Cobram** Austr.
101 E2 **Coburg** Ger.
152 B1 **Cochabamba** Bol.
100 C2 **Cochem** Ger.
73 B4 **Cochin** India
128 C2 **Cochrane** *Alta* Can.
130 B3 **Cochrane** *Ont.* Can.
153 A4 **Cochrane** Chile
52 A2 **Cockaleechie** Austr.
52 B2 **Cockburn** Austr.
 **Cockburn Town** Turks and Caicos Is *see* **Grand Turk**
98 B2 **Cockermouth** U.K.
50 B3 **Cocklebiddy** Austr.
122 B3 **Cockscomb** *mt.* S. Africa
146 B3 **Coco** *r.* Hond./Nic.
125 J9 **Coco, Isla de** *i.* N. Pacific Ocean
159 F4 **Cocos Basin** *sea feature* Indian Ocean
58 A3 **Cocos Islands** *terr.* Indian Ocean
144 B2 **Cocula** Mex.
150 B2 **Cocuy, Sierra Nevada del** *mt.* Col.
139 C3 **Cod, Cape** U.S.A.
150 C3 **Codajás** Brazil
108 B2 **Codigoro** Italy
131 D2 **Cod Island** Can.
151 E3 **Codó** Brazil
136 B2 **Cody** U.S.A.
51 D1 **Coen** Austr.
100 C2 **Coesfeld** Ger.

113 I6 **Coëtivy** i. Seychelles
134 C1 **Coeur d'Alene** U.S.A.
100 C1 **Coevorden** Neth.
123 C3 **Coffee Bay** S. Africa
137 D3 **Coffeyville** U.S.A.
52 A2 **Coffin Bay** Austr.
53 D2 **Coffs Harbour** Austr.
123 C3 **Cofimvaba** S. Africa
104 B2 **Cognac** France
118 A2 **Cogo** Equat. Guinea
52 B3 **Cohuna** Austr.
146 B4 **Coiba, Isla de** i. Panama
153 A4 **Coihaique** Chile
73 B3 **Coimbatore** India
106 B1 **Coimbra** Port.
152 B1 **Coipasa, Salar de** salt flat Bol.
52 B3 **Colac** Austr.
155 D1 **Colatina** Brazil
136 C3 **Colby** U.S.A.
99 D4 **Colchester** U.K.
129 C2 **Cold Lake** Can.
96 C3 **Coldstream** U.K.
53 C2 **Coleambally** Austr.
143 D2 **Coleman** U.S.A.
52 B3 **Coleraine** Austr.
97 C1 **Coleraine** U.K.
123 C3 **Colesberg** S. Africa
153 A3 **Colico** Chile
144 B3 **Colima** Mex.
144 B3 **Colima, Nevado de** vol. Mex.
96 A2 **Coll** i. U.K.
53 C1 **Collarenebri** Austr.
143 D2 **College Station** U.S.A.
53 C1 **Collerina** Austr.
50 A3 **Collie** Austr.
50 B1 **Collier Bay** Austr.
138 C2 **Collingwood** Can.
54 B2 **Collingwood** N.Z.
126 F2 **Collinson Peninsula** Can.
101 F2 **Collmberg** hill Ger.
108 A3 **Collo** Alg.
97 B1 **Collooney** Ireland
105 D2 **Colmar** France
98 B3 **Colne** U.K.
100 C2 **Cologne** Ger.
        **Colomb-Béchar** Alg. see Béchar
154 C2 **Colômbia** Brazil
150 B2 **Colombia** country S. America
73 B4 **Colombo** Sri Lanka
104 C2 **Colomiers** France
152 C3 **Colón** Arg.
146 C4 **Colón** Panama
59 D2 **Colonia** Micronesia
153 B4 **Colonia Las Heras** Arg.
109 C3 **Colonna, Capo** c. Italy
96 A2 **Colonsay** i. U.K.
153 B3 **Colorado** r. Arg.
142 A2 **Colorado** r. Mex./U.S.A.
143 D3 **Colorado** r. U.S.A.
136 B3 **Colorado** state U.S.A.
135 C4 **Colorado Desert** U.S.A.
135 B3 **Colorado Plateau** U.S.A.
136 C3 **Colorado Springs** U.S.A.
144 B2 **Colotlán** Mex.
152 B1 **Colquiri** Bol.
136 B1 **Colstrip** U.S.A.
138 B3 **Columbia** KY U.S.A.
139 D3 **Columbia** MD U.S.A.
137 E3 **Columbia** MO U.S.A.
141 D2 **Columbia** SC U.S.A.
140 C1 **Columbia** TN U.S.A.
134 B1 **Columbia** r. U.S.A.
128 C2 **Columbia, Mount** Can.
134 D1 **Columbia Falls** U.S.A.
128 B2 **Columbia Mountains** Can.
134 C1 **Columbia Plateau** U.S.A.
141 D2 **Columbus** GA U.S.A.
138 B3 **Columbus** IN U.S.A.
140 C2 **Columbus** MS U.S.A.
134 E1 **Columbus** MT U.S.A.
137 D2 **Columbus** NE U.S.A.
142 B2 **Columbus** NM U.S.A.
138 C3 **Columbus** OH U.S.A.
143 D3 **Columbus** TX U.S.A.
134 C1 **Colville** U.S.A.
126 B2 **Colville** r. U.S.A.
126 D2 **Colville Lake** Can.
98 B3 **Colwyn Bay** U.K.
108 B2 **Comacchio** Italy
145 C3 **Comalcalco** Mex.
110 C1 **Comăneşti** Romania
130 C2 **Comencho, Lac** l. Can.
97 C2 **Comeragh Mountains** hills Ireland
143 D2 **Comfort** U.S.A.
75 D2 **Comilla** Bangl.
108 A2 **Comino, Capo** c. Sardinia Italy
145 C3 **Comitán de Domínguez** Mex.
105 C2 **Commentry** France
143 D2 **Commerce** U.S.A.
127 G2 **Committee Bay** Can.
108 A1 **Como** Italy
        **Como, Lago di** Italy see
        **Como, Lake**
108 A1 **Como, Lake** l. Italy
153 B4 **Comodoro Rivadavia** Arg.
145 B2 **Comonfort** Mex.
121 D2 **Comoros** country Africa
128 B3 **Comox** Can.
105 C2 **Compiègne** France
144 B2 **Compostela** Mex.
90 B2 **Comrat** Moldova
114 A4 **Conakry** Guinea
104 B2 **Concarneau** France
155 E1 **Conceição da Barra** Brazil
151 E3 **Conceição do Araguaia** Brazil

155 D1 **Conceição do Mato Dentro** Brazil
152 B2 **Concepción** Arg.
153 A3 **Concepción** Chile
144 B2 **Concepción** Mex.
135 B4 **Conception, Point** U.S.A.
154 C2 **Conchas** Brazil
142 C1 **Conchas Lake** U.S.A.
144 B2 **Conchos** r. Mex.
145 C2 **Conchos** r. Mex.
135 B3 **Concord** CA U.S.A.
139 E2 **Concord** NH U.S.A.
152 C3 **Concordia** Arg.
122 A2 **Concordia** S. Africa
137 D3 **Concordia** U.S.A.
53 C2 **Condobolin** Austr.
104 C3 **Condom** France
134 B1 **Condon** U.S.A.
108 B1 **Conegliano** Italy
51 E1 **Conflict Group** is P.N.G.
104 C2 **Confolens** France
135 D3 **Confusion Range** mts U.S.A.
75 C2 **Congdü** China
98 B3 **Congleton** U.K.
118 B3 **Congo** country Africa
118 B3 **Congo** r. Congo/Dem. Rep. Congo
118 C3 **Congo, Democratic Republic of the** country Africa
118 C3 **Congo Basin** Dem. Rep. Congo
        **Congo (Brazzaville)** country Africa see **Congo**
        **Congo Free State** country Africa see **Congo, Democratic Republic of Congo (Kinshasa)** country Africa see **Congo, Democratic Republic of the**
129 C2 **Conklin** Can.
97 B1 **Conn, Lough** l. Ireland
97 B2 **Connaught** reg. Ireland
139 E2 **Connecticut** r. U.S.A.
139 E2 **Connecticut** state U.S.A.
96 B2 **Connel** U.K.
97 B2 **Connemara** reg. Ireland
134 D1 **Conrad** U.S.A.
159 D7 **Conrad Rise** sea feature Southern Ocean
143 D2 **Conroe** U.S.A.
155 D2 **Conselheiro Lafaiete** Brazil
155 D1 **Conselheiro Pena** Brazil
100 B3 **Consenvoye** France
98 C2 **Consett** U.K.
63 B3 **Côn Son** i. Vietnam
        **Constance** Ger. see **Konstanz**
105 D2 **Constance, Lake** Ger./Switz.
110 C2 **Constanţa** Romania
106 B2 **Constantina** Spain
115 C1 **Constantine** Alg.
134 D2 **Contact** U.S.A.
155 D2 **Contagalo** Brazil
150 B3 **Contamana** Peru
153 A5 **Contreras, Isla** i. Chile
126 E2 **Contwoyto Lake** Can.
140 B1 **Conway** AR U.S.A.
139 E2 **Conway** NH U.S.A.
51 C2 **Coober Pedy** Austr.
        **Cooch Behar** India see **Koch Bihar**
        **Cook, Mount** mt. N.Z. see **Aoraki**
141 C1 **Cookeville** U.S.A.
126 B2 **Cook Inlet** sea chan. U.S.A.
49 K5 **Cook Islands** terr. S. Pacific Ocean
131 E2 **Cook's Harbour** Can.
97 C1 **Cookstown** U.K.
54 B2 **Cook Strait** N.Z.
51 D1 **Cooktown** Austr.
53 C2 **Coolabah** Austr.
53 C2 **Coolamon** Austr.
53 D1 **Coolangatta** Austr.
50 B3 **Coolgardie** Austr.
53 C3 **Cooma** Austr.
52 B2 **Coombah** Austr.
53 C2 **Coonabarabran** Austr.
52 A3 **Coonalpyn** Austr.
53 C2 **Coonamble** Austr.
53 C1 **Coongoola** Austr.
137 E1 **Coon Rapids** U.S.A.
52 A1 **Cooper Creek** watercourse Austr.
141 E3 **Cooper's Town** Bahamas
134 B2 **Coos Bay** U.S.A.
53 C2 **Cootamundra** Austr.
97 C1 **Cootehill** Ireland
145 C3 **Copainalá** Mex.
145 C3 **Copala** Mex.
93 F4 **Copenhagen** Denmark
109 C2 **Copertino** Italy
53 D1 **Copeton Reservoir** Austr.
152 A2 **Copiapó** Chile
143 D2 **Copperas Cove** U.S.A.
138 B1 **Copper Harbor** U.S.A.
        **Coppermine** Can. see **Kugluktuk**
126 E2 **Coppermine** r. Can.
122 B2 **Copperton** S. Africa
        **Coquilhatville** Dem. Rep. Congo see **Mbandaka**
152 A2 **Coquimbo** Chile
152 A2 **Coquimbo, Bahía de** b. Chile
110 B2 **Corabia** Romania
155 D1 **Coração de Jesus** Brazil
150 B4 **Coracora** Peru
53 D1 **Coraki** Austr.
50 A2 **Coral Bay** Austr.
127 G2 **Coral Harbour** Can.
51 E1 **Coral Sea** S. Pacific Ocean
48 G5 **Coral Sea Islands Territory** terr. Austr.
137 E2 **Coralville** U.S.A.
52 B3 **Corangamite, Lake** Austr.

99 C3 **Corby** U.K.
        **Corcaigh** Ireland see **Cork**
135 C3 **Corcoran** U.S.A.
153 A4 **Corcovado, Golfo de** sea chan. Chile
141 D2 **Cordele** U.S.A.
64 B2 **Cordilleras Range** mts Phil.
155 D1 **Cordisburgo** Brazil
152 B3 **Córdoba** Arg.
145 C3 **Córdoba** Mex.
106 C2 **Córdoba** Spain
153 B3 **Córdoba, Sierras de** mts Arg.
126 C2 **Cordova** U.S.A.
51 D2 **Corfield** Austr.
111 A3 **Corfu** i. Greece
154 B1 **Corguinho** Brazil
106 B2 **Coria** Spain
106 B2 **Coria del Río** Spain
53 D2 **Coricudgy** mt. Austr.
111 B3 **Corinth** Greece
140 C2 **Corinth** U.S.A.
        **Corinth, Gulf of** sea chan. Greece see **Gulf of Corinth**
155 D1 **Corinto** Brazil
97 B3 **Cork** Ireland
111 C2 **Çorlu** Turkey
154 B2 **Cornélio Procópio** Brazil
131 E2 **Corner Brook** Can.
53 C3 **Corner Inlet** b. Austr.
135 B3 **Corning** CA U.S.A.
139 D2 **Corning** NY U.S.A.
        **Corn Islands** is Nic. see **Maíz, Islas del**
108 B2 **Corno, Monte** mt. Italy
130 C3 **Cornwall** Can.
126 F1 **Cornwallis Island** Can.
150 C1 **Coro** Venez.
155 D1 **Coroaci** Brazil
154 C1 **Coromandel** Brazil
73 C3 **Coromandel Coast** India
54 C1 **Coromandel Peninsula** N.Z.
64 B2 **Coron** Phil.
129 C2 **Coronation** Can.
126 E2 **Coronation Gulf** Can.
55 B3 **Coronation Island** S. Atlantic Ocean
155 D1 **Coronel Fabriciano** Brazil
152 C2 **Coronel Oviedo** Para.
154 B1 **Coronel Ponce** Brazil
153 B3 **Coronel Pringles** Arg.
154 A2 **Coronel Sapucaia** Brazil
153 B3 **Coronel Suárez** Arg.
109 D2 **Çorovodë** Albania
145 D3 **Corozal** Belize
143 D3 **Corpus Christi** U.S.A.
152 B1 **Corque** Bol.
151 E4 **Corrente** Brazil
154 B1 **Correntes** Brazil
151 E4 **Correntina** Brazil
97 B2 **Corrib, Lough** l. Ireland
152 C2 **Corrientes** Arg.
153 C3 **Corrientes, Cabo** c. Arg.
144 B2 **Corrientes, Cabo** c. Mex.
143 E2 **Corrigan** U.S.A.
53 C3 **Corryong** Austr.
        **Corse** i. France see **Corsica**
105 D3 **Corse, Cap** c. Corsica France
105 D3 **Corsica** i. France
143 D2 **Corsicana** U.S.A.
105 D3 **Corte** Corsica France
106 B2 **Cortegana** Spain
136 B3 **Cortez** U.S.A.
108 B1 **Cortina d'Ampezzo** Italy
139 D2 **Cortland** U.S.A.
108 B2 **Cortona** Italy
106 B2 **Coruche** Port.
80 B1 **Çoruh** Turkey
        **Çoruh** Turkey see **Artvin**
151 D4 **Corumbá** Brazil
154 C1 **Corumbá** r. Brazil
154 C1 **Corumbá de Goiás** Brazil
        **Corunna** Spain see **A Coruña**
134 B2 **Corvallis** U.S.A.
99 B3 **Corwen** U.K.
        **Cos** i. Greece see **Kos**
144 B2 **Cosalá** Mex.
145 C3 **Cosamaloapan** Mex.
109 C3 **Cosenza** Italy
105 C2 **Cosne-Cours-sur-Loire** France
152 B3 **Cosquín** Arg.
107 C2 **Costa Blanca** coastal area Spain
107 D1 **Costa Brava** coastal area Spain
106 B2 **Costa de la Luz** coastal area Spain
107 C2 **Costa del Azahar** coastal area Spain
106 B2 **Costa del Sol** coastal area Spain
146 B3 **Costa de Mosquitos** coastal area Nic.
107 D1 **Costa Dorada** coastal area Spain
150 C4 **Costa Marques** Brazil
154 B1 **Costa Rica** Brazil
146 B3 **Costa Rica** country Central America
144 B2 **Costa Rica** Mex.
        **Costermansville** Dem. Rep. Congo see **Bukavu**
110 B2 **Costeşti** Romania
64 B3 **Cotabato** Phil.
137 D1 **Coteau des Prairies** slope U.S.A.
136 C1 **Coteau du Missouri** slope U.S.A.
147 C3 **Coteaux** Haiti
105 D3 **Côte d'Azur** coastal area France
114 B4 **Côte d'Ivoire** country Africa
        **Côte Française de Somalis** country Africa see **Djibouti**

105 C2 **Côtes de Meuse** ridge France
150 B3 **Cotopaxi, Volcán** vol. Ecuador
99 B4 **Cotswold Hills** U.K.
134 B2 **Cottage Grove** U.S.A.
102 C1 **Cottbus** Ger.
105 D3 **Cottian Alps** mts France/Italy
104 B2 **Coubre, Pointe de la** pt France
52 A3 **Coüedic, Cape de** Austr.
105 C2 **Coulommiers** France
137 D2 **Council Bluffs** U.S.A.
88 B2 **Courland Lagoon** b. Lith./Rus. Fed.
100 A3 **Courmelles** France
128 B3 **Courtenay** Can.
104 B2 **Coutances** France
104 B2 **Coutras** France
100 B2 **Couvin** Belgium
99 C3 **Coventry** U.K.
106 B1 **Covilhã** Port.
141 D2 **Covington** GA U.S.A.
138 C3 **Covington** KY U.S.A.
138 C3 **Covington** VA U.S.A.
50 B3 **Cowan, Lake** salt flat Austr.
96 C2 **Cowdenbeath** U.K.
52 A2 **Cowell** Austr.
53 C3 **Cowes** Austr.
134 B1 **Cowlitz** r. U.S.A.
53 C2 **Cowra** Austr.
154 B1 **Coxim** Brazil
154 B1 **Coxim** r. Brazil
75 D2 **Cox's Bazar** Bangl.
145 B3 **Coyuca de Benítez** Mex.
145 C2 **Cozumel** Mex.
145 C2 **Cozumel, Isla de** i. Mex.
52 A2 **Cradock** Austr.
123 C3 **Cradock** S. Africa
136 B2 **Craig** U.S.A.
102 C2 **Crailsheim** Ger.
110 B2 **Craiova** Romania
129 C2 **Cranberry Portage** Can.
53 C3 **Cranbourne** Austr.
128 C3 **Cranbrook** Can.
151 E3 **Crateús** Brazil
151 F3 **Crato** Brazil
154 C1 **Cravinhos** Brazil
136 C2 **Crawford** U.S.A.
138 B2 **Crawfordsville** U.S.A.
99 C4 **Crawley** U.K.
134 D1 **Crazy Mountains** U.S.A.
129 D2 **Cree** r. Can.
144 B2 **Creel** Mex.
129 D2 **Cree Lake** Can.
129 D2 **Creighton** Can.
104 C2 **Creil** France
100 B1 **Creil** Neth.
108 A1 **Crema** Italy
108 B1 **Cremona** Italy
108 B1 **Cres** i. Croatia
134 B2 **Crescent City** U.S.A.
53 D2 **Crescent Head** Austr.
135 E3 **Crescent Junction** U.S.A.
128 C3 **Creston** Can.
137 E2 **Creston** U.S.A.
140 C2 **Crestview** U.S.A.
111 B3 **Crete** i. Greece
107 D1 **Creus, Cap de** c. Spain
107 C2 **Crevillente** Spain
98 B3 **Crewe** U.K.
96 B2 **Crianlarich** U.K.
152 D2 **Criciúma** Brazil
96 C2 **Crieff** U.K.
108 B1 **Crikvenica** Croatia
91 B1 **Crimea** pen. Ukr.
101 F2 **Crimmitschau** Ger.
96 B2 **Crinan** U.K.
118 B2 **Cristal, Monts de** mts Equat. Guinea/Gabon
154 C1 **Cristalina** Brazil
110 B1 **Crişul Alb** r. Romania
101 E1 **Crivitz** Ger.
109 C2 **Crna Gora** aut. rep. Serb. and Mont.
109 C1 **Črnomelj** Slovenia
97 B2 **Croagh Patrick** hill Ireland
109 C1 **Croatia** country Europe
61 C1 **Crocker, Banjaran** mts Malaysia
143 D2 **Crockett** U.S.A.
59 C3 **Croker Island** Austr.
96 B2 **Cromarty** U.K.
99 D3 **Cromer** U.K.
54 A3 **Cromwell** N.Z.
147 C2 **Crooked Island** Bahamas
137 D1 **Crookston** U.S.A.
53 C2 **Crookwell** Austr.
53 D1 **Croppa Creek** Austr.
136 C1 **Crosby** U.S.A.
141 D3 **Cross City** U.S.A.
140 B2 **Crossett** U.S.A.
98 B2 **Cross Fell** hill U.K.
129 E2 **Cross Lake** Can.
141 C1 **Crossville** U.S.A.
109 C3 **Crotone** Italy
134 E1 **Crow Agency** U.S.A.
99 D4 **Crowborough** U.K.
140 B2 **Crowley** U.S.A.
53 D1 **Crows Nest** Austr.
128 C3 **Crowsnest Pass** Can.
159 D7 **Crozet, Îles** is Indian Ocean
146 B3 **Cruz, Cabo** c. Cuba
152 C2 **Cruz Alta** Brazil
152 B3 **Cruz del Eje** Arg.
155 D3 **Cruzeiro** Brazil
150 B3 **Cruzeiro do Sul** Brazil
52 A2 **Crystal Brook** Austr.
143 D3 **Crystal City** U.S.A.
138 B1 **Crystal Falls** U.S.A.
140 B2 **Crystal Springs** U.S.A.

103 E2 Csongrád Hungary
103 D2 Csorna Hungary
121 C2 Cuamba Moz.
120 B2 Cuando r. Angola/Zambia
120 A2 Cuangar Angola
118 B3 Cuango r. Angola/Dem. Rep. Congo
120 A1 Cuanza r. Angola
144 B2 Cuatro Ciénegas Mex.
144 B2 Cuauhtémoc Mex.
145 C3 Cuautla Mex.
146 B2 Cuba country West Indies
120 A2 Cubal Angola
120 B2 Cubango r. Angola/Namibia
150 B2 Cúcuta Col.
73 B3 Cuddalore India
73 B3 Cuddapah India
50 A2 Cue Austr.
106 C1 Cuéllar Spain
120 A2 Cuemba Angola
150 B3 Cuenca Ecuador
107 C1 Cuenca Spain
107 C1 Cuenca, Serranía de mts Spain
145 C3 Cuernavaca Mex.
143 D3 Cuero U.S.A.
104 C3 Cugnaux France
151 D4 Cuiabá Brazil
151 D4 Cuiabá r. Brazil
96 A2 Cuillin Sound sea chan. U.K.
120 A1 Cuilo Angola
120 B2 Cuito r. Angola
120 A2 Cuito Cuanavale Angola
60 B1 Cukai Malaysia
64 B2 Culasi Phil.
53 C3 Culcairn Austr.
100 B2 Culemborg Neth.
53 C1 Culgoa Austr.
144 B2 Culiacán Mex.
64 A2 Culion i. Phil.
107 C2 Cullera Spain
140 C2 Cullman U.S.A.
97 C1 Cullybackey U.K.
139 D3 Culpeper U.S.A.
151 D4 Culuene r. Brazil
54 B2 Culverden N.Z.
150 C1 Cumaná Venez.
139 D3 Cumberland U.S.A.
138 B3 Cumberland r. U.S.A.
141 D2 Cumberland Island U.S.A.
129 D2 Cumberland Lake Can.
127 H2 Cumberland Peninsula Can.
140 C1 Cumberland Plateau U.S.A.
127 H2 Cumberland Sound sea chan. Can.
96 C3 Cumbernauld U.K.
135 B3 Cummings U.S.A.
96 B3 Cumnock U.K.
144 B1 Cumpas Mex.
145 C3 Cunduacán Mex.
120 A2 Cunene r. Angola/Namibia
108 A2 Cuneo Italy
53 C1 Cunnamulla Austr.
108 A1 Cuorgnè Italy
96 C2 Cupar U.K.
110 B2 Čuprija Serb. and Mont.
147 D3 Curaçao i. Neth. Antilles
150 B3 Curaray r. Ecuador
153 A3 Curicó Chile
154 C3 Curitiba Brazil
52 A2 Curnamona Austr.
135 C3 Currant U.S.A.
51 D3 Currie Austr.
135 D2 Currie U.S.A.
51 E2 Curtis Island Austr.
151 D3 Curuá r. Brazil
60 B2 Curup Indon.
151 E3 Cururupu Brazil
155 D1 Curvelo Brazil
150 B4 Cusco Peru
97 C1 Cushendun U.K.
143 D1 Cushing U.S.A.
136 C2 Custer U.S.A.
134 D1 Cut Bank U.S.A.
140 B3 Cut Off U.S.A.
75 C2 Cuttack India
120 A2 Cuvelai Angola
101 D1 Cuxhaven Ger.
64 B2 Cuyo Islands Phil.
Cuzco Peru see Cusco
99 B4 Cwmbrân U.K.
119 C3 Cyangugu Rwanda
111 B3 Cyclades is Greece
129 C3 Cypress Hills Can.
80 B2 Cyprus country Asia
80 B2 Cyprus i. Asia
102 C2 Czech Republic country Europe
103 D1 Czersk Pol.
103 D1 Częstochowa Pol.

**D**

Đa, Sông r. Vietnam see Black River
69 D2 Daban China
103 D2 Dabas Hungary
114 A3 Dabola Guinea
103 D1 Dąbrowa Górnicza Pol.
110 B2 Dăbuleni Romania
Dacca Bangl. see Dhaka
102 C2 Dachau Ger.
Dachuan China see Dazhou
141 D3 Dade City U.S.A.
Dadong China see Donggang
Dadra India see Achalpur
74 B2 Dadra and Nagar Haveli
union terr. India

74 A2 Dadu Pak.
Daegu S. Korea see Taegu
64 B2 Daet Phil.
114 A3 Dagana Senegal
119 D2 Daga Post Sudan
88 C2 Dagda Latvia
64 B2 Dagupan Phil.
Dahalach, Isole is Eritrea see
Dahlak Archipelago
74 B3 Dahanu India
69 D2 Da Hinggan Ling mts China
116 C3 Dahlak Archipelago is Eritrea
100 C2 Dahlem Ger.
78 B3 Dahm, Ramlat des.
Saudi Arabia/Yemen
74 B2 Dahod India
Dahomey country Africa see Benin
Dahra Senegal see Dara
81 C2 Dahŭk Iraq
60 B2 Daik Indon.
106 C2 Daimiel Spain
Dairen China see Dalian
51 C2 Dajarra Austr.
70 A2 Dajing China
114 A3 Dakar Senegal
117 C4 Daketa Shet' watercourse Eth.
116 A2 Dākhilah, Wāḩāt ad Egypt
Dakhla Oasis Egypt see Dākhilah,
Wāḩāt ad
63 A3 Dakoank India
88 C3 Dakol'ka r. Belarus
109 D2 Đakovica Serb. and Mont.
109 C1 Đakovo Croatia
120 B2 Dala Angola
70 A1 Dalain Hob China
93 G3 Dalälven r. Sweden
111 C3 Dalaman Turkey
111 C3 Dalaman r. Turkey
68 C2 Dalandzadgad Mongolia
64 B2 Dalanganem Islands Phil.
63 B2 Đa Lat Vietnam
74 A2 Dalbandin Pak.
96 C3 Dalbeattie U.K.
53 D1 Dalby Austr.
93 E3 Dale Norway
141 C1 Dale Hollow Lake U.S.A.
53 C3 Dalgety Austr.
143 C1 Dalhart U.S.A.
131 D3 Dalhousie Can.
62 B1 Dali China
70 C2 Dalian China
96 C3 Dalkeith U.K.
143 D2 Dallas U.S.A.
128 A2 Dall Island U.S.A.
Dalmacija reg. Croatia see
Dalmatia
96 B2 Dalmally U.K.
109 C2 Dalmatia reg. Croatia
96 B3 Dalmellington U.K.
66 C2 Dal'negorsk Rus. Fed.
66 B1 Dal'nerechensk Rus. Fed.
Dalny China see Dalian
114 B4 Daloa Côte d'Ivoire
71 A3 Dalou Shan mts China
51 D2 Dalrymple, Mount Austr.
92 ☐A3 Dalsmynni Iceland
75 C2 Daltenganj India
141 D2 Dalton U.S.A.
Daltonganj India see Daltenganj
60 B1 Daludalu Indon.
71 B3 Daluo Shan mt. China
92 ☐B2 Dalvík Iceland
96 B2 Dalwhinnie U.K.
50 C1 Daly r. Austr.
51 C1 Daly Waters Austr.
74 B2 Daman India
74 B2 Daman and Diu union terr. India
116 B1 Damanhūr Egypt
59 C3 Damar i. Indon.
118 B2 Damara C.A.R.
80 B2 Damascus Syria
115 D3 Damaturu Nigeria
76 B3 Damāvand, Qolleh-ye mt. Iran
120 A1 Damba Angola
118 B3 Damboa Nigeria
81 D2 Damghan Iran
Damietta Egypt see Dumyāṭ
79 C2 Dammam Saudi Arabia
101 D1 Damme Ger.
75 B2 Damoh India
114 B4 Damongo Ghana
50 A2 Dampier Austr.
59 C3 Dampir, Selat sea chan. Indon.
75 D1 Damxung China
114 B4 Danané Côte d'Ivoire
63 B2 Đa Nẵng Vietnam
139 E2 Danbury U.S.A.
70 C1 Dandong China
117 B3 Dangila Eth.
146 B3 Dangriga Belize
70 B2 Dangshan China
89 F2 Danilov Rus. Fed.
89 E2 Danilovskaya Vozvyshennost' hills
Rus. Fed.
70 B2 Danjiangkou China
79 C2 Ḏank Oman
89 E3 Dankov Rus. Fed.
146 B3 Danlí Hond.
101 E1 Dannenberg (Elbe) Ger.
54 C2 Dannevirke N.Z.
62 B2 Dan Sai Thai.
70 B2 Dantu China
110 A1 Danube r. Europe

110 C1 Danube Delta Romania
138 B2 Danville IL U.S.A.
138 C3 Danville KY U.S.A.
139 D3 Danville VA U.S.A.
71 A4 Danxian China see Danzhou
Danzhou China
Danzig, Gulf of Pol./Rus. Fed. see
Gdańsk, Gulf of
Daojiang China see Daoxian
115 D2 Dao Timmi Niger
Daoud Alg. see Aïn Beïda
114 B4 Daoukro Côte d'Ivoire
71 B3 Daoxian China
64 B3 Dapa Phil.
114 C4 Dapaong Togo
68 C2 Da Qaidam Zhen China
69 E1 Daqing China
114 A3 Dara Senegal
80 B2 Dar'ā Syria
81 D3 Dārāb Iran
115 D1 Daraj Libya
81 D2 Dārān Iran
63 B2 Đa Răng, Sông r. Vietnam
109 D2 Đaravica mt. Serb. and Mont.
75 C2 Darbhanga India
Dardo China see Kangding
117 A3 Darfur reg. Sudan
119 D3 Dar es Salaam Tanz.
74 B1 Dargai Pak.
54 B1 Dargaville N.Z.
53 C3 Dargo Austr.
68 D1 Darhan Mongolia
150 D1 Darién, Golfo del g. Col.
Darjeeling India see Darjiling
75 C2 Darjiling India
68 C2 Darlag China
52 B2 Darling r. Austr.
53 C1 Darling Downs hills Austr.
50 A3 Darling Range hills Austr.
98 C2 Darlington U.K.
53 C2 Darlington Point Austr.
103 D1 Darłowo Pol.
101 D3 Darmstadt Ger.
115 E1 Darnah Libya
52 B2 Darnick Austr.
55 H3 Darnley, Cape Antarctica
107 C1 Daroca Spain
99 C3 Dartford U.K.
99 A4 Dartmoor hills U.K.
131 D3 Dartmouth Can.
99 B4 Dartmouth U.K.
59 D3 Daru P.N.G.
59 C2 Daruba Indon.
50 C1 Darwin Austr.
153 C5 Darwin Falkland Is
79 C2 Dārzīn Iran
65 A1 Dashiqiao China
Dashkhovuz Turkm. see Dashoguz
76 B2 Dashoguz Turkm.
74 A2 Dasht r. Pak.
61 C1 Datadian Indon.
111 C3 Datça Turkey
66 D2 Date Japan
71 B3 Datian China
70 B1 Datong China
64 B3 Datu Piang Phil.
74 B1 Daud Khel Pak.
88 B2 Daugava r. Latvia
88 C2 Daugavpils Latvia
100 C2 Daun Ger.
129 D2 Dauphin Can.
129 E2 Dauphin Lake Can.
73 B3 Davangere India
64 B3 Davao Phil.
64 B3 Davao Gulf Phil.
137 E2 Davenport U.S.A.
99 C3 Daventry U.K.
123 C2 Daveyton S. Africa
146 B4 David Panama
129 D2 Davidson Can.
126 F3 Davidson Lake Can.
135 B3 Davis U.S.A.
131 D2 Davis Inlet Can.
55 I3 Davis Sea sea Antarctica
127 I2 Davis Strait str. Can./Greenland
105 D2 Davos Switz.
88 C3 Davyd-Haradok Belarus
79 C3 Dawqah Oman
78 B3 Dawqah Saudi Arabia
126 C2 Dawson r. Austr.
141 D2 Dawson U.S.A.
128 B2 Dawson Creek Can.
128 B2 Dawsons Landing Can.
68 C2 Dawu China
Dawukou China see Shizuishan
79 C2 Dawwah Oman
104 B3 Dax France
Daxian China see Dazhou
68 C2 Da Xueshan mts China
52 B3 Daylesford Austr.
Dayong China see Zhangjiajie
81 C2 Dayr az Zawr Syria
75 D3 Dayton U.S.A.
141 D3 Daytona Beach U.S.A.
71 B3 Dayu China
70 B2 Da Yunhe canal China
70 A2 Dazhou China
122 B3 De Aar S. Africa
141 D3 Deadman Bay U.S.A.
80 B2 Dead Sea salt l. Asia
99 D4 Deal U.K.
71 B3 De'an China
152 B3 Deán Funes Arg.
128 B2 Dease Lake Can.
126 E2 Dease Strait Can.

135 C3 Death Valley depr. U.S.A.
104 C2 Deauville France
61 C1 Debak Sarawak Malaysia
111 B2 Debar Macedonia
103 E1 Dębica Pol.
103 E1 Dęblin Pol.
114 B3 Débo, Lac l. Mali
103 E2 Debrecen Hungary
117 B3 Debre Markos Eth.
119 D2 Debre Sina Eth.
117 B3 Debre Tabor Eth.
117 B4 Debre Zeyit Eth.
140 C2 Decatur AL U.S.A.
138 B3 Decatur IL U.S.A.
73 B3 Deccan plat. India
53 D1 Deception Bay Austr.
71 A3 Dechang China
102 C1 Děčín Czech Rep.
137 E2 Decorah U.S.A.
154 C2 Dedo de Deus mt. Brazil
88 C2 Dedovichi Rus. Fed.
121 C2 Dedza Malawi
99 B3 Dee r. England/Wales U.K.
96 C2 Dee r. Scotland U.K.
130 C3 Deep River Can.
53 D1 Deepwater Austr.
131 E3 Deer Lake Can.
134 D1 Deer Lodge U.S.A.
138 C2 Defiance U.S.A.
140 C2 De Funiak Springs U.S.A.
68 C2 Dêgê China
117 C4 Degeh Bur Eth.
139 F1 Dégelis Can.
102 C2 Deggendorf Ger.
91 E2 Degtevo Rus. Fed.
81 D2 Deh Bid Iran
81 C2 Dehlorān Iran
74 B1 Dehra Dun India
75 C2 Dehri India
69 E2 Dehui China
100 A2 Deinze Belgium
110 B1 Dej Romania
138 B2 De Kalb U.S.A.
116 B3 Dekemhare Eritrea
118 C3 Dekese Dem. Rep. Congo
118 B2 Dékoa C.A.R.
141 D3 De Land U.S.A.
135 C3 Delano U.S.A.
135 D3 Delano Peak U.S.A.
48 I3 Delap-Uliga-Djarrit Marshall Is
74 A1 Delārām Afgh.
123 C2 Delareyville S. Africa
129 D2 Delaronde Lake Can.
138 C2 Delaware U.S.A.
139 D3 Delaware r. U.S.A.
139 D3 Delaware state U.S.A.
139 D3 Delaware Bay U.S.A.
53 C3 Delegate Austr.
118 C2 Délembé C.A.R.
105 D2 Delémont Switz.
100 B1 Delft Neth.
100 C1 Delfzijl Neth.
121 D2 Delgado, Cabo c. Moz.
68 C2 Delhi China
74 B2 Delhi India
60 B2 Deli i. Indon.
128 B1 Déline Can.
Delingha China see Delhi
101 F2 Delitzsch Ger.
107 C4 Dellys Alg.
135 C4 Del Mar U.S.A.
101 D1 Delmenhorst Ger.
109 B1 Delnice Croatia
136 B3 Del Norte U.S.A.
83 L1 De-Longa, Ostrova is Rus. Fed.
De Long Islands Rus. Fed. see
De-Longa, Ostrova
De Long Strait Rus. Fed. see
Longa, Proliv
129 D3 Deloraine Can.
111 B3 Delphi tourist site Greece
141 D3 Delray Beach U.S.A.
143 C3 Del Rio U.S.A.
136 B3 Delta CO U.S.A.
135 D3 Delta UT U.S.A.
126 C2 Delta Junction U.S.A.
109 D3 Delvinë Albania
106 C1 Demanda, Sierra de la mts Spain
Demavend mt. Iran see
Damāvand, Qolleh-ye
118 C3 Demba Dem. Rep. Congo
119 D1 Dembech'a Eth.
117 B4 Dembī Dolo Eth.
Demerara Guyana see
Georgetown
91 C3 Demerdzhi mt. Ukr.
89 D2 Demidov Rus. Fed.
142 B2 Deming U.S.A.
111 C3 Demirci Turkey
111 C3 Demirköy Turkey
102 C1 Demmin Ger.
140 C2 Demopolis U.S.A.
60 B2 Dempo, Gunung vol. Indon.
89 D2 Demyansk Rus. Fed.
122 B3 De Naawte S. Africa
117 C3 Denakil reg. Eritrea/Eth.
98 B3 Denbigh U.K.
100 B1 Den Burg Neth.
62 B2 Den Chai Thai.
61 B2 Dendang Indon.
100 B2 Dendermonde Belgium
100 B2 Dendre r. Belgium
Dengjiabu China see Yujiang
70 A1 Dengkou China
Dengxian China see Dengzhou

Dengzhou
176

70 B2 Dengzhou China
Dengzhou China see Penglai
Den Haag Neth. see The Hague
50 A2 Denham Austr.
100 B1 Den Helder Neth.
107 D2 Denia Spain
52 B3 Deniliquin Austr.
134 C2 Denio U.S.A.
137 D2 Denison IA U.S.A.
143 D2 Denison TX U.S.A.
111 C3 Denizli Turkey
53 D2 Denman Austr.
50 A3 Denmark Austr.
93 E4 Denmark country Europe
84 B2 Denmark Strait Greenland/Iceland
77 C3 Denov Uzbek.
61 C2 Denpasar Indon.
143 D2 Denton U.S.A.
50 A3 D'Entrecasteaux, Point Austr.
59 E3 D'Entrecasteaux Islands P.N.G.
141 D2 Dentsville U.S.A.
136 B3 Denver U.S.A.
75 C2 Deogarh Orissa India
74 B2 Deogarh Rajasthan India
75 C2 Deoghar India
138 B2 De Pere U.S.A.
83 K2 Deputatskiy Rus. Fed.
62 A1 Dêqên China
140 B2 De Queen U.S.A.
74 A2 Dera Bugti Pak.
74 B1 Dera Ghazi Khan Pak.
74 B1 Dera Ismail Khan Pak.
87 D4 Derbent Rus. Fed.
50 B1 Derby Austr.
99 C3 Derby U.K.
137 D3 Derby U.S.A.
99 D3 Dereham U.K.
97 B2 Derg, Lough l. Ireland
91 D1 Derhachi Ukr.
140 B2 De Ridder U.S.A.
91 D2 Derkul r. Rus. Fed./Ukr.
75 B1 Dêrub China
116 B3 Derudeb Sudan
122 B3 De Rust S. Africa
109 C2 Derventa Bos.-Herz.
98 C3 Derwent r. England U.K.
98 C3 Derwent r. England U.K.
98 B2 Derwent Water l. U.K.
77 C1 Derzhavinsk Kazakh.
Derzhavinskiy Kazakh. see Derzhavinsk
152 B1 Desaguadero r. Bol.
49 M5 Désappointement, Îles du is Fr. Polynesia
129 D2 Deschambault Lake Can.
134 B1 Deschutes r. U.S.A.
117 B3 Desē Eth.
153 B4 Deseado Arg.
153 B4 Deseado r. Arg.
142 A2 Desemboque Mex.
137 E2 Des Moines U.S.A.
137 E2 Des Moines r. U.S.A.
91 C1 Desna r. Rus. Fed./Ukr.
89 D3 Desnogorsk Rus. Fed.
101 F2 Dessau Ger.
Dessye Eth. see Desē
128 A1 Destruction Bay Can.
149 C5 Desventurados, Islas de los is S. Pacific Ocean
128 C1 Detah Can.
120 B2 Dete Zimbabwe
101 D2 Detmold Ger.
138 C2 Detroit U.S.A.
137 D1 Detroit Lakes U.S.A.
Dett Zimbabwe see Dete
100 B2 Deurne Neth.
110 B1 Deva Romania
100 C1 Deventer Neth.
96 C2 Deveron r. U.K.
103 D2 Devét Skal hill Czech Rep.
137 D1 Devil's Lake U.S.A.
128 A2 Devil's Paw mt. U.S.A.
99 C4 Devizes U.K.
74 B2 Devli India
110 C2 Devnya Bulg.
128 C2 Devon Can.
126 F1 Devon Island Can.
51 D4 Devonport Austr.
74 B2 Dewas India
137 F3 Dexter U.S.A.
70 A2 Deyang China
59 D3 Deyong, Tanjung pt Indon.
79 C2 Deyyer Iran
81 C2 Dezfūl Iran
70 B2 Dezhou China
79 C2 Dhahran Saudi Arabia
75 D2 Dhaka Bangl.
78 B3 Dhamār Yemen
75 C2 Dhamtari India
75 C2 Dhanbad India
74 B2 Dhandhuka India
75 C2 Dhankuta Nepal
74 B2 Dhar India
75 D2 Dharmanagar India
73 B3 Dharmapuri India
75 C2 Dharmjaygarh India
114 B3 Ḍhar Oualâta hills Maur.
114 B3 Ḍhar Tîchît hills Maur.
73 B3 Dharwad India
Dharwar India see Dharwad
74 B2 Dhasa India
75 C2 Dhaulagiri mt. Nepal
78 B3 Dhubāb Yemen
74 B2 Dhule India
Dhulia India see Dhule
117 C4 Dhuusa Marreeb Somalia
144 A1 Diablo, Picacho del mt. Mex.
142 B2 Diablo Plateau U.S.A.
121 C2 Diaca Moz.
51 C2 Diamantina watercourse Austr.
155 D1 Diamantina Brazil
151 E4 Diamantina, Chapada plat. Brazil
159 F6 Diamantina Deep sea feature Indian Ocean
154 B1 Diamantino Brazil
151 D4 Diamantino Brazil
71 B3 Dianbai China
151 E4 Dianópolis Brazil
114 B4 Dianra Côte d'Ivoire
114 C3 Diapaga Burkina
79 C2 Dibā al Ḥiṣn U.A.E.
79 C2 Ḍibab Oman
118 C3 Dibaya Dem. Rep. Congo
122 B2 Dibeng S. Africa
72 D2 Dibrugarh India
136 C1 Dickinson U.S.A.
140 C1 Dickson U.S.A.
Dicle r. Turkey see Tigris
105 D3 Die France
Diedenhofen France see Thionville
129 D2 Diefenbaker, Lake Can.
Diégo Suarez Madag. see Antsirañana
114 B3 Diéma Mali
101 D2 Diemel r. Ger.
62 B1 Điện Biên Phu Vietnam
62 B2 Diên Châu Vietnam
101 D1 Diepholz Ger.
104 C2 Dieppe France
100 B2 Diest Belgium
115 D3 Diffa Niger
131 D3 Digby Can.
105 D3 Digne-les-Bains France
105 C2 Digoin France
64 B3 Digos Phil.
59 D3 Digul r. Indon.
105 D2 Dijon France
115 D4 Dik Chad
117 C3 Dikhil Djibouti
111 C3 Dikili Turkey
100 A2 Diksmuide Belgium
82 G2 Dikson Rus. Fed.
115 D3 Dikwa Nigeria
117 B4 Dīla Eth.
59 C3 Dili East Timor
101 D2 Dillenburg Ger.
117 A3 Dilling Sudan
126 B3 Dillingham U.S.A.
134 D1 Dillon MT U.S.A.
141 E2 Dillon SC U.S.A.
118 C4 Dilolo Dem. Rep. Congo
72 D2 Dimapur India
Dimashq Syria see Damascus
52 B3 Dimboola Austr.
110 C2 Dimitrovgrad Bulg.
87 D3 Dimitrovgrad Rus. Fed.
Dimitrovo Bulg. see Pernik
64 B2 Dinagat i. Phil.
75 C2 Dinajpur Bangl.
104 B2 Dinan France
100 B2 Dinant Belgium
111 D3 Dinar Turkey
81 D2 Dīnār, Kūh-e mt. Iran
104 B2 Dinard France
Dinbych U.K. see Denbigh
73 B3 Dindigul India
118 B1 Dindima Nigeria
123 D1 Dindiza Moz.
101 E2 Dingelstädt Ger.
97 A2 Dingle Ireland
97 A2 Dingle Bay Ireland
71 B3 Dingnan China
102 C2 Dingolfing Ger.
114 A3 Dinguiraye Guinea
96 B2 Dingwall U.K.
70 A2 Dingxi China
75 C2 Dinngyê China
123 C1 Dinokwe Botswana
91 D2 Dinskaya Rus. Fed.
100 C2 Dinslaken Ger.
135 C3 Dinuba U.S.A.
114 B3 Dioïla Mali
154 B3 Dionísio Cerqueira Brazil
114 A3 Diourbel Senegal
75 D2 Diphu India
64 B3 Dipolog Phil.
74 B1 Dir Pak.
51 D1 Direction, Cape Austr.
117 C4 Dirē Dawa Eth.
120 B2 Dirico Angola
50 A2 Dirk Hartog Island Austr.
53 C1 Dirranbandi Austr.
78 B3 Ḍirs Saudi Arabia
153 E5 Disappointment, Cape S. Georgia
134 B1 Disappointment, Cape U.S.A.
50 B2 Disappointment, Lake salt flat Austr.
52 B3 Discovery Bay Austr.
Disko i. Greenland see Qeqertarsuaq
141 E1 Dismal Swamp U.S.A.
99 D3 Diss U.K.
108 B3 Dittaino r. Sicily Italy
74 B2 Diu India
155 D2 Divinópolis Brazil
87 D4 Divnoye Rus. Fed.
114 B4 Divo Côte d'Ivoire
80 B2 Divriği Turkey
74 A2 Diwana Pak.
138 B2 Dixon U.S.A.
128 A2 Dixon Entrance sea chan. Can./U.S.A.
81 C2 Diyarbakır Turkey
74 A2 Diz Pak.
115 D2 Djado Niger
115 D2 Djado, Plateau du Niger
Djakarta Indon. see Jakarta
118 B3 Djambala Congo
115 C2 Djanet Alg.
115 D3 Djédaa Chad
115 C1 Djelfa Alg.
119 C2 Djéma C.A.R.
114 B3 Djenné Mali
114 B3 Djibo Burkina
117 C3 Djibouti country Africa
117 C3 Djibouti Djibouti
Djidjelli Alg. see Jijel
118 C2 Djolu Dem. Rep. Congo
114 C4 Djougou Benin
118 B2 Djoum Cameroon
115 D3 Djourab, Erg du des. Chad
92 □C3 Djúpivogur Iceland
89 F3 Dmitriyevka Rus. Fed.
89 E3 Dmitriyev-L'govskiy Rus. Fed.
Dmitriyevsk Ukr. see Makiyivka
89 E2 Dmitrov Rus. Fed.
Dmytriyevs'k Ukr. see Makiyivka
Dnepr r. Rus. Fed. see Dnieper
89 D3 Dnieper r. Rus. Fed.
91 C2 Dnieper r. Ukr.
90 B2 Dniester r. Ukr.
Dnipro r. Ukr. see Dnieper
91 C2 Dniprodzerzhyns'k Ukr.
91 D2 Dnipropetrovs'k Ukr.
91 C2 Dniprorudne Ukr.
Dnister r. Ukr. see Dniester
90 C2 Dnistrov'ky Lyman l. Ukr.
88 C2 Dno Rus. Fed.
121 C2 Doa Moz.
115 D4 Doba Chad
88 B2 Dobele Latvia
101 F2 Döbeln Ger.
59 C3 Doberai, Jazirah pen. Indon.
Doberai Peninsula Indon. see Doberai, Jazirah
59 C3 Dobo Indon.
109 C2 Doboj Bos.-Herz.
103 E1 Dobre Miasto Pol.
110 C2 Dobrich Bulg.
89 F3 Dobrinka Rus. Fed.
89 E3 Dobroye Rus. Fed.
89 D3 Dobrush Belarus
86 E3 Dobryanka Rus. Fed.
155 E1 Doce r. Brazil
145 B2 Doctor Arroyo Mex.
144 B2 Doctor Belisario Domínguez Mex.
Doctor Petru Groza Romania see Ştei
111 C3 Dodecanese is Greece
Dodekanisos is Greece see Dodecanese
136 C3 Dodge City U.S.A.
119 D3 Dodoma Tanz.
100 C1 Doesburg Neth.
100 C2 Doetinchem Neth.
59 C3 Dofa Indon.
75 C1 Dogai Coring salt l. China
128 B2 Dog Creek Can.
67 B3 Dōgo i. Japan
115 C3 Dogondoutchi Niger
81 C2 Doğubeyazıt Turkey
79 C2 Doha Qatar
62 A2 Doi Saket Thai.
81 D2 Dokali Iran
100 B1 Dokkum Neth.
88 C3 Dokshytsy Belarus
91 D2 Dokuchayevs'k Ukr.
59 D3 Dolak, Pulau i. Indon.
142 A1 Dolan Springs U.S.A.
130 C3 Dolbeau Can.
104 B2 Dol-de-Bretagne France
105 D2 Dole France
91 D2 Dolgaya, Kosa spit Rus. Fed.
99 B3 Dolgellau U.K.
89 E3 Dolgorukovo Rus. Fed.
89 E3 Dolgoye Rus. Fed.
69 F1 Dolinsk Rus. Fed.
103 D2 Dolný Kubín Slovakia
108 B1 Dolomites mts Italy
Dolomiti mts Italy see Dolomites
Dolonnur China see Duolun
117 C4 Dolo Odo Eth.
144 A2 Dolores Mex.
126 E2 Dolphin and Union Strait Can.
90 A2 Dolyna Ukr.
102 C2 Domažlice Czech Rep.
93 E3 Dombås Norway
103 D2 Dombóvár Hungary
Dombrovitsa Ukr. see Dubrovytsya
Dombrowa Pol. see Dąbrowa Górnicza
128 B2 Dome Creek Can.
147 D3 Dominica country West Indies
147 C3 Dominican Republic country West Indies
118 C3 Domiongo Dem. Rep. Congo
117 C4 Domo Eth.
89 E2 Domodedovo Rus. Fed.
111 B3 Domokos Greece
61 C2 Dompu Indon.
153 A3 Domuyo, Volcán vol. Arg.
142 B3 Don Mex.
89 E3 Don r. Rus. Fed.
96 C2 Don r. U.K.
97 D1 Donaghadee U.K.
52 B3 Donald Austr.
Donau r. Austria/Ger. see Danube
102 C2 Donauwörth Ger.
106 B2 Don Benito Spain
98 C3 Doncaster U.K.
120 A1 Dondo Angola
121 C2 Dondo Moz.
73 C4 Dondra Head hd Sri Lanka
97 B1 Donegal Ireland
97 B1 Donegal Bay Ireland
91 D2 Donets'k Ukr.
91 D2 Donets'kyy Kryazh hills Rus. Fed./Ukr.
118 B2 Donga Nigeria
50 A2 Dongara Austr.
71 A3 Dongchuan China
71 A4 Dongfang China
66 B1 Dongfanghong China
61 C2 Donggala Indon.
65 A2 Donggang China
Donggou China see Donggang
71 B3 Dongguan China
62 B2 Đông Ha Vietnam
Dong Hai sea N. Pacific Ocean see East China Sea
62 B2 Đông Hơi Vietnam
116 B3 Dongola Sudan
118 B2 Dongou Congo
Dong Phaya Yen Range mts Thai. see San Khao Phang Hoei
63 B2 Dong Phraya Yen esc. Thai.
Dongping China see Anhua
71 B3 Dongshan China
Dongsheng China see Ordos
70 C2 Dongtai China
71 B3 Dongting Hu l. China
Dong Ujimqin Qi China see Uliasta
71 C3 Dongyang China
70 B2 Dongying China
143 D3 Donna U.S.A.
54 B1 Donnellys Crossing N.Z.
100 C3 Donnersberg hill Ger.
107 C1 Donostia - San Sebastián Spain
81 D1 Donyztau, Sor dry lake Kazakh.
51 C1 Doomadgee Austr.
138 B2 Door Peninsula U.S.A.
117 C4 Dooxo Nugaaleed val. Somalia
50 B2 Dora, Lake salt flat Austr.
99 B4 Dorchester U.K.
122 A1 Dordabis Namibia
104 B2 Dordogne r. France
100 B2 Dordrecht Neth.
123 C3 Dordrecht S. Africa
122 A1 Doreenville Namibia
129 D2 Doré Lake Can.
101 D1 Dorfmark Ger.
114 B3 Dori Burkina
122 A3 Doring r. S. Africa
100 C2 Dormagen Ger.
96 B2 Dornoch U.K.
96 B2 Dornoch Firth est. U.K.
114 B3 Doro Mali
89 D3 Dorogobuzh Rus. Fed.
110 C1 Dorohoi Romania
68 C1 Döröö Nuur salt l. Mongolia
92 G3 Dorotea Sweden
50 A2 Dorre Island Austr.
53 D2 Dorrigo Austr.
118 B2 Dorsale Camerounaise slope Cameroon/Nigeria
100 C2 Dorsten Ger.
100 C2 Dortmund Ger.
100 C2 Dortmund-Ems-Kanal canal Ger.
153 B4 Dos Bahías, Cabo c. Arg.
101 F1 Dosse r. Ger.
114 C3 Dosso Niger
141 C2 Dothan U.S.A.
101 D1 Dötlingen Ger.
105 C1 Douai France
118 A2 Douala Cameroon
104 B2 Douarnenez France
105 D2 Doubs r. France/Switz.
54 A3 Doubtful Sound N.Z.
114 B3 Douentza Mali
98 A2 Douglas Isle of Man
122 B2 Douglas S. Africa
128 A2 Douglas AK U.S.A.
142 B2 Douglas AZ U.S.A.
141 D2 Douglas GA U.S.A.
136 B2 Douglas WY U.S.A.
104 C1 Doullens France
154 B1 Dourada, Serra hills Brazil
154 B2 Dourados Brazil
154 B2 Dourados r. Brazil
154 B2 Dourados, Serra dos hills Brazil
106 B1 Douro r. Port.
99 D4 Dover U.K.
139 D3 Dover U.S.A.
95 D3 Dover, Strait of France/U.K.
139 F1 Dover-Foxcroft U.S.A.
121 C2 Dowa Malawi
81 D3 Dowlatābād Iran
79 C2 Dowlatābād Iran
97 D1 Downpatrick U.K.
81 C2 Dow Rūd Iran
77 C3 Dowshī Afgh.
67 B3 Dōzen is Japan
130 C3 Dozois, Réservoir resr Can.
154 B2 Dracena Brazil
100 C1 Drachten Neth.
110 B2 Drăgănești-Olt Romania
110 B2 Drăgășani Romania
105 D3 Draguignan France
88 C3 Drahichyn Belarus

53 D1 **Drake** Austr.
123 C2 **Drakensberg** *mts* Lesotho/S. Africa
123 C2 **Drakensberg** *mts* S. Africa
149 C8 **Drake Passage** S. Atlantic Ocean
111 B2 **Drama** Greece
93 F4 **Drammen** Norway
109 C1 **Drava** *r.* Europe
128 C2 **Drayton Valley** Can.
101 D2 **Dreieich** Ger.
111 B3 **Drepano, Akra** *pt* Greece
102 C1 **Dresden** Ger.
104 C2 **Dreux** France
100 B1 **Driemond** Neth.
98 C2 **Driffield** U.K.
137 D1 **Drift Prairie** *reg.* U.S.A.
109 C2 **Drina** *r.* Bos.-Herz./Serb. and Mont.
140 B2 **Driskill Mountain** *hill* U.S.A.
**Drissa** Belarus *see* **Vyerkhnyadzvinsk**
109 C2 **Drniš** Croatia
110 B2 **Drobeta-Turnu Severin** Romania
90 B2 **Drochia** Moldova
101 D1 **Drochtersen** Ger.
97 C2 **Drogheda** Ireland
90 A2 **Drohobych** Ukr.
99 B3 **Droitwich Spa** U.K.
**Drokiya** Moldova *see* **Drochia**
97 B1 **Dromahair** Ireland
97 C1 **Dromore** U.K.
100 B1 **Dronten** Neth.
74 B1 **Drosh** Pak.
53 C3 **Drouin** Austr.
128 C2 **Drumheller** Can.
138 C1 **Drummond Island** U.S.A.
131 C3 **Drummondville** Can.
96 B2 **Drummore** U.K.
96 B2 **Drumnadrochit** U.K.
**Druskieniki** Lith. *see* **Druskininkai**
88 B3 **Druskininkai** Lith.
88 C2 **Druya** Belarus
91 D2 **Druzhkivka** Ukr.
88 D2 **Druzhnaya Gorka** Rus. Fed.
89 D3 **Drybin** Belarus
130 A3 **Dryden** Can.
50 B1 **Drysdale** *r.* Austr.
147 C3 **Duarte, Pico** *mt.* Dom. Rep.
78 A2 **Dubā** Saudi Arabia
79 C2 **Dubai** U.A.E.
90 B2 **Dubăsari** Moldova
129 D1 **Dubawnt Lake** Can.
**Dubayy** U.A.E. *see* **Dubai**
78 A2 **Dubbagh, Jabal ad** *mt.* Saudi Arabia
53 C2 **Dubbo** Austr.
97 C2 **Dublin** Ireland
141 D2 **Dublin** U.S.A.
89 E2 **Dubna** Rus. Fed.
90 B1 **Dubno** Ukr.
139 D2 **Du Bois** U.S.A.
**Dubossary** Moldova *see* **Dubăsari**
114 A4 **Dubréka** Guinea
109 C2 **Dubrovnik** Croatia
90 B1 **Dubrovytsya** Ukr.
89 D3 **Dubrowna** Belarus
137 E2 **Dubuque** U.S.A.
135 D2 **Duchesne** U.S.A.
129 D2 **Duck Bay** Can.
63 B2 **Đưc Trong** Vietnam
101 E2 **Duderstadt** Ger.
82 G2 **Dudinka** Rus. Fed.
99 B3 **Dudley** U.K.
106 B1 **Duero** *r.* Spain
48 H4 **Duff Islands** Solomon Is
131 C2 **Duffreboy, Lac** *l.* Can.
96 C2 **Dufftown** U.K.
109 C2 **Dugi Otok** *i.* Croatia
109 C2 **Dugi Rat** Croatia
100 C2 **Duisburg** Ger.
123 D1 **Duiwelskloof** S. Africa
123 C3 **Dukathole** S. Africa
117 B4 **Duk Fadiat** Sudan
79 C2 **Dukhān** Qatar
89 D2 **Dukhovshchina** Rus. Fed.
**Dukou** China *see* **Panzhihua**
88 C2 **Dūkštas** Lith.
68 C2 **Dulan** China
152 B3 **Dulce** *r.* Arg.
142 B1 **Dulce** U.S.A.
97 C2 **Duleek** Ireland
100 C2 **Dülmen** Ger.
110 C2 **Dulovo** Bulg.
137 E1 **Duluth** U.S.A.
64 B1 **Dumaguete** Phil.
60 B1 **Dumai** Indon.
64 B2 **Dumaran** *i.* Phil.
140 C1 **Dumas** *AR* U.S.A.
143 C1 **Dumas** *TX* U.S.A.
96 B3 **Dumbarton** U.K.
103 D2 **Ďumbier** *mt.* Slovakia
96 C3 **Dumfries** U.K.
89 E3 **Duminichi** Rus. Fed.
75 C2 **Dumka** India
55 L3 **Dumont d'Urville Sea** Antarctica
116 B1 **Dumyāṭ** Egypt
**Duna** *r.* Hungary *see* **Danube**
**Dūnaburg** Latvia *see* **Daugavpils**
103 D2 **Dunakeszi** Hungary
97 C2 **Dunany Point** Ireland
**Dunărea** *r.* Romania *see* **Danube**
**Dunării, Delta** Romania *see* **Danube Delta**
103 D2 **Dunaújváros** Hungary
**Dunav** *r.* Bulg./Croatia/Serb. and Mont. *see* **Danube**

90 B2 **Dunayivtsi** Ukr.
96 C1 **Dunbar** U.K.
96 C1 **Dunbeath** U.K.
128 B3 **Duncan** Can.
143 D2 **Duncan** U.S.A.
96 C1 **Duncansby Head** *hd* U.K.
88 B2 **Dundaga** Latvia
97 C1 **Dundalk** Ireland
139 D3 **Dundalk** U.S.A.
97 C2 **Dundalk Bay** Ireland
127 H1 **Dundas** Greenland
**Dún Dealgan** Ireland *see* **Dundalk**
123 D2 **Dundee** S. Africa
96 C2 **Dundee** U.K.
97 C1 **Dundrum Bay** U.K.
54 B3 **Dunedin** N.Z.
53 C2 **Dunedoo** Austr.
96 C2 **Dunfermline** U.K.
97 C1 **Dungannon** U.K.
74 B2 **Dungarpur** India
97 C2 **Dungarvan** Ireland
99 D4 **Dungeness** *hd* U.K.
97 C1 **Dungiven** U.K.
53 D2 **Dungog** Austr.
119 C2 **Dungu** Dem. Rep. Congo
60 B1 **Dungun** Malaysia
116 B2 **Dungunab** Sudan
69 E2 **Dunhua** China
68 C2 **Dunhuang** China
96 C2 **Dunkeld** U.K.
**Dunkerque** France *see* **Dunkirk**
104 C1 **Dunkirk** France
139 D2 **Dunkirk** U.S.A.
97 C2 **Dún Laoghaire** Ireland
97 B3 **Dunmanway** Ireland
97 D1 **Dunmurry** U.K.
96 C1 **Dunnet Head** *hd* U.K.
96 C3 **Duns** U.K.
134 B2 **Dunsmuir** U.S.A.
99 C4 **Dunstable** U.K.
100 B3 **Dun-sur-Meuse** France
96 A2 **Dunvegan** U.K.
70 B1 **Duolun** China
**Duperré** Alg. *see* **Aïn Defla**
110 B2 **Dupnitsa** Bulg.
136 C1 **Dupree** U.S.A.
**Duque de Bragança** Angola *see* **Calandula**
138 B3 **Du Quoin** U.S.A.
50 B1 **Durack** *r.* Austr.
105 C3 **Durance** *r.* France
144 B2 **Durango** Mex.
106 C1 **Durango** Spain
136 B3 **Durango** U.S.A.
143 D2 **Durant** U.S.A.
153 C3 **Durazno** Uru.
**Durazzo** Albania *see* **Durrës**
123 D2 **Durban** S. Africa
105 C3 **Durban-Corbières** France
122 A3 **Durbanville** S. Africa
100 B2 **Durbuy** Belgium
100 C2 **Düren** Ger.
75 C2 **Durg** India
98 C2 **Durham** U.K.
141 E1 **Durham** U.S.A.
60 B1 **Duri** Indon.
109 C2 **Durmitor** *mt.* Serb. and Mont.
96 B1 **Durness** U.K.
109 C2 **Durrës** Albania
97 A3 **Dursey Island** Ireland
111 C3 **Dursunbey** Turkey
117 C4 **Durukhsi** Somalia
59 D3 **D'Urville, Tanjung** *pt* Indon.
54 B2 **D'Urville Island** N.Z.
71 A3 **Dushan** China
77 C3 **Dushanbe** Tajik.
100 C2 **Düsseldorf** Ger.
**Dutch East Indies** country Asia *see* **Indonesia**
**Dutch Guiana** country S. America *see* **Suriname**
**Dutch West Indies** terr. West Indies *see* **Netherlands Antilles**
**Duvno** Bos.-Herz. *see* **Tomislavgrad**
71 A3 **Duyun** China
80 B1 **Düzce** Turkey
91 D2 **Dvorichna** Ukr.
74 A2 **Dwarka** India
123 C1 **Dwarsberg** S. Africa
134 C1 **Dworshak Reservoir** U.S.A.
89 D3 **Dyat'kovo** Rus. Fed.
96 C2 **Dyce** U.K.
127 H2 **Dyer, Cape** Can.
140 C1 **Dyersburg** U.S.A.
99 B3 **Dyfi** *r.* U.K.
**Dyfrdwy** *r.* U.K. *see* **Dee**
103 D2 **Dyje** *r.* Austria/Czech Rep.
103 D1 **Dylewska Góra** *hill* Pol.
91 D2 **Dymytrov** Ukr.
123 C3 **Dyoki** S. Africa
51 D2 **Dysart** Austr.
123 B3 **Dysselsdorp** S. Africa
87 E3 **Dyurtyuli** Rus. Fed.
69 D2 **Dzamin Üüd** Mongolia
121 D2 **Dzaoudzi** Mayotte
91 D2 **Dzerzhyns'k** Ukr.
**Dzhaltyr** Kazakh. *see* **Zhaltyr**
**Dzhambul** Kazakh. *see* **Taraz**
81 D1 **Dzhanga** Turkm.
76 B1 **Dzhangala** Kazakh.
91 C2 **Dzhankoy** Ukr.
81 D2 **Dzhebel** Turkm.
**Dzhetygara** Kazakh. *see* **Zhitikara**

**Dzhezkazgan** Kazakh. *see* **Zhezkazgan**
**Dzhizak** Uzbek. *see* **Jizzax**
91 D3 **Dzhubga** Rus. Fed.
83 K3 **Dzhugdzhur, Khrebet** *mts* Rus. Fed.
77 D2 **Dzhungarskiy Alatau, Khrebet** *mts* China/Kazakh.
76 C2 **Dzhusaly** Kazakh.
103 E1 **Działdowo** Pol.
145 D2 **Dzilam de Bravo** Mex.
69 D1 **Dzuunmod** Mongolia
88 C3 **Dzyarzhynsk** Belarus
88 C3 **Dzyatlavichy** Belarus

**E**

131 E2 **Eagle** *r.* Can.
134 C1 **Eagle Cap** *mt.* U.S.A.
130 A3 **Eagle Lake** Can.
134 B2 **Eagle Lake** U.S.A.
143 C3 **Eagle Pass** U.S.A.
126 C2 **Eagle Plain** Can.
**Eap** *i.* Micronesia *see* **Yap**
130 A2 **Ear Falls** Can.
135 C3 **Earlimart** U.S.A.
96 C2 **Earn** *r.* U.K.
55 J2 **East Antarctica** *reg.* Antarctica
**East Bengal** country Asia *see* **Bangladesh**
99 D4 **Eastbourne** U.K.
59 D2 **East Caroline Basin** *sea feature* N. Pacific Ocean
69 E2 **East China Sea** N. Pacific Ocean
54 B1 **East Coast Bays** N.Z.
**East Dereham** U.K. *see* **Dereham**
129 D3 **Eastend** Can.
157 G7 **Easter Island** S. Pacific Ocean
123 C3 **Eastern Cape** *prov.* S. Africa
116 B2 **Eastern Desert** Egypt
73 B3 **Eastern Ghats** *mts* India
**Eastern Samoa** *terr.* S. Pacific Ocean *see* **American Samoa**
**Eastern Sayan Mountains** Rus. Fed. *see* **Vostochnyy Sayan**
**Eastern Transvaal** *prov.* S. Africa *see* **Mpumalanga**
129 E2 **Easterville** Can.
153 C5 **East Falkland** *i.* Falkland Is
100 A1 **East Frisian Islands** Ger.
135 C3 **Eastgate** U.S.A.
137 D1 **East Grand Forks** U.S.A.
96 B3 **East Kilbride** U.K.
138 C2 **East Lansing** U.S.A.
99 C4 **Eastleigh** U.K.
96 C3 **East Linton** U.K.
138 C2 **East Liverpool** U.S.A.
123 C3 **East London** S. Africa
130 C2 **Eastmain** Can.
130 C2 **Eastmain** *r.* Can.
141 D2 **Eastman** U.S.A.
157 G8 **East Pacific Rise** *sea feature* N. Pacific Ocean
**East Pakistan** country Asia *see* **Bangladesh**
**East Sea** N. Pacific Ocean *see* **Japan, Sea of**
83 K2 **East Siberian Sea** Rus. Fed.
138 A3 **East St Louis** U.S.A.
59 C3 **East Timor** country Asia
53 C2 **East Toorale** Austr.
139 D2 **East York** Can.
138 A2 **Eau Claire** U.S.A.
130 C2 **Eau Claire, Lac à l'** *l.* Can.
59 D2 **Eauripik** *atoll* Micronesia
145 C2 **Ebano** Mex.
99 B4 **Ebbw Vale** U.K.
118 B2 **Ebebiyin** Equat. Guinea
102 C1 **Eberswalde-Finow** Ger.
66 D2 **Ebetsu** Japan
77 E2 **Ebinur Hu** *salt l.* China
118 C2 **Ebola** *r.* Dem. Rep. Congo
109 C2 **Eboli** Italy
118 B2 **Ebolowa** Cameroon
107 D1 **Ebro** *r.* Spain
114 C1 **Ech Chélif** Alg.
**Echeng** China *see* **Ezhou**
144 A2 **Echeverria, Pico** *mt.* Mex.
129 E2 **Echoing** *r.* Can.
100 C3 **Echternach** Lux.
52 B3 **Echuca** Austr.
106 B2 **Écija** Spain
102 B1 **Eckernförde** Ger.
127 G2 **Eclipse Sound** *sea chan.* Can.
150 B3 **Ecuador** country S. America
116 C3 **Ed** Eritrea
96 C1 **Eday** *i.* U.K.
117 A3 **Ed Da'ein** Sudan
117 B3 **Ed Damazin** Sudan
116 B3 **Ed Damer** Sudan
116 B3 **Ed Debba** Sudan
51 D4 **Eddystone Point** Austr.
100 B1 **Ede** Neth.
118 B2 **Edéa** Cameroon
154 C1 **Edéia** Brazil
53 C3 **Eden** Austr.
98 B2 **Eden** *r.* U.K.
143 D2 **Eden** U.S.A.
123 C3 **Edenburg** S. Africa
97 C2 **Edenderry** Ireland
52 B3 **Edenhope** Austr.

141 E1 **Edenton** U.S.A.
111 B2 **Edessa** Greece
139 E2 **Edgartown** U.S.A.
**Edge Island** Svalbard *see* **Edgeøya**
82 C1 **Edgeøya** *i.* Svalbard
141 D3 **Edgewater** U.S.A.
138 C2 **Edinboro** U.S.A.
143 D3 **Edinburg** U.S.A.
96 C3 **Edinburgh** U.K.
90 B2 **Edineț** Moldova
111 C2 **Edirne** Turkey
**Edith Ronne Land** *ice feature* Antarctica *see* **Ronne Ice Shelf**
128 C2 **Edmonton** Can.
131 D3 **Edmundston** Can.
111 C3 **Edremit** Turkey
111 C3 **Edremit Körfezi** *b.* Turkey
128 C2 **Edson** Can.
119 C3 **Edward, Lake** Dem. Rep. Congo/Uganda
**Edwardesabad** Pak. *see* **Bannu**
143 D2 **Edwards Plateau** U.S.A.
55 C2 **Edward VII Peninsula** Antarctica
96 C2 **Edzell** U.K.
100 A2 **Eeklo** Belgium
135 B2 **Eel** *r.* U.S.A.
100 C1 **Eemskanaal** *canal* Neth.
100 C1 **Eenrum** Neth.
138 B3 **Effingham** U.S.A.
135 C3 **Egan Range** U.S.A.
103 E2 **Eger** Hungary
93 E4 **Egersund** Norway
100 B2 **Eghezée** Belgium
92 □C2 **Egilsstaðir** Iceland
80 B2 **Eğirdir** Turkey
80 B2 **Eğirdir Gölü** *l.* Turkey
104 C2 **Égletons** France
**Egmont, Mount** *vol.* N.Z. *see* **Taranaki, Mount**
83 M2 **Egvekinot** Rus. Fed.
116 A2 **Egypt** country Africa
70 A2 **Ehen Hudag** China
106 C1 **Eibar** Spain
100 C1 **Eibergen** Neth.
100 C2 **Eifel** *hills* Ger.
96 A2 **Eigg** *i.* U.K.
73 B4 **Eight Degree Channel** India/Maldives
50 B1 **Eighty Mile Beach** Austr.
80 B3 **Eilat** Israel
101 F2 **Eilenburg** Ger.
101 D2 **Einbeck** Ger.
100 B2 **Eindhoven** Neth.
160 N4 **Eirik Ridge** *sea feature* N. Atlantic Ocean
150 B3 **Eirunepé** Brazil
120 B2 **Eiseb** *watercourse* Namibia
101 E2 **Eisenach** Ger.
101 F2 **Eisenberg** Ger.
101 F2 **Eisenhüttenstadt** Ger.
103 D2 **Eisenstadt** Austria
101 E2 **Eisleben Lutherstadt** Ger.
**Eivissa** Spain *see* **Ibiza**
**Eivissa** *i.* Spain *see* **Ibiza**
107 C1 **Ejea de los Caballeros** Spain
121 □D3 **Ejeda** Madag.
**Ejin Qi** China *see* **Dalain Hob**
93 H4 **Ekenäs** Fin.
77 D1 **Ekibastuz** Kazakh.
93 F4 **Eksjö** Sweden
122 A2 **Eksteenfontein** S. Africa
130 B2 **Ekwan** *r.* Can.
62 A2 **Ela** Myanmar
**El Aaiún** Western Sahara *see* **Laâyoune**
123 C2 **Elandsdoorn** S. Africa
**El Araïche** Morocco *see* **Larache**
**El Asnam** Alg. *see* **Ech Chélif**
111 B3 **Elassona** Greece
**Elat** Israel *see* **Eilat**
80 B2 **Elazığ** Turkey
108 B2 **Elba, Isola d'** *i.* Italy
150 B2 **El Banco** Col.
109 D2 **Elbasan** Albania
150 C2 **El Baúl** Venez.
114 C1 **El Bayadh** Alg.
101 D1 **Elbe** *r.* Ger.
136 B3 **Elbert, Mount** U.S.A.
141 D2 **Elberton** U.S.A.
104 C2 **Elbeuf** France
80 B2 **Elbistan** Turkey
103 D1 **Elbląg** Pol.
153 A4 **El Bolsón** Arg.
87 D4 **El'brus** *mt.* Rus. Fed.
81 C2 **Elburz Mountains** *mts* Iran
150 C2 **El Callao** Venez.
143 D3 **El Campo** U.S.A.
135 C4 **El Centro** U.S.A.
152 B1 **El Cerro** Bol.
107 C2 **Elche-Elx** Spain
145 C3 **El Chichónal** *vol.* Mex.
107 C2 **Elda** Spain
119 D2 **Eldama Ravine** Kenya
137 E3 **Eldon** U.S.A.
154 B3 **Eldorado** Arg.
154 C2 **Eldorado** Brazil
144 B2 **El Dorado** Mex.
140 B2 **El Dorado** *AR* U.S.A.
137 D3 **El Dorado** *KS* U.S.A.
134 B2 **Electric Peak** U.S.A.
114 B2 **El Eglab** *plat.* Alg.
106 C2 **El Ejido** Spain
89 E2 **Elektrostal'** Rus. Fed.
150 B1 **El Encanto** Col.
146 C2 **Eleuthera** *i.* Bahamas

| 116 A3 | El Fasher Sudan |
| 144 B2 | El Fuerte Mex. |
| 117 A3 | El Fula Sudan |
| 116 A3 | El Geneina Sudan |
| 116 B3 | El Geteina Sudan |
| 96 C2 | Elgin U.K. |
| 138 B2 | Elgin U.S.A. |
| 83 K2 | El'ginskiy Rus. Fed. |
| | El Gîza Egypt see Giza |
| 115 C1 | El Goléa Alg. |
| 144 A1 | El Golfo de Santa Clara Mex. |
| 119 D2 | Elgon, Mount Uganda |
| 108 A3 | El Hadjar Alg. |
| 114 A2 | El Hammâmi reg. Maur. |
| 114 B2 | El Hank esc. Mali/Maur. |
| 114 A2 | El Hierro i. Canary Is |
| 145 C2 | El Higo Mex. |
| 114 C2 | El Homr Alg. |
| | Elichpur India see Achalpur |
| 126 B2 | Elim U.S.A. |
| | Élisabethville Dem. Rep. Congo see Lubumbashi |
| | El Iskandarîya Egypt see Alexandria |
| 87 D4 | Elista Rus. Fed. |
| 139 E2 | Elizabeth U.S.A. |
| 141 E1 | Elizabeth City U.S.A. |
| 138 B3 | Elizabethtown U.S.A. |
| 114 B1 | El Jadida Morocco |
| 103 E1 | Ełk Pol. |
| 108 A3 | El Kala Alg. |
| 88 C2 | Elkas kalns hill Latvia |
| 143 D1 | Elk City U.S.A. |
| 114 B1 | El Kelaâ des Srarhna Morocco |
| 128 C2 | Elkford Can. |
| 138 B2 | Elkhart U.S.A. |
| | El Khartûm Sudan see Khartoum |
| 110 C2 | Elkhovo Bulg. |
| 139 D3 | Elkins U.S.A. |
| 128 C3 | Elko Can. |
| 134 C2 | Elko U.S.A. |
| 129 C2 | Elk Point Can. |
| 137 E1 | Elk River U.S.A. |
| 126 F1 | Ellef Ringnes Island Can. |
| 137 D1 | Ellendale U.S.A. |
| 134 B1 | Ellensburg U.S.A. |
| 54 B2 | Ellesmere, Lake N.Z. |
| 127 G1 | Ellesmere Island Can. |
| 98 B3 | Ellesmere Port U.K. |
| 126 F2 | Ellice r. Can. |
| | Ellice Islands country S. Pacific Ocean see Tuvalu |
| 123 C3 | Elliotdale S. Africa |
| 138 C1 | Elliot Lake Can. |
| 96 C2 | Ellon U.K. |
| 139 F2 | Ellsworth U.S.A. |
| 55 R2 | Ellsworth Mountains Antarctica |
| 111 C3 | Elmalı Turkey |
| 115 C1 | El Meghaïer Alg. |
| 139 D2 | Elmira U.S.A. |
| 107 C2 | El Moral Spain |
| 101 D1 | Elmshorn Ger. |
| 117 A3 | El Muglad Sudan |
| 150 B2 | El Nevado, Cerro mt. Col. |
| 64 A2 | El Nido Phil. |
| 116 B3 | El Obeid Sudan |
| 144 B2 | El Oro Mex. |
| 115 C1 | El Oued Alg. |
| 142 A2 | Eloy U.S.A. |
| | El Paso U.S.A. see Derby |
| 142 B2 | El Paso U.S.A. |
| 145 D3 | El Pinalón, Cerro mt. Guat. |
| 144 B1 | El Porvenir Mex. |
| 107 D1 | El Prat de Llobregat Spain |
| 146 B3 | El Progreso Hond. |
| 106 B2 | El Puerto de Santa María Spain |
| | El Qâhira Egypt see Cairo |
| | El Quds Israel/West Bank see Jerusalem |
| 143 D1 | El Reno U.S.A. |
| 128 A1 | Elsa Can. |
| 145 B2 | El Salado Mex. |
| 144 B2 | El Salto Mex. |
| 146 B3 | El Salvador country Central America |
| 152 B2 | El Salvador Chile |
| 145 B2 | El Salvador Mex. |
| 142 B3 | El Sauz Mex. |
| 144 A1 | El Socorro Mex. |
| 142 B3 | El Sueco Mex. |
| | El Suweis Egypt see Suez |
| 108 A3 | El Tarf Alg. |
| 106 B1 | El Teleno mt. Spain |
| 145 C2 | El Temascal Mex. |
| 150 C2 | El Tigre Venez. |
| 147 D4 | El Tocuyo Venez. |
| | El Uqsur Egypt see Luxor |
| 73 C3 | Eluru India |
| 88 C2 | Elva Estonia |
| 106 B2 | Elvas Port. |
| 93 F3 | Elverum Norway |
| 119 E2 | El Wak Kenya |
| 99 D3 | Ely U.K. |
| 137 E1 | Ely MN U.S.A. |
| 135 D3 | Ely NV U.S.A. |
| 81 D2 | Emāmrūd Iran |
| 93 G4 | Emån r. Sweden |
| 76 B2 | Emba Kazakh. |
| 76 B2 | Emba r. Kazakh. |
| 123 C2 | Embalenhle S. Africa |
| 118 B2 | Embondo Dem. Rep. Congo |
| 154 C1 | Emborcação, Represa de resr Brazil |
| 119 D3 | Embu Kenya |
| 100 C1 | Emden Ger. |

| 51 D2 | Emerald Austr. |
| 129 E3 | Emerson Can. |
| 111 C3 | Emet Turkey |
| 123 D2 | eMgwenya S. Africa |
| 123 D2 | eMijindini S. Africa |
| 115 D3 | Emi Koussi mt. Chad |
| 145 C3 | Emiliano Zapata Mex. |
| 110 C2 | Emine, Nos pt Bulg. |
| 80 B2 | Emirdağ Turkey |
| 88 B2 | Emmaste Estonia |
| 100 B1 | Emmeloord Neth. |
| 100 C2 | Emmelshausen Ger. |
| 100 C1 | Emmen Neth. |
| 143 C3 | Emory Peak U.S.A. |
| 144 A2 | Empalme Mex. |
| 123 D2 | Empangeni S. Africa |
| 156 D2 | Emperor Trough sea feature N. Pacific Ocean |
| 108 B2 | Empoli Italy |
| 111 C3 | Emponas Greece |
| 137 D3 | Emporia KS U.S.A. |
| 139 D3 | Emporia VA U.S.A. |
| | Empty Quarter des. Saudi Arabia see Rub' al Khālī |
| 100 C1 | Ems r. Ger. |
| 100 C1 | Emsdetten Ger. |
| 88 C2 | Emumägi hill Estonia |
| 123 C2 | Emzinoni S. Africa |
| 59 D3 | Enarotali Indon. |
| 144 B2 | Encarnación Mex. |
| 152 C2 | Encarnación Para. |
| 155 D1 | Encruzilhada Brazil |
| 61 D2 | Ende Indon. |
| 55 G2 | Enderby Land reg. Antarctica |
| 126 B2 | Endicott Mountains U.S.A. |
| 50 A2 | Eneabba Austr. |
| 91 C2 | Enerhodar Ukr. |
| 111 C2 | Enez Turkey |
| 97 C2 | Enfield Ireland |
| 87 D3 | Engel's Rus. Fed. |
| 60 B2 | Enggano i. Indon. |
| 99 C3 | England admin. div. U.K. |
| 130 C3 | Englehart Can. |
| 141 D3 | Englewood U.S.A. |
| 130 A2 | English r. Can. |
| | English Bazar India see Ingraj Bazar |
| 95 C4 | English Channel France/U.K. |
| 143 D1 | Enid U.S.A. |
| | Enkeldoorn Zimbabwe see Chivhu |
| 100 B1 | Enkhuizen Neth. |
| 93 G4 | Enköping Sweden |
| 108 B3 | Enna Sicily Italy |
| 129 D1 | Ennadai Lake Can. |
| 116 A3 | En Nahud Sudan |
| 115 E3 | Ennedi, Massif mts Chad |
| 53 C1 | Enngonia Austr. |
| 97 B2 | Ennis Ireland |
| 143 D2 | Ennis U.S.A. |
| 97 C2 | Enniscorthy Ireland |
| 97 C2 | Enniskerry Ireland |
| 97 C1 | Enniskillen Ireland |
| 97 B2 | Ennistymon Ireland |
| 102 C2 | Enns Austria |
| 102 C2 | Enns r. Austria |
| 92 J3 | Eno Fin. |
| 92 H2 | Enontekiö Fin. |
| 53 C3 | Ensay Austr. |
| 100 C1 | Enschede Neth. |
| 144 A1 | Ensenada Mex. |
| 70 A2 | Enshi China |
| 119 D2 | Entebbe Uganda |
| 128 C1 | Enterprise Can. |
| 140 C2 | Enterprise AL U.S.A. |
| 134 C1 | Enterprise OR U.S.A. |
| 152 B2 | Entre Ríos Bol. |
| 106 B2 | Entroncamento Port. |
| 115 C4 | Enugu Nigeria |
| 150 B3 | Envira Brazil |
| 118 B2 | Epéna Congo |
| 105 C2 | Épernay France |
| 135 D3 | Ephraim U.S.A. |
| 134 C1 | Ephrata U.S.A. |
| 105 D2 | Épinal France |
| 99 D4 | Epping U.K. |
| 99 C4 | Epsom U.K. |
| 118 A2 | Equatorial Guinea country Africa |
| 104 B2 | Équerdreville-Hainneville France |
| 101 D3 | Erbach Ger. |
| 101 F3 | Erbendorf Ger. |
| 100 C1 | Erbeskopf hill Ger. |
| 81 C2 | Erciş Turkey |
| 80 B2 | Erciyes Dağı mt. Turkey |
| 103 E2 | Érd Hungary |
| | Erdaobaihe China see Baihe |
| 65 B1 | Erdao Jiang r. China |
| 111 C2 | Erdek Turkey |
| 80 B2 | Erdemli Turkey |
| 154 B2 | Eré, Campos hills Brazil |
| 55 M2 | Erebus, Mount vol. Antarctica |
| 152 C2 | Erechim Brazil |
| 69 D1 | Ereentsav Mongolia |
| 80 B2 | Ereğli Turkey |
| 80 B1 | Ereğli Turkey |
| 69 D2 | Erenhot China |
| | Erevan Armenia see Yerevan |
| 101 E2 | Erfurt Ger. |
| 80 B2 | Ergani Turkey |
| 114 B2 | 'Erg Chech des. Alg./Mali |
| 111 C2 | Ergene r. Turkey |
| 78 A3 | Erheib Sudan |
| 96 B2 | Ericht, Loch l. U.K. |
| 138 C2 | Erie U.S.A. |
| 138 C2 | Erie, Lake Can./U.S.A. |
| 66 D2 | Erimo-misaki c. Japan |

| 116 B3 | Eritrea country Africa |
| 101 E3 | Erlangen Ger. |
| 50 C2 | Erldunda Austr. |
| 123 C2 | Ermelo S. Africa |
| 80 B2 | Ermenek Turkey |
| 111 B3 | Ermoupoli Greece |
| 73 B4 | Ernakulam India |
| 97 B1 | Erne r. Ireland/U.K. |
| 73 B3 | Erode India |
| 100 B2 | Erp Neth. |
| 114 B1 | Er Rachidia Morocco |
| 116 B3 | Er Rahad Sudan |
| 97 B1 | Errigal hill Ireland |
| 97 A1 | Erris Head hd Ireland |
| 48 H5 | Erromango i. Vanuatu |
| 109 D2 | Ersekë Albania |
| 89 F3 | Ertil' Rus. Fed. |
| 101 D2 | Erwitte Ger. |
| 101 F2 | Erzgebirge mts Czech Rep./Ger. |
| 80 B2 | Erzincan Turkey |
| 81 C2 | Erzurum Turkey |
| 66 D2 | Esashi Japan |
| 93 E4 | Esbjerg Denmark |
| 135 D3 | Escalante U.S.A. |
| 135 D3 | Escalante Desert U.S.A. |
| 144 B2 | Escalón Mex. |
| 138 B1 | Escanaba U.S.A. |
| 145 C3 | Escárcega Mex. |
| 107 C1 | Escatrón Spain |
| 100 A2 | Escaut r. Belgium |
| 101 E1 | Eschede Ger. |
| 100 B3 | Esch-sur-Alzette Lux. |
| 101 E2 | Eschwege Ger. |
| 100 C2 | Eschweiler Ger. |
| 135 C4 | Escondido U.S.A. |
| 144 B2 | Escuinapa Mex. |
| 111 C3 | Eşen Turkey |
| 81 D2 | Eşfahān Iran |
| 123 D2 | Eshowe S. Africa |
| 123 D2 | Esikhawini S. Africa |
| 98 B2 | Esk r. U.K. |
| 131 D2 | Esker Can. |
| 92 □C2 | Eskifjörður Iceland |
| 93 G4 | Eskilstuna Sweden |
| | Eskimo Point Can. see Arviat |
| 111 D3 | Eskişehir Turkey |
| 81 C2 | Eslāmābād-e Gharb Iran |
| 111 C3 | Esler Dağı mt. Turkey |
| 111 C3 | Eşme Turkey |
| 146 C2 | Esmeralda Cuba |
| 150 B2 | Esmeraldas Ecuador |
| 79 D2 | Espakeh Iran |
| 105 C3 | Espalion France |
| 130 B3 | Espanola Can. |
| 142 B1 | Espanola U.S.A. |
| 50 B3 | Esperance Austr. |
| 153 A5 | Esperanza Arg. |
| 144 B2 | Esperanza Mex. |
| 106 B2 | Espichel, Cabo c. Port. |
| 154 B3 | Espigão, Serra do mts Brazil |
| 143 C3 | Espinazo Mex. |
| 155 D1 | Espinhaço, Serra do mts Brazil |
| 151 E4 | Espinosa Brazil |
| | Espírito Santo Brazil see Vila Velha |
| 48 H5 | Espíritu Santo i. Vanuatu |
| 144 A2 | Espíritu Santo, Isla i. Mex. |
| 93 H3 | Espoo Fin. |
| 153 A4 | Esquel Arg. |
| 114 B1 | Essaouira Morocco |
| 114 A2 | Es Semara Western Sahara |
| 100 C2 | Essen Ger. |
| 150 D2 | Essequibo r. Guyana |
| 139 E2 | Essex Junction U.S.A. |
| 83 L3 | Esso Rus. Fed. |
| 106 B1 | Estaca de Bares, Punta da pt Spain |
| 153 B5 | Estados, Isla de los i. Arg. |
| 81 D3 | Eştahbān Iran |
| 151 F4 | Estância Brazil |
| 123 C2 | Estcourt S. Africa |
| 107 C1 | Estella Spain |
| 106 B2 | Estepona Spain |
| 106 C1 | Esteras de Medinaceli Spain |
| 129 D2 | Esterhazy Can. |
| 152 B2 | Esteros Para. |
| 136 B2 | Estes Park U.S.A. |
| 129 D3 | Estevan Can. |
| 138 B2 | Estherville U.S.A. |
| 129 D2 | Eston Can. |
| 88 C2 | Estonia country Europe |
| | Estonskaya S.S.R. admin. reg. Europe see Estonia |
| 106 B1 | Estrela, Serra da mts Port. |
| 106 B2 | Estremoz Port. |
| 52 A1 | Etadunna Austr. |
| 104 C2 | Étampes France |
| 104 C1 | Étaples France |
| 75 B2 | Etawah India |
| 123 D2 | eThandakukhanya S. Africa |
| 122 B2 | E'Thembini S. Africa |
| 117 B4 | Ethiopia country Africa |
| | Etna, Monte vol. Italy see Etna, Mount |
| 109 C3 | Etna, Mount vol. Sicily Italy |
| 93 E4 | Etne Norway |
| 128 A2 | Etolin Island U.S.A. |
| 120 A2 | Etosha Pan salt pan Namibia |
| 110 B2 | Etropole Bulg. |
| 100 C3 | Ettelbruck Lux. |
| 100 B2 | Etten-Leur Neth. |
| 107 C1 | Etxarri-Aranatz Spain |
| 99 D4 | Eu France |
| 53 C2 | Euabalong Austr. |
| | Euboea i. Greece see Evvoia |
| 50 B3 | Eucla Austr. |

| 138 C2 | Euclid U.S.A. |
| 141 C2 | Eufaula U.S.A. |
| 143 D1 | Eufaula Lake resr U.S.A. |
| 134 B2 | Eugene U.S.A. |
| 144 A2 | Eugenia, Punta pt Mex. |
| 53 C1 | Eulo Austr. |
| 53 C1 | Eumungerie Austr. |
| 143 C2 | Eunice U.S.A. |
| 81 C2 | Euphrates r. Asia |
| 134 B2 | Eureka CA U.S.A. |
| 134 C1 | Eureka MT U.S.A. |
| 135 C3 | Eureka NV U.S.A. |
| 52 B2 | Euriowie Austr. |
| 53 C3 | Euroa Austr. |
| 106 B2 | Europa Point Gibraltar |
| 140 C2 | Eutaw U.S.A. |
| 128 B2 | Eutsuk Lake Can. |
| 123 C2 | Evander S. Africa |
| 130 C2 | Evans, Lac l. Can. |
| 53 D1 | Evans Head Austr. |
| 127 G2 | Evans Strait Can. |
| 138 B2 | Evanston IL U.S.A. |
| 136 A2 | Evanston WY U.S.A. |
| 138 B3 | Evansville U.S.A. |
| | Eva Perón Arg. see La Plata |
| 123 C2 | Evaton S. Africa |
| 79 C2 | Evaz Iran |
| 83 L2 | Evensk Rus. Fed. |
| 50 C2 | Everard Range hills Austr. |
| 75 C2 | Everest, Mount China/Nepal |
| 134 B1 | Everett U.S.A. |
| 100 A2 | Evergem Belgium |
| 141 D3 | Everglades swamp U.S.A. |
| 140 C2 | Evergreen U.S.A. |
| 99 C3 | Evesham U.K. |
| 118 B2 | Evinayong Equat. Guinea |
| 93 E4 | Evje Norway |
| 106 B2 | Évora Port. |
| 69 F1 | Evoron, Ozero l. Rus. Fed. |
| 111 B2 | Evosmo Greece |
| 104 C2 | Évreux France |
| 111 C2 | Evros r. Greece/Turkey |
| 111 B3 | Evrotas r. Greece |
| 104 C2 | Évry France |
| 80 B2 | Evrychou Cyprus |
| 111 B3 | Evvoia i. Greece |
| 119 E2 | Ewaso Ngiro r. Kenya |
| 152 B1 | Exaltación Bol. |
| 99 B4 | Exe r. U.K. |
| 99 B4 | Exeter U.K. |
| 99 B4 | Exmoor hills U.K. |
| 50 A2 | Exmouth Austr. |
| 99 B4 | Exmouth U.K. |
| 50 A2 | Exmouth Gulf Austr. |
| 106 B2 | Extremadura reg. Spain |
| 146 C2 | Exuma Cays is Bahamas |
| 91 D2 | Eya r. Rus. Fed. |
| 118 C3 | Eyangu Dem. Rep. Congo |
| 119 D3 | Eyasi, Lake salt l. Tanz. |
| 96 C3 | Eyemouth U.K. |
| 92 □B2 | Eyjafjörður inlet Iceland |
| 117 C4 | Eyl Somalia |
| 52 A1 | Eyre, Lake salt flat Austr. |
| 52 A2 | Eyre Peninsula Austr. |
| 94 B1 | Eysturoy i. Faroe Is |
| 123 C2 | Ezakheni S. Africa |
| 123 C2 | Ezenzeleni S. Africa |
| 70 B2 | Ezhou China |
| 86 E2 | Ezhva Rus. Fed. |
| 111 C3 | Ezine Turkey |

## F

| 102 C1 | Faaborg Denmark |
| 142 B2 | Fabens U.S.A. |
| 108 B2 | Fabriano Italy |
| 115 D3 | Fachi Niger |
| 114 C3 | Fada-N'Gourma Burkina |
| 108 B2 | Faenza Italy |
| | Faeroes terr. N. Atlantic Ocean see Faroe Islands |
| 59 C3 | Fafanlap Indon. |
| 110 B1 | Făgăraş Romania |
| 49 J5 | Fagatogo American Samoa |
| 93 E3 | Fagernes Norway |
| 93 G4 | Fagersta Sweden |
| 153 B5 | Fagnano, Lago l. Arg./Chile |
| 114 B3 | Faguibine, Lac l. Mali |
| 92 □B3 | Fagurhólsmýri Iceland |
| 126 C2 | Fairbanks U.S.A. |
| 137 D2 | Fairbury U.S.A. |
| 135 B3 | Fairfield CA U.S.A. |
| 138 C3 | Fairfield OH U.S.A. |
| 96 □ | Fair Isle i. U.K. |
| 137 E2 | Fairmont MN U.S.A. |
| 138 C3 | Fairmont WV U.S.A. |
| 128 C2 | Fairview Can. |
| 128 A2 | Fairweather, Mount Can./U.S.A. |
| 59 D2 | Fais i. Micronesia |
| 74 B1 | Faisalabad Pak. |
| 136 C1 | Faith U.S.A. |
| 75 C2 | Faizabad India |
| 156 E6 | Fakaofo atoll Tokelau |
| 99 D3 | Fakenham U.K. |
| 59 C3 | Fakfak Indon. |
| 65 A1 | Faku China |
| 114 A4 | Falaba Sierra Leone |
| 97 B1 | Falcarragh Ireland |
| 143 D3 | Falcon Lake Mex./U.S.A. |
| | Faleshty Moldova see Fălești |
| 90 B2 | Fălești Moldova |
| 143 D3 | Falfurrias U.S.A. |
| 128 C2 | Falher Can. |

101 F2 **Falkenberg** Ger.
93 F4 **Falkenberg** Sweden
101 F1 **Falkensee** Ger.
96 C3 **Falkirk** U.K.
158 D8 **Falkland Escarpment** *sea feature*
S. Atlantic Ocean
153 C5 **Falkland Islands** *terr.*
S. Atlantic Ocean
157 I9 **Falkland Plateau** *sea feature*
S. Atlantic Ocean
93 F4 **Falköping** Sweden
101 D1 **Fallingbostel** Ger.
135 C3 **Fallon** U.S.A.
139 E2 **Fall River** U.S.A.
137 D2 **Falls City** U.S.A.
99 A4 **Falmouth** U.K.
122 A3 **False Bay** S. Africa
144 B2 **Falso, Cabo** *c.* Mex.
93 F5 **Falster** *i.* Denmark
110 C1 **Fălticeni** Romania
93 G3 **Falun** Sweden
152 B2 **Famailla** Arg.
121 □D3 **Fandriana** Madag.
**Fangcheng** China *see*
**Fangchenggang**
71 A3 **Fangchenggang** China
71 C3 **Fangshan** Taiwan
66 A1 **Fangzheng** China
108 B2 **Fano** Italy
62 B1 **Fan Si Pan** *mt.* Vietnam
119 C2 **Faradje** Dem. Rep. Congo
121 □D3 **Farafangana** Madag.
116 A2 **Farāfirah, Wāḥāt al** Egypt
**Farafra Oasis** Egypt *see*
**Farāfirah, Wāḥāt al**
76 C3 **Farāh** Afgh.
114 A3 **Faranah** Guinea
79 C3 **Fararah** Oman
78 B3 **Farasān, Jazā'ir** *is* Saudi Arabia
59 D2 **Faraulep** *atoll* Micronesia
127 J2 **Farewell, Cape** *c.* Greenland
54 B2 **Farewell, Cape** N.Z.
137 D1 **Fargo** U.S.A.
77 D2 **Farg'ona** Uzbek.
137 E2 **Faribault** U.S.A.
130 C2 **Faribault, Lac** *l.* Can.
74 B2 **Faridabad** India
75 C2 **Faridpur** Bangl.
139 E2 **Farmington** *ME* U.S.A.
142 B1 **Farmington** *NM* U.S.A.
139 D3 **Farmville** U.S.A.
99 C4 **Farnborough** U.K.
128 C2 **Farnham, Mount** Can.
128 A1 **Faro** Can.
106 B2 **Faro** Port.
88 A2 **Fårö** *i.* Sweden
147 C3 **Faro, Punta** *pt* Col.
106 B1 **Faro, Serra de** *mts* Spain
94 B1 **Faroe Islands** *terr.*
N. Atlantic Ocean
113 I6 **Farquhar Group** *atoll* Seychelles
81 D3 **Farrāshband** Iran
**Farrukhabad** India *see* **Fatehgarh**
79 C3 **Fartak, Ra's** *c.* Yemen
154 B3 **Fartura, Serra da** *mts* Brazil
143 C2 **Farwell** U.S.A.
79 C2 **Fāryāb** Iran
79 C2 **Fāryāb** Iran
81 D3 **Fasā** Iran
109 C2 **Fasano** Italy
90 B1 **Fastiv** Ukr.
119 D2 **Fataki** Dem. Rep. Congo
75 B2 **Fatehgarh** India
75 C2 **Fatehpur** India
114 A3 **Fatick** Senegal
131 D3 **Fatima** Can.
123 C2 **Fauresmith** S. Africa
92 G2 **Fauske** Norway
92 □A3 **Faxaflói** *b.* Iceland
92 G3 **Faxälven** *r.* Sweden
115 D3 **Faya** Chad
140 B1 **Fayetteville** *AR* U.S.A.
141 E1 **Fayetteville** *NC* U.S.A.
140 C1 **Fayetteville** *TN* U.S.A.
74 B1 **Fazilka** India
114 A2 **Fdérik** Maur.
141 E2 **Fear, Cape** U.S.A.
54 C2 **Featherston** N.Z.
104 C2 **Fécamp** France
**Federated Malay States** *country*
Asia *see* **Malaysia**
48 G3 **Federated States of Micronesia**
*country* N. Pacific Ocean
102 C1 **Fehmarn** *i.* Ger.
101 F1 **Fehrbellin** Ger.
155 D2 **Feia, Lagoa** *lag.* Brazil
150 B3 **Feijó** Brazil
54 C2 **Feilding** N.Z.
151 F4 **Feira de Santana** Brazil
107 D2 **Felanitx** Spain
101 F1 **Feldberg** Ger.
145 C2 **Felipe C. Puerto** Mex.
155 D1 **Felixlândia** Brazil
99 D4 **Felixstowe** U.K.
101 D2 **Felsberg** Ger.
108 B1 **Feltre** Italy
93 F3 **Femunden** *l.* Norway
**Fénérive** Madag. *see*
**Fenoarivo Atsinanana**
**Fengcheng** China *see* **Fengshan**
71 B3 **Fengcheng** *Jiangxi* China
65 A1 **Fengcheng** *Liaoning* China
62 A1 **Fengqing** China
71 A3 **Fengshan** China

**Fengshan** China *see* **Fengqing**
70 B2 **Fengxian** *Jiangsu* China
70 A2 **Fengxian** *Shaanxi* China
**Fengxian** China *see* **Lincang**
**Fengyi** China *see* **Zheng'an**
71 C3 **Fengyüan** Taiwan
70 B1 **Fengzhen** China
105 D3 **Feno, Capo di** *c.* Corsica France
121 □D2 **Fenoarivo Atsinanana** Madag.
70 B2 **Fenyang** China
91 D2 **Feodosiya** Ukr.
108 A3 **Fer, Cap de** *c.* Alg.
137 D1 **Fergus Falls** U.S.A.
51 E1 **Fergusson Island** P.N.G.
114 B4 **Ferkessédougou** Côte d'Ivoire
108 B2 **Fermo** Italy
131 D2 **Fermont** Can.
106 B1 **Fermoselle** Spain
97 B2 **Fermoy** Ireland
141 D2 **Fernandina Beach** U.S.A.
154 B2 **Fernandópolis** Brazil
**Fernando Poó** *i.* Equat. Guinea *see*
**Bioco**
134 B1 **Ferndale** U.S.A.
99 C4 **Ferndown** U.K.
128 C3 **Fernie** Can.
135 C3 **Fernley** U.S.A.
97 C2 **Ferns** Ireland
**Ferozepore** India *see* **Firozpur**
108 B2 **Ferrara** Italy
154 B2 **Ferreiros** Brazil
108 A2 **Ferro, Capo** *c.* Sardinia Italy
106 B1 **Ferrol** Spain
**Ferryville** Tunisia *see*
**Menzel Bourguiba**
100 B1 **Ferwert** Neth.
114 B1 **Fès** Morocco
118 B3 **Feshi** Dem. Rep. Congo
137 E3 **Festus** U.S.A.
110 C2 **Feteşti** Romania
97 C2 **Fethard** Ireland
111 C3 **Fethiye** Turkey
96 □ **Fetlar** *i.* U.K.
130 C2 **Feuilles, Rivière aux** *r.* Can.
77 D3 **Feyzābād** Afgh.
**Fez** Morocco *see* **Fès**
121 □D3 **Fianarantsoa** Madag.
115 D4 **Fianga** Chad
117 B4 **Fichē** Eth.
109 C2 **Fier** Albania
96 C2 **Fife Ness** *pt* U.K.
104 C3 **Figeac** France
106 B1 **Figueira da Foz** Port.
107 D1 **Figueres** Spain
114 B1 **Figuig** Morocco
49 I5 **Fiji** *country* S. Pacific Ocean
152 B2 **Filadelfia** Para.
55 B2 **Filchner Ice Shelf** Antarctica
98 C2 **Filey** U.K.
108 B3 **Filicudi, Isola** *i.* Italy
114 C3 **Filingué** Niger
111 B3 **Filippiada** Greece
93 F4 **Filipstad** Sweden
92 E3 **Fillan** Norway
135 D3 **Fillmore** U.S.A.
119 E2 **Filtu** Eth.
55 D2 **Fimbull Ice Shelf** Antarctica
96 C2 **Findhorn** *r.* U.K.
138 C2 **Findlay** U.S.A.
51 D4 **Fingal** Austr.
139 D2 **Finger Lakes** U.S.A.
111 D3 **Finike** Turkey
106 B1 **Finisterre, Cape** *c.* Spain
93 I3 **Finland** *country* Europe
93 H4 **Finland, Gulf of** Europe
128 B2 **Finlay** *r.* Can.
53 C3 **Finley** Austr.
134 C1 **Finley** U.S.A.
101 E2 **Finne** *ridge* Ger.
92 H2 **Finnmarksvidda** *reg.* Norway
92 G2 **Finnsnes** Norway
93 G4 **Finspång** Sweden
97 C1 **Fintona** U.K.
96 A2 **Fionnphort** U.K.
105 C2 **Firminy** France
74 B2 **Firozabad** India
74 B1 **Firozpur** India
81 D3 **Fīrūzābād** Iran
122 A2 **Fish** *watercourse* Namibia
122 B3 **Fish** *r.* S. Africa
129 F1 **Fisher Strait** Can.
99 A4 **Fishguard** U.K.
105 C2 **Fismes** France
**Fisterra, Cabo** Spain *see*
**Finisterre, Cape**
139 E2 **Fitchburg** U.S.A.
128 C2 **Fitzgerald** Can.
141 D2 **Fitzgerald** U.S.A.
50 B1 **Fitzroy Crossing** Austr.
**Fiume** Croatia *see* **Rijeka**
54 A3 **Five Rivers** N.Z.
108 B2 **Fivizzano** Italy
119 C3 **Fizi** Dem. Rep. Congo
93 F3 **Fjällnäs** Sweden
92 G3 **Fjällsjöälven** *r.* Sweden
123 C3 **Flagstaff** S. Africa
142 A1 **Flagstaff** U.S.A.
130 C2 **Flaherty Island** Can.
98 C2 **Flamborough Head** *hd* U.K.
101 F1 **Fläming** *hills* Ger.
136 B2 **Flaming Gorge Reservoir** U.S.A.
134 D1 **Flathead** *r.* U.S.A.
134 D1 **Flathead Lake** U.S.A.

51 D1 **Flattery, Cape** Austr.
134 B1 **Flattery, Cape** U.S.A.
98 B3 **Fleetwood** U.K.
93 E4 **Flekkefjord** Norway
102 B1 **Flensburg** Ger.
100 B2 **Flers** France
100 B2 **Fleurus** Belgium
104 C2 **Fleury-les-Aubrais** France
51 D1 **Flinders** *r.* Austr.
50 A3 **Flinders Bay** Austr.
51 D3 **Flinders Island** Austr.
52 A2 **Flinders Ranges** *mts* Austr.
129 D2 **Flin Flon** Can.
98 B3 **Flint** U.K.
138 C2 **Flint** U.S.A.
49 L5 **Flint Island** Kiribati
101 F2 **Flöha** Ger.
107 D2 **Florac** France
100 C3 **Florange** France
108 B2 **Florence** Italy
140 C2 **Florence** *AL* U.S.A.
142 A2 **Florence** *AZ* U.S.A.
134 B2 **Florence** *OR* U.S.A.
141 E2 **Florence** *SC* U.S.A.
150 B2 **Florencia** Col.
146 B3 **Flores** Guat.
61 □ **Flores** *i.* Indon.
61 C2 **Flores, Laut** Indon.
**Floreshty** Moldova *see* **Floreşti**
**Flores Sea** Indon. *see* **Flores, Laut**
151 F3 **Floresta** Brazil
90 B2 **Floreşti** Moldova
143 D3 **Floresville** U.S.A.
151 E3 **Floriano** Brazil
152 D2 **Florianópolis** Brazil
153 C3 **Florida** Uru.
141 D3 **Florida** *state* U.S.A.
141 D4 **Florida, Straits of** Bahamas/U.S.A.
141 D4 **Florida Bay** U.S.A.
141 D4 **Florida Keys** *is* U.S.A.
111 B2 **Florina** Greece
93 E3 **Florø** Norway
129 D2 **Foam Lake** Can.
109 C2 **Foča** Bos.-Herz.
110 C1 **Focşani** Romania
71 B3 **Fogang** China
109 C2 **Foggia** Italy
131 E3 **Fogo Island** Can.
104 C3 **Foix** France
89 D3 **Fokino** Rus. Fed.
130 B3 **Foleyet** Can.
108 B2 **Foligno** Italy
99 D4 **Folkestone** U.K.
141 D2 **Folkston** U.S.A.
108 B2 **Follonica** Italy
129 D2 **Fond-du-Lac** Can.
129 D2 **Fond du Lac** *r.* Can.
138 B2 **Fond du Lac** U.S.A.
106 B1 **Fondevila** Spain
108 B2 **Fondi** Italy
146 B3 **Fonseca, Golfo do** *b.*
Central America
150 C3 **Fonte Boa** Brazil
104 B2 **Fontenay-le-Comte** France
92 □C2 **Fontur** *pt* Iceland
53 C2 **Forbes** Austr.
75 C2 **Forbesganj** India
101 E3 **Forchheim** Ger.
93 E3 **Førde** Norway
53 C1 **Fords Bridge** Austr.
140 C2 **Fordyce** U.S.A.
140 C2 **Forest** U.S.A.
53 C3 **Forest Hill** Austr.
131 D3 **Forestville** Can.
96 C2 **Forfar** U.K.
134 B1 **Forks** U.S.A.
108 B2 **Forlì** Italy
107 D2 **Formentera** *i.* Spain
107 D2 **Formentor, Cap de** *c.* Spain
155 C2 **Formiga** Brazil
152 C2 **Formosa** Arg.
**Formosa** Asia *see* **Taiwan**
154 C1 **Formosa** Brazil
**Formosa Strait** China/Taiwan *see*
**Taiwan Strait**
**Føroyar** *terr.* N. Atlantic Ocean *see*
**Faroe Islands**
96 C2 **Forres** U.K.
50 B3 **Forrest** Austr.
140 B2 **Forrest City** U.S.A.
51 D1 **Forsayth** Austr.
93 H3 **Forssa** Fin.
53 C2 **Forster** Austr.
136 B1 **Forsyth** U.S.A.
74 B2 **Fort Abbas** Pak.
130 B2 **Fort Albany** Can.
151 F3 **Fortaleza** Brazil
**Fort Archambault** Chad *see* **Sarh**
128 C2 **Fort Assiniboine** Can.
96 B2 **Fort Augustus** U.K.
123 C3 **Fort Beaufort** S. Africa
134 D1 **Fort Benton** U.S.A.
**Fort Brabant** Can. *see*
**Tuktoyaktuk**
135 B3 **Fort Bragg** U.S.A.
**Fort Carnot** Madag. *see* **Ikongo**
**Fort Charlet** Alg. *see* **Djanet**
**Fort Chimo** Can. *see* **Kuujjuaq**
129 D2 **Fort Chipewyan** Can.
136 B2 **Fort Collins** U.S.A.
**Fort Crampel** C.A.R. *see*
**Kaga Bandoro**
**Fort-Dauphin** Madag. *see*
**Tôlañaro**

147 D3 **Fort-de-France** Martinique
**Fort de Polignac** Alg. *see* **Illizi**
137 E2 **Fort Dodge** U.S.A.
139 D2 **Fort Erie** Can.
**Fort Flatters** Alg. *see*
**Bordj Omer Driss**
**Fort Foureau** Cameroon *see*
**Kousséri**
130 A3 **Fort Frances** Can.
**Fort Franklin** Can. *see* **Déline**
**Fort Gardel** Alg. *see* **Zaouatallaz**
**Fort George** Can. *see* **Chisasibi**
126 D2 **Fort Good Hope** Can.
**Fort Gouraud** Maur. *see* **Fdérik**
96 C2 **Forth** *r.* U.K.
96 C2 **Forth, Firth of** *est.* U.K.
**Fort Hall** Kenya *see* **Murang'a**
**Fort Hertz** Myanmar *see* **Putao**
152 C2 **Fortín** Madrejón Para.
**Fort Jameson** Zambia *see*
**Chipata**
**Fort Johnston** Malawi *see*
**Mangochi**
**Fort Lamy** Chad *see* **Ndjamena**
**Fort Laperrine** Alg. *see*
**Tamanrasset**
141 D3 **Fort Lauderdale** U.S.A.
128 B1 **Fort Liard** Can.
128 C2 **Fort Mackay** Can.
137 E2 **Fort Madison** U.S.A.
**Fort Manning** Malawi *see* **Mchinji**
128 C2 **Fort McMurray** Can.
126 D2 **Fort McPherson** Can.
136 C2 **Fort Morgan** U.S.A.
141 D3 **Fort Myers** U.S.A.
128 B2 **Fort Nelson** Can.
128 B2 **Fort Nelson** *r.* Can.
**Fort Norman** Can. *see* **Tulita**
140 C2 **Fort Payne** U.S.A.
136 B1 **Fort Peck** U.S.A.
136 B1 **Fort Peck Reservoir** U.S.A.
141 D3 **Fort Pierce** U.S.A.
119 D2 **Fort Portal** Uganda
128 B1 **Fort Providence** Can.
129 D2 **Fort Qu'Appelle** Can.
128 C1 **Fort Resolution** Can.
98 B2 **Fortrose** U.K.
**Fort Rosebery** Zambia *see* **Mansa**
**Fort Rousset** Congo *see* **Owando**
**Fort Rupert** Can. *see* **Waskaganish**
**Fort Sandeman** Pak. *see* **Zhob**
128 C2 **Fort Saskatchewan** Can.
137 E3 **Fort Scott** U.S.A.
130 B2 **Fort Severn** Can.
76 B2 **Fort-Shevchenko** Kazakh.
128 B1 **Fort Simpson** Can.
128 C1 **Fort Smith** Can.
140 B1 **Fort Smith** U.S.A.
128 B2 **Fort St James** Can.
128 B2 **Fort St John** Can.
143 C2 **Fort Stockton** U.S.A.
142 C2 **Fort Sumner** U.S.A.
**Fort Trinquet** Maur. *see*
**Bîr Mogreïn**
134 B2 **Fortuna** U.S.A.
131 E3 **Fortune Bay** Can.
128 C2 **Fort Vermilion** Can.
**Fort Victoria** Zimbabwe *see*
**Masvingo**
**Fort Walton** U.S.A. *see*
**Fort Walton Beach**
140 C2 **Fort Walton Beach** U.S.A.
136 B2 **Fort Washakie** U.S.A.
138 B2 **Fort Wayne** U.S.A.
96 B2 **Fort William** U.K.
143 D2 **Fort Worth** U.S.A.
126 C2 **Fort Yukon** U.S.A.
71 B3 **Foshan** China
92 F3 **Fosna** *pen.* Norway
93 E3 **Fosnavåg** Norway
92 □B3 **Foss** Iceland
92 □A2 **Fossá** Iceland
108 A2 **Fossano** Italy
137 D1 **Fosston** U.S.A.
53 C3 **Foster** Austr.
118 B3 **Fougamou** Gabon
104 B2 **Fougères** France
96 □ **Foula** *i.* U.K.
99 D4 **Foulness Point** U.K.
118 B2 **Foumban** Cameroon
111 C3 **Fournoi** *i.* Greece
114 A3 **Fouta Djallon** *reg.* Guinea
54 A3 **Foveaux Strait** N.Z.
136 C3 **Fowler** U.S.A.
50 C3 **Fowlers Bay** Austr.
81 D2 **Fowman** Iran
128 C2 **Fox Creek** Can.
127 G2 **Foxe Basin** *g.* Can.
127 G2 **Foxe Channel** Can.
127 G2 **Foxe Peninsula** Can.
54 B2 **Fox Glacier** N.Z.
128 C2 **Fox Lake** Can.
128 A1 **Fox Mountain** Can.
54 C2 **Foxton** N.Z.
129 D2 **Fox Valley** Can.
97 C1 **Foyle** *r.* Ireland/U.K.
97 C1 **Foyle, Lough** *b.* Ireland/U.K.
97 B2 **Foynes** Ireland
154 B2 **Foz de Areia, Represa de** *resr*
Brazil
120 A2 **Foz do Cunene** Angola
154 B3 **Foz do Iguaçu** Brazil
107 C1 **Fraga** Spain
100 A2 **Frameries** Belgium
154 C2 **Franca** Brazil

109 C2 Francavilla Fontana Italy
104 C2 France country Europe
118 B3 Franceville Gabon
137 D2 Francis Case, Lake U.S.A.
155 D1 Francisco Sá Brazil
120 B3 Francistown Botswana
128 B2 François Lake Can.
100 B1 Franeker Neth.
101 D2 Frankenberg (Eder) Ger.
101 D3 Frankenthal (Pfalz) Ger.
101 E2 Frankenwald mts Ger.
138 C3 Frankfort KY U.S.A.
138 B2 Frankfort MI U.S.A.
Frankfurt Ger. see
Frankfurt am Main
101 D2 Frankfurt am Main Ger.
102 C1 Frankfurt an der Oder Ger.
102 C2 Fränkische Alb hills Ger.
101 E3 Fränkische Schweiz reg. Ger.
139 E2 Franklin NH U.S.A.
139 D2 Franklin PA U.S.A.
140 C1 Franklin TN U.S.A.
126 D2 Franklin Bay Can.
134 C1 Franklin D. Roosevelt Lake U.S.A.
128 B1 Franklin Mountains Can.
126 F2 Franklin Strait Can.
53 C3 Frankston Austr.
82 E1 Frantsa-Iosifa, Zemlya is Rus. Fed.
54 B2 Franz Josef Glacier N.Z.
Franz Josef Land is Rus. Fed. see Frantsa-Iosifa, Zemlya
108 A3 Frasca, Capo della c. Sardinia Italy
128 B3 Fraser r. B.C. Can.
131 D2 Fraser r. Nfld and Lab. Can.
122 B3 Fraserburg S. Africa
96 C2 Fraserburgh U.K.
130 B3 Fraserdale Can.
51 E2 Fraser Island Austr.
128 B2 Fraser Lake Can.
128 B2 Fraser Plateau Can.
153 C3 Fray Bentos Uru.
93 E4 Fredericia Denmark
143 D2 Frederick U.S.A.
143 D2 Fredericksburg TX U.S.A.
139 D3 Fredericksburg VA U.S.A.
128 A2 Frederick Sound sea chan. U.S.A.
131 D3 Fredericton Can.
Frederikshåb Greenland see Paamiut
93 F4 Frederikshavn Denmark
Fredrikshamn Fin. see Hamina
93 F4 Fredrikstad Norway
138 B2 Freeport IL U.S.A.
143 D3 Freeport TX U.S.A.
146 C2 Freeport City Bahamas
143 D3 Freer U.S.A.
123 C2 Free State prov. S. Africa
114 A4 Freetown Sierra Leone
106 B2 Fregenal de la Sierra Spain
104 B2 Fréhel, Cap c. France
102 B2 Freiburg im Breisgau Ger.
102 C2 Freising Ger.
102 C2 Freistadt Austria
105 D3 Fréjus France
50 A3 Fremantle Austr.
135 B3 Fremont CA U.S.A.
137 D2 Fremont NE U.S.A.
138 C2 Fremont OH U.S.A.
French Congo country Africa see Congo
151 D2 French Guiana terr. S. America
French Guinea country Africa see Guinea
134 E1 Frenchman r. U.S.A.
49 M5 French Polynesia terr. S. Pacific Ocean
French Somaliland country Africa see Djibouti
French Sudan country Africa see Mali
French Territory of the Afars and Issas country Africa see Djibouti
151 D3 Fresco r. Brazil
144 B2 Fresnillo Mex.
135 C3 Fresno U.S.A.
107 D2 Freu, Cap des c. Spain
105 D2 Freyming-Merlebach France
114 A3 Fria Guinea
152 B2 Frias Arg.
101 D2 Friedberg (Hessen) Ger.
102 B2 Friedrichshafen Ger.
101 F1 Friesack Ger.
100 C1 Friesoythe Ger.
143 C2 Friona U.S.A.
136 B3 Frisco U.S.A.
Frobisher Bay Can. see Iqaluit
127 H2 Frobisher Bay b. Can.
101 F2 Frohburg Ger.
87 D4 Frolovo Rus. Fed.
103 D1 Frombork Pol.
99 B4 Frome U.K.
52 A2 Frome, Lake salt flat Austr.
52 A2 Frome Downs Austr.
100 C2 Fröndenberg Ger.
143 C3 Frontera Mex.
145 C3 Frontera Mex.
144 B1 Fronteras Mex.
139 D3 Front Royal U.S.A.
108 B2 Frosinone Italy
92 E3 Frøya i. Norway
Frunze Kyrg. see Bishkek
154 C2 Frutal Brazil
105 D2 Frutigen Switz.
103 D2 Frýdek-Místek Czech Rep.

71 B3 Fu'an China
71 C3 Fuding China
106 C1 Fuenlabrada Spain
152 C2 Fuerte Olimpo Para.
114 A2 Fuerteventura i. Canary Is
64 B2 Fuga i. Phil.
79 C2 Fujairah U.A.E.
67 C3 Fuji Japan
71 B3 Fujian prov. China
67 C3 Fujinomiya Japan
67 C3 Fuji-san vol. Japan
Fukien prov. China see Fujian
67 A4 Fukue Japan
67 A4 Fukue-jima i. Japan
67 C3 Fukui Japan
67 B4 Fukuoka Japan
67 D3 Fukushima Japan
101 D2 Fulda Ger.
101 D2 Fulda r. Ger.
70 A3 Fuling China
137 E3 Fulton U.S.A.
105 C2 Fumay France
49 I4 Funafuti atoll Tuvalu
114 A1 Funchal Madeira
155 D1 Fundão Brazil
106 B1 Fundão Port.
131 D3 Fundy, Bay of g. Can.
121 C3 Funhalouro Moz.
70 B2 Funing Jiangsu China
71 A3 Funing Yunnan China
115 C3 Funtua Nigeria
79 C2 Fürgun, Küh-e mt. Iran
89 F2 Furmanov Rus. Fed.
Furmanovka Kazakh. see Moyynkum
Furmanovo Kazakh. see Zhalpaktal
155 E3 Furnas, Represa resr Brazil
51 D4 Furneaux Group is Austr.
Furong China see Wan'an
100 C1 Fürstenau Ger.
101 E3 Fürth Ger.
66 D3 Furukawa Japan
127 G2 Fury and Hecla Strait Can.
70 C1 Fushun China
65 B1 Fusong China
79 C2 Fuwayrit Qatar
Fuxian China see Wafangdian
70 A2 Fuxian China
70 C1 Fuxin China
70 B2 Fuyang China
69 E1 Fuyu China
Fuyu China see Songyuan
68 B1 Fuyun China
71 B3 Fuzhou China
71 B3 Fuzhou China
93 F4 Fyn i. Denmark
96 B3 Fyne, Loch inlet U.K.
F.Y.R.O.M. country Europe see Macedonia

**G**

117 C4 Gaalkacyo Somalia
120 A2 Gabela Angola
Gaberones Botswana see Gaborone
115 D1 Gabès Tunisia
115 D1 Gabès, Golfe de g. Tunisia
118 B3 Gabon country Africa
123 C1 Gaborone Botswana
79 C2 Gäbrik Iran
110 C2 Gabrovo Bulg.
114 A3 Gabú Guinea-Bissau
73 B3 Gadag India
75 C2 Gadchiroli India
101 E1 Gadebusch Ger.
143 C2 Gadsden U.S.A.
118 B2 Gadzi C.A.R.
110 C2 Găești Romania
108 B2 Gaeta Italy
108 B2 Gaeta, Golfo di g. Italy
141 D1 Gaffney U.S.A.
115 C1 Gafsa Tunisia
89 E2 Gagarin Rus. Fed.
109 C3 Gagliano del Capo Italy
114 B4 Gagnoa Côte d'Ivoire
131 D2 Gagnon Can.
Gago Coutinho Angola see Lumbala N'guimbo
81 C1 Gagra Georgia
122 A2 Gaiab watercourse Namibia
104 C3 Gaillac France
Gaillimh Ireland see Galway
141 D3 Gainesville FL U.S.A.
141 D2 Gainesville GA U.S.A.
143 D2 Gainesville TX U.S.A.
98 C3 Gainsborough U.K.
52 A2 Gairdner, Lake salt flat Austr.
96 B2 Gairloch U.K.
122 B2 Gakarosa mt. S. Africa
119 E3 Galana r. Kenya
103 D2 Galanta Slovakia
Galápagos, Islas is Pacific Ocean see Galapagos Islands
125 I10 Galapagos Islands is Pacific Ocean
157 G6 Galapagos Rise sea feature Pacific Ocean
96 C3 Galashiels U.K.
110 C1 Galaţi Romania
93 E3 Galdhøpiggen mt. Norway
145 B2 Galeana Mex.

128 C2 Galena Bay Can.
138 A2 Galesburg U.S.A.
122 B2 Galeshewe S. Africa
89 F2 Galich Rus. Fed.
106 B1 Galicia reg. Spain
80 B2 Galilee, Sea of l. Israel
78 A3 Gallabat Sudan
140 C1 Gallatin U.S.A.
73 C4 Galle Sri Lanka
157 G6 Gallego Rise sea feature Pacific Ocean
150 B1 Gallinas, Punta pt Col.
109 C2 Gallipoli Italy
111 C2 Gallipoli Turkey
92 H2 Gällivare Sweden
142 B1 Gallup U.S.A.
114 A2 Galtat Zemmur Western Sahara
97 B2 Galtymore hill Ireland
143 E3 Galveston U.S.A.
143 E3 Galveston Bay U.S.A.
143 E3 Galveston Island U.S.A.
97 B2 Galway Ireland
97 B2 Galway Bay Ireland
154 C1 Gamá Brazil
123 D3 Gamalakhe S. Africa
117 B4 Gambēla Eth.
114 A3 Gambia r. Gambia
114 A3 Gambia, The country Africa
49 N6 Gambier, Îles is Fr. Polynesia
52 A3 Gambier Islands Austr.
131 E3 Gambo Can.
118 B3 Gamboma Congo
92 H2 Gammelstaden Sweden
142 B1 Ganado U.S.A.
81 D3 Ganäveh Iran
81 C1 Gäncä Azer.
61 C2 Gandadiwata, Bukit mt. Indon.
118 C3 Gandajika Dem. Rep. Congo
106 B1 Gándara Spain
131 E3 Gander Can.
131 E3 Gander r. Can.
101 D1 Ganderkesee Ger.
107 D1 Gandesa Spain
74 B2 Gandhidham India
74 B2 Gandhinagar India
74 B2 Gandhi Sagar resr India
107 C2 Gandía Spain
Ganga r. Bangl./India see Ganges
153 B4 Gangán Arg.
74 B2 Ganganagar India
62 A1 Gangaw Myanmar
68 C2 Gangca China
75 C1 Gangdisê Shan mts China
75 D2 Ganges r. Bangl./India
105 C3 Ganges France
75 C2 Ganges, Mouths of the Bangl./India
159 E2 Ganges Cone sea feature Indian Ocean
75 C2 Gangtok India
75 C3 Ganjam India
71 B3 Gan Jiang r. China
71 A3 Ganluo China
105 C2 Gannat France
136 B2 Gannett Peak U.S.A.
122 A3 Gansbaai S. Africa
70 A1 Gansu prov. China
115 D4 Ganye Nigeria
71 B3 Ganzhou China
114 B3 Gao Mali
Gaoleshan China see Xianfeng
114 B3 Gaoua Burkina
114 A3 Gaoual Guinea
70 B2 Gaoyou China
70 B2 Gaoyou Hu l. China
105 D3 Gap France
64 B2 Gapan Phil.
107 C2 Gap Carbon hd Alg.
75 C1 Gar China
72 C1 Gar China
97 B2 Gara, Lough l. Ireland
117 C4 Garacad Somalia
53 C1 Garah Austr.
151 F3 Garanhuns Brazil
123 C2 Ga-Rankuwa S. Africa
118 C1 Garar, Plaine de plain Chad
117 C4 Garbahaarrey Somalia
135 B2 Garberville U.S.A.
81 D2 Garbosh, Küh-e mt. Iran
101 D1 Garbsen Ger.
154 C2 Garça Brazil
154 B2 Garcias Brazil
108 B1 Garda, Lake l. Italy
108 A3 Garde, Cap de c. Alg.
101 E1 Gardelegen Ger.
136 C3 Garden City U.S.A.
129 E2 Garden Hill Can.
77 C3 Gardēz Afgh.
139 F2 Gardiner U.S.A.
Gardner atoll Micronesia see Faraulep
135 C3 Gardnerville U.S.A.
136 B3 Garfield U.S.A.
88 B2 Gargždai Lith.
123 C3 Gariep Dam resr S. Africa
122 A3 Garies S. Africa
119 D3 Garissa Kenya
88 B2 Garkalne Latvia
143 D2 Garland U.S.A.
102 C2 Garmisch-Partenkirchen Ger.
52 B2 Garnpung Lake imp. l. Austr.
104 B3 Garonne r. France
117 C4 Garoowe Somalia
74 B2 Garoth India

118 B2 Garoua Cameroon
118 B2 Garoua Boulai Cameroon
Garqêntang China see Sog
96 B2 Garry r. U.K.
81 D2 Garrygala Turkm.
126 F2 Garry Lake Can.
119 E3 Garsen Kenya
122 A2 Garub Namibia
60 B2 Garut Indon.
138 B2 Gary U.S.A.
145 B2 Garza García Mex.
68 C2 Garzê China
Gascogne reg. France see Gascony
Gascogne, Golfe de g. France/Spain see Gascony, Gulf of
104 B3 Gascony reg. France
104 B3 Gascony, Gulf of France/Spain
50 A2 Gascoyne r. Austr.
118 B2 Gashaka Nigeria
115 D3 Gashua Nigeria
59 D3 Gasmata P.N.G.
131 D3 Gaspé Can.
131 D3 Gaspé, Péninsule de pen. Can.
141 E1 Gaston, Lake U.S.A.
141 D1 Gastonia U.S.A.
107 C2 Gata, Cabo de c. Spain
88 D2 Gatchina Rus. Fed.
98 C2 Gateshead U.K.
143 D2 Gatesville U.S.A.
139 D1 Gatineau Can.
130 C3 Gatineau r. Can.
Gatooma Zimbabwe see Kadoma
53 D1 Gatton Austr.
129 E2 Gauer Lake Can.
93 E4 Gausta mt. Norway
123 C2 Gauteng prov. S. Africa
79 C2 Gävbandi Iran
111 B3 Gavdos i. Greece
104 B3 Gave r. France
93 G3 Gävle Sweden
93 G3 Gävlebukten b. Sweden
89 F2 Gavrilov Posad Rus. Fed.
89 F2 Gavrilov-Yam Rus. Fed.
122 A2 Gawachab Namibia
62 A1 Gawai Myanmar
52 A2 Gawler Austr.
52 A2 Gawler Ranges hills Austr.
75 C2 Gaya India
114 C3 Gaya Niger
114 C3 Gayéri Burkina
138 C1 Gaylord U.S.A.
86 F2 Gayny Rus. Fed.
116 B1 Gaza terr. Asia
80 B2 Gaza Gaza
76 C2 Gaz-Achak Turkm.
76 B3 Gazandzhyk Turkm.
80 B2 Gaziantep Turkey
114 B4 Gbarnga Liberia
118 A2 Gboko Nigeria
103 D1 Gdańsk Pol.
88 A3 Gdańsk, Gulf of Pol./Rus. Fed.
88 C2 Gdov Rus. Fed.
103 D1 Gdynia Pol.
116 B3 Gedaref Sudan
101 D2 Gedern Ger.
111 C3 Gediz Turkey
111 C3 Gediz r. Turkey
102 C1 Gedser Denmark
100 B2 Geel Belgium
52 B3 Geelong Austr.
101 E1 Geesthacht Ger.
75 C1 Gê'gyai China
129 C2 Geikie r. Can.
93 E3 Geilo Norway
119 D3 Geita Tanz.
71 A3 Gejiu China
108 B3 Gela Sicily Italy
108 B3 Gela, Golfo di g. Sicily Italy
91 D3 Gelendzhik Rus. Fed.
Gelibolu Turkey see Gallipoli
100 C2 Gelsenkirchen Ger.
118 C2 Gemena Dem. Rep. Congo
111 C2 Gemlik Turkey
108 B1 Gemona del Friuli Italy
117 C4 Genalē Wenz r. Eth.
153 B3 General Acha Arg.
153 B3 General Alvear Arg.
153 C3 General Belgrano Arg.
144 B2 General Cepeda Mex.
General Freire Angola see Muxaluando
General Machado Angola see Camacupa
153 B3 General Pico Arg.
153 B3 General Roca Arg.
154 B2 General Salgado Brazil
64 B3 General Santos Phil.
139 D2 Genesee r. U.S.A.
138 A2 Geneseo IL U.S.A.
139 D2 Geneseo NY U.S.A.
105 D2 Geneva Switz.
139 D2 Geneva U.S.A.
105 D2 Geneva, Lake l. France/Switz.
Genève Switz. see Geneva
106 B2 Genil r. Spain
100 B2 Genk Belgium
53 C2 Genoa Austr.
108 A2 Genoa Italy
108 A2 Genoa, Gulf of g. Italy
Genova Italy see Genoa
Gent Belgium see Ghent
61 C2 Genteng i. Indon.
101 F1 Genthin Ger.
50 A3 Geographe Bay Austr.

131 D2 George *r.* Can.
122 B3 George S. Africa
52 A3 George, Lake Austr.
141 D3 George, Lake *FL* U.S.A.
139 E2 George, Lake *NY* U.S.A.
146 C2 George Town Bahamas
114 A3 Georgetown Gambia
151 D2 Georgetown Guyana
60 B1 George Town Malaysia
138 C3 Georgetown *KY* U.S.A.
141 E2 Georgetown *SC* U.S.A.
143 D2 Georgetown *TX* U.S.A.
55 L2 George V Land *reg.* Antarctica
81 C1 Georgia *country* Asia
139 D2 Georgia *state* U.S.A.
130 B3 Georgian Bay Can.
51 C2 Georgina *watercourse* Austr.
Georgiu-Dezh Rus. Fed. *see* Liski
77 E2 Georgiyevka Kazakh.
87 D4 Georgiyevsk Rus. Fed.
101 F2 Gera Ger.
151 E4 Geral de Goiás, Serra *hills* Brazil
54 B2 Geraldine N.Z.
50 A2 Geraldton Austr.
80 B1 Gerede Turkey
76 C3 Gereshk Afgh.
102 C2 Geretsried Ger.
135 C2 Gerlach U.S.A.
103 E2 Gerlachovský štit *mt.* Slovakia
139 D3 Germantown U.S.A.
102 C1 Germany *country* Europe
100 C2 Gerolstein Ger.
101 E3 Gerolzhofen Ger.
53 D2 Gerringong Austr.
101 D2 Gersfeld (Rhön) Ger.
Géryville Alg. *see* El Bayadh
75 C2 Gêrzê China
106 C1 Getafe Spain
139 D3 Gettysburg *PA* U.S.A.
136 D1 Gettysburg *SD* U.S.A.
55 P2 Getz Ice Shelf Antarctica
111 B2 Gevgelija Macedonia
111 C3 Geyikli Turkey
122 B2 Ghaap Plateau S. Africa
Ghadamés Libya *see* Ghadāmis
75 C2 Ghadāmis Libya
75 C2 Ghaghara *r.* India
76 C2 Ghalkarteniz, Solonchak *salt marsh* Kazakh.
114 B4 Ghana *country* Africa
120 B3 Ghanzi Botswana
115 C1 Ghardaïa Alg.
78 A2 Ghārib, Jabal *mt.* Egypt
115 D1 Gharyān Libya
115 D2 Ghāt Libya
75 B2 Ghatal India
75 B2 Ghaziabad *Uttar Prad.* India
75 C2 Ghazipur India
77 C3 Ghaznī Afgh.
78 B2 Ghazzālah Saudi Arabia
100 A2 Ghent Belgium
Gheorghe Gheorghiu-Dej
Romania *see* Oneşti
110 C1 Gheorgheni Romania
110 B1 Gherla Romania
105 D3 Ghisonaccia *Corsica* France
74 B2 Ghotaru India
74 A2 Ghotki Pak.
75 C2 Ghuari *r.* India
76 C3 Ghurian Afgh.
91 E3 Giaginskaya Rus. Fed.
97 C1 Giant's Causeway *lava field* U.K.
61 C2 Gianyar Indon.
109 C3 Giarre *Sicily* Italy
108 A1 Giaveno Italy
122 A2 Gibeon Namibia
106 B2 Gibraltar *terr.* Europe
106 B2 Gibraltar, Strait of Morocco/Spain
140 B2 Gibsland U.S.A.
50 B2 Gibson Desert Austr.
68 C1 Gichgeniyn Nuruu *mts*
Mongolia
117 B4 Gidolē Eth.
105 C2 Gien France
101 E2 Gießen Ger.
101 E1 Gifhorn Ger.
128 C2 Gift Lake Can.
67 C3 Gifu Japan
96 C2 Gigha *i.* U.K.
76 C2 G'ijduvon Uzbek.
106 B1 Gijón-Xixón Spain
142 A2 Gila *r.* U.S.A.
142 A2 Gila Bend U.S.A.
51 D1 Gilbert *r.* Austr.
48 I4 Gilbert Islands *country*
Pacific Ocean
156 D5 Gilbert Ridge *sea feature*
Pacific Ocean
151 E3 Gilbués Brazil
134 D1 Gildford U.S.A.
Gilf Kebir Plateau Egypt *see*
Haḍabat al Jilf al Kabir
53 C2 Gilgandra Austr.
74 B1 Gilgit Jammu and Kashmir
74 B1 Gilgit *r.* Jammu and Kashmir
53 C2 Gilgunnia Austr.
129 E2 Gillam Can.
136 B2 Gillette U.S.A.
99 D4 Gillingham U.K.
130 C2 Gilmour Island Can.
135 C3 Gilroy U.S.A.
129 E2 Gimli Can.
64 B3 Gingoog Phil.
117 C4 Ginir Eth.
109 C2 Ginosa Italy

109 C2 Gioia del Colle Italy
53 C3 Gippsland *reg.* Austr.
74 A2 Girdar Dhor *r.* Pak.
79 D1 Girdi Iran
80 B1 Giresun Turkey
Girgenti Italy *see* Agrigento
53 C2 Girilambone Austr.
Giron Sweden *see* Kiruna
107 D1 Girona Spain
104 B2 Gironde *est.* France
53 C2 Girral Austr.
96 B3 Girvan U.K.
54 C1 Gisborne N.Z.
93 F4 Gislaved Sweden
119 C3 Gitarama Rwanda
119 C3 Gitega Burundi
Giuba *r.* Somalia *see* Jubba
108 B2 Giulianova Italy
110 C2 Giurgiu Romania
110 C1 Giuvala, Pasul *pass* Romania
105 C2 Givors France
123 D1 Giyani S. Africa
119 D2 Giyon Eth.
116 B2 Giza Egypt
103 E1 Giżycko Pol.
109 D2 Gjirokastër Albania
126 F2 Gjoa Haven Can.
93 F3 Gjøvik Norway
131 E3 Glace Bay Can.
134 B1 Glacier Peak *vol.* U.S.A.
143 E2 Gladewater U.S.A.
51 D1 Gladstone *Qld* Austr.
52 A2 Gladstone *S.A.* Austr.
92 □A2 Gláma *mts* Iceland
109 C2 Glamoč Bos.-Herz.
100 C3 Glan *r.* Ger.
97 B2 Glanaruddery Mountains *hills*
Ireland
96 B3 Glasgow U.K.
138 B3 Glasgow *KY* U.S.A.
136 B1 Glasgow *MT* U.S.A.
99 B4 Glastonbury U.K.
101 F2 Glauchau Ger.
86 E3 Glazov Rus. Fed.
89 E3 Glazunovka Rus. Fed.
123 D2 Glencoe S. Africa
96 B2 Glen Coe *val.* U.K.
142 A2 Glendale *AZ* U.S.A.
138 B2 Glendale *WI* U.S.A.
53 D2 Glen Davis Austr.
51 D2 Glenden Austr.
136 C1 Glendive U.S.A.
52 B3 Glenelg *r.* Austr.
96 B2 Glenfinnan U.K.
53 D1 Glen Innes Austr.
96 B2 Glen More *val.* U.K.
53 C1 Glenmorgan Austr.
126 C2 Glennallen U.S.A.
134 C2 Glenns Ferry U.S.A.
136 B2 Glenrock U.S.A.
96 C2 Glenrothes U.K.
139 E2 Glens Falls U.S.A.
96 C2 Glen Shee *val.* U.K.
97 B1 Glenties Ireland
142 B2 Glenwood U.S.A.
136 B3 Glenwood Springs U.S.A.
101 E1 Glinde Ger.
103 D1 Gliwice Pol.
142 A2 Globe U.S.A.
103 D1 Głogów Pol.
93 F3 Glomfjord Norway
93 F4 Glomma *r.* Norway
53 D2 Gloucester Austr.
99 B4 Gloucester U.K.
131 E3 Glovertown Can.
101 F1 Glöwen Ger.
77 E1 Glubokoye Kazakh.
101 D1 Glückstadt Ger.
103 C2 Gmünd Austria
102 C2 Gmunden Austria
101 D1 Gnarrenburg Ger.
103 D1 Gniezno Pol.
109 D2 Gnjilane Serb. and Mont.
75 D2 Goalpara India
96 B3 Goat Fell *hill* U.K.
117 C4 Goba Eth.
122 A1 Gobabis Namibia
153 A4 Gobernador Gregores Arg.
152 C2 Gobernador Virasoro Arg.
68 D2 Gobi *des.* China/Mongolia
67 C4 Gobō Japan
100 C2 Goch Ger.
122 A1 Gochas Namibia
74 B3 Godavari *r.* India
73 C3 Godavari, Mouths of the India
75 C2 Godda India
117 C4 Godē Eth.
130 B3 Goderich Can.
Godhavn Greenland *see*
Qeqertarsuaq
74 B2 Godhra India
129 E2 Gods *r.* Can.
129 E2 Gods Lake Can.
Godthåb Greenland *see* Nuuk
Godwin-Austen, Mount
China/Jammu and Kashmir *see* K2
Goedgegun Swaziland *see*
Nhlangano
130 C3 Goéland, Lac au *l.* Can.
131 D2 Goélands, Lac aux *l.* Can.
100 A2 Goes Neth.
138 B1 Gogebic Range *hills* U.S.A.
88 C1 Gogland, Ostrov *i.* Rus. Fed.
Gogra *r.* India *see* Ghaghara
119 C2 Gogrial Sudan

154 C1 Goiandira Brazil
154 C1 Goianésia Brazil
154 C1 Goiânia Brazil
154 B1 Goiás Brazil
154 C2 Goiatuba Brazil
154 B2 Goio-Erê Brazil
111 C2 Gökçeada *i.* Turkey
111 C3 Gökçedağ Turkey
121 B2 Gokwe Zimbabwe
93 E3 Gol Norway
62 A1 Golaghat India
111 C2 Gölcük Turkey
103 E1 Gołdap Pol.
101 F1 Goldberg Ger.
Gold Coast *country* Africa *see* Ghana
53 D1 Gold Coast Austr.
114 B4 Gold Coast *coastal area* Ghana
128 C2 Golden Can.
54 B2 Golden Bay N.Z.
134 B1 Goldendale U.S.A.
128 B3 Golden Hinde *mt.* Can.
97 B2 Golden Vale *lowland* Ireland
135 C3 Goldfield U.S.A.
128 B3 Gold River Can.
141 E1 Goldsboro U.S.A.
103 C1 Goleniów Pol.
135 C4 Goleta U.S.A.
Golfe du St-Laurent *g.* Can. *see*
St Lawrence, Gulf of
75 D1 Golmud China
81 D2 Golpāyegān Iran
96 C2 Golspie U.K.
Golyshi Rus. Fed. *see*
Vetluzhskiy
119 C3 Goma Dem. Rep. Congo
75 C2 Gomati *r.* India
115 D3 Gombe Nigeria
115 D3 Gombi Nigeria
Gomel' Belarus *see* Homyel'
144 B2 Gómez Palacio Mex.
81 D2 Gomīshān Iran
75 C1 Gomo China
147 C3 Gonaïves Haiti
147 C3 Gonâve, Île de la *i.* Haiti
81 D2 Gonbad-e Kavus Iran
74 B2 Gondal India
116 B3 Gondar Eth. *see* Gonder
75 C2 Gonder Eth.
75 C2 Gondia India
111 C2 Gönen Turkey
62 A1 Gonggar China
70 A3 Gongga Shan *mt.* China
68 C2 Gonghe China
115 D4 Gongola *r.* Nigeria
53 C2 Gongolgon Austr.
Gongtang China *see* Damxung
123 C3 Gonubie S. Africa
145 C2 Gonzáles Mex.
143 D3 Gonzales U.S.A.
122 A3 Good Hope, Cape of S. Africa
134 D2 Gooding U.S.A.
136 C3 Goodland U.S.A.
53 C1 Goodooga Austr.
98 C3 Goole U.K.
53 C2 Goolgowi Austr.
52 A3 Goolwa Austr.
53 D1 Goondiwindi Austr.
134 B2 Goose Lake U.S.A.
102 B2 Göppingen Ger.
75 C2 Gorakhpur India
109 C2 Goražde Bos.-Herz.
111 C3 Gördes Turkey
89 D3 Gordeyevka Rus. Fed.
136 C2 Gordon U.S.A.
51 D4 Gordon, Lake Austr.
115 D4 Goré Chad
117 B4 Gore Eth.
54 A3 Gore N.Z.
97 C2 Gorey Ireland
81 D2 Gorgān Iran
81 C1 Gori Georgia
100 B2 Gorinchem Neth.
108 B1 Gorizia Italy
Gor'kiy Rus. Fed. *see*
Nizhniy Novgorod
89 F2 Gor'kovskoye Vodokhranilishche
*resr* Rus. Fed.
103 E2 Gorlice Pol.
103 C1 Görlitz Ger.
Gorna Dzhumaya Bulg. *see*
Blagoevgrad
109 D2 Gornji Milanovac Serb. and Mont.
109 C2 Gornji Vakuf Bos.-Herz.
77 E1 Gorno-Altaysk Rus. Fed.
86 F2 Gornopravdinsk Rus. Fed.
110 C2 Gornotrakiyska Nizina *lowland*
Bulg.
66 D1 Gornozavodsk Rus. Fed.
77 E1 Gornyak Rus. Fed.
59 D3 Goroka P.N.G.
52 B3 Goroke Austr.
114 B3 Gorom Gorom Burkina
121 C2 Gorongosa Moz.
61 D1 Gorontalo Indon.
89 E3 Gorshechnoye Rus. Fed.
97 B2 Gorumna Island Ireland
91 B2 Goryachiy Klyuch Rus. Fed.
103 D1 Gorzów Wielkopolski Pol.
59 D3 Goschen Strait P.N.G.
53 D2 Gosford Austr.
74 A2 Goshanak Pak.
66 D2 Goshogawara Japan
101 E2 Goslar Ger.

109 C2 Gospić Croatia
99 C4 Gosport U.K.
111 B2 Gostivar Macedonia
Göteborg Sweden *see* Gothenburg
101 E2 Gotha Ger.
93 F4 Gothenburg Sweden
136 C2 Gothenburg U.S.A.
93 G4 Gotland *i.* Sweden
111 B2 Gotse Delchev Bulg.
93 H4 Gotska Sandön *i.* Sweden
67 B4 Gōtsu Japan
101 E2 Göttingen Ger.
128 B2 Gott Peak Can.
Gottwaldov Czech Rep. *see* Zlín
100 B1 Gouda Neth.
114 A3 Goudiri Senegal
115 D3 Goudoumaria Niger
158 E7 Gough Island S. Atlantic Ocean
130 C3 Gouin, Réservoir Can.
53 C2 Goulburn Austr.
53 D2 Goulburn *r. N.S.W.* Austr.
53 C3 Goulburn *r. Vic.* Austr.
114 B3 Goundam Mali
107 D2 Gouraya Alg.
114 B3 Gourcy Burkina
104 C2 Gourdon France
115 D3 Gouré Niger
122 B3 Gourits *r.* S. Africa
114 B3 Gourma-Rharous Mali
53 C3 Gourock Range *mts* Austr.
155 D1 Governador Valadares Brazil
141 E3 Governor's Harbour Bahamas
68 C2 Goví Altayn Nuruu *mts* Mongolia
75 C2 Govind Ballash Pant Sagar *resr*
India
76 C4 Gowd-e Zereh *plain* Afgh.
99 A3 Gower *pen.* U.K.
152 C2 Goya Arg.
81 C1 Göyçay Azer.
80 B1 Göynük Turkey
115 E3 Goz-Beïda Chad
75 C1 Gozha Co *salt l.* China
122 B3 Graaf-Reinet S. Africa
122 A3 Graafwater S. Africa
101 E1 Grabow Ger.
109 C2 Gračac Croatia
87 E3 Grachevka Rus. Fed.
109 C2 Gradačac Bos.-Herz.
104 B3 Gradignan France
101 F2 Gräfenhainichen Ger.
53 D1 Grafton Austr.
137 D1 Grafton U.S.A.
143 D2 Graham *r.* Can.
142 B2 Graham, Mount U.S.A.
Graham Bell Island Rus. Fed. *see*
Greem-Bell, Ostrov
128 A2 Graham Island Can.
55 A3 Graham Land *reg.* Antarctica
123 C3 Grahamstown S. Africa
97 C2 Graiguenamanagh Ireland
151 E3 Grajaú Brazil
103 E1 Grajewo Pol.
111 B2 Grammos *mt.* Greece
96 B2 Grampian Mountains U.K.
146 B3 Granada Nic.
106 C2 Granada Spain
97 C2 Granard Ireland
139 E1 Granby Can.
114 A2 Gran Canaria *i.* Canary Is
152 B3 Gran Chaco *reg.* Arg./Para.
136 C3 Grand *r. MO* U.S.A.
136 C1 Grand *r. SD* U.S.A.
146 C2 Grand Bahama *i.* Bahamas
131 E3 Grand Bank Can.
158 D2 Grand Banks of Newfoundland
*sea feature* N. Atlantic Ocean
Grand Canal *canal* China *see*
Da Yunhe
Grand Canary *i.* Canary Is *see*
Gran Canaria
142 A1 Grand Canyon U.S.A.
142 A1 Grand Canyon *gorge* U.S.A.
146 B3 Grand Cayman *i.* Cayman Is
129 C2 Grand Centre Can.
134 C1 Grand Coulee U.S.A.
152 B1 Grande *r. Bol.*
154 B2 Grande *r.* Brazil
153 B5 Grande, Bahía *b.* Arg.
155 D2 Grande, Ilha *i.* Brazil
150 C2 Grande, Serra *mt.* Brazil
128 C2 Grande Cache Can.
Grande Comore *i.* Comoros *see*
Njazidja
128 C2 Grande Prairie Can.
115 D3 Grand Erg de Bilma *des.* Niger
114 B1 Grand Erg Occidental *des.* Alg.
115 C2 Grand Erg Oriental *des.* Alg.
131 D3 Grande-Rivière Can.
152 B3 Grandes, Salinas *salt marsh* Arg.
131 D3 Grand Falls *N.B.* Can.
131 E3 Grand Falls *Nfld and Lab.* Can.
128 C2 Grand Forks Can.
137 D1 Grand Forks U.S.A.
138 B2 Grand Haven U.S.A.
128 C1 Grandin, Lac *l.* Can.
137 D2 Grand Island U.S.A.
140 B3 Grand Isle U.S.A.
136 B3 Grand Junction U.S.A.
114 B4 Grand-Lahou Côte d'Ivoire
131 D3 Grand Lake *N.B.* Can.
131 E3 Grand Lake *Nfld and Lab.* Can.
137 E1 Grand Marais U.S.A.
130 C3 Grand-Mère Can.
106 B2 Grândola Port.

129 E2 Grand Rapids Can.
138 B2 Grand Rapids *MI* U.S.A.
137 E1 Grand Rapids *MN* U.S.A.
136 A2 Grand Teton *mt.* U.S.A.
147 D3 Grand Turk Turks and Caicos Is
129 D2 Grandview Can.
134 C1 Grandview U.S.A.
134 C1 Grangeville U.S.A.
128 B2 Granisle Can.
137 D2 Granite Falls U.S.A.
134 E1 Granite Peak *MT* U.S.A.
134 C2 Granite Peak *NV* U.S.A.
108 B3 Granitola, Capo *c.* Sicily Italy
93 F4 Gränna Sweden
101 F1 Gransee Ger.
99 C3 Grantham U.K.
96 C2 Grantown-on-Spey U.K.
142 B1 Grants U.S.A.
134 B2 Grants Pass U.S.A.
104 B2 Granville France
129 D2 Granville Lake Can.
155 D1 Grão Mogol Brazil
123 C1 Graskop S. Africa
105 D3 Grasse France
50 B3 Grass Patch Austr.
107 D1 Graus Spain
92 F2 Gravdal Norway
104 B2 Grave, Pointe de *pt* France
129 D3 Gravelbourg Can.
130 C3 Gravenhurst Can.
53 D1 Gravesend Austr.
99 D4 Gravesend U.K.
105 D2 Gray France
141 D1 Gray U.S.A.
138 C2 Grayling U.S.A.
99 D4 Grays U.K.
103 D2 Graz Austria
146 C2 Great Abaco *i.* Bahamas
50 B3 Great Australian Bight *g.* Austr.
146 C2 Great Bahama Bank *sea feature*
    Bahamas
54 C1 Great Barrier Island N.Z.
51 D1 Great Barrier Reef Austr.
135 C3 Great Basin U.S.A.
128 C1 Great Bear Lake Can.
93 F4 Great Belt *sea chan.* Denmark
137 D3 Great Bend U.S.A.
63 A2 Great Coco Island Cocos Is
53 B3 Great Dividing Range *mts* Austr.
    Great Eastern Erg *des.* Alg. see
    Grand Erg Oriental
146 B2 Greater Antilles *is*
    Caribbean Sea
    Greater Khingan Mountains
    China see Da Hinggan Ling
134 D1 Great Falls U.S.A.
123 C3 Great Fish *r.* S. Africa
123 C3 Great Fish Point S. Africa
147 C2 Great Inagua *i.* Bahamas
122 B3 Great Karoo *plat.* S. Africa
123 C3 Great Kei *r.* S. Africa
99 B3 Great Malvern U.K.
122 A2 Great Namaqualand *reg.* Namibia
73 D4 Great Nicobar *i.* India
98 B3 Great Ormes Head *hd* U.K.
99 D3 Great Ouse *r.* U.K.
136 C2 Great Plains U.S.A.
119 D3 Great Rift Valley Africa
119 D3 Great Ruaha *r.* Tanz.
134 D2 Great Salt Lake U.S.A.
134 D2 Great Salt Lake Desert U.S.A.
116 A2 Great Sand Sea *des.* Egypt/Libya
50 B2 Great Sandy Desert Austr.
128 C1 Great Slave Lake Can.
141 D1 Great Smoky Mountains U.S.A.
99 A4 Great Torrington U.K.
50 B2 Great Victoria Desert Austr.
70 B1 Great Wall *tourist site* China
    Great Western Erg *des.* Alg. see
    Grand Erg Occidental
99 D3 Great Yarmouth U.K.
    Grebenkovskiy Ukr. see Hrebinka
106 B1 Gredos, Sierra de *mts* Spain
111 B3 Greece *country* Europe
136 C2 Greeley U.S.A.
82 F1 Greem-Bell, Ostrov *i.* Rus. Fed.
138 F1 Green *r.* Can.
138 C3 Green *r. KY* U.S.A.
136 B3 Green *r. WY* U.S.A.
138 B2 Green Bay U.S.A.
138 B1 Green Bay *b.* U.S.A.
138 C2 Greenbrier *r.* U.S.A.
138 B3 Greencastle U.S.A.
141 D1 Greeneville U.S.A.
139 E2 Greenfield U.S.A.
129 D2 Green Lake Can.
127 J2 Greenland *terr.* N. America
160 L2 Greenland Basin *sea feature*
    Arctic Ocean
160 R2 Greenland Sea *sea*
    Greenland/Svalbard
96 C3 Greenock U.K.
97 C1 Greenore Ireland
135 D3 Green River *UT* U.S.A.
136 B2 Green River *WY* U.S.A.
138 B3 Greensburg *IN* U.S.A.
139 D2 Greensburg *PA* U.S.A.
141 E2 Green Swamp U.S.A.
142 A2 Green Valley U.S.A.
114 B4 Greenville Liberia
140 C2 Greenville *AL* U.S.A.
139 F1 Greenville *ME* U.S.A.
140 B2 Greenville *MS* U.S.A.
141 E1 Greenville *NC* U.S.A.
141 D2 Greenville *SC* U.S.A.

143 D2 Greenville *TX* U.S.A.
53 D2 Greenwell Point Austr.
131 D3 Greenwood Can.
140 B2 Greenwood *MS* U.S.A.
141 D2 Greenwood *SC* U.S.A.
50 B2 Gregory, Lake *salt flat* Austr.
51 D1 Gregory Range *hills* Austr.
102 C1 Greifswald Ger.
101 F2 Greiz Ger.
86 C2 Gremikha Rus. Fed.
93 F4 Grenå Denmark
140 C2 Grenada U.S.A.
147 D3 Grenada *country* West Indies
104 C3 Grenade France
93 F4 Grenen *spit* Denmark
53 C2 Grenfell Austr.
129 D2 Grenfell Can.
105 D2 Grenoble France
51 D1 Grenville, Cape Austr.
134 B1 Gresham U.S.A.
140 B3 Gretna *LA* U.S.A.
139 D3 Gretna *VA* U.S.A.
100 C1 Greven Ger.
111 B2 Grevena Greece
100 C2 Grevenbroich Ger.
101 E1 Grevesmühlen Ger.
136 B2 Greybull U.S.A.
128 A1 Grey Hunter Peak Can.
131 E2 Grey Islands Can.
54 B2 Greymouth N.Z.
52 B1 Grey Range *hills* Austr.
97 C2 Greystones Ireland
123 D2 Greytown S. Africa
91 E1 Gribanovskiy Rus. Fed.
118 B2 Gribingui *r.* C.A.R.
101 D3 Griesheim Ger.
141 D2 Griffin U.S.A.
53 C2 Griffith Austr.
88 C3 Grigiškės Lith.
118 C2 Grimari C.A.R.
101 F2 Grimma Ger.
102 C1 Grimmen Ger.
98 C3 Grimsby U.K.
128 C2 Grimshaw Can.
92 □B2 Grímsstaðir Iceland
93 E4 Grimstad Norway
92 □A3 Grindavík Iceland
93 E4 Grindsted Denmark
137 E2 Grinnell U.S.A.
123 C3 Griqualand East *reg.* S. Africa
122 B3 Griqualand West *reg.* S. Africa
122 B2 Griquatown S. Africa
127 G1 Grise Fiord Can.
    Grishino Ukr. see Krasnoarmiys'k
99 D4 Gris Nez, Cap *c.* France
96 C1 Gritley U.K.
123 C2 Groblersdal S. Africa
122 B2 Groblershoop S. Africa
    Grodno Belarus see Hrodna
103 D1 Grodzisk Wielkopolski Pol.
92 □A3 Gröf Iceland
104 B3 Groix, Île de *i.* France
100 C1 Gronau (Westfalen) Ger.
92 F3 Grong Norway
100 C1 Groningen Neth.
122 B3 Groot Brakrivier S. Africa
122 B2 Grootdrink S. Africa
51 C1 Groote Eylandt *i.* Austr.
120 A2 Grootfontein Namibia
122 A2 Groot Karas Berg *plat.* Namibia
122 B3 Groot Swartberge *mts* S. Africa
122 B2 Grootvloer *salt pan* S. Africa
123 C3 Groot Winterberg *mt.* S. Africa
101 D2 Großenlüder Ger.
101 E2 Großer Beerberg *hill* Ger.
102 C2 Großer Rachel *mt.* Ger.
103 C2 Grosser Speikkogel *mt.* Austria
108 B2 Grosseto Italy
101 D3 Groß-Gerau Ger.
102 C2 Großglockner *mt.* Austria
100 C1 Groß-Hesepe Ger.
101 E2 Großlohra Ger.
122 A1 Gross Ums Namibia
136 A2 Gros Ventre Range *mts* U.S.A.
131 E2 Groswater Bay Can.
130 B3 Groundhog *r.* Can.
135 B3 Grover Beach U.S.A.
140 B3 Groves U.S.A.
139 E2 Groveton U.S.A.
87 D4 Groznyy Rus. Fed.
109 C1 Grubišno Polje Croatia
    Grudovo Bulg. see Sredets
103 D1 Grudziądz Pol.
122 A2 Grünau Namibia
92 □A3 Grundarfjörður Iceland
    Gruzinskaya S.S.R. *admin. reg.*
    Asia see Georgia
89 E3 Gryazi Rus. Fed.
89 F2 Gryazovets Rus. Fed.
103 D1 Gryfice Pol.
102 C1 Gryfino Pol.
153 E5 Grytviken S. Georgia
146 C2 Guacanayabo, Golfo de *b.* Cuba
144 B2 Guadalajara Mex.
106 C1 Guadalajara Spain
48 H4 Guadalcanal *i.* Solomon Is
107 C2 Guadalope *r.* Spain
106 B2 Guadalquivir *r.* Spain
132 B2 Guadalupe *i.* Mex.
106 B2 Guadalupe, Sierra de *mts* Spain
142 B2 Guadalupe Peak U.S.A.
144 B2 Guadalupe Victoria Mex.
144 B2 Guadalupe y Calvo Mex.
106 C1 Guadarrama, Sierra de *mts*
    Spain

147 D3 Guadeloupe *terr.* West Indies
147 D3 Guadeloupe Passage
    Caribbean Sea
106 B2 Guadiana *r.* Port./Spain
106 C2 Guadix Spain
154 B2 Guaíra Brazil
147 C3 Guajira, Península de la *pen.* Col.
150 B3 Gualaceo Ecuador
59 D2 Guam *terr.* N. Pacific Ocean
144 B2 Guamúchil Mex.
144 B2 Guanacevi Mex.
151 E4 Guanambi Brazil
150 C2 Guanare Venez.
146 B2 Guane Cuba
70 A2 Guang'an China
71 B3 Guangchang China
71 B3 Guangdong *prov.* China
    Guanghua China see Laohekou
71 A3 Guangxi Zhuangzu Zizhiqu
    *aut. reg.* China
70 A2 Guangyuan China
71 B3 Guangzhou China
155 D1 Guanhães Brazil
147 D4 Guanipa *r.* Venez.
71 A3 Guanling China
65 A1 Guanshui China
    Guansuo China see Guanling
147 C2 Guantánamo Cuba
155 C2 Guapé Brazil
150 C4 Guaporé *r.* Bol./Brazil
155 C2 Guarapari Brazil
154 B3 Guarapuava Brazil
154 C3 Guaraqueçaba Brazil
155 C2 Guaratinguetá Brazil
154 C3 Guaratuba Brazil
106 B1 Guarda Port.
    Guardafui, Cape Somalia see
    Gwardafuy, Gees
154 C1 Guarantã do Norte Brazil
106 C1 Guardo Spain
155 C2 Guarujá Brazil
144 B2 Guasave Mex.
146 A3 Guatemala *country*
    Central America
    Guatemala Guat. see
    Guatemala City
157 G5 Guatemala Basin *sea feature*
    N. Pacific Ocean
146 A3 Guatemala City Guat.
150 C2 Guaviare *r.* Col.
155 C2 Guaxupé Brazil
150 B3 Guayaquil Ecuador
150 A3 Guayaquil, Golfo de *g.* Ecuador
152 B1 Guayaramerín Bol.
144 A2 Guaymas Mex.
117 B3 Guba Eth.
86 E1 Guba Dolgaya Rus. Fed.
108 B2 Gubbio Italy
89 E3 Gubkin Rus. Fed.
73 C3 Gudivada India
105 D2 Guebwiller France
    Guecho Spain see Algorta
114 A2 Guelb er Rîchât *hill* Maur.
115 C1 Guelma Alg.
114 A2 Guelmine Morocco
130 B3 Guelph Can.
145 C2 Guémez Mex.
104 B2 Guérande France
115 E2 Guerende Libya
104 C2 Guéret France
95 C4 Guernsey *i.* Channel Is
95 C4 Guernsey *terr.* Channel Is
144 A2 Guerrero Negro Mex.
131 D2 Guers, Lac *l.* Can.
158 D4 Guiana Basin *sea feature*
    N. Atlantic Ocean
150 C2 Guiana Highlands *mts*
    Guyana/Venez.
    Guichi China see Chizhou
118 B2 Guider Cameroon
108 B2 Guidonia-Montecelio Italy
71 A3 Guigang China
100 A3 Guignicourt France
123 D1 Guija Moz.
99 C4 Guildford U.K.
71 B3 Guilin China
130 C2 Guillaume-Delisle, Lac *l.* Can.
106 B1 Guimarães Port.
114 A3 Guinea *country* Africa
113 D5 Guinea, Gulf of Africa
114 A3 Guinea-Bissau *country* Africa
104 B2 Guingamp France
104 B2 Guipavas France
154 B1 Guiratinga Brazil
150 C1 Güiria Venez.
151 D2 Guisanbourg Fr. Guiana
98 C2 Guisborough U.K.
100 A3 Guise France
64 B2 Guiuan Phil.
71 A3 Guiyang China
71 A3 Guizhou *prov.* China
104 B3 Gujan-Mestras France
74 B2 Gujarat *state* India
    Gujerat *state* India see Gujarat
74 B1 Gujranwala Pak.
74 B1 Gujrat Pak.
91 D2 Gukovo Rus. Fed.
70 A2 Gulang China
53 C2 Gulargambone Austr.
73 B3 Gulbarga India
88 C2 Gulbene Latvia
79 C2 Gulf, The Asia
    Gulf of California Mex. see
    California, Gulf of
    Gulf of Chihli China see Bo Hai

111 B3 Gulf of Corinth *sea chan.* Greece
140 C2 Gulfport U.S.A.
53 C2 Gulgong Austr.
69 E1 Gulian China
77 C2 Guliston Uzbek.
    Gulja China see Yining
129 D2 Gull Lake Can.
111 C3 Güllük Turkey
    Gulü China see Xincai
119 D2 Gulu Uganda
120 B2 Gumare Botswana
76 B3 Gumdag Turkm.
115 C3 Gumel Nigeria
75 C2 Gumla India
100 C2 Gummersbach Ger.
87 C4 Gümüşhane Turkey
74 B2 Guna India
    Gunan China see Qijiang
53 C3 Gundagai Austr.
111 C3 Güney Turkey
118 B3 Gungu Dem. Rep. Congo
129 E2 Gunisao *r.* Can.
53 C2 Gunnedah Austr.
136 B3 Gunnison *CO* U.S.A.
135 D3 Gunnison *UT* U.S.A.
136 B3 Gunnison *r.* U.S.A.
73 B3 Guntakal India
73 C3 Guntur India
51 C1 Gununa Austr.
60 A1 Gunungsitoli Indon.
60 A1 Gunungtua Indon.
102 C2 Günzburg Ger.
102 C2 Gunzenhausen Ger.
70 B2 Guojiaba China
    Guoluezhen China see Lingbao
74 B2 Gurgaon India
151 E3 Gurgueia *r.* Brazil
150 C2 Guri, Embalse de *resr* Venez.
154 C1 Gurinhatã Brazil
121 C2 Guro Moz.
151 E4 Gurupi Brazil
151 E3 Gurupi *r.* Brazil
74 B2 Guru Sikhar *mt.* India
121 C2 Guruve Zimbabwe
    Gur'yev Kazakh. see Atyrau
115 C3 Gusau Nigeria
88 B3 Gusev Rus. Fed.
65 A2 Gushan China
74 A1 Gushgy Turkm.
70 B2 Gushi China
83 I3 Gusinoozersk Rus. Fed.
89 F2 Gus'-Khrustal'nyy Rus. Fed.
108 A3 Guspini *Sardinia* Italy
128 A2 Gustavus U.S.A.
101 F1 Güstrow Ger.
101 D2 Gütersloh Ger.
143 D1 Guthrie U.S.A.
152 B1 Gutiérrez Bol.
121 C2 Gutu Zimbabwe
75 D2 Guwahati India
150 D2 Guyana *country* S. America
    Guyi China see Sanjiang
143 C1 Guymon U.S.A.
53 C2 Guyra Austr.
70 A2 Guyuan China
    Guzhou China see Rongjiang
144 B1 Guzmán Mex.
144 B1 Guzmán, Lago de *l.* Mex.
77 C3 G'uzor Uzbek.
88 B3 Gvardeysk Rus. Fed.
74 A2 Gwadar Pak.
    Gwador Pak. see Gwadar
74 B2 Gwalior India
121 B3 Gwanda Zimbabwe
117 D3 Gwardafuy, Gees *c.* Somalia
97 B1 Gweebarra Bay Ireland
97 B1 Gweedore Ireland
    Gwelo Zimbabwe see Gweru
121 C2 Gweru Zimbabwe
115 C3 Gwoza Nigeria
53 D2 Gwydir *r.* Austr.
    Gya'gya China see Saga
    Gyandzha Azer. see Gäncä
    Gyangkar China see Dinngyê
    Gyangtse China see Gyangzê
71 C1 Gyangzê China
75 C2 Gyaring Co *l.* China
68 C2 Gyaring Hu *l.* China
86 G1 Gydan Peninsula *pen.* Rus. Fed.
    Gydanskiy Poluostrov *pen.*
    Rus. Fed. see Gydan Peninsula
    Gyêgu China see Yushu
62 A1 Gyigang China
51 E2 Gyimpie Austr.
62 A2 Gyobingauk Myanmar
103 D2 Gyöngyös Hungary
103 D2 Győr Hungary
136 B3 Gypsum U.S.A.
129 E2 Gypsumville Can.
131 D2 Gyrfalcon Islands Can.
111 B3 Gytheio Greece
103 E2 Gyula Hungary
81 C1 Gyumri Armenia
76 B3 Gyzylarbat Turkm.
    Gzhatsk Rus. Fed. see Gagarin

**H**

88 B2 Haapsalu Estonia
100 B1 Haarlem Neth.
122 B3 Haarlem S. Africa
101 C2 Haarstrang *ridge* Ger.

54 A2 **Haast** N.Z.
74 A2 **Hab** r. Pak.
79 C3 **Habarūt** Oman
78 B3 **Habbān** Yemen
81 C2 **Ḩabbānīyah, Hawr al** l. Iraq
70 B1 **Habirag** China
67 C4 **Hachijō-jima** i. Japan
66 D2 **Hachinohe** Japan
67 C3 **Hachiōji** Japan
121 C3 **Hacufera** Moz.
116 A1 **Ḩaḑabat al Jilf al Kabīr** Egypt
79 C2 **Ḩadd, Ra's al** pt Oman
96 C1 **Haddington** U.K.
115 D3 **Hadejia** Nigeria
93 E4 **Haderslev** Denmark
78 B2 **Ḩāḑhah** Saudi Arabia
79 B3 **Ḩaḑramawt** reg. Yemen
79 B3 **Ḩaḑramawt, Wādī** watercourse Yemen
91 C1 **Hadyach** Ukr.
65 B2 **Haeju** N. Korea
65 B3 **Haeju-man** b. N. Korea
65 B3 **Haenam** S. Korea
78 B2 **Ḩafar al Bāţin** Saudi Arabia
74 B1 **Hafizabad** Pak.
75 D2 **Haflong** India
92 □A3 **Hafnarfjörður** Iceland
78 A3 **Hagar Nish Plateau** Eritrea
59 D2 **Hagåtña** Guam
101 C1 **Hagelberg** hill Ger.
100 C2 **Hagen** Ger.
101 E1 **Hagenow** Ger.
128 B2 **Hagensborg** Can.
139 D3 **Hagerstown** U.S.A.
93 F3 **Hagfors** Sweden
134 D1 **Haggin, Mount** U.S.A.
67 B4 **Hagi** Japan
62 B1 **Ha Giang** Vietnam
97 B2 **Hag's Head** hd Ireland
104 B2 **Hague, Cap de la** c. France
69 F3 **Hahajima-rettō** is Japan
119 D3 **Hai** Tanz.
  **Haicheng** China see **Haifeng**
70 C1 **Haicheng** China
62 B1 **Hai Dương** Vietnam
80 B2 **Haifa** Israel
71 B3 **Haifeng** China
  **Haikang** China see **Leizhou**
71 B3 **Haikou** China
78 B2 **Ḩā'il** Saudi Arabia
  **Hailar** China see **Hulun Buir**
  **Hailong** China see **Meihekou**
92 H2 **Hailuoto** i. Fin.
69 D3 **Hainan** i. China
71 A4 **Hainan** prov. China
128 A2 **Haines** U.S.A.
128 A1 **Haines Junction** Can.
101 E2 **Hainich** ridge Ger.
101 E2 **Hainleite** ridge Ger.
62 B1 **Hai Phong** Vietnam
  **Haiphong** Vietnam see **Hai Phong**
147 L5 **Haiti** country West Indies
116 B3 **Haiya** Sudan
103 E2 **Hajdúböszörmény** Hungary
103 E2 **Hajdúszoboszló** Hungary
67 C3 **Hajiki-zaki** pt Japan
78 B3 **Ḩajjah** Yemen
79 D2 **Ḩājjīābād** Iran
103 E1 **Hajnówka** Pol.
62 A1 **Haka** Myanmar
81 C2 **Hakkâri** Turkey
66 D2 **Hakodate** Japan
122 B2 **Hakseen Pan** salt pan S. Africa
  **Ḩalab** Syria see **Aleppo**
78 B2 **Ḩalabān** Saudi Arabia
81 C2 **Halabja** Iraq
116 B2 **Halaib** Sudan
78 A2 **Halaib Triangle** terr. Egypt/Sudan
79 C3 **Ḩalānīyāt, Juzur al** is Oman
78 A2 **Ḩālat 'Ammār** Saudi Arabia
68 C1 **Halban** Mongolia
101 E2 **Halberstadt** Ger.
64 B2 **Halcon, Mount** Phil.
93 F4 **Halden** Norway
101 E1 **Haldensleben** Ger.
75 D2 **Haldwani** India
79 C2 **Hāleh** Iran
54 A3 **Halfmoon Bay** N.Z.
139 D1 **Haliburton Highlands** hills Can.
131 D3 **Halifax** Can.
98 C3 **Halifax** U.K.
139 D3 **Halifax** U.S.A.
65 B3 **Halla-san** mt. S. Korea
127 G2 **Hall Beach** Can.
100 B2 **Halle** Belgium
102 C2 **Hallein** Austria
101 E2 **Halle-Neustadt** Ger.
101 E2 **Halle (Saale)** Ger.
48 G3 **Hall Islands** Micronesia
137 D1 **Hallock** U.S.A.
127 H2 **Hall Peninsula** Can.
50 B1 **Halls Creek** Austr.
59 C2 **Halmahera** i. Indon.
93 F4 **Halmstad** Sweden
  **Hälsingborg** Sweden see **Helsingborg**
100 B2 **Halsteren** Neth.
98 B2 **Haltwhistle** U.K.
67 B4 **Hamada** Japan
81 C2 **Hamadān** Iran
80 B2 **Ḩamāh** Syria
67 C4 **Hamamatsu** Japan
93 F3 **Hamar** Norway

116 B2 **Ḩamāţah, Jabal** mt. Egypt
73 C4 **Hambantota** Sri Lanka
101 D1 **Hamburg** Ger.
123 C3 **Hamburg** S. Africa
140 B2 **Hamburg** U.S.A.
78 A2 **Ḩamḑ, Wādī al** watercourse Saudi Arabia
78 B3 **ḩamḑah** Saudi Arabia
139 E2 **Hamden** U.S.A.
93 H3 **Hämeenlinna** Fin.
101 D1 **Hameln** Ger.
50 A2 **Hamersley Range** mts Austr.
65 B1 **Hamgyŏng-sanmaek** mts N. Korea
65 B2 **Hamhŭng** N. Korea
68 C2 **Hami** China
116 B2 **Hamid** Sudan
52 B3 **Hamilton** Austr.
130 C3 **Hamilton** Can.
  **Hamilton** r. Can. see **Churchill**
54 C1 **Hamilton** N.Z.
96 B3 **Hamilton** U.K.
140 C2 **Hamilton** AL U.S.A.
134 D1 **Hamilton** MT U.S.A.
138 C3 **Hamilton** OH U.S.A.
115 E1 **Hamim, Wādī al** watercourse Libya
93 I3 **Hamina** Fin.
100 C2 **Hamm** Ger.
114 B2 **Hammada du Drâa** plat. Alg.
115 D1 **Hammamet, Golfe de g.** Tunisia
81 C2 **Ḩammār, Hawr al** imp. l. Iraq
101 D2 **Hammelburg** Ger.
92 G3 **Hammerdal** Sweden
92 H1 **Hammerfest** Norway
140 B2 **Hammond** U.S.A.
139 E3 **Hammonton** U.S.A.
139 D3 **Hampton** U.S.A.
139 E2 **Hampton Bays** U.S.A.
79 C2 **Hāmūn-e Jaz Mūrīān** salt marsh Iran
74 A2 **Hamun-i-Lora** dry lake Pak.
74 A2 **Hamun-i-Mashkel** salt flat Pak.
78 A2 **Ḩanak** Saudi Arabia
66 D3 **Hanamaki** Japan
101 D2 **Hanau** Ger.
70 B2 **Hancheng** China
138 B1 **Hancock** U.S.A.
70 B2 **Handan** China
119 D3 **Handeni** Tanz.
135 C3 **Hanford** U.S.A.
68 C1 **Hangayn Nuruu** mts Mongolia
  **Hangchow** China see **Hangzhou**
  **Hanggin Houqi** China see **Xamba**
  **Hangö** Fin. see **Hanko**
70 B2 **Hangu** China
70 C2 **Hangzhou** China
70 C2 **Hangzhou Wan** b. China
79 B2 **Ḩanīdh** Saudi Arabia
  **Hanjia** China see **Pengshui**
  **Hanjiang** China see **Yangzhou**
93 H4 **Hanko** Fin.
135 D3 **Hanksville** U.S.A.
54 B2 **Hanmer Springs** N.Z.
128 C2 **Hanna** Can.
136 B2 **Hanna** U.S.A.
137 E3 **Hannibal** U.S.A.
101 D1 **Hannover** Ger.
101 D2 **Hannoversch Münden** Ger.
93 F4 **Hanöbukten** b. Sweden
62 B1 **Ha Nôi** Vietnam
  **Hanoi** Vietnam see **Ha Nôi**
130 B3 **Hanover** Can.
122 B3 **Hanover** S. Africa
139 E2 **Hanover** NH U.S.A.
139 D3 **Hanover** PA U.S.A.
92 G2 **Hansnes** Norway
93 E4 **Hanstholm** Denmark
88 C3 **Hantsavichy** Belarus
75 C2 **Hanumana** India
74 B2 **Hanumangarh** India
70 A2 **Hanzhong** China
49 M5 **Hao** atoll Fr. Polynesia
75 C2 **Haora** India
92 H2 **Haparanda** Sweden
100 B2 **Hapert** Neth.
131 D2 **Happy Valley-Goose Bay** Can.
78 A2 **Ḩaql** Saudi Arabia
79 B2 **Ḩaraḑh** Saudi Arabia
88 C2 **Haradok** Belarus
78 B3 **Ḩarajā** Saudi Arabia
121 C2 **Harare** Zimbabwe
79 C3 **Ḩarāsīs, Jiddat al** des. Oman
69 D1 **Har-Ayrag** Mongolia
115 D3 **Haraze-Mangueigne** Chad
114 A4 **Harbel** Liberia
69 E1 **Harbin** China
138 C2 **Harbor Beach** U.S.A.
131 E3 **Harbour Breton** Can.
74 B2 **Harda** India
92 E4 **Hardangerfjorden** sea chan. Norway
61 C1 **Harden, Bukit** mt. Indon.
100 C1 **Hardenberg** Neth.
100 B1 **Harderwijk** Neth.
122 A3 **Hardeveld** mts S. Africa
134 E1 **Hardin** U.S.A.
128 C1 **Hardisty Lake** Can.
93 E3 **Hareid** Norway
100 C1 **Haren (Ems)** Ger.
117 C4 **Härer** Eth.
117 C4 **Hargeysa** Somalia
110 C1 **Harghita-Mădăraş, Vârful** mt. Romania

68 C2 **Har Hu** l. China
88 B2 **Hari kurk** sea chan. Estonia
74 B1 **Haripur** Pak.
74 A1 **Hari Rūd** r. Afgh./Iran
110 C1 **Hârlău** Romania
100 B1 **Harlingen** Neth.
143 D3 **Harlingen** U.S.A.
99 D4 **Harlow** U.K.
134 E1 **Harlowton** U.S.A.
134 C1 **Harney Basin** U.S.A.
134 C2 **Harney Lake** U.S.A.
93 G3 **Härnösand** Sweden
69 E1 **Har Nur** China
68 C1 **Har Nuur** l. Mongolia
96 □ **Haroldswick** U.K.
114 B4 **Harper** Liberia
101 D1 **Harpstedt** Ger.
130 C2 **Harricanaw** r. Can.
53 D2 **Harrington** Austr.
131 E2 **Harrington Harbour** Can.
96 A2 **Harris** pen. U.K.
96 A2 **Harris, Sound of** sea chan. U.K.
138 B3 **Harrisburg** IL U.S.A.
139 D2 **Harrisburg** PA U.S.A.
123 C2 **Harrismith** S. Africa
140 B1 **Harrison** U.S.A.
131 E2 **Harrison, Cape** Can.
126 B2 **Harrison Bay** U.S.A.
139 D3 **Harrisonburg** U.S.A.
128 B3 **Harrison Lake** Can.
137 E3 **Harrisonville** U.S.A.
98 C3 **Harrogate** U.K.
110 C2 **Hârşova** Romania
92 G2 **Harstad** Norway
122 B2 **Hartbees** watercourse S. Africa
103 D2 **Hartberg** Austria
139 E2 **Hartford** CT U.S.A.
137 D2 **Hartford** SD U.S.A.
99 A4 **Hartland Point** U.K.
98 C2 **Hartlepool** U.K.
  **Hartley** Zimbabwe see **Chegutu**
128 B2 **Hartley Bay** Can.
123 C3 **Harts** r. S. Africa
141 D2 **Hartwell Reservoir** U.S.A.
68 C1 **Har Us Nuur** l. Mongolia
136 C1 **Harvey** U.S.A.
99 D4 **Harwich** U.K.
74 B2 **Haryana** state India
101 E2 **Harz** hills Ger.
101 E2 **Harzgerode** Ger.
78 B2 **Ḩasan, Jabal** hill Saudi Arabia
80 B2 **Hasan Dağı** mts Turkey
99 C4 **Haslemere** U.K.
73 B3 **Hassan** India
100 B2 **Hasselt** Belgium
101 E2 **Haßfurt** Ger.
115 C2 **Hassi Bel Guebbour** Alg.
115 C1 **Hassi Messaoud** Alg.
93 F4 **Hässleholm** Sweden
100 B2 **Hastière-Lavaux** Belgium
53 C3 **Hastings** Vic. Austr.
54 C1 **Hastings** N.Z.
99 D4 **Hastings** U.K.
137 E2 **Hastings** MN U.S.A.
137 D2 **Hastings** NE U.S.A.
  **Hatay** Turkey see **Antakya**
142 B2 **Hatch** U.S.A.
129 D2 **Hatchet Lake** Can.
110 B1 **Haţeg** Romania
52 B2 **Hatfield** Austr.
68 C1 **Hatgal** Mongolia
62 B2 **Ha Tinh** Vietnam
52 B2 **Hattah** Austr.
141 E1 **Hatteras, Cape** U.S.A.
157 H3 **Hatteras Abyssal Plain** sea feature S. Atlantic Ocean
140 C2 **Hattiesburg** U.S.A.
100 C2 **Hattingen** Ger.
63 B3 **Hat Yai** Thai.
117 C4 **Haud** reg. Eth.
93 E4 **Haugesund** Norway
93 E4 **Haukeligrend** Norway
92 I2 **Haukipudas** Fin.
54 C1 **Hauraki Gulf** N.Z.
54 A3 **Hauroko, Lake** N.Z.
114 B1 **Haut Atlas** mts Morocco
131 D3 **Hauterive** Can.
  **Haute-Volta** country Africa see **Burkina**
114 B1 **Hauts Plateaux** Alg.
146 B2 **Havana** Cuba
99 C4 **Havant** U.K.
101 E1 **Havel** r. Ger.
54 B2 **Havelberg** Ger.
54 B2 **Havelock** N.Z.
  **Havelock** Swaziland see **Bulembu**
54 C1 **Havelock North** N.Z.
99 A4 **Haverfordwest** U.K.
100 C2 **Havixbeck** Ger.
103 D2 **Havlíčkův Brod** Czech Rep.
92 H1 **Havøysund** Norway
111 C3 **Havran** Turkey
134 E1 **Havre** U.S.A.
131 D3 **Havre Aubert** Can.
131 D2 **Havre-St-Pierre** Can.
49 L2 **Hawai'i** i. U.S.A.
156 E4 **Hawai'ian Islands** is N. Pacific Ocean
78 B2 **Ḩawallī** Kuwait
98 B3 **Hawarden** U.K.
54 A2 **Hawea, Lake** N.Z.
54 B1 **Hawera** N.Z.
98 B2 **Hawes** U.K.
96 C3 **Hawick** U.K.

54 C1 **Hawke Bay** N.Z.
52 A2 **Hawker** Austr.
52 B1 **Hawkers Gate** Austr.
122 A3 **Hawston** S. Africa
135 C3 **Hawthorne** U.S.A.
52 B2 **Hay** Austr.
128 C1 **Hay** r. Can.
100 C3 **Hayange** France
81 C2 **Ḩaydarābād** Iran
134 C1 **Hayden** U.S.A.
129 E2 **Hayes** r. Man. Can.
126 F2 **Hayes** r. Nunavut Can.
79 C3 **Haymā'** Oman
77 C2 **Hayotboshi tog'i** mt. Uzbek.
111 C2 **Hayrabolu** Turkey
128 C1 **Hay River** Can.
137 D3 **Hays** U.S.A.
78 B3 **Hays** Yemen
90 B2 **Haysyn** Ukr.
135 B3 **Hayward** U.S.A.
99 C4 **Haywards Heath** U.K.
74 A1 **Hazārajāt** reg. Afgh.
138 C3 **Hazard** U.S.A.
75 C2 **Hazaribāgh** India
75 C2 **Hazaribagh Range** mts India
104 C1 **Hazebrouck** France
128 B2 **Hazelton** Can.
139 D2 **Hazleton** U.S.A.
135 B3 **Healdsburg** U.S.A.
53 C3 **Healesville** Austr.
159 E7 **Heard Island** Indian Ocean
143 D2 **Hearne** U.S.A.
130 B3 **Hearst** Can.
55 A3 **Hearst Island** Antarctica
70 B2 **Hebei** prov. China
53 C1 **Hebel** Austr.
140 B1 **Heber Springs** U.S.A.
70 B2 **Hebi** China
131 D2 **Hebron** Can.
128 A2 **Hecate Strait** Can.
71 A3 **Hechi** China
100 B2 **Hechtel** Belgium
54 C2 **Hector, Mount** N.Z.
93 F3 **Hede** Sweden
100 C1 **Heerde** Neth.
100 B1 **Heerenveen** Neth.
100 B1 **Heerhugowaard** Neth.
100 B2 **Heerlen** Neth.
  **Hefa** Israel see **Haifa**
70 B2 **Hefei** China
70 B3 **Hefeng** China
69 E1 **Hegang** China
119 D2 **Heiban** Sudan
102 B1 **Heide** Ger.
122 A1 **Heide** Namibia
101 D3 **Heidelberg** Ger.
122 B3 **Heidelberg** S. Africa
69 E1 **Heihe** China
102 B2 **Heilbronn** Ger.
69 E1 **Heilong Jiang** r. China/Rus. Fed.
93 I3 **Heinola** Fin.
  **Hejaz** reg. Saudi Arabia see **Hijaz**
92 A3 **Hekla** vol. Iceland
92 F3 **Helagsfjället** mt. Sweden
70 A2 **Helan Shan** mts China
140 B2 **Helena** AR U.S.A.
134 D1 **Helena** MT U.S.A.
96 B2 **Helensburgh** U.K.
102 B1 **Helgoland** i. Ger.
102 B1 **Helgoländer Bucht** b. Ger.
  **Heligoland** i. Ger. see **Helgoland**
  **Heligoland Bight** b. Ger. see **Helgoländer Bucht**
  **Helixi** China see **Ningguo**
92 □A3 **Hella** Iceland
100 B1 **Hellevoetsluis** Neth.
107 C2 **Hellín** Spain
  **Hell-Ville** Madag. see **Andoany**
76 B3 **Helmand** r. Afgh.
101 E2 **Helmbrechts** Ger.
122 A2 **Helmeringhausen** Namibia
100 B2 **Helmond** Neth.
96 C1 **Helmsdale** U.K.
96 C1 **Helmsdale** r. U.K.
98 C2 **Helmsley** U.K.
101 E1 **Helmstedt** Ger.
65 B2 **Helong** China
143 D3 **Helotes** U.S.A.
93 F4 **Helsingborg** Sweden
  **Helsingfors** Fin. see **Helsinki**
93 F4 **Helsingør** Denmark
93 H3 **Helsinki** Fin.
99 A4 **Helston** U.K.
97 C2 **Helvick Head** hd Ireland
99 C4 **Hemel Hempstead** U.K.
101 D1 **Hemmoor** Ger.
92 F2 **Hemnesberget** Norway
70 B2 **Henan** prov. China
111 D2 **Hendek** Turkey
138 B3 **Henderson** KY U.S.A.
141 E1 **Henderson** NC U.S.A.
135 D3 **Henderson** NV U.S.A.
143 E2 **Henderson** TX U.S.A.
49 O6 **Henderson Island** Pitcairn Is
141 D1 **Hendersonville** U.S.A.
99 C4 **Hendon** U.K.
62 A1 **Hengduan Shan** mts China
100 C1 **Hengelo** Neth.
  **Hengnan** China see **Hengyang**
71 B3 **Hengshan** China
70 B2 **Hengshui** China
71 A3 **Hengxian** China
71 B3 **Hengyang** China
  **Hengzhou** China see **Hengxian**
91 C2 **Heniches'k** Ukr.

**139** D3 Henlopen, Cape U.S.A.
**100** C2 Hennef (Sieg) Ger.
**130** B2 Henrietta Maria, Cape Can.
Henrique de Carvalho Angola *see*
Saurimo
**139** D3 Henry, Cape U.S.A.
**143** D1 Henryetta U.S.A.
**127** H2 Henry Kater, Cape Can.
**101** D1 Henstedt-Ulzburg Ger.
**120** A3 Hentiesbaai Namibia
**101** D3 Heppenheim (Bergstraße) Ger.
**71** A3 Hepu China
**76** C3 Herāt Afgh.
**129** D2 Herbert Can.
**54** C2 Herbertville N.Z.
**101** D2 Herbstein Ger.
**109** C2 Herceg-Novi Serb. and Mont.
**99** B3 Hereford U.K.
**143** C2 Hereford U.S.A.
**101** D1 Herford Ger.
**100** C2 Herkenbosch Neth.
**96** □ Herma Ness *hd* U.K.
**122** A4 Hermanus S. Africa
**53** C2 Hermidale Austr.
**134** C1 Hermiston U.S.A.
**59** D3 Hermit Islands P.N.G.
**144** A2 Hermosillo Mex.
**154** B3 Hernandarias Para.
**100** C2 Herne Ger.
**93** E4 Herning Denmark
**104** B2 Hérouville-St-Clair France
**106** B2 Herrera del Duque Spain
**139** D2 Hershey U.S.A.
**99** C4 Hertford U.K.
**123** C2 Hertzogville S. Africa
**51** E2 Hervey Bay Austr.
**101** F2 Herzberg Ger.
**101** E3 Herzogenaurach Ger.
**71** A3 Heshan China
**135** C4 Hesperia U.S.A.
**128** A1 Hess *r.* Can.
**101** E1 Hessen Ger.
**101** D2 Hessisch Lichtenau Ger.
**136** C1 Hettinger U.S.A.
**101** E2 Hettstedt Ger.
**98** B2 Hexham U.K.
**98** B2 Heysham U.K.
**71** B3 Heyuan China
**52** B3 Heywood Austr.
**70** B2 Heze China
**71** B3 Hezhou China
**141** D3 Hialeah U.S.A.
**137** D3 Hiawatha U.S.A.
**137** E1 Hibbing U.S.A.
**141** D1 Hickory U.S.A.
**54** C1 Hicks Bay N.Z.
**66** D2 Hidaka-sanmyaku *mts* Japan
**143** D3 Hidalgo Mex.
**145** C2 Hidalgo Mex.
**144** B2 Hidalgo del Parral Mex.
**154** C1 Hidrolândia Brazil
**67** A4 Higashi-suidō *sea chan.* Japan
High Atlas *mts* Morocco *see*
Haut Atlas
**134** B2 High Desert U.S.A.
**128** C2 High Level Can.
**141** E1 High Point U.S.A.
**128** C2 High Prairie Can.
**128** C2 High River Can.
**129** D2 Highrock Lake Can.
High Tatras *mts* Pol./Slovakia *see*
Tatry
**99** C4 High Wycombe U.K.
**88** B2 Hiiumaa *i.* Estonia
**78** A2 Hijaz *reg.* Saudi Arabia
**54** C1 Hikurangi *mt.* N.Z.
**101** E2 Hildburghausen Ger.
**100** C2 Hilden Ger.
**101** E2 Hilders Ger.
**101** D1 Hildesheim Ger.
**81** C2 Hillah Iraq
**100** B1 Hillegom Neth.
**100** C2 Hillesheim Ger.
**138** C3 Hillsboro *OH* U.S.A.
**143** D2 Hillsboro *TX* U.S.A.
**53** C2 Hillston Austr.
**96** □ Hillswick U.K.
**49** L2 Hilo U.S.A.
**141** D2 Hilton Head Island U.S.A.
**100** B1 Hilversum Neth.
**74** B1 Himachal Pradesh *state* India
**68** B2 Himalaya *mts* Asia
**74** B2 Himatnagar India
**67** B4 Himeji Japan
**123** C2 Himeville S. Africa
**67** C3 Himi Japan
Ḩimş Syria *see* Homs
**147** C3 Hinche Haiti
**51** D1 Hinchinbrook Island Austr.
**52** B3 Hindmarsh, Lake *dry lake* Austr.
**74** A1 Hindu Kush *mts* Afgh./Pak.
**73** B3 Hindupur India
**134** C2 Hines U.S.A.
**141** D2 Hinesville U.S.A.
**74** B2 Hinganghat India
**81** C2 Hınıs Turkey
**92** G2 Hinnøya *i.* Norway
**106** B2 Hinojosa del Duque Spain
**100** C1 Hinte Ger.
**62** A2 Hinthada Myanmar
**128** C2 Hinton Can.
**75** C2 Hirakud Reservoir India
Hîrlău Romania *see* Hârlău
**66** D2 Hiroo Japan
**66** D2 Hirosaki Japan

**67** B4 Hiroshima Japan
**101** E3 Hirschaid Ger.
**101** E2 Hirschberg Ger.
**105** C2 Hirson France
Hîrşova Romania *see* Hârşova
**93** E4 Hirtshals Denmark
**74** B2 Hisar India
**147** C2 Hispaniola *i.* Caribbean Sea
**81** C2 Ḩīt Iraq
**67** D3 Hitachi Japan
**67** D3 Hitachinaka Japan
**92** E3 Hitra *i.* Norway
**49** N4 Hiva Oa *i.* Fr. Polynesia
**93** G4 Hjälmaren *l.* Sweden
**129** D1 Hjalmar Lake Can.
**93** F4 Hjørring Denmark
**123** D2 Hlabisa S. Africa
**92** □B2 Hlíð Iceland
**91** C2 Hlobyne Ukr.
**123** C2 Hlohlowane S. Africa
**123** C2 Hlotse Lesotho
**91** C1 Hlukhiv Ukr.
**88** C3 Hlusk Belarus
**88** C2 Hlybokaye Belarus
**114** C4 Ho Ghana
**122** A1 Hoachanas Namibia
**120** A2 Hoanib *watercourse* Namibia
**120** A2 Hoarusib *watercourse* Namibia
**51** D4 Hobart Austr.
**143** D1 Hobart U.S.A.
**143** C2 Hobbs U.S.A.
**93** E4 Hobro Denmark
**117** C4 Hobyo Somalia
Hô Chi Minh Vietnam *see*
Ho Chi Minh City
**63** B2 Ho Chi Minh City Vietnam
**114** B3 Hôd *reg.* Maur.
**117** C3 Hodda *mt.* Somalia
**78** B3 Hodeidah Yemen
**103** E2 Hódmezővásárhely Hungary
Hoek van Holland Neth. *see*
Hook of Holland
**65** B2 Hoeyang N. Korea
**101** E2 Hof Ger.
**101** E2 Hofheim in Unterfranken Ger.
**92** □B3 Höfn Sweden
**92** □A2 Höfn Iceland
**92** □B3 Hofsjökull *ice cap* Iceland
**67** B4 Hōfu Japan
**115** C2 Hoggar *plat.* Alg.
**93** G4 Högsby Sweden
**93** E3 Høgste Breakulen *mt.* Norway
**101** D2 Hohe Rhön *mts* Ger.
**100** C2 Hohe Venn *moorland* Belgium
**70** B1 Hohhot China
**75** C1 Hoh Xil Shan *mts* China
**63** B2 Hôi An Vietnam
**119** D2 Hoima Uganda
**63** B2 Hôi Xuân Vietnam
**75** D2 Hojai India
**54** B2 Hokitika N.Z.
**66** D2 Hokkaidō *i.* Japan
**91** C2 Hola Prystan' Ukr.
**128** B2 Holberg Can.
**53** C3 Holbrook Austr.
**142** A2 Holbrook U.S.A.
**137** D2 Holdrege U.S.A.
**146** C2 Holguín Cuba
**92** □B2 Hóll Iceland
**103** D1 Hollabrunn Austria
**138** B2 Holland U.S.A.
Hollandia Indon. *see*
Jayapura
**135** B3 Hollister U.S.A.
**103** E2 Hollóháza Hungary
**93** I3 Hollola Fin.
**100** B1 Hollum Neth.
**140** C2 Holly Springs U.S.A.
**134** C4 Hollywood U.S.A.
**141** D3 Hollywood U.S.A.
**92** F2 Holm Norway
**126** E2 Holman Can.
**92** H3 Holmsund Sweden
**122** A2 Holoog Namibia
**93** E4 Holstebro Denmark
**141** D1 Holston *r.* U.S.A.
**98** A3 Holyhead U.K.
**98** A3 Holy Island *England* U.K.
**98** A3 Holy Island *Wales* U.K.
**136** C2 Holyoke U.S.A.
Holy See Europe *see* Vatican City
**101** D2 Holzminden Ger.
**62** A1 Homalin Myanmar
**101** D2 Homberg (Efze) Ger.
**114** B3 Hombori Mali
**100** C3 Homburg Ger.
**127** H2 Home Bay Can.
**140** B2 Homer U.S.A.
**141** D3 Homestead U.S.A.
**92** F3 Hommelvik Norway
**141** D3 Homosassa Springs U.S.A.
**80** B2 Homs Syria
**89** D3 Homyel' Belarus
Honan *prov.* China *see* Henan
**122** A3 Hondeklipbaai S. Africa
**145** D3 Hondo *r.* Belize/Mex.
**142** B2 Hondo *NM* U.S.A.
**143** D3 Hondo *TX* U.S.A.
**146** B3 Honduras *country* Central America
**146** B3 Honduras, Gulf of Belize/Hond.
**93** F3 Hønefoss Norway
**135** B3 Honey Lake U.S.A.
**104** C2 Honfleur France
**62** B1 Hông Gai Vietnam
**70** B3 Honghu China

**71** A3 Hongjiang China
**71** B3 Hong Kong China
**71** B3 Hong Kong *special admin. reg.*
China
**131** D3 Hongqizhen China *see* Wuzhishan
**65** B1 Hongwŏn N. Korea
**70** B2 Hongze Hu *l.* China
**48** H4 Honiara Solomon Is
**99** B4 Honiton U.K.
**66** D3 Honjō Japan
**92** I1 Honningsvåg Norway
**49** L1 Honolulu U.S.A.
**67** B3 Honshū *i.* Japan
**134** B1 Hood, Mount *vol.* U.S.A.
**50** A3 Hood Point Austr.
**134** B1 Hood River U.S.A.
**100** B2 Hoogerheide Neth.
**100** C1 Hoogeveen Neth.
**100** C1 Hoogezand-Sappemeer Neth.
**100** C2 Hoogstraten Neth.
**100** B2 Hook of Holland Neth.
**128** A2 Hoonah U.S.A.
**123** C2 Hoopstad S. Africa
**100** B1 Hoorn Neth.
**49** J5 Hoorn, Îles de *is*
Wallis and Futuna Is
**128** B3 Hope Can.
**140** B2 Hope U.S.A.
**83** N2 Hope, Point U.S.A.
**131** D2 Hopedale Can.
**145** D3 Hopelchén Mex.
**131** D2 Hope Mountains Can.
Hopes Advance Bay Can. *see*
Aupaluk
**52** A2 Hopetoun Austr.
**122** B2 Hopetown S. Africa
**139** D3 Hopewell U.S.A.
**130** C2 Hopewell Islands Can.
**50** B2 Hopkins, Lake *salt flat* Austr.
**138** B3 Hopkinsville U.S.A.
**134** B1 Hoquiam U.S.A.
**81** C1 Horasan Turkey
**93** F4 Hörby Sweden
**89** D3 Horki Belarus
**91** D2 Horlivka Ukr.
**79** D2 Hormak Iran
**79** C2 Hormuz, Strait of Iran/Oman
**103** D2 Horn Austria
**92** □A2 Horn *c.* Iceland
**153** B5 Horn, Cape Chile
**139** D2 Hornell U.S.A.
**130** B3 Hornepayne Can.
Hornos, Cabo de *c.* Chile *see*
Horn, Cape
**53** D2 Hornsby Austr.
**98** C3 Hornsea U.K.
**90** B2 Horodenka Ukr.
**91** C1 Horodnya Ukr.
**90** B2 Horodok Ukr.
**90** A2 Horodok Ukr.
**90** A1 Horokhiv Ukr.
Horqin Youyi Qianqi China *see*
Ulanhot
**131** E2 Horse Islands Can.
**52** B3 Horsham Austr.
**99** C4 Horsham U.K.
**93** F4 Horten Norway
**126** D2 Horton *r.* Can.
**117** B4 Hosa'ina Eth.
**74** A2 Hoshab Pak.
**74** B1 Hoshiarpur India
**142** B1 Hosta Butte *mt.* U.S.A.
**75** C1 Hotan China
**122** B2 Hotazel S. Africa
**92** G3 Hoting Sweden
**140** B2 Hot Springs *AR* U.S.A.
Hot Springs *SD* U.S.A. *see*
Truth or Consequences
**136** C2 Hot Springs *SD* U.S.A.
**128** C1 Hottah Lake Can.
**100** B2 Houffalize Belgium
**138** B1 Houghton U.S.A.
**139** F1 Houlton U.S.A.
**70** B2 Houma China
**140** B3 Houma U.S.A.
**128** B2 Houston Can.
**143** D3 Houston U.S.A.
**50** A2 Houtman Abrolhos *is* Austr.
**122** A3 Houwater S. Africa
**68** C1 Hovd Mongolia
**99** C4 Hove U.K.
**90** A2 Hoverla, Hora *mt.* Ukr.
**68** C1 Hövsgöl Nuur *l.* Mongolia
**68** C2 Hövüün Mongolia
**116** A3 Howar, Wadi *watercourse* Sudan
**98** C3 Howden U.K.
**53** C3 Howe, Cape Austr.
**123** C2 Howick S. Africa
**49** J3 Howland Island *terr.*
N. Pacific Ocean
**53** C3 Howlong Austr.
Howrah India *see* Haora
**140** B1 Hoxie U.S.A.
**101** D2 Höxter Ger.
**96** C1 Hoy *i.* U.K.
**93** E3 Høyanger Norway
**102** C1 Hoyerswerda Ger.
**62** A1 Hpapun Myanmar
**103** D1 Hradec Králové Czech Rep.
**109** C2 Hrasnica Bos.-Herz.
**92** □B2 Hraun Iceland
**91** C1 Hrebinka Ukr.

**88** B3 Hrodna Belarus
**62** A1 Hsi-hseng Myanmar
**71** C3 Hsinchu Taiwan
**71** C3 Hsinying Taiwan
**62** A1 Hsipaw Myanmar
**70** A2 Huachi China
**150** B4 Huacho Peru
**70** B1 Huade China
**65** B1 Huadian China
**70** B2 Huai'an China
**70** B2 Huaibei China
**70** B2 Huai He *r.* China
**71** A3 Huaihua China
**70** B2 Huainan China
**70** B2 Huaiyang China
**145** C3 Huajuápan de León Mex.
**59** C3 Huaki Indon.
**71** C3 Hualien Taiwan
**150** B3 Huallaga *r.* Peru
**120** A2 Huambo Angola
**150** B4 Huancavelica Peru
**150** B4 Huancayo Peru
Huangcaoba China *see* Xingyi
**70** B2 Huangchuan China
Huang Hai *sea* N. Pacific Ocean
*see* Yellow Sea
Huang He *r.* China *see* Yellow River
**71** A4 Huangliu China
**70** B2 Huangshan China
**70** B2 Huangshi China
**70** A2 Huangtu Gaoyuan *plat.* China
**71** C3 Huangyan China
**70** A2 Huangyuan China
**65** B1 Huanren China
**150** B3 Huánuco Peru
**152** B1 Huanuni Bol.
**150** B4 Huaral Peru
**150** B4 Huaráz Peru
**150** B4 Huarmey Peru
**152** A2 Huasco Chile
**152** A2 Huasco *r.* Chile
**144** B2 Huatabampo Mex.
**145** C3 Huatusco Mex.
**71** A3 Huayuan China
**62** B1 Huayxay Laos
**70** B2 Hubei *prov.* China
**73** B3 Hubli India
**100** C2 Hückelhoven Ger.
**99** C3 Hucknall U.K.
**98** C3 Huddersfield U.K.
**93** G3 Hudiksvall Sweden
**139** E2 Hudson *r.* U.S.A.
**129** D2 Hudson Bay Can.
**127** G3 Hudson Bay *sea* Can.
**128** B2 Hudson's Hope Can.
**127** H2 Hudson Strait Can.
**63** B2 Huê Vietnam
**146** A3 Huehuetenango Guat.
**144** B2 Huehueto, Cerro *mt.* Mex.
**145** C2 Huejutla Mex.
**106** B2 Huelva Spain
**107** C2 Huércal-Overa Spain
**107** C1 Huesca Spain
**106** C2 Huéscar Spain
**51** D2 Hughenden Austr.
**50** B3 Hughes Austr.
**75** C2 Hugli *r. mouth* India
**143** D2 Hugo U.S.A.
Huhehot China *see* Hohhot
**122** B2 Huhudi S. Africa
**122** A2 Huib-Hoch Plateau Namibia
**71** B3 Huichang China
Huicheng China *see* Huilai
**65** B1 Huich'ŏn N. Korea
**71** B3 Huilai China
**120** A2 Huíla Plateau Angola
**71** A3 Huili China
**70** B2 Huinan China
**69** E2 Huinan China
Huinan China *see* Nanhui
**93** H3 Huittinen Fin.
**145** C3 Huixtla Mex.
**71** A3 Huize China
**68** C1 Hujirt Mongolia
**78** B2 Hujr Saudi Arabia
**122** B1 Hukuntsi Botswana
**78** B2 Ḩulayfah Saudi Arabia
**66** B1 Hulin China
**130** C3 Hull Can.
**70** C1 Huludao China
**69** D1 Hulun Buir China
**69** D1 Hulun Nur *l.* China
**91** D2 Hulyaypole Ukr.
**69** E1 Huma China
**150** C3 Humaitá Brazil
**122** B3 Humansdorp S. Africa
**98** C2 Humber *est.* U.K.
**143** D3 Humble U.S.A.
**129** D2 Humboldt Can.
**135** C2 Humboldt *NV* U.S.A.
**140** C1 Humboldt *TN* U.S.A.
**135** C2 Humboldt *r.* U.S.A.
**103** E2 Humenné Slovakia
**53** C3 Hume Reservoir Austr.
**142** A1 Humphreys Peak U.S.A.
**115** D2 Hūn Libya
**92** □A2 Húnaflói *b.* Iceland
**71** B3 Hunan *prov.* China
**65** C1 Hunchun China
**110** B1 Hunedoara Romania
**101** D2 Hünfeld Ger.
**103** D2 Hungary *country* Europe
**52** B1 Hungerford Austr.
**65** B2 Hŭngnam N. Korea
**65** A1 Hun He *r.* China

99 D3 Hunjiang China see Baishan
101 D1 Hunstanton U.K.
48 I6 Hunter Island S. Pacific Ocean
51 D4 Hunter Islands Austr.
99 C3 Huntingdon U.K.
138 B2 Huntington IN U.S.A.
138 C3 Huntington WV U.S.A.
135 C4 Huntington Beach U.S.A.
54 C1 Huntly N.Z.
96 C2 Huntly U.K.
130 C3 Huntsville Can.
140 C2 Huntsville AL U.S.A.
143 D2 Huntsville TX U.S.A.
Hunyani r. Moz./Zimbabwe see Manyame
59 D3 Huon Peninsula P.N.G.
Huoxian China see Huozhou
70 B2 Huozhou China
Hupeh prov. China see Hubei
Hurghada Egypt see Al Ghurdaqah
137 D2 Huron U.S.A.
138 C2 Huron, Lake Can./U.S.A.
135 D3 Hurricane U.S.A.
100 C2 Hürth Ger.
92 □B2 Húsavík Iceland
110 C1 Huşi Romania
126 B2 Huslia U.S.A.
78 B3 Husn Āl 'Abr Yemen
102 B1 Husum Ger.
68 C1 Hutag Mongolia
60 A1 Hutanopan Indon.
137 D3 Hutchinson U.S.A.
141 D3 Hutchinson Island U.S.A.
70 B2 Hutuo He r. China
100 B2 Huy Belgium
70 C2 Huzhou China
92 □C3 Hvalnes Iceland
92 □B3 Hvannadalshnúkur vol. Iceland
109 C2 Hvar Croatia
109 C2 Hvar i. Croatia
91 C2 Hvardiys'ke Ukr.
120 B2 Hwange Zimbabwe
Hwang Ho r. China see Yellow River
136 C2 Hyannis U.S.A.
68 C1 Hyargas Nuur salt l. Mongolia
50 A3 Hyden Austr.
73 B3 Hyderabad India
74 A2 Hyderabad Pak.
Hydra i. Greece see Ydra
105 D3 Hyères France
105 D3 Hyères, Îles d' is France
65 B1 Hyesan N. Korea
128 B2 Hyland Post Can.
67 B3 Hyōno-sen mt. Japan
99 D4 Hythe U.K.
67 B4 Hyūga Japan
93 H3 Hyvinkää Fin.

## I

114 B2 Iabès, Erg des. Alg.
150 C3 Iaco r. Brazil
110 C2 Ialomiţa r. Romania
110 C1 Ianca Romania
110 C1 Iaşi Romania
64 A2 Iba Phil.
115 C4 Ibadan Nigeria
150 B2 Ibagué Col.
154 B2 Ibaiti Brazil
150 B2 Ibarra Ecuador
78 B3 Ibb Yemen
100 C1 Ibbenbüren Ger.
115 C4 Ibi Nigeria
107 C2 Ibi Spain
155 C1 Ibiá Brazil
155 D1 Ibiaí Brazil
155 D1 Ibiraçu Brazil
107 D2 Ibiza Spain
107 D2 Ibiza i. Spain
151 E4 Ibotirama Brazil
79 C2 Ibrā' Oman
79 C2 Ibrī Oman
150 B4 Ica Peru
Icaria i. Greece see Ikaria
İçel Turkey see Mersin
92 □B2 Iceland country Europe
160 M4 Iceland Basin sea feature N. Atlantic Ocean
160 L3 Icelandic Plateau sea feature N. Atlantic Ocean
66 D3 Ichinoseki Japan
91 C1 Ichnya Ukr.
65 B2 Ich'ŏn N. Korea
151 F3 Icó Brazil
155 D2 Iconha Brazil
143 E2 Idabel U.S.A.
115 C4 Idah Nigeria
134 D2 Idaho state U.S.A.
134 D2 Idaho Falls U.S.A.
100 C3 Idar-Oberstein Ger.
68 C1 Ideriyn Gol r. Mongolia
116 B2 Idfū Egypt
115 C4 Idhān Awbārī des. Libya
115 D2 Idhān Murzūq des. Libya
Idi Amin Dada, Lake Dem. Rep. Congo/Uganda see Edward, Lake
118 B3 Idiofa Dem. Rep. Congo
80 B2 Idlib Syria
123 C3 Idutywa S. Africa
88 B2 Iecava Latvia

154 B2 Iepê Brazil
100 A2 Ieper Belgium
111 C3 Ierapetra Greece
121 □D3 Ifanadiana Madag.
119 D3 Ifakara Tanz.
115 C4 Ife Nigeria
114 C3 Ifôghas, Adrar des hills Mali
118 C3 Ifumo Dem. Rep. Congo
61 C1 Igan Sarawak Malaysia
119 D2 Iganga Uganda
154 C2 Igarapava Brazil
82 G2 Igarka Rus. Fed.
74 B3 Igatpuri India
81 C2 Iğdır Turkey
108 A3 Iglesias Sardinia Italy
127 G2 Igloolik Can.
Igluligaarjuk Can. see Chesterfield Inlet
130 A3 Ignace Can.
88 C2 Ignalina Lith.
111 C2 İğneada Turkey
110 C2 İğneada Burnu pt Turkey
111 B3 Igoumenitsa Greece
86 E3 Igra Rus. Fed.
86 F2 Igrim Rus. Fed.
154 B3 Iguaçu r. Brazil
154 B3 Iguaçu Falls Arg./Brazil
145 C3 Iguala Mex.
107 D1 Igualada Spain
154 C2 Iguape Brazil
154 B2 Iguatemi Brazil
154 B2 Iguatemi r. Brazil
151 F3 Iguatu Brazil
118 A3 Iguéla Gabon
114 B2 Iguidi, Erg des. Alg./Maur.
119 D3 Igunga Tanz.
121 □D2 Iharaña Madag.
69 D2 Ihbulag Mongolia
121 □D3 Ihosy Madag.
92 I2 Iijoki r. Fin.
92 I3 Iisalmi Fin.
67 B4 Iizuka Japan
115 C4 Ijebu-Ode Nigeria
100 B1 IJmuiden Neth.
100 B1 IJssel r. Neth.
100 B1 IJsselmeer l. Neth.
152 C2 Ijuí Brazil
Ikaahuk Can. see Sachs Harbour
123 C2 Ikageleng S. Africa
123 C2 Ikageng S. Africa
111 C3 Ikaria i. Greece
118 C3 Ikela Dem. Rep. Congo
110 B2 Ikhtiman Bulg.
67 A4 Iki i. Japan
118 A2 Ikom Nigeria
121 □D3 Ikongo Madag.
65 B2 Iksan S. Korea
119 D3 Ikungu Tanz.
114 C2 Ilaferh, Oued watercourse Alg.
64 B2 Ilagan Phil.
81 C2 Īlām Iran
75 C2 Ilam Nepal
103 D1 Iława Pol.
79 C2 Ilazārān, Kūh-e mt. Iran
129 D2 Île-à-la-Crosse Can.
129 D2 Île-à-la-Crosse, Lac l. Can.
118 C3 Ilebo Dem. Rep. Congo
119 D2 Ileret Kenya
99 D4 Ilford U.K.
99 A4 Ilfracombe U.K.
155 D2 Ilhabela Brazil
155 D2 Ilha Grande, Baía da b. Brazil
155 D2 Ilha Grande, Represa resr Brazil
154 B2 Ilha Solteira, Represa resr Brazil
106 B1 Ílhavo Port.
151 F4 Ilhéus Brazil
Ili Kazakh. see Kapchagay
126 B3 Iliamna Lake U.S.A.
64 B3 Iligan Phil.
Iliysk Kazakh. see Kapchagay
98 C3 Ilkley U.K.
152 A3 Illapel Chile
90 C2 Illichivs'k Ukr.
138 A3 Illinois r. U.S.A.
138 B3 Illinois state U.S.A.
90 B2 Illintsi Ukr.
115 C2 Illizi Alg.
89 D2 Il'men', Ozero l. Rus. Fed.
101 E2 Ilmenau Ger.
150 B4 Ilo Peru
64 B2 Iloilo Phil.
92 J3 Ilomantsi Fin.
115 C4 Ilorin Nigeria
87 D4 Ilovlya Rus. Fed.
53 D1 Iluka Austr.
127 I2 Ilulissat Greenland
Iman Rus. Fed. see Dal'nerechensk
66 B1 Iman r. Rus. Fed.
67 A4 Imari Japan
93 I3 Imatra Fin.
imeni Petra Stuchki Latvia see Aizkraukle
117 C4 Īmī Eth.
65 B2 Imjin-gang r. N. Korea/S. Korea
141 D3 Immokalee U.S.A.
108 B2 Imola Italy
151 E3 Imperatriz Brazil
108 A2 Imperia Italy
136 C2 Imperial U.S.A.
118 B2 Impfondo Congo
72 D2 Imphal India
111 C2 İmroz Turkey
67 C3 Ina Japan
150 C4 Inambari r. Peru

115 C2 In Aménas Alg.
115 C2 In Amguel Alg.
54 B2 Inangahua Junction N.Z.
59 C3 Inanwatan Indon.
92 I2 Inari Fin.
92 I2 Inarijärvi l. Fin.
67 D3 Inawashiro-ko l. Japan
80 B1 İnce Burun pt Turkey
65 B2 Inch'ŏn S. Korea
121 C2 Inchope Moz.
123 D2 Incomati r. Moz.
116 B3 Inda Silasē Eth.
144 B2 Indé Mex.
135 C2 Independence CA U.S.A.
137 E2 Independence IA U.S.A.
137 D3 Independence KS U.S.A.
137 E3 Independence MO U.S.A.
134 C2 Independence Mountains U.S.A.
76 B2 Inderborskiy Kazakh.
72 B2 India country Asia
139 D2 Indiana U.S.A.
138 B2 Indiana state U.S.A.
138 B3 Indianapolis U.S.A.
129 D2 Indian Head Can.
159 Indian Ocean
137 E2 Indianola IA U.S.A.
140 B2 Indianola MS U.S.A.
135 D3 Indian Peak U.S.A.
135 C3 Indian Springs U.S.A.
86 D2 Indiga Rus. Fed.
83 K2 Indigirka r. Rus. Fed.
109 D1 Indija Serb. and Mont.
135 C4 Indio U.S.A.
58 B3 Indonesia country Asia
74 B2 Indore India
60 B2 Indramayu, Tanjung pt Indon.
Indrapura, Gunung vol. Indon. see Kerinci, Gunung
75 C3 Indravati r. India
104 C2 Indre r. France
74 A2 Indus r. China/Pak.
74 A2 Indus, Mouths of the Pak.
159 E2 Indus Cone sea feature Indian Ocean
80 B1 İnebolu Turkey
111 C2 İnegöl Turkey
Infantes Spain see Villanueva de los Infantes
144 B2 Infiernillo, Presa resr Mex.
51 D1 Ingham Austr.
53 D1 Inglewood Austr.
102 C2 Ingolstadt Ger.
75 C2 Ingraj Bazar India
123 D2 Ingwavuma S. Africa
120 B2 Ingwe Zambia
123 D2 Inhaca Moz.
121 C2 Inhambane Moz.
121 C2 Inhaminga Moz.
151 D2 Inini Fr. Guiana
Inis Ireland see Ennis
97 A2 Inishbofin i. Ireland
97 B2 Inishmore i. Ireland
97 C1 Inishowen pen. Ireland
54 B2 Inland Kaikoura Range mts N.Z.
Inland Sea Japan see Seto-naikai
102 C2 Inn r. Europe
127 G2 Innaanganeq c. Greenland
52 B1 Innamincka Austr.
70 A1 Inner Mongolia aut. reg. China
96 B2 Inner Sound sea chan. U.K.
51 D1 Innisfail Austr.
102 C2 Innsbruck Austria
97 C2 Inny r. Ireland
154 B1 Inocência Brazil
118 B3 Inongo Dem. Rep. Congo
111 D3 İnönü Turkey
Inoucdjouac Can. see Inukjuak
103 D1 Inowrocław Pol.
114 C2 In Salah Alg.
62 A2 Insein Myanmar
110 C2 Însurăţei Romania
86 F2 Inta Rus. Fed.
105 D2 Interlaken Switz.
137 E1 International Falls U.S.A.
63 A2 Interview Island India
130 C2 Inukjuak Can.
126 D2 Inuvik Can.
96 B2 Inveraray U.K.
96 C2 Inverbervie U.K.
54 A3 Invercargill N.Z.
53 D1 Inverell Austr.
96 B2 Invergordon U.K.
128 C2 Invermere Can.
131 D3 Inverness Can.
96 B2 Inverness U.K.
96 C2 Inverurie U.K.
159 F4 Investigator Ridge sea feature Indian Ocean
52 A3 Investigator Strait Austr.
77 E1 Inya Rus. Fed.
Inyanga Zimbabwe see Nyanga
119 D3 Inyonga Tanz.
87 D3 Inza Rus. Fed.
111 B3 Ioannina Greece
137 D3 Iola U.S.A.
96 A2 Iona i. U.K.
111 B3 Ionian Islands Greece
109 C3 Ionian Sea Greece/Italy
Ionioi Nisoi is Greece see Ionian Islands
111 C3 Ios i. Greece
137 E2 Iowa state U.S.A.
137 E2 Iowa City U.S.A.
154 C1 Ipameri Brazil
155 D1 Ipatinga Brazil
81 D2 Ipatovo Rus. Fed.

123 C2 Ipelegeng S. Africa
150 B2 Ipiales Col.
151 F4 Ipiaú Brazil
154 B3 Ipiranga Brazil
150 B3 Ipixuna Brazil
60 B1 Ipoh Malaysia
154 B1 Iporá Brazil
118 C2 Ippy C.A.R.
111 C2 İpsala Turkey
53 D1 Ipswich Austr.
99 D3 Ipswich U.K.
127 H2 Iqaluit Can.
152 A2 Iquique Chile
150 B3 Iquitos Peru
Irakleio Greece see Iraklion
111 C3 Iraklion Greece
81 D2 Iran country Asia
61 C1 Iran, Pegunungan mts Indon.
79 D2 Īrānshahr Iran
144 B2 Irapuato Mex.
81 C2 Iraq country Asia
154 B3 Irati Brazil
88 B2 Irbe Strait Estonia/Latvia
80 B2 Irbid Jordan
86 F3 Irbit Rus. Fed.
151 E4 Irecê Brazil
97 C2 Ireland country Europe
118 C3 Irema Dem. Rep. Congo
76 C2 Irgiz Kazakh.
Iri S. Korea see Iksan
Irian Jaya reg. Indon. see Papua
115 E3 Iriba Chad
114 B3 Irígui reg. Mali/Maur.
119 D3 Iringa Tanz.
151 D3 Iriri r. Brazil
Irish Free State country Europe see Ireland
95 B3 Irish Sea Ireland/U.K.
68 C1 Irkutsk Rus. Fed.
160 M4 Irminger Basin sea feature N. Atlantic Ocean
139 D2 Irondequoit U.S.A.
52 A2 Iron Knob Austr.
138 B1 Iron Mountain U.S.A.
138 C3 Ironton U.S.A.
138 A1 Ironwood U.S.A.
130 B3 Iroquois Falls Can.
64 B2 Irosin Phil.
67 C4 Irō-zaki pt Japan
90 C1 Irpin' Ukr.
62 A2 Irrawaddy r. Myanmar
63 A2 Irrawaddy, Mouths of the Myanmar
86 F2 Irtysh r. Kazakh./Rus. Fed.
107 C1 Irún Spain
96 B3 Irvine U.K.
143 D2 Irving U.S.A.
64 B3 Isabela Phil.
146 B3 Isabelia, Cordillera mts Nic.
92 □A2 Ísafjarðardjúp est. Iceland
92 □A2 Ísafjörður Iceland
67 B4 Isahaya Japan
102 C2 Isar r. Ger.
96 □ Isbister U.K.
108 B2 Ischia, Isola d' i. Italy
67 C4 Ise Japan
118 C2 Isengi Dem. Rep. Congo
105 C3 Isère r. France
100 C2 Iserlohn Ger.
101 D1 Isernhagen Ger.
67 C4 Ise-wan b. Japan
114 C4 Iseyin Nigeria
Isfahan Iran see Eşfahān
66 D2 Ishikari-wan b. Japan
77 D1 Ishim r. Kazakh./Rus. Fed.
82 F3 Ishim Rus. Fed.
67 D3 Ishinomaki Japan
67 D3 Ishioka Japan
67 B4 Ishizuchi-san mt. Japan
74 B1 Ishkoshim Tajik.
138 B1 Ishpeming U.S.A.
111 C2 Işıklar Dağı mts Turkey
111 C3 Işıklı Turkey
123 D2 Isipingo S. Africa
119 C2 Isiro Dem. Rep. Congo
80 B2 İskenderun Turkey
82 G3 Iskitim Rus. Fed.
110 B2 Iskŭr r. Bulg.
117 D3 Iskushuban Somalia
128 A2 Iskut r. Can.
74 B1 Islamabad Pak.
141 D4 Islamorada U.S.A.
52 A2 Island Lagoon salt flat Austr.
129 E2 Island Lake Can.
54 B1 Islands, Bay of N.Z.
Islas Canarias is N. Atlantic Ocean see Canary Islands
96 A3 Islay i. U.K.
98 A2 Isle of Man i. Irish Sea
Ismail Ukr. see Izmayil
77 D3 Ismoili Somoní, Qullai mt. Tajik.
116 B2 Isnā Egypt
121 □D3 Isoanala Madag.
121 □D3 Isoka Zambia
93 H3 Isokyrö Fin.
109 C3 Isola di Capo Rizzuto Italy
Ispahan Iran see Eşfahān
80 B2 Isparta Turkey
110 B2 Isperikh Bulg.
Ispisar Tajik. see Khüjand
80 B2 Israel country Asia
50 B3 Israelite Bay Austr.
105 C2 Issoire France
Issyk-Kul' Kyrg. see Balykchy

111 C2 **İstanbul** Turkey
**İstanbul Boğazı** str. Turkey see Bosporus
103 D2 **Isten dombja** hill Hungary
111 B3 **Istiaia** Greece
141 D3 **Istokpoga, Lake** U.S.A.
105 C3 **Istra** pen. Croatia see Istria
105 C3 **Istres** France
108 B1 **Istria** pen. Croatia
155 D2 **Itabapoana** Brazil
151 E4 **Itaberaí** Brazil
154 C2 **Itaberaí** Brazil
155 D1 **Itabira** Brazil
155 D2 **Itabirito** Brazil
151 F4 **Itabuna** Brazil
150 D3 **Itacoatiara** Brazil
155 D2 **Itaguaí** Brazil
154 B2 **Itaguajé** Brazil
154 C2 **Itaí** Brazil
154 C3 **Itaiópolis** Brazil
154 B3 **Itaipu, Represa de** resr Brazil
151 D3 **Itaituba** Brazil
154 C3 **Itajaí** Brazil
155 D2 **Itajubá** Brazil
108 B2 **Italy** country Europe
155 E1 **Itamaraju** Brazil
155 D1 **Itamarandiba** Brazil
155 D1 **Itambacuri** Brazil
155 D1 **Itambé, Pico de** mt. Brazil
75 D2 **Itanagar** India
154 C2 **Itanhaém** Brazil
155 D1 **Itanhém** Brazil
155 D1 **Itaobím** Brazil
154 C1 **Itapajipe** Brazil
155 E1 **Itapebi** Brazil
155 D2 **Itapemirim** Brazil
155 D2 **Itaperuna** Brazil
155 D1 **Itapetinga** Brazil
154 C2 **Itapetininga** Brazil
154 C2 **Itapeva** Brazil
151 F4 **Itapicuru** r. Brazil
151 E3 **Itapicuru Mirim** Brazil
155 C2 **Itapira** Brazil
154 C2 **Itaporanga** Brazil
154 C1 **Itapuranga** Brazil
154 C2 **Itararé** Brazil
74 B2 **Itarsi** India
154 B1 **Itarumã** Brazil
155 D2 **Itaúna** Brazil
155 E1 **Itaúnas** Brazil
64 B1 **Itbayat** i. Phil.
139 D2 **Ithaca** U.S.A.
101 D1 **Ith Hils** ridge Ger.
118 C2 **Itimbiri** r. Dem. Rep. Congo
155 D1 **Itinga** Brazil
154 B1 **Itiquira** Brazil
154 A1 **Itiquira** r. Brazil
67 C4 **Itō** Japan
154 C2 **Itu** Brazil
150 B3 **Ituí** r. Brazil
154 C1 **Ituiutaba** Brazil
119 C3 **Itula** Dem. Rep. Congo
154 C1 **Itumbiara** Brazil
154 C1 **Itumbiara, Barragem** resr Brazil
154 B1 **Iturama** Brazil
101 D1 **Itzehoe** Ger.
83 N2 **Iul'tin** Rus. Fed.
155 D2 **Iúna** Brazil
154 B2 **Ivaí** r. Brazil
92 I2 **Ivalo** Fin.
88 C3 **Ivanava** Belarus
109 C1 **Ivanec** Croatia
**Ivangrad** Serb. and Mont. see Berane
52 B2 **Ivanhoe** Austr.
90 B1 **Ivankiv** Ukr.
90 A2 **Ivano-Frankivs'k** Ukr.
89 F2 **Ivanovo** Rus. Fed.
88 C3 **Ivatsevichy** Belarus
111 C2 **Ivaylovgrad** Bulg.
86 F2 **Ivdel'** Rus. Fed.
110 C1 **Iveşti** Romania
154 B2 **Ivinheima** Brazil
154 B2 **Ivinheima** r. Brazil
127 I2 **Ivittuut** Greenland
**Iviza** i. Spain see Ibiza
89 E3 **Ivnya** Rus. Fed.
**Ivory Coast** country Africa see Côte d'Ivoire
108 A1 **Ivrea** Italy
111 C3 **İvrindi** Turkey
**Ivugivik** Can. see Ivujivik
127 G2 **Ivujivik** Can.
67 G2 **Iwaki** Japan
67 B4 **Iwakuni** Japan
66 D2 **Iwamizawa** Japan
66 D2 **Iwanai** Japan
66 D3 **Iwate-san** vol. Japan
88 C3 **Iwye** Belarus
123 D3 **Ixopo** S. Africa
144 B2 **Ixtlán** Mex.
146 B3 **Izabal, Lago de** l. Guat.
145 D2 **Izamal** Mex.
81 C1 **Izberbash** Rus. Fed.
86 E3 **Izhevsk** Rus. Fed.
86 E2 **Izhma** Rus. Fed.
**Izhma** Rus. Fed. see Sosnogorsk
89 E3 **Izmalkovo** Rus. Fed.
90 B2 **Izmayil** Ukr.
111 C3 **İzmir** Turkey
111 C2 **İzmit** Turkey
111 C2 **İznik Gölü** l. Turkey
67 A4 **Izuhara** Japan
67 B3 **Izumo** Japan

156 C4 **Izu-Ogasawara Trench** sea feature N. Pacific Ocean
67 C4 **Izu-shotō** is Japan
90 B1 **Izyaslav** Ukr.
91 D2 **Izyum** Ukr.

**J**

74 A1 **Jabal as Sirāj** Afgh.
106 C2 **Jabalón** r. Spain
75 B2 **Jabalpur** India
50 C1 **Jabiru** Austr.
109 C2 **Jablanica** Bos.-Herz.
151 E2 **Jaboatão** Brazil
154 C2 **Jaboticabal** Brazil
107 C1 **Jaca** Spain
145 C2 **Jacala** Mex.
151 D3 **Jacareacanga** Brazil
155 C2 **Jacareí** Brazil
154 B1 **Jaciara** Brazil
155 C1 **Jacinto** Brazil
139 E1 **Jackman** U.S.A.
140 C2 **Jackson** AL U.S.A.
138 C2 **Jackson** MI U.S.A.
140 B2 **Jackson** MS U.S.A.
140 C1 **Jackson** TN U.S.A.
136 A2 **Jackson** WY U.S.A.
54 A2 **Jackson Head** hd N.Z.
140 B2 **Jacksonville** AR U.S.A.
141 D2 **Jacksonville** FL U.S.A.
138 A3 **Jacksonville** IL U.S.A.
141 E2 **Jacksonville** NC U.S.A.
143 D2 **Jacksonville** TX U.S.A.
147 C3 **Jacmel** Haiti
74 A2 **Jacobabad** Pak.
151 E4 **Jacobina** Brazil
131 D3 **Jacques Cartier, Mont** mt. Can.
151 E3 **Jacunda** Brazil
154 C2 **Jacupiranga** Brazil
101 D1 **Jadebusen** b. Ger.
**Jadotville** Dem. Rep. Congo see Likasi
109 C2 **Jadovnik** mt. Bos.-Herz.
150 B3 **Jaén** Peru
106 C2 **Jaén** Spain
**Jaffa** Israel see Tel Aviv-Yafo
52 A3 **Jaffa, Cape** Austr.
73 B4 **Jaffna** Sri Lanka
75 C3 **Jagdalpur** India
123 C2 **Jagersfontein** S. Africa
79 C2 **Jaghin** Iran
152 C3 **Jaguarão** Uru.
154 C2 **Jaguariaíva** Brazil
81 D3 **Jahrom** Iran
74 B2 **Jaipur** India
74 B2 **Jaisalmer** India
74 B2 **Jaitgarh** hill India
75 C2 **Jajarkot** Nepal
109 C2 **Jajce** Bos.-Herz.
**Jajnagar** state India see Orissa
60 B2 **Jakarta** Indon.
128 A1 **Jakes Corner** Can.
92 G2 **Jäkkvik** Sweden
**Jakobshavn** Greenland see Ilulissat
92 H3 **Jakobstad** Fin.
77 D3 **Jalālābād** Afgh.
77 D2 **Jalal-Abad** Kyrg.
74 B1 **Jalandhar** India
145 C3 **Jalapa** Mex.
154 B2 **Jales** Brazil
74 B2 **Jalgaon** India
115 D4 **Jalingo** Nigeria
74 B3 **Jalna** India
74 B2 **Jalore** India
144 B2 **Jalostotitlán** Mex.
144 B2 **Jalpa** Mex.
75 C2 **Jalpaiguri** India
145 C2 **Jalpan** Mex.
115 E2 **Jālū** Libya
146 C3 **Jamaica** country West Indies
146 C3 **Jamaica Channel** Haiti/Jamaica
75 C2 **Jamalpur** Bangl.
60 B2 **Jambi** Indon.
137 D2 **James** r. ND/SD U.S.A.
139 D3 **James** r. VA U.S.A.
130 B2 **James Bay** Can.
52 A2 **Jamestown** Austr.
**Jamestown** Can. see Wawa
123 C3 **Jamestown** S. Africa
137 D1 **Jamestown** ND U.S.A.
139 D2 **Jamestown** NY U.S.A.
74 B1 **Jammu** Jammu and Kashmir
74 B1 **Jammu and Kashmir** terr. Asia
74 B2 **Jamnagar** India
74 B2 **Jampur** Pak.
93 I3 **Jämsä** Fin.
78 A2 **Jamsah** Egypt
75 C2 **Jamshedpur** India
75 C2 **Jamuna** r. Bangl.
75 C2 **Janakpur** Nepal
155 D1 **Janaúba** Brazil
81 D2 **Jandaq** Iran
114 A2 **Jandia** hill Canary Islands
135 C2 **Janesville** CA U.S.A.
138 B2 **Janesville** WI U.S.A.
154 A2 **Jango** Brazil
82 A2 **Jan Mayen** i. Arctic Ocean
122 A3 **Jansenville** S. Africa
155 D1 **Januária** Brazil
74 B2 **Jaora** India
67 C3 **Japan** country Asia
66 B3 **Japan, Sea of** N. Pacific Ocean

150 C3 **Japurá** r. Brazil
154 C1 **Jaraguá** Brazil
154 C3 **Jaraguá, Serra** mts Brazil
154 C3 **Jaraguá do Sul** Brazil
154 B2 **Jaraguari** Brazil
152 C2 **Jardim** Brazil
69 D1 **Jargalant** Mongolia
103 D1 **Jarocin** Pol.
103 E1 **Jarosław** Pol.
92 F3 **Järpen** Sweden
70 A2 **Jartai** China
150 C4 **Jarú** Brazil
**Jarud** China see Lubei
88 C2 **Järvenpää** Fin.
49 K4 **Jarvis Island** terr. S. Pacific Ocean
93 G3 **Järvsö** Sweden
79 C2 **Jāsk** Iran
103 E2 **Jasło** Pol.
55 A3 **Jason Peninsula** Antarctica
128 C2 **Jasper** Can.
140 C2 **Jasper** AL U.S.A.
138 B3 **Jasper** IN U.S.A.
143 E2 **Jasper** TX U.S.A.
**Jassy** Romania see Iaşi
103 D2 **Jastrzębie-Zdrój** Pol.
103 D2 **Jászberény** Hungary
154 B1 **Jataí** Brazil
74 A2 **Jati** Pak.
154 C2 **Jaú** Brazil
150 C3 **Jaú** r. Brazil
145 C2 **Jaumave** Mex.
75 C2 **Jaunpur** India
154 B1 **Jauru** Brazil
61 B2 **Java** i. Indon.
107 C1 **Javalambre, Sierra de** mts Spain
69 D1 **Javarthushuu** Mongolia
61 B2 **Java Sea** Indon. see Laut Jawa
156 B6 **Java Trench** sea feature Indian Ocean
**Jawa** i. Indon. see Java
117 C4 **Jawhar** Somalia
103 D1 **Jawor** Pol.
103 D1 **Jaworzno** Pol.
59 D3 **Jaya, Puncak** mt. Indon.
59 D3 **Jayapura** Indon.
79 C2 **Jazirat Maşirah** i. Oman
128 B1 **Jean Marie River** Can.
131 D2 **Jeannin, Lac** l. Can.
**Jebel, Bahr el** r. Sudan/Uganda see White Nile
116 A3 **Jebel Abyad Plateau** Sudan
96 C3 **Jedburgh** U.K.
78 A2 **Jeddah** Saudi Arabia
108 A3 **Jedeida** Tunisia
101 E1 **Jeetze** r. Ger.
137 E2 **Jefferson** U.S.A.
135 C3 **Jefferson, Mount** U.S.A.
137 E3 **Jefferson City** U.S.A.
122 B3 **Jeffrey's Bay** S. Africa
88 C2 **Jēkabpils** Latvia
103 D1 **Jelenia Góra** Pol.
88 B2 **Jelgava** Latvia
61 C2 **Jemaja** i. Indon.
61 C2 **Jember** Indon.
101 E2 **Jena** Ger.
**Jengish Chokusu** mt. China/Kyrg. see Pobeda Peak
80 B2 **Jenīn** West Bank
140 B2 **Jennings** U.S.A.
151 E4 **Jequié** Brazil
155 D1 **Jequitaí** Brazil
155 D1 **Jequitinhonha** Brazil
155 E1 **Jequitinhonha** r. Brazil
147 C3 **Jérémie** Haiti
144 B2 **Jerez** Mex.
106 B2 **Jerez de la Frontera** Spain
109 D3 **Jergucat** Albania
115 C1 **Jerid, Chott el** salt l. Tunisia
134 D2 **Jerome** U.S.A.
95 C4 **Jersey** i. Channel Is
95 C4 **Jersey** terr. Channel Is
151 E3 **Jerumenha** Brazil
80 B2 **Jerusalem** Israel/West Bank
53 D3 **Jervis Bay Territory** admin. div. Austr.
108 B1 **Jesenice** Slovenia
108 B2 **Jesi** Italy
**Jesselton** Malaysia see Kota Kinabalu
101 F2 **Jessen** Ger.
75 C2 **Jessore** Bangl.
141 D2 **Jesup** U.S.A.
145 C3 **Jesús, Mount** hill U.S.A.
145 C3 **Jesús Carranza** Mex.
100 C1 **Jever** Ger.
74 B2 **Jhalawar** India
74 B1 **Jhang** Pak.
74 B2 **Jhansi** India
75 C2 **Jharkhand** state India
75 C2 **Jharsuguda** India
74 B1 **Jhelum** r. India/Pak.
74 B1 **Jhelum** Pak.
74 B2 **Jhunjhunun** India
69 E1 **Jiading** China
71 B3 **Jiamusi** China
71 B3 **Ji'an** Jiangxi China
65 B1 **Ji'an** Jilin China
**Jianchang** China see Nancheng
62 A1 **Jianchuan** China
70 B3 **Jiande** China
**Jiangling** China see Jingzhou
71 B3 **Jiangmen** China
70 B2 **Jiangsu** prov. China
71 B3 **Jiangxi** prov. China
70 A2 **Jiangyou** China

70 B3 **Jianli** China
70 B2 **Jianqiao** Hebei China
71 B3 **Jianyang** Fujian China
70 A2 **Jianyang** Sichuan China
69 E2 **Jiaohe** Jilin China
**Jiaojiang** China see Taizhou
70 C2 **Jiaozhou** China
70 B2 **Jiaozuo** China
**Jiashan** China see Mingguang
70 C2 **Jiaxing** China
68 C2 **Jiayuguan** China
**Jiddah** Saudi Arabia see Jeddah
92 G2 **Jiehkkevárri** mt. Norway
70 B2 **Jiexiu** China
103 D2 **Jihlava** Czech Rep.
115 C1 **Jijel** Alg.
117 C4 **Jijiga** Eth.
117 C4 **Jilib** Somalia
69 E2 **Jilin** China
65 B1 **Jilin** prov. China
65 A1 **Jilin Hada Ling** mts China
117 B4 **Jīma** Eth.
110 B1 **Jimbolia** Romania
144 B2 **Jiménez** Mex.
143 C3 **Jiménez** Mex.
145 C2 **Jiménez** Mex.
70 B2 **Jinan** China
70 A2 **Jinchang** China
70 B2 **Jincheng** China
**Jinchuan** China see Jinchang
53 C3 **Jindabyne** Austr.
103 D2 **Jindřichův Hradec** Czech Rep.
**Jin'e** China see Longchang
70 A2 **Jingbian** China
71 B3 **Jingdezhen** China
62 B1 **Jingdong** China
53 C3 **Jingellic** Austr.
71 B3 **Jinggangshan** China
62 B1 **Jinghong** China
70 B2 **Jingmen** China
70 A2 **Jingning** China
**Jingsha** China see Jingzhou
70 A2 **Jingtai** China
71 A3 **Jingxi** China
**Jingxian** China see Jingzhou
70 A2 **Jingyuan** China
70 B2 **Jingzhou** China
70 B2 **Jingzhou** Hubei China
71 A3 **Jingzhou** Hunan China
71 B3 **Jinhua** China
70 B1 **Jining** Nei Mongol China
70 B2 **Jining** Shandong China
119 D2 **Jinja** Uganda
117 B4 **Jinka** Eth.
146 B3 **Jinotega** Nic.
146 B3 **Jinotepe** Nic.
71 A3 **Jinping** China
**Jinsha Jiang** r. China see Yangtze
**Jinshi** China see Xinning
70 B3 **Jinshi** China
**Jinxi** China see Lianshan
70 B2 **Jinzhong** China
70 C1 **Jinzhou** China
150 C3 **Jiparaná** r. Brazil
75 C1 **Jirang** India
116 B2 **Jirjā** Egypt
79 C2 **Jiroft** Iran
79 C2 **Jirwān** Saudi Arabia
71 A3 **Jishou** China
110 B1 **Jiu** r. Romania
70 A2 **Jiuding Shan** mt. China
70 B3 **Jiujiang** China
**Jiulian** China see Mojiang
79 C2 **Jiwani** Pak.
66 B1 **Jixi** China
78 B3 **Jīzān** Saudi Arabia
77 C2 **Jizzax** Uzbek.
155 D1 **Joaíma** Brazil
151 F3 **João Pessoa** Brazil
155 C1 **João Pinheiro** Brazil
74 B2 **Jodhpur** India
92 I3 **Joensuu** Fin.
67 C3 **Jōetsu** Japan
121 C3 **Jofane** Moz.
88 C2 **Jõgeva** Estonia
**Jogjakarta** Indon. see Yogyakarta
123 C2 **Johannesburg** S. Africa
134 C2 **John Day** U.S.A.
134 B1 **John Day** r. U.S.A.
128 C2 **John d'Or Prairie** Can.
141 E1 **John H. Kerr Reservoir** U.S.A.
96 C1 **John o'Groats** U.K.
141 D1 **Johnson City** U.S.A.
128 A1 **Johnson's Crossing** Can.
50 B3 **Johnston, Lake** salt flat Austr.
49 J2 **Johnston Atoll** N. Pacific Ocean
96 B3 **Johnstone** U.K.
**Johnstone Lake** Can. see Old Wives Lake
139 D2 **Johnstown** U.S.A.
60 B1 **Johor Bahru** Malaysia
88 C2 **Jõhvi** Estonia
154 C3 **Joinville** Brazil
105 D2 **Joinville** France
55 B3 **Joinville Island** Antarctica
92 G2 **Jokkmokk** Sweden
92 □B2 **Jökulsá á Fjöllum** r. Iceland
138 B2 **Joliet** U.S.A.
130 C3 **Joliette** Can.
64 B3 **Jolo** Phil.

Karabalyk 187


64 B3 **Jolo** *i.* Phil.
61 C2 **Jombang** Indon.
75 C2 **Jomsom** Nepal
88 B2 **Jonava** Lith.
140 B1 **Jonesboro** *AR* U.S.A.
140 B2 **Jonesboro** *LA* U.S.A.
139 F2 **Jonesport** U.S.A.
127 G1 **Jones Sound** *sea chan.* Can.
93 F4 **Jönköping** Sweden
131 C3 **Jonquière** Can.
145 C3 **Jonuta** Mex.
137 E3 **Joplin** U.S.A.
80 B2 **Jordan** *country* Asia
80 B2 **Jordan** *r.* Asia
134 E1 **Jordan** U.S.A.
155 D1 **Jordânia** Brazil
134 C2 **Jordan Valley** U.S.A.
72 D2 **Jorhat** India
101 D1 **Jork** Ger.
93 E4 **Jørpeland** Norway
115 C4 **Jos** Nigeria
145 C3 **José Cardel** Mex.
131 D2 **Joseph, Lac** *l.* Can.
50 B1 **Joseph Bonaparte Gulf** Austr.
115 C4 **Jos Plateau** Nigeria
93 E3 **Jotunheimen** *mts* Norway
122 B3 **Joubertina** S. Africa
123 C2 **Jouberton** S. Africa
104 C2 **Joué-lès-Tours** France
93 I3 **Joutseno** Fin.
134 B1 **Juan de Fuca Strait** Can./U.S.A.
149 B6 **Juan Fernández Islands** S. Pacific Ocean
**Juanshui** China *see* **Tongcheng**
145 B2 **Juaréz** Mex.
144 A1 **Juárez, Sierra de** *mts* Mex.
151 E3 **Juàzeiro** Brazil
151 F3 **Juàzeiro do Norte** Brazil
117 B4 **Juba** Sudan
117 C5 **Jubba** *r.* Somalia
78 B2 **Jubbah** Saudi Arabia
**Jubbulpore** India *see* **Jabalpur**
107 C2 **Júcar** *r.* Spain
145 C3 **Juchitán** Mex.
155 E1 **Jucuruçu** Brazil
102 C2 **Judenburg** Austria
155 E1 **Juerana** Brazil
101 D2 **Jühnde** Ger.
146 B3 **Juigalpa** Nic.
150 D4 **Juína** Brazil
100 C1 **Juist** *i.* Ger.
155 D2 **Juiz de Fora** Brazil
136 C2 **Julesburg** U.S.A.
150 B4 **Juliaca** Peru
**Julianatop** *mt.* Indon. *see* **Mandala, Puncak**
151 D2 **Juliana Top** *mt.* Suriname
**Jullundur** India *see* **Jalandhar**
107 C2 **Jumilla** Spain
75 C2 **Jumla** Nepal
**Jumna** *r.* India *see* **Yamuna**
74 B2 **Junagadh** India
143 D2 **Junction** U.S.A.
137 D3 **Junction City** U.S.A.
154 C2 **Jundiaí** Brazil
128 A2 **Juneau** U.S.A.
53 C2 **Junee** Austr.
105 D2 **Jungfrau** *mt.* Switz.
139 D2 **Juniata** *r.* U.S.A.
153 B3 **Junín** Arg.
92 G3 **Junsele** Sweden
134 C2 **Juntura** U.S.A.
**Junxi** China *see* **Datian**
**Junxian** China *see* **Danjiangkou**
154 B2 **Jupía, Represa** *resr* Brazil
141 D3 **Jupiter** U.S.A.
154 C2 **Juquiá** Brazil
117 A4 **Jur** *r.* Sudan
105 D2 **Jura** *mts* France/Switz.
96 B2 **Jura** *i.* U.K.
96 B3 **Jura, Sound of** *sea chan.* U.K.
88 B2 **Jurbarkas** Lith.
88 B2 **Jūrmala** Latvia
150 C3 **Juruá** *r.* Brazil
150 D3 **Juruena** *r.* Brazil
154 C2 **Jurumirim, Represa de** *resr* Brazil
151 D3 **Juruti** Brazil
154 B1 **Jussara** Brazil
150 C3 **Jutaí** *r.* Brazil
101 F2 **Jüterbog** Ger.
154 B2 **Juti** Brazil
145 D3 **Jutiapa** Guat.
93 E4 **Jutland** *pen.* Denmark
146 B2 **Juventud, Isla de la** *i.* Cuba
70 B2 **Juxian** China
81 D3 **Jūyom** Iran
122 B1 **Jwaneng** Botswana
**Jylland** *pen.* Denmark *see* **Jutland**
93 I3 **Jyväskylä** Fin.


## K


74 B1 **K2** *mt.* China/Jammu and Kashmir
**Kaakhka** Turkm. *see* **Kaka**
92 I2 **Kaamanen** Fin.
61 D2 **Kabaena** *i.* Indon.
119 C3 **Kabalo** Dem. Rep. Congo
119 C3 **Kabambare** Dem. Rep. Congo
119 C3 **Kabare** Dem. Rep. Congo
119 C3 **Kabemba** Dem. Rep. Congo
130 B3 **Kabinakagami Lake** Can.
118 C3 **Kabinda** Dem. Rep. Congo
118 B2 **Kabo** C.A.R.
120 B2 **Kabompo** Zambia
119 C3 **Kabongo** Dem. Rep. Congo
77 C3 **Kābul** Afgh.
64 B3 **Kaburuang** *i.* Indon.
121 B2 **Kabwe** Zambia
109 D2 **Kačanik** Serb. and Mont.
74 A2 **Kachchh, Gulf of** India
83 I3 **Kachug** Rus. Fed.
81 C1 **Kaçkar Dağı** *mt.* Turkey
111 C2 **Kadıköy** Turkey
52 A2 **Kadina** Austr.
114 B3 **Kadiolo** Mali
**Kadiyevka** Ukr. *see* **Stakhanov**
73 B3 **Kadmat** *i.* India
89 F2 **Kadnikov** Rus. Fed.
121 B2 **Kadoma** Zimbabwe
63 A2 **Kadonkani** Myanmar
117 A3 **Kadugli** Sudan
115 C3 **Kaduna** Nigeria
89 E2 **Kaduy** Rus. Fed.
86 E2 **Kadzherom** Rus. Fed.
114 A3 **Kaédi** Maur.
118 B1 **Kaélé** Cameroon
65 B2 **Kaesŏng** N. Korea
118 C3 **Kafakumba** Dem. Rep. Congo
114 A3 **Kaffrine** Senegal
111 B3 **Kafireas, Akra** *pt* Greece
80 B2 **Kafr ash Shaykh** Egypt
121 B2 **Kafue** Zambia
120 B2 **Kafue** *r.* Zambia
67 C3 **Kaga** Japan
118 B2 **Kaga Bandoro** C.A.R.
91 E2 **Kagal'nitskaya** Rus. Fed.
**Kaganovichi Pervyye** Ukr. *see* **Polis'ke**
60 A2 **Kagologolo** Indon.
67 B4 **Kagoshima** Japan
**Kagul** Moldova *see* **Cahul**
119 D3 **Kahama** Tanz.
90 C2 **Kaharlyk** Ukr.
61 C2 **Kahayan** *r.* Indon.
118 B3 **Kahemba** Dem. Rep. Congo
101 E2 **Kahla** Ger.
79 C2 **Kahnūj** Iran
92 H2 **Kahperusvaarat** *mts* Fin.
80 B2 **Kahramanmaraş** Turkey
79 C2 **Kahūrak** Iran
59 C3 **Kai, Kepulauan** *is* Indon.
115 C4 **Kaiama** Nigeria
54 B2 **Kaiapoi** N.Z.
59 C3 **Kai Besar** *i.* Indon.
70 B2 **Kaifeng** China
**Kaihua** China *see* **Wenshan**
122 B2 **Kaiingveld** *reg.* S. Africa
59 C3 **Kai Kecil** *i.* Indon.
54 B2 **Kaikoura** N.Z.
114 A4 **Kailahun** Sierra Leone
**Kailas Range** *mts* China *see* **Gangdisê Shan**
71 A3 **Kaili** China
59 C3 **Kaimana** Indon.
54 C1 **Kaimanawa Mountains** N.Z.
72 C2 **Kaimur Range** *hills* India
88 B2 **Käina** Estonia
67 C4 **Kainan** Japan
115 C3 **Kainji Reservoir** Nigeria
54 B1 **Kaipara Harbour** N.Z.
74 B2 **Kairana** India
115 D1 **Kairouan** Tunisia
100 C3 **Kaiserslautern** Ger.
55 I2 **Kaiser Wilhelm II Land** *reg.* Antarctica
54 B1 **Kaitaia** N.Z.
54 C1 **Kaitawa** N.Z.
**Kaitong** China *see* **Tongyu**
59 C3 **Kaiwatu** Indon.
65 A1 **Kaiyuan** *Liaoning* China
71 A3 **Kaiyuan** *Yunnan* China
92 I3 **Kajaani** Fin.
51 D2 **Kajabbi** Austr.
76 B3 **Kaka** Turkm.
122 B2 **Kakamas** S. Africa
119 D2 **Kakamega** Kenya
114 A4 **Kakata** Liberia
91 C2 **Kakhovka** Ukr.
91 C2 **Kakhovs'ke Vodoskhovyshche** *resr* Ukr.
**Kakhul** Moldova *see* **Cahul**
73 C3 **Kakinada** India
128 C1 **Kakisa** Can.
67 B4 **Kakogawa** Japan
119 C3 **Kakoswa** Dem. Rep. Congo
126 C2 **Kaktovik** U.S.A.
**Kalaallit Nunaat** *terr.* N. America *see* **Greenland**
59 C3 **Kalabahi** Indon.
120 B2 **Kalabo** Zambia
91 E1 **Kalach** Rus. Fed.
119 D2 **Kalacha Dida** Kenya
87 D4 **Kalach-na-Donu** Rus. Fed.
62 A1 **Kaladan** *r.* India/Myanmar
120 B3 **Kalahari Desert** Africa
92 H3 **Kalajoki** Fin.
123 C1 **Kalamare** Botswana
111 B2 **Kalamaria** Greece
111 B3 **Kalamata** Greece
138 B2 **Kalamazoo** U.S.A.
111 B3 **Kalampaka** Greece
88 B2 **Kalana** Estonia
91 C2 **Kalanchak** Ukr.
61 D2 **Kalao** *i.* Indon.
61 D2 **Kalaotoa** *i.* Indon.
63 B2 **Kalasin** Thai.
77 C3 **Kalāt** Afgh.
79 C2 **Kalāt** Iran
74 A2 **Kalat** Pak.
50 A2 **Kalbarri** Austr.
111 C3 **Kale** Turkey
80 B1 **Kalecik** Turkey
118 C3 **Kalema** Dem. Rep. Congo
119 C3 **Kalemie** Dem. Rep. Congo
62 A1 **Kalemyo** Myanmar
86 C2 **Kalevala** Rus. Fed.
**Kalgan** China *see* **Zhangjiakou**
50 B3 **Kalgoorlie** Austr.
109 C2 **Kali** Croatia
110 C2 **Kaliakra, Nos** *pt* Bulg.
60 A2 **Kaliet** Indon.
119 C3 **Kalima** Dem. Rep. Congo
61 C2 **Kalimantan** *reg.* Indon.
**Kalinin** Rus. Fed. *see* **Tver'**
88 B3 **Kaliningrad** Rus. Fed.
91 D2 **Kalininskaya** Rus. Fed.
88 C3 **Kalinkavichy** Belarus
134 D1 **Kalispell** U.S.A.
103 D1 **Kalisz** Pol.
91 E2 **Kalitva** *r.* Rus. Fed.
92 H2 **Kalix** Sweden
92 H2 **Kalixälven** *r.* Sweden
111 C3 **Kalkan** Turkey
120 A3 **Kalkfeld** Namibia
100 C2 **Kall** Ger.
92 I3 **Kallavesi** *l.* Fin.
92 F3 **Kallsjön** *l.* Sweden
93 G4 **Kalmar** Sweden
93 G4 **Kalmarsund** *sea chan.* Sweden
73 C4 **Kalmunai** Sri Lanka
119 C3 **Kalole** Dem. Rep. Congo
120 B2 **Kalomo** Zambia
128 B2 **Kalone Peak** Can.
74 B1 **Kalpa** India
73 B3 **Kalpeni** *i.* India
75 B2 **Kalpi** India
126 B2 **Kaltag** U.S.A.
101 D1 **Kaltenkirchen** Ger.
118 B2 **Kaltungo** Nigeria
89 E3 **Kaluga** Rus. Fed.
93 F4 **Kalundborg** Denmark
74 B1 **Kalur Kot** Pak.
90 A2 **Kalush** Ukr.
74 B3 **Kalyan** India
89 E2 **Kalyazin** Rus. Fed.
111 C3 **Kalymnos** Greece
111 C3 **Kalymnos** *i.* Greece
119 C3 **Kama** Dem. Rep. Congo
62 A2 **Kama** Myanmar
86 E3 **Kama** *r.* Rus. Fed.
66 D3 **Kamaishi** Japan
80 B2 **Kaman** Turkey
120 A2 **Kamanjab** Namibia
78 B3 **Kamarān** *i.* Yemen
**Kamaran Island** Yemen *see* **Kamarān**
74 A2 **Kamarod** Pak.
50 B3 **Kambalda** Austr.
119 C4 **Kambove** Dem. Rep. Congo
160 C4 **Kamchatka Basin** *sea feature* Bering Sea
83 L3 **Kamchatka Peninsula** Rus. Fed.
110 C2 **Kamchiya** *r.* Bulg.
108 B2 **Kamenjak, Rt** *pt* Croatia
76 B1 **Kamenka** Kazakh.
86 D2 **Kamenka** Rus. Fed.
87 D3 **Kamenka** Rus. Fed.
66 C2 **Kamenka** Rus. Fed.
91 D1 **Kamenka** Rus. Fed.
**Kamenka-Strumilovskaya** Ukr. *see* **Kam"yanka-Buz'ka**
91 E3 **Kamennomostskiy** Rus. Fed.
91 E2 **Kamenolomni** Rus. Fed.
**Kamenongue** Angola *see* **Camanongue**
83 M2 **Kamenskoye** Rus. Fed.
**Kamenskoye** Ukr. *see* **Dniprodzerzhyns'k**
91 E2 **Kamensk-Shakhtinskiy** Rus. Fed.
86 F3 **Kamensk-Ural'skiy** Rus. Fed.
89 F2 **Kameshkovo** Rus. Fed.
75 B1 **Kamet** *mt.* China
72 C1 **Kamet** *mt.* China
122 A3 **Kamiesberge** *mts* S. Africa
122 A3 **Kamieskroon** S. Africa
129 D1 **Kamilukuak Lake** Can.
119 C3 **Kamina** Dem. Rep. Congo
129 E1 **Kaminak Lake** Can.
90 A1 **Kamin'-Kashyrs'kyy** Ukr.
119 C3 **Kamituga** Dem. Rep. Congo
128 B2 **Kamloops** Can.
54 B1 **Kamo** N.Z.
116 B3 **Kamob Sanha** Sudan
118 C3 **Kamonia** Dem. Rep. Congo
119 D2 **Kampala** Uganda
60 B1 **Kampar** *r.* Indon.
60 B1 **Kampar** Malaysia
100 B1 **Kampen** Neth.
119 C3 **Kampene** Dem. Rep. Congo
63 A2 **Kamphaeng Phet** Thai.
63 B2 **Kâmpóng Cham** Cambodia
63 B2 **Kâmpóng Chhnăng** Cambodia
**Kâmpóng Saôm** Cambodia *see* **Sihanoukville**
63 B2 **Kâmpóng Spœ** Cambodia
63 B2 **Kâmpôt** Cambodia
**Kampuchea** *country* Asia *see* **Cambodia**
129 D2 **Kamsack** Can.
86 E3 **Kamskoye Vodokhranilishche** *resr* Rus. Fed.
117 C4 **Kamsuuma** Somalia
90 B2 **Kam"yanets'-Podil's'kyy** Ukr.
90 A1 **Kam"yanka-Buz'ka** Ukr.
88 B3 **Kamyanyets** Belarus
91 D2 **Kamyshevatskaya** Rus. Fed.
87 D3 **Kamyshin** Rus. Fed.
135 D3 **Kanab** U.S.A.
118 C3 **Kananga** Dem. Rep. Congo
87 D3 **Kanash** Rus. Fed.
138 C3 **Kanawha** *r.* U.S.A.
67 C3 **Kanazawa** Japan
62 A1 **Kanbalu** Myanmar
63 A2 **Kanchanaburi** Thai.
73 B3 **Kanchipuram** India
77 C3 **Kandahār** Afgh.
86 C2 **Kandalaksha** Rus. Fed.
61 C2 **Kandangan** Indon.
74 A2 **Kandhkot** Pak.
114 C3 **Kandi** Benin
74 A2 **Kandiaro** Pak.
74 B2 **Kandla** India
53 C2 **Kandos** Austr.
121 □D2 **Kandreho** Madag.
73 C4 **Kandy** Sri Lanka
76 B2 **Kandyagash** Kazakh.
127 H1 **Kane Bassin** *b.* Greenland
91 D2 **Kanevskaya** Rus. Fed.
122 B1 **Kang** Botswana
127 I2 **Kangaatsiaq** Greenland
114 B3 **Kangaba** Mali
80 B2 **Kangal** Turkey
79 C2 **Kangān** Iran
60 B1 **Kangar** Malaysia
52 A3 **Kangaroo Island** Austr.
93 H3 **Kangasala** Fin.
81 C2 **Kangāvar** Iran
75 C2 **Kangchenjunga** *mt.* India/Nepal
70 A2 **Kangding** China
65 B2 **Kangdong** N. Korea
61 C2 **Kangean, Kepulauan** *is* Indon.
119 D2 **Kangen** *r.* Sudan
127 J2 **Kangeq** *c.* Greenland
127 J2 **Kangerlussuaq** *inlet* Greenland
127 I2 **Kangerlussuaq** *inlet* Greenland
127 I2 **Kangersuatsiaq** Greenland
65 B1 **Kanggye** N. Korea
131 D2 **Kangiqsualujjuaq** Can.
127 H2 **Kangiqsujuaq** Can.
131 C1 **Kangirsuk** Can.
75 C2 **Kangmar** China
65 B2 **Kangnŭng** S. Korea
65 A1 **Kangping** China
72 D2 **Kangto** *mt.* China/India
62 A1 **Kani** Myanmar
118 C3 **Kaniama** Dem. Rep. Congo
61 C1 **Kanibongan** *Sabah* Malaysia
86 D2 **Kanin, Poluostrov** *pen.* Rus. Fed.
86 D2 **Kanin Nos** Rus. Fed.
86 D2 **Kanin Nos, Mys** *c.* Rus. Fed.
91 C2 **Kaniv** Ukr.
52 B3 **Kaniva** Austr.
93 H3 **Kankaanpää** Fin.
138 B2 **Kankakee** U.S.A.
114 B3 **Kankan** Guinea
75 C2 **Kanker** India
**Kannur** India *see* **Cannanore**
115 C3 **Kano** Nigeria
122 B3 **Kanonpunt** *pt* S. Africa
67 B4 **Kanoya** Japan
75 C2 **Kanpur** India
136 C3 **Kansas** *r.* U.S.A.
137 D3 **Kansas** *state* U.S.A.
137 E3 **Kansas City** *KS* U.S.A.
137 E3 **Kansas City** *MO* U.S.A.
83 H3 **Kansk** Rus. Fed.
**Kansu** *prov.* China *see* **Gansu**
63 B2 **Kantaralak** Thai.
114 C3 **Kantchari** Burkina
91 D2 **Kantemirovka** Rus. Fed.
49 J4 **Kanton** *i.* Kiribati
97 B2 **Kanturk** Ireland
123 D2 **KaNyamazane** S. Africa
123 C1 **Kanye** Botswana
71 C3 **Kaohsiung** Taiwan
120 A2 **Kaokoveld** *plat.* Namibia
114 A3 **Kaolack** Senegal
120 B2 **Kaoma** Zambia
118 C3 **Kapanga** Dem. Rep. Congo
88 C3 **Kapatkyevichy** Belarus
77 D2 **Kapchagay** Kazakh.
77 D2 **Kapchagayskoye Vodokhranilishche** *resr* Kazakh.
100 B2 **Kapellen** Belgium
121 B2 **Kapiri Mposhi** Zambia
127 I2 **Kapisillit** Greenland
130 B2 **Kapiskau** *r.* Can.
61 C1 **Kapit** *Sarawak* Malaysia
63 A3 **Kapoe** Thai.
117 B4 **Kapoeta** Sudan
103 D2 **Kaposvár** Hungary
102 B1 **Kappeln** Ger.
65 B1 **Kapsan** N. Korea
**Kapsukas** Lith. *see* **Marijampolė**
61 B2 **Kapuas** *r.* Indon.
52 A2 **Kapunda** Austr.
130 B3 **Kapuskasing** Can.
53 D2 **Kaputar** *mt.* Austr.
103 D2 **Kapuvár** Hungary
88 C3 **Kapyl'** Belarus
77 D3 **Kaqung** China
114 C4 **Kara** Togo
111 C3 **Kara Ada** *i.* Turkey
77 D2 **Kara-Balta** Kyrg.
76 C1 **Karabalyk** Kazakh.

76 C3 Karabil', Vozvyshennost' *hills* Turkm.
Kara-Bogaz-Gol Turkm. *see* Karabogazkel'
76 B2 Kara-Bogaz-Gol, Zaliv *b.* Turkm.
76 B2 Karabogazkel' Turkm.
80 B1 Karabük Turkey
76 C2 Karabutak Kazakh.
111 C2 Karacabey Turkey
111 C2 Karaçaköy Turkey
81 C1 Karachayevsk Rus. Fed.
89 D3 Karachev Rus. Fed.
74 A2 Karachi Pak.
77 D2 Karaganda Kazakh.
77 D2 Karagayly Kazakh.
83 L3 Karaginskiy Zaliv *b.* Rus. Fed.
81 D2 Karaj Iran
Kara-Kala Turkm. *see* Garrygala
64 B3 Karakelong *i.* Indon.
Karaklis Armenia *see* Vanadzor
77 D2 Kara-Köl Kyrg.
77 D2 Karakol Kyrg.
74 B1 Karakoram Range *mts* Asia
72 B1 Karakoram Range *mts* Asia
117 B3 Kara K'orë Eth.
Karakum, Peski *des.* Kazakh. *see* Karakum Desert
76 B2 Karakum Desert des.
76 C3 Karakum Desert Turkm.
Karakumy, Peski *des.* Turkm. *see* Karakum Desert
80 B2 Karaman Turkey
77 E2 Karamay China
54 B2 Karamea N.Z.
54 B2 Karamea Bight *b.* N.Z.
80 B2 Karapınar Turkey
122 A2 Karasburg Namibia
86 F1 Kara Sea Rus. Fed.
92 I2 Karasjok Norway
Kara Strait Rus. Fed. *see* Karskiye Vorota, Proliv
111 D2 Karasu Turkey
Karasubazar Ukr. *see* Bilohirs'k
77 D1 Karasuk Rus. Fed.
77 D2 Karatau Kazakh.
77 C2 Karatau, Khrebet *mts* Kazakh.
86 F2 Karatayka Rus. Fed.
67 A4 Karatsu Japan
111 B3 Karavas Greece
60 B2 Karawang Indon.
81 C2 Karbalā' Iraq
103 E2 Karcag Hungary
Kardeljevo Croatia *see* Ploče
111 B3 Karditsa Greece
88 C2 Kärdla Estonia
122 B3 Kareeberge *mts* S. Africa
75 B2 Kareli India
88 C3 Karelichy Belarus
92 H2 Karesuando Sweden
Karghalik China *see* Yecheng
74 B1 Kargil Jammu and Kashmir
Kargilik China *see* Yecheng
86 C2 Kargopol' Rus. Fed.
118 B1 Kari Nigeria
121 B2 Kariba Zimbabwe
121 B2 Kariba, Lake *resr* Zambia/Zimbabwe
60 B2 Karimata, Pulau-pulau *is* Indon.
60 B2 Karimata, Selat *str.* Indon.
73 B3 Karimnagar India
61 C2 Karimunjawa, Pulau-pulau *is* Indon.
91 C2 Karkinits'ka Zatoka *g.* Ukr.
91 D2 Karlivka Ukr.
Karl-Marx-Stadt Ger. *see* Chemnitz
109 C1 Karlovac Croatia
102 C1 Karlovy Vary Czech Rep.
Karlsburg Romania *see* Alba Iulia
93 F4 Karlshamn Sweden
93 F4 Karlskoga Sweden
93 G4 Karlskrona Sweden
102 B2 Karlsruhe Ger.
93 F4 Karlstad Sweden
101 D3 Karlstadt Ger.
89 D3 Karma Belarus
93 E4 Karmøy *i.* Norway
75 D2 Karnafuli Reservoir Bangl.
74 B2 Karnal India
110 C2 Karnobat Bulg.
74 A2 Karodi Pak.
121 B2 Karoi Zimbabwe
121 C1 Karonga Malawi
116 B3 Karora Eritrea
111 C3 Karpathos Greece
111 C3 Karpathos *i.* Greece
111 B3 Karpenisi Greece
Karpilovka Belarus *see* Aktsyabrski
86 D2 Karpogory Rus. Fed.
50 A2 Karratha Austr.
81 C1 Kars Turkey
88 C2 Kärsava Latvia
76 B2 Karshi Turkm.
Karshi Uzbek. *see* Qarshi
111 C3 Karşıyaka Turkey
86 E2 Karskiye Vorota, Proliv *str.* Rus. Fed.
Karskoye More *sea* Rus. Fed. *see* Kara Sea
101 E1 Karstädt Ger.
111 C2 Kartal Turkey
87 F3 Kartaly Rus. Fed.
81 C2 Kārūn, Rūd-e *r.* Iran

73 B3 Karwar India
83 I1 Karymskoye Rus. Fed.
111 B3 Karystos Greece
111 C3 Kaş Turkey
130 B2 Kasabonika Lake Can.
118 C2 Kasaï, Plateau du Dem. Rep. Congo
118 C4 Kasaji Dem. Rep. Congo
121 C2 Kasama Zambia
120 B2 Kasane Botswana
118 B3 Kasangulu Dem. Rep. Congo
73 B3 Kasaragod India
129 C1 Kasba Lake Can.
120 B2 Kasempa Zambia
119 C4 Kasenga Dem. Rep. Congo
119 C3 Kasese Dem. Rep. Congo
119 D2 Kasese Uganda
Kasevo Rus. Fed. *see* Neftekamsk
81 D2 Kāshān Iran
77 D3 Kashi China
67 D3 Kashima-nada *b.* Japan
89 E2 Kashin Rus. Fed.
89 E3 Kashira Rus. Fed.
89 E3 Kashirskoye Rus. Fed.
67 C3 Kashiwazaki Japan
81 D2 Kāshmar Iran
Kashmir *terr.* Asia *see* Jammu and Kashmir
74 A2 Kashmor Pak.
119 C3 Kashyukulu Dem. Rep. Congo
89 F3 Kasimov Rus. Fed.
138 B3 Kaskaskia *r.* U.S.A.
93 H3 Kaskinen Fin.
119 C3 Kasongo Dem. Rep. Congo
118 C4 Kasongo-Lunda Dem. Rep. Congo
111 C3 Kasos *i.* Greece
Kaspiyskiy Rus. Fed. *see* Lagan'
116 B3 Kassala Sudan
101 D2 Kassel Ger.
115 C1 Kasserine Tunisia
80 B1 Kastamonu Turkey
111 B3 Kastelli Greece
Kastellorizon *i.* Greece *see* Megisti
111 B2 Kastoria Greece
89 D3 Kastsyukovichy Belarus
119 D3 Kasulu Tanz.
121 C2 Kasungu Malawi
139 F1 Katahdin, Mount U.S.A.
118 C3 Katako-Kombe Dem. Rep. Congo
119 D2 Katakwi Uganda
50 A3 Katanning Austr.
63 A3 Katchall *i.* India
111 B2 Katerini Greece
119 D3 Katesh Tanz.
128 A2 Kate's Needle *mt.* Can./U.S.A.
121 C2 Katete Zambia
62 A1 Katha Myanmar
50 C1 Katherine Austr.
50 C1 Katherine *r.* Austr.
74 B2 Kathiawar *pen.* India
123 C2 Kathlehong S. Africa
75 C2 Kathmandu Nepal
122 B2 Kathu S. Africa
74 B1 Kathua Jammu and Kashmir
114 B3 Kati Mali
75 C2 Katihar India
54 C1 Katikati N.Z.
123 C3 Kati-Kati S. Africa
120 B2 Katima Mulilo Namibia
114 B4 Katiola Côte d'Ivoire
Katmandu Nepal *see* Kathmandu
111 B3 Kato Achaïa Greece
119 C3 Katompi Dem. Rep. Congo
53 D2 Katoomba Austr.
103 D1 Katowice Pol.
80 B3 Kātrīnā, Jabal *mt.* Egypt
93 G4 Katrineholm Sweden
115 C3 Katsina Nigeria
115 C3 Katsina-Ala Nigeria
67 D3 Katsuura Japan
77 C3 Kattaqo'rg'on Uzbek.
93 F4 Kattegat *str.* Denmark/Sweden
100 B1 Katwijk aan Zee Neth.
101 D3 Katzenbuckel *hill* Ger.
49 L1 Kaua'i *i.* U.S.A.
93 H3 Kauhajoki Fin.
88 B3 Kaunas Lith.
115 C3 Kaura-Namoda Nigeria
Kaushany Moldova *see* Căuşeni
92 H2 Kautokeino Norway
109 D2 Kavadarci Macedonia
109 D2 Kavajë Albania
111 B2 Kavala Greece
66 C2 Kavalerovo Rus. Fed.
73 C3 Kavali India
73 B3 Kavaratti *i.* India
110 C2 Kavarna Bulg.
59 E3 Kavieng P.N.G.
81 D2 Kavir, Dasht-e *des.* Iran
67 C3 Kawagoe Japan
54 B1 Kawakawa N.Z.
121 B1 Kawambwa Zambia
67 C3 Kawanishi Japan
130 C3 Kawartha Lakes Can.
67 C3 Kawasaki Japan
54 C1 Kawerau N.Z.
63 A3 Kawkareik Myanmar
62 A1 Kawlin Myanmar
63 A2 Kawmapyin Myanmar
116 B2 Kawm Umbū Egypt
63 A2 Kawthaung Myanmar
Kaxgar China *see* Kashi
77 D3 Kaxgar He *r.* China

114 B3 Kaya Burkina
111 C3 Kayacı Dağı *hill* Turkey
121 C1 Kayambi Zambia
61 C1 Kayan *r.* Indon.
136 B2 Kaycee U.S.A.
Kaydanovo Belarus *see* Dzyarzhynsk
142 A1 Kayenta U.S.A.
114 A3 Kayes Mali
77 D2 Kaynar Kazakh.
80 B2 Kayseri Turkey
134 D2 Kaysville U.S.A.
60 B2 Kayuagung Indon.
Kazakhskaya S.S.R. *admin. reg.* Asia *see* Kazakhstan
77 D1 Kazakhskiy Melkosopochnik *plain* Kazakh.
76 B2 Kazakhskiy Zaliv *b.* Kazakh.
76 C2 Kazakhstan *country* Asia
Kazakhstan Asia *see* Aksay
87 D3 Kazan' Rus. Fed.
Kazandzhik Turkm. *see* Gazandzhyk
110 C2 Kazanlŭk Bulg.
Kazan-rettō Japan *see* Volcano Islands
76 B2 Kazbek *mt.* Georgia/Rus. Fed.
81 D3 Kāzerūn Iran
103 E2 Kazincbarcika Hungary
118 C3 Kazumba Dem. Rep. Congo
66 D2 Kazuno Japan
86 F2 Kazymskiy Mys Rus. Fed.
111 B3 Kea *i.* Greece
97 C1 Keady U.K.
137 D2 Kearney U.S.A.
142 A2 Kearny U.S.A.
115 C1 Kebili Tunisia
116 A3 Kebkabiya Sudan
92 G2 Kebnekaise *mt.* Sweden
117 C4 K'ebrī Dehar Eth.
60 B2 Kebumen Indon.
128 B2 Kechika *r.* Can.
113 D3 Keçiborlu Turkey
103 D2 Kecskemét Hungary
88 B2 Kėdainiai Lith.
114 A3 Kédougou Senegal
103 D1 Kędzierzyn-Koźle Pol.
128 B1 Keele *r.* Can.
128 A1 Keele Peak Can.
Keelung Taiwan *see* Chilung
139 E2 Keene U.S.A.
122 A2 Keetmanshoop Namibia
129 E3 Keewatin Can.
Kefallonia *i.* Greece *see* Cephalonia
59 C3 Kefamenanu Indon.
92 □A3 Keflavik Iceland
77 D2 Kegen Kazakh.
128 C2 Keg River Can.
88 C2 Kehra Estonia
62 A1 Kehsi Mansam Myanmar
98 C3 Keighley U.K.
88 B2 Keila Estonia
122 B2 Keimoes S. Africa
92 I3 Keitele *l.* Fin.
52 B3 Keith Austr.
96 C2 Keith U.K.
128 B1 Keith Arm *b.* Can.
134 B2 Keizer U.S.A.
103 E2 Kékes *mt.* Hungary
117 C4 K'elafo Eth.
Kelang Malaysia *see* Klang
92 J2 Keles-Uayv, Gora *hill* Rus. Fed.
102 C2 Kelheim Ger.
76 C3 Kelifskiy Uzboy *marsh* Turkm.
80 B1 Kelkit *r.* Turkey
128 B1 Keller Lake Can.
134 C1 Kellogg U.S.A.
92 I2 Kelloselkä Fin.
97 C2 Kells Ireland
88 B2 Kelmė Lith.
115 D4 Kelo Chad
128 C3 Kelowna Can.
96 C3 Kelso U.K.
134 B1 Kelso U.S.A.
60 B1 Keluang Malaysia
129 D2 Kelvington Can.
86 C2 Kem' Rus. Fed.
Ke Macina Mali *see* Massina
128 B2 Kemano Can.
118 C2 Kembé C.A.R.
111 C3 Kemer Turkey
82 G3 Kemerovo Rus. Fed.
92 H2 Kemi Fin.
92 I2 Kemijärvi Fin.
92 I2 Kemijärvi *l.* Fin.
92 I2 Kemijoki *r.* Fin.
136 A2 Kemmerer U.S.A.
92 I3 Kempele Fin.
55 G2 Kemp Land *reg.* Antarctica
55 A2 Kemp Peninsula Antarctica
53 D2 Kempsey Austr.
130 C2 Kempt, Lac *l.* Can.
102 C2 Kempten (Allgäu) Ger.
123 C2 Kempton Park S. Africa
61 C2 Kemujan *i.* Indon.
126 B2 Kenai U.S.A.
129 D2 Kenaston Can.
98 B2 Kendal U.K.
141 D3 Kendall U.S.A.
61 D2 Kendari Indon.
60 C2 Kendawangan Indon.
115 D4 Kendégué Chad
114 A4 Kenema Sierra Leone
118 B3 Kenge Dem. Rep. Congo

62 A1 Kengtung Myanmar
122 B2 Kenhardt S. Africa
114 B1 Kénitra Morocco
97 B3 Kenmare Ireland
136 C1 Kenmare U.S.A.
97 A3 Kenmare River *inlet* Ireland
100 C3 Kenn Ger.
143 C2 Kenna U.S.A.
139 F2 Kennebec *r.* U.S.A.
Kennedy, Cape U.S.A. *see* Canaveral, Cape
140 B3 Kenner U.S.A.
99 C4 Kennet *r.* U.K.
137 E3 Kennett U.S.A.
130 A3 Kennewick U.S.A.
138 B2 Kenora Can.
138 B2 Kenosha U.S.A.
142 C2 Kent U.S.A.
77 C2 Kentau Kazakh.
138 B3 Kentucky *r.* U.S.A.
138 C3 Kentucky *state* U.S.A.
138 B3 Kentucky Lake U.S.A.
140 B2 Kentwood U.S.A.
119 D2 Kenya *country* Africa
119 D3 Kenya, Mount *mt.* Kenya
60 B1 Kenyir, Tasik *resr* Malaysia
137 E2 Keokuk U.S.A.
75 C2 Keonjhar India
111 C3 Kepsut Turkey
52 B3 Kerang Austr.
91 C2 Kerch Ukr.
59 D3 Kerema P.N.G.
128 C3 Keremeos Can.
116 B3 Keren Eritrea
81 C2 Kerend Iran
159 E7 Kerguélen, Îles *is* Indian Ocean
159 E7 Kerguelen Plateau *sea feature* Indian Ocean
119 D3 Kericho Kenya
54 B1 Kerikeri N.Z.
60 B2 Kerinci, Gunung *vol.* Indon.
Kerintji *vol.* Indon. *see* Kerinci, Gunung
100 C2 Kerkrade Neth.
111 A3 Kerkyra Greece
Kerkyra *i.* Greece *see* Corfu
116 B3 Kerma Sudan
49 J7 Kermadec Islands S. Pacific Ocean
79 C1 Kermān Iran
81 C2 Kermānshāh Iran
Kermine Uzbek. *see* Navoiy
143 C2 Kermit U.S.A.
135 C3 Kern *r.* U.S.A.
114 B4 Kérouané Guinea
100 C2 Kerpen Ger.
129 D2 Kerrobert Can.
143 D2 Kerrville U.S.A.
97 B3 Kerry Head *hd* Ireland
Keryneia Cyprus *see* Kyrenia
130 B2 Kesagami Lake Can.
111 C2 Keşan Turkey
66 D3 Kesennuma Japan
74 B2 Keshod India
100 C2 Kessel Neth.
98 B2 Keswick U.K.
103 D2 Keszthely Hungary
82 G3 Ket' *r.* Rus. Fed.
60 C2 Ketapang Indon.
128 A2 Ketchikan U.S.A.
134 D2 Ketchum U.S.A.
114 B4 Kete Krachi Ghana
118 B2 Kétté Cameroon
99 C3 Kettering U.K.
138 C3 Kettering U.S.A.
134 C1 Kettle River Range *mts* U.S.A.
93 H3 Keuruu Fin.
100 C2 Kevelaer Ger.
138 B2 Kewanee U.S.A.
138 B1 Keweenaw Bay U.S.A.
138 B1 Keweenaw Peninsula U.S.A.
141 D3 Key Largo U.S.A.
99 B4 Keynsham U.K.
139 D3 Keyser U.S.A.
141 D4 Key West U.S.A.
123 C2 Kgotsong S. Africa
69 F1 Khabarovsk Rus. Fed.
91 D2 Khadyzhensk Rus. Fed.
75 D2 Khagrachari Bangl.
74 A2 Khairpur Pak.
122 B1 Khakhea Botswana
76 B3 Khalilabad Iran
86 F2 Khal'mer-Yu Rus. Fed.
68 C1 Khamar-Daban, Khrebet *mts* Rus. Fed.
74 B2 Khambhat India
74 B3 Khambhat, Gulf of India
74 B2 Khamgaon India
79 C2 Khamir Iran
78 B3 Khamir Yemen
78 B3 Khamis Mushayt Saudi Arabia
77 C3 Khānābād Afgh.
74 B2 Khandwa India
83 K2 Khandyga Rus. Fed.
74 B1 Khanewal Pak.
Khan Hung Vietnam *see* Soc Trăng
83 J3 Khani Rus. Fed.
66 B2 Khanka, Lake China/Rus. Fed.
115 C2 Khannfoussa *hill* Alg.
74 B2 Khanpur Pak.
77 D2 Khantau Kazakh.
83 H2 Khantayskoye, Ozero *l.* Rus. Fed.
86 F2 Khanty-Mansiysk Rus. Fed.
63 A3 Khao Chum Thong Thai.
63 A2 Khao Laem Reservoir Thai.

74 B1 **Khapalu** Jammu and Kashmir
87 D4 **Kharabali** Rus. Fed.
75 C2 **Kharagpur** India
79 C2 **Khārān** r. Iran
**Kharga Oasis** Egypt see **Khārijah, Wāḩāt al**
74 B2 **Khargon** India
116 B2 **Khārijah, Wāḩāt al** Egypt
91 D2 **Kharkiv** Ukr.
**Khar'kov** Ukr. see **Kharkiv**
111 C2 **Kharmanli** Bulg.
89 F2 **Kharovsk** Rus. Fed.
116 B3 **Khartoum** Sudan
87 D4 **Khasav'yurt** Rus. Fed.
79 D2 **Khāsh** Iran
86 F2 **Khashgort** Rus. Fed.
78 A3 **Khashm el Girba** Sudan
78 A3 **Khashm el Girba Dam** Sudan
81 C1 **Khashuri** Georgia
75 D2 **Khasi Hills** India
111 C2 **Khaskovo** Bulg.
83 H2 **Khatanga** Rus. Fed.
123 C3 **Khayamnandi** S. Africa
78 A2 **Khaybar** Saudi Arabia
122 A3 **Khayelitsha** S. Africa
62 B2 **Khê Bo** Vietnam
107 D2 **Khemis Miliana** Alg.
63 B2 **Khemmarat** Thai.
115 C1 **Khenchela** Alg.
81 D3 **Kherāmeh** Iran
91 C2 **Kherson** Ukr.
83 H2 **Kheta** r. Rus. Fed.
69 D1 **Khilok** Rus. Fed.
89 E2 **Khimki** Rus. Fed.
89 E3 **Khlevnoye** Rus. Fed.
63 B2 **Khlung** Thai.
90 B2 **Khmel'nyts'kyy** Ukr.
**Khmer Republic** country Asia see **Cambodia**
76 B1 **Khobda** Kazakh.
**Khodzheyli** Uzbek. see **Xoʻjayli**
89 E3 **Khokhol'skiy** Rus. Fed.
74 B2 **Khokhropar** Pak.
74 A1 **Kholm** Afgh.
89 D2 **Kholm** Rus. Fed.
89 D2 **Kholm-Zhirkovskiy** Rus. Fed.
122 A1 **Khomas Highland** hills Namibia
89 E3 **Khomutovo** Rus. Fed.
79 C2 **Khonj** Iran
63 B2 **Khon Kaen** Thai.
62 A1 **Khonsa** India
83 K2 **Khonuu** Rus. Fed.
86 F2 **Khoreyver** Rus. Fed.
69 D1 **Khorinsk** Rus. Fed.
120 A3 **Khorixas** Namibia
66 B2 **Khorol** Rus. Fed.
91 C2 **Khorol** Ukr.
81 C2 **Khorramābād** Iran
81 C2 **Khorramshahr** Iran
77 D3 **Khorugh** Tajik.
**Khotan** China see **Hotan**
90 B2 **Khotyn** Ukr.
114 B1 **Khouribga** Morocco
77 C3 **Khowst** Afgh.
88 C2 **Khoyniki** Belarus
62 A1 **Khreum** Myanmar
76 B1 **Khromtau** Kazakh.
**Khrushchev** Ukr. see **Svitlovods'k**
90 B2 **Khrystynivka** Ukr.
123 B1 **Khudumelapye** Botswana
77 C2 **Khŭjand** Tajik.
63 B2 **Khu Khan** Thai.
78 A2 **Khulays** Saudi Arabia
75 C2 **Khulna** Bangl.
**Khūnīnshahr** Iran see **Khorramshahr**
81 D2 **Khunsar** Iran
79 B2 **Khurayş** Saudi Arabia
74 B1 **Khushab** Pak.
90 A2 **Khust** Ukr.
123 C2 **Khutsong** S. Africa
74 A2 **Khuzdar** Pak.
81 D3 **Khvormūj** Iran
81 C2 **Khvoy** Iran
89 D2 **Khvoynaya** Rus. Fed.
77 D2 **Khyber Pass** Afgh./Pak.
53 D2 **Kiama** Austr.
64 B3 **Kiamba** Phil.
119 C3 **Kiambi** Dem. Rep. Congo
**Kiangsi** prov. China see **Jiangxi**
**Kiangsu** prov. China see **Jiangsu**
119 D3 **Kibaha** Tanz.
119 D3 **Kibaya** Tanz.
119 D3 **Kibiti** Tanz.
119 C3 **Kibombo** Dem. Rep. Congo
119 D3 **Kibondo** Tanz.
119 D2 **Kibre Mengist** Eth.
119 D3 **Kibungo** Rwanda
111 B2 **Kičevo** Macedonia
114 C3 **Kidal** Mali
99 B3 **Kidderminster** U.K.
114 A3 **Kidira** Senegal
74 B1 **Kidmang** Jammu and Kashmir
54 C1 **Kidnappers, Cape** N.Z.
102 C1 **Kiel** Ger.
103 E1 **Kielce** Pol.
98 D2 **Kielder Water** resr U.K.
119 C4 **Kienge** Dem. Rep. Congo
90 C1 **Kiev** Ukr.
114 A3 **Kiffa** Maur.
119 C3 **Kigali** Rwanda
119 C3 **Kigoma** Tanz.
88 B2 **Kihnu** i. Estonia
92 I2 **Kiiminki** Fin.

67 B4 **Kii-suidō** sea chan. Japan
109 D1 **Kikinda** Serb. and Mont.
119 C3 **Kikondja** Dem. Rep. Congo
59 D3 **Kikori** P.N.G.
59 D3 **Kikori** r. P.N.G.
118 B3 **Kikwit** Dem. Rep. Congo
65 B1 **Kilchu** N. Korea
97 C2 **Kilcock** Ireland
97 C2 **Kildare** Ireland
118 B3 **Kilembe** Dem. Rep. Congo
143 E2 **Kilgore** U.S.A.
119 D3 **Kilifi** Kenya
119 D3 **Kilimanjaro** vol. Tanz.
119 D3 **Kilindoni** Tanz.
80 B2 **Kilis** Turkey
90 B2 **Kiliya** Ukr.
97 B2 **Kilkee** Ireland
97 D1 **Kilkeel** U.K.
97 C2 **Kilkenny** Ireland
111 B2 **Kilkis** Greece
97 B1 **Killala** Ireland
97 B1 **Killala Bay** Ireland
97 B2 **Killaloe** Ireland
128 C2 **Killam** Can.
97 B2 **Killarney** Ireland
143 D2 **Killeen** U.S.A.
96 B2 **Killin** U.K.
131 D1 **Killiniq** Can.
97 B2 **Killorglin** Ireland
97 B1 **Killybegs** Ireland
96 B3 **Kilmarnock** U.K.
53 B3 **Kilmore** Austr.
119 D3 **Kilosa** Tanz.
97 B2 **Kilrush** Ireland
119 C3 **Kilwa** Dem. Rep. Congo
119 D3 **Kilwa Masoko** Tanz.
119 D3 **Kimambi** Tanz.
52 A2 **Kimba** Austr.
136 C2 **Kimball** U.S.A.
59 E3 **Kimbe** P.N.G.
128 C3 **Kimberley** Can.
122 B2 **Kimberley** S. Africa
50 B1 **Kimberley Plateau** Austr.
65 B2 **Kimch'aek** N. Korea
65 B2 **Kimch'ŏn** S. Korea
65 B2 **Kimhae** S. Korea
127 H2 **Kimmirut** Can.
89 E2 **Kimovsk** Rus. Fed.
118 C3 **Kimpanga** Dem. Rep. Congo
118 B3 **Kimpese** Dem. Rep. Congo
89 E2 **Kimry** Rus. Fed.
61 C1 **Kinabalu, Gunung** mt. Sabah Malaysia
128 C2 **Kinbasket Lake** Can.
96 C1 **Kinbrace** U.K.
130 B3 **Kincardine** Can.
62 A1 **Kinchang** Myanmar
119 C3 **Kinda** Dem. Rep. Congo
98 C3 **Kinder Scout** hill U.K.
129 D2 **Kindersley** Can.
114 A3 **Kindia** Guinea
119 C3 **Kindu** Dem. Rep. Congo
89 F2 **Kineshma** Rus. Fed.
118 B3 **Kingandu** Dem. Rep. Congo
51 E2 **Kingaroy** Austr.
135 B3 **King City** U.S.A.
130 C2 **King George Islands** Can.
88 C2 **Kingisepp** Rus. Fed.
51 D3 **King Island** Austr.
**Kingisseppa** Estonia see **Kuressaare**
50 B1 **King Leopold Ranges** hills Austr.
142 A1 **Kingman** U.S.A.
135 B3 **Kings** r. U.S.A.
52 A3 **Kingscote** Austr.
97 C2 **Kingscourt** Ireland
99 D3 **King's Lynn** U.K.
50 B1 **King Sound** b. Austr.
134 D2 **Kings Peak** U.S.A.
141 D1 **Kingsport** U.S.A.
51 D4 **Kingston** Austr.
130 C3 **Kingston** Can.
146 C3 **Kingston** Jamaica
139 E2 **Kingston** U.S.A.
52 A3 **Kingston South East** Austr.
98 C3 **Kingston upon Hull** U.K.
147 D3 **Kingstown** St Vincent
143 D3 **Kingsville** U.S.A.
99 B4 **Kingswood** U.K.
96 B2 **Kingussie** U.K.
126 F2 **King William Island** Can.
123 C3 **King William's Town** S. Africa
67 D3 **Kinka-san** i. Japan
96 B2 **Kinlochleven** U.K.
93 F4 **Kinna** Sweden
97 B3 **Kinsale** Ireland
118 B3 **Kinshasa** Dem. Rep. Congo
141 E1 **Kinston** U.S.A.
88 B2 **Kintai** Lith.
114 B4 **Kintampo** Ghana
96 C2 **Kintore** U.K.
96 B3 **Kintyre** pen. U.K.
119 D3 **Kiomboi** Tanz.
130 C3 **Kipawa, Lac** l. Can.
119 D3 **Kipembawe** Tanz.
119 D3 **Kipengere Range** mts Tanz.
129 D2 **Kipling** Can.
**Kipling Station** Can. see **Kipling**
119 C4 **Kipushi** Dem. Rep. Congo
119 C4 **Kipushia** Dem. Rep. Congo
101 D2 **Kirchhain** Ger.
101 D3 **Kirchheim-Bolanden** Ger.
83 I3 **Kirenga** r. Rus. Fed.
83 I3 **Kirensk** Rus. Fed.
89 E3 **Kireyevsk** Rus. Fed.

**Kirghizia** country Asia see **Kyrgyzstan**
77 D2 **Kirghiz Range** mts Asia
**Kirgizskaya S.S.R.** admin. reg. Asia see **Kyrgyzstan**
49 J4 **Kiribati** country Pacific Ocean
80 B2 **Kırıkkale** Turkey
89 E2 **Kirillov** Rus. Fed.
**Kirin** China see **Jilin**
**Kirin** prov. China see **Jilin**
**Kirinyaga** Kenya see **Kenya, Mount**
89 D2 **Kirishi** Rus. Fed.
48 L3 **Kiritimati** i. Kiribati
111 C3 **Kırkağaç** Turkey
98 B3 **Kirkby** U.K.
98 B3 **Kirkby Stephen** U.K.
96 C2 **Kirkcaldy** U.K.
96 B3 **Kirkcudbright** U.K.
92 J2 **Kirkenes** Norway
88 B1 **Kirkkonummi** Fin.
130 B3 **Kirkland Lake** Can.
111 C2 **Kırklareli** Turkey
137 E2 **Kirksville** U.S.A.
81 C2 **Kirkūk** Iraq
96 C1 **Kirkwall** U.K.
**Kirov** Kazakh. see **Balpyk Bi**
89 D3 **Kirov** Rus. Fed.
86 D3 **Kirov** Rus. Fed.
**Kirovabad** Azer. see **Gäncä**
**Kirovakan** Armenia see **Vanadzor**
**Kirovo** Ukr. see **Kirovohrad**
86 E3 **Kirovo-Chepetsk** Rus. Fed.
**Kirovo-Chepetskiy** Rus. Fed. see **Kirovo-Chepetsk**
91 C2 **Kirovohrad** Ukr.
86 C2 **Kirovsk** Rus. Fed.
91 D2 **Kirovs'ke** Ukr.
**Kirovskiy** Kazakh. see **Balpyk Bi**
66 B1 **Kirovskiy** Rus. Fed.
96 C2 **Kirriemuir** U.K.
86 E3 **Kirs** Rus. Fed.
87 D3 **Kirsanov** Rus. Fed.
80 B2 **Kırşehir** Turkey
74 A2 **Kirthar Range** mts Pak.
92 H2 **Kiruna** Sweden
67 C3 **Kiryū** Japan
89 E2 **Kirzhach** Rus. Fed.
119 D3 **Kisaki** Tanz.
119 C3 **Kisangani** Dem. Rep. Congo
118 B3 **Kisantu** Dem. Rep. Congo
60 A1 **Kisaran** Indon.
82 G3 **Kiselevsk** Rus. Fed.
75 C2 **Kishanganj** India
115 C4 **Kishi** Nigeria
**Kishinev** Moldova see **Chişinău**
67 C4 **Kishiwada** Japan
77 D1 **Kishkenekol'** Kazakh.
75 D2 **Kishoreganj** Bangl.
74 B1 **Kishtwar** Jammu and Kashmir
119 D3 **Kisii** Kenya
103 D2 **Kiskunfélegyháza** Hungary
103 D2 **Kiskunhalas** Hungary
87 D4 **Kislovodsk** Rus. Fed.
117 C5 **Kismaayo** Somalia
**Kismayu** Somalia see **Kismaayo**
119 C3 **Kisoro** Uganda
114 A4 **Kissidougou** Guinea
141 D3 **Kissimmee** U.S.A.
141 D3 **Kissimmee, Lake** U.S.A.
129 D2 **Kississing Lake** Can.
**Kistna** r. India see **Krishna**
103 E2 **Kisvárda** Hungary
**Kisykkamys** Kazakh. see **Dzhangala**
114 B3 **Kita** Mali
67 D3 **Kitaibaraki** Japan
66 D3 **Kitakami** Japan
66 D3 **Kitakami-gawa** r. Japan
67 B4 **Kita-Kyūshū** Japan
119 D2 **Kitale** Kenya
66 D2 **Kitami** Japan
130 B3 **Kitchener** Can.
93 J3 **Kitee** Fin.
119 D2 **Kitgum** Uganda
128 B2 **Kitimat** Can.
118 B3 **Kitona** Dem. Rep. Congo
92 H2 **Kittilä** Fin.
141 E1 **Kitty Hawk** U.S.A.
119 D3 **Kitunda** Tanz.
128 B2 **Kitwanga** Can.
121 B2 **Kitwe** Zambia
102 C2 **Kitzbühel** Austria
101 E3 **Kitzingen** Ger.
59 D3 **Kiunga** P.N.G.
92 I3 **Kiuruvesi** Fin.
92 I2 **Kivalo** ridge Fin.
90 B1 **Kivertsi** Ukr.
88 C2 **Kiviõli** Estonia
91 D2 **Kivsharivka** Ukr.
119 C3 **Kivu, Lake** Dem. Rep. Congo/Rwanda
111 C2 **Kıyıköy** Turkey
111 C3 **Kizel** Rus. Fed.
111 C3 **Kızılca Dağ** mt. Turkey
80 B1 **Kızılırmak** r. Turkey
87 D4 **Kizlyar** Rus. Fed.
**Kizyl-Arbat** Turkm. see **Gyzylarbat**
92 I1 **Kjøllefjord** Norway
92 G2 **Kjøpsvik** Norway
102 C1 **Kladno** Czech Rep.
102 C2 **Klagenfurt** Austria
88 B2 **Klaipėda** Lith.
94 B1 **Klaksvík** Faroe Is

134 B2 **Klamath** r. U.S.A.
134 B2 **Klamath Falls** U.S.A.
134 B2 **Klamath Mountains** U.S.A.
60 B1 **Klang** Malaysia
102 C2 **Klatovy** Czech Rep.
122 A3 **Klawer** S. Africa
128 A2 **Klawock** U.S.A.
122 B2 **Kleena Kleene** Can.
122 B2 **Kleinbegin** S. Africa
122 A2 **Klein Karas** Namibia
122 A2 **Kleinsee** S. Africa
123 C2 **Klerksdorp** S. Africa
90 B1 **Klesiv** Ukr.
89 D3 **Kletnya** Rus. Fed.
100 C2 **Kleve** Ger.
88 C3 **Klichaw** Belarus
89 D3 **Klimavichy** Belarus
89 D3 **Klimovo** Rus. Fed.
89 E2 **Klimovsk** Rus. Fed.
89 E2 **Klin** Rus. Fed.
101 F2 **Klingenthal** Ger.
101 F2 **Klínovec** mt. Czech Rep.
93 G4 **Klintehamn** Sweden
89 D3 **Klintsy** Rus. Fed.
109 C2 **Ključ** Bos.-Herz.
103 D1 **Kłodzko** Pol.
100 C1 **Kloosterhaar** Neth.
103 D2 **Klosterneuburg** Austria
101 E1 **Klötze (Altmark)** Ger.
128 A1 **Kluane Lake** Can.
**Kluang** Malaysia see **Keluang**
103 D1 **Kluczbork** Pol.
**Klukhori** Rus. Fed. see **Karachayevsk**
128 A2 **Klukwan** U.S.A.
74 A2 **Klupro** Pak.
89 F2 **Klyaz'ma** r. Rus. Fed.
88 C3 **Klyetsk** Belarus
83 L3 **Klyuchi** Rus. Fed.
98 C2 **Knaresborough** U.K.
93 F3 **Knästen** hill Sweden
129 E2 **Knee Lake** Can.
101 E1 **Knesebeck** Ger.
101 E3 **Knetzgau** Ger.
109 C2 **Knin** Croatia
103 C2 **Knittelfeld** Austria
109 D2 **Knjaževac** Serb. and Mont.
**Knob Lake** Can. see **Schefferville**
97 B3 **Knockaboy** hill Ireland
100 A2 **Knokke-Heist** Belgium
141 D1 **Knoxville** U.S.A.
127 H1 **Knud Rasmussen Land** reg. Greenland
122 B3 **Knysna** S. Africa
60 B2 **Koba** Indon.
67 C4 **Kōbe** Japan
**København** Denmark see **Copenhagen**
100 C2 **Koblenz** Ger.
59 C3 **Kobroōr** i. Indon.
88 B3 **Kobryn** Belarus
**Kocaeli** Turkey see **İzmit**
111 B2 **Kočani** Macedonia
111 C2 **Kocasu** r. Turkey
109 B1 **Kočevje** Slovenia
75 C2 **Koch Bihar** India
89 F3 **Kochetovka** Rus. Fed.
**Kochi** India see **Cochin**
67 B4 **Kōchi** Japan
87 D4 **Kochubey** Rus. Fed.
75 C2 **Kodarma** India
126 B3 **Kodiak** U.S.A.
126 B3 **Kodiak Island** U.S.A.
123 C1 **Kodibeleng** Botswana
117 B4 **Kodok** Sudan
90 B2 **Kodyma** Ukr.
111 C2 **Kodzhaele** mt. Bulg./Greece
122 A2 **Koës** Namibia
122 C2 **Koffiefontein** S. Africa
114 B4 **Koforidua** Ghana
67 C3 **Kōfu** Japan
131 D2 **Kogaluk** r. Can.
114 B3 **Kogoni** Mali
74 B1 **Kohat** Pak.
72 D2 **Kohima** India
88 C2 **Kohtla-Järve** Estonia
128 A1 **Koidern** Can.
**Kokand** Uzbek. see **Qoʻqon**
88 B2 **Kōkar** Fin.
**Kokchetav** Kazakh. see **Kokshetau**
122 A2 **Koerboom** Namibia
88 C3 **Kokhanava** Belarus
89 F2 **Kokhma** Rus. Fed.
92 H3 **Kokkola** Fin.
88 C2 **Kokomo** Latvia
138 B2 **Kokomo** U.S.A.
122 B1 **Kokong** Botswana
123 C2 **Kokosi** S. Africa
77 E2 **Kokpekti** Kazakh.
77 C1 **Kokshetau** Kazakh.
131 D2 **Koksoak** r. Can.
123 C3 **Kokstad** S. Africa
**Koktokay** China see **Fuyun**
61 D2 **Kolaka** Indon.
86 C2 **Kola Peninsula** Rus. Fed.
92 H2 **Kolari** Fin.
**Kolarovgrad** Bulg. see **Shumen**
114 A3 **Kolda** Senegal
93 E4 **Kolding** Denmark
119 C2 **Kole** Dem. Rep. Congo
107 D2 **Koléa** Alg.
86 D2 **Kolguyev, Ostrov** i. Rus. Fed.
73 B3 **Kolhapur** India
88 B2 **Kolkasrags** pt Latvia

**75** C2 Kolkata India
Kollam India *see* Quilon
**100** C1 Kollum Neth.
Köln Ger. *see* Cologne
**103** D1 Koło Pol.
**103** D1 Kołobrzeg Pol.
**114** B3 Kolokani Mali
**89** E2 Kolomna Rus. Fed.
**90** B2 Kolomyya Ukr.
**114** B3 Kolondiéba Mali
**61** D2 Kolonedale Indon.
**122** B2 Kolonkwane Botswana
**82** G3 Kolpashevo Rus. Fed.
**89** E3 Kolpny Rus. Fed.
Kol'skiy Poluostrov *pen.* Rus. Fed.
*see* Kola Peninsula
**78** B3 Koluli Eritrea
**92** F3 Kolvereid Norway
**119** C4 Kolwezi Dem. Rep. Congo
**83** L2 Kolyma *r.* Rus. Fed.
Kolyma Lowland Rus. Fed. *see*
Kolymskaya Nizmennost'
Kolyma Range *mts* Rus. Fed. *see*
Kolymskiy, Khrebet
**83** L2 Kolymskaya Nizmennost' *lowland*
Rus. Fed.
**83** M2 Kolymskiy, Khrebet *mts* Rus. Fed.
**122** A2 Komaggas S. Africa
**67** C3 Komaki Japan
**83** M3 Komandorskiye Ostrova *is*
Rus. Fed.
**103** D2 Komárno Slovakia
**123** D2 Komati *r.* Swaziland
**123** D2 Komatipoort S. Africa
**67** C3 Komatsu Japan
**120** A2 Kombat Namibia
**119** C3 Kombe Dem. Rep. Congo
Komintern Ukr. *see* Marhanets'
**90** C1 Kominternivs'ke Ukr.
**109** C2 Komiža Croatia
**103** D2 Komló Hungary
Kommunarsk Ukr. *see* Alchevs'k
**118** B3 Komono Congo
**111** C3 Komotini Greece
Kompong Som Cambodia *see*
Sihanoukville
Komrat Moldova *see* Comrat
**122** B3 Komsberg *mts* S. Africa
**83** H1 Komsomolets, Ostrov *i.* Rus. Fed.
**89** F2 Komsomol'sk Rus. Fed.
**91** C2 Komsomol's'k Ukr.
**83** M2 Komsomol'skiy Rus. Fed.
Komsomol'skiy Rus. Fed. *see*
Yugorsk
**87** D4 Komsomol'skiy Rus. Fed.
**83** K3 Komsomol'sk-na-Amure Rus. Fed.
**89** E2 Konakovo Rus. Fed.
**75** C3 Kondagaon India
**86** F2 Kondinskoye Rus. Fed.
Kondinskoye Rus. Fed. *see*
Oktyabr'skoye
**119** D3 Kondoa Tanz.
**86** C2 Kondopoga Rus. Fed.
**89** E3 Kondrovo Rus. Fed.
**127** J2 Kong Christian IX Land *reg.*
Greenland
**127** K2 Kong Christian X Land *reg.*
Greenland
**127** J2 Kong Frederik VI Kyst
*coastal area* Greenland
**65** B2 Kongju S. Korea
**119** C3 Kongolo Dem. Rep. Congo
**93** E4 Kongsberg Norway
**93** F3 Kongsvinger Norway
**77** D3 Kongur Shan *mt.* China
**100** C2 Königswinter Ger.
**103** D1 Konin Pol.
**109** C2 Konjic Bos.-Herz.
**122** A2 Konkiep *watercourse* Namibia
**86** D2 Konosha Rus. Fed.
**91** C1 Konotop Ukr.
**103** E1 Końskie Pol.
Konstantinograd Ukr. *see*
Krasnohrad
**102** B2 Konstanz Ger.
**115** C3 Kontagora Nigeria
**63** B2 Kon Tum Vietnam
**63** B2 Kontum, Plateau du Vietnam
**80** B2 Konya Turkey
**77** D2 Konyrat Kazakh.
**100** C3 Konz Ger.
**86** E3 Konzhakovskiy Kamen', Gora *mt.*
Rus. Fed.
**134** C1 Kooskia U.S.A.
**128** C3 Kootenay Lake Can.
**53** D2 Kootingal Austr.
**122** B3 Kootjieskolk S. Africa
**92** □B2 Kópasker Iceland
**108** B1 Koper Slovenia
**93** G4 Köping Sweden
**123** C1 Kopong Botswana
**93** G4 Kopparberg Sweden
**109** C1 Koprivnica Croatia
**89** F3 Korablino Rus. Fed.
**73** C3 Koraput India
**75** C2 Korba India
**101** D2 Korbach Ger.
**109** D2 Korçë Albania
**109** C2 Korčula Croatia
**109** C2 Korčula *i.* Croatia
**65** B1 Korea, North *country* Asia
**65** B2 Korea, South *country* Asia
**70** C2 Korea Bay *g.* China/N. Korea
**65** B3 Korea Strait Japan/S. Korea
**89** D3 Korenevo Rus. Fed.

**91** D2 Korenovsk Rus. Fed.
Korenovskaya Rus. Fed. *see*
Korenovsk
**90** B1 Koryda Ukr.
**111** C1 Körfez Turkey
**114** B4 Korhogo Côte d'Ivoire
Korinthos Greece *see* Corinth
**103** D2 Kõris-hegy *hill* Hungary
**109** D2 Koritnik *mt.* Albania
Koritsa Albania *see* Korçë
**67** D3 Kōriyama Japan
**87** F3 Korkino Rus. Fed.
**111** D3 Korkuteli Turkey
**77** E2 Korla China
**103** D2 Körmend Hungary
**49** I5 Koro *i.* Fiji
**114** B3 Koro Mali
**131** D2 Koroc *r.* Can.
**91** D1 Korocha Rus. Fed.
**119** D3 Korogwe Tanz.
**59** C2 Koror Palau
**103** E2 Körös *r.* Romania
**90** B1 Korosten' Ukr.
**90** B1 Korostyshiv Ukr.
**115** D3 Koro Toro Chad
**93** H3 Korpo Fin.
**66** D1 Korsakov Rus. Fed.
**91** C2 Korsun'-Shevchenkivs'kyy Ukr.
**103** E1 Korsze Pol.
**116** B3 Korti Sudan
**100** A2 Kortrijk Belgium
**83** L3 Koryakskaya, Sopka *vol.* Rus. Fed.
**83** M2 Koryakskiy Khrebet *mts* Rus. Fed.
**86** D2 Koryazhma Rus. Fed.
**65** B2 Koryŏng S. Korea
**91** C1 Koryukivka Ukr.
**111** C3 Kos Greece
**111** C3 Kos *i.* Greece
**91** D2 Kosa Biryuchyy Ostriv *i.* Ukr.
**65** B2 Kosan N. Korea
**103** D1 Kościan Pol.
Kosciusko, Mount Austr. *see*
Kosciuszko, Mount
**53** C2 Kosciuszko, Mount Austr.
**77** E2 Kosh-Agach Rus. Fed.
**67** A4 Koshikijima-rettō *is* Japan
**103** E2 Košice Slovakia
**92** H2 Koskullskulle Sweden
**65** B2 Kosŏng N. Korea
**109** D2 Kosovo *prov.* Serb. and Mont.
**109** D2 Kosovska Mitrovica
Serb. and Mont.
**48** H3 Kosrae *atoll* Micronesia
**114** B4 Kossou, Lac de *l.* Côte d'Ivoire
**76** C1 Kostanay Kazakh.
**110** B2 Kostenets Bulg.
**123** C2 Koster S. Africa
**116** B3 Kosti Sudan
**92** J3 Kostomuksha Rus. Fed.
**90** B1 Kostopil' Ukr.
**89** F2 Kostroma Rus. Fed.
**89** F2 Kostroma *r.* Rus. Fed.
**102** C1 Kostrzyn Pol.
**91** D2 Kostyantynivka Ukr.
**103** D1 Koszalin Pol.
**103** D2 Kőszeg Hungary
**74** B2 Kota India
**60** B2 Kotaagung Indon.
**61** C2 Kotabaru Indon.
**61** C1 Kota Belud *Sabah* Malaysia
**60** B1 Kota Bharu Malaysia
**60** B2 Kotabumi Indon.
**61** C1 Kota Kinabalu *Sabah* Malaysia
**75** C2 Kotaparh India
**61** C1 Kota Samarahan *Sarawak*
Malaysia
**86** D3 Kotel'nich Rus. Fed.
**87** D4 Kotel'nikovo Rus. Fed.
**83** K1 Kotel'nyy, Ostrov *i.* Rus. Fed.
**91** C1 Kotel'va Ukr.
**101** E2 Köthen (Anhalt) Ger.
**119** D2 Kotido Uganda
**93** I3 Kotka Fin.
**86** D2 Kotlas Rus. Fed.
**126** B2 Kotlik U.S.A.
**115** C4 Kotorkoshi Nigeria
**109** C2 Kotor Varoš Bos.-Herz.
**87** D3 Kotovo Rus. Fed.
**91** E1 Kotovsk Rus. Fed.
**90** B2 Kotovs'k Ukr.
**73** C3 Kottagudem India
**118** C2 Kotto *r.* C.A.R.
**83** H2 Kotuy *r.* Rus. Fed.
**126** B2 Kotzebue U.S.A.
**126** B2 Kotzebue Sound *sea chan.* U.S.A.
**114** A3 Koubia Guinea
**100** A2 Koudekerke Neth.
**114** B3 Koudougou Burkina
**122** B3 Kougaberge *mts* S. Africa
**118** B3 Koulamoutou Gabon
**114** B3 Koulikoro Mali
**118** B2 Koum Cameroon
**118** B2 Koumra Chad
**114** A3 Koundâra Guinea
Kounradskiy Kazakh. *see* Konyrat
**151** D2 Kourou Fr. Guiana
**114** B3 Kouroussa Guinea
**115** D3 Kousséri Cameroon
**114** B3 Koutiala Mali
**93** I3 Kouvola Fin.
**109** D1 Kovačica Serb. and Mont.
**92** J2 Kovdor Rus. Fed.
**90** A1 Kovel' Ukr.
Kovno Lith. *see* Kaunas
**89** F2 Kovrov Rus. Fed.

**51** D1 Kowanyama Austr.
**54** B2 Kowhitirangi N.Z.
**111** C3 Köyceğiz Turkey
**86** D2 Koyda Rus. Fed.
**126** B2 Koyukuk *r.* U.S.A.
**111** B2 Kozani Greece
**90** C1 Kozelets' Ukr.
**89** E3 Kozel'sk Rus. Fed.
Kozhikode India *see* Calicut
**90** B2 Kozyatyn Ukr.
**63** A3 Kra, Isthmus of Thai.
**63** A3 Krabi Thai.
**63** A2 Kra Buri Thai.
**63** B2 Krâchéh Cambodia
**93** E4 Kragerø Norway
**100** B1 Kraggenburg Neth.
**109** D2 Kragujevac Serb. and Mont.
**60** B2 Krakatau *i.* Indon.
**103** D1 Kraków Pol.
**109** D2 Kraljevo Serb. and Mont.
**91** D2 Kramators'k Ukr.
**93** G3 Kramfors Sweden
**111** B3 Kranidi Greece
**102** C2 Kranj Slovenia
**123** D2 Kranskop S. Africa
**86** E1 Krasino Rus. Fed.
**88** C2 Krāslava Latvia
**101** F2 Kraslice Czech Rep.
**89** D3 Krasnapollye Belarus
**89** D3 Krasnaya Gora Rus. Fed.
**89** F2 Krasnaya Gorbatka Rus. Fed.
Krasnoarmeysk Kazakh. *see*
Tayynsha
**87** D3 Krasnoarmeysk Rus. Fed.
Krasnoarmeyskaya Rus. Fed. *see*
Poltavskaya
**91** D2 Krasnoarmiys'k Ukr.
**86** D2 Krasnoborsk Rus. Fed.
**91** D2 Krasnodar Rus. Fed.
**91** D2 Krasnodon Ukr.
**88** C2 Krasnogorodskoye Rus. Fed.
**91** D1 Krasnogvardeyskoye Rus. Fed.
**91** C2 Krasnohvardiys'ke Ukr.
**86** E3 Krasnokamsk Rus. Fed.
**89** D2 Krasnomayskiy Rus. Fed.
**91** C2 Krasnoperekops'k Ukr.
**87** D3 Krasnoslobodsk Rus. Fed.
**86** F3 Krasnotur'insk Rus. Fed.
**86** E3 Krasnoufimsk Rus. Fed.
**86** E2 Krasnovishersk Rus. Fed.
Krasnovodsk Turkm. *see*
Turkmenbashi
**83** H3 Krasnoyarsk Rus. Fed.
**89** E3 Krasnoye Rus. Fed.
**83** M2 Krasnoye, Ozero *l.* Rus. Fed.
**89** F2 Krasnoye-na-Volge Rus. Fed.
**103** E1 Krasnystaw Pol.
**89** D3 Krasnyy Rus. Fed.
Krasnyy Kamyshanik Rus. Fed.
*see* Komsomol'skiy
**89** E2 Krasnyy Kholm Rus. Fed.
**91** D2 Krasnyy Luch Ukr.
**91** E2 Krasnyy Sulin Rus. Fed.
**90** B2 Krasyliv Ukr.
Kraulshavn Greenland *see*
Nuussuaq
**100** C2 Krefeld Ger.
**91** C2 Kremenchuk Ukr.
**91** C2 Kremenchuts'ka
Vodoskhovyshche *resr* Ukr.
**90** B1 Kremenets' Ukr.
**103** D1 Křemešník *hill* Czech Rep.
Kremges Ukr. *see* Svitlovods'k
**91** D2 Kreminna Ukr.
**136** B2 Kremmling U.S.A.
**103** D2 Krems an der Donau Austria
**89** D2 Kresttsy Rus. Fed.
**88** B2 Kretinga Lith.
**100** C2 Kreuzau Ger.
**101** C2 Kreuztal Ger.
**118** A2 Kribi Cameroon
**123** C2 Kriel S. Africa
**111** B3 Krikellos Greece
**66** D1 Kril'on, Mys *c.* Rus. Fed.
**111** B3 Krios, Akra *pt* Greece
**73** C3 Krishna *r.* India
**73** C3 Krishna, Mouths of the India
**75** C2 Krishnanagar India
**93** E4 Kristiansand Norway
**93** F4 Kristianstad Sweden
**92** E3 Kristiansund Norway
**93** F4 Kristinehamn Sweden
Kristinopol' Ukr. *see*
Chervonohrad
Kriti *i.* Greece *see* Crete
**110** B2 Kriva Palanka Macedonia
Krivoy Rog Ukr. *see* Kryvyy Rih
**109** C1 Križevci Croatia
**108** B1 Krk *i.* Croatia
**92** F3 Krokom Sweden
**91** C1 Krolevets' Ukr.
**89** E3 Kromy Rus. Fed.
**101** E2 Kronach Ger.
**63** B2 Krŏng Kaôh Kŏng Cambodia
**127** J2 Kronprins Frederik Bjerge
*nunataks* Greenland
**123** C3 Kroonstad S. Africa
**91** E2 Kropotkin Rus. Fed.
**103** D1 Krosno Pol.
**103** D1 Krotoszyn Pol.
**60** B2 Krui Indon.
**122** B3 Kruisfontein S. Africa
**109** C2 Krujë Albania
**111** C2 Krumovgrad Bulg.

Krung Thep Thai. *see* Bangkok
**88** C3 Krupki Belarus
**109** D2 Kruševac Serb. and Mont.
**101** E2 Krušné Hory *mts* Czech Rep.
**128** A2 Kruzof Island U.S.A.
**89** D3 Krychaw Belarus
**91** D2 Krylovskaya Rus. Fed.
**91** D3 Krymsk Rus. Fed.
Krymskaya Rus. Fed. *see*
Krymsk
Kryms'kyy Pivostriv *pen.* Ukr. *see*
Crimea
Krystynopol Ukr. *see*
Chervonohrad
**111** C3 Krytiko Pelagos *sea* Greece
**91** C2 Kryvyy Rih Ukr.
**90** B2 Kryzhopil' Ukr.
**114** B2 Ksabi Alg.
**107** D2 Ksar el Boukhari Alg.
**114** B1 Ksar el Kebir Morocco
Ksar-es-Souk Morocco *see*
Er Rachidia
**89** E3 Kshenskiy Rus. Fed.
**78** B2 Kū', Jabal al *hill* Saudi Arabia
**61** C1 Kuala Belait Brunei
Kuala Dungun Malaysia *see*
Dungun
**60** B1 Kuala Kangsar Malaysia
**60** B1 Kuala Kerai Malaysia
**60** B1 Kuala Lipis Malaysia
**60** B1 Kuala Lumpur Malaysia
**61** C2 Kualapembuang Indon.
**60** B1 Kuala Terengganu Malaysia
**60** B2 Kualatungal Indon.
**61** C1 Kuamut *Sabah* Malaysia
**65** A1 Kuandian China
**60** B1 Kuantan Malaysia
**91** D2 Kuban' *r.* Rus. Fed.
**89** E2 Kubenskoye, Ozero *l.* Rus. Fed.
**110** C2 Kubrat Bulg.
**60** B2 Kubu Indon.
**61** C1 Kubuang Indon.
**60** C1 Kuching *Sarawak* Malaysia
**109** C2 Kuçovë Albania
**61** C1 Kudat *Sabah* Malaysia
**61** C2 Kudus Indon.
**102** C2 Kufstein Austria
**127** G2 Kugaaruk Can.
**91** D2 Kugey Rus. Fed.
**126** E2 Kugluktuk Can.
**126** D2 Kugmallit Bay Can.
**92** I3 Kuhmo Fin.
**79** C2 Kührän, Küh-e *mt.* Iran
**122** A1 Kuis Namibia
Kuitin China *see* Kuytun
**120** A2 Kuito Angola
**92** I2 Kuivaniemi Fin.
**65** B2 Kujang N. Korea
**66** D2 Kuji Japan
**67** B4 Kujū-san *vol.* Japan
**109** D2 Kukës Albania
**76** B3 Kukurtli Turkm.
**111** C3 Kula Turkey
**89** G3 Kula Kangri *mt.* Bhutan
**76** B2 Kulandy Kazakh.
**88** B2 Kuldīga Latvia
Kuldja China *see* Yining
**122** B1 Kule Botswana
**101** E2 Kulmbach Ger.
**77** C3 Kŭlob Tajik.
**76** B2 Kul'sary Kazakh.
**111** D3 Kulübe Tepe *mt.* Turkey
**77** D1 Kulunda Rus. Fed.
**77** D1 Kulundinskoye, Ozero *salt l.*
Rus. Fed.
**127** J2 Kulusuk Greenland
**67** C3 Kumagaya Japan
**67** B4 Kumamoto Japan
**67** C4 Kumano Japan
**110** B2 Kumanovo Macedonia
**114** B4 Kumasi Ghana
**118** A2 Kumba Cameroon
Kum-Dag Turkm. *see* Gumdag
**78** B2 Kumdah Saudi Arabia
**87** E3 Kumertau Rus. Fed.
**65** B2 Kumi S. Korea
**119** D2 Kumi Uganda
**111** C3 Kumkale Turkey
**93** G4 Kumla Sweden
**115** D3 Kumo Nigeria
**62** A1 Kumon Range *mts* Myanmar
**62** B2 Kumphawapi Thai.
Kumul China *see* Hami
**120** A2 Kunene *r.* Angola/Namibia
**77** D2 Kungei Alatau *mts*
Kazakh./Kyrg.
**93** F4 Kungsbacka Sweden
**118** C3 Kungu Dem. Rep. Congo
**86** E3 Kungur Rus. Fed.
**62** A1 Kunhing Myanmar
**62** A1 Kunlong Myanmar
**75** B1 Kunlun Shan *mts* China
**71** A3 Kunming China
**65** B2 Kunsan S. Korea
**50** B1 Kununurra Austr.
**101** D3 Künzelsau Ger.
**92** I3 Kuopio Fin.
**109** C1 Kupa *r.* Croatia/Slovenia
**59** C3 Kupang Indon.
**88** B2 Kupiškis Lith.
**111** C2 Küplü Turkey
**128** A2 Kupreanof Island U.S.A.
**91** D2 Kup"yans'k Ukr.
**77** E2 Kuqa China
**81** C2 Kür *r.* Azer.

67 B4 **Kurashiki** Japan
75 C2 **Kurasia** India
67 B3 **Kurayoshi** Japan
89 E3 **Kurchatov** Rus. Fed.
77 E2 **Kurchum** Kazakh.
111 C2 **Kürdzhali** Bulg.
67 B4 **Kure** Japan
57 T7 **Kure Atoll** U.S.A.
88 B2 **Kuressaare** Estonia
87 F3 **Kurgan** Rus. Fed.
**Kuria Muria Islands** Oman *see* Ḥalāniyāt, Juzur al
93 H3 **Kurikka** Fin.
156 C2 **Kuril Basin** *sea feature* Sea of Okhotsk
69 F1 **Kuril Islands** *is* Rus. Fed.
69 F1 **Kuril'sk** Rus. Fed.
**Kuril'skiye Ostrova** Rus. Fed. *see* Kuril Islands
156 C3 **Kuril Trench** *sea feature* N. Pacific Ocean
89 E3 **Kurkino** Rus. Fed.
**Kurmashkino** Kazakh. *see* Kurchum
117 B3 **Kurmuk** Sudan
73 B3 **Kurnool** India
67 D3 **Kuroiso** Japan
101 E2 **Kurort Schmalkalden** Ger.
53 D2 **Kurri Kurri** Austr.
88 B2 **Kuršėnai** Lith.
78 B2 **Kursh, Jabal** *hill* Saudi Arabia
89 E3 **Kursk** Rus. Fed.
109 D2 **Kuršumlija** Serb. and Mont.
122 B2 **Kuruman** S. Africa
122 B2 **Kuruman** *watercourse* S. Africa
67 B4 **Kurume** Japan
83 I3 **Kurumkan** Rus. Fed.
73 C4 **Kurunegala** Sri Lanka
81 D1 **Kuryk** Kazakh.
111 C3 **Kuşadası** Turkey
111 C3 **Kuşadası Körfezi** *b.* Turkey
111 C2 **Kuş Gölü** *l.* Turkey
91 D2 **Kushchevskaya** Rus. Fed.
66 D2 **Kushiro** Japan
**Kushka** Turkm. *see* Gushgy
76 C1 **Kushmurun** Kazakh.
75 C2 **Kushtia** Bangl.
126 B2 **Kuskokwim** *r.* U.S.A.
126 B2 **Kuskokwim Mountains** U.S.A.
66 D2 **Kussharo-ko** *l.* Japan
**Kustanay** Kazakh. *see* Kostanay
63 B2 **Kut, Ko** *i.* Thai.
111 C3 **Kütahya** Turkey
81 C1 **K'ut'aisi** Georgia
**Kutaraja** Indon. *see* Banda Aceh
**Kutch, Gulf of** India *see* Kachchh, Gulf of
109 C2 **Kutjevo** Croatia
103 D1 **Kutno** Pol.
118 B3 **Kutu** Dem. Rep. Congo
116 A3 **Kutum** Sudan
126 E2 **Kuujjua** *r.* Can.
131 D2 **Kuujjuaq** Can.
130 C2 **Kuujjuarapik** Can.
92 I2 **Kuusamo** Fin.
120 A2 **Kuvango** Angola
89 D2 **Kuvshinovo** Rus. Fed.
78 B2 **Kuwait** *country* Asia
78 B2 **Kuwait** Kuwait
82 G3 **Kuybyshev** Rus. Fed.
**Kuybyshev** Rus. Fed. *see* Samara
91 D2 **Kuybysheve** Ukr.
**Kuybyshevka-Vostochnaya** Rus. Fed. *see* Belogorsk
87 D3 **Kuybyshevskoye Vodokhranilishche** *resr* Rus. Fed.
77 E2 **Kuytun** China
111 C3 **Kuyucak** Turkey
87 D3 **Kuznetsk** Rus. Fed.
90 B1 **Kuznetsovs'k** Ukr.
86 C2 **Kuzomen'** Rus. Fed.
92 H1 **Kvalsund** Norway
123 D2 **KwaMashu** S. Africa
61 D1 **Kwandang** Indon.
**Kwangchow** China *see* Guangzhou
65 B2 **Kwangju** S. Korea
**Kwangtung** *prov.* China *see* Guangdong
65 B1 **Kwanmo-bong** *mt.* N. Korea
123 C3 **Kwanobuhle** S. Africa
123 C3 **KwaNojoli** S. Africa
122 B3 **Kwanonzame** S. Africa
123 C3 **Kwatinidubu** S. Africa
123 C2 **KwaZamokhule** S. Africa
122 B3 **Kwazamukucinga** S. Africa
123 C2 **KwaZanele** S. Africa
123 D2 **Kwazulu-Natal** *prov.* S. Africa
**Kweichow** *prov.* China *see* Guizhou
**Kweiyang** China *see* Guiyang
121 B2 **Kwekwe** Zimbabwe
118 B3 **Kwenge** *r.* Dem. Rep. Congo
123 C3 **Kwezi-Naledi** S. Africa
103 D1 **Kwidzyn** Pol.
59 D3 **Kwikila** P.N.G.
118 B3 **Kwilu** *r.* Angola/Dem. Rep. Congo
59 C3 **Kwoka** *mt.* Indon.
118 B2 **Kyabé** Chad
53 C3 **Kyabram** Austr.
62 A2 **Kyaikto** Myanmar
63 A2 **Kya-in Seikkyi** Myanmar
68 D1 **Kyakhta** Rus. Fed.
52 B3 **Kyancutta** Austr.
62 A1 **Kyaukpadaung** Myanmar
62 A2 **Kyaukpyu** Myanmar

88 B3 **Kybartai** Lith.
62 A2 **Kyebogyi** Myanmar
54 B3 **Kyeburn** N.Z.
62 A2 **Kyeintali** Myanmar
74 B1 **Kyelang** India
**Kyiv** Ukr. *see* Kiev
**Kyklades** *is* Greece *see* Cyclades
129 D2 **Kyle** Can.
96 B2 **Kyle of Lochalsh** U.K.
100 C3 **Kyll** *r.* Ger.
111 B3 **Kyllini** *mt.* Greece
111 B3 **Kymi** Greece
52 B3 **Kyneton** Austr.
119 D2 **Kyoga, Lake** Uganda
53 D1 **Kyogle** Austr.
65 B2 **Kyŏnggi-man** *b.* S. Korea
65 B2 **Kyŏngju** S. Korea
67 C4 **Kyōto** Japan
111 B3 **Kyparissia** Greece
111 B3 **Kyparissiakos Kolpos** *b.* Greece
111 B3 **Kyra Panagia** *i.* Greece
80 B2 **Kyrenia** Cyprus
77 D2 **Kyrgyzstan** *country* Asia
101 F1 **Kyritz** Ger.
93 H3 **Kyrönjoki** *r.* Fin.
86 E2 **Kyrta** Rus. Fed.
86 D2 **Kyssa** Rus. Fed.
83 J2 **Kytalyktakh** Rus. Fed.
111 B3 **Kythira** *i.* Greece
111 B3 **Kythnos** *i.* Greece
128 B2 **Kyuquot** Can.
67 B4 **Kyūshū** *i.* Japan
110 B2 **Kyustendil** Bulg.
62 A2 **Kywebwe** Myanmar
90 C1 **Kyyivs'ke Vodoskhovyshche** *resr* Ukr.
92 H3 **Kyyjärvi** Fin.
68 C1 **Kyzyl** Rus. Fed.
76 C2 **Kyzylkum Desert** Kazakh./Uzbek.
77 C2 **Kyzylorda** Kazakh.
**Kzyl-Orda** Kazakh. *see* Kyzylorda
**Kzyltu** Kazakh. *see* Kishkenekol'

## L

145 C3 **La Angostura, Presa de** *resr* Mex.
117 C4 **Laascaanood** Somalia
117 C3 **Laasgoray** Somalia
150 C1 **La Asunción** Venez.
114 A2 **Laâyoune** Western Sahara
87 D4 **Laba** *r.* Rus. Fed.
144 B3 **La Babia** Mex.
61 D2 **Labala** Indon.
152 B2 **La Banda** Arg.
61 C1 **Labang** *Sarawak* Malaysia
104 B2 **La Baule-Escoublac** France
102 C1 **Labe** *r.* Czech Rep.
114 A3 **Labé** Guinea
128 A1 **Laberge, Lake** Can.
128 C2 **La Biche, Lac** *l.* Can.
108 B1 **Labin** Croatia
87 D4 **Labinsk** Rus. Fed.
64 B2 **Labo** Phil.
104 B3 **Labouheyre** France
153 B3 **Laboulaye** Arg.
131 D2 **Labrador** *reg.* Can.
131 D2 **Labrador City** Can.
127 I2 **Labrador Sea** Can./Greenland
150 C3 **Lábrea** Brazil
61 C1 **Labuan** Malaysia
61 D2 **Labuhanbajo** Indon.
60 B1 **Labuhanbilik** Indon.
59 C3 **Labuna** Indon.
63 A2 **Labutta** Myanmar
86 F2 **Labytnangi** Rus. Fed.
109 C2 **Laç** Albania
**La Calle** Alg. *see* El Kala
105 C2 **La Capelle** France
73 B3 **Laccadive Islands** India
129 E2 **Lac du Bonnet** Can.
146 B3 **La Ceiba** Hond.
52 A3 **Lacepede Bay** Austr.
134 B1 **La Crosse** U.S.A.
105 C2 **La Chaux-de-Fonds** Switz.
53 B2 **Lachlan** *r.* Austr.
146 C4 **La Chorrera** Panama
139 E1 **Lachute** Can.
105 D3 **La Ciotat** France
128 C2 **Lac La Biche** Can.
**La Martre** Can. *see* Wha Ti
139 E1 **Lac-Mégantic** Can.
128 C2 **Lacombe** Can.
146 B4 **La Concepción** Panama
145 C3 **La Concordia** Mex.
108 A3 **Laconi** *Sardinia* Italy
139 E2 **Laconia** U.S.A.
128 C2 **La Crete** Can.
138 A2 **La Crosse** U.S.A.
144 B2 **La Cruz** Mex.
144 B2 **La Cuesta** Mex.
155 D1 **Ladainha** Brazil
74 B1 **Ladakh Range** *mts* India
123 C3 **Ladismith** S. Africa
79 D2 **Lādīz** Iran
89 D1 **Ladoga, Lake** Rus. Fed.
**Ladozhskoye Ozero** *l.* Rus. Fed. *see* Ladoga, Lake
141 D2 **Ladson** U.S.A.
123 C3 **Lady Grey** S. Africa
128 B3 **Ladysmith** Can.
123 C2 **Ladysmith** S. Africa
59 D3 **Lae** P.N.G.

143 C3 **La Encantada, Sierra** *mts* Mex.
152 B2 **La Esmeralda** Bol.
93 F4 **Læsø** *i.* Denmark
**Lafayette** Alg. *see* Bougaa
141 C2 **La Fayette** U.S.A.
138 B2 **Lafayette** *IN* U.S.A.
140 B2 **Lafayette** *LA* U.S.A.
115 C4 **Lafia** Nigeria
104 B2 **La Flèche** France
141 D1 **La Follette** U.S.A.
130 C2 **Laforge** Can.
79 C2 **Läft** Iran
108 A3 **La Galite** *i.* Tunisia
87 D4 **Lagan'** Rus. Fed.
151 F4 **Lagarto** Brazil
118 B2 **Lagdo, Lac de** *l.* Cameroon
119 E2 **Lagh Bor** *watercourse* Kenya/Somalia
115 C1 **Laghouat** Alg.
155 D1 **Lagoa Santa** Brazil
114 A2 **La Gomera** *i.* Canary Is
114 C4 **Lagos** Nigeria
106 B2 **Lagos** Port.
134 C1 **La Grande** U.S.A.
130 C2 **La Grande 2, Réservoir** *resr* Can.
130 C2 **La Grande 3, Réservoir** *resr* Can.
130 C2 **La Grande 4, Réservoir** *resr* Can.
50 B1 **Lagrange** Austr.
141 C2 **La Grange** U.S.A.
150 C2 **La Gran Sabana** *plat.* Venez.
152 D2 **Laguna** Brazil
144 A2 **Laguna, Picacho de la** *mt.* Mex.
150 B4 **Lagunas** Peru
147 C3 **Lagunillas** Venez.
**La Habana** Cuba *see* Havana
61 C1 **Lahad Datu** *Sabah* Malaysia
60 B2 **Lahat** Indon.
78 B3 **Laḥij** Yemen
81 C2 **Lāhījān** Iran
100 C2 **Lahnstein** Ger.
74 B1 **Lahore** Pak.
74 A2 **Lahri** Pak.
93 I3 **Lahti** Fin.
115 D4 **Laï** Chad
53 D1 **Laidley** Austr.
104 C2 **L'Aigle** France
122 B3 **Laingsburg** S. Africa
92 H2 **Lainioälven** *r.* Sweden
96 B1 **Lairg** U.K.
108 B1 **Laives** Italy
70 B2 **Laiwu** China
70 C2 **Laiyang** China
70 B2 **Laiyuan** China
70 B2 **Laizhou** China
70 B2 **Laizhou Wan** *b.* China
50 C1 **Lajamanu** Austr.
152 C2 **Lajes** Brazil
136 C3 **La Junta** Mex.
136 C3 **La Junta** U.S.A.
117 B4 **Lake Abaya** *l.* Eth.
103 D2 **Lake Balaton** *l.* Hungary
53 C2 **Lake Cargelligo** Austr.
53 D2 **Lake Cathie** Austr.
140 B2 **Lake Charles** U.S.A.
141 D2 **Lake City** *FL* U.S.A.
141 E2 **Lake City** *SC* U.S.A.
128 B3 **Lake Cowichan** Can.
**Lake Harbour** Can. *see* Kimmirut
142 A2 **Lake Havasu City** U.S.A.
143 D3 **Lake Jackson** U.S.A.
50 A3 **Lake King** Austr.
141 D3 **Lakeland** U.S.A.
128 C2 **Lake Louise** Can.
134 B1 **Lake Oswego** U.S.A.
54 A2 **Lake Paringa** N.Z.
140 B2 **Lake Providence** U.S.A.
53 C3 **Lakes Entrance** Austr.
117 B4 **Lake Tana** *l.* Eth.
134 B2 **Lakeview** U.S.A.
137 E2 **Lakeville** U.S.A.
136 B3 **Lakewood** *CO* U.S.A.
139 E2 **Lakewood** *NJ* U.S.A.
141 D3 **Lake Worth** U.S.A.
74 A2 **Lakhpat** India
74 B1 **Lakki** Pak.
111 B3 **Lakonikos Kolpos** *b.* Greece
114 B4 **Lakota** Côte d'Ivoire
92 H1 **Lakselv** Norway
146 A3 **La Libertad** Guat.
106 B1 **Lalín** Spain
106 B2 **La Línea de la Concepción** Spain
74 B2 **Lalitpur** India
**Lalitpur** Nepal *see* Patan
129 D2 **La Loche** Can.
100 B2 **La Louvière** Belgium
108 A2 **La Maddalena** *Sardinia* Italy
61 C1 **Lamag** *Sabah* Malaysia
**La Manche** *str.* France/U.K. *see* English Channel
136 C3 **Lamar** U.S.A.
79 C2 **Lamard** Iran
108 A3 **La Marmora, Punta** *mt.* Sardinia Italy
128 C2 **La Martre, Lac** *l.* Can.
104 B2 **Lamballe** France
118 B3 **Lambaréné** Gabon
122 A3 **Lambert's Bay** S. Africa
92 □A2 **Lambeyri** Iceland
106 B1 **Lamego** Port.
131 D3 **Lamèque, Île** *l.* Can.
150 B4 **La Merced** Peru
52 B3 **Lameroo** Austr.
143 C2 **Lamesa** U.S.A.
111 B3 **Lamia** Greece
137 E2 **Lamoni** U.S.A.

62 A2 **Lampang** Thai.
143 D2 **Lampasas** U.S.A.
145 B2 **Lampazos** Mex.
99 A3 **Lampeter** U.K.
62 A2 **Lamphun** Thai.
119 E3 **Lamu** Kenya
105 D3 **La Mure** France
96 C3 **Lanark** U.K.
63 A2 **Lanbi Kyun** *i.* Myanmar
62 A1 **Lancang** China
**Lancang Jiang** *r.* China *see* Mekong
98 B2 **Lancaster** U.K.
135 C4 **Lancaster** *CA* U.S.A.
138 C3 **Lancaster** *OH* U.S.A.
139 D2 **Lancaster** *PA* U.S.A.
141 D2 **Lancaster** *SC* U.S.A.
127 G2 **Lancaster Sound** *str.* Can.
50 A3 **Lancelin** Austr.
**Lanchow** China *see* Lanzhou
102 C2 **Landeck** Austria
136 B2 **Lander** U.S.A.
99 A4 **Land's End** *pt* U.K.
102 C2 **Landshut** Ger.
93 F4 **Landskrona** Sweden
141 C2 **Lanett** U.S.A.
122 B3 **Langberg** *mts* S. Africa
137 D1 **Langdon** U.S.A.
93 F4 **Langeland** *i.* Denmark
101 D1 **Langen** Ger.
100 C1 **Langeoog** Ger.
100 C1 **Langeoog** *i.* Ger.
82 G2 **Langepas** Rus. Fed.
70 B2 **Langfang** China
101 D2 **Langgöns** Ger.
96 C3 **Langholm** U.K.
92 □A3 **Langjökull** *ice cap* Iceland
60 A1 **Langkawi** *i.* Malaysia
105 C3 **Langogne** France
104 B3 **Langon** France
106 B1 **Langreo** Spain
105 C2 **Langres** France
60 A1 **Langsa** Indon.
62 B1 **Lang Son** Vietnam
105 C3 **Languedoc** *reg.* France
101 D1 **Langwedel** Ger.
129 D2 **Lanigan** Can.
153 A3 **Lanín, Volcán** *vol.* Arg./Chile
81 C2 **Länkäran** Azer.
104 B2 **Lannion** France
138 B1 **L'Anse** U.S.A.
139 E1 **L'Anse-St-Jean** Can.
138 C2 **Lansing** U.S.A.
71 B3 **Lanxi** China
117 B4 **Lanya** Sudan
114 A2 **Lanzarote** *i.* Canary Is
70 A2 **Lanzhou** China
64 B2 **Laoag** Phil.
62 B1 **Lao Cai** Vietnam
70 B2 **Laohekou** China
**Laojunmiao** China *see* Yumen
65 B1 **Laoling** China
65 B1 **Lao Ling** *mts* China
105 C2 **Laon** France
62 B2 **Laos** *country* Asia
65 B1 **Laotougou** China
66 A2 **Laoye Ling** *mts* China
154 C3 **Lapa** Brazil
114 A2 **La Palma** *i.* Canary Is
146 C4 **La Palma** Panama
150 C2 **La Paragua** Venez.
152 B1 **La Paz** Bol.
145 A2 **La Paz** Mex.
144 A2 **La Paz** Mex.
150 C3 **La Pedrera** Col.
138 C2 **Lapeer** U.S.A.
66 D1 **La Pérouse Strait** Japan/Rus. Fed.
145 C2 **La Pesca** Mex.
144 B2 **La Piedad** Mex.
153 C3 **La Plata** Arg.
153 C3 **La Plata, Río de** *sea chan.* Arg./Uru.
92 H3 **Lappajärvi** *l.* Fin.
93 I3 **Lappeenranta** Fin.
92 G2 **Lappland** *reg.* Europe
111 C2 **Lâpseki** Turkey
**Laptevo** Rus. Fed. *see* Yasnogorsk
83 J1 **Laptev Sea** Rus. Fed.
**Laptevykh, More** *sea* Rus. Fed. *see* Laptev Sea
93 H3 **Lapua** Fin.
152 B3 **La Quiaca** Arg.
108 B2 **L'Aquila** Italy
135 C4 **La Quinta** U.S.A.
79 C2 **Lār** Iran
114 A1 **Larache** Morocco
136 B2 **Laramie** U.S.A.
136 B2 **Laramie Mountains** U.S.A.
154 B3 **Laranjeiras do Sul** Brazil
61 D2 **Larantuka** Indon.
59 C3 **Larat** *i.* Indon.
107 D2 **Larba** Alg.
**L'Ardenne, Plateau de** Belgium *see* Ardennes
106 C1 **Laredo** Spain
143 D3 **Laredo** U.S.A.
141 D3 **Largo** U.S.A.
96 B3 **Largs** U.K.
115 D1 **L'Ariana** Tunisia
108 A2 **La Rioja** Arg.
111 B3 **Larisa** Greece
74 A2 **Larkana** Pak.
80 B2 **Larnaca** Cyprus

**Larnaka** Cyprus see **Larnaca**
97 D1 **Larne** U.K.
100 B2 **La Roche-en-Ardenne** Belgium
104 B2 **La Rochelle** France
104 B2 **La Roche-sur-Yon** France
107 C2 **La Roda** Spain
147 D3 **La Romana** Dom. Rep.
129 D2 **La Ronge** Can.
129 D2 **La Ronge, Lac** l. Can.
50 C1 **Larrimah** Austr.
55 A3 **Larsen Ice Shelf** Antarctica
93 F4 **Larvik** Norway
136 C3 **Las Animas** U.S.A.
**Las Anod** Somalia see **Laascaanood**
130 C3 **La Sarre** Can.
142 B2 **Las Cruces** U.S.A.
152 A2 **La Serena** Chile
153 C3 **Las Flores** Arg.
153 B3 **Las Heras** Arg.
62 A1 **Lashio** Myanmar
76 B3 **Lashkar Gāh** Afgh.
109 C3 **La Sila** reg. Italy
152 B2 **Las Lomitas** Arg.
106 B2 **Las Marismas** marsh Spain
144 B2 **Las Nieves** Mex.
114 A2 **Las Palmas de Gran Canaria** Canary Is
108 A2 **La Spezia** Italy
153 C3 **Las Piedras** Uru.
153 B4 **Las Plumas** Arg.
155 D1 **Lassance** Brazil
129 D2 **Last Mountain Lake** Can.
152 B2 **Las Tórtolas, Cerro** mt. Chile
118 B3 **Lastoursville** Gabon
109 C2 **Lastovo** i. Croatia
144 A2 **Las Tres Vírgenes, Volcán** vol. Mex.
146 C1 **Las Tunas** Cuba
144 B2 **Las Varas** Mex.
144 B2 **Las Varas** Mex.
142 B1 **Las Vegas** NM U.S.A.
135 C3 **Las Vegas** NV U.S.A.
131 E2 **La Tabatière** Can.
80 B2 **Latakia** Syria
104 B3 **La Teste** France
108 B2 **Latina** Italy
147 D3 **La Tortuga, Isla** i. Venez.
64 B2 **La Trinidad** Phil.
89 E2 **Latskoye** Rus. Fed.
130 C3 **La Tuque** Can.
88 B2 **Latvia** country Europe
**Latviyskaya S.S.R.** admin. reg. Europe see **Latvia**
59 E3 **Lau** P.N.G.
102 C1 **Lauchhammer** Ger.
101 E3 **Lauf an der Pegnitz** Ger.
105 D2 **Laufen** Switz.
92 □A3 **Laugarás** Iceland
127 H1 **Lauge Koch Kyst** reg. Greenland
142 C1 **Laughlin Peak** U.S.A.
51 D4 **Launceston** Austr.
99 A4 **Launceston** U.K.
62 A1 **Launggyaung** Myanmar
153 A4 **La Unión** Chile
51 D1 **Laura** Austr.
140 C2 **Laurel** MS U.S.A.
134 E1 **Laurel** MT U.S.A.
96 C2 **Laurencekirk** U.K.
109 C2 **Lauria** Italy
141 E2 **Laurinburg** U.S.A.
105 D2 **Lausanne** Switz.
60 B1 **Laut** i. Indon.
61 C2 **Laut** i. Indon.
61 C2 **Laut Bali** Indon.
101 D2 **Laut Jawa** Indon.
101 E2 **Lautersbach (Hessen)** Ger.
60 C2 **Laut Jawa** Indon.
61 C2 **Laut Kecil, Kepulauan** is Indon.
59 C3 **Laut Maluku** Indon.
61 D2 **Laut Sawu** Indon.
59 C3 **Laut Seram** Indon.
100 C1 **Lauwersmeer** l. Neth.
139 E1 **Laval** Can.
104 B2 **Laval** France
81 D2 **Lāvar Meydān** salt marsh Iran
50 B2 **Laverton** Austr.
155 D2 **Lavras** Brazil
123 C2 **Lavumisa** Swaziland
61 C1 **Lawas** Sarawak Malaysia
78 B3 **Lawdar** Yemen
62 A1 **Lawksawk** Myanmar
114 B3 **Lawra** Ghana
138 B3 **Lawrence** IN U.S.A.
137 D3 **Lawrence** KS U.S.A.
139 E2 **Lawrence** MA U.S.A.
140 C1 **Lawrenceburg** U.S.A.
141 D2 **Lawrenceville** U.S.A.
143 D2 **Lawton** U.S.A.
78 A2 **Lawz, Jabal al** mt. Saudi Arabia
93 F4 **Laxå** Sweden
122 B2 **Laxey** S. Africa
78 B2 **Laylá** Saudi Arabia
109 D2 **Lazarevac** Serb. and Mont.
144 A1 **Lázaro Cárdenas** Mex.
144 B3 **Lázaro Cárdenas** Mex.
88 B3 **Lazdijai** Lith.
66 B2 **Lazo** Rus. Fed.
83 K2 **Lazo** Rus. Fed.
136 C2 **Lead** U.S.A.
129 D2 **Leader** Can.
136 B2 **Leadville** U.S.A.
**Leaf Bay** Can. see **Tasiujaq**
129 D2 **Leaf Rapids** Can.
143 D2 **League City** U.S.A.
143 D3 **Leakey** U.S.A.

99 C3 **Leamington Spa, Royal** U.K.
97 B2 **Leane, Lough** l. Ireland
137 E3 **Leavenworth** U.S.A.
64 B3 **Lebak** Phil.
80 B2 **Lebanon** country Asia
137 E3 **Lebanon** MO U.S.A.
139 E2 **Lebanon** NH U.S.A.
134 B2 **Lebanon** OR U.S.A.
139 D2 **Lebanon** PA U.S.A.
140 C1 **Lebanon** TN U.S.A.
89 E3 **Lebedyan'** Rus. Fed.
91 C1 **Lebedyn** Ukr.
130 C1 **Lebel-sur-Quévillon** Can.
104 C2 **Le Blanc** France
103 D1 **Lębork** Pol.
123 C1 **Lebowakgomo** S. Africa
106 B2 **Lebrija** Spain
153 A3 **Lebu** Chile
104 C3 **Le Bugue** France
109 C2 **Lecce** Italy
108 A1 **Lecco** Italy
102 C2 **Lech** r. Austria/Ger.
111 B3 **Lechaina** Greece
71 B3 **Lechang** China
102 B1 **Leck** Ger.
140 B2 **Lecompte** U.S.A.
105 C2 **Le Creusot** France
106 B1 **Ledesma** Spain
104 C2 **Le Dorat** France
128 C2 **Leduc** Can.
97 B3 **Lee** r. Ireland
137 E1 **Leech Lake** U.S.A.
98 C1 **Leeds** U.K.
99 B3 **Leek** U.K.
97 B2 **Leenane** Ireland
100 C1 **Leer (Ostfriesland)** Ger.
141 D3 **Leesburg** U.S.A.
140 B2 **Leesville** U.S.A.
53 C2 **Leeton** Austr.
122 B3 **Leeu-Gamka** S. Africa
100 B1 **Leeuwarden** Neth.
50 A3 **Leeuwin, Cape** Austr.
147 D3 **Leeward Islands** Caribbean Sea
111 B3 **Lefkada** Greece
111 B3 **Lefkada** i. Greece
**Lefkosia** Cyprus see **Nicosia**
64 B2 **Legaspi** Phil.
103 E1 **Legionowo** Pol.
108 B1 **Legnago** Italy
103 D1 **Legnica** Pol.
74 B1 **Leh** Jammu and Kashmir
104 C2 **Le Havre** France
101 E1 **Lehre** Ger.
122 B1 **Lehututu** Botswana
74 B1 **Leiah** Pak.
103 D2 **Leibnitz** Austria
99 C3 **Leicester** U.K.
51 C1 **Leichhardt** r. Austr.
51 D2 **Leichhardt Range** mts Austr.
100 B1 **Leiden** Neth.
100 A2 **Leie** r. Belgium
52 A2 **Leigh Creek** Austr.
97 C2 **Leighlinbridge** Ireland
99 C4 **Leighton Buzzard** U.K.
93 E3 **Leikanger** Norway
101 D1 **Leine** r. Ger.
50 B2 **Leinster** Austr.
97 C2 **Leinster** Ireland
97 C2 **Leinster, Mount** hill Ireland
101 F2 **Leipzig** Ger.
92 F2 **Leiranger** Norway
106 B2 **Leiria** Port.
93 E4 **Leirvik** Norway
97 C2 **Leixlip** Ireland
71 B3 **Leiyang** China
71 B3 **Leizhou** China
71 A3 **Leizhou Bandao** pen. China
118 B3 **Lékana** Congo
122 A2 **Lekkersing** S. Africa
140 B2 **Leland** U.S.A.
**Leli** China see **Tianlin**
100 B1 **Lelystad** Neth.
153 B5 **Le Maire, Estrecho de** sea chan. Arg.
**Léman, Lac** France/Switz. see **Geneva, Lake**
104 C2 **Le Mans** France
137 D2 **Le Mars** U.S.A.
102 B2 **Lemberg** hill Ger.
154 C2 **Leme** Brazil
**Lemesos** Cyprus see **Limassol**
101 D1 **Lemförde** Ger.
127 H2 **Lemieux Islands** Can.
136 C1 **Lemmon** U.S.A.
135 C3 **Lemoore** U.S.A.
131 D2 **Le Moyne, Lac** l. Can.
62 A1 **Lemro** r. Myanmar
109 C2 **Le Murge** hills Italy
83 J2 **Lena** r. Rus. Fed.
100 C1 **Lengerich** Ger.
70 A2 **Lenglong Ling** mts China
71 B3 **Lengshuijiang** China
71 B3 **Lengshuitan** China
**Leninabad** Tajik. see **Khŭjand**
**Leninakan** Armenia see **Gyumri**
91 D2 **Lenine** Ukr.
**Leningrad** Rus. Fed. see **St Petersburg**
91 D2 **Leningradskaya** Rus. Fed.
**Leninobod** Tajik. see **Khŭjand**
77 D3 **Leninogorsk** Kazakh.
**Lenin Peak** Kyrg./Tajik. see **Lenin Peak**
**Leninsk** Kazakh. see **Baykonyr**
89 E3 **Leninskiy** Rus. Fed.

53 D1 **Lennox Head** Austr.
141 D1 **Lenoir** U.S.A.
100 A2 **Lens** Belgium
105 C1 **Lens** France
83 I2 **Lensk** Rus. Fed.
103 D2 **Lenti** Hungary
109 C3 **Lentini** Sicily Italy
114 B3 **Léo** Burkina
103 D2 **Leoben** Austria
99 B3 **Leominster** U.K.
144 B2 **León** Mex.
146 B3 **León** Nic.
106 B1 **León** Spain
122 A1 **Leonardville** Namibia
108 B3 **Leonforte** Sicily Italy
53 C3 **Leongatha** Austr.
50 B2 **Leonora** Austr.
**Léopold II, Lac** l. Dem. Rep. Congo see **Mai-Ndombe, Lac**
155 D2 **Leopoldina** Brazil
**Léopoldville** Dem. Rep. Congo see **Kinshasa**
90 B2 **Leova** Moldova
**Leovo** Moldova see **Leova**
123 C1 **Lephalale** S. Africa
123 C1 **Lephepe** Botswana
123 C3 **Lephoi** S. Africa
71 B3 **Leping** China
77 D2 **Lepsy** Kazakh.
105 C2 **Le Puy-en-Velay** France
123 C1 **Lerala** Botswana
123 C2 **Leratswana** S. Africa
150 B3 **Lérida** Col.
**Lérida** Spain see **Lleida**
106 C1 **Lerma** Spain
111 C3 **Leros** i. Greece
130 C2 **Le Roy, Lac** l. Can.
93 F4 **Lerum** Sweden
96 □ **Lerwick** U.K.
111 C3 **Lesbos** i. Greece
147 C3 **Les Cayes** Haiti
104 C3 **Les Escaldes** Andorra
139 F1 **Les Escoumins** Can.
107 D1 **Le Seu d'Urgell** Spain
70 A3 **Leshan** China
104 B2 **Les Herbiers** France
86 D2 **Leshukonskoye** Rus. Fed.
**Leskhimstroy** Ukr. see **Syeverodonets'k**
109 D2 **Leskovac** Serb. and Mont.
104 B2 **Lesneven** France
**Lesnoy** Rus. Fed. see **Umba**
89 E2 **Lesnoye** Rus. Fed.
83 H3 **Lesosibirsk** Rus. Fed.
123 C2 **Lesotho** country Africa
66 B1 **Lesozavodsk** Rus. Fed.
104 B2 **Les Sables-d'Olonne** France
147 D3 **Lesser Antilles** is Caribbean Sea
81 C1 **Lesser Caucasus** mts Asia
**Lesser Khingan Mountains** China see **Xiao Hinggan Ling**
128 C2 **Lesser Slave Lake** Can.
105 C3 **Les Vans** France
**Lesvos** i. Greece see **Lesbos**
103 D1 **Leszno** Pol.
123 D1 **Letaba** S. Africa
99 C4 **Letchworth** U.K.
128 C3 **Lethbridge** Can.
150 D2 **Lethem** Guyana
59 C3 **Leti, Kepulauan** is Indon.
150 C3 **Leticia** Col.
120 B3 **Letlhakane** Botswana
123 C1 **Letlhakeng** Botswana
104 C1 **Le Touquet-Paris-Plage** France
99 D4 **Le Tréport** France
123 D1 **Letsitele** S. Africa
63 A2 **Letsok-aw Kyun** i. Myanmar
123 C2 **Letsopa** S. Africa
97 C1 **Letterkenny** Ireland
105 C3 **Leucate, Étang de** l. France
**Leukas** Greece see **Lefkada**
60 A1 **Leuser, Gunung** mt. Indon.
100 B2 **Leuven** Belgium
111 B3 **Levadeia** Greece
92 F3 **Levanger** Norway
143 C2 **Levelland** U.S.A.
50 B1 **Lévêque, Cape** Austr.
96 A2 **Leverburgh** U.K.
100 C2 **Leverkusen** Ger.
103 D2 **Levice** Slovakia
54 C2 **Levin** N.Z.
131 C3 **Lévis** Can.
139 E2 **Levittown** U.S.A.
89 E3 **Lev Tolstoy** Rus. Fed.
99 D4 **Lewes** U.K.
96 A1 **Lewis, Isle of** i. U.K.
139 D2 **Lewisburg** PA U.S.A.
140 C1 **Lewisburg** TN U.S.A.
138 C3 **Lewisburg** WV U.S.A.
134 C1 **Lewis Range** mts U.S.A.
134 C1 **Lewiston** ID U.S.A.
139 F2 **Lewiston** ME U.S.A.
134 E1 **Lewistown** U.S.A.
138 C3 **Lexington** KY U.S.A.
137 D2 **Lexington** NE U.S.A.
143 D1 **Lexington** OK U.S.A.
139 D3 **Lexington** VA U.S.A.
64 B2 **Leyte** i. Phil.
109 C2 **Lezhë** Albania
89 F2 **Lezhnevo** Rus. Fed.
89 E3 **L'gov** Rus. Fed.
75 C2 **Lhagoi Kangri** mt. China

75 D1 **Lharigarbo** China
75 D2 **Lhasa** China
75 C2 **Lhazê** China
60 A1 **Lhokseumawe** Indon.
67 B3 **Lhûnzê** China see **Xingba**
**Liancourt Rocks** i. N. Pacific Ocean
**Liangzhou** China see **Wuwei**
70 B2 **Liangzi Hu** l. China
**Lianhe** China see **Qianjiang**
71 B3 **Lianhua** China
71 B3 **Lianjiang** China
**Lianran** China see **Anning**
70 C1 **Lianshan** China
**Liantang** China see **Nanchang**
**Lianxian** China see **Lianzhou**
70 B2 **Lianyungang** China
71 B3 **Lianzhou** China
**Lianzhou** China see **Hepu**
70 C2 **Liaocheng** China
70 C1 **Liaodong Bandao** pen. China
70 C1 **Liaodong Wan** b. China
65 A1 **Liao He** r. China
70 C1 **Liaoning** prov. China
70 C1 **Liaoyang** China
65 B1 **Liaoyuan** China
128 B1 **Liard** r. Can.
134 C1 **Libby** U.S.A.
118 B2 **Libenge** Dem. Rep. Congo
136 C3 **Liberal** U.S.A.
103 D1 **Liberec** Czech Rep.
114 B4 **Liberia** country Africa
146 B3 **Liberia** Costa Rica
150 C2 **Libertad** Venez.
137 E3 **Liberty** U.S.A.
100 B3 **Libin** Belgium
64 B2 **Libmanan** Phil.
71 A3 **Libo** China
123 C3 **Libode** S. Africa
119 E2 **Liboi** Kenya
104 B3 **Libourne** France
100 B3 **Libramont** Belgium
142 A3 **Libre, Sierra** mts Mex.
118 A2 **Libreville** Gabon
115 D2 **Libya** country Africa
115 E2 **Libyan Desert** Egypt/Libya
116 A1 **Libyan Plateau** Egypt
108 B3 **Licata** Sicily Italy
**Licheng** China see **Lipu**
99 C3 **Lichfield** U.K.
121 C2 **Lichinga** Moz.
101 E2 **Lichte** Ger.
123 C2 **Lichtenburg** S. Africa
101 E2 **Lichtenfels** Ger.
88 C3 **Lida** Belarus
93 F4 **Lidköping** Sweden
50 C2 **Liebig, Mount** Austr.
105 D2 **Liechtenstein** country Europe
100 B2 **Liège** Belgium
92 J3 **Lieksa** Fin.
119 C2 **Lienart** Dem. Rep. Congo
102 C2 **Lienz** Austria
88 B2 **Liepāja** Latvia
100 B2 **Lier** Belgium
102 C2 **Liezen** Austria
97 C2 **Liffey** r. Ireland
97 C1 **Lifford** Ireland
53 C1 **Lightning Ridge** Austr.
121 C2 **Ligonha** r. Moz.
105 D3 **Ligurian Sea** France/Italy
119 C4 **Likasi** Dem. Rep. Congo
118 C2 **Likati** Dem. Rep. Congo
128 C2 **Likely** Can.
**Likhachevo** Ukr. see **Pervomays'kyy**
**Likhachyovo** Ukr. see **Pervomays'kyy**
89 E2 **Likhoslavl'** Rus. Fed.
60 B1 **Liku** Indon.
105 D3 **L'Île-Rousse** Corsica France
71 B3 **Liling** China
93 F4 **Lilla Edet** Sweden
100 B2 **Lille** Belgium
105 C1 **Lille** France
**Lille Bælt** sea chan. Denmark see **Little Belt**
93 F3 **Lillehammer** Norway
93 F4 **Lillestrøm** Norway
128 B2 **Lillooet** Can.
121 C2 **Lilongwe** Malawi
64 B3 **Liloy** Phil.
150 B4 **Lima** Peru
138 C2 **Lima** U.S.A.
155 D2 **Lima Duarte** Brazil
79 C2 **Limah** Oman
80 B2 **Limassol** Cyprus
97 C1 **Limavady** U.K.
153 B3 **Limay** r. Arg.
101 F2 **Limbach-Oberfrohna** Ger.
88 B2 **Limbaži** Latvia
118 A2 **Limbe** Cameroon
101 D2 **Limburg an der Lahn** Ger.
122 B2 **Lime Acres** S. Africa
154 C2 **Limeira** Brazil
97 B2 **Limerick** Ireland
93 E4 **Limfjorden** sea chan. Denmark
92 I3 **Liminka** Fin.
111 C3 **Limnos** i. Greece
104 C2 **Limoges** France
136 C3 **Limon** U.S.A.
104 C2 **Limousin, Plateaux du** France
104 C3 **Limoux** France
123 C1 **Limpopo** prov. S. Africa
121 C3 **Limpopo** r. S. Africa/Zimbabwe
64 A2 **Linapacan** i. Phil.

153 A3 **Linares** Chile
145 C2 **Linares** Mex.
106 C2 **Linares** Spain
108 A3 **Linas, Monte** *mt. Sardinia* Italy
62 B1 **Lincang** China
**Linchuan** China *see* Fuzhou
98 C3 **Lincoln** U.K.
138 B2 **Lincoln** *IL* U.S.A.
139 F1 **Lincoln** *ME* U.S.A.
137 D2 **Lincoln** *NE* U.S.A.
134 B2 **Lincoln City** U.S.A.
151 D2 **Linden** Guyana
140 C1 **Linden** U.S.A.
119 C2 **Lindi** *r.* Dem. Rep. Congo
119 D3 **Lindi** Tanz.
**Lindisfarne** *i.* U.K. *see* Holy Island
111 C3 **Lindos** Greece
130 C3 **Lindsay** Can.
48 K3 **Line Islands** Kiribati
70 B2 **Linfen** China
64 B2 **Lingayen** Phil.
70 B2 **Lingbao** China
**Lingcheng** China *see* Lingshan
**Lingcheng** China *see* Lingshui
123 C3 **Lingelethu** S. Africa
123 C3 **Lingelihle** S. Africa
100 C1 **Lingen (Ems)** Ger.
60 B2 **Lingga** *i.* Indon.
60 B2 **Lingga, Kepulauan** *is* Indon.
71 A3 **Lingshan** China
71 A4 **Lingshui** China
114 A3 **Linguère** Senegal
155 D1 **Linhares** Brazil
70 A1 **Linhe** China
**Linjiang** China *see* Shanghang
65 B1 **Linjiang** China
93 G4 **Linköping** Sweden
66 B1 **Linkou** China
71 B3 **Linli** China
96 B2 **Linnhe, Loch** *inlet* U.K.
70 B2 **Linqing** China
154 C2 **Lins** Brazil
136 C1 **Linton** U.S.A.
69 D2 **Linxi** China
70 A2 **Linxia** China
70 B2 **Linyi** *Shandong* China
70 B2 **Linyi** *Shandong* China
70 B2 **Linying** China
102 C2 **Linz** Austria
90 A1 **Lioboml'** Ukr.
105 C3 **Lion, Golfe du** *g.* France
**Lions, Gulf of** France *see*
Lion, Golfe du
109 B3 **Lipari** Italy
108 B3 **Lipari, Isole** *is* Italy
89 E3 **Lipetsk** Rus. Fed.
110 B1 **Lipova** Romania
101 D2 **Lippstadt** Ger.
53 C2 **Liptrap, Cape** Austr.
71 B3 **Lipu** China
119 C2 **Lira** Uganda
108 B2 **Liri** *r.* Italy
76 C1 **Lisakovsk** Kazakh.
118 C2 **Lisala** Dem. Rep. Congo
**Lisboa** Port. *see* Lisbon
106 B2 **Lisbon** Port.
97 C1 **Lisburn** U.K.
97 B2 **Liscannor Bay** Ireland
97 B2 **Lisdoonvarna** Ireland
71 B3 **Lishui** China
104 C2 **Lisieux** France
99 A4 **Liskeard** U.K.
89 E3 **Liski** Rus. Fed.
53 D1 **Lismore** Austr.
97 C2 **Lismore** Ireland
97 C1 **Lisnaskea** U.K.
97 B2 **Listowel** Ireland
71 A3 **Litang** *Guangxi* China
68 C2 **Litang** *Sichuan* China
138 B3 **Litchfield** *IL* U.S.A.
137 E1 **Litchfield** *MN* U.S.A.
53 D2 **Lithgow** Austr.
111 B3 **Lithino, Akra** *pt* Greece
88 B2 **Lithuania** *country* Europe
111 B2 **Litochoro** Greece
102 C1 **Litoměřice** Czech Rep.
**Litovskaya S.S.R.** *admin. reg.*
Europe *see* Lithuania
146 C2 **Little Abaco** *i.* Bahamas
73 D3 **Little Andaman** *i.* India
141 E3 **Little Bahama Bank** *sea feature*
Bahamas
93 E4 **Little Belt** *sea chan.* Denmark
146 B3 **Little Cayman** *i.* Cayman Is
142 A1 **Little Colorado** *r.* U.S.A.
138 C1 **Little Current** U.S.A.
137 E1 **Little Falls** U.S.A.
143 C2 **Littlefield** U.S.A.
99 C4 **Littlehampton** U.K.
122 A2 **Little Karas Berg** *plat.* Namibia
122 B3 **Little Karoo** *plat.* S. Africa
96 A2 **Little Minch** *sea chan.* U.K.
136 C1 **Little Missouri** *r.* U.S.A.
73 D4 **Little Nicobar** *i.* India
140 B2 **Little Rock** U.S.A.
139 E2 **Littleton** U.S.A.
121 C2 **Litunde** Moz.
90 B2 **Lityn** Ukr.
**Liuchow** China *see* Liuzhou
70 B2 **Liujiachang** China
**Liupanshui** China *see* Lupanshui
121 C2 **Liupo** Moz.
71 A3 **Liuzhou** China
88 C2 **Līvāni** Latvia

141 D2 **Live Oak** U.S.A.
50 B1 **Liveringa** Austr.
142 C2 **Livermore, Mount** U.S.A.
53 D2 **Liverpool** Can.
131 D3 **Liverpool** Can.
98 B3 **Liverpool** U.K.
127 G2 **Liverpool, Cape** Can.
53 C2 **Liverpool Range** *mts* Austr.
96 C3 **Livingston** U.K.
134 D1 **Livingston** *MT* U.S.A.
143 E2 **Livingston** *TX* U.S.A.
143 D3 **Livingston, Lake** U.S.A.
120 B2 **Livingstone** Zambia
55 A3 **Livingston Island** Antarctica
109 C2 **Livno** Bos.-Herz.
89 E3 **Livny** Rus. Fed.
138 C2 **Livonia** U.S.A.
108 B2 **Livorno** Italy
119 D3 **Liwale** Tanz.
99 A5 **Lizard Point** U.K.
108 B1 **Ljubljana** Slovenia
93 G3 **Ljungan** *r.* Sweden
93 F4 **Ljungby** Sweden
93 G3 **Ljusdal** Sweden
93 G3 **Ljusnan** *r.* Sweden
99 B4 **Llandeilo** U.K.
99 B4 **Llandovery** U.K.
99 B4 **Llandrindod Wells** U.K.
98 B3 **Llandudno** U.K.
99 A4 **Llanelli** U.K.
106 C1 **Llanes** Spain
98 A3 **Llangefni** U.K.
99 B3 **Llangollen** U.K.
99 B3 **Llangurig** U.K.
143 C2 **Llano Estacado** *plain* U.S.A.
150 C2 **Llanos** *reg.* Col./Venez.
107 D1 **Lleida** Spain
99 A3 **Lleyn Peninsula** U.K.
107 C2 **Lliria** Spain
106 C1 **Llodio** Spain
128 B2 **Lloyd George, Mount** Can.
129 D2 **Lloyd Lake** Can.
129 C2 **Lloydminster** Can.
152 B2 **Llullaillaco, Volcán** *vol.* Chile
154 B2 **Loanda** Brazil
123 C2 **Lobatse** Botswana
103 D1 **Łobez** Pol.
120 A2 **Lobito** Angola
101 F1 **Loburg** Ger.
96 B2 **Lochaber** *mts* U.K.
96 B2 **Lochaline** U.K.
96 A1 **Loch a' Tuath** U.K.
**Loch Baghasdail** U.K. *see*
Lochboisdale
96 A2 **Lochboisdale** U.K.
104 C2 **Loches** France
96 B2 **Lochgilphead** U.K.
96 A2 **Lochinver** U.K.
96 A2 **Lochmaddy** U.K.
96 C2 **Lochnagar** *mt.* U.K.
**Loch nam Madadh** U.K. *see*
Lochmaddy
96 B3 **Lochranza** U.K.
52 A2 **Lock** Austr.
96 C3 **Lockerbie** U.K.
53 C3 **Lockhart** Austr.
143 D3 **Lockhart** U.S.A.
51 D1 **Lockhart River** Austr.
139 D2 **Lock Haven** U.S.A.
139 D2 **Lockport** U.S.A.
63 B2 **Lộc Ninh** Vietnam
105 C3 **Lodève** France
86 C2 **Lodeynoye Pole** Rus. Fed.
74 B2 **Lodhran** Pak.
108 A1 **Lodi** Italy
135 B3 **Lodi** U.S.A.
92 G2 **Loding** Norway
92 G2 **Lødingen** Norway
118 C3 **Lodja** Dem. Rep. Congo
119 D2 **Lodwar** Kenya
103 D1 **Łódź** Pol.
62 B2 **Loei** Thai.
122 A3 **Loeriesfontein** S. Africa
92 F2 **Lofoten** *is* Norway
134 D2 **Logan** U.S.A.
128 A1 **Logan, Mount** Can.
138 B2 **Logansport** U.S.A.
108 B1 **Logatec** Slovenia
115 D3 **Logone** *r.* Africa
106 C1 **Logroño** Spain
93 H3 **Lohja** Fin.
101 D1 **Löhne** Ger.
101 D1 **Lohne (Oldenburg)** Ger.
62 A2 **Loikaw** Myanmar
62 A2 **Loi Lan** *mt.* Myanmar/Thai.
93 H3 **Loimaa** Fin.
104 B2 **Loire** *r.* France
150 B2 **Loja** Ecuador
106 C2 **Loja** Spain
92 I2 **Lokan tekojärvi** *l.* Fin.
100 B2 **Lokeren** Belgium
122 B1 **Lokgwabe** Botswana
91 C1 **Lokhvytsya** Ukr.
119 D2 **Lokichar** Kenya
119 D2 **Lokichokio** Kenya
93 E4 **Løkken** Denmark
89 D2 **Loknya** Rus. Fed.
115 C4 **Lokoja** Nigeria
89 D3 **Lokot'** Rus. Fed.
88 C2 **Loksa** Estonia
127 H2 **Loks Land** *i.* Can.
114 B4 **Lola** Guinea
93 F5 **Lolland** *i.* Denmark
119 D3 **Lollondo** Tanz.
118 C2 **Lolo** Dem. Rep. Congo

122 B2 **Lolwane** S. Africa
110 B2 **Lom** Bulg.
93 E3 **Lom** Norway
119 C2 **Lomami** *r.* Dem. Rep. Congo
153 C4 **Lomas de Zamora** Arg.
50 B1 **Lombardina** Austr.
61 C2 **Lombok** *i.* Indon.
61 C2 **Lombok, Selat** *sea chan.* Indon.
114 C4 **Lomé** Togo
118 C3 **Lomela** *r.* Dem. Rep. Congo
100 B2 **Lommel** Belgium
96 B2 **Lomond, Loch** *l.* U.K.
88 C2 **Lomonosov** Rus. Fed.
160 A1 **Lomonosov Ridge** *sea feature*
Arctic Ocean
61 C2 **Lompobattang, Gunung** *mt.*
Indon.
135 B4 **Lompoc** U.S.A.
63 B2 **Lom Sak** Thai.
103 E1 **Łomża** Pol.
130 B3 **London** Can.
99 C4 **London** U.K.
138 C3 **London** U.S.A.
97 C1 **Londonderry** U.K.
50 B1 **Londonderry, Cape** Austr.
154 B2 **Londrina** Brazil
135 C3 **Lone Pine** U.S.A.
83 M2 **Longa, Proliv** *sea chan.* Rus. Fed.
61 C1 **Long Akah** *Sarawak* Malaysia
141 E2 **Long Bay** U.S.A.
135 C4 **Long Beach** U.S.A.
71 A3 **Longchang** China
99 C3 **Long Eaton** U.K.
97 C2 **Longford** Ireland
96 C1 **Longhope** U.K.
119 D3 **Longido** Tanz.
61 C2 **Longiram** Indon.
147 C3 **Long Island** Bahamas
130 C2 **Long Island** Can.
59 D3 **Long Island** P.N.G.
139 E2 **Long Island** U.S.A.
130 B3 **Longlac** Can.
130 B3 **Long Lake** Can.
71 A3 **Longli** China
71 A3 **Longming** China
136 B2 **Longmont** U.S.A.
**Longping** China *see* Luodian
138 C2 **Long Point** Can.
71 B3 **Longquan** China
131 E3 **Long Range Mountains** Can.
51 D2 **Longreach** Austr.
**Longshan** China *see* Longli
99 C3 **Long Stratton** U.K.
98 B2 **Longtown** U.K.
105 D2 **Longuyon** France
143 E2 **Longview** *TX* U.S.A.
134 B1 **Longview** *WA* U.S.A.
61 C1 **Longwai** Indon.
70 A2 **Longxi** China
**Longxian** China *see* Wengyuan
71 B3 **Longxi Shan** *mt.* China
63 B2 **Long Xuyên** Vietnam
71 B3 **Longyan** China
82 C1 **Longyearbyen** Svalbard
108 B1 **Lonigo** Italy
100 C1 **Löningen** Ger.
105 D2 **Lons-le-Saunier** France
141 E2 **Lookout, Cape** U.S.A.
119 D3 **Loolmalasin** *vol. crater* Tanz.
50 B2 **Loongana** Austr.
97 B2 **Loop Head** *hd* Ireland
63 B2 **Lop Buri** Thai.
64 B2 **Lopez** Phil.
118 A3 **Lopez, Cap** *c.* Gabon
68 C2 **Lop Nur** *salt l.* China
118 B2 **Lopori** *r.* Dem. Rep. Congo
92 H1 **Lopphavet** *b.* Norway
106 B2 **Lora del Río** Spain
138 C2 **Lorain** U.S.A.
74 A2 **Loralai** Pak.
107 C2 **Lorca** Spain
51 E3 **Lord Howe Island** Austr.
142 B2 **Lordsburg** U.S.A.
155 C2 **Lorena** Brazil
59 D3 **Lorengau** P.N.G.
59 C3 **Lorentz** *r.* Indon.
152 B1 **Loreto** Bol.
144 A2 **Loreto** Mex.
104 B2 **Lorient** France
96 B2 **Lorn, Firth of** *est.* U.K.
52 B3 **Lorne** Austr.
105 D2 **Lorraine** *reg.* France
142 B1 **Los Alamos** U.S.A.
143 D3 **Los Aldamas** Mex.
153 A3 **Los Ángeles** Chile
135 C4 **Los Angeles** U.S.A.
135 B3 **Los Banos** U.S.A.
152 B2 **Los Blancos** Arg.
89 F3 **Losevo** Rus. Fed.
108 B2 **Lošinj** *i.* Croatia
144 B2 **Los Mochis** Mex.
118 B2 **Losombo** Dem. Rep. Congo
106 B2 **Los Pedroches** *plat.* Spain
147 D3 **Los Roques, Islas** *is* Venez.
96 C2 **Lossiemouth** U.K.
150 C1 **Los Teques** Venez.
59 E3 **Losuia** P.N.G.
152 A3 **Los Vilos** Chile
104 C3 **Lot** *r.* France
96 C1 **Loth** U.K.
134 D1 **Lothair** U.S.A.
**Lothringen** *reg.* France *see*
Lorraine
119 D2 **Lotikipi Plain** Kenya

118 C3 **Loto** Dem. Rep. Congo
89 E2 **Lotoshino** Rus. Fed.
62 B1 **Louangnamtha** Laos
62 B2 **Louangphabang** Laos
118 B3 **Loubomo** Congo
104 B2 **Loudéac** France
71 B3 **Loudi** China
118 B3 **Loudima** Congo
114 A3 **Louga** Senegal
99 C2 **Loughborough** U.K.
97 B2 **Loughrea** Ireland
105 D2 **Louhans** France
97 B2 **Louisburgh** Ireland
51 E1 **Louisiade Archipelago** *is* P.N.G.
140 B2 **Louisiana** *state* U.S.A.
123 C1 **Louis Trichardt** S. Africa
138 B3 **Louisville** *KY* U.S.A.
140 C2 **Louisville** *MS* U.S.A.
86 C2 **Loukhi** Rus. Fed.
118 B3 **Loukoléla** Congo
106 B2 **Loulé** Port.
118 A2 **Loum** Cameroon
130 C2 **Loups Marins, Lacs des** *lakes*
Can.
104 B3 **Lourdes** France
151 C2 **Lourenço** Brazil
**Lourenço Marques** Moz. *see*
Maputo
106 B1 **Lousã** Port.
53 C2 **Louth** Austr.
98 C3 **Louth** U.K.
**Louvain** Belgium *see* Leuven
122 A1 **Louwater-Suid** Namibia
89 D2 **Lovat'** *r.* Rus. Fed.
110 B2 **Lovech** Bulg.
136 B2 **Loveland** U.S.A.
136 B2 **Lovell** U.S.A.
135 C2 **Lovelock** U.S.A.
88 C1 **Loviisa** Fin.
143 C2 **Lovington** U.S.A.
86 C2 **Lovozero** Rus. Fed.
119 C3 **Lowa** Dem. Rep. Congo
139 E2 **Lowell** U.S.A.
119 D2 **Lowelli** Sudan
128 C3 **Lower Arrow Lake** Can.
**Lower California** *pen.* Mex. *see*
Baja California
54 B2 **Lower Hutt** N.Z.
97 C1 **Lower Lough Erne** *l.* U.K.
128 B2 **Lower Post** Can.
137 E1 **Lower Red Lake** U.S.A.
**Lower Tunguska** *r.* Rus. Fed. *see*
Nizhnyaya Tunguska
99 D3 **Lowestoft** U.K.
103 D1 **Łowicz** Pol.
139 D2 **Lowville** U.S.A.
52 B2 **Loxton** Austr.
**Loyang** China *see* Luoyang
48 H6 **Loyauté, Îles** New Caledonia
89 D3 **Loyew** Belarus
92 F2 **Leypskardtinden** *mt.* Norway
109 C2 **Loznica** Serb. and Mont.
91 D2 **Lozova** Ukr.
120 B2 **Luacano** Angola
70 B2 **Lu'an** China
120 A1 **Luanda** Angola
63 B3 **Luang, Thale** *lag.* Thai.
121 C2 **Luangwa** *r.* Zambia
121 C2 **Luanshya** Zambia
**Luao** Angola *see* Luau
106 B1 **Luarca** Spain
120 B2 **Luau** Angola
103 C1 **Lubaczów** Pol.
103 D1 **Lubań** Pol.
64 A2 **Lubang Islands** Phil.
120 A2 **Lubango** Angola
119 C3 **Lubao** Dem. Rep. Congo
103 E1 **Lubartów** Pol.
101 D1 **Lübbecke** Ger.
102 C1 **Lübben** Ger.
143 C2 **Lubbock** U.S.A.
101 E1 **Lübeck** Ger.
69 E2 **Lubei** China
76 B1 **Lubenka** Kazakh.
119 C3 **Lubero** Dem. Rep. Congo
103 D1 **Lubin** Pol.
103 E1 **Lublin** Pol.
91 C1 **Lubny** Ukr.
61 C1 **Lubok Antu** *Sarawak* Malaysia
101 E1 **Lübow** Ger.
101 E1 **Lübtheen** Ger.
119 C3 **Lubudi** Dem. Rep. Congo
60 B2 **Lubuklinggau** Indon.
119 C4 **Lubumbashi** Dem. Rep. Congo
120 B2 **Lubungu** Zambia
119 C3 **Lubutu** Dem. Rep. Congo
120 A1 **Lucala** Angola
97 C2 **Lucan** Ireland
120 B1 **Lucapa** Angola
108 B2 **Lucca** Italy
96 B3 **Luce Bay** U.K.
154 B2 **Lucélia** Brazil
64 B1 **Lucena** Phil.
106 C2 **Lucena** Spain
103 D2 **Lučenec** Slovakia
109 C2 **Lucera** Italy
105 D2 **Lucerne** Switz.
66 B1 **Luchegorsk** Rus. Fed.
101 E1 **Lüchow** Ger.
120 A1 **Lucira** Angola
**Łuck** Ukr. *see* Luts'k
101 F1 **Luckenwalde** Ger.
122 B2 **Luckhoff** S. Africa
75 C2 **Lucknow** India
120 A1 **Lucunga** Angola

Lucusse

194

120 B2 Lucusse Angola
Lüda China see Dalian
100 C2 Lüdenscheid Ger.
101 E1 Lüder Ger.
120 A3 Lüderitz Namibia
119 D4 Ludewa Tanz.
74 B1 Ludhiana India
138 B2 Ludington U.S.A.
99 B3 Ludlow U.K.
135 C4 Ludlow U.S.A.
110 C2 Ludogorie reg. Bulg.
93 G3 Ludvika Sweden
102 B2 Ludwigsburg Ger.
101 F1 Ludwigsfelde Ger.
101 D3 Ludwigshafen am Rhein Ger.
101 E1 Ludwigslust Ger.
88 C2 Ludza Latvia
118 C3 Luebo Dem. Rep. Congo
120 A2 Luena Angola
70 A2 Lüeyang China
71 B3 Lufeng China
119 C3 Lufira r. Dem. Rep. Congo
143 E2 Lufkin U.S.A.
88 C2 Luga Rus. Fed.
88 C2 Luga r. Rus. Fed.
105 D2 Lugano Switz.
121 C2 Lugenda r. Moz.
106 B1 Lugo Spain
110 B1 Lugoj Romania
91 D2 Luhans'k Ukr.
119 D3 Luhombero Tanz.
90 B1 Luhyny Ukr.
120 B2 Luiana Angola
Luichow Peninsula China see Leizhou Bandao
118 C3 Luilaka r. Dem. Rep. Congo
Luimneach Ireland see Limerick
105 D2 Luino Italy
92 I2 Luiro r. Fin.
118 C3 Luiza Dem. Rep. Congo
70 B2 Lujiang China
Lukapa Angola see Lucapa
109 C2 Lukavac Bos.-Herz.
118 B3 Lukenie r. Dem. Rep. Congo
142 A2 Lukeville U.S.A.
89 E3 Lukhovitsy Rus. Fed.
Lukou China see Zhuzhou
103 E1 Łuków Pol.
120 B2 Lukulu Zambia
92 H2 Luleå Sweden
92 H2 Luleälven r. Sweden
111 C2 Lüleburgaz Turkey
70 B2 Lüliang Shan mts China
143 D3 Luling U.S.A.
Luluabourg Dem. Rep. Congo see Kananga
61 C2 Lumajang Indon.
75 C1 Lumajangdong Co salt l. China
Lumbala Angola see Lumbala Kaquengue
Lumbala Angola see Lumbala N'guimbo
120 B2 Lumbala Kaquengue Angola
120 B2 Lumbala N'guimbo Angola
140 C2 Lumberton MS U.S.A.
141 E2 Lumberton NC U.S.A.
61 C1 Lumbis Indon.
106 B1 Lumbrales Spain
63 B2 Lumphăt Cambodia
129 D2 Lumsden Can.
54 A3 Lumsden N.Z.
93 F4 Lund Sweden
121 C2 Lundazi Zambia
99 A4 Lundy U.K.
101 E1 Lüneburg Ger.
101 E1 Lüneburger Heide reg. Ger.
100 C2 Lünen Ger.
105 D2 Lunéville France
120 B2 Lunga r. Zambia
114 A4 Lungi Sierra Leone
Lungleh India see Lunglei
75 D2 Lunglei India
97 C2 Lungnaquilla Mountain hill Ireland
120 B2 Lungwebungu r. Zambia
74 B2 Luni r. India
88 C3 Luninyets Belarus
104 C3 L'Union France
114 A4 Lunsar Sierra Leone
77 E2 Luntai China
71 A3 Luodian China
71 B3 Luoding China
70 B2 Luohe China
70 B2 Luoyang China
118 B3 Luozi Dem. Rep. Congo
121 B2 Lupane Zimbabwe
71 A3 Lupanshui China
110 B1 Lupeni Romania
121 C2 Lupilichi Moz.
101 F2 Luppa Ger.
95 B3 Lurgan U.K.
Luring China see Gêrzê
121 D2 Lúrio Moz.
121 D2 Lurio r. Moz.
92 F2 Lurøy Norway
121 B2 Lusaka Zambia
118 C3 Lusambo Dem. Rep. Congo
109 C2 Lushnjë Albania
70 C2 Lüshun China
123 C3 Lusikisiki S. Africa
136 C2 Lusk U.S.A.
Luso Angola see Luena
76 B3 Lut, Dasht-e des. Iran
101 F2 Lutherstadt Wittenberg Ger.
99 C4 Luton U.K.
61 C1 Lutong Sarawak Malaysia
129 C1 Łutselk'e Can.
90 B1 Luts'k Ukr.
55 F3 Lützow-Holm Bay Antarctica
122 B2 Lutzputs S. Africa
122 A3 Lutzville S. Africa
117 C4 Luuq Somalia
137 D2 Luverne U.S.A.
119 C3 Luvua r. Dem. Rep. Congo
120 B2 Luvuei Angola
123 D1 Luvuvhu r. S. Africa
119 D3 Luwegu r. Tanz.
119 D2 Luwero Uganda
61 D2 Luwuk Indon.
100 C3 Luxembourg country Europe
100 C3 Luxembourg Lux.
105 D2 Luxeuil-les-Bains France
62 A1 Luxi China
123 C3 Luxolweni S. Africa
116 B2 Luxor Egypt
100 B2 Luyksgestel Neth.
86 D2 Luza Rus. Fed.
Luzern Switz. see Lucerne
62 B1 Luzhai China
71 A3 Luzhi China
71 A3 Luzhou China
154 C1 Luziânia Brazil
151 E3 Luzilândia Brazil
64 B2 Luzon i. Phil.
64 B1 Luzon Strait Phil.
109 C3 Luzzi Italy
90 A2 L'viv Ukr.
L'vov Ukr. see L'viv
Lwów Ukr. see L'viv
88 C3 Lyakhavichy Belarus
Lyallpur Pak. see Faisalabad
89 D2 Lychkovo Rus. Fed.
92 G3 Lycksele Sweden
55 C2 Lyddan Island Antarctica
123 D2 Lydenburg S. Africa
88 C3 Lyel'chytsy Belarus
88 C3 Lyepyel' Belarus
136 A2 Lyman U.S.A.
99 B4 Lyme Bay U.K.
99 B4 Lyme Regis U.K.
139 D3 Lynchburg U.S.A.
52 A2 Lyndhurst Austr.
129 D2 Lynn Lake Can.
134 B1 Lynnwood U.S.A.
129 D1 Lynx Lake Can.
105 C2 Lyon France
Lyons France see Lyon
89 D2 Lyozna Belarus
103 E1 Łysica hill Pol.
86 E3 Lys'va Rus. Fed.
91 D2 Lysychans'k Ukr.
87 D3 Lysyye Gory Rus. Fed.
98 B3 Lytham St Anne's U.K.
88 C3 Lyuban' Belarus
90 C2 Lyubashivka Ukr.
89 E2 Lyubertsy Rus. Fed.
90 B1 Lyubeshiv Ukr.
89 F2 Lyubim Rus. Fed.
91 D2 Lyubotyn Ukr.
89 D2 Lyubytino Rus. Fed.
89 D3 Lyudinovo Rus. Fed.

## M

80 B2 Ma'ān Jordan
70 B2 Ma'anshan China
88 C2 Maardu Estonia
78 B3 Ma'ārid, Banī des. Saudi Arabia
80 B2 Ma'arrat an Nu'mān Syria
100 B1 Maarssen Neth.
100 B2 Maas r. Neth.
100 B2 Maaseik Belgium
64 B2 Maasin Phil.
100 B2 Maastricht Neth.
121 C3 Mabalane Moz.
78 B3 Ma'bar Yemen
150 D2 Mabaruma Guyana
98 D3 Mablethorpe U.K.
123 C2 Mabopane S. Africa
121 C3 Mabote Moz.
122 B2 Mabule Botswana
122 B1 Mabutsane Botswana
155 D2 Macaé Brazil
121 C2 Macaloge Moz.
126 F2 MacAlpine Lake Can.
151 D2 Macapá Brazil
150 B3 Macará Ecuador
155 D1 Macarani Brazil
Macassar Indon. see Makassar
Macassar Strait Indon. see Makassar, Selat
121 C2 Macatanja Moz.
151 F3 Macau Brazil
71 B3 Macau special admin. reg. China
121 C3 Maccaretane Moz.
98 B3 Macclesfield U.K.
50 B2 Macdonald, Lake salt flat Austr.
50 C2 Macdonnell Ranges mts Austr.
130 A2 MacDowell Lake Can.
96 C2 Macduff U.K.
106 B1 Macedo de Cavaleiros Port.
52 B3 Macedon mt. Austr.
111 B2 Macedonia country Europe
151 F3 Maceió Brazil
108 B2 Macerata Italy
52 A2 Macfarlane, Lake salt flat Austr.
97 B3 Macgillycuddy's Reeks mts Ireland
74 A2 Mach Pak.
155 C2 Machado Brazil
121 C3 Machaila Moz.
119 D3 Machakos Kenya
150 B3 Machala Ecuador
121 C3 Machanga Moz.
Machaze Moz. see Chitobe
70 B2 Macheng China
138 B2 Machesney Park U.S.A.
139 F2 Machias U.S.A.
73 C3 Machilipatnam India
121 C2 Machinga Malawi
150 B1 Machiques Venez.
150 B4 Machupicchu Peru
99 B3 Machynlleth U.K.
123 D2 Macia Moz.
Macias Nguema i. Equat. Guinea see Bioco
110 C1 Măcin Romania
53 D1 Macintyre r. Austr.
51 D2 Mackay Austr.
50 B2 Mackay, Lake salt flat Austr.
128 C1 MacKay Lake Can.
128 B2 Mackenzie Can.
128 A1 Mackenzie r. Can.
Mackenzie Guyana see Linden
Mackenzie atoll Micronesia see Ulithi
55 H3 Mackenzie Bay Antarctica
126 C2 Mackenzie Bay Can.
126 E1 Mackenzie King Island Can.
128 A1 Mackenzie Mountains Can.
Mackillop, Lake salt flat Austr. see Yamma Yamma, Lake
129 D2 Macklin Can.
53 D2 Macksville Austr.
53 D1 Maclean Austr.
123 C3 Maclear S. Africa
50 A2 MacLeod, Lake imp. l. Austr.
138 A2 Macomb U.S.A.
108 A2 Macomer Sardinia Italy
121 D2 Macomia Moz.
105 C2 Mâcon France
141 D2 Macon GA U.S.A.
137 E3 Macon MO U.S.A.
140 C2 Macon MS U.S.A.
53 C2 Macquarie r. Austr.
48 G9 Macquarie Island S. Pacific Ocean
53 C2 Macquarie Marshes Austr.
53 C2 Macquarie Mountain Austr.
156 D9 Macquarie Ridge sea feature S. Pacific Ocean
55 H2 Mac. Robertson Land reg. Antarctica
97 B3 Macroom Ireland
52 A1 Macumba watercourse Austr.
145 C3 Macuspana Mex.
144 B2 Macuzari, Presa resr Mex.
123 D2 Madadeni S. Africa
121 □D3 Madagascar country Africa
159 D5 Madagascar Ridge sea feature Indian Ocean
115 D2 Madama Niger
111 B2 Madan Bulg.
59 D3 Madang P.N.G.
139 D1 Madawaska r. Can.
62 A1 Madaya Myanmar
150 D3 Madeira r. Brazil
114 A1 Madeira terr. N. Atlantic Ocean
131 D3 Madeleine, Îles de la is Can.
99 B3 Madeley U.K.
144 B2 Madera Mex.
135 B3 Madera U.S.A.
73 B3 Madgaon India
74 B2 Madhya Pradesh state India
123 C2 Madibogo S. Africa
118 B3 Madingou Congo
121 □D2 Madirovalo Madag.
138 B3 Madison IN U.S.A.
137 D2 Madison SD U.S.A.
138 B2 Madison WI U.S.A.
138 C3 Madison WV U.S.A.
134 D1 Madison r. U.S.A.
138 B3 Madisonville U.S.A.
61 C2 Madiun Indon.
119 D2 Mado Gashi Kenya
68 C2 Madoi China
88 C2 Madona Latvia
78 A2 Madrakah Saudi Arabia
79 C3 Madrakah, Ra's c. Oman
Madras India see Chennai
134 B2 Madras U.S.A.
145 C2 Madre, Laguna lag. Mex.
143 D3 Madre, Laguna lag. U.S.A.
150 C4 Madre de Dios r. Peru
145 B3 Madre del Sur, Sierra mts Mex.
144 B2 Madre Occidental, Sierra mts Mex.
145 B2 Madre Oriental, Sierra mts Mex.
106 C1 Madrid Spain
106 C2 Madridejos Spain
61 C2 Madura i. Indon.
61 C2 Madura, Selat sea chan. Indon.
73 B4 Madurai India
121 B2 Madziwadzido Zimbabwe
67 C3 Maebashi Japan
62 A2 Mae Hong Son Thai.
62 A1 Mae Sai Thai.
62 A2 Mae Sariang Thai.
99 B4 Maesteg U.K.
62 A2 Mae Suai Thai.
121 □D2 Maevatanana Madag.
Mafeking S. Africa see Mafikeng
123 C2 Mafeteng Lesotho
53 C3 Maffra Austr.
119 D3 Mafia Island Tanz.
123 C2 Mafikeng S. Africa
119 D3 Mafinga Tanz.
154 C3 Mafra Brazil
83 L3 Magadan Rus. Fed.
Magallanes Chile see Punta Arenas
Magallanes, Estrecho de Chile see Magellan, Strait of
150 B2 Magangue Col.
140 B1 Magazine Mountain hill U.S.A.
114 A4 Magburaka Sierra Leone
69 E1 Magdagachi Rus. Fed.
144 A1 Magdalena Mex.
142 B2 Magdalena U.S.A.
144 A2 Magdalena, Bahía b. Mex.
101 E1 Magdeburg Ger.
153 A5 Magellan, Strait of sea chan. Chile
Maggiore, Lago Italy see Maggiore, Lake
108 A1 Maggiore, Lake l. Italy
116 B2 Maghāghah Egypt
97 C1 Magherafelt U.K.
87 E3 Magnitogorsk Rus. Fed.
140 B2 Magnolia U.S.A.
121 C2 Màgoé Moz.
130 C3 Magog Can.
131 D2 Magpie, Lac l. Can.
114 A3 Magṭa' Laḥjar Maur.
119 D3 Magu Tanz.
151 E3 Maguarinho, Cabo c. Brazil
123 D2 Magude Moz.
90 B2 Măgura, Dealul hill Moldova
62 A1 Magwe Myanmar
81 C2 Mahābād Iran
74 B2 Mahajan India
121 □D2 Mahajanga Madag.
61 C2 Mahakam r. Indon.
123 C1 Mahalapye Botswana
121 □D2 Mahalevona Madag.
75 C2 Mahanadi r. India
121 □D2 Mahanoro Madag.
74 B3 Maharashtra state India
63 B2 Maha Sarakham Thai.
121 □D2 Mahavavy r. Madag.
68 B3 Mahbubnagar India
78 B2 Mahd adh Dhahab Saudi Arabia
107 D2 Mahdia Alg.
150 D2 Mahdia Guyana
113 I6 Mahé i. Seychelles
75 C3 Mahendragiri mt. India
119 D3 Mahenge Tanz.
54 B3 Maheno N.Z.
74 B2 Mahesana India
74 B2 Mahi r. India
54 C1 Mahia Peninsula N.Z.
89 D3 Mahilyow Belarus
107 D2 Mahón Spain
114 B3 Mahou Mali
Mahsana India see Mahesana
74 B2 Mahuva India
111 C2 Mahya Dağı mt. Turkey
106 B1 Maia Port.
Maiaia Moz. see Nacala
147 C3 Maicao Col.
129 D2 Maidstone Can.
99 D4 Maidstone U.K.
115 D3 Maiduguri Nigeria
75 D2 Maijdi Bangl.
75 C2 Mailani India
101 D2 Main r. Ger.
118 B3 Mai-Ndombe, Lac l. Dem. Rep. Congo
101 E3 Main-Donau-Kanal canal Ger.
139 F1 Maine state U.S.A.
131 D3 Maine, Gulf of Can./U.S.A.
62 A1 Maingkwan Myanmar
96 C1 Mainland i. Orkney Is, Scotland U.K.
96 □ Mainland i. Shetland Is, Scotland U.K.
121 □D2 Maintirano Madag.
101 D2 Mainz Ger.
150 C1 Maiquetía Venez.
120 B3 Maitengwe Botswana
53 D2 Maitland N.S.W. Austr.
52 A2 Maitland S.A. Austr.
146 B3 Maíz, Islas del is Nic.
67 C3 Maizuru Japan
109 C2 Maja Jezercë mt. Albania
61 C2 Majene Indon.
119 D2 Majī Eth.
107 D2 Majorca i. Spain
Majunga Madag. see Mahajanga
123 C2 Majwemasweu S. Africa
118 B3 Makabana Congo
61 C2 Makale Indon.
119 C3 Makamba Burundi
77 E2 Makanchi Kazakh.
118 B2 Makanza Dem. Rep. Congo
90 B1 Makariv Ukr.
69 F1 Makarov Rus. Fed.
160 B1 Makarov Basin sea feature Arctic Ocean
109 C2 Makarska Croatia
61 C2 Makassar Indon.
61 C2 Makassar, Selat Indon.
76 B2 Makat Kazakh.
119 D3 Makatapora Tanz.
123 D2 Makatini Flats lowland S. Africa
114 A4 Makeni Sierra Leone
120 B3 Makgadikgadi salt pan Botswana
87 D4 Makhachkala Rus. Fed.
76 B2 Makhambet Kazakh.
119 D3 Makindu Kenya
77 D1 Makinsk Kazakh.
91 D2 Makiyivka Ukr.

**Makkah** Saudi Arabia *see* **Mecca**
131 E2 **Makkovik** Can.
103 E2 **Makó** Hungary
118 B2 **Makokou** Gabon
119 D3 **Makongolosi** Tanz.
122 B2 **Makopong** Botswana
119 C3 **Makoro** Dem. Rep. Congo
118 B3 **Makoua** Congo
111 B3 **Makrakomi** Greece
79 D2 **Makran** *reg.* Iran/Pak.
74 A2 **Makran Coast Range** *mts* Pak.
89 E2 **Maksatikha** Rus. Fed.
81 C2 **Mākū** Iran
62 A1 **Makum** India
67 B4 **Makurazaki** Japan
115 C4 **Makurdi** Nigeria
92 G2 **Malå** Sweden
146 B4 **Mala, Punta** *pt* Panama
73 B3 **Malabar Coast** India
118 A2 **Malabo** Equat. Guinea
155 D1 **Malacacheta** Brazil
**Malacca** Malaysia *see* **Melaka**
60 A1 **Malacca, Strait of** Indon./Malaysia
134 D2 **Malad City** U.S.A.
88 C3 **Maladzyechna** Belarus
106 C2 **Málaga** Spain
**Malagasy Republic** *country* Africa *see* **Madagascar**
121 □D3 **Malaimbandy** Madag.
48 H4 **Malaita** *i.* Solomon Is
117 B4 **Malakal** Sudan
48 H5 **Malakula** *i.* Vanuatu
61 C2 **Malamala** Indon.
61 C2 **Malang** Indon.
**Malange** Angola *see* **Malanje**
120 A1 **Malanje** Angola
93 G4 **Mälaren** *l.* Sweden
153 B3 **Malargüe** Arg.
130 C3 **Malartic** Can.
88 C3 **Malaryta** Belarus
80 B2 **Malatya** Turkey
121 C2 **Malawi** *country* Africa
**Malawi, Lake** Africa *see* **Nyasa, Lake**
89 D2 **Malaya Vishera** Rus. Fed.
64 B3 **Malaybalay** Phil.
81 C2 **Malāyer** Iran
60 B1 **Malaysia** *country* Asia
81 C2 **Malazgirt** Turkey
103 D1 **Malbork** Pol.
101 F1 **Malchin** Ger.
100 A2 **Maldegem** Belgium
48 L4 **Malden Island** Kiribati
56 C5 **Maldives** *country* Indian Ocean
99 D4 **Maldon** U.K.
56 I9 **Male** Maldives
111 B3 **Maleas, Akra** *pt* Greece
103 D2 **Malé Karpaty** *hills* Slovakia
119 C3 **Malela** Dem. Rep. Congo
134 C4 **Malheur Lake** U.S.A.
114 B3 **Mali** *country* Africa
114 B3 **Mali** Guinea
59 C3 **Maliana** East Timor
58 D3 **Malili** Indon.
97 C1 **Malin** Ireland
119 E3 **Malindi** Kenya
97 C1 **Malin Head** *hd* Ireland
97 B1 **Malin More** Ireland
111 C2 **Malkara** Turkey
88 C3 **Mal'kavichy** Belarus
110 C2 **Malko Tŭrnovo** Bulg.
53 C3 **Mallacoota** Austr.
53 C3 **Mallacoota Inlet** *b.* Austr.
96 B2 **Mallaig** U.K.
116 B2 **Mallawi** Egypt
129 E1 **Mallery Lake** Can.
**Mallorca** *i.* Spain *see* **Majorca**
97 B2 **Mallow** Ireland
92 F3 **Malm** Norway
92 H2 **Malmberget** Sweden
100 C2 **Malmédy** Belgium
122 A3 **Malmesbury** S. Africa
93 F4 **Malmö** Sweden
71 A3 **Malong** China
118 C4 **Malonga** Dem. Rep. Congo
86 C2 **Maloshuyka** Rus. Fed.
93 E3 **Måløy** Norway
89 E2 **Maloyaroslavets** Rus. Fed.
89 E2 **Maloye Borisovo** Rus. Fed.
86 D2 **Malozemel'skaya Tundra** *lowland* Rus. Fed.
125 J9 **Malpelo, Isla de** *i.* N. Pacific Ocean
84 F5 **Malta** *country* Europe
88 C2 **Malta** Latvia
134 E1 **Malta** U.S.A.
122 A1 **Maltahöhe** Namibia
98 C2 **Malton** U.K.
**Maluku** *is* Indon. *see* **Moluccas**
93 F3 **Malung** Sweden
123 C3 **Maluti Mountains** Lesotho
73 B3 **Malvan** India
140 B2 **Malvern** U.S.A.
117 B4 **Malwal** Sudan
90 B1 **Malyn** Ukr.
83 L2 **Malyy Anyuy** *r.* Rus. Fed.
**Malyy Kavkaz** *mts* Asia *see* **Lesser Caucasus**
83 K2 **Malyy Lyakhovskiy, Ostrov** *i.* Rus. Fed.
123 C2 **Mamafubedu** S. Africa
151 F3 **Mamanguape** Brazil
64 B3 **Mambajao** Phil.

119 C2 **Mambasa** Dem. Rep. Congo
118 B2 **Mambéré** *r.* C.A.R.
64 B2 **Mamburao** Phil.
123 C2 **Mamelodi** S. Africa
118 A2 **Mamfe** Cameroon
135 C3 **Mammoth Lakes** U.S.A.
88 A3 **Mamonovo** Rus. Fed.
150 C4 **Mamoré** *r.* Bol./Brazil
114 A3 **Mamou** Guinea
114 B4 **Mampong** Ghana
61 C2 **Mamuju** Indon.
114 B4 **Man** Côte d'Ivoire
98 A2 **Man, Isle of** *i.* Irish Sea
150 C2 **Manacapuru** Brazil
107 D2 **Manacor** Spain
59 C2 **Manado** Indon.
146 B3 **Managua** Nic.
121 □D3 **Manakara** Madag.
78 B3 **Manākhah** Yemen
79 C2 **Manama** Bahrain
59 D3 **Manam Island** P.N.G.
121 □D3 **Mananara** *r.* Madag.
121 □D2 **Mananara Avaratra** Madag.
121 □D3 **Mananjary** Madag.
114 A3 **Manantali, Lac de** *l.* Mali
54 A3 **Manapouri, Lake** N.Z.
77 E2 **Manas Hu** *l.* China
75 C2 **Manaslu** *mt.* Nepal
**Manastir** Macedonia *see* **Bitola**
59 C3 **Manatuto** East Timor
62 A2 **Man-aung Kyun** Myanmar
150 C2 **Manaus** Brazil
80 B2 **Manavgat** Turkey
116 A3 **Manawashei** Sudan
98 B3 **Manchester** U.K.
139 E2 **Manchester** CT U.S.A.
139 E2 **Manchester** NH U.S.A.
140 C1 **Manchester** TN U.S.A.
81 D3 **Mand, Rūd-e** *r.* Iran
117 B3 **Manda, Jebel** *mt.* Sudan
121 □D3 **Mandabe** Madag.
93 E4 **Mandal** Norway
59 D3 **Mandala, Puncak** *mt.* Indon.
62 A1 **Mandalay** Myanmar
68 C1 **Mandalgovi** Mongolia
136 C1 **Mandan** U.S.A.
118 B1 **Mandara Mountains** Cameroon/Nigeria
108 A3 **Mandas** Sardinia Italy
119 E2 **Mandera** Kenya
100 C2 **Manderscheid** Ger.
74 B1 **Mandi** India
114 B3 **Mandiana** Guinea
74 B1 **Mandi Burewala** Pak.
**Mandidzuzure** Zimbabwe *see* **Chimanimani**
75 C2 **Mandla** India
121 □D2 **Mandritsara** Madag.
74 B2 **Mandsaur** India
50 A3 **Mandurah** Austr.
73 B3 **Mandya** India
108 B1 **Manerbio** Italy
90 B1 **Manevychi** Ukr.
109 C2 **Manfredonia** Italy
109 C2 **Manfredonia, Golfo di** *g.* Italy
114 B3 **Manga** Burkina
118 B3 **Mangai** Dem. Rep. Congo
49 L6 **Mangaia** *i.* Cook Is
54 C1 **Mangakino** N.Z.
110 C2 **Mangalia** Romania
73 B3 **Mangalore** India
123 C2 **Mangaung** S. Africa
60 B2 **Manggar** Indon.
**Manggyshlaq** Kazakh. *see* **Mangystau**
61 C1 **Mangkalihat, Tanjung** *pt* Indon.
68 C2 **Mangnai** China
121 C2 **Mangochi** Malawi
121 □D3 **Mangoky** *r.* Madag.
59 C3 **Mangole** *i.* Indon.
54 B1 **Mangonui** N.Z.
**Mangshi** China *see* **Luxi**
106 B1 **Mangualde** Port.
154 B3 **Mangueirinha** Brazil
69 E1 **Mangui** China
**Mangyshlak** Kazakh. *see* **Mangystau**
76 B2 **Mangystau** Kazakh.
137 D3 **Manhattan** U.S.A.
121 C3 **Manhica** Moz.
121 □D2 **Manhuaçu** Brazil
121 □D2 **Mania** *r.* Madag.
108 B1 **Maniago** Italy
121 C2 **Maniamba** Moz.
150 C3 **Manicoré** Brazil
131 D3 **Manicouagan** *r.* Can.
131 D2 **Manicouagan, Réservoir** *resr* Can.
79 B2 **Manifah** Saudi Arabia
49 K5 **Manihiki** *atoll* Cook Is
64 B2 **Manila** Phil.
53 D2 **Manilla** Austr.
**Manipur** India *see* **Imphal**
111 C3 **Manisa** Turkey
107 C2 **Manises** Spain
98 A2 **Man, Isle of** *i.* Irish Sea
138 B2 **Manistee** U.S.A.
138 B1 **Manistique** U.S.A.
129 E2 **Manitoba** *prov.* Can.
129 E2 **Manitoba, Lake** Can.
138 B1 **Manitou Islands** U.S.A.
130 B3 **Manitoulin Island** Can.
136 C3 **Manitou Springs** U.S.A.
130 B3 **Manitouwadge** Can.
138 B2 **Manitowoc** U.S.A.
130 C3 **Maniwaki** Can.

150 B2 **Manizales** Col.
121 □D3 **Manja** Madag.
121 C3 **Manjacaze** Moz.
137 E2 **Mankato** U.S.A.
114 B4 **Mankono** Côte d'Ivoire
129 D3 **Mankota** Can.
73 C4 **Mankulam** Sri Lanka
74 B2 **Manmad** India
52 A2 **Mannahill** Austr.
73 B4 **Mannar** Sri Lanka
73 B4 **Mannar, Gulf of** India/Sri Lanka
101 D2 **Mannheim** Ger.
128 C2 **Manning** Can.
52 A2 **Mannum** Austr.
129 C2 **Mannville** Can.
59 C3 **Manokwari** Indon.
119 C3 **Manono** Dem. Rep. Congo
63 A2 **Manoron** Myanmar
105 D3 **Manosque** France
131 C2 **Manouane, Lac** *l.* Can.
65 B1 **Manp'o** N. Korea
107 D1 **Manresa** Spain
121 B2 **Mansa** Zambia
127 G2 **Mansel Island** Can.
92 I2 **Mansel'kya** *ridge* Fin./Rus. Fed.
53 C3 **Mansfield** Austr.
98 C3 **Mansfield** U.K.
140 B1 **Mansfield** AR U.S.A.
140 B2 **Mansfield** LA U.S.A.
138 C2 **Mansfield** OH U.S.A.
139 D2 **Mansfield** PA U.S.A.
150 A3 **Manta** Ecuador
64 A3 **Mantalingajan, Mount** Phil.
155 D1 **Mantena** Brazil
141 E1 **Manteo** U.S.A.
104 C2 **Mantes-la-Jolie** France
155 C2 **Mantiqueira, Serra da** *mts* Brazil
**Mantova** Italy *see* **Mantua**
88 C1 **Mäntsälä** Fin.
108 B1 **Mantua** Italy
86 D3 **Manturovo** Rus. Fed.
151 D3 **Manuelzinho** Brazil
61 D2 **Manui** *i.* Indon.
54 B1 **Manukau** N.Z.
59 D3 **Manus Island** P.N.G.
140 B2 **Many** U.S.A.
121 C2 **Manyame** *r.* Moz./Zimbabwe
119 D3 **Manyara, Lake** *salt l.* Tanz.
**Manyas Gölü** *l.* Turkey *see* **Kuş Gölü**
87 D4 **Manych-Gudilo, Ozero** *l.* Rus. Fed.
142 B1 **Many Farms** U.S.A.
119 D3 **Manyoni** Tanz.
106 C2 **Manzanares** Spain
146 C2 **Manzanillo** Cuba
144 B3 **Manzanillo** Mex.
119 C3 **Manzanza** Dem. Rep. Congo
69 D1 **Manzhouli** China
123 D2 **Manzini** Swaziland
115 D3 **Mao** Chad
**Maó** Spain *see* **Mahón**
59 D3 **Maoke, Pegunungan** *mts* Indon.
123 C2 **Maokeng** S. Africa
65 A1 **Maokui Shan** *mt.* China
70 A2 **Maomao Shan** *mt.* China
71 B3 **Maoming** China
121 C2 **Mapai** Moz.
75 C1 **Mapam Yumco** *l.* China
61 D2 **Mapane** Indon.
145 C2 **Mapastepec** Mex.
144 B2 **Mapimí** Mex.
144 B2 **Mapimí, Bolsón de** *des.* Mex.
64 A3 **Mapin** *i.* Phil.
121 C3 **Mapinhane** Moz.
129 D3 **Maple Creek** Can.
156 D4 **Mapmakers Seamounts** *sea feature* N. Pacific Ocean
59 D3 **Maprik** P.N.G.
123 D1 **Mapulanguene** Moz.
121 C3 **Maputo** Moz.
123 D2 **Maputo** *r.* Moz./S. Africa
123 C2 **Maputsoe** Lesotho
114 A2 **Maqteïr** *reg.* Maur.
75 C2 **Maquan He** *r.* China
120 A1 **Maquela do Zombo** Angola
153 B4 **Maquinchao** Arg.
137 E2 **Maquoketa** U.S.A.
123 C2 **Mara** S. Africa
150 C3 **Maraã** Brazil
151 E3 **Maraba** Brazil
151 D2 **Maracá, Ilha de** *i.* Brazil
150 B1 **Maracaibo** Venez.
**Maracaibo, Lago de** Venez. *see* **Maracaibo, Lake**
150 B2 **Maracaibo, Lake** *l.* Venez.
154 A2 **Maracaju** Brazil
154 A2 **Maracaju, Serra de** *hills* Brazil
150 C1 **Maracay** Venez.
115 D2 **Marādah** Libya
115 C3 **Maradi** Niger
81 C2 **Marāgheh** Iran
150 C2 **Marahuaca, Cerro** *mt.* Venez.
151 E3 **Marajó, Baía de** *est.* Brazil
151 D3 **Marajó, Ilha de** *i.* Brazil
79 C2 **Marākī** Iran
119 D2 **Maralal** Kenya
**Maralbashi** China *see* **Bachu**
52 A2 **Maralinga** Austr.
**Maralwexi** China *see* **Bachu**
142 A2 **Marana** U.S.A.
81 C2 **Marand** Iran
**Marandellas** Zimbabwe *see* **Marondera**
150 B3 **Marañón** *r.* Peru
**Maraş** Turkey *see* **Kahramanmaraş**

110 C1 **Mărăşeşti** Romania
130 B3 **Marathon** Can.
141 D4 **Marathon** U.S.A.
106 C2 **Marbella** Spain
50 A2 **Marble Bar** Austr.
123 C1 **Marble Hall** S. Africa
123 C1 **Marburg** S. Africa
101 D2 **Marburg an der Lahn** Ger.
103 D2 **Marcali** Hungary
137 E3 **Marceline** U.S.A.
99 D3 **March** U.K.
100 B2 **Marche-en-Famenne** Belgium
106 B2 **Marchena** Spain
152 B3 **Mar Chiquita, Laguna** *l.* Arg.
150 B4 **Marcona** Peru
139 E2 **Marcy, Mount** U.S.A.
74 B1 **Mardan** Pak.
153 C3 **Mar del Plata** Arg.
81 C2 **Mardin** Turkey
96 B2 **Maree, Loch** *l.* U.K.
51 C1 **Mareeba** Austr.
108 B3 **Marettimo, Isola** *i.* Sicily Italy
89 D2 **Marevo** Rus. Fed.
142 C2 **Marfa** U.S.A.
**Margao** India *see* **Madgaon**
50 A3 **Margaret River** Austr.
150 C1 **Margarita, Isla de** *i.* Venez.
123 D3 **Margate** S. Africa
99 D4 **Margate** U.K.
62 A1 **Margherita** India
**Margherita, Lake** Eth. *see* **Lake Abaya**
119 C2 **Margherita Peak** Dem. Rep. Congo/Uganda
76 C3 **Mārgow, Dasht-e** *des.* Afgh.
91 C2 **Marhanets'** Ukr.
62 A1 **Mari** Myanmar
152 B2 **María Elena** Chile
156 C5 **Mariana Trench** *sea feature* N. Pacific Ocean
**Mariánica, Cordillera** *mts* Spain *see* **Morena, Sierra**
140 B2 **Marianna** AR U.S.A.
141 C2 **Marianna** FL U.S.A.
102 C2 **Mariánské Lázně** Czech Rep.
144 B2 **Marías, Islas** *is* Mex.
78 B3 **Ma'rib** Yemen
109 C1 **Maribor** Slovenia
117 B3 **Maridi** Sudan
117 A4 **Maridi** *watercourse* Sudan
55 P2 **Marie Byrd Land** *reg.* Antarctica
147 D3 **Marie-Galante** *i.* Guadeloupe
93 G3 **Mariehamn** Fin.
122 A1 **Mariental** Namibia
93 F4 **Mariestad** Sweden
141 D2 **Marietta** GA U.S.A.
138 C2 **Marietta** OH U.S.A.
105 D3 **Marignane** France
83 K3 **Marii, Mys** *pt* Rus. Fed.
88 B3 **Marijampolė** Lith.
154 C2 **Marília** Brazil
106 B1 **Marín** Spain
135 B3 **Marina** U.S.A.
109 C3 **Marina di Gioiosa Ionica** Italy
88 C3 **Mar"ina Horka** Belarus
138 B1 **Marinette** U.S.A.
154 B2 **Maringá** Brazil
106 B2 **Marinha Grande** Port.
138 B2 **Marion** IN U.S.A.
138 C2 **Marion** OH U.S.A.
141 E2 **Marion** SC U.S.A.
138 C3 **Marion** VA U.S.A.
141 D2 **Marion, Lake** U.S.A.
52 A3 **Marion Bay** Austr.
152 B3 **Mariscal José Félix Estigarribia** Para.
105 D3 **Maritime Alps** *mts* France/Italy
110 C2 **Maritsa** *r.* Bulg.
91 D2 **Mariupol'** Ukr.
117 C4 **Marka** Somalia
68 C3 **Markam** China
123 C1 **Marken** S. Africa
100 B1 **Markermeer** *l.* Neth.
98 C3 **Market Rasen** U.K.
98 C3 **Market Weighton** U.K.
83 I2 **Markha** *r.* Rus. Fed.
139 C2 **Markham** Can.
91 D2 **Markivka** Ukr.
118 B2 **Markounda** C.A.R.
140 B2 **Marksville** U.S.A.
101 D3 **Marktheidenfeld** Ger.
101 F2 **Marktredwitz** Ger.
100 C2 **Marl** Ger.
51 C2 **Marla** Austr.
100 A3 **Marle** France
143 D2 **Marlin** U.S.A.
53 C3 **Marlo** Austr.
104 C3 **Marmande** France
111 C2 **Marmara, Sea of** *g.* Turkey
**Marmara Denizi** *g.* Turkey *see* **Marmara, Sea of**
111 C3 **Marmaris** Turkey
105 C2 **Marne** *r.* France
105 C2 **Marne-la-Vallée** France
118 B2 **Maro** Chad
121 □D2 **Maroantsetra** Madag.
54 B1 **Marokopa** N.Z.
101 E2 **Maroldsweisach** Ger.
121 □D2 **Maromokotro** *mt.* Madag.
121 C2 **Marondera** Zimbabwe
151 D2 **Maroni** *r.* Fr. Guiana
51 E2 **Maroochydore** Austr.
61 C2 **Maros** Indon.
49 M6 **Marotiri** *is* Fr. Polynesia

118 B1 **Maroua** Cameroon
121 □D2 **Marovoay** Madag.
49 N4 **Marquesas Islands** Fr. Polynesia
141 D4 **Marquesas Keys** *is* U.S.A.
155 D2 **Marquês de Valença** Brazil
138 B1 **Marquette** U.S.A.
116 A3 **Marra, Jebel** *mt.* Sudan
123 D2 **Marracuene** Moz.
114 B1 **Marrakech** Morocco
**Marrakesh** Morocco *see*
Marrakech
116 A3 **Marra Plateau** Sudan
52 A1 **Marree** Austr.
86 F2 **Marresale** Rus. Fed.
121 C2 **Marromeu** Moz.
121 C2 **Marrupa** Moz.
116 B2 **Marsá al 'Alam** Egypt
115 D1 **Marsa al Burayqah** Libya
119 D2 **Marsabit** Kenya
78 A2 **Marsa Delwein** Sudan
108 B3 **Marsala** *Sicily* Italy
116 A1 **Marsá Maṭrūḥ** Egypt
101 D2 **Marsberg** Ger.
108 B2 **Marsciano** Italy
53 C2 **Marsden** Austr.
100 B1 **Marsdiep** *sea chan.* Neth.
105 D3 **Marseille** France
**Marseilles** France *see* **Marseille**
140 B1 **Marshall** AR U.S.A.
137 D2 **Marshall** MN U.S.A.
137 E3 **Marshall** MO U.S.A.
143 E2 **Marshall** TX U.S.A.
48 H2 **Marshall Islands** country
N. Pacific Ocean
137 E2 **Marshalltown** U.S.A.
138 A2 **Marshfield** U.S.A.
146 C2 **Marsh Harbour** Bahamas
140 B3 **Marsh Island** U.S.A.
93 G4 **Märsta** Sweden
**Martaban, Gulf of** Myanmar *see*
Mottama, Gulf of
61 C2 **Martapura** Indon.
60 B2 **Martapura** Indon.
139 E2 **Martha's Vineyard** *i.* U.S.A.
105 D2 **Martigny** Switz.
103 D2 **Martin** Slovakia
136 C2 **Martin** U.S.A.
145 C2 **Martínez** Mex.
141 D2 **Martínez** U.S.A.
155 C1 **Martinho Campos** Brazil
147 D3 **Martinique** *terr.* West Indies
147 D3 **Martinique Passage**
Dominica/Martinique
139 D3 **Martinsburg** U.S.A.
138 B3 **Martinsville** U.S.A.
54 C2 **Marton** N.Z.
107 D1 **Martorell** Spain
106 C2 **Martos** Spain
76 B3 **Martuk** Kazakh.
81 D3 **Marv Dasht** Iran
105 C3 **Marvejols** France
76 C3 **Mary** Turkm.
51 E2 **Maryborough** Austr.
122 B2 **Marydale** S. Africa
139 D3 **Maryland** *state* U.S.A.
98 B2 **Maryport** U.K.
137 D3 **Marysville** U.S.A.
137 E2 **Marysville** MO U.S.A.
141 D1 **Maryville** TN U.S.A.
119 D3 **Masai Steppe** *plain* Tanz.
119 D3 **Masaka** Uganda
61 C2 **Masalembu Besar** *i.* Indon.
61 D2 **Masamba** Indon.
65 B2 **Masan** S. Korea
119 D4 **Masasi** Tanz.
64 B2 **Masbate** Phil.
64 B2 **Masbate** *i.* Phil.
107 D2 **Mascara** Alg.
155 E1 **Mascote** Brazil
123 C3 **Maseru** Lesotho
**Mashaba** Zimbabwe *see* **Mashava**
121 C3 **Mashava** Zimbabwe
76 B3 **Mashhad** Iran
123 C3 **Masibambane** S. Africa
79 C3 **Maşīlah, Wādī al** *watercourse*
Yemen
123 C2 **Masilo** S. Africa
118 B3 **Masi-Manimba** Dem. Rep. Congo
119 D2 **Masindi** Uganda
122 B3 **Masinyusane** S. Africa
**Masira, Gulf of** Oman *see*
Maşīrah, Khalīj
79 C3 **Maşīrah, Khalīj** Oman
81 C2 **Masjed Soleymān** Iran
97 B2 **Mask, Lough** *l.* Ireland
121 □E2 **Masoala, Tanjona** *c.* Madag.
137 E2 **Mason City** U.S.A.
**Masqaṭ** Oman *see* Muscat
108 B2 **Massa** Italy
139 E2 **Massachusetts** *state* U.S.A.
139 E2 **Massachusetts Bay** U.S.A.
115 D3 **Massaguet** Chad
115 D3 **Massakory** Chad
121 C3 **Massangena** Moz.
120 A1 **Massango** Angola
116 B3 **Massawa** Eritrea
139 E2 **Massena** U.S.A.
115 D3 **Massenya** Chad
128 A2 **Masset** Can.
105 C2 **Massif Central** *mts* France
115 C3 **Massif de l'Aïr** *mts* Niger
138 C2 **Massillon** U.S.A.
114 B3 **Massina** Mali
121 C3 **Massinga** Moz.
123 D1 **Massingir** Moz.

78 A2 **Mastābah** Saudi Arabia
54 C2 **Masterton** N.Z.
74 B1 **Mastuj** Pak.
74 A2 **Mastung** Pak.
78 A2 **Mastūrah** Saudi Arabia
88 B3 **Masty** Belarus
67 B2 **Masuda** Japan
**Masuku** Gabon *see* Franceville
121 C3 **Masvingo** Zimbabwe
119 D3 **Maswa** Tanz.
118 B3 **Matadi** Dem. Rep. Congo
146 B3 **Matagalpa** Nic.
130 C3 **Matagami** Can.
130 C3 **Matagami, Lac** *l.* Can.
143 D3 **Matagorda Island** U.S.A.
143 D3 **Matagorda Peninsula** U.S.A.
120 A2 **Matala** Angola
114 A3 **Matam** Senegal
54 C1 **Matamata** N.Z.
144 B2 **Matamoros** Mex.
145 C2 **Matamoros** Mex.
119 D3 **Matandu** *r.* Tanz.
131 D3 **Matane** Can.
146 B2 **Matanzas** Cuba
**Matapan, Cape** *pt* Greece *see*
Tainaro, Akra
73 C4 **Matara** Sri Lanka
61 C2 **Mataram** Indon.
50 C1 **Mataranka** Austr.
107 D1 **Mataró** Spain
123 C3 **Matatiele** S. Africa
54 A3 **Mataura** N.Z.
54 A3 **Mataura** *r.* N.Z.
54 C1 **Matawai** N.Z.
152 B1 **Mategua** Bol.
145 B2 **Matehuala** Mex.
109 C2 **Matera** Italy
108 A3 **Mateur** Tunisia
129 C2 **Matheson Island** Can.
143 D3 **Mathis** U.S.A.
74 B2 **Mathura** India
64 B3 **Mati** Phil.
145 C2 **Matías Romero** Mex.
98 C3 **Matlock** U.K.
150 D4 **Mato Grosso** Brazil
154 B1 **Mato Grosso, Planalto do** *plat.*
Brazil
123 D2 **Matola** Moz.
106 B1 **Matosinhos** Port.
**Matou** China *see* Pingguo
79 C2 **Maṭraḥ** Oman
67 B2 **Matsue** Japan
66 D2 **Matsumae** Japan
67 C3 **Matsumoto** Japan
67 C4 **Matsusaka** Japan
71 C3 **Matsu Tao** *i.* Taiwan
67 B4 **Matsuyama** Japan
130 B2 **Mattagami** *r.* Can.
130 C3 **Mattawa** Can.
105 D2 **Matterhorn** *mt.* Italy/Switz.
134 C2 **Matterhorn** *mt.* U.S.A.
141 D1 **Matthews** U.S.A.
79 C2 **Maṭṭī, Sabkhat** *salt pan*
Saudi Arabia
138 B3 **Mattoon** U.S.A.
150 B2 **Maturín** Venez.
91 D2 **Matveyev Kurgan** Rus. Fed.
123 C2 **Matwabeng** S. Africa
105 C1 **Maubeuge** France
104 C3 **Maubourguet** France
55 E3 **Maud Seamount** *sea feature*
S. Atlantic Ocean
49 L1 **Maui** *i.* U.S.A.
141 D2 **Mauldin** U.S.A.
138 C2 **Maumee** *r.* U.S.A.
61 D2 **Maumere** Indon.
120 B2 **Maun** Botswana
75 C2 **Maunath Bhanjan** India
123 C1 **Maunatlala** Botswana
62 A1 **Maungdaw** Myanmar
75 B2 **Mau Ranipur** India
50 C2 **Maurice, Lake** *salt flat* Austr.
114 A3 **Mauritania** country Africa
113 I8 **Mauritius** country Indian Ocean
120 B2 **Mavinga** Angola
123 C3 **Mavuya** S. Africa
78 B2 **Māwān, Khashm** *hill* Saudi Arabia
118 B3 **Mawanga** Dem. Rep. Congo
71 B3 **Mawei** China
62 A1 **Mawkmai** Myanmar
62 A1 **Mawlaik** Myanmar
63 A2 **Mawlamyaing** Myanmar
78 B2 **Mawqaq** Saudi Arabia
55 L3 **Mawson Peninsula** Antarctica
78 B3 **Mawza** Yemen
108 A3 **Maxia, Punta** *mt. Sardinia* Italy
121 C3 **Maxixe** Moz.
54 B1 **Maxwell** N.Z.
83 J2 **Maya** *r.* Rus. Fed.
147 C2 **Mayaguana** *i.* Bahamas
147 D3 **Mayagüez** Puerto Rico
81 D2 **Mayamey** Iran
96 B3 **Maybole** U.K.
116 B3 **Maych'ew** Eth.
117 C3 **Maydh** Somalia
100 C2 **Mayen** Ger.
104 B2 **Mayenne** France
104 B2 **Mayenne** *r.* France
128 C2 **Mayerthorpe** Can.
138 B3 **Mayfield** U.S.A.
91 D3 **Maykop** Rus. Fed.
128 A1 **Mayo** Can.
118 B3 **Mayoko** Congo
**Mayo Landing** Can. *see* Mayo
64 B2 **Mayon** *vol.* Phil.

121 D2 **Mayotte** *terr.* Africa
83 J3 **Mayskiy** Rus. Fed.
138 C3 **Maysville** U.S.A.
118 B3 **Mayumba** Gabon
137 D1 **Mayville** U.S.A.
120 C2 **Mazabuka** Zambia
**Mazagan** Morocco *see* El Jadida
151 D3 **Mazagão** Brazil
104 C3 **Mazamet** France
74 B1 **Mazar** China
108 B3 **Mazara del Vallo** *Sicily* Italy
77 C3 **Mazār-e Sharīf** Afgh.
107 C2 **Mazarrón** Spain
107 C2 **Mazarrón, Golfo de** *b.* Spain
144 A2 **Mazatán** Mex.
146 A3 **Mazatenango** Guat.
144 B2 **Mazatlán** Mex.
88 B2 **Mažeikiai** Lith.
88 B2 **Mazirbe** Latvia
121 B3 **Mazunga** Zimbabwe
103 E1 **Mazurskie, Pojezierze** *reg.* Pol.
88 C3 **Mazyr** Belarus
123 D2 **Mbabane** Swaziland
118 B2 **Mbaïki** C.A.R.
118 B2 **Mbakaou, Lac de** *l.* Cameroon
121 B3 **Mbalabala** Zimbabwe
119 D2 **Mbale** Uganda
118 B2 **Mbalmayo** Cameroon
118 B3 **Mbandaka** Dem. Rep. Congo
118 B2 **Mbandjok** Cameroon
118 A2 **Mbanga** Cameroon
120 A1 **M'banza Congo** Angola
118 B3 **Mbanza-Ngungu** Dem. Rep. Congo
119 D3 **Mbarara** Uganda
118 B2 **Mbé** Cameroon
119 D3 **Mbeya** Tanz.
119 D4 **Mbinga** Tanz.
119 D3 **Mbizi Mountains** Tanz.
119 C2 **Mboki** C.A.R.
118 B2 **Mbomo** Congo
118 B2 **Mbouda** Cameroon
114 A3 **Mbour** Senegal
114 A3 **Mbout** Maur.
118 C3 **Mbuji-Mayi** Dem. Rep. Congo
119 D3 **Mbuyuni** Tanz.
139 F1 **McAdam** Can.
143 D2 **McAlester** U.S.A.
143 D3 **McAllen** U.S.A.
128 B2 **McBride** Can.
134 C2 **McCall** U.S.A.
143 C2 **McCamey** U.S.A.
126 F2 **McClintock Channel** Can.
126 E2 **McClure Strait** Can.
140 B2 **McComb** U.S.A.
136 C2 **McConaughy, Lake** U.S.A.
136 C2 **McCook** U.S.A.
134 C2 **McDermitt** U.S.A.
159 E7 **McDonald Islands** Indian Ocean
134 D1 **McDonald Peak** U.S.A.
135 D3 **McGill** U.S.A.
126 B2 **McGrath** U.S.A.
134 D1 **McGuire, Mount** U.S.A.
121 C2 **Mchinji** Malawi
140 C1 **McKenzie** U.S.A.
51 D2 **McKinlay** Austr.
134 B2 **McKinleyville** U.S.A.
128 C2 **McLennan** Can.
128 B2 **McLeod Lake** Can.
134 B1 **McMinnville** OR U.S.A.
140 C1 **McMinnville** TN U.S.A.
137 D3 **McPherson** U.S.A.
128 C1 **McTavish Arm** *b.* Can.
123 C3 **Mdantsane** S. Africa
135 D3 **Mead, Lake** *resr* U.S.A.
136 C3 **Meade** U.S.A.
129 C2 **Meadow Lake** Can.
138 C2 **Meadville** U.S.A.
66 D2 **Meaken-dake** *vol.* Japan
106 B1 **Mealhada** Port.
131 E2 **Mealy Mountains** Can.
128 C2 **Meander River** Can.
78 A2 **Mecca** Saudi Arabia
139 D3 **Mechanicsville** U.S.A.
100 B2 **Mechelen** Belgium
100 B2 **Mechelen** Neth.
100 C2 **Mechernich** Ger.
100 C2 **Meckenheim** Ger.
101 E1 **Mecklenburgische Seenplatte**
*reg.* Ger.
106 B1 **Meda** Port.
60 A1 **Medan** Indon.
153 B4 **Medanosa, Punta** *pt* Arg.
73 C4 **Medawachchiya** Sri Lanka
107 D2 **Médéa** Alg.
150 B2 **Medellín** Col.
115 D1 **Medenine** Tunisia
134 B2 **Medford** U.S.A.
110 C2 **Medgidia** Romania
110 B1 **Mediaș** Romania
136 B2 **Medicine Bow Mountains** U.S.A.
136 B2 **Medicine Bow Peak** U.S.A.
129 C2 **Medicine Hat** Can.
137 D3 **Medicine Lodge** U.S.A.
155 D1 **Medina** Brazil
78 A2 **Medina** Saudi Arabia
106 C1 **Medinaceli** Spain
106 C1 **Medina del Campo** Spain
106 B1 **Medina de Rioseco** Spain
75 C2 **Medinipur** India
84 E5 **Mediterranean Sea**
129 C2 **Medley** Can.
87 E3 **Mednogorsk** Rus. Fed.
62 A1 **Mêdog** China
88 B2 **Medvėgalio kalnis** *hill* Lith.

83 L2 **Medvezh'i, Ostrova** *is* Rus. Fed.
86 C2 **Medvezh'yegorsk** Rus. Fed.
50 A2 **Meekatharra** Austr.
136 B2 **Meeker** U.S.A.
74 B2 **Meerut** India
100 A2 **Meetkerke** Belgium
119 D2 **Mēga** Eth.
60 B2 **Mega** *i.* Indon.
119 D2 **Mega Escarpment** Eth./Kenya
111 B3 **Megalopoli** Greece
75 D2 **Meghalaya** *state* India
75 C2 **Meghasani** *mt.* India
111 C3 **Megisti** *i.* Greece
92 I1 **Mehamn** Norway
50 A2 **Meharry, Mount** Austr.
137 E3 **Mehlville** U.S.A.
79 C2 **Mehrān** *watercourse* Iran
74 B1 **Mehtar Lām** Afgh.
119 D3 **Meia Meia** Tanz.
154 C1 **Meia Ponte** *r.* Brazil
118 B2 **Meiganga** Cameroon
65 B1 **Meihekou** China
**Meijiang** China *see* Ningdu
62 A1 **Meiktila** Myanmar
101 E2 **Meiningen** Ger.
102 C1 **Meißen** Ger.
**Meixian** China *see* Meizhou
71 B3 **Meizhou** China
152 B2 **Mejicana** *mt.* Arg.
152 A2 **Mejillones** Chile
118 B2 **Mékambo** Gabon
116 B3 **Mek'elē** Eth.
114 C2 **Mekerrhane, Sebkha** *salt pan* Alg.
114 B1 **Meknès** Morocco
63 B3 **Mekong** *r.* Asia
63 B3 **Mekong, Mouths of the** Vietnam
60 B1 **Melaka** Malaysia
156 D6 **Melanesia** *is* Pacific Ocean
156 D5 **Melanesian Basin** *sea feature*
Pacific Ocean
53 B3 **Melbourne** Austr.
141 D3 **Melbourne** U.S.A.
108 A2 **Mele, Capo** *c.* Italy
**Melekess** Rus. Fed. *see*
Dimitrovgrad
89 F2 **Melenki** Rus. Fed.
131 C2 **Mélèzes, Rivière aux** *r.* Can.
115 D3 **Mélfi** Chad
109 C2 **Melfi** Italy
129 D2 **Melfort** Can.
92 F3 **Melhus** Norway
106 B1 **Melide** Spain
114 B1 **Melilla** N. Africa
129 D3 **Melita** Can.
91 D2 **Melitopol'** Ukr.
119 D2 **Melka Guba** Eth.
101 D1 **Melle** Ger.
93 F4 **Mellerud** Sweden
101 E2 **Mellrichstadt** Ger.
101 D1 **Mellum** *i.* Ger.
123 D2 **Melmoth** S. Africa
152 C3 **Melo** Uru.
115 C1 **Melrhir, Chott** *salt l.* Alg.
96 C3 **Melrose** U.K.
**Melsetter** Zimbabwe *see*
Chimanimani
52 B3 **Melton** Austr.
99 C3 **Melton Mowbray** U.K.
105 C2 **Melun** France
129 D2 **Melville** Can.
51 D1 **Melville, Cape** Austr.
131 E2 **Melville, Lake** Can.
50 C1 **Melville Island** Austr.
126 E1 **Melville Island** Can.
127 G2 **Melville Peninsula** Can.
61 C2 **Memboro** Indon.
102 C2 **Memmingen** Ger.
60 B1 **Mempawah** Indon.
80 B3 **Memphis** *tourist site* Egypt
140 B1 **Memphis** TN U.S.A.
143 C2 **Memphis** TX U.S.A.
91 C1 **Mena** Ukr.
140 B2 **Mena** U.S.A.
121 □D3 **Menabe** *mts* Madag.
114 C3 **Ménaka** Mali
**Mènam Khong** *r.* Laos/Thai. *see* Mekong
105 C3 **Mende** France
117 B4 **Mendebo Mountains** Eth.
116 B3 **Mendefera** Eritrea
160 B1 **Mendeleyev Ridge** *sea feature* Arctic Ocean
145 C2 **Mendez** Mex.
117 B4 **Mendī** Eth.
59 D3 **Mendi** P.N.G.
99 B4 **Mendip Hills** U.K.
138 B2 **Mendota** U.S.A.
153 B3 **Mendoza** Arg.
111 C3 **Menemen** Turkey
100 A2 **Menen** Belgium
70 B2 **Mengcheng** China
60 B2 **Menggala** Indon.
71 A3 **Mengzi** China
131 D2 **Menihek** Can.
52 B2 **Menindee** Austr.
52 B2 **Menindee Lake** Austr.
52 A3 **Meningie** Austr.
104 C2 **Mennecy** France
138 B1 **Menominee** U.S.A.
120 A2 **Menongue** Angola
**Menorca** *i.* Spain *see* Minorca
61 C1 **Menonala** Indon.
60 A1 **Mentawai, Kepulauan** *is* Indon.
60 B2 **Mentok** Indon.
61 C1 **Menyapa, Gunung** *mt.* Indon.

108 A3 **Menzel Bourguiba** Tunisia
50 B2 **Menzies** Austr.
144 B2 **Meoqui** Mex.
100 C1 **Meppel** Neth.
100 C1 **Meppen** Ger.
121 C3 **Mepuze** Moz.
123 C2 **Meqheleng** S. Africa
138 B2 **Mequon** U.S.A.
108 B1 **Merano** Italy
59 D3 **Merauke** Indon.
52 B2 **Merbein** Austr.
 **Merca** Somalia see **Marka**
107 D2 **Mercadal** Spain
135 B3 **Merced** U.S.A.
152 C2 **Mercedes** Arg.
143 D3 **Mercedes** U.S.A.
127 H2 **Mercy, Cape** Can.
143 C1 **Meredith, Lake** U.S.A.
91 D2 **Merefa** Ukr.
116 A3 **Merga Oasis** Sudan
63 A2 **Mergui Archipelago** is Myanmar
110 C2 **Meriç** r. Greece/Turkey
111 C2 **Meriç** Turkey
145 D2 **Mérida** Mex.
106 B2 **Mérida** Spain
150 B2 **Mérida** Venez.
147 C4 **Mérida, Cordillera de** mts Venez.
134 C2 **Meridian** ID U.S.A.
140 C2 **Meridian** MS U.S.A.
143 D2 **Meridian** TX U.S.A.
104 B3 **Mérignac** France
93 H3 **Merikarvia** Fin.
53 C3 **Merimbula** Austr.
88 B3 **Merkinė** Lith.
116 B3 **Merowe** Sudan
50 A3 **Merredin** Austr.
96 B3 **Merrick** hill U.K.
138 B1 **Merrill** U.S.A.
136 C2 **Merrillville** U.S.A.
136 C2 **Merriman** U.S.A.
128 B2 **Merritt** Can.
53 C2 **Merrygoen** Austr.
116 C3 **Mersa Fatma** Eritrea
100 C3 **Mersch** Lux.
101 E2 **Merseburg (Saale)** Ger.
98 B2 **Mersey** r. U.K.
80 B2 **Mersin** Turkey
60 B1 **Mersing** Malaysia
99 D4 **Mers-les-Bains** France
74 B2 **Merta** India
99 B4 **Merthyr Tydfil** U.K.
119 D2 **Merti Plateau** Kenya
106 B2 **Mértola** Port.
76 B2 **Mertvyy Kultuk, Sor** dry lake Kazakh.
119 D3 **Meru** vol. Tanz.
122 B3 **Merweville** S. Africa
80 B1 **Merzifon** Turkey
101 D3 **Merzig** Ger.
142 A2 **Mesa** AZ U.S.A.
142 C2 **Mesa** NM U.S.A.
137 E1 **Mesabi Range** hills U.S.A.
109 C2 **Mesagne** Italy
142 B2 **Mescalero** U.S.A.
143 C2 **Mescalero Ridge** U.S.A.
101 D2 **Meschede** Ger.
89 E3 **Meshchovsk** Rus. Fed.
 **Meshed** Iran see **Mashhad**
91 E2 **Meshkovskaya** Rus. Fed.
142 B2 **Mesilla** U.S.A.
111 B3 **Mesimeri** Greece
111 B3 **Mesolongi** Greece
115 C1 **Messaad** Alg.
121 D2 **Messalo** r. Moz.
109 C3 **Messina** Sicily Italy
109 C3 **Messina, Strait of** str. Italy
 **Messina, Stretta di** Italy see **Messina, Strait of**
111 B3 **Messini** Greece
111 B3 **Messiniakos Kolpos** b. Greece
111 B3 **Mesta** r. Bulg.
 **Mesta** r. Greece see **Nestos**
150 C2 **Meta** r. Col./Venez.
130 C3 **Métabetchouan** Can.
127 H2 **Meta Incognita Peninsula** Can.
140 B3 **Metairie** U.S.A.
152 B3 **Metán** Arg.
111 B3 **Methoni** Greece
109 C2 **Metković** Croatia
121 C2 **Metoro** Moz.
60 B2 **Metro** Indon.
100 C3 **Mettlach** Ger.
135 D3 **Mettler** U.S.A.
117 B4 **Metu** Eth.
105 D2 **Metz** France
100 B2 **Meuse** r. Belgium/France
143 D2 **Mexia** U.S.A.
144 A1 **Mexicali** Mex.
144 B2 **Mexico** country Central America
 **México** Mex. see **Mexico City**
137 E3 **Mexico** U.S.A.
125 I7 **Mexico, Gulf of** Mex./U.S.A.
145 C3 **Mexico City** Mex.
81 D2 **Meybod** Iran
101 F1 **Meyenburg** Ger.
76 C3 **Meymaneh** Afgh.
83 M2 **Meynypil'gyno** Rus. Fed.
86 D2 **Mezen'** Rus. Fed.
86 D2 **Mezen'** r. Rus. Fed.
86 E1 **Mezhdusharskiy, Ostrov** i. Rus. Fed.
103 E2 **Mezőtúr** Hungary
132 C4 **Mezquital** r. Mex.
144 B2 **Mezquitic** Mex.
88 C2 **Mežvidi** Latvia

121 C2 **Mfuwe** Zambia
89 D3 **Mglin** Rus. Fed.
123 D2 **Mhlume** Swaziland
74 B2 **Mhow** India
145 C3 **Miahuatlán** Mex.
106 B2 **Miajadas** Spain
141 D3 **Miami** FL U.S.A.
143 E1 **Miami** OK U.S.A.
141 D3 **Miami Beach** U.S.A.
81 C2 **Miandowāb** Iran
121 □D2 **Miandrivazo** Madag.
81 C2 **Miāneh** Iran
71 A3 **Mianning** China
74 B1 **Mianwali** Pak.
 **Mianyang** China see **Xiantao**
70 A2 **Mianyang** China
121 □D2 **Miarinarivo** Madag.
87 F3 **Miass** Rus. Fed.
103 D1 **Miastko** Pol.
103 E2 **Michalovce** Slovakia
138 B1 **Michigan** state U.S.A.
138 B1 **Michigan, Lake** U.S.A.
138 B2 **Michigan City** U.S.A.
130 B3 **Michipicoten Bay** Can.
130 B3 **Michipicoten Island** Can.
130 B3 **Michipicoten River** Can.
 **Michurin** Bulg. see **Tsarevo**
89 F3 **Michurinsk** Rus. Fed.
156 D5 **Micronesia** is Pacific Ocean
48 G3 **Micronesia, Federated States of** country N. Pacific Ocean
158 E6 **Mid-Atlantic Ridge** sea feature Atlantic Ocean
100 A2 **Middelburg** Neth.
123 C3 **Middelburg** E. Cape S. Africa
123 C2 **Middelburg** Mpumalanga S. Africa
100 B2 **Middelharnis** Neth.
134 B2 **Middle Alkali Lake** U.S.A.
73 D3 **Middle Andaman** i. India
 **Middle Congo** country Africa see **Congo**
136 D2 **Middle Loup** r. U.S.A.
138 C3 **Middlesboro** U.S.A.
98 C2 **Middlesbrough** U.K.
139 E2 **Middletown** NY U.S.A.
138 C3 **Middletown** OH U.S.A.
78 B3 **Midi** Yemen
130 C3 **Midland** Can.
138 C2 **Midland** MI U.S.A.
143 C2 **Midland** TX U.S.A.
97 B3 **Midleton** Ireland
 **Midnapore** India see **Medinipur**
94 B1 **Miðvágur** Faroe Is
57 T7 **Midway Islands** terr. N. Pacific Ocean
 **Midway** Oman see **Thamarīt**
109 D2 **Midzhur** mt. Bulg./Serb. and Mont.
103 E1 **Mielec** Pol.
110 C1 **Miercurea-Ciuc** Romania
106 B1 **Mieres** Spain
101 E1 **Mieste** Ger.
75 D1 **Migriggyangzham Co** l. China
145 C3 **Miguel Alemán, Presa** resr Mex.
144 B2 **Miguel Auza** Mex.
144 B2 **Miguel Hidalgo, Presa** resr Mex.
63 A2 **Migyaunglaung** Myanmar
67 B4 **Mihara** Japan
89 E3 **Mikhaylov** Rus. Fed.
66 B2 **Mikhaylovgrad** Bulg. see **Montana**
87 D3 **Mikhaylovka** Rus. Fed.
77 D1 **Mikhaylovka** Rus. Fed.
 **Mikhaylovskiy** Rus. Fed. see **Kimovsk**
93 I3 **Mikkeli** Fin.
86 E2 **Mikun'** Rus. Fed.
67 C3 **Mikuni-sanmyaku** mts Japan
67 C4 **Mikura-jima** i. Japan
73 B4 **Miladhunmadulu Atoll** Maldives
108 A1 **Milan** Italy
121 C2 **Milange** Moz.
 **Milano** Italy see **Milan**
111 C3 **Milas** Turkey
137 D1 **Milbank** U.S.A.
99 D3 **Mildenhall** U.K.
52 B2 **Mildura** Austr.
71 A3 **Mile** China
136 B1 **Miles City** U.S.A.
139 D3 **Milford** DE U.S.A.
135 D3 **Milford** UT U.S.A.
99 A4 **Milford Haven** U.K.
54 A2 **Milford Sound** N.Z.
 **Milḥ, Baḥr al** l. Iraq see **Razāzah, Buḩayrat ar**
107 D2 **Miliana** Alg.
50 C1 **Milikapiti** Austr.
51 C1 **Milingimbi** Austr.
134 E1 **Milk** r. U.S.A.
116 B3 **Milk, Wadi el** watercourse Sudan
83 L3 **Mil'kovo** Rus. Fed.
128 C3 **Milk River** Can.
105 C3 **Millau** France
141 D2 **Milledgeville** U.S.A.
137 E1 **Mille Lacs** lakes U.S.A.
130 A3 **Mille Lacs, Lac des** l. Can.
 **Millennium Island** Kiribati see **Caroline Island**
137 D2 **Miller** U.S.A.
91 E2 **Millerovo** Rus. Fed.
52 A2 **Millers Creek** Austr.
96 B3 **Milleur Point** U.K.
52 B3 **Millicent** Austr.
140 C1 **Millington** U.S.A.
139 F1 **Millinocket** U.S.A.

55 J3 **Mill Island** Antarctica
53 D1 **Millmerran** Austr.
98 B2 **Millom** U.K.
136 B2 **Mills** U.S.A.
113 B3 **Mills Lake** Can.
111 B3 **Milos** i. Greece
89 E3 **Miloslavskoye** Rus. Fed.
91 E2 **Milove** Ukr.
52 B1 **Milparinka** Austr.
54 A3 **Milton** N.Z.
99 C3 **Milton Keynes** U.K.
138 B2 **Milwaukee** U.S.A.
158 C3 **Milwaukee Deep** sea feature Caribbean Sea
104 B3 **Mimizan** France
118 B3 **Mimongo** Gabon
155 D2 **Mimoso do Sul** Brazil
79 C2 **Mināb** Iran
61 D1 **Minahasa, Semenanjung** pen. Indon.
 **Minahassa Peninsula** Indon. see **Minahasa, Semenanjung**
79 C2 **Mina Jebel Ali** U.A.E.
 **Minaker** Can. see **Prophet River**
60 B1 **Minas** Indon.
153 C3 **Minas** Uru.
79 B2 **Minā' Sa'ūd** Kuwait
145 D3 **Minas, Cerro de las** mt. Hond.
155 D1 **Minas Novas** Brazil
145 C3 **Minatitlán** Mex.
62 A1 **Minbu** Myanmar
64 B3 **Mindanao** i. Phil.
52 B2 **Mindarie** Austr.
101 D1 **Minden** Ger.
140 B2 **Minden** LA U.S.A.
137 D2 **Minden** NE U.S.A.
64 B2 **Mindoro** i. Phil.
64 A2 **Mindoro Strait** Phil.
118 B3 **Mindouli** Congo
99 B4 **Minehead** U.K.
154 B1 **Mineiros** Brazil
143 D2 **Mineral Wells** U.S.A.
75 C1 **Minfeng** China
119 C4 **Minga** Dem. Rep. Congo
81 C1 **Mingäçevir** Azer.
131 D2 **Mingan** Can.
52 B2 **Mingary** Austr.
70 B2 **Mingguang** China
62 A1 **Mingin** Myanmar
107 C2 **Minglanilla** Spain
119 D4 **Mingoyo** Tanz.
69 E1 **Mingshui** China
96 A2 **Mingulay** i. U.K.
71 B3 **Mingxi** China
 **Mingzhou** China see **Suide**
70 A2 **Minhe** China
73 B4 **Minicoy** i. India
50 A2 **Minilya** Austr.
114 B3 **Mininian** Côte d'Ivoire
131 D2 **Minipi Lake** Can.
130 A2 **Miniss Lake** Can.
52 A2 **Minlaton** Austr.
115 C4 **Minna** Nigeria
137 E2 **Minneapolis** U.S.A.
129 E2 **Minnedosa** Can.
137 E2 **Minnesota** r. U.S.A.
137 E1 **Minnesota** state U.S.A.
106 B1 **Miño** r. Port./Spain
107 D1 **Minorca** i. Spain
136 C1 **Minot** U.S.A.
88 C3 **Minsk** Belarus
103 E1 **Mińsk Mazowiecki** Pol.
96 D2 **Mintlaw** U.K.
131 D3 **Minto** Can.
130 C2 **Minto, Lac** l. Can.
68 C1 **Minusinsk** Rus. Fed.
62 A1 **Minutang** India
70 A2 **Minxian** China
155 D1 **Mirabela** Brazil
155 D1 **Miralta** Brazil
131 D2 **Miramichi** Can.
111 C3 **Mirampelou, Kolpos** b. Greece
152 C2 **Miranda** Brazil
152 C1 **Miranda** r. Brazil
 **Miranda** Moz. see **Macaloge**
106 C1 **Miranda de Ebro** Spain
106 B1 **Mirandela** Port.
154 B2 **Mirandópolis** Brazil
154 B2 **Mirante, Serra do** hills Brazil
79 C2 **Mirbāţ** Oman
61 C1 **Miri** Sarawak Malaysia
153 C3 **Mirim, Lagoa** l. Brazil
79 D2 **Mirjāveh** Iran
89 D3 **Mirnyy** Rus. Fed.
83 I2 **Mirnyy** Rus. Fed.
101 F1 **Mirow** Ger.
74 A2 **Mirpur Khas** Pak.
 **Mirtoan Sea** Greece see **Mirtoö Pelagos**
 **Mirtoö Pelagos** sea Greece see **Murzechirla**
111 B3 **Mirtoö Pelagos** sea Greece
65 B2 **Miryang** S. Korea
 **Mirzachirla** Turkm. see **Murzechirla**
 **Mirzachul** Uzbek. see **Guliston**
75 C2 **Mirzapur** India
77 E3 **Misalay** China
66 B1 **Mishan** China
51 E1 **Misima Island** P.N.G.
146 B3 **Miskitos, Cayos** is Nic.
103 E2 **Miskolc** Hungary
59 C3 **Misoöl** i. Indon.
115 D1 **Mişrātah** Libya
130 B3 **Missinaibi** r. Can.
130 B3 **Missinaibi Lake** Can.
128 B3 **Mission** Can.

130 B2 **Missisa Lake** Can.
140 C3 **Mississippi** r. U.S.A.
140 C2 **Mississippi** state U.S.A.
140 C3 **Mississippi Delta** U.S.A.
140 C2 **Mississippi Sound** sea chan. U.S.A.
 **Missolonghi** Greece see **Mesolongi**
134 D1 **Missoula** U.S.A.
137 E3 **Missouri** r. U.S.A.
137 E3 **Missouri** state U.S.A.
130 C3 **Mistassibi** r. Can.
130 C2 **Mistassini, Lac** l. Can.
131 D2 **Mistastin Lake** Can.
103 D2 **Mistelbach** Austria
131 D2 **Mistinibi, Lac** l. Can.
130 C2 **Mistissini** Can.
51 D1 **Mitchell** Austr.
51 D1 **Mitchell** r. Austr.
136 C2 **Mitchell** NE U.S.A.
137 D2 **Mitchell** SD U.S.A.
97 B2 **Mitchelstown** Ireland
74 A2 **Mithi** Pak.
67 D3 **Mito** Japan
119 D3 **Mitole** Tanz.
53 D2 **Mittagong** Austr.
101 E2 **Mittelhausen** Ger.
101 D1 **Mittellandkanal** canal Ger.
101 F3 **Mitterteich** Ger.
 **Mittimatalik** Can. see **Pond Inlet**
150 B2 **Mitú** Col.
119 C4 **Mitumba, Chaîne des** mts Dem. Rep. Congo
119 C3 **Mitumba, Monts** mts Dem. Rep. Congo
118 B3 **Mitwaba** Dem. Rep. Congo
118 B3 **Mitzic** Gabon
78 B2 **Miyah, Wādī al** watercourse Saudi Arabia
67 C4 **Miyake-jima** i. Japan
66 D3 **Miyako** Japan
67 B4 **Miyakonojō** Japan
76 B2 **Miyaly** Kazakh.
 **Miyang** China see **Mile**
67 B4 **Miyazaki** Japan
67 C3 **Miyazu** Japan
115 D1 **Mizdah** Libya
97 B3 **Mizen Head** hd Ireland
90 A2 **Mizhhir"ya** Ukr.
 **Mizo Hills** state India see **Mizoram**
75 D2 **Mizoram** state India
93 G4 **Mjölby** Sweden
93 F3 **Mjøsa** l. Norway
119 D3 **Mkomazi** Tanz.
103 C1 **Mladá Boleslav** Czech Rep.
109 D2 **Mladenovac** Serb. and Mont.
103 E1 **Mława** Pol.
109 C2 **Mljet** i. Croatia
123 C3 **Mlungisi** S. Africa
90 B1 **Mlyniv** Ukr.
123 C2 **Mmabatho** S. Africa
123 C2 **Mmathethe** Botswana
93 E3 **Mo** Norway
135 B3 **Moab** U.S.A.
123 C3 **Moamba** Moz.
54 B2 **Moana** N.Z.
118 B3 **Moanda** Gabon
97 C2 **Moate** Ireland
119 C3 **Moba** Dem. Rep. Congo
118 C2 **Mobayi-Mbongo** Dem. Rep. Congo
137 E3 **Moberly** U.S.A.
140 C2 **Mobile** U.S.A.
140 C2 **Mobile Bay** U.S.A.
140 C2 **Mobile Point** U.S.A.
136 C1 **Mobridge** U.S.A.
 **Mobutu, Lake** Dem. Rep. Congo/Uganda see **Albert, Lake**
 **Mobutu Sese Seko, Lake** Dem. Rep. Congo/Uganda see **Albert, Lake**
121 C2 **Moçambicano, Planalto** plat. Moz.
121 D2 **Moçambique** Moz.
 **Moçâmedes** Angola see **Namibe**
62 B1 **Môc Châu** Vietnam
78 B3 **Mocha** Yemen
123 C1 **Mochudi** Botswana
121 D2 **Mocimboa da Praia** Moz.
101 E2 **Möckmühl** Ger.
150 B2 **Mocoa** Col.
154 C2 **Mococa** Brazil
144 B2 **Mocorito** Mex.
144 B1 **Moctezuma** Mex.
145 B2 **Moctezuma** Mex.
144 B2 **Moctezuma** Mex.
121 C2 **Mocuba** Moz.
105 D2 **Modane** France
122 B2 **Modder** r. S. Africa
108 B2 **Modena** Italy
135 B3 **Modesto** U.S.A.
109 C3 **Modica** Sicily Italy
123 C1 **Modimolle** S. Africa
53 C3 **Moe** Austr.
 **Moero, Lake** Dem. Rep. Congo/Zambia see **Mweru, Lake**
100 C2 **Moers** Ger.
96 C2 **Moffat** U.K.
117 C4 **Mogadishu** Somalia
 **Mogador** Morocco see **Essaouira**
106 B2 **Mogadouro, Serra de** mts Port.
123 C2 **Mogalakwena** r. S. Africa
62 A1 **Mogaung** Myanmar
 **Mogilev** Belarus see **Mahilyow**
154 C2 **Mogi-Mirim** Brazil
83 I3 **Mogocha** Rus. Fed.

123 C1 **Mogoditshane** Botswana
62 A1 **Mogok** Myanmar
142 A2 **Mogollon Plateau** U.S.A.
103 D2 **Mohács** Hungary
123 C3 **Mohale's Hoek** Lesotho
107 D2 **Mohammadia** Alg.
142 A2 **Mohave Mountains** U.S.A.
139 E2 **Mohawk** *r.* U.S.A.
62 A1 **Mohnyin** Myanmar
119 D3 **Mohoro** Tanz.
90 B2 **Mohyliv Podil's'kyy** Ukr.
123 C1 **Moijabana** Botswana
110 C1 **Moinești** Romania
       **Mointy** Kazakh. *see* **Moyynty**
92 F2 **Mo i Rana** Norway
88 C2 **Mõisaküla** Estonia
104 C3 **Moissac** France
135 C3 **Mojave** U.S.A.
135 C3 **Mojave Desert** U.S.A.
62 B1 **Mojiang** China
155 C2 **Moji das Cruzes** Brazil
154 C2 **Moji-Guaçu** *r.* Brazil
109 C2 **Mojkovac** Serb. and Mont.
54 B1 **Mokau** N.Z.
123 C2 **Mokhotlong** Lesotho
83 J2 **Mokhsogollokh** Rus. Fed.
118 B1 **Mokolo** Cameroon
123 C1 **Mokopane** S. Africa
65 B3 **Mokp'o** S. Korea
109 C2 **Mola di Bari** Italy
145 C2 **Molango** Mex.
       **Moldavia** *country* Europe *see*
       **Moldova**
       **Moldavskaya S.S.R.** *admin. reg.*
       Europe *see* **Moldova**
93 E3 **Molde** Norway
90 B2 **Moldova** *country* Europe
110 B2 **Moldova Nouă** Romania
110 B1 **Moldoveanu, Vârful** *mt.* Romania
110 B1 **Moldovei, Podişul** *plat.* Romania
90 B2 **Moldovei Centrale, Podişul** *plat.*
       Moldova
123 C1 **Molepolole** Botswana
88 C2 **Molėtai** Lith.
109 C2 **Molfetta** Italy
       **Molière** Alg. *see* **Bordj Bounaama**
107 C1 **Molina de Aragón** Spain
107 C2 **Molina de Segura** Spain
119 D3 **Moliro** Dem. Rep. Congo
150 B4 **Mollendo** Peru
93 F4 **Mölnlycke** Sweden
91 D2 **Molochna** *r.* Ukr.
89 E2 **Molokovo** Rus. Fed.
53 C2 **Molong** Austr.
122 B2 **Molopo** *watercourse*
       Botswana/S. Africa
       **Molotov** Rus. Fed. *see* **Perm'**
       **Molotovsk** Rus. Fed. *see*
       **Severodvinsk**
       **Molotovsk** Rus. Fed. *see* **Nolinsk**
118 B2 **Moloundou** Cameroon
59 C3 **Moluccas** *is* Indon.
       **Molucca Sea** Indon. *see*
       **Laut Maluku**
52 B2 **Momba** Austr.
119 D3 **Mombasa** Kenya
154 B1 **Mombuca, Serra da** hills Brazil
111 C2 **Momchilgrad** Bulg.
93 F4 **Møn** *i.* Denmark
105 D3 **Monaco** *country* Europe
96 B2 **Monadhliath Mountains** U.K.
97 C1 **Monaghan** Ireland
143 C2 **Monahans** U.S.A.
147 D3 **Mona Passage**
       Dom. Rep./Puerto Rico
120 A1 **Mona Quimbundo** Angola
       **Monastir** Macedonia *see* **Bitola**
89 D3 **Monastyrshchina** Rus. Fed.
90 B2 **Monastyryshche** Ukr.
118 B2 **Monatélé** Cameroon
66 D2 **Monbetsu** Japan
108 A1 **Moncalieri** Italy
86 C2 **Monchegorsk** Rus. Fed.
100 C2 **Mönchengladbach** Ger.
144 B2 **Monclova** Mex.
131 D3 **Moncton** Can.
106 B1 **Mondego** *r.* Port.
118 C2 **Mondjamboli** Dem. Rep. Congo
123 D2 **Mondlo** S. Africa
108 A2 **Mondovì** Italy
106 C1 **Mondragón-Arrasate** Spain
111 B3 **Monemvasia** Greece
66 D1 **Moneron, Ostrov** *i.* Rus. Fed.
139 D1 **Monet** Can.
137 E3 **Monett** U.S.A.
108 B1 **Monfalcone** Italy
106 B1 **Monforte** Spain
119 D2 **Mongbwalu** Dem. Rep. Congo
62 B1 **Mông Cai** Vietnam
62 A1 **Mong Hang** Myanmar
       **Monghyr** India *see* **Munger**
75 C2 **Mongla** Bangl.
62 B1 **Mong Lin** Myanmar
62 A1 **Mong Nawng** Myanmar
115 D3 **Mongo** Chad
68 C1 **Mongolia** *country* Asia
74 B2 **Mongora** Pak.
62 A1 **Mong Pawk** Myanmar
62 A1 **Mong Ping** Myanmar
120 B2 **Mongu** Zambia
135 C3 **Monitor Range** *mts* U.S.A.
103 E1 **Mońki** Pol.
99 B4 **Monmouth** U.K.
114 C4 **Mono** *r.* Togo
135 C3 **Mono Lake** U.S.A.

109 C2 **Monopoli** Italy
107 C1 **Monreal del Campo** Spain
140 B2 **Monroe** *LA* U.S.A.
138 C2 **Monroe** *MI* U.S.A.
138 B2 **Monroe** *WI* U.S.A.
140 C2 **Monroeville** U.S.A.
114 A4 **Monrovia** Liberia
100 A2 **Mons** Belgium
155 E1 **Monsarás, Ponta de** *pt* Brazil
100 C2 **Montabaur** Ger.
122 B3 **Montagu** S. Africa
109 C3 **Montalto** *mt.* Italy
110 B2 **Montana** Bulg.
134 E1 **Montana** *state* U.S.A.
105 C2 **Montargis** France
104 C3 **Montauban** France
139 E2 **Montauk Point** U.S.A.
123 C2 **Mont-aux-Sources** *mt.* Lesotho
105 C2 **Montbard** France
105 D2 **Montbéliard** France
105 D2 **Mont Blanc** *mt.* France/Italy
105 C2 **Montbrison** France
100 B3 **Montcornet** France
104 B3 **Mont-de-Marsan** France
104 C2 **Montdidier** France
151 D3 **Monte Alegre** Brazil
154 C2 **Monte Alegre de Minas** Brazil
139 E1 **Montebello** Can.
154 B3 **Montecarlo** Arg.
105 D3 **Monte-Carlo** Monaco
154 C1 **Monte Carmelo** Brazil
152 C3 **Monte Caseros** Arg.
123 C1 **Monte Christo** S. Africa
108 B2 **Montecristo, Isola di** *i.* Italy
146 C3 **Montego Bay** Jamaica
105 C3 **Montélimar** France
109 C2 **Montella** Italy
145 C2 **Montemorelos** Mex.
104 B2 **Montendre** France
       **Montenegro** *aut. rep.*
       Serb. and Mont. *see* **Crna Gora**
121 C2 **Montepuez** Moz.
108 B2 **Montepulciano** Italy
135 B3 **Monterey** U.S.A.
135 B3 **Monterey Bay** U.S.A.
150 B2 **Montería** Col.
152 B1 **Montero** Bol.
145 B2 **Monterrey** Mex.
109 C2 **Montesano sulla Marcellana**
       Italy
109 C2 **Monte Sant'Angelo** Italy
151 F4 **Monte Santo** Brazil
108 A2 **Monte Santu, Capo di** *c.* Sardinia
155 D1 **Montes Claros** Brazil
153 C3 **Montevideo** Uru.
137 D2 **Montevideo** U.S.A.
136 B3 **Monte Vista** U.S.A.
140 C2 **Montgomery** U.S.A.
100 B3 **Monthermé** France
105 D2 **Monthey** Switz.
140 B3 **Monticello** *AR* U.S.A.
141 D3 **Monticello** *FL* U.S.A.
135 E3 **Monticello** *UT* U.S.A.
104 C2 **Montignac** France
100 B2 **Montignies-le-Tilleul** Belgium
106 B2 **Montijo** Port.
106 B2 **Montijo** Spain
106 C2 **Montilla** Spain
154 B1 **Montividiu** Brazil
131 D3 **Mont-Joli** Can.
130 C3 **Mont-Laurier** Can.
104 C2 **Montluçon** France
131 D3 **Montmagny** Can.
104 C2 **Montmorillon** France
51 D2 **Monto** Austr.
134 D2 **Montpelier** *ID* U.S.A.
139 E2 **Montpelier** *VT* U.S.A.
105 C3 **Montpellier** France
130 C3 **Montréal** Can.
129 D2 **Montreal Lake** Can.
129 D2 **Montreal Lake** *l.* Can.
99 D4 **Montreuil** France
105 D2 **Montreux** Switz.
96 C2 **Montrose** U.K.
136 B3 **Montrose** U.S.A.
147 D3 **Montserrat** *terr.* West Indies
62 A1 **Monywa** Myanmar
108 A1 **Monza** Italy
107 D1 **Monzón** Spain
123 C1 **Mookane** Botswana
52 A1 **Moolawatana** Austr.
52 B1 **Moomba** Austr.
53 D1 **Moonie** Austr.
53 C1 **Moonie** *r.* Austr.
52 A2 **Moonta** Austr.
50 A3 **Moora** Austr.
50 A2 **Moore, Lake** *salt flat* Austr.
137 D1 **Moorhead** U.S.A.
53 C3 **Mooroopna** Austr.
122 A3 **Moorreesburg** S. Africa
130 B3 **Moose** *r.* Can.
130 B2 **Moose Factory** Can.
139 F1 **Moosehead Lake** U.S.A.
129 D2 **Moose Jaw** Can.
137 E1 **Moose Lake** U.S.A.
129 D2 **Moosomin** Can.
130 B2 **Moosonee** Can.
52 B2 **Mootwingee** Austr.
107 D2 **M'Ooukal** Alg.
123 C1 **Mopane** S. Africa
114 B3 **Mopti** Mali
150 B4 **Moquegua** Peru
103 D2 **Mór** Hungary
118 B1 **Mora** Cameroon

93 F3 **Mora** Sweden
137 E1 **Mora** U.S.A.
74 B2 **Moradabad** India
121 □D2 **Morafenobe** Madag.
121 □D2 **Moramanga** Madag.
136 A2 **Moran** U.S.A.
51 D2 **Moranbah** Austr.
103 D2 **Morava** *r.* Europe
96 B2 **Moray Firth** *b.* U.K.
100 C3 **Morbach** Ger.
74 B2 **Morbi** India
93 G4 **Mörbylånga** Sweden
104 B3 **Morcenx** France
69 E1 **Mordaga** China
129 E3 **Morden** Can.
89 F3 **Mordovo** Rus. Fed.
98 B2 **Morecambe** U.K.
98 B2 **Morecambe Bay** U.K.
53 C1 **Moree** Austr.
59 D3 **Morehead** P.N.G.
138 C3 **Morehead** U.S.A.
141 E2 **Morehead City** U.S.A.
145 B3 **Morelia** Mex.
107 C1 **Morella** Spain
74 B2 **Morena** India
106 B2 **Morena, Sierra** *mts* Spain
110 C2 **Moreni** Romania
142 A3 **Moreno** Mex.
128 A2 **Moresby, Mount** Can.
128 A2 **Moresby Island** Can.
53 D1 **Moreton Island** Austr.
52 A2 **Morgan** Austr.
140 B3 **Morgan City** U.S.A.
141 D1 **Morganton** U.S.A.
139 D3 **Morgantown** U.S.A.
105 D2 **Morges** Switz.
68 C2 **Mori** China
66 D2 **Mori** Japan
53 C1 **Moriarty's Range** *hills* Austr.
128 A2 **Morice Lake** Can.
66 D3 **Morioka** Japan
53 D2 **Morisset** Austr.
104 B2 **Morlaix** France
98 C3 **Morley** U.K.
157 G9 **Mornington Abyssal Plain**
       *sea feature* S. Atlantic Ocean
51 C1 **Mornington Island** Austr.
59 D3 **Morobe** P.N.G.
114 B1 **Morocco** *country* Africa
119 D3 **Morogoro** Tanz.
64 B3 **Moro Gulf** Phil.
122 B2 **Morokweng** S. Africa
121 □D3 **Morombe** Madag.
68 C1 **Mörön** Mongolia
121 □D3 **Morondava** Madag.
106 B2 **Morón de la Frontera** Spain
121 C2 **Moroni** Comoros
59 C2 **Morotai** *i.* Indon.
119 D2 **Moroto** Uganda
98 C2 **Morpeth** U.K.
140 B1 **Morrilton** U.S.A.
154 C1 **Morrinhos** Brazil
54 C1 **Morrinsville** N.Z.
129 E3 **Morris** Can.
137 D1 **Morris** U.S.A.
141 D1 **Morristown** U.S.A.
154 C2 **Morro Agudo** Brazil
155 E1 **Morro d'Anta** Brazil
55 K3 **Morse, Cape** Antarctica
87 D3 **Morshanka** Rus. Fed.
       **Morshansk** Rus. Fed. *see*
       **Morshanka**
151 C3 **Mortes, Rio das** *r.* Brazil
52 B3 **Mortlake** Austr.
48 G3 **Mortlock Islands** Micronesia
138 B2 **Morton** U.S.A.
53 C2 **Morundah** Austr.
53 D3 **Moruya** Austr.
96 B2 **Morvern** *reg.* U.K.
       **Morvi** India *see* **Morbi**
53 C2 **Morwell** Austr.
101 D3 **Mosbach** Ger.
89 E2 **Moscow** Rus. Fed.
134 C1 **Moscow** U.S.A.
100 C3 **Mosel** *r.* Ger.
122 B2 **Moselebe** *watercourse* Botswana
105 D2 **Moselle** *r.* France
134 C1 **Moses Lake** U.S.A.
92 □A3 **Mosfellsbær** Iceland
54 B3 **Mosgiel** N.Z.
88 C2 **Moshchnyy, Ostrov** *i.* Rus. Fed.
89 D2 **Moshenskoye** Rus. Fed.
119 D3 **Moshi** Tanz.
92 F2 **Mosjøen** Norway
       **Moskva** Rus. Fed. *see* **Moscow**
89 E2 **Moskva** *r.* Rus. Fed.
103 D2 **Mosonmagyaróvár** Hungary
146 B4 **Mosquitos, Golfo de los** *b.*
       Panama
93 F4 **Moss** Norway
       **Mossâmedes** Angola *see* **Namibe**
122 B3 **Mossel Bay** S. Africa
122 B3 **Mossel Bay** *b.* S. Africa
118 B3 **Mossendjo** Congo
52 B2 **Mossgiel** Austr.
51 D1 **Mossman** Austr.
151 F3 **Mossoró** Brazil
53 D2 **Moss Vale** Austr.
102 C1 **Most** Czech Rep.
114 C1 **Mostaganem** Alg.
109 C2 **Mostar** Bos.-Herz.
152 C3 **Mostardas** Brazil
106 C1 **Móstoles** Spain
81 C2 **Mosul** Iraq
145 D3 **Motagua** *r.* Guat.

93 G4 **Motala** Sweden
123 C2 **Motetema** S. Africa
96 C3 **Motherwell** U.K.
75 C2 **Motihari** India
107 C2 **Motilla del Palancar** Spain
122 B1 **Motokwe** Botswana
106 C2 **Motril** Spain
110 B2 **Motru** Romania
136 C1 **Mott** U.S.A.
63 A2 **Mottama** Myanmar
63 A2 **Mottama, Gulf of** Myanmar
54 B2 **Motueka** N.Z.
145 D2 **Motul** Mex.
49 L5 **Motu One** *atoll* Fr. Polynesia
114 A3 **Moudjéria** Maur.
111 C3 **Moudros** Greece
118 B3 **Mouila** Gabon
52 B3 **Moulamein** Austr.
105 C2 **Moulins** France
141 D2 **Moultrie** U.S.A.
141 E2 **Moultrie, Lake** U.S.A.
138 B3 **Mound City** U.S.A.
115 D4 **Moundou** Chad
138 C3 **Moundsville** U.S.A.
137 E3 **Mountain Grove** U.S.A.
140 B1 **Mountain Home** *AR* U.S.A.
134 C2 **Mountain Home** *ID* U.S.A.
141 D1 **Mount Airy** U.S.A.
123 C3 **Mount Ayliff** S. Africa
52 A3 **Mount Barker** Austr.
53 C3 **Mount Beauty** Austr.
97 B2 **Mount Bellew** Ireland
121 C2 **Mount Darwin** Zimbabwe
139 F2 **Mount Desert Island** U.S.A.
123 C3 **Mount Fletcher** S. Africa
123 C3 **Mount Frere** S. Africa
52 B3 **Mount Gambier** Austr.
59 D3 **Mount Hagen** P.N.G.
53 C2 **Mount Hope** Austr.
51 C2 **Mount Isa** Austr.
52 A3 **Mount Lofty Range** *mts* Austr.
50 A2 **Mount Magnet** Austr.
52 B2 **Mount Manara** Austr.
54 C1 **Mount Maunganui** N.Z.
97 C2 **Mountmellick** Ireland
111 B2 **Mount Olympus** *mt.* Greece
137 E2 **Mount Pleasant** *IA* U.S.A.
138 C2 **Mount Pleasant** *MI* U.S.A.
141 E2 **Mount Pleasant** *SC* U.S.A.
143 E2 **Mount Pleasant** *TX* U.S.A.
135 D3 **Mount Pleasant** *UT* U.S.A.
99 A4 **Mount's Bay** U.K.
134 B2 **Mount Shasta** U.S.A.
54 B2 **Mount Somers** N.Z.
138 B3 **Mount Vernon** *IL* U.S.A.
138 C2 **Mount Vernon** *OH* U.S.A.
134 B1 **Mount Vernon** *WA* U.S.A.
51 D2 **Moura** Austr.
106 B2 **Moura** Port.
115 E3 **Mourdi, Dépression du** *depr.*
       Chad
97 C1 **Mourne Mountains** *hills* U.K.
100 A2 **Mouscron** Belgium
115 D3 **Moussoro** Chad
61 D1 **Moutong** Indon.
115 C2 **Mouydir, Monts du** *plat.* Alg.
100 B3 **Mouzon** France
97 B1 **Moy** *r.* Ireland
117 B4 **Moyale** Eth.
       **Moyen Congo** *country* Africa *see*
       **Congo**
123 C3 **Moyeni** Lesotho
76 B2 **Mo'ynoq** Uzbek.
119 D2 **Moyo** Uganda
77 D2 **Moyynkum** Kazakh.
77 D2 **Moyynty** Kazakh.
121 C3 **Mozambique** *country* Africa
113 G8 **Mozambique Channel** Africa
81 C1 **Mozdok** Rus. Fed.
89 E2 **Mozhaysk** Rus. Fed.
119 D3 **Mpanda** Tanz.
121 C2 **Mpika** Zambia
118 B2 **Mpoko** *r.* C.A.R.
121 C1 **Mporokoso** Zambia
123 C2 **Mpumalanga** *prov.* S. Africa
119 D3 **Mpwapwa** Tanz.
62 A1 **Mrauk-U** Myanmar
115 C1 **M'Saken** Tunisia
119 D3 **Msambweni** Kenya
119 D3 **Msata** Tanz.
88 C2 **Mshinskaya** Rus. Fed.
115 C1 **M'Sila** Alg.
89 D2 **Msta** *r.* Rus. Fed.
89 D2 **Mstinskiy Most** Rus. Fed.
89 D3 **Mstsislaw** Belarus
       **Mtoko** Zimbabwe *see* **Mutoko**
89 E3 **Mtsensk** Rus. Fed.
123 D2 **Mtubatuba** S. Africa
119 E4 **Mtwara** Tanz.
151 E3 **Muana** Brazil
118 B3 **Muanda** Dem. Rep. Congo
62 B1 **Muang Hiam** Laos
62 B2 **Muang Hinboun** Laos
63 B2 **Muang Không** Laos
63 B2 **Muang Khôngxédôn** Laos
62 B1 **Muang Ngoy** Laos
62 B2 **Muang Pakbeng** Laos
63 B2 **Muang Phalan** Laos
62 B2 **Muang Phôn-Hông** Laos
62 B1 **Muang Sing** Laos
62 B2 **Muang Vangviang** Laos
60 B1 **Muar** Malaysia
60 B2 **Muarabungo** Indon.
60 B2 **Muaradua** Indon.
61 C2 **Muaralaung** Indon.

Narnaul
199

60 A2 **Muarasiberut** Indon.
60 B2 **Muaratembesi** Indon.
61 C2 **Muarateweh** Indon.
**Muara Tuang** Malaysia *see* Kota Samarahan
119 D2 **Mubende** Uganda
115 D3 **Mubi** Nigeria
120 B2 **Muconda** Angola
120 A2 **Mucope** Angola
121 C2 **Mucubela** Moz.
155 E1 **Mucuri** Brazil
155 E1 **Mucuri** *r.* Brazil
66 A2 **Mudanjiang** China
66 A1 **Mudan Jiang** *r.* China
111 C2 **Mudanya** Turkey
136 B2 **Muddy Gap** U.S.A.
101 E1 **Müden (Örtze)** Ger.
53 C2 **Mudgee** Austr.
63 A2 **Mudon** Myanmar
80 B1 **Mudurnu** Turkey
121 C2 **Mueda** Moz.
121 B2 **Mufulira** Zambia
120 B2 **Mufumbwe** Zambia
111 C3 **Muğla** Turkey
116 B2 **Muhammad Qol** Sudan
**Muhammarah** Iran *see* Khorramshahr
101 F2 **Mühlberg** Ger.
101 E2 **Mühlhausen (Thüringen)** Ger.
88 B2 **Muhu** *i.* Estonia
63 B3 **Mui Ca Mau** *c.* Vietnam
97 C2 **Muine Bheag** Ireland
96 B3 **Muirkirk** U.K.
121 C2 **Muite** Moz.
65 B2 **Muju** S. Korea
**Mukačevo** Ukr. *see* **Mukacheve**
90 A2 **Mukacheve** Ukr.
61 C1 **Mukah** *Sarawak* Malaysia
79 B3 **Mukalla** Yemen
63 B2 **Mukdahan** Thai.
**Mukden** China *see* **Shenyang**
**Mukhtuya** Rus. Fed. *see* **Lensk**
50 A3 **Mukinbudin** Austr.
60 B2 **Mukomuko** Indon.
121 C2 **Mulanje, Mount** Malawi
101 F2 **Mulde** *r.* Ger.
119 D3 **Muleba** Tanz.
144 A2 **Mulegé** Mex.
143 C2 **Muleshoe** U.S.A.
106 C2 **Mulhacén** *mt.* Spain
100 C2 **Mülheim an der Ruhr** Ger.
105 D2 **Mulhouse** France
62 B1 **Muli** China
66 B2 **Muling** China
66 B1 **Muling He** *r.* China
96 B2 **Mull** *i.* U.K.
53 C2 **Mullaley** Austr.
136 C2 **Mullen** U.S.A.
61 C1 **Muller, Pegunungan** *mts* Indon.
50 A2 **Mullewa** Austr.
97 C2 **Mullingar** Ireland
96 B3 **Mull of Galloway** *c.* U.K.
96 B3 **Mull of Kintyre** *hd* U.K.
96 A3 **Mull of Oa** *hd* U.K.
53 D1 **Mullumbimby** Austr.
120 B2 **Mulobezi** Zambia
74 B1 **Multan** Pak.
86 F2 **Mulym'ya** Rus. Fed.
74 B3 **Mumbai** India
120 B2 **Mumbeji** Zambia
120 B2 **Mumbwa** Zambia
61 D2 **Muna** *i.* Indon.
145 D2 **Muna** Mex.
101 E2 **Münchberg** Ger.
**München** Ger. *see* Munich
**München-Gladbach** Ger. *see* Mönchengladbach
138 B2 **Muncie** U.S.A.
50 B3 **Mundrabilla** Austr.
138 B3 **Munfordville** U.S.A.
119 C2 **Mungbere** Dem. Rep. Congo
75 C2 **Munger** India
52 A1 **Mungeranie** Austr.
53 C1 **Mungindi** Austr.
102 C2 **Munich** Ger.
155 D2 **Muniz Freire** Brazil
101 E1 **Münster** Ger.
100 C2 **Münster** Ger.
97 B2 **Munster** *reg.* Ireland
100 C2 **Münsterland** *reg.* Ger.
62 B1 **Mương Nhie** Vietnam
92 H2 **Muonio** Fin.
92 H2 **Muonioälven** *r.* Fin./Sweden
**Muqdisho** Somalia *see* **Mogadishu**
155 D2 **Muqui** Brazil
103 D2 **Mur** *r.* Austria
67 C3 **Murakami** Japan
119 C3 **Muramvya** Burundi
119 D3 **Murang'a** Kenya
86 D3 **Murashi** Rus. Fed.
81 B2 **Murat** *r.* Turkey
111 C2 **Muratlı** Turkey
67 D3 **Murayama** Japan
50 A2 **Murchison** *watercourse* Austr.
107 C2 **Murcia** Spain
107 C2 **Murcia** *reg.* Spain
136 C2 **Murdo** U.S.A.
131 D3 **Murdochville** Can.
111 C2 **Mürefte** Turkey
110 B1 **Mureşul** *r.* Romania
104 C3 **Muret** France
140 C1 **Murfreesboro** U.S.A.
77 C3 **Murghab** *r.* Afgh.
77 D3 **Murghob** Tajik.
155 D2 **Muriaé** Brazil
120 B1 **Muriege** Angola
101 F1 **Müritz** *l.* Ger.
92 J2 **Murmansk** Rus. Fed.
86 C2 **Murmanskiy Bereg** *coastal area* Rus. Fed.
87 D3 **Murom** Rus. Fed.
66 D2 **Muroran** Japan
106 B1 **Muros** Spain
67 B4 **Muroto** Japan
67 B4 **Muroto-zaki** *pt* Japan
141 D1 **Murphy** U.S.A.
53 C1 **Murra Murra** Austr.
52 A3 **Murray** *r.* Austr.
128 B2 **Murray** *r.* Can.
138 B3 **Murray** U.S.A.
59 D3 **Murray, Lake** P.N.G.
141 D2 **Murray, Lake** U.S.A.
52 A3 **Murray Bridge** Austr.
122 B3 **Murraysburg** S. Africa
52 B3 **Murrayville** Austr.
52 B2 **Murrumbidgee** *r.* Austr.
53 C2 **Murrumburrah** Austr.
121 C2 **Murrupula** Moz.
53 D2 **Murrurundi** Austr.
109 C1 **Murska Sobota** Slovenia
54 C1 **Murupara** N.Z.
49 N6 **Mururoa** *atoll* Fr. Polynesia
75 C2 **Murwara** India
53 D1 **Murwillumbah** Austr.
76 C3 **Murzechirla** Turkm.
115 D2 **Murzūq** Libya
103 D2 **Mürzzuschlag** Austria
81 C2 **Muş** Turkey
110 B2 **Musala** *mt.* Bulg.
65 B1 **Musan** N. Korea
78 B3 **Musaymir** Yemen
79 C2 **Muscat** Oman
**Muscat and Oman** *country* Asia *see* **Oman**
137 E2 **Muscatine** U.S.A.
50 C2 **Musgrave Ranges** *mts* Austr.
118 B3 **Mushie** Dem. Rep. Congo
60 B2 **Musi** *r.* Indon.
123 D1 **Musina** S. Africa
138 B2 **Muskegon** U.S.A.
138 B2 **Muskegon** *r.* U.S.A.
138 C3 **Muskingum** *r.* U.S.A.
143 D1 **Muskogee** U.S.A.
139 D1 **Muskoka, Lake** Can.
128 B2 **Muskwa** *r.* Can.
74 A1 **Muslimbagh** Pak.
116 B3 **Musmar** Sudan
119 D3 **Musoma** Tanz.
59 D3 **Mussau Island** P.N.G.
96 C3 **Musselburgh** U.K.
117 C4 **Mustahīl** Eth.
88 B2 **Mustjala** Estonia
53 D2 **Muswellbrook** Austr.
116 A2 **Mūţ** Egypt
121 C2 **Mutare** Zimbabwe
121 C2 **Mutoko** Zimbabwe
66 D2 **Mutsu** Japan
66 D2 **Mutsu-wan** *b.* Japan
121 C2 **Mutuali** Moz.
155 D1 **Mutum** Brazil
92 I2 **Muurola** Fin.
70 A2 **Mu Us Shamo** *des.* China
120 A1 **Muxaluando** Angola
86 C2 **Muyezerskiy** Rus. Fed.
119 D3 **Muyinga** Burundi
74 B1 **Muzaffargarh** Pak.
75 C2 **Muzaffarpur** India
123 D1 **Muzamane** Moz.
155 C2 **Muzambinho** Brazil
144 B2 **Múzquiz** Mex.
75 C1 **Muz Tag** *mt.* China
117 A4 **Mvolo** Sudan
119 C3 **Mwanza** Dem. Rep. Congo
119 D3 **Mwanza** Tanz.
118 C3 **Mweka** Dem. Rep. Congo
121 B2 **Mwenda** Zambia
118 C3 **Mwene-Ditu** Dem. Rep. Congo
121 C3 **Mwenezi** Zimbabwe
121 C3 **Mwenezi** *r.* Zimbabwe
119 C3 **Mweru, Lake** Dem. Rep. Congo/Zambia
121 B1 **Mweru Wantipa, Lake** Zambia
118 C3 **Mwimba** Dem. Rep. Congo
120 B2 **Mwinilunga** Zambia
88 C3 **Myadzyel** Belarus
62 A2 **Myanaung** Myanmar
62 A1 **Myanmar** *country* Asia
63 A2 **Myaungmya** Myanmar
63 A2 **Myeik** Myanmar
**Mergui Archipelago** *is* Myanmar *see* **Mergui Archipelago**
62 A1 **Myingyan** Myanmar
62 A1 **Myitkyina** Myanmar
90 A2 **Mykolayiv** Ukr.
91 C2 **Mykolayiv** Ukr.
111 C3 **Mykonos** Greece
111 C3 **Mykonos** *i.* Greece
86 E2 **Myla** Rus. Fed.
75 D2 **Mymensingh** Bangl.
65 B1 **Myŏnggan** N. Korea
88 C2 **Myory** Belarus
92 □B3 **Mýrdalsjökull** *ice cap* Iceland
92 G2 **Myre** Norway
91 C2 **Myrhorod** Ukr.
111 C3 **Myrina** Greece
90 C2 **Myronivka** Ukr.
141 E2 **Myrtle Beach** U.S.A.
53 C3 **Myrtleford** Austr.
134 B2 **Myrtle Point** U.S.A.
89 E2 **Myshkin** Rus. Fed.
**Myshkino** Rus. Fed. *see* **Myshkin**
103 C1 **Myślibórz** Pol.
73 B3 **Mysore** India
83 N2 **Mys Shmidta** Rus. Fed.
63 B2 **My Tho** Vietnam
111 C3 **Mytilini** Greece
89 E3 **Mytishchi** Rus. Fed.
123 C3 **Mzamomhle** S. Africa
121 C2 **Mzimba** Malawi
121 C2 **Mzuzu** Malawi

## N

101 F3 **Naab** *r.* Ger.
100 B1 **Naarden** Neth.
97 C2 **Naas** Ireland
122 A2 **Nababeep** S. Africa
87 E3 **Naberezhnyye Chelny** Rus. Fed.
59 D3 **Nabire** Indon.
80 B2 **Nāblus** West Bank
123 C1 **Naboomspruit** S. Africa
121 D2 **Nacala** Moz.
119 D4 **Nachingwea** Tanz.
103 D1 **Náchod** Czech Rep.
73 D3 **Nachuge** India
143 E2 **Nacogdoches** U.S.A.
144 B1 **Nacozari de García** Mex.
**Nada** China *see* **Danzhou**
74 B2 **Nadiad** India
90 A2 **Nadvirna** Ukr.
86 C2 **Nadvoitsy** Rus. Fed.
86 G2 **Nadym** Rus. Fed.
93 F4 **Næstved** Denmark
111 B3 **Nafpaktos** Greece
111 B3 **Nafplio** Greece
115 D1 **Nafūsah, Jabal** *hills* Libya
78 B2 **Nafy** Saudi Arabia
64 B2 **Naga** Phil.
130 B2 **Nagagami** *r.* Can.
67 C3 **Nagano** Japan
67 C3 **Nagaoka** Japan
75 D2 **Nagaon** India
74 B1 **Nagar** India
74 B2 **Nagar Parkar** Pak.
67 A4 **Nagasaki** Japan
67 B4 **Nagato** Japan
74 B2 **Nagaur** India
73 B4 **Nagercoil** India
74 A2 **Nagha Kalat** Pak.
74 B2 **Nagina** India
67 C3 **Nagoya** Japan
75 B2 **Nagpur** India
75 D1 **Nagqu** China
141 E1 **Nags Head** U.S.A.
82 E1 **Nagurskoye** Rus. Fed.
103 D2 **Nagyatád** Hungary
103 D2 **Nagykanizsa** Hungary
128 B1 **Nahanni Butte** Can.
81 C2 **Nahāvand** Iran
101 E1 **Nahrendorf** Ger.
153 A4 **Nahuel Huapí, Lago** *l.* Arg.
141 D2 **Nahunta** U.S.A.
131 D2 **Nain** Can.
81 D2 **Nā'īn** Iran
121 C2 **Naiopué** Moz.
96 C2 **Nairn** U.K.
119 D3 **Nairobi** Kenya
**Naissus** Serb. and Mont. *see* **Niš**
119 D3 **Naivasha** Kenya
81 D2 **Najafābād** Iran
78 B2 **Najd** *reg.* Saudi Arabia
106 C1 **Nájera** Spain
65 C1 **Najin** N. Korea
78 B3 **Najrān** Saudi Arabia
119 D2 **Nakasongola** Uganda
67 C3 **Nakatsugawa** Japan
78 A3 **Nakfa** Eritrea
66 B2 **Nakhodka** Rus. Fed.
63 B2 **Nakhon Nayok** Thai.
63 B2 **Nakhon Pathom** Thai.
62 B2 **Nakhon Phanom** Thai.
63 B2 **Nakhon Ratchasima** Thai.
63 B2 **Nakhon Sawan** Thai.
63 A3 **Nakhon Si Thammarat** Thai.
**Nakhrachi** Rus. Fed. *see* Kondinskoye
130 B2 **Nakina** Can.
126 B3 **Naknek** U.S.A.
121 C1 **Nakonde** Zambia
93 F5 **Nakskov** Denmark
119 D3 **Nakuru** Kenya
128 C2 **Nakusp** Can.
75 D2 **Nalbari** India
87 D4 **Nal'chik** Rus. Fed.
115 D1 **Nālūt** Libya
123 D2 **Namaacha** Moz.
123 C2 **Namahadi** S. Africa
81 D2 **Namak, Daryācheh-ye** *salt flat* Iran
76 B3 **Namak, Kavīr-e** *salt flat* Iran
79 C1 **Namakzar-e Shadad** *salt flat* Iran
77 D2 **Namangan** Uzbek.
119 D3 **Namanyere** Tanz.
122 A2 **Namaqualand** *reg.* S. Africa
51 E2 **Nambour** Austr.
53 D2 **Nambucca Heads** Austr.
63 B3 **Năm Căn** Vietnam
75 D1 **Nam Co** *salt l.* China
62 B1 **Nam Đinh** Vietnam
121 C2 **Namialo** Moz.
120 A3 **Namib Desert** Namibia
120 A2 **Namibe** Angola
120 A3 **Namibia** *country* Africa
72 D2 **Namjagbarwa Feng** *mt.* China
59 C3 **Namlea** Indon.
62 B2 **Nam Ngum Reservoir** Laos
53 C2 **Namoi** *r.* Austr.
134 C2 **Nampa** U.S.A.
114 B3 **Nampala** Mali
65 B2 **Namp'o** N. Korea
121 C2 **Nampula** Moz.
72 D2 **Namrup** India
62 A1 **Namsang** Myanmar
92 F3 **Namsos** Norway
92 F3 **Namsskogan** Norway
63 A2 **Nam Tok** Thai.
83 J2 **Namtsy** Rus. Fed.
62 A1 **Namtu** Myanmar
121 C2 **Namuno** Moz.
100 B2 **Namur** Belgium
120 B2 **Namwala** Zambia
65 B2 **Namwŏn** S. Korea
62 A1 **Namya Ra** Myanmar
62 B2 **Nan** Thai.
128 B3 **Nanaimo** Can.
71 B3 **Nan'an** China
122 A1 **Nananib Plateau** Namibia
**Nan'ao** China *see* **Dayu**
67 C3 **Nanao** Japan
71 B3 **Nanchang** *Jiangxi* China
71 B3 **Nanchang** *Jiangxi* China
71 B3 **Nancheng** China
70 A2 **Nanchong** China
63 A3 **Nancowry** *i.* India
105 D2 **Nancy** France
75 C1 **Nanda Devi** *mt.* India
71 A3 **Nandan** China
74 B3 **Nanded** India
**Nander** India *see* **Nanded**
53 D2 **Nandewar Range** *mts* Austr.
74 B2 **Nandurbar** India
73 B3 **Nandyal** India
71 B3 **Nanfeng** China
62 A1 **Nang** China
118 B2 **Nanga Eboko** Cameroon
61 C2 **Nangahpinoh** Indon.
77 D3 **Nanga Parbat** *mt.* Jammu and Kashmir
61 C2 **Nangatayap** Indon.
63 A2 **Nangin** Myanmar
65 B1 **Nangnim-sanmaek** *mts* N. Korea
70 B2 **Nangong** China
119 D3 **Nangulangwa** Tanz.
70 C2 **Nanhui** China
70 B2 **Nanjing** China
**Nanking** China *see* **Nanjing**
67 B4 **Nankoku** Japan
120 A2 **Nankova** Angola
70 B2 **Nanle** China
71 B3 **Nan Ling** *mts* China
71 A3 **Nanning** China
127 I2 **Nanortalik** Greenland
71 A3 **Nanpan Jiang** *r.* China
75 C2 **Nanpara** India
71 B3 **Nanping** China
**Nanpu** China *see* **Pucheng**
**Nansei-shotō** Japan *see* Ryukyu Islands
160 I1 **Nansen Basin** *sea feature* Arctic Ocean
126 F1 **Nansen Sound** *sea chan.* Can.
104 B2 **Nantes** France
70 C2 **Nantong** China
139 E2 **Nantucket** U.S.A.
139 F2 **Nantucket Island** U.S.A.
99 B3 **Nantwich** U.K.
49 I4 **Nanumea** *i.* Tuvalu
155 D1 **Nanuque** Brazil
64 B3 **Nanusa, Kepulauan** *is* Indon.
71 B3 **Nanxiong** China
70 B2 **Nanyang** China
119 D3 **Nanyuki** Kenya
70 B2 **Nanzhang** China
**Nanzhao** China *see* **Zhao'an**
107 D2 **Nao, Cabo de la** *c.* Spain
131 C2 **Naococane, Lac** *l.* Can.
74 A2 **Naokot** Pak.
71 B3 **Naozhou Dao** *i.* China
135 B3 **Napa** U.S.A.
126 E2 **Napaktulik Lake** Can.
139 D2 **Napanee** Can.
127 I2 **Napasoq** Greenland
137 F2 **Naperville** U.S.A.
54 C1 **Napier** N.Z.
108 B2 **Naples** Italy
141 D3 **Naples** U.S.A.
150 B3 **Napo** *r.* Ecuador
**Napoli** Italy *see* **Naples**
**Napug** China *see* **Gê'gyai**
114 B3 **Nara** Mali
88 C3 **Narach** Belarus
52 B3 **Naracoorte** Austr.
53 C2 **Naradhan** Austr.
145 C2 **Naranjos** Mex.
63 B3 **Narathiwat** Thai.
74 B3 **Narayangaon** India
105 C3 **Narbonne** France
63 A2 **Narcondam Island** India
127 H1 **Nares Strait** Can./Greenland
103 E1 **Narew** *r.* Pol.
122 A1 **Narib** Namibia
87 D4 **Narimanov** Rus. Fed.
67 D3 **Narita** Japan
74 B2 **Narmada** *r.* India
74 B2 **Narnaul** India

108 B2 **Narni** Italy
86 F2 **Narodnaya, Gora** *mt.* Rus. Fed.
90 B1 **Narodychi** Ukr.
89 E2 **Naro-Fominsk** Rus. Fed.
53 D3 **Narooma** Austr.
88 C3 **Narowlya** Belarus
93 H3 **Närpes** Fin.
53 C2 **Narrabri** Austr.
53 C2 **Narrandera** Austr.
53 C2 **Narromine** Austr.
67 B4 **Naruto** Japan
88 C2 **Narva** Estonia
88 C2 **Narva Bay** Estonia/Rus. Fed.
92 G2 **Narvik** Norway
88 C2 **Narvskoye Vodokhranilishche** *resr* Estonia/Rus. Fed.
86 E2 **Nar'yan-Mar** Rus. Fed.
77 E2 **Naryn** Kyrg.
74 B2 **Nashik** India
139 E2 **Nashua** U.S.A.
140 C1 **Nashville** U.S.A.
137 E1 **Nashwauk** U.S.A.
109 C1 **Našice** Croatia
117 B4 **Nasir** Sudan
**Nasirabad** Bangl. *see* Mymensingh
119 C4 **Nasondoye** Dem. Rep. Congo
76 B3 **Naşrābād** Iran
128 C2 **Nass** *r.* Can.
146 C2 **Nassau** Bahamas
116 B2 **Nasser, Lake** *resr* Egypt
93 F4 **Nässjö** Sweden
130 C2 **Nastapoca** *r.* Can.
130 C2 **Nastapoka Islands** Can.
89 D2 **Nasva** Rus. Fed.
120 B3 **Nata** Botswana
151 F3 **Natal** Brazil
60 A1 **Natal** Indon.
**Natal** *prov.* S. Africa *see* Kwazulu-Natal
159 D6 **Natal Basin** *sea feature* Indian Ocean
143 D3 **Natalia** U.S.A.
131 D2 **Natashquan** Can.
131 D2 **Natashquan** *r.* Can.
140 B2 **Natchez** U.S.A.
140 B2 **Natchitoches** U.S.A.
53 C3 **Nathalia** Austr.
107 D1 **Nati, Punta** *pt* Spain
114 C3 **Natitingou** Benin
151 E4 **Natividade** Brazil
67 D3 **Natori** Japan
119 D3 **Natron, Lake** *salt l.* Tanz.
60 B1 **Natuna, Kepulauan** *is* Indon.
60 B1 **Natuna Besar** *i.* Indon.
122 A1 **Nauchas** Namibia
101 F1 **Nauen** Ger.
64 B2 **Naujan** Phil.
88 B2 **Naujoji Akmenė** Lith.
101 E2 **Naumburg (Saale)** Ger.
48 H34 **Nauru** *country* S. Pacific Ocean
150 B3 **Nauta** Peru
145 C2 **Nautla** Mex.
88 C2 **Navahrudak** Belarus
106 B2 **Navalmoral de la Mata** Spain
106 B2 **Navalvillar de Pela** Spain
97 C2 **Navan** Ireland
**Navangar** India *see* Jamnagar
88 C2 **Navapolatsk** Belarus
83 M2 **Navarin, Mys** *c.* Rus. Fed.
153 B5 **Navarino, Isla** *i.* Chile
107 C1 **Navarra** *reg.* Spain
**Navarre** *aut. comm.* Spain *see* Navarra
96 B1 **Naver** *r.* U.K.
89 D3 **Navlya** Rus. Fed.
110 C2 **Năvodari** Romania
77 C2 **Navoiy** Uzbek.
144 B2 **Navojoa** Mex.
144 B2 **Navolato** Mex.
74 A2 **Nawabshah** Pak.
75 C2 **Nawada** India
62 A1 **Nawnghkio** Myanmar
62 A1 **Nawngleng** Myanmar
81 C2 **Naxçıvan** Azer.
111 C3 **Naxos** Greece
111 C3 **Naxos** *i.* Greece
144 B2 **Nayar** Mex.
66 D2 **Nayoro** Japan
80 B2 **Nazareth** Israel
144 B2 **Nazas** Mex.
144 B2 **Nazas** *r.* Mex.
150 B4 **Nazca** Peru
157 H7 **Nazca Ridge** *sea feature* S. Pacific Ocean
111 C3 **Nazilli** Turkey
117 B4 **Nazrēt** Eth.
79 C2 **Nazwá** Oman
121 B1 **Nchelenge** Zambia
122 B1 **Ncojane** Botswana
120 A1 **N'dalatando** Angola
118 C2 **Ndélé** C.A.R.
118 B3 **Ndendé** Gabon
115 D3 **Ndjamena** Chad
118 A3 **Ndogo, Lagune** *lag.* Gabon
121 B2 **Ndola** Zambia
97 C1 **Neagh, Lough** *l.* U.K.
50 C2 **Neale, Lake** *salt flat* Austr.
111 B3 **Neapoli** Greece
111 B2 **Nea Roda** Greece
99 B4 **Neath** U.K.
119 D2 **Nebbi** Uganda
53 C1 **Nebine Creek** *r.* Austr.
150 C2 **Neblina, Pico da** *mt.* Brazil
135 D3 **Nebo, Mount** U.S.A.

89 D2 **Nebolchi** Rus. Fed.
136 C2 **Nebraska** *state* U.S.A.
137 D2 **Nebraska City** U.S.A.
108 B3 **Nebrodi, Monti** *mts* Sicily Italy
143 E3 **Neches** *r.* U.S.A.
156 E4 **Necker Island** U.S.A.
153 C3 **Necochea** Arg.
143 E3 **Nederland** U.S.A.
100 B2 **Neder Rijn** *r.* Neth.
130 C2 **Nedlouc, Lac** *l.* Can.
139 E2 **Needham** U.S.A.
135 D4 **Needles** U.S.A.
74 B2 **Neemuch** India
129 E2 **Neepawa** Can.
87 E3 **Neftekamsk** Rus. Fed.
82 F2 **Nefteyugansk** Rus. Fed.
108 A3 **Nefza** Tunisia
120 A1 **Negage** Angola
117 B4 **Negēlē** Eth.
109 D2 **Negotin** Serb. and Mont.
111 B2 **Negotino** Macedonia
150 A3 **Negra, Punta** *pt* Peru
155 D1 **Negra, Serra** *mts* Brazil
63 A2 **Negrais, Cape** Myanmar
153 B4 **Negro** *r.* Arg.
152 C3 **Negro** *r.* S. America
152 C3 **Negro** *r.* Uru.
106 B2 **Negro, Cabo** *c.* Morocco
64 B3 **Negros** *i.* Phil.
79 D1 **Nehbandān** Iran
69 E1 **Nehe** China
70 A3 **Neijiang** China
129 D2 **Neilburg** Can.
150 B2 **Neiva** Col.
129 E2 **Nejanilini Lake** Can.
**Nejd** *reg.* Saudi Arabia *see* Najd
117 B4 **Nek'emtē** Eth.
89 E2 **Nekrasovskoye** Rus. Fed.
89 D2 **Nelidovo** Rus. Fed.
73 B3 **Nellore** India
128 C3 **Nelson** Can.
129 E2 **Nelson** *r.* Can.
54 B2 **Nelson** N.Z.
52 B3 **Nelson, Cape** Austr.
53 D2 **Nelson Bay** Austr.
129 D2 **Nelson House** Can.
134 E1 **Nelson Reservoir** U.S.A.
123 C2 **Nelspruit** S. Africa
114 B3 **Néma** Maur.
88 B2 **Neman** Rus. Fed.
105 C2 **Nemours** France
66 D2 **Nemuro** Japan
90 B2 **Nemyriv** Ukr.
97 B2 **Nenagh** Ireland
99 D3 **Nene** *r.* U.K.
69 E1 **Nenjiang** China
137 E3 **Neosho** U.S.A.
75 C2 **Nepal** *country* Asia
75 C2 **Nepalganj** Nepal
139 D1 **Nepean** Can.
135 D3 **Nephi** U.S.A.
97 B1 **Nephin** *hill* Ireland
97 B1 **Nephin Beg Range** *hills* Ireland
131 D3 **Nepisiguit** *r.* Can.
119 C2 **Nepoko** *r.* Dem. Rep. Congo
139 E2 **Neptune** U.S.A.
108 B2 **Nera** *r.* Italy
104 C3 **Nérac** France
53 D1 **Nerang** Austr.
69 D1 **Nerchinsk** Rus. Fed.
89 F2 **Nerekhta** Rus. Fed.
109 C2 **Neretva** *r.* Bos.-Herz./Croatia
120 B2 **Neriquinha** Angola
88 B3 **Neris** *r.* Lith.
89 E2 **Nerl'** *r.* Rus. Fed.
86 F2 **Nerokhi** Rus. Fed.
154 C1 **Nerópolis** Brazil
83 J3 **Neryungri** Rus. Fed.
92 □C2 **Neskaupstaður** Iceland
96 B2 **Ness, Loch** *l.* U.K.
136 D3 **Ness City** U.S.A.
**Nesterov** Ukr. *see* Zhovkva
111 B2 **Nestos** *r.* Greece
100 B1 **Netherlands** *country* Europe
147 D3 **Netherlands Antilles** *terr.* West Indies
127 H2 **Nettilling Lake** Can.
101 F1 **Neubrandenburg** Ger.
105 D2 **Neuchâtel** Switz.
105 D2 **Neuchâtel, Lac de** *l.* Switz.
100 C2 **Neuerburg** Ger.
100 B3 **Neufchâteau** Belgium
105 D2 **Neufchâteau** France
104 C2 **Neufchâtel-en-Bray** France
101 D2 **Neuhof** Ger.
101 E3 **Neumarkt in der Oberpfalz** Ger.
102 B1 **Neumünster** Ger.
100 C3 **Neunkirchen** Ger.
153 B3 **Neuquén** Arg.
153 B3 **Neuquén** *r.* Arg.
101 F1 **Neuruppin** Ger.
100 C2 **Neuss** Ger.
101 D1 **Neustadt am Rübenberge** Ger.
101 E3 **Neustadt an der Aisch** Ger.
**Neustadt an der Hardt** Ger. *see* Neustadt an der Weinstraße
101 D3 **Neustadt an der Weinstraße** Ger.
101 E1 **Neustadt-Glewe** Ger.
101 F1 **Neustrelitz** Ger.
99 D5 **Neuville-lès-Dieppe** France
100 C2 **Neuwied** Ger.
137 E3 **Nevada** U.S.A.
135 C3 **Nevada** *state* U.S.A.
106 C2 **Nevada, Sierra** *mts* Spain
135 B2 **Nevada, Sierra** *mts* U.S.A.

88 C2 **Nevaišių kalnis** *hill* Lith.
105 E2 **Nevel'** Rus. Fed.
105 C2 **Nevers** France
53 C2 **Nevertire** Austr.
109 C2 **Nevesinje** Bos.-Herz.
87 D4 **Nevinnomyssk** Rus. Fed.
80 B2 **Nevşehir** Turkey
99 C4 **New Addington** U.K.
128 B2 **New Aiyansh** Can.
119 D4 **Newala** Tanz.
138 B3 **New Albany** U.S.A.
151 D2 **New Amsterdam** Guyana
139 E2 **Newark** *NJ* U.S.A.
138 C2 **Newark** *OH* U.S.A.
99 C3 **Newark-on-Trent** U.K.
139 E2 **New Bedford** U.S.A.
141 E1 **New Bern** U.S.A.
138 B1 **Newberry** *MI* U.S.A.
141 D2 **Newberry** *SC* U.S.A.
143 E2 **New Boston** U.S.A.
143 D3 **New Braunfels** U.S.A.
97 C2 **Newbridge** Ireland
59 D3 **New Britain** *i.* P.N.G.
131 D3 **New Brunswick** *prov.* Can.
99 C4 **Newbury** U.K.
48 H6 **New Caledonia** *terr.* S. Pacific Ocean
156 D7 **New Caledonia Trough** *sea feature* Tasman Sea
53 D2 **Newcastle** Austr.
123 C2 **Newcastle** S. Africa
97 D1 **Newcastle** U.K.
138 C2 **New Castle** U.S.A.
136 C2 **Newcastle** U.S.A.
99 B3 **Newcastle-under-Lyme** U.K.
98 C2 **Newcastle upon Tyne** U.K.
51 C1 **Newcastle Waters** Austr.
97 B2 **Newcastle West** Ireland
74 B2 **New Delhi** India
128 C2 **New Denver** Can.
53 D2 **New England Range** *mts* Austr.
157 H3 **New England Seamounts** *sea feature* N. Atlantic Ocean
131 E1 **Newfoundland** *i.* Can.
131 E2 **Newfoundland and Labrador** *prov.* Can.
96 B3 **New Galloway** U.K.
48 G4 **New Georgia Islands** Solomon Is
131 D3 **New Glasgow** Can.
59 D3 **New Guinea** *i.* Indon./P.N.G.
78 A3 **New Halfa** Sudan
139 E2 **New Hampshire** *state* U.S.A.
59 E3 **New Hanover** *i.* P.N.G.
139 E2 **New Haven** U.S.A.
128 C2 **New Hazelton** Can.
**New Hebrides** *country* S. Pacific Ocean *see* Vanuatu
156 D7 **New Hebrides Trench** *sea feature* S. Pacific Ocean
140 B2 **New Iberia** U.S.A.
59 E3 **New Ireland** *i.* P.N.G.
139 E3 **New Jersey** *state* U.S.A.
130 C3 **New Liskeard** Can.
138 B2 **New London** U.S.A.
50 A2 **Newman** Austr.
54 C2 **Newman** N.Z.
97 C2 **Newmarket** Ireland
99 D3 **Newmarket** U.K.
97 C2 **Newmarket-on-Fergus** Ireland
142 B1 **New Mexico** *state* U.S.A.
141 D2 **Newnan** U.S.A.
140 B3 **New Orleans** U.S.A.
138 C2 **New Philadelphia** U.S.A.
54 B1 **New Plymouth** N.Z.
99 C4 **Newport** England U.K.
99 B3 **Newport** Wales U.K.
140 B1 **Newport** *AR* U.S.A.
134 B2 **Newport** *OR* U.S.A.
139 E2 **Newport** *RI* U.S.A.
141 D1 **Newport** *TN* U.S.A.
139 E2 **Newport** *VT* U.S.A.
134 C1 **Newport** *WA* U.S.A.
139 D3 **Newport News** U.S.A.
141 E3 **New Providence** *i.* Bahamas
99 A4 **Newquay** U.K.
140 B2 **New Roads** U.S.A.
97 C2 **New Ross** Ireland
97 C1 **Newry** U.K.
83 K1 **New Siberia Islands** Rus. Fed.
52 B2 **New South Wales** *state* Austr.
137 E2 **Newton** *IA* U.S.A.
137 D3 **Newton** *KS* U.S.A.
99 B4 **Newton Abbot** U.K.
98 C2 **Newton Aycliffe** U.K.
96 B3 **Newton Mearns** U.K.
96 C3 **Newtonmore** U.K.
96 B3 **Newton Stewart** U.K.
97 B2 **Newtown** Ireland
99 B3 **Newtown** U.K.
136 C2 **New Town** U.S.A.
97 D1 **Newtownabbey** U.K.
97 D1 **Newtownards** U.K.
**Newtownbarry** Ireland *see* Bunclody
97 C1 **Newtownbutler** U.K.
96 C3 **Newtown St Boswells** U.K.
97 C1 **Newtownstewart** U.K.
137 E2 **New Ulm** U.S.A.
139 E2 **New York** U.S.A.
139 D2 **New York** *state* U.S.A.
54 B2 **New Zealand** *country* Oceania
86 D3 **Neya** Rus. Fed.
81 D3 **Neyrīz** Iran
76 B3 **Neyshābūr** Iran
145 C3 **Nezahualcóyotl, Presa** *resr* Mex.

60 B1 **Ngabang** Indon.
118 B3 **Ngabé** Congo
75 C2 **Ngamring** China
119 D2 **Ngangala** Sudan
75 C1 **Ngangla Ringco** *salt l.* China
75 C1 **Nganglong Kangri** *mt.* China
75 C1 **Nganglong Kangri** *mts* China
75 C1 **Ngangzê Co** *salt l.* China
62 A2 **Ngao** Thai.
118 B2 **Ngaoundal** Cameroon
118 B2 **Ngaoundéré** Cameroon
54 C1 **Ngaruawahia** N.Z.
62 A2 **Ngathainggyaung** Myanmar
**Ngiva** Angola *see* Ondjiva
118 B3 **Ngo** Congo
63 B2 **Ngoc Linh** *mt.* Vietnam
115 D4 **Ngol Bembo** Nigeria
115 D3 **Ngourti** Niger
115 D3 **Nguigmi** Niger
59 D2 **Ngulu** *atoll* Micronesia
61 C2 **Ngunut** Indon.
**Ngunza** Angola *see* Sumbe
**Ngunza-Kabolu** Angola *see* Sumbe
115 D3 **Nguru** Nigeria
62 B1 **Nguyên Bình** Vietnam
123 C2 **Ngwathe** S. Africa
123 D2 **Ngwelezana** S. Africa
121 C2 **Nhamalabué** Moz.
120 A2 **N'harea** Angola
63 B2 **Nha Trang** Vietnam
52 B3 **Nhill** Austr.
123 D2 **Nhlangano** Swaziland
51 C1 **Nhulunbuy** Austr.
139 D2 **Niagara Falls** Can.
114 C3 **Niamey** Niger
119 C2 **Niangara** Dem. Rep. Congo
114 B3 **Niangay, Lac** *l.* Mali
119 C2 **Nia-Nia** Dem. Rep. Congo
60 A1 **Nias** *i.* Indon.
88 C2 **Nica** Latvia
146 B3 **Nicaragua** *country* Central America
**Nicaragua, Lago de** Nic. *see* Nicaragua, Lake
146 B3 **Nicaragua, Lake** *l.* Nic.
109 C3 **Nicastro** Italy
105 D3 **Nice** France
73 D4 **Nicobar Islands** India
80 B2 **Nicosia** Cyprus
146 B4 **Nicoya, Golfo de** *b.* Costa Rica
88 B2 **Nida** Lith.
103 E1 **Nidzica** Pol.
102 B1 **Niebüll** Ger.
101 D2 **Niederaula** Ger.
118 B2 **Niefang** Equat. Guinea
101 F1 **Niemegk** Ger.
101 D1 **Nienburg (Weser)** Ger.
103 D1 **Niesky** Ger.
100 B1 **Nieuwegein** Neth.
100 B1 **Nieuwe-Niedorp** Neth.
151 D2 **Nieuw Nickerie** Suriname
122 A3 **Nieuwoudtville** S. Africa
100 A2 **Nieuwpoort** Belgium
80 B2 **Niğde** Turkey
115 C3 **Niger** *country* Africa
115 C4 **Niger** *r.* Africa
115 C4 **Niger, Mouths of the** Nigeria
115 C4 **Nigeria** *country* Africa
130 B3 **Nighthawk Lake** Can.
111 B2 **Nigrita** Greece
67 C3 **Niigata** Japan
67 B4 **Niihama** Japan
67 C4 **Nii-jima** *i.* Japan
67 B4 **Niimi** Japan
67 C3 **Niitsu** Japan
107 C2 **Níjar** Spain
100 B1 **Nijkerk** Neth.
100 B2 **Nijmegen** Neth.
100 C1 **Nijverdal** Neth.
92 J2 **Nikel'** Rus. Fed.
**Nikolayev** Ukr. *see* Mykolayiv
87 D3 **Nikolayevsk** Rus. Fed.
**Nikolayevskiy** Rus. Fed. *see* Nikolayevsk
86 D3 **Nikol'sk** Rus. Fed.
**Nikol'skiy** Kazakh. *see* Satpayev
83 M3 **Nikol'skoye** Rus. Fed.
**Nikol'skoye** Rus. Fed. *see* Sheksna
91 C2 **Nikopol'** Ukr.
80 B1 **Niksar** Turkey
79 D2 **Nīkshahr** Iran
109 C2 **Nikšić** Serb. and Mont.
**Nīl, Bahr el** *r.* Africa *see* Nile
135 C4 **Niland** U.S.A.
116 B1 **Nile** *r.* Africa
138 B2 **Niles** U.S.A.
**Nimach** India *see* Neemuch
105 C3 **Nîmes** France
53 C3 **Nimmitabel** Austr.
117 B4 **Nimule** Sudan
**Nimwegen** Neth. *see* Nijmegen
53 C1 **Nindigully** Austr.
73 B4 **Nine Degree Channel** India
53 C3 **Ninety Mile Beach** Austr.
54 B1 **Ninety Mile Beach** N.Z.
70 C3 **Ningbo** China
71 B3 **Ningde** China
71 B3 **Ningdu** China
70 B2 **Ningguo** China
71 C3 **Ninghai** China
72 D2 **Ninging** India
**Ningjiang** China *see* Songyuan
68 C2 **Ningjing Shan** *mts* China
70 A2 **Ningxia Huizu Zizhiqu** *aut. reg.* China

Nyzhn'ohirs'kyy
201


70 B2 **Ningyang** China
62 B1 **Ninh Binh** Vietnam
63 B2 **Ninh Hoa** Vietnam
66 D2 **Ninohe** Japan
137 D2 **Niobrara** *r.* U.S.A.
62 A1 **Nioko** India
114 B3 **Niono** Mali
114 B3 **Nioro** Mali
104 B2 **Niort** France
129 D2 **Nipawin** Can.
130 B3 **Nipigon** Can.
130 B3 **Nipigon, Lake** Can.
131 D2 **Nipishish Lake** Can.
130 C3 **Nipissing, Lake** Can.
135 C3 **Nipton** U.S.A.
151 E4 **Niquelândia** Brazil
74 B3 **Nirmal** India
109 D2 **Niš** Serb. and Mont.
109 D2 **Nišava** *r.* Serb. and Mont.
108 B3 **Niscemi** *Sicily* Italy
67 B4 **Nishino-omote** Japan
90 B2 **Nisporeni** Moldova
155 D2 **Niterói** Brazil
96 C3 **Nith** *r.* U.K.
103 D2 **Nitra** Slovakia
49 K5 **Niue** *terr.* S. Pacific Ocean
92 H3 **Nivala** Fin.
100 B2 **Nivelles** Belgium
73 B3 **Nizamabad** India
87 E3 **Nizhnekamsk** Rus. Fed.
87 E3 **Nizhnekamskoye Vodokhranilishche** *resr* Rus. Fed.
83 H3 **Nizhneudinsk** Rus. Fed.
82 G2 **Nizhnevartovsk** Rus. Fed.
**Nizhnevolzhsk** Rus. Fed. *see* Narimanov
83 K2 **Nizhneyansk** Rus. Fed.
**Nizhniye Kresty** Rus. Fed. *see* Cherskiy
**Nizhniye Ustriki** Pol. *see* Ustrzyki Dolne
89 F3 **Nizhniy Kislyay** Rus. Fed.
87 D3 **Nizhniy Lomov** Rus. Fed.
87 D3 **Nizhniy Novgorod** Rus. Fed.
86 E2 **Nizhniy Odes** Rus. Fed.
86 E3 **Nizhniy Tagil** Rus. Fed.
83 G2 **Nizhnyaya Tunguska** *r.* Rus. Fed.
86 E3 **Nizhnyaya Tura** Rus. Fed.
91 C1 **Nizhyn** Ukr.
103 E1 **Nizina Mazowiecka** *reg.* Pol.
121 D2 **Njazidja** *i.* Comoros
119 D3 **Njinjo** Tanz.
119 D3 **Njombe** Tanz.
118 B2 **Nkambe** Cameroon
119 D4 **Nkhata Bay** Malawi
121 C2 **Nkhotakota** Malawi
118 A3 **Nkomi, Lagune** *lag.* Gabon
119 D3 **Nkondwe** Tanz.
118 A2 **Nkongsamba** Cameroon
123 C3 **Nkululeko** S. Africa
123 C3 **Nkwenkwezi** S. Africa
67 B4 **Nobeoka** Japan
138 B2 **Noblesville** U.S.A.
52 B1 **Noccundra** Austr.
144 A1 **Nogales** Mex.
142 A2 **Nogales** U.S.A.
104 C2 **Nogent-le-Rotrou** France
83 H2 **Noginsk** Rus. Fed.
89 E2 **Noginsk** Rus. Fed.
83 K3 **Nogliki** Rus. Fed.
74 B2 **Nohar** India
100 C3 **Nohfelden** Ger.
104 B2 **Noires, Montagnes** *hills* France
104 B2 **Noirmoutier, Île de** *i.* France
104 B2 **Noirmoutier-en-l'Île** France
67 C4 **Nojima-zaki** *c.* Japan
74 B2 **Nokha** India
93 H3 **Nokia** Fin.
74 A2 **Nok Kundi** Pak.
118 B2 **Nola** C.A.R.
86 D3 **Nolinsk** Rus. Fed.
126 A2 **Nome** U.S.A.
123 C3 **Nomonde** S. Africa
123 D2 **Nondweni** S. Africa
**Nonghui** China *see* **Guang'an**
62 B2 **Nong Khai** Thai.
75 D2 **Nongstoin** India
52 A2 **Nonning** Austr.
144 B2 **Nonoava** Mex.
65 B2 **Nonsan** S. Korea
63 B2 **Nonthaburi** Thai.
122 B3 **Nonzwakazi** S. Africa
100 B1 **Noordwijk-Binnen** Neth.
77 C3 **Norak** Tajik.
130 C3 **Noranda** Can.
82 C1 **Nordaustlandet** *i.* Svalbard
128 C2 **Nordegg** Can.
100 C1 **Norden** Ger.
83 H1 **Nordenshel'da, Arkhipelag** *is* Rus. Fed.
**Nordenskjold Archipelago** *is* Rus. Fed. *see* **Nordenshel'da, Arkhipelag**
100 C1 **Norderney** Ger.
100 C1 **Norderney** *i.* Ger.
101 E1 **Norderstedt** Ger.
93 E3 **Nordfjordeid** Norway
**Nordfriesische Inseln** Ger. *see* North Frisian Islands
101 E2 **Nordhausen** Ger.
101 D1 **Nordholz** Ger.
100 C1 **Nordhorn** Ger.
**Nordkapp** Norway *see* **North Cape**
92 F3 **Nordli** Norway
102 C2 **Nördlingen** Ger.
92 G3 **Nordmaling** Sweden
94 B1 **Norðoyar** *i.* Faroe Is
97 C2 **Nore** *r.* Ireland
88 B3 **Noreikiškės** Lith.
137 D2 **Norfolk** *NE* U.S.A.
139 D3 **Norfolk** *VA* U.S.A.
48 H6 **Norfolk Island** *terr.* S. Pacific Ocean
93 E3 **Norheimsund** Norway
82 G2 **Noril'sk** Rus. Fed.
75 C2 **Norkyung** China
143 D1 **Norman** U.S.A.
**Normandes, Îles** *is* English Chan. *see* **Channel Islands**
150 D2 **Normandia** Brazil
**Normandie** *reg.* France *see* Normandy
104 B2 **Normandy** *reg.* France
51 D1 **Normanton** Austr.
128 B1 **Norman Wells** Can.
93 G4 **Norrköping** Sweden
93 G4 **Norrtälje** Sweden
50 B3 **Norseman** Austr.
92 G3 **Norsjö** Sweden
55 M2 **North, Cape** Antarctica
98 C2 **Northallerton** U.K.
50 A3 **Northam** Austr.
50 A2 **Northampton** Austr.
99 C3 **Northampton** U.K.
73 D3 **North Andaman** *i.* India
159 F4 **North Australian Basin** *sea feature* Indian Ocean
129 D2 **North Battleford** Can.
130 C3 **North Bay** Can.
130 C2 **North Belcher Islands** Can.
96 C2 **North Berwick** U.K.
**North Borneo** *state* Malaysia *see* Sabah
92 I1 **North Cape** *c.* Norway
54 B1 **North Cape** N.Z.
130 A2 **North Caribou Lake** Can.
141 E1 **North Carolina** *state* U.S.A.
130 B3 **North Channel** *lake channel* Can.
96 A3 **North Channel** U.K.
141 E2 **North Charleston** U.S.A.
128 B3 **North Cowichan** Can.
136 C1 **North Dakota** *state* U.S.A.
99 C4 **North Downs** *hills* U.K.
157 E3 **Northeast Pacific Basin** *sea feature* N. Pacific Ocean
141 E3 **Northeast Providence Channel** Bahamas
101 D2 **Northeim** Ger.
122 A2 **Northern Cape** *prov.* S. Africa
**Northern Dvina** *r.* Rus. Fed. *see* Severnaya Dvina
129 E2 **Northern Indian Lake** Can.
97 C1 **Northern Ireland** *prov.* U.K.
59 D1 **Northern Mariana Islands** *terr.* N. Pacific Ocean
**Northern Rhodesia** *country* Africa *see* **Zambia**
50 C1 **Northern Territory** *admin. div.* Austr.
**Northern Transvaal** *prov.* S. Africa *see* **Limpopo**
96 C2 **North Esk** *r.* U.K.
137 E2 **Northfield** U.S.A.
99 D4 **North Foreland** *c.* U.K.
102 B1 **North Frisian Islands** *is* Ger.
54 B1 **North Island** N.Z.
129 E2 **North Knife Lake** Can.
65 B1 **North Korea** *country* Asia
72 D2 **North Lakhimpur** India
**North Land** *is* Rus. Fed. *see* Severnaya Zemlya
128 B1 **North Nahanni** *r.* Can.
136 C2 **North Platte** U.S.A.
136 C2 **North Platte** *r.* U.S.A.
96 C1 **North Ronaldsay** *i.* U.K.
129 D2 **North Saskatchewan** *r.* Can.
94 D2 **North Sea** Europe
63 A2 **North Sentinel Island** India
130 A2 **North Spirit Lake** Can.
53 D1 **North Stradbroke Island** Austr.
131 D3 **North Sydney** Can.
54 B1 **North Taranaki Bight** *b.* N.Z.
130 C2 **North Twin Island** Can.
98 B2 **North Tyne** *r.* U.K.
96 A2 **North Uist** *i.* U.K.
131 D3 **Northumberland Strait** Can.
99 D3 **North Walsham** U.K.
123 C2 **North West** *prov.* S. Africa
158 D1 **Northwest Atlantic Mid-Ocean Channel** *sea chan.* N. Atlantic Ocean
50 A2 **North West Cape** Austr.
156 D3 **Northwest Pacific Basin** *sea feature* N. Pacific Ocean
141 E3 **Northwest Providence Channel** Bahamas
131 E2 **North West River** Can.
128 B1 **Northwest Territories** *admin. div.* Can.
98 C2 **North York Moors** *moorland* U.K.
138 C3 **Norton** U.S.A.
121 C2 **Norton** Zimbabwe
**Norton de Matos** Angola *see* Balombo
126 B2 **Norton Sound** *sea chan.* U.S.A.
55 D2 **Norvegia, Cape** Antarctica
138 C2 **Norwalk** U.S.A.
93 F3 **Norway** *country* Europe
129 E2 **Norway House** Can.
160 L3 **Norwegian Basin** *sea feature* N. Atlantic Ocean
92 E2 **Norwegian Sea** N. Atlantic Ocean
99 D3 **Norwich** U.K.
139 E2 **Norwich** *CT* U.S.A.
139 D2 **Norwich** *NY* U.S.A.
66 D2 **Noshiro** Japan
91 C1 **Nosivka** Ukr.
122 B2 **Nosop** *watercourse* Africa
86 E2 **Nosovaya** Rus. Fed.
79 C2 **Noşratābād** Iran
121 □D2 **Nosy Bé** *i.* Madag.
121 □E2 **Nosy Boraha** *i.* Madag.
103 D1 **Noteć** *r.* Pol.
93 E4 **Notodden** Norway
67 C3 **Noto-hantō** *pen.* Japan
131 D3 **Notre Dame, Monts** *mts* Can.
131 E3 **Notre Dame Bay** Can.
130 C2 **Nottaway** *r.* Can.
99 C3 **Nottingham** U.K.
114 A2 **Nouâdhibou** Maur.
114 A3 **Nouakchott** Maur.
114 A3 **Nouâmghâr** Maur.
63 B2 **Nouei** Vietnam
48 H6 **Nouméa** New Caledonia
114 B3 **Nouna** Burkina
122 B3 **Noupoort** S. Africa
**Nouveau-Comptoir** Can. *see* Wemindji
**Nouvelle Anvers** Dem. Rep. Congo *see* **Makanza**
**Nouvelles Hébrides** *country* S. Pacific Ocean *see* **Vanuatu**
**Nova Chaves** Angola *see* Muconda
154 B2 **Nova Esperança** Brazil
**Nova Freixa** Moz. *see* **Cuamba**
155 D2 **Nova Friburgo** Brazil
109 C1 **Nova Gradiška** Croatia
154 C2 **Nova Granada** Brazil
155 D2 **Nova Iguaçu** Brazil
91 C2 **Nova Kakhovka** Ukr.
155 D1 **Nova Lima** Brazil
**Nova Lisboa** Angola *see* Huambo
154 B2 **Nova Londrina** Brazil
91 C2 **Nova Odesa** Ukr.
150 C2 **Nova Paraiso** Brazil
154 C1 **Nova Ponte** Brazil
108 A1 **Novara** Italy
151 E3 **Nova Remanso** Brazil
131 D3 **Nova Scotia** *prov.* Can.
155 D1 **Nova Venécia** Brazil
83 K1 **Novaya Sibir', Ostrov** *i.* Rus. Fed.
86 E1 **Novaya Zemlya** *is* Rus. Fed.
107 C2 **Novelda** Spain
103 D2 **Nové Zámky** Slovakia
**Novgorod** Rus. Fed. *see* Velikiy Novgorod
91 C1 **Novhorod-Sivers'kyy** Ukr.
110 B2 **Novi Iskŭr** Bulg.
66 D1 **Novikovo** Rus. Fed.
108 A2 **Novi Ligure** Italy
109 D2 **Novi Pazar** Serb. and Mont.
109 C1 **Novi Sad** Serb. and Mont.
**Novoalekseyevka** Kazakh. *see* Khobda
87 D3 **Novoanninskiy** Rus. Fed.
150 C3 **Novo Aripuanã** Brazil
91 D2 **Novoazovs'k** Ukr.
91 E2 **Novocherkassk** Rus. Fed.
89 D2 **Novodugino** Rus. Fed.
86 D2 **Novodvinsk** Rus. Fed.
**Novoekonomicheskoye** Ukr. *see* Dymytrov
152 C2 **Novo Hamburgo** Brazil
154 C2 **Novo Horizonte** Brazil
90 B1 **Novohrad-Volyns'kyy** Ukr.
**Novokazalinsk** Kazakh. *see* Ayteke Bi
91 E1 **Novokhopersk** Rus. Fed.
68 B1 **Novokuznetsk** Rus. Fed.
109 C1 **Novo Mesto** Slovenia
91 D3 **Novomikhaylovskiy** Rus. Fed.
89 E3 **Novomoskovsk** Rus. Fed.
91 D2 **Novomoskovs'k** Ukr.
91 C2 **Novomyrhorod** Ukr.
**Novonikolayevsk** Rus. Fed. *see* Novosibirsk
91 C2 **Novooleksiyivka** Ukr.
91 E2 **Novopokrovskaya** Rus. Fed.
91 D2 **Novopskov** Ukr.
**Novo Redondo** Angola *see* **Sumbe**
91 D3 **Novorossiysk** Rus. Fed.
88 C2 **Novorzhev** Rus. Fed.
87 E3 **Novosergiyevka** Rus. Fed.
91 D2 **Novoshakhtinsk** Rus. Fed.
82 G3 **Novosibirsk** Rus. Fed.
**Novosibirskiye Ostrova** *is* Rus. Fed. *see* **New Siberia Islands**
89 E3 **Novosil'** Rus. Fed.
89 D2 **Novosokol'niki** Rus. Fed.
91 C2 **Novotroyits'ke** Ukr.
91 C2 **Novoukrayinka** Ukr.
90 A1 **Novovolyns'k** Ukr.
89 E3 **Novovoronezh** Rus. Fed.
**Novovoronezhskiy** Rus. Fed. *see* Novovoronezh
89 D3 **Novozybkov** Rus. Fed.
103 D2 **Nový Jičín** Czech Rep.
86 E2 **Novyy Bor** Rus. Fed.
91 C2 **Novyy Buh** Ukr.
**Novyy Donbass** Ukr. *see* **Dymytrov**
**Novyye Petushki** Rus. Fed. *see* Petushki
**Novyy Margelan** Uzbek. *see* Farg'ona
89 E2 **Novyy Nekouz** Rus. Fed.
91 D1 **Novyy Oskol** Rus. Fed.
86 G2 **Novyy Port** Rus. Fed.
86 G2 **Novyy Urengoy** Rus. Fed.
69 E1 **Novyy Urgal** Rus. Fed.
**Novyy Uzen'** Kazakh. *see* Zhanaozen
103 D1 **Nowogard** Pol.
**Noworadomsk** Pol. *see* **Radomsko**
53 D2 **Nowra** Austr.
81 D2 **Now Shahr** Iran
74 B1 **Nowshera** Pak.
103 E2 **Nowy Sącz** Pol.
103 E2 **Nowy Targ** Pol.
82 G2 **Noyabr'sk** Rus. Fed.
105 C2 **Noyon** France
121 C2 **Nsanje** Malawi
121 B2 **Nsombo** Zambia
118 B3 **Ntandembele** Dem. Rep. Congo
123 C2 **Ntha** S. Africa
118 A2 **Ntoum** Gabon
119 D3 **Ntungamo** Uganda
**Nuanetsi** *r.* Zimbabwe *see* Mwenezi
79 C2 **Nu'aym** *reg.* Oman
116 B2 **Nubian Desert** Sudan
150 B4 **Nudo Coropuna** *mt.* Peru
143 D3 **Nueces** *r.* U.S.A.
129 E1 **Nueltin Lake** Can.
150 B2 **Nueva Loja** Ecuador
153 A4 **Nueva Lubecka** Arg.
145 B2 **Nueva Rosita** Mex.
144 B1 **Nuevo Casas Grandes** Mex.
144 B2 **Nuevo Ideal** Mex.
145 C2 **Nuevo Laredo** Mex.
117 C4 **Nugaal** *watercourse* Somalia
105 C2 **Nuits-St-Georges** France
**Nu Jiang** *r.* China/Myanmar *see* Salween
**Nukha** Azer. *see* **Şäki**
49 J6 **Nuku'alofa** Tonga
49 M4 **Nuku Hiva** *i.* Fr. Polynesia
48 G4 **Nukumanu Islands** P.N.G.
76 B2 **Nukus** Uzbek.
50 B2 **Nullagine** Austr.
50 C3 **Nullarbor** Austr.
50 B3 **Nullarbor Plain** Austr.
115 D4 **Numan** Nigeria
67 C3 **Numazu** Japan
51 C1 **Numbulwar** Austr.
93 E3 **Numedal** *val.* Norway
59 C3 **Numfoor** *i.* Indon.
53 C3 **Numurkah** Austr.
**Nunap Isua** *c.* Greenland *see* **Farewell, Cape**
127 G2 **Nunavik** *reg.* Can.
129 E1 **Nunavut** *admin. div.* Can.
99 C3 **Nuneaton** U.K.
127 G2 **Nunavik** *reg.* Can.
126 A3 **Nunivak Island** U.S.A.
106 B1 **Nuñomoral** Spain
108 A2 **Nuoro** *Sardinia* Italy
78 B2 **Nuqrah** Saudi Arabia
77 C1 **Nura** *r.* Kazakh.
101 E3 **Nuremberg** Ger.
52 A2 **Nuriootpa** Austr.
92 I3 **Nurmes** Fin.
**Nürnberg** Ger. *see* **Nuremberg**
53 C2 **Nurri, Mount** *hill* Austr.
62 A1 **Nu Shan** *mts* China
74 A2 **Nushki** Pak.
127 I2 **Nuuk** Greenland
127 I2 **Nuussuaq** Greenland
127 I2 **Nuussuaq** *pen.* Greenland
80 B3 **Nuwaybi' al Muzayyinah** Egypt
122 A3 **Nuwerus** S. Africa
122 B3 **Nuweveldberge** *mts* S. Africa
86 F2 **Nyagan'** Rus. Fed.
75 D1 **Nyainqêntanglha Feng** *mt.* China
75 D2 **Nyainqêntanglha Shan** *mts* China
**Nyakh** Rus. Fed. *see* **Nyagan'**
117 A3 **Nyala** Sudan
119 D4 **Nyamtumbo** Tanz.
**Nyande** Zimbabwe *see* **Masvingo**
86 D2 **Nyandoma** Rus. Fed.
118 B3 **Nyanga** Congo
118 B3 **Nyanga** *r.* Gabon
121 C2 **Nyanga** Zimbabwe
121 C1 **Nyasa, Lake** Africa
**Nyasaland** *country* Africa *see* Malawi
88 C3 **Nyasvizh** Belarus
62 A2 **Nyaunglebin** Myanmar
93 F4 **Nyborg** Denmark
92 I1 **Nyborg** Norway
93 G4 **Nybro** Sweden
**Nyenchen Tanglha Range** *mts* China *see* **Nyainqêntanglha Shan**
119 D3 **Nyeri** Kenya
75 C1 **Nyima** China
68 C3 **Nyingchi** China
103 E2 **Nyíregyháza** Hungary
93 F5 **Nykøbing** Denmark
93 G4 **Nyköping** Sweden
53 C2 **Nymagee** Austr.
93 G4 **Nynäshamn** Sweden
53 C2 **Nyngan** Austr.
88 B3 **Nyoman** *r.* Belarus/Lith.
105 D3 **Nyons** France
86 E2 **Nyrob** Rus. Fed.
103 D1 **Nysa** Pol.
134 C2 **Nyssa** U.S.A.
119 C3 **Nyunzu** Dem. Rep. Congo
83 I2 **Nyurba** Rus. Fed.
91 C2 **Nyzhni Sirohozy** Ukr.
91 C2 **Nyzhn'ohirs'kyy** Ukr.

118 B3 **Nzambi** Congo
119 D3 **Nzega** Tanz.
114 B4 **Nzérékoré** Guinea
120 A1 **N'zeto** Angola

# O

136 C2 **Oahe, Lake** U.S.A.
49 L1 **O'ahu** i. U.S.A.
52 B2 **Oakbank** Austr.
140 B2 **Oakdale** U.S.A.
53 D1 **Oakey** Austr.
138 B3 **Oak Grove** U.S.A.
99 C3 **Oakham** U.K.
134 B1 **Oak Harbor** U.S.A.
138 C3 **Oak Hill** U.S.A.
135 B3 **Oakland** CA U.S.A.
139 D3 **Oakland** MD U.S.A.
138 B2 **Oak Lawn** U.S.A.
136 C3 **Oakley** U.S.A.
50 B2 **Oakover** r. Austr.
134 B2 **Oakridge** U.S.A.
141 D1 **Oak Ridge** U.S.A.
54 B3 **Oamaru** N.Z.
64 B2 **Oas** Phil.
145 C3 **Oaxaca** Mex.
86 F2 **Ob'** r. Rus. Fed.
**Ob, Gulf of** sea chan. Rus. Fed.
see **Obskaya Guba**
88 C2 **Obal'** Belarus
118 B2 **Obala** Cameroon
96 B2 **Oban** U.K.
106 B1 **O Barco** Spain
**Obbia** Somalia see **Hobyo**
136 C3 **Oberlin** U.S.A.
53 C2 **Oberon** Austr.
101 F3 **Oberviechtach** Ger.
59 C3 **Obi** i. Indon.
151 D3 **Óbidos** Brazil
66 C2 **Obihiro** Japan
69 E1 **Obluch'ye** Rus. Fed.
89 E2 **Obninsk** Rus. Fed.
119 C2 **Obo** C.A.R.
117 C3 **Obock** Djibouti
103 D1 **Oborniki** Pol.
118 B3 **Obouya** Congo
89 E3 **Oboyan'** Rus. Fed.
86 D2 **Obozerskiy** Rus. Fed.
144 B2 **Obregón, Presa** resr Mex.
109 D2 **Obrenovac** Serb. and Mont.
134 B2 **O'Brien** U.S.A.
87 E3 **Obshchiy Syrt** hills Rus. Fed.
86 F2 **Obskaya Guba** sea chan. Rus. Fed.
114 B4 **Obuasi** Ghana
90 C1 **Obukhiv** Ukr.
86 D2 **Ob"yachevo** Rus. Fed.
141 D3 **Ocala** U.S.A.
144 B2 **Ocampo** Mex.
106 C2 **Ocaña** Spain
150 B2 **Occidental, Cordillera** mts Col.
150 A3 **Occidental, Cordillera** mts Peru
139 D3 **Ocean City** MD U.S.A.
139 E3 **Ocean City** NJ U.S.A.
128 B2 **Ocean Falls** Can.
135 C4 **Oceanside** U.S.A.
91 C2 **Ochakiv** Ukr.
86 E3 **Ocher** Rus. Fed.
101 E3 **Ochsenfurt** Ger.
110 B1 **Ocna Mureş** Romania
90 B2 **Ocniţa** Moldova
141 D2 **Oconee** r. U.S.A.
145 C3 **Ocosingo** Mex.
141 E1 **Ocracoke Island** U.S.A.
**October Revolution Island**
Rus. Fed. see
**Oktyabr'skoy Revolyutsii, Ostrov**
59 C3 **Ocussi** enclave East Timor
116 B2 **Oda, Jebel** mt. Sudan
66 D2 **Ōdate** Japan
67 C3 **Odawara** Japan
93 E3 **Odda** Norway
106 B2 **Odemira** Port.
111 C3 **Ödemiş** Turkey
93 F4 **Odense** Denmark
101 D3 **Odenwald** reg. Ger.
102 C1 **Oder** r. Ger.
102 C1 **Oderbucht** b. Ger.
90 C2 **Odesa** Ukr.
143 C2 **Odessa** U.S.A.
114 B4 **Odienné** Côte d'Ivoire
89 E3 **Odoyev** Rus. Fed.
103 D1 **Odra** r. Pol.
151 E3 **Oeiras** Brazil
101 D2 **Oelde** Ger.
136 C2 **Oelrichs** U.S.A.
101 F2 **Oelsnitz** Ger.
100 B1 **Oenkerk** Neth.
137 E3 **O'Fallon** U.S.A.
109 C2 **Ofanto** r. Italy
101 D2 **Offenbach am Main** Ger.
102 B2 **Offenburg** Ger.
66 C2 **Oga** Japan
117 C4 **Ogadēn** reg. Eth.
66 C2 **Oga-hantō** pen. Japan
67 C3 **Ōgaki** Japan
136 C2 **Ogallala** U.S.A.
**Ogasawara-shotō** Japan see
**Bonin Islands**
115 C4 **Ogbomosho** Nigeria
134 D2 **Ogden** U.S.A.
139 D2 **Ogdensburg** U.S.A.
126 C2 **Ogilvie** r. Can.
126 C2 **Ogilvie Mountains** Can.

141 D2 **Oglethorpe, Mount** U.S.A.
130 B2 **Ogoki** r. Can.
130 B2 **Ogoki Reservoir** Can.
88 B2 **Ogre** Latvia
109 C1 **Ogulin** Croatia
81 D2 **Ogurchinskiy, Ostrov** i. Turkm.
115 C2 **Ohanet** Alg.
138 B3 **Ohio** r. U.S.A.
138 C2 **Ohio** state U.S.A.
101 E2 **Ohrdruf** Ger.
101 F2 **Ohře** r. Czech Rep.
111 B2 **Ohrid** Macedonia
151 D2 **Oiapoque** Brazil
139 D2 **Oil City** U.S.A.
100 A3 **Oise** r. France
67 B4 **Ōita** Japan
144 B2 **Ojinaga** Mex.
152 B2 **Ojos del Salado, Nevado** mt. Arg./Chile
89 F3 **Oka** r. Rus. Fed.
120 A3 **Okahandja** Namibia
120 A3 **Okakarara** Namibia
128 C3 **Okanagan Falls** Can.
128 C3 **Okanagan Lake** Can.
134 C1 **Okanogan** U.S.A.
134 C1 **Okanogan** r. U.S.A.
74 B1 **Okara** Pak.
120 B2 **Okavango** r. Botswana/Namibia
120 B2 **Okavango Delta** swamp Botswana
67 C3 **Okaya** Japan
67 B4 **Okayama** Japan
67 C4 **Okazaki** Japan
141 D3 **Okeechobee** U.S.A.
141 D3 **Okeechobee, Lake** U.S.A.
141 D2 **Okefenokee Swamp** U.S.A.
99 A4 **Okehampton** U.K.
115 C4 **Okene** Nigeria
101 E1 **Oker** r. Ger.
74 A2 **Okha** India
83 K3 **Okha** Rus. Fed.
75 C2 **Okhaldhunga** Nepal
83 K3 **Okhotka** r. Rus. Fed.
83 K3 **Okhotsk** Rus. Fed.
83 K3 **Okhotsk, Sea of** Japan/Rus. Fed.
**Okhotskoye More** sea Japan/Rus. Fed. see **Okhotsk, Sea of**
91 C1 **Okhtyrka** Ukr.
69 E3 **Okinawa** i. Japan
67 B3 **Oki-shotō** is Japan
143 D1 **Oklahoma** state U.S.A.
143 D1 **Oklahoma City** U.S.A.
143 D1 **Okmulgee** U.S.A.
**Oknitsa** Moldova see **Ocniţa**
78 A2 **Oko, Wadi** watercourse Sudan
118 B3 **Okondja** Gabon
128 C2 **Okotoks** Can.
89 D3 **Okovskiy Les** for. Rus. Fed.
118 B3 **Okoyo** Congo
92 H1 **Øksfjord** Norway
62 A2 **Oktwin** Myanmar
**Oktyabr'** Kazakh. see **Kandyagash**
**Oktyabr'sk** Kazakh. see **Kandyagash**
86 D2 **Oktyabr'skiy** Rus. Fed.
83 L3 **Oktyabr'skiy** Rus. Fed.
87 E3 **Oktyabr'skiy** Rus. Fed.
86 F2 **Oktyabr'skoye** Rus. Fed.
83 H1 **Oktyabr'skoy Revolyutsii, Ostrov** i. Rus. Fed.
89 D2 **Okulovka** Rus. Fed.
66 C2 **Okushiri-tō** i. Japan
92 ☐B2 **Ólafsfjörður** Iceland
92 ☐A3 **Ólafsvík** Iceland
88 B2 **Olaine** Latvia
93 G4 **Öland** i. Sweden
52 B2 **Olary** Austr.
136 B3 **Olathe** CO U.S.A.
137 E3 **Olathe** KS U.S.A.
153 B3 **Olavarría** Arg.
103 D1 **Oława** Pol.
108 A2 **Olbia** Sardinia Italy
126 C2 **Old Crow** Can.
101 D1 **Oldenburg** Ger.
102 C1 **Oldenburg in Holstein** Ger.
100 C1 **Oldenzaal** Neth.
98 B3 **Oldham** U.K.
97 B3 **Old Head of Kinsale** hd Ireland
96 C2 **Oldmeldrum** U.K.
128 C2 **Olds** Can.
129 D2 **Old Wives Lake** Can.
139 D2 **Olean** U.S.A.
103 E1 **Olecko** Pol.
83 J2 **Olekminsk** Rus. Fed.
91 C2 **Oleksandrivka** Ukr.
**Oleksandrivs'k** Ukr. see **Zaporizhzhya**
91 C2 **Oleksandriya** Ukr.
86 C2 **Olenegorsk** Rus. Fed.
83 I2 **Olenek** Rus. Fed.
83 I2 **Olenek** r. Rus. Fed.
89 D2 **Olenino** Rus. Fed.
**Olenivs'ki Kar"yery** Ukr. see **Dokuchayevs'k**
**Olenya** Rus. Fed. see **Olenegorsk**
**Oleshky** Ukr. see **Tsyurupyns'k**
103 D1 **Oleśno** Pol.
90 B1 **Olevs'k** Ukr.
106 B2 **Olhão** Port.
123 D1 **Olifants** r. Moz./S. Africa
122 A2 **Olifants** watercourse Namibia
123 D1 **Olifants** S. Africa
122 A3 **Olifants** r. S. Africa
122 B2 **Olifantshoek** S. Africa
154 C2 **Olímpia** Brazil

151 F3 **Olinda** Brazil
123 C1 **Oliphants Drift** S. Africa
107 C1 **Oliva** Spain
155 D2 **Oliveira** Spain
**Olivença** Moz. see **Lupilichi**
106 B2 **Olivenza** Spain
140 B2 **Olla** U.S.A.
152 B2 **Ollagüe** Chile
77 C2 **Olmaliq** Uzbek.
106 C1 **Olmedo** Spain
105 D3 **Olmeto** Corsica France
150 B3 **Olmos** Peru
138 B3 **Olney** U.S.A.
103 D2 **Olomouc** Czech Rep.
86 C2 **Olonets** Rus. Fed.
64 B2 **Olongapo** Phil.
104 B3 **Oloron-Ste-Marie** France
107 D1 **Olot** Spain
69 D1 **Olovyannaya** Rus. Fed.
100 C2 **Olpe** Ger.
103 E1 **Olsztyn** Pol.
110 B2 **Olt** r. Romania
110 C2 **Olteniţa** Romania
143 C2 **Olton** U.S.A.
81 C1 **Oltu** Turkey
**Ol'viopol'** Ukr. see **Pervomays'k**
111 B3 **Olympia** tourist site Greece
134 B1 **Olympia** U.S.A.
**Olympus, Mount** Greece see **Mount Olympus**
134 B1 **Olympus, Mount** U.S.A.
83 M2 **Olyutorskiy** Rus. Fed.
83 M3 **Olyutorskiy, Mys** c. Rus. Fed.
66 D2 **Ōma** Japan
97 C1 **Omagh** U.K.
137 D2 **Omaha** U.S.A.
79 C2 **Oman** country Asia
79 C2 **Oman, Gulf of** Asia
54 A2 **Omarama** N.Z.
120 A3 **Omaruru** Namibia
120 B2 **Omatako** watercourse Namibia
122 B2 **Omaweneno** Botswana
116 B3 **Omdurman** Sudan
53 C3 **Omeo** Austr.
145 C3 **Ometepec** Mex.
78 A3 **Om Hajēr** Eritrea
81 C2 **Omīdīyeh** Iran
128 B2 **Omineca Mountains** Can.
120 A3 **Omitara** Namibia
67 C3 **Ōmiya** Japan
100 C1 **Ommen** Neth.
83 L2 **Omolon** r. Rus. Fed.
100 B3 **Omont** France
82 F3 **Omsk** Rus. Fed.
83 L2 **Omsukchan** Rus. Fed.
110 C1 **Omu, Vârful** mt. Romania
67 A4 **Ōmura** Japan
138 A2 **Onalaska** U.S.A.
139 D3 **Onancock** U.S.A.
138 C1 **Onaping Lake** Can.
131 C3 **Onatchiway, Lac** l. Can.
63 A2 **Onbingwin** Myanmar
120 A2 **Oncócua** Angola
122 B3 **Onderstedorings** S. Africa
120 A2 **Ondjiva** Angola
69 D1 **Öndörhaan** Mongolia
122 B1 **One Botswana**
86 C2 **Onega** Rus. Fed.
86 C2 **Onega** r. Rus. Fed.
86 C2 **Onega, Lake** Rus. Fed.
128 B3 **100 Mile House** Can.
139 D2 **Oneida Lake** U.S.A.
137 D2 **O'Neill** U.S.A.
139 D2 **Oneonta** U.S.A.
110 C1 **Oneşti** Romania
**Onezhskoye Ozero** l. Rus. Fed. see **Onega, Lake**
122 B2 **Ongers** watercourse S. Africa
65 B2 **Ongjin** N. Korea
73 C3 **Ongole** India
121 ☐D3 **Onilahy** r. Madag.
115 C4 **Onitsha** Nigeria
120 A3 **Onjati Mountain** Namibia
67 C3 **Ōno** Japan
122 A2 **Onseepkans** S. Africa
50 A2 **Onslow** Austr.
141 E2 **Onslow Bay** U.S.A.
130 A2 **Ontario** prov. Can.
134 C2 **Ontario** U.S.A.
139 D2 **Ontario, Lake** Can./U.S.A.
107 C2 **Ontinyent** Spain
51 C2 **Oodnadatta** Austr.
**Oostende** Belgium see **Ostend**
100 C1 **Oosterhout** Neth.
100 A2 **Oosterschelde** est. Neth.
100 B1 **Oost-Vlieland** Neth.
128 B2 **Ootsa Lake** Can.
128 B2 **Ootsa Lake** l. Can.
118 C3 **Opala** Dem. Rep. Congo
130 C2 **Opataca, Lac** l. Can.
103 D2 **Opava** Czech Rep.
141 C2 **Opelika** U.S.A.
140 B2 **Opelousas** U.S.A.
117 A4 **Opienge** Dem. Rep. Congo
130 C2 **Opinaca, Réservoir** resr Can.
131 D2 **Opiscotéo, Lac** l. Can.
88 C2 **Opochka** Rus. Fed.
144 B2 **Opodepe** Mex.
103 D1 **Opole** Pol.
106 B1 **Oporto** Port.
54 C1 **Opotiki** N.Z.
93 E3 **Oppdal** Norway
134 C1 **Opportunity** U.S.A.
54 B1 **Opunake** N.Z.
120 A2 **Opuwo** Namibia

110 B1 **Oradea** Romania
109 D2 **Orahovac** Serb. and Mont.
114 B1 **Oran** Alg.
152 B2 **Orán** Arg.
65 B1 **Ŏrang** N. Korea
53 C2 **Orange** Austr.
105 C3 **Orange** France
122 A2 **Orange** r. Namibia/S. Africa
143 E2 **Orange** U.S.A.
141 D2 **Orangeburg** U.S.A.
**Orange Free State** prov. S. Africa see **Free State**
141 D2 **Orange Park** U.S.A.
138 C2 **Orangeville** Can.
145 D3 **Orange Walk** Belize
101 F1 **Oranienburg** Ger.
122 A2 **Oranjemund** Namibia
147 D3 **Oranjestad** Aruba
120 B3 **Orapa** Botswana
110 B1 **Orăştie** Romania
**Oraşul Stalin** Romania see **Braşov**
108 B2 **Orbetello** Italy
53 C3 **Orbost** Austr.
141 D3 **Orchid Island** U.S.A.
111 B3 **Orchomenos** Greece
50 B1 **Ord, Mount** hill Austr.
106 B1 **Ordes** Spain
70 B2 **Ordos** China
80 B1 **Ordu** Turkey
**Ordzhonikidze** Rus. Fed. see **Vladikavkaz**
91 C2 **Ordzhonikidze** Ukr.
93 G4 **Örebro** Sweden
134 B2 **Oregon** state U.S.A.
134 B1 **Oregon City** U.S.A.
141 E1 **Oregon Inlet** U.S.A.
87 C3 **Orekhovo-Zuyevo** Rus. Fed.
89 E3 **Orel** Rus. Fed.
83 K3 **Orel', Ozero** l. Rus. Fed.
135 D2 **Orem** U.S.A.
111 C3 **Ören** Turkey
87 E3 **Orenburg** Rus. Fed.
54 A3 **Orepuki** N.Z.
111 C2 **Orestiada** Greece
93 F4 **Øresund** str. Denmark/Sweden
**Oretana, Cordillera** mts Spain see **Toledo, Montes de**
99 D3 **Orford Ness** hd U.K.
89 F2 **Orgtrud** Rus. Fed.
74 A1 **Orgūn** Afgh.
111 C3 **Orhaneli** Turkey
111 C2 **Orhangazi** Turkey
68 D1 **Orhon Gol** r. Mongolia
152 B1 **Oriental, Cordillera** mts Bol.
150 B2 **Oriental, Cordillera** mts Col.
150 B4 **Oriental, Cordillera** mts Peru
107 C2 **Orihuela** Spain
91 C2 **Orikhiv** Ukr.
130 C3 **Orillia** Can.
93 I3 **Orimattila** Fin.
150 C2 **Orinoco** r. Col./Venez.
150 C2 **Orinoco Delta** Venez.
75 C2 **Orissa** state India
88 B2 **Orissaare** Estonia
108 A3 **Oristano** Sardinia Italy
93 I3 **Orivesi** l. Fin.
151 D3 **Oriximiná** Brazil
145 C3 **Orizaba** Mex.
145 C3 **Orizaba, Pico de** vol. Mex.
154 C1 **Orizona** Brazil
92 E3 **Orkanger** Norway
93 F4 **Örkelljunga** Sweden
93 E3 **Orkla** r. Norway
96 C1 **Orkney Islands** U.K.
154 B1 **Orlândia** Brazil
141 D3 **Orlando** U.S.A.
104 C2 **Orléans** France
139 F2 **Orleans** U.S.A.
139 E1 **Orléans, Île d'** i. Can.
**Orléansville** Alg. see **Ech Chélif**
74 A2 **Ormara** Pak.
64 B2 **Ormoc** Phil.
141 D3 **Ormond Beach** U.S.A.
98 B3 **Ormskirk** U.K.
104 B2 **Orne** r. France
92 F2 **Ørnes** Norway
92 G3 **Örnsköldsvik** Sweden
114 B3 **Orodara** Burkina
134 C1 **Orofino** U.S.A.
139 F2 **Orono** U.S.A.
64 B3 **Oroquieta** Phil.
108 A2 **Orosei** Sardinia Italy
108 A2 **Orosei, Golfo di** b. Sardinia Italy
103 E2 **Orosháza** Hungary
135 B3 **Oroville** U.S.A.
52 A2 **Orroroo** Austr.
93 F3 **Orsa** Sweden
89 D3 **Orsha** Belarus
87 E3 **Orsk** Rus. Fed.
110 B2 **Orşova** Romania
93 E3 **Ørsta** Norway
106 B1 **Ortegal, Cabo** c. Spain
104 B3 **Orthez** France
106 B1 **Ortigueira** Spain
108 B1 **Ortles** mt. Italy
108 B2 **Ortona** Italy
137 D1 **Ortonville** U.S.A.
83 J2 **Orulgan, Khrebet** mts Rus. Fed.
**Orūmīyeh** Iran see **Urmia**
**Orūmīyeh, Daryācheh-ye** salt l. Iran see **Urmia, Lake**
152 B1 **Oruro** Bol.
104 B2 **Orvault** France

Pardo
203

108 B2 Orvieto Italy
93 F3 Os Norway
146 B4 Osa, Península de pen. Costa Rica
137 E3 Osage r. U.S.A.
137 D3 Osage City U.S.A.
67 C4 Ōsaka Japan
77 D1 Osakarovka Kazakh.
101 E1 Oschersleben (Bode) Ger.
108 A2 Oschiri Sardinia Italy
138 C2 Oscoda U.S.A.
89 E3 Osetr r. Rus. Fed.
139 D1 Osgoode Can.
77 D2 Osh Kyrg.
120 A2 Oshakati Namibia
130 C3 Oshawa Can.
120 A2 Oshikango Namibia
66 C2 Ō-shima i. Japan
67 C4 Ō-shima i. Japan
138 B2 Oshkosh U.S.A.
81 C2 Oshnovīyeh Iran
115 C4 Oshogbo Nigeria
118 B3 Oshwe Dem. Rep. Congo
109 C1 Osijek Croatia
128 B2 Osilinka r. Can.
108 B2 Osimo Italy
Osipenko Ukr. see Berdyans'k
123 D2 Osizweni S. Africa
137 E2 Oskaloosa U.S.A.
93 G4 Oskarshamn Sweden
89 E3 Oskol r. Rus. Fed.
93 F4 Oslo Norway
93 F4 Oslofjorden sea chan. Norway
80 B1 Osmancık Turkey
111 C2 Osmaneli Turkey
80 B2 Osmaniye Turkey
88 C2 Os'mino Rus. Fed.
101 D1 Osnabrück Ger.
153 A4 Osorno Chile
106 C1 Osorno Spain
128 C3 Osoyoos Can.
100 B2 Oss Neth.
51 D4 Ossa, Mount Austr.
83 L3 Ossora Rus. Fed.
89 D2 Ostashkov Rus. Fed.
101 D1 Oste r. Ger.
100 A2 Ostend Belgium
101 E1 Osterburg (Altmark) Ger.
93 F3 Österdalälven l. Sweden
101 D1 Osterholz-Scharmbeck Ger.
101 E2 Osterode am Harz Ger.
92 F3 Östersund Sweden
Ostfriesische Inseln is Ger. see East Frisian Islands
100 C1 Ostfriesland reg. Ger.
93 G3 Östhammar Sweden
103 D2 Ostrava Czech Rep.
103 D1 Ostróda Pol.
89 E3 Ostrogozhsk Rus. Fed.
90 B1 Ostroh Ukr.
103 E1 Ostrołęka Pol.
101 F2 Ostrov Czech Rep.
88 C2 Ostrov Rus. Fed.
Ostrovets Pol. see Ostrowiec Świętokrzyski
89 F2 Ostrovskoye Rus. Fed.
103 E1 Ostrowiec Świętokrzyski Pol.
103 E1 Ostrów Mazowiecka Pol.
Ostrowo Pol. see Ostrów Wielkopolski
103 D1 Ostrów Wielkopolski Pol.
109 C2 Ostuni Italy
110 B2 Osŭm r. Bulg.
67 B4 Ōsumi-kaikyō sea chan. Japan
67 B4 Ōsumi-shotō is Japan
106 B2 Osuna Spain
139 D2 Oswego U.S.A.
99 B3 Oswestry U.K.
67 C3 Ōta Japan
54 B3 Otago Peninsula N.Z.
54 C2 Otaki N.Z.
77 D2 Otar Kazakh.
66 D2 Otaru Japan
120 A2 Otavi Namibia
67 D3 Ōtawara Japan
92 G2 Oteren Norway
134 C1 Othello U.S.A.
120 A3 Otjiwarongo Namibia
109 C2 Otočac Croatia
Otog Qi China see Ulan
117 B3 Otoro, Jebel mt. Sudan
Otpor Rus. Fed. see Zabaykal'sk
93 E4 Otra r. Norway
109 C2 Otranto, Strait of Albania/Italy
67 C3 Ōtsu Japan
93 E3 Otta Norway
130 C3 Ottawa Can.
130 C3 Ottawa r. Can.
138 B2 Ottawa IL U.S.A.
137 D3 Ottawa KS U.S.A.
130 B2 Ottawa Islands Can.
98 B2 Otterburn U.K.
130 B2 Otter Rapids Can.
100 B2 Ottignies Belgium
137 E2 Ottumwa U.S.A.
150 B3 Otuzco Peru
52 B3 Otway, Cape Austr.
140 B2 Ouachita r. U.S.A.
140 B2 Ouachita, Lake U.S.A.
140 B2 Ouachita Mountains U.S.A.
118 C2 Ouadda C.A.R.
115 D3 Ouaddaï reg. Chad
114 B3 Ouagadougou Burkina
114 B3 Ouahigouya Burkina
114 B3 Oualâta Maur.
118 C2 Ouanda-Djailé C.A.R.
114 B2 Ouarâne reg. Maur.
115 C1 Ouargla Alg.
114 B1 Ouarzazate Morocco
100 A2 Oudenaarde Belgium
122 B3 Oudtshoorn S. Africa
107 C2 Oued Tlélat Alg.
114 B1 Oued Zem Morocco
104 A2 Ouessant, Île d' i. France
118 B2 Ouesso Congo
97 B2 Oughterard Ireland
118 B2 Ouham r. C.A.R./Chad
114 B1 Oujda Morocco
92 H3 Oulainen Fin.
107 D2 Ouled Farès Alg.
92 I2 Oulu Fin.
92 I3 Oulujärvi l. Fin.
108 A1 Oulx Italy
115 E3 Oum-Chalouba Chad
115 D3 Oum-Hadjer Chad
115 E3 Ounianga Kébir Chad
100 B2 Oupeye Belgium
100 C3 Our r. Lux.
106 B1 Ourense Spain
154 C2 Ourinhos Brazil
155 D2 Ouro Preto Brazil
100 B2 Ourthe r. Belgium
98 C3 Ouse r. U.K.
Outaouais, Rivière des r. Can. see Ottawa
131 D3 Outardes r. Can.
131 D2 Outardes Quatre, Réservoir resr Can.
96 A2 Outer Hebrides is U.K.
Outer Mongolia country Asia see Mongolia
120 A3 Outjo Namibia
129 D2 Outlook Can.
92 I3 Outokumpu Fin.
52 B3 Ouyen Austr.
108 A2 Ovace, Punta d' mt. Corsica France
152 A3 Ovalle Chile
106 B1 Ovar Port.
92 H2 Överkalix Sweden
137 E3 Overland Park U.S.A.
135 D3 Overton U.S.A.
92 H2 Övertorneå Sweden
106 B1 Oviedo Spain
141 D3 Oviedo U.S.A.
88 B2 Ovišrags hd Latvia
93 E3 Øvre Årdal Norway
93 F3 Øvre Rendal Norway
90 B1 Ovruch Ukr.
118 B3 Owando Congo
67 C4 Owase Japan
143 D1 Owasso U.S.A.
137 E2 Owatonna U.S.A.
139 D2 Owego U.S.A.
138 B3 Owensboro U.S.A.
135 C3 Owens Lake U.S.A.
130 B3 Owen Sound Can.
51 D1 Owen Stanley Range mts P.N.G.
115 C4 Owerri Nigeria
115 C4 Owo Nigeria
138 C2 Owosso U.S.A.
134 C2 Owyhee U.S.A.
134 C2 Owyhee r. U.S.A.
129 D3 Oxbow Can.
54 B2 Oxford N.Z.
99 C4 Oxford U.K.
140 C2 Oxford U.S.A.
129 E2 Oxford Lake Can.
145 D2 Oxkutzcab Mex.
52 B2 Oxley Austr.
Ox Mountains hills Ireland see Slieve Gamph
135 C4 Oxnard U.S.A.
67 C3 Oyama Japan
118 B2 Oyem Gabon
129 C2 Oyen Can.
105 D2 Oyonnax France
77 C2 Oyoqquduq Uzbek.
64 B3 Ozamiz Phil.
140 C2 Ozark AL U.S.A.
137 E3 Ozark MO U.S.A.
137 E3 Ozark Plateau U.S.A.
137 E3 Ozarks, Lake of the U.S.A.
83 L3 Ozernovskiy Rus. Fed.
88 B3 Ozersk Rus. Fed.
89 E3 Ozery Rus. Fed.
87 D3 Ozinki Rus. Fed.

## P

127 I2 Paamiut Greenland
122 A3 Paarl S. Africa
103 D1 Pabianice Pol.
75 C2 Pabna Bangl.
88 C3 Pabradė Lith.
74 A2 Pab Range mts Pak.
150 B3 Pacasmayo Peru
142 B3 Pacheco Mex.
109 C3 Pachino Sicily Italy
145 C2 Pachuca Mex.
135 B3 Pacifica U.S.A.
157 E9 Pacific-Antarctic Ridge sea feature S. Pacific Ocean
156 Pacific Ocean
61 C2 Pacitan Indon.
52 B2 Packsaddle Austr.
103 D1 Paczków Pol.
60 B2 Padang Indon.
60 B1 Padang Endau Malaysia
60 B2 Padangpanjang Indon.
60 A1 Padangsidimpuan Indon.
101 D2 Paderborn Ger.
Padova Italy see Padua
143 D3 Padre Island U.S.A.
99 A4 Padstow U.K.
52 B3 Padthaway Austr.
108 B1 Padua Italy
138 B3 Paducah KY U.S.A.
143 C2 Paducah TX U.S.A.
65 B1 Paegam N. Korea
Paektu-san mt. China/N. Korea see Baotou Shan
65 A2 Paengnyŏng-do i. S. Korea
54 C1 Paeroa N.Z.
Pafos Cyprus see Paphos
109 C2 Pag Croatia
109 B2 Pag i. Croatia
64 B3 Pagadian Phil.
60 B2 Pagai Selatan i. Indon.
60 B2 Pagai Utara i. Indon.
59 D1 Pagan i. N. Mariana Is
61 C2 Pagatan Indon.
142 A1 Page U.S.A.
88 B2 Pagėgiai Lith.
153 E5 Paget, Mount S. Georgia
136 B3 Pagosa Springs U.S.A.
88 C2 Paide Estonia
99 B4 Paignton U.K.
93 I3 Päijänne l. Fin.
75 C2 Paikü Co l. China
60 B2 Painan Indon.
138 C2 Painesville U.S.A.
142 A1 Painted Desert U.S.A.
Paint Hills Can. see Wemindji
96 B3 Paisley U.K.
92 H2 Pajala Sweden
150 A3 Paján Ecuador
150 C2 Pakaraima Mountains mts Brazil
150 D2 Pakaraima Mountains Guyana
74 A2 Pakistan country Asia
62 A1 Pakokku Myanmar
88 B2 Pakruojis Lith.
103 D2 Paks Hungary
130 A2 Pakwash Lake Can.
62 B2 Pakxan Laos
63 B2 Pakxé Laos
115 D4 Pala Chad
60 B2 Palabuhanratu, Teluk b. Indon.
111 C3 Palaikastro Greece
111 B3 Palaiochora Greece
Palakkat India see Palghat
122 B1 Palamakoloi Botswana
107 D1 Palamós Spain
83 L3 Palana Rus. Fed.
64 B2 Palanan Phil.
61 C2 Palangkaraya Indon.
74 B2 Palanpur India
123 C1 Palapye Botswana
83 L2 Palatka Rus. Fed.
141 D3 Palatka U.S.A.
59 C2 Palau country N. Pacific Ocean
63 A2 Palaw Myanmar
64 A3 Palawan i. Phil.
64 A3 Palawan Passage str. Phil.
88 B2 Paldiski Estonia
89 F2 Palekh Rus. Fed.
60 B2 Palembang Indon.
106 C1 Palencia Spain
145 C3 Palenque Mex.
108 B3 Palermo Sicily Italy
143 D2 Palestine U.S.A.
62 A1 Paletwa Myanmar
73 B3 Palghat India
74 B2 Pali India
48 G4 Palikir Micronesia
109 C2 Palinuro, Capo c. Italy
111 B3 Paliouri, Akra pt Greece
100 B3 Paliseul Belgium
92 I3 Paljakka hill Fin.
88 C2 Palkino Rus. Fed.
73 B4 Palk Strait India/Sri Lanka
Palla Bianca mt. Austria/Italy see Weißkugel
54 C2 Palliser, Cape N.Z.
157 F7 Palliser, Îles is Fr. Polynesia
106 B2 Palma del Río Spain
107 D2 Palma de Mallorca Spain
154 B3 Palmas Brazil
151 E4 Palmas Tocantins Brazil
154 B3 Palmas, Campos de hills Brazil
114 B4 Palmas, Cape Liberia
141 D3 Palm Bay U.S.A.
135 C4 Palmdale U.S.A.
154 C3 Palmeira Brazil
151 E3 Palmeirais Brazil
126 C2 Palmer U.S.A.
55 A2 Palmer Land reg. Antarctica
49 K5 Palmerston atoll Cook Is
54 C2 Palmerston North N.Z.
109 C3 Palmi Italy
145 C2 Palmillas Mex.
150 B2 Palmira Col.
154 B2 Palmital Brazil
135 C4 Palm Springs U.S.A.
Palmyra Syria see Tadmur
49 K3 Palmyra Atoll N. Pacific Ocean
135 B3 Palo Alto U.S.A.
117 B3 Paloich Sudan
145 C3 Palomares Mex.
61 D2 Palopo Indon.
107 C2 Palos, Cabo de c. Spain
92 I3 Paltamo Fin.
61 C2 Palu Indon.
83 M2 Palyavaam r. Rus. Fed.
150 B3 Pamar Col.
121 C3 Pambarra Moz.
104 C3 Pamiers France
77 D3 Pamir mts Asia
141 E1 Pamlico Sound sea chan. U.S.A.
152 B1 Pampa Grande Bol.
153 B3 Pampas reg. Arg.
150 B2 Pamplona Col.
107 C1 Pamplona Spain
111 D2 Pamukova Turkey
60 B2 Panaitan i. Indon.
73 B3 Panaji India
146 B4 Panama country Central America
Panamá Panama see Panama City
Panamá, Golfo de Panama see Panama, Gulf of
146 C4 Panama, Gulf of g. Panama
146 C4 Panama Canal canal Panama
146 C4 Panama City Panama
140 C2 Panama City U.S.A.
135 C3 Panamint Range mts U.S.A.
60 B1 Panarik Indon.
64 B2 Panay i. Phil.
109 D2 Pančevo Serb. and Mont.
64 B2 Pandan Phil.
64 B2 Pandan Phil.
75 C2 Pandaria India
73 B3 Pandharpur India
88 B2 Panevėžys Lith.
Panfilov Kazakh. see Zharkent
61 C2 Pangkalanbuun Indon.
60 A1 Pangkalansusu Indon.
60 B2 Pangkalpinang Indon.
61 D2 Pangkalsiang, Tanjung pt Indon.
127 H2 Pangnirtung Can.
86 G2 Pangody Rus. Fed.
89 F3 Panino Rus. Fed.
74 B2 Panipat India
74 A2 Panjgur Pak.
Panjim India see Panaji
118 A2 Pankshin Nigeria
65 C1 Pan Ling mts China
75 C2 Panna India
50 A2 Pannawonica Austr.
154 B2 Panorama Brazil
65 B1 Panshi China
152 C1 Pantanal reg. Brazil
145 C2 Pánuco Mex.
145 C2 Pánuco r. Mex.
71 A3 Panxian China
62 B1 Panzhihua China
109 C3 Paola Italy
118 B2 Paoua C.A.R.
63 B2 Paôy Pêt Cambodia
103 D2 Pápa Hungary
54 B1 Papakura N.Z.
145 C2 Papantla Mex.
96 □ Papa Stour i. U.K.
54 B1 Papatoetoe N.Z.
49 M5 Papeete Fr. Polynesia
100 C1 Papenburg Ger.
80 B2 Paphos Cyprus
137 D2 Papillion U.S.A.
59 D3 Papua reg. Indon.
59 D3 Papua, Gulf of P.N.G.
59 D3 Papua New Guinea country Oceania
89 F3 Para r. Rus. Fed.
50 A2 Paraburdoo Austr.
154 C1 Paracatu Brazil
155 C1 Paracatu r. Brazil
52 A2 Parachilna Austr.
109 D2 Paraćin Serb. and Mont.
155 D1 Pará de Minas Brazil
151 D2 Paradise Guyana
135 B3 Paradise U.S.A.
140 B1 Paragould U.S.A.
151 D3 Paraguai r. Brazil
147 D3 Paraguaná, Península de pen. Venez.
152 C2 Paraguay r. Arg./Para.
152 C2 Paraguay country S. America
155 D2 Paraíba do Sul r. Brazil
154 B1 Paraíso Brazil
145 C3 Paraíso Mex.
114 C4 Parakou Benin
52 A2 Parakylia Austr.
151 D2 Paramaribo Suriname
83 L3 Paramushir, Ostrov i. Rus. Fed.
152 B3 Paraná Arg.
154 A3 Paraná r. S. America
154 C1 Paraná, Serra do hills Brazil
154 C3 Paranaguá Brazil
154 B1 Paranaíba Brazil
154 B2 Paranaíba r. Brazil
154 B2 Paranapanema r. Brazil
154 B2 Paranapiacaba, Serra mts Brazil
154 B2 Paranavaí Brazil
90 A2 Parângul Mare, Vârful mt. Romania
54 B2 Paraparaumu N.Z.
155 D2 Parati Brazil
52 A2 Paratoo Austr.
151 D3 Parauaquara, Serra hill Brazil
154 B1 Paraúna Brazil
105 C2 Paray-le-Monial France
74 B2 Parbati r. India
74 B3 Parbhani India
101 E1 Parchim Ger.
103 E1 Parczew Pol.
155 E1 Pardo r. Brazil
154 B2 Pardo r. Brazil

Pardo
204

154 C2 Pardo r. Brazil
103 D1 Pardubice Czech Rep.
152 C1 Parecis, Serra dos hills Brazil
130 C3 Parent Can.
130 C3 Parent, Lac l. Can.
61 C2 Parepare Indon.
89 D2 Parfino Rus. Fed.
111 B3 Parga Greece
109 C3 Parghelia Italy
147 D3 Paria, Gulf of Trin. and Tob./Venez.
150 C2 Parima, Serra mts Brazil
151 D3 Parintins Brazil
104 C2 Paris France
140 C1 Paris TN U.S.A.
143 D2 Paris TX U.S.A.
93 H3 Parkano Fin.
142 A2 Parker U.S.A.
138 C3 Parkersburg U.S.A.
53 C2 Parkes Austr.
138 A1 Park Falls U.S.A.
134 B1 Parkland U.S.A.
137 D1 Park Rapids U.S.A.
106 C1 Parla Spain
108 B2 Parma Italy
134 C2 Parma U.S.A.
151 E3 Parnaíba Brazil
151 E3 Parnaíba r. Brazil
111 B3 Parnassos mt. Greece
54 B2 Parnassus N.Z.
111 B3 Parnon mts Greece
88 B2 Pärnu Estonia
65 B2 P'aro-ho l. S. Korea
52 B2 Paroo watercourse Austr.
76 C3 Paropamisus mts Afgh.
111 C3 Paros i. Greece
135 D3 Parowan U.S.A.
153 A3 Parral Chile
53 D2 Parramatta Austr.
144 B2 Parras Mex.
126 D2 Parry, Cape Can.
126 E1 Parry Islands Can.
130 B3 Parry Sound Can.
137 D3 Parsons U.S.A.
108 B3 Partanna Sicily Italy
101 D2 Partenstein Ger.
104 B2 Parthenay France
108 B3 Partinico Sicily Italy
66 B2 Partizansk Rus. Fed.
97 B2 Partry Mountains hills Ireland
151 D3 Paru r. Brazil
131 E3 Pasadena Can.
135 C4 Pasadena CA U.S.A.
143 D3 Pasadena TX U.S.A.
62 A2 Pasawng Myanmar
140 C2 Pascagoula U.S.A.
110 C1 Paşcani Romania
134 C1 Pasco U.S.A.
155 E1 Pascoal, Monte hill Brazil
Pascua, Isla de i. S. Pacific Ocean see Easter Island
Pas de Calais str. France/U.K. see Dover, Strait of
102 C1 Pasewalk Ger.
129 D2 Pasfield Lake Can.
89 D1 Pasha Rus. Fed.
64 B2 Pasig Phil.
60 B1 Pasir Putih Malaysia
103 D1 Pasłęk Pol.
74 A2 Pasni Pak.
153 A4 Paso Río Mayo Arg.
135 B3 Paso Robles U.S.A.
97 B3 Passage West Ireland
155 D2 Passa Tempo Brazil
102 C2 Passau Ger.
152 C2 Passo Fundo Brazil
155 C2 Passos Brazil
88 C2 Pastavy Belarus
150 B3 Pastaza r. Peru
150 B2 Pasto Col.
74 B1 Pasu Jammu and Kashmir
61 C2 Pasuruan Indon.
88 B2 Pasvalys Lith.
103 D2 Pásztó Hungary
153 A5 Patagonia reg. Arg.
75 C2 Patan Nepal
54 B1 Patea N.Z.
139 E2 Paterson U.S.A.
74 B1 Pathankot India
Pathein Myanmar see Bassein
136 B2 Pathfinder Reservoir U.S.A.
61 C2 Pati Indon.
74 B1 Patiala India
62 A1 Patkai Bum mts India/Myanmar
111 C3 Patmos i. Greece
75 C2 Patna India
81 C2 Patnos Turkey
154 B3 Pato Branco Brazil
152 C3 Patos, Lagoa dos l. Brazil
155 C1 Patos de Minas Brazil
152 B3 Patquía Arg.
Patra Greece see Patras
111 B3 Patras Greece
75 C2 Patratu India
154 C1 Patrocínio Brazil
63 B3 Pattani Thai.
63 B2 Pattaya Thai.
128 B2 Pattullo, Mount Can.
129 D2 Patuanak Can.
146 B3 Patuca r. Hond.
144 B3 Pátzcuaro Mex.
104 B3 Pau France
104 B2 Pauillac France
150 C3 Pauini Brazil
62 A1 Pauk Myanmar
126 D2 Paulatuk Can.
Paulis Dem. Rep. Congo see Isiro
151 E3 Paulistana Brazil
151 F3 Paulo Afonso Brazil
123 D2 Paulpietersburg S. Africa
143 D2 Pauls Valley U.S.A.
62 A2 Paungde Myanmar
155 D1 Pavão Brazil
108 A1 Pavia Italy
88 B2 Pāvilosta Latvia
110 C2 Pavlikeni Bulg.
77 D1 Pavlodar Kazakh.
91 D2 Pavlohrad Ukr.
91 E1 Pavlovsk Rus. Fed.
91 D2 Pavlovskaya Rus. Fed.
139 E2 Pawtucket U.S.A.
111 B3 Paxoi i. Greece
60 B2 Payakumbuh Indon.
134 C2 Payette U.S.A.
134 C2 Payette r. U.S.A.
86 F2 Pay-Khoy, Khrebet hills Rus. Fed.
Payne Can. see Kangirsuk
130 C2 Payne, Lac l. Can.
152 C3 Paysandú Uru.
81 C1 Pazar Turkey
110 B2 Pazardzhik Bulg.
111 C3 Pazarköy Turkey
108 B1 Pazin Croatia
63 A2 Pe Myanmar
128 C2 Peace r. Can.
128 C2 Peace River Can.
53 C2 Peak Hill N.S.W. Austr.
50 A2 Peak Hill W.A. Austr.
135 E3 Peale, Mount U.S.A.
140 C2 Pearl r. U.S.A.
71 B3 Pearl River r. China
143 D3 Pearsall U.S.A.
126 F1 Peary Channel Can.
121 C2 Pebane Moz.
109 D2 Peć Serb. and Mont.
155 D1 Peçanha Brazil
154 C3 Peças, Ilha das i. Brazil
92 J2 Pechenga Rus. Fed.
86 E2 Pechora Rus. Fed.
86 E2 Pechora r. Rus. Fed.
Pechora Sea Rus. Fed. see Pechorskoye More
86 E2 Pechorskoye More sea Rus. Fed.
88 C2 Pechory Rus. Fed.
142 B1 Pecos NM U.S.A.
143 C2 Pecos TX U.S.A.
143 C3 Pecos r. U.S.A.
103 D2 Pécs Hungary
142 B3 Pedernales Mex.
155 D1 Pedra Azul Brazil
154 C2 Pedregulho Brazil
151 E3 Pedreiras Brazil
73 C4 Pedro, Point Sri Lanka
151 E3 Pedro Afonso Brazil
152 B2 Pedro de Valdivia Chile
154 B1 Pedro Gomes Brazil
152 C2 Pedro Juan Caballero Para.
106 B1 Pedroso Port.
96 C3 Peebles U.K.
141 E2 Pee Dee r. U.S.A.
126 D2 Peel r. Can.
98 A2 Peel Isle of Man
128 C2 Peerless Lake Can.
54 B2 Pegasus Bay N.Z.
101 E3 Pegnitz Ger.
62 A2 Pegu Myanmar
62 A2 Pegu Yoma mts Myanmar
153 B3 Pehuajó Arg.
101 E1 Peine Ger.
88 C2 Peipus, Lake Estonia/Rus. Fed.
Peiraias Greece see Piraeus
154 B2 Peixe r. Brazil
155 C2 Peixoto, Represa resr Brazil
151 D4 Peixoto de Azevedo Brazil
123 C2 Peka Lesotho
60 B2 Pekalongan Indon.
60 B1 Pekan Malaysia
60 B1 Pekanbaru Indon.
Peking China see Beijing
130 B3 Pelee Island Can.
61 D2 Peleng i. Indon.
103 D2 Pelhřimov Czech Rep.
92 I2 Pelkosenniemi Fin.
122 A2 Pella S. Africa
137 E2 Pella U.S.A.
59 D3 Pelleluhu Islands P.N.G.
92 H2 Pello Fin.
128 A1 Pelly r. Can.
Pelly Bay Can. see Kugaaruk
128 A1 Pelly Mountains Can.
152 C3 Pelotas Brazil
152 C2 Pelotas, Rio das r. Brazil
139 F1 Pemadumcook Lake U.S.A.
60 B1 Pemangkat Indon.
60 A1 Pematangsiantar Indon.
121 D2 Pemba Moz.
120 B2 Pemba Zambia
119 D3 Pemba Island Tanz.
128 B2 Pemberton Can.
137 D1 Pembina r. Can.
137 D1 Pembina r. U.S.A.
130 C3 Pembroke Can.
99 A4 Pembroke U.K.
141 D3 Pembroke Pines U.S.A.
106 C1 Peñalara mt. Spain
154 B2 Penápolis Brazil
106 B1 Peñaranda de Bracamonte Spain
107 C1 Peñarroya mt. Spain
106 B2 Peñarroya-Pueblonuevo Spain
106 B1 Peñas, Cabo de c. Spain
153 A4 Penas, Golfo de g. Chile
106 B1 Peña Ubiña mt. Spain
111 C2 Pendik Turkey
134 C1 Pendleton U.S.A.
128 B2 Pendleton Bay Can.
134 C1 Pend Oreille Lake U.S.A.
Penfro U.K. see Pembroke
74 B3 Penganga r. India
118 C3 Penge Dem. Rep. Congo
123 D1 Penge S. Africa
70 C2 Penglai China
71 A3 Pengshui China
106 B2 Peniche Port.
96 C3 Penicuik U.K.
60 B1 Peninsular Malaysia pen. Malaysia
108 B2 Penne Italy
52 A3 Penneshaw Austr.
98 B2 Pennines hills U.K.
139 D2 Pennsylvania state U.S.A.
127 H2 Penny Icecap Can.
89 D2 Peno Rus. Fed.
139 F2 Penobscot r. U.S.A.
52 B3 Penola Austr.
50 C3 Penong Austr.
157 E6 Penrhyn Basin sea feature S. Pacific Ocean
53 D2 Penrith Austr.
98 B2 Penrith U.K.
140 C2 Pensacola U.S.A.
55 B1 Pensacola Mountains Antarctica
61 C1 Pensiangan Sabah Malaysia
128 C3 Penticton Can.
96 C1 Pentland Firth sea chan. U.K.
99 B3 Penygadair hill U.K.
87 D3 Penza Rus. Fed.
99 A4 Penzance U.K.
83 L2 Penzhinskaya Guba b. Rus. Fed.
142 A2 Peoria AZ U.S.A.
138 B2 Peoria IL U.S.A.
107 C1 Perales del Alfambra Spain
111 B3 Perama Greece
131 D3 Percé Can.
50 B2 Percival Lakes salt flat Austr.
51 E2 Percy Isles Austr.
107 D1 Perdido, Monte mt. Spain
154 C1 Perdizes Brazil
86 F2 Peregrebnoye Rus. Fed.
150 B2 Pereira Col.
154 B2 Pereira Barreto Brazil
Pereira de Eça Angola see Ondjiva
90 A2 Peremyshlyany Ukr.
89 E2 Pereslavl'-Zalesskiy Rus. Fed.
91 C1 Pereyaslav-Khmel'nyts'kyy Ukr.
153 B3 Pergamino Arg.
92 H3 Perhonjoki r. Fin.
131 C2 Péribonka, Lac l. Can.
152 B2 Perico Arg.
144 B2 Pericos Mex.
104 C2 Périgueux France
150 B2 Perija, Sierra de mts Venez.
111 B3 Peristerio Greece
153 A4 Perito Moreno Arg.
101 E1 Perleberg Ger.
86 E3 Perm' Rus. Fed.
109 D2 Përmet Albania
Pernambuco Brazil see Recife
52 A2 Pernatty Lagoon salt flat Austr.
110 B2 Pernik Bulg.
Pernov Estonia see Pärnu
105 C2 Péronne France
145 C3 Perote Mex.
105 C3 Perpignan France
99 A4 Perranporth U.K.
Perrégaux Alg. see Mohammadia
141 D2 Perry FL U.S.A.
141 D2 Perry GA U.S.A.
137 E2 Perry IA U.S.A.
143 D1 Perry OK U.S.A.
138 C2 Perrysburg U.S.A.
143 C1 Perryton U.S.A.
137 F3 Perryville U.S.A.
Pershnotravnevoye Ukr. see Pershotravens'k
99 B3 Pershore U.K.
91 D2 Pershotravens'k Ukr.
Persia country Asia see Iran
Persian Gulf Asia see The Gulf
50 A3 Perth Austr.
96 C2 Perth U.K.
159 F5 Perth Basin sea feature Indian Ocean
86 C2 Pertominsk Rus. Fed.
105 D3 Pertuis France
108 A2 Pertusato, Capo c. Corsica France
150 B3 Peru country S. America
138 B2 Peru U.S.A.
157 H6 Peru Basin sea feature S. Pacific Ocean
157 H7 Peru-Chile Trench sea feature S. Pacific Ocean
108 B2 Perugia Italy
154 C2 Peruíbe Brazil
100 A2 Péruwelz Belgium
90 C2 Pervomays'k Ukr.
91 C2 Pervomays'ke Ukr.
Pervomayskiy Rus. Fed. see Novodvinsk
89 F3 Pervomayskiy Rus. Fed.
91 D2 Pervomays'kyy Ukr.
108 B2 Pesaro Italy
108 B2 Pescara Italy
108 B2 Pescara r. Italy
74 B1 Peshawar Pak.
109 D2 Peshkopi Albania
109 C1 Pesnica Slovenia
104 B3 Pessac France
89 E2 Pestovo Rus. Fed.
140 C2 Petal U.S.A.
100 B3 Pétange Lux.
147 D3 Petare Venez.
144 B3 Petatlán Mex.
121 C2 Petauke Zambia
130 C3 Petawawa Can.
138 B2 Petenwell Lake U.S.A.
52 A2 Peterborough Austr.
130 C3 Peterborough Can.
99 C3 Peterborough U.K.
96 D2 Peterhead U.K.
55 R3 Peter I Island Antarctica
129 E1 Peter Lake Can.
50 B2 Petermann Ranges mts Austr.
129 D2 Peter Pond Lake Can.
128 A2 Petersburg AK U.S.A.
139 D3 Petersburg VA U.S.A.
101 D1 Petershagen Ger.
Peter the Great Bay Rus. Fed. see Petra Velikogo, Zaliv
Petitjean Morocco see Sidi Kacem
131 D2 Petit Lac Manicouagan l. Can.
131 E2 Petit Mécatina r. Can.
145 D2 Peto Mex.
138 C1 Petoskey U.S.A.
80 B2 Petra tourist site Jordan
66 B2 Petra Velikogo, Zaliv b. Rus. Fed.
111 B2 Petrich Bulg.
Petroaleksandrovsk Uzbek. see To'rtko'l
88 C2 Petrodvorets Rus. Fed.
Petrokov Pol. see Piotrków Trybunalski
151 E3 Petrolina Brazil
77 C1 Petropavlovsk Kazakh.
83 L3 Petropavlovsk-Kamchatskiy Rus. Fed.
110 B1 Petroşani Romania
Petrovskoye Rus. Fed. see Svetlograd
89 F3 Petrovskoye Rus. Fed.
89 E2 Petrovskoye Rus. Fed.
69 D1 Petrovsk-Zabaykal'skiy Rus. Fed.
86 C2 Petrozavodsk Rus. Fed.
123 C2 Petrusburg S. Africa
123 C2 Petrus Steyn S. Africa
122 B3 Petrusville S. Africa
Petsamo Rus. Fed. see Pechenga
87 F3 Petukhovo Rus. Fed.
89 E2 Petushki Rus. Fed.
60 A1 Peureula Indon.
83 M2 Pevek Rus. Fed.
102 B2 Pforzheim Ger.
102 C2 Pfunds Austria
101 D3 Pfungstadt Ger.
123 C2 Phahameng Free State S. Africa
123 C1 Phahameng Limpopo S. Africa
123 D1 Phalaborwa S. Africa
74 B2 Phalodi India
63 A3 Phangnga Thai.
63 B2 Phan Rang Vietnam
63 B2 Phan Thiêt Vietnam
63 B3 Phatthalung Thai.
62 A2 Phayao Thai.
129 D2 Phelps Lake Can.
141 C2 Phenix City U.S.A.
63 A2 Phet Buri Thai.
63 B2 Phetchabun Thai.
63 B2 Phichit Thai.
139 D3 Philadelphia U.S.A.
136 C2 Philip U.S.A.
Philip Atoll Micronesia see Sorol
Philippeville Alg. see Skikda
100 B2 Philippeville Belgium
51 C2 Philippi, Lake salt flat Austr.
100 A2 Philippine Neth.
156 C4 Philippine Basin sea feature N. Pacific Ocean
64 B2 Philippines country Asia
64 B2 Philippine Sea N. Pacific Ocean
126 C2 Philip Smith Mountains U.S.A.
122 B3 Philipstown S. Africa
53 C3 Phillip Island Austr.
137 D3 Phillipsburg U.S.A.
63 B2 Phimun Mangsahan Thai.
123 C2 Phiritona S. Africa
63 B2 Phitsanulok Thai.
63 B2 Phnom Penh Cambodia
Phnum Pénh Cambodia see Phnom Penh
142 A2 Phoenix U.S.A.
49 J4 Phoenix Islands Kiribati
63 B2 Phon Thai.
62 B2 Phong Nha Vietnam
62 B1 Phôngsali Laos
62 B1 Phong Thô Vietnam
62 B2 Phrae Thai.
Phu Cuong Vietnam see Thu Dâu Môt
120 B3 Phuduhudu Botswana
63 A3 Phuket Thai.
63 B2 Phumĭ Kâmpóng Trâlach Cambodia
63 B2 Phumĭ Sâmraông Cambodia
63 B2 Phu Nhơn Vietnam
63 B2 Phu Quôc, Đao i. Vietnam
123 C2 Phuthaditjhaba S. Africa
Phu Vinh Vietnam see Tra Vinh
62 A2 Phyu Myanmar
108 A1 Piacenza Italy

108 B2 Pianosa, Isola i. Italy
110 C1 Piatra Neamţ Romania
151 E3 Piauí r. Brazil
108 B1 Piave r. Italy
117 A4 Pibor r. Sudan
117 B4 Pibor Post Sudan
Picardie reg. France see Picardy
104 C2 Picardy reg. France
140 D2 Picayune U.S.A.
152 B2 Pichanal Arg.
144 A2 Pichilingue Mex.
98 C2 Pickering U.K.
130 A2 Pickle Lake Can.
151 E3 Picos Brazil
153 B4 Pico Truncado Arg.
53 D2 Picton Austr.
54 B2 Picton N.Z.
73 C4 Pidurutalagala mt. Sri Lanka
154 C2 Piedade Brazil
145 C3 Piedras Negras Guat.
145 B2 Piedras Negras Mex.
150 C4 Piedras, Río de las r. Peru
93 I3 Pieksämäki Fin.
92 I3 Pielinen l. Fin.
136 C2 Pierre U.S.A.
105 C3 Pierrelatte France
123 D2 Pietermaritzburg S. Africa
Pietersaari Fin. see Jakobstad
Pietersburg S. Africa see Polokwane
123 D2 Piet Retief S. Africa
110 B1 Pietrosa mt. Romania
110 C1 Pietrosu, Vârful mt. Romania
128 C2 Pigeon Lake Can.
137 F1 Pigeon River U.S.A.
153 B3 Pigüé Arg.
93 I3 Pihlajavesi l. Fin.
92 I3 Pihtipudas Fin.
145 C3 Pijijiapan Mex.
130 A2 Pikangikum Can.
136 C3 Pikes Peak U.S.A.
122 A3 Piketberg S. Africa
138 C3 Pikeville U.S.A.
103 D1 Piła Pol.
153 C3 Pilar Arg.
152 C2 Pilar Para.
75 B2 Pilibhit India
53 C2 Pilliga Austr.
154 C3 Pilões, Serra dos mts Brazil
150 C4 Pimenta Bueno Brazil
88 C3 Pina r. Belarus
153 C3 Pinamar Arg.
60 B1 Pinang i. Malaysia
80 B2 Pınarbaşı Turkey
146 B2 Pinar del Río Cuba
64 B2 Pinatubo, Mount vol. Phil.
103 E1 Pińczów Pol.
151 E3 Pindaré r. Brazil
Pindos Greece see Pindus Mountains
111 B2 Pindus Mountains mts Greece
140 B2 Pine Bluff U.S.A.
136 C2 Pine Bluffs U.S.A.
50 C1 Pine Creek Austr.
136 B2 Pinedale U.S.A.
86 D2 Pinega Rus. Fed.
129 D2 Pinehouse Lake Can.
111 B3 Pineios r. Greece
141 D3 Pine Islands FL U.S.A.
141 D4 Pine Islands FL U.S.A.
128 C1 Pine Point Can.
136 C2 Pine Ridge U.S.A.
108 A2 Pinerolo Italy
Pines, Isle of i. Cuba see Juventud, Isla de la
123 D2 Pinetown S. Africa
140 B2 Pineville U.S.A.
70 B2 Pingdingshan China
70 B2 Pingdu China
62 B1 Pingguo China
71 B3 Pingjiang China
70 A2 Pingliang China
70 B1 Pingquan China
71 C3 P'ingtung Taiwan
Pingxi China see Yuping
71 A3 Pingxiang Guangxi China
71 B3 Pingxiang Jiangxi China
70 B2 Pingyin China
155 C2 Pinhal Brazil
151 E3 Pinheiro Brazil
52 B3 Pinnaroo Austr.
101 D1 Pinneberg Ger.
Pinos, Isla de i. Cuba see Juventud, Isla de la
145 C3 Pinotepa Nacional Mex.
48 H6 Pins, Île des i. New Caledonia
88 C3 Pinsk Belarus
152 B2 Pinto Arg.
135 D3 Pioche U.S.A.
119 C3 Piodi Dem. Rep. Congo
108 B2 Piombino Italy
86 F2 Pionerskiy Rus. Fed.
103 E1 Pionki Pol.
103 D1 Piotrków Trybunalski Pol.
137 D2 Pipestone U.S.A.
131 C3 Pipmuacan, Réservoir resr Can.
154 B2 Piquiri r. Brazil
154 C1 Piracanjuba Brazil
154 C2 Piracicaba Brazil
155 D1 Piracicaba r. Brazil
154 C2 Piraçununga Brazil
111 B3 Piraeus Greece
154 C3 Piraí do Sul Brazil
154 C2 Piraju Brazil

154 C2 Pirajuí Brazil
154 B1 Piranhas Brazil
151 F3 Piranhas r. Brazil
155 D1 Pirapora Brazil
154 C1 Pirenópolis Brazil
154 C1 Pires do Rio Brazil
Pirineos mts Europe see Pyrenees
151 E3 Piripiri Brazil
109 D2 Pirot Serb. and Mont.
59 C3 Piru Indon.
108 B2 Pisa Italy
152 A1 Pisagua Chile
150 B4 Pisco Peru
102 C2 Písek Czech Rep.
79 D2 Pishin Iran
74 A1 Pishin Pak.
145 D2 Pisté Mex.
109 C2 Pisticci Italy
108 B2 Pistoia Italy
106 C1 Pisuerga r. Spain
134 B2 Pit r. U.S.A.
114 A3 Pita Guinea
154 B2 Pitanga Brazil
155 D1 Pitangui Brazil
49 O6 Pitcairn Island S. Pacific Ocean
49 O6 Pitcairn Islands terr. S. Pacific Ocean
92 H2 Piteå Sweden
92 H2 Piteälven r. Sweden
110 B2 Piteşti Romania
75 C2 Pithoragarh India
142 A2 Pitiquito Mex.
86 C2 Pitkyaranta Rus. Fed.
96 C2 Pitlochry U.K.
128 B2 Pitt Island Can.
137 E3 Pittsburg U.S.A.
138 D2 Pittsburgh U.S.A.
139 E2 Pittsfield U.S.A.
53 D1 Pittsworth Austr.
155 C2 Piumhi Brazil
150 A3 Piura Peru
143 C2 Plains U.S.A.
143 C1 Plainview U.S.A.
60 B2 Plaju Indon.
61 C1 Plampang Indon.
154 C1 Planaltina Brazil
137 D2 Plankinton U.S.A.
143 D2 Plano U.S.A.
154 C2 Planura Brazil
140 B2 Plaquemine U.S.A.
106 B1 Plasencia Spain
109 C1 Plaški Croatia
147 C4 Plato Col.
137 D2 Platte r. U.S.A.
138 A2 Platteville U.S.A.
139 E2 Plattsburgh U.S.A.
101 F1 Plau Ger.
101 F2 Plauen Ger.
101 F1 Plauer See l. Ger.
89 E3 Plavsk Rus. Fed.
106 B2 Playa de Castilla coastal area Spain
63 B2 Plây Cu Vietnam
129 E2 Playgreen Lake Can.
153 B3 Plaza Huincul Arg.
143 D3 Pleasanton U.S.A.
54 C2 Pleasant Point N.Z.
138 B3 Pleasure Ridge Park U.S.A.
104 C2 Pleaux France
130 B2 Pledger Lake Can.
54 C1 Plenty, Bay of g. N.Z.
136 C1 Plentywood U.S.A.
86 D2 Plesetsk Rus. Fed.
131 C2 Plétipi, Lac l. Can.
100 C2 Plettenberg Ger.
122 B3 Plettenberg Bay S. Africa
110 B2 Pleven Bulg.
Plevna Bulg. see Pleven
109 C2 Pljevlja Serb. and Mont.
108 A2 Ploaghe Sardinia Italy
109 C2 Ploče Croatia
103 D1 Płock Pol.
109 C2 Pločno mt. Bos.-Herz.
104 B2 Ploemeur France
Ploeşti Romania see Ploieşti
110 C2 Ploieşti Romania
89 F2 Ploskoye Rus. Fed.
104 B2 Plouzané France
110 B2 Plovdiv Bulg.
Plozk Pol. see Płock
121 B3 Plumtree Zimbabwe
88 B2 Plungė Lith.
144 B2 Plutarco Elías Calles, Presa resr Mex.
88 C3 Plyeshchanitsy Belarus
147 D3 Plymouth Montserrat
99 A4 Plymouth U.K.
138 B2 Plymouth U.S.A.
99 B3 Plynlimon hill U.K.
88 C2 Plyussa Rus. Fed.
102 C2 Plzeň Czech Rep.
114 B3 Pô Burkina
108 B1 Po r. Italy
61 C1 Po, Tanjung pt Malaysia
77 E2 Pobeda Peak China/Kyrg.
Pobedy, Pik mt. China/Kyrg. see Pobeda Peak
140 B3 Pocahontas U.S.A.
134 D2 Pocatello U.S.A.
90 B1 Pochayiv Ukr.

89 D3 Pochep Rus. Fed.
89 D3 Pochinok Rus. Fed.
145 C3 Pochutla Mex.
139 D3 Pocomoke City U.S.A.
155 C2 Poços de Caldas Brazil
89 D2 Poddor'ye Rus. Fed.
91 D1 Podgorenskiy Rus. Fed.
109 C2 Podgorica Serb. and Mont.
82 G3 Podgornoye Rus. Fed.
83 H2 Podkamennaya Tunguska r. Rus. Fed.
89 E2 Podol'sk Rus. Fed.
109 D2 Podujevo Serb. and Mont.
122 A2 Pofadder S. Africa
89 D3 Pogar Rus. Fed.
105 E3 Poggibonsi Italy
109 D2 Pogradec Albania
66 B2 Pogranichnyy Rus. Fed.
Po Hai g. China see Bo Hai
65 B2 P'ohang S. Korea
48 G3 Pohnpei atoll Micronesia
90 B2 Pohrebyshche Ukr.
110 B2 Poiana Mare Romania
118 C3 Poie Dem. Rep. Congo
118 B3 Pointe-Noire Congo
160 B3 Point Hope U.S.A.
128 C1 Point Lake Can.
138 C3 Point Pleasant U.S.A.
104 C2 Poitiers France
104 C2 Poitou, Plaines et Seuil du plain France
74 B2 Pokaran India
53 C1 Pokataroo Austr.
75 C2 Pokhara Nepal
119 C2 Poko Dem. Rep. Congo
83 J2 Pokrovsk Rus. Fed.
91 D2 Pokrovskoye Rus. Fed.
Pola Croatia see Pula
142 A1 Polacca U.S.A.
106 B1 Pola de Lena Spain
106 B1 Pola de Siero Spain
103 D1 Poland country Europe
55 C1 Polar Plateau Antarctica
80 B2 Polatlı Turkey
88 C2 Polatsk Belarus
77 C3 Pol-e Khomrī Afgh.
61 C2 Polewali Indon.
118 B2 Poli Cameroon
102 C1 Police Pol.
109 C2 Policoro Italy
105 D2 Poligny France
64 B2 Polillo Islands Phil.
80 B2 Polis Cyprus
90 B1 Polis'ke Ukr.
109 C2 Polistena Italy
103 D1 Polkowice Pol.
107 D2 Pollença Spain
109 C3 Pollino, Monte mt. Italy
86 F2 Polnovat Rus. Fed.
91 D2 Polohy Ukr.
123 C1 Polokwane S. Africa
90 B1 Polonne Ukr.
134 D1 Polson U.S.A.
91 C2 Poltava Ukr.
66 B2 Poltavka Rus. Fed.
91 D2 Poltavskaya Rus. Fed.
88 C2 Põltsamaa Estonia
88 C2 Põlva Estonia
Polyanovgrad Bulg. see Karnobat
92 J2 Polyarnyy Rus. Fed.
86 C2 Polyarnyye Zori Rus. Fed.
111 B3 Polygyros Greece
111 B2 Polykastro Greece
156 E6 Polynesia is Pacific Ocean
106 B2 Pombal Port.
108 B2 Pomezia Italy
92 I2 Pomokaira reg. Fin.
110 C2 Pomorie Bulg.
102 C1 Pomorska, Zatoka b. Pol.
155 D1 Pompéu Brazil
143 D1 Ponca City U.S.A.
147 D3 Ponce Puerto Rico
73 B3 Pondicherry India
127 G2 Pond Inlet Can.
Ponds Bay Can. see Pond Inlet
106 B1 Ponferrada Spain
117 A4 Pongo watercourse Sudan
123 D2 Pongola r. S. Africa
123 D2 Pongolapoort Dam l. S. Africa
128 C2 Ponoka Can.
154 B3 Ponta Grossa Brazil
154 C1 Pontalina Brazil
105 D2 Pont-à-Mousson France
154 A2 Ponta Porã Brazil
105 D2 Pontarlier France
102 C2 Pontcharra France
140 B2 Pontchartrain, Lake U.S.A.
154 B1 Ponte de Pedra Brazil
106 B2 Ponte de Sor Port.
154 B1 Ponte do Rio Verde Brazil
98 C3 Pontefract U.K.
129 D3 Ponteix Can.
155 D2 Ponte Nova Brazil
150 D4 Pontes-e-Lacerda Brazil
106 B1 Pontevedra Spain
Ponthierville Dem. Rep. Congo see Ubundu
138 B2 Pontiac IL U.S.A.
138 C2 Pontiac MI U.S.A.
60 B2 Pontianak Indon.
Pontine Islands is Italy see Ponziane, Isole
104 B2 Pontivy France
104 B2 Pontoetoe Suriname

104 C2 Pontoise France
129 E2 Ponton Can.
99 B4 Pontypool U.K.
99 B4 Pontypridd U.K.
108 B2 Ponziane, Isole is Italy
99 C4 Poole U.K.
Poona India see Pune
52 B2 Pooncarie Austr.
152 B1 Poopó, Lago de l. Bol.
150 B2 Popayán Col.
83 I2 Popigay r. Rus. Fed.
52 B2 Popiltah Austr.
129 E2 Poplar r. Can.
137 E3 Poplar Bluff U.S.A.
145 C3 Popocatépetl, Volcán vol. Mex.
118 B3 Popokabaka Dem. Rep. Congo
Popovichskaya Rus. Fed. see Kalininskaya
110 C2 Popovo Bulg.
103 E2 Poprad Slovakia
151 E4 Porangatu Brazil
74 A2 Porbandar India
126 C2 Porcupine r. Can./U.S.A.
108 B1 Pordenone Italy
108 B1 Poreč Croatia
154 B2 Porecatu Brazil
114 C3 Porga Benin
93 H3 Pori Fin.
54 B2 Porirua N.Z.
88 C2 Porkhov Rus. Fed.
104 B2 Pornic France
83 K3 Poronaysk Rus. Fed.
75 C2 Porong China
111 B3 Poros Greece
92 I1 Porsangerfjorden sea chan. Norway
93 E4 Porsgrunn Norway
111 D3 Porsuk r. Turkey
97 C1 Portadown U.K.
97 D1 Portaferry U.K.
138 B2 Portage U.S.A.
129 E3 Portage la Prairie Can.
128 B3 Port Alberni Can.
106 B2 Portalegre Port.
143 C2 Portales U.S.A.
128 A2 Port Alexander U.S.A.
128 B2 Port Alice U.S.A.
140 B2 Port Allen U.S.A.
134 B1 Port Angeles U.S.A.
97 C2 Portarlington Ireland
51 D4 Port Arthur Austr.
Port Arthur China see Lüshun
143 E3 Port Arthur U.S.A.
96 A3 Port Askaig U.K.
52 A2 Port Augusta Austr.
147 C3 Port-au-Prince Haiti
131 E2 Port aux Choix Can.
122 B3 Port Beaufort S. Africa
73 D3 Port Blair India
52 B3 Port Campbell Austr.
131 D2 Port-Cartier Can.
54 B3 Port Chalmers N.Z.
141 D3 Port Charlotte U.S.A.
147 C3 Port-de-Paix Haiti
128 A2 Port Edward Can.
155 D1 Porteirinha Brazil
151 D3 Portel Brazil
130 B3 Port Elgin Can.
123 C3 Port Elizabeth S. Africa
96 A3 Port Ellen U.K.
98 A2 Port Erin Isle of Man
122 A3 Porterville S. Africa
135 C3 Porterville U.S.A.
Port Étienne Maur. see Nouâdhibou
52 B3 Port Fairy Austr.
54 C1 Port Fitzroy N.Z.
Port Francqui Dem. Rep. Congo see Ilebo
118 A3 Port-Gentil Gabon
115 C4 Port Harcourt Nigeria
128 B2 Port Hardy Can.
Port Harrison Can. see Inukjuak
131 D3 Port Hawkesbury Can.
99 B4 Porthcawl U.K.
50 A2 Port Hedland Austr.
Port Herald Malawi see Nsanje
99 A3 Porthmadog U.K.
131 E2 Port Hope Simpson Can.
138 C2 Port Huron U.S.A.
106 B2 Portimão Port.
Port Keats Austr. see Wadeye
53 C2 Portland N.S.W. Austr.
52 B3 Portland Vic. Austr.
139 E2 Portland ME U.S.A.
134 B1 Portland OR U.S.A.
143 D3 Portland TX U.S.A.
99 B4 Portland, Isle of pen. U.K.
128 A2 Portland Canal inlet Can.
97 C2 Portlaoise Ireland
143 D3 Port Lavaca U.S.A.
52 A2 Port Lincoln Austr.
114 A4 Port Loko Sierra Leone
113 I8 Port Louis Mauritius
Port-Lyautrey Morocco see Kénitra
52 B3 Port MacDonnell Austr.
53 D2 Port Macquarie Austr.
Portmadoc U.K. see Porthmadog
128 B2 Port McNeill Can.
131 D3 Port-Menier Can.
59 D3 Port Moresby P.N.G.
96 A3 Portnahaven U.K.
96 A1 Port Ness U.K.

**Port Nis** U.K. see Port Ness
122 A2 **Port Nolloth** S. Africa
**Port-Nouveau-Québec** Can. see Kangiqsualujjuaq
**Porto** Port. see Oporto
150 C2 **Porto Acre** Brazil
154 C3 **Porto Alegre** Brazil
152 C3 **Porto Alegre** Brazil
**Porto Alexandre** Angola see Tombua
**Porto Amélia** Moz. see Pemba
151 D4 **Porto Artur** Brazil
154 B2 **Porto Camargo** Brazil
151 D4 **Porto dos Gaúchos Óbidos** Brazil
150 D4 **Porto Esperidião** Brazil
108 B2 **Portoferraio** Italy
151 E3 **Porto Franco** Brazil
147 D3 **Port of Spain** Trin. and Tob.
108 B1 **Portogruaro** Italy
108 B2 **Portomaggiore** Italy
154 B2 **Porto Mendes** Brazil
152 C2 **Porto Murtinho** Brazil
151 E4 **Porto Nacional** Brazil
114 C4 **Porto-Novo** Benin
154 B2 **Porto Primavera, Represa** resr Brazil
134 B2 **Port Orford** U.S.A.
151 D3 **Porto Santana** Brazil
154 B2 **Porto São José** Brazil
108 A3 **Portoscuso** Sardinia Italy
155 E1 **Porto Seguro** Brazil
108 B2 **Porto Tolle** Italy
108 A2 **Porto Torres** Sardinia Italy
154 B3 **Porto União** Brazil
105 D3 **Porto-Vecchio** Corsica France
150 C3 **Porto Velho** Brazil
150 A3 **Portoviejo** Ecuador
96 B3 **Portpatrick** U.K.
52 B2 **Port Phillip Bay** Austr.
52 A2 **Port Pirie** Austr.
96 A2 **Portree** U.K.
128 B3 **Port Renfrew** Can.
97 C1 **Portrush** U.K.
116 B2 **Port Said** Egypt
123 D3 **Port Shepstone** S. Africa
99 C4 **Portsmouth** U.K.
139 E2 **Portsmouth** NH U.S.A.
138 C3 **Portsmouth** OH U.S.A.
139 D3 **Portsmouth** VA U.S.A.
153 B5 **Port Stephens** Falkland Is
97 C1 **Portstewart** U.K.
141 D3 **Port St Joe** U.S.A.
123 C3 **Port St Johns** S. Africa
141 D3 **Port St Lucie City** U.S.A.
116 B3 **Port Sudan** Sudan
140 C3 **Port Sulphur** U.S.A.
99 B4 **Port Talbot** U.K.
134 B1 **Port Townsend** U.S.A.
106 B2 **Portugal** country Europe
**Portugália** Angola see Chitato
**Portuguese Guinea** country Africa see Guinea-Bissau
**Portuguese Timor** country Asia see East Timor
**Portuguese West Africa** country Africa see Angola
97 B2 **Portumna** Ireland
105 C3 **Port-Vendres** France
48 H5 **Port Vila** Vanuatu
52 A2 **Port Wakefield** Austr.
50 B1 **Port Warrender** Austr.
153 A5 **Porvenir** Chile
93 I3 **Porvoo** Fin.
65 B2 **Poryŏng** S. Korea
152 C2 **Posadas** Arg.
89 E2 **Poshekhon'ye** Rus. Fed.
**Poshekon'ye-Volodarsk** Rus. Fed. see Poshekhon'ye
92 I2 **Posio** Fin.
61 D2 **Poso** Indon.
151 E4 **Posse** Brazil
101 E2 **Pößneck** Ger.
143 C2 **Post** U.S.A.
**Poste-de-la-Baleine** Can. see Kuujjuarapik
122 B2 **Postmasburg** S. Africa
108 B1 **Postojna** Slovenia
114 C2 **Post Weygand** Alg.
**Postysheve** Ukr. see Krasnoarmiys'k
109 C2 **Posušje** Bos.-Herz.
123 C2 **Potchefstroom** S. Africa
143 E1 **Poteau** U.S.A.
109 C2 **Potenza** Italy
108 B2 **Potenza** r. Italy
151 E3 **Poti** r. Brazil
81 C1 **P'ot'i** Georgia
155 E1 **Potiraguá** Brazil
115 D3 **Potiskum** Nigeria
139 D3 **Potomac, South Branch** r. U.S.A.
152 B1 **Potosí** Bol.
64 B2 **Pototan** Phil.
142 C3 **Potrero del Llano** Mex.
101 F1 **Potsdam** Ger.
139 E2 **Potsdam** U.S.A.
139 D2 **Pottstown** U.S.A.
139 D2 **Pottsville** U.S.A.
131 E3 **Pouch Cove** Can.
139 E2 **Poughkeepsie** U.S.A.
98 B3 **Poulton-le-Fylde** U.K.
155 C3 **Pouso Alegre** Brazil
63 B2 **Poŭthisăt** Cambodia
103 D2 **Považská Bystrica** Slovakia
109 C2 **Povlen** mt. Serb. and Mont.
106 B1 **Póvoa de Varzim** Port.

136 B2 **Powell** U.S.A.
135 D3 **Powell, Lake** resr U.S.A.
128 B3 **Powell River** Can.
154 B1 **Poxoréu** Brazil
**Poyang** China see Boyang
71 B3 **Poyang Hu** l. China
109 D2 **Požarevac** Serb. and Mont.
145 C2 **Poza Rica** Mex.
109 C1 **Požega** Croatia
109 D2 **Požega** Serb. and Mont.
79 D2 **Pozm Tiāb** Iran
103 D1 **Poznań** Pol.
106 C2 **Pozoblanco** Spain
152 C2 **Pozo Colorado** Para.
109 B3 **Pozzallo** Sicily Italy
108 B2 **Pozzuoli** Italy
60 B2 **Prabumulih** Indon.
102 C2 **Prachatice** Czech Rep.
63 A2 **Prachuap Khiri Khan** Thai.
103 D1 **Praděd** mt. Czech Rep.
104 C3 **Prades** France
155 E1 **Prado** Brazil
102 C1 **Prague** Czech Rep.
**Praha** Czech Rep. see Prague
143 C2 **Prairie Dog Town Fork** r. U.S.A.
138 A2 **Prairie du Chien** U.S.A.
60 A1 **Prapat** Indon.
154 C1 **Prata** Brazil
108 B2 **Prato** Italy
137 D3 **Pratt** U.S.A.
140 C2 **Prattville** U.S.A.
61 C2 **Praya** Indon.
63 B2 **Preăh Vihéar** Cambodia
89 F2 **Prechistoye** Rus. Fed.
129 D2 **Preeceville** Can.
88 C2 **Preiļi** Latvia
53 C2 **Premer** Austr.
105 C2 **Prémery** France
101 F1 **Premnitz** Ger.
102 C1 **Prenzlau** Ger.
66 B2 **Preobrazheniye** Rus. Fed.
63 A2 **Preparis Island** Cocos Is
63 A2 **Preparis North Channel** Cocos Is
63 A2 **Preparis South Channel** Cocos Is
103 D2 **Přerov** Czech Rep.
142 A2 **Prescott** U.S.A.
142 A2 **Prescott Valley** U.S.A.
109 D2 **Preševo** Serb. and Mont.
152 B2 **Presidencia Roque Sáenz Peña** Arg.
151 E3 **Presidente Dutra** Brazil
154 B2 **Presidente Epitácio** Brazil
154 B1 **Presidente Murtinho** Brazil
155 C1 **Presidente Olegário** Brazil
154 B2 **Presidente Prudente** Brazil
142 C3 **Presidio** U.S.A.
103 E2 **Prešov** Slovakia
111 B2 **Prespa, Lake** Europe
139 F1 **Presque Isle** U.S.A.
**Pressburg** Slovakia see Bratislava
101 F2 **Pressel** Ger.
98 B3 **Preston** U.K.
134 D2 **Preston** U.S.A.
96 B3 **Prestwick** U.K.
155 C1 **Preto** r. Brazil
123 C2 **Pretoria** S. Africa
**Pretoria-Witwatersrand-Vereeniging** prov. S. Africa see Gauteng
111 B3 **Preveza** Greece
63 B2 **Prey Vêng** Cambodia
124 A4 **Pribilof Islands** U.S.A.
109 C2 **Priboj** Serb. and Mont.
135 D3 **Price** U.S.A.
140 C2 **Prichard** U.S.A.
106 C2 **Priego de Córdoba** Spain
88 B3 **Prienai** Lith.
122 B2 **Prieska** S. Africa
103 D2 **Prievidza** Slovakia
109 C2 **Prijedor** Bos.-Herz.
109 C2 **Prijepolje** Serb. and Mont.
**Prikaspiyskaya Nizmennost'** lowland Kazakh./Rus. Fed. see Caspian Lowland
111 B2 **Prilep** Macedonia
101 F3 **Přimda** Czech Rep.
91 D2 **Primorsko-Akhtarsk** Rus. Fed.
129 D2 **Primrose Lake** Can.
129 D2 **Prince Albert** Can.
122 B3 **Prince Albert** S. Africa
126 E2 **Prince Albert Peninsula** Can.
122 B3 **Prince Albert Road** S. Africa
126 D2 **Prince Alfred, Cape** Can.
122 A3 **Prince Alfred Hamlet** S. Africa
127 G2 **Prince Charles Island** Can.
55 H2 **Prince Charles Mountains** Antarctica
131 D3 **Prince Edward Island** prov. Can.
128 B2 **Prince George** Can.
51 D1 **Prince of Wales Island** Austr.
126 F2 **Prince of Wales Island** Can.
128 A2 **Prince of Wales Island** U.S.A.
126 E2 **Prince of Wales Strait** Can.
126 E1 **Prince Patrick Island** Can.
126 F2 **Prince Regent Inlet** sea chan. Can.
128 A2 **Prince Rupert** Can.
51 D1 **Princess Charlotte Bay** Austr.
55 H2 **Princess Elizabeth Land** reg. Antarctica
128 B2 **Princess Royal Island** Can.
128 B3 **Princeton** Can.
138 B3 **Princeton** IN U.S.A.
137 E2 **Princeton** MO U.S.A.
134 B2 **Prineville** U.S.A.

86 C2 **Priozersk** Rus. Fed.
**Pripet** r. Belarus see Prypyats'
90 A1 **Pripet Marshes** Belarus/Ukr.
109 D2 **Priština** Serb. and Mont.
101 F1 **Pritzwalk** Ger.
105 C3 **Privas** France
109 C2 **Privlaka** Croatia
89 F2 **Privolzhsk** Rus. Fed.
109 D2 **Prizren** Serb. and Mont.
151 D2 **Professor van Blommestein Meer** resr Suriname
145 C2 **Progreso** Mex.
81 C1 **Prokhladnyy** Rus. Fed.
109 D2 **Prokuplje** Serb. and Mont.
**Prome** Myanmar see Pyè
154 C2 **Promissão** Brazil
154 C2 **Promissão, Represa** resr Brazil
126 D3 **Prophet** r. Can.
128 B2 **Prophet River** Can.
51 D2 **Proserpine** Austr.
103 D2 **Proskurov** Ukr. see Khmel'nyts'kyy
89 E3 **Protvino** Rus. Fed.
110 C2 **Provadiya** Bulg.
105 D3 **Provence** reg. France
139 E2 **Providence** U.S.A.
146 B3 **Providencia, Isla de** i. Caribbean Sea
83 N2 **Provideniya** Rus. Fed.
105 C2 **Provins** France
135 D2 **Provo** U.S.A.
129 C2 **Provost** Can.
91 C2 **Prubiynyy, Mys** pt Ukr.
154 B3 **Prudentópolis** Brazil
126 C2 **Prudhoe Bay** U.S.A.
100 C2 **Prüm** Ger.
105 D3 **Prunelli-di-Fiumorbo** Corsica France
103 D1 **Pruszcz Gdański** Pol.
103 E1 **Pruszków** Pol.
110 C1 **Prut** r. Europe
88 B3 **Pruzhany** Belarus
91 C1 **Pryazovs'ke** Ukr.
91 C1 **Pryluky** Ukr.
91 D2 **Prymors'k** Ukr.
91 D2 **Prymors'kyy** Ukr.
143 D1 **Pryor** U.S.A.
90 B1 **Prypyats'** r. Belarus/Ukr.
103 E2 **Przemyśl** Pol.
103 E1 **Przeworsk** Pol.
**Przheval'sk** Kyrg. see Karakol
111 C3 **Psara** i. Greece
81 C1 **Psebay** Rus. Fed.
91 D3 **Pshekha** r. Rus. Fed.
88 C2 **Pskov** Rus. Fed.
88 C2 **Pskov, Lake** Estonia/Rus. Fed.
111 B2 **Ptolemaïda** Greece
109 C1 **Ptuj** Slovenia
150 B3 **Pucallpa** Peru
71 B3 **Pucheng** China
65 B2 **Puch'ŏn** S. Korea
103 D1 **Puck** Pol.
92 I2 **Pudasjärvi** Fin.
70 C2 **Pudong** China
86 C2 **Pudozh** Rus. Fed.
**Puduchcheri** India see Pondicherry
145 C3 **Puebla** Mex.
136 C3 **Pueblo** U.S.A.
153 B3 **Puelén** Arg.
153 A3 **Puente Alto** Chile
106 C2 **Puente-Genil** Spain
153 A4 **Puerto Aisén** Chile
152 B1 **Puerto Alegre** Bol.
145 C3 **Puerto Ángel** Mex.
146 B4 **Puerto Armuelles** Panama
150 C2 **Puerto Ayacucho** Venez.
146 B3 **Puerto Barrios** Guat.
146 B3 **Puerto Cabezas** Nic.
153 A4 **Puerto Cisnes** Chile
144 A2 **Puerto Cortés** Mex.
145 C3 **Puerto Escondido** Mex.
152 B1 **Puerto Frey** Bol.
150 C2 **Puerto Inírida** Col.
152 C1 **Puerto Isabel** Bol.
150 B3 **Puerto Leguizamo** Col.
146 B3 **Puerto Lempira** Hond.
144 A2 **Puerto Libertad** Mex.
146 B3 **Puerto Limón** Costa Rica
106 C2 **Puertollano** Spain
153 B4 **Puerto Madryn** Arg.
150 C4 **Puerto Maldonado** Peru
**Puerto México** Mex. see Coatzacoalcos
147 D3 **Puerto Miranda** Venez.
153 A4 **Puerto Montt** Chile
153 A5 **Puerto Natales** Chile
150 C2 **Puerto Nuevo** Col.
150 C2 **Puerto Páez** Venez.
144 A1 **Puerto Peñasco** Mex.
152 C2 **Puerto Pinasco** Para.
147 C3 **Puerto Plata** Dom. Rep.
150 B3 **Puerto Portillo** Peru
**Puerto Presidente Stroessner** Para. see Ciudad del Este
64 A3 **Puerto Princesa** Phil.
154 A3 **Puerto Rico** Arg.
147 D3 **Puerto Rico** terr. West Indies
158 C3 **Puerto Rico Trench** sea feature Caribbean Sea
146 A3 **Puerto San José** Guat.
153 B5 **Puerto Santa Cruz** Arg.
152 C2 **Puerto Sastre** Para.
144 B2 **Puerto Vallarta** Mex.
87 D3 **Pugachev** Rus. Fed.

74 B2 **Pugal** India
54 B2 **Pukaki, Lake** N.Z.
49 K5 **Pukapuka** atoll Cook Is
129 D2 **Pukatawagan** Can.
65 B1 **Pukchin** N. Korea
65 B1 **Pukch'ŏng** N. Korea
109 C2 **Pukë** Albania
54 B1 **Pukekohe** N.Z.
65 B1 **Puksubaek-san** mt. N. Korea
**Pula** China see Nyingchi
108 B2 **Pula** Croatia
108 A3 **Pula** Sardinia Italy
152 B2 **Pulacayo** Bol.
103 E1 **Puławy** Pol.
92 I3 **Pulkkila** Fin.
134 C1 **Pullman** U.S.A.
64 B2 **Pulog, Mount** Phil.
64 B3 **Pulutan** Indon.
150 A3 **Puná, Isla** i. Ecuador
54 B2 **Punakaiki** N.Z.
123 D1 **Punda Maria** S. Africa
73 B3 **Pune** India
65 B1 **P'ungsan** N. Korea
121 C2 **Púnguè** r. Moz.
119 C3 **Punia** Dem. Rep. Congo
74 B1 **Punjab** state India
153 B3 **Punta Alta** Arg.
153 A5 **Punta Arenas** Chile
108 A2 **Punta Balestrieri** mt. Sardinia Italy
153 C3 **Punta del Este** Uru.
146 B3 **Punta Gorda** Belize
146 B3 **Puntarenas** Costa Rica
150 B1 **Punto Fijo** Venez.
92 I3 **Puolanka** Fin.
**Puqi** China see Chibi
82 G2 **Pur** r. Rus. Fed.
75 C3 **Puri** India
100 B1 **Purmerend** Neth.
**Purnea** India see Purnia
75 C2 **Purnia** India
75 C2 **Puruliya** India
150 C3 **Purus** r. Peru
61 B2 **Purwakarta** Indon.
61 C2 **Purwodadi** Indon.
65 B1 **Puryŏng** N. Korea
74 B2 **Pusad** India
65 B2 **Pusan** S. Korea
89 E3 **Pushchino** Rus. Fed.
**Pushkino** Azer. see Biläsuvar
89 E2 **Pushkino** Rus. Fed.
88 C2 **Pushkinskiye Gory** Rus. Fed.
88 C2 **Pustoshka** Rus. Fed.
62 A1 **Putao** Myanmar
71 B3 **Putian** China
**Puting** China see De'an
61 C2 **Puting, Tanjung** pt Indon.
101 F1 **Putlitz** Ger.
60 B1 **Putrajaya** Malaysia
122 B2 **Putsonderwater** S. Africa
102 C1 **Puttgarden** Ger.
150 B3 **Putumayo** r. Col.
61 C1 **Putusibau** Indon.
90 B2 **Putyla** Ukr.
91 C1 **Putyvl'** Ukr.
93 I3 **Puula** l. Fin.
130 C1 **Puvirnituq** Can.
70 B2 **Puyang** China
104 C3 **Puylaurens** France
119 C3 **Pweto** Dem. Rep. Congo
99 A3 **Pwllheli** U.K.
92 J2 **Pyaozerskiy** Rus. Fed.
63 A2 **Pyapon** Myanmar
83 G2 **Pyasina** r. Rus. Fed.
87 D4 **Pyatigorsk** Rus. Fed.
91 C2 **P"yatykhatky** Ukr.
62 A2 **Pyè** Myanmar
88 C3 **Pyetrykaw** Belarus
93 H3 **Pyhäjärvi** l. Fin.
92 H3 **Pyhäjoki** r. Fin.
92 I3 **Pyhäsalmi** Fin.
62 A1 **Pyingaing** Myanmar
62 A2 **Pyinmana** Myanmar
62 A1 **Pyin-U-Lwin** Myanmar
65 B2 **Pyŏksŏng** N. Korea
65 B1 **P'yŏngsan** N. Korea
65 B2 **P'yŏngsan** N. Korea
65 B2 **P'yŏngsong** N. Korea
65 B2 **P'yŏngt'aek** S. Korea
65 B2 **P'yŏngyang** N. Korea
135 C2 **Pyramid Lake** U.S.A.
80 B3 **Pyramids of Giza** tourist site Egypt
107 D1 **Pyrenees** mts Europe
111 B3 **Pyrgetos** Greece
111 C3 **Pyrgi** Greece
111 B3 **Pyrgos** Greece
91 C1 **Pyryatyn** Ukr.
103 C1 **Pyrzyce** Pol.
88 C2 **Pytalovo** Rus. Fed.
111 B3 **Pyxaria** mt. Greece

**Q**

**Qaanaaq** Greenland see Thule
**Qabqa** China see Gonghe
123 C2 **Qacha's Nek** Lesotho
69 D2 **Qagan Nur** China
**Qahremānshahr** Iran see Kermānshāh
68 C2 **Qaidam Pendi** basin China
79 C2 **Qalamat Abū Shafrah** Saudi Arabia

78 A2 Qal'at al Aẓlam Saudi Arabia
78 A2 Qal'at al Mu'aẓẓam Saudi Arabia
78 B2 Qal'at Bishah Saudi Arabia
76 C3 Qal'eh-ye Now Afgh.
129 E1 **Qamanirjuaq Lake** Can.
Qamanittuaq Can. see Baker Lake
79 C3 Qamar, Ghubbat al b. Yemen
68 C2 Qamdo China
78 B3 Qam Ḩadīl Saudi Arabia
127 I2 Qaqortoq Greenland
80 A3 Qārah Egypt
Qarkilik China see Ruoqiang
Qarqan China see Qiemo
77 C3 Qarshi Uzbek.
78 B2 Qaryat al Ulyā Saudi Arabia
127 I2 Qasigiannguit Greenland
116 A2 Qaşr al Farāfirah Egypt
79 D2 Qaşr-e Qand Iran
81 C2 Qaşr-e Shīrīn Iran
127 I2 Qassimiut Greenland
79 C2 Qaṭabah Yemen
79 C2 Qatar country Asia
116 A2 Qattāra Depression Egypt
76 B3 Qāyen Iran
81 C1 Qazax Azer.
81 C1 Qazımämmäd Azer.
81 C2 Qazvīn Iran
Qena Egypt see Qinā
127 I2 Qeqertarsuaq Greenland
127 I2 Qeqertarsuaq i. Greenland
127 I2 Qeqertarsuatsiaat Greenland
127 I2 Qeqertarsuup Tunua b. Greenland
79 C2 Qeshm Iran
74 A1 Qeysār, Kūh-e mt. Afgh.
70 A3 Qianjiang Chongqing China
70 B2 Qianjiang Hubei China
69 E1 Qianjin China
65 A1 Qian Shan mts China
71 A3 Qianxi China
72 B2 Qidong China
77 E3 Qiemo China
68 C2 Qijiang China
68 C2 Qijiaojing China
127 H2 Qikiqtarjuaq Can.
74 A2 Qila Ladgasht Pak.
68 C2 Qilian Shan mts China
127 J2 Qillak i. Greenland
70 B3 Qimen China
127 H1 Qimusseriarsuaq b. Greenland
116 B2 Qinā Egypt
Qincheng China see Nanfeng
70 C2 Qingdao China
68 C2 Qinghai Hu salt l. China
68 C2 Qinghai Nanshan mts China
Qingjiang China see Huai'an
Qingjiang China see Zhangshu
70 B2 Qingshuihe China
70 A2 Qingtongxia China
70 C2 Qingyang China
71 B3 Qingyuan Guangdong China
Qingyuan China see Yizhou
65 A1 Qingyuan Liaoning China
68 B2 Qingzang Gaoyuan plat. China
70 B2 Qingzhou China
70 B2 Qinhuangdao China
Qinjiang China see Shicheng
70 A2 Qin Ling mts China
Qinting China see Lianhua
70 B2 Qinyang China
71 A3 Qinzhou China
71 B4 Qionghai China
70 A2 Qionglai Shan mts China
71 B4 Qiongshan China
71 A4 Qiongzhong China
69 E1 Qiqihar China
81 D3 Qīr Iran
Qishan China see Qimen
79 C3 Qishn Yemen
66 B1 Qitaihe China
70 B2 Qixian Henan China
70 B2 Qixian Shanxi China
Qogir Feng mt.
China/Jammu and Kashmir see K2
81 D2 Qom Iran
Qomishēh Iran see Shahrezā
Qomolangma Feng mt.
China/Nepal see Everest, Mount
76 B2 Qo'ng'irot Uzbek.
Qoqek China see Tacheng
77 D2 Qo'qon Uzbek.
76 B2 Qoraqalpog'iston Uzbek.
80 B2 Qornet es Saouda mt. Lebanon
81 C2 Qorveh Iran
79 C2 Qoṭbābād Iran
101 C1 Quakenbrück Ger.
53 C2 Quambone Austr.
63 B2 Quang Ngai Vietnam
63 B2 Quang Tri Vietnam
Quan Long Vietnam see Ca Mau
Quan Phu Quoc i. Vietnam see
Phu Quôc, Đao
71 B3 Quanzhou Fujian China
71 B3 Quanzhou Guangxi China
108 A3 Quartu Sant'Elena Sardinia Italy
142 A2 Quartzsite U.S.A.
81 C1 Quba Azer.
76 B3 Quchan Iran
53 C3 Queanbeyan Austr.
131 C3 Québec Can.
131 C2 Québec prov. Can.
101 E2 Quedlinburg Ger.
Queen Adelaide Islands Chile see
Reina Adelaida,
Archipiélago de la

128 A2 Queen Charlotte Can.
128 A2 Queen Charlotte Islands Can.
128 B2 Queen Charlotte Sound sea chan. Can.
128 B2 Queen Charlotte Strait Can.
126 E1 Queen Elizabeth Islands Can.
55 I2 Queen Mary Land reg. Antarctica
126 F2 Queen Maud Gulf Can.
55 E2 Queen Maud Land reg. Antarctica
55 P1 Queen Maud Mountains Antarctica
52 B3 Queenscliff Austr.
52 B1 Queensland state Austr.
51 D4 Queenstown Austr.
54 A3 Queenstown N.Z.
Queenstown Ireland see Cóbh
123 C3 Queenstown S. Africa
121 C2 Quelimane Moz.
153 A4 Quellón Chile
Quelpart Island S. Korea see Cheju-do
142 B2 Quemado U.S.A.
Que Que Zimbabwe see Kwekwe
154 B1 Querência do Norte Brazil
145 B2 Querétaro Mex.
101 E2 Querfurt Ger.
128 B2 Quesnel Can.
128 B2 Quesnel Lake Can.
74 A1 Quetta Pak.
146 A3 Quetzaltenango Guat.
64 A3 Quezon Phil.
64 B2 Quezon City Phil.
120 A2 Quibala Angola
150 B2 Quibdó Col.
104 B2 Quiberon France
120 A2 Quilengues Angola
104 C3 Quillan France
153 C3 Quilmes Arg.
73 B4 Quilon India
51 D2 Quilpie Austr.
153 A3 Quilpué Chile
120 A1 Quimbele Angola
152 B2 Quimili Arg.
104 B2 Quimper France
104 B2 Quimperlé France
135 B3 Quincy CA U.S.A.
141 D2 Quincy FL U.S.A.
137 E3 Quincy IL U.S.A.
139 E2 Quincy MA U.S.A.
63 B2 Qui Nhon Vietnam
107 C1 Quinto Spain
121 D2 Quionga Moz.
120 A2 Quirima Angola
53 D2 Quirindi Austr.
154 B1 Quirinópolis Brazil
131 D3 Quispamsis Can.
121 C3 Quissico Moz.
120 A2 Quitapa Angola
150 B3 Quito Ecuador
151 F3 Quixadá Brazil
71 A3 Qujing China
75 D1 Qumar He r. China
123 C3 Qumrha S. Africa
115 E1 Qunayyin, Sabkhat al salt marsh Libya
129 E1 Quoich r. Can.
52 A2 Quorn Austr.
79 C2 Qurayat Oman
77 C3 Qürghonteppa Tajik.
Quxar China see Lhazê
Quyang China see Jingzhou
71 B3 Quzhou China
Qyteti Stalin Albania see Kuçovë
Qyzyltü Kazakh. see Kishkenekol'

# R

103 D2 Raab r. Austria
92 H3 Raahe Fin.
100 C1 Raalte Neth.
61 C2 Raas i. Indon.
61 C2 Raba Indon.
114 B1 Rabat Morocco
59 E3 Rabaul P.N.G.
50 C2 Rabbit Flat Austr.
78 A2 Rābigh Saudi Arabia
103 D2 Rabka Pol.
Râbniţa Moldova see Rîbniţa
Rabyânah, Ramlat des. Libya see Rebiana Sand Sea
131 E3 Race, Cape Can.
140 B3 Raceland U.S.A.
139 E2 Race Point U.S.A.
63 B3 Rach Gia Vietnam
103 D1 Racibórz Pol.
138 B2 Racine U.S.A.
110 C1 Rădăuţi Romania
138 B3 Radcliff U.S.A.
74 B2 Radhanpur India
130 C2 Radisson Can.
103 E1 Radom Pol.
103 D1 Radomsko Pol.
90 B1 Radomyshl' Ukr.
111 B2 Radoviš Macedonia
88 B2 Radviliškis Lith.
78 A2 Raḍwá, Jabal mt. Saudi Arabia
90 B1 Radyvyliv Ukr.
75 C2 Rae Bareli India
128 C1 Rae-Edzo Can.
128 C1 Rae Lakes Can.
100 C2 Raeren Belgium
54 C1 Raetihi N.Z.

78 A2 Rāf hill Saudi Arabia
152 B3 Rafaela Arg.
118 C2 Rafaï C.A.R.
78 B2 Rafḩā' Saudi Arabia
79 C1 Rafsanjān Iran
117 B3 Raga Sudan
64 B3 Ragang, Mount vol. Phil.
109 B3 Ragusa Sicily Italy
61 D2 Raha Indon.
88 D3 Rahachow Belarus
78 A3 Rahad r. Sudan
74 B2 Rahimyar Khan Pak.
73 B3 Raichur India
75 C2 Raigarh India
128 C2 Rainbow Lake Can.
134 B1 Rainier, Mount vol. U.S.A.
130 A3 Rainy Lake Can.
129 E3 Rainy River Can.
75 C2 Raipur India
93 H3 Raisio Fin.
88 C2 Raja Estonia
73 C3 Rajahmundry India
61 C1 Rajang r. Sarawak Malaysia
74 B2 Rajanpur Pak.
73 B4 Rajapalaiyam India
74 B2 Rajasthan state India
74 B2 Rajasthan Canal canal India
74 B2 Rajgarh India
60 B2 Rajik Indon.
74 B2 Rajkot India
74 B2 Raj Nandgaon India
74 B2 Rajpur India
75 C2 Rajshahi Bangl.
54 B2 Rakaia r. N.Z.
74 B1 Rakaposhi mt. Jammu and Kashmir
90 A2 Rakhiv Ukr.
91 D1 Rakitnoye Rus. Fed.
88 C2 Rakke Estonia
88 C2 Rakvere Estonia
141 E1 Raleigh U.S.A.
141 E2 Raleigh Bay U.S.A.
48 H3 Ralik Chain is Marshall Is
75 C2 Ramanuj Ganj India
123 C2 Ramatlabama S. Africa
104 C2 Rambouillet France
99 A4 Rame Head U.K.
97 C1 Ramelton Ireland
89 E2 Rameshki Rus. Fed.
74 B2 Ramgarh India
81 C2 Rāmhormoz Iran
110 C1 Râmnicu Sărat Romania
110 B1 Râmnicu Vâlcea Romania
89 E3 Ramon' Rus. Fed.
135 C4 Ramona U.S.A.
123 C1 Ramotswa Botswana
75 C2 Rampur India
62 A2 Ramree Island Myanmar
98 A2 Ramsey Isle of Man
130 B3 Ramsey Lake Can.
99 D3 Ramsgate U.K.
81 C2 Rāmshīr Iran
62 A1 Ramsing India
75 C2 Ranaghat India
61 C1 Ranau Sabah Malaysia
153 A3 Rancagua Chile
154 B2 Rancharia Brazil
75 C2 Ranchi India
93 F4 Randers Denmark
63 B3 Rangae Thai.
75 D2 Rangapara North India
54 B2 Rangiora N.Z.
49 M5 Rangiroa atoll Fr. Polynesia
54 C1 Rangitaiki r. N.Z.
60 B2 Rangkasbitung Indon.
63 A2 Rangoon Myanmar
75 C2 Rangpur Bangl.
129 E1 Rankin Inlet Can.
53 C2 Rankin's Springs Austr.
Rankovićevo Serb. and Mont. see Kraljevo
96 B2 Rannoch Moor moorland U.K.
74 B2 Rann of Kachchh marsh India
63 A3 Ranong Thai.
59 C3 Ransiki Indon.
61 C2 Rantaupanjang Indon.
60 A1 Rantauprapat Indon.
61 C2 Rantepao Indon.
92 I2 Ranua Fin.
93 E4 Ranum Denmark
78 B2 Ranyah, Wādī watercourse Saudi Arabia
49 J6 Raoul Island Kermadec Is
49 M6 Rapa i. Fr. Polynesia
108 A2 Rapallo Italy
136 C2 Rapid City U.S.A.
88 B2 Rapla Estonia
74 A2 Rapur India
49 L6 Rarotonga i. Cook Is
153 B4 Rasa, Punta pt Arg.
Ras al Khaimah U.A.E. see Ra's al Khaymah
79 C2 Ra's al Khaymah U.A.E.
116 B3 Ras Dejen mt. Eth.
88 B2 Raseiniai Lith.
116 B2 Ra's Ghārib Egypt
81 C2 Rasht Iran
74 A2 Ras Koh mt. Pak.
110 C1 Râşnov Romania
88 C2 Rasony Belarus
79 C2 Ra's Şirāb Oman
108 B3 Rass Jebel Tunisia
87 D3 Rasskazovo Rus. Fed.
79 C2 Ras Tannūrah Saudi Arabia
101 D1 Rastede Ger.

48 I2 Ratak Chain is Marshall Is
93 F3 Rätan Sweden
123 C2 Ratanda S. Africa
74 B2 Ratangarh India
63 A2 Rat Buri Thai.
62 A1 Rathedaung Myanmar
101 F1 Rathenow Ger.
97 C1 Rathfriland U.K.
97 C1 Rathlin Island U.K.
97 C1 Rathluirc Ireland
100 C2 Ratingen Ger.
74 B2 Ratlam India
73 B3 Ratnagiri India
73 C4 Ratnapura Sri Lanka
90 A1 Ratne Ukr.
142 C1 Raton U.S.A.
96 D2 Rattray Head hd U.K.
93 G3 Rättvik Sweden
101 E1 Ratzeburg Ger.
78 B2 Raudhatain Kuwait
92 □B2 Raufarhöfn Iceland
54 C1 Raukumara Range mts N.Z.
93 H3 Rauma Fin.
88 C2 Rauna Latvia
61 C2 Raung, Gunung vol. Indon.
75 C2 Raurkela India
66 D2 Rausu Japan
90 B2 Rāut r. Moldova
134 D1 Ravalli U.S.A.
81 C2 Ravānsar Iran
108 B2 Ravenna Italy
102 B2 Ravensburg Ger.
50 B3 Ravensthorpe Austr.
74 B1 Ravi r. Pak.
74 B1 Rawalpindi Pak.
103 D1 Rawicz Pol.
50 B3 Rawlinna Austr.
136 B2 Rawlins U.S.A.
153 B4 Rawson Arg.
75 C3 Rayagada India
69 E1 Raychikhinsk Rus. Fed.
78 B3 Raydah Yemen
87 E3 Rayevskiy Rus. Fed.
134 B1 Raymond U.S.A.
53 D2 Raymond Terrace Austr.
143 D3 Raymondville U.S.A.
129 D2 Raymore Can.
145 C2 Rayón Mex.
63 B2 Rayong Thai.
78 A2 Rayyis Saudi Arabia
104 B2 Raz, Pointe du pt France
81 C2 Razāzah, Buḩayrat ar l. Iraq
110 C2 Razgrad Bulg.
110 C2 Razim, Lacul lag. Romania
111 B2 Razlog Bulg.
Raz"yezd 3km Rus. Fed. see Novyy Urgal
104 B2 Ré, Île de i. France
99 C4 Reading U.K.
138 C3 Reading OH U.S.A.
139 D2 Reading PA U.S.A.
123 C2 Reagile S. Africa
115 E2 Rebiana Sand Sea des. Libya
66 D1 Rebun-tō i. Japan
50 B3 Recherche, Archipelago of the is Austr.
89 D3 Rechytsa Belarus
151 F3 Recife Brazil
123 C3 Recife, Cape S. Africa
100 C2 Recklinghausen Ger.
152 C2 Reconquista Arg.
137 D1 Red r. Can./U.S.A.
140 B2 Red r. U.S.A.
100 B3 Redange Lux.
141 C1 Red Bank U.S.A.
Red Basin China see Sichuan Pendi
131 E2 Red Bay Can.
135 B2 Red Bluff U.S.A.
98 C2 Redcar U.K.
129 C2 Redcliff Can.
121 B2 Redcliff Zimbabwe
52 B2 Red Cliffs Austr.
128 C2 Red Deer Can.
126 C2 Red Deer r. Can.
129 D2 Red Deer Lake Can.
135 B2 Redding U.S.A.
99 C3 Redditch U.K.
137 D2 Redfield U.S.A.
137 D3 Red Hills U.S.A.
130 A2 Red Lake Can.
130 A2 Red Lake l. Can.
137 E1 Red Lakes U.S.A.
134 E1 Red Lodge U.S.A.
134 B2 Redmond U.S.A.
137 D2 Red Oak U.S.A.
104 B2 Redon France
106 B1 Redondela Spain
106 B2 Redondo Port.
78 A3 Red Sea Africa/Asia
128 B1 Redstone r. Can.
100 B1 Reduzum Neth.
128 C2 Redwater Can.
137 E2 Red Wing U.S.A.
137 D2 Redwood Falls U.S.A.
97 C2 Ree, Lough l. Ireland
134 B2 Reedsport U.S.A.
54 B2 Reefton N.Z.
143 D3 Refugio U.S.A.
102 C2 Regen Ger.
155 E1 Regência Brazil
102 C2 Regensburg Ger.
114 C2 Reggane Alg.
109 C3 Reggio di Calabria Italy
108 B2 Reggio nell'Emilia Italy

**110** B1 **Reghin** Romania
**129** D2 **Regina** Can.
**154** C2 **Registro** Brazil
**122** A1 **Rehoboth** Namibia
 **80** B2 **Rehovot** Israel
**101** F2 **Reichenbach** Ger.
**141** E1 **Reidsville** U.S.A.
 **99** C4 **Reigate** U.K.
**105** C2 **Reims** France
**153** A5 **Reina Adelaida,**
     **Archipiélago de la** is Chile
**101** C1 **Reinbek** Ger.
**129** D2 **Reindeer** r. Can.
**129** E2 **Reindeer Island** Can.
**129** D2 **Reindeer Lake** Can.
 **92** F2 **Reine** Norway
**106** C1 **Reinosa** Spain
**100** C3 **Reinsfeld** Ger.
**123** C2 **Reitz** S. Africa
**122** B2 **Reivilo** S. Africa
**129** D1 **Reliance** Can.
**107** D2 **Relizane** Alg.
 **52** A2 **Remarkable, Mount** hill Austr.
 **79** C2 **Remeshk** Iran
**105** D2 **Remiremont** France
**100** C2 **Remscheid** Ger.
**102** B1 **Rendsburg** Ger.
**139** D1 **Renfrew** Can.
 **60** B2 **Rengat** Indon.
 **90** B2 **Reni** Ukr.
 **52** B2 **Renmark** Austr.
 **48** H5 **Rennell** i. Solomon Is
**101** D2 **Rennerod** Ger.
**104** B2 **Rennes** France
**129** D1 **Rennie Lake** Can.
**108** B2 **Reno** r. Italy
**135** C3 **Reno** U.S.A.
 **70** A3 **Renshou** China
**138** B2 **Rensselaer** U.S.A.
 **75** C2 **Renukut** India
 **54** B2 **Renwick** N.Z.
 **61** D2 **Reo** Indon.
**136** D3 **Republican** r. U.S.A.
**127** G2 **Repulse Bay** Can.
**150** B3 **Requena** Peru
**107** C2 **Requena** Spain
 **60** B2 **Resag, Gunung** mt. Indon.
**111** B2 **Resen** Macedonia
**154** B2 **Reserva** Brazil
 **91** C2 **Reshetylivka** Ukr.
**152** C2 **Resistencia** Arg.
**110** B1 **Reşiţa** Romania
**126** F2 **Resolute** Can.
**127** H2 **Resolution Island** Can.
**155** D1 **Resplendor** Brazil
**145** C3 **Retalhuleu** Guat.
 **98** C3 **Retford** U.K.
**105** C2 **Rethel** France
**111** B3 **Rethymno** Greece
**113** I8 **Réunion** terr. Indian Ocean
**107** D1 **Reus** Spain
     **Reut** r. Moldova see **Răut**
**102** B2 **Reutlingen** Ger.
 **86** C2 **Revda** Rus. Fed.
**128** C2 **Revelstoke** Can.
**144** A3 **Revillagigedo, Islas** is Mex.
**128** A2 **Revillagigedo Island** U.S.A.
 **75** C2 **Rewa** India
**134** D2 **Rexburg** U.S.A.
**135** B3 **Reyes, Point** U.S.A.
**160** M4 **Reykjanes Ridge** sea feature
     N. Atlantic Ocean
 **92** □A3 **Reykjanestá** pt Iceland
 **92** □A3 **Reykjavík** Iceland
**145** C2 **Reynosa** Mex.
     **Rezā'īyeh** Iran see **Urmia**
     **Rezā'īyeh, Daryācheh-ye** salt l.
     Iran see **Urmia, Lake**
 **88** C2 **Rēzekne** Latvia
     **Rheims** France see **Reims**
     **Rhein** r. Ger. see **Rhine**
**100** C1 **Rheine** Ger.
**101** F1 **Rheinsberg** Ger.
     **Rhin** r. France see **Rhine**
**100** C2 **Rhine** r. Europe
**138** B1 **Rhinelander** U.S.A.
**101** F1 **Rhinluch** marsh Ger.
**101** F1 **Rhinow** Ger.
**108** A1 **Rho** Italy
**139** E2 **Rhode Island** state U.S.A.
**111** C3 **Rhodes** Greece
**111** C3 **Rhodes** i. Greece
     **Rhodesia** country Africa see
     **Zimbabwe**
**111** B2 **Rhodope Mountains** Bulg./Greece
**105** C3 **Rhône** r. France/Switz.
     **Rhum** i. U.K. see **Rum**
     **Rhuthun** U.K. see **Ruthin**
 **98** B3 **Rhyl** U.K.
**155** D1 **Riacho dos Machados** Brazil
**154** C1 **Rialma** Brazil
**154** C1 **Rianópolis** Brazil
 **60** B1 **Riau, Kepulauan** is Indon.
**106** B1 **Ribadeo** Spain
**106** B1 **Ribadesella** Spain
**154** B2 **Ribas do Rio Pardo** Brazil
**121** C2 **Ribáuè** Moz.
 **98** B3 **Ribble** r. U.K.
 **93** E4 **Ribe** Denmark
**154** C2 **Ribeira** r. Brazil
**154** C2 **Ribeirão Preto** Brazil
**104** C2 **Ribérac** France
**152** B1 **Riberalta** Bol.
 **90** B2 **Ribniţa** Moldova
**102** C1 **Ribnitz-Damgarten** Ger.

**138** A1 **Rice Lake** U.S.A.
**123** D2 **Richards Bay** S. Africa
**143** D2 **Richardson** U.S.A.
**126** C2 **Richardson Mountains** Can.
**135** D3 **Richfield** U.S.A.
**134** C1 **Richland** U.S.A.
**138** A2 **Richland Center** U.S.A.
 **53** D2 **Richmond** N.S.W. Austr.
 **51** D2 **Richmond** Qld Austr.
**134** B1 **Richmond** Can.
 **54** B2 **Richmond** N.Z.
**122** B3 **Richmond** S. Africa
 **98** C2 **Richmond** U.K.
**138** C3 **Richmond** IN U.S.A.
**138** C3 **Richmond** KY U.S.A.
**139** D3 **Richmond** VA U.S.A.
**141** D2 **Richmond Hill** U.S.A.
 **53** D1 **Richmond Range** hills Austr.
**130** C3 **Rideau Lakes** Can.
**135** C3 **Ridgecrest** U.S.A.
**140** B2 **Ridgeland** U.S.A.
**102** C1 **Riesa** Ger.
**101** D1 **Rieste** Ger.
**123** B2 **Riet** r. S. Africa
**101** D2 **Rietberg** Ger.
**122** B2 **Rietfontein** S. Africa
**108** B2 **Rieti** Italy
**136** B3 **Rifle** U.S.A.
 **88** B2 **Riga** Latvia
 **88** B2 **Riga, Gulf of** Estonia/Latvia
 **79** C2 **Rīgān** Iran
**134** D2 **Rigby** U.S.A.
**131** E2 **Rigolet** Can.
 **93** H3 **Riihimäki** Fin.
 **55** D2 **Riiser-Larsen Ice Shelf**
     Antarctica
**108** B1 **Rijeka** Croatia
**134** C2 **Riley** U.S.A.
**105** C2 **Rillieux-la-Pape** France
 **78** B2 **Rimah, Wādī al** watercourse
     Saudi Arabia
**103** E2 **Rimavská Sobota** Slovakia
**128** C2 **Rimbey** Can.
**108** B2 **Rimini** Italy
     **Rîmnicu Sărat** Romania see
     **Râmnicu Sărat**
     **Rîmnicu Vîlcea** Romania see
     **Râmnicu Vâlcea**
**131** D3 **Rimouski** Can.
**144** B2 **Rincón de Romos** Mex.
 **93** F3 **Ringebu** Norway
 **93** E4 **Ringkøbing** Denmark
 **92** G2 **Ringvassøya** i. Norway
 **99** C4 **Ringwood** U.K.
**101** D1 **Rinteln** Ger.
**154** B3 **Rio Azul** Brazil
**150** B3 **Riobamba** Ecuador
**155** D2 **Rio Bonito** Brazil
**150** C4 **Rio Branco** Brazil
**154** C3 **Rio Branco do Sul** Brazil
**154** B2 **Rio Brilhante** Brazil
**155** D2 **Rio Casca** Brazil
**154** C2 **Rio Claro** Brazil
**153** B3 **Río Colorado** Arg.
**153** B4 **Río Cuarto** Arg.
**155** D2 **Rio de Janeiro** Brazil
**153** B5 **Río Gallegos** Arg.
**153** B5 **Río Grande** Arg.
**152** C3 **Río Grande** Brazil
**144** B2 **Río Grande** Mex.
**143** D3 **Rio Grande** r. Mex./U.S.A.
**143** D3 **Rio Grande City** U.S.A.
**150** B1 **Riohacha** Col.
**150** B2 **Rioja** Peru
**145** D2 **Río Lagartos** Mex.
**151** F3 **Rio Largo** Brazil
**105** C2 **Riom** France
**152** B1 **Río Mulatos** Bol.
**154** C3 **Rio Negro** Brazil
**155** D1 **Rio Pardo de Minas** Brazil
**154** C1 **Rio Preto, Serra do** hills Brazil
**142** B1 **Rio Rancho** U.S.A.
**150** B3 **Rio Tigre** Ecuador
 **64** A3 **Rio Tuba** Phil.
**154** B1 **Rio Verde** Brazil
**145** C2 **Río Verde** Mex.
**154** B1 **Rio Verde de Mato Grosso** Brazil
 **90** C1 **Ripky** Ukr.
 **99** C3 **Ripley** U.K.
**107** D1 **Ripoll** Spain
 **98** C2 **Ripon** U.K.
 **66** D1 **Rishiri-tō** i. Japan
     **Rîşnov** Romania see **Râşnov**
 **93** E4 **Risør** Norway
**122** B2 **Ritchie** S. Africa
 **73** D3 **Ritchie's Archipelago** is India
**134** C1 **Ritzville** U.S.A.
**152** B2 **Rivadavia** Arg.
**108** B1 **Riva del Garda** Italy
**146** B3 **Rivas** Nic.
**152** C3 **Rivera** Uru.
**114** B4 **River Cess** Liberia
**129** D2 **Riverhurst** Can.
 **52** C2 **Riverina** reg. Austr.
**122** B3 **Riversdale** S. Africa
**135** C4 **Riverside** U.S.A.
**136** B2 **Riverton** U.S.A.
**131** D3 **Riverview** Can.
**105** C3 **Rivesaltes** France
**131** D3 **Rivière-au-Renard** Can.
**131** D3 **Rivière-du-Loup** Can.
**139** F1 **Rivière-Ouelle** Can.
 **90** B1 **Rivne** Ukr.
**108** A1 **Rivoli** Italy
**120** B2 **Rivungo** Angola

 **54** B2 **Riwaka** N.Z.
 **78** B2 **Riyadh** Saudi Arabia
 **81** C1 **Rize** Turkey
 **70** B2 **Rizhao** China
**105** C2 **Roanne** France
**138** D3 **Roanoke** U.S.A.
**141** E1 **Roanoke** r. U.S.A.
**141** E1 **Roanoke Rapids** U.S.A.
**135** E3 **Roan Plateau** U.S.A.
**146** B3 **Roatán** Hond.
 **52** A3 **Robe** Austr.
 **52** B2 **Robe, Mount** hill Austr.
**101** F1 **Röbel** Ger.
 **53** D1 **Roberts, Mount** Austr.
 **92** H3 **Robertsfors** Sweden
**122** A3 **Robertson** S. Africa
**114** A4 **Robertsport** Liberia
     **Robert Williams** Angola see **Caála**
**130** C3 **Roberval** Can.
 **50** A2 **Robinson Range** hills Austr.
 **52** B2 **Robinvale** Austr.
**129** D2 **Roblin** Can.
**128** C2 **Robson, Mount** Can.
**143** D3 **Robstown** U.S.A.
     **Roçadas** Angola see **Xangongo**
**108** B3 **Rocca Busambra** mt. Sicily Italy
**153** C3 **Rocha** Uru.
 **98** B3 **Rochdale** U.K.
**154** B1 **Rochedo** Brazil
**100** B2 **Rochefort** Belgium
**104** B2 **Rochefort** France
 **52** B3 **Rochester** Austr.
**137** E2 **Rochester** MN U.S.A.
**139** E2 **Rochester** NH U.S.A.
**139** D2 **Rochester** NY U.S.A.
 **94** A2 **Rockall** i. N. Atlantic Ocean
**160** L4 **Rockall Bank** sea feature
     N. Atlantic Ocean
**138** B2 **Rockford** U.S.A.
 **51** E2 **Rockhampton** Austr.
**141** D2 **Rock Hill** U.S.A.
 **50** A3 **Rockingham** Austr.
**138** A2 **Rock Island** U.S.A.
**136** B1 **Rock Springs** MT U.S.A.
**143** C3 **Rocksprings** U.S.A.
**136** B2 **Rock Springs** WY U.S.A.
**141** D1 **Rockwood** U.S.A.
**136** C3 **Rocky Ford** U.S.A.
**141** E1 **Rocky Mount** U.S.A.
**128** C2 **Rocky Mountain House** Can.
**124** F4 **Rocky Mountains** U.S.A.
**100** B3 **Rocroi** France
**102** C1 **Rødbyhavn** Denmark
**131** E2 **Roddickton** Can.
**104** C3 **Rodez** France
     **Rodi** i. Greece see **Rhodes**
 **89** F2 **Rodniki** Rus. Fed.
     **Rodos** Greece see **Rhodes**
     **Rodos** i. Greece see **Rhodes**
     **Rodosto** Turkey see **Tekirdağ**
 **50** A2 **Roebourne** Austr.
 **50** B1 **Roebuck Bay** Austr.
**123** C1 **Roedtan** S. Africa
**100** B2 **Roermond** Neth.
**100** A2 **Roeselare** Belgium
**127** G2 **Roes Welcome Sound** sea chan.
     Can.
**128** C2 **Rogers** Can.
**140** B1 **Rogers** U.S.A.
**138** C3 **Rogers, Mount** U.S.A.
**138** C1 **Rogers City** U.S.A.
**157** G8 **Roggeveen Basin** sea feature
     S. Pacific Ocean
**122** B3 **Roggeveldberge** esc. S. Africa
 **92** G2 **Rognan** Norway
**134** B2 **Rogue** r. U.S.A.
 **74** B2 **Rohtak** India
 **49** M5 **Roi Georges, Îles du** is
     Fr. Polynesia
 **88** B2 **Roja** Latvia
 **60** B1 **Rokan** r. Indon.
 **88** C2 **Rokiškis** Lith.
 **90** B1 **Rokytne** Ukr.
**154** B2 **Rolândia** Brazil
**137** E3 **Rolla** U.S.A.
**143** C2 **Rolling Prairies** reg. U.S.A.
 **51** D2 **Roma** i. Austr.
 **59** C3 **Roma** i. Indon.
     **Roma** Italy see **Rome**
**123** C2 **Roma** Lesotho
**143** D3 **Roma** U.S.A.
**141** E2 **Romain, Cape** U.S.A.
**110** C1 **Roman** Romania
**158** E5 **Romanche Gap** sea feature
     S. Atlantic Ocean
**110** B1 **Romania** country Europe
 **91** C3 **Roman-Kosh** mt. Ukr.
 **69** D1 **Romanovka** Rus. Fed.
**105** D2 **Romans-sur-Isère** France
**105** D2 **Rombas** France
 **64** B2 **Romblon** Phil.
**108** B2 **Rome** Italy
**141** C2 **Rome** GA U.S.A.
**139** D2 **Rome** NY U.S.A.
 **99** D4 **Romford** U.K.
**105** C2 **Romilly-sur-Seine** France
 **91** C1 **Romny** Ukr.
**104** C2 **Romorantin-Lanthenay** France
 **99** C4 **Romsey** U.K.
**134** D1 **Ronan** U.S.A.
 **96** □ **Ronas Hill** U.K.
**151** D4 **Roncador, Serra do** hills Brazil
**106** B2 **Ronda** Spain
**154** B2 **Rondon** Brazil
**154** B1 **Rondonópolis** Brazil

 **74** B1 **Rondu** Jammu and Kashmir
 **71** A3 **Rong'an** China
     **Rongcheng** China see **Rongxian**
     **Rongcheng** China see **Jianli**
 **71** A3 **Rongjiang** China
 **62** A1 **Rongklang Range** mts Myanmar
     **Rongmei** China see **Hefeng**
 **71** B3 **Rongxian** China
 **93** F4 **Rønne** Denmark
 **93** G4 **Ronneby** Sweden
 **55** A2 **Ronne Ice Shelf** Antarctica
**101** D1 **Ronnenberg** Ger.
**100** A2 **Ronse** Belgium
     **Rooke Island** P.N.G. see **Umboi**
 **74** B2 **Roorkee** India
**100** B2 **Roosendaal** Neth.
**135** E2 **Roosevelt** U.S.A.
**128** B2 **Roosevelt, Mount** Can.
 **55** N2 **Roosevelt Island** Antarctica
**104** B3 **Roquefort** France
**150** C2 **Roraima, Mount** Guyana
 **93** F3 **Røros** Norway
 **90** C2 **Ros'** r. Ukr.
**142** B3 **Rosa, Punta** pt Mex.
**106** B2 **Rosal de la Frontera** Spain
**153** B3 **Rosario** Arg.
**144** A1 **Rosario** Mex.
**144** B2 **Rosario** Mex.
**144** B2 **Rosario** Mex.
**147** C3 **Rosario** Venez.
**152** B2 **Rosario de la Frontera** Arg.
**151** D4 **Rosário Oeste** Brazil
**144** A2 **Rosarito** Mex.
**144** A1 **Rosarito** Mex.
**142** A3 **Rosarito** Mex.
**109** C3 **Rosarno** Italy
**104** B2 **Roscoff** France
 **97** B2 **Roscommon** Ireland
 **97** C2 **Roscrea** Ireland
**147** D3 **Roseau** Dominica
**137** D1 **Roseau** U.S.A.
**134** B2 **Roseburg** U.S.A.
 **96** C2 **Rosehearty** U.K.
**143** D3 **Rosenberg** U.S.A.
**101** D1 **Rosengarten** Ger.
**102** C2 **Rosenheim** Ger.
**129** D2 **Rosetown** Can.
**122** A2 **Rosh Pinah** Namibia
**110** C2 **Roşiori de Vede** Romania
 **93** F4 **Roskilde** Denmark
 **89** D3 **Roslavl'** Rus. Fed.
**134** B1 **Roslyn** U.S.A.
**109** C3 **Rossano** Italy
 **97** B1 **Rossan Point** Ireland
 **51** E1 **Rossel Island** P.N.G.
 **55** N1 **Ross Ice Shelf** Antarctica
**131** D3 **Rossignol, Lake** Can.
**128** C3 **Rossland** Can.
 **97** C2 **Rosslare** Ireland
 **97** C2 **Rosslare Harbour** Ireland
**101** F2 **Roßlau** Ger.
**101** E2 **Roßleben** Ger.
**114** A3 **Rosso** Maur.
**105** D3 **Rosso, Capo** c. Corsica France
 **99** B4 **Ross-on-Wye** U.K.
 **91** D1 **Rossosh'** Rus. Fed.
**128** A1 **Ross River** Can.
 **55** N2 **Ross Sea** Antarctica
 **92** F2 **Røssvatnet** l. Norway
 **81** D3 **Rostāq** Iran
**129** D2 **Rosthern** Can.
**102** C1 **Rostock** Ger.
 **89** E2 **Rostov** Rus. Fed.
 **91** D2 **Rostov-na-Donu** Rus. Fed.
     **Rostov-on-Don** Rus. Fed. see
     **Rostov-na-Donu**
**104** B2 **Rostrenen** France
 **92** G2 **Røsvik** Norway
 **92** H2 **Rosvik** Sweden
**142** C1 **Roswell** U.S.A.
 **59** D2 **Rota** i. N. Mariana Is
 **59** C3 **Rote** i. Indon.
**101** D1 **Rotenburg (Wümme)** Ger.
**101** E3 **Roth** Ger.
 **98** C2 **Rothbury** U.K.
**101** E3 **Rothenburg ob der Tauber** Ger.
 **98** C3 **Rotherham** U.K.
 **96** C2 **Rothes** U.K.
 **96** B3 **Rothesay** U.K.
 **53** C2 **Roto** Austr.
**105** D3 **Rotondo, Monte** mt. Corsica
     France
 **54** C1 **Rotorua** N.Z.
 **54** C1 **Rotorua, Lake** N.Z.
**101** E2 **Rottenbach** Ger.
**102** C2 **Rottenmann** Austria
**100** B2 **Rotterdam** Neth.
**102** B2 **Rottweil** Ger.
 **49** I5 **Rotuma** i. Fiji
**105** C1 **Roubaix** France
**104** C2 **Rouen** France
     **Roulers** Belgium see **Roeselare**
 **53** D2 **Round Mountain** Austr.
**131** E3 **Round Pond** l. Can.
**143** D2 **Round Rock** U.S.A.
**134** E1 **Roundup** U.S.A.
 **96** C1 **Rousay** i. U.K.
**130** C3 **Rouyn-Noranda** Can.
     **Rouyuanchengzi** China see **Huachi**
 **92** I2 **Rovaniemi** Fin.
 **91** D2 **Roven'ki** Rus. Fed.
 **91** D2 **Roven'ky** Ukr.
**108** B1 **Rovereto** Italy
 **63** B2 **Rôviěng Tbong** Cambodia

Salem
209

108 B1 Rovigo Italy
108 B1 Rovinj Croatia
53 C1 Rowena Austr.
Równe Ukr. see Rivne
64 B3 Roxas Phil.
64 B2 Roxas Phil.
64 A2 Roxas Phil.
64 B2 Roxas Phil.
52 A2 Roxby Downs Austr.
142 C1 Roy NM U.S.A.
134 D2 Roy UT U.S.A.
138 B1 Royale, Isle i. U.S.A.
104 B2 Royan France
99 C3 Royston U.K.
90 C2 Rozdil'na Ukr.
91 C2 Rozdol'ne Ukr.
103 E2 Rožňava Slovakia
100 B3 Rozoy-sur-Serre France
87 D3 Rtishchevo Rus. Fed.
Ruanda country Africa see Rwanda
54 C1 Ruapehu, Mount vol. N.Z.
54 A3 Ruapuke Island N.Z.
89 D2 Ruba Belarus
79 B3 Rub' al Khālī des. Saudi Arabia
119 D3 Rubeho Mountains Tanz.
91 D2 Rubizhne Ukr.
77 E1 Rubtsovsk Rus. Fed.
126 B2 Ruby U.S.A.
135 C2 Ruby Mountains U.S.A.
76 C3 Rudbar Afgh.
66 C2 Rudnaya Pristan' Rus. Fed.
89 D3 Rudnya Rus. Fed.
76 C1 Rudnyy Kazakh.
Rudolf, Lake salt l. Eth./Kenya see Turkana, Lake
82 E1 Rudol'fa, Ostrov i. Rus. Fed.
Rudolph Island Rus. Fed. see Rudol'fa, Ostrov
101 E2 Rudolstadt Ger.
116 B3 Rufa'a Sudan
119 D3 Rufiji r. Tanz.
153 B3 Rufino Arg.
121 B2 Rufunsa Zambia
70 C2 Rugao China
99 C3 Rugby U.K.
136 C1 Rugby U.S.A.
102 C1 Rügen i. Ger.
119 C3 Ruhengeri Rwanda
101 E2 Ruhla Ger.
88 B2 Ruhnu i. Estonia
100 C2 Ruhr r. Ger.
71 C3 Rui'an China
142 B2 Ruidoso U.S.A.
144 B2 Ruiz Mex.
119 D3 Rukwa, Lake Tanz.
96 A2 Rum i. U.K.
109 C1 Ruma Serb. and Mont.
78 B2 Rumāh Saudi Arabia
117 A4 Rumbek Sudan
147 C2 Rum Cay i. Bahamas
139 E2 Rumford U.S.A.
103 D1 Rumia Pol.
105 D2 Rumilly France
50 C1 Rum Jungle Austr.
66 D2 Rumoi Japan
121 C2 Rumphi Malawi
54 B2 Runanga N.Z.
98 B3 Runcorn U.K.
120 A2 Rundu Namibia
119 C2 Rungu Dem. Rep. Congo
119 D3 Rungwa Tanz.
68 B2 Ruoqiang China
130 C2 Rupert r. Can.
134 D2 Rupert U.S.A.
130 C2 Rupert Bay Can.
Rusaddir N. Africa see Melilla
121 C2 Rusape Zimbabwe
110 C2 Ruse Bulg.
137 E1 Rush City U.S.A.
121 C2 Rushinga Zimbabwe
77 D3 Rushon Tajik.
136 C2 Rushville U.S.A.
53 C3 Rushworth Austr.
129 D2 Russell Can.
54 B1 Russell N.Z.
137 D3 Russell U.S.A.
140 C2 Russellville AL U.S.A.
140 B1 Russellville AR U.S.A.
138 B3 Russellville KY U.S.A.
101 D2 Rüsselsheim Ger.
82 F2 Russian Federation country Asia/Europe
81 C1 Rust'avi Georgia
123 C2 Rustenburg S. Africa
140 B2 Ruston U.S.A.
61 D2 Ruteng Indon.
98 B3 Ruthin U.K.
139 E2 Rutland U.S.A.
Rutog China see Dêrub
119 C3 Rutshuru Dem. Rep. Congo
119 E4 Ruvuma r. Moz./Tanz.
79 C2 Ruweis U.A.E.
89 E2 Ruza Rus. Fed.
77 C1 Ruzayevka Kazakh.
87 D3 Ruzayevka Rus. Fed.
119 C3 Rwanda country Africa
89 E3 Ryazan' Rus. Fed.
89 F3 Ryazhsk Rus. Fed.
86 C2 Rybachiy, Poluostrov pen. Rus. Fed.
Rybach'ye Kyrg. see Balykchy
89 E2 Rybinsk Rus. Fed.
89 E2 Rybinskoye Vodokhranilishche resr Rus. Fed.
103 D1 Rybnik Pol.
Rybnitsa Moldova see Rîbnița
89 E3 Rybnoye Rus. Fed.
99 D4 Rye U.K.
Rykovo Ukr. see Yenakiyeve
89 D3 Ryl'sk Rus. Fed.
Ryojun China see Lüshun
67 C3 Ryōtsu Japan
69 E3 Ryukyu Islands is Japan
89 D3 Ryzhikovo Rus. Fed.
103 E1 Rzeszów Pol.
91 E1 Rzhaksa Rus. Fed.
89 D2 Rzhev Rus. Fed.

## S

79 C2 Sa'ādatābād Iran
101 E2 Saale r. Ger.
101 E2 Saalfeld Ger.
134 B1 Saanich Can.
100 C3 Saar r. Ger.
102 B2 Saarbrücken Ger.
88 B2 Sääre Estonia
88 B2 Saaremaa i. Estonia
92 I2 Saarenkylä Fin.
93 I3 Saarijärvi Fin.
100 C3 Saarlouis Ger.
80 B2 Sab' Ābār Syria
107 D1 Sabadell Spain
67 C3 Sabae Japan
61 C1 Sabah state Malaysia
61 C2 Sabalana i. Indon.
146 B2 Sabana, Archipiélago de is Cuba
150 B1 Sabanalarga Col.
60 A1 Sabang Indon.
155 D1 Sabará Brazil
108 B2 Sabaudia Italy
122 B3 Sabelo S. Africa
119 D2 Sabena Desert Kenya
115 D2 Sabhā Libya
123 D2 Sabie r. Moz./S. Africa
123 D2 Sabie S. Africa
145 B2 Sabinas Mex.
145 B2 Sabinas Hidalgo Mex.
143 E3 Sabine r. U.S.A.
131 D3 Sable, Cape Can.
141 D3 Sable, Cape U.S.A.
131 E3 Sable Island Can.
106 B1 Sabugal Port.
78 B3 Şabyā Saudi Arabia
76 B3 Sabzevār Iran
107 D2 Sa Cabaneta Spain
137 D2 Sac City U.S.A.
120 A2 Sachanga Angola
130 A2 Sachigo Lake Can.
65 B3 Sach'on S. Korea
126 D2 Sachs Harbour Can.
154 C1 Sacramento Brazil
135 B3 Sacramento U.S.A.
135 B3 Sacramento r. U.S.A.
142 B2 Sacramento Mountains U.S.A.
135 B2 Sacramento Valley U.S.A.
110 B1 Săcueni Romania
123 C3 Sada S. Africa
107 C1 Sádaba Spain
Sá da Bandeira Angola see Lubango
78 B3 Şa'dah Yemen
63 B3 Sadao Thai.
79 B3 Şadārah Yemen
63 B2 Sa Đec Vietnam
74 B2 Sadiqabad Pak.
72 D2 Sadiya India
67 C3 Sadoga-shima i. Japan
107 D2 Sa Dragonera i. Spain
93 F4 Säffle Sweden
142 B2 Safford U.S.A.
99 D3 Saffron Walden U.K.
114 B1 Safi Morocco
155 D1 Safiras, Serra das mts Brazil
86 D2 Safonovo Rus. Fed.
89 D2 Safonovo Rus. Fed.
78 B2 Safrā' as Sark esc. Saudi Arabia
75 C2 Saga China
67 B4 Saga Japan
62 A1 Sagaing Myanmar
67 C3 Sagamihara Japan
74 B2 Sagar India
Sagarmatha mt. China/Nepal see Everest, Mount
138 C2 Saginaw U.S.A.
138 C2 Saginaw Bay U.S.A.
Saglouc Can. see Salluit
106 B2 Sagres Port.
146 B2 Sagua la Grande Cuba
139 F1 Saguenay r. Can.
107 C2 Sagunto Spain
76 B2 Sagyndyk, Mys pt Kazakh.
106 B1 Sahagún Spain
114 C3 Sahara des. Africa
Saharan Atlas mts Alg. see Atlas Saharien
74 B2 Saharanpur India
75 C2 Saharsa India
114 B3 Sahel reg. Africa
74 B1 Sahiwal Pak.
144 B2 Sahuayo Mex.
78 B2 Şāḩūq reg. Saudi Arabia
114 C1 Saïda Alg.
Saïda Lebanon see Sidon
75 C2 Saidpur Bangl.
67 B3 Saigō Japan
Saigon Vietnam see Ho Chi Minh City
75 D2 Saiha India
70 B1 Saihan Tal China
67 B4 Saiki Japan
93 I3 Saimaa l. Fin.
144 B2 Sain Alto Mex.
96 C3 St Abb's Head hd U.K.
131 E3 St Alban's Can.
99 C4 St Albans U.K.
138 C3 St Albans U.S.A.
99 B4 St Alban's Head hd U.K.
St Aldhelm's Head hd U.K. see St Alban's Head
St-André, Cap pt Madag. see Vilanandro, Tanjona
96 C2 St Andrews U.K.
131 E2 St Anthony Can.
134 D2 St Anthony U.S.A.
52 B3 St Arnaud Austr.
131 E2 St-Augustin Can.
131 E2 St Augustin r. Can.
141 D3 St Augustine U.S.A.
99 A4 St Austell U.K.
104 C2 St-Avertin France
147 D3 St-Barthélemy i. West Indies
98 B2 St Bees Head hd U.K.
105 D3 St-Bonnet-en-Champsaur France
99 A4 St Bride's Bay U.K.
104 B2 St-Brieuc France
130 C3 St Catharines Can.
141 D2 St Catherines Island U.S.A.
99 C4 St Catherine's Point U.K.
137 E3 St Charles U.S.A.
138 C2 St Clair, Lake Can./U.S.A.
105 D2 St-Claude France
99 A4 St Clears U.K.
137 E1 St Cloud U.S.A.
138 A1 St Croix r. U.S.A.
147 D3 St Croix Virgin Is (U.S.A.)
99 A4 St David's U.K.
99 A4 St David's Head hd U.K.
113 I8 St-Denis Can.
104 C2 St-Denis France
St-Denis-du-Sig Alg. see Sig
105 D2 St-Dié France
105 C2 St-Dizier France
130 C3 Ste-Adèle Can.
131 D3 Ste-Anne-des-Monts Can.
139 E1 Ste-Foy Can.
105 D2 St-Égrève France
128 A1 St Elias Mountains Can.
131 D2 Ste-Marguerite r. Can.
139 E1 Ste-Marie Can.
Ste-Marie, Cap c. Madag. see Vohimena, Tanjona
Sainte-Marie, Île i. Madag. see Nosy Boraha
Ste-Rose-du-Dégelé Can. see Dégelis
129 E2 Ste Rose du Lac Can.
104 B2 Saintes France
105 C2 St-Étienne France
104 C2 St-Étienne-du-Rouvray France
130 C3 St-Félicien Can.
97 D1 Saintfield U.K.
105 D3 St-Florent Corsica France
105 C2 St-Flour France
136 C3 St Francis U.S.A.
104 C3 St-Gaudens France
53 C1 St George Austr.
135 D3 St George U.S.A.
141 D3 St George Island U.S.A.
131 C3 St-Georges Can.
147 D3 St George's Grenada
131 E3 St George's Bay Can.
97 C3 St George's Channel Ireland/U.K.
105 D2 St Gotthard Pass pass Switz.
113 C7 St Helena terr. S. Atlantic Ocean
122 A3 St Helena Bay S. Africa
122 A3 St Helena Bay b. S. Africa
98 B3 St Helens U.K.
134 B1 St Helens, Mount vol. U.S.A.
95 C4 St Helier Channel Is
100 B2 St-Hubert Belgium
139 E1 St-Hyacinthe Can.
138 C1 St Ignace U.S.A.
130 B3 St Ignace Island Can.
99 A4 St Ives U.K.
St Jacques, Cap Vietnam see Vung Tau
128 A2 St James, Cape Can.
130 C3 St-Jean, Lac l. Can.
104 B2 St-Jean-d'Angély France
104 B3 St-Jean-de-Luz France
104 B2 St-Jean-de-Monts France
130 C3 St-Jean-sur-Richelieu Can.
139 E1 St-Jérôme Can.
134 C1 St Joe r. U.S.A.
131 D3 Saint John Can.
137 D3 St John U.S.A.
139 F1 St John r. U.S.A.
147 D3 St John's Antigua
131 E3 St John's Can.
142 B2 St Johns U.S.A.
141 D2 St Johns r. U.S.A.
139 E2 St Johnsbury U.S.A.
137 E3 St Joseph U.S.A.
130 A2 St Joseph, Lake Can.
St-Joseph-d'Alma Can. see Alma
130 B3 St Joseph Island Can.
139 E1 St-Jovité Can.
104 C2 St-Junien France
94 B2 St Kilda i. U.K.
147 D3 St Kitts and Nevis country West Indies
151 D2 St-Laurent-du-Maroni Fr. Guiana
131 E3 St Lawrence Can.
131 D3 St Lawrence inlet Can.
131 D3 St Lawrence, Gulf of Can.
126 A2 St Lawrence Island U.S.A.
104 B2 St-Lô France
114 A3 St-Louis Senegal
137 E3 St Louis U.S.A.
137 E1 St Louis r. U.S.A.
147 D3 St Lucia country West Indies
147 D3 St Lucia Channel Martinique/St Lucia
123 D2 St Lucia Estuary S. Africa
147 D3 St Maarten i. West Indies
96 □ St Magnus Bay U.K.
104 B2 St-Malo France
104 B2 St-Malo, Golfe de g. France
147 C3 St-Marc Haiti
St Mark's S. Africa see Cofimvaba
147 D3 St-Martin i. West Indies
122 A3 St Martin, Cape S. Africa
129 E2 St Martin, Lake Can.
139 D2 St Marys U.S.A.
124 A3 St Matthew Island U.S.A.
59 D3 St Matthias Group is P.N.G.
130 C3 St-Maurice r. Can.
130 C3 St-Michel-des-Saints Can.
104 B2 St-Nazaire France
104 C1 St-Omer France
129 C2 St Paul Can.
137 E2 St Paul U.S.A.
156 A8 St-Paul, Île i. Indian Ocean
137 E2 St Peter U.S.A.
95 C4 St Peter Port Channel Is
141 D3 St Petersburg U.S.A.
131 E3 St-Pierre St Pierre and Miquelon
139 E1 St-Pierre, Lac l. Can.
131 E3 St Pierre and Miquelon terr. N. America
104 B2 St-Pierre-d'Oléron France
105 C2 St-Pourçain-sur-Sioule France
131 D3 St Quentin Can.
105 C2 St-Quentin France
105 D3 St-Raphaël France
122 B3 St Sebastian Bay S. Africa
104 B2 St-Sébastien-sur-Loire France
131 D3 St-Siméon Can.
129 E2 St Theresa Point Can.
130 B3 St Thomas Can.
105 D3 St-Tropez France
105 D3 St-Tropez, Cap de c. France
St Vincent, Cape Port. see São Vicente, Cabo de
52 A3 St Vincent, Gulf Austr.
147 D3 St Vincent and the Grenadines country West Indies
147 D3 St Vincent Passage St Lucia/St Vincent
129 D2 St Walburg Can.
104 C2 St-Yrieix-la-Perche France
59 D1 Saipan i. N. Mariana Is
152 B1 Sajama, Nevado mt. Bol.
122 B2 Sak watercourse S. Africa
67 C4 Sakai Japan
67 B4 Sakaide Japan
78 B2 Sakākah Saudi Arabia
136 C1 Sakakawea, Lake U.S.A.
Sakarya Turkey see Adapazarı
111 D2 Sakarya r. Turkey
66 C3 Sakata Japan
65 B1 Sakchu N. Korea
66 D1 Sakhalin i. Rus. Fed.
123 C2 Sakhile S. Africa
81 C1 Şäki Azer.
88 B3 Šakiai Lith.
69 E3 Sakishima-shotō is Japan
62 B2 Sakon Nakhon Thai.
74 A2 Sakrand Pak.
122 B3 Sakrivier S. Africa
67 D3 Sakura Japan
91 C2 Saky Ukr.
93 G4 Sala Sweden
130 C3 Salaberry-de-Valleyfield Can.
88 B2 Salacgrīva Latvia
109 C2 Sala Consilina Italy
135 C4 Salada, Laguna salt l. Mex.
152 C2 Saladas Arg.
152 B3 Salado r. Arg.
145 C2 Salado r. Mex.
153 B3 Salado o Chadileo r. Arg.
114 B4 Salaga Ghana
122 B1 Salajwe Botswana
79 C2 Salakh, Jabal mt. Oman
115 D3 Salal Chad
78 A2 Salâla Sudan
79 C3 Şalālah Oman
145 B2 Salamanca Mex.
106 B1 Salamanca Spain
139 D2 Salamanca U.S.A.
106 B1 Salas Spain
63 B2 Salavan Laos
59 C3 Salawati i. Indon.
61 D2 Salayar i. Indon.
157 G7 Sala y Gómez, Isla i. S. Pacific Ocean
Salazar Angola see N'dalatando
104 C2 Salbris France
88 C3 Šalčininkai Lith.
106 C1 Saldaña Spain
122 A3 Saldanha S. Africa
88 B2 Saldus Latvia
53 C3 Sale Austr.
86 F2 Salekhard Rus. Fed.
73 B3 Salem India
138 B3 Salem IL U.S.A.

137 E3 Salem *MO* U.S.A.
134 B2 Salem *OR* U.S.A.
137 D2 Salem *SD* U.S.A.
96 B2 Salem U.K.
109 B2 Salerno Italy
108 B2 Salerno, Golfo di *g.* Italy
98 B3 Salford U.K.
151 E2 Salgado *r.* Brazil
103 D2 Salgótarján Hungary
151 F3 Salgueiro Brazil
136 B3 Salida U.S.A.
111 C3 Salihli Turkey
88 C3 Salihorsk Belarus
121 C2 Salima Malawi
121 C2 Salimo Moz.
137 D3 Salina *KS* U.S.A.
135 D3 Salina *UT* U.S.A.
109 B3 Salina, Isola *i.* Italy
145 C3 Salina Cruz Mex.
155 D1 Salinas Brazil
144 B2 Salinas Mex.
135 B3 Salinas U.S.A.
135 B3 Salinas *r.* U.S.A.
107 D2 Salines, Cap de ses *c.* Spain
151 E2 Salinópolis Brazil
99 C4 Salisbury U.K.
139 D3 Salisbury *MD* U.S.A.
141 D1 Salisbury *NC* U.S.A.
Salisbury Zimbabwe *see* Harare
99 B4 Salisbury Plain U.K.
151 E3 Salitre *r.* Brazil
92 I2 Salla Fin.
143 E1 Sallisaw U.S.A.
127 G2 Salluit Can.
75 C2 Sallyana Nepal
81 C2 Salmäs Iran
128 C3 Salmo Can.
134 D1 Salmon U.S.A.
134 C1 Salmon *r.* U.S.A.
128 C2 Salmon Arm Can.
134 C2 Salmon River Mountains U.S.A.
100 C3 Salmtal Ger.
118 B2 Salo C.A.R.
93 H3 Salo Fin.
105 D3 Salon-de-Provence France
Salonica Greece *see* Thessaloniki
110 B1 Salonta Romania
87 D4 Sal'sk Rus. Fed.
122 B3 Salt *watercourse* S. Africa
107 D1 Salt Spain
142 A2 Salt *r.* U.S.A.
152 B2 Salta Arg.
99 A4 Saltash U.K.
96 B3 Saltcoats U.K.
145 B2 Saltillo Mex.
134 D2 Salt Lake City U.S.A.
154 C2 Salto Brazil
152 C3 Salto Uru.
155 E1 Salto da Divisa Brazil
154 B2 Salto del Guairá Para.
135 C4 Salton Sea *salt l.* U.S.A.
154 B3 Salto Osório, Represa *resr* Brazil
154 B3 Salto Santiago, Represa de *resr* Brazil
141 D2 Saluda U.S.A.
76 B3 Saluq, Küh-e *mt.* Iran
108 A2 Saluzzo Italy
151 F4 Salvador Brazil
79 C2 Salwah Saudi Arabia
62 A2 Salween *r.* China/Myanmar
81 C2 Salyan Azer.
138 C3 Salyersville U.S.A.
122 A1 Salzbrunn Namibia
102 C2 Salzburg Austria
101 E1 Salzgitter Ger.
101 D2 Salzkotten Ger.
101 E1 Salzwedel Ger.
144 B1 Samalayuca Mex.
66 D2 Samani Japan
64 B2 Samar *i.* Phil.
87 E3 Samara Rus. Fed.
Samarahan Malaysia *see* Sri Aman
59 B3 Samarai P.N.G.
61 C2 Samarinda Indon.
77 C3 Samarqand Uzbek.
81 C2 Sämarrä' Iraq
81 C1 Samaxı Azer.
119 C3 Samba Dem. Rep. Congo
61 C1 Sambaliung *mts* Indon.
75 C2 Sambalpur India
60 C2 Sambar, Tanjung *pt* Indon.
60 B1 Sambas Indon.
121 □E2 Sambava Madag.
74 B2 Sambhar India
90 A2 Sambir Ukr.
61 C2 Sambo Indon.
61 C2 Samboja Indon.
153 C3 Samborombón, Bahía *b.* Arg.
65 B2 Samch'ŏk S. Korea
Samch'ŏnp'o S. Korea *see* Sach'on
81 C2 Samdi Dag *mt.* Turkey
119 D3 Same Tanz.
121 B2 Samfya Zambia
78 B2 Samirah Saudi Arabia
65 B1 Samjiyön N. Korea
Sam Neua Laos *see* Xam Nua
48 J5 Samoa *country* S. Pacific Ocean
156 E6 Samoa Basin *sea feature* S. Pacific Ocean
Samoa i Sisifo *country* S. Pacific Ocean *see* Samoa
109 C1 Samobor Croatia
110 B2 Samokov Bulg.
111 C3 Samos *i.* Greece

Samothrace *i.* Greece *see* Samothraki
111 C2 Samothraki Greece
111 C2 Samothraki *i.* Greece
61 C2 Sampit Indon.
119 C3 Sampwe Dem. Rep. Congo
143 E2 Sam Rayburn Reservoir U.S.A.
62 B2 Sâm Son Vietnam
80 B1 Samsun Turkey
81 C1 Samtredia Georgia
63 B3 Samui, Ko *i.* Thai.
63 B2 Samut Songkhram Thai.
114 B3 San Mali
78 B3 Şan'ä' Yemen
118 A2 Sanaga *r.* Cameroon
81 D2 Sanandaj Iran
146 B3 San Andrés, Isla de *i.* Caribbean Sea
106 B1 San Andrés del Rabanedo Spain
142 B3 San Andres Mountains U.S.A.
145 C3 San Andrés Tuxtla Mex.
143 C2 San Angelo U.S.A.
143 D3 San Antonio U.S.A.
135 C4 San Antonio, Mount U.S.A.
107 C2 San Antonio Abad Spain
152 B2 San Antonio de los Cobres Arg.
153 B4 San Antonio Oeste Arg.
108 B2 San Benedetto del Tronto Italy
144 A3 San Benedicto, Isla *i.* Mex.
135 C4 San Bernardino U.S.A.
135 C4 San Bernardino Mountains U.S.A.
142 B3 San Blas Mex.
141 C3 San Blas, Cape U.S.A.
146 C4 San Blas, Punta *pt* Panama
152 B1 San Borja Bol.
144 B2 San Buenaventura Mex.
64 B2 San Carlos Phil.
147 D4 San Carlos Venez.
153 A4 San Carlos de Bariloche Arg.
147 C4 San Carlos del Zulia Venez.
104 C2 Sancerrois, Collines du *hills* France
135 C4 San Clemente U.S.A.
135 C4 San Clemente Island U.S.A.
105 C2 Sancoins France
150 B2 San Cristóbal Venez.
145 C3 San Cristóbal de las Casas Mex.
146 C2 Sancti Spíritus Cuba
123 D1 Sand *r.* S. Africa
61 C1 Sandakan Sabah Malaysia
93 E3 Sandane Norway
111 B2 Sandanski Bulg.
114 A3 Sandaré Mali
96 C1 Sanday *i.* U.K.
143 C2 Sanderson U.S.A.
150 C4 Sandia Peru
135 C4 San Diego U.S.A.
111 D3 Sandıklı Turkey
93 E4 Sandnes Norway
92 F2 Sandnessjøen Norway
118 C3 Sandoa Dem. Rep. Congo
103 E1 Sandomierz Pol.
89 E2 Sandovo Rus. Fed.
94 B1 Sandoy *i.* Faroe Is
134 C1 Sandpoint U.S.A.
71 B3 Sandu China
94 B1 Sandur Faroe Is
138 C2 Sandusky U.S.A.
122 A3 Sandveld *mts* S. Africa
122 A2 Sandverhaar Namibia
93 F4 Sandvika Norway
93 G3 Sandviken Sweden
131 E2 Sandwich Bay Can.
135 D2 Sandy U.S.A.
129 D2 Sandy Bay Can.
51 E2 Sandy Cape Austr.
130 A2 Sandy Lake Can.
130 A2 Sandy Lake *l.* Can.
141 D2 Sandy Springs U.S.A.
144 A1 San Felipe Mex.
145 B2 San Felipe Mex.
150 C1 San Felipe Venez.
144 A2 San Fernando Mex.
145 C2 San Fernando Mex.
64 B2 San Fernando Phil.
64 B2 San Fernando Phil.
106 B2 San Fernando Spain
147 D3 San Fernando Trin. and Tob.
150 C2 San Fernando de Apure Venez.
141 D3 Sanford *FL* U.S.A.
139 E2 Sanford *ME* U.S.A.
141 E1 Sanford *NC* U.S.A.
152 B3 San Francisco Arg.
135 B3 San Francisco U.S.A.
107 D2 San Francisco Javier Spain
74 B3 Sangamner India
83 J2 Sangar Rus. Fed.
108 A3 San Gavino Monreale *Sardinia* Italy
101 E2 Sangerhausen Ger.
61 C1 Sanggau Indon.
118 B3 Sangha *r.* Congo
109 C3 San Giovanni in Fiore Italy
59 C2 Sangir *i.* Indon.
59 C2 Sangir, Kepulauan *is* Indon.
65 B2 Sangju S. Korea
63 A2 Sangkhla Buri Thai.
61 C1 Sangkulirang Indon.
73 B3 Sangli India
118 B2 Sangmélima Cameroon
121 C3 Sango Zimbabwe
San Gottardo, Passo del *pass* Switz. *see* St Gotthard Pass

136 B3 Sangre de Cristo Range *mts* U.S.A.
75 C2 Sangsang China
144 A2 San Hipólito, Punta *pt* Mex.
145 D3 San Ignacio Belize
152 B1 San Ignacio Bol.
144 A2 San Ignacio Mex.
130 C2 Sanikiluaq Can.
71 A3 Sanjiang China
67 C3 Sanjō Japan
Sanjiang China *see* Jinping
135 B3 San Joaquin *r.* U.S.A.
153 B4 San Jorge, Golfo de *g.* Arg.
146 B4 San José Costa Rica
64 B2 San Jose Phil.
64 B2 San Jose Phil.
135 B3 San Jose U.S.A.
144 A2 San José, Isla *i.* Mex.
144 B2 San José de Bavícora Mex.
64 B2 San Jose de Buenavista Phil.
144 A2 San José de Comondú Mex.
144 B2 San José del Cabo Mex.
150 B2 San José del Guaviare Col.
152 B3 San Juan Arg.
146 B3 San Juan *r.* Costa Rica/Nic.
147 C3 San Juan Dom. Rep.
147 D3 San Juan Puerto Rico
152 C3 San Juan *r.* U.S.A.
152 C3 San Juan Bautista Para.
107 D2 San Juan Bautista Spain
145 C3 San Juan Bautista Tuxtepec Mex.
147 D4 San Juan de los Morros Venez.
145 C2 San Juan del Río Mex.
134 B1 San Juan Islands U.S.A.
144 B2 San Juanito Mex.
136 B3 San Juan Mountains U.S.A.
153 B4 San Julián Arg.
75 C2 Sankh *r.* India
63 B2 San Khao Phang Hoei *mts* Thai.
100 C2 St Augustin Ger.
105 D2 St Gallen Switz.
105 D2 St Moritz Switz.
Sankt-Peterburg Rus. Fed. *see* St Petersburg
89 D2 St Petersburg Rus. Fed.
102 C2 Sankt Veit an der Glan Austria
111 C3 Şanlıurfa Turkey
142 B3 San Lorenzo Mex.
106 B2 Sanlúcar de Barrameda Spain
144 B2 San Lucas Mex.
153 B3 San Luis Arg.
145 B2 San Luis de la Paz Mex.
142 A2 San Luisito Mex.
135 B3 San Luis Obispo U.S.A.
135 B3 San Luis Obispo U.S.A.
145 B2 San Luis Potosí Mex.
144 A1 San Luis Río Colorado Mex.
143 D3 San Marcos U.S.A.
108 B2 San Marino *country* Europe
108 B2 San Marino San Marino
144 B2 San Martín de Bolaños Mex.
153 A4 San Martín de los Andes Arg.
135 B3 San Mateo U.S.A.
153 B4 San Matías, Golfo *g.* Arg.
70 B2 Sanmenxia China
146 B3 San Miguel El Salvador
152 B3 San Miguel de Tucumán Arg.
135 B4 San Miguel Island U.S.A.
145 C3 San Miguel Sola de Vega Mex.
71 B3 Sanming China
153 B3 San Nicolás de los Arroyos Arg.
135 C4 San Nicolas Island U.S.A.
110 B1 Sânnicolau Mare Romania
123 C2 Sannieshof S. Africa
114 B4 Sanniquellie Liberia
103 E2 Sanok Pol.
64 B2 San Pablo Phil.
144 B2 San Pablo Balleza Mex.
152 B1 San Pedro Bol.
152 B1 San Pedro Bol.
114 B4 San-Pédro Côte d'Ivoire
144 A2 San Pedro *watercourse* U.S.A.
106 B2 San Pedro, Sierra de *mts* Spain
144 B2 San Pedro de las Colonias Mex.
152 C2 San Pedro de Ycuamandyyú Para.
142 A3 San Pedro el Saucito Mex.
146 B3 San Pedro Sula Hond.
108 A3 San Pietro, Isola di *i.* *Sardinia* Italy
96 C3 Sanquhar U.K.
144 A1 San Quintín, Cabo *c.* Mex.
153 B3 San Rafael Arg.
108 A2 San Remo Italy
143 D2 San Saba U.S.A.
147 C3 San Salvador *i.* Bahamas
146 B3 San Salvador El Salvador
152 B2 San Salvador de Jujuy Arg.
108 B2 Sansepolcro Italy
109 C2 San Severo Italy
109 C2 Sanski Most Bos.-Herz.
152 B1 Santa Ana Bol.
146 B3 Santa Ana El Salvador
144 A1 Santa Ana Mex.
135 C4 Santa Ana U.S.A.
152 B1 Santa Ana de Yacuma Bol.
144 B2 Santa Bárbara Mex.
135 C4 Santa Barbara U.S.A.
154 B2 Santa Bárbara, Serra de *hills* Brazil
152 B2 Santa Catalina Chile
135 C4 Santa Catalina Island U.S.A.
150 C3 Santa Clara Col.
146 C2 Santa Clara Cuba

135 B3 Santa Clara U.S.A.
135 C4 Santa Clarita U.S.A.
107 D1 Santa Coloma de Gramanet Spain
Santa Comba Angola *see* Waku-Kungo
109 C3 Santa Croce, Capo *c.* *Sicily* Italy
153 B5 Santa Cruz *r.* Arg.
152 B1 Santa Cruz Bol.
64 B2 Santa Cruz Phil.
135 B3 Santa Cruz U.S.A.
145 C3 Santa Cruz Barillas Guat.
155 E1 Santa Cruz Cabrália Brazil
107 C2 Santa Cruz de Moya Spain
114 A2 Santa Cruz de Tenerife Canary Is
152 C2 Santa Cruz do Sul Brazil
135 C4 Santa Cruz Island U.S.A.
48 H5 Santa Cruz Islands Solomon Is
107 D2 Santa Eulalia del Río Spain
152 B3 Santa Fé Arg.
142 B1 Santa Fe U.S.A.
154 B2 Santa Fé do Sul Brazil
154 B1 Santa Helena de Goiás Brazil
153 B3 Santa Isabel Arg.
Santa Isabel Equat. Guinea *see* Malabo
48 G4 Santa Isabel *i.* Solomon Is
154 B1 Santa Luisa, Serra de *hills* Brazil
151 E3 Santa Luzia Brazil
144 A2 Santa Margarita, Isla *i.* Mex.
152 C2 Santa María *r.* Mex.
144 B1 Santa María *r.* Mex.
135 B4 Santa Maria U.S.A.
123 D2 Santa Maria, Cabo de *c.* Moz.
106 B2 Santa Maria, Cabo de *c.* Port.
155 C1 Santa Maria, Chapadão de *hills* Brazil
151 E3 Santa Maria das Barreiras Brazil
109 C3 Santa Maria di Leuca, Capo *c.* Italy
155 D1 Santa Maria do Suaçuí Brazil
150 B1 Santa Marta Col.
135 C4 Santa Monica U.S.A.
151 E4 Santana Brazil
110 B1 Sântana Romania
106 C1 Santander Spain
108 A3 Sant'Antioco *Sardinia* Italy
108 A3 Sant'Antioco, Isola di *i.* *Sardinia* Italy
151 D3 Santarém Brazil
106 B2 Santarém Port.
154 B1 Santa Rita do Araguaia Brazil
153 B3 Santa Rosa Arg.
152 C2 Santa Rosa Brazil
135 B3 Santa Rosa *CA* U.S.A.
142 C2 Santa Rosa *NM* U.S.A.
146 B3 Santa Rosa de Copán Hond.
135 B4 Santa Rosa Island *CA* U.S.A.
140 C2 Santa Rosa Island *FL* U.S.A.
144 A2 Santa Rosalía Mex.
134 C2 Santa Rosa Range *mts* U.S.A.
106 B1 Santa Uxía de Ribeira Spain
154 B1 Santa Vitória Brazil
107 D1 Sant Carles de la Ràpita Spain
135 C4 Santee U.S.A.
152 C2 Santiago Brazil
153 A3 Santiago Chile
147 C3 Santiago Dom. Rep.
152 B2 Santiago Mex.
146 B4 Santiago Panama
64 B2 Santiago Phil.
106 B1 Santiago de Compostela Spain
146 C2 Santiago de Cuba Cuba
145 C2 Santiago Ixcuintla Mex.
144 B2 Santiago Papasquiaro Mex.
106 C1 Santillana Spain
107 D1 Sant Jordi, Golf de *g.* Spain
155 C2 Santo Amaro de Campos Brazil
154 B2 Santo Anastácio Brazil
155 C2 Santo André Brazil
152 C2 Santo Ângelo Brazil
154 B2 Santo Antônio da Platina Brazil
151 F4 Santo Antônio de Jesus Brazil
150 C3 Santo Antônio do Içá Brazil
155 C2 Santo Antônio do Monte Brazil
147 D3 Santo Domingo Dom. Rep.
144 A2 Santo Domingo Mex.
142 B1 Santo Domingo Pueblo U.S.A.
Santorini *i.* Greece *see* Thira
155 C2 Santos Brazil
157 I7 Santos Dumont Brazil
Santos Plateau *sea feature* S. Atlantic Ocean
152 C2 Santo Tomé Arg.
153 A4 San Valentín, Cerro *mt.* Chile
146 B3 San Vicente El Salvador
144 A1 San Vicente Mex.
64 B2 San Vicente Phil.
150 B4 San Vicente de Cañete Peru
108 B2 San Vincenzo Italy
108 B3 San Vito, Capo *c.* *Sicily* Italy
71 A4 Sanya China
155 C2 São Bernardo do Campo Brazil
152 C2 São Borja Brazil
154 C2 São Carlos Brazil
155 C1 São Felipe, Serra de *hills* Brazil
151 D4 São Félix Brazil
151 D3 São Félix Brazil
155 D2 São Fidélis Brazil
155 D1 São Francisco Brazil
151 F4 São Francisco *r.* Brazil
154 C3 São Francisco, Ilha de *i.* Brazil
154 C3 São Francisco do Sul Brazil
152 C3 São Gabriel Brazil
155 D2 São Gonçalo Brazil

Serpa Pinto
211

155 C1 **São Gonçalo do Abaeté** Brazil
155 C1 **São Gotardo** Brazil
154 B1 **São Jerônimo, Serra de** *hills* Brazil
155 D2 **São João da Barra** Brazil
155 C2 **São João da Boa Vista** Brazil
106 B1 **São João da Madeira** Port.
155 D1 **São João da Ponte** Brazil
155 D2 **São João del Rei** Brazil
155 D1 **São João do Paraíso** Brazil
155 D1 **São João Evangelista** Brazil
155 D2 **São João Nepomuceno** Brazil
154 C2 **São Joaquim da Barra** Brazil
152 D2 **São José** Brazil
154 C2 **São José do Rio Preto** Brazil
155 C2 **São José dos Campos** Brazil
154 C3 **São José dos Pinhais** Brazil
154 A1 **São Lourenço** Brazil
155 C2 **São Lourenço** Brazil
151 E3 **São Luís** Brazil
154 C2 **São Manuel** Brazil
154 C1 **São Marcos** *r.* Brazil
151 E3 **São Marcos, Baía de** *b.* Brazil
155 E1 **São Mateus** Brazil
154 B3 **São Mateus do Sul** Brazil
105 C2 **Saône** *r.* France
155 C2 **São Paulo** Brazil
155 D2 **São Pedro da Aldeia** Brazil
151 E3 **São Raimundo Nonato** Brazil
155 C1 **São Romão** Brazil
**São Salvador** Angola *see* **M'banza Congo**
**São Salvador do Congo** Angola *see* **M'banza Congo**
155 C2 **São Sebastião, Ilha do** *i.* Brazil
154 C2 **São Sebastião do Paraíso** Brazil
154 B1 **São Simão** Brazil
154 B1 **São Simão, Barragem de** *resr* Brazil
59 C2 **Sao-Siu** Indon.
13 D5 **São Tomé** São Tomé and Príncipe
13 D5 **São Tomé** *i.* São Tomé and Príncipe
155 D2 **São Tomé, Cabo de** *c.* Brazil
13 D5 **São Tomé and Príncipe** *country* Africa
155 C2 **São Vicente** Brazil
106 B2 **São Vicente, Cabo de** *c.* Port.
59 C3 **Saparua** Indon.
107 D2 **Sa Pobla** Spain
89 F3 **Sapozhok** Rus. Fed.
66 D2 **Sapporo** Japan
109 C2 **Sapri** Italy
143 D1 **Sapulpa** U.S.A.
81 C2 **Saqqez** Iran
81 C2 **Sarāb** Iran
63 B2 **Sara Buri** Thai.
**Saragossa** Spain *see* **Zaragoza**
89 F3 **Sarai** Rus. Fed.
109 C2 **Sarajevo** Bos.-Herz.
87 E3 **Saraktash** Rus. Fed.
62 A1 **Saramati** *mt.* India/Myanmar
139 E2 **Saranac Lake** U.S.A.
109 D3 **Sarandë** Albania
64 B3 **Sarangani Islands** Phil.
87 D3 **Saransk** Rus. Fed.
87 E3 **Sarapul** Rus. Fed.
141 D3 **Sarasota** U.S.A.
90 B2 **Sarata** Ukr.
136 B2 **Saratoga** U.S.A.
139 E2 **Saratoga Springs** U.S.A.
61 C1 **Saratok** *Sarawak* Malaysia
87 D3 **Saratov** Rus. Fed.
79 D2 **Saravan** Iran
61 C1 **Sarawak** *state* Malaysia
111 C2 **Saray** Turkey
111 C3 **Sarayköy** Turkey
79 D2 **Sarbāz** Iran
76 B3 **Sarbīsheh** Iran
74 B2 **Sardarshahr** India
**Sardegna** *i.* Italy *see* **Sardinia**
108 A2 **Sardinia** *i.* Italy
92 G2 **Sarektjåkkå** *mt.* Sweden
77 C3 **Sar-e Pol** Afgh.
158 C3 **Sargasso Sea** *sea* Atlantic Ocean
74 B1 **Sargodha** Pak.
115 D4 **Sarh** Chad
79 D2 **Sarhad** *reg.* Iran
81 D2 **Sārī** Iran
111 C3 **Sarıgöl** Turkey
81 C1 **Sarıkamış** Turkey
61 C1 **Sarikei** *Sarawak* Malaysia
51 D2 **Sarina** Austr.
115 D2 **Sarīr Tibesti** *des.* Libya
65 B2 **Sariwŏn** N. Korea
111 C2 **Sarıyer** Turkey
77 D2 **Sarkand** Kazakh.
111 C2 **Şarköy** Turkey
104 C3 **Sarlat-la-Canéda** France
59 D3 **Sarmi** Indon.
153 B4 **Sarmiento** Arg.
138 C2 **Sarnia** Can.
90 B1 **Sarny** Ukr.
60 B2 **Sarolangun** Indon.
111 B3 **Saronikos Kolpos** *g.* Greece
111 C2 **Saros Körfezi** *b.* Turkey
103 E2 **Sárospatak** Hungary
87 D3 **Sarova** Rus. Fed.
**Sarpan** *i.* N. Mariana Is *see* **Rota**
105 D2 **Sarrebourg** France
106 B1 **Sarria** Spain
107 C1 **Sarrión** Spain
105 D3 **Sartène** *Corsica* France
**Sartu** China *see* **Daqing**
111 C3 **Saruhanlı** Turkey
103 D2 **Sárvár** Hungary
81 D3 **Sarvestān** Iran
76 B2 **Sarykamyshskoye Ozero** *salt l.* Turkm./Uzbek.
77 D2 **Saryozek** Kazakh.
77 D2 **Saryshagan** Kazakh.
77 C2 **Sarysu** *watercourse* Kazakh.
77 D3 **Sary-Tash** Kyrg.
75 C2 **Sasaram** India
67 A4 **Sasebo** Japan
129 D2 **Saskatchewan** *prov.* Can.
129 D2 **Saskatchewan** *r.* Can.
129 D2 **Saskatoon** Can.
83 I2 **Saskylakh** Rus. Fed.
123 C2 **Sasolburg** S. Africa
87 D3 **Sasovo** Rus. Fed.
114 B4 **Sassandra** Côte d'Ivoire
108 A2 **Sassari** *Sardinia* Italy
102 C1 **Sassnitz** Ger.
114 A3 **Satadougou** Mali
136 C3 **Satanta** U.S.A.
73 B3 **Satara** India
123 D1 **Satara** S. Africa
87 E3 **Satka** Rus. Fed.
75 C2 **Satna** India
77 C2 **Satpayev** Kazakh.
74 B2 **Satpura Range** *mts* India
63 B2 **Sattahip** Thai.
110 B1 **Satu Mare** Romania
63 B3 **Satun** Thai.
144 B2 **Saucillo** Mex.
93 E4 **Sauda** Norway
92 □B2 **Sauðárkrókur** Iceland
78 B2 **Saudi Arabia** *country* Asia
105 C3 **Saugues** France
137 E1 **Sauk Center** U.S.A.
105 C2 **Saulieu** France
88 B2 **Saulkrasti** Latvia
130 B3 **Sault Sainte Marie** Can.
138 C1 **Sault Sainte Marie** U.S.A.
77 C1 **Saumalkol'** Kazakh.
59 C3 **Saumlakki** Indon.
104 B2 **Saumur** France
120 B1 **Saurimo** Angola
109 D2 **Sava** *r.* Europe
49 J5 **Savai'i** *i.* Samoa
91 E1 **Savala** *r.* Rus. Fed.
114 C4 **Savalou** Benin
141 D2 **Savannah** *GA* U.S.A.
140 C1 **Savannah** *TN* U.S.A.
141 D2 **Savannah** *r.* U.S.A.
63 B2 **Savannakhét** Laos
130 A2 **Savant Lake** Can.
111 C3 **Savaştepe** Turkey
114 C4 **Savè** Benin
105 D2 **Saverne** France
89 F2 **Savino** Rus. Fed.
86 D2 **Savinskiy** Rus. Fed.
**Savoie** *reg.* France *see* **Savoy**
108 A2 **Savona** Italy
93 I3 **Savonlinna** Fin.
105 D2 **Savoy** *reg.* France
93 F4 **Sävsjö** Sweden
59 C3 **Savu** *i.* Indon.
92 I2 **Savukoski** Fin.
**Savu Sea** Indon. *see* **Laut Sawu**
74 B2 **Sawai Madhopur** India
62 A1 **Sawan** Myanmar
62 A2 **Sawankhalok** Thai.
136 B3 **Sawatch Range** *mts* U.S.A.
116 B2 **Sawhāj** Egypt
121 B2 **Sawmills** Zimbabwe
79 C3 **Şawqirah, Dawḩat** *b.* Oman
**Şawqirah Bay** Oman *see* **Şawqirah, Dawḩat**
53 D2 **Sawtell** Austr.
134 C2 **Sawtooth Range** *mts* U.S.A.
68 C1 **Sayano-Shushenskoye Vodokhranilishche** *resr* Rus. Fed.
76 C3 **Sayat** Turkm.
79 C3 **Sayḩūt** Yemen
93 I3 **Säynätsalo** Fin.
69 D2 **Saynshand** Mongolia
139 D2 **Sayre** U.S.A.
144 B3 **Sayula** Mex.
145 C3 **Sayula** Mex.
128 B2 **Sayward** Can.
**Sayyod** Turkm. *see* **Sayat**
89 E2 **Sazonovo** Rus. Fed.
114 B2 **Sbaa** Alg.
98 B2 **Scafell Pike** *hill* U.K.
109 C3 **Scalea** Italy
96 □ **Scalloway** U.K.
108 B2 **Scandicci** Italy
96 C1 **Scapa Flow** *inlet* U.K.
96 B2 **Scarba** *i.* U.K.
130 C3 **Scarborough** Can.
147 D3 **Scarborough** Trin. and Tob.
98 C2 **Scarborough** U.K.
64 A2 **Scarborough Shoal** *sea feature* Phil.
96 A2 **Scarinish** U.K.
**Scarpanto** *i.* Greece *see* **Karpathos**
100 B2 **Schaerbeek** Belgium
105 D2 **Schaffhausen** Switz.
100 B1 **Schagen** Neth.
102 C2 **Schärding** Austria
100 A2 **Scharendijke** Neth.
101 D1 **Scharhörn** *sea feature* Ger.
101 D1 **Scheeßel** Ger.
131 D2 **Schefferville** Can.
135 D3 **Schell Creek Range** *mts* U.S.A.
139 E2 **Schenectady** U.S.A.
143 D3 **Schertz** U.S.A.
101 E3 **Scheßlitz** Ger.
100 C1 **Schiermonnikoog** *i.* Neth.
100 B2 **Schilde** Belgium
108 B1 **Schio** Italy
101 F2 **Schkeuditz** Ger.
101 E1 **Schladen** Ger.
102 C2 **Schladming** Austria
101 E2 **Schleiz** Ger.
102 B1 **Schleswig** Ger.
101 D2 **Schloss Holte-Stukenbrock** Ger.
101 D2 **Schlüchtern** Ger.
101 E3 **Schlüsselfeld** Ger.
101 D2 **Schmallenberg** Ger.
**Schmidt Island** Rus. Fed. *see* **Shmidta, Ostrov**
101 F2 **Schmölln** Ger.
101 D1 **Schneverdingen** Ger.
101 E1 **Schönebeck (Elbe)** Ger.
101 E1 **Schöningen** Ger.
100 B2 **Schoonhoven** Neth.
59 D3 **Schouten Islands** P.N.G.
97 B3 **Schull** Ireland
101 E3 **Schwabach** Ger.
102 B2 **Schwäbische Alb** *mts* Ger.
101 F3 **Schwandorf** Ger.
61 C2 **Schwaner, Pegunungan** *mts* Indon.
101 E1 **Schwarzenbek** Ger.
101 F2 **Schwarzenberg** Ger.
122 A2 **Schwarzrand** *mts* Namibia
**Schwarzwald** *mts* Ger. *see* **Black Forest**
102 C2 **Schwaz** Austria
102 C1 **Schwedt an der Oder** Ger.
101 E2 **Schweinfurt** Ger.
101 E1 **Schwerin** Ger.
101 E1 **Schweriner See** *l.* Ger.
105 D2 **Schwyz** Switz.
108 B3 **Sciacca** *Sicily* Italy
95 B4 **Scilly, Isles of** U.K.
138 C3 **Scioto** *r.* U.S.A.
136 B1 **Scobey** U.S.A.
53 D2 **Scone** Austr.
110 B2 **Scorniceşti** Romania
55 C3 **Scotia Ridge** *sea feature* S. Atlantic Ocean
149 F8 **Scotia Sea** S. Atlantic Ocean
96 C2 **Scotland** *admin. div.* U.K.
128 B2 **Scott, Cape** Can.
123 D3 **Scottburgh** S. Africa
136 C3 **Scott City** U.S.A.
136 C2 **Scottsbluff** U.S.A.
140 C2 **Scottsboro** U.S.A.
96 B1 **Scourie** U.K.
139 D2 **Scranton** U.S.A.
98 C3 **Scunthorpe** U.K.
105 E2 **Scuol** Switz.
**Scutari** Albania *see* **Shkodër**
99 D4 **Seaford** U.K.
98 C2 **Seaham** U.K.
129 E2 **Seal** *r.* Can.
122 B3 **Seal, Cape** S. Africa
52 B3 **Sea Lake** Austr.
143 D3 **Sealy** U.S.A.
140 B1 **Searcy** U.S.A.
98 B2 **Seascale** U.K.
134 B1 **Seattle** U.S.A.
139 E2 **Sebago Lake** U.S.A.
144 A2 **Sebastián Vizcaíno, Bahía** *b.* Mex.
**Sebastopol** Ukr. *see* **Sevastopol'**
**Sebenico** Croatia *see* **Šibenik**
110 B1 **Sebeş** Romania
60 B2 **Sebesi** *i.* Indon.
88 C2 **Sebezh** Rus. Fed.
80 B1 **Şebinkarahisar** Turkey
141 D3 **Sebring** U.S.A.
61 C2 **Sebuku** *i.* Indon.
128 B3 **Sechelt** Can.
150 A3 **Sechura** Peru
73 B3 **Secunderabad** India
137 E3 **Sedalia** U.S.A.
105 C2 **Sedan** France
54 B2 **Seddon** N.Z.
114 A3 **Sédhiou** Senegal
142 A2 **Sedona** U.S.A.
101 E2 **Seeburg** Ger.
101 E1 **Seehausen (Altmark)** Ger.
122 A2 **Seeheim** Namibia
104 C2 **Sées** France
101 E2 **Seesen** Ger.
101 E1 **Seevetal** Ger.
114 A4 **Sefadu** Sierra Leone
123 C1 **Sefare** Botswana
93 F3 **Segalstad** Norway
60 B1 **Segamat** Malaysia
86 C2 **Segezha** Rus. Fed.
114 B3 **Ségou** Mali
106 C1 **Segovia** Spain
86 C2 **Segozerskoye, Ozero** *resr* Rus. Fed.
115 D2 **Séguédine** Niger
114 B4 **Séguéla** Côte d'Ivoire
143 D3 **Seguin** U.S.A.
107 C2 **Segura** *r.* Spain
106 C2 **Segura, Sierra de** *mts* Spain
120 B3 **Sehithwa** Botswana
93 H3 **Seinäjoki** Fin.
104 C2 **Seine** *r.* France
104 B2 **Seine, Baie de** *b.* France
105 C2 **Seine, Val de** *val.* France
103 E1 **Sejny** Pol.
60 B2 **Sekayu** Indon.
114 B4 **Sekondi** Ghana
134 B1 **Selah** U.S.A.
59 C3 **Selaru** *i.* Indon.
61 C2 **Selatan, Tanjung** *pt* Indon.
126 B2 **Selawik** U.S.A.
98 C3 **Selby** U.K.
136 C1 **Selby** U.S.A.
111 C3 **Selçuk** Turkey
120 B3 **Selebi-Phikwe** Botswana
**Selebi-Pikwe** Botswana *see* **Selebi-Phikwe**
105 D2 **Sélestat** France
**Seletyteniz, Oz.** *salt l.* Kazakh. *see* **Siletiteniz, Ozero**
92 □A3 **Selfoss** Iceland
114 A3 **Sélibabi** Maur.
142 A1 **Seligman** U.S.A.
116 A2 **Selîma Oasis** Sudan
111 C3 **Selimiye** Turkey
114 B3 **Sélingué, Lac de** *l.* Mali
89 D2 **Selizharovo** Rus. Fed.
93 E4 **Seljord** Norway
129 E2 **Selkirk** Can.
96 C3 **Selkirk** U.K.
128 C2 **Selkirk Mountains** Can.
142 A2 **Sells** U.S.A.
140 C2 **Selma** *AL* U.S.A.
135 C3 **Selma** *CA* U.S.A.
105 D2 **Selongey** France
99 C4 **Selsey Bill** *hd* U.K.
89 D3 **Sel'tso** Rus. Fed.
**Selukwe** Zimbabwe *see* **Shurugwi**
150 B3 **Selvas** *reg.* Brazil
134 C1 **Selway** *r.* U.S.A.
129 D1 **Selwyn Lake** Can.
128 A1 **Selwyn Mountains** Can.
51 C2 **Selwyn Range** *hills* Austr.
60 B2 **Semangka, Teluk** *b.* Indon.
61 C2 **Semarang** Indon.
60 B1 **Sematan** *Sarawak* Malaysia
118 B2 **Sembé** Congo
81 C2 **Şemdinli** Turkey
91 C1 **Semenivka** Ukr.
87 D3 **Semenov** Rus. Fed.
61 C2 **Semeru, Gunung** *vol.* Indon.
91 E2 **Semikarakorsk** Rus. Fed.
89 E3 **Semiluki** Rus. Fed.
136 B2 **Seminoe Reservoir** U.S.A.
143 C2 **Seminole** U.S.A.
141 D2 **Seminole, Lake** U.S.A.
77 E1 **Semipalatinsk** Kazakh.
61 C1 **Semitau** Indon.
**Sem Kolodezey** Ukr. *see* **Lenine**
81 D2 **Semnān** Iran
61 C1 **Semporna** *Sabah* Malaysia
105 C2 **Semur-en-Auxois** France
**Semyonovskoye** Rus. Fed. *see* **Bereznik**
**Semyonovskoye** Rus. Fed. *see* **Ostrovskoye**
150 C3 **Sena Madureira** Brazil
120 B2 **Senanga** Zambia
67 B4 **Sendai** Japan
67 D3 **Sendai** Japan
141 D2 **Seneca** U.S.A.
114 A3 **Senegal** *country* Africa
114 A3 **Sénégal** *r.* Maur./Senegal
102 C1 **Senftenberg** Ger.
119 D3 **Sengerema** Tanz.
151 E4 **Senhor do Bonfim** Brazil
103 D2 **Senica** Slovakia
108 B2 **Senigallia** Italy
109 B2 **Senj** Croatia
92 G2 **Senja** *i.* Norway
122 B2 **Senlac** S. Africa
105 C2 **Senlis** France
63 B2 **Senmonorom** Cambodia
116 B3 **Sennar** Sudan
130 C3 **Senneterre** Can.
123 C3 **Senqu** *r.* Lesotho
105 C2 **Sens** France
109 D1 **Senta** Serb. and Mont.
128 B2 **Sentinel Peak** Can.
75 B2 **Seoni** India
65 B2 **Seoul** S. Korea
155 D2 **Sepetiba, Baía de** *b.* Brazil
59 D3 **Sepik** *r.* P.N.G.
61 C1 **Sepinang** Indon.
131 D2 **Sept-Îles** Can.
87 D4 **Serafimovich** Rus. Fed.
100 B2 **Seraing** Belgium
59 C3 **Seram** *i.* Indon.
60 B2 **Serang** Indon.
60 B1 **Serasan, Selat** *sea chan.* Indon.
**Serbia** *aut. rep.* Serb. and Mont. *see* **Srbija**
109 D2 **Serbia and Montenegro** *country* Europe
117 C3 **Serdo** Eth.
89 E3 **Serebryanyye Prudy** Rus. Fed.
60 B1 **Seremban** Malaysia
119 D3 **Serengeti Plain** Tanz.
121 C2 **Serenje** Zambia
90 B2 **Seret** *r.* Ukr.
87 D3 **Sergach** Rus. Fed.
86 F2 **Sergino** Rus. Fed.
89 E2 **Sergiyev Posad** Rus. Fed.
**Sergo** Ukr. *see* **Stakhanov**
61 C1 **Seria** Brunei
61 C1 **Serian** *Sarawak* Malaysia
111 B3 **Serifos** *i.* Greece
80 B2 **Serik** Turkey
59 C3 **Sermata, Kepulauan** *is* Indon.
**Sernyy Zavod** Turkm. *see* **Kukurtli**
86 F3 **Serov** Rus. Fed.
120 B3 **Serowe** Botswana
106 B2 **Serpa** Port.
**Serpa Pinto** Angola *see* **Menongue**

| | | |
|---|---|---|
| 89 E3 | Serpukhov Rus. Fed. | |

89 E3 Serpukhov Rus. Fed.
155 D2 Serra Brazil
155 C1 Serra das Araras Brazil
108 A3 Serramanna Sardinia Italy
154 B1 Serranópolis Brazil
100 A3 Serre r. France
111 B2 Serres Greece
151 F4 Serrinha Brazil
155 D1 Sêrro Brazil
154 C2 Sertãozinho Brazil
59 D3 Serui Indon.
120 B3 Serule Botswana
61 C2 Seruyan r. Indon.
68 C2 Sêrxü China
120 A2 Sesfontein Namibia
108 B2 Sessa Aurunca Italy
108 A2 Sestri Levante Italy
105 C3 Sète France
155 D1 Sete Lagoas Brazil
92 G2 Setermoen Norway
93 E4 Setesdal val. Norway
115 C1 Sétif Alg.
67 B4 Seto-naikai sea Japan
114 B1 Settat Morocco
98 B2 Settle U.K.
106 B2 Setúbal Port.
106 B2 Setúbal, Baía de b. Port.
130 A2 Seul, Lac l. Can.
81 C1 Sevan Armenia
76 A2 Sevan, Lake Armenia
Sevana Lich l. Armenia see Sevan, Lake
91 C3 Sevastopol' Ukr.
Seven Islands Can. see Sept-Îles
131 C2 Seven Islands Bay Can.
99 D4 Sevenoaks U.K.
105 C3 Sévérac-le-Château France
130 B2 Severn r. Can.
122 B2 Severn S. Africa
99 B4 Severn r. U.K.
86 D2 Severnaya Dvina r. Rus. Fed.
83 H1 Severnaya Zemlya is Rus. Fed.
86 D2 Severnyy Rus. Fed.
86 F2 Severnyy Rus. Fed.
83 I3 Severobaykal'sk Rus. Fed.
86 C2 Severodvinsk Rus. Fed.
83 L3 Severo-Kuril'sk Rus. Fed.
92 J2 Severomorsk Rus. Fed.
86 C2 Severoonezhsk Rus. Fed.
83 H2 Severo-Yeniseyskiy Rus. Fed.
91 D3 Severskaya Rus. Fed.
135 D3 Sevier r. U.S.A.
135 D3 Sevier Lake U.S.A.
Sevilla Spain see Seville
106 B2 Seville Spain
Sevlyush Ukr. see Vynohradiv
89 D3 Sevsk Rus. Fed.
126 C2 Seward U.S.A.
126 B2 Seward Peninsula U.S.A.
128 A2 Sewell Inlet Can.
128 C2 Sexsmith Can.
144 B2 Sextín r. Mex.
86 G1 Seyakha Rus. Fed.
113 I6 Seychelles country Indian Ocean
92 □C2 Seyðisfjörður Iceland
Seyhan Turkey see Adana
80 B2 Seyhan r. Turkey
91 C1 Seym r. Rus. Fed./Ukr.
83 L2 Seymchan Rus. Fed.
53 C3 Seymour Austr.
123 C3 Seymour S. Africa
138 B3 Seymour IN U.S.A.
143 D2 Seymour TX U.S.A.
105 C2 Sézanne France
108 B2 Sezze Italy
111 B3 Sfakia Greece
110 C1 Sfântu Gheorghe Romania
115 D1 Sfax Tunisia
Sfîntu Gheorghe Romania see Sfântu Gheorghe
's-Gravenhage Neth. see The Hague
96 A2 Sgurr Alasdair hill U.K.
70 A2 Shaanxi prov. China
Shabani Zimbabwe see Zvishavane
91 D2 Shabel'sk Rus. Fed.
77 D3 Shache China
55 C1 Shackleton Range mts Antarctica
74 A2 Shadadkot Pak.
86 F3 Shadrinsk Rus. Fed.
99 B4 Shaftesbury U.K.
126 B2 Shageluk U.S.A.
Shāhābād Iran see Eslāmābād-e Gharb
75 C2 Shahdol India
77 C2 Shah Fuladi mt. Afgh.
75 B2 Shahjahanpur India
76 B3 Shāh Kūh mt. Iran
81 D2 Shahr-e Bābak Iran
81 D2 Shahr-e Kord Iran
81 D2 Shahreză Iran
77 C3 Shahrisabz Uzbek.
Shāhrūd Iran see Emāmrūd
79 B2 Shaj'ah, Jabal hill Saudi Arabia
89 E2 Shakhovskaya Rus. Fed.
Shakhterskoye Ukr. see Pershotravens'k
Shakhty Rus. Fed. see Gusinoozersk
91 E2 Shakhty Rus. Fed.
Shakhtyorskoye Ukr. see Pershotravens'k
86 D3 Shakhun'ya Rus. Fed.
114 C4 Shaki Nigeria
66 D2 Shakotan-hantō pen. Japan

66 D2 Shakotan-misaki c. Japan
76 B2 Shalkar Kazakh.
68 C2 Shaluli Shan mts China
129 E2 Shamattawa Can.
143 C1 Shamrock U.S.A.
70 A2 Shandan China
70 B2 Shandong prov. China
70 C2 Shandong Bandao pen. China
121 B2 Shangani Zimbabwe
121 B2 Shangani r. Zimbabwe
70 B1 Shangdu China
70 C2 Shanghai China
70 C2 Shanghai mun. China
71 B3 Shanghang China
70 A2 Shangluo China
70 B2 Shangnan China
71 B3 Shangrao China
70 B2 Shangshui China
77 E2 Shangyou Shuiku resr China
70 C2 Shangyu China
69 E1 Shangzhi China
Shangzhou China see Shangluo
134 B1 Shaniko U.S.A.
97 B2 Shannon r. Ireland
97 B2 Shannon, Mouth of the Ireland
62 A1 Shan Plateau Myanmar
Shansi prov. China see Shanxi
71 B3 Shantou China
Shantung prov. China see Shandong
70 B2 Shanxi prov. China
71 B3 Shaoguan China
70 C2 Shaowu China
70 C2 Shaoxing China
70 B2 Shaoyang China
96 C1 Shapinsay i. U.K.
116 C2 Shaqrā' Saudi Arabia
90 B2 Sharhorod Ukr.
79 C2 Sharjah U.A.E.
88 C2 Sharkawshchyna Belarus
50 A1 Shark Bay Austr.
78 A2 Sharm ash Shaykh Egypt
138 C2 Sharon U.S.A.
86 D3 Shar'ya Rus. Fed.
121 B3 Shashe r. Botswana/Zimbabwe
117 B4 Shashemenē Eth.
Shashi China see Jingzhou
134 B2 Shasta, Mount vol. U.S.A.
134 B2 Shasta Lake U.S.A.
115 D2 Shāṭi', Wādī ash watercourse Libya
Shatilki Belarus see Svyetlahorsk
89 E2 Shatura Rus. Fed.
129 D3 Shaunavon Can.
138 B2 Shawano U.S.A.
130 C3 Shawinigan Can.
143 D1 Shawnee U.S.A.
83 M2 Shayboveyem r. Rus. Fed.
50 B2 Shay Gap Austr.
89 E3 Shchekino Rus. Fed.
89 E2 Shchelkovo Rus. Fed.
Shcherbakov Rus. Fed. see Rybinsk
Shcherbinovka Ukr. see Dzerzhyns'k
89 E3 Shchigry Rus. Fed.
91 C1 Shchors Ukr.
88 B3 Shchuchyn Belarus
91 D1 Shebekino Rus. Fed.
77 C3 Sheberghān Afgh.
138 B2 Sheboygan U.S.A.
91 D3 Shebsh r. Rus. Fed.
97 C2 Sheelin, Lough l. Ireland
136 B3 Sheep Mountain U.S.A.
99 D4 Sheerness U.K.
98 C3 Sheffield U.K.
143 C2 Sheffield U.S.A.
Sheikh Othman Yemen see Ash Shaykh 'Uthman
Shekhem West Bank see Nāblus
89 E2 Sheksna Rus. Fed.
89 E2 Sheksninskoye Vodokhranilishche resr Rus. Fed.
83 M2 Shelagskiy, Mys pt Rus. Fed.
131 D3 Shelburne Can.
138 B2 Shelby MI U.S.A.
134 D1 Shelby MT U.S.A.
141 D1 Shelby NC U.S.A.
138 B3 Shelbyville IL U.S.A.
140 C2 Shelbyville TN U.S.A.
83 L2 Shelikhova, Zaliv g. Rus. Fed.
126 B3 Shelikof Strait U.S.A.
129 D2 Shellbrook Can.
Shelter Bay Can. see Port-Cartier
134 B1 Shelton U.S.A.
137 D2 Shenandoah U.S.A.
139 D3 Shenandoah r. U.S.A.
139 D3 Shenandoah Mountains U.S.A.
118 A2 Shendam Nigeria
Shengli Feng mt. China/Kyrg. see Pobeda Peak
86 D2 Shenkursk Rus. Fed.
70 B2 Shenmu China
Shensi prov. China see Shaanxi
70 C1 Shenyang China
71 B3 Shenzhen China
90 B1 Shepetivka Ukr.
53 C3 Shepparton Austr.
99 D4 Sheppey, Isle of i. U.K.
131 D3 Sherbrooke N.S. Can.
130 C3 Sherbrooke Que. Can.
97 C2 Shercock Ireland
116 B3 Shereiq Sudan
136 B2 Sheridan U.S.A.
52 A2 Sheringa Austr.

86 F2 Sherkaly Rus. Fed.
143 D2 Sherman U.S.A.
100 B2 's-Hertogenbosch Neth.
96 □ Shetland Islands U.K.
76 B2 Shetpe Kazakh.
Shevchenko Kazakh. see Aktau
91 D2 Shevchenkove Ukr.
137 D1 Sheyenne r. U.S.A.
79 B3 Shibām Yemen
67 C3 Shibata Japan
66 D2 Shibetsu Japan
Shibotsu-jima i. Rus. Fed. see Zelenyy, Ostrov
71 B3 Shicheng China
70 C2 Shidao China
96 B2 Shiel, Loch l. U.K.
Shigatse China see Xigazê
77 E2 Shihezi China
Shihkiachwang China see Shijiazhuang
Shijiao China see Fogang
70 B2 Shijiazhuang China
Shijiusuo China see Rizhao
74 A2 Shikarpur Pak.
67 B4 Shikoku i. Japan
66 D2 Shikotsu-ko l. Japan
86 D2 Shilega Rus. Fed.
75 C2 Shiliguri India
97 C2 Shillelagh Ireland
75 D2 Shillong India
89 F3 Shilovo Rus. Fed.
69 E1 Shimanovsk Rus. Fed.
117 C3 Shimbiris mt. Somalia
67 C3 Shimizu Japan
74 B1 Shimla India
67 C4 Shimoda Japan
73 B3 Shimoga India
66 D2 Shimokita-hantō pen. Japan
67 B4 Shimonoseki Japan
89 D2 Shimsk Rus. Fed.
96 B1 Shin, Loch l. U.K.
62 A1 Shingbwiyang Myanmar
67 C4 Shingū Japan
123 D1 Shingwedzi S. Africa
123 D1 Shingwedzi r. S. Africa
66 D3 Shinjō Japan
119 D3 Shinyanga Tanz.
67 D3 Shiogama Japan
67 C4 Shiono-misaki c. Japan
71 A3 Shiping China
98 C3 Shipley U.K.
142 B1 Shiprock U.S.A.
71 A3 Shiqian China
Shiqizhen China see Zhongshan
70 A2 Shiquan China
78 B2 Shi'r, Jabal hill Saudi Arabia
67 C3 Shirane-san mt. Japan
67 C3 Shirane-san vol. Japan
81 D3 Shīrāz Iran
66 D2 Shiretoko-misaki c. Japan
66 D2 Shiriya-zaki c. Japan
76 B3 Shirvān Iran
74 B2 Shiv India
74 B2 Shivpuri India
70 B2 Shiyan China
70 A2 Shizuishan China
67 C4 Shizuoka Japan
89 D3 Shklow Belarus
109 C2 Shkodër Albania
83 H1 Shmidta, Ostrov i. Rus. Fed.
67 D2 Shōbara Japan
Sholapur India see Solapur
158 F8 Shona Ridge sea feature S. Atlantic Ocean
77 C3 Sho'rchi Uzbek.
74 B1 Shorkot Pak.
135 C3 Shoshone CA U.S.A.
134 D2 Shoshone ID U.S.A.
135 C3 Shoshone Mountains U.S.A.
123 C1 Shoshong Botswana
91 C1 Shostka Ukr.
70 B2 Shouxian China
78 A3 Showak Sudan
142 A2 Show Low U.S.A.
91 C2 Shpola Ukr.
140 B2 Shreveport U.S.A.
99 B3 Shrewsbury U.K.
77 D2 Shu Kazakh.
Shuangjiang China see Tongdao
62 A1 Shuangjiang China
Shuangxi China see Shunchang
66 B1 Shuangyashan China
87 E4 Shubarkuduk Kazakh.
116 B1 Shubrā al Khaymah Egypt
89 D2 Shugozero Rus. Fed.
Shuidong China see Dianbai
120 B2 Shumba Zimbabwe
110 C2 Shumen Bulg.
87 F3 Shumikha Rus. Fed.
88 C2 Shumilina Belarus
143 C1 Shumla U.S.A.
89 D3 Shumyachi Rus. Fed.
71 B3 Shunchang China
126 B2 Shungnak U.S.A.
78 B3 Shuqrah Yemen
121 C2 Shurugwi Zimbabwe
89 F2 Shushkodom Rus. Fed.
81 C2 Shushtar Iran
128 C2 Shuswap Lake Can.
89 F2 Shuya Rus. Fed.
89 F2 Shuyskoye Rus. Fed.
62 A1 Shwebo Myanmar
62 A2 Shwedwin Myanmar
62 A2 Shwegun Myanmar
62 A2 Shwegyin Myanmar

62 A1 Shweli r. Myanmar
77 C2 Shymkent Kazakh.
74 B1 Shyok r. India
91 C2 Shyroke Ukr.
91 C2 Shyryayeve Ukr.
59 C3 Sia Indon.
74 A2 Siahan Range mts Pak.
74 B1 Sialkot Pak.
Siam country Asia see Thailand
Sian China see Xi'an
64 B3 Siargao i. Phil.
64 B3 Siasi Phil.
88 B2 Šiauliai Lith.
123 D1 Sibasa S. Africa
109 C2 Šibenik Croatia
83 G2 Siberia reg. Rus. Fed.
60 A2 Siberut i. Indon.
74 A2 Sibi Pak.
Sibir' reg. Rus. Fed. see Siberia
118 B3 Sibiti Congo
110 B1 Sibiu Romania
60 A1 Sibolga Indon.
62 A1 Sibsagar India
61 C1 Sibu Sarawak Malaysia
118 B2 Sibut C.A.R.
64 A3 Sibutu i. Phil.
64 B2 Sibuyan i. Phil.
64 B2 Sibuyan Sea Phil.
128 C2 Sicamous Can.
63 A3 Sichon Thai.
70 A2 Sichuan prov. China
70 A3 Sichuan Pendi basin China
105 D3 Sicié, Cap c. France
Sicilia i. Italy see Sicily
108 B3 Sicilian Channel Italy/Tunisia
108 B3 Sicily i. Italy
150 B4 Sicuani Peru
74 B2 Siddhapur India
111 C3 Sideros, Akra pt Greece
122 B3 Sidesaviwa S. Africa
75 C2 Sidhi India
107 D2 Sidi Aïssa Alg.
107 D2 Sidi Ali Alg.
114 B1 Sidi Bel Abbès Alg.
114 B1 Sidi Ifni Morocco
114 B1 Sidi Kacem Morocco
60 A1 Sidikalang Indon.
111 B2 Sidirokastro Greece
96 C2 Sidlaw Hills U.K.
99 B4 Sidmouth U.K.
134 B1 Sidney Can.
136 C1 Sidney MT U.S.A.
136 C2 Sidney NE U.S.A.
138 C2 Sidney OH U.S.A.
141 D2 Sidney Lanier, Lake U.S.A.
61 D1 Sidoan Indon.
80 B2 Sidon Lebanon
154 B2 Sidrolândia Brazil
103 E1 Siedlce Pol.
100 C2 Sieg r. Ger.
101 D2 Siegen Ger.
63 B2 Siĕmréab Cambodia
Siem Reap Cambodia see Siĕmréab
108 B2 Siena Italy
103 D1 Sieradz Pol.
142 B2 Sierra Blanca U.S.A.
153 B4 Sierra Grande Arg.
114 A4 Sierra Leone country Africa
158 E4 Sierra Leone Basin sea feature N. Atlantic Ocean
158 E4 Sierra Leone Rise sea feature N. Atlantic Ocean
144 B2 Sierra Mojada Mex.
142 A2 Sierra Vista U.S.A.
105 D2 Sierre Switz.
116 C3 Sifeni Eth.
111 B3 Sifnos i. Greece
107 C2 Sig Alg.
127 I2 Siggup Nunaa pen. Greenland
110 B1 Sighetu Marmației Romania
110 B1 Sighișoara Romania
60 A1 Sigli Indon.
92 □B2 Siglufjörður Iceland
102 B2 Sigmaringen Ger.
100 B3 Signy-l'Abbaye France
106 C1 Sigüenza Spain
114 B3 Siguiri Guinea
88 B2 Sigulda Latvia
63 B2 Sihanoukville Cambodia
92 I3 Siilinjärvi Fin.
80 B2 Siirt Turkey
60 B2 Sijunjung Indon.
74 B2 Sikar India
74 A1 Sikaram mt. Afgh.
114 B3 Sikasso Mali
111 B2 Sikea Greece
137 F3 Sikeston U.S.A.
66 B2 Sikhote-Alin' mts Rus. Fed.
111 C3 Sikinos i. Greece
103 D2 Siklós Hungary
65 A2 Sikuaishi China
88 B2 Šilalė Lith.
144 B2 Silao Mex.
101 D1 Silberberg hill Ger.
75 D2 Silchar India
77 D1 Siletiteniz, Ozero salt l. Kazakh.
75 C2 Silgarhi Nepal
80 B2 Silifke Turkey
75 C1 Siling Co salt l. China
110 C2 Silistra Bulg.
111 C2 Silivri Turkey
93 F3 Siljan l. Sweden
93 E4 Silkeborg Denmark
88 C2 Sillamäe Estonia

98 B2 Silloth U.K.
80 B1 Siloam Springs U.S.A.
123 D2 Silobela S. Africa
60 B1 Siluas Indon.
88 B2 Šilutė Lith.
81 C2 Silvan Turkey
154 C1 Silvânia Brazil
74 B2 Silvassa India
137 E1 Silver Bay U.S.A.
142 B2 Silver City U.S.A.
136 B3 Silverton U.S.A.
62 B1 Simao China
130 C3 Simàrd, Lac l. Can.
111 C3 Simav Turkey
111 C3 Simav Dağları mts Turkey
118 C2 Simba Dem. Rep. Congo
138 C2 Simcoe Can.
139 D2 Simcoe, Lake Can.
78 A3 Simēn Eth.
60 A1 Simeulue i. Indon.
91 C3 Simferopol' Ukr.
75 C2 Simikot Nepal
135 C4 Simi Valley U.S.A.
Simla India see Shimla
110 B1 Şimleu Silvaniei Romania
92 I2 Simo Fin.
129 D2 Simonhouse Can.
60 B2 Simpang Indon.
51 C2 Simpson Desert Austr.
93 F4 Simrishamn Sweden
60 A1 Sinabang Indon.
116 B2 Sinai pen. Egypt
71 A3 Sinan China
65 B2 Sinanju N. Korea
62 A1 Sinbo Myanmar
62 A1 Sinbyugyun Myanmar
150 B2 Sincelejo Col.
60 B2 Sindangbarang Indon.
111 C3 Sındırgı Turkey
86 E2 Sindor Rus. Fed.
81 C2 Sinekçi Turkey
106 B2 Sines Port.
106 B2 Sines, Cabo de c. Port.
116 B3 Singa Sudan
75 C2 Singahi India
60 B1 Singapore country Asia
61 C2 Singaraja Indon.
63 B2 Sing Buri Thai.
119 D3 Singida Tanz.
62 A1 Singkaling Hkamti Myanmar
61 D2 Singkang Indon.
60 B1 Singkawang Indon.
60 B2 Singkep i. Indon.
60 B1 Singkil Indon.
53 D2 Singleton Austr.
Sin'gosan N. Korea see Kosan
62 A1 Singu Myanmar
Sining China see Xining
108 A2 Siniscola Sardinia Italy
109 C2 Sinj Croatia
60 B1 Sinjai Indon.
116 B3 Sinkat Sudan
151 D2 Sinnamary Fr. Guiana
Sânnicolau Mare Romania see
Sânnicolau Mare
Sinoia Zimbabwe see Chinhoyi
80 B1 Sinop Turkey
65 B1 Sinp'o N. Korea
61 C1 Sintang Indon.
100 B2 St Anthonis Neth.
100 A2 St-Laureins Belgium
100 B2 St-Niklaas Belgium
143 D3 Sinton U.S.A.
100 C2 St-Vith Belgium
65 A1 Sinüiju N. Korea
64 B3 Siocon Phil.
103 D2 Siófok Hungary
105 D2 Sion Switz.
137 D2 Sioux Center U.S.A.
137 D2 Sioux City U.S.A.
137 D2 Sioux Falls U.S.A.
130 A2 Sioux Lookout Can.
65 A1 Siping China
129 E2 Sipiwesk Lake Can.
55 P2 Siple, Mount Antarctica
55 P2 Siple Island Antarctica
Sipolilo Zimbabwe see Guruve
60 A2 Sipura i. Indon.
64 B3 Siquijor Phil.
93 E4 Sira r. Norway
Siracusa Italy see Syracuse
51 C1 Sir Edward Pellew Group
is Austr.
110 C1 Siret Romania
110 C1 Siret r. Romania
79 C2 Sīrīk Iran
61 C1 Sirik, Tanjung pt Malaysia
62 B2 Siri Kit Dam Thai.
128 B1 Sir James MacBrien, Mount
Can.
79 C2 Sīrjān Iran
81 C2 Şırnak Turkey
74 B2 Sirohi India
60 A1 Sirombu Indon.
74 B2 Sirsa India
115 D1 Sirte Libya
115 D1 Sirte, Gulf of Libya
88 B2 Širvintos Lith.
109 C1 Sisak Croatia
63 B2 Sisaket Thai.
145 C2 Sisal Mex.
122 B2 Sishen S. Africa
81 C2 Sisian Armenia

127 I2 Sisimiut Greenland
129 D2 Sisipuk Lake Can.
63 B2 Sisôphŏn Cambodia
105 D3 Sisteron France
Sitang China see Sinan
75 C2 Sitapur India
111 C3 Siteia Greece
123 D2 Siteki Swaziland
128 A2 Sitka U.S.A.
100 B2 Sittard Neth.
62 A1 Sittaung Myanmar
62 A2 Sittaung r. Myanmar
62 A1 Sittwe Myanmar
61 C2 Situbondo Indon.
80 B2 Sivas Turkey
111 C3 Sivaslı Turkey
80 B2 Siverek Turkey
88 D2 Siverskiy Rus. Fed.
91 D2 Sivers'kyy Donets' r. Ukr.
80 B2 Sivrihisar Turkey
116 A2 Sīwah Egypt
75 B1 Siwalik Range mts India/Nepal
116 A2 Sīwah, Wāḥāt Egypt
Siwa Oasis Egypt see Sīwah,
Wāḥāt
105 D3 Six-Fours-les-Plages France
70 B2 Sixian China
123 C3 Siyabuswa S. Africa
Sjælland i. Denmark see Zealand
109 D2 Sjenica Serb. and Mont.
92 G2 Sjøvegan Norway
91 C2 Skadovs'k Ukr.
93 F4 Skagen Denmark
93 E4 Skagerrak str. Denmark/Norway
134 B1 Skagit r. U.S.A.
128 A2 Skagway U.S.A.
92 G2 Skaland Norway
93 F4 Skara Sweden
74 B1 Skardu Jammu and Kashmir
103 E1 Skarżysko-Kamienna Pol.
103 D2 Skawina Pol.
114 A2 Skaymat Western Sahara
128 B2 Skeena r. Can.
128 B2 Skeena Mountains Can.
98 D3 Skegness U.K.
92 H3 Skellefteå Sweden
92 H3 Skellefteälven r. Sweden
97 C2 Skerries Ireland
93 F4 Ski Norway
111 B3 Skiathos i. Greece
97 B3 Skibbereen Ireland
92 □B2 Skiðadals-jökull glacier
Iceland
98 B2 Skiddaw hill U.K.
93 E4 Skien Norway
103 E1 Skierniewice Pol.
115 C1 Skikda Alg.
53 C3 Skipton Austr.
98 B3 Skipton U.K.
93 E4 Skive Denmark
92 H1 Skjervøy Norway
Skobelev Uzbek. see Farg'ona
111 B3 Skopelos i. Greece
89 E3 Skopin Rus. Fed.
111 B2 Skopje Macedonia
111 C3 Skoutaros Greece
83 J3 Skövde Sweden
139 F2 Skovorodino Rus. Fed.
92 H2 Skröven Sweden
88 B2 Skrunda Latvia
128 A1 Skukum, Mount Can.
123 D1 Skukuza S. Africa
88 B2 Skuodas Lith.
90 B2 Skvyra Ukr.
96 A2 Skye i. U.K.
111 B3 Skyros Greece
111 B3 Skyros i. Greece
93 F4 Slagelse Denmark
60 B2 Slamet, Gunung vol. Indon.
97 C2 Slaney r. Ireland
88 C2 Slantsy Rus. Fed.
109 C1 Slatina Croatia
110 B2 Slatina Romania
143 C2 Slaton U.S.A.
129 C1 Slave r. Can.
114 C4 Slave Coast Africa
128 C2 Slave Lake Can.
77 D1 Slavgorod Rus. Fed.
88 C2 Slavkovichi Rus. Fed.
Slavonska Požega Croatia see
Požega
109 C1 Slavonski Brod Croatia
90 B1 Slavuta Ukr.
90 C1 Slavutych Ukr.
66 B2 Slavyanka Rus. Fed.
Slavyanskaya Rus. Fed. see
Slavyansk-na-Kubani
91 D2 Slavyansk-na-Kubani Rus. Fed.
89 D3 Slawharad Belarus
103 D1 Sławno Pol.
99 C3 Sleaford U.K.
97 A2 Slea Head hd Ireland
130 C2 Sleeper Islands Can.
97 C1 Slieve Donard hill U.K.
97 B1 Slieve Gamph hills
Ireland
96 A2 Sligachan U.K.
Sligeach Ireland see Sligo
97 B1 Sligo Ireland
97 B1 Sligo Bay Ireland
93 G4 Slite Sweden
110 C2 Sliven Bulg.
Sloboda Rus. Fed. see Ezhva
110 C2 Slobozia Romania

128 C3 Slocan Can.
88 C3 Slonim Belarus
100 B1 Sloten Neth.
99 C4 Slough U.K.
103 D2 Slovakia country Europe
108 B1 Slovenia country Europe
91 D2 Slov"yans'k Ukr.
102 C1 Słubice Pol.
90 B1 Sluch r. Ukr.
100 A2 Sluis Neth.
103 D1 Słupsk Pol.
88 C3 Slutsk Belarus
97 A2 Slyne Head hd Ireland
68 C2 Slyudyanka Rus. Fed.
131 D2 Smallwood Reservoir Can.
88 C3 Smalyavichy Belarus
88 C3 Smarhon' Belarus
129 D2 Smeaton Can.
109 D2 Smederevo Serb. and Mont.
109 D2 Smederevska Palanka
Serb. and Mont.
91 C2 Smila Ukr.
88 C3 Smilavichy Belarus
88 C2 Smiltene Latvia
137 D3 Smith Center U.S.A.
128 B2 Smithers Can.
141 E1 Smithfield NC U.S.A.
135 D3 Smithfield UT U.S.A.
139 D3 Smith Mountain Lake U.S.A.
130 C3 Smiths Falls Can.
53 C3 Smithton Austr.
53 D2 Smoky Cape Austr.
137 D3 Smoky Hills U.S.A.
92 E3 Smøla i. Norway
89 D3 Smolensk Rus. Fed.
89 D3 Smolensko-Moskovskaya
Vozvyshennost' hills Rus. Fed.
111 B2 Smolyan Bulg.
66 B2 Smolyoninovo Rus. Fed.
130 B3 Smooth Rock Falls Can.
Smyrna Turkey see İzmir
91 D2 Smyrnove Ukr.
92 □B3 Snæfell mt. Iceland
98 A2 Snaefell hill Isle of Man
128 A1 Snag Can.
134 C1 Snake r. U.S.A.
134 D2 Snake River Plain U.S.A.
Snare Lakes Can. see Wekweti
92 F3 Snåsvatn l. Norway
100 B1 Sneek Neth.
97 B3 Sneem Ireland
122 B3 Sneeuberge mts S. Africa
Snegurovka Ukr. see Tetiyiv
103 D1 Sněžka mt. Czech Rep.
108 B1 Snežnik mt. Slovenia
103 E1 Śniardwy, Jezioro l. Pol.
Sniečkus Lith. see Visaginas
91 C2 Snihurivka Ukr.
93 E3 Snøhetta mt. Norway
Snovsk Ukr. see Shchors
129 D1 Snowbird Lake Can.
99 A3 Snowdon mt. U.K.
Snowdrift Can. see Łutselk'e
129 C1 Snowdrift r. Can.
142 A2 Snowflake U.S.A.
129 D2 Snow Lake Can.
134 C1 Snowshoe Peak U.S.A.
52 A2 Snowtown Austr.
53 C3 Snowy r. Austr.
53 C3 Snowy Mountains Austr.
143 C2 Snyder U.S.A.
121 □D2 Soalala Madag.
121 □D2 Soanierana-Ivongo Madag.
90 B2 Sob' r. Ukr.
65 B2 Sobaek-sanmaek mts S. Korea
117 B4 Sobat r. Sudan
100 C2 Sobernheim Ger.
89 F2 Sobinka Rus. Fed.
151 E4 Sobradinho, Barragem de resr
Brazil
151 E3 Sobral Brazil
91 D3 Sochi Rus. Fed.
65 B2 Sŏch'ŏn S. Korea
49 L5 Society Islands Fr. Polynesia
150 B2 Socorro Col.
142 B2 Socorro NM U.S.A.
142 B2 Socorro TX U.S.A.
144 A3 Socorro, Isla i. Mex.
56 B4 Socotra i. Yemen
63 B3 Soc Trăng Vietnam
106 C2 Socuéllamos Spain
92 I2 Sodankylä Fin.
134 D2 Soda Springs U.S.A.
93 G3 Söderhamn Sweden
93 G3 Södertälje Sweden
116 A3 Sodiri Sudan
117 B4 Sodo Eth.
93 G3 Södra Kvarken str. Fin./Sweden
123 C1 Soekmekaar S. Africa
Soerabaia Indon. see Surabaya
101 D2 Soest Ger.
53 C2 Sofala Austr.
110 B2 Sofia Bulg.
121 □D2 Sofia r. Madag.
Sofiya Bulg. see Sofia
Sofiyevka Ukr. see Vil'nyans'k
75 D1 Sog China
93 E3 Sognefjorden inlet Norway
111 D2 Söğüt Turkey
Sohâg Egypt see Sawhāj
Sohar Oman see Şuḥār
100 B2 Soignies Belgium
105 C2 Soissons France
90 A1 Sokal' Ukr.
65 B2 Sokch'o S. Korea

111 C3 Söke Turkey
81 C1 Sokhumi Georgia
114 C4 Sokodé Togo
89 F2 Sokol Rus. Fed.
101 F2 Sokolov Czech Rep.
115 C3 Sokoto Nigeria
115 C3 Sokoto r. Nigeria
90 B2 Sokyryany Ukr.
73 B3 Solapur India
135 B3 Soledad U.S.A.
89 F2 Soligalich Rus. Fed.
99 C2 Solihull U.K.
86 E3 Solikamsk Rus. Fed.
87 E3 Sol'-Iletsk Rus. Fed.
100 C2 Solingen Ger.
122 A1 Solitaire Namibia
92 G3 Sollefteå Sweden
93 G4 Sollentuna Sweden
107 D2 Sóller Spain
101 D2 Solling hills Ger.
89 E2 Solnechnogorsk Rus. Fed.
60 B2 Solok Indon.
48 H4 Solomon Islands country
S. Pacific Ocean
48 G4 Solomon Sea P.N.G./Solomon Is
61 D2 Solor, Kepulauan is Indon.
105 D2 Solothurn Switz.
81 D2 Soltānābād Iran
101 D1 Soltau Ger.
89 D2 Sol'tsy Rus. Fed.
96 C3 Solway Firth est. U.K.
120 B2 Solwezi Zambia
111 C3 Soma Turkey
117 C4 Somalia country Africa
120 B1 Sombo Angola
109 C1 Sombor Serb. and Mont.
144 B2 Sombrerete Mex.
138 C3 Somerset U.S.A.
123 C3 Somerset East S. Africa
126 F2 Somerset Island Can.
122 A3 Somerset West S. Africa
110 B1 Someş r. Romania
101 E2 Sömmerda Ger.
146 B3 Somoto Nic.
75 C2 Son r. India
93 E5 Sønderborg Denmark
101 E2 Sondershausen Ger.
Søndre Strømfjord inlet Greenland
see Kangerlussuaq
108 A1 Sondrio Italy
63 B2 Sông Cau Vietnam
62 B1 Sông Da, Hô resr Vietnam
119 D4 Songea Tanz.
65 B1 Sŏnggan N. Korea
65 B1 Songhua Hu resr China
65 B1 Songjianghe China
Sŏngjin N. Korea see Kimch'aek
63 B3 Songkhla Thai.
65 B2 Sŏngnam S. Korea
65 B2 Sŏngnim N. Korea
120 A1 Songo Angola
121 C2 Songo Moz.
Songololo Dem. Rep. Congo see
Mbanza-Ngungu
69 E1 Songyuan China
Sonid Youqi China see Saihan Tal
74 B2 Sonipat India
89 E2 Sonkovo Rus. Fed.
62 B1 Son La Vietnam
74 A2 Sonmiani Pak.
74 A2 Sonmiani Bay Pak.
101 E2 Sonneberg Ger.
142 A2 Sonoita Mex.
144 A2 Sonora r. Mex.
135 B3 Sonora CA U.S.A.
143 C2 Sonora TX U.S.A.
146 B3 Sonsonate El Salvador
Soochow China see Suzhou
117 A4 Sopo watercourse Sudan
103 D2 Sopron Hungary
74 B1 Sopur Jammu and Kashmir
108 B2 Sora Italy
130 C3 Sorel Can.
51 D4 Sorell Austr.
106 C1 Soria Spain
90 B2 Soroca Moldova
154 C2 Sorocaba Brazil
87 E3 Sorochinsk Rus. Fed.
Soroki Moldova see Soroca
59 D2 Sorol atoll Micronesia
59 C3 Sorong Indon.
119 D2 Soroti Uganda
92 H1 Sørøya i. Norway
108 B2 Sorrento Italy
92 G2 Sorsele Sweden
64 B2 Sorsogon Phil.
86 C2 Sortavala Rus. Fed.
92 G2 Sortland Norway
65 B2 Sŏsan S. Korea
123 C2 Soshanguve S. Africa
89 E3 Sosna r. Rus. Fed.
153 B3 Sosneado mt. Arg.
86 E2 Sosnogorsk Rus. Fed.
86 D2 Sosnovka Rus. Fed.
88 C2 Sosnovyy Bor Rus. Fed.
103 D1 Sosnowiec Pol.
91 C1 Sosnytsya Ukr.
86 F3 Sos'va Rus. Fed.
91 C2 Sosyka r. Rus. Fed.
145 C2 Soto la Marina Mex.
118 B2 Souanké Congo
111 B3 Souda Greece
104 C3 Souillac France
Sŏul S. Korea see Seoul
104 B2 Soulac-sur-Mer France

Soulom

214

104 B3 Soulom France
Soûr Lebanon *see* Tyre
107 D2 Sour el Ghozlane Alg.
129 D3 Souris *Man.* Can.
131 D3 Souris *P.E.I.* Can.
129 E3 Souris *r.* Can.
151 F3 Sousa Brazil
115 D1 Sousse Tunisia
104 B3 Soustons France
122 B3 South Africa, Republic of *country* Africa
99 C4 Southampton U.K.
129 F1 Southampton, Cape Can.
129 F1 Southampton Island Can.
73 D3 South Andaman *i.* India
52 A1 South Australia *state* Austr.
140 B2 Southaven U.S.A.
142 B2 South Baldy *mt.* U.S.A.
130 B3 South Baymouth Can.
138 B2 South Bend U.S.A.
141 D2 South Carolina *state* U.S.A.
58 B2 South China Sea N. Pacific Ocean
South Coast Town Austr. *see* Gold Coast
136 C2 South Dakota *state* U.S.A.
99 C4 South Downs *hills* U.K.
159 E6 Southeast Indian Ridge *sea feature* Indian Ocean
55 O2 Southeast Pacific Basin *sea feature* S. Pacific Ocean
129 D2 Southend Can.
99 D4 Southend-on-Sea U.K.
54 B2 Southern Alps *mts* N.Z.
50 A3 Southern Cross Austr.
129 E2 Southern Indian Lake Can.
159 D7 Southern Ocean
141 E1 Southern Pines U.S.A.
Southern Rhodesia *country* Africa *see* Zimbabwe
96 B3 Southern Uplands *hills* U.K.
55 J2 South Geomagnetic Pole Antarctica
149 G8 South Georgia *terr.* S. Atlantic Ocean
149 G8 South Georgia and South Sandwich Islands *terr.* S. Atlantic Ocean
138 B2 South Haven U.S.A.
129 E1 South Henik Lake Can.
119 D2 South Horr Kenya
54 B2 South Island N.Z.
65 B2 South Korea *country* Asia
135 B3 South Lake Tahoe U.S.A.
55 K3 South Magnetic Pole Antarctica
149 F9 South Orkney Islands S. Atlantic Ocean
136 C2 South Platte *r.* U.S.A.
98 B3 Southport U.K.
141 E2 Southport U.S.A.
130 C3 South River Can.
96 C1 South Ronaldsay *i.* U.K.
123 D3 South Sand Bluff *pt* S. Africa
149 H8 South Sandwich Islands S. Atlantic Ocean
55 C4 South Sandwich Trench *sea feature* S. Atlantic Ocean
129 D2 South Saskatchewan *r.* Can.
129 E2 South Seal *r.* Can.
149 E9 South Shetland Islands Antarctica
98 C2 South Shields U.K.
54 B1 South Taranaki Bight *b.* N.Z.
156 C8 South Tasman Rise *sea feature* Southern Ocean
130 C2 South Twin Island Can.
96 A2 South Uist *i.* U.K.
South-West Africa *country* Africa *see* Namibia
Southwest Peru Ridge *sea feature* S. Pacific Ocean *see* Nazca Ridge
53 D2 South West Rocks Austr.
99 D3 Southwold U.K.
109 C3 Soverato Italy
88 B2 Sovetsk Rus. Fed.
86 F2 Sovetskiy Rus. Fed.
91 C2 Sovyets'kyy Ukr.
123 C2 Soweto S. Africa
66 D1 Sōya-misaki *c.* Japan
65 B2 Soyang-ho *l.* S. Korea
104 C2 Soyaux France
90 C1 Sozh *r.* Europe
110 C2 Sozopol Bulg.
100 B2 Spa Belgium
106 C1 Spain *country* Europe
Spalato Croatia *see* Split
99 C3 Spalding U.K.
135 D2 Spanish Fork U.S.A.
Spanish Guinea *country* Africa *see* Equatorial Guinea
97 B2 Spanish Point Ireland
Spanish Sahara *terr.* Africa *see* Western Sahara
146 C3 Spanish Town Jamaica
108 B3 Sparagio, Monte *mt. Sicily* Italy
135 C3 Sparks U.S.A.
138 A2 Sparta U.S.A.
141 D2 Spartanburg U.S.A.
111 B3 Sparti Greece
109 C3 Spartivento, Capo *c.* Italy
89 D3 Spas-Demensk Rus. Fed.
89 F2 Spas-Klepiki Rus. Fed.
66 B2 Spassk-Dal'niy Rus. Fed.
89 F3 Spassk-Ryazanskiy Rus. Fed.
111 B3 Spatha, Akra *pt* Greece
96 B2 Spean Bridge U.K.
136 C2 Spearfish U.S.A.
143 C1 Spearman U.S.A.
Spence Bay Can. *see* Taloyoak
137 D2 Spencer *IA* U.S.A.
134 D2 Spencer *ID* U.S.A.
52 A2 Spencer Gulf *est.* Austr.
98 C2 Spennymoor U.K.
54 B2 Spenser Mountains N.Z.
101 D3 Spessart *reg.* Ger.
96 C2 Spey *r.* U.K.
101 D3 Speyer Ger.
100 C1 Spiekeroog *i.* Ger.
100 B2 Spijkenisse Neth.
100 B3 Spincourt France
128 C2 Spirit River Can.
103 E2 Spišská Nová Ves Slovakia
82 C1 Spitsbergen *i.* Svalbard
102 C2 Spittal an der Drau Austria
93 E3 Spjelkavik Norway
109 C2 Split Croatia
129 E2 Split Lake Can.
129 E2 Split Lake *l.* Can.
134 C1 Spokane U.S.A.
138 A1 Spooner U.S.A.
102 C1 Spree *r.* Ger.
122 A2 Springbok S. Africa
131 E3 Springdale Can.
140 B1 Springdale U.S.A.
101 D1 Springe Ger.
142 C1 Springer U.S.A.
142 B2 Springerville U.S.A.
136 C3 Springfield *CO* U.S.A.
138 B3 Springfield *IL* U.S.A.
139 E2 Springfield *MA* U.S.A.
137 E3 Springfield *MO* U.S.A.
138 C3 Springfield *OH* U.S.A.
134 B2 Springfield *OR* U.S.A.
140 C1 Springfield *TN* U.S.A.
123 C3 Springfontein S. Africa
131 D3 Springhill Can.
141 D3 Spring Hill U.S.A.
54 B2 Springs Junction N.Z.
51 D2 Springsure Austr.
135 D2 Springville U.S.A.
98 D3 Spurn Head *hd* U.K.
128 B3 Squamish Can.
109 C3 Squillace, Golfo di *g.* Italy
109 D2 Srbija *aut. rep.* Serb. and Mont.
108 C2 Srebrenica Bos.-Herz.
110 C2 Sredets Bulg.
83 L3 Sredinnyy Khrebet *mts* Rus. Fed.
83 L2 Srednekolymsk Rus. Fed.
Sredne-Russkaya Vozvyshennost' *hills* Rus. Fed. *see* Central Russian Upland
Sredne-Sibirskoye Ploskogor'ye Rus. Fed. *see* Central Siberian Plateau
110 B2 Srednogorie Bulg.
69 D1 Sretensk Rus. Fed.
61 C1 Sri Aman *Sarawak* Malaysia
73 B4 Sri Jayewardenepura Kotte Sri Lanka
73 C3 Srikakulam India
73 C4 Sri Lanka *country* Asia
74 B1 Srinagar Jammu and Kashmir
73 B3 Srivardhan India
101 D1 Stade Ger.
101 E1 Stadensen Ger.
100 C1 Stadskanaal Neth.
101 D2 Stadtallendorf Ger.
101 D1 Stadthagen Ger.
101 E2 Staffelstein Ger.
99 B3 Stafford U.K.
99 C4 Staines U.K.
91 D2 Stakhanov Ukr.
Stakhanovo Rus. Fed. *see* Zhukovskiy
Stalin Bulg. *see* Varna
Stalinabad Tajik. *see* Dushanbe
Stalingrad Rus. Fed. *see* Volgograd
Staliniri Georgia *see* Ts'khinvali
Stalino Ukr. *see* Donets'k
Stalinogorsk Rus. Fed. *see* Novomoskovsk
Stalinogród Pol. *see* Katowice
Stalinsk Rus. Fed. *see* Novokuznetsk
103 E1 Stalowa Wola Pol.
138 B1 Stambaugh U.S.A.
99 C3 Stamford U.K.
139 E2 Stamford *CT* U.S.A.
143 D2 Stamford *TX* U.S.A.
Stampalia *i.* Greece *see* Astypalaia
122 A1 Stampriet Namibia
92 F2 Stamsund Norway
123 C2 Standerton S. Africa
138 C2 Standish U.S.A.
123 D2 Stanger S. Africa
Stanislav Ukr. *see* Ivano-Frankivs'k
Stanke Dimitrov Bulg. *see* Dupnitsa
153 C5 Stanley Falkland Is
136 C1 Stanley U.S.A.
Stanleyville Dem. Rep. Congo *see* Kisangani
Stann Creek Belize *see* Dangriga
111 B3 Stanos Greece
83 I3 Stanovoye Nagor'ye *mts* Rus. Fed.
83 J3 Stanovoy Khrebet *mts* Rus. Fed.
53 D1 Stanthorpe Austr.
137 E1 Staples U.S.A.
103 E1 Starachowice Pol.
Stara Planina *mts* Bulg./Serb. and Mont. *see* Balkan Mountains
89 D2 Staraya Russa Rus. Fed.
89 D2 Staraya Toropa Rus. Fed.
110 C2 Stara Zagora Bulg.
49 L4 Starbuck Island Kiribati
103 D1 Stargard Szczeciński Pol.
89 D2 Staritsa Rus. Fed.
141 D3 Starke U.S.A.
140 C2 Starkville U.S.A.
102 C2 Starnberg Ger.
91 D2 Starobil's'k Ukr.
89 D3 Starodub Rus. Fed.
103 D1 Starogard Gdański Pol.
90 B2 Starokostyantyniv Ukr.
91 D2 Starominskaya Rus. Fed.
91 D2 Staroshcherbinovskaya Rus. Fed.
91 D2 Starotitarovskaya Rus. Fed.
89 F3 Staroyur'yevo Rus. Fed.
89 E3 Starozhilovo Rus. Fed.
99 B4 Start Point U.K.
88 C3 Staryya Darohi Belarus
86 G2 Staryy Nadym Rus. Fed.
89 E3 Staryy Oskol Rus. Fed.
101 E2 Staßfurt Ger.
103 E1 Staszów Pol.
139 D2 State College U.S.A.
141 D2 Statesboro U.S.A.
141 D1 Statesville U.S.A.
160 L1 Station Nord Greenland
139 D3 Staunton U.S.A.
93 E4 Stavanger Norway
87 D4 Stavropol' Rus. Fed.
Stavropol'-na-Volge Rus. Fed. *see* Tol'yatti
87 D4 Stavropol'skaya Vozvyshennost' *hills* Rus. Fed.
52 B3 Stawell Austr.
123 C2 Steadville S. Africa
136 B2 Steamboat Springs U.S.A.
101 E2 Stedten Ger.
128 C2 Steen River Can.
134 C2 Steens Mountain U.S.A.
100 C1 Steenwijk Neth.
126 E2 Stefansson Island Can.
Stegi Swaziland *see* Siteki
110 B1 Ştei Romania
101 E3 Steigerwald *mts* Ger.
100 B2 Stein Neth.
129 E3 Steinbach Can.
100 C1 Steinfurt Ger.
120 A3 Steinhausen Namibia
92 F3 Steinkjer Norway
122 A2 Steinkopf S. Africa
122 B2 Stella S. Africa
122 A3 Stellenbosch S. Africa
105 D3 Stello, Monte *mt. Corsica* France
105 D2 Stenay France
101 E1 Stendal Ger.
Steornabhagh U.K. *see* Stornoway
Stepanakert Azer. *see* Xankändi
52 B2 Stephens Creek Austr.
129 E2 Stephens Lake Can.
131 E3 Stephenville Can.
143 D2 Stephenville U.S.A.
Stepnoy Rus. Fed. *see* Elista
122 B3 Sterling S. Africa
136 C2 Sterling *CO* U.S.A.
138 B2 Sterling *IL* U.S.A.
136 C1 Sterling *ND* U.S.A.
138 C2 Sterling Heights U.S.A.
87 E3 Sterlitamak Rus. Fed.
101 E1 Sternberg Ger.
128 C2 Stettler Can.
138 C2 Steubenville U.S.A.
99 C4 Stevenage U.K.
129 E2 Stevenson Lake Can.
138 B2 Stevens Point U.S.A.
126 C2 Stevens Village U.S.A.
134 D1 Stevensville U.S.A.
128 B2 Stewart Can.
128 A1 Stewart *r.* Can.
54 A3 Stewart Island N.Z.
127 G2 Stewart Lake Can.
123 C3 Steynsburg S. Africa
102 C2 Steyr Austria
122 B3 Steytlerville S. Africa
128 A2 Stikine *r.* Can.
128 A2 Stikine Plateau Can.
122 B3 Stilbaai S. Africa
137 E1 Stillwater *MN* U.S.A.
143 D1 Stillwater *OK* U.S.A.
135 C3 Stillwater Range *mts* U.S.A.
109 D2 Štip Macedonia
96 C2 Stirling U.K.
52 A2 Stirling North Austr.
92 F3 Stjørdalshalsen Norway
103 D2 Stockerau Austria
93 G4 Stockholm Sweden
98 B3 Stockport U.K.
135 B3 Stockton U.S.A.
98 C2 Stockton-on-Tees U.K.
143 C2 Stockton Plateau U.S.A.
63 B2 Stœng Trêng Cambodia
96 B1 Stoer, Point of U.K.
99 B3 Stoke-on-Trent U.K.
98 C2 Stokesley U.K.
92 F2 Stokmarknes Norway
110 B2 Stol *mt.* Serb. and Mont.
109 C2 Stolac Bos.-Herz.
100 C2 Stolberg (Rheinland) Ger.
82 E2 Stolbovoy Rus. Fed.
88 C3 Stolin Belarus
101 F2 Stollberg Ger.
101 D1 Stolzenau Ger.
96 C2 Stonehaven U.K.
99 C4 Stonehenge *tourist site* U.K.
129 E2 Stonewall Can.
129 D2 Stony Rapids Can.
92 G2 Storavan *l.* Sweden
Store Bælt *sea chan.* Denmark *see* Great Belt
92 F3 Støren Norway
92 I1 Storfjordbotn Norway
92 F2 Storforshei Norway
126 E2 Storkerson Peninsula Can.
137 D2 Storm Lake U.S.A.
93 E3 Stornosa *mt.* Norway
96 A1 Stornoway U.K.
86 E2 Storozhevsk Rus. Fed.
90 B2 Storozhynets' Ukr.
92 F3 Storsjön *l.* Sweden
92 H2 Storslett Norway
92 G2 Storuman Sweden
92 G2 Storuman *l.* Sweden
99 C4 Stour *r. England* U.K.
99 D4 Stour *r. England* U.K.
99 C3 Stour *r. England* U.K.
130 A2 Stout Lake Can.
88 C3 Stowbtsy Belarus
99 D3 Stowmarket U.K.
97 C1 Strabane U.K.
102 C2 Strakonice Czech Rep.
102 C1 Stralsund Ger.
122 A3 Strand S. Africa
93 E3 Stranda Norway
97 D1 Strangford Lough *inlet* U.K.
96 B3 Stranraer U.K.
105 D2 Strasbourg France
130 B3 Stratford Can.
54 B1 Stratford N.Z.
143 C1 Stratford U.S.A.
99 C3 Stratford-upon-Avon U.K.
128 C2 Strathmore Can.
96 C2 Strathspey *val.* U.K.
102 C2 Straubing Ger.
134 C2 Strawberry Mountain U.S.A.
51 C3 Streaky Bay Austr.
138 B2 Streator U.S.A.
99 B4 Street U.K.
110 B2 Strehaia Romania
94 B1 Streymoy *i.* Faroe Is
82 G2 Strezhevoy Rus. Fed.
101 F3 Stříbro Czech Rep.
111 B2 Strimonas *r.* Greece
153 B4 Stroeder Arg.
101 D1 Ströhen Ger.
109 C3 Stromboli, Isola *i.* Italy
96 B2 Stromeferry U.K.
96 C1 Stromness U.K.
92 G3 Strömsund Sweden
96 C1 Stronsay *i.* U.K.
53 D2 Stroud Austr.
99 B4 Stroud U.K.
100 C1 Strücklingen (Saterland) Ger.
111 B2 Struga Macedonia
88 C2 Strugi-Krasnyye Rus. Fed.
122 B3 Struis Bay S. Africa
111 B2 Struma *r.* Bulg.
99 A3 Strumble Head *hd* U.K.
111 B2 Strumica Macedonia
122 B2 Strydenburg S. Africa
93 E3 Stryn Norway
90 A2 Stryy Ukr.
90 A2 Stryy *r.* Ukr.
128 B2 Stuart Lake Can.
53 C2 Stuart Town Austr.
Stuchka Latvia *see* Aizkraukle
Stučka Latvia *see* Aizkraukle
130 A2 Stull Lake Can.
89 E3 Stupino Rus. Fed.
55 M3 Sturge Island Antarctica
138 B2 Sturgeon Bay U.S.A.
130 C3 Sturgeon Falls Can.
130 A3 Sturgeon Lake Can.
138 B2 Sturgis *MI* U.S.A.
136 C2 Sturgis *SD* U.S.A.
52 B1 Sturt, Mount *hill* Austr.
50 B1 Sturt Creek *watercourse* Austr.
50 C1 Sturt Plain Austr.
52 B1 Sturt Stony Desert Austr.
123 C3 Stutterheim S. Africa
102 B2 Stuttgart Ger.
140 B2 Stuttgart U.S.A.
92 □A2 Stykkishólmur Iceland
90 B1 Styr *r.* Belarus/Ukr.
155 D1 Suaçuí Grande *r.* Brazil
116 B3 Suakin Sudan
71 C3 Suao Taiwan
78 A3 Suara, Mount Eritrea
60 B1 Subi Besar *i.* Indon.
109 C1 Subotica Serb. and Mont.
110 C1 Suceava Romania
Suchan Rus. Fed. *see* Partizansk
97 B2 Suck *r.* Ireland
152 B1 Sucre Bol.
154 B2 Sucuriú *r.* Brazil
Suczawa Romania *see* Suceava
89 E2 Suda Rus. Fed.
91 C3 Sudak Ukr.
116 A3 Sudan *country* Africa
130 B3 Sudbury Can.
99 D3 Sudbury U.K.
117 A4 Sudd *swamp* Sudan
89 F2 Sudislavl' Rus. Fed.

89 F2 **Sudogda** Rus. Fed.
94 B1 **Suðuroy** *i.* Faroe Is
89 E3 **Sudzha** Rus. Fed.
107 C2 **Sueca** Spain
116 B2 **Suez** Egypt
116 B2 **Suez, Gulf of** Egypt
80 B2 **Suez Canal** *canal* Egypt
139 D3 **Suffolk** U.S.A.
140 A3 **Sugar Land** U.S.A.
139 E1 **Sugarloaf Mountain** U.S.A.
53 D2 **Sugarloaf Point** Austr.
70 A2 **Suhait** China
70 C2 **Şuḩār** Oman
68 D1 **Sühbaatar** Mongolia
101 E2 **Suhl** Ger.
109 C1 **Suhopolje** Croatia
70 B2 **Suide** China
66 B2 **Suifenhe** China
69 E1 **Suihua** China
70 A2 **Suining** China
70 B2 **Suiping** China
97 C2 **Suir** *r.* Ireland
**Suixian** China *see* Suizhou
70 B2 **Suiyang** China
70 B2 **Suizhou** China
74 B2 **Sujangarh** India
74 B1 **Sujanpur** India
74 A2 **Sujawal** Pak.
60 B2 **Sukabumi** Indon.
60 B2 **Sukadana** Indon.
67 D3 **Sukagawa** Japan
60 C2 **Sukaraja** Indon.
**Sukarnapura** Indon. *see* Jayapura
**Sukarno, Puntjak** *mt.* Indon. *see* Jaya, Puncak
89 E3 **Sukhinichi** Rus. Fed.
89 F2 **Sukhona** *r.* Rus. Fed.
62 A2 **Sukhothai** Thai.
74 A2 **Sukkur** Pak.
89 E2 **Sukromny** Rus. Fed.
59 C3 **Sula, Kepulauan** *is* Indon.
74 A1 **Sulaiman Range** *mts* Pak.
**Sulawesi** *i.* Indon. *see* Celebes
101 D1 **Sulingen** Ger.
150 A3 **Sullana** Peru
138 B3 **Sullivan** *IN* U.S.A.
137 E3 **Sullivan** *MO* U.S.A.
140 B2 **Sulphur** U.S.A.
143 D2 **Sulphur Springs** U.S.A.
138 C1 **Sultan** Can.
**Sultanabad** Iran *see* Arāk
64 B3 **Sulu Archipelago** *is* Phil.
64 A3 **Sulu Sea** N. Pacific Ocean
101 E3 **Sulzbach-Rosenberg** Ger.
79 C2 **Sumāïl** Oman
**Sumatera** *i.* Indon. *see* Sumatra
60 A1 **Sumatra** *i.* Indon.
61 D2 **Sumba** *i.* Indon.
61 C2 **Sumba, Selat** *sea chan.* Indon.
61 C2 **Sumbawa** *i.* Indon.
61 C2 **Sumbawabesar** Indon.
119 D3 **Sumbawanga** Tanz.
120 A2 **Sumbe** Angola
96 □ **Sumburgh** U.K.
96 □ **Sumburgh Head** *hd* U.K.
119 C2 **Sumeih** Sudan
61 C2 **Sumenep** Indon.
67 D4 **Sumisu-jima** *i.* Japan
131 D3 **Summerside** Can.
138 C3 **Summersville** U.S.A.
141 D2 **Summerville** U.S.A.
137 D1 **Summit** U.S.A.
128 B2 **Summit Lake** Can.
103 D2 **Šumperk** Czech Rep.
81 C1 **Sumqayıt** Azer.
141 D2 **Sumter** U.S.A.
91 C1 **Sumy** Ukr.
75 D2 **Sunamganj** Bangl.
65 B2 **Sunan** N. Korea
79 C2 **Şunaynah** Oman
52 B3 **Sunbury** Austr.
139 D2 **Sunbury** U.S.A.
65 B2 **Sunch'ŏn** N. Korea
65 B3 **Sunch'ŏn** S. Korea
123 C2 **Sun City** S. Africa
93 H3 **Sund** Fin.
60 B2 **Sunda, Selat** *str.* Indon.
136 C2 **Sundance** U.S.A.
75 C2 **Sundarbans** *reg.* Bangl./India
74 B1 **Sundarnagar** India
**Sunda Strait** Indon. *see*
**Sunda, Selat**
**Sunda Trench** *sea feature*
Indian Ocean *see* Java Trench
98 C2 **Sunderland** U.K.
128 C2 **Sundre** Can.
93 G3 **Sundsvall** Sweden
123 D2 **Sundumbili** S. Africa
60 B2 **Sungailiat** Indon.
60 B2 **Sungaipenuh** Indon.
60 B1 **Sungai Petani** Malaysia
80 B1 **Sungurlu** Turkey
75 C2 **Sun Kosi** *r.* Nepal
93 E3 **Sunndalsøra** Norway
134 C1 **Sunnyside** U.S.A.
135 B3 **Sunnyvale** U.S.A.
141 D3 **Sunrise** U.S.A.
83 I2 **Suntar** Rus. Fed.
74 A2 **Suntsar** Pak.
114 B4 **Sunyani** Ghana
92 I3 **Suomussalmi** Fin.
67 B4 **Suō-nada** *b.* Japan
86 C2 **Suoyarvi** Rus. Fed.
142 A2 **Superior** *AZ* U.S.A.
137 D2 **Superior** *NE* U.S.A.

138 A1 **Superior** *WI* U.S.A.
138 B1 **Superior, Lake** Can./U.S.A.
63 B2 **Suphan Buri** Thai.
81 C2 **Süphan Dağı** *mt.* Turkey
89 D3 **Suponevo** Rus. Fed.
81 C2 **Sūq ash Shuyūkh** Iraq
70 B2 **Suqian** China
78 A2 **Sūq Suwayq** Saudi Arabia
**Suquṭrā** *i.* Yemen *see* Socotra
79 C2 **Şūr** Oman
74 A2 **Surab** Pak.
61 C2 **Surabaya** Indon.
61 C2 **Surakarta** Indon.
74 B2 **Surat** India
74 B2 **Suratgarh** India
63 A3 **Surat Thani** Thai.
89 D3 **Surazh** Rus. Fed.
109 D2 **Surdulica** Serb. and Mont.
100 C3 **Sûre** *r.* Lux.
74 B2 **Surendranagar** India
82 F2 **Surgut** Rus. Fed.
64 B3 **Surigao** Phil.
63 B2 **Surin** Thai.
151 D2 **Suriname** *country* S. America
75 C3 **Surkhet** Nepal
**Surt** Libya *see* Sirte
**Surt, Khalīj** *g.* Libya *see*
Sirte, Gulf of
60 B2 **Surulangun** Indon.
81 C2 **Süsangerd** Iran
89 F2 **Susanino** Rus. Fed.
135 B2 **Susanville** U.S.A.
80 B1 **Suşehri** Turkey
139 D3 **Susquehanna** *r.* U.S.A.
131 D3 **Sussex** Can.
101 D1 **Süstedt** Ger.
100 C1 **Sustrum** Ger.
83 K2 **Susuman** Rus. Fed.
111 C3 **Susurluk** Turkey
74 B1 **Sutak** Jammu and Kashmir
53 D2 **Sutherland** Austr.
122 B3 **Sutherland** S. Africa
136 C2 **Sutherland** U.S.A.
134 B2 **Sutherlin** U.S.A.
74 B2 **Sutlej** *r.* India/Pak.
138 C3 **Sutton** U.S.A.
99 C3 **Sutton Coldfield** U.K.
98 C3 **Sutton in Ashfield** U.K.
66 D2 **Suttsu** Japan
49 I5 **Suva** Fiji
**Suvalki** Pol. *see* Suwałki
89 E3 **Suvorov** Rus. Fed.
90 B2 **Suvorove** Ukr.
103 E1 **Suwałki** Pol.
141 D3 **Suwanee Sound** *b.* U.S.A.
62 B2 **Suwannaphum** Thai.
141 D3 **Suwannee** *r.* U.S.A.
**Suways, Qanāt as** *canal* Egypt *see*
Suez Canal
65 B2 **Suwŏn** S. Korea
79 C2 **Sūza** Iran
89 F2 **Suzdal'** Rus. Fed.
89 D3 **Suzemka** Rus. Fed.
70 B2 **Suzhou** *Anhui* China
70 C2 **Suzhou** *Jiangsu* China
67 C3 **Suzu** Japan
67 C3 **Suzu-misaki** *pt* Japan
82 B1 **Svalbard** *terr.* Arctic Ocean
90 A2 **Svalyava** Ukr.
92 H2 **Svappavaara** Sweden
91 D2 **Svatove** Ukr.
63 B2 **Svay Riěng** Cambodia
93 F3 **Sveg** Sweden
88 C2 **Švenčionys** Lith.
93 F4 **Svendborg** Denmark
**Sverdlovsk** Rus. Fed. *see*
Yekaterinburg
111 B2 **Sveti Nikole** Macedonia
66 C1 **Svetlaya** Rus. Fed.
88 B3 **Svetlogorsk** Rus. Fed.
87 D4 **Svetlograd** Rus. Fed.
88 B3 **Svetlyy** Rus. Fed.
93 I3 **Svetogorsk** Rus. Fed.
103 E2 **Svidník** Slovakia
111 C3 **Svilengrad** Bulg.
110 B2 **Svinecea Mare, Vârful** *mt.*
Romania
110 C2 **Svishtov** Bulg.
88 B3 **Svislach** Belarus
103 D2 **Svitavy** Czech Rep.
91 C2 **Svitlovods'k** Ukr.
69 E1 **Svobodnyy** Rus. Fed.
110 B2 **Svoge** Bulg.
92 F2 **Svolvær** Norway
88 C3 **Svyetlahorsk** Belarus
141 D2 **Swainsboro** U.S.A.
120 A3 **Swakopmund** Namibia
52 A3 **Swan Hill** Austr.
128 C2 **Swan Hills** Can.
129 D2 **Swan Lake** Can.
97 C2 **Swanlinbar** Ireland
129 D2 **Swan River** Can.
53 D2 **Swansea** Austr.
99 B4 **Swansea** U.K.
122 B3 **Swartkolkvloer** *salt pan* S. Africa
123 C2 **Swartruggens** S. Africa
**Swatow** China *see* Shantou
123 D2 **Swaziland** *country* Africa
93 G3 **Sweden** *country* Europe
143 C2 **Sweetwater** U.S.A.
136 B2 **Sweetwater** *r.* U.S.A.
122 B3 **Swellendam** S. Africa
103 D1 **Świdnica** Pol.
103 E1 **Świdnik** Pol.
103 D1 **Świdwin** Pol.
103 D1 **Świebodzin** Pol.

103 D1 **Świecie** Pol.
129 D2 **Swift Current** Can.
97 C1 **Swilly, Lough** *inlet* Ireland
99 C4 **Swindon** U.K.
102 C1 **Świnoujście** Pol.
105 D2 **Switzerland** *country* Europe
97 C2 **Swords** Ireland
88 C3 **Syanno** Belarus
89 D1 **Syas'troy** Rus. Fed.
89 D2 **Sychevka** Rus. Fed.
53 D2 **Sydney** Austr.
131 D3 **Sydney** Can.
131 D3 **Sydney Mines** Can.
91 D2 **Syeverodonets'k** Ukr.
86 E2 **Syktyvkar** Rus. Fed.
140 C2 **Sylacauga** U.S.A.
75 D2 **Sylhet** Bangl.
102 B1 **Sylt** *i.* Ger.
138 C2 **Sylvania** U.S.A.
51 C1 **Sylvester, Lake** *salt flat* Austr.
111 C3 **Symi** *i.* Greece
91 D2 **Synel'nykove** Ukr.
90 C2 **Synyukha** *r.* Ukr.
109 C3 **Syracuse** *Sicily* Italy
136 C3 **Syracuse** *KS* U.S.A.
139 D2 **Syracuse** *NY* U.S.A.
77 C2 **Syrdar'ya** *r.* Asia
80 B2 **Syria** *country* Asia
80 B2 **Syrian Desert** Asia
111 B3 **Syros** *i.* Greece
91 C2 **Syvash, Zatoka** *lag.* Ukr.
91 C2 **Syvas'ke** Ukr.
87 D3 **Syzran'** Rus. Fed.
102 C1 **Szczecin** Pol.
103 D1 **Szczecinek** Pol.
103 E1 **Szczytno** Pol.
**Szechwan** *prov.* China *see*
Sichuan
103 E2 **Szeged** Hungary
103 D2 **Székesfehérvár** Hungary
103 D2 **Szekszárd** Hungary
103 E2 **Szentes** Hungary
103 D2 **Szentgotthárd** Hungary
103 D2 **Szerencs** Hungary
103 D2 **Szigetvár** Hungary
103 E2 **Szolnok** Hungary
103 D2 **Szombathely** Hungary
**Sztálinváros** Hungary *see*
Dunaújváros

**T**

117 C4 **Taagga Duudka** *reg.* Somalia
64 B2 **Tabaco** Phil.
78 B2 **Tābah** Saudi Arabia
108 A3 **Tabarka** Tunisia
76 B3 **Ṭabas** Iran
79 C1 **Tabāsín** Iran
81 D3 **Tābask, Kūh-e** *mt.* Iran
150 A3 **Tabatinga** Brazil
154 C2 **Tabatinga** Brazil
114 B2 **Tabelbala** Alg.
128 C3 **Taber** Can.
64 B2 **Tablas** *i.* Phil.
102 C2 **Tábor** Czech Rep.
119 D3 **Tabora** Tanz.
114 B4 **Tabou** Côte d'Ivoire
81 C2 **Tabriz** Iran
48 L3 **Tabuaeran** *i.* Kiribati
78 A2 **Tabūk** Saudi Arabia
93 G4 **Täby** Sweden
77 E2 **Tacheng** China
102 C2 **Tachov** Czech Rep.
64 B2 **Tacloban** Phil.
150 B4 **Tacna** Peru
134 B1 **Tacoma** U.S.A.
152 C2 **Tacuarembó** Uru.
142 B3 **Tacupeto** Mex.
114 C2 **Tademaït, Plateau du** Alg.
**Tadjikistan** *country* Asia *see*
Tajikistan
117 C3 **Tadjoura** Djibouti
80 B2 **Tadmur** Syria
129 E2 **Tadoule Lake** Can.
**Tadzhikskaya S.S.R.** *admin. reg.*
Asia *see* Tajikistan
65 B2 **T'aebaek-sanmaek** *mts*
N. Korea/S. Korea
**Taech'ŏn** S. Korea *see* Poryŏng
65 B2 **Taegu** S. Korea
65 B2 **Taejŏn** S. Korea
65 B3 **Taejŏng** S. Korea
65 B2 **T'aepaek** S. Korea
69 E1 **Ta'erqi** China
107 C1 **Tafalla** Spain
152 B2 **Tafí Viejo** Arg.
79 D2 **Taftān, Kūh-e** *mt.* Iran
91 D2 **Taganrog** Rus. Fed.
91 D2 **Taganrog, Gulf of** Rus. Fed./Ukr.
62 A1 **Tagaung** Myanmar
64 B2 **Tagaytay City** Phil.
64 B3 **Tagbilaran** Phil.
64 B2 **Tagudin** Phil.
51 E1 **Tagula Island** P.N.G.
64 B3 **Tagum** Phil.
106 B2 **Tagus** *r.* Port./Spain
60 B1 **Tahan, Gunung** *mt.* Malaysia
115 C2 **Tahat, Mont** *mt.* Alg.
69 E1 **Tahe** China
49 M5 **Tahiti** *i.* Fr. Polynesia
143 E1 **Tahlequah** U.S.A.
135 B3 **Tahoe, Lake** U.S.A.
135 B3 **Tahoe City** U.S.A.

126 E2 **Tahoe Lake** Can.
115 C3 **Tahoua** Niger
79 C2 **Tahrūd** Iran
128 B3 **Tahsis** Can.
116 B2 **Ṭahṭā** Egypt
64 B3 **Tahuna** Indon.
70 B2 **Tai'an** China
70 A2 **Taibai Shan** *mt.* China
**Taibus Qi** China *see* Baochang
71 C3 **T'aichung** Taiwan
70 B2 **Taihang Shan** *mts* China
54 C1 **Taihape** N.Z.
71 B3 **Taihe** China
70 C2 **Tai Hu** *l.* China
52 A3 **Tailem Bend** Austr.
71 C3 **T'ainan** Taiwan
111 B3 **Tainaro, Akra** *pt* Greece
155 D1 **Taiobeiras** Brazil
71 C3 **T'aipei** Taiwan
**Taiping** China *see* Chongzuo
60 B1 **Taiping** Malaysia
**Tairbeart** U.K. *see* Tarbert
71 B3 **Taishan** China
70 B2 **Tai Shan** *hills* China
119 D3 **Taita Hills** Kenya
153 A4 **Taitao, Península de** *pen.* Chile
71 C3 **T'aitung** Taiwan
92 I2 **Taivalkoski** Fin.
92 H2 **Taivaskero** *hill* Fin.
71 C3 **Taiwan** Asia
**Taiwan Shan** *mts* Taiwan *see*
Chungyang Shanmo
71 B3 **Taiwan Strait** China/Taiwan
70 B2 **Taiyuan** China
70 B2 **Taizhou** *Jiangsu* China
71 C3 **Taizhou** *Zhejiang* China
78 B3 **Ta'izz** Yemen
145 C3 **Tajumulco, Volcán de** *vol.* Guat.
77 D3 **Tajikistan** *country* Asia
74 B2 **Taj Mahal** *tourist site* India
**Tajo** *r.* Spain *see* Tagus
63 A2 **Tak** Thai.
54 B2 **Takaka** N.Z.
115 C2 **Takalous, Oued** *watercourse* Alg.
67 B4 **Takamatsu** Japan
67 C3 **Takaoka** Japan
54 B1 **Takapuna** N.Z.
67 C3 **Takasaki** Japan
122 B1 **Takatokwane** Botswana
122 B1 **Takatshwaane** Botswana
67 C3 **Takayama** Japan
67 C3 **Takefu** Japan
60 A1 **Takengon** Indon.
63 B2 **Takêv** Cambodia
**Takhiatash** Uzbek. *see* Taxiatosh
63 B2 **Ta Khmau** Cambodia
74 B1 **Takht-i-Sulaiman** *mt.* Pak.
66 D2 **Takikawa** Japan
128 B2 **Takla Lake** Can.
128 B2 **Takla Landing** Can.
**Takla Makan** *des.* China *see*
Taklimakan Desert
77 E3 **Taklimakan Desert** *des.* China
**Taklimakan Shamo** China *see*
Taklimakan Desert
128 A2 **Taku** *r.* Can./U.S.A.
63 A3 **Takua Pa** Thai.
115 C4 **Takum** Nigeria
88 C3 **Talachyn** Belarus
74 B1 **Talagang** Pak.
146 B4 **Talamanca, Cordillera de** *mts*
Costa Rica
150 A3 **Talara** Peru
59 C2 **Talaud, Kepulauan** *is* Indon.
106 C2 **Talavera de la Reina** Spain
153 A3 **Talca** Chile
153 A3 **Talcahuano** Chile
89 E2 **Taldom** Rus. Fed.
77 D2 **Taldykorgan** Kazakh.
**Taldy-Kurgan** Kazakh. *see*
Taldykorgan
59 C3 **Taliabu** *i.* Indon.
64 B2 **Talisay** Phil.
61 C2 **Taliwang** Indon.
81 C2 **Tall 'Afar** Iraq
141 D2 **Tallahassee** U.S.A.
53 C3 **Tallangatta** Austr.
88 B2 **Tallinn** Estonia
140 B2 **Tallulah** U.S.A.
104 B2 **Talmont-St-Hilaire** France
90 C2 **Tal'ne** Ukr.
117 B3 **Talodi** Sudan
74 A1 **Tāloqān** Afgh.
91 A1 **Talovaya** Rus. Fed.
126 F2 **Taloyoak** Can.
88 B2 **Talsi** Latvia
152 A2 **Taltal** Chile
129 C1 **Taltson** *r.* Can.
60 A1 **Talu** Indon.
53 D2 **Talwood** Austr.
114 B4 **Tamale** Ghana
115 C2 **Tamanrasset** Alg.
99 A4 **Tamar** *r.* U.K.
**Tamatave** Madag. *see*
Toamasina
144 B2 **Tamazula** Mex.
145 C2 **Tamazunchale** Mex.
114 A3 **Tambacounda** Senegal
60 B1 **Tambelan, Kepulauan** *is* Indon.
86 E2 **Tambey** Rus. Fed.
61 C2 **Tambisan** *Sabah* Malaysia
61 C2 **Tambora, Gunung** *vol.* Indon.
91 E1 **Tambov** Rus. Fed.
119 C2 **Tambura** Sudan
62 A1 **Tamenglong** India

145 C2 **Tamiahua, Laguna de** *lag.* Mex.
**Tammerfors** Fin. *see* Tampere
141 D3 **Tampa** U.S.A.
141 D3 **Tampa Bay** U.S.A.
93 H3 **Tampere** Fin.
145 C2 **Tampico** Mex.
69 D1 **Tamsagbulag** Mongolia
102 C2 **Tamsweg** Austria
53 D2 **Tamworth** Austr.
99 C2 **Tamworth** U.K.
119 E3 **Tana** *r.* Kenya
**Tana, Lake** Eth. *see* Lake Tana
67 C4 **Tanabe** Japan
92 I1 **Tana Bru** Norway
60 A2 **Tanahbala** *i.* Indon.
61 C2 **Tanahgrogot** Indon.
61 D2 **Tanahjampea** *i.* Indon.
60 A2 **Tanahmasa** *i.* Indon.
50 C1 **Tanami Desert** Austr.
63 B2 **Tân An** Vietnam
126 B2 **Tanana** U.S.A.
**Tananarive** Madag. *see* Antananarivo
108 A1 **Tanaro** *r.* Italy
65 B3 **Tanch'ŏn** N. Korea
64 B3 **Tandag** Phil.
110 C2 **Ţăndărei** Romania
153 C3 **Tandil** Arg.
74 A2 **Tando Adam** Pak.
74 A2 **Tando Muhammmad Khan** Pak.
52 B2 **Tandou Lake** *imp. l.* Austr.
67 B4 **Tanega-shima** *i.* Japan
114 B2 **Tanezrouft** *reg.* Alg./Mali
119 D3 **Tanga** Tanz.
75 C2 **Tangail** Bangl.
**Tanganyika** *country* Africa *see* Tanzania
119 C3 **Tanganyika, Lake** Africa
55 F3 **Tange Promontory** *hd* Antarctica
**Tanger** *see* Tangier
101 E1 **Tangermünde** Ger.
75 D1 **Tanggulashan** China
75 C1 **Tanggula Shan** *mts* China
114 B1 **Tangier** Morocco
75 C1 **Tangra Yumco** *salt l.* China
70 B2 **Tangshan** China
68 C2 **Taniantaweng Shan** *mts* China
59 C3 **Tanimbar, Kepulauan** *is* Indon.
64 B3 **Tanjay** Phil.
61 C2 **Tanjung** Indon.
60 A1 **Tanjungbalai** Indon.
**Tanjungkarang-Telukbetung** Indon. *see* Bandar Lampung
60 B2 **Tanjungpandan** Indon.
60 B1 **Tanjungpinang** Indon.
61 C1 **Tanjungredeb** Indon.
61 C1 **Tanjungselor** Indon.
74 B1 **Tank** Pak.
48 H5 **Tanna** *i.* Vanuatu
115 C3 **Tanout** Niger
75 C2 **Tansen** Nepal
116 B1 **Ţanţā** Egypt
114 A2 **Tan-Tan** Morocco
145 C2 **Tantoyuca** Mex.
119 D3 **Tanzania** *country* Africa
**Tao'an** China *see* Taonan
**Taocheng** China *see* Yongchun
**Taolanaro** Madag. *see* Tôlañaro
69 E1 **Taonan** China
109 C2 **Taormina** *Sicily* Italy
142 B1 **Taos** U.S.A.
114 B2 **Taoudenni** Mali
114 B1 **Taounate** Morocco
114 B1 **Taourirt** Morocco
88 C2 **Tapa** Estonia
145 C3 **Tapachula** Mex.
151 D3 **Tapajós** *r.* Brazil
60 A1 **Tapaktuan** Indon.
145 C3 **Tapanatepec** Mex.
150 C3 **Tapauá** Brazil
152 C2 **Tapera** Brazil
114 B4 **Tapeta** Liberia
74 B2 **Tapi** *r.* India
139 D3 **Tappahannock** U.S.A.
54 B2 **Tapuaenuku** *mt.* N.Z.
150 C3 **Tapurucuara** Brazil
154 B1 **Taquaral, Serra do** *hills* Brazil
154 A1 **Taquarí** *r.* Brazil
154 B1 **Taquari, Serra do** *hills* Brazil
154 C2 **Taquaritinga** Brazil
53 D1 **Tara** Austr.
115 D4 **Taraba** *r.* Nigeria
**Ţarābulus** Libya *see* Tripoli
54 C1 **Taradale** N.Z.
61 C1 **Tarakan** Indon.
111 D2 **Taraklı** Turkey
88 A3 **Taran, Mys** *pt* Rus. Fed.
54 B1 **Taranaki, Mount** *vol.* N.Z.
106 C1 **Tarancón** Spain
109 C2 **Taranto** Italy
109 C2 **Taranto, Golfo di** *g.* Italy
150 B3 **Tarapoto** Peru
90 C2 **Tarashcha** Ukr.
91 E2 **Tarasovskiy** Rus. Fed.
150 B3 **Tarauacá** Brazil
150 C3 **Tarauacá** *r.* Brazil
48 I3 **Tarawa** *atoll* Kiribati
54 C1 **Tarawera** N.Z.
77 D2 **Taraz** Kazakh.
107 C1 **Tarazona** Spain
77 E2 **Tarbagatay, Khrebet** *mts* Kazakh.
96 C2 **Tarbat Ness** *pt* U.K.
97 B2 **Tarbert** Ireland
96 A2 **Tarbert** *Scotland* U.K.
96 B3 **Tarbert** *Scotland* U.K.

104 C3 **Tarbes** France
96 B2 **Tarbet** U.K.
141 E1 **Tarboro** U.S.A.
51 C3 **Tarcoola** Austr.
53 D2 **Taree** Austr.
110 C2 **Târgovişte** Romania
110 C1 **Târgu Frumos** Romania
110 B1 **Târgu Jiu** Romania
110 B1 **Târgu Lăpuş** Romania
110 B1 **Târgu Mureş** Romania
110 C1 **Târgu Neamţ** Romania
110 C1 **Târgu Ocna** Romania
79 C2 **Tarif** U.A.E.
152 B2 **Tarija** Bol.
79 B3 **Tarim** Yemen
77 E3 **Tarim Basin** *basin* China
119 D3 **Tarime** Tanz.
77 E2 **Tarim He** *r.* China
**Tarim Pendi** China *see* Tarim Basin
77 C3 **Tarin Kowt** Afgh.
59 D3 **Taritatu** *r.* Indon.
123 C1 **Tarkastad** S. Africa
82 G2 **Tarko-Sale** Rus. Fed.
114 B4 **Tarkwa** Ghana
64 B2 **Tarlac** Phil.
105 C3 **Tarn** *r.* France
92 G2 **Tärnaby** Sweden
77 C3 **Tarnak** *r.* Afgh.
110 B1 **Târnăveni** Romania
103 E1 **Tarnobrzeg** Pol.
**Tarnopol** Ukr. *see* Ternopil'
103 E1 **Tarnów** Pol.
51 C2 **Taroom** Austr.
114 B1 **Taroudannt** Morocco
141 D3 **Tarpon Springs** U.S.A.
108 B2 **Tarquinia** Italy
107 D1 **Tarragona** Spain
107 D1 **Tàrrega** Spain
80 B2 **Tarsus** Turkey
152 B2 **Tartagal** Arg.
104 B3 **Tartas** France
88 C2 **Tartu** Estonia
80 B2 **Ţarţūs** Syria
155 D1 **Tarumirim** Brazil
89 E3 **Tarusa** Rus. Fed.
90 B2 **Tarutyne** Ukr.
108 B1 **Tarvisio** Italy
**Tashauz** Turkm. *see* Dashoguz
75 D2 **Tashigang** Bhutan
81 D3 **Tashk, Daryācheh-ye** *l.* Iran
77 C2 **Tashkent** Uzbek.
130 C2 **Tasialujjuaq, Lac** *l.* Can.
130 C2 **Tasiat, Lac** *l.* Can.
131 D2 **Tasiujaq** Can.
77 E2 **Taskesken** Kazakh.
54 B2 **Tasman Bay** N.Z.
51 D4 **Tasmania** *state* Austr.
54 B2 **Tasman Mountains** N.Z.
54 A1 **Tasman Sea** S. Pacific Ocean
115 C2 **Tassili du Hoggar** *plat.* Alg.
115 C2 **Tassili n'Ajjer** *plat.* Alg.
61 D2 **Tataba** Indon.
103 D2 **Tatabánya** Hungary
90 B2 **Tatarbunary** Ukr.
83 K3 **Tatarskiy Proliv** *str.* Rus. Fed.
**Tatar Strait** Rus. Fed. *see* Tatarskiy Proliv
67 C4 **Tateyama** Japan
128 C1 **Tathlina Lake** Can.
78 B3 **Tathlīth** Saudi Arabia
78 B2 **Tathlīth, Wādī** *watercourse* Saudi Arabia
53 C3 **Tathra** Austr.
62 A1 **Tatkon** Myanmar
128 B2 **Tatla Lake** Can.
103 D2 **Tatra Mountains** *mts* Pol./Slovakia
**Tatry** *mts* Pol./Slovakia *see* Tatra Mountains
74 A2 **Tatta** Pak.
154 C2 **Tatuí** Brazil
143 C2 **Tatum** U.S.A.
81 C2 **Tatvan** Turkey
151 E3 **Taua** Brazil
155 C2 **Taubaté** Brazil
101 D3 **Tauberbischofsheim** Ger.
54 C1 **Taumarunui** N.Z.
62 A1 **Taung** S. Africa
62 A1 **Taunggyi** Myanmar
62 A2 **Taung-ngu** Myanmar
62 A2 **Taungup** Myanmar
74 B1 **Taunsa** Pak.
99 B4 **Taunton** U.K.
101 C2 **Taunus** *hills* Ger.
54 C1 **Taupo** N.Z.
54 C1 **Taupo, Lake** N.Z.
88 B2 **Tauragė** Lith.
54 C1 **Tauranga** N.Z.
139 E1 **Taureau, Réservoir** *resr* Can.
80 B2 **Taurus Mountains** *mts* Turkey
111 C3 **Tavas** Turkey
86 F3 **Tavda** Rus. Fed.
106 B2 **Tavira** Port.
99 A4 **Tavistock** U.K.
63 A2 **Tavoy** Myanmar
111 C3 **Tavşanlı** Turkey
99 A4 **Taw** *r.* U.K.
138 C2 **Tawas City** U.S.A.
61 C1 **Tawau** *Sabah* Malaysia
64 A3 **Tawitawi** *i.* Phil.
71 C3 **Tawu** Taiwan
145 C3 **Taxco** Mex.
76 B2 **Taxiatosh** Uzbek.
77 D3 **Taxkorgan** China

96 C2 **Tay** *r.* U.K.
96 C2 **Tay, Firth of** *est.* U.K.
96 B2 **Tay, Loch** *l.* U.K.
128 B2 **Taylor** Can.
138 C2 **Taylor** *MI* U.S.A.
143 D2 **Taylor** *TX* U.S.A.
138 B3 **Taylorville** U.S.A.
78 A2 **Taymā'** Saudi Arabia
83 H2 **Taymura** *r.* Rus. Fed.
83 H2 **Taymyr, Ozero** *l.* Rus. Fed.
**Taymyr, Poluostrov** Rus. Fed. *see* Taymyr Peninsula
83 G2 **Taymyr Peninsula** *pen.* Rus. Fed.
63 B2 **Tây Ninh** Vietnam
96 C2 **Tayport** U.K.
64 A2 **Taytay** Phil.
76 C3 **Tayyebād** Iran
77 C1 **Tayynsha** Kazakh.
82 G2 **Taz** *r.* Rus. Fed.
114 B1 **Taza** Morocco
129 D2 **Tazin Lake** Can.
86 G2 **Tazovskaya Guba** *sea chan.* Rus. Fed.
81 C1 **T'bilisi** Georgia
91 E2 **Tbilisskaya** Rus. Fed.
118 B3 **Tchibanga** Gabon
115 C3 **Tchin-Tabaradene** Niger
118 B2 **Tcholliré** Cameroon
103 D1 **Tczew** Pol.
144 B2 **Teacapán** Mex.
54 A3 **Te Anau** N.Z.
54 A3 **Te Anau, Lake** N.Z.
145 C3 **Teapa** Mex.
54 C1 **Te Awamutu** N.Z.
115 C1 **Tébessa** Alg.
60 B2 **Tebingtinggi** Indon.
60 A1 **Tebingtinggi** Indon.
144 A1 **Tecate** Mex.
114 B4 **Techiman** Ghana
144 B3 **Tecomán** Mex.
144 B2 **Tecoripa** Mex.
145 B3 **Técpan** Mex.
144 B2 **Tecuala** Mex.
110 C1 **Tecuci** Romania
76 C3 **Tedzhen** Turkm.
76 C3 **Tedzhen** *r.* Turkm.
68 C1 **Teeli** Rus. Fed.
98 C2 **Tees** *r.* U.K.
111 C3 **Tefenni** Turkey
60 B2 **Tegal** Indon.
146 B3 **Tegucigalpa** Hond.
115 C3 **Teguidda-n-Tessoumt** Niger
129 E1 **Tehek Lake** Can.
**Teheran** Iran *see* Tehrān
114 B4 **Téhini** Côte d'Ivoire
81 D2 **Tehrān** Iran
145 C3 **Tehuacán** Mex.
**Tehuantepec, Golfo de** Mex. *see* Tehuantepec, Gulf of
145 C3 **Tehuantepec, Gulf of** *g.* Mex.
145 C3 **Tehuantepec, Istmo de** *isth.* Mex.
114 A2 **Teide, Pico del** *vol.* Canary Islands
99 A3 **Teifi** *r.* U.K.
**Teixeira de Sousa** Angola *see* Luau
**Tejo** *r.* Port. *see* Tagus
145 B3 **Tejupilco** Mex.
54 B2 **Tekapo, Lake** N.Z.
145 D2 **Tekax** Mex.
116 B3 **Tekezē Wenz** *r.* Eritrea/Eth.
111 C2 **Tekirdağ** Turkey
54 C1 **Te Kuiti** N.Z.
75 C2 **Tel** *r.* India
81 C1 **T'elavi** Georgia
80 B2 **Tel Aviv-Yafo** Israel
145 D2 **Telchac Puerto** Mex.
128 A2 **Telegraph Creek** Can.
154 B2 **Telêmaco Borba** Brazil
61 C1 **Telen** *r.* Indon.
50 B2 **Telfer Mining Centre** Austr.
99 B3 **Telford** U.K.
128 B2 **Telkwa** Can.
60 A2 **Telo** Indon.
86 E2 **Tel'pos-Iz, Gora** *mt.* Rus. Fed.
88 B2 **Telšiai** Lith.
60 B2 **Telukbatang** Indon.
60 A1 **Telukdalam** Indon.
60 B1 **Teluk Intan** Malaysia
114 C4 **Tema** Ghana
130 C2 **Temagami Lake** Can.
60 C2 **Temanggung** Indon.
123 C2 **Temba** S. Africa
83 H2 **Tembenchi** *r.* Rus. Fed.
60 B2 **Tembilahan** Indon.
123 C2 **Tembisa** S. Africa
120 A1 **Tembo Aluma** Angola
**Tembué** Moz. *see* Chifunde
99 B3 **Teme** *r.* U.K.
135 C4 **Temecula** U.S.A.
63 B3 **Temengor, Tasik** *resr* Malaysia
60 B1 **Temerluh** Malaysia
77 D1 **Temirtau** Kazakh.
139 D1 **Témiscamingue, Lac** *l.* Can.
53 C2 **Temora** Austr.
142 A2 **Tempe** U.S.A.
143 D2 **Temple** U.S.A.
97 C2 **Templemore** Ireland
102 C1 **Templin** Ger.
145 C2 **Tempoal** Mex.
120 A2 **Tempué** Angola
91 D2 **Temryuk** Rus. Fed.
91 D2 **Temryukskiy Zaliv** *b.* Rus. Fed.
153 A3 **Temuco** Chile

54 B2 **Temuka** N.Z.
145 C2 **Tenabo** Mex.
143 E2 **Tenaha** U.S.A.
73 C3 **Tenali** India
63 A2 **Tenasserim** Myanmar
99 A4 **Tenby** U.K.
117 C3 **Tendaho** Eth.
105 D3 **Tende** France
105 D3 **Tende, Col de** *pass* France/Italy
73 D4 **Ten Degree Channel** India
114 A3 **Te-n-Dghâmcha, Sebkhet** *salt marsh* Maur.
67 D3 **Tendō** Japan
114 B3 **Ténenkou** Mali
115 C2 **Ténéré** *reg.* Niger
115 D3 **Ténéré, Erg du** *des.* Niger
115 D2 **Ténéré du Tafassâsset** *des.* Niger
114 A2 **Tenerife** *i.* Canary Is
107 D2 **Ténès** Alg.
61 C2 **Tengah, Kepulauan** *is* Indon.
**Tengcheng** China *see* Tengxian
62 A1 **Tengchong** China
61 C2 **Tenggarong** Indon.
70 A2 **Tengger Shamo** *des.* China
77 C1 **Tengiz, Ozero** *salt l.* Kazakh.
71 B3 **Tengxian** China
119 C4 **Tenke** Dem. Rep. Congo
114 B3 **Tenkodogo** Burkina
51 C1 **Tennant Creek** Austr.
140 C1 **Tennessee** *r.* U.S.A.
140 C1 **Tennessee** *state* U.S.A.
61 C1 **Tenom** *Sabah* Malaysia
145 C3 **Tenosique** Mex.
61 D2 **Tenteno** Indon.
53 D1 **Tenterfield** Austr.
141 D3 **Ten Thousand Islands** U.S.A.
154 B2 **Teodoro Sampaio** Brazil
155 D1 **Teófilo Otôni** Brazil
145 C3 **Teopisca** Mex.
59 C3 **Tepa** Indon.
144 B2 **Tepache** Mex.
54 B1 **Te Paki** N.Z.
144 B3 **Tepalcatepec** Mex.
144 B2 **Tepatitlán** Mex.
144 B2 **Tepehuanes** Mex.
109 D2 **Tepelenë** Albania
144 B2 **Tepic** Mex.
102 C1 **Teplice** Czech Rep.
89 E3 **Teploye** Rus. Fed.
90 B2 **Teplyk** Ukr.
54 C1 **Te Puke** N.Z.
144 B2 **Tequila** Mex.
49 K3 **Teraina** *i.* Kiribati
108 B2 **Teramo** Italy
52 B3 **Terang** Austr.
89 E3 **Terbuny** Rus. Fed.
90 B2 **Terebovlya** Ukr.
87 D4 **Terek** *r.* Rus. Fed.
154 B2 **Terenos** Brazil
151 E3 **Teresina** Brazil
155 D2 **Teresópolis** Brazil
63 A3 **Teressa Island** India
100 A3 **Tergnier** France
80 B1 **Terme** Turkey
108 B3 **Termini Imerese** *Sicily* Italy
145 C3 **Términos, Laguna de** *lag.* Mex.
77 C3 **Termiz** Uzbek.
109 B2 **Termoli** Italy
59 C2 **Ternate** Indon.
100 A2 **Terneuzen** Neth.
66 C1 **Terney** Rus. Fed.
108 B2 **Terni** Italy
90 B2 **Ternopil'** Ukr.
52 A2 **Terowie** Austr.
69 F1 **Terpeniya, Mys** *c.* Rus. Fed.
69 F1 **Terpeniya, Zaliv** *g.* Rus. Fed.
128 B2 **Terrace** Can.
130 B3 **Terrace Bay** Can.
122 B2 **Terra Firma** S. Africa
140 B3 **Terrebonne Bay** U.S.A.
138 B3 **Terre Haute** U.S.A.
131 E3 **Terrenceville** Can.
100 B1 **Terschelling** *i.* Neth.
108 A3 **Tertenia** *Sardinia* Italy
107 C1 **Teruel** Spain
92 H2 **Tervola** Fin.
109 C2 **Tešanj** Bos.-Herz.
116 B3 **Teseney** Eritrea
66 D2 **Teshio** Japan
66 D2 **Teshio-gawa** *r.* Japan
128 A1 **Teslin** Can.
128 A1 **Teslin Lake** Can.
154 B1 **Tesouro** Brazil
115 C3 **Tessaoua** Niger
99 C4 **Test** *r.* U.K.
121 C2 **Tete** Moz.
90 C1 **Teteriv** *r.* Ukr.
101 F1 **Teterow** Ger.
90 B2 **Tetiyiv** Ukr.
114 B1 **Tétouan** Morocco
110 B2 **Tetovo** Macedonia
**Tetyukhe** Rus. Fed. *see* Dal'negorsk
**Teuchezhsk** Rus. Fed. *see* Adygeysk
152 B2 **Teuco** *r.* Arg.
144 B2 **Teul de González Ortega** Mex.
101 D1 **Teutoburger Wald** *hills* Ger.
**Tevere** *r.* Italy *see* Tiber
54 A3 **Teviot** N.Z.
96 C3 **Teviot** *r.* U.K.
96 C3 **Teviothead** U.K.
61 C2 **Tewah** Indon.
51 E2 **Tewantin** Austr.

| | | |
|---|---|---|
| 54 C2 | Te Wharau N.Z. | |
| 99 B4 | Tewkesbury U.K. | |
| 143 E2 | Texarkana U.S.A. | |
| 53 D1 | Texas Austr. | |
| 143 D2 | **Texas** state U.S.A. | |
| 143 E3 | Texas City U.S.A. | |
| 145 C3 | Texcoco Mex. | |
| 100 B1 | Texel i. Neth. | |
| 143 D2 | Texoma, Lake U.S.A. | |
| 123 C2 | Teyateyaneng Lesotho | |
| 89 F2 | Teykovo Rus. Fed. | |
| 89 F2 | Teza r. Rus. Fed. | |
| 75 D2 | Tezpur India | |
| 72 B2 | Tezu India | |
| 129 E1 | Tha-anne r. Can. | |
| 123 C2 | Thabana-Ntlenyana mt. Lesotho | |
| 123 C2 | Thaba Nchu S. Africa | |
| 123 C2 | Thaba Putsoa mt. Lesotho | |
| 123 C2 | Thaba-Tseka Lesotho | |
| 123 C1 | Thabazimbi S. Africa | |
| 123 C2 | Thabong S. Africa | |
| 63 A2 | Thagyettaw Myanmar | |
| 62 B1 | Thai Binh Vietnam | |
| 63 B2 | **Thailand** country Asia | |
| 63 B2 | Thailand, Gulf of Asia | |
| 62 B1 | Thai Nguyên Vietnam | |
| 62 B2 | Thakèk Laos | |
| 74 B1 | Thal Pak. | |
| 63 A2 | Thalang Thai. | |
| 74 B1 | Thal Desert Pak. | |
| 101 E2 | Thale (Harz) Ger. | |
| 62 B2 | Tha Li Thai. | |
| 53 C1 | Thallon Austr. | |
| 123 C1 | Thamaga Botswana | |
| 78 B3 | **Thamar, Jabal** mt. Yemen | |
| 79 C3 | Thamarit Oman | |
| 130 B3 | Thames r. Can. | |
| 54 C1 | Thames N.Z. | |
| 99 D4 | Thames U.K. | |
| 99 D4 | Thames r. U.K. | |
| 79 B3 | Thamūd Yemen | |
| | Thana India see Thane | |
| 63 A2 | Thanbyuzayat Myanmar | |
| 62 A2 | Thandwè Myanmar | |
| 74 B3 | Thane India | |
| 62 B1 | Thanh Hoa Vietnam | |
| 73 B3 | Thanjavur India | |
| 63 A2 | Thanlyin Myanmar | |
| 74 A2 | Thano Bula Khan Pak. | |
| 62 B1 | Than Uyen Vietnam | |
| 74 A2 | Thar Desert India/Pak. | |
| 52 B1 | Thargomindah Austr. | |
| 81 C2 | Tharthār, Buḩayrat ath r. Iraq | |
| 111 B2 | Thasos Greece | |
| 111 B2 | Thasos i. Greece | |
| 62 B1 | Thât Khê Vietnam | |
| 62 A2 | Thaton Myanmar | |
| 62 A1 | Thaungdut Myanmar | |
| 62 A2 | Thayawadi Myanmar | |
| 63 A2 | Thayetchaung Myanmar | |
| 62 A2 | Thayetmyo Myanmar | |
| 62 A1 | Thazi Myanmar | |
| 146 C2 | **The Bahamas** country West Indies | |
| 98 B2 | The Cheviot hill U.K. | |
| 134 B1 | The Dalles U.S.A. | |
| 136 C2 | Thedford U.S.A. | |
| 53 D2 | The Entrance Austr. | |
| 99 C3 | The Fens reg. U.K. | |
| 114 A3 | **The Gambia** country Africa | |
| 52 B1 | The Grampians mts Austr. | |
| | The Great Oasis Egypt see Wāḩāt al Khārijah | |
| 79 C2 | The Gulf Asia | |
| 100 B1 | The Hague Neth. | |
| 129 E1 | Thelon r. Can. | |
| 101 E2 | Themar Ger. | |
| 123 C2 | Thembalihle S. Africa | |
| 96 A1 | The Minch sea chan. U.K. | |
| 97 A1 | The Mullet b. Ireland | |
| 99 C4 | The Needles stack U.K. | |
| 150 D3 | Theodore Roosevelt r. Brazil | |
| 129 D2 | The Pas Can. | |
| 111 B2 | Thermaïkos Kolpos g. Greece | |
| 136 B2 | Thermopolis U.S.A. | |
| 53 C3 | The Rock Austr. | |
| | The Skaw spit Denmark see Grenen | |
| 99 C4 | The Solent str. U.K. | |
| 130 B3 | Thessalon Can. | |
| 111 B2 | Thessaloniki Greece | |
| 99 D3 | Thetford U.K. | |
| 131 C3 | Thetford Mines Can. | |
| 62 A1 | The Triangle mts Myanmar | |
| 147 D3 | The Valley Anguilla | |
| 131 D2 | Thévenet, Lac l. Can. | |
| 99 D3 | The Wash b. U.K. | |
| 99 D4 | The Weald reg. U.K. | |
| 143 D2 | The Woodlands U.S.A. | |
| 140 B3 | Thibodaux U.S.A. | |
| 129 E2 | Thicket Portage Can. | |
| 137 D1 | Thief River Falls U.S.A. | |
| | Thiel Neth. see Tiel | |
| 105 C2 | Thiers France | |
| 114 A3 | Thiès Senegal | |
| 119 D3 | Thika Kenya | |
| 73 B4 | Thiladhunmathi Atoll Maldives | |
| 75 C2 | Thimphu Bhutan | |
| 105 D2 | Thionville France | |
| 111 B3 | Thira Greece | |
| 111 C3 | Thira i. Greece | |
| 98 C2 | Thirsk U.K. | |
| | Thiruvananthapuram India see Trivandrum | |
| 93 E4 | Thisted Denmark | |
| 129 E1 | Thlewiaza r. Can. | |
| 63 B3 | Thô Chu, Đao i. Vietnam | |
| 62 A2 | Thoen Thai. | |
| 123 D1 | Thohoyandou S. Africa | |
| 101 E1 | Thomasburg Ger. | |
| 97 C2 | Thomastown Ireland | |
| 140 C2 | **Thomasville** AL U.S.A. | |
| 141 D2 | **Thomasville** GA U.S.A. | |
| 100 C2 | Thommen Belgium | |
| 129 E2 | Thompson Can. | |
| 128 E3 | Thompson r. U.S.A. | |
| 134 C1 | Thompson Falls U.S.A. | |
| 128 B2 | Thompson Sound Can. | |
| 51 D2 | Thomson watercourse Austr. | |
| 141 D2 | Thomson U.S.A. | |
| 63 A2 | Thon Buri Thai. | |
| 63 A2 | Thongwa Myanmar | |
| 142 B1 | Thoreau U.S.A. | |
| 96 C3 | Thornhill U.K. | |
| 136 C3 | Thornton U.S.A. | |
| 55 F2 | Thorshavnheiane reg. Antarctica | |
| 123 C2 | Thota-ea-Moli Lesotho | |
| 104 B2 | Thouars France | |
| 62 A1 | Thoubal India | |
| 134 D1 | Three Forks U.S.A. | |
| 128 C2 | Three Hills Can. | |
| 63 A2 | Three Pagodas Pass Myanmar/Thai. | |
| 114 B4 | Three Points, Cape Ghana | |
| 138 B2 | **Three Rivers** MI U.S.A. | |
| 143 D3 | **Three Rivers** TX U.S.A. | |
| | Thrissur India see Trichur | |
| 63 B2 | Thu Dâu Môt Vietnam | |
| 100 B2 | Thuin Belgium | |
| | Thule see Qaanaaq | |
| 121 B3 | Thuli Zimbabwe | |
| 102 B2 | Thun Switz. | |
| 130 B3 | Thunder Bay Can. | |
| 130 B3 | Thunder Bay b. Can. | |
| 63 A3 | Thung Song Thai. | |
| 101 E2 | Thüringer Becken reg. Ger. | |
| 101 E2 | Thüringer Wald mts Ger. | |
| | Thuringian Forest mts Ger. see Thüringer Wald | |
| 97 C2 | Thurles Ireland | |
| 59 D3 | Thursday Island Austr. | |
| 96 C1 | Thurso U.K. | |
| 96 C1 | Thurso r. U.K. | |
| 55 R2 | Thurston Island Antarctica | |
| 101 D1 | Thüster Berg hill Ger. | |
| 121 C2 | Thyolo Malawi | |
| | Thysville Dem. Rep. Congo see Mbanza-Ngungu | |
| 79 C2 | Tiāb Iran | |
| 151 E3 | Tianguá Brazil | |
| 70 B2 | Tianjin China | |
| 70 B2 | Tianjin mun. China | |
| 71 A3 | Tianlin China | |
| 70 B2 | Tianmen China | |
| 69 E2 | Tianshan China | |
| 70 A2 | Tianshui China | |
| 70 A2 | Tianzhu China | |
| 107 D2 | Tiaret Alg. | |
| 114 B4 | Tiassalé Côte d'Ivoire | |
| 154 B2 | Tibagi Brazil | |
| 154 B2 | Tibagi r. Brazil | |
| 118 B2 | Tibati Cameroon | |
| 108 B2 | Tiber r. Italy | |
| | Tiberias, Lake Israel see Galilee, Sea of | |
| 115 D2 | Tibesti mts Chad | |
| 75 C1 | Tibet aut. reg. China | |
| | Tibet, Plateau of China see Qingzang Gaoyuan | |
| 52 B1 | Tibooburra Austr. | |
| 144 A2 | Tiburón, Isla i. Mex. | |
| 114 B3 | Tichît Maur. | |
| 114 A2 | Tichla Western Sahara | |
| 105 D2 | Ticino r. Italy/Switz. | |
| 139 E2 | Ticonderoga U.S.A. | |
| 145 D2 | Ticul Mex. | |
| 114 A3 | Tidjikja Maur. | |
| 100 B2 | Tiel Neth. | |
| 70 C1 | Tieling China | |
| 75 B2 | Tielongtan Aksai Chin | |
| 100 A2 | Tielt Belgium | |
| 100 B2 | Tienen Belgium | |
| 68 B2 | Tien Shan mts China/Kyrg. | |
| | Tientsin China see Tianjin | |
| | Tientsin mun. China see Tianjin | |
| 93 G3 | Tierp Sweden | |
| 145 C3 | Tierra Blanca Mex. | |
| 145 C3 | Tierra Colorada Mex. | |
| 153 B5 | Tierra del Fuego, Isla Grande de i. Arg./Chile | |
| 106 B1 | Tiétar, Valle de val. Spain | |
| 154 C2 | Tietê Brazil | |
| 154 B2 | Tietê r. Brazil | |
| 138 C2 | Tiffin U.S.A. | |
| | Tiflis Georgia see T'bilisi | |
| 141 D2 | Tifton U.S.A. | |
| 90 B2 | Tighina Moldova | |
| 75 C2 | Tigiria India | |
| 118 B2 | Tignère Cameroon | |
| 131 D3 | Tignish Can. | |
| 150 B3 | Tigre r. Ecuador/Peru | |
| 81 C2 | Tigris r. Asia | |
| 114 A3 | Tiguent Maur. | |
| 114 B2 | Tiguesmat hills Maur. | |
| 115 D3 | Tigui Chad | |
| 145 C2 | Tihuatlán Mex. | |
| 144 A1 | Tijuana Mex. | |
| 91 E2 | Tikhoretsk Rus. Fed. | |
| 89 D2 | Tikhvin Rus. Fed. | |
| 89 D2 | Tikhvinskaya Gryada ridge Rus. Fed. | |
| 157 F7 | Tiki Basin sea feature S. Pacific Ocean | |
| 54 C1 | Tikokino N.Z. | |
| 81 C2 | Tikrīt Iraq | |
| 83 J2 | Tiksi Rus. Fed. | |
| 100 B2 | Tilburg Neth. | |
| 152 B2 | Tilcara Arg. | |
| 52 B1 | Tilcha Austr. | |
| 114 C3 | Tilemsi, Vallée du watercourse Mali | |
| 114 C3 | Tillabéri Niger | |
| 134 B1 | Tillamook U.S.A. | |
| 63 A3 | Tillanchong Island India | |
| 111 C3 | Tilos i. Greece | |
| 52 B2 | Tilpa Austr. | |
| 86 F2 | Til'tim Rus. Fed. | |
| 89 E3 | Tim Rus. Fed. | |
| 86 D2 | Timanskiy Kryazh ridge Rus. Fed. | |
| 54 B2 | Timaru N.Z. | |
| 91 D2 | Timashevsk Rus. Fed. | |
| | Timashevskaya Rus. Fed. see Timashevsk | |
| 114 B3 | Timbedgha Maur. | |
| 50 C1 | Timber Creek Austr. | |
| 114 B3 | Timbuktu Mali | |
| 115 C3 | Timia Niger | |
| 114 C2 | Timimoun Alg. | |
| 110 B1 | Timiş r. Romania | |
| 110 B1 | Timişoara Romania | |
| 130 B3 | Timmins Can. | |
| 89 E2 | Timokhino Rus. Fed. | |
| 151 E3 | Timon Brazil | |
| 59 C3 | Timor i. Indon. | |
| 59 C3 | Timor Sea Austr./Indon. | |
| | Timor Timur country Asia see East Timor | |
| 93 G3 | Timrå Sweden | |
| 78 B3 | Tin, Jabal hill Saudi Arabia | |
| 114 B2 | Tindouf Alg. | |
| 53 D1 | Tingha Austr. | |
| 75 C2 | Tingri China | |
| 93 F4 | Tingsryd Sweden | |
| 92 E3 | Tingvoll Norway | |
| | Tingzhou China see Changting | |
| 59 D2 | Tinian i. N. Mariana Is | |
| | Tinnelvelly India see Tirunelveli | |
| 152 B2 | Tinogasta Arg. | |
| 111 C3 | Tinos Greece | |
| 111 C3 | Tinos i. Greece | |
| 100 A3 | Tinqueux France | |
| 115 C2 | Tinrhert, Plateau du Alg. | |
| 62 A1 | Tinsukia India | |
| 52 B3 | Tintinara Austr. | |
| 136 C1 | Tioga U.S.A. | |
| 107 D2 | Tipasa Alg. | |
| 97 B2 | Tipperary Ireland | |
| 151 E3 | Tiracambu, Serra do hills Brazil | |
| 109 C2 | Tirana Albania | |
| | Tiranë Albania see Tirana | |
| 108 B1 | Tirano Italy | |
| 52 A1 | Tirari Desert Austr. | |
| 90 B2 | Tiraspol Moldova | |
| 122 A2 | Tiraz Mountains Namibia | |
| 111 C3 | Tire Turkey | |
| 96 A2 | Tiree i. U.K. | |
| | Tîrgovişte Romania see Târgovişte | |
| | Tîrgu Frumos Romania see Târgu Frumos | |
| | Tîrgu Jiu Romania see Târgu Jiu | |
| | Tîrgu Lăpuş Romania see Târgu Lăpuş | |
| | Tîrgu Mureş Romania see Târgu Mureş | |
| | Tîrgu Neamţ Romania see Târgu Neamţ | |
| | Tîrgu Ocna Romania see Târgu Ocna | |
| 74 B1 | Tirich Mir mt. Pak. | |
| | Tîrnăveni Romania see Târnăveni | |
| 155 C1 | Tiros Brazil | |
| 118 C2 | Tiroungoulou C.A.R. | |
| 73 B3 | Tiruchchirappalli India | |
| 73 B4 | Tirunelveli India | |
| 73 B3 | Tirupati India | |
| 73 B3 | Tiruppattur India | |
| 73 B3 | Tiruppur India | |
| 109 D1 | Tisa r. Europe | |
| | Tisa r. Hungary see Tisza | |
| 129 D2 | Tisdale Can. | |
| 107 D2 | Tissemsilt Alg. | |
| 75 C2 | Tista r. India | |
| 103 E2 | Tisza r. Hungary | |
| 55 L1 | Titan Dome ice feature Antarctica | |
| | Titicaca, Lago Bol./Peru see Titicaca, Lake | |
| 152 B2 | Titicaca, Lake l. Bol./Peru | |
| 75 C2 | Titlagarh India | |
| | Titograd Serb. and Mont. see Podgorica | |
| | Titova Mitrovica Serb. and Mont. see Kosovska Mitrovica | |
| | Titovo Užice Serb. and Mont. see Užice | |
| | Titovo Velenje Slovenia see Velenje | |
| | Titov Veles Macedonia see Veles | |
| | Titov Vrbas Serb. and Mont. see Vrbas | |
| 110 C2 | Titu Romania | |
| 141 D3 | Titusville U.S.A. | |
| 99 B3 | Tiverton U.K. | |
| 108 B2 | Tivoli Italy | |
| 79 C2 | Ţīwī Oman | |
| 63 A2 | Ti-ywa Myanmar | |
| 145 D2 | Tizimín Mex. | |
| 107 D2 | Tizi Ouzou Alg. | |
| 114 B2 | Tiznit Morocco | |
| 92 G2 | Tjaktjajaure l. Sweden | |
| | Tjirebon Indon. see Cirebon | |
| 145 C3 | Tlacotalpán Mex. | |
| 144 B2 | Tlahualilo Mex. | |
| 145 C3 | Tlalnepantla Mex. | |
| 145 C3 | Tlapa Mex. | |
| 145 C3 | Tlaxcala Mex. | |
| 145 C3 | Tlaxiaco Mex. | |
| 114 B1 | Tlemcen Alg. | |
| 123 C1 | Tlokweng Botswana | |
| 128 B2 | Toad River Can. | |
| 121 □D2 | Toamasina Madag. | |
| 60 A1 | Toba, Danau l. Indon. | |
| | Toba, Lake Indon. see Toba, Danau | |
| 74 A1 | Toba and Kakar Ranges mts Pak. | |
| 147 D3 | Tobago i. Trin. and Tob. | |
| 59 C2 | Tobelo Indon. | |
| 130 B3 | Tobermory Can. | |
| 96 A2 | Tobermory U.K. | |
| 129 D2 | Tobin Lake Can. | |
| 60 B2 | Toboali Indon. | |
| 76 C1 | Tobol r. Kazakh./Rus. Fed. | |
| 86 F3 | Tobol'sk Rus. Fed. | |
| | Tobruk Libya see Tubruq | |
| 151 E3 | Tocantinópolis Brazil | |
| 151 E3 | Tocantins r. Brazil | |
| 141 D2 | Toccoa U.S.A. | |
| 108 A1 | Toce r. Italy | |
| 152 A2 | Tocopilla Chile | |
| 53 C3 | Tocumwal Austr. | |
| 59 C3 | Todeli Indon. | |
| 108 B2 | Todi Italy | |
| 144 A2 | Todos Santos Mex. | |
| 128 B3 | Tofino Can. | |
| 96 □ | Toft U.K. | |
| 61 D2 | Togian i. Indon. | |
| 61 D2 | Togian, Kepulauan is Indon. | |
| | Togliatti Rus. Fed. see Tol'yatti | |
| 114 C4 | **Togo** country Africa | |
| 74 B2 | Tohana India | |
| 141 D3 | Tohopekaliga, Lake U.S.A. | |
| 126 C2 | Tok U.S.A. | |
| 116 B3 | Tokar Sudan | |
| 69 C3 | Tokara-rettō is Japan | |
| 91 E1 | Tokarevka Rus. Fed. | |
| 80 B1 | Tokat Turkey | |
| 49 J4 | Tokelau terr. S. Pacific Ocean | |
| 91 D2 | Tokmak Ukr. | |
| 77 D2 | Tokmok Kyrg. | |
| 54 C1 | Tokoroa N.Z. | |
| 68 B2 | Toksun China | |
| 67 B4 | Tokushima Japan | |
| 67 C3 | Tōkyō Japan | |
| 121 □D3 | Tôlañaro Madag. | |
| | Tolbukhin Bulg. see Dobrich | |
| 154 B2 | Toledo Brazil | |
| 106 C2 | Toledo Spain | |
| 138 C2 | Toledo U.S.A. | |
| 106 C2 | Toledo, Montes de mts Spain | |
| 140 B2 | Toledo Bend Reservoir U.S.A. | |
| 121 □D3 | Toliara Madag. | |
| | Toling China see Zanda | |
| 61 D1 | Tolitoli Indon. | |
| 108 B1 | Tolmezzo Italy | |
| 108 B1 | Tolmin Slovenia | |
| 103 D2 | Tolna Hungary | |
| 104 B3 | Tolosa Spain | |
| 145 C3 | Toluca Mex. | |
| 87 D3 | Tol'yatti Rus. Fed. | |
| 138 A2 | Tomah U.S.A. | |
| 138 B1 | Tomahawk U.S.A. | |
| 66 D2 | Tomakomai Japan | |
| 61 D2 | Tomali Indon. | |
| 61 C1 | Tomani Sabah Malaysia | |
| 106 B2 | Tomar Port. | |
| 103 E1 | Tomaszów Lubelski Pol. | |
| 103 E1 | Tomaszów Mazowiecki Pol. | |
| 144 B3 | Tomatlán Mex. | |
| 154 C2 | Tomazina Brazil | |
| 140 C2 | Tombigbee r. U.S.A. | |
| 120 A1 | Tomboco Angola | |
| 155 D2 | Tombos Brazil | |
| | Tombouctou Mali see Timbuktu | |
| 142 B2 | Tombstone U.S.A. | |
| 120 A2 | Tombua Angola | |
| 123 C1 | Tom Burke S. Africa | |
| 106 C2 | Tomelloso Spain | |
| 53 C2 | Tomingley Austr. | |
| 61 D2 | Tomini, Teluk g. Indon. | |
| 109 C2 | Tomislavgrad Bos.-Herz. | |
| 103 D2 | Tompa Hungary | |
| 50 A2 | Tom Price Austr. | |
| 82 G3 | Tomsk Rus. Fed. | |
| 93 F4 | Tomtabacken hill Sweden | |
| 83 K2 | Tomtor Rus. Fed. | |
| 145 C3 | Tonalá Mex. | |
| 150 C3 | Tonantins Brazil | |
| 99 D4 | Tonbridge U.K. | |
| 59 C2 | Tondano Indon. | |
| 49 J5 | **Tonga** country S. Pacific Ocean | |
| 123 D2 | Tongaat S. Africa | |
| 49 J6 | Tongatapu Group is Tonga | |
| 71 B3 | Tongcheng China | |
| 70 A2 | Tongchuan China | |
| 71 A3 | Tongdao China | |
| 65 B2 | Tongduch'ŏn S. Korea | |
| 100 B2 | Tongeren Belgium | |
| 65 B2 | Tonghae S. Korea | |
| 71 A3 | Tonghai China | |
| 65 B1 | Tonghua China | |

65 B2 **Tongjosŏn-man** b. N. Korea
62 B1 **Tongking, Gulf of** China/Vietnam
69 E2 **Tongliao** China
70 B2 **Tongling** China
52 B2 **Tongo** Austr.
**Tongquan** China see Malong
71 A3 **Tongren** China
75 D2 **Tongsa** Bhutan
70 B2 **Tongshan** China
**Tongshi** China see Wuzhishan
**Tongtian He** r. China see Yangtze
96 B1 **Tongue** U.K.
**Tongxian** China see Tongzhou
65 B3 **T'ongyŏng** S. Korea
69 E2 **Tongyu** China
65 A1 **Tongyuanpu** China
70 B2 **Tongzhou** China
71 A3 **Tongzi** China
119 C2 **Tonj** Sudan
74 B2 **Tonk** India
81 D2 **Tonkābon** Iran
**Tônlé Sab** l. Cambodia see Tonle Sap
63 B2 **Tonle Sap** l. Cambodia
135 C3 **Tonopah** U.S.A.
93 F4 **Tønsberg** Norway
135 D2 **Tooele** U.S.A.
52 B3 **Tooleybuc** Austr.
53 D1 **Toowoomba** Austr.
137 D3 **Topeka** U.S.A.
144 B2 **Topia** Mex.
144 B2 **Topolobampo** Mex.
86 C2 **Topozero, Ozero** l. Rus. Fed.
134 B1 **Toppenish** U.S.A.
111 C3 **Torbalı** Turkey
76 B3 **Torbat-e Heydariyeh** Iran
76 C3 **Torbat-e Jām** Iran
131 E3 **Torbay** Can.
106 C1 **Tordesillas** Spain
107 C1 **Tordesilos** Spain
92 H2 **Töre** Sweden
107 D1 **Torelló** Spain
100 B1 **Torenberg** hill Neth.
**Toretam** Kazakh. see Baykonyr
101 F2 **Torgau** Ger.
100 A2 **Torhout** Belgium
**Torino** Italy see Turin
67 D4 **Tori-shima** i. Japan
117 B4 **Torit** Sudan
154 E1 **Torixoreu** Brazil
89 D2 **Torkovichi** Rus. Fed.
106 B1 **Tormes** r. Spain
92 H2 **Torneälven** r. Sweden
131 D2 **Torngat Mountains** Can.
92 H2 **Tornio** Fin.
106 B1 **Toro** Spain
130 C3 **Toronto** Can.
89 D2 **Toropets** Rus. Fed.
119 D2 **Tororo** Uganda
**Toros Dağları** Turkey see Taurus Mountains
52 B3 **Torquay** Austr.
99 B4 **Torquay** U.K.
135 C4 **Torrance** U.S.A.
106 B2 **Torrão** Port.
106 B1 **Torre** mt. Port.
107 D1 **Torreblanca** Spain
106 C1 **Torrecerredo** mt. Spain
106 B1 **Torre de Moncorvo** Port.
106 C1 **Torrelavega** Spain
106 C2 **Torremolinos** Spain
52 A2 **Torrens, Lake** salt flat Austr.
107 C2 **Torrent** Spain
144 B2 **Torreón** Mex.
106 B2 **Torres Novas** Port.
156 C6 **Torres Strait** Austr.
106 B2 **Torres Vedras** Port.
107 C2 **Torrevieja** Spain
96 B2 **Torridon** U.K.
96 B2 **Torridon, Loch** b. U.K.
106 C2 **Torrijos** Spain
139 E2 **Torrington** CT U.S.A.
136 C3 **Torrington** WY U.S.A.
107 D1 **Torroella de Montgrí** Spain
94 B1 **Tórshavn** Faroe Is
76 C2 **Toʻrtkoʻl** Uzbek.
108 A3 **Tortolì** Sardinia Italy
108 A2 **Tortona** Italy
107 C1 **Tortosa** Spain
81 D2 **Torūd** Iran
103 D1 **Toruń** Pol.
97 B1 **Tory Island** Ireland
97 B1 **Tory Sound** sea chan. Ireland
89 D2 **Torzhok** Rus. Fed.
67 B4 **Tosashimizu** Japan
122 B2 **Tosca** S. Africa
108 A2 **Toscano, Arcipelago** is Italy
**Toshkent** see Tashkent
89 D2 **Tosno** Rus. Fed.
68 C1 **Tosontsengel** Mongolia
152 B2 **Tostado** Arg.
101 D1 **Tostedt** Ger.
80 B1 **Tosya** Turkey
86 D3 **Tot'ma** Rus. Fed.
151 D2 **Totness** Suriname
67 B3 **Tottori** Japan
114 B4 **Touba** Côte d'Ivoire
114 B1 **Toubkal, Jbel** mt. Morocco
118 B2 **Touboro** Cameroon
114 B3 **Tougan** Burkina
115 C1 **Touggourt** Alg.
105 D2 **Toul** France
71 C3 **Touliu** Taiwan
105 D3 **Toulon** France
104 C3 **Toulouse** France

**Tourane** Vietnam see Đà Nẵng
104 B2 **Tourlaville** France
100 A2 **Tournai** Belgium
115 D2 **Tourndo, Oued** watercourse Alg./Niger
105 C2 **Tournus** France
151 F3 **Touros** Brazil
104 C2 **Tours** France
115 D2 **Tousside, Pic** mt. Chad
122 B3 **Touwsrivier** S. Africa
150 B2 **Tovar** Venez.
66 D2 **Towada** Japan
134 D1 **Towanda** U.S.A.
51 D1 **Townsville** Austr.
61 D2 **Towori, Teluk** b. Indon.
77 E2 **Toxkan He** r. China
66 D2 **Tōya-ko** l. Japan
67 C3 **Toyama** Japan
67 C3 **Toyohashi** Japan
67 C3 **Toyota** Japan
115 C1 **Tozeur** Tunisia
81 C1 **Tqvarch'eli** Georgia
**Trâblous** Lebanon see Tripoli
80 B1 **Trabzon** Turkey
106 B2 **Trafalgar, Cabo** c. Spain
128 C3 **Trail** Can.
88 B3 **Trakai** Lith.
97 B2 **Tralee** Ireland
**Trá Lí** Ireland see Tralee
97 C2 **Tramore** Ireland
93 F4 **Tranås** Sweden
63 A3 **Trang** Thai.
59 C3 **Trangan** i. Indon.
55 L2 **Transantarctic Mountains** Antarctica
110 B1 **Transylvanian Alps** mts Romania
108 B3 **Trapani** Sicily Italy
53 C3 **Traralgon** Austr.
63 B2 **Trat** Thai.
102 C2 **Traunstein** Ger.
54 B2 **Travers, Mount** N.Z.
138 B2 **Traverse City** U.S.A.
63 B3 **Tra Vinh** Vietnam
103 D2 **Třebíč** Czech Rep.
109 C2 **Trebinje** Bos.-Herz.
103 E2 **Trebišov** Slovakia
**Trebizond** Turkey see Trabzon
109 C1 **Trebnje** Slovenia
**Trefynwy** U.K. see Monmouth
153 C3 **Treinta y Tres** Uru.
153 B4 **Trelew** Arg.
93 F4 **Trelleborg** Sweden
130 C3 **Tremblant, Mont** hill Can.
109 C2 **Tremiti, Isole** is Italy
134 D2 **Tremonton** U.S.A.
107 D1 **Tremp** Spain
103 D2 **Trenčín** Slovakia
153 B3 **Trenque Lauquén** Arg.
**Trent** Italy see Trento
98 C3 **Trent** r. U.K.
108 B1 **Trento** Italy
139 D2 **Trenton** Can.
137 E2 **Trenton** MO U.S.A.
139 E2 **Trenton** NJ U.S.A.
131 E3 **Trepassey** Can.
153 B3 **Tres Arroyos** Arg.
155 C2 **Três Corações** Brazil
154 B2 **Três Irmãos, Represa** resr Brazil
154 B2 **Três Lagoas** Brazil
153 A4 **Tres Lagos** Arg.
155 C2 **Três Marias, Represa** resr Brazil
155 C2 **Três Pontas** Brazil
153 B4 **Tres Puntas, Cabo** c. Arg.
155 D2 **Três Rios** Brazil
101 F1 **Treuenbrietzen** Ger.
**Treves** Ger. see Trier
108 A1 **Treviglio** Italy
108 B1 **Treviso** Italy
99 A4 **Trevose Head** hd U.K.
109 C3 **Tricase** Italy
**Trichinopoly** India see Tiruchchirappalli
73 B3 **Trichur** India
53 C2 **Trida** Austr.
100 C3 **Trier** Ger.
108 B1 **Trieste** Italy
108 B1 **Triglav** mt. Slovenia
111 B3 **Trikala** Greece
59 D3 **Trikora, Puncak** mt. Indon.
97 C2 **Trim** Ireland
73 C4 **Trincomalee** Sri Lanka
154 C1 **Trindade** Brazil
148 H5 **Trindade, Ilha da** i. S. Atlantic Ocean
152 B2 **Trinidad** Bol.
147 D3 **Trinidad** i. Trin. and Tob.
136 C3 **Trinidad** U.S.A.
147 D3 **Trinidad and Tobago** country West Indies
143 E3 **Trinity** r. U.S.A.
131 E3 **Trinity Bay** Can.
111 B3 **Tripoli** Greece
80 B2 **Tripoli** Lebanon
115 D1 **Tripoli** Libya
75 D2 **Tripura** state India
113 B9 **Tristan da Cunha** i. S. Atlantic Ocean
73 B4 **Trivandrum** India
108 B2 **Trivento** Italy
103 D2 **Trnava** Slovakia
59 D3 **Trobriand Islands** P.N.G.
92 F2 **Trofors** Norway
109 C2 **Trogir** Croatia
109 C2 **Troia** Italy

100 C2 **Troisdorf** Ger.
106 C2 **Trois Fourches, Cap des** c. Morocco
130 C3 **Trois-Rivières** Can.
87 F3 **Troitsk** Rus. Fed.
86 E2 **Troitsko-Pechorsk** Rus. Fed.
151 D3 **Trombetas** r. Brazil
**Tromelin Island** Micronesia see Fais
123 C3 **Trompsburg** S. Africa
92 G2 **Tromsø** Norway
92 F3 **Trondheim** Norway
96 B3 **Troon** U.K.
89 E3 **Trosna** Rus. Fed.
97 C1 **Trostan** hill U.K.
128 C2 **Trout Lake** Alta Can.
128 B1 **Trout Lake** l. N.W.T. Can.
130 A2 **Trout Lake** l. Ont. Can.
99 B4 **Trowbridge** U.K.
140 C2 **Troy** AL U.S.A.
139 E2 **Troy** NY U.S.A.
105 C2 **Troyes** France
135 C3 **Troy Peak** U.S.A.
109 D2 **Trstenik** Serb. and Mont.
89 D3 **Trubchevsk** Rus. Fed.
**Truc Giang** Vietnam see Bên Tre
106 B1 **Truchas** Spain
**Trucial Coast** country Asia see United Arab Emirates
79 C2 **Trucial Coast** U.A.E.
**Trucial States** country Asia see United Arab Emirates
146 B3 **Trujillo** Hond.
150 B3 **Trujillo** Peru
106 B2 **Trujillo** Spain
147 C4 **Trujillo** Venez.
**Trujillo, Monte** mt. Dom. Rep. see Duarte, Pico
140 B1 **Trumann** U.S.A.
131 D3 **Truro** Can.
99 A4 **Truro** U.K.
61 C1 **Trus Madi, Gunung** mt. Malaysia
142 B2 **Truth or Consequences** U.S.A.
103 D1 **Trutnov** Czech Rep.
93 F3 **Trysil** Norway
103 D1 **Trzebiatów** Pol.
103 D1 **Trzebnica** Pol.
68 B1 **Tsagaannuur** Mongolia
**Tsaidam Basin** China see Qaidam Pendi
121 □D2 **Tsaratanana, Massif du** mts Madag.
110 C2 **Tsarevo** Bulg.
122 A2 **Tsaukaib** Namibia
**Tselinograd** Kazakh. see Astana
**Tsementnyy** Rus. Fed. see Fokino
122 A2 **Tses** Namibia
122 B1 **Tsetseng** Botswana
68 C1 **Tsetserleg** Mongolia
**Tsetserleg** Mongolia see Halban
122 B2 **Tshabong** Botswana
122 B1 **Tshane** Botswana
91 D2 **Tshchikskoye Vodokhranilishche** resr Rus. Fed.
118 B3 **Tshela** Dem. Rep. Congo
118 C3 **Tshikapa** Dem. Rep. Congo
118 C3 **Tshikapa** r. Dem. Rep. Congo
123 C2 **Tshing** S. Africa
123 D1 **Tshipise** S. Africa
118 C3 **Tshitanzu** Dem. Rep. Congo
120 B3 **Tshootsha** Botswana
118 C3 **Tshuapa** r. Dem. Rep. Congo
**Tshwane** S. Africa see Pretoria
87 D4 **Tsimlyanskoye Vodokhranilishche** resr Rus. Fed.
**Tsinan** China see Jinan
**Tsingtao** China see Qingdao
**Tsining** China see Jining
121 □D2 **Tsiroanomandidy** Madag.
**Tsitsihar** China see Qiqihar
76 A2 **Ts'khinvali** Georgia
123 C3 **Tsomo** S. Africa
67 C4 **Tsu** Japan
67 D3 **Tsuchiura** Japan
66 D2 **Tsugarū-kaikyō** str. Japan
**Tsugaru Strait** Japan see Tsugarū-kaikyō
120 A2 **Tsumeb** Namibia
122 A1 **Tsumis Park** Namibia
120 B2 **Tsumkwe** Namibia
66 C3 **Tsuruga** Japan
67 A4 **Tsushima** is Japan
67 C3 **Tsuruoka** Japan
67 C3 **Tsuyama** Japan
123 C2 **Tswelelang** S. Africa
88 C3 **Tsyelyakhany** Belarus
91 C2 **Tsyurupyns'k** Ukr.
**Tthenaagoo** Can. see Nahanni Butte
59 C3 **Tual** Indon.
97 B2 **Tuam** Ireland
54 A3 **Tuapeka Mouth** N.Z.
91 D3 **Tuapse** Rus. Fed.
54 A3 **Tuatapere** N.Z.
142 A1 **Tuba City** U.S.A.
61 C2 **Tuban** Indon.
152 D2 **Tubarão** Brazil
102 B2 **Tübingen** Ger.
115 E1 **Tubruq** Libya
49 L6 **Tubuai Islands** is Fr. Polynesia
144 A1 **Tubutama** Mex.
152 C1 **Tucavaca** Bol.
128 B1 **Tuchitua** Can.

142 A2 **Tucson** U.S.A.
143 C1 **Tucumcari** U.S.A.
150 C2 **Tucupita** Venez.
151 E3 **Tucuruí** Brazil
151 E3 **Tucuruí, Represa** resr Brazil
107 C1 **Tudela** Spain
106 B1 **Tuela** r. Port.
157 F2 **Tufts Abyssal Plain** sea feature N. Pacific Ocean
123 D2 **Tugela** r. S. Africa
64 B2 **Tuguegarao** Phil.
106 B1 **Tui** Spain
59 C3 **Tukangbesi, Kepulauan** is Indon.
126 D2 **Tuktoyaktuk** Can.
88 B2 **Tukums** Latvia
119 D3 **Tukuyu** Tanz.
145 C2 **Tula** Mex.
89 E3 **Tula** Rus. Fed.
**Tulach Mhór** Rep. of Ireland see Tullamore
145 C2 **Tulancingo** Mex.
135 C3 **Tulare** U.S.A.
142 B2 **Tularosa** U.S.A.
110 C1 **Tulcea** Romania
90 B2 **Tul'chyn** Ukr.
**Tuléar** Madag. see Toliara
129 E1 **Tulemalu Lake** Can.
143 C2 **Tulia** U.S.A.
128 B1 **Tulita** Can.
140 C1 **Tullahoma** U.S.A.
53 C2 **Tullamore** Austr.
97 C2 **Tullamore** Ireland
104 C2 **Tulle** France
97 C2 **Tullow** Ireland
51 D1 **Tully** Austr.
143 D1 **Tulsa** U.S.A.
126 B2 **Tuluksak** U.S.A.
83 H3 **Tulun** Rus. Fed.
150 B2 **Tumaco** Col.
123 C2 **Tumahole** S. Africa
93 G4 **Tumba** Sweden
118 B3 **Tumba, Lac** l. Dem. Rep. Congo
61 C2 **Tumbangtiti** Indon.
53 C3 **Tumbarumba** Austr.
150 A3 **Tumbes** Peru
128 B2 **Tumbler Ridge** Can.
52 A2 **Tumby Bay** Austr.
65 B1 **Tumen** China
150 C2 **Tumereng** Guyana
64 A3 **Tumindao** i. Phil.
74 A2 **Tump** Pak.
151 D2 **Tumucumaque, Serra** hills Brazil
53 C3 **Tumut** Austr.
99 D4 **Tunbridge Wells, Royal** U.K.
80 B2 **Tunceli** Turkey
53 D2 **Tuncurry** Austr.
118 A1 **Tundun-Wada** Nigeria
119 D4 **Tunduru** Tanz.
110 C2 **Tundzha** r. Bulg.
128 B1 **Tungsten** Can.
115 D1 **Tunis** Tunisia
108 B3 **Tunis, Golfe de** g. Tunisia
115 C1 **Tunisia** country Africa
150 B2 **Tunja** Col.
92 F3 **Tunnsjøen** l. Norway
**Tunxi** China see Huangshan
154 B2 **Tupã** Brazil
154 C1 **Tupaciguara** Brazil
140 C2 **Tupelo** U.S.A.
152 B2 **Tupiza** Bol.
83 H2 **Tura** Rus. Fed.
86 F3 **Tura** r. Rus. Fed.
78 B2 **Turabah** Saudi Arabia
83 J3 **Turana, Khrebet** mts Rus. Fed.
54 C1 **Turangi** N.Z.
76 B2 **Turan Lowland** Asia
77 D2 **Turar Ryskulov** Kazakh.
78 A1 **Ṭurayf** Saudi Arabia
88 B2 **Turba** Estonia
74 A2 **Turbat** Pak.
150 B2 **Turbo** Col.
110 B1 **Turda** Romania
**Turfan** China see Turpan
76 C2 **Turgay** Kazakh.
76 C1 **Turgayskaya Stolovaya Strana** reg. Kazakh.
110 C2 **Tŭrgovishte** Bulg.
111 C3 **Turgutlu** Turkey
80 B1 **Turhal** Turkey
107 C2 **Turia** r. Spain
108 A1 **Turin** Italy
86 F3 **Turinsk** Rus. Fed.
90 A1 **Turiya** r. Ukr.
90 A1 **Turiys'k** Ukr.
90 A2 **Turka** Ukr.
119 D2 **Turkana, Lake** salt l. Eth./Kenya
77 C2 **Turkestan** Kazakh.
103 E2 **Túrkeve** Hungary
80 B2 **Turkey** country Asia/Europe
50 B1 **Turkey Creek** Austr.
76 C3 **Turkmenabat** Turkm.
76 B2 **Turkmenbashi** Turkm.
76 B2 **Turkmenistan** country Asia
**Turkmeniya** country Asia see Turkmenistan
**Turkmenskaya S.S.R.** admin. reg. Asia see Turkmenistan
147 C2 **Turks and Caicos Islands** terr. West Indies
147 C2 **Turks Islands** Turks and Caicos Is
93 H3 **Turku** Fin.
119 D2 **Turkwel** watercourse Kenya
135 B3 **Turlock** U.S.A.
155 D1 **Turmalina** Brazil
54 C2 **Turnagain, Cape** N.Z.

Valença
219

146 B3 **Turneffe Islands** Belize
100 B2 **Turnhout** Belgium
129 D2 **Turnor Lake** Can.
**Tŭrnovo** Bulg. *see* **Veliko Tŭrnovo**
110 B2 **Turnu Măgurele** Romania
68 B2 **Turpan** China
96 C2 **Turriff** U.K.
64 A3 **Turtle Islands** Phil.
77 D2 **Turugart Pass** China/Kyrg.
82 G2 **Turukhansk** Rus. Fed.
140 C2 **Tuscaloosa** U.S.A.
140 C2 **Tuskegee** U.S.A.
81 C2 **Tutak** Turkey
89 E2 **Tutayev** Rus. Fed.
73 B4 **Tuticorin** India
121 C1 **Tutubu** Tanz.
49 J5 **Tutuila** *i.* American Samoa
120 B3 **Tutume** Botswana
93 H3 **Tuusula** Fin.
49 I4 **Tuvalu** *country* S. Pacific Ocean
78 B2 **Tuwayq, Jabal** *hills* Saudi Arabia
78 B2 **Tuwayq, Jabal** *mts* Saudi Arabia
78 A2 **Tuwwal** Saudi Arabia
144 B2 **Tuxpan** Mex.
145 C2 **Tuxpan** Mex.
145 C3 **Tuxtla Gutiérrez** Mex.
62 B1 **Tuyên Quang** Vietnam
63 B2 **Tuy Hoa** Vietnam
80 B2 **Tuz, Lake** *salt l.* Turkey
**Tuz Gölü** *salt l.* Turkey *see* **Tuz, Lake**
81 C2 **Tuz Khurmātū** Iraq
109 C2 **Tuzla** Bos.-Herz.
91 E2 **Tuzlov** *r.* Rus. Fed.
89 E2 **Tver'** Rus. Fed.
98 B2 **Tweed** *r.* U.K.
53 D1 **Tweed Heads** Austr.
122 A2 **Twee Rivier** Namibia
135 C4 **Twentynine Palms** U.S.A.
131 E3 **Twillingate** Can.
134 D2 **Twin Falls** U.S.A.
54 B2 **Twizel** *South I.* N.Z.
137 E1 **Two Harbors** U.S.A.
128 C2 **Two Hills** Can.
**Tyddewi** U.K. *see* **St David's**
143 D2 **Tyler** U.S.A.
83 J3 **Tynda** Rus. Fed.
**Tyndinskiy** Rus. Fed. *see* **Tynda**
96 B2 **Tyndrum** U.K.
98 C2 **Tyne** *r. England* U.K.
95 C2 **Tyne** *r. Scotland* U.K.
93 F3 **Tynset** Norway
80 B2 **Tyre** Lebanon
69 E1 **Tyrma** Rus. Fed.
111 B3 **Tyrnavos** Greece
52 B3 **Tyrrell, Lake** *dry lake* Austr.
108 B2 **Tyrrhenian Sea** France/Italy
76 B2 **Tyub-Karagan, Mys** *pt* Kazakh.
87 E3 **Tyul'gan** Rus. Fed.
86 F3 **Tyumen'** Rus. Fed.
83 J2 **Tyung** *r.* Rus. Fed.
**Tyuratam** Kazakh. *see* **Baykonyr**
99 A4 **Tywi** *r.* U.K.
123 D1 **Tzaneen** S. Africa

## U

**Uaco Congo** Angola *see* **Waku-Kungo**
120 B2 **Uamanda** Angola
150 C3 **Uarini** Brazil
150 C3 **Uaupés** Brazil
155 D2 **Ubá** Brazil
155 D1 **Ubaí** Brazil
151 F4 **Ubaitaba** Brazil
118 B3 **Ubangi** *r.* C.A.R./Dem. Rep. Congo
**Ubangi-Shari** *country* Africa *see* **Central African Republic**
67 B4 **Ube** Japan
106 C2 **Úbeda** Spain
154 C1 **Uberaba** Brazil
154 C1 **Uberlândia** Brazil
123 D2 **Ubombo** S. Africa
63 B2 **Ubon Ratchathani** Thai.
119 C3 **Ubundu** Dem. Rep. Congo
150 B3 **Ucayali** *r.* Peru
100 B2 **Uccle** Belgium
74 B2 **Uch** Pak.
77 E2 **Ucharal** Kazakh.
66 D2 **Uchiura-wan** *b.* Japan
76 C2 **Uchquduq** Uzbek.
83 J3 **Uchur** *r.* Rus. Fed.
99 D4 **Uckfield** U.K.
128 B3 **Ucluelet** Can.
83 I2 **Udachnyy** Rus. Fed.
74 B2 **Udaipur** India
91 C1 **Uday** *r.* Ukr.
93 F4 **Uddevalla** Sweden
92 G2 **Uddjaure** *l.* Sweden
100 B2 **Uden** Neth.
74 B1 **Udhampur** Jammu and Kashmir
108 B1 **Udine** Italy
89 E2 **Udomlya** Rus. Fed.
62 B2 **Udon Thani** Thai.
73 B3 **Udupi** India
83 K3 **Udyl', Ozero** *l.* Rus. Fed.
67 C3 **Ueda** Japan
61 D2 **Uekuli** Indon.
118 C2 **Uele** *r.* Dem. Rep. Congo
83 N2 **Uelen** Rus. Fed.
101 E1 **Uelzen** Ger.
119 C2 **Uere** *r.* Dem. Rep. Congo
87 E3 **Ufa** Rus. Fed.
119 D3 **Ugalla** *r.* Tanz.
119 D2 **Uganda** *country* Africa
69 F1 **Uglegorsk** Rus. Fed.
89 E2 **Uglich** Rus. Fed.
89 D2 **Uglovka** Rus. Fed.
66 B2 **Uglovoye** Rus. Fed.
89 D3 **Ugra** Rus. Fed.
103 D2 **Uherské Hradiště** Czech Rep.
**Uibhist a' Deas** *i.* U.K. *see* **South Uist**
**Uibhist a' Tuath** *i.* U.K. *see* **North Uist**
101 E2 **Uichteritz** Ger.
96 A2 **Uig** U.K.
120 A1 **Uíge** Angola
65 B2 **Ŭijŏngbu** S. Korea
65 A1 **Ŭiju** N. Korea
135 D2 **Uinta Mountains** U.S.A.
120 A3 **Uis Mine** Namibia
65 B2 **Ŭisŏng** S. Korea
123 C3 **Uitenhage** S. Africa
100 C1 **Uithuizen** Neth.
131 D2 **Uivak, Cape** Can.
**Ujiyamada** Japan *see* **Ise**
74 B2 **Ujjain** India
**Ujung Pandang** Indon. *see* **Makassar**
89 F3 **Ukholovo** Rus. Fed.
**Ukhta** Rus. Fed. *see* **Kalevala**
86 E2 **Ukhta** Rus. Fed.
135 B3 **Ukiah** U.S.A.
127 I2 **Ukkusissat** Greenland
88 B2 **Ukmergė** Lith.
90 C2 **Ukraine** *country* Europe
**Ukrainskaya S.S.R.** *admin. reg.* Europe *see* **Ukraine**
**Ulaanbaatar** Mongolia *see* **Ulan Bator**
68 C1 **Ulaangom** Mongolia
59 E3 **Ulamona** P.N.G.
70 A2 **Ulan** China
69 D1 **Ulan Bator** Mongolia
**Ulanhad** China *see* **Chifeng**
69 E1 **Ulanhot** China
87 D4 **Ulan-Khol** Rus. Fed.
69 D1 **Ulan-Ude** Rus. Fed.
75 D1 **Ulan Ul Hu** *l.* China
65 B2 **Ulchin** S. Korea
**Uleåborg** Fin. *see* **Oulu**
88 C2 **Ülenurme** Estonia
74 B3 **Ulhasnagar** India
69 D1 **Uliastai** China
68 C1 **Uliastay** Mongolia
59 D2 **Ulithi** *atoll* Micronesia
53 D3 **Ulladulla** Austr.
96 B2 **Ullapool** U.K.
98 B2 **Ullswater** *l.* U.K.
65 C2 **Ullŭng-do** *i.* S. Korea
102 B2 **Ulm** Ger.
65 B2 **Ulsan** S. Korea
96 □ **Ulsta** U.K.
97 C1 **Ulster** *reg.* Ireland/U.K.
52 B3 **Ultima** Austr.
145 D3 **Ulúa** *r.* Hond.
111 C3 **Ulubey** Turkey
111 D3 **Uluborlu** Turkey
111 C2 **Uludağ** *mt.* Turkey
123 D2 **Ulundi** S. Africa
77 E2 **Ulungur Hu** *l.* China
**Uluqsaqtuuq** Can. *see* **Holman**
50 C2 **Uluṟu** *hill* Austr.
98 B2 **Ulverston** U.K.
90 C2 **Ul'yanovka** Ukr.
87 D3 **Ul'yanovsk** Rus. Fed.
136 C3 **Ulysses** U.S.A.
90 C2 **Uman'** Ukr.
86 C2 **Umba** Rus. Fed.
59 D3 **Umboi** *i.* P.N.G.
59 D3 **Umbukul** P.N.G.
92 H3 **Umeå** Sweden
92 H3 **Umeälven** *r.* Sweden
123 D2 **Umhlanga Rocks** S. Africa
127 J2 **Umiiviip Kangertiva** *inlet* Greenland
126 E2 **Umingmaktok** Can.
123 D2 **Umlazi** S. Africa
78 A2 **Umm al Birak** Saudi Arabia
79 C2 **Umm as Samīm** *salt flat* Oman
116 A3 **Umm Keddada** Sudan
78 A2 **Umm Lajj** Saudi Arabia
78 A2 **Umm Mukhbār, Jabal** *hill* Saudi Arabia
116 B3 **Umm Ruwaba** Sudan
115 E1 **Umm Sa'ad** Libya
134 B2 **Umpqua** *r.* U.S.A.
120 A2 **Umpulo** Angola
**Umtali** Zimbabwe *see* **Mutare**
123 C3 **Umtata** S. Africa
123 D3 **Umtentweni** S. Africa
154 B2 **Umuarama** Brazil
123 C3 **Umzimkulu** S. Africa
109 C1 **Una** *r.* Bos.-Herz./Croatia
155 E1 **Una** Brazil
154 C1 **Unaí** Brazil
126 B2 **Unalakleet** U.S.A.
78 B2 **'Unayzah** Saudi Arabia
136 B3 **Uncompahgre Peak** U.S.A.
52 B3 **Underbool** Austr.
136 C1 **Underwood** U.S.A.
89 D3 **Unecha** Rus. Fed.
53 C2 **Ungarie** Austr.
52 A2 **Ungarra** Austr.
127 H2 **Ungava, Péninsule d'** *pen.* Can.
131 D2 **Ungava Bay** Can.
**Ungeny** Moldova *see* **Ungheni**
65 C1 **Unggi** N. Korea
90 B2 **Ungheni** Moldova
**Unguja** *i.* Tanz. *see* **Zanzibar Island**
119 E3 **Ungwana Bay** Kenya
154 B3 **União da Vitória** Brazil
150 C3 **Unini** *r.* Brazil
134 C1 **Union** U.S.A.
140 C1 **Union City** U.S.A.
122 B3 **Uniondale** S. Africa
139 D3 **Uniontown** U.S.A.
79 C2 **United Arab Emirates** *country* Asia
**United Arab Republic** *country* Africa *see* **Egypt**
95 C3 **United Kingdom** *country* Europe
**United Provinces** *state* India *see* **Uttar Pradesh**
133 B3 **United States of America** *country* N. America
129 D2 **Unity** Can.
100 C2 **Unna** Ger.
96 □ **Unst** *i.* U.K.
101 E2 **Unstrut** *r.* Ger.
89 E3 **Upa** *r.* Rus. Fed.
119 C3 **Upemba, Lac** *l.* Dem. Rep. Congo
122 B2 **Upington** S. Africa
74 B2 **Upleta** India
49 J5 **Upolu** *i.* Samoa
134 B2 **Upper Alkali Lake** U.S.A.
128 C2 **Upper Arrow Lake** Can.
54 C2 **Upper Hutt** N.Z.
134 B2 **Upper Klamath Lake** U.S.A.
128 B1 **Upper Liard** Can.
97 C1 **Upper Lough Erne** *l.* U.K.
137 E1 **Upper Red Lake** U.S.A.
**Upper Tunguska** *r.* Rus. Fed. *see* **Angara**
**Upper Volta** *country* Africa *see* **Burkina**
93 G4 **Uppsala** Sweden
78 B2 **'Uqlat aş Şuqūr** Saudi Arabia
**Urad Qianqi** China *see* **Xishanzui**
76 B2 **Ural** *r.* Kazakh./Rus. Fed.
53 D2 **Uralla** Austr.
87 E3 **Ural Mountains** Rus. Fed.
76 B1 **Ural'sk** Kazakh.
**Ural'skiy Khrebet** *mts* Rus. Fed. *see* **Ural Mountains**
119 D3 **Urambo** Tanz.
53 C3 **Urana** Austr.
129 D2 **Uranium City** Can.
86 F2 **Uray** Rus. Fed.
98 C2 **Ure** *r.* U.K.
86 D3 **Uren'** Rus. Fed.
82 G2 **Urengoy** Rus. Fed.
144 A2 **Ures** Mex.
**Urfa** Turkey *see* **Şanlıurfa**
76 C2 **Urganch** Uzbek.
100 B1 **Urk** Neth.
111 C3 **Urla** Turkey
110 C2 **Urlaţi** Romania
81 C2 **Urmia** Iran
81 C2 **Urmia, Lake** *salt l.* Iran
109 D2 **Uroševac** Serb. and Mont.
144 B2 **Uruáchic** Mex.
151 E4 **Uruaçu** Brazil
144 B3 **Uruapan** Mex.
150 B4 **Urubamba** *r.* Peru
151 D3 **Urucara** Brazil
151 E3 **Uruçuí** Brazil
151 E3 **Uruçuí, Serra do** *hills* Brazil
151 D3 **Urucurituba** Brazil
152 C2 **Uruguaiana** Brazil
153 C3 **Uruguay** *country* S. America
**Urumchi** China *see* **Ürümqi**
68 B2 **Ürümqi** China
**Urundi** *country* Africa *see* **Burundi**
53 D2 **Urunga** Austr.
78 B3 **'Urūq al Awārik** *des.* Saudi Arabia
119 D3 **Uruwira** Tanz.
110 C2 **Urziceni** Romania
67 B4 **Usa** Japan
86 E2 **Usa** *r.* Rus. Fed.
111 C3 **Uşak** Turkey
120 A3 **Usakos** Namibia
88 C2 **Ushachy** Belarus
82 G1 **Ushakova, Ostrov** *i.* Rus. Fed.
77 D2 **Ushtobe** Kazakh.
**Ush-Tyube** Kazakh. *see* **Ushtobe**
153 B5 **Ushuaia** Arg.
86 E2 **Usinsk** Rus. Fed.
99 B4 **Usk** *r.* U.K.
88 C3 **Uskhodni** Belarus
89 E3 **Usman'** Rus. Fed.
86 D2 **Usogorsk** Rus. Fed.
104 C2 **Ussel** France
66 C1 **Ussuri** *r.* China/Rus. Fed.
66 B2 **Ussuriysk** Rus. Fed.
**Ust'-Abakanskoye** Rus. Fed. *see* **Abakan**
**Ust'-Balyk** Rus. Fed. *see* **Nefteyugansk**
91 E2 **Ust'-Donetskiy** Rus. Fed.
108 B3 **Ustica, Isola di** *i. Sicily* Italy
83 H3 **Ust'-Ilimsk** Rus. Fed.
86 E2 **Ust'-Ilych** Rus. Fed.
102 C1 **Ústí nad Labem** Czech Rep.
**Ustinov** Rus. Fed. *see* **Izhevsk**
103 D1 **Ustka** Pol.
83 L3 **Ust'-Kamchatsk** Rus. Fed.
77 E2 **Ust'-Kamenogorsk** Kazakh.
86 F2 **Ust'-Kara** Rus. Fed.
86 E2 **Ust'-Kulom** Rus. Fed.
83 I3 **Ust'-Kut** Rus. Fed.
91 D2 **Ust'-Labinsk** Rus. Fed.
**Ust'-Labinskaya** Rus. Fed. *see* **Ust'-Labinsk**
88 C2 **Ust'-Luga** Rus. Fed.
86 E2 **Ust'-Nem** Rus. Fed.
83 K2 **Ust'-Nera** Rus. Fed.
83 I2 **Ust'-Olenek** Rus. Fed.
83 K2 **Ust'-Omchug** Rus. Fed.
83 H3 **Ust'-Ordynskiy** Rus. Fed.
103 E2 **Ustrzyki Dolne** Pol.
86 E2 **Ust'-Tsil'ma** Rus. Fed.
86 D2 **Ust'-Ura** Rus. Fed.
76 B2 **Ustyurt Plateau** Kazakh./Uzbek.
89 E2 **Ustyuzhna** Rus. Fed.
146 B3 **Usulután** El Salvador
**Usumbura** Burundi *see* **Bujumbura**
89 D2 **Usvyaty** Rus. Fed.
135 D3 **Utah** *state* U.S.A.
135 D2 **Utah Lake** U.S.A.
88 C2 **Utena** Lith.
119 D3 **Utete** Tanz.
63 B2 **Uthai Thani** Thai.
74 A2 **Uthal** Pak.
139 D2 **Utica** U.S.A.
107 C2 **Utiel** Spain
128 C2 **Utikuma Lake** Can.
93 G4 **Utlängan** *i.* Sweden
100 B1 **Utrecht** Neth.
123 D2 **Utrecht** S. Africa
106 B2 **Utrera** Spain
92 I2 **Utsjoki** Fin.
67 C3 **Utsunomiya** Japan
87 D4 **Utta** Rus. Fed.
62 B2 **Uttaradit** Thai.
75 B1 **Uttaranchal** *state* India
75 B2 **Uttar Pradesh** *state* India
**Uummannaq** Greenland *see* **Dundas**
127 I2 **Uummannaq** Greenland
127 I2 **Uummannaq Fjord** *inlet* Greenland
93 H3 **Uusikaupunki** Fin.
120 A2 **Uutapi** Namibia
143 D3 **Uvalde** U.S.A.
81 D1 **Uval Karabaur** *hills* Uzbek.
119 D3 **Uvinza** Tanz.
123 D3 **Uvongo** S. Africa
68 C1 **Uvs Nuur** *salt l.* Mongolia
67 B4 **Uwajima** Japan
78 A2 **'Uwayriḍ, Ḥarrat al** *lava field* Saudi Arabia
116 A2 **Uweinat, Jebel** *mt.* Sudan
83 H3 **Uyar** Rus. Fed.
115 C4 **Uyo** Nigeria
79 B2 **Uyun** Saudi Arabia
152 B2 **Uyuni** Bol.
152 B2 **Uyuni, Salar de** *salt flat* Bol.
76 C2 **Uzbekistan** *country* Asia
**Uzbekskaya S.S.R.** *admin. reg.* Asia *see* **Uzbekistan**
**Uzbek S.S.R.** *admin.reg.* Asia *see* **Uzbekistan**
104 C2 **Uzerche** France
105 C3 **Uzès** France
90 C1 **Uzh** *r.* Ukr.
90 A2 **Uzhhorod** Ukr.
**Užhorod** Ukr. *see* **Uzhhorod**
109 C2 **Užice** Serb. and Mont.
89 E3 **Uzlovaya** Rus. Fed.
111 C3 **Üzümlü** Turkey
111 C2 **Uzunköprü** Turkey

## V

123 B2 **Vaal** *r.* S. Africa
92 I3 **Vaala** Fin.
123 C2 **Vaal Dam** S. Africa
123 C1 **Vaalwater** S. Africa
92 H3 **Vaasa** Fin.
103 D2 **Vác** Hungary
152 C2 **Vacaria** Brazil
154 B2 **Vacaria, Serra** *hills* Brazil
135 B3 **Vacaville** U.S.A.
74 B2 **Vadodara** India
92 I1 **Vadsø** Norway
105 D2 **Vaduz** Liechtenstein
94 B1 **Vágar** *i.* Faroe Is
94 B1 **Vágur** Faroe Is
103 D2 **Váh** *r.* Slovakia
49 I4 **Vaiaku** Tuvalu
88 B2 **Vaida** Estonia
136 B3 **Vail** U.S.A.
77 C3 **Vakhsh** Tajik.
**Vakhstroy** Tajik. *see* **Vakhsh**
79 C2 **Vakīlābād** Iran
108 B1 **Valdagno** Italy
**Valdai Hills** Rus. Fed. *see* **Valdayskaya Vozvyshennost'**
89 D2 **Valday** Rus. Fed.
89 D2 **Valdayskaya Vozvyshennost'** *hills* Rus. Fed.
106 B2 **Valdecañas, Embalse de** *resr* Spain
93 G4 **Valdemarsvik** Sweden
105 D2 **Val-de-Meuse** France
106 C2 **Valdepeñas** Spain
153 B4 **Valdés, Península** *pen.* Arg.
126 C2 **Valdez** U.S.A.
153 A3 **Valdivia** Chile
130 C3 **Val-d'Or** Can.
141 D2 **Valdosta** U.S.A.
128 C2 **Valemount** Can.
152 E1 **Valença** Brazil

105 C3 **Valence** France
107 C2 **Valencia** Spain
107 C2 **Valencia** *aut. Comm.* Spain
150 C1 **Valencia** Venez.
107 D2 **Valencia, Golfo de** *g.* Spain
106 B1 **Valencia de Don Juan** Spain
97 A3 **Valencia Island** Ireland
105 C1 **Valenciennes** France
136 C2 **Valentine** U.S.A.
64 B2 **Valenzuela** Phil.
150 B2 **Valera** Venez.
88 C2 **Valga** Estonia
109 C2 **Valjevo** Serb. and Mont.
88 C2 **Valka** Latvia
93 H3 **Valkeakoski** Fin.
100 B2 **Valkenswaard** Neth.
91 D2 **Valky** Ukr.
55 G2 **Valkyrie Dome** *ice feature* Antarctica
145 D2 **Valladolid** Mex.
106 C1 **Valladolid** Spain
107 C2 **Vall de Uxó** Spain
93 E4 **Valle** Norway
145 C2 **Vallecillos** Mex.
150 C2 **Valle de la Pascua** Venez.
150 B1 **Valledupar** Col.
145 C2 **Valle Hermoso** Mex.
135 B3 **Vallejo** U.S.A.
152 A2 **Vallenar** Chile
84 F5 **Valletta** Malta
137 D1 **Valley City** U.S.A.
134 B2 **Valley Falls** U.S.A.
128 C2 **Valleyview** Can.
107 D1 **Valls** Spain
129 D3 **Val Marie** Can.
88 C2 **Valmiera** Latvia
104 B2 **Valognes** France
88 C2 **Valozhyn** Belarus
154 B2 **Valparaíso** Brazil
153 A3 **Valparaíso** Chile
105 C3 **Valréas** France
59 D3 **Vals, Tanjung** *c.* Indon.
74 B2 **Valsad** India
122 B2 **Valspan** S. Africa
91 D1 **Valuyki** Rus. Fed.
106 B2 **Valverde del Camino** Spain
81 C2 **Van** Turkey
81 C2 **Van, Lake** *salt l.* Turkey
81 C1 **Vanadzor** Armenia
83 H2 **Vanavara** Rus. Fed.
140 B1 **Van Buren** *AR* U.S.A.
139 F1 **Van Buren** *ME* U.S.A.
**Van Buren** U.S.A. *see* Kettering
128 B3 **Vancouver** Can.
134 B1 **Vancouver** U.S.A.
128 B3 **Vancouver Island** Can.
138 B3 **Vandalia** *IL* U.S.A.
138 C3 **Vandalia** *OH* U.S.A.
123 C2 **Vanderbijlpark** S. Africa
128 B2 **Vanderhoof** Can.
122 B3 **Vanderkloof Dam** *resr* S. Africa
50 C1 **Van Diemen Gulf** Austr.
88 C2 **Vändra** Estonia
**Väner, Lake** Sweden *see* Vänern
93 F4 **Vänern** *l.* Sweden
93 F4 **Vänersborg** Sweden
121 □D3 **Vangaindrano** Madag.
**Van Gölü** *salt l.* Turkey *see* Van, Lake
142 C2 **Van Horn** U.S.A.
59 D3 **Vanimo** P.N.G.
83 K3 **Vanino** Rus. Fed.
104 B2 **Vannes** France
**Vannovka** Kazakh. *see* Turar Ryskulov
59 D3 **Van Rees, Pegunungan** *mts* Indon.
122 A3 **Vanrhynsdorp** S. Africa
93 H3 **Vantaa** Fin.
49 I5 **Vanua Levu** *i.* Fiji
48 H5 **Vanuatu** *country* S. Pacific Ocean
138 C2 **Van Wert** U.S.A.
122 B3 **Vanwyksvlei** S. Africa
122 B2 **Van Zylsrus** S. Africa
75 C2 **Varanasi** India
92 I1 **Varangerfjorden** *sea chan.* Norway
92 I1 **Varangerhalvøya** *pen.* Norway
88 C2 **Varapayeva** Belarus
109 C1 **Varaždin** Croatia
93 F4 **Varberg** Sweden
111 B3 **Varda** Greece
111 B2 **Vardar** *r.* Macedonia
93 E4 **Varde** Denmark
92 I1 **Vardø** Norway
101 D1 **Varel** Ger.
88 B3 **Varėna** Lith.
139 E1 **Varennes** Can.
108 A1 **Varese** Italy
155 C2 **Varginha** Brazil
93 I3 **Varkaus** Fin.
110 C2 **Varna** Bulg.
93 F4 **Värnamo** Sweden
155 D1 **Várzea da Palma** Brazil
86 D2 **Varzino** Rus. Fed.
**Vasa** Fin. *see* Vaasa
88 C3 **Vasilyevichy** Belarus
88 C2 **Vasknarva** Estonia
110 C1 **Vaslui** Romania
93 G4 **Västerås** Sweden
93 G3 **Västerdalälven** *r.* Sweden
88 A2 **Västerhaninge** Sweden
93 G4 **Västervik** Sweden
108 B2 **Vasto** Italy
91 D2 **Vasylivka** Ukr.

90 C1 **Vasyl'kiv** Ukr.
91 D2 **Vasyl'kivka** Ukr.
104 C2 **Vatan** France
111 B3 **Vathia** Greece
108 B2 **Vatican City** Europe
92 □B3 **Vatnajökull** *ice cap* Iceland
110 C1 **Vatra Dornei** Romania
**Vätter, Lake** Sweden *see* Vättern
93 F4 **Vättern** *l.* Sweden
142 B2 **Vaughn** U.S.A.
105 C3 **Vauvert** France
121 □D2 **Vavatenina** Madag.
49 J5 **Vava'u Group** *is* Tonga
88 B3 **Vawkavysk** Belarus
93 F4 **Växjö** Sweden
**Vayenga** Rus. Fed. *see* Severomorsk
86 E1 **Vaygach, Ostrov** *i.* Rus. Fed.
154 C1 **Vazante** Brazil
101 D1 **Vechta** Ger.
110 C2 **Vedea** *r.* Romania
100 C1 **Veendam** Neth.
100 B1 **Veenendaal** Neth.
92 F2 **Vega** *i.* Norway
128 C2 **Vegreville** Can.
106 B2 **Vejer de la Frontera** Spain
93 E4 **Vejle** Denmark
110 B2 **Velbüzhdki Prokhod** *pass* Macedonia
122 A3 **Velddrif** S. Africa
100 B2 **Veldhoven** Neth.
109 C2 **Velebit** *mts* Croatia
100 C2 **Velen** Ger.
109 C1 **Velenje** Slovenia
109 D2 **Veles** Macedonia
106 C2 **Vélez-Málaga** Spain
155 D1 **Velhas** *r.* Brazil
109 D2 **Velika Plana** Serb. and Mont.
88 C2 **Velikaya** *r.* Rus. Fed.
89 D2 **Velikiye Luki** Rus. Fed.
89 D2 **Velikiy Novgorod** Rus. Fed.
86 D2 **Velikiy Ustyug** Rus. Fed.
110 C2 **Veliko Tŭrnovo** Bulg.
108 B2 **Veli Lošinj** Croatia
89 D2 **Velizh** Rus. Fed.
108 B2 **Velletri** Italy
73 B3 **Vellore** India
86 C2 **Vel'sk** Rus. Fed.
101 F1 **Velten** Ger.
91 D1 **Velykyy Burluk** Ukr.
**Velykyy Tokmak** Ukr. *see* Tokmak
159 E4 **Vema Trench** *sea feature* Indian Ocean
108 B2 **Venafro** Italy
154 C2 **Venceslau Bráz** Brazil
104 C2 **Vendôme** France
108 B1 **Veneta, Laguna** *lag.* Italy
89 E3 **Venev** Rus. Fed.
**Venezia** Italy *see* Venice
150 C1 **Venezuela** *country* S. America
150 B1 **Venezuela, Golfo de** *g.* Venez.
108 B1 **Venice** Italy
141 D3 **Venice** U.S.A.
108 B1 **Venice, Gulf of** Europe
100 C2 **Venlo** Neth.
93 E4 **Vennesla** Norway
100 B1 **Venray** Neth.
88 B2 **Venta** *r.* Latvia/Lith.
88 B2 **Venta** Lith.
123 C2 **Ventersburg** S. Africa
123 C3 **Venterstad** S. Africa
108 A2 **Ventimiglia** Italy
99 C4 **Ventnor** U.K.
88 B2 **Ventspils** Latvia
135 C4 **Ventura** U.S.A.
143 C3 **Venustiano Carranza, Presa** *resr* Mex.
107 C2 **Vera** Spain
154 C2 **Vera Cruz** Brazil
145 C3 **Veracruz** Mex.
74 B2 **Veraval** India
108 A1 **Verbania** Italy
108 A1 **Vercelli** Italy
105 D3 **Vercors** *reg.* France
92 F3 **Verdalsøra** Norway
154 B1 **Verde** *r.* Brazil
154 B2 **Verde** *r.* Brazil
144 B2 **Verde** *r.* Mex.
142 A2 **Verde** *r.* U.S.A.
155 D1 **Verde Grande** *r.* Brazil
101 D1 **Verden (Aller)** Ger.
154 B1 **Verdinho, Serra do** *mts* Brazil
105 C3 **Verdon** *r.* France
105 D2 **Verdun** France
123 C2 **Vereeniging** S. Africa
106 B1 **Verín** Spain
91 D2 **Verkhnebakanskiy** Rus. Fed.
89 D3 **Verkhnedneprovskiy** Rus. Fed.
92 J2 **Verkhnetulomskiy** Rus. Fed.
92 J2 **Verkhnetulomskoye Vodokhranilishche** *resr* Rus. Fed.
87 D4 **Verkhniy Baskunchak** Rus. Fed.
91 E1 **Verkhniy Mamon** Rus. Fed.
86 F2 **Verkhnyaya Toyma** Rus. Fed.
89 E3 **Verkhov'ye** Rus. Fed.
90 A2 **Verkhovyna** Ukr.
83 J2 **Verkhoyanskiy Khrebet** *mts* Rus. Fed.
129 C2 **Vermilion** Can.
137 D2 **Vermillion** U.S.A.
130 A3 **Vermillion Bay** Can.
139 E2 **Vermont** *state* U.S.A.
135 E2 **Vernal** U.S.A.
122 B2 **Verneuk Pan** *salt pan* S. Africa

128 C2 **Vernon** Can.
143 D2 **Vernon** U.S.A.
141 D3 **Vero Beach** U.S.A.
111 B2 **Veroia** Greece
108 B1 **Verona** Italy
138 B2 **Verona** U.S.A.
104 C2 **Versailles** France
104 B2 **Vertou** France
123 D2 **Verulam** S. Africa
100 B2 **Verviers** Belgium
105 C2 **Vervins** France
105 D3 **Vescovato** Corsica France
87 E3 **Veselaya, Gora** *mt.* Rus. Fed.
91 C2 **Vesele** Ukr.
91 E2 **Veselyy** Rus. Fed.
105 D2 **Vesoul** France
140 C2 **Vestavia Hills** U.S.A.
92 F2 **Vesterålen** *is* Norway
92 F2 **Vestfjorden** *sea chan.* Norway
94 B1 **Vestmanna** Faroe Is
92 □A3 **Vestmannaeyjar** Iceland
92 □A3 **Vestmannaeyjar** *is* Iceland
93 E3 **Vestnes** Norway
**Vesuvio** *vol.* Italy *see* Vesuvius
108 B2 **Vesuvius** *vol.* Italy
89 E2 **Ves'yegonsk** Rus. Fed.
103 D2 **Veszprém** Hungary
93 G4 **Vetlanda** Sweden
86 D3 **Vetluga** Rus. Fed.
86 D3 **Vetluzhskiy** Rus. Fed.
100 A2 **Veurne** Belgium
119 D2 **Veveno** *r.* Sudan
105 D2 **Vevey** Switz.
91 D1 **Veydelevka** Rus. Fed.
80 B1 **Vezirköprü** Turkey
**Vialar** Alg. *see* Tissemsilt
152 C3 **Viamao** Brazil
151 E3 **Viana** Brazil
106 B1 **Viana do Castelo** Port.
62 B1 **Viangchan** Laos *see* Vientiane
62 B1 **Viangphoukha** Laos
154 C1 **Vianópolis** Brazil
108 B2 **Viareggio** Italy
93 E4 **Viborg** Denmark
**Viborg** Rus. Fed. *see* Vyborg
109 C3 **Vibo Valentia** Italy
107 D1 **Vic** Spain
144 A1 **Vicente Guerrero** Mex.
108 B1 **Vicenza** Italy
89 F2 **Vichuga** Rus. Fed.
105 C2 **Vichy** France
140 B2 **Vicksburg** U.S.A.
155 D2 **Viçosa** Brazil
52 A3 **Victor Harbor** Austr.
50 C1 **Victoria** *r.* Austr.
52 B3 **Victoria** *state* Austr.
**Victoria** Cameroon *see* Limbe
128 B3 **Victoria** Can.
153 A3 **Victoria** Chile
**Victoria** Malaysia *see* Labuan
113 I6 **Victoria** Seychelles
143 D3 **Victoria** U.S.A.
119 D3 **Victoria, Lake** Africa
52 B2 **Victoria, Lake** Austr.
62 A1 **Victoria, Mount** Myanmar
59 D3 **Victoria, Mount** P.N.G.
154 B3 **Victoria, Sierra de la** *hills* Arg.
120 B2 **Victoria Falls** *waterfall* Zambia/Zimbabwe
120 B2 **Victoria Falls** Zimbabwe
126 E2 **Victoria Island** Can.
55 M2 **Victoria Land** *coastal area* Antarctica
50 C1 **Victoria River Downs** Austr.
139 E1 **Victoriaville** Can.
122 B3 **Victoria West** S. Africa
135 C4 **Victorville** U.S.A.
141 D3 **Vidalia** U.S.A.
110 C2 **Videle** Romania
92 □A3 **Viðidalsá** Iceland
110 B2 **Vidin** Bulg.
74 B2 **Vidisha** India
140 B2 **Vidor** U.S.A.
153 B4 **Viedma** Arg.
153 A4 **Viedma, Lago** *l.* Arg.
102 C2 **Viehberg** *mt.* Austria
107 D1 **Vielha** Spain
100 B2 **Vielsalm** Belgium
101 E2 **Vienenburg** Ger.
103 D2 **Vienna** Austria
138 C3 **Vienna** U.S.A.
105 C2 **Vienne** France
104 C2 **Vienne** *r.* France
62 B2 **Vientiane** Laos
100 C2 **Viersen** Ger.
104 C2 **Vierzon** France
144 B2 **Viesca** Mex.
109 C2 **Vieste** Italy
62 B2 **Vietnam** *country* Asia
62 B1 **Viêt Tri** Vietnam
64 B2 **Vigan** Phil.
108 A1 **Vigevano** Italy
106 B1 **Vigo** Spain
**Viipuri** Rus. Fed. *see* Vyborg
73 C3 **Vijayawada** India
92 □B3 **Vík** Iceland
111 B3 **Vikhren** *mt.* Bulg.
128 C2 **Viking** Can.
92 F3 **Vikna** *i.* Norway
**Vila Alferes Chamusca** Moz. *see* Guija
**Vila Arriaga** Angola *see* Bibala
**Vila Bugaço** Angola *see* Camanongue

**Vila Cabral** Moz. *see* Lichinga
**Vila da Ponte** Angola *see* Kuvango
**Vila de Aljustrel** Angola *see* Cangamba
**Vila de Almoster** Angola *see* Chiange
**Vila de João Belo** Moz. *see* Xai-Xai
**Vila de Trego Morais** Moz. *see* Chókwé
**Vila Fontes** Moz. *see* Caia
106 B2 **Vila Franca de Xira** Port.
106 B1 **Vilagarcía de Arousa** Spain
123 D1 **Vila Gomes da Costa** Moz.
106 B1 **Vilalba** Spain
**Vila Luísa** Moz. *see* Marracuene
**Vila Marechal Carmona** Angola *see* Uíge
121 □D2 **Vilanandro, Tanjona** *pt* Madag.
88 C2 **Viļāni** Latvia
106 B1 **Vila Nova de Gaia** Port.
107 D1 **Vilanova i la Geltrú** Spain
**Vila Paiva de Andrada** Moz. *see* Gorongosa
**Vila Pery** Moz. *see* Chimoio
106 B1 **Vila Real** Port.
106 B1 **Vilar Formoso** Port.
**Vila Salazar** Angola *see* N'dalatando
**Vila Salazar** Zimbabwe *see* Sango
**Vila Teixeira de Sousa** Angola *see* Luau
155 D2 **Vila Velha** Brazil
150 B4 **Vilcabamba, Cordillera** *mts* Peru
82 F1 **Vil'cheka, Zemlya** *i.* Rus. Fed.
92 G3 **Vilhelmina** Sweden
150 C4 **Vilhena** Brazil
88 C2 **Viljandi** Estonia
123 C2 **Viljoenskroon** S. Africa
88 B3 **Vilkaviškis** Lith.
83 H1 **Vil'kitskogo, Proliv** *str.* Rus. Fed.
144 B1 **Villa Ahumada** Mex.
106 B1 **Villablino** Spain
102 C2 **Villach** Austria
**Villa Cisneros** Western Sahara *see* Ad Dakhla
144 B2 **Villa de Cos** Mex.
152 B3 **Villa Dolores** Arg.
145 C3 **Villa Flores** Mex.
153 C3 **Villa Gesell** Arg.
145 C2 **Villagrán** Mex.
145 C3 **Villahermosa** Mex.
144 A2 **Villa Insurgentes** Mex.
107 C2 **Villajoyosa - La Vila Joiosa** Spain
152 B3 **Villa María** Arg.
153 B3 **Villa Mercedes** Arg.
152 B2 **Villa Montes** Bol.
144 B2 **Villanueva** Mex.
106 B2 **Villanueva de la Serena** Spain
106 C2 **Villanueva de los Infantes** Spain
152 C2 **Villa Ocampo** Arg.
142 B3 **Villa Ocampo** Mex.
108 A3 **Villaputzu** Sardinia Italy
152 C2 **Villarrica** Para.
106 C2 **Villarrobledo** Spain
**Villasalazar** Zimbabwe *see* Sango
152 B2 **Villa Unión** Arg.
144 B2 **Villa Unión** Mex.
144 B2 **Villa Unión** Mex.
150 B1 **Villavicencio** Col.
152 B2 **Villazon** Bol.
104 C3 **Villefranche-de-Rouergue** France
105 C2 **Villefranche-sur-Saône** France
107 C2 **Villena** Spain
100 A2 **Villeneuve-d'Ascq** France
104 C3 **Villeneuve-sur-Lot** France
140 B2 **Ville Platte** U.S.A.
100 A3 **Villers-Cotterêts** France
105 C2 **Villeurbanne** France
123 C2 **Villiers** S. Africa
102 B2 **Villingen** Ger.
137 E2 **Villisca** U.S.A.
88 C3 **Vilnius** Lith.
91 C2 **Vil'nohirs'k** Ukr.
91 D2 **Vil'nyans'k** Ukr.
100 B2 **Vilvoorde** Belgium
88 C3 **Vilyeyka** Belarus
83 J2 **Vilyuy** *r.* Rus. Fed.
93 G4 **Vimmerby** Sweden
153 A3 **Viña del Mar** Chile
107 D1 **Vinaròs** Spain
138 B3 **Vincennes** U.S.A.
55 J3 **Vincennes Bay** Antarctica
139 D3 **Vineland** U.S.A.
62 B2 **Vinh** Vietnam
63 B2 **Vinh Long** Vietnam
143 D1 **Vinita** U.S.A.
90 B2 **Vinnytsya** Ukr.
55 R2 **Vinson Massif** *mt.* Antarctica
93 E3 **Vinstra** Norway
108 B1 **Vipiteno** Italy
64 B2 **Virac** Phil.
74 B2 **Viramgam** India
80 B2 **Viranşehir** Turkey
129 C3 **Virden** Can.
104 B2 **Vire** France
120 A2 **Virei** Angola
155 D1 **Virgem da Lapa** Brazil
142 A1 **Virgin** *r.* U.S.A.
123 C2 **Virginia** S. Africa
137 E1 **Virginia** U.S.A.
139 D3 **Virginia** *state* U.S.A.
139 D3 **Virginia Beach** U.S.A.

Weißenfels 221


135 C3 **Virginia City** U.S.A.
147 D3 **Virgin Islands (U.K.)** *terr.* West Indies
147 D3 **Virgin Islands (U.S.A.)** *terr.* West Indies
63 B2 **Virôchey** Cambodia
109 C1 **Virovitica** Croatia
100 B3 **Virton** Belgium
88 B2 **Virtsu** Estonia
73 B4 **Virudhunagar** India
109 C2 **Vis** *i.* Croatia
88 C2 **Visaginas** Lith.
135 C3 **Visalia** U.S.A.
74 B2 **Visavadar** India
64 B2 **Visayan Sea** Phil.
93 G4 **Visby** Sweden
126 E2 **Viscount Melville Sound** *sea chan.* Can.
151 E3 **Viseu** Brazil
106 B1 **Viseu** Port.
110 B1 **Vişeu de Sus** Romania
73 C3 **Vishakhapatnam** India
88 C2 **Višķi** Latvia
109 C2 **Visoko** Bos.-Herz.
103 D1 **Vistula** *r.* Pol.
**Vitebsk** Belarus *see* **Vitsyebsk**
108 B2 **Viterbo** Italy
49 I5 **Viti Levu** *i.* Fiji
83 I3 **Vitim** *r.* Rus. Fed.
155 D2 **Vitória** Brazil
151 E4 **Vitória da Conquista** Brazil
106 C1 **Vitoria-Gasteiz** Spain
104 B2 **Vitré** France
105 C2 **Vitry-le-François** France
89 D2 **Vitsyebsk** Belarus
105 D2 **Vittel** France
108 B3 **Vittoria** *Sicily* Italy
108 B1 **Vittorio Veneto** Italy
106 B1 **Viveiro** Spain
136 C2 **Vivian** U.S.A.
**Vizagapatam** India *see* **Vishakhapatnam**
142 A3 **Vizcaíno, Desierto de** *des.* Mex.
144 A2 **Vizcaíno, Sierra** *mts* Mex.
111 C2 **Vize** Turkey
73 C3 **Vizianagaram** India
100 B2 **Vlaardingen** Neth.
87 D4 **Vladikavkaz** Rus. Fed.
89 F2 **Vladimir** Rus. Fed.
66 B2 **Vladivostok** Rus. Fed.
109 D2 **Vlasotince** Serb. and Mont.
100 B1 **Vlieland** *i.* Neth.
100 A2 **Vlissingen** Neth.
109 C2 **Vlorë** Albania
102 C1 **Vltava** *r.* Czech Rep.
102 C2 **Vöcklabruck** Austria
109 C2 **Vodice** Croatia
**Vogelkop Peninsula** Indon. *see* **Doberai, Jazirah**
101 D2 **Vogelsberg** *hills* Ger.
**Vohémar** Madag. *see* **Iharaña**
**Vohibinany** Madag. *see* **Ampasimanolotra**
**Vohimarina** Madag. *see* **Iharaña**
121 □D3 **Vohimena, Tanjona** *c.* Madag.
121 □D3 **Vohipeno** Madag.
119 D3 **Voi** Kenya
105 D2 **Voiron** France
131 D2 **Voisey Bay** Can.
109 C1 **Vojvodina** *prov.* Serb. and Mont.
92 J3 **Voknavolok** Rus. Fed.
**Volcano Bay** Japan *see* **Uchiura-wan**
69 F3 **Volcano Islands** *is* Japan
**Volchansk** Ukr. *see* **Vovchans'k**
89 E2 **Volga** Rus. Fed.
89 F2 **Volga** *r.* Rus. Fed.
87 D4 **Volgodonsk** Rus. Fed.
87 D4 **Volgograd** Rus. Fed.
87 D4 **Volgogradskoye Vodokhranilishche** *resr* Rus. Fed.
89 D2 **Volkhov** Rus. Fed.
89 D1 **Volkhov** *r.* Rus. Fed.
101 E2 **Volkstedt** Ger.
91 D2 **Volnovakha** Ukr.
90 B2 **Volochys'k** Ukr.
91 D2 **Volodars'ke** Ukr.
**Volodarskoye** Kazakh. *see* **Saumalkol'**
90 B1 **Volodars'k-Volyns'kyy** Ukr.
90 B1 **Volodymyrets'** Ukr.
90 A1 **Volodymyr-Volyns'kyy** Ukr.
89 E2 **Vologda** Rus. Fed.
89 E2 **Volokolamsk** Rus. Fed.
91 D1 **Volokonovka** Rus. Fed.
111 B3 **Volos** Greece
88 C2 **Volosovo** Rus. Fed.
89 D2 **Volot** Rus. Fed.
89 E3 **Volovo** Rus. Fed.
87 D3 **Vol'sk** Rus. Fed.
114 C4 **Volta** *r.* Ghana
114 C4 **Volta, Lake** *resr* Ghana
155 D2 **Volta Redonda** Brazil
110 C2 **Voluntari** Romania
87 D4 **Volzhskiy** Rus. Fed.
92 □C2 **Vopnafjörður** Iceland
88 C3 **Voranava** Belarus
160 K3 **Voring Plateau** *sea feature* N. Atlantic Ocean
86 F2 **Vorkuta** Rus. Fed.
88 B2 **Vormsi** *i.* Estonia
83 G2 **Vorogovo** Rus. Fed.
89 E3 **Voronezh** Rus. Fed.
89 E3 **Voronezh** *r.* Rus. Fed.
91 E1 **Vorontsovka** Rus. Fed.
**Voroshilov** Rus. Fed. *see* **Ussuriysk**
**Voroshilovgrad** Ukr. *see* **Luhans'k**
**Voroshilovsk** Rus. Fed. *see* **Stavropol'**
**Voroshilovsk** Ukr. *see* **Alchevs'k**
91 C2 **Vorskla** *r.* Rus. Fed.
88 C2 **Võrtsjärv** *l.* Estonia
88 C2 **Võru** Estonia
122 B3 **Vosburg** S. Africa
105 D2 **Vosges** *mts* France
89 E2 **Voskresensk** Rus. Fed.
93 E3 **Voss** Norway
86 C2 **Vostochnaya Litsa** Rus. Fed.
**Vostochno-Sibirskoye More** *sea* Rus. Fed. *see* **East Siberian Sea**
83 H3 **Vostochnyy Sayan** *mts* Rus. Fed.
66 C1 **Vostok** Rus. Fed.
49 L5 **Vostok Island** Kiribati
86 E3 **Votkinsk** Rus. Fed.
86 E3 **Votkinskoye Vodokhranilishche** *resr* Rus. Fed.
154 C2 **Votuporanga** Brazil
105 C2 **Vouziers** France
91 D1 **Vovchans'k** Ukr.
92 J2 **Voynitsa** Rus. Fed.
86 E2 **Voyvozh** Rus. Fed.
91 C2 **Voznesens'k** Ukr.
76 B2 **Vozrozhdenya Island** *i.* Uzbek.
93 E4 **Vrådal** Norway
90 C2 **Vradiyivka** Ukr.
66 B2 **Vrangel'** Rus. Fed.
83 N2 **Vrangelya, Ostrov** *i.* Rus. Fed.
109 D2 **Vranje** Serb. and Mont.
110 C2 **Vratnik** *pass* Bulg.
110 B2 **Vratsa** Bulg.
109 C1 **Vrbas** *r.* Bos.-Herz.
109 C1 **Vrbas** Serb. and Mont.
122 A3 **Vredenburg** S. Africa
122 A3 **Vredendal** S. Africa
100 B3 **Vresse** Belgium
100 C1 **Vriezenveen** Neth.
109 D1 **Vršac** Serb. and Mont.
122 B2 **Vryburg** S. Africa
123 D2 **Vryheid** S. Africa
89 D1 **Vsevolozhsk** Rus. Fed.
109 D2 **Vučitrn** Serb. and Mont.
109 C1 **Vukovar** Croatia
86 E2 **Vuktyl'** Rus. Fed.
123 C2 **Vukuzakhe** S. Africa
90 B2 **Vulcăneşti** Moldova
109 B3 **Vulcano, Isola** *i.* Italy
**Vulkaneshty** Moldova *see* **Vulcăneşti**
63 B2 **Vung Tau** Vietnam
92 H2 **Vuollerim** Sweden
92 I2 **Vuotso** Fin.
74 B2 **Vyara** India
**Vyarkhowye** Belarus *see* **Ruba**
**Vyatka** Rus. Fed. *see* **Kirov**
89 D2 **Vyaz'ma** Rus. Fed.
88 C1 **Vyborg** Rus. Fed.
88 C1 **Vyborgskiy Zaliv** *b.* Rus. Fed.
86 D2 **Vychegda** *r.* Rus. Fed.
88 C2 **Vyerkhnyadzvinsk** Belarus
89 D3 **Vyetka** Belarus
89 D3 **Vygonichi** Rus. Fed.
86 C2 **Vygozero, Ozero** *l.* Rus. Fed.
87 D3 **Vyksa** Rus. Fed.
90 B2 **Vylkove** Ukr.
90 A2 **Vynohradiv** Ukr.
89 D2 **Vypolzovo** Rus. Fed.
89 D2 **Vyritsa** Rus. Fed.
91 D2 **Vyselki** Rus. Fed.
90 C1 **Vyshhorod** Ukr.
89 D2 **Vyshnevolotskaya Gryada** *ridge* Rus. Fed.
89 D2 **Vyshniy-Volochek** Rus. Fed.
103 D2 **Vyškov** Czech Rep.
89 E2 **Vysokovsk** Rus. Fed.
86 C2 **Vytegra** Rus. Fed.


## W


114 B3 **Wa** Ghana
100 B2 **Waal** *r.* Neth.
100 B2 **Waalwijk** Neth.
119 D2 **Waat** Sudan
128 C2 **Wabasca** *r.* Can.
128 C2 **Wabasca-Desmarais** Can.
138 B3 **Wabash** *r.* U.S.A.
117 C4 **Wabē Gestro** *r.* Eth.
117 C4 **Wabē Shebelē Wenz** *r.* Eth.
129 E2 **Wabowden** Can.
103 D1 **Wąbrzeźno** Pol.
141 D3 **Waccasassa Bay** U.S.A.
101 D2 **Wächtersbach** Ger.
143 D2 **Waco** U.S.A.
74 A2 **Wad** Pak.
115 D2 **Waddān** Libya
**Waddeneilanden** *is* Neth. *see* **West Frisian Islands**
**Wadden Islands** Neth. *see* **West Frisian Islands**
100 B1 **Waddenzee** *sea chan.* Neth.
128 B2 **Waddington, Mount** Can.
100 B1 **Waddinxveen** Neth.
129 D2 **Wadena** Can.
137 D1 **Wadena** U.S.A.
50 B1 **Wadeye** Austr.
**Wadhwan** India *see* **Surendranagar**
116 B2 **Wadi Halfa** Sudan
116 B3 **Wad Medani** Sudan
122 B3 **Waenhuiskrans** S. Africa
70 C2 **Wafangdian** China
100 B2 **Wageningen** Neth.
127 G2 **Wager Bay** Can.
53 C3 **Wagga Wagga** Austr.
137 D2 **Wagner** U.S.A.
74 B1 **Wah** Pak.
137 D2 **Wahoo** U.S.A.
137 D1 **Wahpeton** U.S.A.
54 B2 **Waiau** *r.* N.Z.
59 C3 **Waigeo** *i.* Indon.
61 C2 **Waikabubak** Indon.
54 C1 **Waikaremoana, Lake** N.Z.
52 A2 **Waikerie** Austr.
54 B2 **Waimate** N.Z.
75 B3 **Wainganga** *r.* India
61 D2 **Waingapu** Indon.
129 C2 **Wainwright** Can.
126 B2 **Wainwright** U.S.A.
54 C1 **Waiouru** N.Z.
54 B2 **Waipara** N.Z.
54 C1 **Waipawa** N.Z.
54 B2 **Wairau** *r.* N.Z.
54 C1 **Wairoa** N.Z.
54 B2 **Waitaki** *r.* N.Z.
54 B1 **Waitara** N.Z.
54 B1 **Waiuku** N.Z.
67 C3 **Wajima** Japan
119 E2 **Wajir** Kenya
67 C3 **Wakasa-wan** *b.* Japan
54 A3 **Wakatipu, Lake** N.Z.
129 D2 **Wakaw** Can.
67 C4 **Wakayama** Japan
136 D3 **WaKeeney** U.S.A.
54 B2 **Wakefield** N.Z.
98 C3 **Wakefield** U.K.
**Wakeham** Can. *see* **Kangiqsujuaq**
48 H2 **Wake Island** *terr.* N. Pacific Ocean
66 D1 **Wakkanai** Japan
123 D2 **Wakkerstroom** S. Africa
120 A2 **Waku-Kungo** Angola
103 D1 **Wałbrzych** Pol.
53 D2 **Walcha** Austr.
100 C1 **Walchum** Ger.
103 D1 **Wałcz** Pol.
99 B3 **Wales** *admin. div.* U.K.
53 C2 **Walgett** Austr.
119 C3 **Walikale** Dem. Rep. Congo
135 C3 **Walker Lake** U.S.A.
134 C1 **Wallace** *ID* U.S.A.
141 E2 **Wallace** *NC* U.S.A.
52 A2 **Wallaroo** Austr.
98 B3 **Wallasey** U.K.
134 C1 **Walla Walla** U.S.A.
101 D3 **Walldürn** Ger.
122 A3 **Wallekraal** S. Africa
53 C2 **Wallendbeen** Austr.
49 J5 **Wallis, Îles** *is* Wallis and Futuna Is
49 J5 **Wallis and Futuna Islands** *terr.* S. Pacific Ocean
96 □ **Walls** U.K.
98 B2 **Walney, Isle of** *i.* U.K.
99 C3 **Walsall** U.K.
136 C3 **Walsenburg** U.S.A.
101 D1 **Walsrode** Ger.
141 D2 **Walterboro** U.S.A.
120 A3 **Walvis Bay** Namibia
158 F6 **Walvis Ridge** *sea feature* S. Atlantic Ocean
119 C2 **Wamba** Dem. Rep. Congo
52 B1 **Wanaaring** Austr.
54 A2 **Wanaka** N.Z.
54 A2 **Wanaka, Lake** N.Z.
71 B3 **Wan'an** China
130 B3 **Wanapitei Lake** Can.
154 B3 **Wanda** Arg.
66 B1 **Wanda Shan** *mts* China
62 A1 **Wanding** China
**Wandingzhen** China *see* **Wanding**
54 C1 **Wanganui** N.Z.
54 B1 **Wanganui** *r.* N.Z.
53 C3 **Wangaratta** Austr.
65 B1 **Wangqing** China
62 A1 **Wan Hsa-la** Myanmar
**Wankie** Zimbabwe *see* **Hwange**
71 B4 **Wanning** China
100 B2 **Wanroij** Neth.
99 C4 **Wantage** U.K.
70 A2 **Wanxian** China
70 A2 **Wanyuan** China
117 A4 **Warab** Sudan
73 B3 **Warangal** India
101 D2 **Warburg** Ger.
50 B2 **Warburton** Austr.
52 A1 **Warburton** *watercourse* Austr.
74 B2 **Wardha** India
96 C1 **Ward Hill** U.K.
128 B2 **Ware** Can.
101 F1 **Waren** Ger.
101 C2 **Warendorf** Ger.
53 D1 **Warialda** Austr.
122 A2 **Warmbad** Namibia
135 C3 **Warm Springs** U.S.A.
134 C2 **Warner Lakes** U.S.A.
134 B2 **Warner Mountains** U.S.A.
141 D2 **Warner Robins** U.S.A.
152 B1 **Warnes** Bol.
52 B3 **Warracknabeal** Austr.
53 C3 **Warrandyte** Austr.
53 C2 **Warrego** *r.* Austr.
53 C2 **Warren** Austr.
140 B2 **Warren** *AR* U.S.A.
138 C2 **Warren** *OH* U.S.A.
139 D2 **Warren** *PA* U.S.A.
97 C1 **Warrenpoint** U.K.
137 E3 **Warrensburg** U.S.A.
122 B2 **Warrenton** S. Africa
115 C4 **Warri** Nigeria
98 B3 **Warrington** U.K.
52 B3 **Warrnambool** Austr.
103 E1 **Warsaw** Pol.
138 B2 **Warsaw** U.S.A.
**Warszawa** Pol. *see* **Warsaw**
103 C1 **Warta** *r.* Pol.
53 D1 **Warwick** Austr.
99 C3 **Warwick** U.K.
139 E2 **Warwick** U.S.A.
134 D3 **Wasatch Range** *mts* U.S.A.
135 C3 **Wasco** U.S.A.
136 C1 **Washburn** U.S.A.
139 D3 **Washington** *DC* U.S.A.
137 E2 **Washington** *IA* U.S.A.
138 B2 **Washington** *IL* U.S.A.
138 B3 **Washington** *IN* U.S.A.
137 E3 **Washington** *MO* U.S.A.
141 E1 **Washington** *NC* U.S.A.
138 C2 **Washington** *PA* U.S.A.
135 D3 **Washington** *UT* U.S.A.
134 B1 **Washington** *state* U.S.A.
139 E2 **Washington, Mount** U.S.A.
138 C3 **Washington Court House** U.S.A.
74 A2 **Washuk** Pak.
130 C2 **Waskaganish** Can.
129 E2 **Waskaiowaka Lake** Can.
122 A2 **Wasser** Namibia
101 D2 **Wasserkuppe** *hill* Ger.
130 C3 **Waswanipi, Lac** *l.* Can.
61 D2 **Watampone** Indon.
**Watenstadt-Salzgitter** Ger. *see* Salzgitter
139 E2 **Waterbury** U.S.A.
129 D2 **Waterbury Lake** Can.
97 C2 **Waterford** Ireland
97 C2 **Waterford Harbour** Ireland
100 B2 **Waterloo** Belgium
137 E2 **Waterloo** U.S.A.
99 C4 **Waterlooville** U.K.
123 C1 **Waterpoort** S. Africa
139 D2 **Watertown** *NY* U.S.A.
137 D2 **Watertown** *SD* U.S.A.
138 B2 **Watertown** *WI* U.S.A.
97 A3 **Waterville** Ireland
139 F2 **Waterville** U.S.A.
99 C4 **Watford** U.K.
136 C1 **Watford City** U.S.A.
129 D2 **Wathaman** *r.* Can.
**Watling Island** Bahamas *see* **San Salvador**
143 D1 **Watonga** U.S.A.
129 D2 **Watrous** Can.
119 C2 **Watsa** Dem. Rep. Congo
138 B2 **Watseka** U.S.A.
118 C3 **Watsi Kengo** Dem. Rep. Congo
128 B1 **Watson Lake** Can.
135 B3 **Watsonville** U.S.A.
59 C3 **Watubela, Kepulauan** *is* Indon.
59 D3 **Wau** P.N.G.
117 A4 **Wau** Sudan
53 D2 **Wauchope** Austr.
138 B2 **Waukegan** U.S.A.
138 B2 **Waukesha** U.S.A.
143 D2 **Waurika** U.S.A.
138 B2 **Wausau** U.S.A.
99 D3 **Waveney** *r.* U.K.
137 E2 **Waverly** U.S.A.
130 B3 **Wawa** Can.
141 D2 **Waycross** U.S.A.
137 D2 **Wayne** U.S.A.
141 D2 **Waynesboro** *GA* U.S.A.
139 D3 **Waynesboro** *VA* U.S.A.
137 E3 **Waynesville** *MO* U.S.A.
141 D1 **Waynesville** *NC* U.S.A.
74 B1 **Wazirabad** Pak.
60 A1 **We, Pulau** *i.* Indon.
98 C2 **Wear** *r.* U.K.
143 D1 **Weatherford** *OK* U.S.A.
143 D2 **Weatherford** *TX* U.S.A.
134 B2 **Weaverville** U.S.A.
143 D3 **Webb** U.S.A.
130 B2 **Webequie** Can.
117 C4 **Webi Shabeelle** *r.* Somalia
137 D1 **Webster** U.S.A.
137 E2 **Webster City** U.S.A.
55 C3 **Weddell Abyssal Plain** *sea feature* Southern Ocean
55 B3 **Weddell Sea** Antarctica
123 D2 **Weenen** S. Africa
100 B2 **Weert** Neth.
53 C2 **Weethalle** Austr.
53 C2 **Wee Waa** Austr.
100 C2 **Wegberg** Ger.
103 E1 **Węgorzewo** Pol.
103 E1 **Węgrów** Pol.
70 B1 **Weichang** China
101 F3 **Weiden in der Oberpfalz** Ger.
**Weidongmen** China *see* **Qianjin**
70 B2 **Weifang** China
70 C2 **Weihai** China
70 B2 **Wei He** *r.* China
53 C1 **Weilmoringle** Austr.
101 E2 **Weimar** Ger.
143 D3 **Weimar** U.S.A.
70 A2 **Weinan** China
71 A3 **Weining** China
51 D1 **Weipa** Austr.
53 C1 **Weir** *r.* Austr.
138 C2 **Weirton** U.S.A.
62 B1 **Weishan** China
101 E2 **Weiße Elster** *r.* Ger.
101 E2 **Weißenfels** Ger.

102 C2 **Weißkugel** *mt.* Austria/Italy
71 A3 **Weixin** China
   **Weizhou** China *see* **Wenchuan**
103 D1 **Wejherowo** Pol.
128 C1 **Wekweti** Can.
138 C3 **Welch** U.S.A.
117 B3 **Weldiya** Eth.
123 C3 **Welkom** S. Africa
99 C3 **Welland** *r.* U.K.
51 C1 **Wellesley Islands** Austr.
99 C3 **Wellingborough** U.K.
53 C2 **Wellington** Austr.
54 B2 **Wellington** N.Z.
122 A3 **Wellington** S. Africa
136 B2 **Wellington** *CO* U.S.A.
137 D3 **Wellington** *KS* U.S.A.
135 D3 **Wellington** *UT* U.S.A.
153 A4 **Wellington, Isla** *i.* Chile
53 C2 **Wellington, Lake** Austr.
128 B2 **Wells** Can.
99 B4 **Wells** U.K.
134 D2 **Wells** U.S.A.
50 B2 **Wells, Lake** *salt flat* Austr.
54 B1 **Wellsford** N.Z.
99 D3 **Wells-next-the-Sea** U.K.
142 A2 **Wellton** U.S.A.
102 C2 **Wels** Austria
99 B3 **Welshpool** U.K.
   **Welwitschia** Namibia *see*
   **Khorixas**
123 C2 **Wembesi** S. Africa
130 C2 **Wemindji** Can.
134 B1 **Wenatchee** U.S.A.
71 B4 **Wenchang** China
114 B4 **Wenchi** Ghana
   **Wenchow** China *see* **Wenzhou**
70 A2 **Wenchuan** China
70 C1 **Wendeng** China
101 E1 **Wendisch Evern** Ger.
117 B4 **Wendo** Eth.
135 D2 **Wendover** U.S.A.
71 B3 **Wengyuan** China
   **Wenhua** China *see* **Weishan**
   **Wenlan** China *see* **Mengzi**
   **Wenlin** China *see* **Renshou**
71 C3 **Wenling** China
   **Wenquan** China *see* **Yingshan**
71 A3 **Wenshan** China
52 A3 **Wentworth** Austr.
71 C3 **Wenzhou** China
123 C2 **Wepener** S. Africa
122 B2 **Werda** Botswana
101 F2 **Werdau** Ger.
101 F1 **Werder** Ger.
101 F3 **Wernberg-Köblitz** Ger.
101 E2 **Wernigerode** Ger.
101 D2 **Werra** *r.* Ger.
52 B2 **Werrimull** Austr.
53 D2 **Werris Creek** Austr.
101 D3 **Wertheim** Ger.
100 C2 **Wesel** Ger.
101 E1 **Wesendorf** Ger.
101 D1 **Weser** *r.* Ger.
101 D1 **Weser** *sea chan.* Ger.
51 C1 **Wessel, Cape** Austr.
51 C1 **Wessel Islands** Austr.
123 C2 **Wesselton** S. Africa
55 P2 **West Antarctica** *reg.*
   Antarctica
156 B7 **West Australian Basin**
   *sea feature* Indian Ocean
80 B3 **West Bank** *terr.* Asia
138 B2 **West Bend** U.S.A.
75 C2 **West Bengal** *state* India
99 C3 **West Bromwich** U.K.
139 E2 **Westbrook** U.S.A.
137 E2 **West Des Moines** U.S.A.
100 C2 **Westerburg** Ger.
100 C1 **Westerholt** Ger.
139 E2 **Westerly** U.S.A.
50 A2 **Western Australia** *state* Austr.
122 B3 **Western Cape** *prov.* S. Africa
116 A2 **Western Desert** Egypt
   **Western Dvina** *r.* Europe *see*
   **Zapadnaya Dvina**
73 B3 **Western Ghats** *mts* India
114 A2 **Western Sahara** *terr.* Africa
   **Western Samoa** *country*
   S. Pacific Ocean *see* **Samoa**
   **Western Sayan Mountains** *reg.*
   Rus. Fed. *see* **Zapadnyy Sayan**
100 A2 **Westerschelde** *est.* Neth.
100 C1 **Westerstede** Ger.
101 D2 **Westerwald** *hills* Ger.
153 B6 **West Falkland** *i.* Falkland Is
138 B3 **West Frankfort** U.S.A.
100 B1 **West Frisian Islands** Neth.
96 C2 **Westhill** U.K.
55 I3 **West Ice Shelf** Antarctica
147 D2 **West Indies** *is* Caribbean Sea
100 A2 **Westkapelle** Neth.
96 A1 **West Loch Roag** *b.* U.K.
128 C2 **Westlock** Can.
100 B2 **Westmalle** Belgium
   **Westman Islands** Iceland *see*
   **Vestmannaeyjar**
53 C1 **Westmar** Austr.
156 C4 **West Mariana Basin** *sea feature*
   N. Pacific Ocean
140 B1 **West Memphis** U.S.A.
138 C3 **Weston** U.S.A.
99 B4 **Weston-super-Mare** U.K.
141 D3 **West Palm Beach** U.S.A.
137 E3 **West Plains** U.S.A.
137 D2 **West Point** U.S.A.

54 B2 **Westport** N.Z.
97 B2 **Westport** Ireland
129 D2 **Westray** Can.
96 C1 **Westray** *i.* U.K.
82 G2 **West Siberian Plain** *plain*
   Rus. Fed.
100 B1 **West-Terschelling** Neth.
136 A2 **West Thumb** U.S.A.
97 B1 **West Town** Ireland
135 D2 **West Valley City** U.S.A.
138 C3 **West Virginia** *state* U.S.A.
53 C2 **West Wyalong** Austr.
134 D2 **West Yellowstone** U.S.A.
59 C3 **Wetar** *i.* Indon.
128 C2 **Wetaskiwin** Can.
119 D3 **Wete** Tanz.
101 D2 **Wetzlar** Ger.
59 D3 **Wewak** P.N.G.
97 C2 **Wexford** Ireland
97 C2 **Wexford Harbour** *b.* Ireland
129 D2 **Weyakwin** Can.
129 D3 **Weyburn** Can.
101 D1 **Weyhe** Ger.
99 B4 **Weymouth** U.K.
54 C1 **Whakatane** N.Z.
129 E1 **Whale Cove** Can.
96 □ **Whalsay** *i.* U.K.
98 C3 **Wharfe** *r.* U.K.
143 D3 **Wharton** U.S.A.
128 C1 **Wha Ti** Can.
136 B2 **Wheatland** U.S.A.
140 C2 **Wheeler Lake** *resr* U.S.A.
142 B1 **Wheeler Peak** *NM* U.S.A.
135 D2 **Wheeler Peak** *NV* U.S.A.
138 C2 **Wheeling** U.S.A.
98 B2 **Whernside** *hill* U.K.
128 B2 **Whistler** Can.
98 C2 **Whitby** U.K.
128 A1 **White** *r.* Can./U.S.A.
140 B2 **White** *r.* *AR* U.S.A.
138 C3 **White** *r.* *IN* U.S.A.
50 B2 **White, Lake** *salt flat* Austr.
131 E3 **White Bay** Can.
136 C1 **White Butte** *mt.* U.S.A.
52 B2 **White Cliffs** Austr.
128 C2 **Whitecourt** Can.
134 D1 **Whitefish** U.S.A.
98 B2 **Whitehaven** U.K.
97 D1 **Whitehead** U.K.
128 A1 **Whitehorse** Can.
140 B2 **White Lake** U.S.A.
51 D4 **Whitemark** Austr.
135 C3 **White Mountain Peak** U.S.A.
116 B3 **White Nile** *r.* Sudan/Uganda
   **White Russia** *country* Europe *see*
   **Belarus**
86 C2 **White Sea** Rus. Fed.
134 D1 **White Sulphur Springs** U.S.A.
141 E2 **Whiteville** U.S.A.
114 B3 **White Volta** *watercourse*
   Burkina/Ghana
136 B3 **Whitewater** U.S.A.
142 B2 **Whitewater Baldy** *mt.* U.S.A.
130 B2 **Whitewater Lake** Can.
129 D2 **Whitewood** Can.
96 B3 **Whithorn** U.K.
54 C1 **Whitianga** N.Z.
135 C3 **Whitney, Mount** U.S.A.
99 D4 **Whitstable** U.K.
51 D2 **Whitsunday Island** Austr.
53 C3 **Whittlesea** Austr.
52 A2 **Whyalla** Austr.
62 A2 **Wiang Pa Pao** Thai.
100 A2 **Wichelen** Belgium
137 D3 **Wichita** U.S.A.
143 D2 **Wichita Falls** U.S.A.
143 D2 **Wichita Mountains** U.S.A.
96 C1 **Wick** U.K.
142 A2 **Wickenburg** U.S.A.
97 C2 **Wicklow** Ireland
97 C2 **Wicklow Head** *hd*
   Ireland
97 C2 **Wicklow Mountains** Ireland
98 B3 **Widnes** U.K.
101 D2 **Wiehengebirge** *hills* Ger.
100 C2 **Wiehl** Ger.
103 D1 **Wieluń** Pol.
   **Wien** Austria *see* **Vienna**
103 D2 **Wiener Neustadt** Austria
100 B1 **Wieringerwerf** Neth.
101 D2 **Wiesbaden** Ger.
100 C1 **Wiesmoor** Ger.
103 D1 **Wieżyca** *hill* Pol.
98 B3 **Wigan** U.K.
99 C3 **Wight, Isle of** *i.* U.K.
96 B3 **Wigtown** U.K.
100 B2 **Wijchen** Neth.
130 B3 **Wikwemikong** Can.
52 B2 **Wilcannia** Austr.
   **Wilczek Land** *i.* Rus. Fed. *see*
   **Vil'cheka, Zemlya**
123 C3 **Wild Coast** S. Africa
101 D1 **Wildeshausen** Ger.
136 C2 **Wild Horse Hill** *mt.* U.S.A.
123 C2 **Wilge** *r.* S. Africa
48 F4 **Wilhelm, Mount** P.N.G.
101 D1 **Wilhelmshaven** Ger.
139 D2 **Wilkes-Barre** U.S.A.
55 K3 **Wilkes Land** *reg.* Antarctica
129 C2 **Wilkie** Can.
134 B1 **Willamette** *r.* U.S.A.

134 B1 **Willapa Bay** U.S.A.
142 B2 **Willcox** U.S.A.
100 B2 **Willebroek** Belgium
147 D3 **Willemstad** Neth. Antilles
52 A1 **William, Mount** Austr.
52 A1 **William Creek** Austr.
142 A1 **Williams** U.S.A.
138 C3 **Williamsburg** *KY* U.S.A.
139 D3 **Williamsburg** *VA* U.S.A.
128 B2 **Williams Lake** Can.
138 C3 **Williamson** U.S.A.
139 D2 **Williamsport** U.S.A.
141 E1 **Williamston** U.S.A.
122 B3 **Williston** S. Africa
136 C1 **Williston** U.S.A.
128 B2 **Williston Lake** Can.
135 B3 **Willits** U.S.A.
137 D1 **Willmar** U.S.A.
122 B3 **Willowmore** S. Africa
135 B3 **Willows** U.S.A.
123 C3 **Willowvale** S. Africa
50 B2 **Wills, Lake** *salt flat* Austr.
52 A3 **Willunga** Austr.
52 A2 **Wilmington** Austr.
139 D3 **Wilmington** *DE* U.S.A.
141 E2 **Wilmington** *NC* U.S.A.
138 C3 **Wilmington** *OH* U.S.A.
141 D2 **Wilmington Island** U.S.A.
101 D2 **Wilnsdorf** Ger.
101 D1 **Wilseder Berg** *hill* Ger.
141 E1 **Wilson** U.S.A.
53 C3 **Wilson's Promontory** *pen.* Austr.
100 B3 **Wiltz** Lux.
50 B2 **Wiluna** Austr.
99 D4 **Wimereux** France
123 C2 **Winburg** S. Africa
99 B4 **Wincanton** U.K.
99 C4 **Winchester** U.K.
138 C3 **Winchester** *KY* U.S.A.
139 D3 **Winchester** *VA* U.S.A.
98 B2 **Windermere** *l.* U.K.
122 A1 **Windhoek** Namibia
137 D2 **Windom** U.S.A.
51 D2 **Windorah** Austr.
136 B2 **Wind River Range** *mts* U.S.A.
53 D2 **Windsor** Austr.
130 B3 **Windsor** Can.
147 D3 **Windward Islands** Caribbean Sea
147 C3 **Windward Passage** Cuba/Haiti
137 D3 **Winfield** U.S.A.
100 A2 **Wingene** Belgium
53 D2 **Wingham** Austr.
130 B2 **Winisk** Can.
130 B2 **Winisk** *r.* Can.
130 B2 **Winisk Lake** Can.
63 A2 **Winkana** Myanmar
129 E3 **Winkler** Can.
114 B4 **Winneba** Ghana
138 B2 **Winnebago, Lake** U.S.A.
134 C2 **Winnemucca** U.S.A.
136 C2 **Winner** U.S.A.
140 B2 **Winnfield** U.S.A.
137 E1 **Winnibigoshish, Lake** U.S.A.
129 E3 **Winnipeg** Can.
129 E2 **Winnipeg** *r.* Can.
129 E2 **Winnipeg, Lake** Can.
129 D2 **Winnipegosis, Lake** Can.
139 E2 **Winnipesaukee, Lake** U.S.A.
140 B2 **Winnsboro** U.S.A.
137 E2 **Winona** *MN* U.S.A.
140 C2 **Winona** *MS* U.S.A.
100 C1 **Winschoten** Neth.
101 D1 **Winsen (Aller)** Ger.
101 E1 **Winsen (Luhe)** Ger.
142 A1 **Winslow** U.S.A.
141 D1 **Winston-Salem** U.S.A.
101 D2 **Winterberg** Ger.
141 D3 **Winter Haven** U.S.A.
100 C2 **Winterswijk** Neth.
105 D2 **Winterthur** Switz.
51 D2 **Winton** Austr.
54 A3 **Winton** N.Z.
52 A2 **Wirrabara** Austr.
52 A2 **Wirraminna** Austr.
99 D3 **Wisbech** U.K.
138 A2 **Wisconsin** *r.* U.S.A.
138 B2 **Wisconsin** *state* U.S.A.
138 B2 **Wisconsin Rapids** U.S.A.
   **Wisła** *r.* Pol. *see* **Vistula**
101 E1 **Wismar** Ger.
123 C2 **Witbank** S. Africa
122 A2 **Witbooisvlei** Namibia
98 C3 **Witham** U.K.
98 D3 **Withernsea** U.K.
100 B1 **Witmarsum** Neth.
99 C4 **Witney** U.K.
123 D2 **Witrivier** S. Africa
123 C3 **Witteberg** *mts* S. Africa
101 E1 **Wittenberge** Ger.
101 E1 **Wittenburg** Ger.
50 A2 **Wittenoom** Austr.
101 E1 **Wittingen** Ger.
100 C3 **Wittlich** Ger.
100 C1 **Wittmund** Ger.
101 F1 **Wittstock** Ger.
122 A1 **Witvlei** Namibia
101 D2 **Witzenhausen** Ger.
103 D1 **Władysławowo** Pol.
103 D1 **Włocławek** Pol.
103 E1 **Włodawa** Pol.
53 C3 **Wodonga** Austr.
59 C3 **Wokam** *i.* Indon.
62 A1 **Wokha** India
99 C4 **Woking** U.K.
101 F2 **Wolfen** Ger.

101 E1 **Wolfenbüttel** Ger.
101 D2 **Wolfhagen** Ger.
136 B1 **Wolf Point** U.S.A.
101 E1 **Wolfsburg** Ger.
100 C3 **Wolfstein** Ger.
131 D3 **Wolfville** Can.
102 C1 **Wolgast** Ger.
102 C1 **Wolin** Pol.
129 D2 **Wollaston Lake** Can.
129 D2 **Wollaston Lake** *l.* Can.
126 E2 **Wollaston Peninsula** Can.
53 D2 **Wollongong** Austr.
101 E2 **Wolmirsleben** Ger.
101 E1 **Wolmirstedt** Ger.
100 C1 **Wolvega** Neth.
99 B3 **Wolverhampton** U.K.
65 B2 **Wŏnju** S. Korea
128 B2 **Wonowon** Can.
65 B2 **Wŏnsan** N. Korea
53 C3 **Wonthaggi** Austr.
52 A2 **Woocalla** Austr.
51 C1 **Woodah, Isle** *i.* Austr.
99 D3 **Woodbridge** U.K.
134 B1 **Woodburn** U.S.A.
136 B3 **Woodland Park** U.S.A.
138 A3 **Wood River** U.S.A.
50 C2 **Woodroffe, Mount** Austr.
51 C1 **Woods, Lake** *salt flat* Austr.
129 E3 **Woods, Lake of the** Can./U.S.A.
53 C3 **Woods Point** Austr.
131 D3 **Woodstock** *N.B.* Can.
138 C2 **Woodstock** Ont. Can.
54 C2 **Woodville** N.Z.
143 D1 **Woodward** U.S.A.
98 B2 **Wooler** U.K.
53 D2 **Woolgoolga** Austr.
52 A2 **Woomera** Austr.
138 C2 **Wooster** U.S.A.
122 A3 **Worcester** S. Africa
99 B3 **Worcester** U.K.
139 E2 **Worcester** U.S.A.
102 C2 **Wörgl** Austria
98 B2 **Workington** U.K.
98 C3 **Worksop** U.K.
136 B2 **Worland** U.S.A.
101 D3 **Worms** Ger.
99 A4 **Worms Head** *hd* U.K.
122 A1 **Wortel** Namibia
99 C4 **Worthing** U.K.
137 D2 **Worthington** U.S.A.
61 D2 **Wotu** Indon.
61 D2 **Wowoni** *i.* Indon.
   **Wrangel Island** *see* **Vrangelya,**
   **Ostrov**
128 A2 **Wrangell** U.S.A.
96 B1 **Wrath, Cape** U.K.
136 C2 **Wray** U.S.A.
122 A2 **Wreck Point** S. Africa
   **Wrecsam** U.K. *see* **Wrexham**
99 B3 **Wrexham** U.K.
136 B2 **Wright** U.S.A.
63 A2 **Wrightmyo** India
142 A2 **Wrightson, Mount** U.S.A.
128 B1 **Wrigley** Can.
103 D1 **Wrocław** Pol.
103 D1 **Września** Pol.
70 B2 **Wu'an** China
   **Wuchow** China *see* **Wuzhou**
70 A2 **Wudu** China
70 A2 **Wuhai** China
70 B2 **Wuhan** China
71 A3 **Wuhu** China
   **Wu Jiang** *r.* China
   **Wujin** China *see* **Changzhou**
115 C4 **Wukari** Nigeria
75 D1 **Wuli** China
62 B1 **Wuliang Shan** *mts* China
59 C3 **Wuliaru** *i.* Indon.
118 B2 **Wum** Cameroon
71 A3 **Wumeng Shan** *mts* China
101 D1 **Wümme** *r.* Ger.
130 B2 **Wunnummin Lake** Can.
101 F2 **Wunsiedel** Ger.
101 D1 **Wunstorf** Ger.
62 A1 **Wuntho** Myanmar
100 C2 **Wuppertal** Ger.
122 A3 **Wuppertal** S. Africa
101 E2 **Wurzbach** Ger.
101 D3 **Würzburg** Ger.
101 F2 **Wurzen** Ger.
101 D2 **Wüstegarten** *hill* Ger.
59 D3 **Wuvulu Island** P.N.G.
70 A2 **Wuwei** China
70 C2 **Wuxi** *Chongqing* China
70 C2 **Wuxi** *Jiangsu* China
   **Wuxing** China *see* **Huzhou**
71 A3 **Wuxuan** China
   **Wuyang** China *see* **Zhenyuan**
69 E1 **Wuyiling** China
71 B3 **Wuyishan** China
71 B3 **Wuyi Shan** *mts* China
70 A1 **Wuyuan** China
71 A4 **Wuzhishan** China
70 A2 **Wuzhong** China
71 B3 **Wuzhou** China
51 D2 **Wyandra** Austr.
53 C2 **Wyangala Reservoir** Austr.
52 B3 **Wycheproof** Austr.
99 B4 **Wye** *r.* U.K.
50 B1 **Wyndham** Austr.
52 B3 **Wyndham-Werribee** Austr.
140 B1 **Wynne** U.S.A.
129 D2 **Wynyard** Can.
138 B2 **Wyoming** U.S.A.
136 B2 **Wyoming** *state* U.S.A.

53 D2 **Wyong** Austr.
103 E1 **Wyszków** Pol.
138 C3 **Wytheville** U.S.A.

## X

117 D3 **Xaafuun** Somalia
62 B2 **Xaignabouli** Laos
121 C3 **Xai-Xai** Moz.
70 A1 **Xamba** China
62 B1 **Xam Nua** Laos
120 A1 **Xá-Muteba** Angola
120 A2 **Xangongo** Angola
81 C2 **Xankändi** Azer.
111 B2 **Xanthi** Greece
154 B3 **Xanxerê** Brazil
150 C4 **Xapuri** Brazil
107 C2 **Xàtiva** Spain
120 B3 **Xhumo** Botswana
**Xiaguan** China see Dali
71 B3 **Xiamen** China
70 A2 **Xi'an** China
70 A3 **Xianfeng** China
65 A1 **Xiangcheng** China
70 B2 **Xiangfan** China
62 A1 **Xianggelila** China
**Xianghuang Qi** China see Xin Bulag
**Xiangjiang** China see Huichang
71 B3 **Xiang Jiang** r. China
62 B2 **Xiangkhoang** Laos
71 B3 **Xiangtan** China
**Xiangyang** China see Xiangfan
71 B3 **Xiangyin** China
70 B2 **Xianning** China
70 B2 **Xiantao** China
70 A2 **Xianyang** China
70 B2 **Xiaogan** China
69 E1 **Xiao Hinggan Ling** mts China
70 C2 **Xiaoshan** China
70 B2 **Xiaowutai Shan** mt. China
**Xiayingpan** China see Luzhi
**Xibu** China see Dongshan
71 A3 **Xichang** China
145 C2 **Xicohténcatl** Mex.
70 A2 **Xifeng** Gansu China
71 A3 **Xifeng** Guizhou China
**Xifengzhen** China see Xifeng
75 C2 **Xigazê** China
71 A3 **Xilin** China
69 D2 **Xilinhot** China
68 C2 **Ximiao** China
70 B3 **Xin'anjiang Shuiku** resr China
70 B1 **Xin Bulag** China
70 B2 **Xincai** China
**Xincun** China see Dongchuan
**Xindi** China see Honghu
71 B3 **Xing'an** China
62 A1 **Xingba** China
68 C2 **Xinghai** China
71 B3 **Xinghua** China
70 A2 **Xingping** China
71 B3 **Xingtai** China
151 D3 **Xingu** r. Brazil
151 D3 **Xinguara** Brazil
71 A3 **Xingyi** China
71 B3 **Xinhua** China
70 A2 **Xining** China
75 C1 **Xinjiang** aut. reg. China
**Xinjing** China see Jingxi
65 A1 **Xinmin** China
71 B3 **Xinning** China
71 A3 **Xinping** China
**Xinshiba** China see Ganluo
70 B2 **Xintai** China
**Xinxian** China see Xinzhou
70 B2 **Xinxiang** China
70 B2 **Xinyang** China
71 A3 **Xinying** China
71 B3 **Xinyu** China
77 E2 **Xinyuan** China
69 D2 **Xinzhou** Shanxi China
70 B2 **Xinzhou** Shanxi China
106 B1 **Xinzo de Limia** Spain
**Xiongshan** China see Zhenghe
**Xiongzhou** China see Nanxiong
70 A2 **Xiqing Shan** mts China
151 E4 **Xique Xique** Brazil
70 A2 **Xishanzui** China
71 A3 **Xiushan** China
**Xiushan** China see Tonghai
71 B3 **Xiushui** China
71 B3 **Xiuying** China
76 B2 **Xixia** China
71 B3 **Xixiang** China
**Xizhou** China see Xuancheng
70 B2 **Xuchang** China
**Xucheng** China see Xuwen
117 C4 **Xuddur** Somalia
**Xuefeng** China see Mingxi
**Xujiang** China see Guangchang
71 B3 **Xun Jiang** r. China
71 B3 **Xunwu** China
71 B3 **Xuwen** China
71 A3 **Xuyong** China
**Xuzhou** China see Tongshan
111 B3 **Xylokastro** Greece
70 A2 **Ya'an** China

## Y

117 B4 **Yabêlo** Eth.
69 D1 **Yablonovyy Khrebet** mts Rus. Fed.
141 D1 **Yadkin** r. U.S.A.
75 C2 **Yadong** China
70 A1 **Yagan** China
55 A4 **Yaghan Basin** sea feature S. Atlantic Ocean
89 E2 **Yagnitsa** Rus. Fed.
83 K2 **Yagodnoye** Rus. Fed.
118 B1 **Yagoua** Cameroon
91 C1 **Yahotyn** Ukr.
144 B2 **Yahualica** Mex.
80 B2 **Yahyalı** Turkey
67 C4 **Yaizu** Japan
134 B1 **Yakima** U.S.A.
134 C1 **Yakima** r. U.S.A.
74 A2 **Yakmach** Pak.
114 B3 **Yako** Burkina
66 D2 **Yakumo** Japan
67 B4 **Yaku-shima** i. Japan
126 C3 **Yakutat** U.S.A.
128 A2 **Yakutat Bay** U.S.A.
83 J2 **Yakutsk** Rus. Fed.
91 C2 **Yakymivka** Ukr.
63 B3 **Yala** Thai.
118 C2 **Yalinga** C.A.R.
53 C3 **Yallourn** Austr.
111 C2 **Yalova** Turkey
90 B2 **Yalpuh, Ozero** l. Ukr.
91 C3 **Yalta** Ukr.
65 A1 **Yalu Jiang** r. China/N. Korea
86 F3 **Yalutorovsk** Rus. Fed.
67 D3 **Yamagata** Japan
67 B4 **Yamaguchi** Japan
**Yamal, Poluostrov** Rus. Fed. see Yamal Peninsula
86 F1 **Yamal Peninsula** pen. Rus. Fed.
**Yamankhalinka** Kazakh. see Makhambet
53 D1 **Yamba** Austr.
150 B2 **Yambi, Mesa de** hills Col.
117 A4 **Yambio** Sudan
110 C2 **Yambol** Bulg.
86 G2 **Yamburg** Rus. Fed.
62 A1 **Yamethin** Myanmar
88 C2 **Yamm** Rus. Fed.
51 D2 **Yamma Yamma, Lake** salt flat Austr.
114 B4 **Yamoussoukro** Côte d'Ivoire
91 C1 **Yampil'** Ukr.
90 B2 **Yampil'** Ukr.
75 C2 **Yamuna** r. India
62 A1 **Yamzho Yumco** l. China
83 K2 **Yana** r. Rus. Fed.
70 A2 **Yan'an** China
150 B4 **Yanaoca** Peru
78 A2 **Yanbu' al Bahr** Saudi Arabia
70 C2 **Yancheng** China
50 A3 **Yanchep** Austr.
114 B3 **Yanfolila** Mali
118 C2 **Yangambi** Dem. Rep. Congo
70 B2 **Yangcheng** China
71 B3 **Yangchun** China
65 B2 **Yangdok** N. Korea
71 B3 **Yangjiang** China
**Yangôn** Myanmar see Rangoon
70 B2 **Yangquan** China
71 B3 **Yangshuo** China
62 B1 **Yangtouyan** China
70 C23 **Yangtze** r. China
70 C2 **Yangtze, Mouth of the** China
**Yangtze Kiang** r. China see Yangtze
70 A2 **Yangxian** China
70 B2 **Yangzhou** China
65 B1 **Yanji** China
137 D2 **Yankton** U.S.A.
83 K2 **Yano-Indigirskaya Nizmennost'** lowland Rus. Fed.
70 B1 **Yanqing** China
71 A3 **Yanshan** China
83 K2 **Yanskiy Zaliv** g. Rus. Fed.
53 C1 **Yantabulla** Austr.
70 C2 **Yantai** China
118 B2 **Yaoundé** Cameroon
59 D2 **Yap** i. Micronesia
59 D3 **Yapen** i. Indon.
59 D3 **Yapen, Selat** sea chan. Indon.
144 A2 **Yaqui** r. Mex.
51 D2 **Yaraka** Austr.
86 D3 **Yaransk** Rus. Fed.
48 H4 **Yaren** Nauru
78 B3 **Yarīm** Yemen
**Yarkand** China see Shache
**Yarkant** China see Shache
77 D3 **Yarkant He** r. China
**Yarlung Zangbo** r. China see Brahmaputra
131 D3 **Yarmouth** Can.
142 A2 **Yarnell** U.S.A.
86 F2 **Yarongo** Rus. Fed.
89 E2 **Yaroslavl'** Rus. Fed.
66 D2 **Yaroslavskiy** Rus. Fed.
53 C3 **Yarra Junction** Austr.
53 C3 **Yarram** Austr.
89 D2 **Yartsevo** Rus. Fed.
89 E3 **Yasnogorsk** Rus. Fed.
63 B2 **Yasothon** Thai.
53 C2 **Yass** Austr.
81 D2 **Yāsūj** Iran
111 C3 **Yatağan** Turkey

119 D3 **Yata Plateau** Kenya
129 E1 **Yathkyed Lake** Can.
67 B4 **Yatsushiro** Japan
150 C3 **Yavari** r. Brazil/Peru
90 A2 **Yavoriv** Ukr.
67 B4 **Yawatahama** Japan
62 A1 **Yawng-hwe** Myanmar
**Yaxian** China see Sanya
81 D2 **Yazd** Iran
140 B2 **Yazoo** r. U.S.A.
140 B2 **Yazoo City** U.S.A.
111 B3 **Ydra** Greece
111 B3 **Ydra** i. Greece
63 A2 **Ye** Myanmar
77 D3 **Yecheng** China
107 C2 **Yecla** Spain
144 B2 **Yécora** Mex.
**Yedintsy** Moldova see Edineţ
89 E3 **Yefremov** Rus. Fed.
91 E2 **Yegorlykskaya** Rus. Fed.
89 E2 **Yegor'yevsk** Rus. Fed.
117 B4 **Yei** Sudan
86 F3 **Yekaterinburg** Rus. Fed.
**Yekaterinodar** Rus. Fed. see Krasnodar
**Yekaterinoslav** Ukr. see Dnipropetrovs'k
**Yekaterinovskaya** Rus. Fed. see Krylovskaya
**Yelenovskiye Kar'yery** Ukr. see Dokuchayevs'k
89 E3 **Yelets** Rus. Fed.
89 D2 **Yeligovo** Rus. Fed.
114 A3 **Yélimané** Mali
96 □ **Yell** i. U.K.
128 C1 **Yellowknife** Can.
53 C1 **Yellow Mountain** hill Austr.
70 B2 **Yellow River** r. China
69 E2 **Yellow Sea** N. Pacific Ocean
136 C1 **Yellowstone** r. U.S.A.
136 A2 **Yellowstone Lake** U.S.A.
88 C3 **Yel'sk** Belarus
78 B3 **Yemen** country Asia
90 B1 **Yemil'chyne** Ukr.
86 E2 **Yemva** Rus. Fed.
91 D2 **Yenakiyeve** Ukr.
62 A1 **Yenangyaung** Myanmar
62 B1 **Yên Bai** Vietnam
114 B4 **Yendi** Ghana
111 C3 **Yenice** Turkey
111 C3 **Yenifoça** Turkey
68 C1 **Yenisey** r. Rus. Fed.
**Yeotmal** India see Yavatmal
53 C2 **Yeoval** Austr.
99 B4 **Yeovil** U.K.
51 E2 **Yeppoon** Austr.
83 I2 **Yerbogachen** Rus. Fed.
81 C1 **Yerevan** Armenia
77 D1 **Yereymentau** Kazakh.
**Yermentau** Kazakh. see Yereymentau
143 C3 **Yermo** Mex.
135 C4 **Yermo** U.S.A.
89 D3 **Yershichi** Rus. Fed.
87 D3 **Yershov** Rus. Fed.
150 B4 **Yerupaja** mt. Peru
**Yerushalayim** Israel/West Bank see Jerusalem
65 B2 **Yesan** S. Korea
77 C1 **Yesil'** Kazakh.
111 C3 **Yeşilova** Turkey
83 H2 **Yessey** Rus. Fed.
99 A4 **Yes Tor** hill U.K.
53 D1 **Yetman** Austr.
62 A1 **Ye-U** Myanmar
104 B2 **Yeu, Île d'** i. France
87 D4 **Yevlax** Azer.
91 C2 **Yevpatoriya** Ukr.
**Yexian** China see Laizhou
91 D2 **Yeysk** Rus. Fed.
88 C2 **Yezyaryshcha** Belarus
**Y Fenni** U.K. see Abergavenny
154 A2 **Ygatimí** Para.
71 A3 **Yibin** China
70 B2 **Yichang** China
69 E1 **Yichun** Heilong. China
71 B3 **Yichun** Jiangxi China
**Yidu** China see Qingzhou
66 A1 **Yilan** China
110 C2 **Yıldız Dağları** mts Turkey
80 B2 **Yıldızeli** Turkey
**Yilong** China see Shiping
70 A2 **Yinchuan** China
65 A2 **Yingchengzi** China
71 B3 **Yingde** China
70 C1 **Yingkou** China
70 B2 **Yingshan** Hubei China
70 A2 **Yingshan** Sichuan China
71 B3 **Yingtan** China
**Yining** China see Xiushui
77 E2 **Yining** China
62 A1 **Yinmabin** Myanmar
70 A1 **Yin Shan** mts China
117 B4 **Yirga Alem** Eth.
119 D2 **Yirga Ch'efê** Eth.
119 D2 **Yirol** Sudan
**Yishan** China see Yizhou
70 B2 **Yishui** China
62 A1 **Yi Tu, Nam** r. Myanmar
68 C2 **Yiwu** China
70 C1 **Yixian** China

70 B2 **Yixing** China
71 B3 **Yiyang** China
71 B3 **Yizhang** China
71 A3 **Yizhou** China
**Yizhou** China see Yixian
92 I2 **Yli-Kitka** l. Fin.
92 H2 **Ylitornio** Fin.
92 H3 **Ylivieska** Fin.
93 H3 **Ylöjärvi** Fin.
83 K2 **Ynykchanskiy** Rus. Fed.
**Ynys Môn** i. U.K. see Anglesey
61 C2 **Yogyakarta** Indon.
118 B2 **Yokadouma** Cameroon
118 B2 **Yoko** Cameroon
67 C3 **Yokohama** Japan
66 D3 **Yokote** Japan
115 D4 **Yola** Nigeria
67 D3 **Yonezawa** Japan
71 B3 **Yong'an** China
**Yongbei** China see Yongsheng
71 B3 **Yongchun** China
70 A2 **Yongdeng** China
65 B2 **Yŏngdŏk** S. Korea
65 B2 **Yŏnghŭng** N. Korea
**Yongjing** China see Xifeng
65 B2 **Yŏngju** S. Korea
71 C3 **Yongkang** China
**Yongning** China see Zhen'an
62 B1 **Yongren** China
62 B1 **Yongsheng** China
71 B3 **Yongzhou** China
139 E2 **Yonkers** U.S.A.
105 C2 **Yonne** r. France
150 B2 **Yopal** Col.
50 A3 **York** Austr.
98 C3 **York** U.K.
140 C2 **York** AL U.S.A.
137 D2 **York** NE U.S.A.
139 D3 **York** PA U.S.A.
51 D1 **York, Cape** Austr.
52 A3 **Yorke Peninsula** Austr.
52 A3 **Yorketown** Austr.
98 C3 **Yorkshire Wolds** hills U.K.
129 D2 **Yorkton** Can.
87 D3 **Yoshkar-Ola** Rus. Fed.
97 C3 **Youghal** Ireland
53 C2 **Young** Austr.
52 A3 **Younghusband Peninsula** Austr.
138 C2 **Youngstown** U.S.A.
114 B3 **Youvarou** Mali
71 B3 **Youyang** China
77 E2 **Youyi Feng** mt. China/Rus. Fed.
80 B2 **Yozgat** Turkey
154 A2 **Ypé-Jhú** Para.
134 B2 **Yreka** U.S.A.
**Yr Wyddfa** mt. U.K. see Snowdon
59 D3 **Ysabel Channel** P.N.G.
105 C2 **Yssingeaux** France
93 F4 **Ystad** Sweden
**Ysyk-Köl** Kyrg. see Balykchy
77 D2 **Ysyk-Köl** salt l. Kyrg.
**Y Trallwng** U.K. see Welshpool
92 □A3 **Ytri-Rangá** r. Iceland
83 J2 **Ytyk-Kyuyel'** Rus. Fed.
71 A3 **Yuanbao Shan** mt. China
71 A3 **Yuanjiang** China
62 B1 **Yuan Jiang** r. China
71 B3 **Yuanling** China
71 A3 **Yuanmou** China
70 B2 **Yuanping** China
135 B3 **Yuba City** U.S.A.
66 D2 **Yūbari** Japan
145 C3 **Yucatán** pen. Mex.
146 B2 **Yucatan Channel** Cuba/Mex.
**Yuci** China see Jinzhong
50 C2 **Yuendumu** Austr.
71 C3 **Yueqing** China
71 B3 **Yueyang** China
86 F2 **Yugorsk** Rus. Fed.
**Yugoslavia** country Europe see Serbia and Montenegro
71 B3 **Yujiang** China
83 L2 **Yukagirskoye Ploskogor'ye** plat. Rus. Fed.
89 E3 **Yukhnov** Rus. Fed.
126 B2 **Yukon** r. Can./U.S.A.
143 D1 **Yukon** U.S.A.
128 A1 **Yukon Territory** admin. div. Can.
50 C2 **Yulara** Austr.
71 B3 **Yulin** Guangxi China
70 A2 **Yulin** Shaanxi China
62 B1 **Yulong Xueshan** mt. China
142 A2 **Yuma** AZ U.S.A.
136 C2 **Yuma** CO U.S.A.
135 D4 **Yuma Desert** U.S.A.
68 C2 **Yumen** China
80 B2 **Yunak** Turkey
70 B2 **Yuncheng** China
71 B3 **Yunfu** China
71 A3 **Yungui Gaoyuan** plat. China
**Yunjinghong** China see Jinghong
**Yunling** China see Yunxiao
71 A3 **Yunnan** prov. China
52 A2 **Yunta** Austr.
71 B3 **Yunxiao** China
70 B2 **Yunyang** China
71 A3 **Yuping** China
**Yuping** China see Libo
82 G3 **Yurga** Rus. Fed.
150 B3 **Yurimaguas** Peru
75 C1 **Yurungkax He** r. China
**Yuryev** Estonia see Tartu
71 C3 **Yü Shan** mt. Taiwan
70 B2 **Yushe** China

68 C2 **Yushu** China
**Yushuwan** China see Huaihua
81 B2 **Yusufeli** Turkey
75 C1 **Yutian** China
71 A3 **Yuxi** China
89 F2 **Yuza** Rus. Fed.
83 K3 **Yuzhno-Sakhalinsk** Rus. Fed.
91 C2 **Yuzhnoukrayinsk** Ukr.
70 B2 **Yuzhou** China
**Yuzovka** Ukr. see Donets'k
105 D2 **Yverdon** Switz.
104 C2 **Yvetot** France

**Z**

100 B1 **Zaandam** Neth.
69 D1 **Zabaykal'sk** Rus. Fed.
119 C2 **Zabia** Dem. Rep. Congo
78 B3 **Zabid** Yemen
79 D1 **Zābol** Iran
79 D2 **Zābolī** Iran
145 C3 **Zacapa** Guat.
144 B3 **Zacapu** Mex.
144 B2 **Zacatecas** Mex.
145 C3 **Zacatepec** Mex.
145 C3 **Zacatlán** Mex.
111 B3 **Zacharo** Greece
91 D2 **Zachepylivka** Ukr.
144 B3 **Zacoalco** Mex.
145 C3 **Zacualtipán** Mex.
109 C2 **Zadar** Croatia
63 A3 **Zadetkyi Kyun** i. Myanmar
89 E3 **Zadonsk** Rus. Fed.
80 B3 **Za'farānah** Egypt
106 B2 **Zafra** Spain
**Zagazig** Egypt see Az Zaqāzīq
114 B1 **Zagora** Morocco
**Zagorsk** Rus. Fed. see
Sergiyev Posad
109 C1 **Zagreb** Croatia
**Zagros, Kūhhā-ye** Iran see
Zagros Mountains
81 C2 **Zagros Mountains** mts Iran
79 D2 **Zāhedān** Iran
80 B2 **Zahlé** Lebanon
78 B3 **Zahrān** Saudi Arabia
**Zaire** country Africa see Congo,
Democratic Republic of the
109 C2 **Zaječar** Serb. and Mont.
121 C3 **Zaka** Zimbabwe
89 E3 **Zakharovo** Rus. Fed.
81 C2 **Zākhō** Iraq
86 C2 **Zakhrebetnoye** Rus. Fed.
111 B3 **Zakynthos** Greece
111 B3 **Zakynthos** i. Greece
103 D2 **Zalaegerszeg** Hungary
110 B1 **Zalău** Romania
78 B2 **Zalim** Saudi Arabia
116 A3 **Zalingei** Sudan
90 B2 **Zalishchyky** Ukr.
78 A2 **Zalmā, Jabal az** mt. Saudi Arabia
128 C2 **Zama City** Can.
**Zambeze** r. Moz. see Zambezi
120 B2 **Zambezi** r. Africa
120 B2 **Zambezi** Zambia
120 B2 **Zambezi Escarpment**
Zambia/Zimbabwe
120 B2 **Zambia** country Africa
64 B3 **Zamboanga** Phil.
64 B3 **Zamboanga Peninsula** Phil.
103 E1 **Zambrów** Pol.
106 B1 **Zamora** Spain
144 B3 **Zamora de Hidalgo** Mex.
103 E1 **Zamość** Pol.
**Zamost'ye** Pol. see Zamość
75 B1 **Zanda** China
100 B2 **Zandvliet** Belgium
100 B1 **Zandvoort** Neth.
138 C2 **Zanesville** U.S.A.
77 D3 **Zangguy** China
75 C1 **Zangsêr Kangri** mt. China
81 C2 **Zanjān** Iran
74 B1 **Zanskar Mountains** India
**Zante** i. Greece see Zakynthos
119 D3 **Zanzibar** Tanz.

119 D3 **Zanzibar Island** Tanz.
89 E3 **Zaokskiy** Rus. Fed.
115 C2 **Zaouatallaz** Alg.
**Zaouet el Kahla** Alg. see
Bordj Omer Driss
70 B2 **Zaoyang** China
83 H3 **Zaozernyy** Rus. Fed.
70 B2 **Zaozhuang** China
89 D2 **Zapadnaya Dvina** r. Europe
89 D2 **Zapadnaya Dvina** Rus. Fed.
**Zapadno-Sibirskaya Ravnina**
Rus. Fed. see West Siberian Plain
68 B1 **Zapadnyy Sayan** reg. Rus. Fed.
143 D3 **Zapata** U.S.A.
92 J2 **Zapolyarnyy** Rus. Fed.
91 D2 **Zaporizhzhya** Ukr.
101 E2 **Zappendorf** Ger.
81 C1 **Zaqatala** Azer.
**Zara** Croatia see Zadar
80 B2 **Zara** Turkey
145 B2 **Zaragoza** Mex.
107 C1 **Zaragoza** Spain
79 C1 **Zarand** Iran
76 C3 **Zaranj** Afgh.
88 C2 **Zarasai** Lith.
89 E3 **Zaraysk** Rus. Fed.
150 C2 **Zaraza** Venez.
115 C3 **Zaria** Nigeria
90 B1 **Zarichne** Ukr.
81 D3 **Zarqān** Iran
66 B2 **Zarubino** Rus. Fed.
103 D1 **Żary** Pol.
115 D1 **Zarzis** Tunisia
88 C3 **Zaslawye** Belarus
123 C3 **Zastron** S. Africa
**Zavitaya** Rus. Fed. see Zavitinsk
69 E1 **Zavitinsk** Rus. Fed.
89 F2 **Zavolzhsk** Rus. Fed.
**Zavolzh'ye** Rus. Fed. see
Zavolzhsk
103 D1 **Zawiercie** Pol.
115 E1 **Zāwiyat Masūs** Libya
77 E2 **Zaysan** Kazakh.
77 E2 **Zaysan, Lake** l. Kazakh.
**Zaysan, Ozero** Kazakh. see
Zaysan, Lake
90 B2 **Zbarazh** Ukr.
90 B1 **Zdolbuniv** Ukr.
93 F4 **Zealand** i. Denmark
100 A2 **Zedelgem** Belgium
100 A2 **Zeebrugge** Belgium
123 C2 **Zeerust** S. Africa
101 F1 **Zehdenick** Ger.
50 C2 **Zeil, Mount** Austr.
101 F2 **Zeitz** Ger.
109 C2 **Zelena Gora** mt. Bos.-Herz.
87 D3 **Zelenodol'sk** Rus. Fed.
88 C1 **Zelenogorsk** Rus. Fed.
89 E2 **Zelenograd** Rus. Fed.
88 B3 **Zelenogradsk** Rus. Fed.
88 B3 **Zel'va** Belarus
119 C2 **Zémio** C.A.R.
107 D2 **Zemmora** Alg.
145 C3 **Zempoaltépetl, Nudo de** mt. Mex.
109 D2 **Zemun** Serb. and Mont.
65 B1 **Zengfeng Shan** mt. China
109 C2 **Zenica** Bos.-Herz.
107 D2 **Zenzach** Alg.
101 F2 **Zerbst** Ger.
105 D2 **Zermatt** Switz.
91 E2 **Zernovoy** Rus. Fed.
**Zernovoy** Rus. Fed. see
Zernograd
101 E2 **Zeulenroda** Ger.
101 D1 **Zeven** Ger.
100 C2 **Zevenaar** Neth.
100 B2 **Zevenbergen** Neth.
83 J3 **Zeya** Rus. Fed.
79 C2 **Zeydābād** Iran
79 C2 **Zeynalābād** Iran
83 J3 **Zeyskoye Vodokhranilishche** resr
Rus. Fed.
103 D1 **Zgierz** Pol.
88 B3 **Zhabinka** Belarus
**Zhabye** Ukr. see Verkhovyna
**Zhaksy Sarysu** watercourse
Kazakh. see Sarysu

76 A2 **Zhalpaktal** Kazakh.
77 C1 **Zhaltyr** Kazakh.
**Zhambyl** Kazakh. see Taraz
76 B2 **Zhanaozen** Kazakh.
**Zhangaqazaly** Kazakh. see
Ayteke Bi
**Zhangde** China see Anyang
**Zhangdian** China see Zibo
66 A1 **Zhangguangcai Ling**
mts China
71 B3 **Zhangjiajie** China
70 B1 **Zhangjiakou** China
71 B3 **Zhangping** China
71 B3 **Zhangshu** China
65 A1 **Zhangwu** China
70 A2 **Zhangxian** China
68 C2 **Zhangye** China
71 B3 **Zhangzhou** China
76 A2 **Zhanibek** Kazakh.
71 B3 **Zhanjiang** China
71 B3 **Zhao'an** China
69 E1 **Zhaodong** China
**Zhaoge** China see Qixian
71 B3 **Zhaoqing** China
71 A3 **Zhaotong** China
75 C1 **Zhari Namco** salt l. China
77 E2 **Zharkent** Kazakh.
89 D2 **Zharkovskiy** Rus. Fed.
77 E2 **Zharma** Kazakh.
90 C2 **Zhashkiv** Ukr.
**Zhaxi** China see Weixin
77 D2 **Zhayrem** Kazakh.
**Zhdanov** Ukr. see Mariupol'
71 C3 **Zhejiang** prov. China
82 F1 **Zhelaniya, Mys** c. Rus. Fed.
**Zheleznodorozhnyy** Rus. Fed. see
Yemva
**Zheleznodorozhnyy** Uzbek. see
Qo'ng'irot
89 E3 **Zheleznogorsk** Rus. Fed.
**Zheltyye Vody** Ukr. see
Zhovti Vody
70 A2 **Zhen'an** China
70 A2 **Zhenba** China
71 A3 **Zheng'an** China
71 B3 **Zhenghe** China
70 B2 **Zhengzhou** China
**Zhenjiang** China see Dantu
71 A3 **Zhenyuan** China
91 E1 **Zherdevka** Rus. Fed.
86 D2 **Zheshart** Rus. Fed.
77 C2 **Zhezkazgan** Kazakh.
77 C2 **Zhezkazgan** Kazakh.
83 J2 **Zhigansk** Rus. Fed.
70 B2 **Zhijiang** China
76 C1 **Zhitikara** Kazakh.
89 D3 **Zhizdra** Rus. Fed.
88 D3 **Zhlobin** Belarus
90 B2 **Zhmerynka** Ukr.
74 A1 **Zhob** Pak.
88 C3 **Zhodzina** Belarus
83 L1 **Zhokhova, Ostrov** i. Rus. Fed.
**Zholkva** Ukr. see Zhovkva
**Zhongba** China see Jiangyou
75 C2 **Zhongba** China
**Zhongduo** China see Youyang
**Zhonghe** China see Xiushan
70 A2 **Zhongning** China
**Zhongping** China see Huize
71 B3 **Zhongshan** China
**Zhongshan** China see
Lupanshui
70 A2 **Zhongwei** China
**Zhongxin** China see
Xianggelila
70 B2 **Zhoukou** China
70 C2 **Zhoushan** China
90 A1 **Zhovkva** Ukr.
91 C2 **Zhovti Vody** Ukr.
65 A2 **Zhuanghe** China
70 B2 **Zhucheng** China
89 D3 **Zhukovka** Rus. Fed.
89 E2 **Zhukovskiy** Rus. Fed.
70 B2 **Zhumadian** China
**Zhuoyang** China see Suiping
71 B3 **Zhuzhou** Hunan China
71 B3 **Zhuzhou** Hunan China

90 A2 **Zhydachiv** Ukr.
88 C3 **Zhytkavichy** Belarus
90 B1 **Zhytomyr** Ukr.
103 D2 **Žiar nad Hronom** Slovakia
70 B2 **Zibo** China
103 D1 **Zielona Góra** Pol.
100 A2 **Zierikzee** Neth.
62 A1 **Zigaing** Myanmar
115 E2 **Zighan** Libya
71 A3 **Zigong** China
**Zigui** China see Guojiaba
114 A3 **Ziguinchor** Senegal
144 B3 **Zihuatanejo** Mex.
103 D2 **Žilina** Slovakia
115 D2 **Zillah** Libya
83 H3 **Zima** Rus. Fed.
145 C2 **Zimapán** Mex.
121 B2 **Zimbabwe** country Africa
114 A4 **Zimmi** Sierra Leone
110 C2 **Zimnicea** Romania
86 C2 **Zimniy Bereg** coastal area
Rus. Fed.
115 C3 **Zinder** Niger
78 B3 **Zinjibār** Yemen
91 C1 **Zin'kiv** Ukr.
**Zinoyevsk** Ukr. see Kirovohrad
150 B2 **Zipaquirá** Col.
103 D2 **Zirc** Hungary
75 D2 **Ziro** India
79 C2 **Zir Rūd** Iran
103 D2 **Zistersdorf** Austria
145 B3 **Zitácuaro** Mex.
103 C1 **Zittau** Ger.
87 E3 **Zlatoust** Rus. Fed.
103 D2 **Zlín** Czech Rep.
115 D1 **Zlīṭan** Libya
103 D1 **Złotów** Pol.
89 D3 **Zlynka** Rus. Fed.
89 E3 **Zmiyevka** Rus. Fed.
91 D2 **Zmiyiv** Ukr.
89 E3 **Znamenka** Rus. Fed.
91 E1 **Znamenka** Rus. Fed.
91 C2 **Znam"yanka** Ukr.
103 D2 **Znojmo** Czech Rep.
122 B3 **Zoar** S. Africa
70 A2 **Zoigê** China
91 D1 **Zolochiv** Ukr.
90 A2 **Zolochiv** Ukr.
91 C2 **Zolotonosha** Ukr.
89 E3 **Zolotukhino** Rus. Fed.
121 C2 **Zomba** Malawi
118 B2 **Zongo** Dem. Rep. Congo
80 B1 **Zonguldak** Turkey
105 D3 **Zonza** Corsica France
114 B3 **Zorgho** Burkina
114 B4 **Zorzor** Liberia
115 D2 **Zouar** Chad
114 A2 **Zouérat** Maur.
109 D1 **Zrenjanin** Serb. and Mont.
89 D2 **Zubtsov** Rus. Fed.
105 D2 **Zug** Switz.
81 C1 **Zugdidi** Georgia
**Zuider Zee** l. Neth. see
IJsselmeer
106 B2 **Zújar** r. Spain
100 C2 **Zülpich** Ger.
100 A2 **Zulte** Belgium
121 C2 **Zumbo** Moz.
145 C3 **Zumpango** Mex.
142 B1 **Zuni Mountains** U.S.A.
71 A3 **Zunyi** China
109 C1 **Županja** Croatia
105 D2 **Zürich** Switz.
105 D2 **Zürichsee** l. Switz.
100 C1 **Zutphen** Neth.
115 D1 **Zuwārah** Libya
90 C2 **Zvenyhorodka** Ukr.
121 C3 **Zvishavane** Zimbabwe
103 D2 **Zvolen** Slovakia
109 C2 **Zvornik** Bos.-Herz.
114 B4 **Zwedru** Liberia
123 C3 **Zwelitsha** S. Africa
103 C2 **Zwettl** Austria
101 F2 **Zwickau** Ger.
100 C1 **Zwolle** Neth.
83 L2 **Zyryanka** Rus. Fed.
77 E2 **Zyryanovsk** Kazakh.

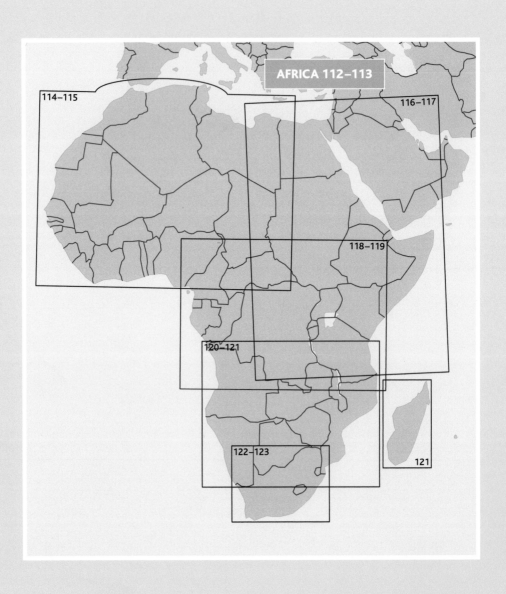

AFRICA 112–113

114–115

116–117

118–119

120–121

121

122–123